Economics
of Transportation

THE IRWIN SERIES IN ECONOMICS

Consulting Editor
LLOYD G. REYNOLDS
Yale University

GORDON *The Investment Financing and Valuation of the Corporation*

GRAMPP & WEILER (eds.) *Economic Policy: Readings in Political Economy* 3d ed.

GROSSMAN, HANSEN, HENDRIKSEN, MCALLISTER, OKUDA, & WOLMAN (eds.) *Readings in Current Economics* rev. ed.

GUTHRIE *Statistical Methods in Economics*

GUTHRIE & WALLACE *Economics* 4th ed.

HAGEN *The Economics of Development*

HARRISS *The American Economy: Principles, Practices, and Policies* 6th ed.

HERBER *Modern Public Finance* rev. ed.

HIGGINS *United Nations and U.S. Foreign Economic Policy*

JOME *Principles of Money and Banking*

KINDLEBERGER *International Economics* 4th ed.

KUHLMAN & SKINNER *The Economic System* rev. ed.

LEE *Macroeconomics: Fluctuations, Growth, and Stability* 5th ed.

LLOYD *Microeconomic Analysis*

LOCKLIN *Economics of Transportation* 7th ed.

LOW *Modern Economic Organization*

MEYERS *Economics of Labor Relations*

PEGRUM *Public Regulation of Business* rev. ed.

PEGRUM *Transportation: Economics and Public Policy* rev. ed.

PETERSON *Principles of Economics: Macro*

PETERSON *Principles of Economics: Micro*

PETERSON & GRAY *Economic Development of the United States*

PHILLIPS *The Economics of Regulation: Theory and Practice in the Transportation and Public Utility Industries* rev. ed.

REYNOLDS *Economics: A General Introduction* 3d ed.

RIMA *Development of Economic Analysis* rev. ed.

SCITOVSKY *Welfare and Competition: The Economics of a Fully Employed Economy* rev. ed.

SIEGEL *Aggregate Economics and Public Policy* 3d ed.

SIRKIN *Introduction to Macroeconomic Theory* 3d ed.

SMITH *Macroeconomics*

SMITH & TEIGEN (eds.) *Readings in Money, National Income, and Stabilization Policy* rev. ed.

SNIDER *Introduction to International Economics* 5th ed.

SPENCER *Managerial Economics: Text, Problems, and Short Cases* 3d ed.

VANEK *International Trade: Theory and Economic Policy*

WILCOX *Public Policies toward Business* 4th ed.

Economics
of Transportation

D. PHILIP LOCKLIN, Ph.D.
Emeritus Professor of Economics
University of Illinois

Seventh Edition • 1972
RICHARD D. IRWIN, INC.   *Homewood, Illinois   60430*
IRWIN-DORSEY LIMITED   *Georgetown, Ontario*

138780

To
the many devoted public servants
past and present
who have sought to shape or administer
transport legislation
for the common good

PREFACE

In this, the seventh edition of *Economics of Transportation*, the author has attempted to bring factual material up to date, noting particularly the developments in public policy as reflected in recent legislation and in the decisions of regulatory bodies and the courts.

In the area of legislative action, developments since 1965 (when the previous edition was published) include three major legislative acts, namely, the Department of Transportation Act, 1966; the Rail Passenger Service Act of 1970; and the Airport and Airway Development Act of 1970.

Events are moving rapidly in the transport field and are likely to continue to do so. It is all the more important, therefore, to understand the past—the development of the various modes of transport, the problems they have created, the attempts to deal with these problems through the regulatory process, and the accomplishments and failures revealed by the story.

The general organization of the earlier editions of this book has been followed, with many of the additions and changes so interspersed in the framework of the previous edition that they may not always be observable at a glance. In order to make room for new material, some deletion and condensation of older material has been necessary.

Only a few changes in the organization of the book have been made. Some descriptive material relating to highway, pipeline, water, and air transport has been transferred from later chapters of the book to Chapter 2 in order to give the reader early in his study a consciousness of the whole transportation system. Another major change is the addition of a final chapter dealing with recent trends in transport policy and the various choices that lie ahead, together with a glance at some problems that each course of action might entail. The chapter on government ownership of railroads which is found in the earlier editions of the book has been deleted as a separate chapter, and some observations about this course of action are incorporated in the final chapter.

One further comment on the organization of the book may be made. The fact that only two chapters are devoted specifically to water transport, four to highway transport, three to air and one to pipelines, while many chapters are concerned primarily with rail transport and its regulation should not lead to the inference that railroad transportation is overemphasized and that the other modes of transport are slighted. When the student has acquired an understanding of railway rate theory and of railway rate structures and rate-making practices, has studied the evolution of the regulatory system as it was first developed for railroads, and has studied some of the major problems of railroad regulation and the policies worked out by regulatory agencies, the other modes of transport can be treated more briefly and with a minimum amount of repetition. Attention can be called briefly to similarities between these modes of transport and the railroads; significant differences can be stressed; and emphasis can be put on the problems peculiar to the mode of transport under consideration. In like manner, differences in regulatory statutes and regulatory policy can be brought out, and particular attention can be given to the regulatory problems peculiar to each mode of transport. This is the plan that has been followed in the present volume.

It should be noted also that we begin the book with chapters relating to transport generally, regardless of the mode utilized, and end the book with chapters dealing specifically with transport coordination and the relationship between the various modes of transport together with some consideration of overall transportation policy.

The author wishes to acknowledge indebtedness to his colleague, Professor Robert W. Harbeson, for the stimulus provided by frequent discussions of matters of mutual interest in the field of transportation. In the preparation of this edition, as of previous editions, the author has had the aid of his wife, Anne Littlefield Locklin, who has carefully read the manuscript in the various stages of its preparation.

May 1972   D. Philip Locklin

CONTENTS

Chapter 1

ECONOMIC SIGNIFICANCE OF IMPROVED TRANSPORTATION

Before the development of railroads the overland transportation of goods was both slow and costly. The carriage of goods by water, however, was performed at less cost than by land. For this reason most of the commerce of the world was carried by water, and the important commercial cities were maritime cities. The invention of the steam engine in the 18th century paved the way for improved transportation facilities. The application of the steam engine to navigation in 1807, and to land transportation, through the invention of the locomotive in 1829, opened an era of cheap transportation. The steamboat greatly reduced the cost of transportation by water, but the steam locomotive was nothing less than revolutionary in its effect on transportation by land. The railroad made cheap transportation possible for vast areas of the earth's surface. This cheap transportation was one of the basic facts on which the economic life of the 19th and 20th centuries was built.

Technological improvements which have been made continuously since the first introduction of railroads have tended to reduce the cost of rail transportation and have improved the services which the railroads provide. There is no reason to believe that the end of this process has been reached, although technological improvement in the railroad industry is naturally slower than when the industry was in the developmental stage. Improvement in transportation facilities, however, has not been confined to railroads. New forms of transport have arisen, and older ones have been improved. Pipelines have been developed for the transportation of petroleum and its products. The motor vehicle and the airplane have appeared upon the scene since the completion of the railroad network. Waterways have been improved, and modern boats and barges have been constructed to operate over them.

Improvements in transportation generally mean reductions in transportation costs to shippers, or greater speed in transport, or some improvement in the nature or quality of the service. From the historical standpoint, reductions in transport costs have probably been the most important. Improvements in speed, however, have also been significant; and air transportation, which has brought great advances in this respect, is

1

having important economic consequences. In this chapter, however, we are concerned primarily with the economic results which flow from reductions in transportation costs to shippers.

TRANSPORTATION AND AVAILABILITY OF GOODS

The most obvious effect of cheap transportation is to make available to a community the goods which must of necessity be produced elsewhere. A community without cheap transportation must be largely self-sufficing. Climatic conditions and available natural resources limit the goods which may be produced, and only those products from other lands can be brought in which will stand high transportation costs. Cheap transportation permits other goods to be brought in, so that the products of other lands and climes may become as commonplace as the articles produced at home. A moment's reflection will reveal dozens of commodities daily consumed in any modern community which are not and could not be produced locally.

PRICE STABILIZATION AND EQUALIZATION

Closely related to the above is another result of cheap transportation. The possibility of an easy movement of goods from one community to another tends to equalize prices. Illustrations of this can be easily found. Fresh fruits and vegetables can be brought into a community when the season is not right for the local product or when the local supply is short. Crop failures, although bringing hardship to the producers, are less serious to a community as a whole if it can obtain supplies from outside. Similarly a local oversupply can be disposed of by shipping to other markets, thus preventing a serious break in local prices. For many commodities, cheap transportation makes possible the establishment of central markets, replacing local markets where local conditions of supply and demand often create wide price fluctuations. A central market, deriving its supply from many sources and disposing of the product to many consumers, is less subject to extreme price fluctuations. For some commodities—those which stand long-distance transportation especially well—world markets and world prices are established. In such cases the price in any producing area is closely related to the world price, varying from that price chiefly by the transportation rates and other costs incident to shipment to the market.

RELATION OF TRANSPORTATION TO LAND VALUES

Another effect of cheap transportation is to extend greatly the area of profitable production for a given market. This is illustrated by the facts given below regarding the production of food supplies for larger cities. Many lands would be unprofitable for agricultural purposes if cheap transportation did not enable the product to be shipped to distant markets. Cheap transportation, therefore, tends to increase land rents and values in remoter regions. The economic history of the United States affords illustrations of this relationship. The high cost of transportation by land prior to the construction of railroads made it impossible to produce agricultural products or to develop natural resources at any great distances from markets. Until cheap transportation made such markets accessible, the rich lands west of the Allegheny Mountains had little value. During the era of railroad building the advantages of railroads were frequently demonstrated by pointing out that, with ordinary roads as a means of transportation, corn could be transported only about 125 miles to market and wheat only 250 miles.[1] For longer distances the cost of

TABLE 1–1. Early Estimates of Value of Wheat and Corn per Ton at Different Distances from Market on a Railroad and on a Common Road

Miles	Railroad		Ordinary Road	
	Wheat	Corn	Wheat	Corn
0	$49.50	$24.75	$49.50	$24.75
10	49.25	24.60	48.00	23.25
20	49.20	24.45	45.50	21.75
30	49.05	24.30	45.00	20.25
40	49.00	24.15	43.50	18.75
50	48.75	24.00	42.00	17.25
100	48.00	23.25	34.50	9.75
150	47.25	22.50	27.00	2.25
160	47.10	22.35	25.50	0.75
170	46.95	22.20	24.00	....
200	46.50	21.75	19.50	....
250	45.75	21.00	12.00	....
300	45.00	20.25	4.50	....
320	44.70	19.95	1.50	....
330	44.55	19.80	....	....

transportation became so great that grain could not be profitably produced in excess of local needs. Figures like those in Table 1–1 were sometimes used to illustrate how the area of profitable cultivation could be increased by rail transportation and how the value of grain would be enhanced along the line of the railroad.[2]

Many of these calculations failed to allow for the fall in prices which was brought about by the great increase in the areas of cultivation. In

[1] Henry V. Poor, *Influence of the Railroads of the United States in the Creation of Its Commerce and Wealth* (New York: Journeymen Printers' Cooperative Association, 1869), pp. 11–12.

[2] This table appeared in 25 *American Railroad Journal* 705 (1852) and in 29 *Merchants' Magazine and Commercial Review* 388 (1853).

spite of such price declines the construction of railroads made millions of acres of land valuable that had been worthless before.

If the building of railroads increased the profitableness of agriculture in areas remote from markets, it made agriculture less profitable on the lands situated nearer the markets. The advantage of nearness to market became less important than formerly. And when the distant lands were fertile and easily tilled and the nearer lands were poorer or difficult to work, the nearer regions suffered greatly. The opening of the Erie Canal in 1825 reduced the cost of transportation from Buffalo to Albany from $100 to $10 and ultimately to $3 per ton.[3] This had the effect of increasing land values in the West and depreciating them in the East. As railroads were constructed, land values changed still more. Agricultural production increased immensely in the West; in New England and the seaboard regions, agriculture declined, and farms were abandoned. The effect of cheap railroad transportation in the United States was felt even in England where prices of grain fell from 40 to 50 percent. This worked a great hardship on English farmers and landowners.[4]

TRANSPORTATION AND PRICES

The most important effect of improved transportation is the reduction in the cost of goods which it brings about. Cheap transportation reduces the price of goods by lowering the cost of producing them. This result is accomplished in several ways.

The most obvious way in which this is brought about is through the reduction in the cost of getting goods from the point of production to the consumer. The freight rates on goods are in reality costs of production. The process of production is not complete until goods are placed in the hands of consumers. This truth is frequently explained by pointing out that production is the creation of utilities, not simply the creation of physical goods, and that transportation produces place utilities. If goods are brought into a community for sale, the price must be high enough to cover the cost incurred in shipping them. High freight rates mean higher prices for the goods which are brought into a community. Low freight rates mean lower prices for these goods. Before railroads or other improved means of transportation had developed in the United States, the settlers who had pushed into the interior had to pay high prices for many essential commodities. Salt could be purchased on the coast for a cent a pound, but it sometimes cost six cents a pound three hundred miles inland because of the cost of transportation.[5] Iron likewise was high in price in

---

[3] Poor, op. cit., p. 8.

[4] J. Stephens Jeans, "American Railroads and British Farmers," 28 *Nineteenth Century* 392, 401 (1890).

[5] Arthur T. Hadley, *Railroad Transportation* (New York: Putnam's, 1885), p. 25.

the interior; at times it was worth as much as twenty-five cents a pound in Pittsburgh.[6]

A second way in which cheap transportation reduces the price of goods is through reducing the cost of assembling the raw materials needed in the manufacturing process. Manufactured articles often contain raw materials which must be assembled from many sources of supply. These transportation expenses increase the cost of producing the manufactured goods. Thus, if the cost of assembling the lumber, the iron and steel, the rubber, and the many other raw materials used in the manufacture of automobiles were to be increased, it would increase the cost of producing automobiles and would tend to increase the prices charged for them. As will be seen in a later chapter,[7] industries sometimes move closer to sources of raw materials in order to avoid increased freight rates; but if a number of raw materials from different sources of supply are used, the high transportation rates on raw materials cannot be wholly avoided. The industry may move toward the source of supply of the raw material on which the freight bill is the largest, but the other raw materials will have to be brought perhaps even longer distances than formerly. There is no escape from the fact that the cost of assembling raw materials is a cost of production. Anything which tends to reduce this cost will tend to reduce the price of the manufactured goods.

TERRITORIAL DIVISION OF LABOR

A third manner in which cheap transportation reduces prices is through the opportunity it makes for geographical division of labor, or territorial specialization. It is in this connection that transportation has wrought the greatest changes in our system of production. By geographical division of labor is meant a system of production in which each geographical area tends to specialize in the production of one or a limited number of commodities.

Geographical division of labor, with resulting exchange of goods between regions, is of two sorts. The simpler case arises when one region, A, can produce a commodity more cheaply than another region, B, and when B can produce something else more cheaply than A. Under these conditions it is certainly to the advantage of all parties that each community produce that for which it is best fitted and exchange with the other. If the costs of transportation between A and B are so great as to offset the advantage which each community has in the production of its specialty, no exchange will take place. As a result, A will find it necessary to devote some of its land, labor, and capital to the production of the

---

[6] Seymour Dunbar, *A History of Travel in America* (Indianapolis: Bobbs-Merrill, 1915), Vol. I, p. 195.

[7] Chapter 4.

commodity which B can produce more cheaply. Community B will have to produce some of the commodity which A can produce more cheaply. Land, labor, and capital are less effectively employed than when each community specializes. High transportation costs, therefore, operate as a barrier to trade and profitable specialization. In this respect, high freight rates act as a protective tariff and compel A and B to produce some goods for which they are not adapted.

But a more complicated situation than the foregoing usually develops if cheap transportation is available. A community will specialize in the production of the goods for which it has the *greatest* advantage. When specialization of this sort takes place, a community sometimes purchases things from outside which it can produce with less cost at home. It does this in order to be free to devote its energies to the production of the things in which its advantages are the greatest. This principle is called the principle of "comparative advantage" or "comparative costs." It has been developed most extensively in connection with studies of international trade.[8] The principle, however, is of much wider application. It applies equally well to trade between sections of the same country. It applies to division of labor between individuals as well as between localities. Thus a lawyer may be able to do his stenographic work better than the stenographer whom he employs. He will devote himself, however, to the tasks which he can do and the stenographer cannot do, unless his business is not extensive enough to permit it. It would be poor business for him to allow stenographic work, which a stenographer can do, to interfere with tasks which the lawyer only can do and which will increase his income. Similarly the manager of a store may be a better salesman than those whom he employs, but he would be foolish to do the work of a salesman if it interfered with the proper management of the store or attention to tasks which he alone can perform satisfactorily.

The principle of comparative advantage does not mean that a community produces all of the things in which it has an advantage over other communities. It simply means that of all the commodities which it can produce, it will produce those which it can produce most cheaply. This may mean producing a commodity that it can produce more cheaply than other communities. It may mean producing a commodity which could be produced more cheaply somewhere else. But in any case the community produces that which it can produce at the greatest advantage. To quote Professor Warren, who has recognized this principle in his studies of types of farming: "Sometimes a product that does not pay well

---

[8] For a statement of the principle see F. W. Taussig, *Principles of Economics* (3d rev. ed.; New York: Macmillan, 1921), Vol. I, chap. xxxiv; also by the same author, *Some Aspects of the Tariff Question* (Cambridge: Harvard University Press, 1915), chap. iii, and *International Trade* (New York: Macmillan, 1927), chap. iv. The principle is also fully developed and given a wider application in John D. Black, *Introduction to Production Economics* (New York: Holt, 1926), chap. v.

must continue to be raised, because there is nothing better."[9] A community in this situation, unfortunate though it may be, is making the most of its limited opportunities. It is not wasting its resources in the production of things which give an even smaller return.

The principle of comparative advantage explains why certain types of farming are carried on in certain localities. This is particularly true of regions devoted to one-crop farming. There are, for instance, many crops besides cotton which could be raised in the South very cheaply. If the South fails to produce them, it is probably because cotton is more profitable. To preach diversification under such circumstances, desirable as diversification might be for some reasons, is to ignore a fundamental law of economics. Farmers will continue to produce that which yields them the greatest return. Corn-belt farming illustrates the same phenomenon. It is said that sugar beets could be grown more cheaply in the corn belt than in the sugar-beet areas of Michigan and Colorado. They are not grown in the corn belt to any appreciable extent because corn is more profitable.[10] As Professor Warren states the principle as applied to types of farming: "It is not sufficient that a crop pay; it must pay better than the other crops with which it competes." And again: "No matter how profitable a product is, it must give way to a competing product that pays better."[11]

The gain to society from territorial division of labor is clearly apparent. There is a greater output at less expenditure of capital and labor if each community can specialize in the lines of activity for which it is best fitted. The high standard of living in the United States is sometimes attributed to the fact that the United States comprises a large area having varied natural resources and climate, yet within which trade is unrestricted by tariff barriers or by high transportation costs.

Territorial specialization and the gains that go with it are dependent upon cheap transportation. A community cannot specialize unless it has a market for its products and unless it can obtain other commodities which it needs. The gain to society from the production of goods where they can be produced most advantageously can easily be offset by high transportation charges, making specialization impossible. Adam Smith's remark that the division of labor is limited by the extent of the market,[12] although true of any form of division of labor, is clearly true of geographical division of labor. Without cheap transportation there can be little territorial division of labor. This relationship is clearly illustrated by early railroad history in the United States. The early specialization

---

[9] G. F. Warren, *Farm Management* (New York: Macmillan, 1913), p. 93.

[10] J. W. Tapp, "The Principle of Comparative Advantage Applied to Farm Management Studies of Regional Competition between Farms," 8 *Journal of Farm Economies* 417, 419 (1926).

[11] Warren, op. cit., pp. 92 and 93.

[12] *Wealth of Nations* (1776), Bk. I, chap. iii.

of the West in agricultural products, of the South in cotton, and of New England in manufactured goods required cheap transportation. Many of the early railroads were projected to further this specialization.

TRANSPORTATION AND LARGE-SCALE PRODUCTION

A fourth manner in which transportation reduces prices is through the encouragement it lends to large-scale production with its resulting economies. By large-scale production we mean production by large production units—the firm, or, in some cases, the plant—rather than by a larger number of small production units. Large-scale production may exist which is not dependent upon cheap transportation. But in many instances large-scale production means that either raw materials or finished products must be transported long distances. This is not possible if freight rates are too high. The milling industry would not be characterized by large-scale operations if high freight rates made impossible the transportation of wheat for long distances. Similarly, high freight rates on flour would make large-scale milling impossible except in regions of dense population. The meat-packing industry likewise could not have been carried on on such a large scale as it was in Chicago for many years if meat packers had been obliged to rely on a local supply of livestock or on a local market for their products.

TRANSPORTATION AND COMPETITION

There is still another way in which cheap transportation tends to reduce prices. As transportation costs are reduced, a larger and larger number of producers are able to sell in a given market. High freight rates, on the other hand, restrict the area within which goods can be distributed. It follows that low freight rates will tend to increase the number of competitors supplying a market. This gives purchasers the benefit of increased competition and tends to keep prices down.

TRANSPORTATION AND URBANIZATION

The growth of large cities is dependent upon cheap transportation. The urbanization of the United States has been one of the characteristic features of the last 100 years. Before the days of railroads, large cities were located where water transportation was available. Lack of transportation facilities hindered the development of large inland cities because, in the absence of cheap transportation, the necessity of deriving a food supply from the immediate locality acted as a limiting factor.

The extent to which the larger cities of the United States derive perishable food products from great distances is shown by figures compiled several years ago by the United States Department of Agriculture.

In 1949, for instance, New York City obtained 32,910 carloads of certain fresh fruits and vegetables from California, more than 3,000 miles away, and 19,623 carloads from Florida. New York obtained 2,341 carloads of carrots from California and 662 from Texas. It obtained 4,878 carloads of lettuce from California and 1,668 from Arizona. It obtained 6,343 carloads of potatoes from Maine, 1,739 from California, and 1,609 from Idaho.[13] Chicago in 1949 received 55,711 carloads of certain fresh fruits and vegetables. These originated in 42 out of the 48 states and in seven foreign countries.[14] Even fresh milk is daily supplied to New York, Boston, and other large cities from farms several hundred miles away. Of course, it would be possible for these cities to derive their food supplies from nearer sources, but these facts indicate how cheap transportation has freed cities from the necessity of relying on a local source of supply.

Cheap transportation not only makes large cities possible, but it has been a positive stimulus to urban concentration. We have noted that improved transportation has stimulated both large-scale production and geographical division of labor. Large-scale production leads to the concentration of manufacturing and the creation of large industrial cities. And both large-scale production and territorial division of labor increase the amount of trade that takes place. The activities that accompany trade, such as storing, processing, packaging, advertising, merchandising, financing, professional risk bearing, and some of the activities related to transportation, all tend to be performed in urban centers and hence lead to the establishment of trade and transportation centers. Thus urbanization is an indirect result of cheap transportation through the latter's stimulus to large-scale production, territorial division of labor, and the resulting exchange of commodities.

LOW FREIGHT RATES IN THE PUBLIC INTEREST

Since cheap transportation contributes to the prosperity of society by making possible the production of more goods at less cost, it follows that the public interest requires the lowest possible freight rates. The lower the rates, the greater will be the benefit to society. Nowhere is this more apparent than in connection with geographical division of labor. Each reduction in transportation charges develops possibilities of specialization and exchange that were not apparent before. Conversely, any increase in transportation charges breaks down geographical division of labor.

There is almost always a possibility of specialized production in a

---

[13] U.S. Department of Agriculture, Production and Marketing Administration, *Carlot Unloads of Certain Fruits and Vegetables in 100 Cities . . . , Calendar Year 1949* (Washington, D.C., 1950), p. 59.

[14] Ibid., p. 17.

given region if transportation charges can be reduced. It is for this reason that the public is constantly seeking lower freight rates and attempting to develop cheaper agencies of transportation. Agitation for the government to improve rivers and develop water transportation is rooted in the same cause. The constant pressure to reduce freight rates is often embarrassing to the railroads because the cost of providing the service imposes limits to the reduction of charges. It is natural for the railroads to meet this situation at times by diverting attention from the rate level and emphasizing the importance of good service.[15] Although the importance to shippers and to the public of adequate service is not to be minimized, it remains true that the interest of the public lies in getting transportation service at the lowest possible cost. If the cost of transportation could be reduced to zero, i.e., if transportation could be put in the class of "free goods," society would be the gainer. The chief obstacle to the production of goods in the most favored locations and under the most favorable conditions would be removed. But this must be forever impossible, since the movement of goods from place to place requires the expenditure of energy and human effort.

LIMITS TO FREIGHT-RATE REDUCTIONS

We have seen that it is clearly in the interest of society to have cheaper and cheaper transportation. It is not to be inferred, however, that the cost of providing the transportation service can be ignored or that freight rates can be reduced below the cost of service. Railroads in the United States are privately owned and must compete with other enterprises for capital. In the absence of a government guaranty this means that investors in and owners of railroads must be rewarded if further capital is to be forthcoming. But even if railroad earnings were guaranteed by the state, or if the government owned the railroads and could support them from the proceeds of taxation, it would still be economically unsound to ignore costs of transportation in fixing rates. If the savings in production costs occasioned by territorial specialization are offset by greater expenditures incurred in transporting the goods, there is an economic loss to society by the process. Professor Taussig has stated the principle thus: "No gain comes from carrying a thing from one place to another unless it can be produced at the first place so much more cheaply that it can afford the cost of carriage to the second. Ability to stand the transportation charge is the test of the utility of the

---

[15] For example, Mr. Howard Elliott, former chairman of the Northern Pacific Railroad Company, once said: ". . . the true interest of the people is not so much in the level of rates—the first cost of transportation—as in the character and adequacy of the service." *The Economics of Modern Transport* (New York: Committee on Public Relations of the Eastern Railroads, 1926), p. 10.

carriage."[16] There is a social loss in the transportation of goods if the cost of transporting them is greater than the saving caused by production under the most favorable conditions.[17]

TREND OF FREIGHT RATES IN THE UNITED STATES

The introduction of railroads greatly reduced transportation charges in the United States. The cost of transporting wheat and corn over ordinary highways was sometimes estimated to have been 20 cents per ton-mile before the era of railroads.[18] Even after railroads were constructed, the possibility of inducing a greater flow of traffic by lower rates and so reducing unit costs of operation was not realized at once. The chart in Figure 1–1, showing the revenue per ton-mile received by the railroads for transportating freight from 1867 to 1970, can be used to indicate the average charge for shipping freight by rail in the United States.[19] The revenue per ton-mile declined from 19 mills in 1867 to 7.2 mills in 1899. The variations were unimportant from 1899 to 1916. Thereafter the revenue per ton-mile rose from 7.2 mills in 1916 to 12.9 mills in 1921. From this level the average revenue per ton-mile decreased to 9.4 mills in 1941, 1942, and 1943. Postwar freight-rate increases brought this figure to a new high of 14.9 mills in 1953. In 1970 the revenue per ton-mile was estimated to be 14.3 mills.

The trends in the volume of freight traffic are shown in Figure 1–2.[20] It is estimated that in 1882 the railroads of the United States transported about 39,300,000,000 ton-miles of freight.[21] In 1890 the railroads carried 76,207,000,000 ton-miles. This figure increased to 450,189,000,000 ton-miles in 1929. The steep decline after 1929 was caused by the severe depression which set in late in that year. The low point reached during

---

[16] Taussig, op. cit., Vol. II, p. 391. The same point is developed in a different manner and more elaborately in H. T. Newcomb, *Railway Economics* (Philadelphia: Railway World Publishing Co., 1898), chaps. xii and xiii.

[17] As will be developed in later chapters, it is not necessary that the charge for a particular service should cover a proportionate share of all the overhead or constant expenditures of a railroad in order to prevent economic waste. Under some conditions no social loss is involved if certain services are performed at a charge that covers only out-of-pocket costs.

[18] Poor, op. cit., p. 11.

[19] Revenue per ton-mile is not a wholly satisfactory index of freight rates, since changes in the proportion of low-grade or high-grade freight or in the ratio of short-haul to long-haul traffic affect the figure although freight rates remain unchanged. The figures prior to 1889 are from H. T. Newcomb, *Changes in the Rates of Charge for Railway and Other Transportation Services*, U.S. Department of Agriculture, Division of Statistics, Bulletin No. 15 (rev. ed., 1901), p. 14. Figures since 1889 are from the Interstate Commerce Commission. Figure for 1970 is estimated.

[20] Figures are from the Interstate Commerce Commission.

[21] Interstate Commerce Commission, Bureau of Statistics, *Railway Statistics before 1890* (mimeographed, 1932).

FIGURE 1–1.   Freight Revenue per Ton-Mile of U.S. Railroads, 1867–1970

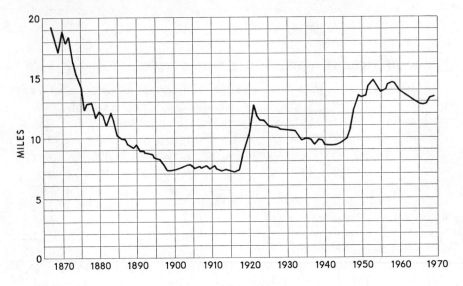

the depression was 235,308,000,000 ton-miles in 1932. The effect of World War II was to increase the ton-miles of freight carried to a high of 740,586,000,000 in 1944. As might be expected, the postwar volume was considerably below the 1944 peak; it reached a low of 529,111,000,-000 in 1949. A new all-time high, however, was attained in 1970 when the total ton-miles reached nearly 794 billion.

The figures shown above relate to railroad traffic. They do not represent the total intercity movement of freight. In fact, the railroad proportion in 1963 was only 41 percent of the total ton-miles. The rest was divided among water carriers, motor carriers, pipelines, and airlines.[22] The total volume of intercity freight in 1970 was over 1.9 trillion ton-miles.

SIZE OF THE TRANSPORTATION INDUSTRY

Since reduced transportation charges greatly increase the amount of freight which is transported, it follows that, as freight rates are reduced, the amount of capital and labor devoted to transportation will tend to increase.

It has been estimated that the investment in privately owned transportation facilities in the United States in 1966 amounted to $192,496,000,000.[23] In addition there is a large amount of public investment in transport facilities—highways, waterways, ports and harbors,

---

[22] See p. 20 *infra* for the division of traffic among the five modes of transport.

[23] Transportation Association of America, *Transportation: Facts and Figures* (Washington: Transportation Association of America, 1971), p. 26.

FIGURE 1–2. Ton-Miles of Freight Carried by Railroads of the United States, 1890–1970

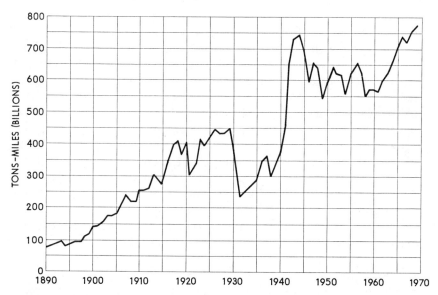

and airway and airport facilities. Unfortunately, the amount invested in public transportation facilities cannot be stated even approximately. This is because public expenditure figures usually do not distinguish between capital investment and operating and maintenance expenditures. Neither is allowance made for depreciation and obsolescence of the older facilities constructed.

The number of persons employed in transportation and related industries in 1968 has been estimated at more than 10,000,000, or over 13 percent of the total labor force.[24] The size and importance of the transportation industry is also revealed by the fact that over 19 percent of our total annual expenditure for goods and services is made directly or indirectly for transportation.[25]

It is clear from the figures given above that very large amounts of capital and labor are devoted to the business of transporting persons and property from place to place. Probably a larger proportion of the total productive energy of society is being expended on transportation today than in any other period of history.

IS TRANSPORTATION WASTEFUL?

Some observers, looking at the enormous quantities of freight hauled long distances in the United States, have concluded that much of this

---

[24] Ibid., p. 22.

[25] Ibid., p. 3.

transportation is unnecessary and wasteful. The waste of energy spent in the useless hauling of goods is held to be an important factor in making prices high. Those who take this position suggest as a remedy the decentralization of industry and local self-sufficiency. The production of flour, for example, by thousands of small mills scattered throughout the grain-growing regions and the slaughter and packaging of meat in small establishments located near the supplies of livestock have been advocated.[26]

Although it must be admitted that there is some wasteful transportation performed by our railroads, the contentions of those who allege an enormous social waste in our transportation system are not justified. The criticism fails to recognize the advantages that accrue from geographical division of labor, large-scale production, and the location of industries at the most favored sites. The decentralization of industry, and production on a small scale over much more extensive areas, would of course reduce the amount of transportation service required and the amounts spent on freight transportation. This would undoubtedly be more than offset by higher costs of production. The decentralization of industry and the creation of a multitude of smaller plants, such as flour mills and packing houses, could easily be brought about by the simple expedient of increasing freight rates. We would be worse off rather than better off if this were done. Increased rates would give local producers an advantage, enabling them to undersell the more distant producers who might be securing the advantages of large-scale production and who might, because of favorable location, have cheaper costs of production.

Increases in freight rates that occurred during and after World War I had a tendency to decentralize certain industries. Rate increases which followed World War II had a similar effect. The Interstate Commerce Commission, in its *Annual Report* in 1949, pointed out that cumulative increases in freight rates following the war, ranging from 53 to 61.5 percent in different parts of the country, had tended to disturb many processes of production and distribution, "with permanent changes in the economic map of the country."[27]

TRANSPORTATION COSTS VERSUS OTHER COSTS OF PRODUCTION

The belief that transportation is wasteful is based upon a misunderstanding of the relation between transportation costs and other expenses of production. In the typical case of geographical division of labor,

---

[26] For a vigorous exposition of this point of view see Henry Ford, *My Life and Works* (Garden City, N.Y.: Doubleday, Page, 1922), pp. 230–33.

[27] Interstate Commerce Commission, *Annual Report, 1949*, pp. 2–3. See also Donnald E. Church, *Effect of Increases in Freight Rates on Agricultural Products*, U.S. Department of Agriculture, Circular No. 847 (Washington, D.C., 1950), pp. 33–34.

transportation costs are in part substituted for other costs of production. This can be illustrated by Figure 1–3.

Suppose there are two places, A and B, either of which can produce all the goods of a certain kind which are consumed in M. Suppose, furthermore, that the cost of producing the goods is $6 per ton at A and $3 per ton at B. The cost of transporting the goods from A to M is $2 per ton and from B to M $6 per ton. Although the goods can be produced at B for $3 per ton, B cannot supply the market at M, for the delivered price would be $9 ($3, cost of production, plus $6, freight), while A can lay the goods down in M for $8 ($6, cost of production, plus $2,

FIGURE 1–3.   Relation of Transportation Costs to Other Costs of Production

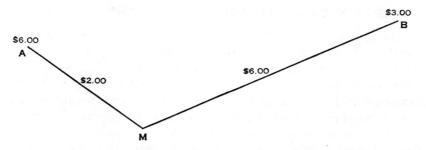

freight). Now suppose rates are reduced by one half. A could now sell the article in M for $7 ($6 plus $1), but B can sell it for $6 ($3 plus $3). As a result, B now supplies the market. The price has been reduced from $8 to $6. The former price of $8 represented a cost of production at A of $6, and $2 for freight. The present price of $6 represents a cost of physical production of $3 and freight of $3. Although the price has been reduced, more is spent on freight than before, and less is spent on the cost of physical production. Transportation costs have been substituted for other costs of production. From this it will be seen that the money spent on transportation is well spent if the saving in cost of production at the producing point is greater than the freight rate.

The situation in Figure 1–3 is perhaps unusual in that the decline in freight charges forces the nearby production point out of business in favor of a more distant producing point. Although this sometimes happens, a more usual situation is for the lowered freight rates to enable a distant producer to share the market with the nearer producer. The nearby producer is not always displaced by a more distant producer but is forced to divide the market with him.

The illustration used above demonstrates another and related result which frequently follows reductions in rates. As the freight rates are reduced, the rate becomes a larger proportion of the delivered price of the good. Thus, in the illustration, when A supplied the market, the freight rate represented one fourth of the delivered price. When the rates were reduced and B began to supply the market, the rate represented one half the delivered price.

The real significance of improved transportation cannot be understood until it is realized that, as transportation rates are reduced, more money is spent for transportation and less for creating form utilities. One of the earliest expositions of this was by a French engineer named Dupuit. After a demonstration of the principle, M. Dupuit said: "The ultimate purpose of a means of transportation ought not to be to reduce the expenses [total expenses] of transportation, but to reduce the expenses of production."[28]

TRANSPORTATION AND ECONOMIC DEVELOPMENT

The analysis which we have presented in this chapter makes it apparent that the development of a transportation system is essential to the economic development of a nation. The eagerness with which governments throughout the world engaged in railroad building in the 19th century is evidence of awareness of that fact. Our own history, with its encouragement of railroad building, and even earlier, with the building of canals and turnpikes, demonstrates public realization of the importance of transportation in the economic development of the country.[29]

In many undeveloped areas in the 19th century, railroads were built, often by colonial powers, to enable the resources of those areas to be developed. In countries like India, Burma, Argentina, and Australia, early railroads were designed largely to connect the interior with seaports and thus provide an outlet for agricultural and other products of the areas and at the same time provide means by which manufactured products from industrialized areas of the world could reach new markets.

The developmental function to be performed by a transport system is evidenced not only by government participation in the construction of transport facilities but also by the motives that often led to private investment in means of transport. Even where railways were built by private capital, investment was often motivated by expectations of indirect economic gains—appreciation of land values, greater profitability of agriculture and other enterprises—rather than by profits of railway operation. Farmers and merchants were often induced to invest in American railroads in anticipation of such gains. It has been estimated that the increase in land values along an eighty-mile strip of the Union Pacific

---

[28] ". . . le but final d'une voie de communication doit être pas de diminuer les frais de transport, mais de diminuer les frais de production." Dupuit, "De la mesure de l'utilité des travaux publics," 8 *Annales des ponts et chaussées*, 2d Ser., 351–52 (1844). The same principle is described in Black, op. cit., pp. 813–14.

[29] See Chapters 5 and 6.

Railroad, attributable solely to the existence of the railroad, amounted to over $152 million in 1880.[30] It has been observed that much of the British capital investment in railroads in Argentina was motivated by the indirect gains expected to flow to the British owners of enterprises engaged in various commercial activities in that country.[31] Nearly everywhere, indirect economic gains have been a factor in investment decisions with respect to railroads.

CHOICE OF A TRANSPORT SYSTEM

In the 19th century the development of a transport system was synonymous with railroad building except where the construction of canals or the improvement of natural waterways was feasible. Undeveloped and underdeveloped areas today have other alternatives. The most important of these is a system of highways adapted to the use of motor vehicles. Air transport provides a further alternative; so likewise do pipelines, although for a very limited use. What form transport investment will take depends on many factors including relative capital costs, relative operating and maintenance costs, the volume of traffic, the nature of the commodities to be carried, the distances they are to be moved, and even the relative demands on the supply of foreign exchange. In many newly developing countries, highways, because of their land-access function and their availability for use by anyone, may be given a preference over other modes of transport. This does not foreclose investment in other modes of transport in special circumstances or under special conditions. In fact, an appropriate mixture of the various modes of transport may be the wisest course of action if care is taken to avoid uneconomic duplication.

SELECTED REFERENCES

References of a general nature dealing with the significance of improved transportation are: Dionysius Lardner, *Railway Economy* (New York: Harper, 1850), chap. i; Frederick A. Cleveland and F. W. Powell, *Railroad Promotion and Capitalization* (New York: Longmans, 1909), chap. v; Harry T. Newcomb, *Railway Economics* (Philadelphia: Railway World Publishing Co., 1898), chap. i; Stuart Daggett, *Principles of Inland Transportation* (4th ed.; New York: Harper, 1955), chap. ii; Truman C. Bigham, *Transportation: Principles and Problems* (New York: McGraw-Hill, 1946), chap. i; Marvin L. Fair and Ernest W. Williams, Jr., *Economics of Transportation* (rev. ed.; New York: Harper, 1959), chaps. i–ii; Charles E. Landon, *Transportation: Principles, Practices, Problems* (New York: Wm. Sloane Associates, 1951),

---

[30] Robert W. Fogel, *The Union Pacific Railroad: A Case in Premature Enterprise* (Baltimore: Johns Hopkins Press, 1960), pp. 99–102.

[31] H. S. Ferns, *Britain and Argentina in the Nineteenth Century* (Oxford: Oxford University Press, 1960), pp. 337–38.

chap. i; Russell E. Westmeyer, *Economics of Transportation* (New York: Prentice-Hall, 1952), chap. i; Alastair M. Milne, *The Economics of Inland Transport* (London: Pitman & Sons, 1955), chaps. i–ii; Dudley F. Pegrum, *Transportation: Economics and Public Policy* (Homewood, Ill.; Richard D. Irwin, Inc., 1963), chap. i.

For a discussion of geographical division of labor and the principle of comparative advantage, any standard text on the principles of economics would be helpful. The following references are especially good on this subject: F. W. Taussig, *Principles of Economics* (3d ed.; New York: Macmillan, 1921), Vol. I, chap. xxxiv; Taussig, *Some Aspects of the Tariff Question* (Cambridge: Harvard University Press, 1915), chap. iii; Taussig, *International Trade* (New York: Macmillan, 1927), chap. iv; John D. Black, *Introduction to Production Economics* (New York: Holt, 1926), chap. v.

On transport planning for underdeveloped countries see Edwin T. Haefele, "Transport Planning for Undeveloped Areas," in *Papers—Fourth Annual Meeting, Transportation Research Forum* (1963), pp. 342–46; also a series of papers on "The Role of Transportation in Economic Development," *American Economic Review*, vol. 52, No. 2 (1962), pp. 386–415. Books on the subject are Wilfred Owen, *Strategy for Mobility* (Washington, D.C.: Brookings Institution, 1964); Gary Fromm, ed., *Transport Investment and Economic Development* (Washington, D.C.: Brookings Institution, 1965); George Wilson, *The Impact of Highway Investment on Development* (Washington, D.C.: The Brookings Institution, 1966); A. R. Prest, *Transport Economics in Developing Countries* (New York: Praeger, 1969).

Chapter 2

THE TRANSPORTATION SYSTEM OF THE UNITED STATES

In the preceding chapter the economic significance of low-cost and efficient transportation was pointed out. It may be worth while at this juncture to take an over-all look at the transportation system that has been created in the United States. In so doing, we shall also point out certain facts about the transportation system and its development which give rise to some of the transportation problems of present concern.

THE FIVE MODES OF TRANSPORT

There are five modes of transport that figure prominently in the intercity movement of persons and property. These are: (1) railroad transportation, (2) transportation by water, (3) motor-vehicle transportation on public highways, (4) pipeline transportation, and (5) transportation by air. The relative importance of these modes of transport can be measured in various ways.

Comparison on Basis of Mileage

Table 2–1 shows the miles of railroads in the United States, the miles of improved waterways, the miles of rural highways, the miles of oil pipelines exclusive of the crude-oil gathering lines, and the miles of airways under the control of the Federal Aviation Administration. The figures given are not all for the same year, but year-to-year changes are so small in relation to the total miles that they do not significantly affect the proportions of the total miles of improved "ways" represented by the various transportation media.

It will be observed that the miles of highways exceed the mileage of all the other transportation media. Even if we confine the comparison to highways with a high-type surface—and most intercity highway transportation is presumably confined to such highways—the mileage still exceeds that of the railroads. The miles of improved waterways are limited somewhat by the mileage of streams that can be made navigable and also by the expenditures of the government in improving them. The mileage of waterways shown in Table 2–1 excludes the coastwise and intercoastal ocean routes and the open water of the Great Lakes.

TABLE 2–1. Miles of Improved Transportation Facilities in the United States

Agency	Mileage	Date
Railroads[a]	207,005	1969
Improved waterways[b]	25,543	1970
Rural highways[c]	3,161,726	1969
Non-surfaced	770,401	
Soil-surfaced, slag, gravel, stone	1,229,486	
Bituminous surfaced, low-grade	656,485	
High-grade surface	505,354	
Pipelines (oil)[d]	149,051	1969
Airways (federal)[e]	278,977	1969
"Low frequency"	155	
"Very-high frequency"	170,651	
Jet routes	108,171	

a Interstate Commerce Commission, *Transport Statistics in the United States, 1969*, Part I, *Railroads*, p. 3.
b American Waterways Operators, Inc., *Inland Waterborne Commerce Statistics, 1970* (Washington, D.C., 1970), p. 1.
c Bureau of Public Roads, *Highway Statistics, 1969*, Table M–3.
d Trunk lines only. From American Petroleum Institute, *Petroleum Facts & Figures, 1971 ed.*, p. 215.
e Federal Aviation Administration, *FAA Statistical Handbook of Aviation, 1970 ed.*, p. 11.

Comparison on Basis of Traffic Volume

The most significant measure of the importance of the different modes of transport is on the basis of traffic carried. When the comparison is on this basis, it is necessary to treat freight and passenger business separately.

Table 2–2 shows the total ton-miles of freight carried by the five transport media in 1969 and the proportion of the total which each car-

TABLE 2–2. Volume of Intercity Freight Traffic, Public and Private by Modes of Transport, 1970*

Agency	Ton-Miles (in millions)	Percent of Total
Railroads (mail & express included)	768,000	39.97
Highways	412,000	21.44
Inland waterways (including Great Lakes)	307,000	15.98
Pipelines (oil)	431,000	22.43
Airways (including mail, express & excess baggage)	3,400	.18
Total	1,921,400	100.00

* From Interstate Commerce Commission, *Annual Report*, 1971, p. 119.

ried. The figures in the table do not include coastwise and intercoastal shipping, for which ton-mile statistics are not regularly compiled. The transportation by water included in the table is that on the inland waterways, including the Great Lakes. The table shows that the railroads carried less than 40 per cent of the total ton-miles. Highways carried about 21 percent of the total. Had the figures been in terms of tons of freight rather than ton-miles, highways would have shown up somewhat better. This is because the average haul by motor vehicles is much less than the average haul by rail. Thus, motor carriers show a smaller proportion of the total ton-miles of freight transported than they do of the tons transported. It will be noted that the proportion of total freight carried by air is very slight.

Table 2–3 shows the relative importance of the various modes of

TABLE 2–3. Intercity Movement of Persons, by Modes of Transport, 1970*

Agency	*Passenger-Miles* *(in millions)*	*Percent* *of Total*	*Percent* *of For-Hire*
Railroads......................	10,900	.92	6.86
Highways:			
Buses......................	25,300	2.14	15.93
Private automobiles............	1,026,000	86.60	. . .
Total highway..............	1,051,300	88.73	
Inland waterways (including			
Great Lakes....................	4,000	.34	2.52
Airways (domestic)...............	118,600	10.01	74.69
Total....................	1,184,800	100.00	100.00

° From Interstate Commerce Commission. Percent of for-hire computed on the assumption that rail, bus, waterway, and air transportation is mostly for hire.

transport in the intercity movement of persons. Pipelines, of course, are omitted from this table. It will be noted that over 86 percent of the intercity movement of persons was by private automobile. If we consider only the for-hire carriers, the railroads accounted for about 7 percent of the passenger-miles. Buses accounted for nearly 16 percent, and airways for nearly 75 percent.[1] The airlines have become more important than the railroads in terms of passenger-miles, in contrast to their still almost negligible position in the movement of the nation's freight.

Table 2–4 shows that the proportion of the total traffic carried by each mode of transport has been undergoing a change over a period of years. In 1940 the railroads carried 61 percent of the total ton-miles of freight; by 1970 the railroad share had dropped to 40 percent. On the other hand, motor transport, which accounted for about 8 percent of

---

[1] The table overstates somewhat the relative position of air transportation in the for-hire segment of the industry, since the number of passenger-miles given in the table includes an undisclosed amount of private-plane travel.

the total ton-miles in 1940, accounted for over 21 percent in 1970. The proportion of intercity passenger-miles transported by the railways in 1940 was nearly 9 percent of the total movement, but by 1970 it had dropped below one percent. The airway share of passenger traffic, on the other hand, increased from less than one half of 1 percent in 1940 to 10 percent in 1970.

In interpreting the changing proportion of traffic carried by the different modes of transport, it should be realized that each mode of transport, as it develops, creates new traffic and does not merely take traffic away from the older forms of transport. Motor-vehicle transportation

TABLE 2–4. Trends in the Distribution of Freight and Passenger Traffic Among the Principal Modes of Transport*

Agency	*Percent of Total Ton-Miles*				*Percent of Total Passenger-Miles*			
	1940	*1950*	*1960*	*1970*	*1940*	*1950*	*1960*	*1970*
Railroads.................	61.34	58.69	43.51	39.97	8.71	8.12	2.86	0.92
Highways................	7.91	12.39	22.50	21.44	90.46	89.57	92.37	88.73
Inland Waterways........	19.13	16.19	16.76	15.98	0.46	0.30	0.27	0.34
Pipelines (oil)............	11.62	12.70	17.18	22.43	—	—	—	—
Airways................	a	0.03	0.06	0.18	0.37	2.01	4.50	10.01

° Interstate Commerce Commission.
a Less than 0.01 percent.

has created a vast amount of intercity movement, particularly of persons, that would not have occurred if the motor vehicle had not developed. Air transport likewise has created a movement of persons and property that would not have occurred if air transport had not been available. The increasing share of the total traffic which is carried by highway and by air, therefore, arises partly from the creation of new traffic and not entirely from the diversion of traffic from the older modes of transport.

Differences in Composition of Traffic

There are differences in the composition of the traffic carried by the different modes of transport. Table 2–5 shows in a general way the differences in the composition of the traffic of railroads, motor carriers, and water carriers. It will be observed that products of mines comprise nearly half of the tonnage carried by railroads and more than half of that carried by water carriers. Manufactured articles, although comprising a substantial proportion of the traffic of all three modes shown in the table, constitute nearly 87 percent of the traffic of motor carriers. We are not able to include airlines in Table 2–5 since no figures are published which show a breakdown of their traffic. It is well known, however, that the preponderance of air freight consists of manufactured articles.

The differences in the nature of the traffic moved by the various modes of transport are the resultant of a number of factors. Important among these are the type of facilities required by the different commodities, the character and quality of the service provided, and the rates charged. The rates charged reflect to some extent the differences in transport costs by the different modes of transport. Thus the high costs of air transport account for the high rates charged; the low rates often

TABLE 2–5. Composition of Freight Traffic—Railroads, Water Carriers, Motor Carriers, 1960*

	Class I Railroads (percent of tons carried, c.l.)	Class A & B Water Carriers (percent of tons carried)	Class I Motor Carriers (intercity) (percent of tons carried, t.l.)
Products of agriculture....................	10.84	7.45	2.80
Animals & products.....................	0.97	0.06	3.17
Products of mines......................	48.60	58.73	5.96
Products of forests.....................	7.04	10.63	0.62
Manufactures & miscellaneous............	32.03	23.11	86.93
Forwarder traffic......................	0.51	0.02	0.53
Total.........................	100.00	100.00	100.00

* From Interstate Commerce Commission, *Transport Statistics in the United States for 1960* and *Motor Carrier Freight Commodity Statistics, Class I Common & Contract Carriers of Property for 1960.*

found in water transportation result in part from economies in the movement of goods by water, and partly from the fact that the costs associated with the construction and maintenance of improved waterways are borne by the taxpayers. Rates are not always based on transport costs, however. Railroads, as we will see later,[2] often make rates on particular articles or for particular movements either higher or lower than cost of service justifies—higher if conditions of demand will permit; lower if conditions of demand require it. The other modes of transport follow a similar policy to a lesser degree. Competition between the different modes of transport also results in rates not strictly related to cost.

TRANSPORTATION SYSTEMS

It seems desirable at this point to turn from an overall look at the five modes of transport to a closer examination of each of the five transport "systems," for each of the five modes is dependent upon a specialized system of "ways," structures, and facilities to enable it to function.

[2] Chapter 7.

THE RAILROAD SYSTEM

Mileage

In 1969 the railroad system of the United States comprised 207,005 miles of road.[3] The miles of track, however, amounted to 341,546. The miles of track exceeds the miles of road, or line, because of the existence of yard tracks and sidings and because some main lines consist of two or more parallel tracks.

The network of railroad lines is shown in Figure 2–1. A glance at the map reveals that the railway mileage is very unequally distributed throughout the country. The lines are thickest in the densely populated and industrialized sections and thinnest in the sparsely populated areas.

Classification of Railroads according to Size

The Interstate Commerce Commission classifies railroads according to size for statistical and accounting purposes into Class I and Class II railroads. Class I railroads are those having annual operating revenues which average $5,000,000 or more over a three-year period. Class II railroads are those with operating revenues under $5,000,000.[4]

In 1970 there were 70 Class I line-haul operating railroads. Class II lines numbered 276. Even the Class I operating railroads vary greatly in size. Table 2–6 groups the Class I operating railroads according to the mileage operated in 1969.

Although there is a large number of small railroads, the larger roads own and operate by far the greatest proportion of the total mileage of the country. The ownership of the 207,005 miles of road in the country in 1969 was distributed as follows:[5]

	Mileage Owned
Class I railways	178,099
Class II railways	9,245
Lessors to Class I railways	16,819
Lessors to Class II railways	280
Others	2,562
Total	207,005

Thus about 86 percent of the mileage was owned by Class I railways, and they also operated another 8 percent which was owned by other

[3] Interstate Commerce Commission, *Transport Statistics in the United States, 1969, Part I, Railroads,* p. 3.

[4] Prior to 1956 the Commission recognized three classes of railroads, viz., Class I, with operating revenues of $1,000,000 or more; Class II, with operating revenues between $100,000 and $1,000,000; and Class III, with operating revenues of less than $100,000. From 1956 to 1965, Class I railroads were those with operating revenues exceeding $3,000,000.

[5] Interstate Commerce Commission, *Transport Statistics in the United States, 1969, Part I, Railroads,* p. 3.

railroads. The number of separate railroad companies tends to become fewer, year by year, as a result of railroad consolidations and abandonments.

Efforts have been made from time to time to encourage the consolidation of the railroads into a few large systems. The Transportation Act of 1920 directed the Interstate Commerce Commission to draw up a plan for the consolidation of the railroads into a limited number of sys-

TABLE 2–6.   Distribution of Class I Operating Railroad Companies According to Mileage Operated, 1969*

Mileage Operated	*Number*
Over 10,000	5
5,000 to 10,000	13
2,000 to 5,000	5
1,000 to 2,000	9
500 to 1,000	15
100 to 500	25
Under 100	1
Total	73

* From Interstate Commerce Commission, *Transport Statistics in the United States, 1969, Part I, Railroads.*

tems.[6] All actual consolidations were to conform to this plan. A plan was drawn up by the Commission in 1929;[7] and a major revision, as far as the East was concerned, was made in 1932.[8] The Commission's plan called for seventeen systems, with a few railroads assigned to the two large Canadian systems, the Canadian National and the Canadian Pacific. Since there was no power given to the Interstate Commerce Commission to compel consolidation, and since the carriers were not anxious to consolidate in accordance with the plan drawn up by the Commission, nothing came of this effort, and the Transportation Act of 1940 repealed the provisions relating to the making of a consolidation plan and requiring that any consolidations occurring should conform to the plan. Other suggestions have been made to consolidate the railroads into an even smaller number than the 19 systems proposed by the Commission.[9]

The low earnings of the railroads and the increased competition that

---

[6] See Chapter 11.

[7] 159 ICC 522.

[8] 185 ICC 403.

[9] See Federal Coordinator of Transportation, *Regulation of Railroads,* 73d Cong., 2d Sess., Senate Doc. No. 119 (1934), pp. 21–29 and 106–23; Carroll Miller, Address, in *Proceedings of the 49th Annual Convention of the National Association of Railroad and Utilities Commissioners, 1937,* p. 25; see also Commissioner Miller's concurring opinion in *Fifteen Percent Case, 1937–1938,* 226 ICC 41, 158; and for more recent proposals see Gilbert Burck, "A Plan to Save the Railroads," *Fortune,* August, 1958, p. 82; J. W. Barriger, *Why Consolidation,* Remarks at Transportation Management Institute, Stanford University (mimeographed, 1959).

FIGURE 2–1.   U.S. Railroads Classified by Number of Tracks and by Train Control Methods

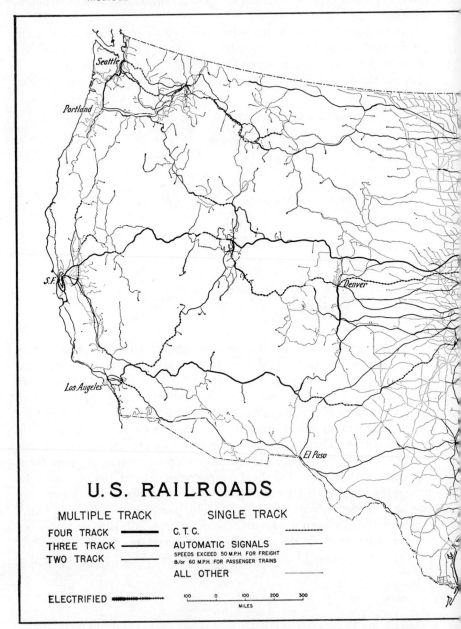

From Edward L. Ullman, *American Commodity Flow* (Seattle: University of Washington Press, 1957). See also large-scale color edition, *U.S. Railroads* (New York: Simmons-Boardman, 1950).

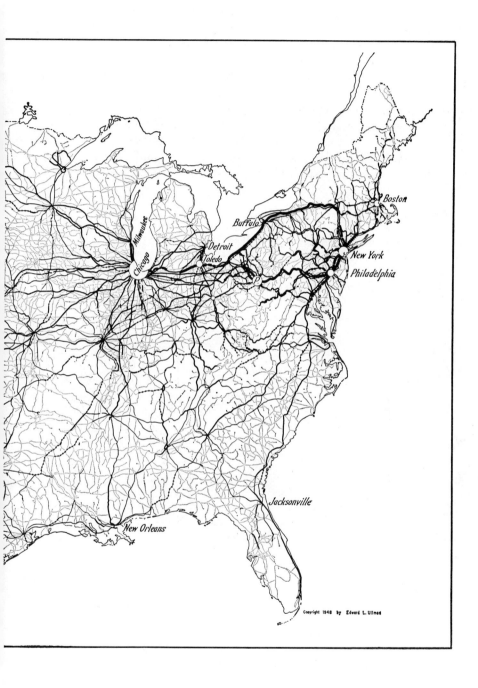

Copyright 1948 by Edward L. Ullman

railroads have faced from other modes of transport led to a revival of consolidation proposals in the early 1960s. These efforts seem to have been motivated by a desire to effect operating economies, to eliminate excess capacity in the industry, and to place the railroads in a stronger position to meet the competition of the other modes of transport. Strategic and defensive considerations relating to possible adverse effects of other proposed consolidations also played a part. Several consolidations, even among larger railroads, have resulted from this movement, as will be noted later in this chapter; and other consolidations of major railroads may occur in the near future. The issues of public policy involved in consolidation proposals will be discussed in a later chapter.[10]

Geographical Grouping of Railroads

The Interstate Commerce Commission groups the railroads into three geographical areas or districts—Eastern, Southern, and Western—for

FIGURE 2–2. Railroad Districts

From Interstate Commerce Commission, *Transport Statistics in the United States, 1968, Part I, Railroads*, p. 2.

statistical purposes. These districts are shown in Figure 2–2. A few rail roads have operations in two or more districts, but in such instances they are assigned to the district in which most of their operations lie. Prior to 1966, each district was divided into "Regions," of which there were

---

[10] Chapter 14.

eight in all. Beginning in 1966, only the districts have been recognized for statistical purposes.

Below are listed the larger railroads or railroad systems in each district. It should be recognized that within a system there may be several separately operated lines controlled through stock ownership, and an operating company may operate properties of another railroad company under a lease.

Eastern District

There are three large systems in the Eastern District, namely:

The Penn Central
The Chesapeake & Ohio—Baltimore & Ohio
The Norfolk & Western

The Penn Central was formed in 1968 by the merger of the Pennsylvania Railroad Co. and the New York Central Railroad Co., both railroads having extensive mileage in Eastern District.[11] Both the New York Central and the Pennsylvania had numerous controlled lines. The Penn Central was required to take over the New York, New Haven & Hartford, a New England road.

A second system in Eastern District centers about the Chesapeake & Ohio Railway Co. which owns over 93 percent of the stock of the Baltimore & Ohio Railroad Co. The two roads jointly control the Western Maryland through stock ownership. The control of the Baltimore & Ohio by the Chesapeake & Ohio was authorized in 1962.[12]

The third large system in Eastern District is the Norfolk & Western. In 1959 this road, which was principally a coal-carrying railroad in the so-called Pocahontas Region, absorbed the Virginian Railway Co. serving the same area. In 1964 and 1967, the Interstate Commerce Commission approved the merger of the New York, Chicago & St. Louis Railroad, commonly known as the Nickel Plate, into the Norfolk & Western and also the lease of the Wabash Railroad and eventually its purchase.[13] The Commission also required the Norfolk & Western to acquire control of the Erie-Lackawanna Railroad Co.,[14] the Delaware & Hudson Railroad Corporation, and the Boston & Maine Corporation. The Boston & Maine later rejected this opportunity to be included in the system.

---

[11] 327 ICC 475 (1966); 328 ICC 304 (1966); 330 ICC 328 (1967); 331 ICC 643 (1967); 331 ICC 754 (1968); 334 ICC 25 (1968).

[12] 317 ICC 261.

[13] 324 ICC 1; 330 ICC 780.

[14] The Erie-Lackawanna Railroad Co. came into existence in 1960 by the merger of the Erie Railroad Co. and the Delaware, Lackawanna & Western.

Southern District

In the Southern District there are three major rail systems, namely:

Seaboard Coastline
Southern Railway
Illinois Central

The Seaboard Coast Line Railroad Co. came into existence in 1967 by the merger of the Atlantic Coast Line Railroad and the Seaboard Air Line Railroad Co. The merger had been approved by the Interstate Commerce Commission in 1964[15] but was the subject of prolonged litigation before it was finally accomplished.[16] The Seaboard Coast Line controls the Louisville & Nashville through ownership of stock. In 1969 the Louisville & Nashville purchased a portion of the line of the Chicago & Eastern Illinois, which, with some additional arrangements, gave the Louisville & Nashville an entrance into Chicago. Merger of the Monon Railroad into the Louisville & Nashville was authorized in 1970.

A second system in the South is the Southern Railway. The Southern controls the Central of Georgia through ownership of nearly all of its stock.

The Illinois Central Railroad Co. is principally a north-south line from Chicago into the South but it is classified with the southern railroad systems. In 1971 the Interstate Commerce Commission authorized the merger of the Illinois Central and the Gulf, Mobile & Ohio Railroad into a new corporation, the Illinois Central Gulf Railroad Company.[17]

Western District

In the Western District we have five so-called "transcontinental" lines, namely:

Burlington Northern Lines
Chicago, Milwaukee, St. Paul & Pacific
Union Pacific
Atchison, Topeka & Santa Fe
Southern Pacific

The Burlington Northern Lines came into existence in 1970 as a result of the merger of the Great Northern Railway Co., the Northern Pacific Railway Co., and the Chicago, Burlington & Quincy Railroad Co., together with some smaller lines in the area. The Burlington had long been controlled by the Northern Pacific and the Great Northern jointly.

---

[15] 320 ICC 122.

[16] *Seaboard Air Line R. Co.* v. *United States*, 382 U.S. 154 (1965).

[17] Finance Docket No. 25103.

The Chicago, Milwaukee, St. Paul & Pacific operates in much the same area as the Burlington Northern, but somewhat south of it in the eastern part of the district.

The Union Pacific Railroad Co. occupies the central transcontinental route. Important subsidiaries are the Los Angeles and Salt Lake Railroad Co., the Oregon Short Line Railroad Co. and the Oregon-Washington Railroad & Navigation Co.

The Atchison, Topeka & Santa Fe, with its subsidiaries, extends from Los Angeles and San Francisco to Chicago.

The Southern Pacific Co., the southernmost of the transcontinental lines, extends from Los Angeles to New Orleans, and also north and south along the Pacific Coast. A subsidiary of the Southern Pacific is the St. Louis Southwestern Railway Co.

In addition to the transcontinentals there are other important railroads in the Western District. Listed below are those operating a thousand miles or more of line and not affiliated with our transcontinental lines.

Chicago & North Western
Chicago, Rock Island & Pacific
Denver & Rio Grande Western
Kansas City Southern
Missouri-Kansas-Texas
Missouri Pacific
St. Louis–San Francisco
Soo Line (controlled by Canadian Pacific)
Texas & Pacific (controlled by Missouri Pacific)
Western Pacific

THE HIGHWAY SYSTEM

Mileage and Type

We have already noted that the total mileage of highways, exclusive of streets in municipalities, was 3,161,726 in 1969. These roads vary from primitive ungraded roads in thinly settled areas to the most modern multilaned divided highways designed to move large numbers of vehicles at high speeds. Over 500,000 miles have a high-grade surface adequate for carrying heavy loads.[18] This represents about 16 percent of the total.

Although about 89 percent of the state primary highways in 1969 were two-lane roads, about 10 percent consisted of four lanes or more.[19]

---

[18] P. 20 *supra*.

[19] Most of the figures concerning highways herein are taken from Bureau of Public Roads, *Highway Statistics, 1969*.

Highway Administration

The rural mileage consists of three systems, if the roads are classified by the governmental unit responsible for their administration. These are (1) local roads, that is, roads under control of local units of government—counties, towns, and townships; (2) state highways, for which the state governments are responsible; and (3) a relatively small mileage under federal control, consisting of roads in national parks, national forests, reservations, and the like. Before the development of the automobile, practically all roads were under the jurisdiction of local governments. Even before the development of the automobile, however, a demand had arisen for better rural highways and for more effective planning and supervision of them. In 1891 New Jersey established a system of state aid to local units of government for highway purposes. New Jersey's example was soon followed by other states. It was soon discovered that something more than state financial aid to local units of government was necessary if better roads were to be provided. Beginning in 1893, state highway commissions or departments were established which were given complete jurisdiction over a system of state highways. Massachusetts was the first state to adopt this plan. Since 1924 all states have had a system of state highways for which the state assumes responsibility. In most states some roads are in the state system, while other roads remain under the control of local units of government. A few states have taken over the management and financing of all rural highways in their jurisdictions. In this group are North Carolina, West Virginia, and Delaware. In Alabama, Virginia, and Nevada much or most of the county road mileage has been taken over by the state.

In 1969, the rural road mileage of the country was divided among administrative jurisdictions as follows:

	Miles
Under state control	704,341
Under county control	1,733,494
Under town or township control	510,692
Other local roads[20]	30,523
Under federal control[21]	182,676
Total	3,161,726

It should be noted that there are also 72,212 miles of roads or streets in municipalities which are under state control as urban extensions of state highways.

---

[20] Principally special highway districts.

[21] Mileage principally in federal parks, forests, reservations, etc.

The Federal-Aid Highway System

The Federal Highway Act of 1921 provided for the designation of a system of "federal-aid highways," originally limited to 7 percent of the total mileage of rural roads in the state. These roads were to be improved with the aid of federal funds, matched by the state, but they were to be maintained by the states. The Federal-Aid Primary System was to include the most important highways in the state, i.e., the main channels of highway traffic.[22] In 1944 there were added to the Federal-Aid Primary System the extensions of these roads through urban communities. The Federal-Aid Highway Act of 1944 created another system of federal-aid highways, which has come to be called the "Federal-Aid Secondary System." The Act refers to these roads as "principal secondary and feeder roads, including farm-to-market roads, rural free delivery mail and public school bus routes." In 1969, the Federal-Aid Primary System comprised 256,499 miles; most was part of state highway systems. The Federal-Aid Secondary System consisted of 633,595 miles.[23]

The "National System of Interstate and Defense Highways"

The Federal-Aid Highway Act of 1944 provided for the selection of a system of highways to be known as the "National System of Interstate Highways," not exceeding 40,000 miles in extent and "so located as to connect by routes, as direct as practicable, the principal metropolitan areas, cities, and industrial centers, to serve the national defense, and to connect at suitable border points with routes of continental importance in the Dominion of Canada and the Republic of Mexico." These routes were selected by the Bureau of Public Roads and by state authorities, and are the most heavily traveled highways in the country. Most of the roads comprising this system were already in the Federal-Aid System, but the Act provided that any mileage in the new system not already included in the federal system should be added thereto without regard to any mileage limitations.

The Federal-Aid Highway Act of 1956 changed the name of this system to the "National System of Interstate and Defense Highways," commonly known as the "Interstate System." A 1958 Act raised the mileage limitation of the system to 42,500. The special provisions for financing the Interstate System and the Federal-Aid highways are described in a later chapter.[24] The Interstate System is scheduled for completion in 1974 or 1975; and the total cost is presently estimated as $56.5

---

[22] There is no necessary relation between the highways which are given U.S. route numbers for the convenience of the motorist and the highways in the Federal-Aid System.

[23] Bureau of Public Roads, *Highway Statistics, 1969*, p. 186.

[24] Chapter 27.

FIGURE 2–3. The "National System of Interstate and Defense Highways"

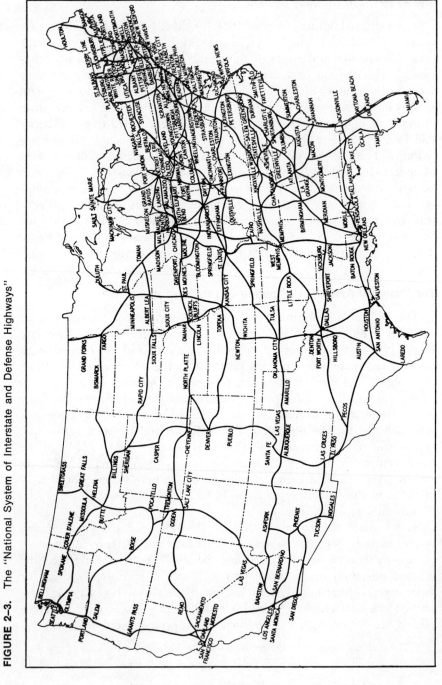

From 25 *Public Roads* 20 (1947).

billion. The location of the roads in the Interstate System is shown on the map in Figure 2–3. When completed, the Interstate System is expected to carry nearly 25 percent of all rural travel.[25]

Serious consideration is being given to further expansion of the Interstate System when the presently planned system is completed. Another proposal is to create a supplemental system, intermediate to the regular Federal-Aid System and the Interstate System.[26]

Motor Vehicles and Highway Use

Table 2–7 shows the growth in the number of passenger motor vehicles registered in the United States over a period of years. The large number of motor vehicles is both a cause and an effect of the highway

TABLE 2–7. Passenger-Car Registrations in the United States, Privately Owned*

Year	Number	Year	Number
1895	4	1935	22,494,884
1900	8,000	1940	27,372,397
1905	77,400	1945	25,694,926
1910	458,377	1950	40,190,632
1915	2,332,426	1955	51,960,532
1920	8,131,522	1960	61,430,862
1925	17,439,701	1965	74,903,163
1930	22,972,745	1968	83,276,317

*Automobile Manufacturers Association, *Automobile Facts and Figures* (Detroit, annual).

construction programs. Improved highways are built to accommodate the growing number of motor vehicles, but the better the highways, the greater is the resort to highway transport. Table 2–8 shows the number of motor trucks registered over a similar period.

TABLE 2–8. Motor-Truck Registrations in the United States, Publicly and Privately Owned*

Year	Number	Year	Number
1910	10,123	1940	4,886,262
1915	158,506	1945	5,076,310
1920	1,107,639	1950	8,598,962
1925	2,569,734	1955	10,288,804
1930	3,674,593	1960	11,914,249
1935	3,919,305	1965	14,795,051
		1969	17,885,836

*Automobile Manufacturers Association, *Motor Truck Facts* (Detroit, annual).

[25] Department of Transportation, *1968 National Highway Needs Report* (Washington, D.C.: Government Printing Office, 1968), p. 44.

[26] Ibid., pp. 41–45.

Intensity of Highway Use

The volume of traffic on the different portions of the highway system varies greatly. The Bureau of Public Roads noted that in 1950 approximately 40 percent of the local rural roads carried fewer than 10 vehicles per day.[27] Whatever the exact figure may be today, it must be obvious to all observers that there are thousand of miles of roads in rural America that carry only a small number of vehicles per day. On the other hand, nearly a third of the Interstate System carries from 5,000 to 10,000 vehicles per day, with a small mileage—117 miles—carrying over 40,000 vehicles per day in 1969.[28]

In terms of vehicle-miles, the greatest use of the highways is made by the private automobile. According to a study by the Bureau of Public Roads, the personal passenger vehicle accounted for 80.1 percent of the total vehicle-miles on the streets and highways in 1968; buses accounted for 0.5 percent; trucks, 19.3 percent.[29]

Use of the highways in private trucking exceeds the use by for-hire truckers. It was found by the Bureau of the Census that in 1967 only 4.4 percent of the trucks inventoried in its survey were for-hire trucks.[30] The others included farm vehicles, trucks used in construction work and manufacturing, in wholesale and retail trade, and in various other activities.

In a later chapter we will have more to say about the organization and characteristics of the for-hire trucking industry.[31]

Highway Standards

The quality of the highways, as we have noted, ranges from ungraded dirt roads to the most modern multiple-lane divided highways constructed to carry large volumes of traffic at high speeds. Of the 3,162,000 miles of rural road in 1969, about 24 percent was unsurfaced; 39 percent had a low-type surface (mostly slag, gravel, or stone); 21 percent had an intermediate-type surface (bituminous or bituminous treated, but of low load-bearing capacity); 16 percent had a high-type surface (bituminous with a high load-bearing capacity, bituminous concrete, Portland cement concrete, etc.).[32]

Where traffic volume is heavy on main traveled routes, it becomes desirable to separate the through and local traffic, since the latter inter-

---

[27] Bureau of Public Roads, *Highways in the United States* (Washington, D.C.: U.S. Government Printing Office, 1951), p. 13.

[28] Bureau of Public Roads, *Highway Statistics, 1969*, p. 209.

[29] Office of Planning, Bureau of Public Roads, "Travel by Motor Vehicles in 1968 and Related Data," 36 *Public Roads* 16 (1970).

[30] Automobile Manufacturers Association, *Motor Truck Facts, 1969*. p. 29.

[31] Chapter 28.

[32] *Highway Statistics in the United States, 1969*, p. 183.

feres with expeditious through movement and increases hazards. For this reason more and more of the heavily traveled through highways are constructed as "freeways" or "limited-access" highways. This means that traffic may enter or leave the highway only at designated points. Cross-traffic at grade is frequently eliminated by the elevation or depression of either the main highway or the crossroads so that cross-traffic can pass over or under the main highway. This feature of the highways and the complicated intersections required to eliminate left turns greatly increase their cost.

Design standards for the National System of Interstate and Defense Highways have been approved by the American Association of State Highway Officials.[33] Much of the system will consist of four-lane divided highways. Crossings at grade will be eliminated except in sparsely settled rural areas. Control of access is required for all sections of the Interstate System.

INLAND WATERWAY SYSTEM

Exclusive of the Great Lakes–St. Lawrence System, the inland waterways of the United States consist of 25,543 miles of improved waterways. The mileage, classified by depth, is as follows:[34]

Depth	Miles
14 feet & over	4,666
12 to 14 feet	4,033
9 to 12 feet	6,976
6 to 9 feet	3,516
Under 6 feet	6,352

Since a depth of nine feet is required for most modern barges, the mileage suitable for the movement of modern barges is limited to 15,675 miles.

The inland waterways consist of five distinct systems: (1) the Great Lakes System, (2) the Mississippi River System, (3) the coastal rivers, (4) the intracoastal waterways, and (5) the New York Barge Canal. These waterways are shown in Figure 2–4.

The Five Waterway Systems

The Great Lakes System. The Great Lakes, including the St. Lawrence outlet, are a natural waterway extending from Duluth, Minne-

---

[33] American Association of State Highway Officials, *A Policy on Design Standards, Interstate System* (Washington, D.C., 1967).

[34] American Waterways Operators, Inc., *Inland Waterborne Commerce Statistics, 1970* (Washington, D.C., 1971), p. 1.

FIGURE 2–4. Principal Waterways of the United States

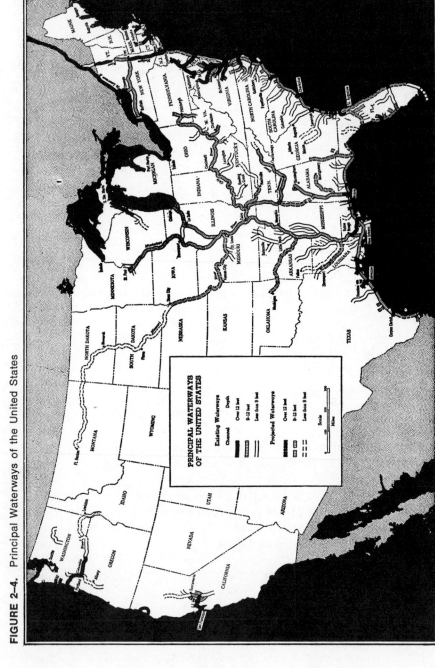

From President's Water Resources Policy Committee, *A Water Policy for the American People* (Washington, D.C.: U.S. Government Printing Office, 1950), Vol. I, pp. 206–7.

sota, and Superior, Wisconsin, at the head of Lake Superior, and from Chicago, Illinois, near the southern extremity of Lake Michigan, to the port of Montreal, Quebec. Part of this route, of course, lies in Canada. Expenditures have been necessary for the construction of locks between Lake Superior and Lake Huron and between Lake Erie and Lake Ontario. Other expenditures have been required to improve connecting channels.

As a result of a cooperative arrangement made between the governments of Canada and the United States, improvement of the St. Lawrence River between Montreal, Quebec, and Ogdensburg, New York, was undertaken in 1954 after many years of unsuccessful efforts to get Congress to authorize the project. This extensive improvement, involving the construction of new and deeper canals, new and larger locks and dams, and the deepening of river channels, provides a twenty-seven-foot channel between Montreal and Lake Ontario, and enables ocean-going vessels of much greater capacity than formerly to enter the Great Lakes. The "St. Lawrence Seaway," as it is called, was formally opened on June 26, 1959. The Seaway principally affects the foreign commerce of the United States and the development of the Lake ports and adjacent areas. Since the deepened channel is mostly in Canada, providing access to the sea, the domestic commerce on the Great Lakes is affected only indirectly by the Seaway.

The Great Lakes have an area of more than 95,000 square miles and have 8,300 miles of shore line. From Duluth to Montreal the distance is 1,340 miles, and from Chicago to Montreal it is 1,260 miles.[35]

Mississippi River System.   This system comprises the Mississippi River, from Minneapolis and St. Paul to its mouth, and certain tributary streams, notably the Ohio, the Missouri, and the Illinois rivers. The canal from Lake Michigan at Chicago to the Illinois River unites this system with the Great Lakes.

Coastal Rivers.   In addition to the Mississippi River System, mention should be made of the numerous other rivers which flow into the Atlantic and Pacific oceans or into the Gulf of Mexico. The map of the waterways of the United States indicates where these navigable streams are found.

Intracoastal Waterways.   The intracoastal waterways consist of a connected series of bays, inlets, canals, and protected channels extending along the Atlantic and Gulf coasts. The Atlantic Intracoastal Waterway extends from Massachusetts Bay to Miami, Florida. The Gulf Intracoastal Waterway extends from St. Marks River, Florida, to the Mexican border.

The New York Barge Canal.   The New York Barge Canal is the old

---

[35] National Resources Planning Board, *Transportation and National Policy* (Washington, D.C.: U.S. Government Printing Office, 1942), p. 50.

Erie Canal, reconstructed and in part relocated, together with certain branch canals. The canal is maintained and operated by the state of New York.

Floating Equipment

The physical characteristics of the various waterways are quite different. As a result, floating equipment which is used on one waterway may not be usable on another. On the Great Lakes, large vessels are used. In fact, special types of vessels have been developed for the Great Lakes traffic which are particularly efficient carriers of such bulk cargoes as grain, coal, and ore. On the Mississippi River and its tributaries, most of the freight is transported in steel barges, which are towed in groups by means of Diesel-powered propelling units. Barges are lashed tightly together and pushed by the towing vessel. Towboats have been developed for use on the Mississippi River System which commonly handle 20 to 30 barges in a single tow. On the Atlantic and Gulf Intracoastal waterways, and in open water along the Atlantic, Gulf, and Pacific coasts where rough water may be encountered, towboats pull the barges, which are attached by a hawser.

Inland Waterway Traffic

Most of the traffic on the inland waterways is in barge lots. It consists largely of bulk commodities, and also of commodities of low value in relation to their weight. In 1970 about 36 percent of the tonnage carried on the inland waterways, exclusive of the Great Lakes, consisted of petroleum and its products; bituminous coal and lignite constituted another 21 percent of the total; sand and gravel constituted 12 percent; grain and grain products including soybeans, 5 percent; chemicals, 5 percent. This leaves only 21 percent for all other commodities.[36]

A large part of the traffic on the inland waterways is "proprietary" traffic, that is, traffic transported by the owners, mostly large industrial concerns. More will be said about inland water transportation in a later chapter.[37]

THE AIR TRANSPORT SYSTEM: AIRWAYS AND AIRPORTS

The Airways

Air transport is dependent upon an elaborate and highly technical system of aids to guide the course of planes in flight and to control their

---

[36] Computed from figures in American Waterways Operators, Inc., *Inland Waterborne Commerce Statistics, 1970* (Washington, D.C., 1971), p. 5.

[37] Chapter 31.

movements in the interest of safety. This is known as the airway system.

In 1969 the airway system consisted of 278,977 miles of routes equipped in varying degrees with such facilities.[38]

Included in the airway system are various facilities provided at airports for the safe arrival and departure of planes. These include airport traffic control towers, various radar facilities, approach lighting systems, and instrument landing facilities. For flight between airports, navigational facilities include traffic control centers, long-range radar, and direct voice communication between pilots and air traffic controllers. The principal navigational aid, largely superseding the older radio range beacons, is the "omnirange," which enables the pilot to determine his precise location at any time. Flight service stations are also provided which house the facilities for the air-ground communications necessary for the air traffic control system and for the air navigation facilities, and which also provide flight assistance that the pilots may require.

The airway facilities are provided by the federal government and are under the control of the Federal Aviation Administration in the Department of Transportation.

The airway facilities are used by commercial airlines, private planes, and the military. In 1969 over 21 million planes were handled at FAA air route traffic control centers. Of these 62 percent were for air carriers, 16 percent for general aviation, and 22 percent for the military.[39]

Airports

Air transportation requires airports as well as airways. At the close of 1969 there were 9,909 civil airports in the United States, if we include those that are used jointly by civil aviation and the military but exclude heliports and seaplane bases.[40] Of the 9,909 airports, 817 were *air carrier* airports, and it is with these that we are principally interested in this book. The other airports are known as *general aviation* airports. The air carrier airports are nearly all publicly owned, that is, owned by cities, counties, states, or the federal government. Some are owned by special airport "authorities," with several cities or other governmental units participating.

Most air carrier airports serve general aviation to some extent. Congestion at some of the larger airports led to the designation of 147 airports in 1968 as "reliever" airports to divert general aviation from the congested airline-served airports.[41]

Airports vary greatly in size, even those that are air carrier airports.

---

[38] Federal Aviation Administration, *FAA Statistical Handbook of Aviation, 1970 ed.*, p. 11.

[39] Ibid., p. 13.

[40] Ibid., p. 45.

[41] Federal Aviation Administration, *FAA Statistical Handbook of Aviation, 1968 ed.*, p. 6.

The largest airports are in the large air traffic "hubs" since these are the points at which air traffic concentrates. O'Hare International Airport in Chicago handled over 29 million passengers in 1968; John F. Kennedy International Airport in New York, over 19 million; Los Angeles International Airport 20 million; San Francisco International Airport, 13.5 million.[42]

The principal users of the federal airways system and of the larger airports are the commercial airlines. The bulk of the domestic air transportation is performed by 11 domestic trunk lines and 9 local service carriers. The organization of the air transport industry and some of its characteristics are reserved for discussion in a later chapter.[43]

PIPELINES

Pipelines constitute a specialized transportation system for the movement of crude oil, gasoline, and other liquid products of petroleum, and natural gas. On a limited scale, pipelines are being used for the transportation of pulverized coal, ores, and other solids in suspension in water. Although some 35 nonliquid products are known to be transported by pipelines, it is not likely that such pipelines will become common carriers unless and until transportation of solid articles through pipelines in capsules becomes feasible.[44] Here, we shall confine our attention to pipelines used for transporting petroleum and its products. An extensive system of pipelines, however, for the transportation of natural gas is also in existence.

As of December 31, 1969, the oil pipeline system of the United States totaled 222,621 miles.[45] Of this total, 149,051 miles consisted of crude-oil lines, and 73,570 were refined-oil or "products" lines. The investment in carrier property of the pipeline companies which report to the Interstate Commerce Commission, that is, interstate lines that have a common-carrier status, was over $3.5 billion in 1970.[46]

Crude-Oil Lines

The crude-oil lines on December 31, 1969 consisted of 73,830 miles of trunklines and 75,221 miles of gathering lines.[47] The latter connect individual oil wells with the trunklines.

Gathering lines range from 2 to 26 inches in diameter, but over 90

---

[42] Ibid., *1969 ed.*, pp. 80, 83, 85. The figures include both arrivals and departures.

[43] Chapter 33.

[44] R. E. Boston, "Some Economic Aspects of Solids Pipelines." In *Papers—Fifth Annual Meeting, Transportation Forum* (1964), p. 34. See also a series of articles in *Papers—Eighth Annual Meeting* (1967), pp. 379–429.

[45] American Petroleum Institute, *Petroleum Facts & Figures, 1971 ed.*, p. 215.

[46] Interstate Commerce Commission, *Annual Report, 1971*, p. 136.

[47] American Petroleum Institute, op. cit., p. 215.

percent of the mileage of gathering lines in 1968 consisted of pipe of 6 inches or less in diameter.[48] Gathering lines are often laid on the surface of the ground. They are easily relocated as new wells are opened and old ones become exhausted.

Trunklines in operation in 1968 varied in diameter from 3 to 42 inches, with 8-inch pipe the predominant size.[49] Pumping stations are located at intervals along the pipeline route, commonly 35 to 40 miles apart, although the distances between them vary with the topography of the country, the size of the pipe, and the viscosity of the oil. Sometimes crude petroleum is heated to lessen its viscosity and to facilitate pumping. Storage tanks are generally a necessary adjunct of the pipeline system. Successive lots of oil, even of different grades and characteristics, can be transported through pipelines without very much mixture of the batches.

Products Lines

As we have noted there were 73,570 miles of refined-oil or products lines in 1969. Product lines, like the crude-oil lines, are mostly controlled by major oil companies. Some mileage, however, is owned by railroad companies.[50]

The importance of pipelines in the transportation system is shown by the fact, pointed out earlier in this chapter, that pipeline traffic represented over 22 percent of the total ton-miles of intercity freight in the United States in 1970.[51]

In 1968, pipelines transported 74.1 percent of the crude oil carried in the United States; water carriers transported 18.6 percent; trucks, 7.1 percent; and railroads, 0.2 percent.[52] Railroad traffic in crude oil is principally from new fields to which pipelines have not been laid, from fields that produce so little oil that the construction of pipelines is not justified, special movements of one sort or another, and some shipments to small refineries.

Pipelines transport large quantities of gasoline and other refinery products, but other forms of transport carry the bulk of this traffic. In 1968 the total tonnage of refined petroleum products carried in domestic transportation was distributed among the various modes of transport as follows: water carriers, 25.7 percent; trucks, 41.4 percent; pipelines, 30.4 percent; and railroads, 2.5 percent.[53]

---

[48] U.S. Department of the Interior, Bureau of Mines, *Mineral Industry Surveys,* Dec. 23, 1968.

[49] Ibid.

[50] See Chapter 36.

[51] P. 20 supra.

[52] American Petroleum Institute, op. cit., p. 273.

[53] Ibid.

HISTORICAL DEVELOPMENT OF THE FIVE MODES OF TRANSPORT

The five modes of transport developed, of course, at different times in our history. This is shown graphically by the chart in Figure 2–5. The period of time covered by the chart is from 1780 to the present, and it thus embraces nearly the whole period of time that the United States has existed as an independent nation. A glance at the chart shows the comparatively recent development of motor-vehicle and air transport.

In 1780 only two of the five modes of intercommunity transport were available—transportation by water and by road. Both of these were quite primitive in character.[54] Steamboats made their appearance in 1807 and

FIGURE 2–5.   Development of the Five Modes of Transport

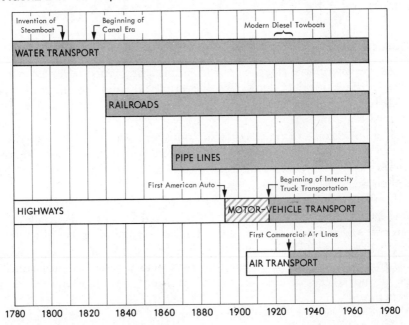

developed rapidly for use on the western rivers. Steamboats on inland rivers, however, declined rapidly after the Civil War. Although the movement of barges in tows, propelled by steam-driven barges, dates back to the early 1850s, modern barge transportation on inland waterways began in the 1920s with the use of the Diesel engine to propel towboats.

The highway transportation of the early decades of our national existence was of little importance, except for that which was carried over

---

[54] Prerailroad transportation is described in Chapter 5.

turnpikes, either public or private. After the coming of the railroads, highway transport was principally local in character until the advent of the automobile made its influence felt in the early 1900s. The development of motor trucks for over-the-road use was greatly stimulated by World War I in 1917, and intercity trucking developed rapidly after the war.

Railroad transportation had its beginning in 1830; pipeline transport in 1865. The invention of the airplane in 1903 ushered in that form of transport, but commercial air transport did not begin until 1926.

The fact that the different modes of transport have developed at different times has had important consequences. It gives rise to the problem of adjustment of the older forms of transportation to the new. The development of railroads brought an end to the era of canal building and caused the decline of steamboating on the inland rivers. The rise of modern barge transport on inland waterways has caused concern to some of the railroads. The development of motor vehicles and improved highways has had serious effects on railroad freight and passenger traffic. Air transportation has had an important effect on the railroads. As previously noted, the proportion of the total freight of the country which is moved by air is almost negligible, but the intercity passenger-miles transported by the airlines is many times that transported by the railroads. In fact, the development of air transport together with the rise in the use of the private automobile threatens the extinction of intercity rail transportation of passengers unless it is revived by public subsidy. As each new form of transport develops, it finds a place in the transportation system, but not without repercussions on the older forms. Some of the problems of the relation between the different modes of transport are discussed in the final chapters of this book.

ORGANIZATION OF THE DIFFERENT MODES OF TRANSPORT

There are certain differences in the organization of the various modes of transport which have important economic consequences and which give rise to some current problems with respect to transportation policy.

In the organization of water, highway, and air transport, there is a separation of the function of providing, owning, and maintaining the basic transport facilities—waterways, highways, and airways and airports—and the function of performing transportation services over them. For the most part, highways are provided by state and local units of government and are financed by them with some federal aid. Inland waterways are mostly under the control of the federal government and are improved and maintained out of Congressional appropriations. Airway facilities are provided, maintained, and operated by the federal government; airports, particularly those used by commercial airlines, are generally municipal undertakings, although financed in part with federal funds. In these forms of transport, therefore, the basic facilities are publicly owned and maintained. Federal, state, and local governments, however, do not generally engage in the business of transporting persons or property for hire over the publicly provided facilities.[55] This is left to private enterprise. Individuals also have the right to use the publicly provided facilities for the purpose of travel or for the transportation of their own property.

Railroads and pipelines are organized on a different basis. Here the functions of providing, owning, and maintaining the basic facilities and the function of performing transportation service over or through them are combined. Railroad companies own their own rights of way, build and maintain their tracks, and transport persons and property over the railroad for hire. Pipeline companies build and maintain pipeline facilities and move petroleum and its products through them.

ECONOMIC RESULTS OF PUBLIC PROVISION OF TRANSPORT FACILITIES

We may now consider some of the economic consequences which flow from the policy of public provision of certain types of transportation facilities and note certain problems to which this policy has given rise.

First, one result of government provision of transportation facilities is that various social and political considerations and indirect economic gains are important factors in determining whether such facilities shall be constructed. The construction of highways is determined largely by considerations of general social benefits—such as farm-town communication, postal service to rural areas, access to schools—and indirect economic gains—such as easier marketing, enlargement of trade areas, effect on land values, and the like. Even national-defense considerations are involved in some highway planning. In the development of waterways, national-defense considerations frequently play a part, and so do the indirect economic gains which may accrue to particular industries or to particular localities. In the development of airway facilities and airports, national defense has been an important consideration. Indirect economic gains to the business interests of particular communities also play a part in the development of municipal airports. In some countries the building of railroads was undertaken by the government for political and national-defense reasons.

A second result of government provision of basic transportation facilities is their more rapid development. This follows from the fact that

---

[55] For many years the federal government owned the Inland Waterways Corporation, which provided water transportation service on certain waterways under the name of the Federal Barge Lines, but this service was sold to a private corporation in 1953. There is also an increasing amount of municipal ownership of urban transportation systems.

social and political considerations and indirect economic benefits rather than profitability of operation are factors in determining whether the facilities shall be provided. Private capital would not, in the absence of subsidy, provide transportation facilities for which the possibility of profitable operation was remote. Our present highway system has developed more rapidly and on a much vaster scale than would have occurred if we had been forced to rely on private toll roads, even for an arterial system of intercity highways. Our inland waterway system is certainly more extensive than private capital would have provided if it had had to reply for its remuneration on a system of tolls. The rapid expansion of air transportation in recent years has been dependent in large measure on the system of federally financed airways and on publicly provided airports. It might be noted also that in some countries the construction of railroads was undertaken by the government because private capital was not able, for one reason or another, to provide railroads as rapidly or as extensively as the public wanted. Even in the United States some railroad construction was undertaken by the states and by local units of government for the same reason,[56] and it was only by heavy subsidy to private companies that we got many of our railroads built into the pioneer West.

Another consequence of government provision of certain transportation facilities is that it makes monopoly in transportation more difficult. Publicly provided waterways, highways, airways, and airports are open to all users. Competing carriers may operate over the same highways, waterways, or airways. A number of airlines can utilize the same airports. No one has a monopoly in the use of publicly provided facilities.[57]

One further result of government provision of waterways, highways, and air transportation facilities should be noted because of its bearing on current transportation problems. Government provision and maintenance of such facilities may result in the taxpayer, rather than the user of the facilities, paying part of the cost of transportation. Whether such a result ensues depends upon the extent and adequacy of special user charges imposed upon the users of these facilities. Part of the cost of transportation by water is borne by the taxpayers, since, with the exception of the Panama Canal and the St. Lawrence Seaway, the federal government exacts no tolls or other charges for the use of the waterways improved and maintained at government expense. Airways are provided, maintained, and operated at the expense of the federal government and, until recently, without any special exaction from the airlines for the use of these facilities.[58] Airlines pay landing fees and other charges for the use of

---

[56] See pp. 121–24, infra.

[57] The number of carriers operating over a particular highway, waterway, or air route may be restricted under regulatory laws requiring certificates of public convenience and necessity or other operating authority of carriers. This device may be used to protect a carrier from competition.

[58] See Chapter 35 for recent developments leading to airway user charges.

publicly provided airports, but it is questionable whether they contribute their fair share of the cost of maintaining and operating them. Whether motor carriers, through special fees and taxes, contribute a fair share of highway costs has long been debated. One of the most controversial issues in recent years has been the question whether user charges should be imposed for the use of publicly provided waterways and airways and whether existing user charges made for the use of public highways are adequate. Problems which arise from the fact that motor carriers, water carriers, and airlines make use of publicly provided facilities, while railroads and pipelines provide their own basic facilities, are discussed in later chapters of this book.[59]

From the broad survey of the transportation system of the country and of some of its peculiarities of organization we may return to a consideration of how transportation costs and the rates which shippers pay affect commodity prices, the location of industries, the size of market areas, and types of agriculture. The next two chapters will concern themselves with these matters.

SELECTED REFERENCES

General descriptions of the transportation system of the United States may be found in the following: Stuart Daggett, *Principles of Inland Transportation* (4th ed.; New York: Harper, 1955), chap. i; Truman C. Bigham and Merrill J. Roberts, *Transportation: Principles and Problems* (New York: McGraw-Hill, 1952), chap. v; Charles E. Landon, *Transportation: Principles, Practices, Problems* (New York: Wm. Sloane Associates, 1951), chap. iii; Roy J. Sampson and Martin T. Farris, *Domestic Transportation: Practice, Theory and Policy* (Boston, Houghton Mifflin, 1966), chaps. 3, 4 and 5. There is much descriptive and factual material relating to all modes of transportation in Martin T. Farris and Paul T. McElhiney, *Modern Transportation: Selected Readings* (Boston: Houghton Mifflin, 1967).

---

[59] See particularly Chapter 36.

Chapter 3

FREIGHT RATES AND PRICES

Certain facts about the relationship between freight rates and the prices of commodities may be inferred from points raised in the first chapter. The subject deserves more detailed attention, however, since there has been much confusion concerning the effect of freight rates, and of changes in freight rates, on the prices of the commodities transported. Although the analysis which follows is in terms of freight rates charged by carriers for hire, the same principles apply when producers, dealers, or consumers perform their own transportation services, provided the term "transport costs" is substituted for the term "freight rates."

It is commonly maintained that the farmer pays the freight on both the things which he buys and the things which he sells. On the goods which he buys, the price is said to be the factory price plus transportation and other costs incurred in getting the goods to the farm. On the things which the farmer sells, the price received is said to be the price at the consuming markets less transportation charges. Thus the farmer pays the freight both ways, it is argued. If this is true, it would seem that on manufactured commodities the freight rate is borne by the consumer but that on the agricultural products it is borne by the producer. But this cannot be true unless one law determines the price of manufactured commodities and a different law determines the price of agricultural products.

FREIGHT RATES AS A COST OF PRODUCTION

The relation of freight charges to prices calls for careful analysis. In approaching the problem, it should be recognized that transportation charges are part of the costs of production. The term "cost of production" is broad enough to cover all the costs necessary to put a commodity in the hands of consumers. Production is often defined as "the creation of utilities," and transportation is recognized as creating "place utilities." If we recognize transportation costs as a part of the cost of production, the conclusion seems incontrovertible that in the long run, transportation costs, like other costs of production, must be included in the price of the good. We must not forget, however, that transportation costs are substitutable, in part, for other costs of production. As was pointed out in the first chapter,[1] a lowering of transportation rates may result in substituting a more distant but cheaper source of supply for a nearer one where costs of production are higher. Conversely an increase in freight rates may shut off the supply of a good from a distant but cheaper source of supply in favor of a nearer and more expensive source.

That freight rates, like other costs of production, must be borne by the consumer is evident in many situations which are daily encountered. When manufactured goods are sold at an F.O.B. factory price, it is obvious that the buyer pays the freight. If he is a dealer, he must recover the cost of the goods, including freight, from his customers, or he will not long remain in business. If the goods are sold at a delivered price which is made up of the factory price plus freight, it is clear that the purchaser pays the freight in the price of the good. The pricing system in the automobile industry illustrates this point. Automobiles are generally sold at retail on the basis of the main-factory price, plus an amount approximating the rail freight charges from the main factory to destination, plus whatever amount is needed to cover the dealer's costs and margin of profit. This basis ordinarily applies, however, regardless of the mode of transportation actually used and whether the automobile is produced at the main factory or at an assembly plant somewhere else.[2]

That freight rates enter into the price of a product may not be so clear in the case of agricultural products produced in a great many different places and shipped to a central market. Different units of the product on the market at a given time come from many different sources of supply. Transportation charges from the different sources of supply may have been widely different, and there is no one freight rate that can be said to enter into the price at the market. It can easily be seen, however, that if freight rates from all sources of supply were increased, the price in the central market would not be unaffected. If freight rates on wheat from all producing areas in the world to Liverpool, the world market, were increased, the price of wheat in Liverpool would rise. If the transportation costs on fluid milk from all farming areas that supply milk to New York or Boston were increased, it would soon bring about changes in the price of milk in those cities.

EFFECT OF FREIGHT-RATE INCREASES

Although freight rates, under the conditions which we have described, enter into the price of a good, it does not follow that an increase

---

[1] Pp. 15–16, supra.

[2] *Chrysler Corp.* v. *Akron, Canton & Youngstown R. Co.*, 279 ICC 377, 383 (1950).

in freight rates will always raise the price by the amount of the increase in freight rates. This is because the increase in the price of a commodity tends to curtail consumption; production must be readjusted to the new conditions of demand, and a new equilibrium of supply and demand must be established.

The effect of increases in freight rates follows exactly the same laws that determine the shifting and incidence of taxes on commodities. The extent to which an increase in freight rates will raise prices will depend upon both the elasticity of demand and the elasticity of supply. The principles can be easily demonstrated by the use of conventional supply-and-demand diagrams familiar to students of economics. In the analysis which follows, it must be assumed that the increase in freight rates will not be evaded by resort to some other agency of transportation or by the relocation of producing centers. It will also be assumed that the goods are produced under competitive conditions and under conditions of increasing costs.

Influence of Elasticity of Demand

The less elastic the demand for a commodity, that is, the less its consumption is affected by price changes, the greater will be the tendency for an increase in freight rates to raise the price of the good.[3] Conversely the more elastic the demand, the less will the price be raised. The situation is illustrated in Figure 3–1.[4]

The demand curve DD in Figure 3–1*A* is steep, which means that the demand is relatively inelastic. That is, an increase in price will only slightly curtail consumption. In Figure 3–1*B* the demand curve is less steep, which means that the demand for the commodity is elastic and that an increase in price will curtail consumption considerably. The supply curves SS are alike in both diagrams. Any differences in the result of a rate increase as shown by the two diagrams will be, therefore, the result of differences in the elasticity of demand and not of differences in elasticity of supply.

The supply curves SS represent the cost of producing various units of the supply, including the cost of transportation. An equilibrium of supply and demand is established, and the price is represented by the distance OP, and the quantity produced by the distance OQ. Now if we assume that the freight rates on the two articles in question are increased by the amount SS′ in such manner that the increase applies equally to each unit produced, there must be a new cost curve S′S′. A new equi-

---

[3] For the purposes of this analysis we are interested in relative elasticity or inelasticity of demand for two different commodities and not whether elasticity is greater or less than unity.

[4] The accompanying diagrams are highly geometricized for the purpose of demonstration.

librium of supply and demand is established. The price becomes OP',
and the quantities produced OQ'. The point to be noted is that the price
was raised more in Figure 3–1A, where demand was inelastic, than in
Figure 3–1B, where demand was elastic. This was because the new
equilibrium was not established in Figure 3–1B until production had
been curtailed considerably. The cost of production is lower on the
smaller quantity now produced. In Figure 3–1B the distance PP' is
considerably less than the distance SS'; in Figure 3–1A the distance PP'
is nearly as great as SS'. In Figures 3–1A and 3–1B the difference be-

FIGURE 3–1. Inelastic and Elastic Demand

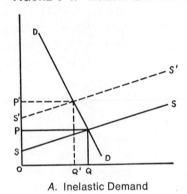

A. Inelastic Demand

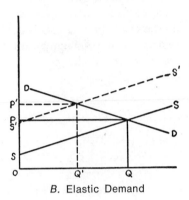

B. Elastic Demand

tween the increase in freight rate and the increase in price is represented
by the lowered cost of producing the marginal supply.

Influence of Elasticity of Supply

The extent to which increased transportation costs will affect prices
to the consumer also depends upon the elasticity of supply. Supply is
elastic if a change in price will result in a considerable change in the
quantity produced, inelastic if such a change in supply does not occur.
Elasticity is largely, but not entirely, a question of the degree to which
costs of producing additional units of supply will be greater than the
cost of producing the former supply. If the supply is elastic, the imposition of an increased freight rate will be shifted to the consumer to a
greater extent than if the supply is inelastic. This is because production
can readily be adjusted to the new conditions in the first case and cannot
be in the second case. This principle is illustrated by Figures 3–2A and
3–2B.

The elasticity of demand is the same in both figures, but the supply
in Figure 3–2A is more elastic than in Figure 3–2B. If both commodities
are subjected to the same rate increase, it is clear that in Figure 3–2A

FIGURE 3–2. Elastic and Inelastic Supply

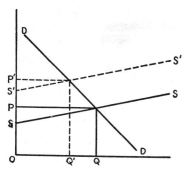

A. Elastic Supply

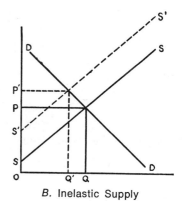

B. Inelastic Supply

more of an increase in price occurs. The distance PP′ in Figure 3–2*A* is greater than PP′ in Figure 3–2*B*.

It can easily be shown that if the cost curve SS were a horizontal line, the price would be increased by the amount of the increase in rates, but the quantity produced would depend upon the elasticity of demand.[5]

Shifting under Noncompetitive Conditions

The foregoing analysis of the influence of elasticity of demand and of supply assumed conditions of competition. It is not to be inferred, however, that the prices of all commodities are so determined. A monopolistic element of greater or lesser degree affects the prices of many commodities. Shifting the burden of a freight-rate increase may be different under pure monopoly from what it is under conditions of competition. At first thought it might appear that in such a case the price would rise by the amount of the increase in rates, since the monopolist can control the price. It must be recalled, however, that the monopolist does not charge a price which yields the highest profit per unit sold but that he will tend to fix a price which will yield the largest total profit. This means that he must consider the quantity of goods that will be taken at different prices and the cost of producing various quantities of the commodity. The extent to which the monopolist will curtail production and raise prices will depend upon the elasticity of demand for the commodity and on the effects of curtailed production on production costs.

Many commodities of everyday use are produced by a small number of producers, that is, under conditions of duopoly or of oligopoly. In the production of other commodities the use of trade-marks, branding,

---

[5] For analysis under other conditions of production see M. Slade Kendrick, *Public Finance* (New York: Houghton Mifflin, 1951), pp. 560–67, where the shifting and incidence of taxes are discussed.

and advertising enables a producer to differentiate his product from that of his competitors and often to obtain a certain limited degree of monopoly power. This situation has been described as "monopolistic competition."[6] Under conditions of duopoly, oligopoly, and monopolistic competition, prices tend to be higher than under conditions of competition and may approach monopoly prices.[7] The effect of a rate increase on commodities produced under these conditions may differ from a rate increase on articles produced under strictly competitive conditions and be similar to the result that would occur under monopoly conditions. In any event the elasticity of demand and the conditions of production will condition the result.

Elasticity of Demand in Rate Cases

In 1938 general rate increases of 10 percent were authorized by the Interstate Commerce Commission on certain commodities, but on anthracite coal an increase of only 5 percent was permitted because it was very doubtful, in the face of the rise of competing fuels, whether anthracite coal could at that time stand a greater increase without severely curtailing consumption.[8] In 1958, when the railroads made selected increases in rates on numerous commodities, bituminous coal rates were increased 10 cents per ton, but lignite coal rates were increased only 5 cents a ton. The smaller increase on lignite was in recognition of the fact that it is a low-grade fuel whose low B.T.U. value required a low price if it was to compete with higher-grade fuels.[9] Similar questions are considered in nearly all general rate level cases.[10]

Are Rate Increases Absorbed by Middlemen?

It is often alleged that increases in freight rates, if small in amount, will be absorbed by producers or by the various jobbers and retailers who handle the goods and that prices will not be increased to the consumer. This contention has sometimes been advanced by the railroads when they are seeking general rate increases. Such increases may be absorbed for a time. Increases and decreases in rates may decrease and increase the profits of producers and middlemen for a while; but as long

---

[6] Edward Chamberlin, *The Theory of Monopolistic Competition* (Cambridge: Harvard University Press, 1936).

[7] Ibid., chaps. iii and v.

[8] *Fifteen Percent Case, 1937–1938,* 226 ICC 41 (1938).

[9] *Increased Freight Rates, 1958,* 304 ICC 289, 330 (1958).

[10] E.g., *Increased Freight Rates, 1967,* 332 ICC 280 (1968); *Increased Freight Rates, 1968,* 332 ICC 714 (1969).

as competition prevails in these lines of endeavor, the consumers will eventually bear the burden of increases and will benefit by reductions in rates.

Are Freight Rates "Pyramided"?

The opposite contention is often advanced by consumers. It is said that freight rates are "pyramided" and that a moderate increase in rates results in increasing prices by a greater amount. This pyramiding process is alleged to result from the practice of middlemen and retailers of selling goods at a certain percentage over cost. Thus, if a retailer's margin is 25 percent of the cost of the goods, a 10 percent increase in freight rates on the goods that he buys would become a 12½ percent increase as far as the consumer is concerned. The more times this process is repeated, the greater becomes the cumulative effect of the rate increase.

This pyramiding may occur as a temporary result of rate increases, but the force of competition tends to eliminate it in the long run. If a dealer prices his goods at a fixed percentage above their cost to him, and an increase in freight rates thus increases the price at which he sells by more than the absolute increase in freight rates, the aggregate profits of the dealer are increased and likewise the profits on the capital invested. In so far as he is subjected to competition, it is likely that these profits will disappear, since our dealer will be forced to shade his prices in order to meet competition.

Goods Sold at a Uniform Price to Consumers

Many manufactured articles are sold throughout the country, or over smaller areas, at uniform prices to consumers. Here, at first sight, there seems to be no relation between freight rates and prices, since differences in freight charges do not result in different prices to consumers. In reality this situation constitutes no exception to the general statement that freight rates enter into the price of goods. The freight has to be paid by someone, and it is a cost of getting the goods to the consumer. If, for instance, a manufacturer is selling goods in different places at uniform delivered prices, he realizes a greater net amount from the sale in nearby territory and a smaller amount from the sale in a distant area. But in the long run he must obtain a price sufficient to cover his manufacturing costs plus the freight charges which he pays. When goods are sold at uniform delivered prices, the consumer near the factory is ordinarily paying more freight than was incurred on his particular purchase, and the consumer located at a distance pays less freight than was incurred on his purchase.

Goods Sold under a Basing-Point Pricing System

A common pricing system which has prevailed in the past in the United States is known as the "basing-point" system.[11] Under this system of pricing, goods were sold at identical delivered prices by all producers, and this price normally consisted of the price at a basing point—usually an important manufacturing point—plus the freight rate from the basing point to the destination of the shipment. The price so determined was applied whether the goods were purchased at the basing point or at some other producing point. An early example of this pricing system was the "Pittsburgh-plus" system of quoting steel prices. While this system was in effect, the price of steel at any point in the United States was the Pittsburgh price plus the freight rate from Pittsburgh. This price obtained whether the steel was purchased in Pittsburgh or at some other steel-producing point, like Chicago. If a buyer of steel purchased it from a point nearer to him than Pittsburgh, the price was still the Pittsburgh price plus freight from Pittsburgh. Hence the seller received a net mill price greater than the Pittsburgh producer would have realized from a sale at the same point. Conversely, if a buyer purchased from a point farther away from him than was Pittsburgh, the seller could only charge the Pittsburgh price plus freight and hence had to absorb part of the freight. This meant that he would receive less for his steel than the Pittsburgh producer would have received if he had sold in the same market. The Pittsburgh-plus system was a single-basing-point system. Other industries have used a system of multiple basing points; in fact, the single-basing-point system in the steel industry gave way to a multiple-basing-point system about 1924.

Under a basing-point pricing system the freight rate paid by the consumer is the freight rate from the basing point. The purchaser pays more freight than was actually incurred on his shipment if he purchases from a source closer than the basing point. He pays less freight than was incurred on his shipment if he purchases from a producer located farther away than the basing point.

RATIOS OF FREIGHT RATES TO PRICES

Since there is some element of freight in the sale price of nearly all goods, it is desirable to have some information that will tell us quantitatively how important the transportation charges are in the prices of ordinary articles of consumption. This becomes particularly important when percentage changes in rates are proposed, for the effect on price will be greater if the freight charge is already a substantial portion of

---

[11] The decision of the Supreme Court of the United States in 1948 in *Federal Trade Commission* v. *The Cement Institute*, 333 U.S. 683, outlawed the basing-point pricing system, at least if it involves collusion or concerted action among producers.

TABLE 3–1.   Relation of Railroad Freight Revenue from Various Commodities to Average Wholesale Price at Destination, 1959*

Commodity	Percent Freight Revenue of Value
Fluxing stone and raw dolomite	57.25
Gravel and sand, n.o.s.ᵃ	54.92
Hay	45.14
Bituminous coal	41.96
Cabbage	38.12
Watermelons	37.53
Common brick	27.72
Potatoes	27.45
Lettuce	27.18
Oranges and grapefruit	23.59
Lumber, shingles and lath	20.74
Iron ore	19.67
Corn	12.18
Gasoline	10.76
Pig iron	8.29
Flour, wheat	7.48
Eggs	6.38
Sugar	6.32
Automobiles, passenger	5.35
Meats, fresh, n.o.s.	4.17
Butter	1.70
Cigarettes	1.04
Copper ore and concentrates	0.65
Business and office machines	0.60
Airplanes, aircraft, and parts	0.17

* Bureau of Transport Economics and Statistics, Interstate Commerce Commission, *Freight Revenue and Wholesale Value at Destination of Commodities Transported by Class I Line-Haul Railroads, 1959* (Washington, D.C., 1961).

ᵃ Means "not otherwise specified."

the price of the article.[12] The Interstate Commerce Commission frequently publishes figures showing the relation of the freight revenue received by the railroads from the transportation of various commodities to the average wholesale prices at destination. Table 3–1 shows these relationships for a number of commodities.

The lowest ratio of freight revenues to value was found on "airplanes, aircraft and parts," where the freight revenues constituted only 0.17 percent of the value at destination; the highest ratio was found on fluxing stone and raw dolomite, where freight represented 57.25 percent of the value at destination.

In drawing conclusions from figures which show the relation between transportation charges and prices, certain cautions should be observed. In the first place, the freight charge is a small proportion of the price of

[12] See R. Vaile, "Some Effects on Certain Agricultural Products of Uniform Percentage Increases in Freight Rates," 36 *Quarterly Journal of Economics* 718 (1922).

articles which have a high value relative to their weight or bulk, such as most manufactured articles; but on the cheaper articles the freight rate is a larger proportion of the price. Second, it should be remembered that the longer the haul, the greater becomes the ratio of freight charges to prices if freight rates increase with distance. Third, the figures usually make no allowance for the rates on raw materials used in the manufacture of the goods. The freight rate on certain iron and steel articles may be a small part of the price; but if the transportation charges on iron ore and pig iron were taken into consideration, the freight element in the price would be increased. Fourth, ratios of freight charges to prices change not only with changes in freight rates, but with changes in prices. In 1920 the transportation and refrigeration charges on deciduous fruits from California to eastern markets were 23 percent of the market price. In 1930 they were 51 percent. Transportation and refrigeration charges had increased only about 2 percent. The change in ratio was due to a decline in prices of fruits in eastern markets of more than 50 percent.[13] Lastly, it should be remembered, as was pointed out in an earlier chapter, that since low freight rates permit production to be carried on in the most advantageous locations, freight rates are sometimes substituted for other costs of production. This means that low rates may increase the ratio of transportation charges to prices, contrary to what is ordinarily expected.[14]

FREIGHT RATES AND THE INDIVIDUAL PRODUCER

Not only are producers interested in the level of rates on the particular commodities which they produce, but each individual producer is interested in the particular rate from his place of production to the market or markets in which he sells. Once the forces of supply and demand have established a price in a given market, the ability of individual producers to sell in that market will often be determined by the freight rates they must pay. If the commodity is one for which central markets are established, the price received by a single producer will approximate the market price minus the costs of transportation. The most obvious illustration of this relationship is found in the case of farm products shipped to commission merchants in the cities. The farmer will receive a check for his produce which is the market price in the city less transportation charges, dealer's commission, and other charges which may be incidental to the sale of the product. It is sometimes asserted that this relationship between the price received by a producer and the freight rate is peculiar to agriculture. A manufacturer, it is asserted, can make

---

[13] Railroad Commission of California, *Brief before the Interstate Commerce Commission, Ex Parte 103* (1931), p. 8.

[14] Pp. 15–16, supra.

the buyer pay the freight or can add the freight rate to the price of the goods. But the position of the individual manufacturer is often no different from that of the individual farmer. If a manufacturer in Chicago wants to sell a commodity in St. Louis in competition with a manufacturer located at St. Louis, he must meet the latter's price. If the costs of manufacture are approximately the same in both cities, the Chicago manufacturer must absorb the freight rate from Chicago to St. Louis. In effect the Chicago manufacturer will receive the St. Louis price less the transportation charge to St. Louis. If the Chicago manufacturer finds this price unremunerative, he must withdraw from the St. Louis market. Similarly, if two competing manufacturers try to sell in a common market which involves a longer haul from one producer than from the other, the one less advantageously located may be forced to absorb the difference between the rate which he must pay and that paid by his competitor. Most rate disputes that arise under the "undue-preference-and-advantage" section of the Interstate Commerce Act furnish abundant proof of the general truth that, once a market price is established, individual producers receive the difference between that price and the rate to that market.

GEOGRAPHY OF PRICES

Ample evidence of the relationship between freight rates and prices received by producers is afforded by studies of the geography of prices. Figure 3–3 shows that the average farm price of potatoes in the United States is lowest in the areas of production most remote from markets.[15] The farm prices increase in the direction of potato shipments, reaching the highest levels in the deficit areas most remote from the producing areas.

The price relationships shown in Figure 3–3 are those of the main crop season. The geography of prices is quite different in the summer, when the new potatoes from the South are put on the market. During this season the prices are lowest in the South and increase along the lines followed by the shipments in their northward movement.[16]

Examples of the relation between freight rates and the geography of prices may be found in abundance. Farm prices of fluid milk in the New York and Boston milksheds decline with distance from market at the same rate as costs of shipping fluid milk increase.[17] The Interstate Com-

---

[15] Holbrook Working, *Factors Determining the Price of Potatoes in St. Paul and Minneapolis,* University of Minnesota Agricultural Experiment Station, Technical Bulletin No. 10 (St. Paul, 1922), p. 6.

[16] Holbrook Working, "Factors Influencing Price Differentials between Potato Markets," 7 *Journal of Farm Economics,* 377, 379 (1925).

[17] John M. Cassels, *Study of Fluid Milk Prices* (Cambridge: Harvard University Press, 1937), p. 162 and map on p. 161.

merce Commission has pointed out that prices paid for cotton in the interior of the South are ordinarily the price in a primary market less the transportation cost to market; and in corn-producing areas the price of corn tends to be the Chicago price less freight to Chicago.[18] The prices of livestock increase as one goes east from Chicago and grow less as one goes west from Chicago toward the areas of livestock production.[19] Hog prices are high in the Pacific Coast states and in the Northeastern states, where populations are large and where hog production is

FIGURE 3–3. Isotims (Lines of Equal Price) of Ten-Year Average Farm Price of Potatoes (1906–15) (Cents per Bushel)

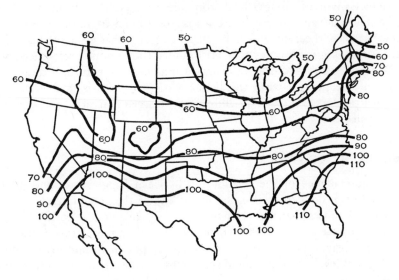

small. The prices of hogs decline from these deficit sections as one moves toward the surplus-producing areas of the North Central states.[20] Wool prices throughout the United States are related to the price in the Boston market. The wool producer ordinarily obtains the Boston price less marketing expenses and the transportation charges to Boston.[21]

The states which have the lowest farm prices of wheat are in the producing regions most remote from markets. Prices increase in the direction of grain movement, that is, toward the Atlantic seaboard, the Gulf,

---

[18] *Cotton from and to Points in the Southwest and Memphis, Tenn.,* 208 ICC 677, 693 (1935); *Corn & Corn Products, Iowa, Nebr., Minn., S. Dak. to Illinois,* 318 ICC 291 (1962).

[19] *Morrell & Co. v. New York Central R. R. Co.,* 104 ICC 104 (1925).

[20] North Central Livestock Marketing Research Committee, *Price Differentials for Slaughter Hogs,* Iowa Agricultural Experiment Station, Bulletin P93 (Ames, 1948), p. 64.

[21] *Wool & Mohair Rates,* 276 ICC 259, 270 (1949).

and the Pacific Coast. Even higher prices are found in regions off the routes of grain movement which produce less grain than they consume. A careful study of farm prices of wheat by counties was published by the United States Department of Agriculture in 1918.[22] The study showed that the lowest wheat prices were found in parts of Montana and Idaho. Prices graduated upward in every direction from this region, following closely the direction of grain shipments. Prices on the Pacific Coast were lower than on the Atlantic Coast because of the remoteness of the Pacific Coast ports from Liverpool, the central wheat market of the world. The highest prices were found in the deficit areas in the Southeast.

The Department of Agriculture has made the following generalizations from price studies of the sort described: first, in a surplus area the price is roughly equivalent to the primary market price less the costs of marketing; second, in a deficit area the price is roughly equivalent to the price in the farthest surplus-producing area from which it draws its supplies, plus the cost of transportation and handling.[23]

For commodities which have a central world market, such as wheat, there is normally a very definite relationship between prices in different parts of the world, and the differences in prices are largely explained by differences in freight rates. The price of wheat in the major surplus-wheat-producing countries of the world tends to be the Liverpool price less transportation costs to Liverpool. The price of wheat in the United States has tended to conform to this pattern. Although this has sometimes been disputed,[24] careful studies substantiate the statement.[25]

When the Liverpool price of wheat exerts a dominating influence on the price of wheat in the United States, one would expect to find that the prices of grain in the various grain markets in the United States would differ and that the differences would correspond closely to the differences in the freight rates to Liverpool. The Federal Trade Commission found such a relationship between grain prices in the different

[22] L. B. Zapoleon, *Geography of Wheat Prices*, U.S. Department of Agriculture, Bulletin No. 594 (1918). Studies were also published of the farm prices of oats and corn, Bulletins Nos. 696 (1918) and 755 (1919).

[23] U.S. Department of Agriculture, *Prices of Farm Products Received by Producers*, Statistical Bulletin No. 17 (1927), pp. 3–4; C. F. Sarle, *Reliability and Adequacy of Farm Price Data*, U.S. Department of Agriculture, Bulletin No. 1480 (1927), p. 3.

[24] Bureau of Railway Economics, *A Study of the Economic Effect of Reductions in Freight Rates on Export Wheat—1929*, Bulletin, Special Series No. 55 (Washington, D.C., 1930); "Wheat Rates and Prices," 87 *Railway Age* 135 (1929); "Wheat Prices and Freight Rates," 87 *Railway Age* 803 (1929); S. O. Dunn, *Is There Economic Justification for Inland Waterway Development?* (an address, 1931), p. 13.

[25] Frank Andrews, "Freight Costs and Market Values," *U.S. Department of Agricultural Yearbook, 1906*, pp. 371–86; Zapoleon, op. cit., p. 16; Federal Trade Commission, *Report on the Grain Trade*, Vol. VI (1924), p. 109; Secretary of Agriculture, *Prices of Wheat to Producers in Kansas*, 63d Cong., 3d Sess., House Doc. No. 1271 (1914).

markets in the United States but noted that the average spreads for rather long periods appeared quite generally to be less than the differences in freight rates. This was explained by the intermittent character of shipments between the large markets and by the influence on averages of the smaller differences in prices that exist when grain is not moving on a strict export basis because local conditions of supply and demand are in control of the markets in this country.[26] The same influence has affected the average spread between Liverpool and American wheat prices.

FIGURE 3–4. Relation of Wheat Prices in Primary Market (St. Louis) to Price at Shipping Points (No. 2 Red Winter Wheat, November, 1899)

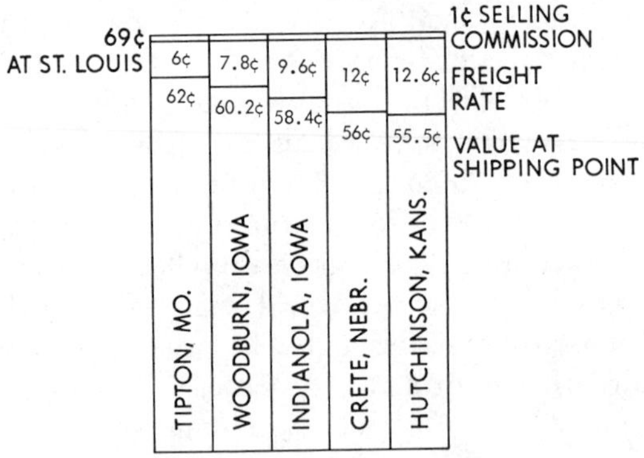

	TIPTON, MO.	WOODBURN, IOWA	INDIANOLA, IOWA	CRETE, NEBR.	HUTCHINSON, KANS.	
69¢ AT ST. LOUIS	6¢	7.8¢	9.6¢	12¢	12.6¢	1¢ SELLING COMMISSION / FREIGHT RATE
	62¢	60.2¢	58.4¢	56¢	55.5¢	VALUE AT SHIPPING POINT

Report of the Industrial Commission, Vol. VI (1901), p. 80.

The difference between the price of grain in the primary grain markets and the price received by the farmer at a country elevator is likewise to be explained by freight rates. Figure 3–4, constructed from data published by the Industrial Commission in 1901, shows the normal relationship between prices at country elevators and in primary grain markets. The farmers at the various country points would receive the sums represented on the diagram as "value at shipping point" less the local elevator margin. This relationship, like the others which we have described, is not an invariable and exact relationship. The presence, or absence, or degree of competition among buying elevators, the existence of temporary shortages of wheat locally or in nearby areas, inability of the elevator to handle all the grain offered at a particular time, and other factors may cause the price paid by the elevator to differ from the terminal market price less transportation charges and elevator margin.

---

[26] Federal Trade Commission, op. cit., p. 108.

Information published several years ago by the Joint Commission of Agricultural Inquiry makes this situation clear.[27]

TYPES OF RATE INCREASES AND THEIR EFFECTS

Two broad conclusions reached earlier in this chapter were (1) that freight charges are a cost of production and enter into the prices of commodities; and (2) that once a price has been established in a particular market, the ability of a particular producer to sell in that market, and the price that he will receive, will depend upon the freight rate to that market. With these conclusions in mind the effects of different methods of increasing freight rates may be examined.

First, it should be noted that an increase in rates on all commodities is more likely to be shifted to consumers than is an increase on a single commodity. This is because there is no possibility in the former case of avoiding the increase by turning to the consumption of substitute articles.

If an increase in freight rates on a commodity or group of commodities is a fixed amount per unit of goods shipped, regardless of the length of the haul, the results will be as indicated in the first part of this chapter. The significant thing about this kind of an increase is that it is the same amount in cents per hundred pounds or per ton for all producers. An increase of this kind is equivalent to raising the cost curve uniformly, and the extent to which the price of the commodity is increased to the consumer will depend upon the relative elasticities of supply and demand. Proposals of the railroads for rate increases in 1958 included many increases of the flat variety. Thus an increase of 10 cents per ton was made on coal regardless of the length of the haul, and an increase of 15 cents per ton on coke.[28]

The effects of a percentage increase in freight rates are in some respects quite different than those resulting from flat increases. A percentage increase will place a greater aggregate increase on the shippers who formerly paid the highest rates. The rate increase will be small to the shippers who paid the lowest rates before. Prices will undoubtedly rise, but it is impossible to say by how much. The cost curve is not raised by a definite amount since the cost of putting some portions of the supply on the market is increased more than that of other portions. The chief difference in the effects of a percentage increase and of a flat increase in rates is that the former changes the relative position of different producers in the market. The long-distance shipper is most adversely affected. The shipper who is near his market is least affected. In fact, the near producer may benefit from the rate increase because his

[27] *Report*, 67th Cong., 1st Sess., House Rep. No. 408 (1922), Part III, pp. 502–5.
[28] *Increased Freight Rates, 1958*, 302 ICC 665, 685 (1958).

distant competitors may be excluded from the market. Many of the general rate increases of recent years have been of the percentage variety. They have met with increasing resistance, however, since they place distant producers at a disadvantage. To ease the burden on distant producers, the Interstate Commerce Commission has frequently made the increases subject to a maximum increase in cents per hundred pounds. This limitation on a percentage increase is commonly called a "hold-down," since it holds down the rates for the longer distances. In a general rate increase case in 1957, increases were authorized which ranged from 9 to 14 percent, but a maximum increase of 11 cents per hundred pounds was prescribed on fresh fruits and vegetables and on canned food products.[29] The Commission pointed out that the hold-down was needed to prevent too great a distortion of rate relations and to permit distant producers to compete with producers nearer their markets.[30] The increases in rates on lumber were also subject to a hold-down to preserve the competitive relation between southern and western lumber.

If an advance in freight rates applies from some producing centers and not from others, the results are quite complex and very difficult to predict. If the areas from which the rates are increased furnish a large part of the supply, or if expansion of production is not easily possible elsewhere, it may be that the price in the market will be raised by nearly the whole amount of the rate increase. If so, the producers whose rates were increased will receive nearly as much as they did before, but the producers whose rates were not increased will receive more than they did before, since the central market price has advanced. Thus the producers subjected to the rate increase may be nearly as well off as before in the absolute sense but worse off in the relative sense. If the supply from the producing area which was subjected to a rate increase is a small portion of the supply, and if it is in no sense the marginal supply, the rate increase will not affect the price in the central market to any great extent. When this situation occurs, the producers subjected to the rate advance will have to accept less for their product, and they will be worse off, in both the absolute and the relative sense.

A practical illustration of the last situation is found in the position of agriculture in the United States after World War I. The increases in railroad freight rates which were made after the war put American agricultural products at a disadvantage in the markets of the world as compared with the products from other countries. According to the United States Department of Commerce, increases in railway rates forced the Middle Western grain farmer to pay from 6 to 12 cents more per

[29] *Increased Freight Rates, Eastern, Southern & Western Territories, 1956,* 300 ICC 633 (1957).

[30] Ibid., p. 688.

bushel to reach world markets than before the war.[31] Foreign farmers produce closer to ocean ports and had to pay but little, if any, more than prewar rates for shipments to European markets. The American grain farmer was therefore at a disadvantage as compared with the Argentine farmer and with farmers in other countries who had easier access to the sea.[32] This situation was frequently pointed out to support the deepening of the Great Lakes–St. Lawrence Waterway in the belief that the reduced transportation costs which would result from making Duluth, Chicago, and other grain-shipping ports on the Great Lakes more accessible to larger ocean-going vessels, would enhance the price of grain to the American farmer.

SELECTED REFERENCES

The general principles governing the incidence of transportation charges are set forth by T. N. Carver in "The Incidence of Costs," 34 *Economic Journal* 576 (1924); and by H. R. Trumbower in "The Incidence of Freight Charges on Agricultural Products," 33 *Journal of Political Economy* 340 (1925). A brief but excellent discussion of who pays the freight is in B. H. Hibbard, *Marketing Agricultural Products* (New York: Appleton, 1921), pp. 54–58; and also in "Effect of Freight Rates on Agricultural Geography," 4 *Journal of Farm Economics* 129, pp. 131–33 (1922). There is a good discussion of the effects of rate changes in M. R. Benedict, *Freight Rates and the South Dakota Farmer*, South Dakota Agricultural Experiment Station, Bulletin 269 (Brookings, S.D., 1932), pp. 17–29; and in Donald E. Church, *Effect of Increases in Freight Rates on Agricultural Products*, U.S. Department of Agriculture, Circular No. 847 (Washington, D.C., 1950). There is a good treatment of prices in different markets as affected by freight costs in Warren C. Waite and Harry C. Trelogan, *Agricultural Market Prices* (New York: Wiley, 1951), chap. vii.

For a discussion of the geography of prices see L. B. Zapoleon, *Geography of Wheat Prices*, U.S. Department of Agriculture, Bulletin No. 594 (1918). For similar studies by Zapoleon, see Bulletin 696, oat prices, and Bulletin 755, corn prices. Grain prices and freight rates are discussed in a great many places, but only a few of these need be listed. The general relationship is set forth in J. W. Strowbridge, *Farm and Terminal Market Prices: Wheat, Corn, and Oats, Crop Movement Year 1920–21*, U.S. Department of Agriculture, Bulletin 1083 (1922); Alfred H. Ritter, *World Wheat Markets, Influence of Transportation Costs on the Wheat Trade of the United States* (Duluth: Great Lakes–Tidewater Association, 1924); and by the same author, *Transportation Economics of the Great Lakes–St. Lawrence Ship Channel*

---

[31] E. S. Gregg and A. L. Cricher, *Great Lakes-to-Ocean Waterways*, Bulletin of the Bureau of Foreign and Domestic Commerce, Domestic Commerce Series No. 4 (1927), p. 4.

[32] Alfred H. Ritter, *Influence of Transportation Costs on the Wheat Trade of the United States* (Duluth: Great Lakes–Tidewater Association, 1924), p. 17.

(Washington, D.C.: Great Lakes–St. Lawrence Tidewater Association, 1925), pp. 216–24; Secretary of Agriculture, *Prices of Wheat to Producers in Kansas,* 63d Cong., 3d Sess., House Doc. No. 1271 (1914).

An excellent study of the geography of milk and butterfat prices is included in John M. Cassels, *A Study of Fluid Milk Prices* (Cambridge: Harvard University Press, 1937).

| Chapter 4 | FREIGHT RATES AND THE LOCATION OF INDUSTRIES AND MARKET CENTERS |

Transportation charges have important effects upon the orientation of industries in relation to markets and raw materials. They also influence the size of the market areas and types of farming. In an earlier chapter[1] it was pointed out that low freight rates enable production to be carried on at points having the lowest costs of production. But in order to analyze the influence of freight charges on the location of industries with respect to markets and raw materials, it is necessary to assume that costs of production at different points, except as they are affected by transportion charges, are the same. The problem may then be stated as follows: Other things being equal, how will transportation charges affect the location of an industry? The illustrations used in the ensuing pages concern charges of railroad companies, but the principles are applicable to the charges made by any transportation agency. When goods are transported by the owner—in his own motor truck, for instance—the same principles will apply if the broader term "cost of transportation" is used instead of the terms "transportation charges" and "freight rates."

LOCATION OF EXTRACTIVE INDUSTRIES

Extractive industries, like mining, agriculture, and lumbering, can be carried on only where the resources to be exploited are located. Freight rates, however, may determine the extent to which the resources of a particular area are utilized, since freight rates may determine the extent to which profitable markets can be reached.

LOCATION OF MANUFACTURING INDUSTRIES

The location of manufacturing industries is not fixed by Nature. Although the location of raw materials may exert a strong influence on the location of manufacturing industries, there is often sufficient freedom of

---

[1] Chapter 1, pp. 5–8.

choice in selecting a location to make freight rates and other factors of very great importance.

In many discussions of the location of manufacturing industries, numerous factors are listed which influence the choice of locations. Among the important factors enumerated are nearness to market, source of raw materials, availability of fuel or power, and labor supply. All but the last of these are partly, if not largely, matters of transportation costs. Except in the case of perishables, nearness to market is nearness in the matter of transportation costs. The same may be said of nearness to raw materials. Availability of a fuel supply or power is also a matter of transportation costs, for power, in the form of coal, fuel oil, electrical energy, or natural gas, can be transported, but only at a cost. Since transportation costs are elements in several of the factors enumerated above, it should be possible to isolate their influence from other elements in order to get a clear understanding of the part they play in the location of industries. In doing this, it should be recognized that we are dealing with only one phase of the problem of the location of industries, albeit an important one.

It must also be recognized that the importance of transportation charges will vary in different industries. If transportation costs are a large factor in the cost of production, and large relative to the value of the commodities produced, they may be the controlling factor in the location of the industry. If transport costs are but a small part of the cost of production, and small relative to the value of the commodities produced, they may exercise practically no influence in the selection of locations. The decline in the manufacturing of cotton goods in New England and its rise in the South are often explained by the nearness of the southern mills to the cotton supply. It does not appear, however, that nearness to raw material was of any appreciable significance in the southward shift of this industry. One analysis of this development showed that the southeastern mills saved from 21 to 34 percent of the freight which New England had to pay on raw cotton; but since the freight was only a small part of the cost of cotton, which in turn was but a small part of the total cost of manufacturing cotton cloth, New England's disadvantage because of higher transportation costs was only from three tenths to seven tenths of 1 percent of the total manufacturing costs.[2] Labor costs were an important factor in the southward shift of this industry. In some other industry a saving of much less than 21 percent of the freight rates on raw material would exert a controlling influence on the location of the industry.

The general principle governing the location of manufacturing industries, in so far as transportation costs are concerned, can be stated simply.

---

[2] C. J. R. Grossman, *The Possibilities of Cotton Manufacturing in Texas*, University of Texas Bulletin No. 2832 (Austin, 1928), pp. 18–20. See also J. H. Burgy, *The New England Cotton Textile Industry* (Baltimore: Waverly Press, 1932), pp. 121–26.

An industry will tend to locate where the aggregate transportation charges are the least. This may be at the source of supply of some important raw material; it may be at the market for the finished product; it may be at the source of fuel supply; or it may be at some intermediate point.

RELATIVE IMPORTANCE OF MARKET AND OF RAW MATERIAL

It will be helpful to ignore fuel supply for the moment and to consider the source of raw materials and the consuming market as they affect the location of the industry. Whether the industry will be drawn toward the raw materials or toward the market for the finished products will depend upon the relative cost of transporting the raw materials and the finished goods. The total cost of transporting the raw materials is the product of the rate on the raw materials and the weight which must be transported. Likewise, the total cost of transporting the finished goods is the product of the rate on the goods and their weight. It follows that whether the industry locates close to the market or close to the raw material depends upon two factors: (1) the loss of weight that results from the manufacturing process and (2) the relation of the rate on the raw materials to the rate on the finished product.

Weight-Losing Materials

Other things being equal, industries may be expected to locate near the source of raw materials which shrink in weight in the process of manufacture. This explains, in part, why sawmills penetrate into the wilderness and why wood-using industries are commonly located near the supplies of growing timber. The migration of the tanning industry from New England to Pennsylvania and the central western states, beginning about 1800, may be explained in the same way. The industry, dependent upon a supply of oak and hemlock bark for the tannin used in the tanning process, migrated from one locality to another as the supplies of bark were exhausted.[3] The bark was a weight-losing raw material, and it did not pay to transport it long distances. In later years the industry was freed from the ties which bound it to the forested areas by leeching the tannin from the bank and shipping the tannin extracts. The manufacture of newsprint paper has been carried on in proximity to the forests of northern United States and Canada from which a supply of pulpwood is obtainable. The loss of weight in the manufacture of newsprint has kept the industry close to the supplies of pulpwood.[4] Other branches of the

---

[3] Frederick S. Hall, "The Localization of Industries," *Twelfth Census of the United States, Manufacturing* (1902), Part I, p. cciii.

[4] John A. Guthrie, *The Newsprint Paper Industry* (Cambridge: Harvard University Press, 1940), p. 180.

paper industry are likewise found close to supplies of suitable wood. The smelting of ores tends to be near the sources of the ore, or else the ore is concentrated near the mines before shipment. In the smelting of copper ore, for instance, from 95 to 99 percent of the weight of the ore is eliminated. Loss of weight in the manufacturing process is also a factor in the location of canning factories and in the preparation of dried fruits, canned fruit juice, and frozen fruit juice, although the perishable nature of many of the fruits and vegetables subjected to these processes is an additional factor tending to draw the industry to the sources of raw materials.

The fact that industries using weight-losing materials tend to develop near the supply of raw material has led some writers to the conclusion that if raw materials are heavy and bulky, the industries will be found at the sources of supply. This, it appears, is an error.[5] If the finished product is as heavy or bulky as the raw material, one may be transported as cheaply as the other, freight rates being the same. It is the loss of weight in the manufacturing process that gives advantage to the concern located near the raw-material supplies. As Weber, a price authority on the subject, says: "Pure materials [that is, those that impart their total weight to the product] can never bind production to their deposits."[6]

Relation of Rates on Raw Material and Finished Products

The relation of the rates on raw material and finished products also affects the location of industries. If the rates on raw materials are higher than on the finished product, there will be an advantage in locating near the raw materials. If the rates on finished products are higher than on the raw materials, there will be an advantage in locating near the centers of consumption, unless this advantage is offset by loss of weight in the manufacturing process. It should be remarked, in passing, that normally the rates on raw materials are lower than on the finished product.

The concentration of agricultural implement and machinery manufacture in Illinois and neighboring states is due to the higher freight rates on the manufactured articles than on the raw materials. Owing to their bulk, these articles have always been charged relatively high rates, and the industry therefore tended to develop in regions most accessible to the farming sections of the country.[7] For a similar reason, tin cans are produced in close proximity to canning regions rather than close to centers of iron and steel production where tin plate is produced.[8] Paper boxes

---

[5] Witold Kryzanowski, "Review of the Literature of the Location of Industries," 35 *Journal of Political Economy* 278 (1927).

[6] C. J. Friedrich, *Alfred Weber's Theory of Location of Industries* (Chicago: University of Chicago Press, 1929), p. 61.

[7] Hall, op. cit., p. cxci; H. H. McCarty, *Industrial Migration in the United States,* Iowa Studies in Business, No. VII (Iowa City, 1930), p. 49.

[8] Carter Goodrich, *Migration and Economic Opportunity* (Philadelphia: University of Pennsylvania Press, 1936), p. 351.

likewise are ordinarily manufactured close to the market for the product, unless they are in collapsible form.[9]

The relation between rates on raw materials and finished products is often involved in rate complaints brought before the Interstate Commerce Commision. In one instance a manufacturer of malt at Minneapolis complained because the rate on malt was higher than on barley. He was competing with plants located at Los Angeles and San Francisco for business on the Pacific Coast. The Minneapolis manufacturer was unable to sell malt on the Pacific Coast in competition with the California producers although the California malt manufacturers bought their barley in Minneapolis. The rate relationship favored the California manufacturer.[10]

Similar controversies have raged over the relationship between the rates on flour and wheat. The conflict of interest between millers located near the wheat fields and those located near the consuming centers resulted in a general equalization of rates on wheat and flour. Thus rates on flour have generally been the same as the rates on wheat. This has been done in disregard of the fact that the cost of transporting flour was probably 25 percent greater than the cost of transporting wheat.[11] It was argued that the mills established in the grain-growing country could not continue in existence if higher rates were imposed on flour. It might appear that even with higher rates on flour the western millers would have an advantage over the eastern millers, since it takes 270 pounds of wheat to manufacture 196 pounds of flour. Wheat, in other words, is a weight-losing material with reference to flour. The percentage of actual waste, however, is very small. The difference between the weight of wheat and the weight of flour is largely represented by bran, shorts, and middlings. In so far as the by-products of flour milling are not consumed in the same areas that provide a market for flour, the by-products market would affect the location of the industry, tending to pull the industry toward the by-products market. In the late 1950s, improved technology in railroad transportation, stimulated by truck-barge competition from some grain-producing areas resulted in lowering the rail rates on grain. Rates on flour, however, were not changed. The creation of this spread between the rates on grain and flour caused much alarm to flour-milling concerns in grain-growing areas since it placed them at a disadvantage in competition with millers located near the large consuming markets.[12]

The relationship between rates on wheat and flour could determine

---

[9] Ibid., p. 360.

[10] *Electric Malting Co. v. Atchinson, Topeka & Santa Fe Ry. Co.*, 23 ICC 378 (1912).

[11] J. B. Eastman, Concurring Opinion in *Rate Structure Investigation, No. 17,000 Part VII, Grain and Grain Products*, 164 ICC 706, 710 (1930).

[12] For an analysis of this situation, see Bruce H. Wright, *Regional and Sectoral Analysis of the Wheat-Flour Economy*. U.S. Department of Agriculture, Economic Research Service (1969).

whether wheat to be consumed as flour in Europe would be milled in the United States or abroad.[13]

The relationship between rates on livestock and on meat has been an important factor in the struggle between rival centers of the packing industry. When the slaughtering business was carried on in the East, the railroads maintained a rate on livestock about one third the rate charged for beef. Chicago packers objected, demanding a lower rate on finished products in order to enable them to sell their product in the East in competition with eastern packers. Later the Chicago packers were found on the other side of the controversy; for when packing establishments sprang up farther west, the Chicago packers needed low rates on livestock to enable them to compete with the newer establishments nearer the cattle ranges, while high rates on meat were a greater disadvantage to the western packers than to the Chicago producers.[14] Controversy over the spread between livestock rates and those on packing-house products has frequently been before the Commission, with the inevitable conflict between producers located near the supply of livestock and those located close to the markets for packing-house products.[15]

Percentage increases in railroad rates that occurred during and after World War I and also those that followed World War II tended to widen the spread between rates on finished products and on raw materials. This made nearness to markets a matter of increasing importance and has been a force working toward a decentralization of manufacturing. A counterforce which has operated since World War I with increasing importance has been the development of motor transport, which has enabled shippers of manufactured goods to avoid paying the relatively high railroad rates commonly charged on high-grade manufactured articles. In many instances, also, the railroads have made substantial reductions in their rates on manufactured goods to prevent further diversion of this traffic to the highways. Thus motor transport, by directly and indirectly reducing the cost to the shipper of transporting manufactured articles, has made nearness to market of less importance for some industries.

Influence of Ubiquitous Materials

There are many materials used in manufacturing that are not localized in certain spots but are available nearly everywhere throughout large areas of the country, at least in sufficient quantities to meet the needs of local industries. Weber calls these materials "ubiquities." Brick clay is

---

[13] See W. Z. Ripley, *Railroads: Rates and Regulation* (New York: Longmans, 1912), pp. 136–38; and *Bulte Milling Co.* v. *Chicago & Alton R. R. Co.*, 15 ICC 351.

[14] Ripley, op. cit., pp. 139–42.

[15] E.g., *Eastern Live Stock Cases of 1926*, 144 ICC 731 (1928); *Ogden Packing & Provision Co.* v. *Denver & Rio Grande R. R. Co.*, 101 ICC 258 (1925), 151 ICC 33 (1929); *Westbound Rates on Meats*, 210 ICC 13 (1935).

available in so many places as to be nearly ubiquitous. Wood and lumber are ubiquities over large expanses of territory.

It might seem that if a raw material is ubiquitous over a large area, it could not affect the location of the industry within the region where it is found. These materials, however, enter into the manufactured product and hence increase the weight to be transported. The total transportation costs will be greater for the establishment which has to ship the finished product a considerable distance, and the tendency will be to combine the ubiquity with the other raw materials near the place of consumption. The effect of ubiquities, then, is to pull the industry toward the market.

The manufacture of soft drinks is an industry that tends to be located near its markets because one of the principal ingredients is water, and water can be obtained nearly everywhere. Brand names are important enough in this industry, however, to enable well-known brands to command a premium price that will permit them to be shipped considerable distances and to compete with the locally bottled product. Somewhat the same situation prevails in the brewery industry where increased decentralization has made inroads on the business of the large breweries of the Middle West in eastern, southwestern, and Pacific Coast markets. To meet this situation, the Middle West concerns have frequently sought lower rates on their product or have established branch plants in their more distant markets.[16]

The manufacture of commercial fertilizer is another industry which is affected by the use of ubiquitous raw materials. In making commercial fertilizer, a considerable amount of ground rock or other filler is commonly combined with the more concentrated ingredients. This circumstance favors manufacture in consuming areas. Trends toward increasing decentralization of this industry, with resulting short hauls on the product, were noted in 1956 in a case before the Interstate Commerce Commission.[17]

Influence of Fuel Supply

It has already been noted that availability of fuel is one factor that affects the location of industries. Theoretically, fuel can be considered as an extreme example of a weight-losing raw material. It is a raw material which does not enter into the weight of the product. According to the principle we have described, the influence of fuel should be to pull strongly toward its source of supply. For many industries, however, the fuel requirements are so small that this influence is outweighed by other

---

[16] See particularly *Transcontinental Rates on Malt Liquors*, 276 ICC 621, 623, 626 (1949); and *Malt Liquors from Illinois, Missouri, Nebraska, & Wisconsin to Texas*, 299 ICC 255 (1956).

[17] *Darling & Co.* v. *Alton & Southern Railroad Co.*, 299 ICC 393, 398 (1956).

factors. For other industries this factor exerts a controlling influence on location.

Illustrations of the influence of fuel on the location of industry are abundant. Proximity to a fuel supply has always been an important factor in the location of the iron and steel industry. Absence of a fuel supply partly explains why there is so little manufacturing in the Dakotas, Kansas, and western Texas. The development of cotton mills in the towns of southern New England rather than in other parts of New England seems to have been due to the cheaper coal available at tidewater. As far as rates on cotton and cotton goods were concerned, southern New England had no advantage over the rest of New England. The "in rates" on cotton and the "out rates" on cotton goods were the same at all points in New England.[18] Fuel is such an important item in the cost of manufacturing glass that the industry has thrived chiefly in the regions where natural gas was available.[19]

EFFECT OF FREIGHT-RATE STRUCTURES

The peculiarities of freight-rate structures exert a profound influence on the location of industries. Some of the more important of these characteristics, and their effects on location, may be mentioned at this point.

Distance-Rate Systems

If freight rates increase with distance, nearness to markets or nearness to raw materials becomes of greater importance than if the rates do not vary with distance. The degree to which rates increase with distance is also of importance. The more rapid the rise in rates with increasing distance, the more the rates will restrict the movement of long-distance traffic, and the stronger becomes the tendency to avoid the high rates by locational changes.

Effect of Group Rates

In a later chapter[20] it will be shown that extensive grouping of origins and destinations is commonly found in railroad freight-rate structures. Rate groups may be small, involving little disregard of distance; or they may include all points over vast areas, disregarding differences in distance of several hundred miles. Grouping points of origin or destination gives all points within a group the same rates and equalizes the advantages of all towns within the same group as far as freight rates are concerned. The

---

[18] M. T. Copeland, *The Cotton Manufacturing Industry in the United States* (Cambridge: Harvard University Press, 1912), pp. 29–30.

[19] Hall, op. cit., p. cxcvii.

[20] Chapter 8, pp. 203–6.

blanketing of rates from all points in New England to destinations in the West long had a decentralizing effect on the location of industries in New England.[21]

Effect of Tapering Rates

As will be pointed out more fully later,[22] railroad freight rates are usually constructed on the tapering principle. This means that although the rates increase with distance, they do not increase in direct proportion to distance. Thus the rate for a distance of 200 miles will be less than twice the rate for 100 miles. The effect that this may have on locational advantage may be seen from the diagram in Figure 4–1.

If A is the source of the principal raw material used in the manufacture of a commodity to be consumed or sold in M, the manufacturer could be located in A, or B, or M. If he is located at A, he must pay the rate AM on the finished product; if he is located at M, he must pay the

FIGURE 4–1. Effect of Tapering Rates on Location of Industries

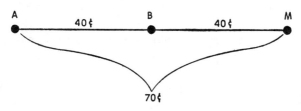

rate AM on his raw material. If the rates on the raw material and on the finished product are the same, and if there is no loss of weight in the manufacturing process, it would be a matter of indifference, as far as freight rates are concerned, whether the manufacturer located at A or at M. A manufacturer at B, however, would be at a disadvantage in comparison with a producer at either A or M, since he would have to pay the rate AB on his raw material and the rate BM on the finished product. Because rates are built on the tapering principle, the rate AB + BM would be greater than the rate AM. If there was weight loss in the manufacturing process, A would be a more favorable location than either B or M. If rates on the finished product were much higher than on the raw material, M would be a better location than either A or B for the manufacturing process to take place. We may conclude that when freight rates are built on the tapering principle, industries tend to be drawn ei-

---

[21] Eliot Jones, *Principles of Railway Transportation* (New York: Macmillan, 1924), p. 157.
[22] Pp. 188–90.

ther to the source of raw material or to the market and that intermediate points are placed at a rate disadvantage.

Transit Privileges

The rate disadvantage suffered by points lying between the source of a raw material and the market for the finished product may be entirely neutralized by the granting of "transit" privileges, of which the milling-in-transit privilege is perhaps the best known. Under this privilege, grain may be shipped from a grain market or a country point to a milling point, ground into flour, and shipped to market at the through rate applicable from the point where the grain originated to the final destination of the finished product. Usually the local rate on grain is paid to the milling point; and when the flour or other product moves out, it goes at "the balance of the through rate," that is, the difference between the rate on grain from point of origin to the final destination and what was paid when the grain was shipped into the milling point. By means of the milling-in-transit arrangement the through rate displaces the combination of rates into and out of the milling point. Since, as we have noted, a through rate is normally less than the sum of intermediate rates, the milling-in-transit privilege places upon an equality all points which lie between the point of origin of the grain and the final consuming point. Were this privilege not granted, the millers located at the grain markets, at consuming centers, or at so-called "rate-breaking points" would have an advantage over others. Those at the grain markets would get a through rate on flour. Those at the consuming points would get a through rate on wheat. Those at the rate-breaking points would pay a combination rate into the milling point and out; but this is the through rate in such instances, since rate-breaking points are points on which through combination rates are made when no single-factor through rate is published. All other millers would find the combination of rates into their milling points plus the rates from there to destination to be in excess of the through rate. The milling-in-transit privilege is thus a device to equalize the sum of the in and out rates at such points as are granted the transit privileges. The granting of this privilege accounts for the multitude of milling points scattered throughout the country.[23]

Similar in-transit arrangements are granted on many other commodities, with a similar purpose in mind. The fabrication-in-transit arrangement on steel was established in 1908 and 1909 at Toledo and Canton, Ohio, thereby substituting the through rate on steel from Pittsburgh for the Toledo combination. This enabled Toledo fabricating plants to compete with plants in the Pittsburgh district.[24]

---

[23] H. B. Vanderblue and K. F. Burgess, *Railroads: Rates, Service, Management* (New York: Macmillan, 1923), pp. 136–37.

[24] Ibid., p. 136.

Rate Adjustments to Meet Market Competition

The railroads, by their power to make and adjust rates, can alter the location of industries. They can maintain industries in unfavorable locations, and they can prevent their establishment at more favored places. This power is limited by the legal requirements that rates must be just and reasonable, not unjustly discriminatory or unduly preferential or prejudicial; but even so, the location of industries is profoundly affected by the rate policies of the carriers. In 1878 an agreement was made between the railroads to charge higher rates from the Middle West to the South than from the East to the South on certain articles manufactured in the East, while maintaining higher rates from the East to the South on certain western products.[25] This arrangement was designed to protect the traffic peculiar to each region and would, of course, have a tendency to retard changes in industrial location.

Railroads are usually interested in stimulating industries along their own lines. Low rates from distant producing points, to enable remote producers to sell goods in a given locality in competition with nearby producers, are to be found by the thousands. This phenomenon, known as "market competition," permeates the rate structure of the country. From New England to points west, rates have for many years been the same as the rates from New York in order to enable New England industries to compete with those in the industrial area about New York.[26] When the manufacture of cotton goods developed in the South, the carriers serving the southern mills found it necessary to lower the rates on cotton piece goods in order to enable the southern mills to sell in Chicago and adjoining territory in competition with New England mills.[27] Relatively low rates on coal from the southern coal fields to Lake Erie ports accounted in part for a shift in coal production from the Pennsylvania and Ohio fields to the southern fields.[28]

LOCATION OF MARKET CENTERS

The general principle governing the location of market centers is identical with that governing the location of manufacturing establishments. In fact, rate relationships play a more important part in the location of market centers than in the location of industries because other factors, such as labor costs, are comparatively unimportant to commercial enterprises. In general, goods will be bought and sold through markets

---

[25] *Freight Bureau v. Cincinnati, New Orleans & Texas Pacific R. R. Co.,* 6 ICC 195, 216, 241–46 (1894).

[26] Jones, op. cit., p. 157.

[27] *Smith Bros. Manufacturing Co. v. Aberdeen & Rockfish Railroad Co.,* 181 ICC 137, 139 (1931).

[28] D. P. Locklin, *Railroad Regulation since 1920* (New York: McGraw-Hill, 1928), pp. 188–98.

established at points having the lowest combination of rates. This probably explains why the important primary grain markets are at rate-breaking points like Chicago, St. Louis, and Minneapolis. In many respects the location of market centers involves fewer complicated rate relationships than those found to affect industrial establishments. The same commodities are shipped in as out; hence there is no such thing as a relationship between the rates on raw materials and finished products. There is no loss of weight, since no manufacturing processes are involved;[29] hence the situation is not complicated by the influence of weight-losing materials. Lastly, fuel supply is not of any importance.

Effect of Spread between Carload and Less-Carload Rates

There is one rate relationship that is of considerable importance in determining the location of jobbing centers. This is the relation between rates on small and large shipments. Jobbers, as a rule, buy in large lots and sell in smaller lots. If the rate per hundred pounds on carload lots is less than the rate per hundred pounds on less-than-carload lots, the jobber located near the consumer is favored. If no such distinction is made and "any-quantity" rates prevail—that is, rates are the same per hundred pounds regardless of the quantity shipped—the distant and local jobbers are upon an equality. When most of the manufacturing was carried on in the East, the maintenance of any-quantity rates enabled the eastern jobbers to sell direct to western retailers. The western jobbers favored the establishment of low carload rates, since such rates would enable them to compete with the eastern jobbers, who had to ship in less-than-carload quantities from the East.[30]

The conflict of interest between the two sets of jobbers is not ended with the adoption of lower rates on carload lots. The controversy then becomes one of the proper spread between the carload and less-than-carload rates. The greater the spread, the greater is the advantage of the jobber located near the consumer. This dispute was once a bone of contention between the Pacific Coast jobbers and those located east of the Missouri River.[31] The wide spread between carload and less-than-carload rates excluded eastern jobbers from business on the Pacific Coast.

MARKET AREAS

Once the market centers are established, rivalry between them takes the form of a struggle to sell (or buy) over the widest possible area.

---

[29] At grain markets, there may be a small loss of weight resulting from cleaning the grain.

[30] Ripley, op. cit., pp. 325–28.

[31] *Business Men's League of St. Louis* v. *Atchison, Topeka & Santa Fe Ry. Co.*, 9 ICC 318 (1902).

Manufacturers and producers of raw materials are also interested in the area in which they are able to sell goods in competition with producers located elsewhere. We are therefore interested in the laws determining the size of market areas. Freight rates play an important part in determining the size of these areas.

In visualizing the conditions to be described, two kinds of markets should be distinguished. Selling markets are those from which goods are sold or distributed to scattered buyers. These have been called "centrifugal markets," since the movement is from a center outward. Buying markets are those which collect goods produced in outlying areas. These have been called "centripetal markets," since the goods are drawn inward toward a center. A jobbing center or a manufacturing center is a selling market. The primary grain markets are buying markets.

The law governing market areas is illustrated by the diagram in Figure 4–2.[32]

FIGURE 4–2. Market Areas

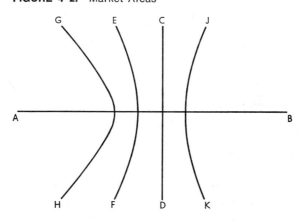

Selling Markets

Assume two markets, A and B. These may be considered as selling markets—markets in which goods of a certain kind are manufactured and sold in the surrounding territory. The division of the territory between the rival producers will depend upon two factors: the factory

---

[32] More elaborate discussions of the theory of market areas may be found in Frank A. Fetter, "The Economic Law of Market Areas," 38 *Quarterly Journal of Economics* 520 (1924), and by the same author, *The Masquerade of Monopoly* (New York: Harcourt, Brace, 1931), chap. xx; see also John D. Black, *Introduction to Production Economics* (New York: Holt, 1926), pp. 923–26. See also J. M. Cassels, *A Study of Fluid Milk Prices* (Cambridge: Harvard University Press, 1937), chaps. iii and iv, and E. M. Hoover, Jr., *Location Theory and the Shoe and Leather Industries* (Cambridge: Harvard University Press, 1937), particularly chaps. ii, iii, and v.

prices of the goods at A and B, respectively (the base prices), and the transportation rates from A and from B. If the base prices are the same, and if freight rates increase with distance and are on the same mileage basis from both A and B, the territory between A and B will be divided equally between the two markets. The line CD will mark the boundary between them. Points on this line can be supplied at the same delivered cost from both A and B. If the freight rates from A toward B are on a higher basis, mile for mile, than from B toward A, the market area of A will be restricted and that of B enlarged. The line of indifference—EF in the diagram—tends to curve about the point having the smaller market. The delivered price from B will be lower than from A in the area between B and the line EF. The area supplied by A would be still smaller if the difference in rates were greater.

If we return to our assumption that freight rates are the same from A and from B for equal distances but assume that the base prices are different in the two markets, the market with the lower base price will supply the larger area. If the goods are manufactured at A and B and the cost of production is less at A than at B, then A can quote a lower base price than B, and B's market area is restricted. If the difference in base prices is greater than the rate between A and B, B will be eliminated as a competitor. The producer at B cannot sell in his own community for less than A can produce the commodity and transport it to B.

It was pointed out above that the line of indifference which marks the boundary between two market areas tends to curve about the market having the smaller area. This is demonstrated in Figure 4–3. A and B are the rival markets. If the base price in B is higher than in A, B's market is smaller than A's. Each concentric circle gives the base price plus transportation costs to points at a given distance from the market.[33] On the line CD, the prices are the same on goods from both A and B. Notice that each additional concentric circle about A encroaches farther on the territory that might seem to be naturally tributary to B. If it is assumed that the rates increase 2 cents for each five miles, the distance between any two circles in Figure 4–3 would be five miles. The lower base price in A enables A to sell at points which are 25 miles farther from A than they are from B. Points on the line CD are all 25 miles farther from A than they are from B. Points at the left of CD are less than 25 miles farther from A than from B and hence are in A's territory; points at the right of the line CD are more than 25 miles farther from A than from B and hence cannot be reached by A at as low a delivered price as they can be reached by B.

---

[33] The diagram is constructed on the assumption that all points equidistant from A or B can be reached at the same transport cost. Actually the lowest transport costs would be on the lines of railways or other modes of transport leading directly from A and B, and transport costs would be greater at off-line points or at points served only by indirect routes.

Thus far we have assumed that the points of indifference which mark the boundary between the two market areas would be represented by a line. As a matter of fact, there are often considerable areas which may be supplied from different markets, and the boundary is not a line but a broad zone. This situation will usually be found to arise from one or more of the following conditions.

First, if the margin of profit to the producers is large, they may cut their prices or absorb part of the freight charges where it is necessary to do so to make sales. This means that the producers or dealers will sell in

FIGURE 4–3.   Unequal Market Areas

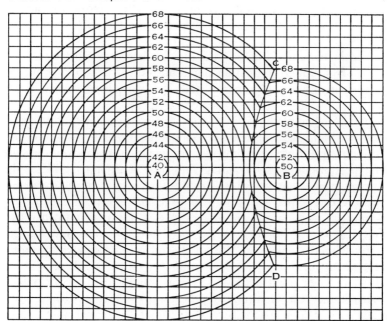

each others' territory near the theoretical line of demarcation between their respective territories.

Second, even greater absorptions in the freight will be made if the commodity is one which is produced under conditions which give rise to large overhead costs, provided there is unused capacity in the plants. Under these conditions the producers may consider it better to cut prices below average costs of production, that is, for that portion of the supply sold in a competitor's market. This will be considered as an extra output, produced at a low additional cost, which need not contribute its share toward the fixed or overhead expenses. Anything that the product will bring over and above the extra expense incurred in producing it will be considered as profit. This practice is identical with the practice of "dumping" in foreign trade. It is a form of price cutting apt to be dangerous to the producer, since his competitors can invade his market in retaliation as easily as he can invade theirs.

A third situation which leads to breaking down the division between market areas is the equalization of freight rates from the different markets to a common destination under the force of "market competition." Railroads might lower the rates in Figure 4–2 from A to points in B's territory in order to enable the producers at A to sell in that territory. Similarly the rates might be reduced from B to points in A's territory. This might even result in rates which, after a given point, decrease as distance increases; that is, the rates from A might increase with distance to points on the line CD and then decline as B is approached; and similarly the rates from B might increase until the line CD is reached and decline beyond.

A fourth reason for blurring the division between market areas is the practice of grouping destination points instead of adhering to a strictly distance scale of rates. This might result in a broad band or area in which both A and B could sell on equal terms.

It has been pointed out that the market area depends upon both freight rates and base prices. Market competition, in its simple forms, seeks to equalize the rates from rival producing areas to given consuming points. Illustrations are not wanting, however, of attempts to offset higher base prices at one center with lower rates than prevail from a rival center. Conversely the points with low base prices may be penalized by higher rates to offset their natural advantages. A case in point is afforded by the famous Eau Claire Lumber Case. Eau Claire, Winona, and La Crosse were rival lumber towns in Wisconsin and Minnesota. After some disagreement among the carriers concerning the rates from these rival towns to Missouri River points, the dispute was submitted to an arbitrator for decision. Under the resulting "Bogue award" in 1884, lower costs of producing lumber at Eau Claire were offset by higher rates in order that Eau Claire should not dominate the market at the Missouri River points and that each town might have a share of the business. The differential in favor of Winona and La Crosse was 5½ cents per hundred pounds.[34]

The illustration on page 79 assumed that rival manufacturers were located at A and B, respectively, and were selling their product in the surrounding territory. The same principles would apply if A and B were rival jobbing centers, drawing their supplies of goods from a common point of origin. But in the latter case the base prices at A and B would not be determined by manufacturing costs but by inbound freight rates. If the "in rates" to A were greater than to B and the "out rates" were the same for equal distances, A's market would be reduced in area, and B's would be enlarged. In the jobbing business, therefore, the in- and

---

[34] *Eau Claire Board of Trade v. Chicago, Milwaukee & St. Paul Ry. Co.,* 4 ICR 65 (1892).

out-rate adjustments will determine the area tributary to a given market.

Controversies over in and out rates at important jobbing centers have often come before the Interstate Commerce Commission.[35] "The question of rates to and from jobbing points has been and is continuously being pressed upon our attention by complaining shippers," said a report of the Commission. "The desire of jobbers located at various points is to have rates into and out of their particular points equalized, so that through rates to consuming territories shall be the same, no matter through which point the traffic moves."[36]

The adjustment of rates to and from the so-called "Colorado Common Points" affords an illustration of such equalization. The Common Points—Denver, Colorado Springs, Pueblo, Walsenburg, and Trinidad—had the same inbound rates from all eastern points; hence the term "Common Points." The in rates were therefore equal. The out rates were so adjusted that each town had a small distributing territory tributary to it; but after a certain distance was reached, the out rates were equalized from all the Common Points.[37] The old Texas intrastate rate structure was built in a somewhat similar manner. Rates increased with distance up to certain limits—245 miles on first-class traffic. Beyond these limits the rates in eastern Texas were the same, regardless of distance. The result was to give many jobbing centers a small area which was their own, but outside this territory all jobbing centers were upon an equality.[38]

The famous Shreveport Cases illustrate the tendency to offset high in rates by low out rates in order to enlarge the market area of towns unfavorably situated.[39] Dallas and Houston were two jobbing centers in Texas. Shreveport, Louisiana, was a rival jobbing town not far from the Texas boundary. Shreveport enjoyed lower rates on manufactured goods from the North and East. To overcome the disadvantage of Dallas and Houston, the Texas Commission had prescribed a scale of intrastate rates in Texas which were lower than the interstate scale from Shreveport into Texas. These lower intrastate rates were later found discriminatory against Shreveport and were brought up to the level of the interstate rates.

Buying Markets

Similar principles apply if A and B are buying markets. Shippers will send goods to the market which will net them the greatest return. This

---

[35] For example, *Mobridge Grocery Co.* v. *Chicago, Milwaukee & St. Paul Ry. Co.*, 52 ICC 307 (1919).

[36] *Wichita Wholesale Furniture Co.* v. *Atchison, Topeka & Santa Fe Ry. Co.*, 44 ICC 339, 343 (1917).

[37] *Pueblo Commerce Club* v. *Denver & Rio Grande R. R. Co.*, 31 ICC 133 (1924).

[38] Ripley, op. cit., p. 394.

[39] 23 ICC 31 (1912).

will depend upon the prices obtainable in the two markets and the freight rates to them. The market with the higher price or with the lower rate will draw from the larger area. If A and B are purchasing a product for which there is a central market, as in the case of grain, the price in A and B will correspond to the price in the central market less transportation and other costs. Here the in-and-out-rate adjustments again become important. The flow of grain in the United States affords a good illustration of these principles. Whether Kansas grain, for instance, moves south to the Gulf for export, or north and east to important interior markets, will depend upon the freight-rate adjustment and the prices of grain in the various markets. But we have learned that when we are on an export basis, the prices in the various markets tend to be the Liverpool price minus the transportation and other costs incurred in handling the grain. Normally the grain from northern Kansas moves northward and eastward to interior centers, while that from southern Kansas moves to the Gulf.[40] Slight changes in prices in the various markets or changes in freight rates may change the direction of grain flow.

Very delicate rate adjustments on export grain determine through which port the grain shall move. The establishment of the "port differentials" was based on the rivalry of the various ports for the export grain business. Originally these differentials were made in order to equalize the in rates to the various ports with the out rates, i.e., the ocean rates from the port to European ports.[41] On grain for export the domestic rate to Baltimore was the key rate. In 1919 the export rate to Philadelphia was made by adding ½ cent per hundred pounds to the Baltimore rate. Rates to New York and Boston were made by adding 1½ cents to the Baltimore rate.[42] From any important grain market, grain could be shipped to Liverpool via a number of ports with but small differences in the total cost.

In the movement of grain to the primary markets from the grain-growing areas of the United States, the important markets, except in unusual cases, draw no grain from areas east of the market. Chicago draws grain mostly from Illinois and Iowa, with some from Minnesota and South Dakota. It derives none from Ohio, Michigan, or Indiana, to the east, or from Missouri, to the south. Minneapolis receipts are from Minnesota, the Dakotas, and some from Montana—all to the west. Duluth receipts come from the same area. The Kansas City supply comes largely from Kansas, to the west; from Nebraska, to the northwest; and from

---

[40] *Prices of Wheat to Producers in Kansas*, 63d Cong., 3d Sess., House Doc. No. 1271 (1914), p. 4.

[41] U.S. Tariff Commission, *Preferential Transportation Rates and Their Relation to Import and Export Traffic of the United States* (1922), p. 35.

[42] Ibid., p. 129.

Iowa, to the north.[43] This phenomenon is easy to explain in terms of our study of the law of market areas. The general movement of grain is from west to east, except in the areas which ship grain to the Pacific Coast. From a given point within the broad area that ships grain to the east, the sum of the in and out rates through a market lying to the west would be greater than through a market lying to the east.

EFFECT OF INDUSTRY PRICING POLICIES

The normal effects of transportation costs on both the size of market areas and the location of industries may be very greatly modified by industry pricing policies. This may be illustrated by reference to the single-basing-point pricing system described in the preceding chapter.

Under a single-basing-point system, it will be recalled, the price at any place in the country is the basing-point price plus freight from the basing point. All other producers, wherever located, are free to meet this price but not to charge less. It appears, therefore, that under this pricing system the producers at the basing point may not be undersold anywhere in the country, since in any market the price must be the basing-point price plus freight from the basing point. Other producers, however, may not be able to sell in markets which are much nearer to the basing point than to these nonbasing-point producers. In such markets the nonbasing-point producer must absorb the differences in freight or not sell in those markets. To markets that are closer to the nonbasing-point producer than to the basing point, the nonbasing-point producer receives a higher factory price than the basing-point producer. It is apparent, however, that under the single-basing-point system the market area of the basing-point producer covers the whole country, while the nonbasing-point producer has a more restricted market area. It would thus appear that the single-basing-point pricing system is likely to result in expansion of production at the basing point and to restrict expansion at other producing points.[44]

The single-basing-point system also affects the location of industries which use as a raw material the products of the industries maintaining a basing-point system. Under the single-basing-point system the price of the product is lowest at the basing point. At all other points, including other producing points, the price is higher than at the basing point. The effect of this pricing system is to draw processing operations to the basing point. Thus the Pittsburgh-plus pricing system would appear to have

---

[43] For further details see Federal Trade Commission, *Report on the Grain Travel*, Vol. I (1920), pp. 132–44. The same situation is indicated in *Report of the Industrial Commission*, Vol. VI (1901), map facing p. 47.

[44] For confirmation of this view as applied to the steel industry see George W. Stocking, *Basing Point Pricing and Regional Development* (Chapel Hill: University of North Carolina Press, 1954), pp. 61–62.

encouraged steel fabrication in the Pittsburgh area rather than at other steel-producing points.[45] In the glucose or corn-syrup industry, where glucose prices were Chicago prices plus freight from Chicago,[46] corn syrup would have been cheaper in Chicago than at any other point, including other producing points like Kansas City, Missouri, or Decatur, Illinois; hence Chicago would appear to have been the most favorable location for an industry using corn syrup as a raw material. The apparent outlawing of basing-point pricing systems in 1948 may prove to have important effects on the location of industries and on regional development.

FREIGHT RATES AND AGRICULTURAL PRODUCTION

It has been shown that manufacturing industries tend to be located where aggregate transportation charges will be the least.[47] The same rule governs the location of the jobbing business and other market centers. Does a similar rule operate in the case of agricultural production? In order to answer this question, two types of agricultural products, garden truck and wheat, may be considered.

It is a commonplace observation that truck gardens are located close to the centers of population and that nearness to market is such an important matter that very high rentals are paid for land suitable for such use. Nearness to market is an advantage because of the bulkiness and perishability of the product. Of course, large quantities of vegetables and fruits are shipped long distances to city markets. Much of this long-distance shipment, however, is seasonal in nature. Fresh fruits and vegetables are sent to northern markets long before a local crop can be produced. It must also be recognized that factors other than transportation costs affect types of agriculture. If certain vegetables can be grown in certain areas more cheaply than near the markets, they will be grown in the advantageous locations and shipped long distances, transportation charges permitting. This is a simple case of geographical division of labor. But in this chapter the effects of transportation charges alone are under consideration, and it is clear that the prevalence of truck gardening in regions close to large cities on high-priced land is to be explained by the savings in freight charges and other advantages of proximity to market. Unless some unusual advantage attaches to a distant location, garden truck can be grown most profitably close to the market. There would seem to be, here, an approximation to the general rule that the

---

[45] Ibid., pp. 63–64.

[46] The pricing policy in the corn-syrup industry is revealed in *Corn Products Refining Co.* v. *Federal Trade Commission*, 324 U.S. 726 (1945), and in *Federal Trade Commission* v. *A. E. Staley Mfg. Co.*, 324 U.S. 746 (1945).

[47] If we disregard nontransportation factors that may affect location.

commodity will be produced where transportation costs, including loss from deterioration, are least.

Wheat, on the other hand, is grown in remote corners of the earth, thousands of miles from consuming markets, and the aggregate transportation charge is large. The location of wheat production is not near the markets where a saving in freight rates would be possible. Wheat production, therefore, does not conform to the rule that production will be carried on where transportation costs are least.

Between these two rather extreme examples are many other agricultural products produced at varying distances from markets. Milk is produced farther away from markets than garden truck but not so far away as butter and cheese, and beef. But it is already apparent why all agricultural products and livestock cannot be produced near consuming areas. There isn't room enough. Agricultural production, unlike manufacturing industries, requires extensive areas of land; and if land is used for one purpose, it cannot be used for another. For some crops, nearness to market is extremely important. For others, it is less important. Producers of the former class of crops will bid higher for the use of the land close to market areas than can the producers of crops for which nearness to market is less important. The crops for which nearness is less essential are therefore forced to occupy areas remoter from the markets.[48] The migration of the wheat belt in the United States is a good illustration of this principle. Wheat raising has always been pushed to the newer and less populated areas. It has been driven from New England and western New York to the Far West. As population advances, the more profitable uses for the land crowd out the wheat.[49]

The principle governing the relation between transportation costs and agricultural production may now be stated. Commodities which cannot stand long-distance transportation, because of bulkiness or perishability, will be produced near consuming markets. Other commodities will be pushed to remoter areas. When the bulky crops are produced in the remoter areas, they are almost always converted into a more concentrated form for shipment. Hay and grain, for instance, will be converted into beef and dairy products.

The agricultural geography of the United States affords many illustrations of the relationship between transportation costs and types of farming. The importance of truck farming in close proximity to large cities has already been noted. Regional variations within the dairying industry itself show the influence of transportation charges and differences in distance from consuming markets. In the area lying about any large industrial center in parts of the United States where dairying is at all

---

[48] The problem of rival uses of the same area is involved in the choice of sites for factories, stores, etc., in any city.

[49] C. W. Thompson, "The Movement of Wheat-Growing: A Study of a Leading State," 18 *Quarterly Journal of Economics* 570 (1904).

feasible, there tend to be three zones of dairying. Closest to the city is a fluid-milk zone; beyond this is a cream zone; and farther out there is a butter-and-cheese zone.[50] The dairying regions of New England market a large part of their product in the form of milk and cream because of the nearness to the centers of population represented by the New York and Boston milk markets. The dairying regions of the Middle West, because of greater distances from large centers of population, are the principal source of butter and cheese.

Professor G. F. Warren pointed out many years ago that the difference between Iowa and Illinois in the production of hogs is to be explained largely by differences in the cost of shipping corn to market. Both Illinois and Iowa produce large quantities of corn, but Illinois had only about half as many hogs.[51] The Illinois farmer, in general, found it more profitable to ship his corn to market. The Iowa farmer, on the other hand, found it more profitable to convert corn into pork. "A difference of 2 cents per bushel in the price of corn," says Warren, "has been sufficient to make this surprising difference in the number of hogs."[52] The difference in price of corn was due to the greater distance of the Iowa farmer from the grain markets. Although the freight rates are higher on hogs than on corn, a pound of pork represents five or six pounds of corn; and it is cheaper for the Iowa farmer to ship corn to market in the form of pork. Another way of looking at this zoning of agricultural production is to say that where feed is cheapest, it will be converted into livestock. But we saw in Chapter 3 that grain, hay, and other products have their lowest value in regions remote from consuming markets because of the high cost of transporting them to market. It is in conformity with this principle, also, that the surplus poultry and egg production of the country is largely in the grain-growing regions, where grain is cheapest.[53]

The influence of freight charges on types of agricultural production is often revealed when rates are changed. The increases in freight rates during and after World War I made it less profitable for the Nebraska farmer to sell corn and more profitable for him to feed it to hogs. The same increases in rates made it less profitable for Ohio and Pennsylvania farmers to raise hogs and more profitable for them to market their crops directly.[54] Similarly the increases in rates on agricultural products after World War II brought complaints of hardships on producing areas that

---

[50] John D. Black, *The Dairy Industry and the AAA* (Washington, D.C.: Brookings Institution, 1935), pp. 153–54; and John M. Cassels, *A Study of Fluid Milk Prices* (Cambridge: Harvard University Press, 1937), pp. 20–24.

[51] G. F. Warren, *Farm Management* (New York: Macmillan, 1913), pp. 55–56.

[52] Ibid., p. 56.

[53] Isaac Lippincott, *Economic Development of the United States* (New York: Appleton, 1921), p. 407.

[54] H. C. Filley, *Hog Prices*, Nebraska Agricultural Experiment Station, Bulletin 208 (Lincoln, Neb., 1925), p. 10.

were remote from their markets.[55] Increases in air-freight rates on cut flowers from California to the East which occurred in 1952 and 1953 were blamed for a decline in the acreage devoted to cut-flower production in Southern California.[56] It is clear that changes in rates on agricultural products, either upward or downward, may bring changes in types of farming to a particular area.

FREIGHT RATES AND ECONOMIC POLICY

Since the level of freight rates on particular commodities affects the ability to exploit the resources of an area, and rate relationships of various sorts may determine the location of industries, it is not strange that governments often manipulate freight rates, or neutralize their effect, in order to foster the development of particular industries or areas, or to bring about some desired pattern of industrial location. This is particularly common where the railroads are government owned. An example of such a policy is afforded by the Crows Nest Pass rates in Canada, dating back to 1897, which were designed to foster the development of the Prairie Provinces by making low rates on grain, their principal product.[57] Canada provides another illustration in the Maritime Freight Rates Act of 1927 which subsidizes shipments to and from the Maritime Provinces in order to overcome the freight-rate handicap of the area.[58] The State of Victoria, in Australia, grants subsidies to industries located, or proposed to be located, in country districts. This is done in an effort to decentralize industry by offsetting the locational disadvantage of interior points as compared with Melbourne, a port city. The disadvantage of interior points is largely a transportation-cost disadvantage.[59]

SELECTED REFERENCES

A classic treatment of the location of industries is Alfred Weber, *Über den Standort der Industrien.* For an English translation see C. J. Friedrich, *Alfred Weber's Theory of the Location of Industries* (Chicago: University of Chicago Press, 1929). Weber's treatment is abstract and highly theoretical. There is an excellent summary and criticism of Weber's theory in Stuart Daggett, *Principles of Inland Transportation* (4th ed.; New York: Harper, 1955), pp. 434–43. A modern book devoted to location of industries is Edgar M.

---

[55] Donald E. Church, *Effect of Increases in Freight Rates on Agricultural Products,* U.S. Department of Agriculture, Circular No. 847 (1950).

[56] Civil Aeronautics Board, *Air Freight Rate Investigation,* 20 CAB 548 (1955).

[57] A. W. Currie, *Economics of Canadian Transportation* (Toronto: University of Toronto Press, 1954), particularly pp. 6, 46–47, 84–87.

[58] Ibid., pp. 93–97.

[59] Described in I. Thomas, "The Influence of Freight Rates on the Location of Industry in New Zealand," 30 *Institute of Transport Journal* 263 (1964).

Hoover, Jr., *The Location of Economic Activity* (New York: McGraw-Hill, 1948). The article by E. A. Ross on "The Location of Industries," 10 *Quarterly Journal of Economics* 247 (1896), is a good general discussion of the subject. So also is the article by Malcolm Keir, "Economic Factors in the Location of Manufacturing Industries," 97 *Annals of the American Academy of Political and Social Science* 83 (1921). For a review of the earlier literature on the subject see Witold Kryzanowski, "Review of the Literature of the Location of Industries," 35 *Journal of Political Economy* 278 (1927). For other general discussions see E. S. Lynch, "The Influence of Transportation on the Location of Economic Activities," in National Resources Planning Board, *Transportation and National Policy* (Washington, D.C.: U.S. Government Printing Office, 1942), pp. 71–86.

The law of market areas is explained by Frank A. Fetter in "The Economic Law of Market Areas," 38 *Quarterly Journal of Economics* 520 (1924). It is further developed by the same author in *The Masquerade of Monopoly* (New York: Harcourt, Brace, 1931). John D. Black also discusses the subject in *Introduction to Production Economics* (New York: Holt, 1926), pp. 923–30. See also Hoover, op. cit., chap. iv; also J. M. Cassels, *A Study of Fluid Milk Prices* (Cambridge: Harvard University Press, 1937), and Warren C. Waite and Harry C. Trelogan, *Agricultural Market Prices* (New York: Wiley, 1951), pp. 162–65.

The relation of transportation costs to agriculture was developed by J. H. von Thunen in *Der Isolierte Staat in Beziehung auf Landwirthschaft und Nationalökonomie* (Berlin: Wiegandt, Hempel and Parey, 1875). For a summary and criticism of Thunen's theory see Daggett, op. cit., pp. 430–34. Chapter ii in G. F. Warren, *Farm Management* (New York: Macmillan, 1913), contains much excellent material relative to the effect of freight rates on types of farming. The article of C. W. Thompson, "The Movement of Wheat-Growing: A Study of a Leading State," 18 *Quarterly Journal of Economics* 570 (1904), develops the principles as they affect wheat growing. For the relation of transportation costs to the dairying industry see J. M. Cassels, op. cit., and also John D. Black, *The Dairy Industry and the AAA* (Washington, D.C.: Brookings Institution, 1935), chap. vi.

Chapter 5   BEFORE RAILROADS

Preceding chapters have shown the economic importance of good transportation and have discussed the relation of transportation costs and freight rates to prices and to the location of economic activity. With these considerations in mind, it is advisable to give some attention to the history of transportation in the United States.

Long before railroads had been thought of, the people of the United States had set about improving their transportation facilities to the best of their abilities. The transportation systems which they constructed were of great importance at the time, although they have been largely forgotten by later generations.

Colonial America relied chiefly upon the ocean and navigable streams for transportation routes. Communication between the colonies was difficult except by sea. The important cities and towns were on the coast or no farther inland than the head of navigation on the numerous streams flowing into the Atlantic.

EARLY RIVER TRANSPORTATION

As settlers penetrated into the interior, the upper reaches of the streams were utilized by small river craft of various sorts for trade with the older towns along the coast. A not insignificant amount of commerce was carried on in this way. Later, as the territory west of the Alleghenies was settled, the Mississippi and Ohio rivers and their tributaries became important avenues of commerce.

Boats of various sizes and descriptions were used on the streams. It is almost impossible to distinguish between the many types of craft, since the types as well as the nomenclature differed in the various parts of the country. The boats were usually propelled by oars in quiet water and by poles when moving against a strong current. The smaller and narrower boats were used for both upstream and downstream traffic; the larger craft were used only for floating traffic downstream.

Huge flatboats were developed, particularly for the downstream traffic on the Mississippi and Ohio rivers. They were square-nosed boats, with perpendicular sides, and were constructed of heavy planks. Flat-boats were unwieldy affairs, and although they had oars for steering, they were propelled by the current. The advantage of the flatboat lay in its large capacity and its ability to float in shallow water. Flatboats were eventually constructed which were 150 feet long and 24 feet wide and capable of carrying 300 tons.[1] They drew from one to two and a half feet of water. Large numbers of these boats carried traffic down the Ohio and Mississippi rivers to New Orleans. No attempt was made to move the flatboats upstream. They were sold for lumber at destination, and the members of the crew made their way back on foot or in smaller boats that went up the river. The flatboats rarely could be sold in New Orleans for more than a tenth of their cost.

Transportation by river boats was slow and dangerous. The trip from Pittsburgh to the mouth of the Ohio took fifteen days under the most favorable conditions.[2] From Cincinnati to New Orleans and return took approximately six months.[3] The risks of transportation were great. Boats were easily wrecked; the rivers were full of snags and sandbars; and sometimes the boats fell into the hands of river pirates.

It is difficult to say exactly what was the cost of transportation on the rivers. In the first place, costs varied greatly, depending upon the river to be navigated and the size of the boats. Much of the traffic, furthermore, was carried by the owner of the goods. This was particularly true in the Middle West. An individual might build a boat, buy up the produce of the region, and set out for New Orleans. Under such conditions no transportation charge was involved. Professor Dixon, however, estimates that the charges levied for upstream transportation on the Mississippi River and its tributaries averaged about 7 cents per ton-mile, while the downstream rate was a little over 1 cent per ton-mile. The latter figure is not far from the average revenue per ton-mile received by United States railroads in the years just prior to World War II.

Notwithstanding the difficulties of river transportation, the volume of traffic transported in this way was surprisingly large. It is estimated that as early as 1790 about 150,000 bushels of grain were floated down the Susquehanna River from Pennsylvania and southern New York for shipment to Philadelphia.[4] During a period of about four months in 1827 a count was made at Harrisburg which showed that 1,631 rafts, 1,370 arks, and 300 keelboats had passed down the Susquehanna. It was esti-

---

[1] Frank H. Dixon, *Traffic History of the Mississippi River* (Washington, D.C.: U.S. Government Printing Office, 1915), p. 13.

[2] Caroline E. MacGill, *History of Transportation in the United States before 1860* (Washington, D.C.: Carnegie Institution, 1917), p. 94.

[3] J. L. Ringwalt, *Development of Transportation Systems in the United States* (Philadelphia: Railway World Office, 1888), p. 14.

[4] Alvin H. Harlow, *Old Towpaths* (New York: Appleton, 1926), p. 37.

mated that the tonnage consisted of approximately 40,000,000 feet of lumber, 468,000 barrels of flour and whiskey, 244,000 bushels of wheat, and 11,000 tons of coal.[5] It is estimated that as early as 1817, 1,500 flatboats and 500 barges went down the Mississippi to New Orleans annually.[6] In the 20s it was not uncommon for a hundred boats a day to pass New Madrid, below the mouth of the Ohio.[7] A single flatboat might carry a cargo worth two or three thousand dollars. Large quantities of pork, bacon, flour, whiskey, apples, cider, and cheese were shipped to New Orleans every year by boats. The value of the cargoes going down the Mississippi was over $3,600,000 in 1801, and about $5,370,000 in 1807.[8] The tonnage upstream on the Mississippi was only about 10 percent of that down. On the Ohio the volume of upstream traffic was relatively greater than on the Mississippi, as the current on the Ohio was not as strong.[9] The upstream traffic consisted largely of coffee, sugar, molasses, and manufactured goods from the East. When the steamboats came upon the scene, they took the upstream traffic; and the keelboats and similar craft practically disappeared from the rivers. The flatboats, however, still continued to carry goods down the streams; in fact, their number increased. River traffic was increasing in volume, and the downstream tonnage was greater than that upstream. Steamboats carried most of the upstream traffic and returned with a load, but supplemental facilities were necessary to carry the downstream tonnage. The flatboat was suited to this task, as the cost of floating the cargoes down the river compared favorably with steamboat charges. It is estimated that between 1820 and 1830, although steamboats were common, as many as 3,000 flatboats annually descended the Ohio.[10] In 1846–47 nearly 2,800 flatboats arrived at New Orleans.[11] After that time there was a steady decline in the flatboat business. The Civil War stopped the traffic completely, and it was not revived to any great extent afterwards.

STEAMBOATS

Robert Fulton is commonly given credit for the first successful steamboat, the "Clermont," which went up the Hudson River from New York to Albany in 1807. There are other contenders for the honor of inventing the steamboat, and it seems necessary to recognize that Fulton was but one of several persons who experimented with some degree of

---

[5] Ibid.
[6] Ibid.
[7] Ibid., p. 38.
[8] MacGill, op. cit., p. 109.
[9] Ibid.
[10] Dixon, op. cit., p. 14.
[11] Ibid.

success in developing a boat propelled by steam power.[12] Fulton, however, probably exercised a greater influence on the development of steamboats and on steamboat transportation than the others, and in his lifetime he designed 21 successful steamboats.[13]

The steamboat made its first appearance on the Ohio River in 1809. In 1811 the steamboat "New Orleans" made its way down the Ohio and Mississippi rivers from Pittsburgh to New Orleans,[14] and in 1815 the "Enterprise" made the trip upstream from New Orleans to Pittsburgh.[15] It was not until 1817, however, that regular service was established on these rivers. A type of steamboat was developed on the western rivers which was quite different from those used in the East. The western boats were ingeniously designed for the peculiar navigation conditions found on these waters.[16] Table 5–1, showing the steamboats built on the Ohio

TABLE 5–1. Steamboats Built on the Ohio River*

1811	1	1820	10
1814	1	1821	5
1815	2	1822	13
1816	3	1823	15
1817	7	1824	16
1818	25	1825	27
1819	34	1826	56
		1827	36

* Caroline E. MacGill, *History of Transportation in the United States before 1860* (Washington, D.C.: Carnegie Institution, 1917), p. 108.

River in different years, indicates the rise of steamboating. The first steamboat appeared on the Great Lakes in 1816, but steamboat traffic did not develop extensively on the Lakes until about 1850.

The early steamboats were flimsily built and recklessly operated and were rarely fit for service after five years.[17] Previous to 1826, 41 percent of all the steamboats constructed on the Mississippi had either been sunk or destroyed.[18] Between 1810 and 1850 the steamboats lost on the Missis-

---

[12] See A. D. Turnbull, *John Stevens, an American Record* (London: Century, 1928); Thomas Boyd, *Poor John Fitch* (New York: Putnam's, 1935); Greville Bathe and Dorothy Bathe, *Oliver Evans: A Chronicle of Early American Engineering* (Philadelphia: Historical Society of Pennsylvania, 1935); Ella M. Turner, *James Rumsey: Pioneer in Steam Navigation* (Scottdale, Pa.: Mennonite Publishing House, 1930); James T. Flexner, *Steamboats Come True: American Inventors in Action* (New York: Viking Press, 1944).

[13] Flexner, op. cit., p. 352.

[14] Louis C. Hunter, *Steamboats on the Western Rivers* (Cambridge: Harvard University Press, 1949), p. 12.

[15] Ibid., pp. 17–18.

[16] Ibid., chaps. ii and iii.

[17] Dixon, op. cit., p. 28.

[18] MacGill, op. cit., p. 108.

sippi numbered 1,070 and represented an investment of over $7,000,000, and the persons killed and injured numbered 4,180.[19]

The speed of the steamboats was slow when compared with the speed of railway transportation today, but better time was made than had been possible in the old boating days. The average rate of speed on the Mississippi and Ohio in 1840 was about 6 miles per hour upstream and 10 or 12 miles per hour downstream.[20]

Steamboat rates fluctuated greatly, varying with the amount of traffic available and the number of boats to carry it. On the Ohio River, rates varied inversely with the height of the river; during seasons of low water the rates were often four times the rates during high water and even became ten times as high.[21] Sometimes the rates represented monopoly charges; at other times, when competition was strong, they were reduced to much lower levels. As a result it is difficult to say what normal charges were. In 1839 the rates from New Orleans to St. Louis were 75 cents per hundred pounds, or 13 mills per ton-mile. Between 1850 and 1860 freight rates from Pittsburgh to St. Louis were frequently from 3.6 to 4.3 cents per ton-mile. At times, however, the rates were less than 1 cent per ton-mile.[22] In 1839 the chief engineer of the James River & Kanawha Canal and Railroad estimated that the rates on steamboats ranged from ½ to 1½ cents per ton-mile.[23] In 1854 the state engineer of New York estimated the average rate per ton-mile on the Mississippi to be from 6 to 8 mills; on the Ohio, 8 mills; and on the Hudson, 7 mills.[24]

The steamboats made the Ohio and Mississippi rivers the principal avenues of commerce in the Middle West. New Orleans, in 1840, ranked fourth among the ports of the world. It was exceeded only by London, Liverpool, and New York in the amount of commerce which it handled.[25] Bogart estimates that the total commerce on the western rivers in 1860 exceeded $300,000,000.[26] The volume of traffic on the rivers is indicated by the steamboat arrivals at New Orleans in various years. These figures are shown in Table 5–2.

If classified by the type of operations in which they were engaged, steamboats on the western rivers were of three classes—transients, packets, and line boats. Transients roamed the rivers, picking up traffic wherever it could be obtained. Packets, on the other hand, made regular trips

---

[19] Dixon, op. cit., p. 28.

[20] Ibid.

[21] Louis C. Hunter, *Studies in the Economic History of the Ohio Valley*, Smith College Studies in History, Vol. XIX (1933–34), p. 8.

[22] Dixon, op. cit., p. 27.

[23] MacGill, op. cit., p. 574.

[24] Ibid., p. 581.

[25] Dixon, op. cit., p. 15.

[26] E. L. Bogart, *Economic History of the American People* (New York: Longmans, 1930), p. 330.

over regular routes at stated intervals. Line boats consisted of two or more packets operating between the same ports under some form of loose organization or agreement.

Steamboat traffic continued to develop until about 1860. Between 1850 and 1860, however, the steamboats began to feel the competition of railroads. Before this time the railroads had been largely passenger carriers; and in so far as they carried freight, they acted as feeders to the waterways. During the 50s, with the consolidation of railroads into longer lines and the construction of additional mileage, the railroads began to divert traffic from the rivers of the Middle West. Traffic that formerly went down the rivers was diverted eastward by rail. When the Civil War broke out, traffic on the Mississippi practically ceased. After the war, traffic revived somewhat, but the steamboats were unable to compete successfully with the railroads. After 1880 steamboating de-

TABLE 5-2. Arrivals of Steamboats at New Orleans*

1814	21	1840	1,573
1815	40	1845	2,530
1820	198	1850	2,784
1825	502	1855	2,763
1830	989	1860	3,566
1835	1,005		

* Frank H. Dixon, *Traffic History of the Mississippi River* (Washington, D.C.: U.S. Government Printing Office, 1915), p. 15.

clined rapidly until the boats practically disappeared from the western rivers.

CANALS

During the early part of the 19th century an extensive system of canals was constructed in the United States. More than 4,400 miles were completed, of which nearly all was constructed during the first half of the century. There had been some canal construction in the 1780s and 1790s, but it consisted largely of short canals around waterfalls or rapids in the rivers. The era of canal building was really ushered in with the completion of the Erie Canal in 1825. This period came to an end with the crisis of 1837, but canal building on a smaller scale continued in the 40s and 50s.

Several of the early canals in the United States were built in Pennsylvania and connected the anthracite coal fields with tidewater. These canals were built by private companies, while most of the canals completed during the era of rapid canal building were state enterprises. Historically, the most important canal built in the United States was the Erie Canal, constructed by the state of New York. This canal extended across the state from Buffalo, on Lake Erie, to Albany, on the Hudson

River, as shown in Figure 5–1. It was 364 miles long and cost about $7 million. The Erie Canal opened a cheap route between the East and the West and diverted eastward much traffic that had formerly gone down the Mississippi to New Orleans. New York City became the important commercial center on the Atlantic Coast and secured an immense advantage over Baltimore and Philadelphia, which had shared in the trade with the West. The canal was an important factor in the development of the West. Financially the Erie Canal was a great success. The revenue from tolls in the first seven years more than covered the entire cost of construction.

The success of the Erie Canal, coupled with the economic need for cheaper and more adequate transportation facilities, resulted in the con-

FIGURE 5–1. The Erie Canal

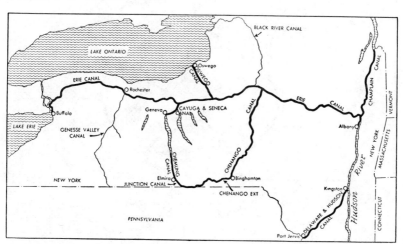

struction of many other canals by the states. In fact, a veritable orgy of canal building occurred after 1825. Many of the projects were unwise and proved to be heavy financial burdens to the states which had constructed them. The principal Eastern canals are shown in Figure 5–2.

Among the more important projects stimulated by the success of the Erie Canal was a system of railroads and canals in Pennsylvania which came to be known as the Pennsylvania Public Works. The main line of this system was projected as a rival of the Erie Canal. The Erie Canal was giving New York a larger share of the trade with the West, to the detriment of Philadelphia. The Pennsylvania Public Works were supposed to recover much of this trade for Philadelphia. Although the system comprised both railroads and canals, it may properly be considered in this chapter, as the canal mileage exceeded the rail mileage and the railroads were considered as a means of portaging freight over difficult sections of the route where a canal was impossible or impracticable. As finally constructed, the Main Line of the system consisted of a railroad from Philadelphia to Columbia, 81 miles; the Eastern Division of the Pennsylvania Canal, from Columbia to Hollidaysburg, 173 miles; the Allegheny Portage Railroad, from Hollidaysburg to Johnstown, 36 miles; and the Western Division of the Pennsylvania Canal, from Johns-

FIGURE 5–2.   Eastern Canals

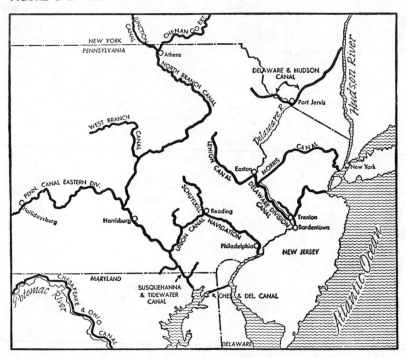

town to Pittsburgh, 105 miles. (See Figure 5–3.) The entire length was 395 miles, of which 278 were by canal. A railroad instead of a canal was constructed from Philadelphia to Columbia because of the hilly country which had to be traversed. The Allegheny Portage Railroad was constructed because of the impossibility of constructing a canal over the mountains. The Portage Railroad consisted of five level stretches and five inclined planes on both eastern and western slopes of the mountains, with a level section at the summit 1½ miles long. Horses at first supplied the motive power on the levels, but locomotives were used later. Stationary engines pulled the cars over the inclined planes by means of cables. The steepest plane rose 10½ feet in every 100 feet. The highest point on the summit was 1,399 feet above the canal at Hollidaysburg and 1,172 feet above the canal at Johnstown.[27] Boats were constructed in sections for use on the Pennsylvania Canal, and each section was mounted on flat cars at the junction with the Portage Railroad and hauled over the mountains, where the sections were assembled and placed in the canal again.

The Main Line of the Pennsylvania Public Works was completed in 1834 at a cost of about $10 million. The route was undoubtedly of great benefit to those sections of the state which it served, but it was not a successful competitor of the Erie Canal. The physical features of the country did not permit as favorable a route through Pennsylvania as through New York. Merchants and manufacturers of Philadelphia found

FIGURE 5–3. Main Line, Pennsylvania Public Works

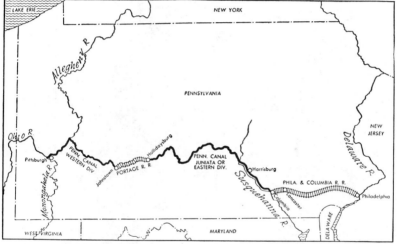

it cheaper to ship goods to New York and thence to the West by the Erie Canal than to patronize the nearer route.

Still other states undertook extensive canal projects during this period. Ohio constructed two canals, both extending from Lake Erie to the Ohio River. The eastern one, known as the Ohio & Erie Canal, connected Cleveland, on Lake Erie, with Portsmouth, on the Ohio River; the western one, the Miami & Erie, extended from Toledo to Cincinnati. (See Figure 5–4.) Indiana also undertook the construction of a number of canals. The most important one completed was the Wabash & Erie, extending from Evansville, on the Ohio River, through Terre Haute,

---

[27] These facts regarding the Allegheny Portage Railroad are taken from a pamphlet, *The Allegheny Portage Railroad*, published by the Pennsylvania Railroad in 1930.

Lafayette, and Fort Wayne to a junction with Ohio's Miami & Erie Canal. Illinois constructed the Illinois & Michigan Canal, connecting Lake Michigan at Chicago with the Illinois River at La Salle, thus making a waterway connection between the Great Lakes and the Mississippi River System.

Evidence of the activity in canal construction which took place in the 20s and 30s can be seen in the figures of state indebtedness at the time. Prior to 1820 no extensive use of public credit had been made by the states. Between 1820 and 1840 the states incurred nearly $200 million of indebtedness.[28] Most of this went into internal improvements—rail-

FIGURE 5–4. The Ohio Canals

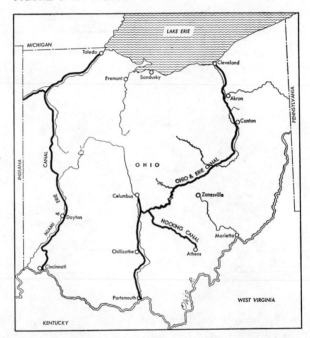

roads, canals, and highways. Some of the canals were absolutely unwarranted. Others would have proved valuable if railroads had not appeared on the scene at about the same time. Others were of immense value for a few decades until the railroads created a superior transportation system.

The canals constructed during this era seem to us today poor excuses for a transportation system, hopelessly inefficient and slow. Often they were mere ditches—the Erie Canal when completed was only 4 feet deep, 40 feet wide at the top, and 28 feet wide at the bottom. No mean engineering skill and ability, however, were spent in building the canals.

---

[28] Bogart, op. cit., p. 336.

Lock construction often proved difficult. The canals did not always follow the streams; sometimes they led along the side of ridges, tunneled hills, or were flung across valleys or streams by huge aqueducts. Providing an adequate supply of water frequently proved a difficult problem also.

Although the canals were eventually superseded by railroads, they served the country well during the period of their existence and carried large quantities of freight. The tolls collected on the Pennsylvania state canals for the first six years of their operation averaged $1,125,000 yearly.[29] The Erie, of course, surpassed them all in volume of traffic. In 1826, the year after the Erie was completed, 50 boats a day commonly left Albany for the West.[30] In 1869 there were 6,870 boats on the New York canals—so many, in fact, as to create a problem of congestion. During this period and for many years after, it was said that one might stand on a bridge over the Erie Canal and see in either direction, as far as the eye could reach, two continuous lines of boats, one moving east, the other west, and during the night the headlights gave the appearance of an endless torchlight procession.[31] The tonnage on the Erie increased long after the other canals were going out of existence. It reached 4,608,651 tons in 1880.[32] After that time the traffic declined. Up to 1870 the tolls from the New York canals averaged over $4 million per year. Toll reductions after that date decreased the earnings, and in 1882 tolls were abolished altogether. In the 60 years of toll gathering the revenue received from the Erie exceeded the cost of construction plus the sums spent on improvement, superintendence, and repairs and left a balance of more than $42,500,000.[33] The branch canals, however, were not profitable.

Comparatively low charges were made for transporting goods on the canals. Ringwalt says that the average tolls on several important canals in 1832 were 2 cents per ton-mile, and the cost of moving the goods 1 cent, making 3 cents per ton-mile the total charge. From 1850 to 1872 the amounts received by carriers on the Erie Canal varied from 6.72 mills to 11.10 mills per ton-mile. The average for the period was 9.14 mills.[34] This figure includes tolls. In 1850 the New York state engineer estimated the average rate per ton-mile on various canals to be as follows: Erie Canal, 11 mills; Pennsylvania Canals, 24 mills; Ohio Canal, 10 mills; Wabash & Erie Canal, 19 mills.[35]

---

[29] Harlow, op. cit., p. 131.
[30] Ibid., p. 66.
[31] Ibid., p. 156.
[32] Ibid.
[33] Ibid., p. 157.
[34] Ringwalt, op. cit., p. 47.
[35] MacGill, op. cit., p. 581.

Even after railroads had been constructed, the canals continued to do a good business. For a time it was an open question whether railroads or canals should be built.[36] Gradually it became clear that the railroads were superior in many respects. The Erie Canal did not reach its peak in tonnage carried until 1880; but even before this it was steadily losing in the proportion of total east-and-west traffic which it carried. A special report on the canals of the United States prepared for the Census of 1880 shows that, of the 4,468 miles of canals which had been constructed, nearly 2,000 miles had been abandoned, and a large portion of the rest was not paying expenses.[37] In 1924 two of the last great canals were abandoned, the Chesapeake & Ohio and the Morris.[38] Even if we consider the New York State Barge Canal as the old Erie, there remain in existence only about 700 miles of canals in the United States, and these are either modern barge canals or ship canals. The old towpath has long since passed into history.[39]

EARLY TRAILS AND THE PACK-HORSE ERA

The transportation system which we have just described made use of waterways, natural or artificial. Where waterways were not available or could not be constructed, agencies for transportation by land had to be developed. In Colonial America there were very few roads that were suitable for wheeled vehicles of any sort. During this period such commerce as could not be carried on by water was largely carried on by means of pack horses. Betwen 1750 and 1790 there were persons in nearly all important communities who made a business of carrying goods by this means. One owner of a pack-horse business in Pennsylvania employed about 200 horses and more than 100 men.[40] Many thousands of persons were employed in this business throughout the country. The cost of transporting goods in this way was prohibitive except for the most valuable or most essential articles. The cost of transportation by pack horse from Philadelphia to Erie was $249 per ton.[41] The business of the pack-horse drivers was threatened when roads were constructed. They naturally opposed the making of wagon roads, and incidents are told of violent treatment of wagoners and coachmen at the hands of the pack-horse people when the construction of roads made the use of wheeled vehicles practicable.

---

[36] See p. 92 of 5th edition.

[37] T. C. Purdy, "Report on the Canals of the United States," *Tenth Census* (1880), Vol. IV, p. 731.

[38] Harlow, op. cit., p. 1.

[39] Modern inland waterway transportation is described in Chapter 31 and pp. 37–40 supra.

[40] Ringwalt, op. cit., p. 24.

[41] Ibid., p. 21.

WAGON ROADS

Gradually the trails, or "tote roads," were widened into wagon roads, and travel by stagecoaches and transportation of goods by wagon became possible. The roads were generally dirt roads, and the cost of transportation was still high. Under very favorable conditions the cost might be as low as 10 cents per ton-mile, but it was usually higher. In 1852 it was said that the average charge for transporting grain by wagon in the United States was 15 cents per ton-mile.[42] In Wisconsin, 20 cents per ton-mile was said to be the average charge for transporting goods by wagon.[43] Where roads were poor, the cost was much higher, as is shown by government contracts for the transportation of army supplies in the West. These costs often averaged from 28 to 35 cents per ton-mile.[44]

TURNPIKES

Inadequate provision for public highways and the wretched condition of such roads as existed in Colonial times created an opportunity for private companies to build good roads, called "turnpikes," and to charge tolls for the use of them. The name "turnpike" is derived from the pole or gate, which turned on a pike and was placed across the road to enforce the payment of tolls before one could proceed. These gates were constructed at intervals along the road. Strictly speaking, a turnpike was a toll road, but the word "turnpike" later came to be used for any improved road, even if it was a public road free of toll.

A few turnpikes were built about 1789, but the Philadelphia & Lancaster Turnpike, completed in 1794, was the first one of importance. This road was a financial success and led to the construction of others. The turnpike movement was well under way by 1800. Within the next few years Pennsylvania chartered 86 turnpike companies, which built about 2,200 miles of road; New York chartered 135 companies, which had built about 1,500 miles by 1811; New England had chartered 180 companies by 1810.[45] Many turnpikes were constructed in Ohio after 1810. Some of the states gave subsidies to turnpike companies. Prior to 1822 Pennsylvania had paid nearly two million dollars in this way. This represented about a thousand dollars a mile, or one third of the total cost of the turnpikes.[46] Ohio subscribed to stock in turnpike companies to the amount of $2 million, and it is estimated that local governments spent as much more.[47]

---

[42] Ibid., pp. 27–28.

[43] Ibid., p. 28.

[44] Ibid.

[45] Bogart, op. cit., p. 324.

[46] A. T. Hadley, *Railroad Transportation* (New York: Putnam, 1885), p. 26.

[47] MacGill, op. cit., p. 125.

Some of the turnpike companies were profitable, but for the most part the stockholders received very moderate returns or nothing at all.[48] This was particularly true after canals and railroads began to take long-distance traffic. After 1830 few turnpikes were built. Most of the turnpikes gradually reverted to public control by abandonment, although a few remained in existence until the early part of the 20th century, when they were bought out and incorporated into the state highway systems that had begun to develop.

One of the most famous turnpikes was the Cumberland Road, or "National Pike." It was begun in 1806 and was constructed by the federal government. In 1818 it extended from Cumberland, Maryland, to Wheeling, on the Ohio River. Later the road was extended westward,

FIGURE 5–5. Route of the Cumberland Road

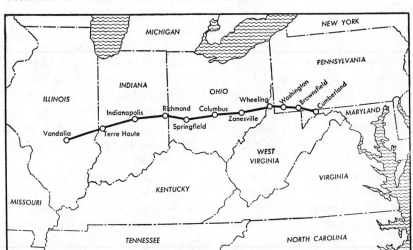

finally reaching Vandalia, Illinois, in 1838. (See Figure 5–5.) The road was to have been continued westward, but the coming of the railroads made its further extension appear unwise. The eastern portion of the road was built more substantially than the western portion. The first contracts called for a layer of stone fifteen inches thick, which was to be covered with gravel and rolled. The last portion, terminating at Vandalia, was simply a dirt road. The cost of the Cumberland Road, including appropriations for maintenance, amounted to $6,800,000. At first, tolls were not charged, as the road was maintained from Congressional appropriations. In 1822 President Monroe vetoed a bill for the collection of tolls for repair of the road, on the grounds that the federal govern-

---

[48] J. A. Durrenberger, *Turnpikes: A Study of the Toll Road Movement in the Middle Atlantic States and Maryland* (Valdosta, Ga.: The author, 1931), pp. 112–16.

ment did not have the power under the Constitution to maintain such a highway through the states. During Jackson's administration the road was transferred to the states through which it passed. The states immediately began to levy tolls. After 1850 Ohio leased portions of the road to private parties.[49] Later the state again took over the road, as the leases were not profitable to the holders.

The Cumberland Road, after it was opened to Wheeling, became an important thoroughfare between the East and the West. Before the road was constructed, eight days were required for a journey from Baltimore to Wheeling, but the time was reduced to three days upon completion of the road. In 1828 more than a thousand wagons went from Wheeling to Baltimore, loaded with the products of the West.[50] One writer, in describing the traffic over the road, says: "Within a mile of the road the country was a wilderness, but on the highway the traffic was as dense and as continuous as in the main street of a large town."[51]

The cost of transporting goods over the turnpikes was somewhat less than over ordinary roads. It is said that, on the average, it cost about $10 per ton for every hundred miles.[52] This is at the rate of 10 cents per ton-mile. Robert Fulton, in a letter to Gallatin, stated that the charge for transporting a barrel of flour (about 200 pounds) on the Lancaster Turnpike from Philadelphia to Columbia was $1. This would be at the rate of about 13.5 cents per ton-mile.[53] MacGill states that the cost of transporting goods over a turnpike averaged 13 cents per ton-mile.[54]

PLANK ROADS

Another type of road that developed in America was the plank road, consisting of heavy planks laid on stringers, or heavy pieces of timber. They were usually constructed by private companies. Plank roads were really turnpikes, since tolls were levied for their use.

Plank roads were supposed to have originated in Russia,[55] but this method of road construction was almost inevitable in any country where timber was plentiful and cheap. One of the first plank roads in North America was built in Toronto in 1835. The first one in the United States was built at Syracuse. Twenty thousand miles of plank roads were constructed in the state of New York, and several thousands of miles were

---

[49] W. F. Gephart, *Transportation and Industrial Development in the Middle West*, Columbia University Studies, Vol. XXXIV (1909), p. 53.

[50] Ringwalt, op. cit., p. 34.

[51] Wm. H. Rideing, "The Old National Pike," 59 *Harper's Magazine* 801, 806 (1879).

[52] Bogart, op. cit., p. 324.

[53] Ringwalt, op. cit., p. 33.

[54] MacGill, op. cit., p. 208.

[55] See quotation in MacGill, op. cit., p. 301, taken from *Debow's Review* (1851).

constructed in other parts of the country. A feverish building of such roads occurred in the United States between 1845 and 1857.

The cost of constructing plank roads was from $1,000 to $2,400 per mile—much less than the cost of constructing macadamized roads. They were subsidized by the states in some instances. Thus, in 1848, North Carolina subscribed one fifth of the capital stock of the Fayette & Western Plank Road.[56]

Some plank roads returned a profit for a time, but in most cases they were unprofitable ventures. The rapid deterioration of the plank surfaces and the rotting of the stringers on which the planks were laid made the cost of upkeep high. Gross revenues were usually insufficient to provide for this replacement.

Plank roads had several advantages over ordinary roads: the cost of constructing them was about half that of macadamized roads; a team could draw heavier loads on them than on a macadamized road; and rains, thaws, and spring mud did not obstruct transportation over them. The plank roads seem to have retarded railroad building in some sections of the country. In other cases they served as feeders to railways.

CONESTOGA WAGONS

The transportation of goods by wagons over roads and turnpikes evolved a special type of wagon which became very popular as a freighter in the eastern part of the country. These wagons were known as "Conestoga wagons," having originated in the Conestoga Valley in Pennsylvania. The western "prairie schooner" was a later adaptation of the Conestoga wagon. A distinguishing feature of the Conestoga wagon was that the wagon "box" or "bed" sagged in the middle, so that a shifting of the load would not throw the weight against the ends but toward the middle of the wagon. The end-boards flared outward, giving the wagon a boat-shaped appearance. The wagons were covered with a white top spread over a series of bows, which followed the sagging contour of the wagon bed and gave the wagon its peculiar silhouette. Conestoga wagons had broad tires—four to six inches wide. They had a capacity of six or eight tons and were usually drawn by six horses. These wagons were abundant on the Philadelphia & Lancaster Turnpike. Inns and taverns sprang up along the roads to care for the wagoners and their teams. In some places the taverns were only a mile apart. About 1817 there were said to be three thousand such wagons regularly engaged in the business of hauling goods between Philadelphia and Pittsburgh.[57] Likewise, most of the hauling over the Cumberland Road was in Conestoga wagons.

---

[56] MacGill, op. cit., p. 300.

[57] John Omwake, *The Conestoga Six-Horse Bell Teams of Eastern Pennsylvania* (Cincinnati: The author, 1930), p. 103.

There seem to have been three kinds of transportation agencies operating these wagons over the National Pike and other roads. First, there were the individual operators, who made a regular business of hauling freight as contract carriers; second, farmers along the road who, in the slack farming season, went into the business temporarily; and third, the large freight companies that owned many wagons and were in fact transportation companies. The last group was the most important of the three.

After 1830 wagoning began to decline. Canals and railroads had appeared on the scene, and they soon put an end to the earlier form of transportation and the various forms of activity that went with it.

SELECTED REFERENCES

The two most complete accounts of the transportation methods in the United States before railroads were built are to be found in J. L. Ringwalt, *The Development of Transportation Systems in the United States* (Philadelphia: Railway World Office, 1888), and Caroline E. MacGill, *History of Transportation in the United States before 1860* (Washington, D.C.: Carnegie Institution, 1917). A. B. Hulbert, *Historic Highways of America* (16 vols.; Cleveland: A. H. Clark Co., 1902–5), is valuable but diffuse. *The Paths of Inland Commerce*, by the same author (New York: Yale University Press, 1921), contains interesting chapters.

An excellent account of steamboat transportation and earlier boating on the Mississippi River and its tributaries is F. H. Dixon, *Traffic History of the Mississippi River* (Washington, D.C.: U.S. Government Printing Office, 1915), a study made for the National Waterways Commission. Additional material may be found in C. H. Ambler, *A History of Transportation in the Ohio Valley* (Glendale, Calif.: A. H. Clark Co., 1931). The most complete and scholarly work on all aspects of steamboat transportation on the western rivers is Louis C. Hunter, *Steamboats on the Western Rivers* (Cambridge: Harvard University Press, 1949). An informative discussion of some aspects of steamboating is Erik F. Haites, "Steamboating on the Mississippi, 1810–1860: A Purely Competitive Industry," 45 *Business History Review* 52 (1971).

Alvin F. Harlow's *Old Towpaths* (New York: Appleton, 1926) is a general treatment of the canal era. A popular and colorful account of canal building and canal life is Madeline S. Waggoner, *The Long Haul West* (New York: Putman, 1958). A brief history of each canal constructed in the United States is found in T. C. Purdy, "Report on the Canals of the United States," in Volume IV of the United States Census report for 1880. The early private canal projects of Pennsylvania are treated in C. L. Jones, *Economic History of the Anthracite-Tidewater Canals*, University of Pennsylvania, Series in Political Economy and Public Law, No. 22 (Philadelphia, 1908). A good history of the Erie Canal is Ronald E. Shaw, *Erie Waters West: A History of the Erie Canal, 1792–1854* (Lexington, Ky.: University of Kentucky Press, 1966). A detailed account of the Pennsylvania Canal is in A. L. Bishop, "State Works of Pennsylvania," published in Volume XIII of the *Transactions of the Connecticut Academy of Arts and Sciences* (New Haven, 1908). An account of the canals in the Middle West is given in W. F. Gephart, *Transportation and Industrial Development in the Middle West*, Columbia University Studies, Vol. XXXIV, No. 1 (New York, 1909). The history of New Jersey and eastern Pennsylvania canals is given in Wheaton J. Lane, *From Indian Trail to Iron Horse—Travel and Transportation in New Jersey, 1620–1860* (Princeton: Princeton University Press, 1939), chap. ix.

A thorough history of the Ohio canals, with emphasis on the economic and political forces behind the movement is Harry N. Scheiber, *Ohio Canal Era: A Case Study of Government and the Economy* (Athens, Ohio: The Ohio University Press, 1969).

An effort to measure the indirect economic gains which resulted from the Ohio Canals from 1837 to 1850 is Roger L. Ransom, "Social Returns from Public Transport Industries: A Case Study of the Ohio Canal," 78 *Journal of Political Economy* 1041 (1970).

The most extensive studies of turnpikes are J. J. Wood, *Turnpikes of New England* (Boston: Marshall Jones Co., 1929), and Joseph A. Durrenberger, *Turnpikes: A Study of the Toll Road Movement in the Middle Atlantic States and Maryland* (Valdosta, Ga.: The author, 1931). A detailed history of the Cumberland Road is told by Thomas B. Searight in *The Old Pike* (Uniontown, Pa.: The author, 1894). An interesting popular account, profusely illustrated, of the Conestoga wagons is afforded by John Omwake, *The Conestoga Six-Horse Bell Teams of Eastern Pennsylvania* (Cincinnati: The author, 1930). Another description of Conestoga wagons and wagoning is H. S. Hill, *The Conestoga Wagon* (Trenton, N.J.: The author, 1930).

The part played by the federal and state governments in early transportation development is told in Carter Goodrich, *Government Promotion of American Canals and Railroads, 1800–1890* (New York: Columbia University Press, 1960), chaps. ii & iii.

Chapter 6 | THE ERA OF RAILROAD BUILDING

The steam locomotive gave the railroad its dominant position among transportation agencies. Railways existed, however, before there were steam locomotives. Over the earliest railroads, cars were drawn by horses or mules. Later, stationary engines were used to haul cars up steep inclines, as was done on the Allegheny Portage Railroad. Even before locomotives were invented, however, railways were an improvement over other means of land transportation because they made use of an important mechanical principle. The resistance offered by a wheeled vehicle when propelled over smooth rails is less than that of a vehicle on the best of ordinary roads. For this reason the primitive railways, or "tramways," as they were called, reduced the cost of transportation. But important as this principle was and still is, the development of steam locomotion was of much greater importance.

EARLY RAILWAYS

Tramways were commonly used in Great Britain in the 18th century, usually for the purpose of transporting coal from the collieries. The first tramway in America is supposed to have been built in 1807 on Beacon Hill, in Boston, by Silas Whitney.[1] A number of other tramways were built in America in succeeding years. Of these the most famous was the Quincy Railroad, a road about four miles long, built in 1826 from the granite quarries at Quincy, Massachusetts, to the Neponset River. The granite used in the construction of the Bunker Hill Monument was carried over this tramway. A number of other primitive railways or tramways were constructed for the purpose of carrying coal. The Mauch Chunk Railroad and the Schuylkill Railroad, both constructed about 1827, were of this variety.[2] Another was built by the Delaware & Hudson Canal Company in 1829 from Carbondale to Honesdale, Pennsylvania. These lines were not intended to be general carriers of freight.

[1] J. L. Ringwalt, *Development of Transportation Systems in the United States* (Philadelphia: Railway World Office, 1888), p. 69.

[2] Ibid., pp. 71–72.

The Baltimore & Ohio Railroad is given credit for being the first railroad in America constructed for general transportation purposes. It was chartered by the state of Maryland in 1827; construction was begun in 1828; and a portion of the road was opened in 1830. The year 1830 may therefore mark the beginning of the railroad era in the United States. Great Britain, however, had preceded the United States in the construction of railroads. The Stockton & Darlington had been opened in 1825, and the Liverpool & Manchester in 1830, the same year that saw the opening of the Baltimore & Ohio on this side of the Atlantic.[3]

INVENTION OF THE LOCOMOTIVE

We cannot proceed further in the discussion of railroad development without reference to the development of steam locomotives. Although there had been a number of successful experiments with steam locomotion before 1829, the first practicable locomotive was George Stephenson's "Rocket," which was tried out on the Liverpool & Manchester Railroad in 1829.[4] The first locomotive tried out on an American railway was the "Stourbridge Lion," operated in 1829 by the Delaware & Hudson Railway and Canal Company. This locomotive was imported from England; and although it functioned successfully, it was not adapted to conditions on this railroad and was not used after the first trip. The "Tom Thumb," constructed by Peter Cooper of New York, was tried out on the Baltimore & Ohio in 1830. This engine was only a model used to demonstrate the practicability of locomotives. Another American locomotive, the "Best Friend," was given a trial on the South Carolina Railroad in 1831. The early locomotives were small and primitive and bore little resemblance to later steam locomotives. Once the locomotive had been proved practicable, improvements were made at a rapid rate. The story of the development of the locomotive cannot be told here, although it must be recognized that without the mechanical improvements on locomotives, as well as on rolling stock and track, the railroads could never have assumed the economic importance which they have attained.

DEVELOPMENT OF THE RAILROAD NET

In 1830 there were not more than 22 miles of railroad in the United States. At the end of 1969 there were 207,005 miles. Figure 6–1 shows the growth in railway mileage from 1830 to 1970.

The chart indicates that the decade of greatest expansion in the rail-

---

[3] Stuart Daggett, *Principles of Inland Transportation* (4th ed.; New York: Harper, 1955), pp. 57–58.

[4] For an account of early experimentation see S. L. Miller, *Inland Transportation* (New York: McGraw-Hill, 1933), pp. 47–51.

way net was the decade of the 80s.[5] By 1890 nearly two thirds of our railway mileage had come into existence; by 1900, more than three fourths. The peak in railway mileage was attained in 1916, when there were 254,037 miles of railroad in the United States.[6] Since then the mileage has declined. In 1969 the mileage was nearly 47,000 miles less than in 1916.

Although the number of miles of line has declined since 1916, there was a continuous growth in the miles of track until 1930, when the figure reached 410,634. In 1969 the miles of track had declined to 341,546. The property investment in railroads increased year by year until 1931, when

FIGURE 6–1. Miles of Railway in the United States, by Decades

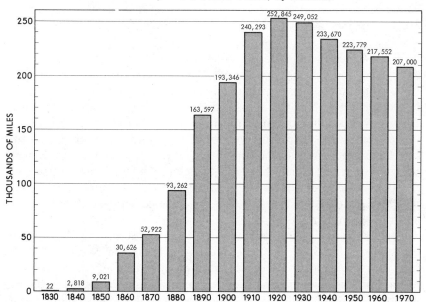

it stood at $26,094,899,000. Thereafter, the figure declined for a number of years, but by 1969 it had risen to $37,383,498,000.

THE COURSE OF RAILROAD EXPANSION, 1830–1910

We have already seen that the Baltimore & Ohio, a portion of which was opened in 1830, was the first railroad to be opened in the United States. The second was the South Carolina Railroad, otherwise known as

---

[5] The statistics of mileage are from the *Statistical Abstract of the United States* and from the Interstate Commerce Commission.

[6] Figures in this and the following paragraph are from Interstate Commerce Commission reports.

the Charleston & Hamburgh. Although this road was not completed until 1833, some of it had been constructed prior to 1830. Railroad construction during the 30s was in the eastern states, especially New York, Pennsylvania, and the New England states. In New England, mileage was built which later became important parts of the Boston & Maine, the New York, New Haven & Hartford, and the Boston & Albany roads. The Philadelphia & Columbia and the Philadelphia & Reading were constructed in Pennsylvania. A number of roads were built in New York which later became parts of the New York Central System. Notwithstanding the very considerable activity in railroad building during this decade, the people did not then foresee the future importance of railroads. As late as 1842 the town of Dorchester, Massachusetts, instructed its representatives in the legislature to do all within their power "to prevent, if possible, so great a calamity to our town as must be the location of any railroad through it."[7]

In the 1840s and the 1850s a number of important railway lines were completed, and others were started. The Erie Railroad, extending westward from New York City through the southern part of the state, was under construction in the 40s. In 1841 a through route from Boston to Albany was established. An all-rail route from Boston to New York was completed in 1849. A through connection between the Atlantic seaboard and Chicago was established in 1853. Other important railroads were being constructed in the Mississippi Valley in the 50s. Among these were the Illinois Central, the Mobile & Ohio, and the Hannibal & St. Joseph which was the first railroad to span the distance between the Mississippi and the Missouri rivers.

During the Civil War, railroad building in the South and West practically ceased, but some construction took place in the North. After the war, railroad building proceeded at a rapid rate. The first transcontinental line was completed in 1869, when the Union Pacific, constructing its line westward from Omaha, and the Central Pacific, building eastward from Sacramento, were joined near Ogden, Utah. During the 70s, railroad construction continued at a rapid rate, notwithstanding the interruption caused by the Panic of 1873. But it was the following decade, the 80s, that surpassed all others, before or since, in point of mileage constructed. More than 70,000 miles of railroad were constructed in this decade. A large portion of the mileage was in the Far West, and the decade was notable for the building of transcontinental lines. Extensive mileage was constructed by the Atchison, Topeka & Santa Fe, the Southern Pacific, the Texas & Pacific, the Northern Pacific, the Oregon Railway & Navigation Company, and the Oregon Short Line Railroad. During the 90s, another transcontinental, the Great Northern, was opened; but the main lines of our transportation system had been laid down, and

---

[7] B. S. Atkinson, *The Development of the American Railroad* (address before the Shreveport Traffic Club, 1927), p. 10.

the railroad-building era was drawing to a close. Only a few lines of major importance were constructed after 1900. Among the more important were the San Pedro, Los Angeles & Salt Lake, opened in 1905; the Pacific Coast extension of the Chicago, Milwaukee & St. Paul, opened in 1909; and the Western Pacific, opened in the same year. Railroad construction declined after 1910. There was less building between 1910 and 1920 than betwen 1850 and 1860. The actual reduction in railroad mileage in operation after 1916 has already been mentioned.

FIGURE 6–2. Railroads in the United States in 1840 and 1850

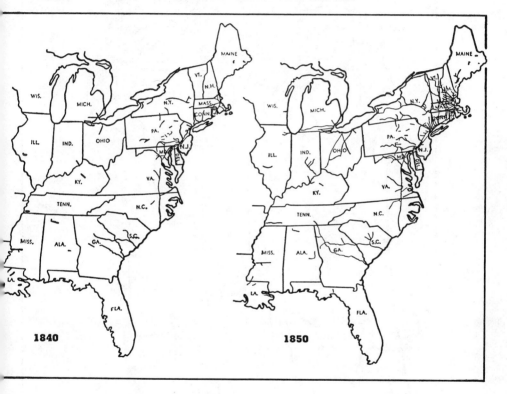

1840   1850

The course of railroad building can be seen from the maps shown in Figures 6–2 to 6–6.[8] These maps show the railroad mileage at the beginning of each decade from 1840 to 1890. What is approximately the present railroad system is shown in Figure 2–4 in Chapter 2.[9]

The development of the railroad system has been presented in terms of the growth of railway mileage. It is apparent upon a moment's con-

---

[8] The maps in Figures 6–2 to 6–6 are taken from Carlton J. Corliss, *Development of Railroad Transportation in the United States* (Washington, D.C.: Association of American Railroads, 1945).

[9] Pp. 26–27, supra.

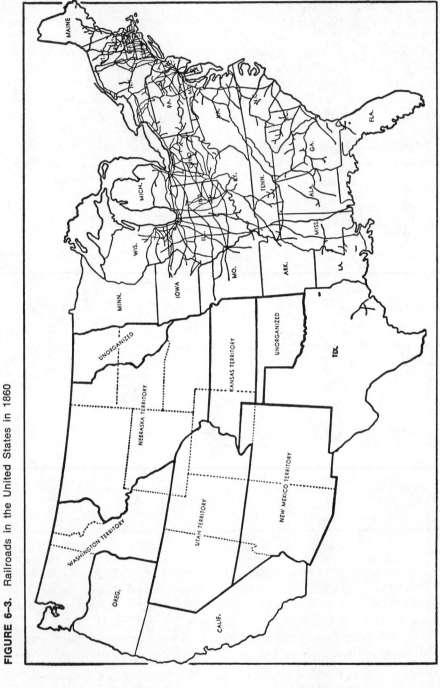

FIGURE 6–3. Railroads in the United States in 1860

FIGURE 6-4. Railroads in the United States in 1870

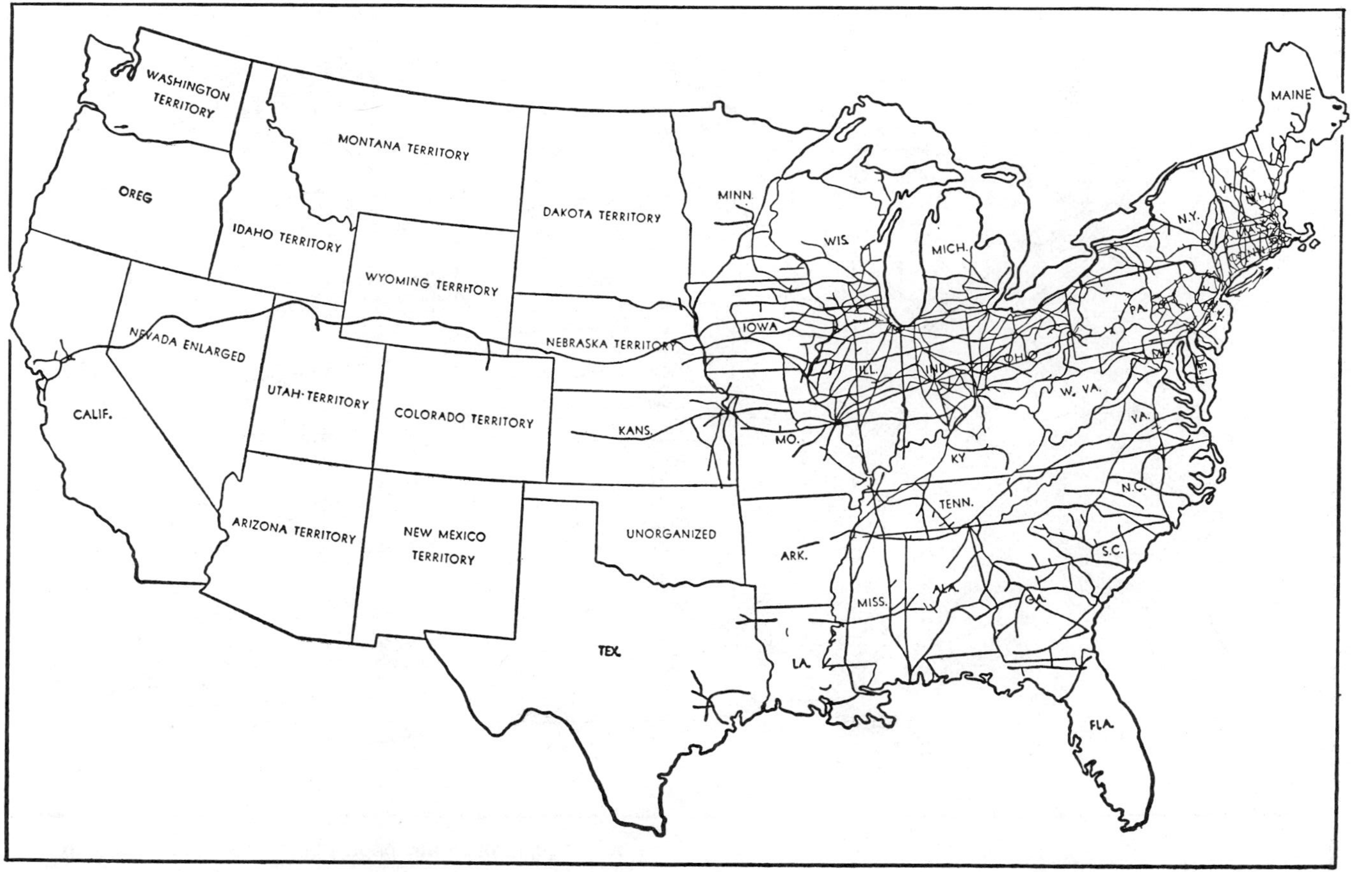

FIGURE 6-5. Railroads in the United States in 1880

FIGURE 6–6. Railroads in the United States in 1890

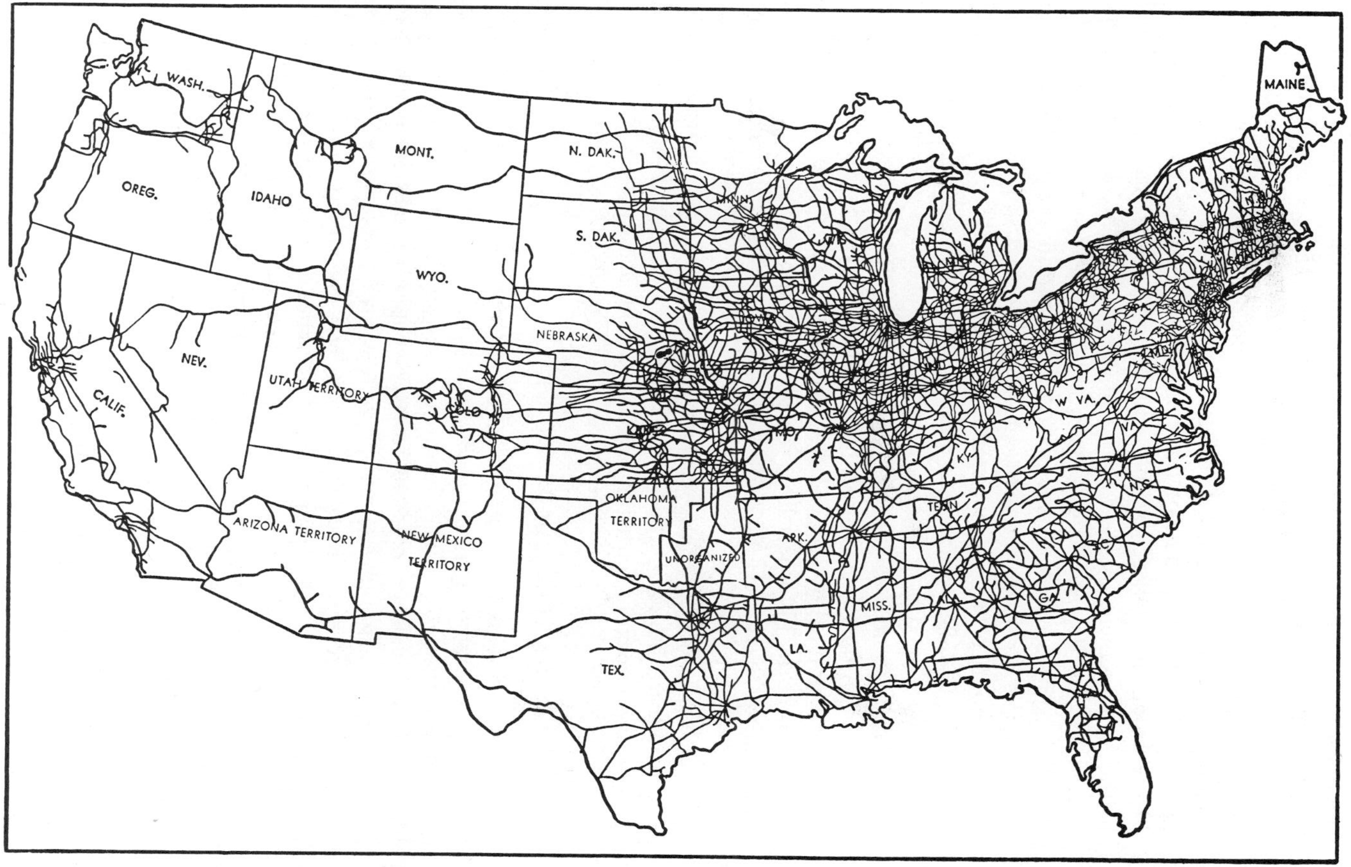

sideration, however, that the expansion of railway mileage has been accompanied by technological improvements of great importance and that the modern railroad is vastly different from the railroad of 100 years ago or even 50 years ago. We are not primarily concerned in this volume with technological features of railroad transportation, but a glance at the dates of some of the more obviously important technological developments will reveal the continuing progress that has occurred in the improvement of the railroad physical plant. Steel rails were imported by the Pennsylvania Railroad to replace iron rails in 1863; the first Pullman sleeping car was placed in service in 1865; Westinghouse invented the air brake in 1869 and the automatic air brake in 1872; standardization of track gauge at 4 feet, 8½ inches was virtually accomplished in 1886;[10] a standard automatic coupler was adopted in 1888; the first electrified train service was started in 1895; all-steel passenger cars were first introduced in 1904; the first Diesel-electric locomotive was placed in operation in 1925 (in switching service); the first Diesel-electric streamlined passenger train was placed in service in 1934.[11] Various types of highly specialized freight cars for the transport of bulk commodities have been developed in recent years, particularly in the 1960s.

We shall now turn to a consideration of various characteristics of the era of railroad building which are of particular economic significance or which have a bearing on later problems which arose.

RAILROADS AS TOLL ROADS

When railroads were new, it was commonly supposed that they would be operated in the manner of toll roads. Any person would be free, it was thought, to haul his own goods on the railway upon paying a toll. Individuals or common carriers could operate over the road. Provisions of early railway charters bear witness to this idea. The charter of the Boston & Providence line authorized the directors "to erect toll houses, establish gates, appoint toll gatherers and demand toll upon the road."[12] Some of the earliest railroads were operated on the toll-road principle for a time, but the special type of equipment required and the difficulty of meeting and passing other users of the railway made the system of operation impracticable. The adoption of steam motive power

---

[10] It is said that in 1871 there were no fewer than 23 different railway gauges in use, ranging from 3 to 6 feet. See Corliss, op. cit., p. 22. Reasons for diversities in gauge and the history of unification of gauge are authoritatively discussed in George R. Taylor and Irene D. Neu, *The American Railroad Network, 1861–1890* (Cambridge: Harvard University Press, 1956).

[11] These dates are for the most part taken from Association of American Railroads, *A Chronology of American Railroads* (Washington, D.C., 1949), and J. H. Parmelee, *The Modern Railway* (New York: Longmans, 1940).

[12] Quoted by F. A. Cleveland and F. W. Powell in *Railroad Promotion and Capitalization in the United States* (New York: Longmans, 1909), p. 161.

imposed other difficulties in the way of this system of operation, and it soon came to be recognized that the railroad company must have a monopoly of transporting over its road. This at once made it clear that such competition as might exist in railway transportation must be competition between different lines and not competition between different carriers over the same road. The fact that a railroad company must have a monopoly of transport over its own line, thus combining the function of providing a transportation "way" and of engaging in transportation over it, has been noted in an earlier chapter.[13] This distinguishes railroad transportation from other modes of transport except pipelines.

Some of the more farsighted individuals of the time foresaw that this characteristic of railways would make them monopolistic in nature. "I consider a long line of railroads," wrote Benjamin White to Congress early in the 30s, "as being odious in this country as a monopoly of the carrying, which it necessarily must be"; and he went on to show that anyone who acquired a boat could operate it over a canal but that a man could not operate his own vehicle over a railroad.[14] The same argument frequently appeared in the controversies over the relative merits of canals and railroads. Railroads continued to develop, however, and the problem of railroad monopoly was left to trouble succeeding generations.

OPPOSITION OF VESTED INTERESTS

Railroad construction encountered serious opposition in the earlier decades of the construction era. Much of the opposition had an economic basis. This was particularly true where vested interests were concerned. It must be remembered that millions of dollars had been spent on canals, turnpikes, and plank roads; that thousands of persons earned their livelihood by transporting persons or property over these routes; and that other thousands kept inns and taverns along the routes of trade. These persons saw their means of livelihood threatened by the new invention. Wagoners feared the direct competition which the railroads would bring. Tavern keepers saw their business going to pieces if railroads were constructed. Farmers feared the loss of markets for horses, hay, and grain. Taxpayers bethought themselves of the state debts incurred in building the canals and foresaw the possibility of increased taxes if canal revenues were reduced. Under these circumstances it is not strange that opposition to railroads was often strong and vociferous.

PROTECTION OF EXISTING TRANSPORTATION AGENCIES

The opposition of vested interests resulted in some instances in the adoption of policies which were designed to protect existing transporta-

---

[13] Pp. 45–46.

[14] L. H. Haney, *A Congressional History of Railways in the United States to 1850,* Bulletin of the University of Wisconsin, No. 211 (Madison, 1908), p. 243.

tion agencies from the competition of the new. In 1838 the Ohio legislature asked the State Board of Public Works if the construction of a railroad from Dayton to Cincinnati would injure the state by diverting traffic from the Miami Canal. The Board reported that the canal did not afford sufficient revenue to pay interest on the investment and that it would therefore be unwise to permit the construction of a railroad which might compete with it.[15] When a charter was granted to the Cincinnati, Hamilton, & Dayton Railroad it was stipulated that when the revenues of the state from the Miami Canal should be diminished as a result of the railroad, tolls should be paid to the state on property transported by railroad. The tolls were to be sufficient to maintain the former earnings of the canal. Other railroads in the state were subject to somewhat similar restrictions.[16] New York, with its huge investment in the Erie and other canals, quite naturally sought to protect canal earnings. The charter of the Utica & Schenectady Railroad prohibited the railroad from carrying property other than the baggage of passengers. In 1844 the railroad was given permission to transport all goods during suspension of canal navigation, but it had to pay the state the same toll that the state would have received had the goods been transported by the Erie Canal. The Auburn & Syracuse Railroad was permitted by its charter to carry property at any time, but it had to pay tolls equal to what would have been paid on the Erie Canal. The Syracuse & Utica Railroad might also carry goods at any time, but it had to pay tolls to the state on such property as it carried when the Erie Canal was navigable. It was not until 1851 that such restrictions were abolished in New York.[17] Later the "Clinton League," organized to protect the canals of New York, proposed to tax the railroads for the movement of freight in order to prevent diversion of the traffic from the canals.[18] Pennsylvania also sought to protect the earnings of the canals. The charter of the Pennsylvania Railroad required the railroad company to pay a tonnage tax of 5 mills per mile between March and December of each year. Later the tax was reduced to 3 mills but was made applicable throughout the year. This tax was not removed until 1861—long after the state had sold the canal to the Pennsylvania Railroad.[19]

---

[15] W. F. Gephart, *Transportation and Industrial Development in the Middle West*, Studies in History, Economics, and Public Law, Columbia University, Vol. XXXIV, No. 1 (New York, 1909), pp. 120–21.

[16] Caroline E. MacGill, *History of Transportation in the United States before 1860* (Washington, D.C.: Carnegie Institution, 1917), p. 490.

[17] Frank W. Stevens, *The Beginnings of the New York Central Railroad* (New York: Putnam, 1926), pp. 267–69, 273.

[18] A. T. Hadley, "American Railroad Legislation," 75 *Harper's Magazine* 141 (1887).

[19] H. W. Schotter, *The Pennsylvania Railroad Company* (Philadelphia: Allen, Lane, and Scott, 1927), pp. 7–8, 47.

GOVERNMENT-OWNED RAILROADS

The railroads of the United States have for the most part been built as private enterprises. Though a number of the earlier railroads were built by the states, the states withdrew from the business of constructing railroads before the era of rapid railroad building began. Whether railroads should be built by the government or by private corporations was an important question in most countries when railroads were new. The question was answered differently in different countries according to the particular circumstances and conditions that existed at the time. In the United States the possibility of the construction of railroads by the federal government was foreclosed by the political situation. Although the federal government had built the National Road and had made appropriations for other internal improvements, a sentiment had grown up that federal participation in internal improvements was an invasion of the rights of the states. With the triumph of Jacksonian Democracy in 1828 the "states' rights" advocates had their way. As a result, when railroads appeared on the scene about 1830, the development of internal improvements was considered an affair for the states and not for the federal government to deal with.

When the question of a transcontinental railroad was brought up in Congress in the 40s and 50s, there was some sentiment in favor of having such a road built by the national government.[20] But as we have seen, the first transcontinental railroad was built by private corporations, although with a heavy government subsidy. Agitation for a government-owned railroad appeared again in 1874, when a committee of Congress reported in favor of the construction of one or more railroads by the government, this time as a means of regulating the rates of privately owned railroads and of preventing monopolistic charges.[21] With minor exceptions, however, the federal government has not built or owned railroads. The two most important exceptions are the Alaska Railroad, 470 miles long, constructed by the government about 1916, and the Panama Railroad, the capital stock of which is owned by the United States government. In 1971 the government took over the Lehigh & New England Railway which had been put up as collateral to secure a government loan to the Central of New Jersey.

Since it was not, in the 30s, considered within the sphere of the federal government to aid internal improvements, the states were the logical government units to engage in railroad building, unless railroad construction was to be left entirely to private corporations. The states did, in a number of instances, engage in railroad building. This was part

---

[20] Haney, op. cit., chap. xxiii.
[21] Senate Rep. No. 307, Part I, 43d Cong., 1st Sess. (1874), pp. 140–61, 242.

of the same movement that had led the states to undertake the construction of canals.

Pennsylvania, we have already seen, constructed two railroads as a part of the Pennsylvania Public Works—the Allegheny Portage Railroad and the Philadelphia & Columbia Railroad. The latter is said to have been the first railroad ever undertaken in any part of the world by a government.[22] The state of Illinois undertook the construction of a number of railroad lines in the 30s, but by 1847 only one road had been completed. The state got into financial difficulties and abandoned its scheme of state railroads. Indiana spent $1,600,000 on a railroad from Madison, on the Ohio River, to Lafayette. The road was turned over to the Madison & Indianapolis Railroad in 1843. Michigan planned the construction of four railroads. In 1846 one of these roads was sold to the Michigan Central for $2,000,000, which represented a loss of from $250,000 to $500,000. Another of the roads was sold to the Michigan Southern in the same year for $509,000, or about half its cost. A third line was turned over to the Port Huron & Northern Michigan after about $100,000 had been spent on the route by the state. The state of Georgia constructed the Western & Atlantic and operated the road successfully from 1851, the date of its completion, until after the Civil War. In 1890 the road was leased to the Nashville, Chattanooga & St. Louis Railroad, but it is still owned by the state of Georgia. Virginia constructed two roads, the Blue Ridge Railroad, a short line across the Blue Ridge Mountains, and the Covington & Ohio, from Covington to the Ohio River. Both of these roads came into the possession of the Chesapeake & Ohio Railroad Company after the Civil War. North Carolina, through stock ownership, held a controlling interest in three railroads and appointed a majority of the directors. These roads were the North Carolina, the Atlantic & North Carolina, and the Western North Carolina railroads.[23]

In addition to these projects undertaken by the states, other railroads came into the hands of the state governments through the failure of private corporations which had built the roads with the aid of state subsidies. In this way the state of North Carolina acquired the Raleigh & Gaston Railroad.[24] Massachusetts took over the Hoosac Tunnel enterprise,[25] and Missouri acquired a number of railroads in that state which had been liberally aided from state funds.[26] As a rule, lines acquired in this manner were sold as soon as possible.

---

[22] Cleveland and Powell, op. cit., p. 103. Unless otherwise indicated, the other facts regarding state construction of railroads are taken from this source.

[23] Cecil K. Brown, *A State Movement in Railroad Development* (Chapel Hill, N.C.: University of North Carolina Press, 1928).

[24] Ibid., p. 278.

[25] Cleveland and Powell, op. cit., p. 102.

[26] J. W. Million, *State Aid to Railways in Missouri* (Chicago: University of Chicago Press, 1896), chap. v.

State building of railroads in this early period is to be explained by the eagerness of the people to obtain improved transportation facilities, the large amounts of capital required to build them, and the reluctance of private capital to embark on such enterprises when the risk of financial loss was great.

The results of state construction of railroads were disappointing. The states found that railroad construction had involved them in financial difficulties; for this reason they finally withdrew from the business and disposed of the roads to private corporations, usually at a loss. North Carolina, however, owns a majority of the capital stock of the North Carolina Railroad Company, and the state of Georgia still owns the Western & Atlantic; these roads are not, however, operated by the states. The burden of indebtedness created by the states in constructing internal improvements became too great; and insolvency and, in some cases, repudiation resulted after the crises of 1837 and 1847. In some instances, state participation in these undertakings was accompanied by graft, corruption, and incompetence. But this was not universally true, and the overexpansion of the period and the inherent unsoundness of the particular projects as business enterprises were more fundamental causes of failure. Many of the private railway projects of the time proved equally unsuccessful.

The financial difficulties of the states, brought about by internal improvement projects, led to the establishment of provisions in the constitutions of the states which prohibited them from engaging in such enterprises. All this happened early in the railroad-building era, that is, when only a few pioneer railways had been constructed. Now that the federal government and the states had successively withdrawn from direct participation in internal improvements, railroad building was left to private corporations.

There were a few instances of railway projects undertaken by municipalities. Several towns in Maine owned a controlling interest in the Knox & Lincoln Railroad, which was completed in 1872.[27] The city of Troy, New York, built a railroad about 20 miles in length—the Schenectady & Troy Railroad. This road was opened in 1842. The town of North Brookfield, Massachusetts, built the North Brookfield Railroad, a road only about four miles long. The Schenectady & Troy Railroad was not a financial success, and it was sold in 1853 and became a part of the New York Central System.[28] The North Brookfield Railroad was leased to the Boston & Albany on terms that enabled the town of North Brookfield to retire the debt incurred in building the road and to derive a considerable income from it.[29] Another example of a municipally

---

[27] E. E. Chase, *Maine Railroads* (Portland: The author, 1926), p. 62.

[28] Harry H. Pierce, *Railroads of New York: A Study of Government Aid, 1826–1875* (Cambridge: Harvard University Press, 1953), p. 20.

[29] F. W. Powell, "Two Experiments in Public Ownership of Steam Railroads,"

owned railroad was the Western Maryland, which was largely financed by the city of Baltimore and was controlled by the city until 1904.[30] A more recent example of railroad building by a municipality is afforded by the City of Prineville Railway, 18 miles in length, built by the town of Prineville, Oregon, in 1918.[31]

The most ambitious of the city-owned railroads was the Cincinnati Southern, which was built and is owned by the city of Cincinnati. This road is over 300 miles long and extends from Cincinnati, Ohio, to Chattanooga, Tennessee. Construction was begun in 1874, and the road was open for traffic in 1877.[32] The road proved successful. It was leased to the Cincinnati, New Orleans & Texas Pacific in 1881, and this lease was renewed in 1902.[33] The railways built or owned by cities or towns were projected primarily for the purpose of giving some trade advantage to the communities concerned rather than for the profits of operation.

RAILROADS AND THE POWER OF EMINENT DOMAIN

In the United States the railroads, from the very beginning, have been given the power of eminent domain, that is, the power to take private property for a public use without the owner's consent. This is a governmental power, but it may be delegated to private corporations. Under our Constitution this power may not be exercised without making "just compensation" to the owners of the property taken. The compensation to be paid when property is taken in this way is determined by a board of appraisers appointed for the purpose or by a court. In this way the railroad corporations are enabled to acquire rights of way and other property at fair prices.

It is to be observed that the power of eminent domain is the power to take the property of others *for a public purpose.* To take the property of one individual for the benefit of another individual would not be a valid exercise of the power of eminent domain. The question very early arose, therefore, whether property taken for the use of a privately owned railroad was being taken for a public or a merely private purpose. The public benefit to be derived from railroads was not doubted; but since the railroads were being operated for private profit, it was not clear that land

---

23 *Quarterly Journal of Economics* 137 (1908). The North Brookfield Railroad Co. now receives no rental for the use of its properties. See *North Brookfield R. R. Co. Operation,* 212 ICC 707 (1936).

[30] Paul Winchester, *The Baltimore and Ohio Railroad* (Baltimore: Maryland County Press Syndicate, 1927), Vol. I, p. 11.

[31] Randall V. Mills, *Railroads down the Valley* (Palo Alto: Pacific Books, 1950), pp. 121–36.

[32] J. H. Hollander, *The Cincinnati Southern Railway: A Study in Municipal Activity,* Johns Hopkins University, Studies in Historical and Political Science, 12th Ser., Nos. 1 and 2 (Baltimore: Johns Hopkins Press, 1894), pp. 39–45.

[33] 65 ICC 581 (1920).

acquired under the power of eminent domain was being taken for a public and not a private use. The courts held, however, that the fact that the railroad was privately owned and was entitled to charge for its services did not alter the public nature of the enterprise. "Because the legislature permitted the company to remunerate itself for the expense of constructing the road, from those who should travel upon it, its private character is not established; it does not destroy the public nature of the road, or convert it from a public to a private use."[34] In the same case the Court went on to show that the owners of the road could be prosecuted if they refused to transport a person or his property without any reasonable excuse, and the Court even asserted the right of the legislature to regulate the charges of the companies. The important thing to notice in connection with these decisions is that judicial sanction of the exercise of the power of eminent domain by rail corporations was based on the public nature of the business. Because the corporation was considered to be constructing a public highway for the people, the power of eminent domain might properly be given.

SOURCES OF CAPITAL

Since capital was comparatively scarce in the United States, particularly during the early years of railroad building, it was natural that much capital from European sources should be invested in American railroads. In the earlier years of railroad construction, when the states were engaging in railroad building, and later, when state bonds were being issued to subsidize private railroad corporations, state securities were sold abroad in large quantities. Stocks and bonds of railroad corporations were also sold in Europe.[35] Investment of foreign capital in American railways was interrupted by each panic, but European interest revived with each succeeding return of prosperity. A number of American railroads were controlled by foreign interests. In others, foreign holders of stocks represented important minority groups. In 1876 about 86 percent of the stock of the Illinois Central was held abroad.[36] Between 1890 and 1896 foreign stockholders held 75 percent of the stock of the Louisville & Nashville. The stock of other important railroads was held abroad in the following proportions: the Reading and Pennsylvania railroads, 52 percent; New York Central & Hudson River, 37 percent; Great North-

---

[34] *Bloodgood* v. *The Mohawk & Hudson Railroad Co.,* 18 Wendell (N.Y.) 9, 21 (1837). For another early case discussing fully the validity of the exercise of the power of eminent domain by railroad corporations see *Beekman* v. *The Saratoga & Schenectady Railroad Co.,* 3 Paige (N.Y.) 45 (1831).

[35] Insight into European attitudes toward American railroad securities is provided in A. W. Currie, "British Attitudes toward Investment in North American Railroads," 34 *Business History Review* 194 (1960).

[36] W. Z. Ripley, *Railroads: Finance and Organization* (New York: Longmans, 1915), p. 4.

ern, 33 percent; Baltimore & Ohio and the Chicago, Milwaukee & St. Paul, 21 percent.[37]

After 1898 the securities of American railroads were purchased from European holders in large quantities. From time to time since then, however, American railroad corporations have found it desirable to float bond issues abroad.

GENERAL RAILWAY INCORPORATION LAWS

All of the early railway companies received their charters directly from the legislatures by special enactment. About 1850 New York and a number of other states passed general incorporation laws under which railroad companies could organize without special legislative sanction. There were several arguments in favor of the substitution of general for special acts of incorporation. Altogether too much time of the legislatures was being taken in the consideration of applications for charters, as each session of the legislature brought requests for charters in great numbers. The practice of granting special charters, furthermore, led to a great deal of favoritism and corruption through the pressure of interested parties for lenient charters and special favors. In addition, it seemed desirable that there should be greater uniformity in railway charters. For these reasons the practice of granting special charters was given up; and general incorporation laws were enacted in all states, although some special charters were granted after the enactment of general incorporation laws.

General incorporation laws were far superior to the system of granting special charters, but the "free railway laws" had one serious disadvantage. Before the enactment of the general laws an important consideration in the granting of any charter was whether the project was for the interests of the state as a whole and whether or not other railroads would be injured thereby. Under free railway laws, projects could be undertaken without regard to the effect on other lines, thus increasing the risks and speculative nature of railroad enterprises. In some states an attempt was made to remedy this situation by requiring a certificate of convenience and necessity from a court or from a commission before a new railroad could be constructed.[38] It must be admitted, however, that the existence of free railway laws was one of the several factors which contributed to the over-building of railroads that characterized the railroad-building era in the United States.

LOCAL AID TO RAILROADS

Although the states withdrew from direct participation in railroad building, private railroad corporations were heavily subsidized, with

---

[37] Ibid., p. 5.

[38] See 68 N.H. 570; 160 N.Y. 202; 227 N.Y. 248.

federal, state, and local governments joining in the granting of subsidies.

Local financial aid was of many kinds. A common form was subscription to stock of railroad companies. County and municipal subscriptions to stock of railroads aggregated more than $91,000,000.[39]

Loans were also made to railroad companies by local units of government. Loans by municipalities and counties to railroads exceeded $19,500,000;[40] and in addition, towns, cities, and counties purchased over $12,000,000 of railroad bonds.[41] Loans to railroads were sometimes in cash; but in many cases, bonds or warrants of the local government were issued to the railroad companies. When railroad bonds were purchased, they were also sometimes paid for in the obligations of the local governments.

Another form of local aid was the guaranty of railroad bonds. The guaranty might extend only to the payment of interest on the bonds, or it might cover both interest and principal. Railroad bonds to the extent of nearly $3,000,000 were guaranteed by cities and counties.[42]

Outright donations constituted another form of financial aid. These might be donations of cash, securities, or land, or of material, equipment, and labor. It has been estimated that railroads received over $30 million in cash donations,[43] but it is impossible to determine what proportion of this consisted of donations by county and municipal governments and what proportion consisted of donations by private individuals, corporations, or associations. County and municipal donations of securities amounted to over $16 million.[44] Donations of land by local governments to railroad companies aggregated over 2,400 acres, most of which was used for right-of-way or other carrier purposes.[45]

Finally, there was some exemption from taxation granted by local units of government.

Local aid to railroad companies usually resulted in the creation of public debt. When municipalities or counties purchased railroad stock, loaned money to railroads, donated cash, or purchased land to give to the railroad companies, the necessary funds were obtained by borrowing. Sometimes, as we have seen, obligations of the local governments were donated to the railroad companies or paid to them in exchange for railroad stocks or bonds.

The load of indebtedness imposed upon themselves by the local gov-

---

[39] Federal Coordinator of Transportation, *Public Aids to Transportation* (Washington, D.C.: U.S. Government Printing Office, 1938), Vol. II. The figure here given is computed from Table 22, pp. 148–59 of the Federal Coordinator's study.

[40] Ibid., p. 60.

[41] Ibid., pp. 148–59.

[42] Ibid., p. 61.

[43] Ibid., p. 133.

[44] Ibid.

[45] Ibid., p. 54.

ernments was often burdensome in the extreme. Instances were said to be not uncommon of municipalities and counties incurring debts in aid of railroads which exceeded the assessed value of all taxable property within the political subdivision.

The explanation of such extravagance is to be found in the dire need for transportation facilities. The people knew very well that the economic future of their communities depended upon transportation facilities, and they were willing to pay almost any price for them. Railroad promoters were expert in working up the enthusiasm of the people along the lines of the proposed railroad with extravagant claims of prosperity that would come with the railroads. In addition to the improvement in the economic condition of a community that the railroads were expected to bring, hope was held out of generous dividends on railroad stocks.

To work up competition in the matter of subsidizing railroads, rival routes were sometimes surveyed. The towns and counties along the different routes were led to bid against each other for the railroad. Perhaps the communities providing the greatest subsidies would get the road; but sometimes the route had already been selected, and the rival routes were for the purpose of increasing the subsidies from the communities through which the route passed. The scheme of surveying rival routes has been attempted in more recent years. In 1926 the Appalachian & Western North Carolina Railroad applied to the Interstate Commerce Commission for authority to construct a line of railroad from a point in North Carolina to a point in Tennessee. Three routes were surveyed, and it was admitted that this was done in order "to develop competition for the location of the route and the maximum financial aid from the communities benefited." The Commission felt that a definite route should have been selected before its approval was sought. For this and other reasons it denied the application until a choice of routes should be made and other information presented concerning the project.[46]

The enthusiasm for railroad connections can be seen in the extreme offers of aid which were sometimes made. In 1880 the Northern Pacific promised to extend its line to Superior, Wisconsin, if the city would give it a right of way into the city and one third of all lands, premises, and real estate in the city. The offer was accepted.[47] Seattle offered the Northern Pacific 7,500 town lots, 3,500 acres of land, $50,000 in money, $200,000 in bonds, and the use of much of the waterfront for terminal purposes if the Northern Pacific would make Seattle its western terminus.[48]

There was some opposition to these orgies of financial aid to railroads, but it was insufficient to stem the tide. Later on, however, when people

---

[46] 111 ICC 557 (1926).

[47] Cleveland and Powell, op. cit., p. 203.

[48] James B. Hedges, *Henry Villard and the Railways of the Northwest* (New Haven: Yale University Press, 1930), p. 26.

began to feel the burden of taxes imposed to pay bonds issued to railroads, public sentiment underwent a decided change. Disillusionment over the benefits which had been anticipated, resentment at the burdens of taxation imposed, and anger for having been tricked into a policy which often lined the pockets of railroad promoters at the expense of the taxpayers led many local governments to repudiate the bonds incurred in aid of railroads. In some cases it was argued that the use of the taxing power to aid private corporations was unlawful because the money was being used for a private and not for a public purpose. The courts held, however, that grants to railroads were not unlawful.[49] In some instances, however, bonds were repudiated because of some irregularity, real or alleged, in their issue. State courts often upheld repudiation in such cases; but the federal courts were more inclined to protect the bondholders, refusing to accept trivial technicalities as an excuse for repudiation.[50]

The policy of local subsidy to railroad corporations proved so burdensome that constitutional provisions were passed in many states prohibiting or severely restricting the granting of aid to railway corporations by local units of government. Such provisions were placed in the constitutions of California, Colorado, Connecticut, Illinois, Mississippi, Missouri, New Hampshire, Texas, Kansas, Arkansas, the Dakotas, and Utah.

STATE AID

The local governments were not alone in their policy of aiding private railway corporations. The states adopted a similar policy. A form of aid which dates from the very beginning of railroads was the granting of special privileges of various sorts to railroad corporations. The power of eminent domain was in reality such a privilege, but the grant of this power was so universally the practice that it was hardly considered a special privilege.

Many of the early railroads were granted monopoly privileges. The Boston & Lowell was given protection from competition for a period of thirty years, and the Western Railroad was given a somewhat similar privilege by the state. The Charleston & Hamburg Railroad was given the exclusive right to construct a railroad between Charleston and Hamburg for 36 years.[51] The grant of monopoly privileges was characteristic of the earlier decades of railroad building and was not a common practice in later decades.

Banking privileges were also given to railroad corporations, but this practice was confined largely to the first decade of railroad building. The idea seemed to be that profits from banking operations were more cer-

---

[49] See *Olcott* v. *The Supervisors*, 83 U.S. 678 (1872).

[50] Pierce, op. cit., chap. v.

[51] These and other illustrations are given in Cleveland and Powell, op. cit., pp. 165–66.

tain than from railroad operations and that the expected profits from banking would attract capital into the joint railway and banking enterprise. Subscription to stock in the bank sometimes was conditioned upon subscribing an equal amount of stock in the affiliated railroad corporation.

Tax exemption was another common form of aid. In a few cases tax exemption was complete. In other cases the exemption was limited to a period of years or until dividends should equal a certain amount. At least 19 states granted tax-exemption privileges to as many as 53 different railroad companies.[52]

If we turn to the direct forms of financial aid in railway building, we find them similar to those described in connection with local aid, namely, stock subscriptions, loans, guaranty of bonds or of interest on bonds, and donations. An unusual form of aid was provided by North Carolina when it turned over gangs of convicts on favorable terms to a number of railroads. The Cape Fear & Yadkin Railroad was constructed entirely by

TABLE 6–1.   State Aid to Railroad Construction*

Form	Amount
Stock subscriptions	$40,102,267
Loans, including purchases of railroad bonds	80,647,579
Guaranty of railroad bonds	45,543,425
Donations:	
Cash	1,575,974
Securities	5,078,120
Land (48,883,372 acres)	47,514,638

* These figures are taken from Federal Coordinator of Transportation, *Public Aids to Transportation* (Washington, D.C.: U.S. Government Printing Office, 1938), Vol. II.

convict labor.[53] Some states made land grants to railroads, but this form of aid was limited, because few states had extensive holdings of land. Maine, however, gave 600,000 acres of land to the European & North America Railroad.[54] Texas gave away for railroads and other internal improvements 32,400,000 acres.[55]

An estimate of the total amount of direct financial aid by the states for railroad construction is given in Table 6–1.

State aid to railroads was as disastrous as local aid proved to be a little later. In some cases, doubtless, the states did not regret the financial aid they had given to railways; but in the majority of instances the debts proved burdensome, and the benefits to the states were either forgotten or proved to be less substantial than had been anticipated. The fraud and

---

[52] Federal Coordinator of Transportation, op. cit., pp. 160–62.

[53] Cleveland and Powell, *Railroad Promotion and Capitalization*, pp. 227–28.

[54] Chase says 700,000 acres (op. cit., p. 49).

[55] Cleveland and Powell, *Railroad Promotion and Capitalization*, p. 229.

corruption caused by the scramble for state aid brought its inevitable reaction. The people considered that they had been tricked by unscrupulous promoters; and when the taxes which had been levied to pay off the indebtedness became burdensome, they refused in some cases to pay the debts. The burden of indebtedness caused by extravagance in the subsidy policy can be seen by comparing the interest on the debts with the income of the states. The interest charge in Florida amounted to $200,000 per year when her total revenue was less than $100,000 per year. In 1870 interest on the debt of Virginia amounted to about $2,000,000, while her income was less than $3,000,000. In North Carolina the interest charges were $700,000, while taxes yielded only a little over $500,000. The interest on Alabama's debt was over $500,000 when the income from taxation was only a little over $800,000.[56]

When the states repudiated their debts, there was no way to compel them to pay. It is a principle of constitutional law that a sovereign government cannot be sued in its own courts without the consent of that government; hence the states could not be sued in the state courts for failure to meet their obligations. And the federal courts have no jurisdiction over suits to compel a state to meet its obligations, since the Eleventh Amendment to the Constitution provides that "the Judicial power of the United States shall not be construed to extend to any suit in law or equity, commenced or prosecuted against one of the United States by Citizens of another State, or by Citizens or Subjects of any Foreign State."

The states which repudiated their debts attempted, for the most part, to justify their action by showing illegality and fraud in the issuance of the bonds. In South Carolina, $2,000,000 in bonds were issued under an act which authorized only $1,000,000. In Georgia, railroad bonds endorsed proved to be second-mortgage bonds, while the constitution provided that endorsement should be of first-mortgage bonds. Such discoveries of illegality provided excuses for repudiation. In some cases the repudiation may have been justified; in most cases it was not. A difficult moral question was involved. Should the loss fall upon defrauded taxpayers or upon bondholders who, in most cases, were innocent holders for value, since they had no part in the fraud practiced upon the state? In some cases the most trivial pretexts were given for repudiation. In Arkansas the bonds were found to have been illegally issued because at the time the legislature authorized the loans the ayes and nays had not been recorded as the constitution of the state provided.[57]

Resentment at the consequences of state aid to railways led to constitutional provisions prohibiting or limiting state aid to private corporations. These prohibitions, in general, came earlier than the prohibitions

---

[56] These figures are taken from W. A. Scott, *The Repudiation of State Debts* (New York: Crowell, 1893), p. 216.

[57] The above illustrations are taken from Scott, op. cit., pp. 200–201.

against local aid and, in fact, led to more local aid than would have otherwise been granted.

FEDERAL AID

The earliest form of federal aid to railways was granted under an act of Congress of 1824 which empowered the President to authorize government surveys of roads and canals. Railroads were not mentioned in the act; but in 1825 and 1826 surveys by the government were made for a railway and canal project which was promoted to unite the headwaters of the Kanawha and James rivers. Similar grants of assistance were made in ensuing years. The act was repealed in 1838 because it had led to logrolling and other abuses. During the period when the act was in force, about 60 railway surveys were made by government engineers.[58]

Another early form of financial aid by the federal government was the remission of duties on railway iron. Rails used on the early railroads were generally imported from England. A high tariff had been put on iron to protect the iron industry, but the duty was a burden to the railroads. In 1832 an act was passed by Congress which permitted a remission of the duties paid on railway iron if the iron was laid down within three years after importation. This act remained in force until 1843. The amount of duty remitted between 1832 and 1843 was nearly $6,000,000. It is estimated that the benefit derived from tariff remission was about $2,000 per mile of road constructed.[59]

Another form of Congressional aid was the grant of rights of way through the public domain, together with sites for depots and terminals, and the right to use timber, stone, and other materials from adjacent public lands. The first of these grants was made in 1835 to the Tallahassee Railroad Company in Florida. In 1852 a law was passed making this form of aid applicable to all railroad, plank-road, and turnpike companies then chartered or to be chartered in ten years. The rights of way granted under this act were to be 100 feet wide.[60] A similar statute enacted in 1875 provided for grants of a 200-foot right of way. Under this act approximately 150 railroad companies obtained rights of way through public lands.[61]

In 1864 Congress departed from its policy of not making loans to railroads and authorized loans to various railroads projected to complete rail routes to the Pacific Coast. Under the terms of this act the roads were to receive United States bonds in amounts varying from $16,000 to

---

[58] For further details of this form of aid see Haney, op. cit., pp. 275–83. See also F. G. Hill, "Government Engineering Aid to Railroads before the Civil War," 11 *Journal of Economic History* 235 (1951).

[59] Haney, op. cit., pp. 304–17.

[60] For additional facts regarding this form of aid see ibid., pp. 335–38, or Federal Coordinator of Transportation, op. cit., pp. 48–49.

[61] Federal Coordinator of Transportation, op. cit., p. 49.

$48,000 per mile. The government accepted a second mortgage on the railways as security. The beneficiaries of this act were the Union Pacific, the Central Pacific, the Kansas Pacific, the Western Pacific, the Central Branch Union Pacific, and the Sioux City & Pacific. Over $64,600,000 in bonds were issued to these companies. Much litigation took place before the United States secured repayment of these loans. They were eventually repaid, with the exception of about $3,700,000 of principal and interest owed by the Central Branch Union Pacific.[62]

LAND GRANTS

Land grants to railroads were the most important form of federal aid. Although the land-grant movement is usually dated from 1850, two early grants of land to the states in aid of canal building were modified by Congress to permit their use in aid of railroads. A grant to Ohio was modified in this manner in 1830, and a grant to Illinois was similarly modified in 1833.[63] The real land-grant era, however, began in 1850 with the grant to the Illinois Central. This grant was typical of the later ones, although considerably more modest in extent. The Illinois Central received a right of way 200 feet wide and six sections of land for each mile of road. These were to be alternate sections of land lying along either side of the road. In case any of the sections falling to the railroad had been occupied, the company could select an equal area within 15 miles of the road. In later grants the right of way was 400 feet wide and the number of sections was increased. Some railroads received 10 sections per mile, some 20, and some 40. No new grants were authorized after 1871. By this time, opposition to the policy had grown so strong that Congress called a halt. The rapid dwindling of the public domain, and the conflict of interest between settlers and the railroads as landowners, explain the change in sentiment.

In all, 89 separate grants were made, 17 of which were later forfeited for failure to carry on the construction work, leaving 72 grants under which land was transferred.[64] Some idea of the magnitude of these grants to individual railroads is shown by the acreage received by the following railroads or predecessor companies: Chicago, Burlington & Quincy, 3,200,000 acres; Illinois Central, 4,600,000; Chicago & North Western, 7,400,000; and Union Pacific, 19,000,000.[65] The largest grant was to the Northern Pacific, which amounted to over 41,000,000 acres.[66]

---

[62] Ibid., p. 59.

[63] M. N. Orfield, *Federal Land Grants to the States with Special Reference to Minnesota,* University of Minnesota Studies in the Social Sciences, No. 2 (Minneapolis, 1915), p. 4.

[64] U.S. Department of the Interior, General Land Office, *Information concerning Land Grants for Roads, Canals, River Improvements and Railroads* (Washington, D.C., 1940), p. 3.

[65] Federal Coordinator of Transportation, op. cit., pp. 107–11.

[66] Ibid., p. 111.

The total acreage patented to railroad companies under these grants was over 130,000,000 acres. This represents an expanse of land equal in size to Michigan, Wisconsin, Illinois, Indiana, and nearly half of Ohio.

Some of the lands granted to the railroads were disposed of as soon as possible and the proceeds used for construction purposes. In other cases the lands were held for future increases in value. Sometimes the lands were mortgaged in order to raise funds for railroad building. The Illinois Central Railroad disposed of part of its land as soon as possible, but about two million acres were mortgaged for about $8 per acre. Since the government lands were being sold at a lower figure—at a minimum price of $2.50—it was necessary for the Illinois Central to hold its mortgaged lands until most of the government lands had been sold before it could hope to sell them for enough to cover the mortgage. It was not until 1856 and 1857 that efforts were made to dispose of the land rapidly. By 1874 most of it had been sold.[67] A number of railroad companies still hold lands—either directly or through subsidiaries—which they acquired under the Congressional grants.

It is often alleged that the land grants cost the government nothing because the selling price of the alternate sections which the government retained was doubled. Thus the lands along the line of the Illinois Central had been on the market at $1.25 per acre and did not sell readily. When the government made the grant for the Illinois Central, it raised the price of the remaining lands within the primary land-grant area to $2.50 per acre. As a matter of fact, however, the government did not obtain the doubled price for all of the alternate sections not granted to the railroads. A considerable amount of the land within the land-grant areas had previously been sold at the lower prices; some had been donated for school purposes; and some was subsequently given to settlers under the Homestead Act of 1862.[68] The argument that the land grants cost the government nothing is also fallacious because it assumes that the railroads would not have been built except for the land grants. In most cases the railroads would have been built, although at a later date, and the government could have eventually sold its lands at an increased price. Or if it had preferred, the government could have sold the lands at the old price, thus giving the settlers the benefit of the increased value due to the construction of the railroads.

The value of the lands at the time that they were granted may be estimated from the price received from the sale of federal public lands during this period. The Federal Coordinator of Transportation found that the average proceeds from the sale of public lands by the govern-

---

[67] Howard G. Brownson, *History of the Illinois Central Railroad to 1870*, University of Illinois Studies in the Social Sciences, Vol. I, Nos. 3 and 4 (Urbana, 1915), pp. 118–19, 136, 139.

[68] See Paul W. Gates, "The Railroad Land-Grant Legend," 14 *Journal of Economic History* 143 (1954).

ment from 1851 to 1871 was 97.2 cents per acre. On this basis the value of the lands granted by the government was approximately $130,-000,000.[69]

How much benefit did the railroads derive from the land grants? This question cannot be answered definitely, but it is clear that the grants were of great value to some of the railroads, while to others the lands netted much less than had been expected. It must be remembered that the government lands were often on the market at $1.25 or $2.50 per acre, and this limited the amount that the railroads could get for their lands unless they waited until the government lands were sold. As we have seen, the Illinois Central followed the latter policy, and so did the Chicago & North Western. It was found from a study of the records of sales of government lands and of railroad lands in Iowa along the line of the Chicago & North Western that the sale of railway land followed the government sales by 20 to 25 years.[70] Prices received by the railroads for their land varied greatly. The Federal Coordinator of Transportation found that the average gross receipts received by the railroads from the sale of lands granted under state and federal land grants were $3.42 per acre.[71] The net proceeds, after paying expenses of administration and sale, including taxes, averaged $2.635 per acre.[72] An estimate by the Board of Investigation and Research, which was set up in 1940 to investigate various transportation problems, placed the actual net proceeds from the sale of lands received under the federal grants at more than $380,000,000.[73] If the value of the lands still held by the railroads is added to this figure, the total value of the land grants to the railroads up to December 31, 1941, was over $440,000,000.[74] These figures do not include large profits which have accrued, or will accrue, to some railroads as a result of sales of land by subsidiary or affiliated companies to which their original holdings were transferred.

The receipts from some of the land grants represented a substantial proportion of the original cost of the railroad. According to one estimate the receipts from the Illinois Central grant were six sevenths of the first cost of the road, and the receipts of the Northern Pacific from land sales were 194 percent of the cost of the road.[75] This estimate is apparently based on gross receipts and not on net receipts from the sales. If net figures were taken, the percentages would be somewhat lower; but it is

---

[69] Federal Coordinator of Transportation, op. cit., p. 36.

[70] B. H. Hibbard, *A History of the Public Land Policies* (New York: Macmillan, 1924), p. 258.

[71] Federal Coordinator of Transportation, op. cit., p. 38.

[72] Ibid.

[73] Board of Investigation and Research, *Land Grants to Railroads and Related Rates* (mimeographed; Washington, D.C., 1944), p. 25.

[74] Ibid., p. 38.

[75] Hibbard, op. cit., pp. 257 and 260.

clear that they would be a substantial proportion of the cost of the road in the first case and much more than the cost of the road in the second case.

In return for the railroad grants, the government secured certain financial benefits. Some land was sold at higher prices than would have been received, but not higher than *could* have been received later; and much land was sold sooner than it otherwise would have been. The government also derived benefits from the grants in reduced transportation charges on mail, troops, and government property. The grants provided that mail should be carried on the land-grant railroads at such rates as should be fixed by Congress. In practice, this came to be 80 percent of the regular rates. Usually the grants required that, over the land-grant railroads, troops and government property should be transported "free from all toll or other charge." The phrase quoted, however, did not mean what might be supposed. In a five-to-four decision in 1877 the United States Supreme Court held that no charge or "toll" should be levied for the use of the road but that a charge might be levied for transporting the troops or property over the road.[76] For this reason the rates charged the government by the land-grant roads were generally 50 percent of the regular charges.

The saving to the government through the reduced-rate provisions of the land grants, together with voluntary equalization of rates by competing nonland-grant railroads, was estimated by the Federal Co-ordinator of Transportation to have amounted to $138,700,000 up to June 30, 1934—a period of 80 years or more. The rapid expansion of government activity, particularly after 1932, greatly increased the amount of traffic entitled to land-grant rates. It was estimated that more than 138 government agencies, some shipping large quantities of freight, such as the Tennessee Valley Authority, the Public Works Administration, and the Federal Surplus Commodities Corporation, were entitled to land-grant rates. It was estimated that in 1937 alone the reduction in rates on government property entitled to the 50 percent rates amounted to about $7,000,000.[77] As a means of financial aid to the railways, Congress, in 1940, relieved the land-grant railroads of the obligation to transport nonmilitary government property and mail at reduced rates.[78] The transportation of persons or property for military or naval establishments, however, was still to be performed by land-grant railroads at the lower rates.

Notwithstanding the elimination of land-grant deductions on non-military traffic, the volume of traffic entitled to deductions increased enormously as a result of the war, the deductions amounting to an

---

[76] *Lake Superior & Mississippi R. R. Co.* v. *United States*, 93 U.S. 442.

[77] *Immediate Relief for Railroads*, 75th Cong., 3d Sess., House Doc. No. 583 (1938), p. 32.

[78] Sec. 321 of Transportation Act of 1940.

estimated $240 million in 1943 alone. The total of all land-grant deductions, including voluntary equalization of rates by competing railroads, from the time of the land grants to June 30, 1943, was estimated at $580 million.[79] It will be noted that this sum was several times the value of the land grants at the time they were made and that it exceeded the sums derived by the railroads from the grants. In 1945 Congress finally relieved the land-grant railroads from any further obligation to transport persons and property for the military and naval establishments at the reduced rates.[80] Under this statute, land-grant rate reductions ceased on October 1, 1946.

CONCLUSIONS ON RAILROAD SUBSIDIES

We have seen that the amount of financial aid given by the federal, state, and local governments to railroad companies was enormous. The Federal Coordinator of Transportation estimated the total amount of public aid for railroad construction at $1,282 billion.[81]

If we summarize the effects of railroad subsidies—local, state, and federal—we find the following results. First, the subsidies accomplished the purpose for which they were intended. They stimulated railroad building and brought about a more rapid expansion of the railway net. In some cases, railroads were probably constructed that would not have been built otherwise; and in many more cases, railroads were built sooner than they would have been without the financial aid provided. A second consequence of railroad subsidies follows from the first. The undeveloped West was settled more rapidly than it could have been otherwise.

But the subsidy policy had other results, results which were not anticipated. The subsidies offered for railroad building by a generous public constituted rich prizes that attracted irresponsible and dishonest schemers into the field of railroad construction. As a result there was much fraud and corruption in connection with the granting of subsidies. A second result of the subsidy policy was the overexpansion of railroad facilities. Many projects were undertaken which, at the time, were not economically justified. There was not traffic enough to support them. The epidemic of railroad failures which afflicted the country is traceable in part to the policy of railroad subsidy. These bankruptcies, which wiped out small investors and left cities, counties, and states holding worthless railroad stocks and bonds, increased the antirailroad feeling which appeared shortly after 1870. The overexpansion of railroad facilities and the rapid settlement of the country were also factors in bring-

---

[79] Board of Investigation & Research, op. cit., p. 42.

[80] 59 Stat. 606.

[81] Federal Coordinator of Transportation, *Public Aids to Transportation* (Washington, D.C.: U.S. Government Printing Office, 1940), Vol. I, p. 19.

ing about the agricultural depression in the 70s and provided the basis for the Granger movement, which subjected the carriers to regulation.

CONSTRUCTION COMPANIES

One more feature of the railroad-building era should be noted, since it plays an important part in explaining the overbuilding that occurred. This was the use of so-called "construction companies" in building the railroads. A construction company was a company standing between the railroad company and the contractors who actually did the work of construction. The construction company seems originally to have been a device to permit the issuance of stock nominally at par but actually below par. Railroads were more or less speculative undertakings, and it was thought to be difficult or impossible for the companies to dispose of their stock at par to secure funds for construction purposes.[82] In some cases the law prohibited the issuance of stock below par. In other cases the issuance of stock for less than par was inexpedient because, in case of the failure of the railroad, the stockholders were held liable for the difference between the par value of their shares and the price at which they had been issued. This position of the courts was based on the theory that the share capital of a company was security for debts of the company. The liability of the shareholders, however, did not extend to third parties. In other words, if the original shareholder sold his shares to another, the latter was not liable for any additional payments even though the stock had been issued for less than par. By use of the construction company the above difficulties were overcome. The railroad company would make a contract with the construction company for the construction of a certain number of miles of road at a certain price per mile, payable in stocks and bonds at par. The contract price, however, would be high enough to enable the construction company to sell the securities at a discount and still realize enough to defray the actual costs of construction and leave a profit. The intervention of the construction company also made the persons who purchased the stock from the construction company third parties and hence not liable for any additional sums in case of the failure of the railroad; and what is more important, the railroad could say that the stock had been issued at par.

The evils of construction-company finance, however, did not arise from this type of construction company but from the "inside construction company." The inside construction company was one organized by "insiders," usually directors of the railroad company, who would vote

---

[82] It may be questioned whether it was necessary for railway companies to issue stock below par. The stockholder has only a proportional interest in the corporation, and this fractional share is the same whether stock is issued at par or whether a larger number of shares is issued at less than par. But the common financial practice was to issue stock at less than par.

themselves—as a construction company—profitable contracts for the construction of the road. The higher the price, the greater would be the profits of the insiders at the expense of the railroad company. Such inside construction companies usually saw to it that they received all the land grants, all the state and local bonds offered as subsidies, and all of the railroad bonds and stock that could be successfully unloaded on the public, in return for constructing the railroad. Not all railroads were constructed by such methods; but the illustrations are all too abundant, and in the 60s and 70s it was considered to be the general practice. The Logan, Crawfordsville & South Western Railroad voted all its municipal subsidy bonds, capital stock, and bonds to the director-contractors. The road actually cost about a million dollars, while $4 million in securities were issued.[83] The Gilman, Clinton & Springfield Railroad was built for $1,500,000, but the construction company received securities in the amount of $3,998,000.[84] The West Shore Railroad was constructed by an inside construction company known as the North River Construction Company. It left the railroad company nearly bankrupt and the insiders rich.[85] One of the most notorious of the inside construction companies, because it besmirched members of Congress, was the Crédit Mobilier, which constructed the Union Pacific. "The members of it are in Congress," wrote Charles Francis Adams, Jr., in 1869; "they are trustees for the bondholders, they are directors, they are stockholders, they are contractors; in Washington they vote the subsidies, in New York they receive them, upon the Plains they expend them, and in the Crédit Mobilier they divide them."[86] As a result the capitalization of the Union Pacific was nearly double the cost of construction. It we take the value of the securities issued to the construction company at their market values, the cash profits of the Crédit Mobilier were over $23 million, according to the report of the Congressional committee which investigated the matter.[87] Other investigators have come up with amounts ranging from $8 million to $17 million.[88] A recent investigator places the profits between a lower limit of $13 million and an upper limit of $16.5 million, which he still considers to have been excessive.[89]

Several results of construction-company financing should be noted. In the first place, it left the railroads with an inflated capitalization and an inflated book value. The impossibility of paying a return upon such an inflated capitalization often resulted in receiverships and reorganiza-

---

[83] Cleveland and Powell, *Railroad Finance*, p. 62.

[84] Ibid.

[85] "The West Shore Enterprise," 11 *Bradstreet's* 274 (1885).

[86] "Railroad Inflation," 108 *North American Review* 130, 148 (1869).

[87] House Rep. No. 78, 42d Cong., 3d Sess. (1873), p. xv.

[88] Summarized in Robert W. Fogel, *The Union Pacific Railroad: A Case in Premature Enterprise* (Baltimore, Johns Hopkins Press, 1960), p. 69.

[89] Ibid., pp. 66–86.

tions, with their attendant losses to security holders. In the second place, the use of construction companies contributed to the tendency, already noted, for overexpansion of railroad facilities. Some railroads were built not for the profits of operation, but for the profits of construction. Under such conditions it was inevitable that railroads should be built without regard to the economic merits of the undertaking. A third result of construction-company financing was that it led to poor standards of construction. The cheaper the construction, the greater were the profits of the insiders. The directors of the road, who secured the profits, were not inclined to insist on proper standards.

SELECTED REFERENCES

The best general material on early railroad history is in J. L. Ringwalt, *Development of Transportation Systems in the United States* (Philadelphia: Railway World Office, 1888), and Caroline E. MacGill, *History of Transportation in the United States before 1860* (Washington, D.C.: Carnegie Institution, 1917). Most general books on transportation contain material on railroad history. We are listing here two that treat the subject with more detail than most, namely: W. Z. Ripley, *Railroads: Rates and Regulation* (New York: Longmans, 1912), chap. i; Sidney L. Miller, *Inland Transportation* (New York: McGraw-Hill, 1933), chaps. iv–vii.

A detailed account of diversity of track gauges and the history of standardization is George R. Taylor and Irene D. Neu, *The American Railroad Network, 1861–1890* (Cambridge: Harvard University Press, 1956).

There are numerous histories of individual railroads ranging from brief pamphlets and magazine articles to detailed studies of one or more volumes. The list of such histories is too long for listing here. There are numerous regional railroad histories. Among these are R. E. Riegel, *The Story of Western Railroads* (New York: Macmillan, 1926); U. B. Phillips, *A History of Transportation in the Eastern Cotton Belt to 1860* (New York: Macmillan, 1913); George P. Baker, *The Formation of the New England Railroad Systems* (Cambridge: Harvard University Press, 1937); Thelma M. Kistler, *The Rise of Railroads in the Connecticut River Valley*, Smith College Studies in History, Vol. XXIII (Northampton, 1938); W. J. Lane, *From Indian Trail to Iron Horse: Travel and Transportation in New Jersey, 1620–1860* (Princeton: Princeton University Press, 1939), chaps. xi–xiii. On the period of railroad building generally see George R. Taylor, *The Transportation Revolution, 1815–1860* (New York: Rinehart, 1951), chap. v.

The best account of state-owned railroads in the United States is in F. A. Cleveland and F. W. Powell, *Railroad Promotion and Capitalization in the United States* (New York: Longmans, 1909), chap. vi. Individual examples of municipally owned projects are described in J. H. Hollander, *The Cincinnati Southern Railway*, Johns Hopkins University Studies in Historical and Political Science, 12th Ser., Nos. 1 and 2 (Baltimore: Johns Hopkins Press, 1894); F. W. Powell, "Two Experiments in Public Ownership of Steam Railroads," 33 *Quarterly Journal of Economics* 137 (1908); and Harry H. Pierce, *Rail-*

roads of New York: A Study of Government Aid, 1826–1875 (Cambridge: Harvard University Press, 1953), chap. iv.

An account of state and local aid to railroad corporations is to be found in Cleveland and Powell, op. cit., chaps. xii–xiv. The most comprehensive accounts of public aid to railroads are Federal Coordinator of Transportation, *Public Aids to Transportation,* Vol. II (Washington, D.C.: U.S. Government Printing Office, 1938); and Board of Investigation and Research, *Public Aids to Domestic Transportation,* 79th Cong., 1st Sess., House Doc. No. 159 (1944), chap. iii. An excellent account of state and local aid in New York is Pierce, op. cit.

Much information about land grants may be found in Federal Coordinator of Transportation, op. cit., and in Board of Investigation and Research, op. cit. The literature relating to land grants is very extensive. See particularly J. B. Sanborn, *Congressional Grants of Land in Aid of Railways,* Economics, Political Science, and History Series, Vol. II, No. 3 (Madison, 1899). A brief account of land grants is in B. H. Hibbard, *A History of the Public Land Policies* (New York: Macmillan, 1924), chap. xiii. For an account of the reaction against land grants and efforts to recover unearned grants see David M. Ellis, "The Forfeiture of Railroad Land Grants, 1867–1894," 33 *Mississippi Valley Historical Review* 27 (1946). A criticism of the treatment of land grants in history textbooks is Robert S. Henry, "The Railroad Land Grant Legend in American History Texts," 32 *Mississippi Valley Historical Review* 171 (1945), to which varied reactions are noted in the same volume, pp. 557–76.

Construction-company finance is described in W. Z. Ripley, *Railroads: Finance and Organization* (New York: Longmans, 1915), pp. 14–18, and in F. A. Cleveland and F. W. Powell, *Railroad Finance* (New York: Appleton, 1912), pp. 59–72.

Chapter

7

THE THEORY OF RAILROAD

RATES

The railroad business requires a large plant, representing a huge investment in fixed and specialized capital. In 1969 the investment in road and equipment of the railroads of the United States was over $37,000,000,000. This is equivalent to over $180,000 per mile of road. This sum also represents capital of a highly specialized sort. The property of a railroad can be used only for transportation purposes. If a railroad proves unprofitable, the plant cannot be used for something else. A large part of the investment is in grading and excavation, and these have no value except as a roadbed for a railroad. Even the land itself, once it has been used for railroad purposes, is largely worthless for any other purpose. But railroad capital is not only specialized; it is fixed capital as well. It is bound to its original location. If a particular railroad fails, it cannot be moved to some other location where the prospects of success may be greater. The rolling stock can be moved away, the rails can be torn up and sold for use elsewhere; but by far the largest part of the investment has been irrevocably sunk in the original site. These characteristics of the railroad business have important economic consequences.

COMPETITION NOT A REGULATOR OF THE RATE LEVEL

Since the original investment in a railroad is large, and since it represents fixed and specialized capital, competition does not keep the earnings of the industry at a normal level. If the capital cannot be withdrawn from the business, a company will continue operations as long as it can make some return on the capital invested. If the railroad is abandoned, practically all the money invested in it is lost. If it can make a small profit by continuing operations, it had better do this than go out of business. Of course, if there is no return on the capital invested, there is no inducement to maintain the property and to replace such units as wear out. The owners will get what they can out of the property before it becomes so deteriorated that it must be abandoned. But even if the return on capital is less than can be secured in other industries, new capital may be put in if the possibility of earning a return on the original investment is improved thereby. A great many railroads in the United States which have been in existence for many years earn very small returns on the capital invested.

A railroad may, on the other hand, earn large profits without inducing capital to build a competing line. At the present time, public authority would not permit the construction of rival railway lines; but even if this were not true, the construction of a competing railroad would be a hazardous undertaking, as many investors learned to their sorrow during the era of railroad building in the United States. Traffic may be sufficient to yield one railroad a handsome profit and at the same time be insufficient to enable two railroads to pay operating expenses.

It must be concluded that the flow of capital into and out of the railroad industry will not take place rapidly and easily enough to act as a regulator of the level of railway charges in any practical sense.

CONSTANT AND VARIABLE EXPENSES

The huge physical plant and the enormous investment therein are largely responsible for another characteristic of the railroad industry. Railroad expenses can be divided into two groups: variable expenses, which tend to vary more or less proportionately with the volume of traffic; and fixed or constant expenses, which, over short periods at least, are independent of the volume of traffic. The latter remain the same whether the railroad is operated to capacity or whether it is only partially utilized. The distinction between the two classes of expenses is of prime importance in explaining the peculiarities of railway rates. The significance of this distinction was pointed out very early in the history of railroads.[1] Variable expenses are frequently called "prime costs" or "direct expenses." Sometimes they are called "out-of-pocket expenses," the term long used by the Interstate Commerce Commission, but suggesting a more restricted meaning than intended. A newer term "incremental cost" is advocated in a study made by the Association of American Railroads; and the Commission has recently announced a preference for the term "variable cost."[2] Constant expenses are commonly called "indirect expenses," "fixed expenses," "supplementary expenses," "overhead expenses," or "burden."

The importance of the distinction between constant and variable expenses warrants an examination of railway expenses for the purpose of determining to what extent they are constant and to what extent variable.

---

[1] See particularly Dupuit, "De la mesure de l'utilité des travaux publics," 8 *Annales des ponts et chaussées*, 2d Ser., 332 (1844), and "De l'influence des péages sur l'utilité des voies de communication," 17 *Annales* . . . 170 (1849); Alphonse Belpaire, *Traité des dépenses d'exploitation aux chemins de fer* (1847); and Dionysius Lardner, *Railway Economy* (New York: Harper, 1850).

[2] Association of American Railroads, Bureau of Railway Economics, *A Guide to Railroad Cost Analysis* (Washington, D.C., 1964), pp. 17–19); *Rules to Govern Assembling and Presenting Cost Evidence*, 337 ICC 298, 324–25 (1970).

First in importance is the interest on the capital invested in the business. If we assume a given physical plant, the interest on the investment is the same regardless of the volume of traffic. That part of the return on capital which is paid out as interest on bonds is clearly a constant expense, for the "fixed charges" (interest on bonds) are the same regardless of the quantity of traffic moved over the railroad. Part of the return on capital is in the form of dividends on stock. Dividends are presumably paid out of earnings. This item might therefore be regarded as a variable expense, or, as the accountants would say, not an expense at all but a distribution of profits. But in discussions of economic theory a return on capital, or so much of it as is a normal return, may properly be considered as a cost of production. This is so because capital must in the long run receive its reward, or additional capital will not be forthcoming when needed. Interest on investment is therefore to be considered as a constant expense. It is sometimes said that in the long run the return on capital is a variable expense. The more traffic there is, the larger the plant becomes, and hence the greater the investment and the greater the sum necessary to pay a return on the capital invested. This is true; but for the purpose of explaining certain characteristics of railway rates, it is necessary to assume a given physical plant. When this is done, interest on investment is clearly a cost which is independent of the traffic handled.

A great many of the expenses of a railway which are classified as operating expenses are independent of the volume of traffic. Many of the items comprising maintenance of way and structures are of this sort. The railroad plant is to a large extent exposed to the action of the elements. Embankments are washed by rains, ditches become filled, rails and rail fastenings rust with exposure to the weather, crossties rot out, and the action of rains and frosts makes expenditures necessary to keep rails in alignment and tracks level. Buildings and bridges require expenditures for upkeep that are in no way related to the quantity of traffic moving over the railroad. Of course, some items in the maintenance-of-way accounts are affected by the volume of traffic. The wear on rails, for instance, increases with the volume of traffic moving over them. It nevertheless remains true that the maintenance-of-way expense is largely independent of the volume of traffic if a given standard of maintenance is assumed. Railroads can, and frequently do, defer maintenance work when business is dull and speed it up when business is good. This practice gives a semblance of variability to maintenance expenses; but the variability is more apparent than real, since deferred maintenance is an expense properly chargeable to the period in which it accrued.

Maintenance of equipment, another important expense of railroads, is more nearly variable than maintenance of way and structures. But even here, many items do not vary with traffic. Freight cars, for instance, are subject to the action of the elements, and repairs become necessary whether the cars are constantly in use or remain standing on sidings for a large part of the time. Depreciation of cars and locomotives is not wholly a function of the use made of them. This is particularly true of that element in depreciation known as obsolescence.

If we turn to the expenses commonly called "transportation expenses," we again find many items which do not vary proportionately with the traffic. Transportation expenses include the wages of train crews and of station and yard forces, fuel consumed, and many other items. If additional traffic can be handled without increasing the number of trains, the wages paid for train crews will remain the same. Neither will fuel expenses increase in proportion to the traffic, since it does not take twice the fuel to pull a train of 50 cars that was required for a train of 25 cars. If the increase in traffic makes necessary an increase in the number of trains, then the wages of train crews and the outlay for fuel may increase in proportion to the traffic increase; but it might not be necessary to increase proportionately the expenditures for station or yard forces. If transportation expenses in the long run tend to vary with the volume of traffic, the railroad is probably justified in apportioning these expenses on the basis of averages; but if particular units of traffic are clearly shown to involve very little extra expense, there is a temptation to consider them as profitable even if they do not contribute their share of all transportation expenses.

The so-called "general expenses" of a railway include the salaries of higher officials and administrative officers, and the expenses of maintaining the general offices of the company. It can be seen at once that these expenses are largely constant.

Finally, mention should be made of taxes, which in 1969 amounted to over $1 billion. Payroll taxes would tend to vary with the volume of traffic. The federal corporation income tax would also be affected by the volume of traffic, since net income tends to vary with the amount of traffic. A large part of railroad taxes, however, are state and local property taxes based on an assessed value of the railroads' property. The taxes levied in this manner have no relation to the volume of traffic carried and may be considered as a constant expense.

In the early development of railway rate theory the fixed expenses were considered to constitute as much as two thirds of the total. These estimates were widely accepted by writers in the field.[3] More recent studies, based on present-day conditions as well as on different assumptions, tend to show that the variable expenses comprise a larger proportion of the total than the earlier writers believed. Reasons for these differences in estimates will be mentioned later in this chapter. At this point the impor-

---

[3] Eliot Jones, *Principles of Railway Transportation* (New York: Macmillan, 1924), pp. 77–78; W. Z. Ripley, *Railroads: Rates and Regulation* (New York: Longmans, 1912), pp. 55–56. For a review of the estimates of many writers who have considered this matter see Ford K. Edwards, *Rail Freight Service Costs in the Various Rate Territories of the United States*, 78th Cong., 1st Sess., Senate Doc. No. 63 (1943), chap. ix.

tant thing to note is that there is a large mass of consant expenses which do not vary with the volume of traffic. It should also be pointed out that it is mathematically impossible for the proportion of either fixed or variable expenses to remain the same after a change in traffic volume has occurred. Suppose, for instance, that on a certain railroad at a certain time, one fourth of the expenses could be classed as variable and three fourths as constant. If the volume of traffic doubled, the variable expenses would become two fifths, and the constant expenses three fifths, of the total.

RAILROADS AND THE LAW OF INCREASING RETURNS

One important result of the invariability of certain railroad expenses is that unit costs—that is, costs per unit of traffic—tend to decline as the volume of traffic increases. This will be true up to the point of most efficient utilization of the existing plant. Beyond this point further increases in traffic will crowd the carrier's facilities, and unit costs will tend to rise. As long as there is a substantial amount of unutilized capacity, however, increases in traffic will lower the unit costs, since the fixed or constant expenses can be spread over a larger amount of business. This situation is commonly expressed by saying that the railroads are subject to the law of increasing returns.[4]

Increasing returns in the railroad industry arise primarily from the economy of more complete plant utilization, whereby constant costs are distributed over a larger volume of traffic. It should be recognized, however, that increasing returns may also arise from the greater economy of a large plant as compared with a smaller one and that over long periods of time this may be an important factor in reducing unit costs if continuous expansion of traffic occurs.

The significance of fixed or constant costs in the railroad industry, and in other industries as well, was pointed out by Dionysius Lardner in 1850. He said:

> The cost of production of the objects of industry may always be regarded as consisting of two parts, one of which is quite independent of the number of articles produced, and being, therefore, equally divided among them, will render one element of their price precisely in the inverse ratio of the number; but still there will be another component, which, depending on the direct application of manual or other labor, and on the immediate consumption of raw material, will be in the direct ratio of the number of articles produced.[5]

---

[4] This does not mean that the railroad industry is necessarily an industry of decreasing costs as that term is used in economic theory. The term "decreasing costs" refers to a situation in which an expansion of the productive facilities in the industry results in lower unit costs, not to a situation in which lower costs result merely from more complete utilization of the existing plant. See Ralph H. Blodgett, *Principles of Economics* (New York: Farrar and Rinehart, 1941), pp. 234 and 251–52.

[5] Lardner, op. cit., p. 192.

Since railroads are subject to increasing returns, they are peculiarly susceptible to fluctuations in earnings when traffic increases or decreases. If an increase in the volume of traffic increases operating expenses only slightly, the increase in traffic will greatly augment the net income of the carrier. Conversely, a decline in the volume of traffic will quickly convert a profit into a loss.[6] This extreme sensitiveness to changes in the volume of traffic is often obscured by the practice of deferring maintenance and postponing property retirements in time of depression and catching up on such expenditures in time of prosperity. It may be a wise policy to defer maintenance and replacements when funds are short and to catch up when funds are abundant, but to do so may give an impression of stability of net earnings which is not real.

DISCRIMINATION

The existence of a large mass of constant or supplementary expenses gives the railroad a motive to vary its charges according to the exigencies of demand. If a particular unit of traffic will not move unless charged a low rate, it is profitable for the railroad to quote a low rate, provided the variable or "out-of-pocket" expenses are covered. If the railroad can get something over the variable expense, this item of traffic is profitable. It covers the extra expense incurred in taking the traffic, and it makes some contribution to the overhead expenses, which must be incurred anyway. If the railroad attempted to charge a normal rate, the traffic would not move.

This practice is called "differential charging" or "discrimination." The terms refer to differences in rates which cannot be explained by differences in cost of service. The practice of differential charging results in a situation which is very confusing to persons unacquainted with railroad economics, for the railroad is found to be carrying some kinds of traffic at less than the full cost of the service, yet is making a profit out of it. For many years the average rate per ton-mile in the United States was close to 10 mills. But much traffic is carried for 6 mills or less, and this traffic is profitable. It will not move at higher rates; it pays the extra expense incurred in taking it; and it makes some contribution to overhead.

If all expenses of a railroad were variable, there would be no incentive to discriminate in this way. If, for instance, it costs 11 mills additional for every ton-mile of freight transported, and no part of this expense was incurred if the traffic did not move, the railroad would never charge less than 11 mills; for if it did, an actual loss would be incurred. The railroad might possibly discriminate by charging certain traffic more than 11 mills. But the characteristic feature of railroad discrimination is that many rates are less than the full cost of the service. The motive for this

---

[6] For a demonstration showing how an increase of 10 percent in traffic might increase net return by over 100 percent see Jones, op. cit., pp. 78–79.

type of discrimination is found in the existence of the large mass of supplementary expenses.

Discrimination between Commodities

The practice of differential charging takes a number of different forms. The first and most obvious type is discrimination between commodities. There is a wide range in the rates on different commodities. The order of the Interstate Commerce Commission in 1945 which required the establishment of a uniform system of freight classification provided for class rates as low as 13 percent of the first-class rates.[7] Thus the first-class rates would be nearly eight times the rates on the lowest class. There may also be "commodity rates" lower than the lowest of the class rates,[8] and provision is made in the classification and the class rates for rates which are as high as four times the first-class rates.

These differences in rates may be explained on two grounds. First, there are differences in the cost of service. Some articles are more expensive to transport than others—some require more expensive types of equipment; some require special facilities of one sort or another; some require expedited service; some are more bulky than others, and hence the cost per unit of weight is greater than when the weight density is greater. Differences in liability and risk also make differences in the cost of service. Cost factors affecting rates will be considered in detail in a subsequent chapter.[9] But differences in rates based on differences in cost of service are not real discriminations. We are interested here in the differences in rates which cannot be explained by differences in cost of service.

These differences are explained by differences in the ability of the traffic to stand high transportation charges. The motive for these discriminations lies in the existence of unused capacity and fixed or overhead expenses. Some commodities will not bear high rates. These will be charged low rates. Others can stand the full cost of transporting them, including a pro rata share of the overhead. These will be charged higher rates. Still other commodities will stand rates which represent more than the cost of service. The carrier, if not restrained by regulation, will exact very high rates on these.

Discrimination between commodities is accomplished by two different devices: (1) the classification of freight, that is, the grouping of commodities into a limited number of classes or groups for the purpose of applying rates; and (2) the granting of special or "commodity" rates on articles for which the regular class rates are not suitable.

The fact that there are many rates which are higher or lower than

---

[7] *Class Rate Investigation, 1939,* 262 ICC 447, 511 (1945).

[8] Class and commodity rates will be discussed more fully in the following chapter. See pp. 171–78, infra.

[9] Chapter 18.

can be justified on the basis of transportation costs alone is clearly revealed by studies which have been made by the staff of the Interstate Commerce Commission. Table 7–1 shows the freight revenue from a large number of carload shipments of different commodities as a percentage of the "fully distributed cost" of transporting these commodities in 1959. The "fully distributed cost" includes not only out-of-pocket costs but an allocation of constant expenses, including an allowance for a return on investment. When the figures in Table 7–1 are less than 100,

TABLE 7–1. Comparison of Carload Freight Revenue from Selected Commodities and Fully Distributed Cost, 1959*

Commodity	Percent of Fully Distributed Cost	Commodity	Percent of Fully Distributed Cost
Wheat	140	Gravel and sand, n.o.s.	54
Corn	111	Lumber, shingles and lath	103
Flour, wheat	76	Pig iron	143
Cotton, in bales	126	Gasoline	84
Cottonseed	90	Drugs and toilet preparations	143
Cottonseed oil	100	Agricultural implements	154
Soybean oil	94	Machinery and machines	212
Oranges and grapefruit	72	Electrical equipment	187
Lettuce	67	Automobiles, passenger	171
Potatoes	73	Refrigerators	145
Cattle and calves (in single-deck cars)	73	Boots, shoes, etc.	158
Butter	109	Airplanes and parts	197
Anthracite coal	93	Liquors, alcoholic	216
Bituminous coal	81	Sugar	122
Iron ore	73	Cigarettes	196

* Interstate Commerce Commission, Bureau of Accounts, Statement No. 2–61, *Distribution of Rail Revenue Contribution by Commodity Groups—1959* (Washington, D.C., 1961).

the revenues are less than the fully distributed cost but are not necessarily less than out-of-pocket costs.[10]

Local Discrimination

Differential charging also results in rates that bear no relation to distance. Since costs of transportation increase with distance, rates that disregard distance disregard costs. They are therefore real discriminations. This type is known as "local discrimination" or "discrimination between places." Local discrimination takes a number of different forms:

[10] On certain of the commodities shown in Table 7–1, namely, oranges and grapefruit, lettuce, potatoes, cattle and calves, and gravel and sand, the revenues did not cover out-of-pocket costs as calculated by the Bureau; but out-of-pocket costs were considered as 80 percent of operating expenses, rents, and taxes, plus 4 percent on 50 percent of the road property and on 100 percent of the investment in equipment. The Association of American Railroads considers that this formula overstates out-of-pocket cost. See Association of American Railroads, op. cit., pp. 17–19.

differences in rates for equal distances;[11] equal rates for unequal distances, such as result from "group" or "blanket" rates; the practice of increasing rates with distance less rapidly than cost of service justifies; and the extreme case of charging higher rates for shorter than for longer hauls over the same line and in the same direction. These are all examples of adjusting rates on particular hauls according to the demand for the service. The cases of market competition mentioned in an earlier chapter show how frequently the conditions of demand may dictate rates that disregard differences in cost of service.[12]

Personal Discrimination

The same motives which cause a railroad to grant special rates on low-grade commodities and on traffic that will not bear high rates lead to the granting of concessions to particular shippers. This practice constitutes personal discrimination. It is highly objectionable, and it is unlawful. A strong motive exists on the part of the carrier, however, to make concessions to particular shippers when necessary to secure their traffic. The additional traffic increases expenses very little, and anything which the carrier can secure above the direct expenses will be considered as profit to it. This subject will be considered more fully in a subsequent chapter;[13] but the point to note here is that, like other forms of discrimination, it finds its motive in the desire to increase traffic and utilize capacity more fully.

RUINOUS COMPETITION

We shall return to the subject of discriminating rates very shortly, but there remains one further characteristic of the railroad business which proceeds from the existence of a large group of supplementary expenses. Competition in the railway industry is ruinous. By this we do not mean simply that some companies will fail, for that happens as a result of normal competition. What we mean is that competition will force rates below the cost of service for the entire industry. Rates cannot continue at this level without destroying the railroads themselves; for if no return is earned on the capital invested, there is no inducement to restore the plant as it wears out.

The reason why competition does not stabilize rates at cost, but forces them below cost, needs a word of explanation. If all costs were variable costs, it would be foolish for a railroad to cut rates below the cost of service. It would be better to close down and let the other road carry the

---

[11] Distance is not always a true measure of differences in the cost of different hauls; hence some differences in rates for equal distances are consistent with the cost-of-service principle.

[12] P. 77, supra.

[13] Chapter 20.

traffic under such conditions; for the greater the volume of traffic carried, the greater would be the loss. But when part of the expenses are constant and part variable, it is better to take traffic that pays less than the full cost of the service than to let a rival carry it. The railroad may lose money in carrying it at a low rate, since the overhead expenses are only partially covered; but if the traffic is not carried by it at all, there is no contribution to overhead whatsoever. In other words, it is often better to carry traffic at a loss than not to carry it and lose more. Competition, then, tends to reduce rates to prime or variable costs. This struggle for traffic, unless checked by some device, will continue as long as there is unused capacity.

Some writers, in discussing ruinous competition, quite properly distinguish between two types of constant expenses.[14] There are the sunk costs, which represent the return on the capital invested; and there are the general expenses of the business, which, although constant, must be regularly made if operations are to continue. Among the latter are the salaries of the executive officers of the railroad, many office expenses, and the like. The latter have more effect on rates than the former. The railroad cannot continue in business if it does not have sufficient income to pay actual expenses of operation. But as we have seen, it may continue in business a long time with scarcely any return on the capital invested. Competition may not, therefore, reduce rates to prime costs without destroying the railroad very quickly, but it can reduce them below the full cost of the service for long periods of time, destroying the railroad by slow degrees.

The same characteristics which cause railroad competition to be ruinous operate in the industrial field, though to a lesser degree. Industries which, like railroads, have a large investment in fixed and specialized capital, and which therefore have large fixed expenses, find themselves subject to the same danger. If competition is not held in check in some way, prices are forced below cost. These are the industries in which the motive to control prices by means of combinations, price agreements, and other devices is the strongest.[15]

CONTROL OF COMPETITION ESSENTIAL TO DISCRIMINATION

The motive for discriminating rates is found in the desire to increase profits by utilizing the plant to capacity. But discriminating rates are not sufficiently explained by pointing out the motive. Regardless of how strong the motive may be, certain conditions must be fulfilled before discrimination can take place.

---

[14] Irving Fisher, *Elementary Principles of Economics* (New York: Macmillan, 1912), pp. 323–28; H. G. Brown, *Transportation Rates and Their Regulation* (New York: Macmillan, 1916), pp. 11–12, 18–24.

[15] An excellent discussion of the extent of ruinous competition in industry is contained in E. Jones, "Is Competition in Industry Ruinous?" 34 *Quarterly Journal of Economics* 473 (1920).

The first condition is that competition must be restrained. In other words, there must be a certain degree of monopoly or control over prices; for if there is not, competition will bring rates to an equality, that is, in so far as direct costs are the same.[16] Suppose a railroad which has been charging discriminating rates finds itself confronted by the competition of a new line. Immediately a struggle for traffic begins. The traffic which is being charged the highest rates and which contributes more than a pro rata share of the overhead costs is the most desirable traffic. In the struggle for tonnage, rates on this traffic will certainly be reduced. Thus the rates which are above cost of service cannot be maintained in the face of competition. But what about the rates which just cover the full cost of the service or are differentially low and contribute less than a pro rata share of all expenses? If there is unused capacity, the rates on this traffic will be forced even lower than they already are. In the desire to obtain traffic, rates will be forced down toward prime costs. Ruinous competition will set in, and such differences in rates as are not based on differences in prime costs will disappear. But long before this happens, combination will occur, or some sort of agreement will be reached, thus restricting competition and permitting discriminating rates to continue. It sometimes happens that there is no agreement between the carriers to maintain rates; but the results are similar, because each carrier is restrained from cutting rates by the knowledge that a cut would be met by a similar reduction in the rates of his rival. This is a common situation when the number of concerns is small. In cases of this sort there is an absence of real price competition between the rival carriers.

There is some concrete evidence to substantiate our conclusion that discriminating rates cannot stand in the face of real competition. During the rate wars of the 1860s and 1870s in Trunk-Line Territory, rate differentiation largely disappeared. During the periods of extremely low rates the rates on all four classes of freight were frequently the same.[17] During the periods of agreement, when more nearly normal rates were

---

[16] The fact that competition would eliminate discriminating rates was pointed out by L. C. Colson in 1890. See *Transports et tarifs* (trans. by Charles Travis), pp. 28–29. The point is also made by H. G. Brown in "The Basis of Rate-Making as Affected by Competition versus Combination of Railroads," 16 *Yale Review* 79 (1907). It was reasserted by A. C. Pigou in his controversy with F. W. Taussig, 27 *Quarterly Journal of Economics* 691 (1913). Taussig disagreed with Pigou on this point, ibid., p. 537. L. H. Haney agrees with Taussig, "Joint Costs with Especial Regard to Railway Rates," 30 ibid. 233 (1916), and so does G. P. Watkins, "The Theory of Differential Rates," ibid., p. 682. We are here following Pigou, who, in reply to Watkins, said: "Reflection . . . shows that, when competition really prevails, seller A must always endeavor to undersell B by offering to serve B's better-paying customers at a rate slightly less than B is charging, and that this process must eventually level rates" (*Economics of Welfare* [London: Macmillan, 1920], p. 257, n.). This point is recognized by John F. Due, when discussing conditions essential for price discrimination generally. See his *Intermediate Economic Analysis* (3d ed.; Homewood, Ill.: Richard D. Irwin, Inc., 1956), p. 249.

[17] Four regular classes of freight were recognized at that time, fewer classes than now prevail.

maintained, differentiation reappeared, and the rates on each of the four classes were different.[18] Recent developments in the competition between railways and motor trucks also point to the conclusion that discriminating rates tend to disappear under the stress of competition. As long as the railroads had a monopoly of transportation, they were able to maintain a considerable degree of discrimination. The very fact that freight classifications are made by classification committees representing all the railroads in the territory concerned and that traffic associations exert a considerable influence in the adjustment of rates implies enough concerted action in rate making to prevent the reduction of rates to equality. But the development of motor-truck competition threatened to break down long-established classifications. In order to meet truck competition, some railroads put into effect special rates on general merchandise in carload lots, regardless of the classification of the articles under the regular freight classification.[19] Another illustration of similar effects of competition is found in the rates charged in connection with the "container-car service" adopted by a number of railroads. Here the rate is on the loaded container, regardless of the nature of the articles in it.[20] Such rates are necessary to meet motor-truck competition. Partly for the same reason some trailer-on-flat-car (TOFC) rates are based on the trailer without regard to the nature of the contents. Motor-truck competition is not likely to destroy completely the railroad classifications, since much of the low-grade traffic moves at such low rates that the trucks cannot compete. The railroads' monopoly of this traffic is therefore unaffected, and the carriers can differentiate between such commodities on the basis of the demand for the service. It is competition with contract motor carriers and private trucking rather than with common carriers by motor vehicle that now exerts the most influence in breaking down railroad classifications, since common carriers by motor vehicle have adopted freight classifications that are not unlike the railroad classifications.

DEMAND PRICES OF DIFFERENT SERVICES MUST BE INDEPENDENT

Control of competition is not the only condition essential to discrimination. Even the monopolist with complete control over his product

---

[18] For actual figures see Albert Fink, *Statistics Regarding the Movement of Eastbound and Westbound Traffic over the Trunk Lines* . . . (New York: Russell Bros., 1884), p. 39.

[19] Leo J. Flynn, *Co-ordination of Motor Transportation*, 72d Cong., 1st Sess., Sen. Doc. No. 43 (1932), p. 72. See also *Selma, Ala., Chamber of Commerce v. Alabama Great Southern R. R. Co.*, 201 ICC 7 (1934); *All Freight, Boston to East Hartford*, 223 ICC 421 (1937); *All Freight from Chicago & St. Louis to Birmingham*, 226 ICC 455 (1938).

[20] See 173 ICC 377 and 185 ICC 787.

may be unable to discriminate. The demand price for one unit of product or kind of service must be to some extent independent of the price at which others are sold.[21] If this situation does not exist, the seller will find that selling a part of his product at a low price will interfere with his ability to sell another part at a higher price. Thus manufacturers often find it necessary to disguise that part of their product which is sold at low prices, say through mail-order houses or chain stores, if they are to continue charging higher prices for the same or similar product sold through other channels of distribution. By thus concealing the practical identity of goods sold at different prices, the demand prices are kept independent. No such deception need be practiced by railroads in order to sell their product—transportation—at different prices to different customers. It can be easily seen that the demand for the transport of one commodity is largely independent of the price at which the transport of other commodities is sold. If one has wheat to ship and finds that the rate on coal is less, he does not purchase coal transport instead of wheat transport. Likewise, transport from A to B and transport from C to D are quite independent, and a higher rate from A to B will not result in substituting shipments from C to D.

Some railroad services, however, are so related that the demand price for one service is affected by the price at which another service is sold. If two commodities are competitive, it may be that a higher rate on one diminishes the demand for the transportation of it and increases that of the other. Similarly a high rate on a raw material and a low rate on a finished product made from it may increase the transport of the latter, and decrease the transport of the former, by increasing the advantage of the producers located near raw materials. And if A and B are two rival producing centers and M is a common market for the product, a higher rate from A to M than from B to M will cause the demand for transport from B to M to increase at the expense of that from A to M. To a large extent, however, the demand for one transportation service is independent of the price at which other services are sold. If this were not true, discrimination would be impossible.

SUMMARY OF RATE THEORY

The theory of railway rates which we have developed involves three main propositions. The first is that the motive to discriminate, in the sense of charging less-than-cost rates, arises from the large mass of constant expenses. If all expenses were variable, there would be no less-

---

[21] This point receives careful consideration in A. C. Pigou, *Wealth and Welfare* (London: Macmillan, 1912), and in *The Economics of Welfare* (London: Macmillan, 1920); it receives some recognition by Douglas Knoop in *Outlines of Railway Economics* (London: Macmillan, 1913), p. 155; and by J. B. Clark in *Essentials of Economic Theory* (New York: Macmillan, 1907), p. 413. See also Due, op. cit., p. 249.

than-cost rates.[22] The second proposition is that discriminating rates would not continue under real competition and that therefore an element of monopoly or some restriction on competition is a further essential in the explanation of discriminating rates.[23] It is essential to note that although discriminating railway rates would not exist under real competition, the presence of monopoly is not a sufficient explanation of discriminating rates, since, in the absence of overhead costs, there would be no downward discrimination in rates, although there might be discrimination upward. The third proposition is that even under monopoly conditions and in the presence of overhead costs, discrimination could not be practiced if the demand prices for different transportation services were not to some extent independent of the price at which other transportation services are sold.[24]

THE DEMAND FOR TRANSPORTATION SERVICE

Discriminating rates are based on the demand for the service rather than on the cost of the service. It is necessary, therefore, to analyze more closely the nature of the demand for transportation service. The discussion is confined to freight service. Transportation service is usually measured in terms of ton-miles; sometimes in terms of car-miles or even train-miles. Transport costs can be expressed in terms of these units. On the demand side, however, and that is the matter under discussion, it must be recognized that a ton-mile, car-mile, or train-mile, is not wanted for itself. People do not purchase ton-miles for the sake of consuming ton-miles. The utility of a transportation service arises from the utility in having a quantity of a certain commodity in B instead of in A. The number of ton-miles of transportation service involved in getting the

---

[22] Except where true jointness of supply exists, as in the case of back hauls.

[23] Again with the exception of cases in which true jointness of supply exists.

[24] The reader familiar with other treatises on transportation will note the absence of any reference to joint costs in the explanation of discriminating rates. The joint-cost theory of railway rates was first put forward in 1891 by Professor Taussig. See "A Contribution to the Theory of Railway Rates," 5 *Quarterly Journal of Economics* 438. Although some doubts were expressed as to the adequacy of this theory, it was widely accepted as an explanation of railway rates. Many writers combined the joint-cost explanation and the overhead-cost explanation. In 1912 and 1913 Professor Pigou criticized the joint-cost theory and maintained that railways did not provide an example of true joint costs. See *Wealth and Welfare* (1912) and the controversy between Pigou and Taussig in 27 *Quarterly Journal of Economics* 378–84, 535–38, 687–94 (1913). The present writer has elsewhere expressed the belief that the joint-cost theory is an inadequate explanation of railway rates and that it confuses "joint-costs" and "constant costs." See D. Philip Locklin, "A Review of the Literature on Railway Rate Theory," 47 ibid. 167 (1933). Real joint costs do exist on railways to some extent; and certain rate phenomena, such as rates on back hauls, can be explained in terms of joint supply. For differentiation between discrimination that is explained by overhead costs or unused capacity and that which is explained by joint costs see D. H. Wallace, "Joint Supply and Overhead Cost and Railway Rate Policy," 48 ibid. 583 (1934).

commodity from A to B is incidental. It represents the obstacle that must be overcome to obtain the utility in having the commodity in B instead of in A. The ton-miles required may be great or small. On the demand side, therefore, we must recognize that the demand for a particular transportation service, unlike the cost of transport, may be quite independent of the number of ton-miles involved, and will be quite different for different commodities, and different for different movements of the same commodity. The railroad industry may be conveniently considered as a multiple-product industry, and one in which the products number in the thousands not only because thousands of commodities are transported but because each may be transported between hundreds of different points. The demand schedule for moving commodity x from A to B may be quite different than the demand schedule for moving y between the same points, and the demand schedule for moving x from A to B may be quite different from the demand schedule for moving it from A to C, or from D to E.

For purposes of rate making, therefore, the demand for transportation service can best be thought of in terms of the movement of a particular commodity between specific points. It is in connection with such movements that we encounter the phrase "the value of the service," which marks the upper limit of the freight charge. If more than this is charged, the traffic will not move. The term "value of service" is sometimes used in the sense of the highest charge that can be levied without diverting traffic to some other transportation agency—another railroad, or motor carriers. Charges made by competing carriers will often limit the charges which another carrier can exact. A demand curve that takes this factor into consideration would be a demand curve for the services of a particular railway or group of railways. In the analysis which follows, we are interested in the demand curve for transportation service, regardless of the agency or agencies which transport it.

At the outset it is well to recognize that the demand for the transportation of a commodity and the demand for the commodity itself are two different but related things. They are related, in that anything which restricts the demand for a commodity restricts the demand for the transportation of that commodity. But the demand for the transportation of a commodity may be restricted without affecting the demand for the commodity itself. To illustrate: Suppose an article can be produced at A at a slightly lower cost than at B, where it is to be consumed. A high freight rate will prevent the production of the commodity in A and its transportation to B but will not prevent consumption of the article. In either case it will be consumed at B; but with a low rate it will be produced in A and transported to B; with a high rate it will be produced at B, and no transportation, except within the community itself, will be involved.

Value of the Service

The value of the service determines the maximum rate that can be charged for the service of transport. The phrase has been defined in many ways in an effort to state precisely what it is that limits the rate that can be charged. A common definition is that the value of the service is the difference in the price of an article in two places. If the price of an article is $1.00 in A and $1.20 in B, the article will not be transported from A to B if the freight rate is greater than 20 cents. It may often happen that the difference in price in two places measures the value of the service of transport; for if a person contemplates buying goods in A to sell in B, he obviously cannot carry out his plan successfully if the price in B is not equal to the price in A plus the transportation charge to B. But in a great many cases the transportation charge itself determines the difference in the price of articles in different places. As we have already seen, the common relationship between wheat prices in the various parts of the United States and of the world illustrates the point. An increase in the freight rate between Chicago and Liverpool on wheat might increase the price in Liverpool or lower it in Chicago, or both. A decrease in the rate would decrease the spread. In other words, the value of the service is whatever the rate happens to be. Clearly, this definition is inadequate.

The adherents to this definition of the value of the service admit, however, that once a rate has been established between two points, prices in the two places will adjust themselves to the rate, and the rate comes to measure the difference in prices. But they maintain that there is a theoretical limit to the rate, which is measured by a sort of natural difference in the prices that would exist if there were no transportation possible between the two points.

If there is any validity to the concept of a natural difference in price in two places, it must relate to differences in cost of production in the two places. The definition thus reduces itself to the difference in the cost of production of an article in two places. Suppose that a commodity can be produced at A for $1.00 and at B, a consuming center, for $1.25. If the freight rate is less than 25 cents, the article will be produced at A and transported to B. The rate cannot be higher than 25 cents without destroying the traffic. This concept of the value of the service fits many cases that arise in practice. It must be recognized, however, that there may be several costs of production at A. This is particularly true if the article is produced by many producers or if different units are produced at different costs. When this situation exists, a marginal shipper or a marginal shipment emerges under almost any rate, whether it be high or low.

An objection to this definition is that it does not cover the situation referred to in an earlier chapter,[25] where comparative costs make it profitable for a community to import a commodity which it *could* produce more cheaply at home but which is *not* produced at home because it would interfere with the production of a more profitable commodity. Suppose A can produce an article for $1.25, and B can produce it for $1.00. The commodity may nevertheless be produced in A and shipped to B, because the production of it at B would interfere with the production of something more profitable. The above definition, however, can be easily modified to cover this case, which is a frequent one. The rate from A to B cannot exceed the difference in cost of production in the two places, including in the cost of production at B the opportunity cost incurred in producing it. (By "opportunity cost" we mean the profit sacrificed by not producing a more profitable commodity.)

But there is still another objection to this definition. It does not cover the case in which a good cannot be produced at all at B or can be produced only at a prohibitive cost. If bananas cannot be produced in New York City, the value of the service in transporting them from Central America to New York can hardly be defined as the difference in the cost of producing bananas in the two localities. And what is the value of the service, under this definition, for transporting coal from a region where it is mined to a region that cannot produce coal because no natural deposits exist? In cases of this sort the effect of the rate upon the price of the commodity, and hence upon the demand for the commodity, becomes the matter of importance.

Another objection to the definition of value of service as the difference in costs of production arises from the fact that although the commodity cannot be produced in B at all, it may be obtained from an alternative source of supply. In this situation the highest rate that can be charged for transporting the article from A to M is not the difference in cost of production in the two places but the difference between the cost at which M can get the product from an alternative source of supply, say B, and the cost of production at A. But the cost of obtaining the article from B resolves itself into the cost of production at B plus the freight from B to M. Thus the highest rate that can be charged from A to M is the cost of production in B, plus freight from B to M, less the cost of production at A. This is the situation with which railroads are confronted in the typical case of "market competition."[26]

No one of the above definitions gives a universal measure of the limit to freight charges. Each definition fits an important group of situations, but none covers them all. We shall therefore be content to define "the value of the service" as the highest charge that can be levied without preventing a shipment from moving, and we shall recognize that the limit

---

[25] Pp. 6–8, supra.
[26] See pp. 200–201, infra.

is determined by no one factor. Sometimes the effect of the rate on the demand for the article sets the limit; sometimes the limit is the difference in prices in two places; sometimes it is the difference in cost of production; sometimes it is the difference in cost of production if the opportunity cost at point of destination is also included; and sometimes the limit is set by the cost of obtaining the commodity from an alternative source of supply. But whatever may determine the limit of the charge, the limit is real and cannot be ignored. It says to the railway manager who is making rates: Thus far shalt thou go and no farther.

Value of Service and Value of Commodity

Valuable articles are quite generally charged higher transportation rates than less valuable commodities. There are two reasons for this. The cost of transporting valuable goods is somewhat greater than the cost of transporting cheap ones, for the railroad's liability is greater. The railroad is liable under the law for the full value of the articles which it carries. But the difference in the rates on valuable and on cheap articles is much greater than can be justified on a cost-of-service basis. Insurance to cover the greater risk on valuable articles, if reduced to cents per hundred pounds, would rarely amount to 1 cent.[27] The more important reason for the differences in rates on cheap and on valuable articles is found in the greater ability of the valuable articles to stand a high rate. In other words, there seems to be a relation between the value of the commodity and the value of the service of transporting it. Sometimes, in fact, it is assumed that basing rates on the value of the service is identical with basing them on the value of the commodity. The two principles are not the same, but they are related. The relationship between the two principles is not difficult to discover. The freight rate on a valuable article, even though high, is a small proportion of the price of the article at destination. The rate on a cheap article, though low, is a substantial proportion of the price. It follows that a high rate will affect the price of, and the demand for, a cheap article much more than it will for a valuable article. And anything which restricts the demand for an article will, as we have noted, restrict the demand for its transportation. Thus high rates restrict the movement of cheap commodities but do not restrict the movement of valuable articles to so great an extent.

There is, however, no necessary relationship between the value of a commodity and its ability to bear high rates. This can be seen when the value of the service is measured by the difference in cost of producing an article in two places. If a very valuable article can be produced almost as cheaply at B, where it is to be consumed, as at A, the demand for the service of transporting it between A and B is very little, as we have pre-

---

[27] Robert W. Woolley, "How Freight Rates Should Be Made," 86 *Annals of the American Academy of Political and Social Science* 156, 165 (1919).

viously shown. The fact that the commodity is of considerable value makes no difference. As Daggett has aptly stated it: "Values and differences in values are obviously distinct."[28]

Value of Service and Distance

As we have previously suggested, there is no necessary relation between distance and the value of the service of transport, though some writers have assumed such a relationship.[29] There is, of course, a relation between distance and cost of service; hence there is often a relation between distance and the rate charged. The reason why discriminating rates so often ignore differences in distance is that there is no necessary relation between distance and the value of the service. Suppose an article may be produced at A, one hundred miles from M, or at B, one thousand miles from M, at the same cost. If we are given a certain market price at M, the value of the service of transporting the article to M is no greater for the thousand-mile haul than for the hundred-mile haul.

"WHAT THE TRAFFIC WILL BEAR"

The railroad rarely attempts to charge the entire value of the service on each commodity or haul. The value of the service sets the upper limit beyond which the traffic will not move. Prime or variable costs, on the other hand, fix the lower limit below which the rate must not fall. But where, between the upper and lower limits, will the rate be fixed? The answer is summed up in the phrase, "charging what the traffic will bear." This is a much-abused phrase. It is often falsely interpreted to mean exacting the highest possible charge that can be extorted from shippers. The policy is more accurately, but more cumbersomely, expressed as "not charging what the traffic will not bear." The practice is one of granting concessions to traffic that will not move at normal rates, although this may, if not controlled in the public interest, lead to higher rates than are necessary on traffic that will stand high rates. To be more precise, charging what the traffic will bear means charging the rate on each commodity or significant traffic movement which, when the volume of traffic is considered, will make the largest total contribution to fixed or overhead expenses.

The principle of charging what the traffic will bear can be easily represented by a diagram. Suppose, in Figure 7–1, that the line DD represents the demand curve for the transportation of a certain article. Let the line CC represent the cost curve. This will be a horizontal line because

---

[28] Stuart Daggett, *Principles of Inland Transportation* (New York: Harper, 1928), p. 364.

[29] See Colson, op. cit., p. 16; also 2 ICR 436, 442 (1889), and 26 ICC 159, 164 (1913).

FIGURE 7–1.   Charging What the Traffic Will Bear

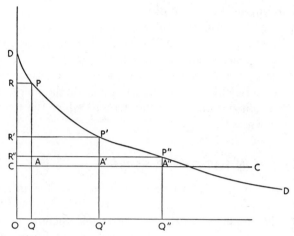

we are here concerned not with total costs, but with prime or variable costs; and as we have pointed out, the variable costs are the same per unit, regardless of the quantity shipped.[30] If the rate OR is charged, the gross revenue will be represented by the area ORPQ, the direct expenses by OCAQ, and the total contribution to overhead by CRPA. If a low rate R″ is charged, the total contribution to overhead will be CR″P″A″. But somewhere between these two extremes, say at the rate OR′, the contribution to overhead will be the largest.

The most profitable rate will be at different points for different commodities or for different hauls of the same commodity. Whether it will

---

[30] Students familiar with modern price theory based on analysis of the individual firm will note that the concept of variable costs, as used here and in most of the literature on railway rate theory, differs somewhat from that with which they have become familiar. In our discussion, expenses which vary with output, but not in direct proportion thereto, are broken down into a fixed and a variable element, and the variable element consists of that portion which varies in proportion to output. This means that the variable-cost curve must be represented as horizontal. The more common expositions of price theory define variable costs as those which vary to some extent with output; and a cost curve representing such costs is usually represented as declining with increasing output until the point of greatest efficiency in the operation of the plant is reached, after which the unit variable cost rises with increasing output. The analysis which we have used to demonstrate railway rate theory is adequate for practical purposes when, as here, we are considering rates on a particular commodity or on a particular haul, which represents a small segment of the carrier's business, since we are concerned with only a small range of output. Over large ranges of output, however, the assumption that unit variable costs remain the same may be unrealistic, at least if rigid assumptions are made with respect to inexpansibility of the plant so that substantial increases in output result in operating the plant considerably beyond its point of greatest efficiency. In fact, however, the assumption of rigid inexpansibility of a railroad's plant is unrealistic. Often comparatively small capital expenditures, where bottlenecks occur, can permit large increases of traffic and greater utilization of other portions of the railway plant with little or no change in unit variable costs.

be high or low will depend upon the price cost of moving the particular commodity and upon the nature of the demand curve. After the rate has been adjusted to the most profitable point, a change either upward or downward will reduce the railroad's profit. The contribution to overhead may be equal to, greater than, or less than the pro rata share of overhead expenses. If the contribution to fixed expenses is less than the pro rata share, it is still inadvisable to increase the rate; for the increase, although increasing the profit per unit of traffic, would reduce the total contribution to fixed expenses.

DISCRIMINATION IN PASSENGER FARES

Discrimination may exist in passenger fares as well as in freight rates. The same forces which cause railroads to classify freight and adjust rates according to the conditions of demand also cause them to provide different classes of passenger service at different fares. In European countries three classes of passenger service have commonly been provided, and the income and social status of the passenger determine to a large extent the class of accommodations which he will purchase. The differences in fares do not always measure differences in cost of service. In the United States there has been less classification in passenger service, although "Pullman" service and coach service represented two distinct classes of service at different prices. Low commutation fares, tourist fares, holiday fares, and other special fares of various sorts are clearly examples of differential pricing. They represent an effort to obtain traffic that would not move at regular rates.

DO PREFERENTIAL RATES BURDEN OTHER TRAFFIC?

Charging what the traffic will bear, although practiced since the beginning of railways, has been severely criticized. The most common criticism is that the low rates on low-grade traffic result in higher rates on other traffic. The low-grade traffic, it is alleged, is subsidized by higher rates on the high-grade traffic. The favored consumers are considered parasitic on other consumers. "If A wants a thing and is prepared to pay its cost," says one writer, "there is . . . no reasonable excuse for refusing to let him have it, [and] it is perfectly inequitable to charge him more than its cost in order that a different thing may be furnished at less than cost to some one else."[31] And as to the preferred traffic the same writer says: "Traffic which will not bear the cost of carrying it ought not to be carried. Its owners have no vested right to live at other people's expense, and that is what happens if they pay only part of the

---

[31] H. W. Edgerton, "Value of the Service as a Factor in Rate Making," 32 *Harvard Law Review* 516, 544–45 (1919).

cost of their service while the utility collects the rest from others."[32] It is clear that the writer quoted believes that the low rates on some traffic throw a burden on other traffic. Of course, it is true that if some traffic is carried at less than average cost, some must be charged more than average cost. But the implication that the low rates on some traffic mean that other traffic must be charged more than it otherwise would have been is entirely erroneous. If the distinction between constant and variable expenses has been fully grasped, it will be apparent that preferential rates relieve rather than increase the burden on other traffic if two conditions are fulfilled. These are (1) that the rate must more than cover the direct costs and (2) that the traffic will not move at higher rates. When these conditions are fulfilled, preferential rates are of benefit to all concerned.

MONOPOLY PROFITS

The second major charge against the practice of charging what the traffic will bear is that it leads to monopoly profits. By exacting the most profitable rate from each class of traffic, the railroad may secure large profits and absorb an unnecessarily large share of the social income. There is no reason why the users of transportation facilities should pay rates in excess of the amount necessary to pay operating expenses and a fair return on the capital invested. In other words, the public can, through government ownership, have transportation at cost, and it will not tolerate a system which requires it to pay much more. This makes it necessary to limit the amount which the railroad may exact for its services. The problem of regulating the general level of rates will be considered more fully in subsequent chapters. It is generally understood that the practice of charging what the traffic will bear is justifiable only as a method of distributing the constant expenses of the business, including the return on capital, over specific items of traffic. It does not justify the exaction of rates which give monopoly profits.[33]

EXCESSIVE RATES ON PARTICULAR COMMODITIES AND HAULS

Low rates on low-grade traffic are justified on the ground that they contribute to the overhead expenses of the railroad and relieve the burden on other traffic. Low rates on low-grade traffic make reductions possible on other traffic. But in the absence of real competition there is no force which compels a lowering of the rates on high-grade traffic, unless it be the action of the state which controls the rates. The principle of

---

[32] Ibid.

[33] This is the view of most economists. See Eliot Jones, *Principles of Railway Transportation*, p. 88; see also John Bauer, *Effective Regulation of Public Utilities* (New York: Macmillan, 1925), p. 280.

charging what the traffic will bear justifies preferential rates on low-grade traffic, and it should bring rate reductions on high-grade traffic. Charging what the traffic will bear does not justify higher rates on high-grade traffic than would be charged if the low-grade traffic did not move. This is evidently what Ripley had in mind when he said that the cost-of-service principle must be used as a check upon the value-of-service principle to prevent rates on high-grade commodities from becoming extortionate. Stated in another way, the practice of discrimination should, in so far as possible, be discrimination downward, and not upward.

It is sometimes alleged that high rates on high-grade traffic are just, even if they are higher than they need to be. It is a mark of justice in the rate structure, according to this view, to charge valuable articles high rates. This idea has its origin in a supposed analogy between railroad rates and taxes. Taxes are often imposed on the principle of ability to pay—a method of taxation which is equitable and just. But the analogy between transportation charges and taxes is not sound. In the first place, valuable articles are not necessarily luxuries consumed by the rich, nor are cheap articles necessarily consumed by the poor. Hence there is no necessary relationship between the value of commodities and the ability of the consumers of such articles to pay taxes. In the second place, even if there were such a relationship, it must be realized that railways are collecting, not taxes, but a charge for a service performed. On economic or on social welfare grounds, it is difficult to see why valuable articles are not entitled to as favorable rates as possible. Valuable articles are often articles which are strictly limited by nature or which can be produced less easily than others. Would it not be a distinct economic gain to the community to have the transportation rates as low upon such goods as on others?[34] To impose a high rate upon these commodities adds another obstacle to the natural difficulties in the way of obtaining a plentiful supply of them.

Our conclusion is that valuable goods should not be charged all that the traffic will bear unless that is necessary to enable the railroad to meet its costs, including a fair return upon the capital invested. Preferential rates may, however, be granted on low-grade commodities, and the contribution which the low-grade commodities make to overhead should enable the railroad to reduce further the rates on other articles.

If the principle of charging what the traffic will bear must be modified to prevent excessive rates on valuable commodities, it must likewise be modified to prevent a railroad from charging excessive rates on particular hauls. If a railroad may vary its charges according to the profits of the shippers, it is in a position to dictate what profits its customers shall receive, and it can absorb differential gains arising from superior location

---

[34] M. H. Robinson, "Railway Freight Rates," 18 *Yale Review* 122, 147 (1909).

and superior business management. A railroad should not be permitted to deprive a locality of its advantages of location by rates that are arbitrarily high.

COST ALLOCATIONS AND RATE MAKING

The principle of charging what the traffic will bear must be modified to prevent the exaction of monopoly profits and to prevent unnecessarily high rates on the traffic that can stand them. There is a school of thought, however, which believes that overhead costs should be allocated to particular kinds and units of traffic and that all rates should be based on these allocations. The advocates of this view maintain that cost accounting has developed into a science and that practically all costs can be allocated.[35] This view seems to rest upon a failure to understand the economic principles involved. It is true that all costs can be allocated; but as one writer has expressed it, "that fact of itself is no more significant than is the possibility of obtaining an arithmetical average of any fortuitous collection of numbers."[36]

The fundamental fallacy in any apportionment of expenses that do not vary with the volume of traffic lies in the fact that the cost depends upon the volume of traffic, and the volume of traffic depends upon the rate charged. To some extent, cost of carriage is a function of the rates, not the rates of the cost; or as Professor Harbeson has put it, "the overhead cost per unit is price determined rather than price determining."[37] "Cost accountants," says G. P. Watkins, "are too likely to assume relations as fixed which may change as a result of prices based upon their cost analysis."[38] If cost apportionments, for instance, result in rates greater than the most profitable rate, the railroad will lose by charging that rate. If the cost allocation should give the most profitable rate, it would be the result of pure chance. The advocates of cost apportionments argue that their method is the only "scientific" way of making rates, but nothing could be more unscientific than an attempt to base rates on cost in disregard of the conditions of demand.

It should not be inferred from the foregoing that cost accounting has

---

[35] Typical expressions of this view are found in *Buell v. Chicago, Milwaukee & St. Paul Ry. Co.*, 1 Wisconsin Railroad Commission 324, 341 (1907); B. H. Meyer, "Memorandum Relating to the Analysis of Operating Expenses of Railway Companies," 19 *Proceedings of the National Association of Railway Commissioners* 103 (1907); Halford Erickson, "The Basis of Reasonable Rates," 9 *American Economic Association Publications* 3d Ser., 95, 100 (1908); M. L. Cooke, "True Cost-Finding —What It Can Do for the Railroads," 86 *Annals of the American Academy of Political and Social Science* 205 (1919).

[36] Watkins, op. cit., pp. 682, 696.

[37] R. W. Harbeson, "The Cost Concept and Economic Control," 17 *Harvard Business Review* 257, 263 (1939).

[38] Watkins, op. cit., p. 697.

no place in railroad rate making. It is often indispensable. From what has already been said, it is apparent that knowledge of out-of-pocket costs of particular traffic movements is of prime importance. Careful cost studies are necessary to provide this information. And even though fully allocated costs are usually of little significance in fixing rates, it is sometimes desirable to know what such costs are. When a particular kind of traffic can bear its full proportion of fixed or overhead costs, there is no reason why it should not do so. We have also pointed out that excessive rates on particular commodities or hauls will result from an unrestricted application of the principle of charging what the traffic will bear. Cost determinations at least provide a standard by which to measure the extent of deviation from cost-of-service rates and so are helpful in keeping deviations within reasonable bounds. The rise of new forms of transport to compete with railways has given further importance to cost finding, especially to find the direct or out-of-pocket costs of particular commodity movements.

IS THE ASSUMPTION OF UNUSED CAPACITY VALID?

The argument for differential charging is based on the assumption of unused capacity. It is sometimes argued that the growth of traffic has brought about a condition in which there is little unused capacity. For this reason the law of increasing returns and the motive to discriminate are said to have lost their force.[39]

If a railroad were not able to expand its plant, the disappearance of unused capacity would mark the beginning of the disappearance of discrimination. The railroad would tend to raise the rates on the low-grade traffic, since the low-grade traffic would interfere with the movement of more profitable traffic. If the growth of traffic continued, it would eventually bring all subnormal rates to a higher level. This situation does not occur in actual practice because the railroad can and will expand its facilities as traffic grows. Comparatively small capital expenditures here and there will enable the railroad to carry additional traffic and to utilize more fully that unused capacity which exists elsewhere on its system. Additional yard tracks or more passing tracks, for instance, may enable the railroad to utilize more fully its existing main-line tracks. Thus capital expenditures are made when and where bottlenecks occur which are restricting the railroad's capacity, and a more or less perpetual condition is maintained which permits additional traffic to be carried without proportionate increases in costs.

-----

[39] This view is taken by R. J. McFall in "Railway Monopoly and Rate Regulation," 69 *Columbia University Studies in History, Economics and Public Law* 1 (1916); also by Owen Ely in *Railway Rates and Cost of Service* (Boston: Houghton Mifflin, 1924).

ARE RAILROAD COSTS LARGELY CONSTANT?

The statement that railroad costs are to a large extent constant or invariable has not gone unchallenged.[40] It has been claimed that railroad expenses are predominantly variable except for very short periods of time. This view is based on the observation that railroads find it possible to vary expenditures in accordance with the traffic carried and the revenues available. Standards of maintenance, it is pointed out, are flexible, and they can be adjusted to the volume of traffic carried. Even the return on capital is said to be variable, except for short periods of time, since the size and character of the physical plant and the capital invested can be adjusted to the volume of traffic available.

Statistical proof of the variability of railroad expenses has been sought in two ways: (1) by showing that over a period of time, railway expenditures have actually fluctuated with traffic volume; and (2) by showing that unit costs of operation are nearly the same on railroads of different traffic densities. In the latter case, however, it is conceded that on lines of very thin traffic, unit costs are higher than on lines having greater traffic density.

Figures showing that railway expenditures vary over a period of time with the volume of traffic must be accepted with some qualification. This is because technical improvements and changes in operating technique affect the figures. So also do changes in wage rates and in the prices of materials and supplies. The practice of deferring maintenance in times of depression is a practice, as has already been noted, which gives an appearance of variability to railroad expenses. Even though standards of maintenance are not rigid, it remains true that much of the deferment of maintenance during lean years represents a consumption of capital. Expenditures and costs are not synonymous.

Figures which tend to show that unit costs are nearly the same on railroads of differing traffic densities demonstrate that operating methods, standards of maintenance, and the size and character of the physical plant can be adjusted to the volume of traffic available. It must be remembered, however, that when a railroad is faced with declining traffic and unused capacity, it will resist any shrinkage in the physical plant. The railroad will endeavor, by discriminating charges, to maximize its return in order to avoid the necessity of shrinking the size of the plant. In other words, although the force of circumstances may ultimately force a reduction in costs somewhat in proportion to the decline in traffic, the railroad, in an effort to avoid this result, will adopt rate-making policies identical to those which would be adopted if expenses and investment could not be reduced.

---

[40] See particularly Kent T. Healy, *The Economics of Transportation* (New York: Ronald Press, 1940), chap. xi; and Herbert Ashton, "Railroad Costs in Relation to the Volume of Traffic," 30 *American Economic Review* 324 (1940).

A study of the variability of railroad expenses in more recent times was made by Dr. Ford K. Edwards while head cost analyst of the Interstate Commerce Commission. He concluded that over a long period of time, between 70 and 80 percent of railroad operating expenses, including rents and taxes, are variable, and that if a 4 percent return on investment is included in the costs, the variable expenses are from 70 to 75 percent of the total.[41] These figures are to be compared with the one third to one half commonly considered in the past to be variable.[42]

The difference between the earlier and the more recent findings can be explained in various ways, but two points require mention in order to avoid confusion. In the first place, the more recent inquiries refer to a longer period of time—in fact, a period long enough to permit changes in the physical plant. The older discussions for the most part assumed a given physical plant and were considering fluctuations of traffic within the capacity of that plant. In the second place, the earlier studies referred to a situation in which the volume of traffic handled by the railroads was much less than that handled by them in recent decades. Even the later studies demonstrate that a much larger proportion of the expenses is constant on lines of thin traffic. At the time the first inquiries into this question were made, the traffic density of the railroads as a whole was much less than it is today. We have already referred to the fact that in the very nature of things the variable expenses must become a larger proportion of the total expenses, and fixed expenses a smaller proportion, as the volume of traffic increases.[43]

Notwithstanding the inherent weaknesses in any attempt to measure the extent of variability of railroad expenses from available statistical data, we may conclude that constant expenses are not so large a share of the total expenses as was formerly thought to be the case, except for very short periods of time or on lines having very light traffic.

The more recent analyses have not undermined the theoretical basis of differential charging. They definitely confirm it, but they find less scope for its exercise than has traditionally been assumed. The conclusions to be drawn from these studies are that more attention should be be paid to the long-run behavior of costs in making rates, particularly in a period when the volume of traffic is growing. Out-of-pocket-cost rate making has probably been overdone, and traffic so acquired has in the long run increased expenses to a greater degree than was assumed would be the case when the rates were made. On lines of light traffic density, however, and on all railroads when unutilized capacity appears, the railroads will continue to find it advantageous to resort to discriminating

---

[41] *Rail Freight Service Costs in the Various Rate Territories of the United States,* 78th Cong., 1st Sess., Senate Doc. No. 63 (1943), p. 75.

[42] See p. 145, supra.

[43] P. 146, supra.

rates to obtain additional traffic or to retain traffic that is in danger of being lost to competing forms of transport.

RATE THEORY AND OTHER MODES OF TRANSPORT

Of fundamental importance in the explanation of discriminating railroad rates is the large mass of constant or fixed expenses which has characterized the industry in the past. This characteristic of the industry still exists, although to a lesser degree than in the early days of the railroads when the density of traffic was much less. The extent to which the theory of rates, developed with respect to railroads, is applicable to the other modes of transport depends upon the extent to which the same cost conditions exist in the motor-carrier, water-carrier, and air-transport industries. This matter will be given attention in the later chapters of the book, where these modes of transport are described.[44]

SELECTED REFERENCES

The literature on railway rate theory is extensive, and only a few of the more important references can be given here. An early treatment of the subject is Dionysius Lardner, *Railway Economy* (New York: Harper, 1850). A. T. Hadley's *Railroad Transportation: Its History and Its Laws* (New York: Putnam, 1885) is classic (for rate theory, chaps. iv–vi and Appendix II). Mention should be made also of W. M. Acworth, "The Theory of Railway Rates," 7 *Economic Journal* 317, 322 (1897).

Among the textbook discussions of the theory are Eliot Jones, *Principles of Railway Transportation* (New York: Macmillan, 1924), chap. iv; Stuart Daggett, *Principles of Inland Transportation* (4th ed.; New York: Harper, 1955), chap. xvi; Truman C. Bigham and Merrill J. Roberts, *Transportation: Principles and Problems* (New York: McGraw-Hill, 1952), pp. 163–81; Marvin L. Fair and Ernest W. Williams, Jr., *Economics of Transportation* (rev. ed.; New York: Harper, 1959), chap. xviii; Russell E. Westmeyer, *Economics of Transportation* (New York: Prentice-Hall, 1952), chap. iv; Emery Troxel, *Economics of Transport* (New York: Rinehart, 1955), chap. xxvi; Dudley F. Pegrum, *Transportation: Economics and Public Policy* (Homewood, Ill.: Richard D. Irwin, Inc., rev. ed., 1968), chaps. vii–viii; Hugh S. Norton, *Modern Transportation Economics* (Columbus, Ohio: Chas. E. Merrill Books, Inc., 1963), chap. vii. Some of the more recent texts express railway rate theory in terms of modern price theory generally instead of in the simpler language of the railway rate theory that developed much earlier than the present-day price theory. In so doing, a desirable integration of railway rate theory and modern price theory is sought, but the exposition may not be helpful to those not thoroughly schooled in microeconomic theory. An interesting article stressing the importance of incremental costs in rate making is Wm. J. Baumol *et al.*, "The Role of Cost in the Minimum Pricing of Railroad Services," 35 *Journal*

---

[44] Chapters 28, 31, and 33.

of Business 357 (1962). Critical responses to the article, with a reply by the authors, are found in 36 *Journal of Business*, pp. 336–51 (1963).

For analyses of railway costs which tend to show greater variability than early writers assumed, see M. O. Lorenz, "Cost and Value of Service in Railroad Rate Making," 30 *Quarterly Journal of Economics* 205 (1916); J. M. Clark, *Studies in the Economics of Overhead Costs* (Chicago: University of Chicago Press, 1923), chaps. xiii–xiv; Kent T. Healy, *The Economics of Transportation* (New York: Ronald Press, 1940), chap. xi; and Herbert Ashton, "Railroad Costs in Relation to the Volume of Traffic," 30 *American Economic Review* 324 (1940). An extensive analysis of the nature of railroad costs was made by Ford K. Edwards in *Rail Freight Service Costs in the Various Rate Territories of the United States*, 78th Cong., 1st Sess., Senate Doc. No. 63 (1943), chaps. ix–xii. A careful re-examination of the variability of railway costs, pointing out the limitations of the Edwards study, has been made under the auspices of the Association of American Railroads and published by the Association under the title, *A Guide to Railroad Cost Analysis* (1964).

The early literature of railway rate theory is reviewed in D. P. Locklin, "A Review of the Literature on Railway Rate Theory," 47 *Quarterly Journal of Economics* 167 (1933). Later discussions of the subject deserving special mention are: D. H. Wallace, "Joint and Overhead Cost and Railway Rate Policy," 48 ibid. 583 (1934); G. Lloyd Wilson and Joseph R. Rose, "Out-of-Pocket Cost in Railroad Freight Rates." 60 ibid. 546 (1946); M. H. Miller, "Decreasing Average Cost and the Theory of Railroad Rates," 21 *Southern Economic Journal* 390 (1955).

Some controversial matters in rate theory are discussed in George W. Wilson, *Essays on Some Unsettled Questions in the Economics of Transportation* (Bloomington, Ind.: Indiana University, 1962). This is distinctly for those thoroughly familiar with modern price theory generally.

Controversy over rate-making under intermodal competition has produced a considerable amount of theoretical analysis of the role of costs in rate-making. Some references on this subject will be found in Chapter 37.

Chapter 8

RAILROAD RATE STRUCTURES

The preceding chapter developed the fact that railroads do not charge the same rate on all articles or a uniform rate per mile for different hauls. To charge on such a basis would be inconsistent with both cost of service and value of service.

Differentiation between commodities is accomplished in two ways: (1) by the freight-classification device, that is, by grouping commodities into a limited number of groups or classes and prescribing rates on the various classes; and (2) by publishing "commodity rates," that is, rates quoted directly on specific commodities without use of the classification device. We shall first consider freight classification.

FREIGHT CLASSIFICATION

We have noted that freight classification, as a process, is the grouping of thousands of commodities into a limited number of classes for purposes of rate making. The result of this process, *a freight classification*, is an alphabetical list of articles, together with the "rating" which each commodity takes. The rating is the class or group into which the article is put for the purpose of quoting freight rates. The rating should be distinguished from the rate. The latter is the amount, usually in cents per hundred pounds, for transporting a commodity or "class" of freight between specific points. The classification gives the rating; to obtain the rate, it is necessary to resort to a freight tariff.

The use of the classification device reduces greatly the number of separate rates to be published and hence reduces the number and size of the freight tariffs in which rates are published. The freight classification provides ratings on over 10,000 different articles or groups of articles;[1] and there are thousands of railroad stations in the United States to and from which rates must be provided. To quote rates on each of these commodities between all stations in the United States, or from such stations as might be points of origin to such points as might be destinations,

---

[1] Board of Investigation and Research, *Report on Interterritorial Freight Rates*, 78th Cong., 1st Sess., House Doc. No. 303 (1943), p. 23.

would make freight tariffs many times more voluminous than they are at present.[2]

The Uniform Freight Classification

The form and manner of use of the classification can be made clearer by examining a sample page of the *Uniform Freight Classification,* shown in Figure 8–1.

It will be noted that articles are listed alphabetically, although many of them are frequently listed under broader groupings printed in large capital letters. For each item in the classification, both less-carload and carload ratings are usually provided. If a carload rating is given, a minimum carload weight is specified. The minimum carload weight is the smallest amount on which a carload rating or rate can be applied. This does not mean, however, that a quantity less than the minimum carload weight must be handled and charged for as a less-carload shipment. On shipments handled as carload shipments but weighing less than the carload minimum weight, the carload rate is applied to the minimum carload weight rather than to the actual weight. On shipments weighing more than the carload minimum, actual weights are used. On some items in the classification the ratings are the same regardless of the size of the shipment. These are known as "any-quantity" rates. In such cases the same rating appears in both the L.C.L. and C.L. columns, and the letters "AQ" appear in the carload minimum column.

It should be noted that the ratings in the Uniform Classification are expressed in relative numbers. Class 100 is the base rating, formerly known as "Class 1." Although, as we have previously noted, the classification gives ratings, not rates, the relative numbers used to designate the various classes indicate the relationship of the rates to the Class 100 rates. Thus a rating of 85, formerly "Class 2," means that the rates on that class are 85 percent of the base, or Class 100, rate. A rating of Class 200 means that the rates are twice the Class 100 rate. Formerly such a rating was known as "D1," or double first class. The use of relative numbers to designate the various classes was introduced with the publication of *Uniform Freight Classification No. 1,* which became effective May 30, 1952.

Certain abbreviations shown on the page of the *Uniform Freight Classification* which is reproduced in Figure 8–1 require explanation. The letter "R" appearing after the minimum carload weight of many of the items means that the item is subject to Rule 34 of the Classification, which provides that the carload minimum varies with the size of the car used. In such instances the minimum weight specified in the body of the Classification applies on shipments loaded in closed cars 40 feet, 7 inches in length or less, or on open cars 41 feet, 6 inches in length or less; and

---

[2] A further reduction in the number of rates to be quoted is obtained through grouping points of origin or of destination.

FIGURE 8–1. Sample Page from *Uniform Freight Classification No. 4*

UNIFORM FREIGHT CLASSIFICATION 4

Item	ARTICLES	Less Carload Ratings	Carload Minimum (Pounds)	Carload Ratings
10690	Bate, tanners', noibn, in barrels or boxes or in packages 76 or 80...........................	70	36,000	30
10700	Battery box compound consisting of a mixture of asphalt or pitch, cotton fibre and inert filler, with or without oil softener, LCL, in barrels, boxes or crates; CL, loose or in packages.......	55	40,000	30
10710	Battery cylinders, frames or plates, copper, lead, steel or zinc, burnt out, in packages; also CL, loose	60	40,000	27½
10720	Battery fillers, rubber, with or without hydrometer for each filler, in boxes....................	100	24,000R	55
10730	Battery fluid, noibn:			
	In carboys..	100	30,000	45
	In glass or 32-ounce synthetic plastic bottles in barrels or boxes....................	70	30,000	40
10740	Battery mix, ground manganese ore and ground graphite combined, dry, LCL, in cloth or paper bags, or in barrels; CL, loose or in packages..	55	50,000	30
10750	Batting (loosely felted sheets), made from cotton, jute or sisal, separate or combined, see Notes 1, 2 and 3, items 10771, 10772 and 10773:			
	In boxes, bundles, paper lined crates, bales not machine-pressed, or in packages 14 or 840.....	125	10,000R	85
	In machine pressed bales or rolls..	85	18,000R	55
10760	Batting (loosely felted sheets), made from cotton, jute or sisal and glass fibre combined, see Note 3, item 10773, with or without binder, in cartons or in wrapped bales or wrapped rolls........	200	10,000R	85
10770	Batting (loosely felted sheets), made from wool or cotton and wool combined, see Notes 1, 2 and 3, items 10771, 10772 or 10773, in bales, boxes or double-walled paper bags, or in cartons in crates	150	10,000R	85
10771	Note 1.—Ratings will also apply on batting as described when sprayed with latex or glazed.			
10772	Note 2.—Ratings will also apply on batting as described cut to dimensions, with or without cloth or paper backing, sufficiently stitched to hold batting in place but not quilted.			
10773	Note 3.—The term "cotton" as used herein refers to cotton fibre in any of its forms, such as cotton linters, cotton waste, cotton motes or cotton card sweepings.			
10780	Bauxite (beauxite), causticized, in paper lined cloth bags or in barrels.........................	55	50,000	30
10790	Bauxite (beauxite) flue dust, LCL, in cloth or paper bags, or in barrels or boxes; CL, in bulk or in packages..	50	40,000	22½
10800	Bayonets, sabres, swords or scabbards, in boxes...	100	30,000	55
10810	Beads, glass, in barrels or boxes...	100	20,000R	70
10820	Beads, wooden, in bags, barrels or boxes..	85	24,000R	55
10830	Beans, castor, LCL, in bags, barrels or boxes; CL, loose or in packages......................	70	36,000	35
10840	Beans, honey (St. John's bread), whole, ground or powdered, in bags, barrels or boxes.........	70	36,000	35
10850	Bed boards, fibreboard, plywood or wallboard, not painted, in boxes, crates or package 763.....	70	30,000	40
10860	Bed rails, bed display, in packages..	70	36,000	45
10870	BEES OR BEE SUPPLIES:			
10880	Bees in hives, see Notes 1 and 2, items 10881 and 10882, loose or in packages................	300	14,000R	85
10881	Note 1.—All openings in hives must be securely covered with wire cloth.			
10882	Note 2.—With shipment of bees, carload, shippers must, at their expense, furnish male adult attendant who will be permitted to accompany such shipments; attendants to pay full fare, unless otherwise provided by tariff of individual carriers, subject to Rule 43.			
10890	Bee hives, wooden:			
	SU, loose or in packages...	150	12,000R	85
	KD, in packages; also CL, loose...	55	30,000	35
10900	Bee hives, SU and KD, in mixed CL, or in mixed CL, with honey section frames, KD..........		30,000	35
10910	Bee hives, steel, insulated, in boxes or crates...	100	20,000R	70
10920	Bee comb or bee comb foundation, in boxes...	100	20,000R	70
10930	Drone traps, in barrels or boxes..	110	20,000R	70
10940	Honey section frames, KD, in packages..	65	30,000	35
10955	Beet slops (beet sugar final molasses residuum):			
	In bulk in barrels...	60	36,000	27½
	In tank cars, Rule 35..			22½
10958	Belts or belting, elevator, conveyor or transmission, other than "V" type, rubber, or rubber and fabric combined, in packages...	70	30,000	40
10960	Belts or belting, noibn, other than chain belts or belting, in packages........................	77½	30,000	45
10970	Belts, cartridge, or hand grenade carriers, in barrels or boxes...............................	100	30,000	70
10980	Belts, conveyor, laundry ironing machine, canvas, in bales or boxes..........................	85	24,000R	55
10990	Berries, juniper or sloe, dried, in bags, barrels or boxes....................................	85	30,000	55
11000	Berries, palmetto, in bags, barrels or boxes...	70	30,000	45
11010	Billboard base or side lattice work, wooden, made of lumber not less than ¾ by 3 inches, in flat sections, loose or in packages..	85	30,000R	50
11020	Billboards or signboards, without advertisement, steel or wood, loose, see Note, item 11021, or in packages..	77½	30,000	40
11021	Note.—LCL shipments may be loose only in lots of 10,000 lbs., subject to minimum charge as for 10,000 lbs.; shipments to be loaded by shipper and unloaded by consignee; shipper to furnish and install all dunnage and packing material; freight charges to be assessed on basis of gross weight of articles and all dunnage or packing material.			
11030	Binders or covers, book or loose leaf, cloth or imitation leather, other than paper or pulpboard, in boxes or crates...	85	30,000	45
11040	Binders or covers, book or loose leaf, noibn, in boxes or crates..............................	100	30,000	55
11050	Binding or gimp, leather or imitation leather, in bales, barrels, boxes or crates................	85	30,000	55
11060	Bins, stone or gravel, wheeled or not wheeled, legs detached or collapsed, wheels on or off, loose or in packages..	100	24,000R	45
11070	Bird food or seed, see Note, item 11071, in bags, barrels or boxes...........................	60	36,000	35
11071	Note.—Each carton in barrels or boxes may contain a piece of cuttlebone. CL shipments in bags may contain not to exceed 2,000 lbs. of cuttlebone in boxes. The weight of the cuttlebone will be charged for in addition to the minimum weight or actual weight if greater on bird food or seed, and must not be used to make up the minimum weight of the bird food or seed.			

higher minima, subject to certain exceptions, apply if the shipment is loaded in or on longer cars, in accordance with a table set forth in Rule 34.

The abbreviations "SU" and "KD," appearing frequently in Figure 8–1, mean "set up" and "knocked down." According to Rule 19 of the Classification, "KD" ratings apply "when article is taken apart in such manner as to materially reduce space occupied." As would be expected, "KD" ratings on an article are lower. than "SU" ratings.

The letters "noibn," frequently appearing in the description of articles, mean "not otherwise indexed by name." An "noibn" item is in a sense a catchall item, embracing all articles included within a broad description unless more specifically listed elsewhere. Item 10960 in Figure 8–1 consists of "Belts or belting, noibn, other than chain belts or belting." Item 10958, however, provides a rating on "Belts or belting, elevator, conveyor or transmission." If elevator, conveyor, or transmission belts had not been given a separate rating, such articles would have come under "Belts or belting, noibn." An "noibn" rating does not apply if there is a more specific description in the Classification.

History of Freight Classification

Freight classification antedates railroads. Freight moving by wagon or by canal had been classified for the purpose of levying charges long before the railroads were built. The railroads, however, developed much more elaborate classifications than were used by the earlier modes of transport. Originally the number of classifications in force was large. Sometimes a different classification was in effect on different portions of a single railroad. At one time there were as many as 138 distinct classifications in use in Eastern Trunk-Line Territory.[3] The confusion caused by this state of affairs led to attempts by the carriers to reduce the number of freight classifications. The railroads were stimulated in this effort by the enactment of the Act to Regulate Commerce in 1887, and by 1889 three major classifications had been established, each applicable within a certain portion of the United States. These three classifications were known as "Official Classification," "Southern Classification," and "Western Classification." The area covered by each classification can be shown by the map of rate territories in Figure 8–6. Official Classification Territory and Southern Classification Territory corresponded to the rate territories of the same name shown on the map. Western Classification applied throughout the rest of the country.

These classifications were made by classification committees, one for each of the three classifications. The committees represented the carriers concerned; they maintained a permanent organization, with machinery

---

[3] This and other information concerning the early history of classification is taken largely from the report of the Interstate Commerce Commission in *Suspension of Western Classification No. 51*, 25 ICC 442, 453–59 (1912).

for classifying new articles of commerce and for considering requests for changes in existing ratings.

The number of classes recognized in the three classifications differed. Just prior to the adoption of the present Uniform Classification, there were 7 regular classes in the Official Classification, 12 in the Southern, and 10 in the Western. The method of designating the classes also differed. In Official Classification the classes were numbered from 1 to 6, with a class inserted between Classes 3 and 4, which was known as "R26," or Rule 26. Southern Classification had 12 classes, numbered from 1 to 12; Western Classification had five numbered classes, 1–5, and five lettered classes, A–E. In addition to the classes enumerated above, there were certain multiple classes in all three classifications. These were 1¼, 1½, 1¾, D1 (double first class), 2½ t 1 (2½ times first class), 3 t 1, and 4 t 1. The practice had also grown up of giving some articles ratings in terms of a percentage of first class—a percentage different from that applying to any of the regular classes in that classification. Thus an article might be given a rating of 37½, which meant that the rate would be 37½ percent of the first-class rate. The relationships of the rates on the various classes to first-class rates were not uniform in the different classifications, although as a result of a number of class-rate cases before the Interstate Commerce Commission between 1925 and 1930 involving the class rates in the different rate territories, Class 2 and Class 3 rates in all territories had become, respectively, 85 and 70 percent of first class.

For many years the three major classifications were published separately. In 1918, when the railroads were being operated by the federal government as a result of the emergency caused by our participation in World War I, an effort was made to consolidate the three classifications into a single volume. This required uniformity in the descriptions of articles so that, after each commodity description, ratings could be shown in three columns, one for each classification. A committee of experienced classification men from the Railroad Administration worked out a proposed "Consolidated Freight Classification." This was adopted by the Director General of Railroads in 1919, with the approval of the Interstate Commerce Commission.[4] Thereafter the three classifications were published in a single volume, known as the *Consolidated Freight Classification.* It is important to realize, however, that although they were published in a single volume, there continued to be three distinct classifications.

The Interstate Commerce Commission, from the beginning of its existence, had pointed out the desirability of establishing a single classification of freight for use throughout the United States. Progress toward this end, however, was slow. Lack of uniformity in ratings in the different classifications was the natural consequence of the fact that the classifications grew up separately. Classification is a matter of judgment, and

---

[4] *Consolidated Classification Case,* 54 ICC 1.

it is hardly to be expected that different persons will arrive at the same conclusions concerning the proper class in which an article should be placed. This is particularly true when the rating assigned is a compromise between various and often conflicting cost-of-service and value-of-service factors. Differences in classification ratings also reflected differences in producer interests in the different territories. The more important a commodity is in the economy of a particular area, the greater will be the pressure by producers to obtain favorable rates on it.

Although a uniform classification was long considered desirable, its attainment was made even more difficult by the differences in the levels of class rates in the different territories. On some commodities, differences in ratings had been established to offset in whole or in part the differences in the levels of the first-class rates. The establishment of a uniform classification and a readjustment in the levels of the class rates had to be undertaken together. In 1939 the Interstate Commerce Commission instituted an investigation into the level of class rates in the different rate territories east of the Rocky Mountains and into the lawfulness of the existing classifications. As a result of this proceeding, known as *Class Rate Investigation, 1939,* the Commission, in 1945, required the carriers to establish a uniform classification of freight for application throughout the United States and a uniform level of class rates to apply east of the Rocky Mountains.[5] The carriers were given the choice of drawing up a uniform classification or of having the Commission do so. The carriers chose to perform the task themselves. This was a time-consuming task, but eventually a new classification was drawn up by the carriers and was made effective on May 30, 1952, simultaneously with new class rates at a level prescribed by the Commission.

The Commission's decision in *Class Rate Investigation, 1939,* required that the new classification contain 30 classes, 7 classes above Class 100, and 22 classes below Class 100. The highest class was to be Class 400; the lowest, Class 13. The carriers, however, have added another class—Class 110—making the total number of classes 31. The sample page from the freight classification shown in Figure 8–1 is from *Uniform Freight Classification No. 4.*

Class rates within Mountain-Pacific Territory and between that territory and the rest of the United States were not covered by the Commission's decision in *Class Rate Investigation, 1939.* These rates therefore remained subject to Western Classification. In a later proceeding, however, *Class Rates, Mountain-Pacific Territory and Class Rates, Transcontinental Rail, 1950,*[6] the Commission required the establishment of a system of class rates in Mountain-Pacific Territory and between that ter-

---

[5] 262 ICC 447 (1945). For a summary and analysis of this decision and of subsequent developments see E. A. Nightingale, "Uniform Freight Classification and Uniform Class Rates," 20 *I.C.C. Practitioners' Journal* 171 (1952).

[6] 296 ICC 555 (1955).

ritory and the rest of the country, and these rates were to be subject to the Uniform Classification.

The Uniform Classification has not entirely displaced the Consolidated Freight Classification. "Exception rates" were not within the scope of the Commission's investigation in the *Class Rate Investigation*. Such "exceptions" were exceptions to the Official, Southern, and Western classifications; and the rates applicable were naturally those published to apply to the various classes in those classifications. Eventually, however, these "exceptions" will presumably be canceled, and the traffic covered by them will be brought under the new system of class rates which are subject to the Uniform Classification. In fact, many of the old "exceptions" have already been canceled by action of the railroads.

"Exceptions to the Classification"

Some further explanation of "Exceptions to the Classification" is required. Individual railroads, or groups of railroads, have long had the right, by publishing "Exceptions to the Classifications," to depart from the classification ratings provided in the regular classifications. These exceptions may have quite limited application, perhaps applying only on the lines of a particular railroad, or they may have a wide application, covering the whole of a major rate territory. The Commission has said, however, that when they become general in their application they should be incorporated in the classification.[7] When an exception rating is published, it takes precedence over the regular classification rating. It is important to note that an exception rating merely substitutes a different rating for the normal one.[8] It is still a "rating" and the class rate applicable to that rating applies.

The establishment of a uniform classification, with a larger number of classes, should reduce the number of exception ratings and, as we have noted, has already done so. In fixing ratings for the Uniform Classification, the carriers sought to incorporate exception ratings into the classification proper, so far as practicable, with the view of canceling many of the exceptions previously in effect. The decision of the Commission in the *Class Rate Investigation* did not prevent continued use of exceptions to the Classification, but the language of the Commission indicated that in the future the establishment of exception ratings would require individual justification.[9]

COMMODITY RATES

Because of the limited number of classes provided by the freight classification, or because of the unsuitability of the class-rate structure for

---

[7] 281 ICC 213, 287 (1951).

[8] Ibid.

[9] 262 ICC 447, 511 (1945).

application to particular commodities, or just because the carriers desire to make special rates to meet particular conditions, "commodity rates" are established. A commodity rate is a rate quoted on an article directly instead of through the medium of a system of freight classification. If there is a commodity rate published on a commodity to apply between particular points, the commodity rate supersedes the class rate. Between points having no commodity rate on the article, the class rates continue to apply. Many important commodities, such as coal, ore, cement, brick, grain, and livestock, practically always move on commodity rates. In 1953, traffic moving on commodity rates accounted for 79 percent of the total revenue from carload freight.[10]

Commodity rates may consist of special point-to-point rates, built upon no systematic basis but adjusted to meet the needs of some particular shippers or communities or to meet some competitive condition. Such commodity rates may be quite isolated, applying only between a very limited number of points. Other commodity rates are more extensive in character and may cover all important movements of a particular commodity. In the latter case the commodity rates may comprise an elaborate rate structure, totally unrelated to the class rates but designed to meet the particular conditions of production, sale, and transportation of the commodity in question. Rates on coal and grain are examples of such rate structures. Other commodity rates are tied to the class-rate structure, usually by being made a percentage of the first-class or Class 100 rates.

FREIGHT TARIFFS

The rates for transporting the various commodities and classes of commodities between specific points are published in freight tariffs. These are of many kinds. Class tariffs contain the rates on the various classes shown in the classification. Commodity tariffs show the commodity rates. Sometimes both class and commodity rates are published in the same tariff. Commodity tariffs may be general or special. If general, they give the rates on many commodities; if special, they contain the rates on one or a number of closely related commodities. Local rates, that is, rates between points on a single railroad, are usually published by the individual railroads in what are known as "local tariffs." Joint rates, that is, the rates between points on different railroads, are commonly published by agents of the participating carriers. These are called "agency tariffs." There are also special tariffs, such as special export or import tariffs, which quote rates to or from the ports on exported or imported articles. The geographical application of tariffs varies widely, some covering extensive areas, while others are quite limited in the area which they cover.

---

[10] Interstate Commerce Commission, Bureau of Transport Economics and Statistics, *Monthly Comment on Transportation Statistics,* March 1955, p. 11.

It was once estimated that there were about 75,000 freight tariffs in current use in the United States, ranging in size from a single page to over 1,200 pages.[11] They are published in accordance with regulations prescribed by the Interstate Commerce Commission[12] and are kept up to date by the issuance of supplements, only a limited number of which may be in effect at one time. Tariffs are constantly being canceled and reissued, or modified by supplement. Several thousand tariff publications containing changes in railroad rates are filed with the Interstate Commerce Commission every year. For the most part, railroad rates in the United States are published as specific point-to-point rates. This accounts for the large number of rates and the size of freight tariffs.

In 1970 the railroads, filed with the Interstate Commerce Commission the first "computerized" tariff, the first step in a plan to computerize all railroad tariffs. Several years will be required to complete the project. Three national computer centers will be established to maintain the tariff data and distribute the magnetic-tape records. The system, although it will benefit both shippers and railroads, will not do away with the printed tariffs, which will be considered the official tariff documents.[13]

Freight tariffs are constructed in different ways, and they are sometimes complicated and difficult for the inexperienced person to use, particularly because of complications arising from restrictions on routing, limitations on the application of rates specified therein, and the fact that the rates may alternate with other rates published in the same or different tariffs. It is generally recognized that there is great need for tariff simplification, and efforts have been made along this line in recent years.[14]

One form of publishing rates is illustrated by Figures 8–2 and 8–3, showing sample pages from *Freight Tariff No. E–1009*, which gives the class rates applicable between points in Central Territory (that part of Eastern Territory west of Buffalo and Pittsburgh) and between Central Territory and points in the rest of Eastern or Official Territory. The sample page shown in Figure 8–2 shows the "rate bases" applicable between a number of points listed across the top of the page and other points listed down the left-hand side of the page. Note that in both cases the points are arranged alphabetically. From this page we find that between Chicago, Illinois, and New York, New York, Rate Basis 890

---

[11] G. L. Wilson, "Are Railroad Freight Rate Structures Obsolete?" 13 *Harvard Business Review* 179, 180 (1935).

[12] *Tariff Circular No. 20.*

[13] This information is from Western Railroad Association, Public Relations Office, *Information*, January 1970.

[14] For discussions of the need for tariff simplification see George P. Shuler and Howard D. Bergen, "Difficulty of Ascertaining Legal Rate Due to Confused State of Many Rail Tariffs," 12 *I.C.C. Practitioners' Journal* 810 (1945); Glenn L. Shinn, "Freight Tariff Improvement," *Traffic World*, October 27, 1951, p. 35; Commissioner Anthony F. Arpaia, *Improvement of Shipper Carrier Relationship* (an address, mimeographed, 1953).

FIGURE 8–2. Sample Page of Rate Bases from *Freight Tariff No. E-1009*

Freight Tariff No. E-1009

SECTION 1
APPLICATION OF RATE BASES

BETWEEN (See Item 100) / AND (See Item 100)	Cheat Bridge...W. Va.	Cheboygan. Mich.	Cherry Tree...Pa.	Chicago......Ill.	Childwold...N. Y.	Chilesburg...Ky.	Chillicothe...Ohio	Cincinnati...Ohio / Cincinnati(N).Ohio	Circleville...Ohio	Clare......Mich.	Claremont..N. H.	Clarks-burg...W. Va.	Clearfield....Pa.	Cleveland...Ohio	Clifford....Mich.	Clinton....Iowa	Coalport......Pa.
	RATE BASES APPLICABLE (For rates, see pages 282 to 337)																
Montpelier..............Vt.	777	897	579	948	202	1004	814	867	794	778	87	742	537	628	687	1086	551
Morehead...............Ky.	395	620	457	425	795	57	135	143	155	485	925	276	477	320	443	532	471
Morris..................Ill.	643	419	597	①	829	393	353	302	348	319	961	519	586	363	336	①	611
Morrison................Ill.	748	478	703	①	933	478	451	389	446	347	1065	624	691	469	431	①	417
Morrisville..............Vt.	786	878	588	929	183	985	795	848	775	759	133	751	553	609	668	1067	560
Mount Clemens........Mich.	492	282	426	289	522	365	251	275	231	163	653	384	410	185	89	427	440
Mt. Morris............N. Y.	482	515	224	561	261	620	430	483	410	395	393	384	195	244	305	699	228
Mt. Sterling............Ky.	427	622	489	394	825	40	166	111	186	487	957	308	408	350	445	500	503
Mount Upton..........N. Y.	496p	655p	304p	704p	152p	759p	569p	622p	549p	536p	272p	461p	263p	383p	445p	842p	270p
Mt. Vernon..............Ill.	675	649	682	①	961	277	373	277	378	518	1093	551	697	487	527	①	696
Mt. Vernon............Ohio	331	435	277	316	589	249	93	159	73	301	721	215	292	115	258	451	291
Muddlety.............W. Va.	182	742	331	612	736	370	303	392	308	607	814	124	362	352	565	748	343
Mullens..............W. Va.	250	708	463	552	801	272	226	294	246	573	834	257	494	381	530	677	470
Muncie.................Ind.	453	441	433	178	701	155	155	105	150	295	833	329	437	227	288	304	447
Murphysboro............Ill.	728	694	730	①	1009	328	425	329	430	563	1141	604	745	535	572	①	744
Muscatine..............Iowa	788	539	745	①	976	517	490	428	485	408	1108	664	733	511	485	①	759
Muskegon.............Mich.	619	251	553	184	697	420	368	330	348	120	828	511	540	312	174	248	567
Nallen...............W. Va.	237	739	470	536	787	256	257	278	236	566	821	288	484	395	524	660	457
Narragansett Pier......R. I.	623b	906b	502b	956b	355b	921b	767b	863b	779b	787b	164b	589b	477b	635b	696b	1094b	474b
Narrowsburg..........N. Y.	476	744	307	790	276	775	604	679	584	624	303	442	274	469	534	928	279
Nashua................N. H.	722	905	574	955	342	1010	820	873	800	786	90	688	539	634	695	1093	546
Natrium..............W. Va.	197	552	201	456	595	317	164	258	169	417	704	69	219	162	375	594	215
Nebo...................Ill.	765	658	753	①	1013	450	463	386	458	528	1145	641	762	539	545	①	767
Newark................Ohio	306	451	263	328	603	237	82	147	61	316	735	190	280	140	274	463	279
New Berlin............N. Y.	547p	645p	349p	694p	101p	749p	559p	612p	539p	526p	233p	512p	314p	373p	435p	832p	321p
New Bethlehem.........Pa.	327	607	103	518	454	489	313	383	292	472	557	229	75	187	427	653	105
New Brunswick........N. J.	445	832	328	855	352	743	589	685	594	712	289	411	311	531	622	991	300
Newburgh.............N. Y.	501	817	360	867	266	799	645	732	637	698	243	467	335	546	607	1005	333
Newburyport..........Mass.	749	938	607	988	387	943	853	906	833	819	133	715	572	667	728	1126	579
New Castle.............Va.	236	838	418	682	701	403	386	425	376	703	735	313	432	511	660	807	405
New Freedom,Pa.-Millers,Md.	304	811	163	749	436	602	448	544	453	691	453	270	215	425	601	885	210
New Haven...........Conn.	572	871	451	921	320	870	716	812	728	752	162	538	426	600	661	1059	423
New London.........Conn.	623	906	502	956	355	921	767	863	779	787	164	589	477	635	696	1094	474
New Market............Va.	291	835	270	737	553	437	411	479	431	681	591	259	284	418	658	862	257
Newport...............Vt.	825	890	627	941	195	997	807	860	787	771	128	786	592	621	680	1079	597
Newton.................Ill.	625	587	612	①	891	270	322	230	317	456	1023	501	627	417	460	①	626
New York.............N. Y.	484	852	363	890	326	782	638	724	633	732	255	450	338	562	642	1028	335
Niles.................Mich.	554	336	494	89	706	331	284	241	264	205	838	430	483	259	214	227	508
Niverton...............Pa.	209	669	121	575	513	491	337	420	325	535	606	163	153	252	492	711	117
Norfolk................Va.	468	1053	485	914	655	634	588	656	608	919	603	477	468	636	861	1039	458
North Adams.........Mass.	623	781	450	831	230	886	696	749	676	662	103	589	415	510	571	969	422
North Manchester......Ind.	500	397	457	123	696	258	211	168	206	255	828	376	445	222	247	252	471
North Vernon..........Ind.	471	528	484	244	776	148	169	73	174	383	908	347	499	302	374	342	498
Norton................Va.	392	758	588	580	897	218	272	304	293	623	908	399	605	457	581	679	601
Norwich..............N. Y.	496	655	304	704	152	759	569	622	549	536	272	461	263	383	445	842	270
Norwood...............Va.	313	915	430	759	679	479	433	501	453	780	648	390	444	578	737	884	417
Oak Hill............W. Va.	231	669	424	513	781	233	187	255	207	534	814	218	455	342	492	638	436
Oakland City..........Ind.	598	623	611	272	896	189	295	199	301	491	1028	474	626	422	482	350	625
Ogdensburg...........N. Y.	648	714	451	765	106	821	631	684	611	595	282	611	416	445	504	903	423
Oil City...............Pa.	359	553	147	464	429	480	297	362	277	419	561	251	116	133	378	597	149
Olcott..............W. Va.	269	663	418	507	796	227	181	249	201	528	880	212	449	336	485	632	430
Old Monroe............Mo.	764	682	751	①	1023	405	461	385	456	551	1156	640	766	550	568	①	765
Olean................N. Y.	413	522	162	538	330	579	391	444	371	402	462	315	126	206	212	674	164
Olive Hill.............Ky.	377	601	439	439	774	75	116	161	136	466	906	258	458	301	424	550	453
Olney.................Ill.	619	606	626	①	905	252	317	221	322	475	1037	495	641	431	479	①	640
Oneonta..............N. Y.	516	702	318	751	170	792	615	669	595	583	225	481	283	430	492	889	290
Orange................Va.	313	912	347	759	759	481	433	503	453	748	565	336	361	495	737	884	334
Orleans Road (B.&O.)..W. Va.-Woodmont (W. Md.)...Md.	190	730	163	636	501	487	333	423	338	596	546	154	179	313	553	772	152
Oswego...............N. Y.	534	590	330	641	186	584	430	526	435	471	318	487	298	321	380	779	308
Owosso...............Mich.	521	217	455	229	580	394	280	304	260	72	711	413	441	214	78	355	469

FIGURE 8–3. Sample Page of Class Rates Shown in *Freight Tariff No. E-1009*

Freight Tariff No. E-1009

SECTION 1
TABLE OF RATES

CLASS RATES IN CENTS PER 100 POUNDS

RATE BASES NUMBERS (Numbers inclusive)	400	300	250	200	175	150	125	110	100	92½	85	77½	70	65	60	55
40	344	258	215	172	151	129	108	95	86	80	73	67	60	56	52	47
41 to 45	356	267	223	178	156	134	111	98	89	82	76	69	62	58	53	49
46 to 50	364	273	228	182	159	137	114	100	91	84	77	71	64	59	55	50
51 to 55	376	282	235	188	165	141	118	103	94	87	80	73	66	61	56	52
56 to 60	384	288	240	192	168	144	120	106	96	89	82	74	67	62	58	53
61 to 65	396	297	248	198	173	149	124	109	99	92	84	77	69	64	59	54
66 to 70	404	303	253	202	177	152	126	111	101	93	86	78	71	66	61	56
71 to 75	412	309	258	206	180	155	129	113	103	95	88	80	72	67	62	57
76 to 80	424	318	265	212	186	159	133	117	106	98	90	82	74	69	64	58
81 to 85	432	324	270	216	189	162	135	119	108	100	92	84	76	70	65	59
86 to 90	440	330	275	220	193	165	138	121	110	102	94	85	77	72	66	61
91 to 95	448	336	280	224	196	168	140	123	112	104	95	87	78	73	67	62
96 to 100	456	342	285	228	200	171	143	125	114	105	97	88	80	74	68	63
101 to 110	472	354	295	236	207	177	148	130	118	109	100	91	83	77	71	65
111 to 120	488	366	305	244	214	183	153	134	122	113	104	95	85	79	73	67
121 to 130	504	378	315	252	221	189	158	139	126	117	107	98	88	82	76	69
131 to 140	516	387	323	258	226	194	161	142	129	119	110	100	90	84	77	71
141 to 150	532	399	333	266	233	200	166	146	133	123	113	103	93	86	80	73
151 to 160	544	408	340	272	238	204	170	150	136	126	116	105	95	88	82	75
161 to 170	560	420	350	280	245	210	175	154	140	130	119	109	98	91	84	77
171 to 180	572	429	358	286	250	215	179	157	143	132	122	111	100	93	86	79
181 to 190	584	438	365	292	256	219	183	161	146	135	124	113	102	95	88	80
191 to 200	596	447	373	298	261	224	186	164	149	138	127	115	104	97	89	82
201 to 210	612	459	383	306	268	230	191	168	153	142	130	119	107	99	92	84
211 to 220	624	468	390	312	273	234	195	172	156	144	133	121	109	101	94	86
221 to 230	636	477	398	318	278	239	199	175	159	147	135	123	111	103	95	87
231 to 240	648	486	405	324	284	243	203	178	162	150	138	126	113	105	97	89
241 to 260	672	504	420	336	294	252	210	185	168	155	143	130	118	109	101	92
261 to 280	692	519	433	346	303	260	216	190	173	160	147	134	121	112	104	95
281 to 300	716	537	448	358	313	269	224	197	179	166	152	139	125	116	107	98
301 to 320	740	555	463	370	324	278	231	204	185	171	157	143	130	120	111	102
321 to 340	760	570	475	380	333	285	238	209	190	176	162	147	133	124	114	105
341 to 360	784	588	490	392	343	294	245	216	196	181	167	152	137	127	118	108
361 to 380	804	603	503	402	352	302	251	221	201	186	171	156	141	131	121	111
381 to 400	824	618	515	412	361	309	258	227	206	191	175	160	144	134	124	113
401 to 420	844	633	528	422	369	317	264	232	211	195	179	164	148	137	127	116
421 to 440	864	648	540	432	378	324	270	238	216	200	184	167	151	140	130	119
441 to 460	884	663	553	442	387	332	276	243	221	204	188	171	155	144	133	122
461 to 480	904	678	565	452	396	339	283	249	226	209	192	175	158	147	136	124
481 to 500	924	693	578	462	404	347	289	254	231	214	196	179	162	150	139	127
501 to 520	944	708	590	472	413	354	295	260	236	218	201	183	165	153	142	130
521 to 540	964	723	603	482	422	362	301	265	241	223	205	187	169	157	145	133
541 to 560	980	735	613	490	429	368	306	270	245	227	208	190	172	159	147	135
561 to 580	1000	750	625	500	438	375	313	275	250	231	213	194	175	163	150	138
581 to 600	1020	765	638	510	446	383	319	281	255	236	217	198	179	166	153	140
601 to 620	1040	780	650	520	455	390	325	286	260	241	221	202	182	169	156	143
621 to 640	1060	795	663	530	464	398	331	292	265	245	225	205	186	172	159	146
641 to 660	1080	810	675	540	473	405	338	297	270	250	230	209	189	176	162	149
661 to 680	1100	825	688	550	481	413	344	303	275	254	234	213	193	179	165	151
681 to 700	1120	840	700	560	490	420	350	308	280	259	238	217	196	182	168	154
701 to 720	1140	855	713	570	499	428	356	314	285	264	242	221	200	185	171	157
721 to 740	1160	870	725	580	508	435	363	319	290	268	247	225	203	189	174	160
741 to 760	1180	885	738	590	516	443	369	325	295	273	251	229	207	192	177	162
761 to 780	1200	900	750	600	525	450	375	330	300	278	255	233	210	195	180	165
781 to 800	1220	915	763	610	534	458	381	336	305	282	259	236	214	198	183	168
801 to 825	1240	930	775	620	543	465	388	341	310	287	264	240	217	202	186	171
826 to 850	1260	945	788	630	551	473	394	347	315	291	268	244	221	205	189	173
851 to 875	1280	960	800	640	560	480	400	352	320	296	272	248	224	208	192	176
876 to 900	1300	975	813	650	569	488	406	358	325	301	276	252	228	211	195	179
901 to 925	1320	990	825	660	578	495	413	363	330	305	281	256	231	215	198	182
926 to 950	1340	1005	838	670	586	503	419	369	335	310	285	260	235	218	201	184
951 to 975	1360	1020	850	680	595	510	425	374	340	315	289	264	238	221	204	187
976 to 1000	1380	1035	863	690	604	518	431	380	345	319	293	267	242	224	207	190
1001 to 1025	1400	1050	875	700	613	525	438	385	350	324	298	271	245	228	210	193
1026 to 1050	1420	1065	888	710	621	533	444	391	355	328	302	275	249	231	213	195

FIGURE 8–4. Sample Page from *National Rate Basis Tariff No. 1-A*

NATIONAL RATE BASIS TARIFF 1-A   VERMONT—VIRGINIA

LIST OF STATIONS AND RATE BASIS APPLICABLE

VERMONT

STATION	RAILROAD	Apply Rates From or To	STATION	RAILROAD	Apply Rates From or To
S			**V**		
St. Albans.........	CVt..............	St. Albans, Vt.	Vergennes..........	Rut.............	Middlebury, Vt.
St. Johnsbury......	CP-E.............		Vernon.............	CVt.............	Greenfield, Mass.
St. Johnsbury......	MeC.............	St. Johnsbury, Vt.			
St. Johnsbury......	StJ&LC..........		**W**		
Salisbury..........	Rut..............	Middlebury, Vt.	Walden.............	StJ&LC..........	St. Johnsbury, Vt.
Sharon.............	CVt..............	Bethel, Vt.	Wallingford........	Rut.............	Rutland, Vt.
Shelburne..........	Rut..............	Burlington, Vt.	Waterbury..........	CVt.............	Montpelier, Vt.
Sheldon............	StJ&LC..........		Websterville.......	Bar&C...........	
Sheldon Jct........	CVt..............	St. Albans, Vt.	Wells River........	B&M.............	
Sheldon Jct........	StJ&LC..........		Wells River........	CP-E............	Wells River, Vt.
Sheldon Springs....	CVt.............		Wells River........	Bar&C...........	
South Hero.........	Rut.............	Burlington, Vt.	Wenlock............	GTE.............	Groveton, N. H.
South Royalton.....	CVt.............	Bethel, Vt.	West Burke.........	CP-E............	St. Johnsbury, Vt.
South Ryegate......	Bar&C...........	Wells River, Vt.	West Danville......	StJ&LC..........	
South Shaftsbury...	Rut.............	Arlington, Vt.	West Hartford......	CVt.............	White River Jct., Vt.
South Vernon.......	B&M.............	Greenfield, Mass.	Westminster........	B&M.............	Bellows Falls, Vt.
South Vernon.......	CVt.............		West Pawlet........	D&H.............	
South Wallingford..	Rut.............	Rutland, Vt.	West Rutland.......	C&Pit..........	Rutland, Vt.
Springfield........	ST...............	Springfield, Vt.	West Rutland.......	D&H.............	
Stevens Mills......	CP-E............	Richford, Vt.	White River Jct....	B&M.............	White River Jct., Vt.
Summit (Essex Co.).	GTE.............	Island Pond, Vt.	White River Jct....	CVt.............	
Swanton (East Side).	CVt.............		Whiting............	Rut.............	Middlebury, Vt.
Swanton (West Side).	CVt.............	St. Albans, Vt.	Wilder.............	B&M.............	White River Jct., Vt.
Swanton............	StJ&LC..........		Williston..........	CVt.............	Burlington, Vt.
			Windsor............	B&M.............	White River Jct., Vt.
T			Windsor............	CVt.............	
Thetford...........	B&M.............	White River Jct., Vt.	Winooski...........	CVt.............	Burlington, Vt.
			Wolcott............	StJ&LC..........	Morrisville, Vt.
			Woodruff...........	CVt.............	Bellows Falls, Vt.

VIRGINIA

STATION	RAILROAD	Apply Rates From or To	STATION	RAILROAD	Apply Rates From or To
A			Appalachia.........	Int.............	
Abert..............	C&O(CD).........	Lynchburg, Va.	Appalachia.........	L&N.............	Appalachia, Va.
Abilene............	Vgn.............	Pamplin, Va.	Appalachia.........	Sou(SRS).......	
Abingdon...........	N&W.............	Bristol, Va.-Tenn.	Applegate..........	Sou(SRS).......	Covesville, Va.
Adams Grove........	A&D.............	Emporia, Va.	Appomattox.........	N&W.............	Pamplin, Va.
Addison............	N&W.............	Petersburg, Va.	Aquia..............	RF&P...........	Fredericksburg, Va.
(Dinwiddie Co.)			Arcadia............	N&W.............	Glasgow, Va.
Adsit..............	Vgn.............	Alberta, Va.	Arkendale..........	RF&P...........	Fredericksburg, Va.
Afton..............	C&O(CD).........	Waynesboro, Va.	Arlinco Siding.....	W&OD...........	Washington, D. C.
Aiken Summit......	Car&NW(SRS)....	Leaksville Jct., Va.	(Arlington)		
Airport............	N&W.............	Petersburg, Va.	Arno...............	Int.............	Appalachia, Va.
Alberta............	SAL.............	Alberta, Va.	Arrington..........	Sou(SRS).......	Covesville, Va.
Alberta............	Vgn.............		Artrip.............	N&W.............	Honaker, Va.
Alexander Park....	SAL.............	Norfolk, Va.	Arvonia............	C&O(CD).........	Bremo, Va.
Alexandria.........	RF&P...........		Ashburn............	W&OD...........	Leesburg, Va.
Alexandria.........	Sou(SRS).......	Washington, D. C.	Ashby (Warren Co.).	N&W.............	Riverton, Va.
Alexandria Jct.....	W&OD...........		Ashcake............	C&O(CD).........	Richmond, Va.
Algren.............	Vgn.............	Suffolk, Va.	Ashland............	RF&P...........	
All................	C&O(CD).........	Eagle Rock, Va.	Aspen..............	Vgn.............	Brookneal, Va.
Alleghany..........	C&O(CD).........	Covington, Va.	Atkins.............	N&W.............	Crockett, Va.
Allen (Dickenson Co.)	CC&O...........	Fremont, Va.	Atlantic Rural Expo-		
Allen Creek........	C&O(CD).........	Norwood, Va.	sition Depot......	C&O(CD).........	Richmond, Va.
Aliens (Henrico Co.).	Sou(SRS)......	Tunstall, Va.	Atlee..............	C&O(CD).........	
Allisonia..........	N&W.............	Pulaski, Va.	Augusta Springs....	C&O(CD).........	Staunton, Va.
Alpha..............	C&O(CD).........	Bremo, Va.	Austinville........	N&W.............	Ivanhoe, Va.
Alpine.............	C&O(CD).........	Glasgow, Va.	Axton..............	Car&NW(SRS)....	Leaksville Jct., Va.
Alsyn..............	Sou(SRS).......	New Market, Va.			
Altavista..........	Sou(SRS).......	Altavista, Va.	**B**		
Altavista..........	Vgn.............		Backbone...........	C&O(CD).........	Covington, Va.
Alton..............	A&D.............	Denniston, Va.	Back Creek.........	Win&W..........	Winchester (N), Va.
Alvarado...........	N&W.............	Damascus, Va.	Bacova Jct.........	C&O(CD).........	Covington, Va.
Amelia.............	Sou(SRS).......	Amelia, Va.	Balcony Falls......	C&O(CD).........	Glasgow, Va.
Amherst............	Sou(SRS).......	Amherst, Va.	Baldwin............	C&O(CD).........	Eagle Rock, Va.
Amoco..............	C&O(CD).........	Williamsburg, Va.	Bandy..............	N&W.............	Welch, W. Va.
Amonate............	N&W.............	Welch, W. Va.	Bangor.............	CC&O...........	Ft. Blackmore, Va.
Ampthill...........	SAL.............	Richmond, Va.	Banner.............	N&W.............	Morton, Va.
Andover............	Int.............	Appalachia, Va.	Barbour's Creek....	C&O(CD).........	New Castle, Va.
Antlers............	A&D.............	Clarkeville, Va.	Barboursville......	Sou(SRS).......	Orange, Va.

FIGURE 8–5. Sample Page from *CTR—Southern Commodity Tariff*

Tariff 128–C

SECTION 1

COMMODITY RATES

ITEM	COMMODITY	FROM	TO	Rates in Cents per 100 Lbs.
		Belle . . . . . W.Va.		69
		Charleston. . W.Va.		69
	ACID, acetic, glacial or liquid, in bulk in aluminum drums, or ·in bulk in barrels, or in carboys, C.L., minimum weight 30,000 pounds, or in tank cars, subject to Rule 35 of Southern Classification.	Dock. . . . . W.Va.		69
		Elk . . . . . W.Va.		69
		Institute . . W.Va.		69
	Subject to intermediate point rules in Items 80 and 85.	Midland . . . Mich.	Charlotte . . .N.C. Chemway . . . .N.C.	98
	Rates will only apply via routes shown in Items 6445 to 6451, to Alberta, Altavista, Va., Elkhorn City, Ky., Lynchburg, Norfolk, Richmond, Va., or Winston-Salem, N.C., thence via routes beyond said gateways as follows:	Owens . . . . W.Va.		69
1000		South Charleston . W.Va.		69
		South Ruffner. . . W.Va.		69
		Spring Hill . W.Va.		69

		TO	
FROM GATEWAYS	Charlotte. . . . . .N.C.		Chemway . . . . .N.C.
	(For explanation of Routes, see Section 3)		
Alberta . . . . Va.	SL2, SL224		SL2211
Altavista . . . . . . Va.	SRS772		SRS511
Elkhorn City. . . . . Ky.	CC33, CC40		CC33, CC40
Lynchburg . . . . . . Va.	SRS772		SRS511
Norfolk . . . . Va.	NS2		NS103
Richmond. . . . . . . Va.	SL2, SL224		SL2211
Winston-Salem . . . .N.C.	SRS2; WS2		SRS510; WS10

	COMMODITY	FROM	TO	
⒡⑩ 1010	ACID, acetic, glacial or liquid, in aluminum drums, in bulk in barrels or carboys, C.L., minimum weight 30,000 pounds, or in tank cars, subject to Rule 35 of Southern Classification. ACETIC ANHYDRIDE, in bulk in barrels or in carboys, C.L., minimum weight 30,000 pounds, or in tank cars, subject to Rule 35 of Southern Classification. Rate will only apply via routes shown in Item 6460.	Belle . . . . W.Va. Charleston. . . W.Va. Dock. . . . . W.Va. Dunbar. . . . W.Va. Elk . . . . . W.Va. Institute . . W.Va. Malden. . . . W.Va. Mound . . . . W.Va. Nitro . . . . W.Va. Owens . . . . W.Va. Reed. . . . . W.Va. Sattes. . . . W.Va. Snow Hill . . W.Va. So.Charleston W.Va. So.Ruffner. . W.Va. West Charleston . W.Va.	Camp Croft . .S.C.	70
⒫⑧⒜ 1020	ACID, acetic, glacial or liquid, in bulk in aluminum drums or in bulk in barrels or carboys, C.L., minimum weight 30,000 pounds, or in tank cars, subject to Rule 35 of Southern Classification. ACETIC ANHYDRIDE, in bulk in barrels or in carboys, C.L., minimum weight 30,000 pounds, or in tank cars, subject to Rule 35 of Southern Classification.	Charleston. . . W.Va. Elk . . . . . W.Va. Institute . . W.Va. Owens . . . . W.Va. South Charleston . W.Va. South Ruffner W.Va.	Decatur. . . .Ala.	80

Rates will only apply via the following routes:
 ① C&O(CD), Louisville, Ky., L&N.
 ① C&O(CD), Lexington, Ky., CNO&TP(SRS), Chattanooga, Tenn., Sou(SRS).
 ① C&O(CD), Elkhorn City, Ky., CC&O, Frisco or Johnson City, Tenn., Sou(SRS).
 ② NYC(W), Charleston, W.Va., C&O(CD), Louisville, Ky., L&N.
 ② NYC(W), Charleston, W.Va., C&O(CD), Lexington, Ky., CNO&TP(SRS), Chattanooga, Tenn., Sou(SRS).
 ③ NYC(W), Columbus, Ohio, NYC(C), Louisville, Ky., L&N.
 ③ NYC(W), Columbus, Ohio, NYC(C), Cincinnati, Ohio, CNO&TP(SRS), Chattanooga, Tenn., Sou(SRS).

① Will not apply from Institute, W.Va.
② Will only apply from Institute, W.Va.
③ Will only apply from Charleston and Institute, W.Va.
For explanation of other reference marks, see concluding pages of this tariff.

applies. If we look in another part of the tariff, a page of which is re-produced in Figure 8–3, we find for each "rate-basis" number the rates on the various classes of freight. From Figure 8–3 it can be seen that the Class 100 rate that goes with Rate Basis 890 is 325 cents per hundred pounds. This, then, is the Class 100 rate between Chicago and New York; or rather, it would be if it were not for the fact that the rates published in this tariff are subject to various increases authorized by the Interstate Commerce Commission in recent years in numerous proceed-ings in which the railroads sought and obtained general increases in their rates to meet increased costs of operation. Resort must be had to another tariff to find the result of the authorized increases on the 325-cent rate shown in *Tariff No. E–1009.*

Although *Tariff No. E–1009* shows the rate bases between several hundred points, there are hundreds of other stations in the area covered by the tariff to and from which rates are not shown. To find the rates to and from such stations, it is necessary to turn to another tariff publica-tion—*National Rate Basis Tariff No. 1–A*—which groups such stations with points which are shown in *Tariff No. E–1009* (see Figure 8–4). This tariff contains an alphabetical list of all stations, grouped by states, and shows the points with which they are grouped for rate purposes.

From *National Rate Basis Tariff No. 1–A* we find, for instance, that Hoopeston, Illinois (not shown on the page reproduced in Figure 8–4), takes the same rates as Danville, Illinois, and that Shelburne, Vermont (shown in Figure 8–4), takes the same rates as Burlington, Vermont. Thus the rates between Hoopeston, Illinois, and Shelburne, Vermont, are those that apply between Danville, Illinois, and Burlington, Vermont. The rates between the latter pair of stations may be found in *Tariff No. E–1009.*

Tariff No. E–1009, from which sample pages are shown in Figures 8–2 and 8–3, is a class tariff. A sample page from a general commodity tariff is shown in Figure 8–5. This tariff publishes commodity rates on a large number of commodities from points in Central Territory to points in Southern Territory. Being a commodity tariff, it publishes rates di-rectly on specifically named commodities. It will be noted from Figure 8–5 that the commodity rates there shown are published from a limited number of origin points to a limited number of destinations. This is characteristic of most commodity rates. In using a commodity tariff, it is important to pay close attention to all of the reference marks, notes, and routing restrictions, such as are shown on the page reproduced in Figure 8–5.

THE RATE-MAKING POWER

The power to make and change rates rests initially with the railroad companies. Usually the carriers in a given area act through "freight associations" or "bureaus" in making and changing rates. Although this is collective action on the part of the carriers, the right of independent action by individual carriers is recognized. In fact, the right of independent action is protected by law.[15]

It is often assumed that all interstate rates are prescribed by the Interstate Commerce Commission or at least that all the rates must be approved by it. Neither assumption is correct. The Interstate Commerce Commission has regulatory powers over the rates; but subject to the requirement that rates must be just and reasonable or not otherwise unlawful, the carriers may prescribe the rates which they please. The importance of the Commission's authority is not to be denied, but thousands of rates are changed each year at the behest of the railroads without any interference by the Commission and without any specific determination of the reasonableness of the new rates. Shippers seeking changes in rates normally bring their proposals before individual railroads or before the appropriate rate bureaus. If satisfactory adjustments are not obtained in this way, resort may be had to the Interstate Commerce Commission or to state regulatory authorities, provided there are grounds for believing that the rates are unreasonable or otherwise unlawful.

RATE SYSTEMS

Freight rates often seem to be constructed most haphazardly and without any attempt to build up a systematic and logical rate structure. This is the natural result of charging what the traffic will bear. The general effect of rate regulation, with its attempt to remove unjustifiable inequalities and discriminations, has been to bring about more systematic rate structures. But even before the development of government regulation the railroads had accomplished something toward this end. A notable example was the Trunk-Line rate structure covering traffic between points in Central Freight Association Territory and the Atlantic ports and other eastern points.[16] This rate structure, so far as the class rates were concerned, was replaced by a new structure as a result of the decision of the Interstate Commerce Commission in *Eastern Class-Rate Investigation*,[17] which in turn has been superseded by the class rates pre-

---

[15] See Section 5a, paragraph 6, of the Interstate Commerce Act. For a description of rate bureaus and their organization and procedures see Board of Investigation and Research, *Report on Rate-Making and Rate-Publishing Procedures of Railroad, Motor, and Water Carriers*, 78th Cong., 1st Sess., House Doc. No. 363 (1944).

[16] This structure is described in W. Z. Ripley, *Railroads: Rates and Regulation* (New York: Longmans, 1912), pp. 356–77; Eliot Jones, *Principles of Railway Transportation* (New York: Macmillan, 1924), pp. 148–57; M. L. Fair and E. W. Williams, Jr., *Economics of Transportation* (rev. ed.; New York: Harper, 1959), pp. 387–89.

[17] 164 ICC 314 (1930).

scribed by the Interstate Commerce Commission in *Class Rate Investigation, 1939.*[18]

There are three general types of freight-rate structures: (1) distance-rate structures, in which the rates are closely related to distance; (2) group-rate structures, in which there is a grouping of origins or destinations, or both; and (3) base-and-related-rate systems, in which the central characteristic is the relating of the rates to some base or key rate. Each type of rate structure will be more fully described in turn. It should be recognized, however, that these types of rate structures overlap, and a particular rate structure may possess characteristics of two, or even of all three, of the types to a limited degree. There has been a tendency for a distinct rate system to develop, or to be prescribed, in certain well-defined rate territories. At this point, therefore, it is well to note the names and locations of these territories.

RATE TERRITORIES

The five major rate territories in the United States are shown in Figure 8–6. They are known as Eastern or Official Territory, Southern

FIGURE 8–6.　The Five Major Freight-Rate Territories

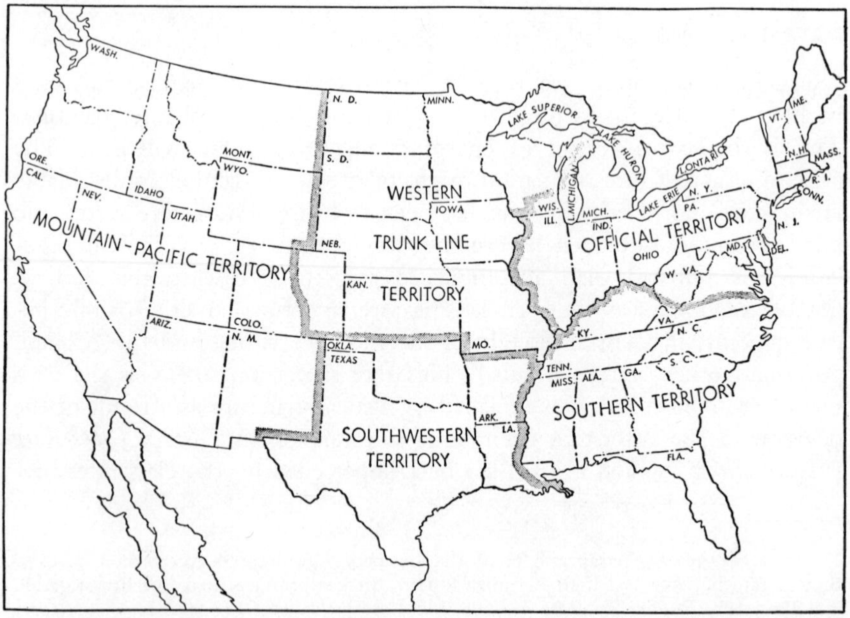

Taken from Interstate Commerce Commission, Bureau of Statistics, *Distribution of the Natural Resources of the United States by Freight Rate Territories,* Exhibit No. 1 in Docket No. 28300 (1941), following p. 3.

---

[18] 262 ICC 447 (1945); 281 ICC 213 (1951). New rates, in compliance with the Commission's orders in this proceeding, became effective May 30, 1952.

Territory, Western Trunk-Line Territory, Southwestern Territory, and Mountain-Pacific Territory. The territories have been important in the class-rate structure, since each of the territories had a distinctive structure and level of class rates for many years. Revision of the class-rate structures following the decisions of the Interstate Commerce Commission in the Class Rate Investigation of 1939 and in the Mountain-Pacific and Transcontinental class-rate case in 1955[19] has resulted in a single class-rate structure throughout the United States, although the level of the rates is higher in Mountain-Pacific Territory than in the rest of the country. Commodity-rate structures and levels may differ in the different rate territories, but some of them disregard traditional territorial boundaries entirely.

In Eastern or Official Territory there are three subterritories, not shown on the map in Figure 8–6, above. These are the New England, Trunk-Line, and Central Freight Association territories. New England Territory comprises the New England states and a small strip of New York east of the Hudson River. Trunk-Line Territory lies west of New England and the Atlantic Coast and extends to a line running southward just east of Buffalo, N.Y., Pittsburgh, Pa., Wheeling, W.Va., and Charleston, W.Va.[20] This line is commonly referred to as the "Buffalo-Pittsburgh line." Central Freight Association Territory, also known as C.F.A. Territory or Central Territory, lies west of the Buffalo-Pittsburgh line.

DISTANCE-RATE SYSTEMS

The simplest form of rate structure is one in which rates are constructed on a distance scale. The class-rate structures prescribed between 1925 and 1935 for application in the various rate territories were predominantly distance-rate systems. So likewise are the class rates which were established as a result of the Class Rate Investigation of 1939. Some commodity-rate structures are also based on distance scales.[21]

Distance-rate systems possess certain characteristics which should be noted.

Distance Blocks

In the typical distance-rate system the rates do not change with each additional mile of distance. Instead a distance-block system is used, with blocks varying in length. In the scale which was prescribed by the Commission in the third supplemental report to *Class Rate Investigation,*

---

[19] 296 ICC 555 (1955).

[20] *Robbins Flooring Co.* v. *Ann Arbor R. Co.,* 256 ICC 129, 130 (1943).

[21] For numerous examples see Board of Investigation and Research, *Report on Interterritorial Freight Rates,* chap. iv.

1939,[22] 5-mile blocks were used for the first 100 miles, then 10-mile blocks up to a distance of 240 miles, then 25-mile blocks up to 2,200 miles, and 50-mile blocks for greater distances.

The Tapering Principle

Most distance rates are constructed on the tapering principle, that is, the rates increase with distance, but not as rapidly as distance increases. In other words, although the total rate is greater for longer than for shorter distances, the rate per mile is less for the longer distances.

When distance rates are plotted on a chart, the tapering character of the scale is revealed. Figure 8–7 shows the scale of Class 100 rates pre-

FIGURE 8–7.   Scale of Class 100 Rates Prescribed in 1951

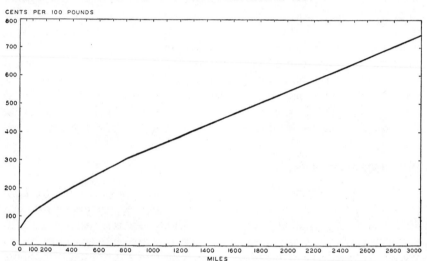

scribed by the Commission in the third supplemental report to *Class Rate Investigation, 1939*. This scale, like many others prescribed by the Commission, is composed of a series of straight lines, each successive line making a smaller angle with the distance axis. In the scale shown in Figure 8–7, it will be observed that there is no further tapering of the scale after 800 miles.[23] Rates of progression can also be shown by stating the increase in rates in each 100 miles. The Class 100 rates shown in Figure 8–7 begin at 58 cents and rise to 114 cents at 100 miles, an in-

---

[22] 281 ICC 213, 328 (1951).

[23] For studies of the rate of progression of scales prescribed by the Interstate Commerce Commission see Interstate Commerce Commission, Bureau of Transport Economics and Statistics, Statement No. 4351, *A Description of the Principal Class Rate Scales Prescribed by the Interstate Commerce Commission* (mimeographed, 1943).

crease of 56 cents. From 100 to 200 miles the increase is 35 cents; from 200 to 300 miles, 30 cents; then it is about 25 cents for each 100 miles up to 800 miles and then 20 cents for each 100 miles throughout the rest of the scale.[24]

It should be observed that the rate of progression of a distance scale can be constant throughout, that is, the scale can be represented by a straight line, and yet the rates per mile will be lower for the longer distances if the initial rate is considerably above zero, as is practically always the case.

There are several reasons for not making freight rates increase in exact proportion to distance. In the first place, terminal costs are the same regardless of the length of the haul.[25] The longer the haul, the greater the distance over which the constant terminal cost can be spread. To use the illustration given by Ripley,[26] suppose there is a terminal cost of 50 cents a ton for handling certain freight, and a haulage or line-haul cost of 0.5 cents per ton-mile. For a haul of 10 miles the rate per mile would be $(50 + 5) \div 10$, or 5.5 cents. For a haul of 500 miles the ton-mile rate would be $(50 + 250) \div 500$, or 0.6 cents.

A second reason for the lower rates per ton-mile for longer hauls is that even the line-haul or conveyance cost is considered to be relatively lower for the longer hauls. This point was discussed by the Commission in the *Southern Class Rate Investigation*. The Commission found that short-haul traffic, particularly that which moved 75 miles or less, was moved in local or "way" freight trains. For longer distances, through freight trains may be used, which make fewer stops and operate more efficiently. For distances in excess of 150 miles, through freights were the general rule, so that on shipments moving long distances the proportion of the haul in expensive way freights was relatively small.[27] This reasoning has not gone unchallenged, however, and it is sometimes maintained that the long hauls require a succession of intermediate yard services which are expensive and which keep the costs more or less proportionate to distance.

A third reason for the use of the tapering principle is to prevent the rates from restricting the movement of long-distance traffic. This point has been previously mentioned.[28] If rates increased in proportion to distance, they would soon become so high as to prevent the movement of traffic. It is in accordance with the value-of-service principle of rate making to keep long-distance rates low enough to enable the traffic to

---

[24] These rates have been subjected to numerous percentage increases since they were originally prescribed.

[25] In the United States, terminal charges are not separately quoted but are included in the freight rate.

[26] Op. cit., p. 104.

[27] 100 ICC 513, 643 (1925).

[28] P. 150, supra.

move. The Interstate Commerce Commission has recognized this as a valid reason for tapering rate scales.[29]

Tapering the rate scale is often carried further than can be justified by cost considerations. The soundness of this practice may sometimes be questioned. If the concession to the long-distance traffic induces the movement of traffic that would not otherwise be carried, of course the railroad gains by the practice; but if the result is only to substitute long hauls for shorter ones, with no gain in tonnage carried, the practice is of doubtful benefit to the railroads.

The Initial Rate

The importance of the terminal charge in the construction of rate scales has already been noted. For the shortest distances a substantial portion of the rate would normally consist of the terminal charge. Strictly speaking, the initial rate in a scale should be based largely on terminal costs. In class-rate scales, however, the scale is of the first-class or Class 100 rates, and the rates on the lower classes are percentages of the first-class or Class 100 rates. This means that if the initial first-class rate were based on terminal costs, the initial rates for the lower classes of freight would not cover such costs unless the traffic moving on the lower ratings actually incurred less-than-average terminal cost.

In the uniform scale of class rates prescribed by the Commission in 1951, the initial Class 100 rate was 58 cents per hundred pounds.[30] The initial rates in commodity-rate scales, applying on carload traffic, are much lower. Initial rates of 13 cents per hundred pounds on packing-house products and of 16 cents on fresh meats are found in scales prescribed in 1948,[31] and an initial rate of 8 cents is found in a brick scale prescribed in 1950.[32]

Rate of Progression

Determination of the rate of progression of distance scales calls for the exercise of judgment. The rate of progression depends in part upon transportation costs and in part upon the ability of traffic to move under high rates. In constructing some rate scales, the Interstate Commerce Commission has relied less upon calculations of transportation costs than upon the practical necessities of fitting the scale into existing rate levels and of joining them to rate structures in bordering territories.[33] In the

---

[29] *Livestock—Western District Rates,* 190 ICC 611, 627–28 (1933).

[30] 281 ICC 213, 328.

[31] *Armour & Co.* v. *Ahnapee & Western Ry. Co.,* 272 ICC 759, 774.

[32] *Mason City Brick & Tile Co.* v. *Chicago & North Western Ry. Co.,* 277 ICC 79, 91.

[33] *Consolidated Southwestern Cases,* 123 ICC 203, 384 (1927).

Southern Class Rate Investigation the carriers proposed a scale built around three "peg" points. The first was an initial rate of 30 cents, supported by cost studies; the second was a rate of $1.45 for 330 miles, the first-class rate and distance from Cairo, Illinois, to Birmingham, Alabama. The third peg was $1.60 for 460 miles, the rate and distance from Atlanta, Georgia, to the Ohio River. The carriers built a scale about these three rates. The Commission did not adopt the particular scale proposed by the carriers; but in this, as in other cases, it was apparently necessary to pay some attention to preexisting rates, as well as to rates in adjoining territories, in order to minimize the disturbance caused by placing rates on a distance basis.[34]

Present class-rate scales have been criticized as not based on the realities of the situation created by motor-truck competition.[35] The effect of this factor would be to make the rates somewhat lower than at present for short hauls where motor-truck competition is most effective. A new rate scale adopted in Argentina in 1961 shows this characteristic.[36]

Computation of Distances

Another problem arising in the application of distance scales is the method of computing mileages. This is not a simple problem when several different routes are available. After experimenting with various rules for determining distances, the Interstate Commerce Commission settled on the rule that distances should be computed over the "shortest possible route over which carload traffic can be interchanged without transfer of lading." Such routes, however, are not necessarily the routes over which shipments actually move. The carriers may use longer routes, but the rate between the two points must be determined by the rule. One objection to this rule is that the establishment of new track connections, the construction of new lines, or the abandonment of old ones may shorten or lengthen a route and require the adjustment of a large number of rates. The Commission, however, finds the plan much more satisfactory than those used previously.[37] An earlier rule that distances should be computed by the "shortest workable route" or, as it came to be stated, by the shortest "economical distance," involved an exercise of

---

[34] For further illustrations of fitting scales to existing rates see S. Daggett, "Mileage Rates and the Interstate Commerce Commission," 46 *Quarterly Journal of Economics* 281, 299–301 (1932).

[35] Herbert O. Whitten, "Maximum Pricing at the Demand Rate Level for Rail Service." In *Papers—Fourth Annual Meeting, Transportation Research Forum, 1963*, p. 200.

[36] Argentina, Ministry of Public Works, Transportation Planning Group, *A Long Range Transportation Plan for Argentina* (Buenos Aires, 1961), Appendix V, p. 36.

[37] The problem is discussed at length in 113 ICC 200 (1926).

judgment on the part of the carriers and led to much controversy with shippers.[38]

Modification of Distance Scales

Many of the distance-rate structures are somewhat modified in their actual application. Rarely, in fact, is there a rigid adherence to the scales prescribed. Three types of departures may be noted. First, a considerable amount of grouping of points of origin or destination may be permitted as a device to reduce the number of rates to be published. Second, there may be deviations from the scale because of competitive forces which require lower rates at particular points than would result from the application of the scale. Distance scales prescribed by the Commission are frequently scales of maximum rates; and the carriers are permitted, within limits, to make adjustments to meet competition of one sort or another. A third type of deviation from a strictly distance basis is sometimes made by the Commission itself. In some cases in which distance scales are prescribed, the Commission fixes specific maximum rates between certain "key points," usually the more important towns and cities, and these rates do not always conform exactly to the distance scales. The carriers are then required to build rates to other points on the basis of the scales prescribed. But in so doing, they use the key-point rates as maxima at intermediate points to avoid violations of the Long-and-Short-Haul Clause. The keypoint rates, in other words, are blanketed back to intermediate points if they are lower than the rate reached by the application of the distance scale.[39]

Differences in Rate Levels

If rates are to be put on a distance basis over any considerable area, the problem arises of determining whether a single scale shall be adopted or whether differences in conditions make it advisable to divide the territory into different areas, with different scales and rate levels for each area. In the major class-rate revisions that were made by the Interstate Commerce Commission between 1925 and 1935 in the various rate territories, the Commission prescribed a single scale of class rates for application over wide areas and introduced a greater degree of uniformity than had previously existed within the territories. Complete uniformity, however, was not attained in any of the territories.

In the *Eastern Class-Rate Investigation* the Commission rejected the plea for a lower level of rates in Central Freight Association Territory, largely on the grounds that more favorable operating conditions were

---

[38] See 109 ICC 300, 310–13 (1926).

[39] For an example see *Eastern Class-Rate Investigation*, 164 ICC 314, 414–15 (1930).

offset by a less favorable traffic density.[40] But higher rates were permitted in New England and also in the northern part of the southern peninsula of Michigan, which was known as "Zone C." For distances in Zone C, "arbitraries" could be added which were about 10 percent of the Eastern basic scale. For New England the Commission established two zones. The Zone A scale, applicable in southern New England, was about 5 percent higher than the basic scale. The Zone B scale, applicable in northern New England, where traffic density was less and operating conditions more difficult, was about 15 percent higher than the basic Eastern scale. Notwithstanding the higher levels prescribed for Zone C in Michigan and for New England, the Eastern class-rate scale was applicable over a large territory, which included areas of diverse traffic and operating characteristics.

In the *Southern Class Rate Investigation*, it was found that traffic densities were somewhat more favorable for the states bordering on Trunk-Line Territory, but the Commission found that it was not possible to draw anything but an arbitrary line between border territory and the more southern areas and that such a line would not coincide with any distinct differences in transportation conditions.[41] The Commission also found that there were greater differences between individual railroads in the same area than between different areas. The Commission therefore prescribed a single scale of class rates for general application throughout Southern Territory, except that higher rates were permitted for that part of Florida south of Jacksonville and River Junction.[42]

In Western Trunk-Line Territory, four scales and levels of class rates were prescribed. The division of the area into zones with different rate levels was found justified, partly by differences in operating and traffic conditions and partly by the necessity of building up the level of rates gradually to the level which had been prescribed in adjacent Southwestern Territory.[43] The Western Trunk-Line zones, together with the extension of Zone IV west of the original boundaries of the territory, are shown in Figure 8–8.

In Southwestern Territory two levels of class rates were prescribed.[44] In the eastern part of the territory the scale was the same as the Western Trunk-Line Zone III scale. A higher scale was prescribed for the western part of the territory, but the carriers established the Zone III basis in this

---

[40] 164 ICC 314, 386 (1930).

[41] 100 ICC 513, 622–23.

[42] A slightly different scale of class rates was later prescribed by the Commission to apply between points in Virginia and points in North Carolina not covered by the *Southern Class Rate Investigation*. See *North Carolina Corporation Commission* v. *Akron, Canton & Youngstown Ry. Co.*, 213 ICC 259 (1935).

[43] *Western Trunk-Line Class Rates*, 164 ICC 1, 198–99 (1930).

[44] *Consolidated Southwestern Cases*, 123 ICC 203 (1927). Rates were revised in the 21st Supplemental Report, 205 ICC 601 (1934).

FIGURE 8–8. Zoning of Western Trunk-Line Territory

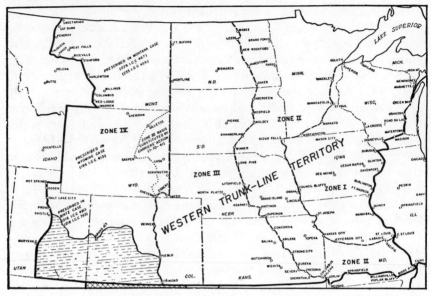

Board of Investigation and Research, *Report on Interterritorial Freight Rates,* adapted from map facing p. 1.

area in 1941, thus making a single scale applicable throughout Southwestern Territory.

Although there had never been a territory-wide revision of class rates in Mountain-Pacific Territory, the so-called "Arizona scale" applied extensively in this area as a result of a long series of Commission decisions dating back to 1911.[45]

Notwithstanding the practice of applying a single distance scale over wide areas, the Commission has made some recognition of differences in transportation conditions by frequently permitting the addition of "arbitraries" for distances on short or weak lines.

Although the result of the major territorial class-rate revisions was to bring about a greater degree of uniformity in class-rate levels within the several territories, considerable differences between the class-rate levels of the different territories remained. If the first-class rates in Eastern Territory were taken as 100, the comparative levels in the various territories prior to about 1947 were as follows:[46]

Eastern.....................................	100
Southern....................................	139
Western Trunk-Line:	
Zone I.....................................	128
Zone II....................................	146

---

[45] Ibid., pp. 15–16.

[46] Ibid., p. 19.

Zone III............................... 161
Zone IV............................... 184
Southwestern........................... 161
Mountain-Pacific........................ 166

These differences in the levels of class rates were brought directly in issue in *Class Rate Investigation, 1939*. By the decision of the Commission in this proceeding in 1945 the establishment of a uniform level of class rates for application throughout the United States east of the Rocky Mountains was ordered.[47] Application of the new rates was deferred, however, pending the establishment of a uniform freight classification to go with the new rates.[48] Since it was apparent that it might take several years to work out the new classification, an interim adjustment of rates was required in order to reduce territorial differences in rate levels. Complete uniformity in the levels of class rates in the different territories, exclusive of Mountain-Pacific Territory and between that territory and the rest of the country, became effective on May 30, 1952, when the Uniform Freight Classification and the revised scale of class rates became effective. It should be noted, however, that under the system of class rates prescribed, the railroads may maintain "arbitraries" for application on short and weak roads.[49]

Distance scales, as we have noted, are not only used in the construction of class rates but are also frequently used in the construction of commodity rates. In some instances, individual railroads have their own scales applicable on a particular commodity. In other instances, scales have been prescribed by the Commission. Some of these have had very limited application; others have applied over wide areas, sometimes coextensive with a major rate territory or even applying over two or more such areas. In some instances a commodity-rate scale originally set up to apply in a limited area, or between a limited number of points, comes to be used as a standard of reasonableness in cases involving other points and areas, and so gradually spreads over a larger area.

Rate between Zones or Areas Having Different Levels

When two or more rate zones are established with a different level or scale of distance rates in each zone, some method has to be found for constructing rates from a point in one zone to a point in another. Various methods have been used for the construction of such rates.

An obvious method of constructing rates in such situations is to apply the scale of each zone for the distance within that zone and to add the rates together. This is equivalent to making rates on a combination basis, the method necessarily used when no through rates are published. A serious weakness in this method of constructing rates between zones is

---

[47] 262 ICC 447.

[48] See p. 176, supra.

[49] 281 ICC 213, 290 (1951).

that it includes the terminal charge twice, or more than twice if more than two zones are involved. As long as distance rates are constructed on the tapering principle, the combination of two or more short-distance rates will be higher than is justified for the whole distance. Prior to the comprehensive class-rate revisions which began in 1925, rates from points in one major rate territory to points in another were usually constructed on the combination basis, and the method is still used in the construction of some commodity rates.[50]

When through rates are to be published from a point in one zone or territory to points in another area having a different level of rates, the problem is to blend the two scales, giving appropriate weight to the proportion of the haul in each zone or territory. Various methods of accomplishing this have been used from time to time.[51] The most widely used method is to apply the lower scale for the whole distance and then to add "arbitraries" or "differentials," that is, specific amounts varying with the length of the haul, in the higher-rated zone. This was the method used by the Interstate Commerce Commission in the *Southern Class Rate Investigation* for the construction of rates to and from points in the Florida peninsula.[52] Thus, on first-class traffic an arbitrary of 6 cents was added when the haul in Florida was 10 miles or less; 7 cents was added when the haul was 25 miles or over 10. It reached a maximum of 25 cents for hauls of over 500 miles in the higher-rated area.[53]

Advantages of Distance Rates

Rates constructed in accordance with the distance principle have certain advantages over rates otherwise constructed. They are comparatively simple and more readily understood, whereas rates constructed primarily in accordance with conditions of demand seem a veritable chaos and arouse suspicions of favoritism that are not easily dispelled.

A second advantage of distance rates is that they conform to the cost-of-service principle, for costs of transportation, generally speaking, increase with distance.

Distance rates are also desirable because they preserve to each locality the advantage of its location. It is for this reason that regulatory authorities are inclined to resort to distance rates to remove preferences and discriminations. This has been called "the rate making of desperation,"[54]

---

[50] This method may be modified by making the rates a combination of "proportional" rates, which are lower than the local rates.

[51] These methods are described in earlier editions of this work. See 1st ed., pp. 177–79; rev. ed., pp. 185–87; 3d ed., pp. 185–88; 4th ed., pp. 191–93.

[52] 100 ICC 513, 625–26 (1925).

[53] 128 ICC 567, 602 (1927).

[54] H. B. Vanderblue and K. F. Burgess, *Railroads: Rates, Service, Management* (New York: Macmillan, 1923), p. 156.

since it is resorted to when the situation involves so many conflicting interests that any other adjustment is bound to result in further complaints of preference or prejudice.

The use of distance scales also tends to stablize the rate structure. If rates are to be adjusted according to commercial and competitive conditions, manufacturers and dealers can never know when the rate system will be disturbed because of changed conditions. Rates constructed on the distance principle have a more permanent basis.

An important social advantage of distance rates is that they discourage wasteful transportation. Rates graded according to distance give an advantage to a producer in the immediately surrounding area. This was pointed out in connection with the discussion of market areas.[55] On the other hand, rates that are the same, without regard to distance, or that are constructed upon the principle of keeping everybody in business, lead to the invasion of one's natural markets by outside producers and permit the local producer to invade the markets of his rivals. This leads to an enormous amount of cross-hauling and the carrying of goods unnecessarily long distances. Rates constructed in accordance with the distance principle tend to prevent this economic waste. The principle is well stated by Professor Ripley: "The transportation of goods great distances at low rates, while economically justifiable in opening up new channels of business, becomes wasteful the moment such carriage, instead of creating new business, merely brings about an exchange between widely separated markets, or an invasion of fields naturally tributary to other centres."[56] Failure to apply a distance system of rates on coal in favor of adjustments which minimize or ignore substantial differences in distance, thus enabling a larger number of coal producers to compete in common markets, is alleged to have been an important factor in the troubles of the coal-mining industry, namely, overexpansion and overcapacity.[57]

A further advantage of distance rates lies in the fact that they interfere less with the natural migration of industries to more favorable locations than do rates which are adjusted in accordance with conditions of demand. Rates should not be used to prevent the development of industries in new and advantageous locations, nor should they be used to continue old centers of production in existence when the reasons which led to the establishment of an industry at that place have ceased to be operative. In the long run, society is best served by a rate structure which permits industries to locate where natural conditions are most favorable.

---

[55] Pp. 78–83, supra.

[56] Ripley, op. cit., p. 277.

[57] See Joseph T. Lambie, *From Mine to Market: The History of Coal Transportation on the Norfolk & Western Railway* (New York: New York University Press, 1954), pp. 329–33.

Disadvantages of Distance Rates

The grading of rates according to distance has certain disadvantages. Such rates, it has been noted, limit the ability of producers seeking to sell goods in distant markets. This is a good thing in many respects, but it sometimes reduces the amount of competition in the production and sale of goods by protecting a local producer from competition.

Another objection to distance rates lies in the fact that to some extent they disregard the conditions of demand. Distance rates are justified largely on a cost-of-service basis; but it is proper to adjust rates, within limits, according to conditions of demand, as has been pointed out in the preceding chapter. Value of service, as we have previously noted, bears no necessary relation to distance.[58]

Increasing Use of Distance Rates

The use of distance rates has increased in the United States in recent years. This is due in part to government regulation of rates. Between 1910 and 1920, for instance, the Interstate Commerce Commission prescribed distance scales in no less than 250 cases.[59] Many additional distance scales have been prescribed since then. It must be remembered, however, that these scales are applied with great flexibility, and exceptions to the scales are numerous. There are still many commodity-rate structures, furthermore, which can hardly be called distance-rate systems.

RAILROAD COMPETITION

One of the strongest forces tending to distort rates and to prevent adherence to strict distance scales is competition. It is desirable, therefore, to consider a number of varieties of competition and their general effect upon the rate structure.

Competition of Routes

Rival railway lines compete with each other for traffic between points which they serve in common. This type of competition is known as "competition of routes." The routes may be nearly parallel, so that the railroads compete at practically all points, or they may diverge to such an extent that the carriers serve entirely different communities except at their termini. Owing to the thick network of rail lines in the United States, the number of possible routes between some points is amazing. Some of the routes may be extremely circuitous, but they may compete

---

[58] P. 160, supra.

[59] Daggett, op. cit., p. 289.

no less actively for traffic. Sometimes, indeed, railroads extending in opposite directions from a common point compete for the same traffic. Lines operating east from Chicago sometimes compete with western lines for transcontinental traffic, the former carrying the traffic to the eastern seaboard for shipment by water via the Panama Canal. Ripley gives a number of examples of competition by extremely circuitous routes. He found that some freight from Boston to Chicago, 1,004 miles, actually moved by a route 1,786 miles long.[60]

Competition of routes affects rates in three ways. It tends to equalize the rates via the various routes regardless of considerable differences in distance. In the second place, if competition is not restrained in some way, it will lead to subnormal rates at the competitive points even over direct routes. The distinction between out-of-pocket and fixed expenses becomes important here. A competitive route that sees the possibility of diverting traffic from another route will be inclined to cut rates below the full cost of the service. The revenue derived from the diverted traffic, is so far as it yields something over out-of-pocket costs, appears to be so much clear profit. A third effect of this type of competition is sometimes to create "differential routes," that is, routes which charge less than the standard rates in order to overcome the natural disadvantages of the route. The differential rate creates the inducement to ship over a route that provides inferior service. Between points in Central Territory and New York and New England points there are "differential" rail routes competing with the "standard" rail routes. The differential routes, consisting in part of lines through Canada, maintain slightly lower rates than the standard lines.[61]

Competition of routes is not always competition between rival rail lines. The railroads often compete with water routes, highways, and pipelines for traffic between the same points.

Cross-Country Competition

Sometimes competition equalizes rates at points which are on different but more or less paralleling lines. This occurs when it is possible to haul goods by truck across country from one line of railroad to another. This has been called "cross-country competition."[62] The influence of cross-country competition is particularly strong in level areas and does not operate in mountainous regions, where cross-country transportation is difficult. It has been an important influence in the western ranch country, where cattle can be driven comparatively long distances. The develop-

---

[60] Ripley, op. cit., p. 115.

[61] 164 ICC 314, 449 (1930).

[62] Vanderblue and Burgess, op. cit., pp. 123–24. For examples see *Grain & Grain Products from Southwest to California*, 190 ICC 257, 258 (1932); and *Corn & Corn Products from Illinois & Indiana to the East*, 319 ICC 568 (1963).

ment of automobiles and improved roads has increased the importance of cross-country competition generally.

Market Competition

Another type of competition, and one which has been mentioned in previous chapters, is market competition. This is the competition between rival producing centers to sell goods in a common market.[63] Although this has been defined as competition between rival producing centers, it is, at the same time, competition between the railroads serving the different producing areas, since each railroad is interested in developing as much traffic for its lines as possible. A simple case of market competition is shown by Figure 8–9.

FIGURE 8–9. Market Competition

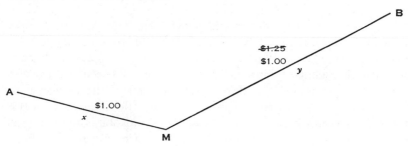

Market competition results in a tendency to lower the rates from more distant sources of supply so that the producers can compete with those more favorably located. It frequently leads to the establishment of group rates, shortly to be described.

There are two types of market competition: primary and secondary, or simple and complex.[64] Primary market competition involves a single commodity shipped directly from producing areas to consuming areas. Potatoes from Maine compete with potatoes from Michigan, and oranges from California compete with oranges from Florida. Salt from Michigan and from Kansas, and sugar from Atlantic seaboard and from Pacific Coast refineries are other examples. Rates from the various sources of supply may not actually be equalized; but there is a tendency in that direction, and the long-haul rates will be depressed to the extent necessary to enable the more distant producers to compete.

---

[63] H. G. Brown, in *Transportation Rates and Their Regulation* (New York: Macmillan, 1916), calls this type of competition "competition of locations." Strictly speaking, Brown's terminology is preferable to the more common term, "market competition," but the latter term is so widely used that we defer to the common practice.

[64] Ripley, op. cit., p. 121.

Secondary market competition involves hauls on two or more commodities, a raw material and the finished product, or on the same commodity into and out of jobbing centers. Here, as has been previously shown, it is the sum of the rates that will tend to equalize.[65]

Market competition usually underlies controversies involving local discrimination or undue preference and prejudice.

Competition of Directions

Market competition was defined as competition of rival producing areas in a common market. There may also be competition of rival markets for the product of a common producing area. This kind of competition is often considered as a kind of market competition, but it seems better to distinguish it as a separate type.[66]

Competition of directions can be illustrated by Figure 8–10. If A is a

FIGURE 8–10. Competition of Directions

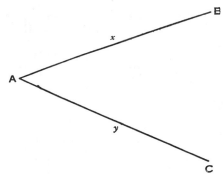

producing center, and B and C are rival markets for the product, the railroad charging the lowest rate may get the traffic.

Competition of directions is involved in the movement of grain from country points to rival grain markets. Ripley refers to a reduction in rates on corn from Kansas to Texas which diverted corn from the rail lines serving Chicago and necessitated a lowering of the rates from Kansas to Chicago.[67] The competition of rival ports for export business may be considered a case of competition of directions if the rail part of the hauls alone is considered. In its larger aspects, however, the competition of ports is a case of competition of routes. Export traffic may move by a number of routes to foreign countries, and different routes lead through different ports.

---

[65] See discussion of in-and-out adjustments, pp. 82–85, supra.

[66] We are here following Brown, op. cit., where the peculiarities of this type of competition are discussed more fully, pp. 50–61.

[67] Ripley, op. cit., pp. 143–44.

Effect of Competition on Distance Scales

Competition makes it very difficult for railroads to observe distance scales strictly. Very frequently, competition creates "basing points" or "basing lines," the rates to and from which exert a dominating influence at other points. The situation can be illustrated by a diagram. Suppose a railroad starts out by charging according to a typical distance scale. This is represented in Figure 8–11 by the curve AB. Suppose, however, that at F the railroad encounters the competition of a shorter rail route or of a water line. Our railroad may be forced to meet the rate set by its rival at this point. As a result the curve of the rates is broken by the notch MSN. But now an impossible situation results. The rate to F is much less than the rate to the nearer point E. To avoid the higher rate at E, ship-

FIGURE 8–11. Effect of Competition on Distance Rates

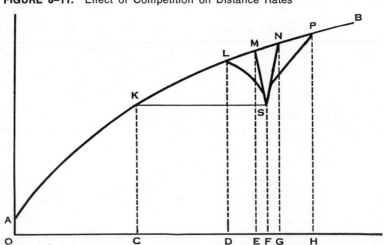

ments will move to F and will then be reconsigned back to E. Thus the maximum rate that it is practicable to charge at E is the rate OF plus the rate FE. The railroad must therefore revise its rates to intermediate points so that they will not exceed the rate to F plus the local rates back. In the same way the rate to points beyond F cannot exceed the low rate to F plus the local rates beyond. As a result the rates are now represented by the curve ALSPB. In other words, the rates to points in the vicinity of F are necessarily based on the rate to F. Point F has become a basing point.

This system of rate construction was characteristic of rates in the South prior to interference by regulatory authorities. A large number of points, mostly competitive points, had been granted favorable rates. These necessarily became basing points, and other rates were combinations to and from the nearest basing point.[68] If there is a series of basing points taking the same rates, the term "basing line" is commonly used. Transcontinental rates long afforded a good illustration of the basing-line system. Transcontinental rates from the East were the same to various Pacific Coast terminals and were made low to meet water competition. Then the rates to points inland from the Pacific Coast were the rates to the Pacific Coast terminals plus local rates back from the Coast. Thus the Pacific Coast became a basing line. Enforcement of the Long-and-Short-Haul Clause of the Interstate Commerce Act eventually forced an abandonment of this system of constructing transcontinental rates. The basing-point and the basing-line system had the peculiar result that as one approached a basing point, the rates decreased as distance increased.

GROUP-RATE SYSTEMS

The characteristic feature of group-rate systems is the grouping of points of origin or destination, or both. All points in a group take the same rate. This means that differences in distance are ignored to some extent. Usually, however, more distant groups take higher rates than less distant groups.

Group-rate systems are numerous, but only a few illustrations need be given. On transcontinental traffic, large rate groups are found. Figure 8–12 shows the grouping of the eastern and central part of the country on traffic to and from the Pacific Coast. The large size of some of the groups will be noted from the map. Thus the rates from a Pacific Coast point are the same to any point in New England, New Jersey, Delaware, Maryland, and most of New York, Pennsylvania, Virginia, and West Virginia. On certain commodities eastbound the whole area east of the Missouri River, in some instances east of Denver, in included within a single destination group. On such traffic the rates from the Pacific Coast to all points in an area over 2,000 miles wide are the same. These rates represent an extreme development of the group-rate principle. Such rates are frequently called "blanket rates."

Figure 8–13 shows destination groups on lumber from an origin group known as the North Pacific Coast Group. The numbers shown on the map are the rates in cents per hundred pounds which at one time applied to all points within the group. In the areas marked G, however, the rates are not on a group basis but are graded according to distance.

Coal rates lend themselves to the group-rate system, since coal-producing points are found clustered together in certain areas where coal is found. Figure 8–14 shows the rate adjustment on coal from producing points in Ohio, Pennsylvania, West Virginia, Virginia, and eastern Ken-

---

[68] For a further description of this rate system see Ripley, op. cit., pp. 238–43, 380–92; see also Jones, op. cit., pp. 157–63.

FIGURE 8–12.   Transcontinental Freight-Rate Groups

FIGURE 8–13.   Lumber Rates from North Pacific Coast

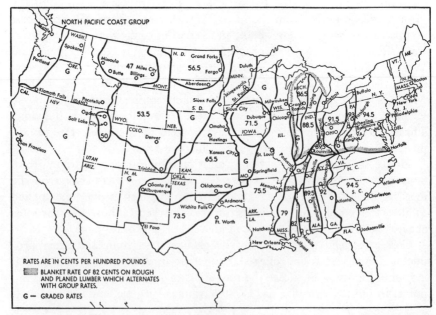

From Board of Investigation and Research, *Report on Interterritorial Freight Rates,* facing p. 210.

FIGURE 8–14.   Map Showing Coal Rates from Ohio, Inner Crescent, and Outer Crescent Groups to Toledo, Ohio

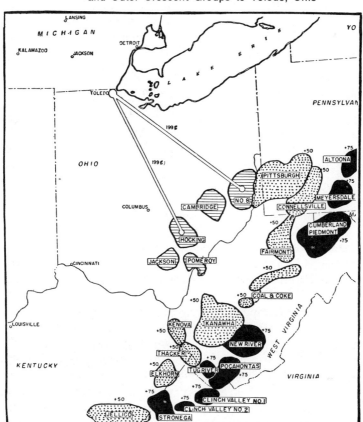

tucky to Toledo, Ohio. The large number of origin groups will be noted.

There are several reasons for the prevalence of group-rate systems. To some extent they are the outgrowth of a desire to simplify traiffs. The grouping of points of origin and destination reduces the number of specific rates that have to be published.

In many cases, group rates are the result of competitive forces. Market competition in particular is responsible for the establishment of many group rates, since group rates put all points in a group upon an equality in the matter of freight rates.

The prohibition of higher charges for shorter than for longer hauls over the same line or route often leads to group rates. This is because a low through rate compelled by competition becomes the maximum that can be lawfully charged at intermediate points. This can be illustrated by the diagram in Figure 8–11. If the law prohibits a higher charge for a shorter than for a longer haul, and the rate at F must be kept low, the railroad will "blanket back" the low rate, and a rate group is formed—including all points between C and F in the diagram. The railroad may, however, choose to give up the competitive traffic, in which case it will maintain a higher rate at the competitive point and thereby avoid a reduction of rates at intermediate points.

BASE-AND-RELATED-RATE ADJUSTMENTS

Many rate systems are characterized by a base rate or rates, with the rates between other points related to the base rate in a definite manner. The most common arrangement is to make the rates fixed differentials over or under the base rate. These adjustments are commonly known as "differential rate systems." Sometimes, however, rates are related to the base rate on a percentage basis.

Prior to the revision of class rates in Eastern Territory that was required by the Commission in 1930, the class rates between Central Freight Association Territory and eastern points were all related to the rates between Chicago and New York.[69] In this instance the rates from any point in Central Freight Association Territory to New York were a percentage of the Chicago–New York rate. The percent of the Chicago–New York rate applying from important points in C.F.A. Territory was calculated according to a formula which gave effect to differences in distance. Other points in surrounding areas would be given the same rate. The result was a series of "percentage groups," of greatly varying size and shape, with every point taking rates that were related to the Chicago–New York rate. Westbound rates were related to the New York–Chicago rate in a similar manner. The map in Figure 8–15 shows these percentage groups as they once existed. This rate structure was abandoned with the revision of the class rates in Eastern Territory after 1930, but some features of the adjustment still characterize some commodity-rate structures in the area.

The use of base rates with fixed differentials is illustrated by the coal-rate adjustment shown in Figure 8–14. In 1942 the rates from the Ohio groups to Toledo were $1.99 per ton. From the so-called "Inner Crescent" groups, the rates were 50 cents per ton higher; and from the "Outer Crescent" groups (shown in black on the map), the rates were 75 cents per ton higher than from the Ohio groups.

Rates on coal from producing points in Illinois, Indiana, and western Kentucky to Chicago illustrate the same sort of adjustment. This adjustment is shown in Figure 8–16. The rates from the various origin groups shown are differentials over or under the rate from the Southern Illinois group to Chicago, which was $2.05 per ton in 1942.

The Atlantic port differentials provide another example of a differen-

---

[69] See n. 16, supra, for references on this rate structure.

tial rate adjustment. Before the revision of class rates in Eastern Territory which followed the Eastern Class-Rate Investigation, rates between Central Freight Association Territory and the Atlantic ports were differentially related to the New York rates. Domestic rates to Philadelphia were 2 cents less than to New York on all six regular classes. To Baltimore they were 3 cents under the New York rate. To Boston the rates on the six regular classes were respectively 7, 6, 5, 4, 3, and 2 cents above New York.

FIGURE 8–15. "Percentage Groups" in the Old Trunk-Line Rate Structure

Adapted from map shown in *Michigan Percentage Cases,* 47 ICC 409 (1917).

Westbound, Boston took the same rates as New York. Philadelphia rates were 6 cents under New York on the first two classes of freight and 2 cents under New York on the other classes. The Baltimore differential under New York was 8 cents on the first two classes and 3 cents on the other classes.[70] These differential relationships were destroyed on domestic shipments as a result of the Eastern Class-Rate Investigation. Until recently a system of differentials still existed, however, on export and import traffic moving through the Atlantic ports.

[70] The port differentials are shown in *Eastern Class-Rate Investigation,* 164 ICC 314, 324, 329–30 (1930).

FIGURE 8–16. Coal Rates—Illinois, Indiana and Western Kentucky to Chicago

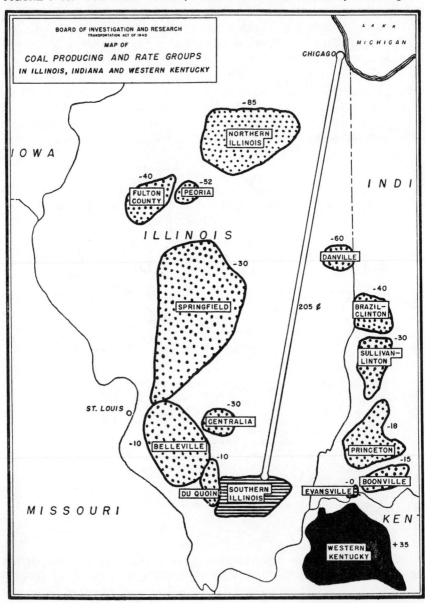

Efforts of the railroads serving the northern ports to do away with the differentials and to equalize the rates on the Baltimore level were blocked by the Interstate Commerce Commission,[71] but this decision was set aside

[71] *Equalization of Rates at North Atlantic Ports*, 311 ICC 689 (1960), 314 ICC 185 (1961).

by the courts.[72] Equality of export rates at North Atlantic ports, however, has not been maintained on all commodities. On paper and paper
articles the Baltimore & Ohio was permitted to make lower rates to
Baltimore than applied at the other ports.[73]

THE STRUCTURE OF PASSENGER FARES

Railroad passenger fares in the United States have been constructed
on the mileage principle. From 1920 to 1933, basic fares of 3.6 cents per
mile were maintained generally throughout the country. The depression
of the 30s led to a considerable reduction in fares and the abandonment
of nationwide uniformity.

Since passenger fares are on the basis of a uniform rate per mile, there
is no recognition of the tapering principle which characterizes the railroad freight-rate structure. In other words, passenger fares are usually
the same per mile for long as for short distances, although in Eastern
Territory round-trip fares were established in 1939 which were at a
lower rate per mile for the longer distances.[74]

American practice has not gone as far as that of some European
countries in setting up several classes of passenger service at different
fares. In the United States there have been essentially two classes of
service—first class, formerly known as Pullman, and coach—with the
higher fares for first class. It should be pointed out that the first-class
passenger must ordinarily purchase a seat, berth, roomette or other
space, in addition to his rail transportation. The railroads also provide a
special "commutation" service at very low fares to accommodate the
daily "commuter" travel into and out of large cities. In addition to these
various classes of service, the railroads generally offer reduced round-
trip fares and still lower fares, at times, for vacation trips, holiday travel,
or special events. Amtrak, which took over operation of most intercity
rail passenger service, on May 1, 1971, initially adopted the preexisting
passenger-fare structure of the railroads.

SELECTED REFERENCES

For material on freight classification and rate making see Eliot Jones, *Principles of Railway Transportation* (New York: Macmillan, 1924), chaps.
viii–ix; S. L. Miller, *Inland Transportation* (New York: McGraw-Hill, 1933),
chaps. xx–xxi; H. B. Vanderblue and Kenneth F. Burgess, *Railroads: Rates,
Service, Management* (New York: Macmillan, 1923), chaps. ix–xii; Stuart
Daggett, *Principles of Inland Transportation* (4th ed.; New York: Harper,

---

[72] *Boston & Maine Railroad v. United States*, 202 F. Supp. 830 (1962), affirmed
by an equally divided court in 373 U.S. 372 (1963).

[73] *Paper, Central Territory to North Atlantic Ports*, 329 ICC 281 (1966).

[74] *Eastern Passenger Fares in Coaches*, 237 ICC 271, 272 (1940).

1955), chaps. xvii–xx; Kent T. Healy, *The Economics of Transportation in America* (New York: Ronald Press, 1940), chaps. xii–xiii; Truman C. Bigham, *Transportation: Principles and Problems* (New York: Harper, 1946), chap. xii; Marvin L. Fair and Ernest W. Williams, Jr., *Economics of Transportation* (rev. ed.; New York: Harper, 1959), chaps. xviii–xx; Russell E. Westmeyer, *Economics of Transportation* (New York: Prentice-Hall, 1952), chaps. xi–xiii; Roy J. Sampson and Martin T. Farris, *Domestic Transportation: Practice, Theory and Policy* (Boston: Houghton Mifflin, 1966), chaps. x–xi.

Class-rate structures applying in each of the major rate territories and interterritorially before the decision in the Class Rate Investigation of 1939 are described in Board of Investigation and Research, *Report on Interterritorial Freight Rates*, 78th Cong., 1st Sess., House Doc. No. 303 (1943), chaps. ii and vi. For descriptions of some commodity-rate structures see *ibid.*, chaps. iv and vii. Class-rate structures are also described in *Class Rate Investigation, 1939*, 262 ICC 447 (1945).

The history of freight classification in the United States and of efforts to attain a uniform classification are told in *Suspension of Western Classification No. 51*, 25 ICC 442 (1912), and in *Class Rate Investigation, 1939*, 262 ICC 447 (1945).

There is an excellent study of transcontinental rate structures in Stuart Daggett and John P. Carter, *The Structure of Transcontinental Railroad Rates* (Berkeley: University of California Press, 1947). The history of the rate structure in the South is authoritatively given in William H. Joubert, *Southern Freight Rates in Transition* (Gainesville: University of Florida Press, 1949). Another rate-structure study is Truman C. Bigham and Merrill J. Roberts, *Citrus Fruit Rates* (Gainesville: University of Florida Press, 1950).

Chapter 9

BEGINNING OF RAILROAD REGULATION

By 1870 a very distinct change in the attitude of the public toward the railroads had occurred. In an earlier chapter we noted the liberality, not to say lavishness, with which financial assistance and other forms of aid were granted to railroad companies. Before railroads were completed, the interests of the railroads and the public were one. The public wanted railroads; the companies wanted to build them. But once the roads were constructed, a conflict of interest appeared. The public wanted the lowest possible rates; the railroads wanted to earn as large profits as possible. This conflict of interest brought about a fundamental change in public attitude toward the railroads. The change followed closely the completion of railroad building in the different parts of the country, and it would have occurred even in the absence of unjustifiable railroad practices.

CHARTER REGULATION

There had been some attempt to regulate railroads prior to the 70s. Early railway charters, which were grants of authority under which the railroad corporations were organized, commonly contained provisions designed to protect the public interest. Sometimes the charters contained schedules of maximum charges. Other charters contained provisions reserving to the state the right to reduce rates when earnings exceeded a certain amount, say 10 percent on the investment. A few charters contained restrictions to prevent discrimination, but usually this problem was not foreseen by the legislatures.

Charter regulations accomplished little to prevent railway abuses. Maximum rates prescribed by charters were generally higher than the railroads found it expedient to charge, so they did not always act as a check on rates even when these were excessive. The prescription of maximum rates, furthermore, did not touch the problem of discrimination at all, since most unjust discriminations resulted from low rates to favored shippers and not from excessive rates to those discriminated against. Attempts to limit earnings often resulted in misrepresentation of accounts in an effort to conceal earnings, and also in stock watering. Regulation through charter provisions was unsatisfactory for other reasons. When charters were granted by special acts of the legislatures, their provisions differed widely. As charters were granted by all the states, any attempt to secure uniformity in railway charters seemed hopeless. Another difficulty arose from the fact that a charter is a contract and cannot be changed without the consent of both parties unless the power to alter it is specifically reserved by the state.[1]

EARLY COMMISSIONS

In some states, railroad commissions were created very early. In the latter part of the 1830s and in the 1840s, commissions were set up in a number of the New England states. The early commissions exerted very little control, and they had no power over rates. The commissions appraised the value of property taken by the railroads under the power of eminent domain. They had charge of the enforcement of laws designed to prevent railroad accidents. They were authorized to investigate the affairs of railroad corporations in order to determine whether charters were being violated, and they had power to require accounting and statistical information from railroad companies.

THE GRANGER MOVEMENT

Positive control over railroad rates was a product of the Granger movement of the early 70s. To be sure, a strong antirailroad feeling had developed in other parts of the country at an earlier date,[2] but strong measures to deal with the problem had not resulted. During the 70s, however, a number of western states, particularly Illinois, Iowa, Wisconsin, and Minnesota, enacted laws subjecting railroads to regulation.

The Granger movement was an agrarian revolt, of which an antirailroad sentiment was but one manifestation. The movement derived its name from the Grange, an organization of farmers which had much to do with giving force to the movement. The Grange did not officially sponsor railroad legislation and attempted to discourage the discussion of the problem in its meetings, but the railroad legislation which resulted has come to be known as the "Granger legislation."

Fundamentally the Granger movement was brought about by a decline in the prices of agricultural products, which caused hardship and distress among the agricultural population. The agricultural depression, in turn, had many causes. Among these were the inflation of the cur-

---

[1] *Dartmouth College Case*, 4 Wheaton 518 (1819).

[2] See Lee Benson, *Merchants, Farmers, and Railroads: Railroad Regulation and New York Politics, 1850–1887* (Cambridge: Harvard University Press, 1955), chap. i, for this development in New York.

rency during the Civil War and the rapid settlement of the West, aided in large measure by the land policy of the government and by rapid railroad construction. Improved methods of agriculture and a decline in the foreign demand for grain were contributing factors. The farmers felt that in some way the railroads were responsible for these difficulties; but even when they knew this was not true, it was natural to turn to the railroads for lower rates as a means of relief.

Grievances against the Railroads

The complaints of the farmers against railroad practices were numerous. For one thing, they believed that freight rates were too high. The decline in the prices of agricultural products had made the burden of existing rates harder to bear. It is impossible, at this time, to pass judgment on this claim, but the farmers were convinced that rates could be reduced.

The farmers were also angered by the gross discriminations practiced by the railroads, particularly the discrimination against noncompeting points. At competitive points, rates were reduced to very low levels, while higher rates were maintained at other places. Indeed the farmers believed that the rates were increased at noncompetitive points to offset the reductions at competitive points. Not versed in the distinction between fixed and variable railroad expenses, they reasoned that if the rates at competing points were profitable, then all traffic could be carried at equally low rates. This reasoning was not sound, but it must be admitted that much of the discrimination was unjustifiable and did work a hardship upon the noncompetitive points.

Personal discrimination also came in for its share of criticism. The railroad companies sometimes gave a practical monopoly to certain individuals or corporations in supplying wood or coal to particular towns and cities. The monopoly was enforced through preferential rates to the favored dealers and higher rates to the independent dealers. In the same way the buying of grain was monopolized by preferential rates to favored shippers. These monopolies could not have long endured if all shippers had been treated equally by the common carriers.

A proper understanding of the Granger sentiment is not to be obtained from a mere recital of the principal charges made against the railroads. Public resentment at railroad practices was not wholly rational. There was a strong emotional element in it. It must be remembered that the farmers had been generous to the railroad companies and had lavished subsidies upon them. In many instances the farmers had personally subscribed to the stock of railroad companies and had often mortgaged their farms to do so. They had been led to expect generous dividends on railroad stock and better prices for farm products. The railroad stock often turned out to be worthless, and the higher prices sometimes failed to materialize. The farmers, as taxpayers, also had to pay off the bonds voted to provide subsidies for railroads, which were now showing their ingratitude by injurious discriminations.

The people felt that they had been tricked by unscrupulous promoters—as was the fact in many cases—and they also felt that they deserved better treatment from the companies which they had so generously aided. In addition to all this, the attitude of the companies toward the public was sometimes most insolent. Travelers and shippers were treated discourteously. Shippers hesitated to demand their legal rights for fear of greater injuries in retaliation. The control of the railroads by eastern capitalists aggravated the situation, for the farmers felt that they were the victims of "absentee ownership." The railroads were pictured as a giant octopus sucking the lifeblood of the people, and railway managers were likened to the robber barons of the Middle Ages. Hadley, referring to the temper of the western people at this time, said they were "dangerously near the point where revolutions begin."[3]

THE GRANGER LAWS

With feeling running high against the railroads, the legislatures of the western states were in no mood to consider carefully and impartially the type of control which it was best to impose upon the railroad companies. It is not strange, therefore, that much of the railroad legislation was unwise and extreme and that much of it had to be modified subsequently. The remarkable thing was that these laws, modified in detail, were sound enough to become the pattern for later legislation, both state and federal.

The railroad laws enacted between 1871 and 1874 by Illinois, Iowa, Wisconsin, and Minnesota are interesting because of the similarities and contrasts to present regulatory laws. For this reason, and for the lessons which they teach, it may be well to summarize their characteristic features.

Provisions of the Granger Laws

Some of the laws prescribed schedules of maximum charges. This was true of the Iowa act of 1874, which prescribed rates for all distances up to 376 miles on various classes of freight and on specific commodities. The Wisconsin law of 1873, known as the Potter law, likewise prescribed scales of maximum rates.

There are many objections to the fixing of maximum rates by statute. The legislature does not have the information necessary to determine what a reasonable scale of rates should be. The complexities of rate

---

[3] A. T. Hadley, *Railroad Transportation* (New York: Putnam, 1885), p. 134.

making are so great, furthermore, that it is practically impossible for a legislative body, changing in personnel, inexperienced with railroad affairs, and concerned with many other things, to acquaint itself with the details of the problem of fixing reasonable rates on thousands of commodities. Political considerations, furthermore, are more likely to become involved in rate making if rates are fixed by legislatures rather than by commissions, which are to some extent protected from political pressures. Rates prescribed by legislative bodies tend also to become rigid and inflexible. Changed conditions require changed rates, but a legislature is not in a position to make the changes with reasonable dispatch. Still another objection to statutory rates is the injustice resulting from any attempt at uniformity. Operating and traffic conditions vary so greatly that uniformity in the rate level may work unfairly. An attempt to meet this objection was made in the Granger acts by classifying railroads and prescribing different scales of rates for each class. But this solution is not satisfactory. Classification of railroads is difficult, and a single railroad may have branches and portions of its lines on which higher or lower rates are justified than would be justified on other portions. The attempt to fix maximum rates by statute has been abandoned as a feature of our regulatory system.

Some of the Granger laws imposed the duty of prescribing a maximum schedule of rates upon the railroad commissions which were set up to administer the laws. This was done, for instance, by the Illinois law of 1873 and the Minnesota law of 1874. The fixing of maximum rates by commissions is an improvement over the practice of direct legislative rate fixing. A commission can act in a semijudicial capacity and is better able to determine what would be reasonable charges. Unlike a legislative body it may be expected to acquire some knowledge of the details and complexities of rate making. It may, in fact, become an expert rate-making body. Also there is greater flexibility in commission-made rates, for a commission can more easily change rates when occasion demands it. Modern regulatory practice, however, favors a system of regulation which prescribes maximum rates only when rates initiated by the railroads have been found unreasonable or otherwise unlawful. This leaves the initiative in rate making with the carriers and brings under more careful scrutiny the rates against which complaints have been made while raising no issues over rates which are not the subject of complaint.

A third feature of the Granger legislation is found in the "pro rata" clauses which they contained. The pro rata clauses provided that rates should not be higher for shorter than for longer hauls. They were the forerunners of modern "long-and-short-haul" clauses, but more drastic. The inclusiveness of the prohibitions contained in early pro rata clauses is illustrated by a provision in the Illinois law of 1871: "No railroad corporation . . . shall charge or collect for the transportation of goods, merchandise or property on its said road, for any distance, the same nor any larger or greater amount as toll or compensation than is at the same time charged or collected for the transportation of similar quantities of the same class of goods, merchandise or property over a greater distance upon the same road."[4] A provision like this does not permit a railroad to maintain a higher scale of rates on branch lines than on main lines, nor does it permit group rates. It will be shown in a subsequent chapter[5] that under some conditions it is not even objectionable to charge more for a shorter than for a longer haul over the same line and in the same direction, but early pro rata clauses made no allowance for such possibilities. Not all the Granger laws, however, were as drastic as the early Illinois law in this respect.

Another feature of the Granger legislation was the attempt to preserve competition by forbidding the combination of competing lines. The policy of attempting to enforce competition between railroads is now considered to have been a mistaken policy, although railroad monopoly could hardly have been accepted until effective means of control had been established. Attempts to preserve competition between railroads have not entirely disappeared from our legislation, but the policy has been greatly modified.

Finally, the Granger laws contained provisions which prohibited railroads from granting free passes to public officials. The railroads had courted the favor of legislators, judges, and other public officials by granting free passes. At first the practice was not considered improper by the public; but it soon proved to be a form of petty bribery which prevented public officials from acting in the interest of the people when the public interest conflicted with that of the railroad companies. It was well that the Granger acts prohibited the practice.

Repeal of the Granger Laws

The Granger laws did not remain on the statute books for very long, except in Illinois. Minnesota substituted a weak and innocuous system of regulation in 1875. Iowa substituted a commission of the advisory type in 1878. The advisory commissions had no power over rates. They were common in the eastern states, and some of them, particularly the Massachusetts commission, were very successful. In Wisconsin the Potter law was repealed in 1876, and an advisory type of commission was set up.

The repeal of the Granger laws was brought about by a number of causes. The Panic of 1873 was perhaps the most important factor in the situation. It brought a halt to railroad building and lent color to the claim that the Granger legislation was frightening capital from railroad enterprises. A second cause for the change in public attitude was the

---

[4] S. J. Buck, *The Granger Movement* (Cambridge: Harvard University Press, 1913), p. 133.

[5] Chapter 21.

vigorous campaign waged by the railroads to convince the people that the Granger legislation was a mistake and was harmful to the business and agricultural interests of the states. The third cause of the repeal of the Granger laws was the unsoundness of some of their provisions. We have shown that some of these were extreme and would not work well in practice. The laws were crude, as there had been little experience upon which to rely in enacting regulatory legislation. It must be remembered also that the laws were passed in the heat of bitter warfare between the agrarians and the railroads and hence in an atmosphere far from conducive to a careful working-out of the problem. The laws should have been modified and the extreme and objectionable features removed. But the pendulum was swinging the other way, and the legislatures went further in the direction of relaxing control than was necessary or desirable. A few years later, in the 80s and 90s, a movement toward more effective control set in, and not only the Granger states, but practically all the states, found it necessary to set up commissions with power to control rates. And in 1887 the Interstate Commerce Commission was created, although its power to fix rates was not established until 1906.

THE GRANGER CASES

The Granger legislation resulted in the Granger cases—decisions of the United States Supreme Court, in 1877, upholding the validity of railroad regulation. These decisions provide the legal basis for our present regulatory system. There were six cases in the series, the most important of which, from the point of view of the discussion of principles, was *Munn* v. *Illinois*.[6] This case did not involve railroads at all, but related to the regulation of warehouses used for the storage of grain. The other five cases concerned the regulation of railroads.

The main argument of the carriers was that regulation was repugnant to the Fourteenth Amendment of the Constitution of the United States, which provides that no state shall "deprive any person of . . . property, without due process of law." A good argument on this score could be made. To limit the charges which one may make for the use of his property will certainly, if the charge does not cover cost, deprive the property of any value. Even if the charge covers the cost of the service rendered, any reduction of charges that reduces earnings will diminish the value of the income-bearing property, for value is dependent upon earnings. The Court, in effect, conceded the validity of this argument so far as ordinary businesses were concerned, but held that it did not apply to a special category of businesses described as "affected with a public interest." The Court pointed out that historically certain classes of busi-

---

[6] 94 U.S. 113.

nesses had been commonly regulated both in England and in this country. "[It] has been customary in England from time immemorial, and in this country from its first colonization, to regulate ferries, common carriers, hackmen, bakers, millers, wharfingers, innkeepers, etc., and in so doing to fix a maximum of charge to be made for services rendered, accommodations furnished, and articles sold."[7] The appeal to the practice of England, or of the American colonies, or of the several states of the United States might not appear to be wholly convincing, since neither England, nor the American colonies, nor the states in the early years of the Republic were bothered by a "Fourteenth Amendment." The Fourteenth Amendment was one of the Civil War amendments adopted in 1868. But the Court circumvented this difficulty by saying: "While this provision of the amendment is new in the Constitution of the United States, as a limitation upon the powers of the States, it is old as a principle of civilized government. It is found in Magna Charta, and in substance if not in form, in nearly or quite all the constitutions that have been from time to time adopted by the several States of the Union."[8] In other words, the principle of the Fourteenth Amendment is old, and it has not in the past prevented regulation of certain types of businesses. If such regulation has not been considered repugnant to the ancient principle, it is not repugnant to the Fourteenth Amendment.

For the distinction between businesses affected with a public interest and ordinary businesses, the Court went back to a discussion by Lord Hale in his treatise *De portibus maris*, written more than two hundred years before, wherein it was pointed out that when private property is "affected with a public interest, it ceases to be *juris privati* only" and its owner must submit to be controlled by the public for the common good. This distinction, which was adopted by the Court, became of great importance in our economic life. Regulation of such businesses as were considered "affected with a public interest" was constitutional; regulation of other businesses was unconstitutional.

The Court, in the Granger cases, made no attempt to define precisely what causes one business to be affected with the public interest while another is not so affected. The language is extremely vague. Property becomes "clothed with a public interest," said the Court, "when used in a manner to make it of public consequence, and affect the community at large."[9]

Mr. Justice Field, in a dissenting opinion, objected to the vague distinction between property affected with a public interest and other property. It would seem, he argued, "that the court holds that property loses something of its private character when employed in such a way as to be

---

[7] Ibid., p. 125.

[8] Ibid., pp. 123–24.

[9] Ibid., p. 126.

generally useful."[10] He went on to say: "The public is interested in the manufacture of cotton, woolen, and silken fabrics, in the construction of machinery, in the printing and publication of books and periodicals, and in the making of utensils of every variety, useful and ornamental; indeed, there is hardly an enterprise or business engaging the attention and labor of any considerable portion of the community, in which the public has not an interest in the sense in which that term is used by the court in its opinion."[11]

Because of the vagueness of the distinction between businesses affected with a public interest and those not so affected, the question of the constitutionality of regulatory legislation has frequently come before the courts. There is a line of decisions in which the Supreme Court of the United States was called upon to determine whether certain businesses were affected with a public interest or not.[12] The courts were loath to extend greatly the list of businesses which might be regulated.[13] No definite rule for distinguishing such businesses was developed, but in many cases the presence or absence of a monopoly element or an element of consumer disadvantage was an important consideration. In *Munn* v. *Illinois* the monopoly character of the warehouse business was pointed out as important in classifying it as a business affected with a public interest. In so far as railroads are concerned, the Court did not mention the monopoly element but merely pointed out that common carriers had been regulated in England as early as 1691 and that railroads, being common carriers, might also be regulated. From an economic point of view, however, it was the monopoly character of railways—or the failure of competition to act as a regulator of rates—coupled with the public importance of the industry, that justified public control.

It should be noted in passing that the division of businesses into two classes—those affected with a public interest, which might constitutionally be regulated, and those not so affected, which might not be regulated—was abandoned by the Supreme Court of the United States in 1934. In *Nebbia* v. *New York* the Supreme Court upheld the New York Milk Control Law of 1933, which provided for the fixing of maximum and minimum retail prices for milk, although the Court said that the industry was not a "public utility."[14] The Court also said: "It is clear that

[10] Ibid., p. 139.

[11] Ibid., p. 141.

[12] For cases in which regulation was upheld see *Budd* v. *New York*, 143 U.S. 517 (1892); *Brass* v. *North Dakota*, 153 U.S. 391 (1894); *German Alliance Insurance Co.* v. *Lewis*, 233 U.S. 389 (1914); *Block* v. *Hirsh*, 256 U.S. 135 (1921).

[13] In the following cases regulation was found invalid: *Wolff Packing Co.* v. *Court of Industrial Relations*, 262 U.S. 522 (1923); *Tyson* v. *Banton*, 273 U.S. 418 (1927); *Ribnik* v. *McBride*, 277 U.S. 350 (1928); *Williams* v. *Standard Oil Co.*, 278 U.S. 235 (1929); *New State Ice Co.* v. *Liebmann*, 285 U.S. 262 (1932).

[14] 291 U.S. 502 (1934). For comments on this decision see Irving B. Goldsmith and Gordon W. Winks, "Price Fixing: From Nebbia to Guffey," 31 *Illinois Law Re-*

there is no closed class or category of businesses affected with a public interest."[15] The decision broke down the traditional classification of businesses into those which could be regulated and those which could not. If there remained any lingering doubt about the effect of this decision, it was dispelled by a later decision, in which the Court specifically said that the former test of the validity of price-fixing legislation—namely, whether or not the industry was "affected with a public interest"—had been "discarded" in the Nebbia case.[16] Long before the Nebbia case was decided, however, the distinction between businesses affected with a public interest and purely private businesses had been invoked in litigation over the constitutionality of regulation of pipelines[17] and of contract carriers by motor vehicle.[18]

In the Granger cases, two justices of the Supreme Court vigorously dissented from the view that railroads could be subjected to regulation. "The principle upon which the opinion of the majority proceeds is, in my judgment," wrote Justice Field, "subversive of the rights of private property, heretofore believed to be protected by constitutional guaranties against legislative interference."[19] "The legislation in question," he added, "is nothing less than a bold assertion of absolute power by the State to control at its discretion the property and business of the citizen and fix the compensation he shall receive."[20] And elsewhere he said: "I deny the power of any legislature under our government to fix the price which one shall receive for his property of any kind."[21]

There was some surprise at the position taken by the Supreme Court in the Granger cases, since it was commonly believed that the Court would invalidate the legislation. If the Court had held that regulation was unconstitutional, the states, and quite likely the federal government also, would have been without power to deal with the railroad abuses which had arisen, as long as the railroads were privately owned. The decision

---

view 179 (1936); R. L. Hale, "The Constitution and the Price System: Some Reflections on Nebbia v. New York," 34 *Columbia Law Review* 401 (1934); Irwin S. Rosenbaum, "Ruling on Milk Price Control," 14 *Public Utilities Fortnightly* 795 (1934); R. W. Harbeson, "The Public Interest Concept in Law and in Economics," 37 *Michigan Law Review* 181 (1938).

[15] 291 U.S. 502, 536 (1934).

[16] *Olsen v. Nebraska*, 313 U.S. 236, 245 (1941). It should not be inferred that the courts will refuse to set aside regulatory laws. In the Nebbia case the Supreme Court said: ". . . the guaranty of due process, as has often been held, demands only that the law shall not be unreasonable, arbitrary or capricious, and that the means selected shall have a real and substantial relation to the object sought to be attained" (291 U.S. 502, 525). Thus there is opportunity for the courts to invalidate regulatory laws that they consider "unreasonable," "arbitrary," "capricious," or not having a "real and substantial relation to the object sought to be attained."

[17] See Chapter 26.

[18] See Chapter 29.

[19] 94 U.S. 113, 136.

[20] Ibid., p. 148.

[21] Ibid., p. 152.

in the Granger cases was a distinct victory for the people. On some points the position taken by the Court in the Granger cases was extreme and was later modified, as will be explained shortly, but from the right of the public to regulate there has been no retreat.

SELECTED REFERENCES

Charter regulation and subsequent general laws relating to railways are described in B. H. Meyer, *Railway Legislation in the United States* (New York: Macmillan, 1903).

The Granger movement and the railroad legislation which accompanied it are described in Eliot Jones, *Principles of Railroad Transportation* (New York: Macmillan, 1924), chap. x; and in Stuart Daggett, *Principles of Inland Transportation* (4th ed.; New York: Harper, 1955), chap. xxviii. The most thorough and scholarly study of the movement is S. J. Buck, *The Granger Movement* (Cambridge: Harvard University Press, 1913). A more popular account by the same author is *The Agrarian Crusade* (New Haven: Yale University Press, 1920), particularly chap. iv. An interesting popular account of the Granger legislation, written shortly after the movement had subsided, is C. F. Adams, "The Granger Movement," 120 *North American Review* 394 (1875). For a study of the movement in particular states see A. E. Paine, "The Granger Movement in Illinois," 1 *University of Illinois Studies* 335 (1905); J. H. Gordon, "Illinois Railway Legislation and Commission Control since 1870," 1 *University of Illinois Studies* 213 (1904); R. S. Saby, "Railroad Legislation in Minnesota, 1849–1873," 15 *Collections of the Minnesota Historical Society* 1 (1915). The excellent article by Charles R. Dietrick, "The Effects of the Granger Acts," 11 *Journal of Political Economy* 237 (1903), should be read before any final judgment is made concerning the effects of the legislation. The Granger decisions and the vigorous dissenting opinions are reported in 94 U.S. 113, pp. 113–87. A very critical treatment of the Supreme Court's reasoning in the Granger cases is Charles Fairman, "The So-Called Granger Cases, Lord Hale, and Justice Bradley," 5 *Stanford Law Review* 587 (1953).

An excellent account of the movement to regulate railroads in New York is Lee Benson, *Merchants, Farmers, and Railroads: Railroad Regulation and New York Politics, 1850–1887* (Cambridge: Harvard University Press, 1955).

FEDERAL LEGISLATION

1887–1920

The Granger movement, which brought about state regulation of railroads, was not without its repercussions in the halls of Congress. Although there was considerable agitation for federal legislation in the 70s and early 80s, Congress did not act for several years.[1]

THE WINDOM REPORT

In 1872 the Senate appointed a special committee to investigate the possibility of securing cheaper transportation between the interior and the seaboard. This committee, known as the Windom Committee, made its report to the Senate in 1874.[2] The defects and abuses of the existing transportation system, according to the Committee, were "insufficient facilities, unfair discriminations, and extortionate charges."[3] Evidently more importance was attached to the first and third of these charges, for the report discussed methods of improving facilities and reducing rates but had little to suggest for the purpose of removing discriminations.

The report reflected the popular view that competition was the best regulator of rates, but the Committee was aware of the fact that competition "invariably ends in combination" and so is not sufficient protection for the public. The Committee concluded that the only means of securing and maintaining reliable and effective competition was through national or state ownership of one or more railroads, "which being unable to enter into combinations, will serve as regulators of other lines."[4] The Committee recommended the construction of one or more such railways to the seaboard and the further development of inland waterways.

---

[1] For a description of early agitation in Congress for legislation see L. H. Haney, *A Congressional History of Railways in the United States, 1850–1887*, Bulletin of the University of Wisconsin, No. 342 (Madison, 1910), chaps. xix, xxi–xxii.

[2] *Transportation Routes to the Seaboard*, 43d Cong., 1st Sess., Senate Rep. No. 307, Part 1.

[3] Ibid., p. 71.

[4] Ibid., p. 242.

THE CULLOM REPORT

No action was taken upon the proposals of the Windom Committee, although the question of regulation was constantly arising before Congress. The House of Representatives passed a bill in 1874 which provided for regulation, and it passed another such bill in 1878. In 1884 the House passed the Reagan bill to regulate interstate commerce, and in the following year the Senate passed the Cullom bill as a substitute. This resulted in a deadlock between the House and the Senate, for the bills were quite different. At this juncture a special committee was appointed to make a thorough investigation of the railroad question. This committee, known as the Cullom Committee, made its report in 1886.[5]

The Cullom report differed from the Windom report of 12 years before in that more emphasis was placed upon the evils of discrimination than upon the level of rates. The Committee favored a system of mild regulation. The Act to Regulate Commerce, passed in 1887, was based largely on the Cullom report. But the divergent views of the House and the Senate had to be compromised before regulatory legislation could be enacted. The House wanted a prohibition of pooling; the Senate did not. The House desired a rigid long-and-short-haul clause; the Senate desired a flexible one. The Senate wished to create a commission to administer the law; the House, wary of administrative boards and executive appointments, wished to leave enforcement to the courts.

THE WABASH CASE

Enactment of a federal law was made necessary by the decision of the United States Supreme Court in *Wabash, St. Louis & Pacific Railway Co.* v. *Illinois* in 1886.[6] It was held in this case that a state could not control rates on interstate traffic. The Wabash, St. Louis & Pacific Railway Company had charged a rate of 15 cents per hundred pounds on certain goods shipped from Peoria, in the state of Illinois, to New York City. At the same time a rate of 25 cents was charged on similar goods from Gilman, also in the state of Illinois, to New York City. Gilman is a point intermediate between Peoria and New York City. The higher rate from Gilman was in violation of a provision in the Illinois statutes prohibiting higher charges for shorter than for longer hauls over the same line. The United States Supreme Court held that this restriction could not apply on the shipments involved since they were interstate shipments, and under the Constitution the power to regulate interstate commerce had been delegated to the federal government. Prior to this decision it had been the common belief that in the absence of federal regulation of interstate com-

---

[5] *Report of the Senate Select Committee on Interstate Commerce*, 49th Cong., 1st Sess., Senate Rep. No. 46.

[6] 118 U.S. 557.

merce, the state could impose its regulations upon the intrastate part of an interstate shipment. In fact, this had been done by the Granger laws, and the United States Supreme Court had found no merit in the contention of the carriers in the Granger cases that such action was an interference with the power of the federal government. The Wabash decision made a sharp distinction between interstate and intrastate commerce. Rates on intrastate commerce were within the control of the state, but rates on interstate commerce were exclusively within the control of the federal government. State restrictions could not apply to interstate commerce, even in the absence of federal regulation. Until the federal government should act, such commerce would remain unregulated. This decision made federal action necessary, since approximately three fourths of the railroad traffic was interstate in character and was beyond the reach of state laws. Whether this decision actually hastened action by Congress is open to question. It may have done so; but at the time of the decision a House and Senate conference committee was attempting to work out a compromise between the Reagan bill, which had passed the House, and the Cullom bill, which had passed the Senate.[7]

THE ACT TO REGULATE COMMERCE, 1887

The Act to Regulate Commerce was approved by President Cleveland on February 4, 1887, and became effective on April 5. Our description of the Act includes minor changes made by amendments in 1889. The Act was made applicable to all common carriers by railroad engaged in interstate or foreign commerce. This meant practically all railroads, since even intrastate railroads engage in interstate commerce, that is, carry traffic moving across state boundaries. The Act did not apply to common carriers wholly by water, although it included common carriers partly by railroad and partly by water when both were used "under a common control, management, or arrangement, for a continuous carriage and shipment." This language is indefinite, and there has been some controversy over the exact scope of the law.[8] It is perhaps needless to say that the provisions of the law applied only to interstate and foreign commerce and not to intrastate commerce.

Reasonableness of Rates

Section 1 of the Act required all rates to be "just and reasonable" and provided that "every unjust and unreasonable charge" was unlawful.

---

[7] Interstate Commerce Commission, Bureau of Statistics, *Interstate Commerce Commission Activities, 1887–1937* (Washington, D.C.: Superintendent of Documents, 1937), pp. 31–32.

[8] See Chapter 32, infra.

This was practically a statutory repetition of the common-law rule that rates of common carriers should be just and reasonable.

Personal Discrimination

Section 2 of the Act prohibited personal discrimination. The language of the section should be carefully noted:

That if any common carrier subject to the provisions of this act shall, directly or indirectly, by any special rate, rebate, drawback, or other device, charge, demand, collect, or receive from any person or persons a greater or less compensation for any service rendered, or to be rendered, in the transportation of passengers or property, subject to the provisions of this act, than it charges, demands, collects or receives from any other person or persons for doing for him or them a like and contemporaneous service in the transportation of a like kind of traffic under substantially similar circumstances and conditions, such common carrier shall be deemed guilty of unjust discrimination, which is hereby prohibited and declared to be unlawful.

Certain exceptions to this blanket prohibition were recognized in later sections of the Act. Thus the carriers were permitted to carry persons or property for the federal, state, or municipal governments, or for charitable purposes, free or at reduced rates, and they were permitted to grant free passes to their employees and to certain other groups of individuals.

Undue Preference or Prejudice

Section 3 proved to be one of the most important provisions of the Act. It prohibited undue preference or prejudice. The section may be called a blanket prohibition of any unjust discrimination, whether between persons, places, or kinds of traffic.[9] The section read as follows:

That it shall be unlawful for any common carrier subject to the provisions of this act to make or give any undue or unreasonable preference or advantage to any particular person, company, firm, corporation, or locality, or any particular description of traffic, in any respect whatsoever, or to subject any particular person, company, firm, corporation, or locality, or any particular description of traffic, to any undue or unreasonable prejudice or disadvantage in any respect whatsoever.[10]

It should be noted that the section did not prohibit all preferential or prejudicial rates but only such as were "undue or unreasonable."

[9] The Commission uses the terms "undue preference and prejudice" to refer to violations of Section 3 to distinguish them from "unjust discrimination," prohibited by Section 2; but both are discriminations in the usual sense of the word.

[10] The scope of Section 3 has been broadened by subsequent amendments. For present language of the section see Chapter 22.

Long-and-Short-Haul Clause

Section 4, the Long-and-Short-Haul Clause, provided:

That it shall be unlawful for any common carrier subject to the provisions of this act to charge or receive any greater compensation in the aggregate for the transportation of passengers or of like kind of property, *under substantially similar circumstances and conditions*,[11] for a shorter than for a longer distance over the same line, in the same direction, the shorter being included within the longer distance.

The Interstate Commerce Commission was authorized to make exception to this prohibition "in special cases."

Pooling

Section 5 of the Act prohibited pooling agreements. This provision represented the popular view that enforced competition was the best protection against unreasonable rates. There was considerable opposition to this provision on the part of those who saw that pooling was necessary to prevent ruinous competition. But the people, fearing railroad monopoly, were unwilling to permit it.

Publication of Rates

Section 6 of the Act required the publication of rates and fares and strict adherence to the rates so published. It also provided that no advance in rates and fares should be made except after ten days' public notice and that no reductions should be made without three days' notice.[12]

The Interstate Commerce Commission

The Act created the Interstate Commerce Commission, which was to consist of five members, to be appointed by the President with the advice and consent of the Senate. The principal powers and duties of the Commission may be described as follows:

1. The Commission was to hear complaints of alleged violations of the Act and to investigate the matters in dispute. If violations of the Act were found, the Commission was to order the carriers to "cease and desist" from the unlawful practice. The Commission also had the

---

[11] Italics ours.

[12] The three-day notice of reductions in rates was put in the Act by the amendments of 1889. It was designed to protect shippers from quick rate reductions, which were often discriminatory in their effects if some shippers were advised in advance of the coming reductions while other shippers were kept ignorant of the pending charges.

power to determine the amount of damages, if any, suffered by any party as a result of violations of the Act.

2. The Commission was given the general power and duty to inquire into the business of common carriers and to keep itself informed of the manner in which their business was conducted. To accomplish this purpose, the Commission might require the attendance and testimony of witnesses and the production of books, papers, contracts, agreements, and documents relating to any matter under investigation.

3. The Commission might require annual reports of the carriers and prescribe a uniform system of accounts.

4. The Commission was to make annual reports to Congress. These reports were to contain such information as might be of value in connection with the regulation of commerce, together with any recommendations for additional legislation that the Commission considered necessary.

Penalties and Enforcement

The Act carried penalties for violation of its provisions, including imprisonment of parties found guilty of unjust discrimination. It should be recognized, however, that penalties were not to be imposed by the Commission but by the courts. The Commission might take part in the prosecution of cases in the courts which involved alleged violations of the Act.

If a carrier failed to obey an order of the Commission requiring it to cease and desist from some unlawful practice, the Commission might apply to a federal court for an injunction or mandamus to enforce compliance with its order. The court might issue such an injunction or mandamus if satisfied that a lawful order of the Commission was being violated.

Carriers were made liable for the full amount of damages sustained by any person in consequence of violations of the Act. Injured shippers had the right to bring action in court to compel the payment of damages awarded by the Commission.[13]

Results of the Act

The Act to Regulate Commerce had very beneficial results. The railroads, generally speaking, endeavored to conform to its provisions and exhibited a disposition to obey the Commission's orders. Weaknesses in the Act soon appeared, however. This situation became apparent when the Commission began to encounter resistance to its orders. As a result

---

[13] This right was not provided by the original Act, but by the amendments of 1889.

of a number of court decisions in 1896 and 1897 the Commission was shorn of much of its authority and importance. To remedy weaknesses and inadequacies of the Act, additional legislation was needed. We shall now turn to a consideration of the more significant amendatory and supplementary legislation enacted in the period prior to 1920.

THE ELKINS ACT, 1903

By 1903 it had become apparent that the law relating to personal discrimination and rebating needed strengthening. The carriers themselves sponsored legislation of this sort because they were losing revenue as a result of the widespread discrimination and departure from published rates. Yet they were unable to stop the practice without the aid of the government. As a result the Elkins Act, dealing solely with the matter of personal discrimination, was passed by Congress without any opposition whatever. The Elkins Act contained four provisions that require emphasis.

First, the railway corporation itself was made liable for prosecution on account of unlawful discriminations and concessions. The courts had held, under the original Act, that the penalties could be imposed upon the officers, agents, and employees of a railroad but not upon the corporation itself. Commenting upon this situation in 1892, the Commission said: "Under this view of the law the corporation itself, the real beneficiary of illegal practices, goes free, and the employees and agents, acting most generally under orders of their superiors, are made scapegoats for corporate delinquencies."[14]

A second provision of the Elkins Act made it unlawful to receive rebates and concessions or even to solicit them. Under the amendments of 1889, shippers might be prosecuted who obtained concessions by underbilling, false classification, and similar practices, or who induced railroads to discriminate in their favor by the use of such devices. But the law had not imposed penalties for receiving rebates when these were given voluntarily by the carrier. The imposition of penalties upon the receiver of a rebate was intended to relieve shipper pressure for rebates or concessions.

A third and important change brought about by the Elkins Act was that it made any departure from the published rate a misdemeanor. The original Act had made it unlawful for carriers to charge more or less than the rates provided in the published tariffs, but the provision seems to have been largely ignored and practically unenforceable because of its interpretation by the courts. The courts would not impose penalties for departure from the published rate, except possibly by a nominal fine, unless there was actual discrimination. And to prove discrimination, it was necessary to show not merely that a rebate had been paid, but that other

---

[14] Interstate Commerce Commission, *Annual Report, 1892*, p. 39.

shippers, shipping the same kind of traffic at the same time under similar conditions, did not receive similar rebates.[15] This made conviction extremely difficult, if not impossible. The Elkins Act, as was emphatically stated by the Supreme Court in 1963, was "intended to prevent any kind of departure from the published rates."[16]

Fourth, the Elkins Act also made certain changes in the penalties for violation of the law and strengthened enforcement provisions by authorizing the courts to enjoin carriers, upon proof of misconduct, from continuing unlawful discriminations or departures from the published rates.

THE HEPBURN ACT, 1906

The Elkins Act dealt only with personal discrimination, and that in its simpler forms. There was need of additional legislation if railroad regulation was to be effective. This was particularly true because of certain Supreme Court decisions which had greatly weakened the Commission's powers. President Theodore Roosevelt, in 1904 and 1905, had recommended more adequate regulation of carriers and, with characteristic vigor, had sought to convince Congress of the necessity for such legislation. The exposure of a number of railway scandals at this time strengthened the President's cause. The final outcome was the Hepburn Act, passed in 1906 notwithstanding bitter opposition from the railroads. The provisions of the Act may now be summarized.

Extension of the Commission's Jurisdiction

Express companies, sleeping-car companies, and pipelines used for the transportation of property other than water and gas were brought within the scope of the Act. A number of accessorial services furnished by the railroads, such as ventilation, refrigeration, and storage, were also brought under the jurisdiction of the Commission. The term "railroad" was defined to include switches, spurs, tracks, and terminal facilities. Privately owned cars were likewise subjected to the Commission's control. This extension of control was necessary for two reasons: (1) the carriers often levied extra charges for these services, and the Commission had no control over them; and (2) instances of discrimination arose that could not be controlled by the Commission without jurisdiction over these services and facilities.

Enlargement of the Commission

The size of the Commission was increased from five to seven members, and their term of office was lengthened from six to seven years.

---

[15] See Interstate Commerce Commission, *Annual Report, 1901*, p. 8.

[16] *United States* v. *Braverman,* 373 U. S. 405, 406.

Rate-Making Power

Perhaps the most important provision of the Hepburn Act was that which empowered the Commission, upon complaint, to prescribe maximum rates. This power was to be exercised only after existing charges had been found unlawful. The significance of this provision cannot be appreciated without a discussion of certain events which occurred in connection with the original Act. The Act to Regulate Commerce had stated that all rates were to be just and reasonable and that all unjust and unreasonable rates were unlawful, and a commission had been set up whose primary function was to hear complaints of violations of the Act and to require the carriers to cease and desist from unlawful practices. The Commission had therefore assumed that if it found a certain rate unreasonable, it could prescribe what, for the future, would be a maximum reasonable rate on the traffic in question. This practice was followed by the Commission from 1887 to 1897. In 68 out of 135 formal cases that had been decided during this time, the Commission had prescribed maximum reasonable rates, and the authority of the Commission to do so had not been questioned.[17] But in 1896 the United States Supreme Court, in the "Social Circle Case"[18] incidentally remarked that it did not find any provision in the Act that "expressly, or by necessary implication," conferred upon the Commission the power to fix rates. In the "Maximum Freight Rate Case," decided in the following year, the matter was directly brought in issue, and the Court held that the Commission was without power to prescribe rates for the future.[19]

The shipper was not entirely without a remedy from the imposition of unjust and unreasonable charges, even though the Commission could not prescribe a rate for the future. He was entitled to reparation if an unreasonable rate had been charged. But there were several reasons why this remedy was inadequate. If the Commission could not state what would be a maximum reasonable rate for the future, the railroad could change a rate ever so little, and it would take another decision by the Commission to determine the lawfulness of the new rate. Reparation for having paid an unreasonable rate in the past is also unsatisfactory since the burden of the rate is not always borne by the party entitled to recover from the carrier.

Without the power to prescribe a maximum reasonable rate for the future, the Commission was unable to give shippers and the public adequate protection from unreasonable charges. In the words of the Commission, it could condemn the wrong but could not prescribe the

---

[17] Interstate Commerce Commission, *Annual Report, 1897*, p. 11.

[18] *Cincinnati, New Orleans & Texas Pacific Railway Co.* v. *Interstate Commerce Commission*, 162 U.S. 184, 196.

[19] *Interstate Commerce Commission* v. *Cincinnati, New Orleans & Texas Pacific Railway Co.*, 167 U.S. 479.

remedy.[20] The effectiveness of regulation was greatly weakened by the decision in the Maximum Freight Rate Case. The Hepburn Act remedied the matter by a definite grant to the Commission of power to prescribe maximum rates.

It is to be noted that the law does not give the Commission power to prescribe rates in the first instance. Rates cannot be prescribed unless existing rates have been found unreasonable or otherwise unlawful. The power of the Commission, furthermore, was limited to the prescription of maximum rates. Neither the precise rate to be charged nor the minimum rate could be fixed by the Commission.

Through Routes and Joint Rates

The Hepburn Act increased the Commission's power over through routes and joint rates. The Commission was given power to establish through routes when the carriers refused to do so and to prescribe maximum joint rates and the division thereof between participating carriers.

Notification of Rate Changes

Since 1889 ten days' notice had been required before increases in rates could take effect, and three days' notice had been required for reductions in rates. The Hepburn Act provided for thirty days' notice for all changes in rates—increases or decreases. The Commission was authorized, however, to allow changes upon shorter notice if circumstances justified them.

Provisions Relating to Discrimination

The extension of the Commission's jurisdiction over accessorial services and various facilities of transportation enabled it to reach certain forms of personal discrimination that could not be reached under the earlier law. But the Hepburn Act, in addition, contained a number of provisions relating specifically to personal discrimination.

1. An antipass provision prohibited the granting of free passes except to certain specified groups of individuals. The original Act had not specifically prohibited free passes, although the provisions forbidding unjust discrimination and undue preference applied to this practice. The Hepburn Act permitted the issuance of free passes to railroad employees and their families, officials and attorneys of the railroads, employees of sleeping-car and express companies, persons engaged in charitable and religious work, inmates of charitable institutions, and

---

[20] Interstate Commerce Commission, *Annual Report, 1904,* p. 6.

to indigent, destitute, and homeless persons and certain other groups.

2. The Hepburn Act also contained the so-called "Commodities Clause." This was aimed at a particular type of discrimination. It had been found that railroads which owned coal mines or engaged in the production of other commodities in competition with independent producers had a distinct advantage over the independents. By charging high rates, the railroad could undersell and force out its competitors and monopolize the production of the commodity in question. If the railroad paid no rates on the goods it produced, its advantage in maintaining high rates on this particular commodity was obvious. If the railroad-owned industry, operating as a subsidiary of the railroad company, paid transportation charges on the goods it shipped, the advantage to the railroad in maintaining high rates was the same, since the payment of the freight charges was simply taking money from one pocket and transferring it to the other. To prevent this type of discrimination, Congress sought to separate the railroad business from other forms of enterprise. In effect the Commodities Clause prohibited a railroad from engaging in the production of goods commercially, but the result was accomplished indirectly. The law prohibited a carrier engaged in interstate commerce from transporting articles in interstate commerce which it had produced or in which it had an interest. Lumber, however, was excepted from the rule because of the many small railroads owned by lumbering concerns and constructed as adjuncts of lumbering operations. The Commodities Clause did not prevent railroads from producing commodities for their own use. The clause was aimed particularly at the monopolization of anthracite coal production by the railroad companies.[21]

3. The penalties for rebating and similar practices were changed in certain respects; and it was provided, by an amendment to the Elkins Act, that the receiver of a rebate should, in addition to other penalties, forfeit to the United States a sum of money three times the amount received as a rebate for the six years previous.[22]

Accounts and Statistics

The Act of 1887 had empowered the Commission to require annual reports of the carriers and had given it authority to require a uniform system of accounts. There was no adequate machinery for enforcing this section of the law, and the carriers in many instances refused to give the

---

[21] For the history of the Commodities Clause see C. A. Miller, *Legislative and Judicial History of the Commodities Clause* (Washington: American Short-Line Railroad Association, 1946).

[22] In its *Annual Report* for 1936, p. 48, the Commission said that the forfeiture provision had been applied in only one case since its enactment.

Commission the information for which it asked. The Hepburn Act strengthened the hand of the Commission by authorizing it to employ agents or examiners for the purpose of inspecting accounts, and it provided penalties for refusal to submit reports in the form stated, or for misrepresentation of accounts.

Enforcement Provisions

Next to the maximum-rate provision, perhaps the most important provision of the Hepburn Act was the change made in the procedure for the enforcement of the Commission's orders. Orders of the Commission under the original Act were not binding upon the carrier unless supported by a court order compelling obedience. This procedure made it necessary for the Commission to bring action in court to get its orders enforced. The procedure was unsatisfactory for several reasons. In the first place, it caused great delay in the enforcement of the Commission's orders. Several years might elapse before the courts compelled the carriers to observe an order. A second objection to this method of enforcement was that it increased the work of the Commission, since that body had to show affirmatively that its order should be enforced. In the third place, this procedure reduced the Commission to an insignificant place in the system of regulation. The question once decided by the Commission had to be redecided by the courts. The Act of 1887 had provided that the Commission's reports and orders were to be prima-facie evidence of the matters therein stated. Although this did not preclude a reconsideration of the facts by the courts nor prevent the consideration of evidence not presented to the Commission, it was probably the intent of the law that the orders of the Commission should be enforced by the courts unless it was plainly evident that there was some reason for not doing so. It was not intended that a court should constitute itself another commission, as it were, to retry the matter once decided by the Commission. The courts, however, frequently reopened the whole proceeding *de novo.* This situation was made even worse by the practice of allowing new evidence to be introduced before the court. This practice discouraged the presentation of evidence before the Commission. Why should the carriers present their evidence before the Commission if the Commission's order was of so little consequence and if the evidence must all be presented again before a court? In commenting upon this situation, the Commission had said in 1897:

The same case is not tried before the court which is tried before the Commission. The trial before the Commission, therefore, with all its attendant expense and consumption of time, goes practically for nothing. The decisions of the Commission are made upon one state of facts, while the decisions of the courts may be, and usually are, upon an entirely different state of facts. When the court refuses to enforce a decree of the Commission, it apparently decides that the order was wrong, although upon the facts before the Commission it might have been absolutely right. . . . A procedure like the present one tends to bring that body into disrepute and is grossly unfair to it and to the complainants who appear before it.[23]

To remedy this state of affairs, the Hepburn Act made the Commission's orders binding upon the carrier.[24] Orders of the Commission were to take effect in not less than thirty days and might continue in effect for two years.[25] For disobeying an order of the Commission, a fine of $5,000 was provided, and each day of a continuing violation was to constitute a separate offense. This procedure made the Commission's orders binding without court action. Should a railroad refuse to obey an order in spite of the penalty attached, the Commission still had the right to seek court action to enforce compliance with its order. And in such case the Act provided that the injunction or mandamus should issue if the order of the Commission "was properly made and duly served." This would seem to restrict the right of judicial review in cases of this type, but there has been no authoritative court decision on this question. Between 1906 and 1930 the Commission found it necessary in only three instances to bring suit to enforce its orders.[26]

The right of judicial review of the Commission's orders was specifically recognized in the Hepburn Act, because the Act provided that the orders of the Commission were binding upon the carrier unless set aside by a court of competent jurisdiction. Carriers objecting to the Commission's orders might bring action in court to set aside the order. This left the way open for a continuance of the practice of reopening cases once decided by the Commission and of allowing new evidence to be introduced. But the courts were soon to limit their own authority in reviewing orders of the Commission, confining themselves largely to questions of law and not of fact.[27]

THE MANN-ELKINS ACT, 1910

The Hepburn Act went a long way toward making regulation effective, but it did not remedy all the weaknesses that had developed in the original law. Further legislation was needed. The platform on which Mr. Taft was elected to the presidency in 1908 was pledged to further regulation. Bills embodying the administration's proposals were introduced in Congress; but the insurgent element took matters into their own

---

[23] Interstate Commerce Commission, *Annual Report, 1897*, pp. 31–32.

[24] Orders for the payment of money were still to be enforced through the courts.

[25] The two-year limit was eliminated in 1920.

[26] Clyde B. Aitchison, *Interstate Commerce Acts Annotated*, 70th Cong., 1st Sess., Senate Doc. No. 166 (1930), p. 2192.

[27] See Chapter 13.

hands, and the bill which was finally passed as the Mann-Elkins Act of 1910 bore little resemblance to President Taft's proposals. Only the major provisions of the Act need be considered here.

Restoration of the Long-and-Short-Haul Clause

The most important provision of the law was the amendment of the Long-and-Short-Haul Clause, which had been rendered ineffective by a decision of the United States Supreme Court in 1897. The original Act provided that railroads could not "under substantially similar circumstances and conditions" exact more for a shorter than for a longer haul over the same line and in the same direction.[28] The Supreme Court held, in *Interstate Commerce Commission* v. *Alabama Midland Ry. Co.*,[29] commonly called the Alabama Midland Case, that the carriers might in the first instance determine for themselves whether conditions at the through and intermediate points were similar or not, and that competition at the through point and not at the intermediate points might create a dissimilarity of circumstances and conditions such that the prohibitions of the section did not apply. The result was a wholesale disregard of Section 4 by the railroads. If called upon to justify higher charges for shorter than for longer hauls, the carriers could defend themselves by showing that competition created circumstances at the through points which were not similar to the circumstances and conditions at the intermediate points. If competition justified lower rates at through points, the Long-and-Short-Haul Clause was absolutely without effect, since it is only when competition forces a low through rate that the railroad maintains higher rates at intermediate points. In other words, the clause could never correct the situations that it was designed to remedy, for each case would be an exception to which the rule did not apply. From 1897 to 1910 the Long-and-Short-Haul Clause was practically a dead letter. The Hepburn Act had made no attempt to revive Section 4, and the Commission was powerless to prevent what Commissioner Knapp had called "the most irritating and obnoxious form of discrimination that has been encountered."[30]

The Mann-Elkins Act restored the Long-and-Short-Haul Clause by striking out the qualifying phrase "under substantially similar circumstances and conditions." This made the prohibition of higher charges for shorter than for longer hauls apply, unless exception was made by the Interstate Commerce Commission. The railroads could no longer disregard the prohibitions of Section 4 and plead dissimilarity of circum-

---

[28] See p. 226, supra.

[29] 168 U.S. 144 (1897).

[30] Quoted in F. H. Dixon, "The Mann-Elkins Act, Amending the Act to Regulate Commerce," 24 *Quarterly Journal of Economics* 593, 598 (1910).

stances and conditions when an attempt was made to enforce the provisions of the law.[31]

Rate-Suspension Power

Under the Hepburn Act the Commission's power to change rates applied only to rates already in effect. The Commission had no power to determine the reasonableness of a proposed rate. After a rate had gone into effect, the Commission might entertain the question of its reasonableness; and if the rate was found to be unreasonable, it could require the rate to be changed, and it could award reparation to the parties who had paid the unreasonable charge. But this remedy was unsatisfactory. The long-established rule regarding reparation is that the shipper who has paid an unreasonable charge may recover, on shipments which have actually moved, the difference between the rate charged and the rate found reasonable. But often the burden of the unreasonable charge is not borne by the shipper. He may have shifted the burden to the consumer of the goods, or he may have shifted it back to the producer of the commodity. But the shipper or consignee is ordinarily the party entitled to recover, and the real sufferers from the unreasonable charge have no remedy. In other cases the shipper who is entitled to recover is not fully compensated for the damages suffered. If the high rate has prevented sales and hence shipments to a given market, the right to recover the difference between the rate charged and the reasonable rate on shipments made is the right to recover nothing. Yet the damage to one's business may have been great. It is therefore desirable to prevent an unreasonable rate from going into effect rather than to award reparation after it has gone into effect.

But if the Commission must approve of the rate before it goes into effect, an injury may be done the railroad; for if an increase in rates is justified but has been delayed for a long time pending a determination of its reasonableness, the carrier has been deprived of revenue to which it is justly entitled.

Congress attempted to meet this situation in a way that would be fair both to the public and to the railroads. The Mann-Elkins Act authorized the Commission to suspend proposed changes in rates for a period of not exceeding 120 days, during which time it was to determine the lawfulness of the proposed rates. An additional suspension period of 6 months was permitted if the first 120 days were insufficient.[32] If the lawfulness of the rates was not determined during the period of suspension, the proposed

---

[31] See Chapter 21.

[32] The rate-suspension period has been changed from time to time and is now seven months.

rates would go into effect; but they might be reduced subsequently if found unreasonable or otherwise unlawful.[33]

It should be noted that the Commission was authorized, but not required, to suspend proposed changes in rates. Thousands of rates are changed every year without suspension and without investigation by the Commission.

The rate-suspension provisions also affected the burden of proof in many rate cases. Proceeding upon the theory that a person proposing a change in rates might reasonably be required to justify the change, the Mann-Elkins Act provided that the burden of proof should be on the railroad to show the reasonableness of any rate proposed to be increased after the passage of the Act, and that in any hearing involving the reasonableness of rates increased after January 1, 1910, the burden of proof should be upon the carrier.

VALUATION ACT, 1913

In 1898 the United States Supreme Court had set up a standard for the determination of the reasonableness of the general level of railroad rates. "We hold," said the Court, "that the basis of all calculations as to the reasonableness of rates to be charged by a corporation maintaining a highway under legislative sanction must be the fair value of the property being used by it for the convenience of the public. . . . What the company is entitled to ask is a fair return upon the value of that which it employs for the public convenience."[34]

If "fair value" was to be made the basis of rate making, it is clear that some authoritative determination of that value was desirable. As early as 1903 the Commission had recommended that a valuation of the railroads be made.[35] The carriers were at first disposed to oppose the Commission in this recommendation; but in two cases arising in 1910 the carriers sought general increases in rates,[36] and the Commission refused to approve of the advances because the carriers had failed to show the reasonableness of the increased rates. One reason for the inability to substantiate the need for higher rates was the lack of any acceptable valuation of the property of the railroads. "It is plain," said the Commission in one of these cases, "that a physical valuation would introduce into the calculation a new element which might lead to a different conclusion."[37] It had

---

[33] For a criticism of the rate-suspension power from a railroad standpoint see Arthur Van Meter, "The I. & S. Proceeding—Its Significance in a System of Modern Rate Making," 11 *I.C.C. Practitioners' Journal* 100 (1943).

[34] *Smyth* v. *Ames*, 169 U.S. 466, 546, 547.

[35] Interstate Commerce Commission, *Annual Report, 1903*, p. 26.

[36] *Advances in Rates—Eastern Case*, 20 ICC 243 (1911), and *Advances in Rates—Western Case*, 20 ICC 307 (1911).

[37] 20 ICC, 243, 305.

now become apparent that it was in the interest of the railroads to have a valuation made of their properties, and opposition to the valuation proposal ceased.

The Valuation Act of 1913 directed the Commission to make a valua- · tion of all the railroad properties in the United States.[38]

COMMISSION DIVISIONS ACT, 1917

An enlargement and reorganization of the Commission was made imperative by the increasing number of duties imposed upon it by the supplementary legislation enacted after 1887 and also by the increasing number of complaints filed with the Commission when it came to be an effective regulatory agency. The result was the enactment of the Commission Divisions Act in 1917.[39]

By the provisions of this Act the size of the Commission was increased from seven to nine members. But more important was the provision authorizing the Commission to organize into divisions of not less than three members each. This enabled the Commission to handle more work, particularly since decisions made by a division were to have the same effect and force as decisions of the whole Commission. Decisions of a division, however, were subject, in the Commission's discretion, to a rehearing before the entire Commission. This made it possible to resolve inconsistencies and conflicts in the decisions of various divisions and also to bring before the whole Commission cases which involved controversial issues. In 1961 the Commission ruled that only cases declared to be "of general transportation importance" could be appealed from a division to the entire Commission.

THE WAR PERIOD

In April 1917, the United States entered World War I. On December 28, by virtue of a proclamation of the President, the operation of the railroads of the United States was taken over by the government, acting through the United States Railroad Administration, which had been created for the purpose. The railroads remained under federal control and operation during the war and until March 1, 1920.[40] This period represents a hiatus in the policy of private operation of railways which had so long been the established policy of the country. With the termination of federal control in 1920 and the return of the railroads to their owners, important modifications in our regulatory policy took place. The Trans-

---

[38] For further details of the Act see Chapter 16.

[39] 40 Stat. 270.

[40] For a history of the period of federal operation of the railroads see F. H. Dixon, *Railroads and Government*, chaps. xii–xiv; or Walker D. Hines, *War History of American Railroads* (New Haven: Yale University Press, 1928).

portation Act of 1920, which embodied these changes, may therefore be considered as opening a new chapter in the history of railroad legislation in the United States.

SELECTED REFERENCES

The reports of the Windom and the Cullom committees give a good picture of the railroad problem as it appeared during the period just prior to federal legislation. The Windom report is entitled *Transportation Routes to the Seaboard*, 43d Cong., 1st Sess., Senate Rep. No. 307 (1874). The Cullom report is entitled *Report of the Senate Select Committee on Interstate Commerce*, 49th Cong., 1st Sess., Senate Rep. No. 46 (1886). The history of early railroad legislation in Congress and attempts at legislation are best described in L. H. Haney, *A Congressional History of Railways in the United States, 1850–1887*, Bulletin of the University of Wisconsin, No. 342 (Madison, 1910). An interesting account of the background and origins of the Act of 1887 may be found in Clyde B. Aitchison, "The Roots of the Act to Regulate Commerce," in *Exercises Commemorating the Fifty Years' Service of the Interstate Commerce Commission* (Washington, D.C.: U.S. Government Printing Office, 1937).

The development of federal legislation applicable to railroads is told in many general works on transportation. W. Z. Ripley's *Railroads: Rates and Regulation* (New York: Longmans, 1912), chaps. xiii–xvii, is especially good and gives somewhat more background than later treatments, doubtless because it was written so shortly after the struggle to bring about effective regulation. Most of the standard texts on transportation give some account of the development of railroad regulation.

A good discussion of the Act to Regulate Commerce, written at the time of the passage of the Act, is by E. R. A. Seligman in "Railway Tariffs and the Interstate Commerce Law," 2 *Political Science Quarterly* 223, 369 (1887). The Hepburn Act is described by F. H. Dixon in "The Interstate Commerce Act as Amended," 21 *Quarterly Journal of Economics* 22 (1906). The legislation of 1910 is also described by F. H. Dixon in "The Mann-Elkins Act, Amending the Act to Regulate Commerce," 24 *Quarterly Journal of Economics* 593 (1910). An excellent review of the Mann-Elkins Act and its administration is in F. H. Dixon, *Railroads and Government* (New York: Scribner, 1922), chaps. ii–vii. A description of federal legislation as it developed prior to 1920 is in I. L. Sharfman, *The Interstate Commerce Commission*, Part I (New York: Commonwealth Fund, 1931), chaps. i and iii. See also Clyde B. Aitchison, "The Evolution of the Interstate Commerce Act, 1887–1937," 5 *George Washington Law Review* 289 (1937), pp. 289–356; and Interstate Commerce Commission, Bureau of Statistics, *Interstate Commerce Commission Activities, 1887–1937* (Washington, D.C.: Superintendent of Documents, 1937), pp. 25–43.

Chapter 11 : THE TRANSPORTATION ACT OF 1920

The occasion for the enactment of the Transportation Act of 1920, otherwise known as the Esch-Cummins Act, was the transition from wartime operation of railroads by the government back to private operation. A certain amount of legislation was needed if the transition was to be made successfully, but Congress seized upon this opportunity to review our entire policy of regulation and to make such modifications in it as seemed desirable. Extensive Congressional hearings on the subject were held in 1919 and 1920. At this time, interested individuals and organizations were given an opportunity to present their views concerning our regulatory system and the changes which should be made.[1]

The resulting legislation, embodied in the Transportation Act of 1920, did two things. It further extended the system of control over railroads, increasing the Commission's power and embracing some matters not theretofore brought within the scope of the Commission's authority. In the second place, the Act radically modified certain policies of regulation which had been followed before that time. Each of these accomplishments merits brief explanation before we turn to a consideration of the details of the new legislation.

INCOMPLETENESS OF REGULATION

Railroad regulation of the prewar period was inadequate in a number of respects. There was no control over railroad capitalization except that which was exercised by state governments. Although the evils of stock watering and overcapitalization had long been subjects of complaint, the theory had generally prevailed that control over rates could prevent excessive charges that might otherwise result from inflated capitalization. But as early as 1907 the Interstate Commerce Commission had urged con-

---

[1] See *Hearings on Extension of Tenure of Government Control of Railroads,* 65th Cong., 3d Sess., and *Hearings on Return of the Railroads to Private Ownership,* 66th Cong., 1st Sess. These plans are summarized in Eliot Jones, *Principles of Railway Transportation* (New York: Macmillan, 1924), chap. xxiii; F. H. Dixon, *Railroads and Government* (New York: Scribner, 1922), chap. xv; and I. L. Sharfman, *The American Railroad Problem* (New York: Century, 1921), pp. 357-74.

trol over railroad capitalization.[2] President Theodore Roosevelt emphasized the necessity for such regulation, and in 1910 President Taft recommended that Congress enact legislation dealing with the subject. But not
until 1920 did Congress see fit to clothe the Interstate Commerce Commission with power over the issuance of new securities by railroad companies.

Control over railroad service was likewise inadequate. Prior to 1920
regulation had been concerned with rates and discrimination and very
little with service. In the years which preceded World War I, the public
frequently suffered great inconveniences on account of car shortages,
traffic congestion, and embargoes on freight. This was partly due to inadequate transportation facilities and partly to failure, under a system of
intense competition, to utilize to best advantage the facilities that were
available. Here was a shortcoming in our system of regulation that called
for some attention. Nearly all proposals submitted to Congress in 1919
recognized the necessity for additional control over railroad service.

A third shortcoming in our system of regulation had been the inadequacy of the machinery for the settlement of railroad labor disputes. The
public can ill afford to permit the interference with transportation service which results from strikes and strained relations between railroads
and their employees. Machinery for the settlement of labor disputes on
railroads had been provided in earlier legislation, but the system had broken down in time of greatest need.[3] Controversies over wages and working conditions were impending in the period after the war, and the necessity of machinery capable of coping with the situation was keenly felt
at the time.

POSITIVE DEFECTS IN THE REGULATORY SYSTEM

In addition to these negative defects in the system of regulation, there
were two positive defects. First, the policy of enforced competition
which had characterized railroad regulation from the beginning was a
mistake; and second, the system of regulation was too restrictive.

The Policy of Enforced Competition

The policy of enforced competition was a natural result of reliance on
competition as a regulator of prices and service throughout industry generally. We have noted, however, that competition between railway lines
cannot be relied upon as a regulator of rates.[4] Competition tends to re-

---

[2] *In re Consolidation of Railroads,* 12 ICC 277 (1907).

[3] This machinery had been provided by the Erdman Act of 1898 and the New-
lands Act of 1913. For a description of this legislation see Jones, op. cit., chap. xx.
This legislation had provided for a system of mediation and voluntary arbitration.

[4] Pp. 142–43 and 150–51, supra.

duce rates to direct or out-of-pocket costs and leaves insufficient revenue
to meet fixed or constant expenses and a return on capital. The public
was slow to realize this and, fearing monopoly, had endeavored to break
up all agreements between railroad companies devised to restrict competition. Provisions of the Granger laws prohibiting combinations of competing railroads and the antipooling provisions of the Act to Regulate
Commerce were indications of the prevailing view. Antitrust laws, when
applied to railroad combinations, represented the same policy.[5]

The policy of enforced competition, although not carried out with
complete success, was unfortunate in many respects. It encouraged the
cutting of rates to unremunerative levels. It resulted in local discrimination, since rates at competitive points were cut to extremely low levels.
Rebating and other forms of personal discrimination were also natural
consequences of the struggle between rival lines for traffic. Competition
resulted in wasteful hauls by circuitous lines, in cross-hauling, and in
other instances of carrying goods unnecessarily long distances. It resulted
in the extension of free privileges to shippers on an excessive scale and in
unjustifiable elaboration of service, thereby increasing the expenses of the
railroads. Lastly, it resulted in the duplication of railroad facilities and
the investment of capital in unnecessary railroad lines.

Restrictive Regulation

Regulation prior to 1920 had been restrictive in its approach. Regulation had originated in an effort to prevent certain abuses. The function of
the Interstate Commerce Commission was to protect the public against
extortionate and unjustly discriminatory charges, and the Commission had
no particular responsibilities toward the carriers. This fact was particularly noticeable after 1910. The Mann-Elkins Act had cast upon the railroads the burden of proof in rate cases involving rates increased after
1910. It chanced that steadily rising prices after 1910 made it necessary
for the carriers to advance rates. Since the law put the burden of proof
upon the carriers, it was difficult for them to prove the reasonableness of
the proposed rates. It was only with extreme difficulty that the carriers
obtained increases, and then they received smaller increases than seemed
necessary to them. The Commission, although not refusing to consider
the financial necessities of the carriers, objected to the efforts of railroad
counsel to establish the Commission *in loco parentis* toward the railroads.

There developed a feeling on the part of railroad executives and investors in railroad securities that the law ought to place upon the Commission some responsibility for giving the railroads an adequate income. But
the immediate cause of the movement to protect railroad earnings grew
out of the impaired credit situation which confronted the carriers after

---

[5] This policy is described more fully later. See Chapter 14.

the war. The gradual rise of prices and the tardy increase in rates had impaired railroad credit prior to our entrance into the war. This had made it difficult for the carriers to obtain needed capital. Financial mismanagement and competitive excesses, with their resulting waste, had contributed to the debacle. The situation was aggravated during the period of federal operation because rates were not increased sufficiently to meet the higher operating cost. This was not a serious matter during the war period, since the railroads were guaranteed a certain income, which came out of the federal treasury when receipts from operation of the railroad did not cover the guaranteed net income. But the situation threatened to be very serious if the roads were turned back to their owners and the financial support of the government were withdrawn. Rate advances would be necessary, and it was essential that they be made with the minimum of delay. In view of this situation, Congress placed upon the Interstate Commerce Commission the responsibility of giving the railroads an opportunity to earn adequate income. In the words of the United States Supreme Court, the railroads were placed under "the fostering guardianship and control of the Commission."[6] And in interpreting the provisions of the Transportation Act, the Court pointed out that the purpose of regulation was not only to protect the shipper against abuses but "to foster, protect and control the commerce with appropriate regard to the welfare of those who are immediately concerned, . . . and to promote its growth and insure its safety."[7] The dominant purpose running through the whole Transportation Act of 1920 was the promotion of an adequate system of transportation for the country. All of the major provisions of the Act were direct to this end.

PROVISIONS OF THE TRANSPORTATION ACT OF 1920

Rule of Rate Making

One of the most important provisions of the Act of 1920 was the Rule of Rate Making, incorporated into the law as Section 15a of the Interstate Commerce Act.[8] Section 15a provided:

In the exercise of its power to prescribe just and reasonable rates the Commission shall initiate, modify, establish or adjust such rates so that carriers as a whole (or as a whole in each of such rate groups or territories as the Commission may from time to time designate) will, under honest, efficient and economical management and reasonable expenditures for maintenance of way, structures and equipment, earn an aggregate annual net railway operating income equal, as nearly as may be, to a fair return upon the ag-

---

[6] *Dayton–Goose Creek Ry. Co.* v. *United States,* 263 U.S. 456, 478 (1924).

[7] Ibid.

[8] After 1920 the Act to Regulate Commerce as amended is referred to as the "Interstate Commerce Act."

gregate value of the railway property of such carriers held for and used in the service of transportation: *Provided,* That the Commission shall have reasonable latitude to modify or adjust any particular rate which it may find to be unjust or unreasonable and to prescribe different rates for different sections of the country.

The Commission was to determine from time to time what should be considered a fair rate of return, but this had to be uniform throughout the country. In fixing the fair rate of return, the Commission was to give due consideration "to the transportation needs of the country and the necessity (under honest, efficient and economical management of existing transportation facilities) of enlarging such facilities in order to provide the people of the United States with adequate transportation." Congress prescribed 5½ percent, however, as the fair rate of return for the first two years that the section was in force, but it authorized the Commission to add an amount not exceeding ½ of 1 percent to make provision for improvements and betterments.[9] The Commission was also to determine the aggregate value of the railroad properties for the purpose of administering the section, but the values found under the Valuation Act of 1913 were to be used when available.

Certain points regarding Section 15a need emphasis. In the first place, the section did not constitute a guaranty. It was certainly not a guaranty in the sense that the government must make good any failure to earn the prescribed return. Neither was it a guaranty in the sense that failure to earn a fair return in a given year required an increase in rates. This is what the Commission had in mind when it said of Section 15a: "It does not constitute a guaranty to the carriers, nor is the obligation cumulative. We are not restricted by past or present statistics of operation and earnings. . . . What is contemplated by the law is that in this exercise of our rate-making power the result shall reflect our best judgment as to the basis which may reasonably be expected for the future to yield the prescribed return."[10]

Another point regarding the Rule of Rate Making which cannot be too strongly emphasized is that it applied to the carriers as a whole, or in rate groups, and not to individual carriers. When rates are based on aggregate property values, an individual carrier may obtain more or less than a fair return. Operating and traffic conditions differ so widely on different roads that a level of rates which gives the carriers, as a whole or in groups, a fair return will be wholly inadequate for certain lines and will give others far more than a fair return.[11]

---

[9] In *Increased Rates, 1920,* 58 ICC 220, the Commission added the ½ of 1 percent and authorized increases intended to give the carriers 6 percent on an estimated value of $18.9 billion. In *Reduced Rates, 1922,* 68 ICC 676, the Commission fixed 5¾ percent as a fair rate of return. No subsequent changes were made in the rate of return deemed "fair."

[10] *Rates on Grain, Grain Products & Hay,* 64 ICC 85, 99 (1921).

[11] This problem is discussed more fully in Chapter 17.

The wording of Section 15a was subsequently changed,[12] but the obligation imposed upon the Commission to consider the revenue needs of the carriers is still a part of the law. The original Section 15a clearly indicated the purpose of Congress to see that railroad earnings were adequate to support railroad credit—an essential part of the broader purpose of securing an adequate transportation system for the country.

The Recapture Clause

Because rates prescribed under the Rule of Rate Making would give some carriers excessive earnings and would leave others with revenues which were inadequate, Congress included in the Act the provisions which came to be known as the Recapture Clause. The recapture provisions provided that one half the earnings of a carrier in any year which were in excess of 6 percent on the value of its property should be paid to the Interstate Commerce Commission and placed in a railroad contingent fund. From this fund, loans were to be made to the carriers for capital expenditures or to refund maturing obligations. As an alternative the Commission might purchase equipment with the recaptured earnings and lease the same to the railroads. Loans from the fund were to bear interest at 6 percent and were to be adequately secured. Rentals of equipment purchased from the fund were to pay a return of at least 6 percent plus depreciation.

The other half of the excess was to be retained by the carrier, but was to be placed in a reserve fund for the payment of interest, dividends, and rentals to the extent that its income in any year fell short of 6 percent on the value of its property, and the fund might not be drawn upon for any other purpose. When the reserve fund amounted to more than 5 percent of the value of its property, the carrier was to be permitted to use its share of further excess earnings for any lawful purpose.

The recapture provisions, we have seen, were a logical part of the system of rate making which bases rates upon aggregate property values. This was made clear by the language of the Act:

Inasmuch as it is impossible . . . to establish uniform rates upon competitive traffic which will adequately sustain all the carriers which are engaged in such traffic and which are indispensable to the communities to which they render the service of transportation, without enabling some of such carriers to receive a net railway operating income substantially and unreasonably in excess of a fair return upon the value of their railway property held for and used in the service of transportation, it is hereby declared that any carrier which receives such an income so in excess of a fair return, shall hold such part of the excess as hereinafter prescribed, as trustee for, and shall pay it to the United States.

---

[12] See pp. 263–64, infra.

The Recapture Clause sought to marshal the earnings for the purpose of supporting the credit of all the railroads. The half retained by the carrier was to be used to stabilize interest and dividend payments, and the half recaptured by the government was to be used for the purpose of making loans to needy railroads, providing them with a new source of credit and perhaps enabling them to improve the earning position of their properties.

The Recapture Clause was eventually repealed;[13] hence it is not now a part of the law. Its provisions should be understood, however, because it represented one of several devices to deal with inequalities in the earnings of railroads which are bound to arise, particularly when rates are made for carriers as a whole or for groups of carriers. This problem was of great concern to Congress at the time Section 15a was enacted.

Division of Joint Rates

The Recapture Clause was not the only provision of the law designed to bring relief to weak carriers. The Transportation Act also contemplated that in the division of joint rates, consideration should be given to the weaker roads. The Mann-Elkins Act had provided that when railroad companies could not agree upon the division of joint rates, the Commission might prescribe the share each was to receive. By the Transportation Act the Commission was directed, in making such divisions, to give consideration to "the amount of revenue required to pay their respective operating expenses, taxes, and a fair return on their railway property held for and used in the service of transportation." The Supreme Court of the United States, in interpreting this section of the law, pointed out that it was intended to help weak lines "by preventing needed revenue from passing to prosperous connections."[14]

Minimum Rates

As early as 1893 the Interstate Commerce Commission had seen the desirability of controlling rate reductions.[15] Congress did not act upon this recommendation until 1920. The Transportation Act empowered the Commission to prescribe minimum rates. The grant of this power is evidence of a change in the policy of enforced competition. The Commission was given this power for the purpose of preventing rate wars and the undermining of a rate level prescribed under Section 15a.

Pooling

The Act of 1920 modified our historic policy toward pooling agreements. The Act of 1887, it will be recalled, contained an absolute prohi-

---

[13] See p. 264, infra.

[14] *The New England Divisions Case*, 261 U.S. 184, 191 (1923).

[15] Interstate Commerce Commission, *Annual Report, 1893*, pp. 38–39, 217–25.

bition of pooling. The wisdom of this drastic provision was questioned at the time and was discussed by the Commission from time to time in its annual reports. The Transportation Act repeated the old prohibition but added a proviso which permitted pooling when approved by the Commission. Under the amended Act the Commission's approval is dependent upon a finding that the pooling agreement (1) "will be in the interest of better service to the public, or economy in operation," and (2) "will not unduly restrain competition." The Commission may authorize pooling upon such terms and conditions as it finds just and reasonable, but the pooling arrangement must have the assent of all of the carriers involved. The "carriers involved" whose assent must be obtained are the carriers which are parties to the proposed pooling agreement. The phrase does not include outside carriers which might be adversely affected by a pooling agreement through diversion of traffic or in some other way.[16]

Restrictions on New Construction

The Transportation Act gave the Interstate Commerce Commission control over new railroad construction. The law provided that "no carrier by railroad subject to this act shall undertake the extension of its line of railroad, or the construction of a new line of railroad . . . unless and until there shall first have been obtained from the Commission a certificate that the present or future public convenience and necessity require or will require the construction . . . of such additional or extended line of railroad."

Senator Cummins, in defending this provision of the bill before the Senate, pointed out the necessity for such a measure. "If there is any one thing from which the transportation system of the country, taken as a whole, is now suffering, it is from the unguided, uncontrolled right of owners to build railroads wherever they may see fit to build them and whenever they can avail themselves of an opportunity to sell at a profit the securities based upon the supposed construction."[17] This provision of the law serves to protect existing lines from competition to some extent. It is also related to Section 15a, for if the public had committed itself to a policy of paying rates which would yield the carriers as a whole an adequate return, it was obviously desirable to prevent the construction of unnecessary lines.

Railroad Consolidations and Acquisitions of Control

The Transportation Act of 1920 contained elaborate provisions relating to railroad consolidations and acquisitions of control of one railroad by another. In view of subsequent changes in the law, it is not necessary

---

[16] *Escanaba & Lake Superior R. R. Co.* v. *United States,* 303 U.S. 315 (1938).

[17] Quoted in Rogers MacVeagh, *The Transportation Act, 1920* (New York: Holt, 1923), p. 221.

to detail these provisions. There was one feature of the law, however, which should be described because it represented an effort, since abandoned, to encourage a planned consolidation of the railroads into a small number of large systems.

The Act directed the Interstate Commerce Commission to prepare and adopt a plan for the consolidation of the railway properties of the United States into a limited number of systems. In drawing up this plan, the Commission was required to observe certain general principles. These were (1) that competition should be preserved "as fully as possible"; (2) that wherever practicable, the existing routes and channels of trade and commerce were to be maintained; and (3) that subject to the foregoing requirements, the systems should be of approximately equal earning power under a uniform level of rates.

The last requirement, although subordinated to the first two, indicated the real purpose of the elaborate consolidation provisions. In the opinion of Congress the problem of supporting all the railroads from earnings which are fair to the railroads as a whole, but which may be too great or too little for particular roads, was ultimately to be solved by the consolidation of the railroads into a limited number of systems of equal earning power. When this object should be accomplished, the Recapture Clause could be repealed and the provisions regarding the division of joint rates would no longer be necessary to marshal earnings in support of the credit of weak lines. The weak lines would have disappeared as separate entities.

The Commission's plan of consolidation was announced in 1929.[18] An extensive revision of the plan for Eastern Territory was made in 1932.[19]

The provisions we have described relate to the drawing-up of a consolidation plan. So far as actual consolidations were concerned, the Act provided that two or more railroads might consolidate under certain conditions.[20] One condition was that the Commission find the consolidation to be in the public interest. Another, and most important, condition was that the consolidation be in conformity with the Commission's plan of consolidation.[21]

When permission was granted railroads to consolidate, or to acquire control of other lines through lease or stock ownership, the carriers were relieved from the operation of the antitrust laws and other restrictions

---

[18] 159 ICC 522.

[19] 185 ICC 403.

[20] The term "consolidation" was used in the Act to refer to combinations which resulted in a single corporation where there were two or more corporations before. Combinations through lease or stock ownership were not required, by the terms of the statute, to be in conformity with the consolidation plan.

[21] A third condition, repealed by the Emergency Transportation Act of 1933, was that the stocks and bonds of the new company might not exceed the value of the consolidated properties as determined by the Commission under the Valuation Act of 1913.

imposed by federal or state law, so far as might be necessary to enable them to do anything authorized or required by the Commission in its order.

It should be noted that consolidation under the Act was to be voluntary. Carriers could not be compelled to combine according to the plan proposed by the Commission; but with certain exceptions, they could be prevented from combining in ways that were contrary to it.[22]

The law did not require that combinations through lease or stock ownership should conform to the consolidation plan; but after the promulgation of its plan the Commission took the position that no acquisition of control should be approved that was not in harmony with it.[23]

Financial Regulation

The Transportation Act of 1920 added Section 20a to the Interstate Commerce Act. This section brought the issuance of securities by railroad companies under the control of the Commission. Stated briefly, this section provided that the approval of the Commission was necessary before a railroad might issue new securities. The Commission was given broad powers in approving or disapproving issues of securities and in attaching terms and conditions.[24]

Regulation of railroad security issues had been undertaken prior to 1920 by a number of states, but Section 20a gave the Interstate Commerce Commission "exclusive and plenary" jurisdiction over the subject, and a carrier may issue securities approved by the Commission without securing the approval of state authorities.

Intrastate Rates

An important provision of the Transportation Act was an amendment to Section 13 of the Interstate Commerce Act to give the Commission power to prescribe intrastate rates when necessary to remove discrimination against interstate commerce. The full significance of this provision is not apparent from a mere consideration of its wording. As interpreted by the Supreme Court of the United States, this section empowers the Interstate Commerce Commission to raise purely intrastate rates to the level of interstate rates if the former are not contributing a fair share of

---

[22] The principal exceptions were (1) consolidations which could be carried out under state laws and which did not therefore require approval of the Commission, 79 ICC 581 (1923); and (2) combinations through holding companies, since these were not within the jurisdiction of the Commission.

[23] See statement of Commissioner Eastman in *Hearings before the Committee on Interstate and Foreign Commerce, House of Representatives, on Regulation of Holding Companies,* 72d Cong., 1st Sess. (1932), p. 59.

[24] See Chapter 24.

the revenue needed to maintain an adequate system of transportation.[25] This provision of the law is therefore closely related to Section 15a. If the Commission, under Section 15a, undertakes to adjust rates for the purpose of giving the railroads a fair return, that object cannot be defeated by the maintenance of low intrastate rates by state regulatory authorities. The federal government can step in and remove the disparity between interstate and intrastate rates by raising the intrastate rates.

Abandonments

The Interstate Commerce Commission was given control over railroad abandonments in 1920. The Act provided that "no carrier by railroad subject to this act shall abandon all or any portion of a line of railroad, or the operation thereof, unless and until there shall first have been obtained from the Commission a certificate that the present or future public convenience and necessity permit of such abandonment." Control over abandonment is for the purpose of protecting the communities which are dependent upon particular railroads.[26] The centralization of control over railroad abandonments in the hands of the Interstate Commerce Commission seems to have had another and broader objective. It freed the railroads to some extent from unduly burdensome requirements for continued operation of unprofitable branches. Prior to 1920 the states exercised some control over abandonments but were often inclined to look upon abandonment from a purely local point of view. The Interstate Commerce Commission is less likely to protect local interests when unprofitable operation of branch lines constitutes a burden upon interstate commerce or a drain upon the resources of a railroad system.

Compulsory Construction of New Lines

A novel provision of the Transportation Act was that which empowered the Commission to require a railroad to extend its line or lines. The exercise of this power was conditioned upon two findings that must be made by the Commission: (1) that the extension was "reasonably required in the interest of public convenience and necessity" and (2) that the expense involved would not "impair the ability of the carrier to perform its duty to the public." Because of a restricted interpretation of this provision by the United States Supreme Court, this power is not likely to prove of much importance.[27]

---

[25] *Railroad Commission of Wisconsin* v. *Chicago, Burlington & Quincy R. R. Co.*, 257 U.S. 563 (1922); *United States* v. *Louisiana*, 290 U.S. 70 (1933); *Florida* v. *United States*, 292 U.S. 1 (1934).

[26] See Chapter 25.

[27] See Chapter 25.

Joint Use of Terminals

The Transportation Act gave the Commission power to require the joint use of terminals. The carrier owning terminal facilities may be compelled to share them with other carriers. The owning carrier is entitled, of course, to reasonable compensation for the use of its facilities by another. The compensation is to be agreed upon by the carriers, if possible; but in case of failure to agree, the Commission may fix the compensation. Before the Commission may require the joint use of terminals, it must find that such use is in the public interest and that it will not impair the ability of the owning carrier to handle its own business.

This power, if exercised, should result in improved service to the public and should strengthen weaker roads which lack adequate terminals. It may also prevent unnecessary duplication of terminal facilities.

Labor Disputes

It was pointed out earlier in the chapter that controversies over wages and working conditions in the railroad industry were impending at the termination of federal operation. This situation, coupled with the realization that more adequate machinery was necessary to deal with railroad labor disputes, led Congress to include elaborate provisions in the Act of 1920 for the settlement of such disputes. Amony these provisions was one which set up a Railroad Labor Board to decide controversies involving wages which could not be settled in conference between the railroads and their employees and to decide certain other classes of labor disputes. The Railroad Labor Board was in the nature of a permanent board of arbitration, but its decisions were not binding.[28] The Labor Board consisted of nine members, three representing the railroads, three representing the employees, and three, the public. A more detailed description of the Labor Board and of the labor provisions of the Transportation Act of 1920 is unnecessary, since these provisions were superseded by the Railway Labor Act of 1926.[29]

Miscellaneous Provisions

A number of miscellaneous provisions in the Transportation Act deserve brief mention:

1. The Interstate Commerce Commission was enlarged from 9 to 11 members.

2. Section 4 of the Interstate Commerce Act—the Long-and-Short-

---

[28] *Pennsylvania Railroad Co.* v. *United States Railroad Labor Board,* 261 U.S. 72, 79–80 (1923).

[29] See pp. 257–59, infra.

Haul Clause—was amended in such manner as to restrict the discretionary power of the Commission in granting relief from the prohibitions of the clause. These changes suggested that a less liberal policy should be followed in the future in granting relief from the operation of the section.[30]

3. We have already noted that the Act of 1920 gave the Commission power to prescribe minimum rates; but in addition, it went further and empowered the Commission to prescribe the actual rate to be charged in lieu of a rate found unlawful.

4. The accounting provisions of the law were changed to the extent of requiring the Interstate Commerce Commission to prescribe the classes of property for which the carriers should set up depreciation reserves and to detemine the amounts thereafter to be charged to operating expenses for depreciation.[31]

5. Interlocking directorates were prohibited. It was made unlawful for any person, after December 31, 1921, to hold the position of officer or director of more than one railroad without special authorization of the Commission upon a showing that neither public nor private interests would be adversely affected thereby.

Transitional Provisions

In addition to the provisions of the Transportation Act which relate to the system of railroad regulation, there were a number of provisions designed to aid the railroads in the difficult period of transition from wartime government operation to operation by their owners. Railroad credit, in particular, needed rehabilitation, and the aid of the government was necessary. Railroad credit had been weak in the years prior to federal operation. Although freight rates had been increased 25 percent during the period of federal operation, this was insufficient to enable the railroads to pay operating expenses and have an adequate net income. While the railroads were being operated by the government, this did not matter, because the carriers were guaranteed a certain net income. But with the support of government resources withdrawn, as would be the case after the return of the railroads to their owners, railroad credit would collapse unless bolstered up in some way pending an increase in earnings.

Measures taken to meet this situation were (1) a six-month guaranty to the railroads of the same income which they received during the period of government control; (2) reimbursement of deficits incurred by short-line railroads which were not operated by the government during the war and which therefore did not benefit from the wartime guaranty of earnings; (3) funding of certain indebtedness of the railroads to the

---

[30] For the details of these changes see Chapter 21.

[31] For administration of this section see Chapter 23.

government which arose out of capital expenditures made on their properties by the government during the war; and (4) direct loans to railroads for the purpose of making capital expenditures or for refunding maturing obligations. Because of their temporary character, the details of these forms of aid do not need to be considered here.[32]

RESULTS OF THE ACT

As a result of the temporary financial aid to railroads provided by the Transportation Act of 1920, the transition from government to private operation was made successfully. The constructive policy of the 1920 Act was helpful to the railroads in the ensuing years. Railroad credit improved, and the position of the railroads was fairly satisfactory during the decade of the twenties. To be sure, some provisions of the Transportation Act did not work out in the manner that had been expected. During this period, also, forces were at work which changed the nature of the transportation problem and defeated some of the objectives which had been sought through the provisions of the Act of 1920. The onslaught of the depression after 1929 intensified these difficulties and ushered in a new period in the history of transportation regulation.

In the next chapter the railroad legislation enacted after 1920 will be described.

SELECTED REFERENCES

A convenient presentation of the railroad problem as it appeared in 1920 may be found in the collection of papers on railroad legislation, 8 *Proceedings of the Academy of Political Science* 513–774 (1920). An excellent and impartial estimate and criticism of the regulatory system prior to 1920 is in I. L. Sharfman, *The Interstate Commerce Commission*, Vol. I (New York: Commonwealth Fund, 1931), chap. ii.

The Act of 1920 has been described in many places. See I. L. Sharfman, *The American Railroad Problem* (New York: Century, 1921), chap. xi; F. H. Dixon, *Railroads and Government* (New York: Scribner, 1923), chaps. xv–xxii; Eliot Jones, *Principles of Railway Transportation* (New York: Macmillan, 1924), chap. xxv; D. P. Locklin, *Railroad Regulation since 1920* (New York: McGraw-Hill, 1928), chaps. i–iv, vi–xi; and Truman C. Bigham, *Transportation: Principles and Problems* (New York: McGraw-Hill, 1946), pp. 171–81. Articles on the subject include: F. Johnston, "The Transportation Act, 1920," 6 *Virginia Law Review* 482 (1920); Edgar J. Rich, "The Transportation Act of 1920," 10 *American Economic Review* 507 (1920); A. Pomerene, "Our Recent Federal Railroad Legislation," 55 *American Law Review* 364 (1921); E. S. Jouett, "Law of Railroad Rate Making," 10 *Virginia Law Review* 618 (1924).

---

[32] A summary of these forms of aid is found in the earlier editions of this book. See pp. 249–51 of the third edition.

The most complete account of the Railroad Labor Board and its work is H. D. Wolf, *The Railroad Labor Board* (Chicago: University of Chicago Press, 1927). Briefer accounts of the settlement of labor disputes under the Transportation Act are found in H. B. Vanderblue and K. F. Burgess, *Railroads: Rates, Service, Management* (New York: Macmillan, 1923), chap. xxv; S. L. Miller, *Railway Transportation: Principles and Point of View* (Chicago: A. W. Shaw Co., 1924), pp. 861–71; Jones, op. cit., pp. 565–88; and Locklin, op. cit., pp. 128–43.

On the consolidation provisions of the Act, their origin, and purpose, see William N. Leonard, *Railroad Consolidation under the Transportation Act of 1920* (New York: Columbia University Press, 1946), chap. iii.

Chapter

12

RAILROAD LEGISLATION
SINCE 1920

After the amendments of 1920 the Interstate Commerce Act remained substantially unmodified for several years. Changed conditions, however, and the partial failure of the Transportation Act to work out as Congress intended brought about amendatory and supplementary legislation which is briefly described in this chapter. This legislation comprises (1) the Hoch-Smith Resolution, (2) the Railway Labor Act, (3) Section 77 of the Bankruptcy Act, (4) the Emergency Transportation Act of 1933, (5) the Transportation Act of 1940, (6) the Railroad Modification Act, (7) the Reed-Bulwinkle Act, (8) the Transportation Act of 1958; (9) the Urban Mass Transportation Act of 1964; (10) the Department of Transportation Act, 1966; and (11) the Rail Passenger Service Act of 1970. These enactments, like earlier railroad legislation, reflect the conditions and problems of the times. This will be brought out in the discussion which follows.

THE HOCH-SMITH RESOLUTION

In 1925 Congress enacted the Hoch-Smith Resolution, which seemed to modify long-standing policies of the Interstate Commerce Commission in regulating freight rates.[1] The provisions of the Resolution may be summarized as follows:

1. The Resolution required the Interstate Commerce Commission, in adjusting freight rates, to take into consideration "the conditions which at any given time prevail in our several industries . . . in so far as it is legally possible to do so, to the end that commodities may freely move."[2]
2. The Interstate Commerce Commission was directed to make a thorough investigation of the rate structure to remove instances of unjust, unreasonable, unjustly discriminatory, and unduly preferential rates.
3. In making rate adjustments as a result of this investigation, the

---

[1] 43 Stat. 801.

[2] More will be said concerning this principle of rate making in a later chapter. See Chapter 18.

Commission was directed to give due regard to three factors: (*a*) the "general and comparative levels in market value of the various classes and kinds of commodities as indicated over a reasonable period of years," (*b*) a natural and proper development of the country as a whole, and (*c*) the maintenance of an adequate system of transportation.

4. The Commission was directed, in view of the existing depression in agriculture, to establish on products of agriculture, including livestock, the "lowest possible lawful rates compatible with the maintenance of adequate transportation service."

The purpose of the Resolution was to help agriculture, which had been in a depressed condition since 1920. There can be no doubt of this, in view of the directive to prescribe the lowest possible lawful rates on the products of agriculture affected by the depression. The history of the measure also reveals this purpose. It was sponsored in Congress by the so-called "farm bloc" in the hope that it would help relieve the agricultural distress.[3]

The Hoch-Smith Resolution was variously interpreted, and it was not clear just what its legal effect would be. At the time of its passage by Congress it appeared to some as a mere political gesture to please the agricultural interests. To others the Resolution seemed to contemplate a revolutionary change in regulatory policy.

It is clear from a study of the Resolution, with its emphasis on the adjustment of rates so that traffic would freely move, that it was intended to justify rate reductions for depressed industries. But since the Resolution did not repeal Section 15a, it is to be presumed that there was no intention of depriving the railroads of a "fair return" as a result of such rate reductions. Rather, it was intended to bring about a moderate shifting of the transportation burden from traffic which it was thought could not stand high rates, at least without undue hardship, to traffic which could stand high rates more easily.

In 1930 the Supreme Court, in *Ann Arbor Railroad Co.* v. *United States*,[4] construed the provisions of the Hoch-Smith Resolution and held that the Resolution did not "purport to make unlawful any rate which under the existing law is a lawful rate, but on the contrary leaves the validity of the rate to be tested by that law." The provision of the Resolution requiring the lowest possible lawful rates on the products of agriculture was described by the Court as "more in the nature of a hopeful characterization of an object deemed desirable, than a rule intended to control rate making."

This decision was commonly considered to have practically nullified

---

[3] The legislative history of the Resolution is told in W. H. Wagner, *The Hoch-Smith Resolution* (Washington: The author, 1929), chap. ii.

[4] 281 U.S. 658 (1930).

the Resolution.[5] At times the Interstate Commerce Commission seems to have shared this view.[6] Subsequently, however, the Commission pointed out that the Resolution is still law,[7] and there are a number of cases in which the Resolution has been invoked to justify comparatively low rates on the products of agriculture.[8]

RAILWAY LABOR ACT, 1926

In the previous chapter it was noted that in the Transportation Act of 1920 Congress set up machinery for the settlement of railway labor disputes. These provisions, however, did not long endure, and they were replaced by the provisions of the Railway Labor Act of 1926. Substantial modifications in this Act were made in 1934. The provisions of the amended Act may be summarized as follows.

Conferences

All disputes between a carrier and its employees must be considered and, if possible, decided in conference between representatives of the two parties. The representatives are to be chosen by the respective parties "without interference, influence, or coercion" by the other party. The majority of any craft or class of employees may determine who shall represent that craft or class.

National Railroad Adjustment Board

Disputes growing out of grievances or out of the interpretation of agreements concerning rates of pay, rules, or working conditions are to be carried to a National Railroad Adjustment Board. This Board is composed of 36 members, 18 selected by the carriers and 18 by the national organizations of employees. It is divided into four divisions, each with jurisdiction over different classes of railroad employment. If any division fails to agree on a decision, it is required to select a neutral referee to sit with the Board until a decision is reached. If the division fails to select a referee, the National Mediation Board is required to appoint one. The decisions of the National Railroad Adjustment Board are final and binding.

---

[5] See note in 17 *Virginia Law Review* 192 (1930); editorial in 45 *Traffic World* 1491 (1930); editorial in 88 *Railway Age* 1405 (1930); and statement of Commissioner Lewis in *Live Stock—Western District Rates*, 176 ICC 159 (1931).

[6] See Interstate Commerce Commission, *Annual Report, 1940*, p. 16.

[7] *Increased Railway Rates, Fares, & Charges, 1942*, 248 ICC 545, 611 (1942).

[8] Ibid.; also *General Commodity Rate Increases, 1937*, 223 ICC 657, 746 (1937); *Fifteen Percent Case, 1937–1938*, 226 ICC 41, 77 (1938); *Wool & Mohair Rates*, 276 ICC 259, 269 (1949); *Increased Freight Rates, Eastern, Western, & Southern Territories*, 300 ICC 633, 686 (1957).

National Mediation Board

Another agency to settle disputes is the National Mediation Board. This Board consists of three members, appointed by the President with the advice and consent of the Senate. The Board has jurisdiction over disputes involving rates of pay or changes in rules and working conditions when such disputes are not settled in conference. The services of the National Mediation Board may be invoked by either party to a dispute; or the Board may, on its own motion in cases of emergency, make efforts to mediate a dispute. The National Mediation Board is not a board of arbitration. It does not decide disputes. It attempts to work out a settlement which will be acceptable to both parties and which will be embodied in a signed agreement between the parties. Another function of the National Mediation Board is to settle disputes concerning the organization which is to represent a class of employees. If it seems desirable, the Board may conduct an election for the purpose of determining the will of a majority of the employees of any craft or class.

Arbitration

If the National Mediation Board is unable to bring about a settlement of a controversy, the dispute may be submitted to arbitration. Arbitration, however, is not compulsory. Both sides must agree to arbitrate if the dispute is to be settled in this manner. Arbitration boards may consist of three or six members. One third of the arbitrators are to be chosen by the carriers, one third by the employees, and the remaining third by the other arbitrators or, in case of failure of the latter to agree, by the National Mediation Board. The boards of arbitration are not permanent organizations like the old Railroad Labor Board. A board is set up for each dispute to be arbitrated and goes out of existence with the completion of its task. When parties to a dispute agree to arbitrate, they must agree to submit to the award of the arbitrators. In other words, the award is binding.

Emergency Boards

If a dispute is not settled by any of the methods described, and if the National Mediation Board has reason to believe that the dispute threatens to interrupt interstate commerce to a degree sufficient to deprive any section of the country of essential transportation service, the Board must notify the President, who may then create an emergency board to investigate the dispute and report its findings to him. The recommendations of Emergency Boards are not binding. The sponsors of the Act believed that the recommendations of such a board, backed by the President, would command sufficient public support to assure acceptance by both sides of a controversy. This has proved not to be the case.

Results of the Act

The procedure for settling railway labor disputes provided by the Railway Labor Act has been instrumental in bringing about a peaceful settlement of thousands of disputes, particularly those involving grievances and the interpretation of existing agreements relating to wages, rules, and working conditions. The National Railroad Adjustment Board, however, which handles such disputes, has been the object of some criticism, particularly by the railroads.[9]

The machinery provided for the settlement of disputes involving wage rates and changes in rules and working conditions has not always proved adequate for the task. The efforts of the National Mediation Board frequently prove unsuccessful; one party or the other will refuse arbitration under the Act; a strike will be called to invoke the appointment of an Emergency Board; the decision of the Emergency Board will be rejected by one side or the other, usually by labor; a strike may then actually occur or perhaps be stalled off by intervention of the President or of Congress. This cannot be considered a satisfactory method for settling disputes in an industry as vital to the functioning of the economy as the railroad industry.

SECTION 77 OF THE BANKRUPTCY ACT

In 1933 Congress added Section 77 to the Bankruptcy Act of 1898 as a means of facilitating the financial reorganization of railroad companies. This section was further amended in 1935.

This measure was an outgrowth of the serious financial condition confronting the carriers as a result of the industrial depression which began in 1929. The decline in business activity that accompanied the depression greatly reduced the volume of traffic. This situation was intensified by the increasing diversion of traffic to other transportation agencies, chiefly motor carriers. Weekly carloadings, which had ranged from 800,000 to nearly 1,000,000 per week in 1930, had fallen to about 550,000 in 1932. In 1932 railways representing 72 percent of our mileage did not earn their fixed charges. Ordinarily the failure of railroad companies to meet interest payments and other fixed obligations would have thrown them into the hands of receivers pending a revision of their capital structure. Only a few companies, however, were placed in the care of receivers during

---

[9] See R. V. Fletcher, *A Sound Transportation Policy*, an address before the Traffic Club of Philadelphia (mimeographed, 1941); S. L. Miller, *The Railways and Labor: What Price Peace?* (Chicago: Associated Traffic Clubs of America, 1941). For other studies of the National Railroad Adjustment Board see Lloyd K. Garrison, "The National Railroad Adjustment Board: A Unique Administrative Agency," 46 *Yale Law Journal* 567 (1937); W. H. Spencer, *The National Railroad Adjustment Board*, University of Chicago Studies in Business Administration, Vol. VIII, No. 3 (Chicago, 1938); H. R. Northrup and M. L. Kahn, "Railroad Grievance Machinery: A Critical Analysis," 5 *Industrial and Labor Relations* 365 (1952).

this period. Receiverships were avoided to a large extent through loans from the Reconstruction Finance Corporation—a government corporation organized to extend aid to distressed banks and industries—and through loans from the Railroad Credit Corporation—a corporation organized by the railroads to extend loans to defaulting railroads out of funds received from the emergency increase in freight rates granted in 1931.[10]

As the depression continued, it became obvious that these forms of aid could not be extended indefinitely and that some railroads would have to undergo a reorganization of their financial structure. A voluntary reorganization of a corporation could not be accomplished without the consent of substantially all creditors. Since it is practically impossible to obtain such consent, the customary procedure is for a railroad to go into receivership and to effect a reorganization by a judicial sale of the property to a new corporation in which security holders participate in such manner and on such terms as have been worked out by reorganization managers with the approval of the courts having jurisdiction over the receivership.

Section 77 set up new procedures for effecting financial reorganization of railroad companies which were in difficulty. It was thought that the new procedures would reduce the delay in completing reorganizations, would result in a sounder capitalization, and would overcome various objections to the older reorganization procedure. The details of this legislation can best be discussed in the chapter dealing with railroad finance.[11] We are concerned here only with its broad purpose and objective.

Since its enactment in 1933 many railroad companies which found themselves in financial difficulties as a result of the depression accomplished a financial reorganization under Section 77 of the Bankruptcy Act. More will be said about these reorganizations later.

EMERGENCY TRANSPORTATION ACT, 1933

The Emergency Transportation Act of 1933,[12] as its name indicates, was to meet emergency conditions in the railroad industry. The emergency conditions were those that led to the enactment of Section 77 of the Bankruptcy Act, namely, declining traffic, reduced earnings, and in some instances, financial distress.

The Act consisted of two parts: Title I, which contained measures of a temporary nature designed to aid the railroads to meet the situation created by the depression; and Title II, which contained important amendments to the Interstate Commerce Act.

---

[10] *Fifteen Per Cent Case, 1931,* 178 ICC 539; 179 ICC 215.

[11] Chapter 24.

[12] 48 Stat. 211.

Emergency Provisions

The emergency provisions of the Act need not be described in detail since they were of a temporary nature. In fact, we would not mention them at all were it not for the fact that valuable lessons may be learned from this effort to bring about a more economical organization of the railroad industry.

Stated briefly, the Act created the office of Federal Coordinator of Transportation, with the Federal Coordinator to be designated by the President from the membership of the Interstate Commerce Commission. This office was held by Commissioner Joseph B. Eastman until the office was terminated in 1936.

Two general duties were imposed upon the Federal Coordinator. The first was to aid the railroads in bringing about economies in railroad operation through cooperative efforts among the railroads. Congress apparently contemplated such things as pooling of equipment, joint use of tracks and terminals, and cooperative effort of many sorts. Initiative in working out such plans was to be taken by regional coordinating committees. Three such committees were set up, each consisting of seven railroad representatives. If the regional committees were unable for any reason, legal or otherwise, to carry out such plans by voluntary action, they were to recommend to the Coordinator that he, by order, require them to be done. Thus any recalcitrant carriers could be forced into line; and the antitrust laws, which might constitute a legal block to voluntary action, could be circumvented, since an order of the Federal Coordinator carried with it exemption from the antitrust laws to the extent necessary to carry out the approved plan.

A second function of the Federal Coordinator was to investigate and consider other means for improving transportation conditions in the country. His recommendations were to be submitted to the Commission, which in turn would submit them with its own comments to the President and to Congress.

Results of the Emergency Provisions

The emergency provisions of the Act proved disappointing so far as bringing about economies in railroad operation are concerned. The Act was based on the belief that if legal obstacles to cooperative action on the part of the carriers were removed and if machinery were devised to bring recalcitrant carriers into line with what the others desired, the railroads would come forward with plans for eliminating competitive waste and for reducing expenses through cooperative action. Events showed, however, that railroad managements could not agree on measures to be undertaken. The railroads are competitive, and the executive officers have grown up in the business with the idea of conflicting interests ingrained in them. "Their habit of mind," said the Coordinator, "is intensely individualistic and suspicious of collective action."[13] There was constant fear that one railroad would obtain an advantage over another in any proposal that might be brought forward. The railroads, therefore, failed to initiate any comprehensive plans for cooperative action.

A second reason for failure of the emergency provisions was the fact that Congress had written into the Act numerous provisions to protect railroad labor which made many coordination projects virtually impossible. For instance, the number of employees in the service of a carrier could not be reduced, by reason of action taken under the Act, below the number in service during May 1933, after deducting the number removed by death, retirement, or resignation. Neither could an employee be deprived of employment such as he had in the month of May or be placed in a worse position in regard to compensation by reason of action taken under the emergency provisions of the Act.

Although the Federal Coordinator issued a large number of reports dealing with methods of eliminating waste through cooperative action of the railroads, they were generally unacceptable to the railroads, and even if undertaken would have run counter to the provisions of the Act designed to protect railroad labor.[14]

Somewhat more effective were the legislative proposals put forward by the Federal Coordinator in the discharge of his obligation to investigate other means for improving transportation conditions. The Motor Carrier Act of 1935 and the provisions of the Transportation Act of 1940 relating to regulation of carriers by water were in general conformity with proposals made by the Federal Coordinator although they did not follow his recommendations in every respect.[15]

Amendments to the Interstate Commerce Act

The amendments to the Interstate Commerce Act included in the Emergency Transportation Act of 1933 comprised (1) a series of changes in the law regarding the combination and consolidation of railroads,

---

[13] *Fourth Report of the Federal Coordinator of Transportation on Transportation Legislation*, 74th Cong., 2d Sess., House Doc. No. 394 (1936), p. 38.

[14] Following are some of the reports in this group: *Freight Traffic Report, Merchandise Traffic Report, Passenger Traffic Report, Report on Freight Car Pooling, Container Report, Report on Economy Possibilities of Regional Coordination Projects, Second Report on Economy Possibilities of Regional Coordination Projects, Railway Traffic Organization Report, Memorandum on the Application of the Clearing House Principle to the Business of the American Railways, Report on Preservative Treatment of Railroad Ties.*

[15] See *Regulation of Railroads*, 73d Cong., 2d Sess., Senate Doc. No. 119 (1934); *Regulation of Transportation Agencies*, 73d Cong., 2d Sess., Senate Doc. No. 152 (1934); *Report of the Federal Coordinator of Transportation, 1934*, 74th Cong., 1st Sess., House Doc. No. 89 (1935); *Fourth Report of the Federal Coordinator of Transportation on Transportation Legislation*, 74th Cong., 2d Sess., House Doc. No. 394 (1936).

(2) the enactment of a different Rule of Rate Making, and (3) the repeal of the Recapture Clause of the Transportation Act of 1920.

Railroad Consolidations and Acquisitions of Control. The most important change in the provisions of the Interstate Commerce Act relating to railroad consolidations and acquisitions of control was that combinations effected by means of holding companies were brought within the scope of the law. Combinations effected by such means were not reached by the law as enacted in 1920. As a result, a number of combinations through holding companies had been accomplished between 1920 and 1933 which might not have been found in the public interest, and which were clearly not in conformity with the plan of consolidation drawn up by the Commission under the provisions of the Act of 1920.[16] The Commission had been powerless to prevent this disregard of its plan of consolidation. The Emergency Transportation Act closed this loophole in the law.

The Rule of Rate Making. The Rule of Rate Making provided by Section 15a of the Interstate Commerce Act was repealed, and a new and simplified rule was substituted.[17] The new rule read as follows:

In the exercise of its power to prescribe just and reasonable rates the Commission shall give due consideration, among other factors, to the effect of rates on the movement of traffic; to the need, in the public interest, of adequate and efficient railway transportation service at the lowest cost consistent with the furnishing of such service; and to the need of revenues sufficient to enable the carriers, under honest, economical, and efficient management, to provide such service.

It will be observed that the Act changed the Rule of Rate Making in several important respects: (1) It removed the "fair-return-on-fair-value" requirement for determining the general level of rates—the standard which had been put into the original Section 15a in 1920. (2) In place of the fair-return-on-fair-value standard is found the more general requirement that in prescribing rates, the Commission shall consider the need of the carriers for revenues sufficient to enable them to provide adequate and efficient railway transportation service. (3) Although revenue need remains an important factor in fixing the level of rates, the Commission is also directed to take into consideration the public's need for transportation service at the lowest cost consistent with furnishing adequate service. (4) The Commission is likewise directed to take into consideration "the effect of rates on the movement of traffic."

In general, it may be said that the new Rule of Rate Making is more

---

[16] See W. M. Leonard, *Railroad Consolidation under the Transportation Act of 1920* (New York: Columbia University Press, 1946), particularly pp. 129, 141, 152, 154, 193–95.

[17] For the old Rule of Rate Making, see pp. 243–44, supra.

flexible than the original Section 15a. It gives the Commission a wider range of discretion in adjusting the level of rates.[18]

Repeal of the Recapture Clause. The Recapture Clause of the Transportation Act of 1920 was repealed retroactively, and the excess earnings paid to the Commission under its provisions were to be distributed among the carriers in proportion to the share each had paid in.

Although the Recapture Clause never worked satisfactorily and was open to criticism on various grounds,[19] its repeal in 1933 was largely a relief measure. There were numerous railroads which had made excess earnings in the decade of the 1920s but which were now suffering from inadequate earnings. Few of these carriers had actually paid to the government any portion of the amounts which would probably be recoverable under the Recapture Clause, and they were contesting the Commission's findings as to the exact amounts due. Pending the outcome of this litigation, the carriers withheld the sums recoverable by the government. These claims, however, constituted a contingent liability hanging over the carriers, some part of which they would ultimately be required to pay. In view of the drastic decline in earnings the payment of these sums might have proved difficult for some of the carriers. Under the circumstances the repeal of the Recapture Clause was clearly a form of financial relief.

THE TRANSPORTATION ACT OF 1940

Enactment of the Transportation Act of 1940 followed prolonged consideration of the transportation problem by House and Senate committees in 1939 and 1940. Like the Emergency Transportation Act of 1933, the 1940 legislation represented an effort to bring some aid to the railroad industry, which had experienced serious difficulties during the depression of the 30s. The Act also reflected the changes in the nature of the transportation problem that had come about since 1920. The increasing importance of transportation by highway, by water, and by pipelines had intensified interagency competition and had brought to the fore many problems concerning the relations between the different modes of transport and concerning their respective places in the transportation system of the country.

The provisions of the Act were influenced by two special reports on the transportation problem which were made in 1938. The first of these reports was that of Commissioners Splawn, Eastman, and Mahaffie of the Interstate Commerce Commission, who had been asked by the President to submit recommendations for means of immediate relief for the railroads. This committee, commonly known as the "Committee of Three,"

---

[18] Objections to the original Section 15a are discussed more fully in a later chapter. See pp. 357–59, infra.

[19] These criticisms are considered more fully in a later chapter. See Chapter 17.

made its report in April, 1938.[20] The other report was made by a committee representing railroad management and railroad labor, also appointed by the President to submit recommendations upon the general transportation situation. This committee, known as the "Committee of Six," made its report in December, 1938.[21]

The Transportation Act of 1940, as finally enacted, was a document of 66 printed pages.[22] Only the more important of its provisions need be mentioned here.

Regulation of Water Transportation

One of the most important features of the law was the extension of the Commission's jurisdiction over water carriers and the setting-up of a regulatory system for them which is comparable in many respects to that applicable to railroads and motor carriers. The new sections dealing with water transportation were added as Part III of the Interstate Commerce Act. Part II of the Interstate Commerce Act is the part relating to motor carriers, which had been enacted in 1935 as the Motor Carrier Act.[23] When Part II was added in 1935, the old Interstate Commerce Act, as amended, which applied principally to railroads, became Part I.[24] A description of the regulatory system provided for water carries is given in a subsequent chapter.[25]

The enactment of legislation setting up a comprehensive system of regulation for water carries was not without significance for the railroads. Although it was not the intention of Congress that water carriers should be regulated for the purpose of protecting railroads, it is undoubtedly true that regulation of carriers by water does incidentally benefit railroads to a limited degree.[26]

Declaration of National Transportation Policy

A declaration of national transportation policy was added to the Interstate Commerce Act. The declaration of policy precedes Parts I, II, and III of the Act—dealing, respectively, with rail, motor, and water transportation—and lays down a general over-all policy to be observed by the Commission in regulating the various forms of transportation.

---

[20] *Immediate Relief for Railroads*, 75th Cong., 3d Sess., House Doc. No. 583.

[21] *Report of Committee Appointed by the President of the United States to Submit Recommendations upon the General Transportation Situation.*

[22] Official print of the law as *Public—No. 785—76th Congress*. For the statute see 54 Stat. 898.

[23] For a description of Part II of the Act see Chapter 29.

[24] Part I also includes pipelines.

[25] Chapter 32.

[26] Interstate Commerce Commission, *Annual Report, 1940*, p. 15.

The National Transportation Policy reads as follows:

It is hereby declared to be the national transportation policy of the Congress to provide for fair and impartial regulation of all modes of transportation subject to the provisions of the Act, so administered as to recognize and
preserve the inherent advantages of each; to promote safe, adequate, economical, and efficient service and foster sound economic conditions in transportation and among the several carriers; to encourage the establishment and
maintenance of reasonable charges for transportation services, without unjust
discriminations, undue preferences or advantages, or unfair or destructive
competitive practices; to cooperate with the several States and the duly
authorized officials thereof; and to encourage fair wages and equitable working conditions;—all to the end of developing, coordinating, and preserving a
national transportation system by water, highway, and rail, as well as other
means, adequate to meet the needs of the commerce of the United States, of
the Postal Service, and of the national defense. All of the provisions of this
Act shall be administered and enforced with a view to carrying out the above
declaration of policy.

Certain language of the declaration of policy will be considered more
fully in later chapters. It is sufficient to note at this point that Congress
has visualized an adequate transportation system as embracing all three
of the major forms of transportation, and that it recognizes that each has
its inherent advantages which should be recognized and preserved.

Railroad Consolidation

Important changes in the provisions of the Interstate Commerce Act
relating to railroad consolidations and other forms of railroad unification
were made by the 1940 legislation.

First, the requirement that railroad consolidations or unifications
should conform to a Commission-made plan of consolidation, drawn up
in advance, was eliminated. The requirement that consolidations must
conform to such a plan had been put into the Act in 1920.[27] It had come
to be felt that this requirement was a hindrance to railroad consolidation,
since the carriers would not voluntarily consolidate according to the
Commission's plan or in accordance with any plan that the Commission
could draw up in compliance with the standards laid down in the Act.
Removal of this requirement from the Act, however, does not mean that
consolidations may take place without the Commission's approval. A proposed consolidation or unification must be found "consistent with the
public interest."

A second change in the law relating to consolidations was the enumeration of certain factors which should be taken into consideration in the
determination of whether a proposed consolidation or unification was in
the public interest. These factors are: "(1) the effect of the proposed

---

[27] Pp. 247–48, supra.

transaction upon adequate transportation service to the public; (2) the effect upon the public interest of the inclusion, or failure to include, other railroads in the territory involved in the proposed transaction; (3) the total fixed charges resulting from the proposed transaction; and (4) the interest of the carrier employees affected."

A third change in the consolidation provisions of the law was the addition of provisions designed to protect railroad labor affected by consolidations. The Commission was directed to require as a condition of its approval of a consolidation or unification that there be a "fair and equitable arrangement" to protect the interests of railroad employees affected. The Act further required that the Commission should include terms and conditions in its order of approval which would provide that for four years the affected employees should not be placed in a worse position with respect to their employment as a result of the consolidation or unification.[28] The Commission may require that labor be protected for a period longer than four years.[29]

Amendment of Section 15a

The provision in Section 15a of the Interstate Commerce Act which requires that in prescribing rates, the Commission shall give due consideration to the "effect of rates on the movement of traffic" was amended by confining such consideration to the movement of traffic "by the carrier or carriers for which the rates are prescribed." The purpose of this modification of Section 15a was to prevent the Commission from prescribing railroad rates which were designed to protect the traffic of another type of carrier. A similar provision is found in corresponding sections of Parts II and III of the Act. The Commission has interpreted the provisions as meaning that "no carrier should be required to maintain rates which would be unreasonable, judged by other standards, for the purpose of protecting the traffic of a competitor."[30]

Rate Changes—Burden of Proof

The Act of 1940 placed the burden of proof upon the railroad in any proceeding involving a change in rates. The law prior to 1940 had placed the burden of proof upon the carrier when an increase in rates was proposed but not when a reduction was proposed. This rather technical provision of the Act is important, since it strengthens the hand of the Commission in controlling competitive rate reductions.

---

[28] An employee who had not been employed by the carrier for four years was entitled to protection only for a period equal to the length of his employment.

[29] *Railway Labor Executives' Assoc.* v. *United States,* 339 U.S. 142 (1950).

[30] *Seatrain Lines, Inc.,* v. *Akron, Canton & Youngstown Ry. Co.,* 243 ICC 199, 214 (1940). But see Chapter 37.

Land-Grant Rates

The Act, as a means of financial aid to the railroads, released the land-grant railroads from the obligation to transport mail and government traffic, other than military and naval property and personnel, at reduced rates,[31] an obligation which dated back to the period of federal land grants to the railroads between 1850 and 1871.[32] This measure was expected to add about $7 million annually to the revenues of the railroads.

Board of Investigation and Research

Recognition by Congress that the transportation problem was not solved by the enactment of the 1940 legislation is found in the provision for the creation of a three-man board, to be known as the Board of Investigation and Research, to investigate transportation problems and to report its findings and recommendations to the President and to Congress.

The Act specifically directed the Board to make studies of three highly controversial matters: (1) "the relative economy and fitness" of rail, motor, and water carriers, with the view of determining the service for which each was especially fitted or unfitted (2) the so-called "subsidy question," or the extent to which rights of way or other transportation facilities have been provided with public funds for the use of each of the three types of carriers without adequate compensation therefor; and (3) the extent to which taxes are imposed upon the three modes of transport. In addition to these specific inquiries the Board was authorized to investigate any other matters relating to transportation which it might deem important to investigate for the improvement of transportation conditions or to further the national transportation policy declared in the Interstate Commerce Act. The Board was of a temporary nature, since its life was to be for only two years unless extended by proclamation of the President. The President extended its life for an additional two years permitted by the statute; but at the expiration of this period, on September 18, 1944, the Board's existence was terminated.[33]

---

[31] In 1945 Congress went further and relieved the land-grant railroads of the obligation to transport even military and naval property and personnel at reduced rates. 59 Stat. 606.

[32] Pp. 136–37, supra.

[33] On the last day of its existence the Board transmitted 13 reports to Congress. Some of these which have been published are: *Federal Regulatory Restrictions upon Motor and Water Carriers*, 79th Cong., 1st Sess., Senate Doc. No. 78 (1944); *Technological Trends in Transportation*, 79th Cong., 1st Sess., Senate Doc. No. 76 (1945); *Public Aids to Domestic Transportation*, 79th Cong., 1st Sess., House Doc. No. 159 (1944); *Comparison of Rail, Motor, and Water Carrier Costs*, 79th Cong., 1st Sess., Senate Doc. No. 84 (1944); *Carrier Taxation*, 79th Cong., 1st Sess., House Doc. No. 160 (1944). Earlier reports of the Board which were published are: *Report on Interterritorial Freight Rates*, 78th Cong., 1st Sess., House Doc. No. 303 (1943); *Report on Rate-Making and Rate-Publishing Procedures of Railroad, Motor, and Water Carriers*, 78th Cong., 1st Sess., House Doc. No. 363 (1944); *Hourly Remu-*

RAILROAD MODIFICATION ACT, 1948

The financial difficulties of the railroads in the 1930s, which forced many into receivership or trusteeship,[34] revealed the need for a method whereby such receiverships or trusteeships could be avoided, particularly if a carrier's financial troubles were of a temporary nature or if drastic financial reorganization was unnecessary. Receiverships or trusteeships can sometimes be avoided by extending the maturity date of bonds, reducing the interest rate on bonds, refunding existing obligations, or by some financial operation that is not strictly in accordance with the terms of existing securities or agreements. Ordinarily the terms of existing securities can be modified only with the consent of all the holders thereof. Consent is often difficult or impossible to obtain.

The Railroad Modification Act,[35] which became Section 20b of the Interstate Commerce Act, authorizes the alteration or modification of the terms of railroad securities or of the instruments pursuant to which they had been issued, if the Commission approves the proposal, and if it is accepted by holders of at least 75 percent of the principal amount or number of shares of each class of securities affected. For the Commission to approve of a modification of the terms of securities or of underlying agreements, it must find (1) that the proposal will be in the public interest; (2) that it will be in the best interests of the carrier, of each class of its stockholders, and of the holders of each class of obligations affected; and (3) that it will not be adverse to the interests of any creditor not affected by the proposal.

The Railroad Modification Act thus provides a method whereby carriers may at any time seek to ward off pending financial difficulties by appropriate measures, provided such measures meet the tests laid down by the Act and receive the assent of the requisite security holders.

REED-BULWINKLE ACT, 1948

The Reed-Bulwinkle Act[36] added Section 5a to the Interstate Commerce Act. The Act legalized rate bureaus through which the railroads have for many years considered proposals for changes in rates submitted by either railroads or shippers. Rate agreements had been held contrary to the Sherman Antitrust Act in 1897[37] and the legality of rate bureaus

---

neration Rates by Occupations in the Transportation Industry, 78th Cong., 2d Sess., House Doc. No. 623 (1944); *Practices and Procedures of Governmental Control*, 78th Cong., 2d Sess., House Doc. No. 678 (1944).

[34] The term "trusteeship" is used in connection with proceedings under Section 77 of the Bankruptcy Act.

[35] 62 Stat. 162. This is often called the "Mahaffie Act," after Commissioner Mahaffie.

[36] 62 Stat. 472.

[37] See pp. 318–19, infra.

was also open to question. The Department of Justice contended that they were in violation of the Sherman Act, and there was reason for believing that the courts might so hold if the question came before them since rate bureaus are an example of collective action in rate making. Rate bureaus, however, perform a useful function; and there was a general belief among those closest to the problems of rate making that a chaotic state of affairs would ensue if there were not some machinery by which proposals for rate changes might be carefully considered, with all interested parties having a right to be heard.

The Act legalized rate bureaus if their rules, regulations, and procedures were approved by the Interstate Commerce Commission. The Commission was empowered to require reports from the rate bureaus; and their accounts, records, files, and memoranda were to be open to inspection by the Commission.

THE TRANSPORTATION ACT OF 1958

At various times during the 1940s and 1950s the problems of the railroads received the attention of government agencies and Congressional committees.[38] In 1954 President Eisenhower set up an Advisory Committee on Transport Policy and Organization to review over-all federal transportation policies and problems and to submit recommendations. This Committee, under the chairmanship of Sinclair Weeks, Secretary of Commerce, made a report in 1955 recommending various changes in the Interstate Commerce Act, some of which represented a sharp break with traditional policy.[39] Congress, however, failed to enact a law which would carry out the recommendations of the Weeks report.

In the early part of 1958 extensive hearings on "the deteriorating railroad situation" were held before subcommittees of the House and Senate committees on interstate and foreign commerce. As a result of these hearings Congress enacted the Transportation Act of 1958.[40] This Act, in addition to providing aid to financially distressed railroads, dealt with specific difficulties which the railroads had encountered in their efforts to adjust rates and services to new conditions brought about principally by the growth of alternative modes of transport.

---

[38] See particularly Secretary of Commerce, *Issues Involved in a Unified and Coordinated Federal Program for Transportation* (Washington, D.C.: U.S. Government Printing Office, 1949), and Senate Committee on Interstate and Foreign Commerce, *Land and Water Transportation,* 82d Cong., 1st Sess., Senate Rep. No. 1039 (1951).

[39] Presidential Advisory Committee on Transport Policy and Organization, *Revision of Federal Transportation Policy* (Washington, D.C.: U.S. Government Printing Office, 1955).

[40] *Public Law 85–625,* 85th Cong.

Guaranty of Loans

The Interstate Commerce Commission was authorized to guarantee loans by public or private institutions to railroad companies for the purpose of financing capital expenditures or for maintenance work. The aggregate amount of loans which the Commission might guarantee could not exceed $500,000,000. The loan provisions were temporary in nature, finally expiring on June 30, 1963 except as to applications before the Commission on that date. Guaranty of nearly $240 million was eventually authorized.[41] The Commission observed in 1963 that some of the eastern railroads had survived since 1958 only with the help of loans guaranteed under the Act.[42]

Relief from Unduly Low Intrastate Rates

Certain changes were made in Section 13 of the Interstate Commerce Act. It will be recalled that an amendment to Section 13, made by the Act of 1920, had empowered the Commission to raise intrastate rates when necessary to remove discrimination against interstate commerce.[43]

Two decisions of the Supreme Court in 1958 threatened to hamper the Commission in Section 13 proceedings. One of these decisions held that an undue burden on interstate commerce resulting from low intrastate commutation fares could not be found from a mere showing that the operations in question were performed at an out-of-pocket loss, but that it must be shown that such losses were not offset by revenues from other intrastate freight and passenger traffic.[44] In another case the Court held that lower intrastate rates than applied on interstate shipments could not be found to create an undue burden on interstate commerce without positive evidence that the relative costs of moving intrastate traffic were as great as the costs of interstate traffic.[45] The decisions would have greatly increased the difficulties of the railroads in obtaining relief from low intrastate rates in a Section 13 proceeding.

Congress sought to remedy this situation by providing that low intrastate rates and fares could be held to cast an undue burden on interstate commerce without proof that losses on the intrastate operations in question were not offset by profits on other intrastate operations, or without a showing that costs of intrastate operations were at least as great as the cost of interstate operations.

---

[41] Interstate Commerce Commission, *Annual Report, 1969*, p. 80.

[42] *Annual Report, 1963*, p. 36. There is a detailed discussion of the loan guaranty provisions and their administration in George W. Hilton, *The Transportation Act of 1958* (Bloomington, Ind., Indiana University Press, 1969), chap. iii.

[43] Pp. 249–50 supra.

[44] *Chicago, Milwaukee, St. Paul & Pacific R. Co.* v. *Illinois*, 355 U.S. 300 (1958).

[45] *Public Service Commission of Utah* v. *United States*, 356 U.S. 421 (1958).

A second change made in Section 13 was designed to expedite procedures under the Section and thus to provide the railroads with quicker relief from unduly low intrastate rates. The Commission had generally taken the position that when increases in interstate rates had been authorized, and the carriers had requested state authorities to make corresponding increases in intrastate rates, a Section 13 proceeding should not be entertained until the state authorities had taken final action. This procedure resulted in long delays before an adjustment in intrastate rates was made. The amended Section 13 directs the Commission, upon petition of the carriers involved, to undertake an investigation of the intrastate rates alleged to be unlawful under Section 13, whether or not the matter is under consideration by any state agency, and to expedite the proceeding.

Discontinuance of Train Service

Prior to the enactment of the Transportation Act of 1958, the Interstate Commerce Commission had been given no authority over passenger-train service. Most states, however, exercised jurisdiction over passenger-train service within their respective states, whether the service was by trains operating across state lines or not. Reluctance of state authorities to permit discontinuance of unprofitable passenger trains had imposed a greater and greater burden on the railroads as public patronage of passenger trains continued to dwindle. A new section, Section 13a, was added to the Interstate Commerce Act by the 1958 legislation to give the railroads some relief from this situation. The section deals separately with trains operating across state lines and those operating wholly within a state.

With respect to interstate trains whose operations were subject to some measure of state control, the Act authorized discontinuance or change in service upon thirty days' notice to the Commission and to the governor of each state involved, the laws of any state to the contrary notwithstanding. The Interstate Commerce Commission, however, was given the power to prevent discontinuance or change of the service for one year, but only upon a finding that the operation of the service was required by public convenience and necessity and would not unduly burden interstate commerce. After the expiration date of such order, however, the state recovered its jurisdiction over the service unless the railroad again invoked the procedure provided by the section. It is to be observed that Section 13a did not require the approval of the Interstate Commerce Commission before a railroad might discontinue interstate passenger-train service; it authorized such discontinuance upon 30 days' notice unless the Commission interfered.

So far as intrastate train operations as concerned, Section 13a provided that when the discontinuance of service of any train or ferry was prevented by state law or by state authorities, or when action on an application for discontinuance or change of service was delayed by state authorities beyond 120 days, the carriers might petition the Interstate Commerce Commission for authority to effect the discontinuance or change. Such authority could be granted only upon findings that public convenience and necessity permitted such discontinuance or change, and that continued operation would constitute an unjust and undue burden upon the interstate operations of the carrier or upon interstate commerce.

The scope of Section 13a has been greatly restricted by developments under the Rail Passenger Service Act of 1970 shortly to be described.

Amendment of Section 15a

Section 15a of the Interstate Commerce Act—the Rule of Rate Making—was amended by adding a new paragraph as follows:

In a proceeding involving competition between carriers of different modes of transportation subject to this Act, the Commission, in determining whether a rate is lower than a reasonable minimum rate, shall consider the facts and circumstances attending the movement of the traffic by the carrier or carriers to which the rate is applicable. Rates of a carrier shall not be held up to a particular level to protect the traffic of any other mode of transportation, giving due consideration to the objectives of the national transportation policy declared by this Act.

We have previously noted that the 1940 amendment to Section 15a had sought to prevent the Commission from holding up the rates of one mode of transport to protect the traffic of another mode.[46] It was the belief of Congress, however, that in the ensuing years the Commission had not consistently adhered to this principle, and that it had often prevented the railroads from making justifiable reductions in rates to meet the competition of other modes of transport.[47] The 1958 amendment of Section 15a, therefore, sought to insure that the Commission would observe greater consistency in this line of cases, and that it would allow the carriers greater freedom to meet the competition of other modes of transport. Nevertheless, Congress found it necessary to qualify its statement that the rates of a carrier should not be held up to a particular level to protect the traffic of another mode by also directing the Commission to give "due consideration to the objectives of the national transportation policy" declared by the Interstate Commerce Act, which includes an express disapproval of "unfair or destructive competitive practices." The effect of the amendment to Section 15a has been to give

---

[46] P. 267, supra.

[47] See *Transportation Act of 1958*, 85th Cong., 2d Sess., Senate Rep. No. 1647, pp. 2–4; also *Transportation Act of 1958*, House Rep. No. 1922, pp. 13–15.

the carriers greater freedom in competitive rate making than the Commission had permitted in numerous instances prior to the amendment. The extent to which the Commission may restrict competitive rate cutting under the amended Act, although still not clearly defined, is discussed in a later chapter.[48]

Amendments to the Motor Carrier Act

The Transportation Act of 1958 also made amendments to Part II of the Interstate Commerce Act, which relates to motor carriers. These amendments may be more appropriately described in connection with motor-carrier regulation, but brief mention needs to be made of them here because of their effect on railroads. One of the amendments is intended to prevent expansion, by judicial interpretation, of the agricultural commodity exemptions from the Motor Carrier Act. The other amendment is designed to stop evasion of regulation by motor carriers masquerading as private carriers when, in reality, they are carriers for hire. Both of these provisions are intended to prevent diversion of traffic from regulated carriers, both rail and motor.

URBAN MASS TRANSPORTATION ACT OF 1964

This Act[49] represents an effort on the part of the federal government to aid states and local governments in solving the growing problem of highway congestion in urban areas. It provides (1) direct grants for comprehensive transportation planning by state and local governments, and (2) low-interest loans to state and local governments and their public instrumentalities to improve mass transportation facilities according to their need. The administration of the Act was originally placed in the hands of the Housing and Home Finance Agency which later became a part of the Department of Housing and Urban Development. Administration of the Urban Mass Transportation Act was later transferred to the newly created Department of Transportation.

DEPARTMENT OF TRANSPORTATION ACT, 1966

In 1966 Congress provided for the creation of a Department of Transportation to be headed by a Secretary of Transportation in the President's Cabinet.[50] The Act transferred to the new Department many activities relating to transportation formerly carried on by other departments and agencies of the government. Among agencies transferred

---

[48] Chapter 37.

[49] Public Law 88–365.

[50] Public Law 89–670.

to the Department were the Federal Aviation Agency, the Bureau of Public Roads, the St. Lawrence Seaway Development Corporation, the United States Coast Guard, the Alaska Railroad, as well as various functions of the Department of Commerce relating to transportation. In 1968, President Johnson, by Executive Order, transferred to the Department of Transportation the mass transportation program administered by the Department of Housing and Urban Development.

As a result of strong opposition from maritime interests Congress did not transfer to the Department of Transportation the Federal Maritime Administration, located in the Department of Commerce, although such a transfer would logically be expected.

The Department of Transportation exercises no regulatory powers over railroads or other modes of transport, save in the matter of safety. It has extensive powers, however, relating to rail, air, pipeline, and highway safety.

The Department of Transportation will function importantly in the areas of broad transportation policy, the encouragement of transport coordination, and the development of criteria for the investment of government funds in transport facilities, although in the last of these matters it is severely restricted and circumscribed by provisions of the Act.[51]

The Secretary of Transportation was given a specific mandate in the field of transport planning and coordination by the Airport and Airway Development Act of 1970.[52] Section 3 of that Act requires the Secretary of Transportation to formulate and present to Congress for approval a "national transportation policy." In formulating such a policy the Secretary is directed to take into consideration "the coordinated development and improvement of all modes of transportation, together with the priority which shall be assigned to the development and improvement of each mode of transportation. . . ."

The Secretary of Transportation has the right to intervene in cases before the Interstate Commerce Commission and other regulatory bodies that involve important questions of policy. When the Secretary does so he has the same standing as any other party to the proceeding.

RAIL PASSENGER SERVICE ACT OF 1970

In referring to the circumstances surrounding the enactment of Section 13a of the Interstate Commerce Act in 1958, we mentioned the financial burden on the railroads caused by unprofitable passenger trains. Between 1958 and 1970 further losses of passenger traffic and larger passenger deficits occurred. The "solely related" deficit in passenger

---

[51] This matter is discussed in a later chapter. See Chapter 36.

[52] The provisions of this Act are described more fully in Chapter 36.

operations increased and was estimated at $200 million for 1969.[53] Large numbers of passenger trains were discontinued as a result of proceedings under Section 13a, and remaining passenger service deteriorated greatly in quality. Congress, alarmed at this situation, was of the opinion that unless something were done immediately, intercity railroad passenger service would soon cease to exist. The Railway Passenger Service Act of 1970[54] was an effort to prevent this from happening and to make possible an upgrading of passenger service to acceptable standards, and provide a viable rail passenger service between major population centers.

The Act created the National Railroad Passenger Corporation, commonly known as "Amtrak"[55] to take over the operation of rail passenger service over a basic intercity system to be selected by the Secretary of Transportation. The Corporation is to contract with the railroads to provide crews and operating facilities, but equipment would be largely owned by the Corporation.

Railroads contracting with the Corporation to provide the necessary service and facilities are relieved of all obligation to provide passenger service either within or without the basic system. Railroads not joining the system must continue to operate all of their existing intercity service until January 1, 1975, after which discontinuance will be subject to the provisions of Section 13a of the Interstate Commerce Act.

The railroads joining the system, and thereby avoiding the losses associated with the passenger trains then being operated, must pay to join. The cost to them is related to the deficits incurred in their passenger service operations in 1969.[56] Payments may be made in cash, equipment, or future services. In return for their payments, the railroads will receive common stock at par in the National Railroad Passenger Corporation.

Amtrak may provide service in addition to that covered by the basic system, but service cannot be reduced below that provided by the basic system until July 1, 1973. If such additional service is operated for two years, it becomes part of the basic system.

State and regional or local authorities may obtain additional transportation service from Amtrak that is not included in the basic plan if they will pay not less than two thirds of the losses solely related to the service.

The National Railroad Passenger Corporation is managed by a board of directors of 15 members. Eight of the directors are appointed by the

---

[53] Western Railroad Association, *Yearbook of Railroad Facts*, 1971 ed., p. 25. In computing the "solely related" deficit, expenses charged against passenger revenues do not include any apportionment of expenses that are common to both freight and passenger services.

[54] Public Law 91–518.

[55] Originally called "Railpax."

[56] Three alternative methods are provided for determining the price to be paid for joining: (1) 50 percent of the "fully distributed passenger deficit" for 1969; (2) 100 percent of the "avoidable loss" on such passenger operations; or (3) 200 percent of the "avoidable loss" on the intercity passenger services it operated over routes within the basic system.

President of the United States with the consent of the Senate; three are elected by the holders of the common stock; and three are elected by holders of preferred stock. Initially, common stock may be issued only to railroads. The Corporation may raise additional capital by borrowing or by the issuance of preferred stock. Congress made an initial appropriation of $200 million to finance the Corporation.

Operation of passenger services by Amtrak was begun on May 1, 1971. The basic system established by the Secretary of Transportation is shown in Figure 12–1.

FIGURE 12–1. Basic Rail Passenger Routes Operated by Amtrak

Whether or not Amtrak will provide a reasonably adequate intercity rail passenger transportation system without heavy subsidies is uncertain.

It should be noted that commuter rail passenger service and other short-haul passenger service in metropolitan and surburban areas is excluded from the provisions of the Rail Passenger Service Act.

RECAPITULATION OF THE DEVELOPMENT OF REGULATION

The Six Periods

The last three chapters have described the evolution of the present system of railroad regulation. Six rather distinct periods may be recognized in this development. These periods are as follows:[57]

---

[57] This classification, with some changes in phraseology, is taken from Clyde B. Aitchison, "The Evolution of the Interstate Commerce Act: 1887–1937," 5 *George Washington Law Review* 289 (1937).

1. *The Initial Period, 1887–97.* This was the period immediately following the enactment of the Act to Regulate Commerce. During this period the machinery of regulation was set up and the enforcement of the Act undertaken with a fair degree of success.

2. *The Doldrums Period, 1897–1906.* This period followed a series of adverse decisions by the Supreme Court of the United States, which severely weakened the Commission and largely destroyed the effectiveness of the original Act. The most important of these decisions were the Alabama Midland Case[58] and the Maximum Freight Rate Case.[59]

3. *Rehabilitation and Extension of Regulation, 1906–17.* The enactment of the Hepburn Act of 1906 brought an end to the Doldrums Period and made regulation effective once more. The Act was further strengthened by the Mann-Elkins Act of 1910 and by other legislation. This period was brought to a close by World War I and the government's decision late in 1917 to take over the operation of the railroads.

4. *The War Interlude, 1917–20.* During this period, government operation of the railroads took the place of our traditional policy of private operation under government regulation. The powers of the Interstate Commerce Commission were somewhat restricted during this time, although the Commission had many extra duties to perform that grew out of the new relations between the government and the railroad corporations.

5. *The Period of Affirmative Control, 1920–33.* Following the return of the railroads to their owners in 1920 and the enactment of the Transportation Act of 1920, a distinctly new period was ushered in. This period was characterized by a less restrictive approach in regulation and by the adoption of the affirmative policy of seeking to build up an adequate national transportation system. The policy of the government was distinctly constructive in nature.

6. *The Period of Interagency Competition and Railroad and Readjustment, 1933 to Date.* The rise of new forms of transport—motor carriers, pipelines, and air carriers—together with a revival of inland water transport, eventually brought us to a new period of regulation. This period has been characterized by an extension of control to include motor carriers, water carriers, and air carriers, and also by numerous measures designed to aid the railoads in a period of readjustment to new conditions. Much of the attention of regulatory agencies has of necessity been concerned with conflicts that have arisen between two or more modes of transport. The central problem in this period is to effectuate a proper coordination of transportation agencies whereby each mode of transport finds its appropriate sphere of activity in a greatly expanded transportation system.

---

[58] See pp. 235–36, supra.
[59] Pp. 230–31, supra.

SOME OBSERVATIONS ON THE DEVELOPMENT OF REGULATION

In examining the details of the various regulatory measures that have been enacted from time to time, attention may have been diverted from certain general but significant facts which the story reveals.

In the first place, it is apparent that the regulatory system did not spring into existence full blown. It is the result of an evolutionary process extending over more than 80 years. Second, each enlargement of the Commission's powers and each extension of its jurisdiction have been in response to well-defined needs. The provisions of the various acts have been designed to remedy specific abuses or to attain specific objectives considered desirable. Third, the transportation problem has been an ever-changing problem. New legislation has been required as new situations developed or new problems arose. There is every reason to believe that this will continue to be the case and that one cannot look for regulation to assume a final or definitive form. Fourth, where the Interstate Commerce Act has proved to be weak or ineffective, Congress has been disposed to strengthen it in order that its objectives might be accomplished. Finally, some statutory provisions have proved unwise or unworkable, or, because of changed conditions, have been deemed no longer useful. Congress has not hesitated to modify or even to eliminate such provisions.

RECENT PROPOSALS FOR REGULATORY CHANGES

We have previously mentioned a report of a Presidential Advisory Committee on Transport Policy and Organization which was made in 1955.[60] Several other reports on the transportation problem with recommendations for changes in regulatory policy have also been made by government agencies.[61] We cannot here analyze the numerous and sometimes diverse recommendations that have been made. If there is any common element in the proposals advanced by the various study groups, it is that greater emphasis should be placed on competition as a control force in the transportation industry. This is a natural outgrowth of the increased competitiveness that has developed among the various modes of transport. It has led some critics to urge substantial, if not complete, deregulation, with sole reliance on competition to protect the public interest. The only significant legislative action which might indicate a

---

[60] P. 270, supra.

[61] U.S. Department of Commerce, *Federal Transportation Policy and Program* (Washington, D.C.: U.S. Government Printing Office, 1960) and *Rationale of Federal Transportation Policy* (Washington, D.C.: U.S. Government Printing Office, 1960); *National Transportation Policy* (Doyle Report), 87th Cong., 1st Sess., Senate Report No. 445 (1961); *Message of the President of the United States Relative to the Transportation System of the Nation*, 87th Cong., 2d Sess., House Doc. No. 384 (1962).

movement toward deregulation was the cautious modification of the Rule of Rate Making in 1958 to permit greater freedom in competitive rate making. On the other hand, various other legislative proposals, aimed at particular inadequacies and shortcomings in the transportation system, are in the direction of further controls over the specific matters considered. If legislative action should take a turn toward substantial deregulation, we will have entered a distinctly new period in the history of regulation.

SELECTED REFERENCES

The most detailed study of the Hoch-Smith Resolution is W. H. Wagner, *The Hoch-Smith Resolution* (Washington, D.C.: The author, 1929). For shorter discussions see G. H. Robinson, "The Hoch-Smith Resolution and the Future of the Interstate Commerce Commission," 42 *Harvard Law Review* 610 (1929); Kenneth F. Burgess, "Conflict in Legislation Respecting Railroad Rates," 7 *Harvard Business Review* 423, and 8 ibid. 24 (1929); H. C. Mansfield, "Hoch-Smith Resolution and the Consideration of Commercial Conditions in Rate Fixing," 16 *Cornell Law Quarterly* 339 (1931).

On the Railway Labor Act of 1926, as amended, see Lloyd K. Garrison, "The National Railroad Adjustment Board: A Unique Administrative Agency," 46 *Yale Law Journal* 567 (1937); E. B. McNatt, "The Amended Railway Labor Act," 5 *Southern Economic Journal* 179 (1938); William H. Spencer, *The National Railroad Adjustment Board*, University of Chicago Studies in Business Administration, Vol. VIII, No. 3 (Chicago, 1938); Leonard A. Lecht, *Experience under Railway Labor Legislation* (New York: Columbia University Press, 1955); National Mediation Board, *Administration of the Railway Labor Act by the National Mediation Board, 1934–1957* (Washington, D.C.: U.S. Government Printing Office, 1958); Allan P. Matthew, "Defects in Railway Labor Act and in Practices Thereunder Can and Must be Remedied," *Traffic World*, Jan. 9, 1960, pp. 52–54, Jan. 16, pp. 72–76, Jan. 23, pp. 68–74.

For a brief description of Section 77 of the Bankruptcy Act see Interstate Commerce Commission, *Annual Report, 1933*, pp. 15–16, and *Annual Report, 1935*, pp. 20–22. For references on critical discussions of Section 77 and of its administration see references at the end of Chapter 24.

The Emergency Act of 1933 is discussed in R. W. Harbeson, "The Emergency Railroad Transportation Act of 1933," 42 *Journal of Political Economy* 106 (1934).

For discussions of the work of the Federal Coordinator see William J. Cunningham, "The Federal Coordinator's Contribution to Railroad Coordination," 15 *Harvard Business Review* 265 (1937); and S. Earnshaw, "The Federal Coordinator of Transportation," 26 *Kentucky Law Journal* 182 and 298 (1938). There is an excellent account of the work of the Federal Coordinator in Claude M. Fuess, *Joseph B. Eastman, Servant of the People* (New York: Columbia University Press, 1952), chaps. xi–xii. A more detailed study of the Federal Coordinator's work with emphasis on the politics of the matter is

Earl Latham, *The Politics of Railroad Coordination, 1933–36* (Cambridge: Harvard University Press, 1959), particularly chaps. vi–xi.

On the Railroad Modification Act and its origin and purpose see Chauncey H. Hand, Jr., and G. Clark Cummings, "The Railroad Modification Law," 48 *Columbia Law Review* 689 (1948).

For a discussion of the controversy over rate bureaus which led to the Reed-Bulwinkle Act, see Board of Investigation and Research, *Report on Rate-Making and Rate-Publishing Procedures of Railroad, Motor, and Water Carriers,* 78th Cong., 1st Sess., House Doc. No. 363 (1944). There is also a good discussion of the subject in Stuart Daggett, "Railroad Traffic Associations and Antitrust Legislation," 38 *American Economic Review* (Proceedings) 452 (1948). On interpretation and administration of the Reed-Bulwinkle Act, see J. Guandola, "Section 5a of the Interstate Commerce Act and its Interpretation and Application by the I.C.C.," 21 *I.C.C. Practitioners' Journal* 585 (1954).

The Transportation Act of 1940 is described in Ralph L. Dewey, "The Transportation Act of 1940," 31 *American Economic Review* 15 (1941); and R. W. Harbeson, "The Transportation Act of 1940," 17 *Journal of Land and Public Utility Economics* 291 (1941).

For background of the Transportation Act of 1958 see 85th Cong., 2d Sess., Senate Report No. 1647 or House Report No. 1922, both entitled *Transportation Act of 1958.* A good discussion of the Act and its administration, although colored throughout by the author's conviction that free competition rather than public regulation should prevail in the transportation industry, is George W. Hilton, *The Transportation Act of 1958* (Bloomington, Ind.: Indiana University Press, 1969).

For a brief analysis of the situation leading to the Mass Transportation Act of 1964 see the President's Transportation Message of 1962, 87th Cong., 2d Sess., House Doc. No. 384, pp. 9–13, or the earlier report of the Senate Committee on Banking and Currency, 86th Cong., 2d Sess., Senate Report No. 1591 (1960). For analysis of the Act see George M. Smerk, "The Urban Mass Transportation Act of 1964: New Hope for American Cities," *Transportation Journal,* Winter, 1965, p. 344.

On the Department of Transportation Act, see Milton E. Douglass, Jr., "A Critical Analysis of the Department of Transportation," 33 *Journal of Air Law & Commerce* 314 (1967).

For a good description and analysis of the Rail Passenger Service Act of 1970, see Robert W. Harbeson, "The Rail Passenger Service Act of 1970," 38 *I.C.C. Practitioners' Journal* 330 (1971).

The text of the Interstate Commerce Act is published in several different forms. One of the most convenient is *The Interstate Commerce Act,* published by the Superintendent of Documents and frequently revised and brought up to date. It also contains supplementary legislation and related acts.

Chapter

13

THE AGENCIES OF CONTROL

The regulation of railroad transportation is carried out through various governmental agencies. The Congress and state legislatures, the Interstate Commerce Commission and 50 state commissions,[1] state and federal courts, and to a certain extent, the executive branches of the state and federal governments partake in the control. It is the purpose of this chapter to explain the part played by each type of agency mentioned.

DIVISION OF AUTHORITY BETWEEN STATE AND FEDERAL GOVERNMENTS

To define the bounds between state and federal authority is our first task. This problem has been of particular importance in the United States because of the federal character of our government. The states existed before the federal government. The federal government was created by the states, and its powers are enumerated in the Constitution of the United States. It has only the powers specifically delegated to it and such others as are "necessary and proper" for carrying out the delegated powers. Among the powers delegated to the federal government is the power "to regulate commerce with foreign nations, and among the several States, and with the Indian tribes."[2] This provision of the Constitution is known as the "Commerce Clause." The power to regulate commerce which is not interstate or foreign, that is, intrastate commerce, is reserved to the states, since, by the Tenth Amendment, the "powers not delegated to the United States by the Constitution, nor prohibited by it to the States, are reserved to the States respectively, or to the people." These two provisions of the Constitution are the basis for the common statement that the federal government regulates interstate and foreign commerce and the states regulate intrastate commerce.

Railroads are interstate in nature. Few operate entirely within the

---

[1] The degree of control varies from state to state.

[2] Art. 1, Sec. 8.

boundaries of a single state, and those railroads which do operate within the confines of a single state are almost always engaged in interstate business and are therefore subject to federal laws. Interstate railroads are engaged in some purely intrastate commerce and in some measure, therefore, come under the control of the states in which they operate. It can readily be seen, therefore, that any attempt to regulate railroads in the United States would give rise to questions of the extent of federal and state powers, respectively, and to conflicts of authority between state and federal agencies. Many cases involving this conflict have come before the United States Supreme Court.

In attempting to draw the line between state and federal power, the courts have recognized three fields of jurisdiction: (1) the field in which the federal power is exclusive; (2) the field in which the state power is exclusive; and (3) the field in which the states and the federal government have "concurrent" power. The third field requires a word of explanation, for the terminology is inapt. By "concurrent powers" we do not mean that both state and federal regulation can operate at the same time. Either may act; but if both legislate on the same subject matter, the federal law supersedes the state law. Only in the absence of federal legislation can the state act in this field.

In railroad regulation the most important example of exclusive federal power is the power to regulate rates on interstate shipments. The federal government, and it alone, can regulate these rates. Such was the decision of the United States Supreme Court in the Wabash Case.[3] It has likewise been held that only the federal government has the power to require certificates of convenience and necessity of persons desiring to operate buses or trucks as common carriers in interstate commerce, except as such certification may be incidental to the enforcement of valid state regulations.[4]

An example of a power which is vested in state authorities is that of regulating rates on intrastate traffic. The states and not the federal government have control over intrastate rates. The Interstate Commerce Commission does not, and could not, have jurisdiction to pass on the reasonableness per se of purely intrastate rates.[5] The power of the states over intrastate rates is somewhat restricted, as will be developed more fully later, when those rates interfere with the regulation of interstate commerce by the federal government. Control over the abandonment of intrastate operations of railroads located entirely within the boundaries of a state is a matter within the jurisdiction of the states.[6] The Supreme Court has held that the federal law relating to control of abandonments

---

[3] 118 U.S. 557 (1886), described on pp. 223–24, supra, and p. 286, infra.

[4] *Buck* v. *Kuykendall*, 267 U.S. 307 (1925); *Bush* v. *Maloy*, 267 U.S. 317 (1925).

[5] *Arkansas R. R. Commission* v. *Chicago, Rock Island & Pacific R. R. Co.*, 274 U.S. 597; *Florida* v. *United States*, 282 U.S. 194 (1931).

[6] See Chapter 25.

by the Interstate Commerce Commission might be unconstitutional if it were interpreted in such a way as to deprive the states of authority over abandonments which were wholly intrastate.[7]

The field within which federal and state governments exercise concurrent powers includes many phases of railroad regulation. State laws affecting interstate commerce which fall within the field of concurrent jurisdiction are of two sorts: (1) those in which the subject matter is local in character and permits or requires diversity of treatment, and (2) those which represent a valid exercise by the state of its police power and which only incidentally affect interstate commerce. In the first group is found regulation of ferries between points in different states. Regulation of these ferries by a state is a regulation of interstate commerce, but it has been upheld because of the local character of the problem.[8] In like manner, quarantine regulations of a state have been upheld, partially on this ground,[9] and so have state pilotage fees.[10] State regulation of the rates at which natural gas is sold to consumers, even though it is transported by pipeline from without the state, has been held valid because of the local nature of the problem.[11]

The second group consists of regulations held valid because their effect upon interstate commerce is only incidental. Such regulations are not regulations of interstate commerce as such, and they are uniformly upheld unless they impose burdens upon interstate commerce.[12] State control over grade crossings has been upheld on this ground,[13] and so has regulation of the size of train crews.[14] Similarly, state legislation is valid that limits the weight of motor trucks, even when applied to vehicles engaged in interstate commerce, for such limitations represent an attempt on the part of the state to protect its highways.[15] Restrictions of this sort must be reasonable and must not discriminate against vehicles used in interstate commerce. Other restrictions are imposed by the states upon motor-vehicle operators, in an attempt either to preserve the highways or

---

[7] See *Texas* v. *Eastern Texas R. R. Co.*, 258 U.S. 204 (1922), pp. 216–18.

[8] See *Port Richmond & Bergen Point Ferry Co.* v. *Board of Chosen Freeholders of Hudson County*, 234 U.S. 317 (1914).

[9] *Morgan* v. *Louisiana*, 118 U.S. 455 (1886).

[10] *Cooley* v. *Board of Wardens of Port of Philadelphia*, 12 Howard 298 (1851).

[11] *Pennsylvania Gas Co.* v. *Public Service Commission*, 252 U.S. 23 (1920).

[12] An Arizona statute limiting train lengths, although defended as a safety measure, was held invalid because it was obstructive to interstate train operation and went beyond what was plainly essential for safety. *Southern Pacific Co.* v. *Arizona*, 325 U.S. 761 (1945). See also *Bibb* v. *Navajo Freight Lines, Inc.*, 359 U.S. 520 (1959).

[13] *New York & New England R. R. Co.* v. *Bristol*, 151 U.S. 556 (1894), and *Missouri Pacific Ry. Co.* v. *Omaha*, 235 U.S. 121 (1914).

[14] *Chicago, Rock Island & Pacific Ry. Co.* v. *Arkansas*, 219 U.S. 453 (1911); *Brotherhood of Locomotive Firemen & Enginemen* v. *Chicago, Rock Island & Pacific R. Co.*, 393 U.S. 129 (1968).

[15] *Morris* v. *Duby*, 274 U.S. 135 (1927); *South Carolina Highway Department* v. *Barnwell Bros., Inc.*, 303 U.S. 177 (1938).

to protect the health, safety, and comfort of the citizens of the state.[16]

But in the field of concurrent powers the authority of the state is dependent upon nonaction by the federal government over the same subject matter. When the federal government steps in, the states must withdraw. In this manner state regulation of many railroad activities has been supplanted by federal regulation. Federal regulation of railroad accounts precludes action by the states in the same sphere. Regulation of security issues was undertaken by the federal government in 1920, and this law supersedes all state regulation on the subject. The consolidation of railroads has been largely brought under the control of the federal government. When the approval of the Interstate Commerce Commission is secured for a particular consolidation or acquisition of control, the combination may be effected, state laws to the contrary notwithstanding. In the field of railroad safety legislation, federal laws have largely taken the place of state laws.

CONFLICT OVER CONTROL OF RATES

The conflict between the state and federal governments in the matter of rate regulation has resulted in a series of Supreme Court decisions which mark a gradual process of evolution, enlarging the authority of the federal government and restricting that of the states.

The Granger Cases, 1877

The controversy first came before the Supreme Court of the United States in the Granger cases, wherein it was argued that the Granger laws were contrary to the Commerce Clause of the Constitution, since they were to some extent a regulation of interstate commerce. The Iowa statute, which was attacked in *Chicago, Burlington & Quincy Railroad Co.* v. *Iowa*,[17] prescribed maximum rates on traffic moving within the state. The maxima applied even on shipments that moved to points outside the state or which came from beyond the state. A somewhat similar system of regulation was involved in *Peik* v. *Chicago & North Western Railway Co.*[18] The application of these rates to interstate traffic was clearly a regulation of interstate commerce. The Supreme Court, however, found this not inconsistent with the Commerce Clause. Said the Court in the Iowa case: ". . . until Congress acts, the State must be permitted to adopt such rules and regulations as may be necessary for the promotion of the general welfare of the people within its own jurisdiction, even though in so doing those without may be indirectly affected."[19]

---

[16] See *Hendrick* v. *Maryland*, 235 U.S. 610 (1915).

[17] 94 U.S. 155 (1877).

[18] 94 U.S. 164 (1877).

[19] 94 U.S. 155, 163.

And in the Peik case the Court said: ". . . until Congress undertakes to legislate for those who are without the State, Wisconsin may provide for those within, even though it may indirectly affect those without."[20]

The Wabash Case, 1886

The next development in this evolutionary process came with the Wabash decision in 1886.[21] This case has already been mentioned because of its relation to the enactment of the Act to Regulate Commerce in 1887.[22] In this decision the Supreme Court held that rates on interstate traffic could be regulated only by the federal government. Even in the absence of federal regulation the states were held to be without authority over rates on interstate commerce. In other words, the regulation of rates on interstate traffic is not within the field of concurrent jurisdiction. The gist of the Court's reasoning is found in the following statement:

It cannot be too strongly insisted upon that the right of continuous transportation from one end of the country to the other is essential in modern times to that freedom of commerce from the restraints which the State might choose to impose upon it, that the commerce clause was intended to secure. This clause, giving to Congress the power to regulate commerce among the States and with foreign nations . . . was among the most important of the subjects which prompted the formation of the Constitution. And it would be a very feeble and almost useless provision, but poorly adapted to secure the entire freedom of commerce among the States which was deemed essential to a more perfect union by the framers of the Constitution, if, at every stage of the transportation of goods and chattels through the country, the State within whose limits a part of this transportation must be done could impose regulations concerning the price, compensation, or taxation, or any other restrictive regulation interfering with and seriously embarrassing this commerce.[23]

The Minnesota and the Shreveport Cases

The next step in the extension of federal authority came as a result of the decisions in the Minnesota Rate Cases and the Shreveport Cases in 1913 and 1914, respectively. The principle established by these cases was that the federal government might change a purely intrastate rate in order to remove unjust discrimination caused by a low intrastate rate which preferred points within the state and discriminated against points without.

The Minnesota Rate Cases involved the validity of certain intrastate

---

[20] 94 U.S. 164, 178.

[21] 118 U.S. 557.

[22] Pp. 223–24, *supra.*

[23] 118 U.S. 557, 572–73.

rates prescribed by the state of Minnesota. It was contended that these rates, when applied to places on or near the boundaries of the state, preferred such points and discriminated against points outside the state which took higher interstate rates. The Supreme Court held that the state rates could not for this reason be found invalid, since the federal government, in the exercise of its authority over interstate rates, had not found the rate adjustment discriminatory against points outside the state. The decision implied, however, that if the federal government should find the rates discriminatory, the state rates would have to yield. This ruling subordinated state control over intrastate rates to federal regulation of interstate rates whenever the two conflict. "There is no room in our scheme of government for the assertion of state power in hostility to the authorized exercise of Federal power."[24]

In the Shreveport Cases the federal government had found a rate adjustment unduly prejudicial to Shreveport, Louisiana, and preferential to Dallas and Houston, Texas. The state of Texas had maintained lower rates from Dallas and Houston eastward toward Shereveport than the interstate rates from Shreveport westward into Texas, thereby giving the Texas cities an advantage over Shreveport as distributing points. The Supreme Court held that the Interstate Commerce Commission could require the removal of the discrimination by a change in the intrastate rates which were so low as to cause the discrimination. The power of the state to prescribe intrastate rates cannot be exercised in such a way as to defeat the legitimate exercise of federal control over interstate commerce. "Wherever the interstate and intrastate transactions of carriers are so related that the government of the one involves the control of the other, it is Congress, and not the State, that is entitled to prescribe the final and dominant rule, for otherwise Congress would be denied the exercise of its constitutional authority and the State, and not the Nation, would be supreme within the national field."[25] In this case, to have given the state the right to maintain the preferentially low rates would have defeated the enforcement of Section 3 of the Act to Regulate Commerce. State authority has to yield, for "a State may not authorize the carrier to do that which Congress is entitled to forbid and has forbidden."[26]

The Wisconsin Passenger Fares Case, 1922

The final step in the growth of federal control over rates was taken in the Wisconsin Passenger Fares Case.[27] This case involved an interpretation of a change made in section 13 of the Interstate Commerce Act in

---

[24] 230 U.S. 352, 399.

[25] 234 U.S. 342, 351–52.

[26] Ibid., p. 354.

[27] 257 U.S. 563.

1920 which has already been referred to.[28] The decision recognized that the federal government has broader powers over intrastate rates than were established by the Shreveport Cases. It recognized that the Interstate Commerce Commission has the power to bring the level of intrastate rates as a whole up to the level of interstate rates, a power not possessed by the Commission before 1920.[29] Power to raise the level of intrastate rates is, as we have seen, definitely related to Section 15a of the Interstate Commerce Act. The constitutionality of the power rests upon the same reasoning as that used in the Shreveport Cases. State control over intrastate rates cannot be used to defeat federal regulation of interstate commerce, in this case, the regulation of the rate level under Section 15a.

It should not be assumed that a mere difference in the levels of interstate and intrastate rates is sufficient to justify federal action to bring intrastate rate levels to interstate levels. The Supreme Court has held that there must be clear evidence of the inadequacy of revenues from intrastate traffic.[30]

In concluding this account of federal versus state authority over rates, the point needs to be emphasized that the Interstate Commerce Commission "is without jurisdiction over intrastate rates except to protect and make effective some regulation of interstate commerce."[31]

DIVISION OF POWER BETWEEN COMMISSIONS AND THE VARIOUS BRANCHES OF THE GOVERNMENT

We have discussed the division of authority between the federal and state governments in the regulation of carriers. We now turn to a discussion of the respective functions of legislatures, commissions, courts, and the executive branch of the government in the scheme of regulation. Illustrations will be drawn largely from the federal government, but a similar system prevails in most of the states. In the regulation of railroads, commissions occupy the center of the stage. The Interstate Commerce Commission is the principal performer in the day-to-day regulation of railroads on the part of the federal government. All of the states have some sort of commission with jurisdiction over railroads and motor carriers. The Interstate Commerce Commission, like most regulatory commissions, is an "independent" agency of the government, that is, it is not attached to any of the regular departments of the executive branch of the government.

---

[28] Pp. 249–50, supra.

[29] *Illinois Central Ry. Co. v. State Public Utilities Commission of Illinois*, 245 U.S. 493 (1918).

[30] *North Carolina v. United States*, 325 U.S. 507 (1945); *Alabama v. United States*, 325 U.S. 535 (1945).

[31] *Illinois Commerce Commission v. Thomson*, 318 U.S. 675, 684 (1943).

Relation of Commissions to the Legislative Authority

The regulatory commission is an administrative body, created by the legislative authority and dependent upon the latter for its powers. It may exercise only such powers as the legislative authority confers upon it. Commissions exercise legislative, executive, and judicial powers. When aiding in the enforcement of the statutes, a commission acts in an executive capacity. When it determines the reasonableness of a rate on past shipments and awards reparations, it exercises judicial powers. When it prescribes a rate for the future, it acts in a legislative capacity.

Our regulatory laws are couched in very general terms. Early attempts to prescribe rates by statute, as we have seen, were not successful.[32] Rates must be "just and reasonable," but the statute does not, and cannot, specify what constitutes a reasonable or an unreasonable rate. The law prohibits "undue preference and advantage." But when is a preference undue, and when is it not? When is a discrimination just and hence lawful, and when is it unjust and hence unlawful? Railroads are required to provide "adequate facilities," but the statute attempts no definition of what constitutes adequate facilities. It is the inclusion of such general language in the statutes, more than any other fact, that makes the commission form of regulation necessary. Regulation through commissions, says Freund, is based largely on "the inability of the legislature to formulate standards sufficiently definite for private guidance." "This inability," he adds, "may be due either to the inherent inapplicability of uniform standards to varying individual cases or to the temporary failure to discover such principles."[33] The words "just" or "unjust" appear more than 40 times in Part I of the Interstate Commerce Act alone, and the words "reasonable" or "unreasonable" over 70 times. The exercise of discretion or judgment is required in the administration of many provisions of the Act, even when the words "just," "reasonable," or "adequate" are not used. The law cannot specify all the circumstances under which an issue of securities is objectionable or unobjectionable. It therefore vests the Interstate Commerce Commission with broad discretionary powers in determining whether particular issues are "compatible with the public interest" or not. Neither can hard and fast rules be laid down to govern the acquisition of control of one carrier by another. For this reason the Commission must determine whether or not a proposed acquisition of control is "consistent with the public interest." The "public-interest" standard, in one form or another, appears more than 20 times in Part I of the Act. Even when the law is specific in its prohibitions, as in the Long-and-Short-Haul Clause or in the antipooling provisions, exceptions are permitted, because it is recognized that exceptions may be justifiable.

---

[32] See 214–15, supra.

[33] Ernst Freund, *Administrative Power over Persons and Property* (Chicago: University of Chicago Press, 1928), p. 29.

In such cases, the Commission is vested with authority to determine whether exceptions may be permitted or not. As a general thing, then, Congress lays down rather broad principles of regulation, and the Commission applies these principles to the many specific instances that arise.

Constitutionality of Commission Regulation

When a commission prescribes a rate or rule of conduct for the future, it is exercising a legislative power. To grant a commission these powers might seem to be contrary to the principle of constitutional law that the legislative power may not be delegated to others. Since the Constitution vests the legislative power in Congress, it is apparent that the delegation of this power to others would represent an abdication by Congress of its authority and might easily lead to an entirely different form of government from that which the Constitution set up. A sweeping delegation of legislative authority without the safeguards of legislative guides or standards to govern the administrative agencies was fatal to the National Industrial Recovery Act, enacted in 1933.[34] The Supreme Court, however, has referred to the delegation of power to the Interstate Commerce Commission to prescribe just and reasonable rates as an example of the kind of delegation of legislative power which is not unconstitutional.[35]

In distinguishing between delegation of legislative power that is unconstitutional and that which is permissible, the courts have stressed the necessity of standards to guide the commission or other administrative agency. "Congress can not delegate any part of its legislative power except under the limitation of a prescribed standard."[36]

Some of the standards found in the Interstate Commerce Act may seem so broad and vague as to constitute no standard at all. The standard "just and reasonable," so often appearing in the Act, would appear to be of this nature. In this connection, however, it was pointed out by Mr. Justice Roberts that the phrase "just and reasonable" when applied to charges exacted by those engaged in a public calling had acquired a legal meaning under the common law prior to the days of statutory regulation.[37] Other equally broad standards in the Interstate Commerce Act have upheld. Thus, in *New York Central Securities Corp.* v. *United States*, the power of the Commission to authorize the acquisition of control of one carrier by another if such acquisition was found to be "in the public interest" was held not to be an unconstitutional delegation of legislative power when viewed in the light of the purposes and objec-

---

[34] See *Schechter Poultry Corp.* v. *United States*, 295 U.S. 495 (1935), and *Panama Refining Co.* v. *Ryan*, 293 U.S. 388 (1935).

[35] See the Schechter Case, p. 539, and the Panama Refining Case, p. 427.

[36] *United States* v. *Chicago, Milwaukee, St. Paul & Pacific R. R. Co.*, 282 U.S. 311, 324 (1931).

[37] See dissenting opinion in *Bowles* v. *Willingham*, 321 U.S. 503, 538–39 (1944).

tives of the Act.[38] Here, as in other legislation in which broad powers have been delegated, standards that, taken by themselves, seem to be no standards at all take on significance in the light of the objectives of the laws of which they are a part.

Some writers are inclined to the view that the courts have sustained such broad delegation of authority that there is little left of the rule that standards must be prescribed if the delegation of legislative power is to be sustained.[39] However that may be, the constitutional question is often raised when orders of the Interstate Commerce Commission or some other regulatory body are challenged.[40] Aside from the constitutional question, the prescription of legislative standards to guide a commission is a protection against arbitrary action and is also the principal method by which Congress exerts control over regulatory policy.

Primary Jurisdiction of the Commission

The importance which commissions have attained in the regulation of carriers is shown by the doctrine announced by the United States Supreme Court in *Texas & Pacific Railway Co.* v. *Abilene Cotton Oil Co.* in 1907.[41] By this decision the courts were shorn of any power to determine the reasonableness of rates in the first instance. A shipper complaining of the unreasonableness of an interstate rate must seek relief from the Interstate Commerce Commission and not from the courts.

It was the intent of Congress, in enacting the law of 1887, to preserve the legal remedies which then existed for protecting the public against unreasonable and discriminatory rates. This is clearly shown by the wording of the Act. Section 9 provides that

any person or persons claiming to be damaged by any common carrier subject to the provisions of this act may either make complaint to the Commission . . . or may bring suit in his or their own behalf for the recovery of the damages for which such common carrier may be liable under the provisions of this act, in any District or Circuit Court of the United States of competent jurisdiction, but such person or persons shall not have the right to pursue

---

[38] 287 U.S. 12 (1932).

[39] See James Hart, "Limits of Legislative Delegation," 221 *Annals of the American Academy of Political and Social Science* 87 (1942); and Kenneth C. Davis, *Administrative Law* (St. Paul: West Publishing Co., 1951), chap. ii; Bernard Schwartz, "A Decade of Administrative Law," 51 *Michigan Law Review* 775 (1953), pp. 776–82.

[40] E.g., *American Trucking Associations, Inc.* v. *United States*, 101 F. Supp. 710 (1951). Judge Goldsboro, dissenting in *Colonial Airlines* v. *Adams*, 87 F. Supp. 242 (1950), pp. 244–45, believed that the provision of the Civil Aeronautics Act allowing the President to grant or deny permits to foreign air carries to operate between the United States and foreign countries was unconstitutional because of the absence of any legislative standard to guide the President.

[41] 204 U.S. 426.

both of said remedies, and must in each case elect which one of the two methods of procedure herein provided he or they will adopt.

And Section 22 of the Act contained the following language: "Nothing in this act contained shall in any way abridge or alter the remedies now existing at common law or by statute, but the provisions of this act are in addition to such remedies." But in the Abilene Case the Supreme Court held that it was improper for a shipper to sue in court for damages caused by charging a rate alleged to be unreasonable without a prior determination of the reasonableness of the rate by the Interstate Commerce Commission.

This decision, although undoubtedly sound, seems so clearly at variance with the express wording and probable intent of Congress that the reasoning of the Court requires attention. The Court held that the existence of the right to resort both to the Commission and to the courts would destroy the Act, and the Act "cannot be held to destroy itself." The primary purpose of the Act to Regulate Commerce was to prevent discrimination and to enforce equality of treatment by common carriers. For this reason the published rate was made the legal rate, from which all departures were prohibited. But if the courts can find a rate unreasonable, there may be divergence between the views of the Commission and of the courts concerning the reasonableness of a rate. A rate found reasonable by the Commission might be found unreasonable by a court, and a conflict would arise which would render the enforcement of identical charges for the same shipment impossible. Furthermore, since several courts might have jurisdiction over a single through rate, different courts might reach opposite conclusions as to the reasonableness of a particular rate, again leading to the enforcement of one rate in one jurisdiction and another in another. Thus the existence of a power in the courts to determine the reasonableness of a rate in the first instance would destroy the prohibitions against preferences and discriminations found in the Act.

This primary jurisdiction of the Commission exists wherever discretionary powers are involved and the exercise of judgment is necessary. Thus resort must be had to the Commission to determine whether a rate is reasonable or unreasonable, whether a rule for the distribution of cars to shippers involves an unreasonable preference or discrimination,[42] and whether rates are unjustly discriminatory or not.[43]

In cases that involve no administrative question, the courts may exercise jurisdiction and award damages for violation of the Act. If a carrier discriminates against shippers by departure from the published tariff, resort may be had to the courts to recover damages without preliminary

---

[42] *Baltimore & Ohio Railroad Co.* v. *Pitcairn Coal Co.*, 215 U.S. 481 (1910); *Morrisdale Coal Co.* v. *Pennsylvania R. R. Co.*, 230 U.S. 304 (1913); *Midland Valley R. R. Co.* v. *Barkley*, 276 U.S. 482 (1928).

[43] *Robinson* v. *Baltimore & Ohio R. R. Co.*, 222 U.S. 506 (1912).

resort to the Commission.[44] This is different from a situation in which the lawfulness or unlawfulness depends upon determination of the reasonableness of the rate or practice—a situation which requires the exercise of administrative discretion. Action may likewise be taken in court for damages due to unequal enforcement of a car-distribution rule.[45] But if the reasonableness of the rule itself were in issue, it would be necessary to have a preliminary determination of that question by the Commission before the courts could entertain the question of damages.

When the question is one of tariff interpretation, the courts may exercise primary jurisdiction. This is because a question of tariff construction is deemed to be a question of law which the courts can settle.[46] An exception to this rule occurs if words used in a freight tariff are used in a peculiar sense, so that consideration by an administrative body acquainted with the technicalities of tariffs and commercial usage is necessary.[47]

Judicial Review

The commissions, we have seen, are vested with broad discretionary powers in applying to concrete situations the rules of guidance found in the statutes. But when an administrative body is set up with broad regulatory powers, a grave danger arises—the danger of arbitrary and unreasonable exercise of power, endangering the rights and liberties of the parties affected. For this reason the courts must act as a check upon the actions of administrative bodies. This check is achieved through the power of judicial review, i.e., the power to review and, if necessary, to set aside and annul orders of the commission. But it is difficult to determine just how far the courts should go in interfering with the acts of administrative bodies; for if the courts insist upon reopening matters supposedly determined by a commission and substitute their judgment for that of the commission, the latter becomes a worthless body which impedes rather than aids in the regulating process.

Findings of Fact of Commissions Ordinarily Conclusive

Difficulties were encountered in the regulation of railroads prior to 1910 by virtue of the unlimited right of review exercised by the courts over the decisions of the Interstate Commerce Commission under the Act to Regulate Commerce. During the debates in Congress leading to the enactment of the Hepburn Act in 1906, there was much controversy over judicial review of the orders of the Commission. One group desired

---

[44] *Pennsylvania R. R. Co.* v. *International Coal Co.,* 230 U.S. 184 (1912).
[45] *Pennsylvania R. R. Co.* v. *Puritan Coal Co.,* 237 U.S. 121 (1915).
[46] *Great Northern Ry. Co.* v. *Merchants Elevator Co.,* 259 U.S. 285 (1922).
[47] Ibid.

to clothe the decisions of the Commission with finality. The railroad spokesmen, on the other hand, believed in broad review. The result was a compromise which left the matter in an uncertain condition, with the general understanding that the advocates of broad review had more nearly obtained what they wanted. In 1910, however, the proper scope of judicial review of orders of the Commission was clarified by a decision of the Supreme Court in which the courts were restricted to the consideration of purely legal and constitutional questions. In *Interstate Commerce Commission* v. *Illinois Central Railroad Co.*, the Supreme Court, recognizing the advantages of commission regulation, held that the courts must confine their review to questions of power and right and not to matters which could be left to the administrative discretion of the Commission.

Beyond controversy, in determining whether an order of the Commission shall be suspended or set aside, we must consider, *a*, all relevant questions of constitutional power or right; *b*, all pertinent questions as to whether the administrative order is within the scope of the delegated authority under which it purports to have been made; and *c*, . . . whether, even although the order be in form within the delegated power, nevertheless it must be treated as not embraced therein, because the exertion of authority which is questioned has been manifested in such an unreasonable manner as to cause it, in truth, to be within the elementary rule that the substance, and not the shadow, determines the validity of the exercise of the power.[48]

But further than this the courts will not go. As the Court phrased it, a court should not usurp merely administrative functions by setting aside a lawful administrative order upon its conception as to whether the administrative power had been wisely exercised. "Power to make the order and not the mere expediency or wisdom of having made it, is the question."[49]

This position of the Court was reaffirmed and stated with more precision in 1912 in *Interstate Commerce Commission* v. *Union Pacific Railroad Co.*[50] Citing an earlier case, the Commission said that to the findings of the Commission were to be ascribed "the strength due to the judgments of a tribunal appointed by law and informed by experience." The Interstate Commerce Commission is a fact-finding body. Whether a rate or a practice is reasonable or unreasonable, whether a discrimination is just or unjust, or whether a preference is undue or not, are questions of fact which the Commission is particularly fitted to determine. The courts will not therefore substitute their judgment for that of the Commission on such matters. If the courts did so, the advantages of commission regulation would be lost, and the Commission would become "a mere instru-

---

[48] 215 U.S. 452, 470 (1910).

[49] Ibid.

[50] 222 U.S. 541 (1912).

ment for the purpose of taking testimony to be submitted to the courts for the ultimate action."[51]

Grounds for Judicial Interference

We now come to consider more specifically the grounds on which orders of the Interstate Commerce Commission will be set aside by the courts. A distinction must be made here between orders for the payment of money, such as arise from reparation cases, and orders which prescribe rates or which require the carriers to do or not to do certain things. It is the latter type of order with which we are concerned at this point.

The courts will set aside orders of commissions if the statute under which they are issued is unconstitutional. This power necessarily follows from the power of the courts to annul a statute which is unconstitutional. The constitutionality of many provisions of the Interstate Commerce Act has been unsuccessfully attacked.[52] Occasionally a statutory provision has been interpreted in a way that was probably not intended by its framers in order to prevent its being found unconstitutional.[53] Some state statutes regulating railroads have been found unconstitutional, and orders made in accordance with them have been set aside.[54]

A second ground for invalidating commission orders exists if a commission exceeds its statutory authority. The Interstate Commerce Commission, as we have seen, is a creature of Congress. It derives its authority from Congress and may exercise only such powers as the statutes provide. The courts must, if necessary, step in to hold the administrative agency in check and prevent an unauthorized assumption of power. But when a commission oversteps its powers, it is usually not because of any desire to extend its control in an unwarranted manner, but is due to a mistaken interpretation of the statute. Thus, in the Maximum Freight Rate Case,[55] the Interstate Commerce Commission believed that it had the power to prescribe rates for the future, but the Supreme Court thought otherwise because there was no specific grant of the power in the statute.[56]

---

[51] *United States* v. *Louisville & Nashville Railroad Co.*, 235 U.S. 314, 321 (1914).

[52] *The Pipe Line Cases*, 234 U.S. 548 (1914); *Wisconsin Railroad Commission* v. *Chicago, Burlington & Quincy R. R. Co.*, 257 U.S. 563 (1922); *Intermountain Rate Cases*, 234 U.S. 476 (1914); *New England Divisions Case*, 261 U.S. 184 (1923); *Dayton–Goose Creek Ry. Co.* v. *United States*, 263 U.S. 456 (1924).

[53] *Texas* v. *Eastern Texas R. R. Co.*, 258 U.S. 204 (1922); *Ann Arbor Railroad Co.* v. *United States*, 281 U.S. 658 (1930); *Interstate Commerce Commission* v. *Oregon-Washington R. R. & Navigation Co.*, 288 U.S. 15 (1933).

[54] *Missouri Pacific Ry. Co.* v. *Nebraska*, 217 U.S. 196 (1910); *Chicago, Milwaukee & St. Paul R. R. Co.* v. *Wisconsin*, 238 U.S. 491 (1915).

[55] 167 U.S. 479 (1897).

[56] For illustrations of orders set aside because not within statutory authority of the Interstate Commerce Commission see *United States* v. *Pennsylvania R. R. Co.*, 242 U.S. 208 (1916); *Texas* v. *Eastern Texas R. R. Co.*, 258 U.S. 204 (1922); *Ann*

Closely related to the above are the cases in which orders of a commission are set aside because they are not supported by the basic or essential findings upon which the commission's exercise of authority is conditioned. Thus, in one case an order of the Interstate Commerce Commission requiring the installation of power reverse gear on locomotives in place of hand reverse gear was held void. The power to make such a requirement was dependent upon a finding that the existing device caused "unnecessary peril to life or limb." This fact was not established by the Commission; hence the order was void.[57]

Orders of a commission may also be set aside if constitutional guaranties are violated. Here we refer not to the unconstitutionality of a statute, but to the violation of specific constitutional guaranties by the action of the commission. Thus the rates prescribed by a commission may be so low as to violate the Fifth or Fourteenth amendments to the Constitution because they result in the confiscation of property. Rates prescribed by state commissions have sometimes been set aside on these grounds.[58] Rarely have orders of the Interstate Commerce Commission been set aside on account of failure to recognize the constitutional rights of the parties affected.[59] Orders of the Commission have frequently been attacked on this ground without success.[60]

Orders of a commission will be set aside if they are based on a misconstruction or misinterpretation of the statute which the commission is administering.[61] The courts, and not a commission, have the final say as to the meaning and construction of a statute. An order of the Interstate Commerce Commission was set aside in which the Commission denied that it had authority to attach conditions to an abandonment authorization to protect displaced workers.[62] In another case an order of the Com-

---

Arbor R. R. Co. v. United States, 281 U.S. 658 (1930); Peoria & Pekin Union Ry. Co. v. United States, 263 U.S. 528 (1924); United States v. Missouri Pacific R. R. Co., 278 U.S. 269 (1929); St. Louis & O'Fallon Ry. Co. v. United States, 279 U.S. 461 (1929); United States v. Idaho, 298 U.S. 105 (1936).

[57] United States v. Baltimore & Ohio R. R. Co., 293 U.S. 454 (1935). See also Florida v. United States, 282 U.S. 194 (1930); United States v. Chicago, Milwaukee, St. Paul & Pacific R. R. Co., 294 U.S. 499 (1935); Atchison, Topeka & Santa Fe Ry. Co. v. United States, 295 U.S. 193 (1935).

[58] See Northern Pacific R. R. Co. v. North Dakota, 236 U.S. 585 (1915); see also the Minnesota Rate Cases, where rates were found unconstitutional so far as the Minneapolis and St. Louis R. R. Co. was concerned, 230 U.S. 352 (1913).

[59] The only example, so far as the writer is aware, is Chicago, Rock Island & Pacific Ry. Co. v. United States, 284 U.S. 80 (1931).

[60] For example, Kansas City Southern Ry. Co. v. United States, 231 U.S. 423 (1913); Pennsylvania Co. v. United States, 236 U.S. 351 (1915).

[61] As previously noted, misinterpretation of a statute may be the cause of a commission's exceeding its statutory powers, but questions of statutory construction may arise that do not involve the charge that the commission has exceeded its powers.

[62] Interstate Commerce Commission v. Railway Labor Executive Assoc., 315 U.S. 373 (1942).

mission was set aside because it had misconstrued certain provisions of Part II of the Act. The Chicago & North Western Railway had provided a motor-freight service between stations on its lines; but instead of providing the service directly, it had entered into contracts with various motor-vehicle operators to transport the freight for it. The question involved was whether or not the railroad was a common carrier by motor vehicle under Part II of the Act. The Commission held that it was not; the Supreme Court held that it was.[63]

Commission orders may be set aside if based on a mistake of law. By a "mistake of law" is meant the failure of the commission to apply some general rule or principle that the courts have come to consider of general applicability and which should control the disposition of the case.[64] It would also be a mistake of law for a commission to refuse to consider matters which the courts consider relevant to the disposition of a case.

Three illustrations of instances in which orders of the Interstate Commerce Commission have been set aside may clarify the nature of a "mistake of law." An error of law was made by the Interstate Commerce Commission in holding, as it once did, that the unreasonableness of a rate could depend upon the fact that it would injure a particular industry which had developed under the stimulus of an exceptionally low rate.[65] An error of law was also made by the Commission when it held that motor carriers could not maintain lower rates on shipments exceeding a truckload than applied on truckload shipments unless lower costs could be shown.[66] This action of the Commission was in apparent disregard of the rule of law that competition might possibly justify such a rate. The Commission made an error of law when it held that discrimination by a railroad against colored passengers in the accommodations provided was not unjust because there was comparatively little such traffic; ". . . the comparative volume of traffic cannot justify the denial of a fundamental right of equality of treatment."[67]

Lastly, orders of a commission will be set aside if made without evidence or contrary to evidence. Reversal of commission decisions on this ground is necessary in order to provide adequate safeguards against arbitrary action by regulatory bodies. In a case which came before the

---

[63] *Thomson* v. *United States*, 321 U.S. 19 (1944). For other examples of an order set aside because based on misconstruction of the statute see *New Orleans Union Passenger Terminal Case*, 339 U.S. 142 (1950); *Interstate Commerce Commission* v. *J-T Transport Co.*, 368 U.S. 81 (1961); *Interstate Commerce Commission* v. *New York, New Haven & Hartford R. R. Co.*, 372 U.S. 744 (1963).

[64] For a discussion of what constitutes a mistake of law see I. L. Sharfman, *The Interstate Commerce Commission*, Vol. II (New York: Commonwealth Fund, 1931), pp. 441–42; and John Dickinson, *Administrative Justice and the Supremacy of Law in the United States* (Cambridge: Harvard University Press, 1927), pp. 168–69, note.

[65] *Southern Pacific Co.* v. *Interstate Commerce Commission*, 219 U.S. 433 (1911).

[66] *Eastern Central Motor Carriers Assoc.* v. *United States*, 321 U.S. 194 (1944).

[67] *Mitchell* v. *United States*, 313 U.S. 80, 97 (1941).

Supreme Court in 1912,[68] the government contended that since the Hepburn Act empowered the Commission to prescribe a rate if the Commission was "of the opinion" that the existing charge was unreasonable, the courts could not interfere even if the finding of the Commission was wholly without evidence to support it. To this the Court replied:

But the statute gave the right to a full hearing, and that conferred the privilege of introducing testimony, and at the same time imposed the duty of deciding in accordance with the facts proved. A finding without evidence is arbitrary and baseless. And if the Government's contention is correct, it would mean that the Commission had a power possessed by no other officer, administrative body, or tribunal under our Government. It would mean that where rights depended upon facts, the Commission could disregard all rules of evidence, and capriciously make findings by administrative fiat. Such authority, however beneficially exercised in one case, could be injuriously exerted in another; is inconsistent with rational justice, and comes under the Constitution's condemnation of all arbitrary exercise of power.[69]

If the courts are to set aside orders of commissions because the order is based on insufficient evidence or is contrary to evidence, examination by the court of the evidence on which the Commission made its decision is necessary. This might easily lead to a retrial of the case before the court, a practice which largely explains the ineffectiveness of the Interstate Commerce Commission before 1906. The courts, however, are careful to confine their inquiry to a determination of whether there was enough evidence before the Commission to permit reasonable men to arrive at the decision which the Commission reached. The courts will not weigh the evidence or reach an independent conclusion on the questions of fact. The position of the courts was clearly stated in *Interstate Commerce Commission* v. *Union Pacific Railroad Co.*[70] as follows: ". . . the court confines itself to the ultimate question as to whether the Commission acted within its power. It will not consider the expediency or wisdom of the order, or whether, on like testimony, it would have made a similar ruling."[71] The conclusion of the Commission is subject to review, but when supported by evidence is accepted as final.

The Supreme Court has held that an order of the Commission cannot stand if supported by a mere "scintilla of proof," but there must be "substantial evidence" to support it. This comes very close to a re-examination of the evidence and an independent conclusion, but still the Court is careful not to substitute its judgment for that of the Commis-

---

[68] *Interstate Commerce Commission* v. *Louisville & Nashville R. R. Co.*, 227 U.S. 88 (1913).

[69] Ibid., p. 91. For another example of a case in which an order of the Commission was set aside because the Court did not feel that there was sufficient evidence to sustain the order, see *North Carolina* v. *United States*, 325 U.S. 507 (1945).

[70] 222 U.S. 541 (1912).

[71] Ibid., p. 547.

sion.[72] "The judicial function is exhausted when there is found to be a rational basis for the conclusions approved by the administrative body."[73]

Determination of whether there is "substantial evidence" to support an order of the Commission, however, must be based on the record "as a whole," and is not satisfied merely by showing that there is evidence which, taken by itself, would support the Commission's finding. Examination of the whole record is required by the Administrative Procedure Act which was passed in 1946 to govern procedures of administrative agencies of the government.[74] This requirement comes close to, but falls short of, judicial weighing of the evidence and substitution of the judgment of the court for that of the Commission.

Review in Reparation Cases

Orders of the Interstate Commerce Commission for the payment of money, such as arise from reparation cases, are treated differently from administrative orders prescribing a rule for the future. If a carrier fails to comply with a reparation order of the Commission, the injured party must bring suit in a court to recover. The findings of the Commission as to the injury sustained and the amount of damage are not clothed with finality, as in other cases. The Commission's findings are only prima-facie evidence of the facts. This means that there is a rebuttable presumption in favor of the Commission's conclusions. But the carrier is free to present evidence to rebut the conclusions of the Commission, and the court may reach a conclusion different from that of the Commission.[75] The reason for this treatment of reparation orders rests upon the difference in the nature of the Commission's power in reparation cases. Here the Commission is acting in a judicial capacity, and it is natural that the courts should reserve the right of review.

Functions of the Courts in Regulation

The foregoing discussion of the powers of commissions and of the limitations of their power makes it clear that one important function of the courts in railroad regulation is to review and, if necessary, to set aside orders of commissions.

---

[72] For examples of orders of the Interstate Commerce Commission set aside for lack of evidence, see *Florida East Coast Ry. Co.* v. *United States,* 234 U.S. 267 (1914); *United States* v. *New York Central R. R. Co.,* 263 U.S. 603 (1924); *Florida* v. *United States,* 282 U.S. 194 (1931); *Chicago Junction Case,* 264 U.S. 258 (1924).

[73] *Mississippi Valley Barge Co.* v. *United States,* 292 U.S. 282, 286–87 (1934).

[74] See *Universal Camera Corporation* v. *Labor Board,* 340 U.S. 474 (1951). See also *Illinois Central R. Co.* v. *Norfolk & Western Ry. Co.,* 385 U.S. 57, 66 (1966).

[75] See *Meeker* v. *Lehigh Valley R. R. Co.,* 236 U.S. 412 (1915); *Mills* v. *Lehigh Valley R. R. Co.,* 238 U.S. 473 (1915); *Pennsylvania R. R. Co.* v. *Jacoby & Co.,* 242 U.S. 89 (1916).

A second function of the courts is to hear cases in which carriers or shippers are being prosecuted for alleged violations of the Interstate Commerce Act and related acts, and to impose the appropriate penalties in case of conviction.

The courts also consider civil suits brought to recover damages caused by violation of the law. It must be remembered, however, that the Interstate Commerce Commission may also award damages; but when it does, resort to the courts may later be necessary, for if the carrier refuses to pay, the party who is entitled to receive reparation must sue to compel payment. When a proceeding is brought to recover damages in a court instead of before the Interstate Commerce Commission, the doctrine of the Abilene Case requires that if the question of violation depends upon the determination of whether a rate or practice is reasonable or unreasonable or whether it is unjustly discriminatory or not, prior determination of that fact by the Commission is necessary. If the violation of the law does not involve the exercise of administrative discretion, no prior resort to the Commission is necessary.

Another function of the courts is to enforce the common-law obligations of common carriers where the common law has not been superseded by statutory regulations. The Interstate Commerce Commission has no part in the enforcement of common-law obligations of carriers.

The courts must also determine the constitutionality of regulatory statutes and interpret their provisions. This has already been mentioned in connection with the review of commission orders, but it is clear that the question of the constitutionality of a regulatory act or its proper interpretation may arise otherwise than in connection with a commission order.

Another function of the courts is to compel observance of orders of commissions and compliance with the provisions of the law by injunction or mandamus. The Interstate Commerce Act, for instance, specifically authorizes the courts to issue injunctions to prevent violation of orders of the Commission, and the Elkins Act provides that the courts may enforce observance of published tariffs and require the discontinuance of discriminations forbidden by law.

Lastly, the courts may compel the Commission to perform its duties under the law. Thus, in one case the Commission was required by the courts to ascertain certain items called for by the Valuation Act of 1913. The Act directed the Commission to find, among other things, the cost of reacquiring land over and above its present value. The Commission, relying upon a Supreme Court decision to the effect that the cost of reacquiring land was not a proper element to be considered in a valuation proceeding, refused to ascertain the sum when valuing the properties of the Kansas City Southern Railway. The Supreme Court required the Commission to ascertain the sum, since the Commission had no authority to disobey the express command of the statute.[76]

---

[76] *United States ex rel. Kansas City Southern Ry. Co. v. Interstate Commerce Commission,* 252 U.S. 178 (1920).

Relation of Commissions to the Executive Branch of the Government

The executive branch of the government comes into contact with regulation principally in three ways. First, the President, with the advice and consent of the Senate, appoints the members of the regulatory commissions. Second, the President is charged with the enforcement of the laws and has some responsibilities in connection with the enforcement of the acts regulating carriers. Third, the President exercises some influence on the Commission's budget.

The President can do much to make regulation effective by the quality of his appointees to the Interstate Commerce Commission. Political considerations, unfortunately, often play a part in the appointments to the Commission;[77] but notwithstanding this fact, it is generally recognized that the appointments have usually been of high quality.[78]

Although the President appoints the members of the Interstate Commerce Commission, he does not have the power to remove them except for specified causes. During their term of office—seven years—members of the Commission may be removed only for "inefficiency, neglect of duty, or malfeasance in office." The fact that the President may not remove members of independent regulatory commissions at will is of great importance. This was pointed out by the United States Supreme Court in 1935 when President Roosevelt removed Commissioner Humphrey from the Federal Trade Commission. The Court pointed out that the independent commissions, like the Federal Trade Commission, the Interstate Commerce Commission, and others, were to be independent in fact and in no way beholden to the executive. The following statement of the Court, although referring to the Federal Trade Commission, applies equally to the Interstate Commerce Commission: "The commission is to be nonpartisan; and it must, from the very nature of its duties, act with entire impartiality. It is charged with the enforcement of no policy except the policy of the law. Its duties are neither political nor executive, but predominantly quasi-judicial and quasi-legislative."[79] Such independence cannot be attained if the tenure of office of the commissioners is dependent upon the will of another, for as the Court said, "It is quite evident that one who holds his office only during the pleasure of another, cannot be depended upon to maintain an attitude of independence against the latter's will."[80]

The second point of contact between the executive branch of the

[77] See E. Pendleton Herring, *Federal Commissioners: A Study of Their Careers and Qualifications* (Cambridge: Harvard University Press, 1936), chap. vii; also Sharfman, op. cit., Vol. IV (1937), pp. 22–25.

[78] Sharfman, op. cit., pp. 27–35. For a biographical sketch of the first 55 members of the Interstate Commerce Commission see Clarence A. Miller, *The Lives of the Interstate Commerce Commissioners and the Commission's Secretaries* (reprinted from *I.C.C. Practitioners' Journal*, 1946).

[79] *Humphrey's Executor* v. *United States*, 295 U.S. 602, 624 (1935).

[80] Ibid., p. 629.

government and the Commission is through the enforcement of the Interstate Commerce Act. Although orders of the Interstate Commerce Commission are binding upon the carriers unless set aside by the courts, it is through the Department of Justice that action is taken to enforce obedience to the Act. The Bureau of Enforcement of the Commission refers violations of the Act to the appropriate United States attorney for criminal prosecution when such action is necessary. In civil proceedings for the recovery of penalties and in mandamus or other proceedings to compel the filing of tariffs or reports or to compel or restrain some action on the part of the carriers, the information is submitted to the Attorney General for appropriate action. Attorneys of the Commission, however, may aid government attorneys in the preparation and prosecution of cases in the courts.

Not only is the Commission dependent upon the Department of Justice to prosecute carriers and others for violations of the Act, but the Department of Justice is also charged with defending orders of the Commission when they are attacked in the courts. The Commission has a statutory right to intervene in such proceedings and regularly does so. The Commission has been embarrassed on a number of occasions by the refusal of the Department to defend the Commission's orders in court or by its open attack on such orders. Situations of this sort may arise as a result of difference between the views of the Commission and the Department of Justice with respect to the extent to which the policies of the antitrust laws may properly be overridden by other considerations in the administration of the Interstate Commerce Act. Refusal of the Department of Justice to defend orders of the Commission may also arise when some other department of the government, in its capacity as a shipper or consignee, may object to a decision of the Commission, or when the Department of Agriculture, representing the interests of agriculture, disagrees with a Commission decision or policy. The Commission has recommended that the law be changed so that actions to set aside orders of the Commission be brought against the Commission instead of against the United States, and that the Commission rather than the Department of Justice have the responsibility for defending the Commission's orders.[81] The Department of Justice would be granted the right to intervene in such a proceeding and urge its views on the propriety of the Commission's order. By such an amendment to present laws the Commission would not be dependent upon the Department of Justice to defend its orders in court.

The third point of contact between the President and the independent regulatory commissions is through budgetary control. Although Congress ultimately determines the amount of appropriations for the regulatory agencies, the budgets of the agencies are first submitted to the Office of

---

[81] Interstate Commerce Commission, *Annual Report, 1958*, pp. 140–41.

Management and Budget, formerly the Bureau of the Budget, which is part of the executive establishment. The federal budget is prepared by this Office and is submitted by the President to Congress. The Office of Management and Budget not only exerts a great deal of influence in determining the amount of money which a regulatory agency may receive, but it may approve or not approve of funds for particular bureaus and activities of the administrative agency. Thus a hostile or unsympathetic President or budget office can severely cripple the activities of a commission. Congress, of course, may increase or reduce the appropriations recommended by the President.

The Office of Management and Budget affects the Interstate Commerce Commission in another way also. It, like the other regulatory bodies, must obtain approval of this office before making recommendations for legislative action. This procedure has the potentiality of interference with the Commission in the exercise of its statutory function of making recommendations to Congress for additional legislation that it may deem necessary.

THE CIVIL AERONAUTICS BOARD AND THE FEDERAL MARITIME COMMISSION

The material in this chapter has related principally to the Interstate Commerce Commission, which has jurisdiction over railroads, pipelines, motor carriers, and certain carriers by water. Other federal regulatory bodies dealing with transportation are the Civil Aeronautics Board, regulating air transportation, and the Federal Maritime Commission, regulating certain carriers by water on the high seas.

The Civil Aeronautics Board and the Federal Maritime Commission are "independent" agencies like the Interstate Commerce Commission, and their relation to Congress, the President, and the courts is essentially the same as that of the Interstate Commerce Commission. Certain differences between these two regulatory bodies and the Interstate Commerce Commission will be pointed out in the discussion of the legislation which they administer.[82]

DANGERS AND WEAKNESSES OF COMMISSION REGULATION

Although regulation by administrative bodies or commissions is essential to successful regulation of railroads, there are certain dangers and weaknesses in the system.

The danger of arbitrariness in action and assumption of unwarranted power inheres in all attempts at control through administrative bodies to whom broad powers of regulation are delegated. It is for the purpose of

---

[82] Chapters 32 and 34.

warding off this danger that the right of judicial review is insisted upon. This danger has been effectively eliminated in our federal regulatory system.

A second danger lies in weakness of personnel. The task of regulation is at best a difficult one, and it is essential that commissions consist of able men. Our state commissions have sometimes been criticized for failure in this respect, although some of them have consisted of men of high caliber. In general, a high standard of ability has been maintained in appointments to the Interstate Commerce Commission.[83] From the very beginning the Commission has had some members of outstanding ability and reputation, who have been an honor to the public service and who have played an important part in making regulation a success.

A third danger in regulation by commissions is political interference. A commission is, and must remain, an impartial body. Commissioner Eastman once stated emphatically that commissions "must not be under the domination or influence of either the President or Congress or of anything else than their own independent judgment of the facts and the law."[84] The high esteem which has usually been attached to the Interstate Commerce Commission is due in large measure to its independence and freedom from political influences. In the words of a former member of the Commission, that body has "performed its duties in accord with its conscientious convictions of what was the right thing to do, and has not been swayed by popular clamor, by any political influence, . . . and if the time ever comes when the Interstate Commerce Commission has to consider whether or not a thing is going to be popular, and whether or not it is going to be attacked by one political party or another, its usefulness will be very seriously impaired. . . ."[85] The reason for making the Interstate Commerce Commission an independent body, not subordinate to any of the departments of the executive branch of the government, was to keep it free from political control and the influence of changing administrations. For the most part the executive branch of the government has not attempted to interfere with the Commission or its decisions. President Wilson is reported to have said, at a time when important controversies were before the Commission which affected the country as a whole, that he would as soon think of proffering suggestions to the Supreme Court upon a matter before it as to suggest how the Commis-

---

[83] The Nader report on the Interstate Commerce Commission is critical of appointments to the Commission because of the importance attached to political background and sponsorship in their selection. See Robert C. Fellmath, *The Interstate Commerce Commission* (New York: Grossman Publishers, 1970), pp. 1–5.

[84] J. B. Eastman, "A Twelve Point Primer on the Subject of Administrative Tribunals," in G. Lloyd Wilson (ed.), *The Selected Papers and Addresses of Joseph B. Eastman, 1942–1944* (New York: Simmons-Boardman, 1948), p. 375.

[85] Statement of Edgar E. Clark before the Committee on Interstate Commerce, U.S. Senate (1921). Reprinted by National Association of Owners of Railroad Securities.

sion should decide a case.[86] Later presidents have not always been as particular, and have at times made their wishes known to the Commission, or have made public statements which might be interpreted as prejudging matters before the Commission.[87] Political influences frequently appear in the appointment and confirmation of commissioners. One of the most discouraging incidents of this sort occurred in 1928, when the Senate refused to confirm the reappointment of Commissioner Esch, apparently because of his vote in the famous Lake Cargo Coal Case, a very difficult and bitterly contested case in which opposing sectional interests were involved.[88]

Political interference with the Commission may come from the legislative branch of the government as well as from the executive branch. One of the prime merits of commission regulation is that the Commission is protected from political pressures, and can decide controversies in a semijudicial atmosphere and enforce the policy of the law with complete impartiality. Congress should not destroy this advantage of commission regulation by bringing pressure to bear upon the Commission in an attempt to influence its decisions. In order to protect regulatory commissions from political pressures brought by members of Congress, as well as from pressures emanating from the executive branch of the government, a special subcommittee of the House Committee on Interstate and Foreign Commerce recommended in 1959 that legislation be enacted to require that any written communication received by a commission or by a commission employee from a member of Congress or from any person in the executive branch of the government relating to any matter before the commission be made a part of the public record in the proceeding, and that a memorandum of any nonwritten communication from the same sources also be included in the record.[89]

Although both Congressional and executive pressures upon a commission should be prevented, it should be borne in mind that the policies of the law which the Commission must carry out are policies which have been laid down by the legislative branch of the government. Congress, therefore, may properly concern itself with the actual results of regulation and with the policies adopted by the Commission in carrying out the broad and general standards of the Act. There is a constant stream of bills under consideration by committees of Congress which would modify regulatory policy, or which would specify more definitely the policies which should be observed by the Commission in administering particular

---

[86] W. M. Daniels, *American Railroads: Four Phases of Their History* (Princeton: Princeton University Press, 1932), p. 83.

[87] For illustrations see Sharfman, op. cit., Vol. II, pp. 455–58.

[88] See *Hearings of Senate Committee on Interstate Commerce on Confirmation of Commissioner Esch*, 70th Cong., 1st Sess. (1928).

[89] House of Representatives, Special Subcommittee on Legislative Oversight, Committee on Interstate and Foreign Commerce, *Independent Regulatory Commissions*, 85th Cong., 2d Sess., House Rep. No. 2711 (1959), p. 9.

provisions of the Act. Needless to say, much of the proposed legislation would prove to be unwise, and in fact, very little of it survives the legislative process to become part of the law; but it should be clearly recognized, however, that in a democratic form of government the ultimate responsibility for determining regulatory policy rests in the people acting through their chosen representatives.

A fourth danger in commission regulation is the danger of sectionalism. In a country as large as the United States, there is danger that sectional rivalries may split a commission into factions. This is particularly true if appointments are made on a regional basis. Although there is merit in having wide geographical representation upon a commission, there is danger if the members consider that it is their function to represent the sectional interests of the regions from which they come. As Commissioner Eastman once said: "Selection of the members of an administrative tribunal from different parts of the country has its advantages, but they turn to disadvantages, if the members regard themselves as special pleaders for their respective sections."[90]

Lastly, there is the danger that commissions may fall under the control of the industries which they are supposed to regulate, or at least may become unduly sympathetic with their desires. The Interstate Commerce Commission is generally considered to have been successful in carrying out its recognized duty to administer the law "with equal impartiality to both shippers and carriers, with an outlook as comprehensive as the whole country—in 'coldest neutrality.' "[91] However, it has occasionally been accused of partiality toward the railroads, if not subservience.[92] More often it is criticized by the carriers for being unduly harsh to them. It is not surprising that both points of view are encountered, nor that an array of cases can be assembled which, taken by themselves, can be used to support either judgment. All will agree, however, that it is the Commission's duty to keep the public interest uppermost in mind. It needs to be observed, however, that the public interest requires an adequate transportation system, and the transportation system could not long endure if a regulatory commission ignored the legitimate interests of the carriers.

EFFORTS TO PLACE COMMISSIONS UNDER PRESIDENTIAL CONTROL

We have noted previously that Congress has established the Interstate Commerce Commission as an "independent" agency. It was meant to be

---

[90] In Wilson, op. cit., p. 377.

[91] Published letter of Commissioner Aitchison to the President of the United States in reply to criticisms of the Commission by the Agricultural Conference (1925).

[92] For an extreme example of such criticism see Samuel P. Huntington, "The Marasmus of the ICC: The Commission, the Railroads, and the Public Interest," 61 *Yale Law Journal* 467 (1952); but for a detailed reply see Charles S. Morgan, "A Critique of 'The Marasmus of the ICC,'" 62 *Yale Law Journal* 170 (1953).

free from control by the President. There is a school of thought, however, which holds that regulatory commissions should be under the control of the executive. This view was strongly put in 1937 in a report of the President's Committee on Administrative Management, usually called the Brownlow Committee.[93]

The essence of the Brownlow Committee's views was that the President, as Chief Executive, should have all regulatory agencies under his control, since he is responsible for the execution of the laws of the country. This has been called the "executive management doctrine."[94] Of course, it is inconsistent with such a theory to have the administration of important laws in the hands of independent agencies. But this is exactly what Congress wanted in order to insure continuity of policy and to keep the administration of regulatory legislation insulated as much as possible from political pressures.

The Brownlow Committee, in accordance with its views, recommended that the regulatory agencies be placed in one or another of the executive departments, and be responsible to a Cabinet member and through him to the President. It was recognized by the Brownlow Committee, however, that the judicial work of the regulatory agencies should be carried on without interference from the executive.

Although the proposals of the Brownlow Committee were never seriously considered by Congress, a step in that direction may have been taken when the President was authorized to appoint the chairman of various regulatory commissions from their membership to serve at the President's discretion. This was done in 1950 when President Truman, acting under the provisions of the Reorganization Act of 1947, submitted plans for the reorganization of several regulatory commissions, including the Interstate Commerce Commission. Congress rejected the proposal so far as the Interstate Commerce Commission was involved, but accepted the plan as applied to several regulatory commissions, namely, the Federal Power Commission, the Federal Trade Commission, the Securities and Exchange Commission, the Civil Aeronautics Board, and the National Labor Relations Board.

The argument for a permanent chairman for each of the regulatory commissions, designated by the President from their membership, is that it would provide more effective leadership, facilitate communication between the President and the commissions on matters of mutual concern, and would facilitate coordination of various plans and programs of the government.

Objection to vesting the President with authority to designate the chairman of the regulatory commissions has been based on the belief that

---

[93] *Reorganization of the Executive Departments*, 75th Cong., 1st Sess., Senate Doc. No. 8 (1937), pp. 67–71.

[94] Frederick F. Blachly and Miriam E. Oatman, *Federal Regulatory Action and Control* (Washington, D.C.: Brookings Institution, 1940), chap. ix.

it would open the way for executive pressure on the commissions and would compromise their independence. In 1956, the Select Committee on Small Business of the House of Representatives contended that the regulatory commissions which have a chairman appointed by the President had fallen too much under executive influence and become vulnerable to political pressure.[95]

In 1969 it was again proposed, this time by President Nixon, that the President be authorized to designate the chairman of the Interstate Commerce Commission. This was accomplished by Reorganization Plan No. 1 of 1969, which met little opposition and was accepted by Congress. The plan became effective on January 1, 1970. This method of appointing the chairman of the Interstate Commerce Commission replaces the former method of selecting the chairman annually by the Commission under a system of rotation. The plan has advantages, as previously noted, and it is hoped that it will not lead to interference by the President with the independence of the Commission in carrying out its duties in accordance with the requirements of the Interstate Commerce Act.

THE DEPARTMENT OF TRANSPORTATION

Among the agencies of control mention should be made of the Department of Transportation[96] although its regulatory powers are confined to matters relating to safety. The Secretary of Transportation is charged with the duty of developing national transportation policies to be presented to the President and to Congress for their consideration. The Department may therefore be influential in bringing about changes in transportation policy.

The Secretary of Transportation may also intervene in proceedings before the regulatory bodies—the Interstate Commerce Commission, the Civil Aeronautics Board, and the Federal Maritime Commission—as various government departments have done in the past. The Secretary of Transportation, however, cannot dictate policy to the regulatory bodies; they have the responsibility for carrying out the provisions of the regulatory statutes which they administer in accordance with such policies as Congress has laid down therein. Presumably, the testimony and argument of the Department of Transportation will be given the same consideration as that of any other party to a proceeding. It is likely, however, that the intervention of the Department of Transportation in important cases will sometimes bring broader considerations to bear on a particular proceeding than would otherwise have been done.

---

[95] See *The Organization and Procedures of the Federal Regulatory Commissions and Agencies and Their Effect on Small Business*, 84th Cong., 2d Sess., House Rep. No. 2967 (1956).

[96] See pp. 274–75 supra for provisions of the Department of Transportation Act.

SELECTED REFERENCES

The most complete account of the function of the Interstate Commerce Commission and its relation to the other agencies of government is I. L. Sharfman, *The Interstate Commerce Commission*, Vol. II (New York: Commonwealth Fund, 1931). Other excellent studies of commission regulation in general are John Dickinson, *Administrative Justice and the Supremacy of Law* (Cambridge: Harvard University Press, 1927); and Robert E. Cushman, *The Independent Regulatory Commissions* (New York: Oxford University Press, 1941); Kenneth C. Davis, *Administrative Law* (St. Paul: West Publishing Co., 1951); Henry J. Friendly, *The Federal Administrative Agencies* (Cambridge: Harvard University Press, 1962). Among government-sponsored studies of regulatory agencies which have great merit are Board of Investigation and Research, *Report on Practices and Procedures of Governmental Control of Transportation*, 78th Cong., 2d Sess., House Doc. No. 678 (1944); James M. Landis, *Report on Regulatory Agencies to the President-Elect* (Washington, D.C.: U.S. Government Printing Office, 1960). For a discussion of the Landis Report, see Carl McFarland, "Landis Report: The Voice of One Crying in the Wilderness," 47 *Virginia Law Review* 374 (1961). The administrative process is thoroughly examined in Lee Loevinger, "The Administrative Agency as a Paradigm of Government—A Survey of the Administrative Process," 40 *Indiana Law Journal* 287 (1965).

All students of regulatory commissions should read J. B. Eastman's "A Twelve Point Primer on the Subject of Administrative Tribunals," in G. Lloyd Wilson (ed.), *Selected Papers and Addresses of Joseph B. Eastman, 1942-1944* (New York: Simmons-Boardman, 1948), pp. 375–77.

On delegation of legislative authority to commissions and the constitutional question raised thereby, the following are good: James Hart, "Limits of Legislative Delegation," 221 *Annals of the American Academy of Political and Social Science* 87 (1942); Louis L. Jaffe, "An Essay on Delegation of Legislative Power," 47 *Columbia Law Review* 561 (1947); Kenneth C. Davis, op. cit., chap. ii.

The most exhaustive study of the conflict between state and federal authority in the regulation of interstate commerce is George G. Reynolds, *The Distribution of Power to Regulate Interstate Commerce between the Nation and the State* (New York: Columbia University Press, 1928). There is a considerable volume of periodical literature on the subject. Good discussions are by W. C. Coleman, "The Evolution of Federal Regulation of Intrastate Rates: The Shreveport Rate Cases," 28 *Harvard Law Review* 34 (1914); P. S. Peyser, "Authority of the Interstate Commerce Commission over Intrastate Rates," 17 *Georgetown Law Journal* 39 (1928).

For interesting material on group and political pressures as they have affected the Interstate Commerce Commission, see E. Pendleton Herring, *Public Administration and the Public Interest* (New York: McGraw-Hill, 1936), chaps. xi–xii; and by the same author, *Federal Commissioners: A Study of Their Careers and Qualifications* (Cambridge: Harvard University Press, 1936), chap. vii.

On the necessity of maintaining the independence of the regulatory commissions, see Sharfman, op. cit., Vol. IV (1937), pp. 254–74; Geo. H. Mortimer, "Should the Interstate Commerce Commission Remain an Independent Tribunal?" 5 *George Washington Law Review* 701 (1937). Relevant to this matter are the points brought out in A. E. MacIntyre, "Status of Regulatory Independence," 29 *Federal Bar Journal* 1 (1969).

The question of judicial review has been frequently discussed in law periodicals. The following are good discussions of various aspects of the subject: T. P. Hardman, "Judicial Review as a Requirement of Due Process in Rate Regulation," 30 *Yale Law Journal* 681 (1921); H. B. Brown, "Functions of Courts and Commissions in Public Utility Regulation," 38 *Harvard Law Review* 141 (1924); Sharfman, op. cit., Vol. IV, chap. xvi; Martin Tollefson, "Judicial Review of the Decisions of the Interstate Commerce Commission," 5 *George Washington Law Review* 543 (1937); Eugene D. Anderson, "Judicial Review of Decisions of the Interstate Commerce Commission," 31 *George Washington Law Review* 277 (1962).

The relation of the Interstate Commerce Commission to the Department of Justice is discussed in C. H. Johns, "The Interstate Commerce Commission and the Department of Justice," 31 *George Washington Law Review* 242 (1962).

Chapter 14   RAILROAD COMPETITION AND ITS CONTROL

In this chapter we shall discuss the nature of competition among railroads and explain public policy with respect to intrarailroad competition as it has developed over the years. In later chapters we shall consider also competition among motor carriers, carriers by water, and among airlines, while in the last chapters of the book the nature and control of intermodal competition, that is, competition between the different modes of transport, will be discussed.

When railroads were new, there was little thought of subjecting them to an elaborate system of regulation. Competition, which was relied upon to control prices of other goods and services, was expected to control the price of transportation. This attitude was natural enough in view of the prevalent laissez-faire theory of the relation of the state to business enterprises. Competition, furthermore, had worked with some degree of success as a regulator of the charges made for carrying goods over highways, toll roads, canals, and natural waterways. It was eventually discovered that rival common carriers could not haul goods over the same railway, but that the railway company must have a monopoly of carriage over its lines. This made a vast difference in the efficacy of competition. Such competition as might exist would have to be between rival railway lines, and not between rival transportation companies using the same rails and right of way. This fact has certain important consequences. First, economic waste is involved if two railroads are constructed when one can carry all the traffic. And since the cost of building railroads is great, the economic waste involved in duplication is great. To build two railway lines where one is sufficient is as wasteful as building two highways where one will serve the purpose, or two waterways where one is sufficient. In the second place, because of the huge investment necessary for railroad construction and the fixed and specialized nature of that investment, capital cannot flow into and out of the industry easily enough to act as a satisfactory regulator of the rate level.[1]

---

[1] Pp. 142–43, supra.

RUINOUS COMPETITION

There is another peculiarity which results from the fact that railway competition must be competition between rival lines. Competition will reduce particular rates below the cost of the service. This point was made in our discussion of railway rate theory and follows from the fact that to a great extent, railroad expenses are fixed and do not vary with the volume of traffic.[2] Under the stress of competition, railroads will carry traffic at little more than the out-of-pocket costs. As Hadley observed, "It very often involves worse loss to stop producing than to produce below cost."[3] This is what is meant by saying that competition between railroads is ruinous. It means more than the destruction of the weaker rivals; it means that all of the participants in the struggle will eventually succumb because the rates are forced below the full cost of the service.

That unrestricted competition between railroads forces rates to unremunerative levels is amply borne out by experience. Rate wars of a particularly violent nature were common in the 60s and 70s of the last century. Although there is no gain to a railroad in charging less than out-of-pocket costs for the transportation of commodities, it would appear that under the stress of competition, rates often fell below that point. Rates were sometimes so low, it is said, that they scarcely paid for the oil used in lubricating the locomotives and car wheels that transported the goods. At times, cattle were hauled from Chicago to the seaboard for $5 per car, although the normal rate at the time was about $110 per car.[4] Hadley states that in 1873 cattle were carried from Chicago to New York for $1 per car.[5] These are exceptional cases, but reductions far less extreme would result in rates that make little or no contribution to the maintenance of the railway or to a return on the capital invested.

OBJECTIONS TO UNRESTRICTED COMPETITION IN RATES

Unrestricted competition in railway rates is objectionable for three reasons. It depletes the revenues of the railroads, as we have just pointed out; and if continued for any length of time, it will result in bankruptcy. Competition in rates also results in extreme fluctuations in the rates charged. The constant slashing of rates, followed by periods of more normal rates when temporary agreement has been reached, introduces an element of uncertainty that is peculiarly disconcerting to business. A dealer may stock up with goods at one time, only to find that his competitor a few days later pays a lower transportation rate and can undersell him. Or a contractor, making a bid on a piece of construction work, finds

---

[2] Pp. 150–51, supra.

[3] A. T. Hadley, *Railroad Transportation* (New York: Putnam, 1885), p. 70.

[4] J. L. Ringwalt, *Development of Transportation Systems in the United States* (Philadelphia: The author, 1888), p. 251.

[5] A. T. Hadley, "American Railroad Legislation," 75 *Harper's* 141, 147 (1887).

his calculations upset because of a change in the freight rates after the bid has been made. Stability in freight rates is desirable, and unrestrained competition causes numerous and violent fluctuations. Table 14–1 shows the fluctuations in first-class rates between New York and Chicago in the year 1869.

A third objection to competition in rates is that it leads to discrimination. It is usually the uneven character of competition that brings about place discrimination. At competitive points, rates are reduced to levels that cannot be maintained at all points if the railroad is to remain solvent; at noncompetitive points the rates either remain on a normal level or are placed on a monopolistic basis. Rebates and concessions, furthermore, are often given to large shippers who are in a position to divert traffic to

TABLE 14–1. First Class New York–Chicago Rates During 1869*

Date	Cents per Hundred Pounds	Date	Cents per Hundred Pounds
Feb. 4	188	Aug. 23	38
18	45	30	43
24	40	Sept. 22	40
Mar. 15	160	24	35
July 1	188	30	30
31	70	Oct. 4	50
Aug. 2	45	9	75
4	40	13	125
5	30	Nov. 1	140
7	25	29	150

* Albert Fink, *Statistics Regarding the Movement of Eastbound and Westbound Traffic over the Trunk Lines and Connecting Roads* (New York: Russell Bros., 1884), p. 39.

other lines. Making concessions to certain shippers is a more effective means of competition than reducing the published rates because it can be kept secret, for a time at least, and hence does not at once invite a cut by a rival line.

RESTRICTIONS ON COMPETITION AND THEIR LEGAL STATUS

The railroads early discovered that railroad competition was destructive. Some means of holding competition in check was necessary as a means of self-preservation. Various devices were employed to accomplish this purpose.

Agreements to Divide Territory

One such device consisted of agreements to divide territory. Generally these were agreements whereby each carrier promised not to extend its lines into the territory occupied by another, although sometimes the agreements dealt with the solicitation of traffic by rival lines. An agreement to divide territory was made in 1880 by the Southern Pacific, on the one hand, and the roads controlled by the Gould interests, on the other, whereby the northern half of Texas was turned over to the latter and the southern half to the Southern Pacific. The two systems agreed not to build lines into each other's territory.[6] A year earlier an agreement had been made by the three leading railroads in Colorado—the Union Pacific, the Atchison, Topeka & Santa Fe, and the Denver & Rio Grande—allotting certain portions of Colorado to each of the lines in the agreement.[7]

Early Rate Agreements

Agreements to divide territory were effective in preventing the construction of competing lines; but when competitive lines were already in existence, a different type of agreement was usually necessary. The earliest device to meet this situation was the simple rate agreement, whereby the carriers agreed to maintain specific rates. There is some record of rate agreements in the 40s and 50s, but it was not until the further extension of the railway net in the 60s and 70s that they became common.[8] Though various attempts to establish agreed rates in Trunk-Line Territory were made in the early 70s by the principal east-west lines, there was difficulty in bringing all roads into the arrangement, and such agreements as were made proved to be short-lived.[9]

Rate agreements suffered from two weaknesses. The incentive to break away from the agreed rates on the part of individual carriers was too great. Even if the agreement was observed for a time, mutual suspicion on the part of railway officials—often aggravated by the insinuations of shippers looking for concessions—resulted in eventual breakdown. This difficulty might have been overcome if the agreements could have been enforced by the courts. Here the second weakness appears. The legal status of rate agreements was questionable. They were agreements in restraint of trade. There was some difference of opinion as to whether the agreements were so unreasonable as to be unlawful or whether they were reasonable and hence lawful.[10] But their precarious legal position made attempts at enforcement through the courts impracticable.

---

[6] C. S. Potts, *Railroad Transportation in Texas*, Bulletin of the University of Texas, No. 119 (1909), pp. 73–78.

[7] John B. Phillips, "A Colorado Railroad Pool," 5 *University of Colorado Studies* 137, 137–38 (1908).

[8] Caroline E. MacGill, *History of Transportation in the United States before 1860* (Washington, D.C.: Carnegie Institution, 1917), pp. 565–70.

[9] C. S. Langstroth and W. Stilz, *Railway Cooperation*, Publications of the University of Pennsylvania, Studies in Political Economy and Public Law, No. 15 (1899), pp. 20–31.

[10] The legal status of rate agreements under the common law was discussed at length by the United States Supreme Court and by the lower court in the Trans-Missouri Freight Association Case, and in both decisions a minority opinion took issue with the conclusions of the majority. 166 U.S. 290 (1897); 58 Fed. 58 (1893).

Pooling Agreements

The failure of rate agreements to prevent rate wars led to the formation of pooling agreements. A pooling agreement is an agreement between railroads to divide competitive business. They are of two types—traffic pools and money pools.[11] In a traffic pool the competitive traffic is divided among the rival carriers. In a money pool the traffic moves over the various lines without interference, but the receipts from the competitive business, or a portion thereof, are divided among the participating carriers. Traffic pools imply an interference with the privilege of shippers to route their traffic, and it was largely for this reason that the money pool was more common. Sometimes, however, a traffic pool was successfully operated by permitting some large shipper to send his shipments over one route or another in amounts that would even up the total flow of traffic according to agreed percentages. Shippers acting in this capacity were called "eveners," and in return for their services to the railroad companies they received rebates or concessions from the published rates. One of the most famous of these arrangements was the cattle eveners' pool, formed in 1875, in which cattle shipments from Chicago to New York were evened in accordance with agreed proportions by a group of large shippers in return for generous rebates. The Standard Oil Company acted as an evener in connection with shipments of crude petroleum from producing points in Pennsylvania to the seaboard.[12]

The Chicago-Omaha pool, organized in 1870, is often called the first pool in the United States, though others probably existed before that time. This pool divided the Chicago-Omaha business between the Chicago, Burlington & Quincy, the Chicago & North Western, and the Chicago, Rock Island & Pacific. It was reorganized in 1882 and later merged in a larger organization.[13] An elaborate system of pools was maintained by the Southern Railway and Steamship Association in the South.[14] Pooling agreements were very extensive in the 70s and 80s. During 1878 the Illinois Central Railroad participated in more than 20 pools in Iowa and Illinois alone, and the Chicago and Alton was a party to 12 such arrangements.[15]

Pooling arrangements were only partially successful in stabilizing rates. Rate wars frequently broke out, started by some carrier dissatisfied with its allotment of the competitive traffic. Some of the pooling agreements, however, succeeded in maintaining rates at profitable levels.

---

[11] Some writers consider agreements to divide territory as a third type of pool.

[12] Ringwalt, op. cit., p. 273.

[13] For a description see Robert Riegel, "The Omaha Pool," 22 *Iowa Journal of History and Politics* 569 (1924).

[14] Described fully in H. Hudson, "The Southern Railway and Steamship Association," 5 *Quarterly Journal of Economics* 70 (1890).

[15] H. T. Newcomb, "The Present Railway Situation," 165 *North American Review* 591, 595 (1897).

Legal Status of Pools

One reason why pooling agreements were not wholly successful was the difficulty of enforcing observance of them through court action. Pooling agreements were quite generally held to be unreasonable restraints of trade, and the courts would therefore refuse to enforce observance of them.[16] The Supreme Court of Louisiana summed up the common-law status of pooling in 1889 by saying: "American jurisprudence has firmly settled the doctrine that all contracts which have a palpable tendency to stifle competition, either in the market value of commodities or in the carriage or transportation of such commodities, are contrary to public policy, and therefore incapable of conferring upon the parties thereto any rights which a court of justice can recognize or enforce."[17] The philosophy behind this position was revealed somewhat more fully in a similar pronouncement by the Indiana Supreme Court in 1890:

> . . . a contract between corporations charged with a public duty, such as is that of common carriers, providing for the formation of a combination having no other purpose than that of stifling competition, and providing means to accomplish that object, is illegal. The purpose to break down competition poisons the whole contract, and there is here no antidote which will rescue it from legal death. The element which destroys the contract is the purpose to stifle competition, for a combination of rival carriers, moved and controlled by that purpose alone, is destructive of public interests, and, to the last degree, antagonistic to sound public policy.[18]

In the case quoted, as in some other cases, there were guarded statements to the effect that an agreement designed wholly to prevent destructive competition might be lawful, but pooling agreements generally fared badly in the courts. Occasionally a court recognized that competition between railroads was not an unmixed blessing. The New Hampshire Supreme Court in 1890 recognized that railway competition might become ruinous in character:

> While, without doubt, contracts which have a direct tendency to prevent a healthy competition are detrimental to the public and consequently against public policy, it is equally free from doubt that when such contracts prevent an unhealthy competition, and yet furnish the public with adequate facilities at fixed and reasonable rates, they are beneficial, and in accord with sound principles of public policy. For the lessons of experience, as well as the deductions of reason, amply demonstrate that the public interest is not subserved by competition which reduces the rate of transportation below the standard of

---

[16] See *Chicago, Milwaukee & St. Paul Ry. Co.* v. *Wabash, St. Louis & Pacific Ry. Co.,* 61 Fed. 993 (1894).

[17] *Texas & Pacific Ry. Co.* v. *Southern Pacific Ry. Co.,* 6 So. 888, 891.

[18] *Cleveland, Columbus, Cincinnati & Indianapolis Ry. Co.* v. *Closser,* 126 Ind. 348, 361.

fair compensation; and the theory which formerly obtained that the public is benefited by unrestricted competition between railroads has been so emphatically disproved by the results which have generally followed its adoption in practice that the hope of any permanent relief from excessive rates through the competition of a parallel or rival road may, as a rule, be justly characterized as illusory and fallacious.[19]

The extralegal status of railroad pools at common law did not prevent their establishment. The difficulties of enforcing them were overcome in part by strengthening the organizations, usually called "traffic associations," which administered them. It was the Act of 1887 that brought an end to the era of pooling agreements. Section 5 of the Act provided: "That it shall be unlawful for any common carrier subject to the provisions of this act to enter into any contract, agreement, or combination with any other common carrier or carriers for the pooling of freights of different and competing railroads, or to divide between them the aggregate or net proceeds of the earnings of such railroads, or any portion thereof."

Even in 1887 there was much doubt of the wisdom of prohibiting pooling. The Cullom report, on which the act was largely based, had not recommended it. The prohibition was inserted in the law as a result of a number of last-minute compromises and at the insistence of Judge Reagan of Texas.

During the 90s there was continual agitation for relaxing the antipooling provisions. The railroad spokesmen went further, asking that the agreements be given a legal status so that they could be enforced in the courts. They argued that pooling prevented discrimination, stabilized rates, and eliminated ruinous competition. There was no denying that this was true in so far as pooling was successful in actually controlling competition. To a certain extent the antipooling provisions were inconsistent with the rest of the Act. The main purpose of the Act was to prevent discrimination, yet competition existing at some points and not at others was the principal cause of discrimination. As the Commission pointed out in 1898, the Act endeavored "to eradicate the results and to perpetuate the cause."[20] But railway spokesmen also maintained that pooling agreements would not prevent competition and hence that the public had no need to fear monopoly. Undoubtedly there was some truth in the contention that a desire for a larger share of the total traffic in the next allotment caused competition between railroads in a pooling agreement, but it must be remembered that the benefits of pools to the participating carriers resulted from the elimination of competition. In so far as competition was not eliminated, the benefits would not arise; and if the benefits were attained, competition was largely eliminated.

---

[19] *Manchester & Lowell Railroad* v. *Concord Railroad*, 20 Atl. 384 (1890).

[20] Interstate Commerce Commission, *Annual Report, 1898*, p. 16.

Was the antipooling policy a wise or a foolish one? It would have been better to have permitted pooling if, at the same time, adequate public control over rates had been provided. But in the absence of adequate regulation the public was justified in insisting upon competition as further protection. As Commissioner Prouty pointed out in 1897: "Competition gives a low rate; but it produces a succession of evils which are deplorable. Pooling, by removing competition, does away with the evils; but it puts into the hands of the carriers absolute power over the rate; and that power should not be entrusted to them until some effectual restraint is put upon the exercise of it."[21] And the Interstate Commerce Commission, although admitting the evils of unrestrained competition and the benefits of pooling, was even more emphatic in its language. "The members of the Interstate Commerce Commission wish to say in the strongest possible terms that they are unanimous in the opinion that . . . to repeal the fifth section and enact in its place a pooling bill, thereby permitting and inviting unlimited combination between carriers, would be little better than a crime against the people of the United States, unless this tribunal, or some other tribunal, is at the same time invested with adequate powers of control."[22]

Rate Agreements and Traffic Associations

After 1887 the traffic associations which had administered the pooling agreements were reorganized, and the pooling agreements were generally given up. In their stead the carriers resorted to rate agreements. Carefully established rate differentials were sometimes as effective in dividing traffic as pooling arrangements had been. These rate agreements maintained by the carriers were more successful than the ones attempted before pooling had become common. The traffic associations were strong enough to enforce observance, sometimes by a system of fines. But even after 1887 a few arrangements continued in effect which practically constituted pools. One such pool was called the "Buffalo Grain Pool." It divided the grain traffic from Buffalo to New York City between a number of railroads.[23]

Legal Status of Rate Agreements

From 1887 to 1897 stability in rates, in so far as it was attained, was largely due to the rate agreements maintained through traffic associations. The common-law status of these agreements remained uncertain, as we have already pointed out. As far as the Act to Regulate Commerce was concerned, rate agreements were neither authorized nor prohibited, since

---

[21] 24 *Forum* 446, 454 (1897).

[22] Interstate Commerce Commission, *Annual Report, 1897*, p. 50.

[23] Interstate Commerce Commission, *Annual Report, 1900*, pp. 21–23.

the Act made no mention of them. But in 1890 the Sherman Antitrust Act was adopted. Section 1 provided that "Every contract, combination in the form of trust or otherwise, or conspiracy, in restraint of trade or commerce among the several States, or with foreign nations," is illegal. Section 2 declared that "Every person who shall monopolize, or attempt to monopolize, or combine or conspire with any other person or persons, to monopolize any part of the trade or commerce among the several States, or with foreign nations, shall be deemed guilty of a misdemeanor." In 1897 the United States Supreme Court, in *United States* v. *Trans-Missouri Freight Association*,[24] held that the Trans-Missouri Freight Association, which had maintained rates in the territory immediately west of the Missouri River, was a combination prohibited by the Sherman Act. In the following year a similar decision was reached regarding the Joint Traffic Association, which maintained rates in Trunk-Line Territory.[25] In the Trans-Missouri Case a majority of the Court held that the rate agreements were agreements in restraint of trade and so fell within the prohibitions of the Sherman law. A minority held that the agreement was a reasonable one and that the Sherman Act was not intended to apply to *all* combinations in restraint of trade but only to unreasonable ones such as were condemned by the common law.

Rate Bureaus

The outlawing of rate agreements did not result in complete independence in rate making on the part of the railroads. In fact, this would have been impossible since so many rates are joint rates, involving participation by two or more carriers. Some form of cooperation among carriers is essential. Traffic associations and rate bureaus continued to exist, and through them were channeled proposals for changing rates. The rate bureaus are organized on a regional basis, each concerned with traffic moving within or between certain areas.[26] Proposals for changes in rates, under their procedures, receive careful consideration by committees

---

[24] 166 U.S. 290.

[25] *United States* v. *Joint Traffic Association*, 171 U.S. 505.

[26] The principal rate bureaus, excluding those concerned exclusively with tariff publication, and the headquarters of each, are as follows: Central Freight Association, Chicago; Coal, Coke, and Iron Ore Committee, C.F.A. Territory, Pittsburgh; Coal and Coke Committee, Trunk-Line Territory, New York; The Colorado-Utah Freight Bureau, Denver; Illinois Freight Association, Chicago; New England Freight Association, Boston; North Pacific Coast Freight Bureau, Seattle; Southern Freight Association, Atlanta; The Southern Ports Foreign Freight Committee, Chicago; Southwestern Freight Bureau, St. Louis; Texas-Louisana Freight Bureau, Dallas; Trans-Continental Freight Bureau, Chicago; Trunk-Line Association, New York: Western Trunk-Line Committee, Chicago. This list is taken from Board of Investigation and Research, *Report on Rate-Making and Rate-Publishing Procedures of Railroad, Motor, and Water Carriers*, 78th Cong., 1st Sess., House Doc. No. 363 (1944), p. 41.

representing the railroads involved, after hearings at which shippers and interested parties are given an opportunity to be heard. Recommendations with respect to proposed rate changes are made by committees, but it has been the general practice to recognize the right of individual carriers to take independent action if they are dissatisfied with the recommendations of carrier committees. Rate-bureau procedure, however, is a form of collective action in rate making in which rate changes are not made without careful consideration of the wishes of all the carriers concerned.

Rate bureaus functioned for many years without any attack upon their legality. But in 1944 their lawfulness was challenged by the Department of Justice. As a result Congress enacted legislation to legalize them.[27]

Consolidation and Combination

In the late 90s a nationwide movement toward railroad consolidation and combination set in. Combination of railroads was no new thing, since our large railroad systems had been built up by the combination of numerous independent railroad companies. Thus the New Haven Railroad was said to be a combination of 203 separate companies,[28] the Chicago, Burlington & Quincy of approximately 200 different companies,[29] and the Pennsylvania Railroad System of over 600.[30] But the consolidations of the 90s and the following decade were not so much for the purpose of building up railroad systems which would be strong from an operating and a traffic standpoint as for the purpose of eliminating competition.

A brief description of the more important combinations of the period will indicate the extent to which elimination of competition was taking place. In the 90s the New York, New Haven & Hartford had obtained control of all lines in southern New England, and the Boston & Maine had built up another system in northern New England. In 1907 the New Haven acquired practically a controlling interest in the Boston & Maine. The two systems had been separated by the Boston & Albany, extending westward across Massachusetts. In 1911 an arrangement was made whereby the profits or losses of the Boston & Albany were to be shared equally by the New York Central and the New Haven. The New Haven had also acquired control of the Rutland Railroad, and it had earlier obtained control of the Central New England and the New York, Ontario & Western, giving it access to the anthracite coal fields of Pennsylvania

---

[27] See pp. 269–70, supra, and pp. 325–26, infra.

[28] J. J. Pelley, *Motor Bus and Motor Truck Competition* (an address, 1932).

[29] Walter R. McFarland, "Unification of Carriers under the Interstate Commerce Act," 9 *I.C.C. Practitioners' Journal* 325 (1942).

[30] H. W. Schotter, *The Pennsylvania Railroad Company* (Philadelphia: Allen, Lane, and Scott, 1927), p. 438.

and an outlet to the Great Lakes. Numerous electric railways in New England and steamship lines operating along the coast were also brought into the system, thus giving the New Haven a practical monopoly.

In Trunk-Line Territory, two large systems had grown up prior to 1900. These were the New York Central and the Pennsylvania. Between 1900 and 1902 the Pennsylvania bought a large amount of stock in the Baltimore & Ohio, the Chesapeake & Ohio, and the Norfolk & Western. The New York Central also had a large interest in the Chesapeake & Ohio. The Reading Railroad and the Central Railroad of New Jersey came into the group when the Reading Company, controlling both of these rail-roads, was acquired partly by the Baltimore & Ohio and partly by a sub-sidiary of the New York Central. Many smaller lines in Trunk-Line Ter-ritory were held individually or jointly by the New York Central and the Pennsylvania or their subsidiaries. These arrangements left the New York Central and the Pennsylvania in control of the lines in Eastern Territory.

In Southern Territory the Morgan financial interests acquired the Southern Railway and the Atlantic Coast Line–Louisville & Nashville system. The latter system was effected in 1902 by the acquisition of over 300,000 shares of Louisville & Nashville stock by the Atlantic Coast Line Railroad Company. Numerous small lines were brought under the control of the two systems or were jointly controlled by them. This arrangement eliminated serious competition in the South, or at least brought it under control.

In the West there were numerous combinations during this period, but the most striking development was the attempt of E. H. Harriman to monopolize the transcontinental routes. The Union Pacific, which had come under the control of Harriman, controlled the Oregon Short Line and the Oregon Railroad & Navigation Company. In 1901 the Union Pacific acquired a large stock interest in the Southern Pacific, which in turn controlled both the Central Pacific Railroad and the Pacific Mail Steamship Company. Later the Union Pacific acquired a half interest in the San Pedro, Los Angeles & Salt Lake and about 13 percent of the stock of the Santa Fe. The stock held in the latter was far short of a controlling interest, but it was enough to prevent serious competition. To the north of the Union Pacific system lay the Hill lines—the Great Northern and the Northern Pacific. In 1901 these two roads had purchased about 97 percent of the stock of the Chicago, Burlington & Quincy Railroad. Harriman attempted at about this time to obtain control of the Northern Pacific. He failed in this attempt, and in 1902 the Great Northern and the Northern Pacific were brought together by the creation of the Northern Securities Company—a holding company which obtained control of both roads by exchanging its stock for the shares of the Great Northern and the Northern Pacific. Harriman, because of his large holdings of North-ern Pacific stock, became a large stockholder in the Northern Securities

Company. The result of these various transactions was to bring the transcontinental lines under Harriman's control or influence and to prevent serious competition.

The Sherman Act and Railroad Consolidations

These railroad combinations were viewed with alarm by the public, which still relied upon competition for protection against excessive rates. In 1907 the Interstate Commerce Commission, reporting on the combinations effected by Harriman, said, "Competition between railways as well as between other industries is the established policy of the nation."[31] At that time about 40 states had laws or constitutional provisions prohibiting the combination of competing lines. It was not strange that the Sherman Antitrust Act was invoked in an effort to break up the railroad monopolies. There followed a series of prosecutions by the Department of Justice which destroyed, in part, some of the combinations formed during the period. The more important of these decisions deserve mention. In 1904 the United States Supreme Court required the dissolution of the Northern Securities Company, which had effected the combination of the Great Northern and the Northern Pacific railways.[32] In the dissolution of the company, the assets, consisting of Northern Pacific and Great Northern shares, were distributed ratably to the shareholders of the Northern Securities Company. This meant that for a time, at least, the same stockholders would control both railroads. It cannot be said, therefore, that the dissolution restored competition between the two systems. In 1912 the Supreme Court held that the ownership by the Union Pacific of 46 percent of the stock of the Southern Pacific also violated the Antitrust Act.[33] In a subsequent proceeding the Court refused to permit the Union Pacific to distribute its Southern Pacific shares to its stockholders because it would leave the Union Pacific shareholders in control of both roads.[34] In 1922 a further dissolution of the Harriman combination was required by breaking up the control of the Central Pacific by the Southern Pacific,[35] but this decree was never carried out because the Southern Pacific obtained the permission of the Interstate Commerce Commission to retain control of the Central Pacific under the provisions of the Transportation Act of 1920.[36] The influence of the antitrust laws was shown in the dissolution of the New Haven monopoly in New England. Threatened prosecution resulted in an agreement between the New Haven and the Department of Justice whereby the New Haven surrendered control of

---

[31] *Consolidations and Combinations of Carriers*, 12 ICC 277, 305 (1907).

[32] 193 U.S. 197.

[33] 226 U.S. 61 (1912).

[34] 226 U.S. 470 (1913).

[35] 259 U.S. 214.

[36] 76 ICC 508 (1923).

the Boston & Maine and disposed of its holdings of stock in various trolley lines and steamship companies.

In some of the arguments before the Court the wisdom of trying to enforce competition between carriers was questioned, if not seriously condemned, but the Court was disposed to consider this as a question for Congress to settle. In the Northern Securities Case the Court said:

Whether the free operation of the normal laws of competition is a wise and wholesome rule for trade and commerce is an economic question which this court need not consider or determine. Undoubtedly, there are those who think that the general business interests and prosperity of the country will be best promoted if the rule of competition is not applied. . . . Be all this as it may, Congress has, in effect, recognized the rule of free competition by declaring illegal every combination or conspiracy in restraint of interstate and international commerce. As in the judgment of Congress the public convenience and the general welfare will be best subserved when the natural laws of competition are left undisturbed by those engaged in interstate commerce, and as Congress has embodied that rule in a statute, that must be, for all, the end of the matter, if this is to remain a government of laws, and not of men.[37]

The Clayton Act, 1914

In addition to the Sherman Antitrust Act, Congress has enacted other measures which relate to railroad combinations. One of these was the Clayton Act of 1914. Section 7 of the Clayton Act provided "That no corporation engaged in commerce shall acquire, directly or indirectly, the whole or any part of the stock or other share capital of another corporation engaged also in commerce, where the effect of such acquisition may be to substantially lessen competition between the corporation whose stock is so acquired and the corporation making the acquisition, or to restrain such commerce in any section or community, or to create a monopoly in any line of commerce." It should be noted that the Clayton Act applies to all corporations engaged in commerce, not merely to railroad corporations. Another section of the Act prevents the acquisition of the stock of competing corporations by holding companies. Under the Clayton Act the Interstate Commerce Commission compelled a number of railroad companies, or controlled holding companies, to divest themselves of stock in other railroad companies. In 1929 the Baltimore & Ohio, the New York Central, and the Nickel Plate were ordered to dispose of stock of the Wheeling & Lake Erie.[38] In 1930 the Baltimore & Ohio was also ordered to dispose of stock of the Western Maryland,[39] and the Pennsylvania Company and the Pennsylvania Railroad Company were ordered to divest themselves of their holdings of the stock of the

---

[37] 193 U.S. 197, 337–38 (1904).

[38] 152 ICC 721; 156 ICC 607.

[39] 160 ICC 785; 183 ICC 165.

Lehigh Valley[40] The order of the Commission in the latter proceeding, however, was set aside by the courts.[41] It should be noted that the prohibitions of the Clayton Act do not apply when holdings of stock are for investment only, and not for control.

Prohibition of Interlocking Directorates

A provision in the Transportation Act of 1920 prohibits interlocking directorates among railroads.[42] The Section provides that "After December 31, 1921, it shall be unlawful for any person to hold the position of officer or director of more than one carrier, unless such holding shall have been authorized by order of the Commission, upon due showing, in form and manner prescribed by the Commission, that neither public nor private interests will be adversely affected thereby."

Appraisal of the Policy toward Combination

Prohibiting the combination of competing railways is open to the same criticism and justification as the policy toward pooling agreements. The policy was based on the mistaken belief that unrestricted competition between railroads was desirable. At the same time the public can hardly be criticized for refusing to surrender the protection afforded by competition when the powers of regulatory bodies over railroad rates and practices were insufficient to prevent the exercise of monopoly power. This was particularly true in the last decade of the 19th century and the first of the 20th, when the system of regulation was weak. The United States Supreme Court remarked in 1896, when it blocked a combination of the Great Northern and the Northern Pacific as contrary to the laws of Minnesota, that public regulation alone would be "but a feeble protection against the monopoly thus created if the combination were effected."[43] As regulatory control over railroads developed, there came to be less reason for maintaining this attitude. This undoubtedly explains the relaxation of restrictions on combination after 1920.

MODIFICATION OF POLICY TOWARD COMPETITION

The 1920 Legalization of Pooling and Consolidation

The historic policy toward competition and combination was modified by the Transportation Act of 1920. This Act, as we have elsewhere shown, legalized pooling agreements when approved by the Commission,

---

[40] 169 ICC 618.

[41] 66 F. 2d 37 (1933); 291 U.S. 651 (1934).

[42] Par. 12, Sec. 20a.

[43] *Pearsall* v. *Great Northern Ry. Co.*, 161 U.S. 646 (1896).

endeavored to bring about the consolidation of railroads into a limited number of systems, and provided for the exemption of the carriers from the antitrust laws, state and federal, in so far as was necessary to effect any combination authorized by the Commission. The new policy was sometimes hailed as a reversal of the previous policy.[44] As a matter of fact the policy was not reversed. Pooling was permitted, to be sure, but only when it did not "unduly restrain competition" and the requirement that competition be preserved "as fully as possible" was put foremost in the instructions to the Commission for drawing up a plan of consolidation. It was clearly the intent of Congress that the limited number of systems to be created were to be competitive systems.[45]

Although the Commission has granted numerous applications of railroads to enter into pooling agreements, it cannot be said that pooling has been extensively used to hold competition in check. The reason presumably lies in the efficacy of other methods of stabilizing rates. Pooling, however, has eliminated some wasteful duplication of service such as often accompanies competition between carriers.[46]

Legalization of Rate Bureaus in 1948

The legalization of rate bureaus by the enactment of the Reed-Bulwinkle Act in 1948[47] may be considered as another step in the relaxation of the policy of enforced competition among railroads, although the exact legal status of the rate-bureau method of rate making had never been determined by the courts.

We have already noted that the methods and procedures of rate bureaus clearly represent a form of collective action in rate making that may have been in violation of the antitrust laws. The legality of rate-bureau methods, however, was not brought in issue until 1944, when the Department of Justice brought suit against the Western Association of Railway Executives, the Association of American Railroads, and certain individual railroads, alleging that the rate-bureau method of rate making

---

[44] See S. W. Moore, "Our Lagging Railway Mergers," 16 *Virginia Law Review* 743 (1929); J. B. McDonough, "Consolidation of Railroads," 16 ibid. 149 (1929); Eliot Jones, "Status of Railroad Problems," 219 *North American Review* 592, 598 (1924); Walker D. Hines, "The Public Interest in Railroad Unification and Consolidation," 13 *Proceedings of the Academy of Political Science* 329 (1929).

[45] For a discussion of Congressional intent see W. C. Green, *Preliminary Report of Study of Railroad Consolidation and Unifications*, 71st Cong., 3d Sess., Part I (1931), pp. 15–24.

[46] For some examples of pooling agreements authorized, see *Puget Sound–Portland Joint Passenger-Train Service*, 96 ICC 116 (1925); *Twin Cities–Head of Lakes Joint Passenger-Train Service*, 107 ICC 493 (1926); *Pooling of Ore Traffic in Wisconsin & Michigan*, 201 ICC 13 (1934); *Pooling of Merchandise Traffic from St. Louis, Mo. to Los Angeles*, 276 ICC 424 (1949); *Pooling, LCL Freight Service, New York to Miami*, 283 ICC 171 (1951).

[47] See pp. 269–70, supra.

used by the western railroads was in violation of the Sherman Antitrust Act. In the same year the state of Georgia instituted a suit in the Supreme Court of the United States alleging conspiracy on the part of the railroads against Georgia, and the South generally, in the making of freight rates. In this case, also, the legality of the rate-bureau method of fixing rates was questioned.[48] The view that rate-bureau activities were in violation of the law was based on the position taken by the Supreme Court in anti-trust cases that price-fixing devices in industry are in violation of the Sherman Act.[49] And in *Georgia* v. *Pennsylvania Railroad Co.*, the decision in which the Supreme Court decided to take jurisdiction over Georgia's complaint of conspiracy in the fixing of rates, the Court stated clearly that the railroads were subject to the antitrust laws. It pointed out that Congress had given the Commission power "to lift the ban of the anti-trust laws in favor of carriers who merge or consolidate," but that Congress had not given the Commission authority "to remove rate-fixing combinations from the prohibitions contained in the anti-trust laws."[50]

It was because of the questionable legality of the rate bureaus and the general belief among carriers, shippers, and regulatory bodies that the rate bureaus performed very necessary functions in rate making that Congress passed the Reed-Bulwinkle Act in 1948, which legalized rate bureaus but placed them under the control of the Interstate Commerce Commission. Rate bureaus and their operations are now lawful. Their rules and procedures, however, are under the control of the Commission, and the Act specifically requires that the bureaus recognize the right of individual carriers to take independent action in making rates if they do not wish to follow the recommendations of carrier committees.

REGULATORY CHECKS ON COMPETITION

Thus far in our discussion of checks on competition we have referred to those devised by the railroads themselves. Regulation, however, imposes certain checks on free competition.

In the first place, the fact that rates must be published and cannot be changed except after 30 days' notice prevents active competition in rates of the sort that was common in the 70s, when rates might fluctuate from day to day or week to week. Legislation against discrimination provides another deterrent to competition, for rate reductions often take the form of concessions and rebates to shippers wherever this is necessary to hold traffic to a given line. Similarly the Long-and-Short-Haul Clause, with its restrictions on the reduction of rates at competitive points without similar reductions at intermediate points, has deterred the railroads from

---

[48] This case was dismissed by the Supreme Court in 1950.

[49] *United States* v. *Socony-Vacuum Oil Co.*, 310 U.S. 150 (1940).

[50] 324 U.S. 439, 456 (1945).

rate cutting. To some extent the same may be said of Section 3, with its broad prohibitions of undue preference and prejudice.[51]

The power to prescribe minimum rates, a power given the Interstate Commerce Commission in 1920, created another, and very important, regulatory check on competition. The provision was intended to check disastrous rate cutting. The Commission had pointed out the need for this power as early as 1893.[52]

Another important check upon competition is found in the provisions of the Act of 1920 which gave the Interstate Commerce Commission control over new construction by railroad companies.[53] In the period when the railroad net was being expanded in the United States, there was little restriction on new construction. A few states had found it desirable to prevent indiscriminate railway building, but generally speaking, the attitude of the public was: The more railroads, the better. Railroads were often built for the purpose of selling them to a competing line, or they were constructed for the profits to be derived from construction rather than from successful operation. Even when they were undertaken with a view to profits of operation, strategic considerations arising from struggles with competing lines often dictated the expansion program without consideration of economic need. Two examples will illustrate the point. The construction of the Western Pacific Railroad from Salt Lake City to San Francisco in the years 1905 to 1911—a line which followed nearly the same route as the Central Pacific—was a project not justified by available traffic. It was projected by the Gould interests, controlling the Denver & Rio Grande and the Missouri Pacific railroads, and was undertaken for the purpose of giving that system an outlet to the Pacific Coast which would be independent of the lines controlled by E. H. Harriman. The line cost over $79 million and although necessary for the success of the proposed Gould transcontinental system, it was not economically justified at the time and resulted in the wrecking of the companies which had attempted to finance it.[54] Another illustration is found in the construction of the Puget Sound extension of the Chicago, Milwaukee & St. Paul Railway after 1905. The failure of the St. Paul in 1925 was due in large measure to this expansion. The extension from the Missouri River to the Pacific Coast, costing more than $250 million, was not justified from an economic point of view as there was an excess of transcontinental rail facilities at the time, and the country did not develop fast enough to support all the lines. But from the point of view of the strategy of the situation, the project seemed essential, for without it the St. Paul was likely to be bottled up by the expansion of other railroad systems.

---

[51] Notwithstanding the fact that competition at some points and not at others may justify a discrimination between places under Section 3. See Chapter 22.

[52] *Annual Report, 1893*, pp. 38–39, 220–23.

[53] P. 247, supra.

[54] *Denver & Rio Grande Investigation*, 113 ICC 75 (1926).

RAILROAD COMPETITION TODAY

Competition in Rates

It is sometimes said that competition in railroad rates no longer exists and that only competition in service remains. In a sense this is true, but it is not wholly true. Railroad rates possess a degree of stability not known in the competitive days of the 70s and 80s. Railroads do not seek traffic by indiscriminately cutting rates or by granting concessions and rebates to every shipper that is in a position to bargain for preferential treatment. But as Professor Daniels pointed out, "To argue that stabilized rates . . . evidence the non-existence of competition is analogous to saying that physical bodies in equilibrium argue the absence of the law of gravitation."[55] Competition, as we have shown in a previous chapter, greatly modifies the rate structure, and this is true even though rate making is carried on through rate bureaus. The all-pervading influence of competition on rates will be further demonstrated in the chapters on discrimination between places and on long-and-short-haul discrimination.

Competition in Service

Competition in service is generally held to be desirable, although the necessity for limiting competition in rates has long been accepted. On the affirmative side it can be said that the struggle for traffic operates strongly and more effectively than the hand of regulation to bring about adequate and efficient transportation service and improvements in facilities. Railroads have often shown a genuine interest in the development of the communities which they serve. But there is another side of the picture. Competition in rates and competition in service are not unlike. In the one case, competition results in the giving of a certain service at a less price; in the other it results in giving more service at the same price. Either may adversely affect the revenues of the carriers. Competition in service often leads to provision of duplicating and unprofitable services. We have already noted that pooling agreements have been made by competing railroads in certain instances to reduce wasteful services that had been brought about by competition. Competition in service has often led to wasteful capital expenditures through the construction of duplicating facilities. Waste of this sort was shown by the report of the Commission in an investigation of produce terminals at Philadelphia and Buffalo. In 1926 the Baltimore & Ohio and the Reading railroads jointly opened a produce terminal in Philadelphia costing approximately $3.1 million. Not to be outdone, the Pennsylvania Railroad opened a competing terminal, which cost about $6.5 million. Both were used at less than half their

---

[55] "Economic Purposes and Limitations of Consolidation," 14 *American Economic Review* (Supplement), 43, 47 (1924).

capacity, and either alone would have been adequate for the needs of the city.[56] In Buffalo, the Erie and Nickel Plate railroads engaged in a contest with the New York Central to provide terminals. The former spent about $6.7 million and the New York Central about $2.7 million in providing rival facilities.[57] Competition between railroads at New York and other ports also resulted in the furnishing of warehousing service by carriers for shippers at nominal charges, which resulted in large losses to the railroads and constituted a drain upon their resources.[58] Competition in service has resulted in the payment by railroads of allowances to industry-owned railroads for switching and spotting services performed by the industry-controlled roads.[59]

An attempt to eliminate many of the wastes of competition was undertaken in the United States by the Railroad Administration when the government was operating the railroads during World War I. During this period, traffic was routed over the shortest routes, terminals were unified, competitive passenger trains were eliminated or "staggered," ticket offices were consolidated, solicitation of traffic was discontinued, and advertising was abandoned. With the return of the railroads to their owners in 1920, many of the wasteful practices were revived. The acute depression which began in 1929 called attention to many of these wastes again. The primary purpose of the Emergency Railroad Transportation Act of 1933 was to enable the railroads, through cooperative effort, to eliminate many of these practices. Recalcitrant carriers were to be brought into line through the powers given the Federal Coordinator, and exemption from antitrust laws was granted, in so far as necessary, to permit concerted action authorized or required by the Coordinator. These provisions of the Emergency Act, however, were of a temporary nature, and they are no longer effective.[60]

POLICY OF THE INTERSTATE COMMERCE COMMISSION TOWARD COMPETITION

Since confusion and uncertainty exist concerning the advisability of adhering to competition in the railroad field or of abandoning it in favor of monopoly, it is not out of place to inquire into the attitude of the Commission on the question as expressed in its decisions and as followed in the administration of certain provisions of the law. In so doing, we must remember that the Commission must faithfully carry out the policies of Congress in so far as they have been expressed in the law. On the

---

[56] *Duplication of Produce Terminals*, 188 ICC 323, 324 (1932).

[57] Ibid., pp. 333–34.

[58] *Propriety of Operating Practices—New York Warehousing*, 198 ICC 134 (1933); 216 ICC 291 (1936); 220 ICC 102 (1937).

[59] *Industrial Railways Case*, 29 ICC 212 (1914).

[60] See p. 268, supra.

other hand, sufficient discretion is given the Commission in the administration of the Act to make significant its attitude toward competition.
The issue of competition versus monopoly may arise in many types of
proceedings, but the most important cases in which they arise are (1)
those involving proposed new construction; (2) those involving the exercise of the Commission's minimum-rate power, and (3) those involving
railroad consolidations and acquisitions of control. The Commission's
attitude toward railroad competition will be considered in each of these
three types of cases.

Control of New Construction

Congress clearly intended to put some check on the building of unnecessary railroad mileage by enacting the provision in the law which
requires a certificate of public convenience and necessity before new lines
or extensions may be built. The Commission has frequently denied authority to construct additional rail lines when the added facilities were
unnecessary, or would merely divert traffic from one railroad to another.[61] The Commission has specifically stated that there is no good reason why a railroad should be constructed for the purpose of taking traffic
away from another "unless its service is inadequate or it is unwilling to
publish rates which will enable the traffic to reach destinations in all
available territory on reasonable terms."[62]

At the same time the Commission does not recognize that the first
carrier entering a territory has a monopoly of the area and that other
carriers must be excluded.[63] The courts have upheld the Commission on
this point.[64] If a new line or extension will perform a useful service, serve
new communities or areas, shorten routes, or provide needed capacity,
the mere fact that it will result in diverting traffic from other railroads is
not sufficient to prevent authorization.

In a number of cases the Commission has permitted the extension of
lines into territory theretofore served by other lines. In most, if not all,
cases of this sort the new lines would improve transportation service in
the region and therefore had some justification other than the introduction of competition, but the Commission nevertheless spoke approvingly
of the increased competition that would result. In a case authorizing a
railroad to build into territory served by the Great Northern, the Com-

---

[61] *Chicago, Burlington & Quincy R. Co. Construction*, 282 ICC 725 (1953);
Southern Ry. Co. Construction, 275 ICC 792 (1951); *Northern Pacific Ry. Co. Construction*, 295 ICC 281 (1956); *Nashville, Chattanooga & St. Louis Ry. Construction*,
295 ICC 363 (1956).

[62] *Elizabeth Southern Ry. Proposed Construction*, 166 ICC 105, 114 (1930).

[63] *Oregon Electric Ry. Construction*, 189 ICC 262 (1932); *St. Louis–San Francisco Ry. Co. Construction*, 271 ICC 282 (1948).

[64] *Pennsylvania Railroad Co. v. United States*, 40 F. 2d 921 (1930); *Indian Valley
Railroad v. United States*, 52 F. 2d 485 (1931).

mission said: "It is probable that the competition afforded would stimulate the Great Northern to further improve its service. Competition, within reason, rather than monopoly, is in the public interest."[65]

Many of the more recent cases involving new construction consist of applications to build short extensions or branches to serve newly developed agricultural areas, new mines, new industrial locations or newly developed ports. In these cases there are often two or more lines seeking access to these new sources of traffic when one line alone would be sufficient. Here the Commission frequently grants the authority to one railroad and denies it to others in the interest of preventing unnecessary duplication of facilities and waste of resources.[66]

Minimum-Rate Cases

The minimum-rate power is most frequently exercised at the present time to control competition between the different modes of transport. The power was originally given the Commission for the purpose of controlling rate cutting among railroads, and it is this aspect of minimum-rate control that we are concerned with at this point.

The Commission will, of course, exercise its minimum-rate power to prevent the establishment of rates that do not cover the direct or out-of-pocket costs of providing the service.[67] However, if the Commission's power to condemn rates as too low were confined to situations in which the rates did not cover out-of-pocket costs, its power to control ruinous competition among railroads would be very largely ineffective. Rate reduction, counterreductions by a competitor, and further cuts by the first carrier in retaliation could go on unchecked until the rates reached the level of out-of-pocket costs. The Commission's minimum-rate power is not so limited. In 1928 a federal court said: ". . . since the passage of the Transportation Act of 1920, the Commission has the right to prescribe minimum rates, and we agree with the Commission that a construction of the law is too narrow which limits its rights to prescribe such rates to cases where the rates proposed are unreasonable per se, or are so low as to a cast a burden on other traffic."[68] The Court specifically held that the Commission could prescribe minimum rates to prevent ruin-

---

[65] *Construction of Line by Wenatchee Southern Ry. Co.*, 90 ICC 237, 257 (1924). For other cases in which the desirability of maintaining competition is expressed, see *Construction by San Antonio & Aransas Pass Ry.*, 111 ICC 483 (1926); *Construction by Virginia & Western Ry.*, 145 ICC 167 (1928); *Construction of Railroad Lines in Eastern Oregon*, 111 ICC 3 (1926).

[66] E.g., *Monon Railroad Construction & Operation*, 324 ICC 208 (1965); *Atlantic Coast Line R. Co.* v. *United States*, 243 F. Supp. 945 (1965); *Northern Pacific Ry. Co. Construction Mesa-Mattawa, Wash.*, 331 ICC 71 (1965).

[67] *Cocoanut Oil from Pacific Coast to Eastbound Transcontinental Destinations*, 167 ICC 599 (1930); *Ex-Lake Grain to North Atlantic Ports*, 235 ICC 415 (1939); *Iron Ore from Eastern Ports to C.F.A. Points*, 300 ICC 102 (1957).

[68] *Anchor Coal Co.* v. *United States*, 25 F. 2d 462, 471 (1928).

ous rate wars and to protect the earnings of the railroads. In 1935 the Supreme Court upheld an order of the Commission in which minimum rates were prescribed to prevent the disruption of a rate structure which had been found reasonable.[69]

Although the Commission's power to prescribe minimum rates to halt or prevent rate wars, or to protect a rate structure which is designed to yield the carriers adequate revenue, is firmly established, the Commission has repeatedly asserted that the minimum-rate power should be exercised sparingly, and "only in cases where it clearly appears that its exercise is necessary in order that substantial public injury may be avoided."[70] This is the only policy consistent with another long-established principle, namely, that carriers have a right to considerable freedom in adjusting their rates to meet competitive conditions.[71]

Consolidation and Control Cases

Probably the most important cases involving the issue of competition between railroads are those relating to consolidation and acquisition of control. In these cases the Commission's early policy undoubtedly reflected Congressional policy as expressed in the provisions of the Transportation Act of 1920. It will be recalled that in the "plan" of consolidation which was to be drawn up by the Commission, competition was to be preserved as fully as possible. Acquisitions of control short of technical consolidation, however, were not, under the 1920 Act, subject to any requirement that competition be preserved, but the Commission recognized that Congress had declared itself in favor of preserving competition between railroads.[72] In both consolidation cases and those involving acquisition of control through lease or stock ownership, the Commission recognized the Congressional policy that competition be preserved.[73] On the other hand, in some rather important instances acquisitions of control were authorized which would otherwise have been in violation of the antitrust laws. One of the outstanding examples was the authorization of the combination of the Great Northern and the Northern Pacific, although the Supreme Court had found such a combination illegal under the antitrust laws.[74] This decision divided the Commission

---

[69] *Youngstown Sheet & Tube Co.* v. *United States*, 295 U.S. 476 (1935).

[70] *Sugar Cases of 1922*, 81 ICC 448, 472 (1926). See also *Iron & Steel from Utah to Pacific Coast Points*, 276 ICC 221, 246 (1949).

[71] See Chapter 19.

[72] The Commission's position on this point was made clear in *Control of Central Pacific by Southern Pacific*, 76 ICC 508, 516 (1923); and in *Control of Alabama & Vicksburg Ry. and Vicksburg, Shreveport & Pacific Ry.*, 111 ICC 161, 170 (1926).

[73] *Control of Virginian Railway*, 117 ICC 67 (1926).

[74] *Great Northern Pacific Ry. Co. Acquisition*, 162 ICC 37 (1930). This combination was not carried out because of the inability or unwillingness of the carriers to comply with certain conditions required by the Commission. These two railroads

and aroused considerable public protest. Another instance in which the Commission authorized a combination formerly held in violation of the Antitrust Act was in permitting the control of the Central Pacific by the Southern Pacific.[75] The position of the Commission in authorizing such combinations was shown in the Nickel Plate Unification Case where the Commission said: "A greater amount of actual and effective competition in service may be assured by a limited number of well-articulated systems than by a greater number of systems less complete."[76] In another case the Commission said: "A certain amount of interference with competition is involved in nearly every railroad combination that may be formed, but if this interference is not unduly great, if effective competition is preserved at all important points, and particularly if the tendency of the combination is to increase and promote other competition to compensate for that destroyed or lessened, the combination may well merit our approval, if it is otherwise shown to be in the public interest."[77] To hold that any elimination of existing competition must require the denial of an application would prevent us from obtaining any of the benefits sought in railroad consolidations and combinations. The Transportation Act of 1940 removed the provision in the Act relating to a "plan" of consolidation, and with it, the Congressional directive that competition shall be preserved as fully as possible. This change in the law did not necessarily indicate that competition between railroads was to be considered less important in determining whether a proposed consolidation was or was not in the public interest. It is still a factor to be considered.

The relevance of competition and of antitrust policy in considering whether consolidations are in the public interest was brought out by the Supreme Court of the United States in *Minneapolis & St. Louis Railroad Co.* v. *United States*[78] and followed an earlier decision involving the consolidation of motor carriers.[79] The Court held that the Commission may not ignore the policy of the antitrust laws, but that it is not to measure consolidation proposals by the standards of the antitrust laws. The Commission is obligated to appraise the effects of curtailment of competition that may result from a proposed consolidation and to weigh them along with the advantages of improved service and other matters favorable to the unification. This the Commission has done in numerous cases and doubtless would have done so even if the Supreme Court had not specifically said that it must.

---

eventually came together, however, as major parts of the Burlington Northern which was created in 1970 with the approval of the Interstate Commerce Commission and of the Supreme Court. 331 ICC 228 (1967); 396 U.S. 491 (1970).

[75] 76 ICC 508 (1923).

[76] *Nickel Plate Unification*, 105 ICC 425, 440 (1926).

[77] *Unification of Southwestern Lines*, 124 ICC 410, 417 (1927).

[78] 361 U.S. 173 (1959).

[79] *McLean Trucking Co.* v. *United States*, 321 U.S. 67 (1944).

As noted elsewhere,[80] a period of renewed activity in railroad consolidation began in the late 1950s and early 1960s. The movement represented an effort by the railroads to eliminate excess capacity and reduce operating costs so that they might compete more effectively with other modes of transport. Several of the proposed consolidations would have had the effect of reducing railroad competition; hence the question arose as to the extent to which a policy of preserving competition among railroads should stand in the way of such consolidations. The degree to which competition would be affected differed greatly in the different consolidations proposed. In some the effect on competition would be negligible.[81] In others it was of major importance.[82]

It is clear that the major consolidation decisions resulting from the merger movement of the 1950s and 1960s show that the Commission attaches less weight to competition between railroads than formerly and stresses the importance of intermodal competition in protecting the public interest. This was mentioned in the Seaboard Air Line—Atlantic Coast Line case where the Commission said:

> While we recognize in general the desirability of preserving intramodal rail competition, it is no longer the all-important factor that it once was in the days when the railroads had a virtual monopoly on all intercity freight traffic. With the development of intense competition in recent years from other modes of transport, the preservation of intramodal rail competition has lost much of its significance in the furtherance of the overall national transportation policy.[83]

The extent to which the Commission is required by the Act to be governed by the policies of the antitrust laws in railroad merger cases, although seemingly settled by the Supreme Court in the Minneapolis & St. Louis case,[84] was raised in several other merger cases of the 1960s. The Department of Justice argued that the effect of rail mergers on competition between railroads should be given major if not controlling weight by the Commission. The Commission has been upheld, however, in holding that the effects on competition may be outweighed by other considerations.[85]

---

[80] P. 28, supra.

[81] See *Chesapeake & Ohio Ry. Co.-Control-Baltimore & Ohio R. Co.*, 317 ICC 261, 292 (1962), and *Norfolk & Western Ry. Co. & New York, Chicago & St. Louis R. Co. Merger*, 324 ICC 1 (1964).

[82] See *Pennsylvania Railroad Co.-Merger-New York Central Railroad Co.*, 327 ICC 475 (1966); *Great Northern Pacific & Burlington Lines, Merger-Great Northern*, 331 ICC 228 (1967).

[83] *Seaboard Air Line R. Co.-Merger-Atlantic Coast Line R. Co.*, 320 ICC 122, 166 (1963).

[84] See footnote 78.

[85] See particularly *Seaboard Air Line R. Co. v. United States*, 382 U.S. 154, 155–157 (1965); *Penn-Central Merger Cases*, 389 U.S. 486, 498–502 (1968); *Northern Lines Merger Cases*, 396 U.S. 491, 506–514 (1970).

Regardless of the legal aspects of the question, the weight that should, as a matter of policy, be given to effects on competition between railroads is subject to great diversity of opinion. One student of the subject has concluded that competition between railroads is no longer of importance and that the Act should be amended to specifically eliminate this factor as an element of the public interest in disposing of consolidation cases.[86] Another careful scholar advocates amendment of the Act to indicate that maintenance of intramodal competition is of crucial importance. He further recommends that the Act establish a presumption in favor of competition which could be overcome only by a showing that the advantages of the merger outweigh the possible advantages of maintaining competition.[87] The present writer's view is that the maintenance of intromodal rail competition should continue to be recognized as a relevant consideration in consolidation cases, but that under present conditions of intense intermodal competition less importance should be attached to it; and that concern over possible reduction or elimination of competition between railroads should not stand in the way of railroad consolidations that will result in a much more economical organization of the railroad industry.

SUMMARY OF POLICY TOWARD RAILROAD COMPETITION

To summarize present policy toward railroad competition is not easy. It is clear that we have abandoned unrestricted competition among railroads. It is equally clear that we have not turned to a policy of monopoly in the railroad industry.

"Controlled competition" is perhaps the best characterization of present policy. We still have a considerable amount of railroad competition. It is competition, however, which is controlled both by government regulation and by carrier action under the supervision of the Commission. Restriction of new construction, the prescription of minimum rates, and the requirements that rates be published and strictly observed are regulatory checks on competition. Carrier devices to keep competition within bounds consist of pooling agreements, consolidations and acquisitions of control, and the rate-bureau method of making rates. All of these carrier devices to control competition are under the watchful eye of the Interstate Commerce Commission to see that they are exercised in a manner that is in accordance with the public interest. Railroads are subject to the antitrust laws to some degree; to some extent they are exempt from these laws. Pooling agreements, rate-bureau procedures, and consolidations and combinations of railroads are all exempt from the prohibitions of the

[86] Michael Conant, "Railroad Consolidations and the Antitrust Laws," 14 *Stanford Law Review* 489 (1962).

[87] Carl H. Fulda, "Antitrust Aspects of Recent Transportation Mergers," 48 *Minnesota Law Review* 723 (1964).

antitrust laws if approved by the Commission. The Commission, however, cannot approve of pooling agreements that "unduly restrain competition." Rate-bureau procedures, although by their very nature a check upon individual-carrier rate making, must still preserve the right of the individual carrier to act independently if it does not wish to accept the rate recommendations of carrier committees which are part of the rate-bureau machinery. Approval of consolidations and combinations that would otherwise violate the antitrust laws is possible; yet in determining whether a proposed consolidation is "consistent with the public interest," the policy of the antitrust laws must be given consideration.

SELECTED REFERENCES

General discussions of competition and combination in the railroad field are Eliot Jones, *Principles of Railway Transportation* (New York: Macmillan, 1924), chap. v; Stuart Daggett, *Principles of Inland Transportation* (4th ed.; New York: Harper, 1955), chap. xxv; S. L. Miller, *Inland Transportation* (New York: McGraw-Hill, 1933), chaps. xxiv–xxv.

A good discussion of the waste of the competitive system is W. Z. Ripley, "Economic Wastes in Transportation," 21 *Political Science Quarterly* 381 (1906).

The best treatments of ruinous competition are A. T. Hadley, *Railroad Transportation* (New York: Putnam, 1885), pp. 63–74; E. Jones, op. cit., pp. 91–95; and by the same author, "Is Competition in Industry Ruinous?" 34 *Quarterly Journal of Economics* 473 (1920).

There is an immense amount of literature on pooling, but much of it is partisan. The following are among the best early treatments, and the approach is impartial, although the conclusions are not identical: C. A. Prouty, "Pooling Arrangements from the People's Point of View," 24 *Forum* 446 (1897); A. T. Hadley, "Prohibition of Pooling," 4 *Quarterly Journal of Economics* 158 (1890); W. Z. Ripley, *Railroads: Finance and Organization* (New York: Longmans, 1915), chap. xviii. For a description of actual pools see Henry Hudson, "The Southern Railway and Steamship Association," 5 *Quarterly Journal of Economics* 70 (1890); John B. Phillips, "A Colorado Railroad Pool," 5 *University of Colorado Studies* 137 (1908); R. E. Riegel, "The Southwestern Pool," 19 *Missouri Historical Review* 12 (1924); and "The Omaha Pool," 22 *Iowa Journal of History and Politics* 569 (1924); and Julius Grodinsky, *The Iowa Pool: A Study in Railroad Competition* (Chicago: University of Chicago Press, 1950). There is an excellent discussion of pooling and its historical setting in D. T. Gilchrist, "Albert Fink and the Pooling System," 34 *Business History Review* 24 (1960).

The combination movement of the 90s is described in Ripley, *Railroads: Finance and Organization,* chaps. xiv–xv. The official source for the Harriman combination is the Interstate Commerce Commission report, *Consolidations and Combinations of Carriers,* 12 ICC 277 (1907). Dissolutions under the Antitrust Act are treated in Ripley, *Railroads: Finance and Organization,* chap. xvii.

For a history of legislation on railroad consolidation see J. Stanley Payne,

"History of the 'Consolidation' Provisions of the Interstate Commerce Act," 19 *I.C.C. Practitioners' Journal* 453 (1952). For treatment of the Commission's policy in administering Section 5 of the Interstate Commerce Act, see S. P. Simpson, "The Interstate Commerce Commission and Railroad Consolidation," 43 *Harvard Law Review* 192 (1929); and I. L. Sharfman, *The Interstate Commerce Commission*, Vol. III–A (New York: Commonwealth Fund, 1935), pp. 430–501. Two books dealing with the consolidation provisions of the Transportation Act of 1920 and their administration are W. M. W. Splawn, *Consolidation of Railroads* (New York: Macmillan, 1925); and Wm. N. Leonard, *Railroad Consolidation under the Transportation Act of 1920* (New York: Columbia University Press, 1946). An analysis of the railroad consolidation problem and a review of past policy may be found in the Senate Committee on Interstate & Foreign Commerce report entitled *National Transportation Policy*, 87th Cong., 1st Sess., Senate Report No. 445 (1961), pp. 229–72. On the recent consolidation movement and legal and economic questions raised thereby see Michael Conant, "Railroad Consolidations and the Antitrust Laws," 14 *Stanford Law Review* 489 (1962); Carl H. Fulda, "Antitrust Aspects of Recent Transportation Mergers," 48 *Minnesota Law Review* 723 (1964), pp. 723–42; Phil C. Beverly, "Railroad Mergers: The Forces of Intermodal Competition," 50 *American Bar Association Journal* 641 (1964); Charles F. Phillips, Jr., "Railroad Mergers: Competition, Monopoly and Antitrust," 19 *Washington & Lee Law Review* 1 (1962); Robert W. Harbeson, "New Patterns in Railway Consolidation," *Quarterly Review of Economics & Business*, Vol. 2, No. 1, (1962), p. 7; Wm. H. Tucker and John H. O'Brien, "The Public Interest in Railroad Mergers," 42 *Boston University Law Review* 160 (1962); Eugene T. Lipfert, "Consolidation and Competition in Transportation: The Need for an Effective and Consistent Policy," 31 *George Washington Law Review* 106 (1962).

On controlling competitive railroad construction, see Sharfman, op. cit., pp. 348–67.

For a brief discussion of the minimum-rate power see D. P. Locklin, "Current Problems in Rate Making and Regulation with Emphasis on Public Policy," in National Resources Planning Board, *Transportation and National Policy* (Washington, D.C.: U.S. Government Printing Office, 1942), pp. 108–10. For a more complete discussion see I. L. Sharfman, op. cit., Vol. III–B, pp. 626–56.

Chapter 15 THE RAILROAD RATE LEVEL

In the chapter on the theory of railway rates it was pointed out that railroads tend to adjust rates on particular traffic movements in such a way as to obtain the largest possible revenue over direct or out-of-pocket costs. This principle is limited and modified in practice by the necessity of observing some system or consistency in the rate structure and by the necessity of complying with the provisions of law and with orders of regulatory bodies. The principle is also limited by lack of positive knowledge, in many situations, of just what the most profitable rate would be. Notwithstanding these limitations, the principle is applied in a broad way. The adjustment of particular rates in an effort to maximize returns will sometimes result in total railway revenues far in excess of the needs of the carrier. One object of government regulation of railway rates is to prevent such exploitation of the public through rates that are in excess of the revenue needs of the carriers. This function of regulation has become less important with the rise of competing modes of transport which have effectively held rates down on a large proportion of traffic movements and have limited railroad earnings to less than an adequate return.

Not only must regulation seek to prevent monopoly profits in the railroad industry, but it must at times concern itself with the question of whether railroad earnings are adequate for the maintenance of a satisfactory transportation system and fair to those who have invested capital in the railroad industry. It might be argued that if particular rates have been adjusted in such a way as to maximize carrier net revenues, there is not much that can be done if the resulting earnings are inadequate. Changes in the volume of traffic or in the conditions of demand for transportation service, however, may render the revenues of the railways inadequate to meet operating expenses and to pay a return on invested capital. Under these circumstances a reexamination of rates and a raising or a lowering of the rate level may become necessary in order to increase railway earnings. Most of the requests of the railroads for increased rates, however, are based on increases in operating expenses occasioned by rising prices.

338

Proceedings which involve efforts to raise or lower rates generally in order to increase or reduce railroad revenues are known as "general rate-level cases" or "revenue cases." In this chapter we are concerned with efforts to set up standards to govern the disposition of cases of this type. The rate-level problem is not peculiar to railroads and in later chapters we will consider the extent to which the same or different standards are used in proceedings involving other modes of transport.

SOURCES OF RAILROAD REVENUE

In a consideration of freight-rate levels it should be pointed out that the railroads derive revenue from various kinds of services which they perform; hence the full burden of supporting the carriers does not fall upon the freight business or upon freight and passenger business combined. In 1970, however, over 90 percent of the revenues of the Class I railroads was derived from their freight business. Table 15–1 shows the principal sources of revenue of the railroads.

TABLE 15–1. Sources of Operating Revenues, Class I Railroads, 1970*

Source	Amount (in millions)	Percent of Total
Freight	$10,914	91.1
Passenger	420	3.5
Mail	161	1.3
Express	22	0.2
All other	465	3.9
Total	$11,982	100.0

* Association of American Railroads, *Yearbook of Railroad Facts, 1971 edition*, p. 7.

In addition to the above, railways receive a considerable nonoperating income. This amounted to $498 million for Class I railways in 1970 and consisted largely of interest and dividends on securities held. Income from such sources does not enter into the calculations of the rate level.

RAILROAD EXPENSES

In the long run the revenues received by the railroads must cover operating expenses, taxes, and some sort of a return upon the capital invested. Operating expenses are the most important element in determining the level of railway rates, since they take a larger proportion of the railroads' revenues than does the return on investment. The importance of the operating expenses in the revenue requirements of the railroads is indicated by figures showing the operating ratio of the railroads over a period of years. The operating ratio is the proportion of operating revenues required to pay operating expenses. Table 15–2 shows the operating ratios of Class I line-haul railways from 1940 to 1970. The operating ratios during the period ranged from 61.6 to 83.4 percent. The difference between 100 and these figures gives the proportion of total operating revenues that represents taxes and return on investment. Since the railroads earned less than would be considered a desirable rate of return during this period, except in 1942 and 1943, the operating ratios slightly exaggerate the relative importance of operating expenses and understate the importance of the return-on-investment element in determining the

TABLE 15–2.   Operating Ratio, Class I Line-Haul Railways, 1940–70*

Year	Percentage	Year	Percentage
1940	71.9	1956	76.9
1941	68.5	1957	78.4
1942	61.6	1958	78.9
1943	62.5	1959	78.4
1944	66.6	1960	79.5
1945	75.2	1961	79.2
1946	83.4	1962	78.6
1947	78.3	1963	77.9
1948	77.3	1964	78.5
1949	80.3	1965	76.9
1950	74.5	1966	76.2
1951	77.4	1967	79.1
1952	76.1	1968	79.0
1953	76.3	1969	79.2
1954	78.8	1970	80.6
1955	75.7		

* Interstate Commerce Commission, *Annual Reports.*

level of rates. The importance of operating expenses in determining the rate level is illustrated by the rate-level cases which followed World War II.[1] In these cases a large amount of the evidence related to increases in railroad operating expenses brought about by higher wages and higher prices.

Regulatory bodies have practically no control over prices and wages paid by the railroads. Their level is determined largely by economic forces. Railroad wages are determined by bargaining between the railways and their employees and are presumably not long out of line with the wages paid by other industries for labor of similar grades. If we turn to other items of railroad expense, we also see the play of economic forces. The railroads presumably pay market prices for fuel and for ma-

---

[1] For a list of these cases see notes 95 and 96, infra.

terials and supplies. Only occasionally does some question arise regarding the propriety of prices paid by carriers.[2]

Railway operating expenses, however, are determined not only by the prices paid for materials, supplies, fuel, labor, and other things, but also by the efficiency of management and the workers. There is ample statistical evidence of steady improvement in the operating efficiency of American railroads[3] and of increasing productivity of railroad labor.[4] Further technological developments, aggressive managerial action, and greater cooperation among railroads to eliminate competitive wastes may result in even greater improvement in the future.

Forces making for improvement in railroad efficiency are competition between railroads[5] and between the railroads and other modes of transport, the pressure arising from less-than-desirable profits, a certain amount of prodding from the Interstate Commerce Commission[6] and from other government agencies, and also from shippers interests, which quickly seize upon evidence of inefficiency when they appear before regulatory bodies in opposition to increases in rates. Forces that operate to slow down improvements in efficiency are managerial inertia, "featherbedding" such as arises from methods of computing a day's pay for train service employees that are not appropriate under modern operating methods,[7] the attitude of railroad labor, a tendency for the railroads in the past to rely too heavily on rate increases to overcome inadequate earnings, and difficulties in financing capital outlays that would reduce operating expenses or improve service.

Taxes

In 1970 the Class I railroads paid out 4.1 percent of their operating revenues for taxes excluding payroll taxes. Here is an element which the

[2] See *Construction and Repair of Railway Equipment,* 66 ICC 694 (1922); 66 ICC 727 (1922). There are many other reports in this series of investigations. See also *In the Matter of Reciprocity in Purchasing and Routing,* 188 ICC 417 (1932); Federal Coordinator of Transportation, *Regulation of Railroads,* 73d Cong., 2d Sess., Senate Doc. 119 (1934), pp. 68, 69; and also Bureau of Transport Economics and Statistics, Interstate Commerce Commission, Statement No. 4428, *Use and Cost of Railway Fuel and Problems in Fuel Statistics* (Washington, D.C., 1944).

[3] Bureau of Railway Economics, Association of American Railroads, *A Review of Railway Operations* (Washington, D.C., published annually); James C. Nelson, *Railroad Transportation and Public Policy* (Washington, D.C.: Brookings Institution, 1959), chap. viii.

[4] Harold Barger, *The Transportation Industries, 1889–1946:A Study of Output, Employment, and Productivity* (New York: National Bureau of Economic Research, 1951), chap. iv.

[5] Competition is a constant spur to improved service and greater efficiency notwithstanding the fact that it is itself the cause of some important wastes.

[6] See n. 60 in this chapter.

[7] For the railroad point of view on this matter see Association of American Railroads, *Facts about Featherbedding in the Railway Industry* (Washington, D.C., 1959).

public might control. In fact, the railroads could be made completely tax exempt if it seemed desirable to do so. There is not much likelihood that this will be done, because so many communities derive a considerable portion of their revenue from taxes levied upon railroad property. But in the larger sense the taxes upon railroads represent a special tax imposed upon the users of the railroads and might be abolished if they made railroad rates too high or prevented the railroads from earning an adequate return.

A question might be raised as to whether railroad taxes are borne by the owners of the road or whether they are borne by the shippers through higher freight rates. An examination of the accounting system of the railroads[8] will reveal that taxes are deducted before net railway operating income—the figure which is supposed to be an adequate return—is reached. This is equivalent to charging taxes to operating expenses and represents an effort to place the burden of such taxes on the shipping public. In so far as the taxes paid by railroads are general property taxes, this practice is consistent with the generally accepted belief that general property taxes on business enterprises are in large measure shifted to consumers.

The practice of treating railroad taxes as an operating expense, however, is not confined to taxes which are levied as a part of the general property tax. Federal corporation income taxes are treated in the same way; yet originally the theory of the corporation income tax was that it should be borne by the corporation and not be shifted to the consumer. To the extent that the railroads are given a rate level which enables them to earn a fair return after federal corporate income taxes, it would appear that they have succeeded in shifting that tax, along with other taxes, to the users of their services. The Supreme Court of the United States has held that all taxes, including the federal corporation income tax, are deductible as an expense in any computation of the net income which a public utility is entitled to earn.[9] Although the Interstate Commerce Commission considers that it is bound by these decisions to treat federal corporation income taxes as an expense, it refused to follow a similar policy with respect to war-time excess-profits taxes, saying: "It is not fair or just that these excess-profits taxes should be shifted through rates to the shipper."[10] The treatment of federal corporation income taxes was reviewed by the Commission in *Increased Freight Rates, 1951*, and the Commission again held that although income taxes must be considered as an expense, excess-profits taxes should not.[11] The Commission also held

---

[8] See Chapter 23.

[9] *Galveston Electric Co.* v. *Galveston*, 258 U.S. 388, 389 (1923); *Georgia Ry. & Power Co.* v. *Railroad Commission of Georgia*, 262 U.S. 625, 633 (1923).

[10] *Minnelusa Oil Corp.* v. *Continental Pipe Line Co.*, 258 ICC 41, 49 (1944).

[11] 284 ICC 589, 613–17 (1952). The excess-profits tax law was subsequently repealed.

that taxes on income derived by railroads from nontransportation operations should not be considered as an expense.[12]

The fact that railroad taxes are treated as an operating expense means that an effort is made to shift them to the consumer, but it does not follow that this effort is always successful. If a railroad or group of railroads earns less than a fair return, as often happens, the taxes are borne, in part at least, by the owners. This can be shown by the fact that in such instances a removal of the taxes would not necessarily mean a lowering of transportation rates, but merely that the carriers might now earn a fair return when they did not do so before. Broadly speaking, however, railroad taxes are to a considerable extent shifted to the shipping public, and they constitute an element which enters into the level of rates.

Depreciation

Depreciation, including retirements, comprised 8.8 percent of the operating expenses of the railroads in 1970. This is not a particularly large item, but certain comments about it are desirable.

Depreciation is a relatively constant amount from year to year. This results from the fact that the annual depreciation charges are based on the cost of depreciable property and its estimated service life. In other words, a certain portion of the cost of depreciable property is charged to operating expenses each year until the cost of the unit of property has been recovered.[13] Prior to the introduction of depreciation accounting on the railroads, the cost of a unit of property consumed in service was charged to operating expenses when the unit was retired from service. By varying from year to year the amount of property retired, a greater degree of flexibility in these charges was possible.

In 1930, in *United Railways* v. *West*,[14] the Supreme Court of the United States held that the annual depreciation charge of public utilities should be based on the "present value" instead of on the original cost of the depreciable property. This was contrary to long-established accounting practice. If the railroad accounting regulations had been revamped to comply with the views of the Court, annual depreciation charges would have become less stable. They would have risen as the price level rose and fallen as prices declined. It would have been extremely difficult to calculate the proper depreciation charge, and other difficulties would have appeared. The Supreme Court subsequently overruled the United Railways

---

[12] Ibid.

[13] The Canadian Pacific Railway follows a policy of varying depreciation charges with the amount of use of the property rather than putting them on a strictly time basis, but this is contrary to practice in the United States. See *Railway Age*, June 11, 1951, p. 50; and ibid., June 18, 1951, p. 50.

[14] 280 U.S. 234.

Case on this point,[15] and railway depreciation charges are based on the actual cost of depreciable property, not on estimated replacement costs.

The contention that depreciation charges should be based on replacement costs instead of on actual costs makes its appearance in periods of rising prices. The argument is that depreciation funds should enable the company to finance replacement of worn-out property at the new and higher costs.[16] To base depreciation rates on original costs of depreciable property places the actual cost of capital consumed upon the users, whether prices are rising or falling. On the other hand, to base depreciation rates on replacement costs in times of rising prices forces the patrons of railroads and public utilities to contribute the new capital required by the added cost of replacing property which is worn out.[17] In times of falling prices, to base depreciation on reproduction costs does not permit the utility to recover the cost of capital which has been consumed in service.

THE PROFIT ELEMENT

Railway revenues should be sufficient, as we have pointed out, to pay necessary operating expenses, taxes, and a return on the capital invested. A difficulty arises, however, in determining what the "profit" element, or return on capital, should be. Most of the controversy over standards of adequacy of the rate level has centered about the "profit" or return-on-investment element. The problem is to prevent exploitation of the public by common carriers, and also to see that railway earnings are adequate.

THE RATE LEVEL AS AN ECONOMIC PROBLEM

Determination of the adequacy of railroad earnings is essentially an economic problem, although, as we shall see, it is not without its ethical aspects also.

Attraction of Capital

That the rate-level problem is essentially an economic problem is revealed by the common assertion that the rate level must permit earnings sufficient to attract capital if private capital is to be relied upon to supply

---

[15] *Federal Power Commission* v. *Hope Natural Gas Co.*, 320 U.S. 591, 606–7 (1944).

[16] See Arthur K. Atkinson, "Depreciation Charges Should Vary with Replacement Costs," 126 *Railway Age* 224 (1949); Paul Grady, "Impact of Price Level Changes on Utility Depreciation Costs," 49 *Public Utilities Fortnightly* 819 (1952), and 50 ibid. 31 (1952); George J. Eder, "Depreciation—and Inflation," ibid., p. 617. For defense of traditional practice see Charles W. Smith, "Public Utility Depreciation," ibid., p. 625; and National Association of Railroad and Utilities Commissioners, *Report of Committee on Depreciation, 1954* (Washington, D.C., 1954).

[17] This was the reasoning of Chief Justice Hughes in *Lindheimer* v. *Illinois Bell Telephone Co.*, 292 U.S. 151, 168–69 (1934).

railroad facilities. To attract private capital, it is said, a fair return must be allowed upon the capital already invested in the enterprise. This statement, however, requires some qualification. In so far as railroad capital is of a fixed and specialized sort, irrevocably sunk in the enterprise, a return would not have to be paid. This is so because the capital cannot be withdrawn from the enterprise. To the extent, however, that the property is consumed in service and must eventually be replaced, there must be a prospect of a return, or there will be no inducement to replace the property either through new capital issues or out of a depreciation fund. But certainly a return does not have to be paid on the capital which represents a permanent investment in property that cannot be withdrawn from the particular enterprise. This, however, is no reason for denying such a return. Fairness and justice require that a return be permitted on such capital if it is possible for the property to earn it.

When a railroad is unable to earn a return on all the capital invested in it, it may be necessary for it to undergo financial reorganization. Presumably the company will emerge with a much smaller capitalization. The ability of that company to attract new capital will then depend not upon its ability to pay a return upon the capital originally invested in the railroad, but upon its ability to pay interest and dividends. If it can pay interest and dividends, it can probably obtain new capital on favorable terms, notwithstanding the fact that it does not earn an adequate return upon the money originally invested. But this, again, is hardly justification for denying a carrier a return on the original investment if, under a new management or changed conditions, it finds it possible to earn it.

Notwithstanding the above qualifications, it remains true that some sort of return must be permitted if private capital is to be enticed into railroad enterprises. Although this truth is generally acknowledged, it is sometimes contended that the railroad industry is no longer an expanding industry because of the rise of competing modes of transport which are diverting traffic from the railroads in increasing quantities. It is then argued that new capital is no longer needed in the railroad industry, at least beyond the amounts needed to replace such portions of the railroad plant as will continue to be needed. Of course, a return sufficient to attract capital into an industry is not an economic necessity if new capital is not needed. But there is still a moral or ethical reason for permitting those who have provided railroad capital to derive a fair return therefrom if economic circumstances will allow it. However, the assumption cannot be accepted that new capital is not needed in the railroad industry. The other modes of transport, desirable and necessary as they may be, cannot replace the railroads. The very fact that railroads must meet the competition of newer modes of transport may require capital outlays to improve their service, reduce expenses, and meet the challenge of competition. There may be extensive railroad facilities that no longer serve a useful purpose, but the need for new capital continues. Railroad capital expenditures have averaged over a billion dollars a year during the period from 1959 to 1969.[18] We must therefore conclude that from an economic standpoint, railroad earnings should be sufficient to enable the railroad companies to raise new capital.

Railroad Users Not Required to Provide New Capital

To say that railroad earnings should be sufficient to enable railroads to raise new capital is not the same as saying that earnings should be high enough to provide the new capital directly. It is sometimes argued that railroad earnings should be sufficient not only to pay a fair return on capital invested, but also to provide for needed additions and betterments. But investors, not shippers, should provide new capital. Of course, it has long been the practice of American railroads to reinvest part of their earnings in the business. If railroad stockholders are willing to have part of their earnings reinvested in the business, it may be in their interest, as well as in the public interest, for them to do so. The policy, however, does not justify earnings sufficient to pay a fair return on investment and also to provide new capital. If shippers were called upon to provide new capital as needed, there would be no economic necessity for paying a return to owners sufficient to attract new capital; and certainly, railroad owners could not in the name of economics or fair play demand a return on capital furnished not by themselves, but by the shipping public. The fact that railroads commonly reinvest part of their earnings in the business should not lead to the conclusion that the rate level should be high enough to provide a fair return on investment and to contribute new capital also.[19]

Objections to Limiting Profits

Although it is generally agreed that the rate level should be regulated and adjusted to give the carriers an adequate but not excessive return, there are some writers who have taken the position that there should be no limitation on carrier profits. According to this view, the carriers should be permitted to follow the practice of charging what the traffic will bear without reference to the profits accruing to them.[20] This view

---

[18] See Association of American Railroads, *Railroad Review and Outlook* (Washington, D.C., 1970), p. 11.

[19] For recognition of this principle by the Civil Aeronautics Board, see *Capital Gains Proceeding*, 27 CAB 79, 83–84 (1958). The principle has also been emphatically stated by the Interstate Commerce Commission. See *Increased Rates & Charges, Middlewest Territory*, 335 ICC 142, 147 (1969).

[20] Philip Cabot, "Public Utility Rate Regulation," 7 *Harvard Business Review* 257, 413 (1929); and "Four Fallacious Dogmas of Utility Regulation," 7 *Public Utilities Fortnightly* 719 (1931); A. T. Hadley, "Principles and Methods of Rate Regulation," 16 *Yale Review* 417 (1927), Hadley's views are also described and criticized by James C. Bonbright in *Report of Commission on Revision of the Public Service Commissions Law* (Albany, 1930), pp. 374–77.

rests upon three grounds. The first is that the present method of regulation is a cost-plus arrangement that removes all incentive to efficiency and technical progress. In part this accusation is justified, as we shall point out shortly; but it is doubtful whether the remedy lies in abandoning regulation and permitting carriers to take advantage of their monopoly, where such monopoly exists.

The second basis for abandoning the practice of limiting profits is the belief that a "fair" or "normal" return is insufficient to attract capital into the railroad enterprise. This was the view of Hadley. To lower the price effectively, we must remove scarcity, he said. This requires capital; and in order to get the capital, we must allow a profit commensurate with the risk involved.

If the government says to the company, "If you succeed, you are limited to a normal rate of profit; if you fail, your shareholders must stand the loss"— it is obvious that the experiment will not be made at all. The country that limits rates to "a fair return" on prudently invested capital discourages just the sort of industrial enterprise which is the most effective measure of lowering public service charges and keeping the nation in the forefront of progress.[21]

It is obvious that Hadley was laboring under a misapprehension regarding the fair-return idea. A fair return is not pure interest, nor is it a normal profit without allowance for risk. Both courts and commissions recognize that a rate of return, to be "fair," must include compensation for risk and that it must be sufficient to attract capital.

The third argument for permitting unrestricted profits is based on the idea that the interests of the railroad and its patrons are identical. It is urged that the railroad will find it in its own interest to encourage traffic by reducing rates to the lowest possible point, since this policy will increase profits. To support this contention, it is pointed out that the railroad operates under conditions of decreasing unit cost as the volume of traffic increases, and that the demand for transportation services is elastic. High rates are held to discourage patronage by turning consumers to substitute services. This view has been ably answered by Bonbright. "It is doubtless true that competition by the use of substitute or alternative services does fix an upper limit of prices above which a public utility, in its own pecuniary self-interest, cannot go in fixing rates"; but this force does not prevent the railroad or utility "from charging more than it needs to charge in order to perform the service and to attract necessary capital for extensions and improvements."[22] He correctly concludes that "there is not the slightest ground in economic theory for supposing that this point of 'maximum profits' is the . . . point at which rates should be fixed in the *public* interest."[23]

---

[21] Hadley, op. cit., p. 424.
[22] Bonbright, op. cit., p. 375.
[23] Ibid.

CONSTITUTIONAL LIMITATIONS—JUDICIAL STANDARDS OF REASONABLENESS

Regulatory commissions have not had a completely free hand in fixing the general level of rates. The courts, in order to protect the constitutional rights of the carriers, have imposed limitations on the power of commissions to reduce railway rates. It becomes important, therefore, to study the standards which have been laid down by the courts in their efforts to protect the carriers from arbitrary action by rate-making bodies. Before these judge-made standards are described, however, it would be well to consider the process by which the courts came to interfere in rate making.

Development of Judicial Review

It was not until more than 20 years after the states began to regulate railway rates that the courts asserted the right to review and, if deemed necessary, to set aside rates which had been prescribed by legislatures or by commissions. The courts at first took the position that regulation was a legislative, and not a judicial, function and that it was improper for the courts to interfere. In one of the Granger cases the Supreme Court, in referring to the power of the legislature to control rates, said: "We know that this is a power which may be abused; but that is no argument against its existence. For protection against abuses by legislatures the people must resort to the polls, not to the courts."[24] In another of the Granger cases the Court said: "Where property has been clothed with a public interest, the legislature may fix the limit to that which shall in law be reasonable for its use. This limit binds the courts as well as the people. If it has been improperly fixed, the legislature, not the courts, must be appealed to for the change."[25] By maintaining this position, the courts barred the way to any relief from unreasonably low rates prescribed by legislatures or commissions.

The position taken by the courts on this question hardly seems consistent with the theory of our government. The Fourteenth Amendment to the Constitution provides that "no State shall deprive a person of property without due process of law." A similar prohibition against the federal government is found in the Fifth Amendment. It is one of the functions of American courts to protect the rights guaranteed by the Constitution. But if the courts would not review the rates prescribed by legislative authority, even if property rights were infringed, the Constitution would not be affording protection to railroad property. As the Supreme Court said in *Smyth* v. *Ames:* "The duty rests upon all courts, Federal and state, when their jurisdiction is properly invoked, to see that

---

[24] *Munn* v. *Illinois*, 94 U.S. 113, 134 (1877).

[25] *Peik* v. *Chicago & North Western R. R. Co.*, 94 U.S. 164, 178 (1877).

no right secured by the supreme law of the land is impaired or destroyed by legislation. This function and duty of the judiciary distinguishes the American system from all other systems of government."[26] It is not strange, therefore, that the doctrine of noninterference with the regulative powers of the legislative branch of the government was soon modified by the Supreme Court.

The first intimation of judicial interference with the legislative power to fix rates occurred in *Stone* v. *Farmers' Loan & Trust Co.* in 1886. Here the Court said:

From what has been said, it is not to be inferred that this power of limitation or regulation is itself without limit. This power to regulate is not a power to destroy, and limitation is not the equivalent of confiscation. Under pretence of regulating fares and freights, the State cannot require a railroad corporation to carry persons or property without reward; neither can it do that which in law amounts to a taking of private property for public use without just compensation, or without due process of law.[27]

But it was in *Chicago, Milwaukee & St. Paul Ry. Co.* v. *Minnesota*, decided in 1890,[28] that the right of judicial review of rates prescribed by legislative authority was clearly established. The right was again asserted in *Reagan* v. *Farmers' Loan & Trust Co.*, in 1894,[29] and has been consistently maintained since that time. In later years, however, some justices of the Supreme Court have taken the position that the Court should revert to its earlier position and hold that the courts do not have the right to interfere with rates fixed by legislatures or commissions.[30]

The Rule of Smyth v. Ames

By 1890 the courts had asserted that they had the power and duty to set aside rates fixed by public authority if those rates were so low as to be confiscatory. The courts, however, had not yet drawn the line between rates that are confiscatory and rates that are not confiscatory. In the famous case of *Smyth* v. *Ames*, decided in 1898,[31] the Supreme Court of the United States attempted to draw the line between confiscatory rates and rates that avoided confiscation; and in so doing, the Court set up a standard for the determination of rate levels that has largely dominated

---

[26] 169 U.S. 446, 527–28 (1898).

[27] 116 U.S. 307, 331.

[28] 134 U.S. 418.

[29] 154 U.S. 362, 397.

[30] See concurring opinion of Justices Black, Douglas, and Murphy in *Federal Power Commission* v. *Natural Gas Pipeline Co.*, 315 U.S. 575 (1942), pp. 599–601; separate opinion of Justices Black and Murphy in *Federal Power Commission* v. *Hope Natural Gas Co.*, 320 U.S. 591 (1944), pp. 619–20; and dissenting opinion of Justice Black in *McCart* v. *Indianapolis Water Co.*, 302 U.S. 419 (1938), pp. 427–28.

[31] 169 U.S. 466.

railroad and public utility rate making since that time in cases in which the general level of rates is under consideration.

In the *Smyth* v. *Ames* decision the Court said:

> We hold that the basis of all calculations as to the reasonableness of rates to be charged by a corporation maintaining a highway under legislative sanction must be the fair value of the property being used by it for the convenience of the public. . . . What the company is entitled to ask is a fair return upon the value of that which it employs for the public convenience. On the other hand, what the public is entitled to demand is that no more be exacted from it for the use of a public highway than the services rendered by it are reasonably worth.[32]

Here we seem to have two standards suggested: (1) cost of service, i.e., operating expenses and a fair return on the value of the property; and (2) the value of the service, or what the services are reasonably worth to shippers. The second of these standards seems to be a limitation on the first, that is, it usually becomes operative only when it is impossible to carry out the first. When we refer, therefore, to the rule of *Smyth* v. *Ames*, we shall have in mind the rule that rates should afford the carrier a fair return on the fair value of its property.

Reasonable Rates and Nonconfiscatory Rates

The fair-value rule was evolved as a means of protecting the carriers against unreasonably low rates prescribed by legislative authority. It was intended primarily to protect the carriers against confiscation. But the *Smyth* v. *Ames* rule came to be not merely a minimum below which rates should not fall, but a real standard of reasonableness. In other words, commissions have endeavored to adjust rates so that the carriers will earn a fair return, but they do not intend to permit higher rates than this. Commissions have sometimes been severely criticized for directing their attention to the fixing of rates that will just avoid confiscation, and for not recognizing that higher rates may be justified.[33] It is argued that the *Smyth* v. *Ames* decision gives a rule for prescribing nonconfiscatory rates, not a rule for prescribing "reasonable" rates.

It is true that a commission, in prescribing "just and reasonable" rates, may make them higher than is necessary to avoid confiscation if it so desires. In the words of the United States Supreme Court:

> A commission or other legislative body, in its discretion, may determine to be reasonable and just a rate that is substantially higher than one merely sufficient to justify a judicial finding in a confiscation case that it is high enough to yield a just and reasonable return on the value of the property used to per-

---

[32] Ibid., p. 377.

[33] C. M. Updegraff, "Deductions from the Economic Basis of Public Utility Rates," 12 *Iowa Law Review* 249 (1927); C. E. Brown, "Economic Aspects of Rate Regulation," 18 *American Bar Association Journal* 473, 474 (1932).

form the service covered by the rate. The mere fact that a rate is non-confiscatory does not indicate that it must be deemed to be just and reasonable.[34]

Although commissions may consider that rates, in order to be reasonable, should be substantially higher than merely nonconfiscatory rates, there is no warrant for the conclusion that rates, in order to be reasonable, *must* be higher than those resulting from the *Smyth* v. *Ames* standard. The United States Supreme Court has clearly indicated that the fair-value standard is a standard of reasonableness and not merely of nonconfiscatoriness. "By investment in a business dedicated to the public service the owner must recognize that, as compared with investment in private business, he cannot expect either high or speculative dividends but that his obligation limits him to only fair or reasonable profit."[35] This seems to support the contention that the *Smyth* v. *Ames* rule prescribes a standard of reasonableness and does not merely fix a minimum below which rates should not fall.

There is another consideration which points to the conclusion that the level of rates suggested by the *Smyth* v. *Ames* rule is reasonable and adequate. A fair rate of return, as will be pointed out later, has been considered by the courts as a return which would be adequate to attract capital. From an economic point of view there is certainly no need of giving a larger return; rates should enable carriers to earn a "fair return" on their fair value, but they do not need to be higher. The *Smyth* v. *Ames* standard is properly a standard for determining a reasonable level of rates.[36]

Dividends and the Fair-Value Rule

Two common misconceptions about the fair-value doctrine should be dispelled in order to avoid confusion of thought.

The first misunderstanding is that the fair-value rule restricts dividends to a certain rate. The fair-value rule is directed toward the return earned upon the property value and not toward the dividends paid or earned. A carrier which is conservatively capitalized may earn less than 6 percent, for instance, upon the value of its property and yet be able to pay dividends on stock at a much higher rate. On the other hand, an overcapitalized road may earn more than a fair return and yet be able to pay scarcely any dividends at all.

Table 15–3 lists some of the railroads which earned a net railway operating income in 1925 of less than 5¾ percent on their book value

---

[34] *Banton* v. *Belt Line Ry. Corp.*, 268 U.S. 413, 422–23 (1925). For other citations in support of this principle see Nathaniel T. Guernsey, "The Test of Reasonable Rates," 14 *Virginia Law Review* 1 (1927).

[35] *Dayton–Goose Creek Ry. Co.* v. *United States*, 263 U.S. 456, 481 (1924).

[36] M. A. Merrill, "On the Distinction between a Non-Confiscatory Rate and a Just and Reasonable Rate," 14 *Cornell Law Quarterly* 447, 455–56 (1929).

but whose net earnings per share, after paying interest and rentals, were liberal. In studying Table 15–3, it should be noted that the return given in the first column is the return upon book value, not the return upon what the Commission would consider "fair value." The "fair value" may be greater or less than the book value.

The fact that carriers can make good earnings per share when earning less than a fair return may be due to three factors. The first and least important is that they may have additional income, such as income from other property or from securities held. The figures in the first column of the above table represent only the net income from railroad operations, while the figures in the second column may include income from

TABLE 15–3.   Net Railway Operating Income and Net Income, Selected Railroads, 1925*

Carrier	Ratio of Net Ry. Operating Income to Book Value Plus Cash, Materials, and Supplies	Ratio of Net Income to Capital Stock after Paying Fixed Charges
Akron, Canton & Youngstown	5.1%	29.8%
Atchison, Topeka & Santa Fe	5.0	12.3
Baltimore & Ohio	5.1	9.9
Bangor & Aroostook	5.1	9.9
Chicago & North Western	4.0	6.4
Chicago, Burlington & Quincy	4.6	12.4
Delaware, Lackawanna & Western	5.5	16.9
Delaware & Hudson	5.3	12.3
Florida East Coast	5.4	10.2
Illinois Central	4.6	11.4
Lehigh Valley	5.0	13.3
New York, Chicago & St. Louis	5.2	11.5

* Taken from Interstate Commerce Commission, *Statistics of Railways of the United States, 1925,* pp. xcii–xciii.

other sources. A second cause is a small capitalization. A railroad with a low capitalization, that is, with securities outstanding which are less than the value of its property, can earn a small return upon its value but have a larger return on its capitalization. But the third and most important reason why earnings per share tend to be larger than the rate of return on the value of the carrier's property is that a considerable proportion of the railroad's capitalization may be in the form of bonds bearing a low rate of interest. This concentrates upon a comparatively small amount of stock the net earnings remaining after interest is paid. An extreme illustration of comparatively moderate earnings upon book value but of enormous earnings per share of stock is afforded by the Bessemer & Lake Erie, which had a net railway operating income of 7.9 percent upon its book value in 1925 but, after paying fixed charges, earned 853 percent on its capital stock. The book value of the road was over $67 million; its capitalization was only a little more than $6.5 million; and only $500 thousand of its capitalization was represented by common stock. These figures should make it clear that the rule of *Smyth* v. *Ames* is not inconsistent with generous dividends.

No Guaranty of a Fair Return

Another erroneous opinion regarding the fair-value doctrine is that it practically guarantees a railroad a fair return. There are many railroads in the United States that have never received a fair return upon the value of their property and probably never will. The most important reason for this situation is the economic impossibility of charging rates that will yield a fair return. Some are in competition with stronger roads which can and do charge rates lower than are reasonable for the weaker line; some serve sparsely settled sections of the country where traffic is light. In the one case, higher rates divert traffic to the other line; in the other case, high rates may exceed the value of the service. For these reasons it is often impossible for a railroad to secure a fair return. The rule of *Smyth* v. *Ames* will protect the carrier against the arbitrary action of rate-making authorities, but it will not protect the carriers from the operation of economic forces. The United States Supreme Court has clearly stated that the fair-value rule cannot protect a carrier from all business hazards:

The due process clause of the Fourteenth Amendment safeguards against the taking of private property, or the compelling of its use, for the service of the public without just compensation. But it does not assure to public utilities the right under all circumstances to have a return upon the value of the property so used. The loss of, or the failure to obtain, patronage, due to competition, does not justify the imposition of charges that are exorbitant and unjust to the public. The clause of the Constitution here invoked does not protect public utilities against such business hazards.[37]

And in *Market Street Railway Co.* v. *Railroad Commission of California* the Supreme Court of the United States said: "The due process clause has been applied to prevent governmental destruction of existing economic values. It has not and cannot be applied to insure values or to restore values that have been lost by the operation of economic forces."[38]

The fact that many railroads in the United States earn less than a fair return while others regularly earn more than a fair return is proof that

---

[37] *Public Service Commission of Montana* v. *Great Northern Utilities Co.*, 289 U.S. 130, 135 (1933). In *Federal Power Commission* v. *Natural Gas Pipeline Co.*, the Supreme Court said: ". . . regulation does not insure that the business shall produce net revenues." 315 U.S. 575, 590 (1942).

[38] 324 U.S. 548, 567 (1945).

the *Smyth* v. *Ames* rule cannot be applied with success to individual railroads. Of 131 Class I line-haul railways, 16 actually operated at a deficit in 1940, while 8 others earned less than 1 percent on the estimated value of their properties. On the other hand, 11 earned more than 10 percent on their estimated value, and 2 of these earned approximately 18 percent. Table 15–4 shows the grouping of the 131 carriers according to the rates of return which they earned.

TABLE 15–4. Grouping of Railroads According to Rate of Return Earned on Estimated Value of Their Properties, 1940*

Rate of Return (percent)	No. of Class I Railroads
Deficit	16
Less than 1	8
1–1.9	11
2–2.9	25
3–3.9	19
4–4.9	13
5–5.9	10
6–6.9	7
7–7.9	5
8–8.9	4
9–9.9	2
10–14.9	9
15–19.9	2
	131

* Computed from data in Bureau of Statistics, Interstate Commerce Commission, Statement No. 4142, *Rate of Return on Value of Property of All Operating Steam Railway Companies, Calendar Year 1940.*

The Credit Standard

The Supreme Court has not always resorted to the fair-return-on-fair-value standard in determining whether the rates prescribed by regulatory authorities are confiscatory. It has sometimes applied what might be called a "credit standard." In other words, the Court has brushed aside matters relating to "fair value" and its determination, and has looked merely at net earnings in relation to interest and dividend requirements and perhaps to the desirability of building up a surplus out of earnings. The primary consideration under this standard is whether the companies have earnings sufficient to maintain their credit and to attract capital to the industry.

The fair-return-on-fair-value standard and the credit standard may be quite different in particular instances. This is because the fair-return-on-fair-value standard concentrates attention on the relation of earnings to investment, or to some measure of the "fair value" of the property of the carrier, while the credit standard emphasizes the relation of earnings to capitalization, i.e., stocks and bonds outstanding. As previously pointed out, an overcapitalized road may earn more than a fair return on fair value and have insufficient earnings to pay interest and dividends. On the other hand, a very conservatively capitalized railroad may have excellent credit although it earns less than a fair return on the fair value of its property.

The Supreme Court resorted to the credit standard in 1934 in *Lindheimer* v. *Illinois Bell Telephone Co.*[39] In that case the Supreme Court reversed a decision of a lower court which had enjoined a reduction of telephone rates required by the Illinois Commerce Commission. The Supreme Court rejected the conclusion of the lower court that the rates were confiscatory, not as a result of considering the fair value of the company's property, but by observing that if the reduced rates were confiscatory so also were existing rates; but under these rates the company had excellent credit, had paid interest on its debt and 8 percent dividends on its stock, had built up large depreciation and other reserves, and had greatly increased its surplus and undivided profits.

Not only has the Commission occasionally applied the credit standard of reasonableness, but in *Federal Power Commission* v. *Hope Natural Gas Co.*, decided in 1944,[40] the Court seems to set up the credit standard as the ultimate test which is to be applied by the courts in determining whether rates are confiscatory or not. In this case the Supreme Court refused to go into the question of whether a valuation made by the Federal Power Commission had been properly determined, but contented itself with observing that the rates prescribed were adequate under the credit test and would not, therefore, be disturbed by the Court.

From the investor or company point of view it is important that there be enough revenue not only for operating expenses but also for the capital costs of the business. These include service on the debt and dividends on the stock. . . . By that standard the return to the equity owners should be commensurate with returns on investments in other enterprises having corresponding risks. That return, moreover, should be sufficient to assure confidence in the financial integrity of the enterprise, so as to maintain its credit and to attract capital.[41]

In a later case the Court referred approvingly to the standard set up in the *Hope* case as "a standard of finance resting on stubborn facts."[42]

The credit standard avoids the problem of valuation and the determination of a rate base, a problem which has been so troublesome in the past. The chief objection to the credit standard is that it is a "capitali-

---

[39] 292 U.S. 151 (1934).

[40] 320 U.S. 591 (1944).

[41] Ibid., p. 603.

[42] *Colorado Interstate Gas Co.* v. *Federal Power Commission*, 325 U.S. 581, 605 (1945).

zation" standard and disregards questions of the propriety of the capitalization. It looks to the liabilities side of the balance sheet and not to the assets devoted to transportation or public utility purposes. Unless subjected to further refinement, it could, under some circumstances, unduly burden the rate-paying public; under others it might not be fair to those who have invested in the enterprise in the past.

It should be noted that the credit standard was adopted by the Supreme Court for its own use in determining whether rates were confiscatory or not. The credit standard is not forced upon regulatory bodies. They may continue to use the fair-value standard, or other standards, for determining the reasonableness of the rate level. If rates so determined are challenged as confiscatory, however, the courts will presumably decide that question by resorting to the credit standard.

STATUTORY STANDARDS

We have described the *Smyth* v. *Ames* or fair-return-on-fair-value standard of reasonableness and also the more recently established credit standard, both of which have been devised by the courts in their efforts to prevent confiscatory rates. The *Smyth* v. *Ames* standard has naturally served as a guide to regulatory commissions, as we have pointed out; but in the future the credit standard may come to be used by commissions in lieu of the older standard. In addition to these judge-made standards the legislative branch of the government has attempted to prescribe standards to be observed by regulatory bodies. In railroad rate making the Congressional standards have been those prescribed in the so-called "Rule of Rate Making"—Section 15a of the Interstate Commerce Act.

The Original Section 15a

Section 15a was added to the Interstate Commerce Act in 1920 as a result of a general feeling that the statute should impose upon the Interstate Commerce Commission the affirmative duty of prescribing rates which would afford the carriers adequate revenues.[43] As previously pointed out, the section, as originally enacted, directed the Interstate Commerce Commission to:

initiate, modify, establish or adjust . . . rates so that carriers as a whole (or as a whole in each of such rate groups or territories as the Commission may from time to time designate) will, under honest, efficient and economical management and reasonable expenditures for maintenance of way, structures, and equipment, earn an aggregate annual net railway operating income equal, as nearly as may be, to a fair return upon the aggregate value of the railway property of such carriers held for and used in the service of transportation.

---

[43] Pp. 242–43, supra.

The section made use of the fair-return-on-fair-value concept, and it might be thought that the section was merely incorporating into the statute the *Smyth* v. *Ames* doctrine. It is important to note, however, that the *Smyth* v. *Ames* rule, as evolved by the courts, applied to individual railroads, while Section 15a applied to the carriers "as a whole," or as a whole in rate groups. The right of the individual carrier to a fair return—a constitutional right—was not impaired by the existence of the new rule requiring rates to be based on aggregate property values. But the constitutional right is of little value to a weak carrier, since higher rates than are maintained by other carriers in the group will usually reduce its earnings still further. To the stronger lines, Section 15a gave a right not possessed before. It gave them a right to a rate level high enough to yield the railroads as a whole a fair return upon their aggregate property values and not simply a rate level sufficient for their individual needs.

The Revised Rule of Rate Making

Section 15a underwent complete revision in 1933.[44] All mention of fair return on fair value was eliminated from the section. The new rule required the Commission, in prescribing reasonable rates, to give due consideration, among other factors,

to the effect of rates on the movement of traffic; to the need, in the public interest, of adequate and efficient railway transportation service at the lowest cost consistent with the furnishing of such service; and to the need for revenues sufficient to enable the carriers, under honest, economical, and efficient management, to provide such service.

The complete removal of any reference to fair return on fair value was due to a number of circumstances. One of these was the difficulty involved in the ascertainment of "fair value," a difficulty which will become more evident to the reader in the following chapter.

Another reason for removing the specific direction to the Commission to prescribe a certain rate level was that such a requirement seemed to place the revenue needs of the carriers ahead of all other considerations in fixing rates. The carriers were constantly urging upon the Commission the view that whenever earnings fell below the contemplated fair return on fair value, the Commission was under legal obligation to grant increases in rates requested by the carriers, regardless of other considerations. The Commission had refused to accept this interpretation of Section 15a,[45] but the language of the section gave some color to the contentions of the railroads. To further insure that revenue needs of the

---

[44] Pp. 263–64, supra.

[45] See *Reduced Rates, 1922*, 68 ICC 676, 730 (1922); and *Fifteen Per Cent Case, 1931*, 178 ICC 539, 575–77 (1931).

carriers would not be the sole consideration in rate-level cases, Congress provided in the revised Section 15a that the Commission should give consideration "to the need, in the public interest, of adequate and efficient railway transportation service at the lowest cost consistent with the furnishing of such service."

A third criticism of the original Section 15a was clearly revealed during the depression years following 1929. The Rule of Rate Making implied that railroad earnings could be stabilized, whereas earnings are subject to wide variations due to changes in the volume of traffic, which in turn are dependent upon general business conditions. The Interstate Commerce Commission recognized that railroad earnings would fluctuate with changes in business activity and refused to adopt a policy which would make rates vary inversely with the volume of business. Thus, in the *Fifteen Per Cent Case, 1931,* the Commission refused a substantial increase in rates during a depression, saying:

> It is only necessary to have in mind the incongruous results which would follow an attempt to adjust rates so that a stable rate of return would be realized, notwithstanding general business conditions and the rise and fall of traffic in consonance therewith, to realize the unreasonableness and impracticability of any such policy.[46]

Notwithstanding this interpretation placed upon Section 15a by the Commission, the language of the section seemed to imply higher rates in periods of depression in order to carry out the mandate of the law. This was undoubtedly a factor in causing Congress to modify the language of Section 15a.

The revised Section 15a does not neglect the revenue needs of the carriers. Revenue need is specifically enumerated as one of the factors to be considered by the Commission, but it becomes one of three factors specified instead of the only one mentioned in the section. The language of the revised Section 15a strongly suggests a credit standard, since emphasis is put upon revenues necessary to enable the railroads to maintain an adequate transportation system.

The removal of all mention of fair return on fair value from Section 15a does not prevent the Commission from making use of that standard in rate-level cases if it wishes to do so. The Commission has, in fact, continued to make use of valuation data in such cases.[47] In one case the Commission said that value of the carriers' properties devoted to common-carrier services was "a necessary factor to be examined."[48] Although the rate of return earned by the railroads as a whole, or in groups, may

---

[46] 178 ICC 539, 565.

[47] *Railway Rates, Fares & Charges, 1946,* 264 ICC 695, 726–29 (1946); *Increased Freight Rates, 1947,* 269 ICC 33, 47–48 (1947); *Increased Freight Rates, 1948,* 276 ICC 9, 17–18 (1949); *Increased Freight Rates, 1951,* 284 ICC 589, 608 (1952).

[48] *Increased Freight Rates, 1951,* 284 ICC 589, 607 (1952).

serve as a useful guide in evaluating the adequacy of the rate level, the Commission has specifically noted that "there is no statutory requirement or statement of policy requiring the making of rates to yield a certain rate of return on investment either in the United States as a whole, or in various rate territories."[49] Two members of the Commission, however, felt that a return-on-investment approach to the problem of the rate level was not authorized by law, and was inappropriate anyway because of duplication of facilities and service and the rise of competing modes of transport.[50] It is quite possible that less use will be made of the fair-return-on-fair-value standard in the future and greater use of the credit standard in rate-level cases.

"Effect of Rates on the Movement of Traffic"

The effect of rates on the movement of traffic is mentioned as one factor to be considered by the Commission in prescribing rates. Prior to the change in Section 15a, there had been some controversy whether the Commission should consider the effect of proposed rates on the movement of traffic in carrying out the Rule of Rate Making. The position of the railroads was that the Commission should not question the judgment of the carriers that proposed increases in rates would increase revenues, or that reductions in rates would reduce revenues. The Commission, however, had adopted the view that it could and should inquire into the probable revenue effects of a proposed change in rates. It was partly on the theory that a reduction of rates would increase the volume of traffic that the 10 percent reduction in rates was ordered in *Reduced Rates, 1922.*[51] Considerations of this nature were also important in the granting of only small increases in rates in the *Fifteen Per Cent Case, 1931.*[52]

Listing "the effect of rates on the movement of traffic" among the factors to be considered by the Commission in rate-level cases has disposed of the matter for the present. This factor has become of major importance in rate-level cases. Increased costs of railway operation have pushed freight rates higher and higher, particularly since World War II; and the higher they become, the more serious becomes the question of the effect of further increases upon the movement of traffic. The railroads feel strongly, however, that the Interstate Commerce Commission should not have the power to question the revenue effects of increases in rates proposed by the carriers, and they have asked that Section 15a be amended by eliminating "the effect of rates on the movement of

---

[49] *Increased Freight Rates, Eastern, Western, and Southern Territories, 1956,* 300 ICC 633, 662 (1957).

[50] Ibid., pp. 702–3.

[51] 68 ICC 676, 733–34.

[52] 178 ICC 539, 575.

traffic" as a factor to be considered by the Commission.[53] A similar view has been expressed by others.[54] Bills to accomplish this effect and to give the railroads greater freedom in increasing rates to meet increasing costs of operation were introduced in Congress in 1952 but were not passed.

As long as the Commission is charged with responsibility for maintaining a level of rates that is adequate for the carriers, it would be entirely unrealistic for the Commission to ignore the revenue effects of proposed changes in rates. The views of railroad managers as to the probable consequences of increases or reductions in rates should not be disregarded or treated lightly, but the Commission cannot intelligently carry out the general policy of the law without considering the probable effects of proposed rate changes. Even if the Commission were relieved of any responsibility for maintaining a level of rates adequate for the carriers and were to confine its attention to the prevention of excessive rates, it could hardly ignore the effect of rates on the movement of traffic. It could not be presumed that rates were not excessive merely because earnings were not excessive, when there was the possibility that rates were restricting the movement of traffic.

PROBLEMS IN THE REGULATION OF THE RATE LEVEL

Whatever the standards of reasonableness applied in the determination of the rate level, certain problems and difficulties are encountered. A number of these problems are discussed below.

Adequacy of Accounts

One question which arises at the outset is that of the truthfulness of railroad accounts and of the propriety of the accounting methods used. If the adequacy or propriety of the net railway operating income of a carrier or group of carriers is under consideration, there must be assurance that the net railway operating income shown in the accounts is in fact what it purports to be. Railroad accounts must be kept according to a sound and uniform system.

---

[53] *Report of Committee Appointed September 20, 1938, by the President of the United States to Submit Recommendations upon the Transportation Situation,* pp. 14–15; Statements of R. V. Fletcher in *Hearings before Committee on Interstate and Foreign Commerce, House of Representatives, on Omnibus Transportation Bill* (1939), Vol. I, pp. 389–90, 563–66; Testimony of W. S. Franklin in *Hearings before the Committee on Interstate and Foreign Commerce, U.S. Senate, on Bills Relative to Domestic Land and Water Transportation* (1952), p. 868 *et seq.,* and of J. Carter Fort, p. 1026 *et seq.*

[54] Emory R. Johnson, "Government Regulation of Railroads in the United States," 201 *Annals of the American Academy of Political and Social Science* 165, 169 (1939); Jervis Langdon, Jr., "Should the Regulation of Railroad Rates Be 'Streamlined' Too?" 24 *Cornell Law Quarterly* 309 (1939); Charles L. Dearing and Wilfred Owen, *National Transportation Policy* (Washington, D.C.: Brookings Institution, 1949), chap. xiii.

Before railroad accounts were regulated by the government, the greatest confusion existed in the methods used. No careful distinction was drawn between the expenditures chargeable to capital account, which affect the reported investment in road and equipment but which do not affect the operating expenses, and those expenditures which should be paid from current earnings and are called "operating expenses." A railroad which charged additions and betterments to operating expenses would be overstating its expenses; it would show a smaller net return than it should and a smaller investment in its property. On the other hand, a railroad which charged replacements and maintenance to cost of road and equipment would be inflating its investment account and, by an understatement of operating expenses, would show a net income which was wholly or partly fictitious. Prior to 1907 lack of definite accounting regulation made possible the manipulation of accounts and the falsification of statements of earnings. Not only was willful falsification possible, but there were honest differences of opinion in regard to accounting practice. For instance, it is not always easy to draw the line between expenses which should be charged to operating expenses and those which should be charged to capital. If old rails are torn up and replaced with new but heavier rails, how much of the expenditure is chargeable to operating expenses, and how much represents new investment in the property? Or if old rails are replaced by new ones of the same kind but which cost more than the old ones, is the entire cost to be considered as an operating expense, or is the excess cost of the new rails over the old to be considered as a further investment and therefore chargeable to capital? Different answers to these questions as well as to many others would cause differences in reported net income. Government supervision and regulation of accounts is indispensable if rate regulation is to be successful.[55]

Fluctuating Earnings

We have already noted that the fair-return-on-fair-value rule as incorporated in the original Section 15a seemed to imply the possibility of stabilizing railroad earnings. In practice this was found impossible. Our study of the fixed nature of many railroad expenses has made it clear why railroad earnings would be expected to fluctuate from year to year. It is wholly unrealistic to assume that railway rates can be adjusted to give the railroads the desired income in each and every year. This principle has been forcefully stated by Professor Sharfman as follows:

In an economic system in which progressive change in existing arrangements and the chaotic succession of cyclical fluctuations create a large measure of instability, instability must, for the most part, be the lot of the railroads

---

[55] Accounting regulation of railroads is discussed in Chapter 23.

also. The hope that rate regulation will at all times afford earnings adequate but not excessive—that a formula involving property value and a rate of return thereon will mark out for the railroads a calm course through troubled economic waters—is obviously an illusory one; and any attempt to maintain a steady flow of railroad income by adjusting rates inversely to the volume of traffic is not only bound to prove impracticable, but is clearly unwarranted in its presumption that the philosophy of regulation bestows upon the carriers so preferred a status in the ranks of industry.[56]

"Honest, Efficient, and Economical Management"

The adjustment of the rate level to cover operating expenses and a definite return on capital is not conducive to the greatest efficiency and economy in the operation and management of the industry. If a railroad were assured of earnings sufficient to yield a fair return under all circumstances, there would be little incentive for the railroad to strive for the greatest possible efficiency in the operation of its system or to introduce improved operating methods.

This problem is of less importance in regulating railways than public utilities because railroad rates must be fixed for carriers as a whole, as we shall presently see. Once the general level is fixed for the railroads as a whole, or for a particular group of carriers, each individual railroad may be able to improve its position by exertion in behalf of efficiency and economy. If it is earning less than an adequate return, it can hope to attain the desired level only by its own efforts and not by appeal to regulatory bodies. If it is earning a fair return or more, it will not be deprived of additional profits that may be obtained through even greater efficiency.

Regulatory authorities do not have direct control over railroad expenditures or over the operating methods and business practices of railroads. Thus the Interstate Commerce Commission has said: ". . . while we may . . . take the character of management and operation into consideration in fixing the level of rates, we are unable to find any provision of the act which authorizes us by order to require a carrier to conduct its affairs along lines which may seem to us more efficient and economical than those now followed."[57] In another case the Commission commented upon the fact that it could not insure or enforce honest, efficient, and economical management.[58] A federal court has also found that Section 15a "gives no power of directly supervising carrier expenditures."[59]

---

[56] I. L. Sharfman, *The Interstate Commerce Commission*, Vol. III–B (New York: Commonwealth Fund, 1936), p. 295.

[57] *New Mexico Central Ry. Co.* v. *Atchison, Topeka & Santa Fe Ry. Co.*, 81 ICC 718, 722 (1923).

[58] *Missouri-Kansas-Texas R. R. Co.* v. *Kansas City Terminal Ry. Co.*, 104 ICC 203, 224 (1925).

[59] *Missouri Pacific R. Co.* v. *Norwood*, 42 F. 2d 765, 773 (1930).

What, then, can regulatory authorities do to enforce the requirement of "honest, economical, and efficient management" mentioned in Section 15a? First, when the occasion demands it, the Commission can admonish the carriers and advise them to introduce certain economies or to improve their methods of operation. This the Commission has done in a few cases.[60] Another thing which the Commission may do, and has done, to discourage wasteful and uneconomical practices is to make public such examples as may be revealed by its investigations.[61]

In a few instances the Commission has held that certain expenditures were improper and should be excluded in determining rates. Thus, in a report on the construction and repair of equipment of the New Haven Railroad, the Commission said: "The record compels us to regard a substantial portion of the extraordinary expenditures incurred by respondent in this outside repair work as improvident and of a character which should be considered when fixing rates to yield the standard return as provided by the act."[62] The difficulty in any attempt to penalize railroads for inefficient management through regulation of the rate level lies in the fact that a particular carrier cannot be singled out in this way. Rates must be made for the carriers as a whole or in groups, and to penalize one through the rate level penalizes all within the group.

Rates for Individual Roads or for Groups of Roads

Mention has been made of the necessity of making rates for railroads as a whole or in groups. This fact requires further consideration. It is a major problem in railroad regulation, although not often encountered in the regulation of other public utilities.

The impossibility of maintaining a different level of rates on railroads that are strictly competitive is obvious. Yet differences in operating conditions and traffic density on the different roads may be so great that a level of rates proper for one carrier is higher than another needs to charge and is entirely inadequate for a third. A similar situation may exist between railroads which seemingly possess a monopoly of the regions they serve. Higher rates in one region than in another tend to discourage industry and agriculture in that area, while lower rates have the opposite effect. As a result it is often impossible to maintain different rate levels on different railways. This means that some compromise must be effected.

This problem has often been encountered by the Interstate Com-

---

[60] See *The Five Per Cent Case*, 31 ICC 351, 408–14 (1914); *Fifteen Per Cent Case, 1931*, 178 ICC 539, 585 (1931); *General Rate Level Investigation*, 195 ICC 5, 55 (1933); *Increased Freight Rates, 1948*, 276 ICC 9, 112 (1949); *Annual Report, 1947*, pp. 4–5.

[61] See n. 2, this chapter.

[62] *Construction & Repair of Railway Equipment*, 107 ICC 721, 735 (1926).

merce Commission when adjusting rate levels or in determining the reasonableness of rates between specific points. In considering rates on grain in Trunk-Line Territory in 1903, the Commission faced this problem and decided to determine the reasonableness of the rates with respect to the two largest railway systems between the East and West: the New York Central and the Pennsylvania.[63] This was thought to be fair also to the Baltimore & Ohio. The situation was again before the Commission in 1909 when it was considering rates from St. Paul to Seattle and Spokane in the Northwest. Two points of view were presented to the Commission concerning the road which was to be used for setting the rates. One view was that the least expensive route was to be used as a standard, "even though the rates thus established when applied to the business of its competitors would deprive them of a fair return upon their investment."[64] The defendant railroads, however, argued otherwise. In reply, the Commission said:

> They urge that a railroad is entitled to a fair return upon its investment, and that this rule applies to all railroads alike. This is the right of the railroad laboring under disadvantages of location and operation, as well as of that one more favorably circumstanced. Hence the Commission must consider that railroad whose net earnings will be the least, for if it established rates which only yield fair returns to the road most favorably situated, it of necessity knowingly and intentionally deprives every other road of a fair return upon the value of its property.[65]

The Commission compromised by considering the railroads as a whole. A similar policy has been followed by the Commission in other cases involving particular rates[66] and also in cases which involved the general rate level.[67] This was the only practicable course to follow.

The policy of considering railroads as a whole in fixing rates received Congressional sanction in 1920. Section 15a of the Act provided that the Commission should prescribe rates that would give the carriers as a whole, or as a whole in such rate groups as the Commission should prescribe, a fair return upon the aggregate value of their properties. The Rule of Rate Making was supplemented by the Recapture Clause as a means of preventing some railroads from earning inordinately large returns and of aiding the weaker roads to improve their earning position.[68]

---

[63] *Re Proposed Advances in Freight Rates,* 9 ICC 382, 426 (1903).

[64] *City of Spokane* v. *Northern Pacific Ry. Co.,* 15 ICC 376, 392 (1909).

[65] Ibid., p. 392.

[66] *Kindel* v. *New York, New Haven & Hartford R. R. Co.,* 15 ICC 555, 563 (1909); *Receivers & Shippers Assoc.* v. *Cincinnati, New Orleans & Texas Pacific Ry. Co.,* 18 ICC 440, 464 (1910); *Newport Mining Co.* v. *Chicago & North Western Ry. Co.,* 33 ICC 646, 656 (1915).

[67] See *Advances in Rates, Eastern Case,* 20 ICC 243, 274 (1911); *The Five Per Cent Case,* 31 ICC 351 (1914).

[68] See pp. 245–46, supra.

The Act of 1933 repealed the Recapture Clause and substituted a new Rule of Rate Making. The new Section 15a makes no reference to the railroads as a whole or in rate groups. In a footnote in a Supreme Court decision in 1945, Mr. Justice Black, in referring to the revised Rule of Rate Making, said: ". . . the rates were no longer to be treated on a national basis as though all railroads constituted one system. Railroads were to be treated on an individual basis."[69] It is extremely doubtful whether this interpretation of the revised Rule of Rate Making is correct. The Interstate Commerce Commission has not accepted the view that under the present law it is without power to consider the railroads as a whole or in groups in determining the rate level.[70] As a practical matter the Commission must consider the roads in this manner. The Commission found this to be true long before the original Section 15a was enacted. When a rate level is prescribed which is adequate for the railroads as a whole or in rate groups, there will almost always be some railroads which will earn much more than they need, and others which will earn much less than they need. This is the so-called "weak-and-strong-road problem," which is considered in a later chapter.[71]

General versus Selective Increases

In the great majority of rate-level cases that have occurred since the enactment of Section 15a in 1920, the carriers have sought general increases, although some traffic might be excepted from the proposed increases or be subject to lesser increases than proposed generally. Such general or across-the-board increases disregard conditions of demand; and if they are percentage increases, they also result in greater aggregate increases upon the traffic which already bears the highest rates.

From time to time the Commission has questioned the wisdom of this method of seeking additional revenues. Accordingly the rate increases proposed by the carriers in *Increased Freight Rates, 1958*,[72] were selective in character. Some flat increases in cents per hundred pounds or per ton were proposed; some percentage increases of varying amounts were proposed; and in some instances percentage increases subject to maximum increases in cents per hundred pounds, or per ton, were contemplated.[73] Selective increases are more in accordance with rate theory since consideration is given to demand factors as well as to cost-of-service factors. In emergencies, however, when increases in revenues are urgent, percentage increases may be the only way to obtain needed revenues quickly. Individual adjustments can be made later.

[69] *North Carolina* v. *United States*, 325 U.S. 507, 515 (1945), n. 4.

[70] *Increased Freight Rates, 1951*, 284 ICC 589, 606 (1952).

[71] Chapter 17.

[72] 302 ICC 665 (1958).

[73] Ibid., pp. 679–95.

Percentage Increases and "Hold-Downs"

In an earlier chapter we noted that percentage increases in freight rates result in greater absolute increases in long-distance rates and often disturb existing patterns of production and marketing.[74] For this reason a conflict often appears in rate-level cases between long-distance shippers and those closer to their markets. The former object to a percentage increase in rates, if an increase has to be made, and prefer an increase that affects all shippers alike, that is, an increase in cents per hundred pounds or per ton applying equally to all shippers. Producers located closer to their markets, on the other hand, prefer a percentage increase in rates, since it will be less burdensome to them. In many rate-level cases the Commission has granted percentage increases but has often imposed a maximum increase in cents per hundred pounds or per ton on many items. This has the effect of holding down long-distance rates and is designed to overcome the more serious effects of straight percentage increases.

In a 1970 decision the Commission departed from its usual practice and refused to apply "hold-downs" in connection with a six percent increase in freight rates that was permitted to become effective. The Commission said that in an inflationary period "a horizontal increase applied to all rates is the fairest means of distributing the burden of providing the additional needed revenue."[75] This ignores the fact that where long-distance shippers are competing with those having shorter hauls, it is very largely the *absolute* difference in rates that determines ability to compete, and a uniform percentage increase results in increasing absolute differences in rates. In *Increased Freight Rates, 1970 and 1971*, however, the Commission reverted to its traditional use of "hold-downs" and prescribed them on many specific commodities and groups of commodities, recognizing that "a straight percentage increase places a greater burden generally on higher-rated commodities and longer-haul traffic."[76]

The Problem of Delay

In periods of rapidly rising costs of operation the railroads have experienced difficulty because of the slowness with which authorization is obtained for rate increases. The machinery of regulation is slow and must necessarily consume a considerable amount of time if all interested parties are given a right to be heard. At one time the railroads estimated that they would have had more than a billion dollars additional revenues in the period from 1946 to 1952 if rate increases which were ultimately allowed by the Commission had become effective within 60 days from

---

[74] Pp. 63–65, supra.

[75] *Increased Freight Rates, 1969*, 337 ICC 436, 479 (1970). Statements to the same effect also appear on pp. 447 and 460 of the decision.

[76] 339 ICC 125, 192 (1971).

the time the requests were made.[77] In 1952 and 1953, bills were introduced in Congress which were intended to force more rapid consideration of rate increase cases. These bills were not enacted, but the Commission has made notable progress in speeding up consideration of such cases. It frequently grants "interim" increases early in the proceedings, with final disposition of the case only after more thorough hearing and argument. This procedure reduces the loss of revenue that would otherwise result, and at the same time it gives shippers some protection from hasty increases that might not prove to be justified.

Value of Service

Mention has already been made of the fact that in the *Smyth* v. *Ames* decision, which laid down the fair-return-on-fair-value rule, the Supreme Court also set up a value-of-service standard by saying that "what the public is entitled to demand is that no more be exacted from it for the use of a public highway than the services rendered by it are reasonably worth." The Interstate Commerce Commission's refusal to grant a 15 percent increase in rates in 1931 was based in part on this doctrine. The Commission quoted with approval a statement in *Corpus Juris* that "the public is entitled to demand that no more be exacted from it than the services rendered are reasonably worth, and this right takes precedence even over the right of the carrier to a fair return on its investment when the two can not stand together."[78] Such judicial support as there is for this doctrine comes largely from the decision of the Supreme Court of the United States in *Covington & Lexington Turnpike Co.* v. *Sandford*,[79] decided in 1896. In this case the Court said:

It cannot be said that a corporation is entitled, as of right, and without reference to the interests of the public, to realize a given percent upon its capital stock. When the question arises whether the legislature has exceeded its constitutional power in prescribing rates to be charged by a corporation controlling a public highway, stockholders are not the only persons whose rights or interests are to be considered. The rights of the public are not to be ignored. It is alleged here that the rates prescribed are unreasonable and unjust to the company and its stockholders. But that involves an inquiry as to what is reasonable and just for the public. If the establishment of new lines of transportation should cause a diminution in the number of those who need to use a turnpike road, and, consequently, a diminution in the tolls collected, that is not, in itself, a sufficient reason why the corporation, operating the road, should be allowed to maintain rates that would be unjust to those who must or do use its property. The public cannot properly be subjected to unreasonable rates in order simply that stockholders may earn dividends.[80]

---

[77] See Nelson, op. cit., p. 126.
[78] Quoted in *Fifteen Per Cent Case, 1931*, 178 ICC 539, 563 (1931).
[79] 164 U.S. 578.
[80] Ibid., p. 596.

This doctrine was quoted approvingly by Justices Black, Douglas, and Murphy in a more recent case.[81] But in the Market Street Railway Case the Supreme Court said: ". . . we do not need to pronounce upon the abstract doctrine as to the validity of the 'value of service' theory as justifying rates that do not yield a fair return."[82] The Court thus implied that this was still an open question.

Value of service is not a meaningful concept when applied to the general level of rates. It has meaning only when related to specific transportation services, where it often does limit the rate that can be charged for such a service. When courts and commissions invoke the value-of-service principle in general rate-level cases, they are usually faced with a situation in which conditions of demand make the application of the fair-return doctrine impossible. In other words, increases in rates would result in rates on particular commodities and hauls which would effectually stop such shipments or would reduce the volume of traffic and result in less revenue for the railroads. The rise of competing modes of transportation, business recession, changes in the location of industries, or exhaustion of natural resources may create conditions such that a railroad or group of railroads cannot earn a fair return under any circumstances. The apparent conflict between the fair-return standard of reasonableness and the value-of-service standard is usually not a conflict between two independent standards of reasonableness but a conflict between the fair-return standard and stubborn economic facts. When the conflict appears, the fair-return standard has to yield, because the conditions of demand impose limitations on what can be charged.[83]

HISTORY OF RATE-LEVEL CASES

From 1910 to 1920

The first great rate-level cases which came before the Interstate Commerce Commission were in 1910, when the railroads sought general increases in freight rates to meet rising costs of operation. After the outbreak of World War I in 1914, rapidly rising operating costs made further applications necessary.[84]

---

[81] *Federal Power Commission* v. *Natural Gas Pipeline Co.*, 315 U.S. 575, 607 (1942).

[82] *Market Street Ry. Co.* v. *Railroad Commission of California*, 324 U.S. 548, 562 (1945).

[83] There may also be situations in which there is a lack of adjustment of facilities to traffic and where high rates, although economically possible, would be deemed unjust and reasonable because of the overcapacity in the industry. The fair-return doctrine can be adjusted to this situation, however, by making allowance in the rate-making values for the condition of overcapacity.

[84] The principal cases were *Advances in Rates, Eastern Case*, 20 ICC 243 (1911); *Advances in Rates, Western Case*, 20 ICC 307 (1911); *The Five Per Cent Case*, 31 ICC 351 (1914), 32 ICC 325 (1914); *1915 Western Rate Advance Case*, 35 ICC 497 (1915); *Fifteen Per Cent Case*, 45 ICC 303 (1917).

As a result of these cases the carriers obtained advances in rates, although not so great as they desired and felt necessary in view of rising costs of operation. The public, accustomed for many years to declining rates, was not sympathetic with the attempts of the carriers to increase rates, and the Interstate Commerce Commission was slow to assume much responsibility for protecting railroad earnings. It must be remembered that the Commission had been created to protect the public from unreasonably high and discriminatory rates, and not to protect the carriers from low rates. The whole machinery and processes of regulation, designed to protect the public from excessive charges, operated to delay the process of increasing rates, although increases were made necessary by rising costs of operation.

In 1918, after the government had taken over the operation of the railroads, the Director General of Railroads ordered a 25 percent increase in rates.

The earnings of the railways in the period 1910 to 1920 ranged from a high of 6.17 percent in 1916 to a low of 2.64 percent in 1919, with an average annual rate of return for the decade of 4.65 percent. The earnings are expressed as a percentage of book value or recorded investment in road and equipment, with certain adjustments. It should be recognized that the investment figures for much railroad property antedate effective accounting regulation and are therefore unreliable and often inflated. Neither do the investment figures make adequate allowance for actual depreciation. If adjustments could be made for these shortcomings, the earnings of the railroads would show up somewhat better than the figures indicate.

The rate cases between 1910 and 1917 showed clearly the need of an authoritative valuation of railroad property. Although the Supreme Court had enunciated the fair-value doctrine in 1898, the Commission had to decide the rate level cases without the aid of reliable figures on railroad valuation. The Commission had frequently recommended to Congress that it authorize such a valuation, but no action was taken until 1913, when the Valuation Act was passed.[85]

From 1920 to 1930

In 1920 railway operations produced a return of only 0.35 percent. It should be recognized, however, that this was not such a serious matter to stockholders and bondholders as might be assumed because the railways were still subject to a war-time government guaranty of earnings based on earnings of a three-year period prior to the war.

Upon the termination of government operation of the railroads in 1920 an increase in rates and fares was clearly necessary if the railroads

---

[85] See particularly *Annual Reports* for 1903, 1905, 1907, 1908; and *Advances in Rates, Eastern Case*, 20 ICC 243, 305 (1911).

were to be self-supporting. In *Increased Rates, 1920*,[86] the Commission, in conformity with the mandates of the newly enacted Section 15a, prescribed further increases in freight rates. Increases were authorized of 40 percent in the East, 25 percent in the South and in Mountain-Pacific Territory, and 35 percent in the West. Interregional rates were increased 33⅓ percent. A general reduction of about 10 percent from these peak levels was required in *Reduced Rates, 1922*.[87] An unsuccessful effort was made by the western railroads to obtain an increase in rates in 1926 in *Revenues in Western District*.[88] In *Increased Rates, 1920*, the Commission considered the value of the railroads to be $18.9 billion and 6 percent as the fair rate of return.[89] In *Reduced Rates, 1922*, a 5¾ percent return was held to be a fair rate of return.

The rate of return earned by the railroads in the 1920s ranged from 3.04 percent in 1921 to 5.31 in 1929. The average for the period was 4.66 percent.

From 1930 to 1940: The Depression Period

The depression of the thirties greatly reduced the volume of railway traffic and created a crisis in railroad affairs. The situation was aggravated by the development of competing forms of transport, principally motor carriers. In the *Fifteen Per Cent Case, 1931*,[90] a 15 percent increase in rates was denied, but the Commission authorized small increases in the form of surcharges which were to be levied temporarily. The Commission originally attached a condition that the proceeds of the surcharges should be pooled and used for the support of railroads which could not meet their interest payments and which were therefore in danger of going into the hands of receivers. The Commission later withdrew this condition,[91] but the railroads agreed that the proceeds of the surcharges should be paid over by the railroads to the Railroad Credit Corporation, a corporation created for the purpose, and that from these funds loans would be made to railroads in danger of default upon their interest payments. The emergency charges were in effect from January 4, 1932, to September 30, 1933. An unsuccessful effort was made by various interests to bring about a general reduction in rates in 1933; but the Commission, in *General Rate Level Investigation, 1933*,[92] found that existing rates were not unreasonable.

---

[86] 58 ICC 220 (1920).

[87] 68 ICC 676 (1922).

[88] 113 ICC 3 (1926).

[89] The Act of 1920 fixed 5½ percent as the rate of return deemed fair for a period of two years, but the Commission was empowered to add one half of 1 percent to make provision for new capital requirements.

[90] 178 ICC 539 (1931).

[91] 179 ICC 215 (1931). A further supplemental report is in 191 ICC 361 (1933).

[92] 195 ICC 5 (1933).

Between 1935 and the outbreak of World War II the railroads sought additional rate increases. Such increases as were granted were for the purpose of avoiding further railroad bankruptcies.[93] There was general recognition of the fact that the railroads could not, under the conditions of general economic depression and increased competition from other modes of transport, expect to earn a fair return upon any conventional measure of their fair value.

Earnings of the railroads in the period 1930 to 1939 varied from a high of 3.62 percent in 1930 to a low of 1.37 percent in 1932. The average for the 10-year period was only 2.43 percent.

War and Postwar Period

Following an increase in railroad wages in 1941 and rising costs of certain materials and supplies occasioned by World War II, the carriers sought an increase in rates of 10 percent. In *Increased Railway Rates, Fares, & Charges, 1942*,[94] the Commission authorized a 6 percent increase in freight rates, again with numerous exceptions, and an increase of 10 percent in passenger fares. Because these increases were based on the emergency created by the war, they were to expire six months after the termination of the war. Because of the large volume of traffic and increased revenues of the railroads which grew out of war conditions, these increases were temporarily suspended on May 15, 1943, and the suspension was subsequently renewed from time to time.[95]

In 1946 a series of rate-level cases began which brought rate levels to a new high.[96] The Bureau of Transport Economics and Statistics estimated that the cumulative increases authorized from 1946 to 1960, taking into consideration the various exceptions and "hold-downs," averaged 115.2 percent.[97] The postwar increases were made necessary by higher operating costs brought about by higher wages, material costs, and taxes.

---

[93] The rate-level cases during this period were *Emergency Freight Charges, 1935*, 208 ICC 4 (1935), 215 ICC 439 (1936), 219 ICC 565 (1936); *General Commodity Rate Increases, 1937*, 223 ICC 657 (1937); *Fifteen Percent Case, 1937–1938*, 226 ICC 41 (1938).

[94] 248 ICC 545 (1942).

[95] 255 ICC 357 (1943); 256 ICC 502 (1943); 258 ICC 455 (1944); 259 ICC 159 (1944).

[96] *Increased Railway Rates, Fares & Charges, 1946*, 264 ICC 695 (1946), 266 ICC 537 (1946); *Increased Freight Rates, 1947*, 269 ICC 33 (1947), 270 ICC 93 (1948); *Increased Freight Rates, 1948*, 272 ICC 695 (1948), 276 ICC 9 (1949); *Increased Freight Rates, 1951*, 280 ICC 179 (1951), 281 ICC 557 (1951), 284 ICC 589 (1952), 289 ICC 395 (1953), 297 ICC 17 (1955); *Increased Freight Rates, 1956*, 298 ICC 279 (1956); *Increased Freight Rates, Eastern & Western Territories, 1956*, 299 ICC 429 (1956), 299 ICC 557 (1957), 300 ICC 633 (1957); *Increased Freight Rates, 1958*, 302 ICC 665 (1958), 304 ICC 289 (1958); *Increased Freight Rates, 1960*, 311 ICC 373 (1960), 313 ICC 471 (1961), 313 ICC 519 (1961), 313 ICC 549 (1961), 313 ICC 563 (1961).

[97] *Transport Economics*, December, 1961, p. 3.

Following the 1960–61 increases, there were no general increases for a number of years. Then, beginning in 1967, there occurred several general increases over a period of about five years.[98] These increases, like the earlier ones, were made necessary by the inflationary tendencies of the period.

Returns earned by the railroads in the war and postwar period are shown in Table 15–5.

TABLE 15–5. Railroad Earnings, 1940–1970*

Year	Rate of Return on Property Investment	Year	Rate of Return on Property Investment
1940	3.02%	1956	4.27
1941	4.41	1957	3.62
1942	6.58	1958	2.91
1943	6.03	1959	2.86
1944	4.87	1960	2.23
1945	3.90	1961	2.04
1946	2.82	1962	2.77
1947	3.53	1963	3.07
1948	4.36	1964	3.22
1949	2.91	1965	3.73
1950	4.34	1966	3.92
1951	4.16	1967	2.48
1952	4.54	1968	2.52
1953	4.55	1969	2.38
1954	3.51	1970	1.75 (prelim.)
1955	4.54		

* Figures for 1940 to 1950 computed from data in Interstate Commerce Commission, *Transport Statistics in the United States;* figures since 1950 from Interstate Commerce Commission, *Annual Reports.*

CRITICISMS OF RATE-LEVEL CONTROL

Criticism of the Commission's performance in rate-level cases varies from the charge that the Commission has been too lenient, if not subservient, to the railroads because it has permitted increase after increase in railway rates,[99] to the charge that it has been niggardly in not allowing even greater increases and is therefore responsible in large measure for the low level of railroad earnings.[100]

It is difficult to see how increased operating costs of the railroads, particularly in the period following World War II, could have been

---

[98] *Increased Freight Rates, 1967,* 329 ICC 854 (1967), 332 ICC 280 (1968); *Increased Freight Rates, 1968,* 332 ICC 590 (1968), 332 ICC 714 (1969); *Increased Freight Rates, 1969,* 337 ICC 436 (1970); *Increased Freight Rates, 1970 and 1971,* 339 ICC 125 (1971).

[99] Bernard Schwartz, *The Professor and the Commissions* (New York: Knopf, 1959), pp. 120–21; Samuel P. Huntington, "The Marasmus of the ICC: The Commission, the Railroads, and the Public Interest," 61 *Yale Law Journal* 467, 481–87 (1952).

[100] Dearing and Owen, op. cit., chap. xiii; Nelson, op. cit., pp. 129–30.

surmounted without substantial increases in rates. The rate of return earned by the railroads during recent years indicates that earnings have been less than desirable. Whether greater increases in rates would have made net earnings greater, particularly in the long run, cannot be positively determined. They might have done so; or on the other hand, they might have resulted in even greater diversion of traffic to other modes of transport, stimulated transportation-saving shifts in the location of industries, restricted the market areas of sellers and buyers, and otherwise dried up revenue-producing traffic.

Those who consider that the Commission is partly, if not largely, responsible for the inadequacy of railroad earnings place part of the blame on the provisions of the Act which require the Commission to consider the effects of rates on the movement of traffic, since these provisions empower the Commission to substitute its judgment for that of management concerning the revenue effect of proposed increases. We have already noted the desire of the railroads to have this provision removed from the Act. Since this authority is a natural concomitant of the obligation to see that the rate level yields the railroads adequate revenue, some students of the problem contend that the Commission should be relieved of any responsibility to see that the rate level yields adequate returns, thus removing the divided responsibility that exists under the present statute.[101]

Regardless of whether railroad management, or the Interstate Commerce Commission, or both, have been responsible for the low level of railroad earnings in the recent past, and regardless of whether Section 15a has aided or hampered efforts to improve the situation, the principal cause of inadequacy of earnings lies in the rise of competing forms of transport. The railroads' problem cannot be solved by rate policies alone, although improved methods of pricing their services, involving both increases and reductions in rates, should occupy an important place in any attack on the problem. This is primarily a function of management. It is not likely that the Interstate Commerce Commission will interpose any obstacles to such efforts other than such as may be incidental to its obligation to see that the resulting rates do not violate any provisions of the Act.

Increases in transportation rates, like other price increases, are now subject to review by the Price Commission established under the wage-price stabilization program instituted by President Nixon in 1971. These controls are intended to be of a temporary nature.

SELECTED REFERENCES

General treatments of the rate-level problem may be found in Kent T. Healy, *The Economics of Transportation in America* (New York: Ronald

---

[101] Dearing and Owen, op. cit., pp. 293–304.

Press, 1940), pp. 507–19; Truman C. Bigham, *Transportation: Principles and Problems* (New York: McGraw-Hill, 1946), chap. ix; Marvin L. Fair and Ernest W. Williams, Jr., *Economics of Transportation* (rev. ed.; New York: Harper, 1959), chap. xxvii; Russell E. Westmeyer, *Economics of Transportation* (New York: Prentice-Hall, 1952), chap. x; Hugh S. Norton, *Modern Transportation Economics* (Columbus, Ohio: Chas. E. Merrill, 1963), chap. xvii.

A thorough treatment of the Commission's handling of rate-level cases prior to World War II is I. L. Sharfman, *The Interstate Commerce Commission*, Vol. III–B (New York: Commonwealth Fund, 1936), chap. xiv. A somewhat critical account of later rate-level cases is Charles L. Dearing and Wilfred Owen, *National Transportation Policy* (Washington, D.C.: Brookings Institution, 1949), chap. xiii. The problem of the rate level is also discussed in James C. Nelson, *Railroad Transportation and Public Policy* (Washington, D.C.: Brookings Institution, 1959), pp. 125–31 and 336–44. A sharply critical review of rate-level proceedings is Merrill J. Roberts, "Maximum Freight Rate Regulation and Railroad Earnings Control," 35 *Land Economics* 125 (1959).

Chapter 16

FAIR VALUE AND RATE OF RETURN

Although the Supreme Court of the United States declared in *Smyth* v. *Ames* that the basis of all calculations as to the reasonableness of the rate level was the "fair value" of the carrier's property, it did not specify very definitely what constituted "fair value." An enormous amount of controversy and litigation has ensued over the meaning of "fair value," and how it can be ascertained.

Some aspects of the controversy, both economic and legal, are discussed in the present chapter. Controversy over the determination of "fair value" was at its height, as far as railroads are concerned, when the Commission was making its valuations under the Valuation Act of 1913, and again in the administration of the Recapture Clause in the Act of 1920. Since the provisions of the Recapture Clause called for recovery by the Government of one half of the earnings of individual railroads in excess of six percent on the value of their properties, determination of the precise amount to be recovered required an exact determination of "value."

In recent years controversy over railroad valuation has subsided. This may be explained by three circumstances: (1) the repeal of the Recapture Clause in 1933; (2) the rise of competing modes of transport which have made it virtually impossible in recent years for the railroads to increase rates sufficiently to earn an adequate return on any conventional rate base; and (3) refusal of the courts in late years to concern themselves with methods of valuation, thus eliminating much litigation over the question in the courts were major battles over valuation had long been fought. The last of these points will be explained more fully later in this chapter.

It should be recognized, however, that valuation for rate-making purposes is still of significance. Wherever rates are tested by the relation of earnings to so-called "value," the propriety of the valuation used is pertinent. In major railroad rate-level cases the Commission makes use of valuation data—usually investment data—and earnings in relation thereto, to appraise the urgency of the railroads' need for increased revenues.[1] Use of valuation data is also made in cases of narrower scope such as commutation fares in metropolitan areas.[2] Value determinations are also used in deciding contests between railroads over the division of joint rates.[3] Valuation for rate-making purposes, furthermore, is not a problem peculiar to the railroads. It has been used in determining the reasonableness of pipeline rates,[4] and in recent years, in motor-carrier rate level cases.[5] The Civil Aeronautics Board relies on the rate-base approach in determining the adequacy of airline fares,[6] and has been obliged to consider the propriety of items sought to be included in the rate base. The Federal Maritime Board has puzzled over the question whether original cost, replacement cost, or "fair market value" of ships should be used in determining the reasonableness of steamship rates subject to its control.[7]

Under these circumstances, it is desirable to give some consideration to issues involved in the determination of the rate base and how these issues have been resolved.

FAIR VALUE AND MARKET VALUE

In approaching the valuation problem, one thing must be made clear at the outset: "fair value" is not value in the economic sense. To the economist, value is exchange value or market value; hence the value of a railroad or of any income-producing property is dependent upon the earnings it yields. To a buyer or to a seller, a railroad is worth the capitalized value of the income which it can be expected to produce. But the income which a railroad will produce depends upon the rates charged. We cannot base rates on a value which is dependent upon the rates. If market value were used as a rate base, it would tend to legalize existing rates, whether they were high or low.

Although rates cannot be based on value in the ordinary sense of the word without destroying the right to regulate, railroads and public utilities argued for a long time that value for rate-making purposes is value in the economic sense, unless perchance the earnings are so low that market value is less than the cost of reproducing the road at current

---

[1] E.g., *Increased Freight Rates, 1967*, 329 ICC 854, 870–72 (1967).

[2] E.g., *New Jersey-New York Commutation Fares*, 277 ICC 459, 468 (1950); *Illinois Central Multiple Fares in Chicago Area*, 281 ICC 537, 548 (1951).

[3] E.g., *Official-Southern Divisions*, 325 ICC 1, 49 (1965).

[4] *Reduced Pipe Line Rates & Charges*, 243 ICC 115 (1940).

[5] E.g., *Increased Rates & Charges, Middlewest Territory*, 335 ICC 142 (1969); *Rate Increases & Charges, Southwestern States*, 335 ICC 361 (1969).

[6] See particularly, *General Passenger Fare Investigation*, 32 CAB 291 (1960).

[7] See *General Increase in Hawaiian Rates*, 5 FMB 347 (1957); *General Increases in Alaskan Rates & Charges*, 5 FMB 486 (1958); *Commonwealth of Puerto Rico* v. *Federal Maritime Board*, 288 F. 2d 419 (1961).

prices.[8] From a purely legalistic point of view this position is logical. The fair-value doctrine was based on a supposed analogy between rate making and condemnation of property under the right of eminent domain. If the government takes private property for a public use, it must pay the owners just compensation. This means the value of the property in the ordinary sense of the word: market value or exchange value. It is logical, therefore, to urge that the same kind of value fixes the limits below which rates cannot be reduced by regulatory authorities without confiscating property.[9] But logical as this reasoning may be, the fact remains that to base rates on value in the economic sense would be to legalize existing rates and to deny the right of the state to interfere with them.

Recognizing that circular reasoning was involved if "fair value" was affected by earnings, the Supreme Court came to reject earning power as a measure of value. In the Los Angeles Gas Case, in 1933, the Court said: ". . . when rates themselves are in dispute, earnings produced by rates do not afford a standard for decision."[10] The Supreme Court has also excluded from consideration in valuation cases certain intangible elements of value because of their dependence upon earnings.[11] Notwithstanding the Court's rejection of elements of value that are important in determining value in the economic sense, the Court continued to maintain that it was trying to find the value of the property, even though the usual measure of value had to be rejected. Since earning power had to be excluded from consideration because of the circular reasoning involved, the Court fell back on original cost and cost of reproduction as indicators of value, although both are largely irrelevant if real value is sought. By using these inferior measures of value instead of earning power, the courts thought that they had avoided the circular reasoning involved in basing rates on earnings. However, if by using an inferior measure of value, they should hit upon real value, the result would be the same as if rates had been based on earnings. If the use of the inferior measure of value resulted in a rate base different from real value, value would not have been found.

The fact that value for rate-making purposes is not and cannot be value in the usual sense was finally recognized and pointed out by the

---

[8] See N. T. Guernsey, *The Regulation of Public Utilities*, an address (1916), pp. 28–29; and "Value in Confiscation Cases," 77 *University of Pennsylvania Law Review* 575 (1929); Pierce Butler, "Valuation of Railroad Property for Purposes of Rate Regulation," 23 *Journal of Political Economy* 17 (1915); W. L. Ransom, "Some Aspects of the Valuation of Private Property for Public Uses," 2 *Journal of Land and Public Utility Economics* 1 (1926); Leslie Craven, "Railroad Valuation— A Statement of the Problem," 9 *American Bar Association Journal* 681, 801 (1923).

[9] The condemnation analogy was reiterated by the Supreme Court as late as 1935 in *West v. Chesapeake & Potomac Telephone Co.*, 295 U.S. 662, 671.

[10] *Los Angeles Gas Co. v. Railroad Commission of California*, 289 U.S. 287, 305 (1933). See also *The Minnesota Rate Cases*, 230 U.S. 352, 461 (1913).

[11] See pp. 390–91, infra.

Supreme Court in 1944. In *Federal Power Commission* v. *Hope Natural Gas Co.* the Court said:

The fixing of prices, like other applications of the police power, may reduce the value of the property which is being regulated. But the fact that the value is reduced does not mean that the regulation is invalid. It does, however, indicate that "fair value" is the end product of the process of rate-making, not the starting point as the Circuit Court of Appeals held. The heart of the matter is that rates cannot be made to depend upon "fair value" when the value of the going enterprise depends on earnings under whatever rates may be anticipated.[12]

Somewhat earlier, in a railroad reorganization case, the Supreme Court had anticipated this recognition that value for rate-making purposes was a different thing from value in the economic sense of the word. The Court, in distinguishing value in a reorganization case from value for rate-making purposes, said: "Thus the question in a valuation for rate making is how much a utility will be allowed to earn. The basic question in a valuation for reorganization purposes is how much the enterprise in all probability can earn."[13] Thus the Supreme Court finally came to recognize that in a valuation proceeding for rate-making purposes a commission or court is not *finding* value; it is deciding what the value ought to be. In so far as rates can be adjusted to yield a fair return on such value, the commission or court is *making* value, not *finding* it. Much confusion of thought can be avoided if this point is kept in mind.

The fact that fair value is not value in the economic sense has resulted in a tendency to substitute the phrase "rate base" for "value," thereby avoiding the confusion of thought engendered by using the word "value" when true value is not sought.

ELEMENTS OF VALUE

In the *Smyth* v. *Ames* decision the Court specified a number of factors to be considered in reaching a conclusion as to fair value. These included (1) the original cost of construction and the amount expended in permanent improvements, (2) the present as compared with the original cost of construction, (3) the amount of stocks and bonds, (4) the value of stocks and bonds, and (5) the probable earning capacity of the property. Then, lest something might have been omitted from the enumeration, the Court added: "We do not say that there may not be other matters to be regarded in estimating the value of the property."[14]

We have already noted that the courts have subsequently rejected earning capacity as a factor to be considered because of the circularity

---

[12] 320 U.S. 591, 601.

[13] *Institutional Investors* v. *Chicago, Milwaukee, St. Paul & Pacific R. R. Co.*, 318 U.S. 523, 540 (1943).

[14] 169 U.S. 466, 547.

of reasoning involved. The value of stocks and bonds must be rejected for the same reason. The value of the stocks and bonds is obviously dependent upon the company's earnings, and the earnings are dependent upon the rates charged.

The amount of stocks and bonds, taken at par or face values, has also been rejected, as it must be. It was specifically rejected by the Supreme Court in the Knoxville Water Case.[15] To allow the amount of stocks and bonds outstanding to affect a valuation for rate-making purposes would obviously put a premium on stock watering and overcapitalization and would penalize the conservatively capitalized road. The *Smyth* v. *Ames* decision is itself authority for not considering capitalization except under special circumstances. The Court said: "If a railroad corporation has bonded its property for an amount that exceeds its fair value, or if its capitalization is largely fictitious, it may not impose upon the public the burden of such increased rates as may be required for the purpose of realizing profits upon such excessive valuation and fictitious capitalization. . . ."[16] But capitalization is excessive if it exceeds the investment or the real value of the property.[17] This is equivalent to rejecting capitalization as an independent factor in determining the rate base. It is useful only as indicating what the investment in the property probably was.

If we rule out the elements mentioned in *Smyth* v. *Ames* which are generally recognized as being entitled to no weight in a valuation case, there remain but two items: (1) original cost, including additions and betterments; and (2) replacement cost, or cost of reproduction. Although by no means confined to this issue, the debate between original cost and reproduction cost has largely dominated the valuation controversy.

Original Cost versus Cost of Reproduction

Concerning the merits of these two bases of valuation, a long and bitter controversy has been waged. It will now be our task to review the arguments advanced in behalf of each and the objections that are raised thereto. In doing so, we shall first consider the problem from a strictly economic point of view. We shall consider the problem as an open one, that is, we shall assume that commissions are free to choose the basis of valuation which seems to promise the most desirable economic results. This is, in fact, the present situation, except where the statutes under which a commission functions restrict the commission's power in this

---

[15] *Knoxville* v. *Knoxville Water Co.*, 212 U.S. 1, 11 (1909).

[16] 169 U.S. 466, 544.

[17] Whether the proper capitalization should be measured by investment, reproduction cost, fair value, or something else is discussed in Chapter 24.

respect. For a long time, however, as will be pointed out shortly, the courts had a great deal to say about the ascertainment of fair value.

Before entering upon a discussion of the rival bases of valuation, our terminology should be made clear. We shall use the terms "actual cost" and "original cost" synonymously. This will mean the expenditure, in cash or its equivalent, for construction of the property, including all additions and betterments which have been made. It will be assumed, furthermore, that all retirements and abandonments will be deducted. In other words, "actual cost" will mean the cost of the present property. Sometimes the term "prudent investment" is used in order to make provision for the deduction from actual cost of fraudulent, unwise, or extravagant expenditures which ought not to be a burden upon the public. What is said in following paragraphs will be equally as applicable to the prudent-investment basis as to the actual-cost basis.

The term "cost of reproduction," or "replacement cost," means the cost that would be incurred if the railway were to be constructed at the present time and at present prices. Sometimes the term "cost of reproduction" is considered as the cost of duplicating the service, i.e., the cost of building a wholly modern plant capable of rendering the same service as the old one. We shall use the term in the former and more usual sense unless we indicate to the contrary.

On the issue of original cost versus reproduction cost the position of the various contestants has been largely opportunistic. For many years the representatives of the railroads and public utilities urged that cost of reproduction was the proper basis. Representatives of the public urged original cost or prudent investment. In general, prices rose from late in the 90s until a peak was reached about 1920. Although lower prices prevailed during the 20s and 30s, a period of rapidly rising prices occurred after World War II. It is not strange, therefore, that the cost-of-reproduction basis of valuation usually gives railroads and public utilities a higher rate base than would original cost. The positions of shipper and carrier were just the opposite when the case of *Smyth* v. *Ames* was before the courts in 1898. Prices had been declining since the period of Civil War inflation. The original cost of the properties was greater than the cost of reproduction; hence the public favored cost of reproduction, and the carriers favored either original cost or outstanding capitalization.

Arguments for Actual Cost

The basic argument for original cost is that it is the best basis to attract capital into the industry. There is no better way of inducing people to put their money into an enterprise than by paying them a stable return on what they have already put in. The original-cost basis does this. Investors will consider themselves fairly treated if they are allowed a return on what they have put into railroad properties, and they will be willing to put more dollars in on the same terms. On the other hand, the cost-of-reproduction basis would pay investors a return not on what they have put in, but on what they would have to put in to construct a new plant at the present time. Sometimes this will be more than the actual investment; sometimes it will be less. The real investor, as distinguished from the speculator, will hesitate to invest money in railroad properties if uncertain that he will be allowed a return on what he has put in. This has been stated very clearly by Professor Eliot Jones: "If an investor were offered his choice between (1) 5 percent on $1000 and (2) 5 percent on $900 or $1100, a toss of the coin to determine whether it would be $900 or $1100, he would choose 5 percent on the $1000; if he did not, he would not be an investor, but a speculator."[18] And it might be added that it is upon investors, rather than speculators, that we should rely for a steady supply of capital.

Two other arguments, but of a secondary nature, are advanced in behalf of original cost. First, it makes for more stable rates than the cost-of-reproduction basis. Original cost changes only as changes are made in investment; cost of reproduction changes with changing prices. The other argument for use of original cost is that it can be more easily kept up to date. Once a valuation has been made, careful accounting will indicate all changes to be made in the rate base. Cost of reproduction, on the other hand, requires frequent revaluations. These are extremely costly as well as time-consuming. We speak of these two arguments for the original-cost basis as secondary because, although they are of great practical significance, they would carry no weight if original cost were unfair or unjust.

Cost of Reproduction

The most persuasive argument for cost of reproduction as a rate base is commonly called the depreciated-dollar argument.[19] Use of cost of reproduction, it is urged, is necessary to compensate investors for changes in the purchasing power of money. If it cost $10 million to build a certain railroad originally, but would cost $20 million to build it at the present time, a return upon the latter is necessary in order to give the owners the same income in terms of purchasing power that they got formerly. The statement is largely true, but a number of limitations must be made.

In the first place, the argument assumes that the cost of reproducing a railroad is a good index of changes in the purchasing power of the dollar. The purchasing power of the dollar is measured by fluctuations in the prices of hundreds of commodities, not merely the changes in the prices of materials and services entering into the construction of a rail-

---

[18] Eliot Jones, *Principles of Railway Transportation* (New York: Macmillan, 1924), p. 283.

[19] Other arguments for cost of reproduction are analyzed in earlier editions of this book. See particularly the sixth edition, pp. 357–62.

way. If we wish to give investors in railways a stable return in terms of purchasing power, the use of standard index numbers of price changes would be fairer, less expensive, and more logical than the use of cost of reproduction as a rate base.

It may also be pointed out, in answer to the depreciated-dollar argument, that it is by no means certain that investors desire a variable monetary return or would think themselves fairly treated if given a return that adjusted their compensation to the changes in the purchasing power of money. Bonds on which the payment of interest and principal is adjusted to the purchasing power of money are not particularly popular with investors. This bears witness to the preference of investors for a fixed monetary return. Perhaps this will be changed as investors become more enlightened as to the uncertainties attendant upon contract obligations which call for future payments of fixed monetary sums.

There is another weakness in the depreciated-dollar argument. To double the rate-making value because cost of reproduction is twice original cost benefits only stockholders and not bondholders. Bonds and preferred stock comprise nearly two thirds of the outstanding railroad securities. Double the return to the company because of high reproduction costs, and the stockholders reap all the reward, since the holders of bonds and preferred stock receive a fixed or limited return. On the other hand, if prices should fall and cost of reproduction decline, the loss would fall upon the stockholders. Thus the use of the cost-of-reproduction basis would impose heavy losses upon stockholders if prices declined, and would give them speculative profits if prices rose. This result is hardly desirable in the interest of stabilizing returns to investors. Certainly it cannot be argued that such a result is required in order to be fair to investors. There would be much point to the depreciated-dollar argument if railroads were capitalized entirely by issues of common stock. But why ignore the facts? When these facts are recognized, the depreciated-dollar argument falls to the ground. Not only is the argument negatived, but wholly undesirable consequences result from the fluctuating income because of the manner in which it is divided between the stockholders and the bondholders. One object of regulation is to remove risks as far as possible from public utility enterprises, to the end that capital may be obtained on the most favorable terms. Obviously any method of valuation which concentrates upon the stockholders the gains and losses arising from changes in rates tends to increase risks and introduces a speculative element in the provision for capital that is not conducive to obtaining capital at the lowest cost.

Conclusion regarding the Rate Base

As a result of considering various arguments in behalf of original cost and cost of reproduction, respectively, many of which could not be analyzed in the preceding pages without unduly lengthening the present discussion, the author is inclined to the view that actual cost or prudent investment is to be preferred as a rate base. Some modification of this basis may be made, however, if it is found necessary or desirable to compensate stockholders for changes in the value of money on that part of the property represented by stockholders' equity. This result might be worked out by giving some weight to cost of reproduction. A preferable method of dealing with the problem, however, would be to use an index number of changes in the price level and apply it to that portion of the rate base represented by equity capital.

POSITION OF THE COURTS

We now turn to the legal status of the rival bases of valuation. The discussion will be confined to the pronouncements of the Supreme Court of the United States. It is necessary to recognize two distinct periods in the attitude of the Court on this question. The first period extends from the *Smyth* v. *Ames* decision in 1898 to the decision in *Federal Power Commission* v. *Natural Gas Pipeline Co.* in 1942.[20] The second period is that following the decision in the Natural Gas Pipeline Case.

Cost of Reproduction as an "Element of Value"

The first period may be characterized as one in which the Court insisted that cost of reproduction must be considered in valuation proceedings. Cost of reproduction, as we have already noted, was one of the "elements of value" mentioned in *Smyth* v. *Ames*. There is some difference of opinion whether the Court meant that cost of reproduction must be given some weight in the final valuation figure, or whether the regulating body could give it such weight, if any, as seemed just and right under the circumstances. Court decisions may be cited to support either of these interpretations.[21]

In *St. Louis & O'Fallon Ry. Co.* v. *United States*,[22] the Supreme Court overthrew a decision of the Interstate Commerce Commission arising under the Recapture Clause of the Act of 1920 because the Court believed that the Commission had not "considered" cost of reproduction. This decision seemed to end the contention that cost of reproduction could be given such weight as seemed appropriate to the regulatory body under the circumstances. The decision was interpreted to mean that cost of reproduction must be given weight regardless of circumstances. Following this decision, the Interstate Commerce Commission

[20] 315 U.S. 575. The leading Supreme Court decisions of the first period are reviewed in earlier editions of this book. See sixth edition, pp. 363–69.

[21] 279 U.S. 461 (1929) and dissenting opinions therein.

[22] Ibid.

and most state public utility commissions frequently gave about equal weight to original cost and cost of reproduction in their valuations.

Criticism of Reproduction Cost as an Element of Value

The view that cost of reproduction was an element which must be considered in arriving at fair value was not unanimously accepted by the Supreme Court. Perhaps the most famous criticism of the Court's position was the separate opinion of Justice Brandeis in the Southwestern Bell Telephone Case, an expression in which Justice Holmes concurred, Justice Brandeis characterized the *Smyth* v. *Ames* rule of determining fair value as "legally and economically unsound."[23] In arguing for prudent investment as a rate base, Brandeis said: "The thing devoted by the investor to the public use is not specific property, tangible or intangible, but capital embarked in the enterprise. Upon the capital so invested the Federal Constitution guarantees to the utility the opportunity to earn a fair return."[24] Dissatisfaction with the view that fair value was compounded of actual cost, cost of reproduction, and perhaps other factors, was later asserted by Justices Frankfurter and Black. Justice Frankfurter characterized the rule of *Smyth* v. *Ames* regarding valuation as "a mischievous formula for fixing utility rates," and "useless as a guide to adjudication."[25]

Cost of reproduction as a measure of fair value had also met with criticism from public utility commissions and students of regulation. The Interstate Commerce Commission, in *Excess Income of St. Louis & O'Fallon Railway,* had taken occasion to criticize it and to defend original cost or prudent investment as a rate base.[26] Dissatisfaction with the fair-value doctrine was based on experience in the attempts to apply it. It may be well to summarize the reasons why the rule had not worked satisfactorily.

The first and most important reason for difficulty arose from the indefiniteness of the concept of fair value and the fact that no real standard of valuation had been set up. The Court had refused to say that original cost was the proper basis of valuation; it had likewise refused to hold that cost of reproduction was the correct basis. It required that both be considered but refused to say what weight should be given to each or what criteria should guide a commission in combining these two "elements of value." The Court was doubtless motivated by a desire not to lay down a rigid rule which would work injustice in particular instances. Because there was no rule for combining these elements, and because of the wide spread between original cost and cost of reproduction in many instances,

---

[23] 262 U.S. 276, 290 (1923).

[24] Ibid.

[25] Concurring opinion in *Driscoll* v. *Edison,* 307 U.S. 104, 122 (1939).

[26] 124 ICC 3, 26–39 (1927).

there was so much latitude within which judgment was to be exercised by the commission that valuations came to depend upon the bias, whim, or caprice of the persons making the valuations. The wide range of estimates of the fair value of the same property is illustrated by the New York Telephone Case. A majority of the New York Public Service Commission found the value of the company's property to be approximately $367 million. A federal court, to which the case had been appealed, held the value to be $397 million. A minority of the Commission thought the value was $405.5 million. The "Master," appointed by the court to hear the evidence in the case, believed that the fair value was $518 million. Two independent appraisals resulted in still higher figures, one of $529 million, the other of $615 million.[27] In the St. Louis & O'Fallon Case the Interstate Commerce Commission pointed out that if the railroads of the United States were valued on the basis of 1914 prices, their value would have been approximately $18 billion; but in 1920, on the basis of cost of reproduction, the value would have become $41 billion, and in 1923 it would have dropped to $31 billion.[28]

A second difficulty with the rule that cost of reproduction must be considered was that cost of reproduction itself is often a matter of conjecture. It depends upon conditions assumed to exist when the hypothetical rebuilding of the property takes place. Mr. Justice Stone once observed that "in assuming the task of determining judicially the present fair replacement value of the vast properties of public utilities, courts have been projected into the most speculative undertaking imposed upon them in the entire history of English jurisprudence."[29] Justice Black remarked that "commissions and courts passing upon rates for public utilities are driven to listen to conjectures, speculations, estimates and guesses, all under the name of 'reproduction costs.' "[30]

The third objection to the rule was a consequence of those which we have just mentioned. Both the difficulty of determining cost of reproduction and the indefiniteness of the rule for determining fair value provoked controversy and litigation. There was a tendency for railroads and utilities to appeal to the courts for a more generous valuation than that of the regulatory commission. The resulting litigation caused delay and expense. Two examples of such delay were pointed out by Justice Brandeis in the St. Joseph Stock Yards Case. A rate investigation of Chicago telephone rates instituted by the Illinois Commerce Commission in 1921 resulted in an order reducing rates in 1923, but it was not until 1934

---

[27] Related in recommendations of Commissioners Walsh, Bonbright, and Adie in *Report of [New York] Commission on Revision of the Public Service Commissions Law* (Albany, 1930), p. 266.

[28] 124 ICC 3, 31–32 (1927).

[29] Dissenting opinion in *West* v. *Chesapeake & Potomac Telephone Co.*, 295 U.S. 662, 689 (1935).

[30] Dissenting opinion in *McCart* v. *Indianapolis Water Co.*, 302 U.S. 419, 429 (1938).

that the Commission's order was finally upheld by the courts.[31] In 1920 the Public Service Commission of New York began hearings on telephone rates in New York City, and in 1922 it required certain rates to be reduced slightly. It was not until 1934 that litigation over the Commission's order was terminated by a decision of the United States Supreme Court.[32]

The Natural Gas Pipeline Case

In 1942 the Supreme Court, in *Federal Power Commission* v. *Natural Gas Pipeline Co.*,[33] opened the way for regulatory commissions to disregard cost of reproduction as an element of value and to adopt original cost or prudent investment, if they chose. The Court did not adopt original cost or prudent investment as the proper rate base, but by implication it left the way clear for commissions to do so. The Court said:

The Constitution does not bind rate-making bodies to the service of any single formula or combination of formulas. . . . Once a fair hearing has been given, proper findings made and other statutory requirements satisfied, the courts cannot intervene in the absence of a clear showing that the limits of due process have been overstepped. If the Commission's order, as applied to the facts before it and viewed in its entirety, produces no arbitrary result, our inquiry is at an end.[34]

The language implies that the courts will no longer inquire into the methods of valuation used by a commission but will concern themselves only with results. The full significance of the decision might not have been fully sensed, because of the use of phrases susceptible of several meanings, had it not been for the interpretation of the decision by Justices Black, Douglas, and Murphy in a concurring opinion. To them the decision started "a new chapter in the regulation of utility rates."[35] "As we read the opinion of the Court, the Commission is now freed from the compulsion of admitting evidence on reproduction cost or of giving any weight to that element of 'fair value.' The Commission may now adopt, if it chooses, prudent investment as a rate base."[36] The majority of the Court did not dispute this interpretation of the decision, but there re-

---

[31] 298 U.S. 38, 88 (1936).

[32] Ibid., pp. 90–91.

[33] 315 U.S. 575.

[34] Ibid., p. 586. There is some language in earlier opinions to the effect that in judicial review of rate cases it is the result reached by the Commission, not the method employed, which the courts are concerned with. See *Los Angeles Gas & Electric Corp.* v. *Railroad Commission*, 289 U.S. 287, 304–5 (1933); *West Ohio Gas Co.* v. *Public Utilities Commission of Ohio*, 294 U.S. 63, 70 (1935). In these cases, however, the Court continued to speak of the necessity of considering reproduction costs in valuation proceedings.

[35] 315 U.S. 575, 602.

[36] Ibid., p. 606.

mained some lingering doubt as to whether the decision threw overboard old standards as completely as Justices Black, Douglas, and Murphy believed. These doubts were dispelled in 1944 in *Federal Power Commission* v. *Hope Natural Gas Co.*[37] A valuation made substantially on an original-cost basis was upheld by the Supreme Court. The Court expanded upon its statement in the Natural Gas Pipeline Case, quoted above, by saying: "It is not the theory but the impact of the rate order which counts. If the total effect of the rate order cannot be said to be unjust and unreasonable, judicial inquiry under the Act is at an end. The fact that the method employed to reach that result may contain infirmities is not then important."[38] Justice Reed, in commenting on the decision of the majority, said: "I agree with the Court in not imposing a rule of prudent investment alone in determining the rate base. This leaves the Commission free, as I understand it, to use any available evidence for its finding of fair value, including both prudent investment and the cost of installing at the present time an efficient system for furnishing the needed utility service."[39] The position of the Court in the Hope Case was reaffirmed in later cases.[40]

We may conclude that so far as constitutional requirements are concerned, commissions are no longer required to consider cost of reproduction in determining the rate base. They are free to use original cost if they wish. The courts, however, still reserve the right to review rates fixed by commissions and to set them aside if the court finds them confiscatory by whatever standard it may set up for the purpose. That standard, as elsewhere pointed out, seems at the present time to be a credit standard.[41]

Valuation of Carrier Lands

Under the original-cost basis of valuation, land would be included on the basis of what the company paid for it. Some question might be raised as to the treatment of donated lands, since they presumably cost the railroad nothing. It might be argued that they should not be included in the rate base; or it might be argued that they should be entered at their fair value at the time that they were given to the railroad.

The basis of valuing land most consistent with the cost-of-reproduction basis would be the estimated cost of reacquiring the land under present conditions. It was not uncommon in some valuations made by

---

[37] 320 U.S. 591.

[38] Ibid., p. 602.

[39] Ibid., p. 623.

[40] *Colorado Interstate Gas Co.* v. *Federal Power Commission*, 324 U.S. 581 (1945); *Panhandle Eastern Pipe Line Co.* v. *Federal Power Commission*, 324 U.S. 635, 649 (1945).

[41] Pp. 354–56, supra.

state commissions to multiply the estimated value of present lands by 2, 2½, or 3, on the theory that a railroad would have to pay more for land than it was really worth if it set out to acquire land for a right of way or other railroad uses. The Valuation Act of 1913 originally directed the Interstate Commerce Commission to find the cost of reacquiring railroad land over and above its present value. In the Minnesota Rate cases, however, the Supreme Court held that railroad companies could not insist on more than the present value of their lands, as measured by the value of adjoining lands, and that it was improper to include anything more on a supposition that a railroad would have to pay more for land than it was worth.[42] The Valuation Act was amended in 1922 to relieve the Commission of the duty of ascertaining the cost of reacquiring land over and above its present value.

The implication of the Supreme Court decision in the Minnesota Rate Cases was that lands should be valued on the basis of their present values. Most state regulatory commissions felt that this was the approved method of valuing land used by railroads and public utilities.[43] It has been pointed out, however, that the Supreme Court has never affirmatively ruled that this is the only acceptable standard for valuing railroad and public utility lands.[44] In the valuations made under the Valuation Act of 1913, land was included on the basis of its values in 1914, that is, when the valuation work was undertaken. These are the values which appear to have been used in calculating the rate base in the various general rate level cases prior to 1964.[45] Since then, land is included in the rate base on an actual-cost basis, estimated in part.[46]

Valuing railroad lands on the basis of present value of adjoining lands, which at one time seemed to be required, would give the railroads the benefit of the unearned increment resulting from increasing land values, a not inconsiderable item when the lands in large city terminals and the rights of way into the city are valued on this basis. Few railroads, if their lines were nonexistent and about to be built, would go to the huge expense involved in securing an entrance into the heart of a great city. The cost would be prohibitive. Usually the city has grown up after the railroad was established. The extent to which unearned increment in land values affected the Commission's valuations, because of the inclusion of land values on the basis of 1914 values, is not easily ascertainable. It would appear to have worked greatly to their advantage. Under certain conditions, however, the practice of valuing lands on the basis of current values of adjoining lands would work to the disadvantage of a railroad.

---

[42] 230 U.S. 352, 451 (1913).

[43] See James C. Bonbright, *The Valuation of Railroad Property* (New York: McGraw Hill, 1937), vol. II, p. 1142.

[44] I. R. Barnes, "Measures of Land Values for Public Utility Regulation," 39 *Michigan Law Review* 37, 58 (1940).

[45] *Increased Freight Rates, 1968*, 332 ICC 590, 605 (1968).

[46] Ibid.

This would happen, for instance, in valuing the right of way through a mountain pass. The adjoining land may have practically no commercial value, but the pass through the mountains is of great value for a railroad right of way, and the railroad may have paid a high price for it. Generally speaking, however, inclusion of railroad lands at the present value of adjoining lands would work to the advantage of the railroads.

Depreciation

That accrued depreciation should be deducted in determining the rate base was clearly established by the Supreme Court in 1909 in *Knoxville* v. *Knoxville Water Co.*[47] The principle was subsequently reaffirmed.[48]

Although it is now accepted that depreciation should be deducted, there has been much controversy over what depreciation really is. In the valuations made by the Interstate Commerce Commission, the carriers argued that "depreciation" was synonymous with "deferred maintenance." Thus, according to this view, if a railroad is kept in 100 percent operating condition, there is no depreciation to deduct. One adherent to this view defines depreciation as "a subnormal or rundown condition of a physical plant—one which is below the proper maximum condition in which the plant can be and should be permanently maintained in order to render adequate service."[49]

The Interstate Commerce Commission, on the other hand, defined depreciation as "exhaustion of capacity for service." The depreciation to be deducted in connection with any item of property is determined from the relation between the total service units in the property when new and the number that have been used up. According to this view, "An article when new contains a certain number of units of service and as those units are exhausted the article depreciates. In order to make any figure, whether of original cost or cost of reproduction, representative of the condition of the property at the time of the inquiry it would seem on principle to be necessary to make due allowance for the expired units of service life."[50] Depreciation in this sense has also been defined as "the consumption of investment in property."[51] Under this concept of depreciation, if the "straight-line" method of depreciation is used, a unit of property having

---

[47] 212 U.S. 1.

[48] *Los Angeles Gas & Electric Corp.* v. *Railroad Commission*, 289 U.S. 287, 312 (1933).

[49] H. E. Riggs, "The Two Radically Different Concepts of Utility 'Depreciation,'" 9 *Public Utilities Fortnightly* 559, 560 (1932). See also by the same author, *Depreciation of Public Utility Properties* (New York: McGraw-Hill, 1922). A similar view of depreciation is taken in W. J. Blood, "The Depreciated Value of Public Utilities," 48 *Stone & Webster Journal* 733 (1931).

[50] *Excess Income of Richmond, Fredericksburg & Potomac R. R. Co.*, 170 ICC 451, 468 (1931).

[51] Staff of the Public Service Commission of Wisconsin, *Depreciation: A Review of Legal and Accounting Problems* (New York: State Law Publishing Co., 1933), p. 14.

a life of 20 years which has seen 10 years of service would be depreciated 50 percent. It will be seen that this concept of depreciation means that there will always be substantial sums to deduct from cost new in arriving at the rate base. This is because a railroad's property is never all new. This concept of depreciation might be termed an "economic" concept of depreciation, since emphasis is put upon the gradual consumption of the capital equipment in the process of production. Adherents to the deferred-maintenance idea of depreciation refer to depreciation in the economic sense as "theoretical" depreciation, as though it were theoretical rather than real because it is not always observable to the eye, as is physical deterioration.

The Interstate Commerce Commission's concept of depreciation is in accordance with the views expressed by the Committee on Depreciation of the National Association of Railroad and Utilities Commissioners in 1943. "Depreciation . . . occurs currently as service life is being consumed in operations. Its progress can be calculated . . . but it cannot be observed, because the entire process is not visible to the naked eye."[52]

The statement that accrued depreciation should be deducted in arriving at the appropriate rate base does not mean that all railroad property is depreciable. A distinction between depreciable and nondepreciable property must always be made. Thus the Interstate Commerce Commission recognized that railway land is not subject to depreciation from age, wear, or use. Grading and excavations are also nondepreciable items, and there are other items which the Commission does not depreciate.

Intangible Values

There remains for consideration the question whether it is proper to include in a rate base various "intangible" elements of value. The most important ones which have been urged from time to time as properly to be included in the rate base are goodwill, franchise value, and going value.

Goodwill is ordinarily understood as the value arising from the preference of customers or patrons for the products or services of one concern over those of another. *Franchise value* is the value of the company's franchise or privilege to do business. If the franchise is exclusive or not granted to all comers, it may result in monopoly powers on the part of the holder. *Going value* has been defined as the "element of value in an assembled and established plant, doing business and earning money, over one not thus advanced."[53] It has also been defined as "the difference in value existing between a plant in successful operation and a similar plant assembled but not yet functioning."[54]

---

[52] *Report of Committee on Depreciation, 1943* (mimeographed ed.), p. x–31.

[53] *Des Moines Gas Co.* v. *Des Moines*, 238 U.S. 153, 165 (1915).

[54] M. C. Waltersdorf, "Going Value in Utility Valuation," 17 *American Economic Review* 26 (1927).

If any of these intangibles have a monetary value, that value is dependent upon the earnings and involves us in the circular reasoning that has caused the courts to reject market value or earning power in the valuation of utilities for rate-making purposes.[55] Their inclusion in the rate base would largely negate any attempt to regulate the rate level.

Although intangibles are ordinarily excluded from the rate base, an exception is recognized under some circumstances in connection with franchise value. If a charge was exacted for the grant of a franchise, its cost may properly be included in the actual investment figure. In the days when street railways were being developed in the United States, some municipalities exacted a price for the concession or privilege of building and operating such a railway in the streets of a city. It has not been the practice, however, for the federal government or state governments to exact a price for the grant of rights to conduct transportation operations.

VALUATIONS BY THE ICC AND OTHER COMMISSIONS

Although the Interstate Commerce Commission has stated that "there is no statutory requirement or statement of policy requiring the making of rates to yield a certain rate of return on investment either in the United States as a whole, or in the various rate territories,"[56] it has been found useful to include return-on-investment figures in the various rate-level cases as an indication of revenue needs of the carriers.[57] The rate base used in recent years is an estimate of original cost, less recorded depreciation, plus an allowance for working capital including supplies. Land, formerly included on the basis of 1914 "present values," is included on the basis of actual cost, although this is partly estimated. The Commission has noted that the use of recorded depreciation probably understates the depreciation which is properly deductible.[58] The Commission has asserted the propriety of its valuations for rate-making purposes against the carriers' contentions that not sufficient weight had been given to reproduction costs.[59] It should be noted that the estimated element in the valuations becomes a smaller proportion of the total as time goes on. The Commission stated in 1968 that approximately 70 percent of the estimates of original cost made under the Valuation Act of 1913 had been written off with the retirement of property which has

---

[55] The nature of these intangibles and their treatment in valuation proceedings are more fully discussed in earlier editions of this book. See particularly the sixth edition, pp. 375–79.

[56] *Increased Freight Rates, Eastern, Western & Southern Territories, 1956,* 300 ICC 633, 656 (1957).

[57] See for example *Increased Freight Rates, 1947,* 269 ICC 33, 47–48 (1947); *Increased Freight Rates, 1956,* 298 ICC 279, 287 (1956).

[58] *Increased Freight Rates, 1951,* 284 ICC 589, 604–5 (1952).

[59] Ibid., p. 608.

been replaced by new property the cost of which is shown in the carrier investment accounts.[60]

An appendix statement in *Increased Freight Rates, 1968*, purporting to show the value figures using the method used by the Commission in prior cases, gives the "net investment" of the Class I railroads in 1968 as $27,817,300,000.[61]

Although in this chapter we are primarily interested in the valuation of railroads, it may be well to compare the valuation methods of the Interstate Commerce Commission with those of other regulatory bodies. The Federal Power Commission has adhered to an original-cost basis.[62] In fact, it was a valuation of the Federal Power Commission on an original-cost basis that was upheld in the Hope Natural Gas Case.[63] Likewise, the Civil Aeronautics Board has adhered to an original-cost or actual-investment basis in regulating airlines.[64] The Federal Maritime Commission has used prudent investment in regulating steamship rates in the domestic off-shore trades.[65]

Several state commissions, even before the Natural Gas Pipeline and Hope cases, adhered to an original-cost or prudent-investment basis of valuation in the regulation of public utilities.[66] Following the Hope Case, numerous other state commissions adopted original cost or prudent investment as the rate base.[67] Some states, although bound by statutory requirements based on the *Smyth* v. *Ames* doctrine to consider various elements of value including reproduction cost, gave original cost predominant weight.[68] In some states the courts have overruled this procedure, holding that under the statutes of the state the commission must give substantial weight to cost of reproduction or "present costs."[69] After a court ruling to this effect in Maine the legislature amended the law

---

[60] *Increased Freight Rates, 1968*, 332 ICC 590, 605 (1968).

[61] Ibid., p. 611.

[62] See F. F. Blachly and M. E. Oatman, "Actual Legitimate Cost as a Basis for Utility Regulation—The Experience of the Federal Power Commission," 36 *Georgetown Law Journal* 487 (1948).

[63] See p. 387, supra.

[64] See Chapter 35, infra.

[65] *Atlantic & Gulf-Puerto Rico General Increase*, 7 FMC 87 (1962); *Investigation of Increased Rates within Hawaii*, 7 FMC 151 (1962); *Pacific-Atlantic/Guam Increases in Rates*, 7 FMC 423 (1962); *Pacific Coast/Puerto Rico Rate Increase*, 7 FMC 525 (1963).

[66] Joseph R. Rose, "The Hope Case and Public Utility Valuation in the States, 54 *Columbia Law Review* 188 (1954), pp. 190–91.

[67] Ibid., p. 204.

[68] Ibid., pp. 200–201.

[69] E.g., *Chesapeake & Potomac Telephone Co. of Baltimore City* v. *Public Service Commission*, 95 PUR NS 129 (1952); *Iowa-Illinois Gas & Electric Co.* v. *City of Fort Dodge*, 20 PUR 3d 159 (1957); *Missouri Water Co.* v. *Missouri Public Service Commission*, 22 PUR 3d 254 (1957).

and excluded "current value" as an element in valuation.[70] In some states, therefore, the original-cost basis of valuation is used by regulatory commissions; in others, cost of reproduction must still be given weight in the valuation of public utilities. Inflationary tendencies have led some states which had used the prudent-investment basis to revert to use of cost of reproduction as a factor in the determination of fair value.[71]

FAIR RATE OF RETURN

Thus far we have discussed questions involved in the determination of the rate base. Nothing has been said about the fair rate of return which should be allowed on the rate base. For many years the question of the fair rate of return received much less attention at the hands of commissions and courts than the matter of "fair value." In recent years, however, the problems of determining a fair rate of return have received increasing attention from state commissions in the regulation of public utilities. In the regulation of railroads, on the other hand, the problem has been considered largely academic. This is because the earnings of the railroads as a whole have been low by any standard, and the problem has been to find ways and means of improving earnings; and it has not been necessary to determine any precise amount which the railroads, either as a whole or in groups, should be permitted to earn. In the airline industry, however, the appropriate rate of return has been of major concern. We need, therefore, to give some attention to the theory and practice involved in the determination of the fair rate of return.

No Single Rate of Return Always Fair

What constitutes a fair rate of return varies with time, place, and circumstance. That the proper rate of return may vary with the times was expressed by the Supreme Court in *Bluefields Water Works & Improvement Co.* v. *Public Service Commission of West Virginia* in 1923. "A rate of return may be reasonable at one time and become too high or too low by changes affecting opportunities for investment, the money market and business conditions generally."[72] That the rate of return may vary with geographical location has also been recognized by the Supreme Court,[73] and is but a reflection of the well-known fact that rates of in-

[70] "The Fair Value Rate Base," 62 *Public Utilities Fortnightly* 489 (1958), p. 491.

[71] See Francis J. and Margadette M. Demet, "Legal Aspects of Rate Base and Rate of Return in Public Utility Regulation," 42 *Marquette Law Review* 331 (1959), pp. 341–42.

[72] 262 U.S. 679, 693 (1923). See also *United Railways* v. *West*, 280 U.S. 234, 249 (1930).

[73] See *Willcox* v. *Consolidated Gas Co.*, 212 U.S. 19, 48–49 (1909); *Denver* v. *Denver Water Co.*, 246 U.S. 178, 194 (1918).

terest are not uniform throughout the world or throughout a single country. Furthermore, what is a fair return in one industry is not necessarily fair in another, because of differences in risk.

Tests for Determining Fair Rate of Return

Two tests of a fair rate of return have been mentioned in court decisions. These are the "comparable earnings" test and the "attraction of capital" or "maintenance of credit" test. Both of these were stated by the Supreme Court of the United States in the Bluefields case. The "comparable earnings" test was indicated in the following language: "A public utility is entitled to such rates as will permit it to earn a return on the value of the property which it employs for the convenience of the public equal to that generally being made at the same time and in the same general part of the country on investments in other business undertakings which are attended by corresponding risks and uncertainties; but it has no constitutional right to profits such as are realized or anticipated in highly profitable enterprises or speculative ventures."[74] The "attraction of capital" test found expression as follows: "The return should be reasonably sufficient to assure confidence in the financial soundness of the utility and should be adequate, under efficient and economical management, to maintain and support its credit and enable it to raise the money necessary for the proper discharge of its public duties."[75] Both of these tests require further comment.

The Comparable Earnings Test

The difficulty with this test is that of finding industries with "corresponding risks." Should the comparison be with other regulated industries or with nonregulated industries? Regulated industries, although subject to many risks, are protected from other risks. They are protected from competition to some extent. Many public utilities, particularly those of a local nature, have a monopoly in the areas they serve. Even railroads and other common carriers are protected from competition to a certain extent through restrictions on entry into the business. Where competition exists, these carriers are protected from the "ruinous" type of competition by interference with rate cutting under the minimum rate power. If earnings are compared with those of other regulated industries of the same kind, in order to compare like with like, we are faced with the fact that the earnings of these other utilities are regulated by the same or different commissions.

If earnings are to be compared with those of unregulated industries, then the great differences in risk among them, and between them as a

---

[74] 262 U.S. 679, 692–93.
[75] Ibid.

group and regulated industries, render comparisons of returns of little significance in determining a fair rate of return. In the American Telephone and Telegraph Investigation of 1967, the company argued that it was legally entitled to earnings comparable to those of unregulated concerns. The Federal Communications Commission rejected the contention although it held that comparison with unregulated industries was one element to be considered.[76]

Capital Attraction Test—Cost of Capital

The "capital attraction" test usually leads to rather elaborate studies of the cost of capital to the firms whose rates are under investigation. Cost-of-capital studies have assumed much importance in proceedings before the Civil Aeronautics Board.[77] Similar studies have been introduced in some recent railroad rate-level cases.[78]

The "cost-of-capital" method of determining a fair rate of return for public utilities was thought at first to be a purely objective method devoid of subjective judgments such as had characterized earlier determinations of an appropriate rate of return. The process seemed to be one that was based on facts that were subject to quantitative measurement.

The method was to determine the cost of borrowed capital which is measured by the interest rates on bonds with adjustment for premiums or discounts at time of issue and a consideration of flotation costs. The cost of capital raised through issues of preferred stock is obtained by substantially the same method. The cost of equity capital is determined by the use of dividend-price ratios (yields), or of earnings-price ratios. The dividend-price ratio is the ratio of dividends to the market price of the common stock, and presumably indicates what yield or rate of return prospective purchasers of stock expect to realize from stock purchased, i.e., the terms on which they are willing to provide equity capital. The earnings-price ratio is based on the same reasoning but includes in the numerator net earnings per share, instead of dividends, on the theory that investors look not only to dividends but also to the increased equity behind their shares which result from reinvested earnings. The earnings-price ratio is used more often than the dividend-price ratio, but when used it becomes necessary to recognize that differences in the pay-out ratio, that is, the proportion of earnings paid out as dividends, will affect the price of the stock. The price of the stock will not be as high, and the earnings-price ratio therefore higher, if the company follows a very conservative dividend policy. Stated in another way, investors will provide equity capital on less favorable terms if a substantial proportion

---

[76] *Re American Telephone & Telegraph Co.,* 70 PUR 3d 129 (1967).

[77] E.g., *Rate of Return, Local Service Carriers Investigation,* 32 CAB 291 (1960).

[78] E.g., *Increased Freight Rates, Eastern, Western & Southern Territories, 1956,* 300 ICC 633 (1957); *Increased Freight Rates, 1968,* 332 ICC 590 (1968).

of the earnings are withheld, even though the stockholders' equity is being increased by the process.

After the respective costs of capital obtained from borrowing and from preferred stock issues are determined and the earnings-price ratio is found as the cost of equity capital, the three figures are averaged, but the average is weighted by the respective proportions of the capital raised by the three methods. Thus, to use a simple example, if the cost of borrowed capital is 5 percent and borrowed capital represents 40 percent of the total capital; and if preferred stock capital cost 7 percent and represents 10 percent of the total capital; and if the earnings-price ratio for common stock is 12 percent and equity capital (common stock and "surplus") represents 50 percent of the total capitalization; the overall cost of capital would be 8.7 percent, according to the following calculation:

$$
\begin{array}{rcl}
5\% \times .40 & = & 2.00\% \\
7\% \times .10 & = & .70\% \\
12\% \times .50 & = & 6.00\% \\
\hline
1.00 & & 8.70\%
\end{array}
$$

If the regulatory body considered the cost of capital, so computed, to be the sole consideration in determining the fair rate of return, this figure would be applied to the rate base to determine the sum needed to reward investors.

In our illustration of the method of computing the overall cost of capital, the cost of debt and preferred stock capital and of equity capital respectively was applied to the actual proportions of capital represented by bonds, preferred stock, common stock and "surplus." It can be argued that a hypothetical and ideal capital structure should be used instead of actual capitalization. Under the ideal capital structure, the combined cost of borrowed and equity capital would be the lowest possible.

In defense of the use of the actual capital structure it can be said that the determination of the appropriate capital structure is a function of management and that the regulatory body ought not to interfere with managerial discretion on this point. It can also be pointed out that the capital structure is the result of capital-raising efforts at various times in the past; and that although the present capital structure may not be ideal, conditions existing at the times when new capital was needed may have dictated the financing methods used; and that management decisions at the time were not objectionable. It can also be argued that since the costs of borrowed and equity capital were calculated under existing capital structures, and since a different capital structure would have produced different costs for both debt and equity capital, it is illogical to apply the costs found to a wholly different capital structure.

Practice among regulatory commissions concerning the use of hypothetical capital structures varies considerably. The Civil Aeronautics Board in the General Passenger Fare Investigation in 1960 used actual capital structure.[79] The Federal Communications Commission, on the other hand, used a hypothetical capital structure in the American Telephone & Telegraph Investigation in 1967, saying that it was the obligation of the company to fix the proportions of debt and equity in the capitalization "in such way as to raise the required capital at the lowest possible cost consistent with overall responsibility to provide modern, efficient service at reasonable rates and to maintain the financial integrity of the enterprise."[80] It was pointed out in a 1960 decision of the Louisiana Supreme Court that 17 state commissions, in addition to Louisiana, had adopted hypothetical debt ratios.[81]

Weaknesses of Cost-of-Capital Studies

The original enthusiasm for cost-of-capital studies, particularly the use of earnings-price ratios, has waned somewhat in view of weaknesses, both theoretical and practical, that have become apparent. Such ratios, however, are considered helpful in efforts to arrive at a fair rate of return.

A theoretical weakness of earnings-price ratios to determine the cost of equity capital is that an element of circular reasoning is involved. If the earnings of an enterprise are very poor, and are likely to continue so, cost-of-capital calculations will indicate that a high rate of return is necessary to attract capital. This is borne out by the fact that the common stocks of corporations that have poor earnings and poor prospects of earnings will sell on a high-yield basis, i.e., will be low in price and will yield a high rate of return on the price of the stock. Conversely, stock of corporations with good earnings and prospect of good earnings will sell on a low-yield basis. Thus, cost-of-capital studies in industries with a record of poor earnings will indicate that a high overall rate of return is necessary; but if such a return were actually earned, perhaps as a result of rate increases, the stock would rise in price and sell on a lower yield basis.[82]

This weakness was brought out in a study of Civil Aeronautics Board policy by Richard E. Caves. The Board, in *Rate of Return, Local Service Carriers*[83] had found that this group of airlines needed a return of 21.35 percent on equity capital. This prompted Caves to ask: "Can anyone believe that firms which *actually* earned this return over a period of time

---

[79] 32 CAB 291.

[80] *Re American Telephone & Telegraph Co.*, 70 PUR 3d 129, 158.

[81] *Southern Bell Telephone & Telegraph Co.* v. *Louisiana Public Service Commission*, 118 So. 2d 372, 381 (1960).

[82] This point was made by H. B. Dorau in "Is Cost of Capital the Fair Rate of Return?", 56 *Public Utilities Fortnightly* 1006, 1007 (1955); and by L. A. O'Connor in "Some Critical Thoughts on Cost of Capital," 62 *Public Utilities Fortnightly* 93, 95 (1958).

[83] 31 CAB 685 (1960).

would find it only sufficient to attract capital?"[84] It is clear that if local service carriers earned any such amount on their equity capital over a period of time, the price of the stock would rise to a level such that the earnings-price ratio would fall to a much more moderate amount.

A second weakness in reliance on earnings-price ratios is that investor appraisal of the worth of stock is based on anticipated earnings whereas earnings-price ratios are based on actual earnings of the past. This point was made by Mr. Minetti, a member of the Civil Aeronautics Board, in a dissenting opinion in the General Passenger Investigation in 1960. Mr. Minetti pointed out that the earnings-price ratios of the "Big Four" airlines were overstated because the earnings for the years included in the computation, 1950 to 1956, were the largest in the history of the airline industry because of the Korean War and investors simply did not believe that such earnings would continue. The real cost of equity capital was not properly measured by the earnings-price ratios of those years.[85]

A third weakness in cost-of-capital studies that rely on earnings-price ratios or on dividend-price ratios is that they are affected by the vagaries of the stock market with its ups and downs, many of which have no rational basis. Earnings-price ratios may even indicate costs of equity capital less than interest on high-grade bonds.

Introduction of a "Growth" Element in Cost of Capital Studies

The phenomenon of absurdly low figures for the cost of equity capital which sometimes results from the use of earnings-price ratios may have been a factor in explaining a more recent development in cost-of-capital studies. This is the introduction of a growth factor in addition to actual earnings of the past in arriving at the earnings-price ratio. The theory here is that the market price of common stock is determined not only by past earnings but by anticipation of additional income resulting from growth—the growth being partly due to reinvested earnings and partly to other factors. Introduction of the growth element into the calculations produces a higher cost of equity capital than is obtained from earnings-price ratios that do not include the growth element in the calculations. The implications and potential results of this modified formula for determining the cost of equity capital should be more thoroughly examined before unqualified acceptance.

Rate of Return and Compensation for the Depreciated Dollar

A question of considerable importance in times of rising prices is whether the rate of return to be allowed stockholders is to be increased

---

[84] Richard E. Caves, *Air Transport and Its Regulators* (Cambridge: Harvard University Press, 1962), p. 402.

[85] 32 CAB 291, 333–34.

because of the depreciation in the value of money. The problem can be considered from either an economic or an ethical standpoint. From an economic point of view it is necessary to give consideration to the depreciated dollar in determining the rate of return only to the extent that inflation affects the cost of obtaining equity capital. If a given rate of dividends is found unsatisfactory by stockholders because of the decline in the purchasing power of the dollar, the price of common stocks in the market will fall, putting them on a higher yield basis than formerly. To bring these stocks to par in the market, a higher dividend rate would be required. The preference of investors for stocks paying stable dividends, however, is such that usually they are willing to invest in public utility stocks on a low-yield basis, and hence the rate of return necessary to attract capital into utility stocks does not seem to be greatly affected by a rising price level.

On ethical grounds a case can be made for increasing the rate of return in a period of inflation sufficiently to give stockholders the same purchasing power that their dividends represented before inflation occurred. The difficulty with this policy is that it treats preferentially the holders of utility stocks, protecting them from the effects of inflation. It disregards the fact that bondholders, and in fact all recipients of fixed incomes in society, also have an ethical claim for protection from the effects of inflation; yet their predicament is made worse by extending protection to holders of utility stocks, since to do so will mean higher utility rates. These considerations have led the Wisconsin Commission to refuse to increase the rate of return to be allowed a public utility beyond an amount that can be justified by the increased cost of obtaining equity capital.[86]

Is a Rate Base Necessary?

We have seen that the modern practice in utility rate cases is to determine the cost of borrowed capital and the cost of equity capital and convert these into an overall rate of return which is then applied to the rate base to determine the sum needed to pay interest and provide an adequate return to equity capital. The question arises whether a rate base and an overall rate of return need to be determined. Why not determine the dollar requirements for interest and the amount needed to cover the cost of equity capital and not bother with finding an overall rate of

---

[86] See *Re Wisconsin Electric Power Co.*, 93 PUR NS 97, 109–10 (1952). For a good discussion of the pros and cons of adjusting the rate of return to compensate holders of equity securities for changes in the value of the dollar see Walter A. Morton, "Rate of Return and the Value of Money in Public Utilities," 28 *Land Economics* 91 (1952); and James C. Bonbright, "Public Utility Rate Control in a Period of Price Inflation," 27 *Land Economics* 16 (1951). See also E. W. Clemens, "Some Aspects of the Rate of Return Problem," 30 *Land Economics* 32 (1954).

return and rate base?[87] The answer is that under some circumstances this might well be done; under other circumstances it would be objectionable.

The use of a rate base is certainly necessary if a utility is also engaged in some nonregulated business activity. Separation of utility and non-utility operations is required unless the patrons of the regulated enterprise are to be called upon to support the unregulated enterprises if the latter are unprofitable, or, conversely, are to be subsidized by the profitable enterprises.

Likewise, many utilities, particularly railroads, have large investments in the securities of other corporations. These investments should neither increase nor reduce the amounts which the patrons of the company should pay for utility or transportation services. Revenue requirements to support the capitalization represented by assets of this sort should not be an element in determining utility or transportation rates.

The use of a rate base, furthermore, enables the regulatory body to exclude from the base property of any kind which is not used or useful in performing the utility or transportation services. Regulatory bodies frequently find it necessary to exclude from the rate base items of this sort. When rates are based on the interest and dividend requirements of a concern there is no opportunity to disallow items on which the rate-paying public should not be called upon to pay a return.

The cost-of-capital approach, without the use of a rate base, is open to the same objection as the "credit standard" for determining the adequacy of the rate level which was mentioned in the preceding chapter.[88] Both stress interest and dividend requirements without questioning the propriety of the capitalization of the company.

THE ICC AND A FAIR RATE OF RETURN

The Transportation Act of 1920 prescribed $5\frac{1}{2}\%$ as the fair rate of return under the Rule of Rate Making for the first two years. However, it gave the Commission the right to add $\frac{1}{2}$ of 1% to this amount. The Commission did so in *Increased Rates, 1920*,[89] the first case to arise under the Rule of Rate Making. In *Reduced Rates, 1922*,[90] the Commission specified 5.75% as a fair rate of return.

Since then, the Commission has not specified what it would consider the appropriate rate of return. In fact, there has been little occasion for it to do so notwithstanding the large number of rate-level cases that have arisen. Increases in rates sought by the railroads have generally been less than would be necessary to earn a return under any reasonable concept

---

[87] For advocacy of this view see Harold M. Somers, " 'The End Result' Approach to Public Utility Regulation," 16 *Buffalo Law Review* 689 (1971).

[88] Pp. 355–56 supra.

[89] 58 ICC 220.

[90] 68 ICC 676.

of a fair rate of return. This situation is attributable largely to increased intermodal competition which effectively holds down rates if additional traffic is not to be diverted to other modes of transport.

In *Increased Freight Rates, 1967*, the Commission, in referring to the low level of railroad earnings, said: "The inadequacy of the present rate of return of less than 4 percent is clear."[91] Later in the same year the Commission again referred to a rate of return of 4 percent as "substandard."[92]

Determination of fair rates of return for other transport industries is discussed in later chapters which deal with the regulatory problems of those modes of transport.

SELECTED REFERENCES

The literature on valuation is so extensive that much excellent material must be omitted from this list. Among books entirely devoted to the subject we mention John H. Gray and J. Levin, *The Valuation and Regulation of Public Utilities* (New York: Harper, 1933); John Bauer and Nathaniel Gold, *Public Utility Valuation for Purposes of Rate Control* (New York: Macmillan, 1934). Extended treatises with special emphasis on the position of courts and commissions are R. H. Whitten, *Valuation of Public Service Corporations* (2d ed.; New York: Banks Law Publishing Co., 1928); and J. C. Bonbright, *The Valuation of Property* (New York: McGraw-Hill, 1937). Both of the latter are in two volumes.

Nearly all general works on public utilities devote one or more chapters to the subject of valuation.

For rather critical discussions of the position of the courts in the past on valuation matters see R. L. Hale, "The Supreme Court's Ambiguous Use of 'Value' in Rate Cases," 18 *Columbia Law Review* 208 (1918); "The 'Physical Value' Fallacy in Rate Cases," 30 *Yale Law Journal* 710, 720 (1931); "Rate Making and the Revision of the Property Concept," 22 *Columbia Law Review* 209 (1922); D. R. Richberg, "The Supreme Court Discusses Value," 37 *Harvard Law Review* 289 (1924); "Value—by Judicial Fiat," 40 *Harvard Law Review* 567 (1927); J. B. Eastman, dissenting opinion in *Excess Income of Richmond, Fredericksburg & Potomac R. R. Co.*, 170 ICC 451, 521–38 (1931).

Cost of reproduction is criticized, and actual cost or some modification thereof is supported in D. R. Richberg, "A Permanent Basis for Rate Regulation," 31 *Yale Law Journal* 263 (1922); J. B. Eastman, dissenting opinion in *San Pedro, Los Angeles & Salt Lake R. R. Co.*, 75 ICC 463, 523–67 (1923), and concurring opinion in *Excess Income of St. Louis & O'Fallon Ry. Co.*, 124 ICC 3, 49–59 (1927); Justice Brandeis in separate opinion in *Southwestern Bell Telephone Co.* v. *Missouri*, 262 U.S. 276, 289–312 (1923); John Bauer, "Rate Base for Effective and Non-Speculative Railroad and Utility Regulation," 34 *Journal of Political Economy* 479 (1926); Interstate Commerce Commission, *Excess Income of St. Louis & O'Fallon Ry. Co.*, 124 ICC 3, 26–41 (1927);

---

[91] 332 ICC 280, 289.
[92] 332 ICC 590, 603.

J. C. Bonbright, "Economic Merits of Original Cost and Reproduction Cost," 41 *Harvard Law Review* 593 (1928); and "Railroad Valuation with Special Reference to the O'Fallon Decision," 18 *American Economic Review* (Supplement) 181 (1928); Joseph R. Rose, "Confusion in Valuation for Public Utility Rate-Making," 47 *Minnesota Law Review* 1 (1962).

For the most comprehensive treatment of depreciation, see National Association of Regulatory Commissioners, *Public Utility Depreciation Practices* (Washington, D.C.: NARUC, 1968).

Cost of reproduction is defended in T. F. Woodlock, dissenting opinion in *Excess Income of St. Louis & O'Fallon Ry. Co.*, 124 ICC 3, 64–66 (1927); H. G. Brown, "Railroad Valuation and Rate Regulation," 33 *Journal of Political Economy* 505 (1925); and "Economic Bases and Limits of Public Utility Regulation," 53 *American Bar Association Proceedings* 717 (1928); F. G. Dorety, "Function of Reproduction Cost in Public Utility Valuation and Rate Making," 27 *Harvard Law Review* 173 (1923); Earl A. Spiller, Jr., "Common Dollar Accounting and the Rate Base," 66 *Public Utilities Fortnightly* 433 (1960).

On going value see M. C. Waltersdorf, "Going Value in Utility Valuation," 17 *American Economic Review* 26 (1927); Ben W. Lewis, "Going-Value—Comments on Its Nature and Legal Status," 17 *American Economic Review* 657 (1927); "Going-Value and Rate Valuation," 26 *Michigan Law Review* 713 (1928); and "Why 'Going-Value' Should Be Discarded in Rate Making," 8 *Public Utilities Fortnightly* 588 (1931); I. R. Barnes, "Shall Going Value Be Included in the Rate Base?" 16 *Journal of Land and Public Utility Economics* 286, 430 (1940).

Interpretation of the decisions of the Supreme Court in the Natural Gas Pipeline and Hope cases may be found in R. W. Harbeson, "Public Utility Regulation: A New Chapter," 20 *Harvard Business Review* 496 (1942); also "The Demise of Fair Value," 42 *Michigan Law Review* 1049 (1944); Martin G. Glaeser, "The United States Supreme Court Redeems Itself," 18 *Journal of Land and Public Utility Economics* 146 (1942); R. L. Hale, "Utility Regulation in the Light of the Hope Natural Gas Case," 44 *Columbia Law Review* 488 (1944); L. Jourolmon, Jr., "The Life and Death of *Smyth* v. *Ames*," 18 *Tennessee Law Review* 663 (1945); Wm. H. Anderson, "The Supreme Court and Public Utility Valuation," 21 *Journal of Land and Public Utility Economics* 12 (1945); Francis X. Welch, "Impact of the Hope Natural Gas Decision on Commission Regulation," 33 *Public Utilities Fortnightly* 139 (1949); John Bauer, *Transforming Public Utility Regulation* (New York: Harper, 1950), chap. vii; Joseph R. Rose, "The *Hope* Case and Public Utility Valuation in the States," 54 *Columbia Law Review* 188 (1954).

The most comprehensive study of the fair rate of return is Nelson L. Smith, *The Fair Rate of Return in Public Utility Regulation* (Boston: Houghton Mifflin, 1932). The subject is dealt with of course in the standard books on public utility regulation.

The literature on the cost-of-capital approach to a determination of a fair return is quite extensive. Useful references are J. Rhoads Foster, "Capital Cost and Fair Return," 53 *Public Utilities Fortnightly* 421 (1954); E. W. Clemens, "Some Aspects of the Rate of Return Problem," 30 *Land Economics* 32 (1954); Fred P. Morrissey, "A Reconsideration of Cost of Capital and a Reasonable Rate of Return," 31 *Land Economics* 229 (1955); Herbert B. Dorau, "Is Cost of Capital the Fair Rate of Return?," 56 *Public Utilities Fortnightly* 1006 (1955); Joseph R. Rose, " 'Cost of Capital' in Public Utility Rate Regulation," 43 *Virginia Law Review* 1079 (1957); Ralph E. Badger, "Important Concepts as to Fair Return and Cost of Money," 66 *Public Utilities Fortnightly* 93 (1960); Lionel W. Thatcher, "Relationship of Capital Structure to Cost of Capital," 67 *Public Utilities Fortnightly* 662 (1961); Harold Leventhal, "Vitality of the Comparable Earnings Standard for the Regulation of Utilities in a Growth Economy," 74 *Yale Law Journal* 989 (1965); Harold M. Somers, " 'The End Result' Approach to Public Utility Regulation," 16 *Buffalo Law Journal* 689 (1967).

On both fair value and rate of return see G. Stanley Joslin and Arthur S. Miller, "Public Utility Rate Regulation: A Re-Examination," 43 *Virginia Law Review* 1027 (1957); Francis J. Demet and Margadette M. Demet, "Legal Aspects of Rate Base and Rate of Return in Public Utility Regulation," 42 *Marquette Law Review* 331 (1959); Charles F. Phillips, Jr., *The Economics of Regulation* (Homewood, Ill.: Richard D. Irwin, Inc., 1965), chaps. viii & ix.

Chapter 17   THE WEAK-AND-STRONG-ROAD PROBLEM

      In the discussion of the general level of rates, the necessity of treating the railroads as a whole, or in rate groups, was pointed out. It is impossible to have different levels of rates for each railroad if the carriers are in any sense competitive. As a practical measure, rate levels must be prescribed with reference to the railroads as a whole or in groups. This was definitely recognized in the original Rule of Rate Making, enacted in 1920. The Commission, it will be recalled, was directed to prescribe rates that would be adequate to yield the railroads as a whole or in rate groups a fair return on the aggregate value of their properties. Although the present Rule of Rate Making makes no specific reference to railroads as a whole or in groups, the practical necessity of so treating them remains. This situation gives rise to the weak-and-strong-road problem. Under any uniform level of rates some railroads will have more-than-adequate earnings, while others will have less-than-adequate earnings. This chapter describes various methods of dealing with this problem which have been tried or which have been suggested.

      It should be noted in passing that a similar problem arises in the regulation of other modes of transport. The extent to which the problem has been recognized and dealt with in the regulation of motor carriers and air carriers will be described in later chapters.

HIGHER RATE LEVEL

      Although we have said that railroads must be treated as a whole or in groups and that more or less uniform levels of rates are required for competing railroads, it is possible to a limited extent to make a somewhat higher level of rates on lines, or in areas, where operating costs are higher than prevail generally. Where this can be done, it is economically sound. From an economic point of view it is desirable that every transportation system pay its own way. Shippers located in regions where transportation costs are high should pay for the transportation which they demand. Uneconomical and wasteful transportation is encouraged if shippers situated in unfavorable locations are relieved of paying the full cost of the transportation service supplied to them. Conversely, profitable and desirable geographical division of labor may be prevented by exacting higher rates on favored lines than the cost of performing the service.[1] Efforts to encourage diffusion of industry and to facilitate the economic development of disadvantaged areas, however, may lead to equalization of rate levels, regardless of differences in transport costs, as a matter of national economic policy. Such a policy should not be condemned out of hand, as it might be if the decision is based on transport costs alone.

The Interstate Commerce Commission has often prescribed somewhat higher rates in certain areas or on particular lines where more difficult operating conditions prevail or where traffic is light.[2] It is on this basis also that the Commission has permitted arbitraries or differentials on short and weak lines.[3] These efforts have not proved wholly successful. In some cases the addition of arbitraries for such areas and lines has apparently driven traffic away from the weak lines and has discouraged the utilization of resources on such lines or has retarded the economic development of those areas.[4] It must be admitted, therefore, that the problem of weak and strong roads cannot be dealt with in this manner, except to a very limited extent. Where the different railroads are competing for traffic between the same points, it is obviously impossible to make rates with respect to the financial needs of each line. The weak-and-strong-road problem, therefore, must be dealt with in other ways.

DISCRIMINATING RATES

A related method of dealing with this problem is to permit high-cost lines to charge high rates where they can obtain them, and then permit them to charge lower rates where necessary to meet the competition of lines maintaining a lower scale of rates. This is very frequently done, but not always as a means of consciously aiding the weaker lines at the expense of the stronger. Illustrations may be found in the granting of relief from the Long-and-Short-Haul Clause to weak lines in order that they may compete at through points with stronger lines without a corresponding reduction in local rates.[5] A similar result follows from the common practice of permitting circuitous lines to meet the rates of more direct

---

[1] This point of view is well set forth in H. G. Brown, "Railroad Valuation and Rate Regulation," 33 *Journal of Political Economy* 505, 522–29 (1925). It is also the view asserted by L. H. Haney, "Advantages and Disadvantages of Railway Consolidation," 14 *American Economic Review* (Supplement) 88, 90 (1924).

[2] Pp. 192–95, supra.

[3] See p. 194, supra.

[4] For examples of instances in which arbitraries or differentials have apparently driven traffic away from weak lines see *Sand, Gravel, Slag & Chert*, 165 ICC 731, 771–72 (1930); and *Rates on Chert, Clay, Sand & Gravel within the State of Georgia*, 197 ICC 215, 220–25, 243–44 (1933).

[5] See Chapter 21.

lines at competitive points without reducing rates at intermediate points on the circuitous lines.[6] This practice permits circuitous lines to participate in competitive traffic that would ordinarily move over more direct routes. It aids the circuitous lines at the expense of the direct route. The practice of granting railroads Fourth-Section relief to meet market competition likewise has this equalizing effect. An undesirable consequence of these practices is that they lead to wasteful transportation and economic loss to society.

DIVISION OF JOINT RATES

Another method of aiding weak lines is through the division of joint rates. This method of dealing with the problem was incorporated into the Transportation Act of 1920.

Paragraph 6 of Section 15 of the Interstate Commerce Act empowers the Commission, in dividing joint rates between participating carriers, to take into consideration the revenue needs of the lines concerned. This power was exercised by the Commission in 1922, when it held that the carriers in New England were entitled to an increase of 15 percent in the divisions which they received on traffic moving into and out of New England from or to the West and South.[7] The increase was granted largely on the basis of the need of the New England carriers for additional revenues.

The close relation between this provision of the law and the system of basing rates on aggregate property values is clearly revealed by the circumstances of the above case. In *Increased Rates, 1920*,[8] the Commission increased freight rates in Eastern Territory by 40 percent. At that time it was estimated that an increase of about 47 percent would have been necessary to give the New England carriers a fair return, while an increase of about 28 percent would have been sufficient for the carriers in Trunk-Line Territory, and an increase of 24 percent for the carriers in Central Freight Association Territory. There was danger, however, that higher rates in New England would have an unfavorable effect upon the volume of traffic in that area. The Commission accordingly grouped together the carriers in the three territories and granted a 40 percent increase in rates. The proceeding in the New England Divisions Case might therefore be deemed as supplementary to the Commission's action in *Increased Rates, 1920*, for it divided revenues from the traffic into and out of New England in such a way that the carriers which needed a larger share of the proceeds would get it.

This action of the Commission was contested in the courts, but the

---

[6] See Chapter 21.

[7] *New England Divisions*, 66 ICC 196 (1922).

[8] 58 ICC 220.

United States Supreme Court upheld the Commission's action. The Court took particular pains to point out that the division of rates according to revenue needs was not "a partition of property." "It is not true, as argued, that the order compels the strong railroads to support the weak. No part of the revenues needed by the New England lines is paid by the western carriers. All is paid by the community pursuant to the single rate increase ordered in *Ex Parte 74*."[9] Throughout the decision the Supreme Court recognized the relation between the practice of making rates on the basis of aggregate property values of groups of carriers and the division of these rates according to revenue needs. Mention was made of the fact that the people would not tolerate greatly increased rates, although no higher than necessary to support the weak lines, if prosperous lines were thereby allowed to earn unreasonably large returns. "The provision concerning divisions was, therefore, an integral part of the machinery for distributing the funds expected to be raised by the new rate-fixing sections. It was, indeed, indispensable."[10]

Since 1920 this provision of the law has been used many times in aid of weak railroads, particularly of the short-line roads. In one instance the Commission went so far as to require the establishment of a joint rate over a certain route to replace a combination of local rates, and it then divided the joint rate in such manner as to aid a financially weak line. The Commission's order in this case was upheld by the Supreme Court.[11]

Although the power to divide joint rates somewhat according to revenue needs is a useful method of distributing earnings which are fair to the carriers in the aggregate, it is subject to certain limitations which restrict its ability to cope with the problem alone.

In the first place, the power is limited, and quite properly so, by the necessity of leaving nonconfiscatory divisions to connecting carriers.[12] Second, the efficacy of divisions as a means of aiding weak railroads depends upon the existence of a substantial amount of traffic interchange. The device can be used only between connecting carriers, and then only when there is sufficient traffic interchange on which an order relating to divisions can operate. It cannot be used to equalize between more or less parallel lines or between connecting lines with little traffic to interchange. A third limitation upon the effectiveness of divisions as a solution of the weak-and-strong-road problem arises from the hesitancy on the part of

---

[9] *New England Divisions Case*, 261 U.S. 184, 196 (1923).

[10] Ibid., p. 191.

[11] *United States* v. *Great Northern Railroad Co.*, 343 U.S. 562 (1952). Where no through route existed, the Commission could not establish one, prescribe a joint rate, and divide it to aid a weak line, since Section 15 (4) of the Act denies the Commission the power to establish through routes and joint rates applicable thereto "for the purpose of assisting any carrier that would participate therein to meet its financial needs." See *Thompson* v. *U.S.*, 343 U.S. 549 (1952).

[12] *United States* v. *Abilene & Southern Ry. Co.*, 265 U.S. 274, 285 (1924); *Baltimore & Ohio R. R. Co.* v. *United States*, 298 U.S. 349, 357 (1936).

short and weak lines about taking any action which would offend their strong connections, on whom they are often dependent for favors of one sort or another. A fourth limitation arises from the possibility that a carrier deprived of its accustomed share of a through rate may defeat the Commission's order by inducing shippers to route their traffic over routes which do not necessitate the use of the line which has attempted to obtain an increase in its divisions. This is possible, of course, only when there are alternative routes available which do not require use of the weak line. Still another circumstance which restricts the usefulness of this device is the possibility of closing through routes. If a weak line is granted a larger share of the through rate than its connections are willing to concede, the through route over which the joint rate is applicable can sometimes be closed—at least, if other routes are available. Although the Interstate Commerce Commission can exercise some control over the closing of through routes, it cannot entirely prevent the use of this device by strong railroads to avoid giving larger divisions to weaker roads.

THE RECAPTURE CLAUSE

Another method of dealing with the weak-road problem is through recovery by the government of excess earnings of strong lines for the benefit of the weak. This method of dealing with the problem was incorporated into the Transportation Act of 1920. The Recapture Clause, it will be recalled, required carriers earning more than 6 percent on the value of their properties to pay one half of the excess into a fund, maintained by the Interstate Commerce Commission, from which loans might be made to needy railroads.[13]

The Recapture Clause was attacked by the railroads as unconstitutional, but it was upheld by the United States Supreme Court in *Dayton–Goose Creek Ry. Co.* v. *United States.*[14] Here again the Court called attention to the group-value system of determining rates and the necessity of supporting all the railroads in the group. "By the recapture clauses Congress is enabled to maintain uniform rates for all shippers and yet keep the net return of railways, whether strong or weak, to the varying percentages which are fair respectively for them. The recapture clauses are thus the key provisions of the whole plan."[15] Elsewhere in the same case the Court said: "The combination of uniform rates with the recapture clauses is necessary to the better development of the country's interstate transportation system as Congress has planned it. The control of the excess profit due to the level of the whole body of rates is the heart of the plan."[16]

---

[13] For a more detailed description of the recapture provisions see pp. 245–46, supra.

[14] 263 U.S. 456 (1924).

[15] Ibid., p. 480.

[16] Ibid., p. 485.

The Court was not impressed by the contention that railroads were entitled to all they could earn under a level of rates prescribed by the Commission:

The carrier owning and operating a railroad, however strong financially, however economical in its facilities, or favorably situated as to traffic, is not entitled as of constitutional right to more than a fair net operating income upon the value of its properties which are being devoted to transportation. By investment in a business dedicated to the public service the owner must recognize that, as compared with investment in private business, he cannot expect either high or speculative dividends but that his obligation limits him to only a fair or reasonable profit.[17]

The argument was also made in the Dayton–Goose Creek Case that if a railroad was entitled only to a fair return, then the shippers using the road ought not to be compelled to pay higher rates than are necessary to give the road such a return. The Court did not accept this view. The rates may be reasonable from the standpoint of the shipper though their net product provides more than a fair return for a particular carrier. "Rates which as a body enable all the railroads necessary to do the business of a rate territory or section, to enjoy not more than a fair net operating income on the aggregate value of their properties therein economically and efficiently operated, are reasonable from the standpoint of the individual shipper in that section."[18] This is because every shipper is interested in an adequate *system* of transportation that will serve the whole area or country. "He may, therefore, properly be required in the rate he pays to share with all other shippers of the same section the burden of maintaining an adequate railway capacity to do their business."[19]

The recapture provisions were frequently criticized on the ground of alleged injustice to the stronger lines, which would be deprived of the advantage of their superior location.[20] This argument failed to recognize the well-established rule that it is legitimate and proper to limit a carrier's return to a fair return. The argument also failed to recognize that the aggregate-return-on-aggregate-value method of rate making, prescribed by the Act of 1920, raised the level of rates on the stronger properties above what they could demand under the *Smyth* v. *Ames* rule. In effect the group-value system enabled the stronger lines to earn a return on the values of the weaker roads which were not able to earn a fair return on their own property.

There was another objection to the recapture provisions which we cannot consider as justified. It was often pointed out that many lines

---

[17] Ibid., p. 481.

[18] Ibid., p. 480.

[19] Ibid.

[20] E.g., see statement of John E. Benton in *Hearings before House Committee on Interstate & Foreign Commerce, 72d Cong., 1st Sess. on H.R. 7116 and 7117—Railroad Legislation* (1931), pp. 140–41.

which were strong financially because their capitalization was low relative to their rate-making value were not subject to the Recapture Clause. A conservative capitalization made these railroads strong, although their earnings were moderate when related to their value. On the other hand, there were many railroads which were financially weak because of excessive capitalization. The earnings of these lines, when related to the value of their properties, might be generous, but their credit nevertheless was poor. Because of this situation it was argued that the Recapture Clause did not always take from the strong but often took from the weak instead.[21] The argument is not sound. Roads which earn less than a fair return on their value, but which may be strong financially because of low capitalization, cannot be equitably deprived of any portion of their earnings; roads which earn more than a fair return on their value, but which may be financially weak because of overcapitalization, have no equitable claim for retention of excess earnings.

Notwithstanding the logic of some sort of recapture provisions to distribute earnings accruing from uniform rates, the recapture provisions of the Transportation Act failed miserably to accomplish the purpose for which they were devised and they were retroactively repealed by the Emergency Railroad Transportation Act of 1933.[22] There were numerous weaknesses in the Recapture Clause that account for its failure.

1. An inherent weakness in the law was that it was inadequate to deal with the problem presented. This was for two reasons. First, it took only half the excess earnings of the stronger lines and thus could never have completely alleviated the inequality in earnings that it sought to remedy, although to have recaptured all excess earnings would have discouraged efficiency and economical management. In the second place, the loaning of the recaptured sums to weaker lines was a dubious form of relief. Under some conditions the borrowing of funds for capital expenditures might have improved the earning position of weak lines; but when the weak position of the road was due to sparsity of traffic or to difficult operating conditions, there could be little prospect of improving earnings through capital expenditures.

2. Another weakness in the law arose from the fact that no averaging of earnings from year to year was possible. Excess earnings of one year could not be offset by inadequate earnings of other years. The law recaptured excess earnings for each and every year in which they appeared. This was particularly burdensome to many small railroads whose earnings fluctuated from year to year. Instances are on record of railroads which were in default in the payment of interest but which had a liability to the government under the Recapture Clause for excess earnings ob-

---

[21] This argument was suggested by Commissioner Eastman in *Hearings on H.R. 7116 and 7117* (1932), p. 10, and by H. G. Moulton in *The American Transportation Problem* (Washington, D.C.: Brookings Institution, 1933), pp. 379–80.

[22] P. 264, supra.

tained in particular years.[23] Various attempts were made to amend the law to exempt the short-line railroads from the provisions of the clause. With the coming of the depression of the 30s, this objection to the Recapture Clause became of importance to the larger and stronger lines— even to those which in normal times would have been considered as permanently in the recapture class. The depression brought home the fact that recapture based on the earnings of each year, considered independently of the earnings of other years, was unfair. This might have been remedied by permitting an averaging of earnings over a period of years, but this would have greatly increased the administrative difficulties of the law. The values and earnings for every year would have to be checked instead of only for years in which a carrier had a probable recapture liability.

3. But the most serious practical objection to the Recapture Clause was due to the fact that recapturable earnings were determined by relating earnings to value. Half the earnings in excess of 6 percent on the "value" of the railroad's property were to be recovered. This at once injected the whole valuation controversy into the administration of the clause. "Fair value" was an indefinite term. Its determination required the exercise of judgment in weighing "elements of value" varying widely in amount, and for that reason it created an administrative difficulty in applying the law. There is every reason to believe, furthermore, that the railroads would have contested nearly every valuation on scores of grounds. The insistence of the courts at that time that current cost of reproduction must be considered in valuation proceedings meant that cost of reproduction would have to be known for every year in which a carrier might be subject to the clause. This would have made the administration of the clause difficult and expensive. After the decision of the United States Supreme Court in the O'Fallon Case, which held that current cost of reproduction must be considered in making valuations under the Recapture Clause, a bill was introduced in Congress prescribing a definite rate base in lieu of value for the purpose of administering the section. This would greatly have simplified the problem of administering the clause but might have involved constitutional difficulties.

The Recapture Clause did not prove workable in the form in which it was originally enacted, and it was swept away by the Emergency Transportation Act of 1933 without adequate consideration of changes which might have made it workable. The financial difficulties of the railroads during the depression had much to do with its repeal. Some railroads which were having financial difficulties had recapture liabilities from earlier years hanging over them. Repeal of the Recapture Clause was a form of financial relief to these carriers. Although the Recapture Clause was repealed, the problem that it was designed to solve remains.

---

[23] See *Hearings on H.R. 7116 and 7117*, pp. 274–319.

CONSOLIDATION

Another method of dealing with the weak-road problem—one also provided by the Transportation Act of 1920—was railroad consolidation. Here, in the estimation of Congress, lay the ultimate solution of the problem. The Recapture Clause and the provisions regarding the division of joint rates were temporary measures and would become unnecessary when the consolidation of railroads into a limited number of well-balanced systems of equal earning power was accomplished. The elaborate provisions of the law relating to consolidation were framed with the definite object of solving this problem.[24] The purpose is clearly revealed in the instructions to the Commission regarding the making of a plan of consolidation. The Commission was directed to establish systems such that, under a uniform level of rates, each system would be able to earn approximately the same rate of return upon the value of its property.

Railroad consolidation was supposed to eliminate the weak-and-strong-road problem in two ways. First, a combination of weak roads with the strong would eliminate, or at least obscure, the inherent weakness of certain lines. Thus the weak lines would be aided by the superior credit of the stronger and would in part be supported by the earnings of the stronger. Second, it would be possible in some cases to build up strong systems by the combination of smaller lines. This is because many weak lines serve small areas or lack access to important points of traffic interchange or to points at which traffic originates. Too often this factor is overlooked, and consolidation is considered as contributing to the solution of the weak-and-strong-road problem only through saddling weak and unprosperous lines upon the stronger.

Consolidation as a solution of the problem of weak railroads has been severely criticized. Some of the more important objections require consideration. One objection was voiced by Professor Daggett.[25] He points out that consolidation remedies no injustice, since there is no equalization between the shareholders of the weak and strong roads. He admits that railroads may be combined in such a way that each system earns about the same rate of return, but consolidation "does not equalize . . . between the human owners of companies."[26] This is because the normal basis for voluntary merger is earning power. If shares in a newly organized corporation are exchanged for the shares of the consolidating corporations, they will normally be exchanged in proportion to the

---

[24] For evidence of this purpose see Rogers MacVeagh, *The Transportation Act, 1920* (New York: Holt, 1923), pp. 275–83; and Albert B. Cummins, "The Senate Committee Railroad Bill," 8 *Proceedings of the Academy of Political Science* 518, 520–21 (1919).

[25] See Stuart Daggett, *Principles of Inland Transportation* (New York: Harper, 1928), pp. 462–63; and "Railroad Consolidation West of the Mississippi River," 11 *University of California Publications in Economics* 127 (1933), pp. 251–52.

[26] *Principles of Inland Transportation*, p. 462.

earnings contributed by each company to the joint undertaking. The shareholders of the weaker company are therefore in no better position than they were before the consolidation. If earnings are distributed after consolidation in the same manner as before, no injustice has been remedied.

The point to which Professor Dagget has called attention is important. Consolidation would not give the stockholders in weak lines the return which they would get if the weak lines could be made to earn a fair return on their cost. It may be seriously questioned, however, whether Congress was concerned with this particular matter. Congress was interested in preserving the existence of weak lines which were considered worth saving. Consolidation might help in this respect. Congress was also interested in creating systems of equal earning power in order to facilitate rate making. Consolidation would accomplish the latter purpose even if it did not equalize between the human owners of the companies.

A second criticism of consolidation as a solution of the weak-road problem is that it is merely a device to preserve lines which cannot pay their own way or which can do so only by charging higher rates than are maintained by more favorably situated lines. Consolidation and rate equalization in such cases, it is argued, subsidize one group of shippers by a tax on others. H. G. Brown has voiced this objection thus: "Any scheme of consolidation of the 'strong' and the 'weak' roads advanced on the assumption that higher earnings of the 'strong' part of the consolidation are going to offset lower earnings of the 'weak' part so as to permit low rates on the latter, is a scheme for an indirect bounty from the more favored regions to encourage the business development of the less favored. . . ."[27]

Consolidation should not be used to preserve railroads which are not economically justified. We have already pointed out, furthermore, that it is desirable to have higher rates on less favorably located lines wherever it is possible to do so, thereby avoiding the charge that the shippers in favorably located regions are subsidizing industry in less favored areas. We have found, however, that this is impossible in many instances. We must also recall that it is justifiable to look at the transportation system as a whole and to recognize that the public has an interest in maintaining an adequate national transportation system, including lines that reach areas that do not furnish a large volume of traffic. As the Supreme Court pointed out in the Dayton–Goose Creek Case, rates high enough to support an adequate system of transportation may reasonably be imposed on shippers. The shipper located on a favorably situated line is interested in having a transportation system that is adequate, and he may therefore be required to pay rates high enough to support the weaker lines as well as the stronger.[28]

---

[27] Brown, op. cit., pp. 505, 522–29.

[28] See pp. 408–9, supra.

The foregoing criticism of consolidation as a solution of the problem under consideration was based on the assumption that the burden of supporting the weak part of a consolidated system would be shifted to the shippers located on the stronger portions. A third criticism of consolidation assumes that the burden of supporting the weak lines is thrown upon the stockholders of the stronger. It is argued that it would be unfair to those who have invested their funds in prosperous lines to be compelled to support the weaker lines through a diversion of funds to the former stockholders of the weak lines. The assumption that the earnings of investors in strong lines would be diluted is implied in the common argument that consolidation would drag down the stronger lines and weaken their credit, or that it is unfair to saddle the weak lines upon the stronger. This would happen, of course, if the acquired road was unable to meet its operating expenses and interest charges and had to be kept in operation by an infusion of funds from the stronger. However, if the weak road regularly earns any net income, its consolidation with a strong road need not burden the stockholders of the latter.

If consolidation proceeded along the lines suggested by Professor Daggett, that is, if the shareholders of the weaker road got no larger share of the joint earnings after consolidation than before, then the absorption of the weak railroads by the strong would not burden the stronger lines or their stockholders. If the weak line was taken in on the basis of its commercial value, that is, the capitalized value of its expected earnings if operated independently, clearly there would be no financial burden placed upon the strong.

Even if the strong railroad pays more for the weak line than its commercial value, this does not necessarily result in diverting funds from the stockholders of the stronger line to stockholders of the weaker. The inclusion of the weak line in the rate base results in higher rates than the strong line would be entitled to demand by itself. Therefore the use of the increased receipts to support the weaker line is no more of an appropriation of funds equitably belonging to the stockholders of the strong than was the recapture of excess earnings under the Recapture Clause or the division of joint rates according to revenue needs, as was done in the New England Divisions Case. The principle is the same in all three instances. Earnings accruing to a strong line solely because the value of the weak line is included in the rate base are distributed to the lines which cannot charge higher rates. The strong are deprived of nothing to which they can justly lay claim.

Although the consolidation of weak railroads with strong would not throw a burden on the stockholders of the strong if consolidation took place on reasonable terms, it is possible that too high a price might be paid for weak lines. If this should occur, it would result in diverting funds from the stockholders of the strong line to those who were stockholders of the weak.

Our conclusion is that consolidation of the weak with the strong roads does not necessarily weaken the strong or work an injustice to the stockholders of the strong. No consolidation of the weak with the strong should be permitted to take place on such terms that the weak line does constitute a drain upon the resources of the stronger.

A fourth objection to consolidation as a remedy for the weak-road problem is that it merely obscures weakness and does not get at the causes of weakness.[29] Thus some roads may be weak because of poor management. Here the remedy does not lie in consolidation but in improved management. Other railroads are weak because of a poor financial structure. Where this is so, the remedy lies in a reorganization or readjustment of the financial structure. In some cases, financial weakness may be due to the fact that a line has outlived its usefulness because of the exhaustion of natural resources or the decline of industries or communities which it served. Abandonment is the remedy in such a situation. Sometimes weakness is to be explained by lack of terminal facilities. In this situation the remedy may consist of opening the terminals of other lines to the use of the weaker line. Weakness may be due to overbuilding and the construction of too many lines. Here again, abandonment of the weaker lines may be desirable.

We find no fault with this argument against consolidation as far as it goes. Consolidation is not a cure-all for every kind of weakness. It is important that causes of weakness be ascertained and the proper remedy applied whenever that is possible. But after all has been said and done, the fact remains that many lines are weak because they cannot charge higher rates than their competitors or their neighbors, and it does not seem equitable to base rates on the necessities of the weaker lines alone.

The consolidation and combination provisions of the Transportation Act of 1920 proved to be a disappointment to those who had hoped to see the weak-and-strong-road problem solved in this manner. Few consolidations occurred under the original provisions of that Act, and in 1940, as elsewhere pointed out,[30] Congress gave up the idea of trying to bring about consolidations that would conform to a Commission-made plan with its emphasis on the creation of a few large systems of approximately equal earning power. Even after this liberalizing of the consolidation provisions to permit mergers that might be more in conformity with railroad wishes only a limited number of consolidations occurred prior to the 1960s.

In the late 1950s and the 1960s railroad merger activity occurred on a large scale. It is possible that this movement when completed will result in a partial solution of the weak-and-strong-road problem. Certainly

---

[29] This argument is used in W. M. W. Splawn, *The Consolidation of Railroads* (New York: Macmillan, 1925), pp. 244–47; and in Haney, op. cit., pp. 89–92.

[30] P. 266 supra.

there will be fewer railroad systems; whether they will be of more equal earning power remains to be seen, and whether a place will be found in the consolidations for weaker roads now independently operated may depend upon the exercise by the Commission of certain powers which it possesses to bring such a result to pass.

This is the power which the Commission has under the present law to require, as a condition of its approval of a particular consolidation, the inclusion of other railroads in the territory involved. In 1931 the Commission attached such a condition to its authorization of the unification of a number of lines by the New York Central.[31] The Commission's power to attach such a condition was upheld by the Supreme Court of the United States.[32]

The most prominent instances of the exercise of this power arose in connection with the merger movement of the 1960s. In approving the merger of the New York Central and the Pennsylvania to form the Penn Central Company, the Commission required the new company to include the New York, New Haven & Hartford Railroad in its system.[33] Also in authorizing the merger of the New York, Chicago & St. Louis Raiload Co. and the Norfolk & Western Railway Co., the Commission directed the inclusion of the Erie-Lackawanna Railroad Co., the Delaware & Hudson Railroad Corporation, and the Boston & Maine Corporation.[34] The action of the Commission in both of these cases was approved by the Supreme Court of the United States.[35] In both cases the terms of the inclusion were initially prescribed by the Commission, but in both instances litigation ensued over the final terms.

GOVERNMENT OWNERSHIP AND OPERATION

The weak-and-strong-road problem could be solved, of course, through government ownership and operation of the railroads, since the roads would be operated as a single system and revenues could be used to support any part of the system which might show a loss if operated separately. The proposal to solve the weak-and-strong-road problem by this method, however, raises a host of questions concerning the desirability or undesirability of government ownership and operation of the railroads. This subject is discussed in Chapter 38.

---

[31] *New York Central Unification*, 150 ICC 278 (1929), 154 ICC 489 (1929); but see 193 ICC 607 (1933).

[32] *New York Central Securities Corp.* v. *United States*, 287 U.S. 12 (1932).

[33] *Pennsylvania R. Co.—Merger—New York Central R. Co.*, 327 ICC 475 (1966); *Penn Central Merger—Inclusion Report*, 331 ICC 643 (1967), 331 ICC 754 (1968), 334 ICC 25 (1968).

[34] *Norfolk & Western Ry. Co. & New York, Chicago & St. Louis R. Co. Merger*, 330 ICC 780 (1967). Concerning the Boston & Maine see p. 29, supra.

[35] *Penn Central & Norfolk & Western Inclusion Cases*, 389 U.S. 486 (1968).

POOLING

Another method of dealing with the weak-and-strong-road problem has been suggested at various times. This is through pooling a portion of the receipts of the railroads and distributing the pooled receipts among the weaker lines according to their needs. This plan was first suggested in 1925 by Mark W. Potter, formerly a member of the Interstate Commerce Commission and then one of the receivers of the Chicago, Milwaukee & St. Paul Railway Company. He proposed a moderate increase in rates in Western Territory, say 5 percent, with the proceeds of the increase to be pooled and distributed among the lines that did not earn a certain return.[36]

It is to be observed that this arrangement would not have equalized earnings but would have prevented the stronger lines from receiving any benefits from the rate increase proposed and would have marshaled the proceeds of the increase for the benefit of the weaker lines. The "Potter Plan" was not adopted. In fact, it received very little serious consideration. A somewhat similar plan appeared in connection with the Fifteen Per Cent Case of 1931 and was supported on brief by the National Industrial Traffic League.[37] The Commission denied the carriers' request for a 15 percent increase in rates but permitted specific increases on a great many commodities. In its original decision in the case of the Commission attached the condition that the proceeds of the increase, or "surcharge," should be pooled and distributed among the carriers which were not earning their fixed charges.[38] The railroads objected to the pooling arrangement. The Commission then modified its order and permitted the carriers to put into effect a modified plan which they had devised as a substitute.[39] The modified plan called for a segregation of the proceeds of the emergency increases but provided that the funds so made available should not be given, but loaned, to the defaulting carriers. The Railroad Credit Corporation was created for the purpose of administering the plan. The plan was discontinued on March 31, 1933.

There was some question concerning the power of the Commission to impose a pooling plan upon the carriers, and this was undoubtedly one reason for the modification of the original order. As a means of relief to the weak lines, however, the original plan of the Commission was superior to the loaning plan finally put into effect. The objection was raised to the Commission's plan that it would take earnings of the strong lines and would turn them over to the weak. This argument has no merit, for

---

[36] *Memorandum on the Subject of Pooling a Portion of Receipts of Rail Carriers, etc.* (1925). The plan is treated favorably in J. S. Eaton, "The St. Paul Plan of Rate Relief," 79 *Railway Age* 137 (1925), and critically by H. T. Newcomb, "The Potter Plan—A Critical Analysis," 27 *Annalist* 5 (1926).

[37] *Brief before the I.C.C. in Ex Parte No. 103* (1931).

[38] 178 ICC 539 (1931).

[39] 179 ICC 215 (1931).

the plan was entirely in accord with the attitude taken by the United States Supreme Court in the New England Divisions Case and in the Dayton–Goose Creek Case. The emergency charges authorized by the Commission in 1931 might properly be considered as a special tax upon the users of the railroads to prevent default of interest payments. It was logical that the proceeds be distributed in such manner as to accomplish the desired result.

Although the attempt in 1931 to use the pooling device to aid the more needy lines failed, the issue was raised again in somewhat different form in 1937. The carriers had proposed certain increases in commodity rates as a means of increasing revenues. They had included an increase on coal, since it is an important item of traffic. It appeared, however, that a large portion of the increased revenues from coal would accrue to three important coal-carrying railroads—the Chesapeake & Ohio, the Norfolk & Western, and the Virginian—which operated largely in the so-called Pocahontas Region and were already earning over 9 percent on their investment in carrier property. But if coal rates were not increased on these three lines, they could not, as a practical matter, be increased on other lines. The Commission authorized temporary increases in the coal rates but suggested that a system of pooling and division of revenues was needed to prevent the revenues from accruing to railroads not in need of additional income.[40] Presumably the continuance of the increased rates on coal was to be contingent upon the establishment of a pooling arrangement. The carriers, however, refused to work out such an arrangement, and the Commission backed down from its stand by allowing the increased rates to continue in effect.[41] Thus ended the Commission's second attempt to exert pressure upon carriers to pool the proceeds of an increase in rates.

A pooling device similar to that proposed by the Commission in the Fifteen Per Cent Case of 1931 might be of considerable aid in the solution of the weak-and-strong-road problem. Such a plan, however, needs positive legislative sanction to remove doubts of its legality. Senator Reed of Kansas introduced a bill to accomplish this purpose in 1942 and again in 1943.[42]

CONCLUSION

The weak-and-strong-road problem has not been dealt with adequately in the past. The Recapture Clause proved impracticable in the form in which it was originally enacted and it was subsequently repealed.

---

[40] *General Commodity Rate Increases, 1937*, 223 ICC 657 (1937), pp. 740–45. See also Commissioner Aitchison's protest at this action, ibid., pp. 758–60.

[41] 229 ICC 435 (1938).

[42] For editorial support of the Reed bill see 69 *Traffic World* 76 and 96, and 71 ibid. 117 and 177.

The division of joint rates to aid weaker lines, although helpful, is not adequate to deal with the problem alone. A pooling device like that proposed by the Commission in the Fifteen Per Cent Case of 1931 might be of considerable aid in the solution of the problem, but it needs legislative authorization if it is to be used.

The greatest hope for solution, or rather partial solution, of the problem lies in the consolidation of railroads into a few large systems, notwithstanding abandonment of the idea of consolidation according to a master plan. This is true particularly if the Commission will exercise its power to require the inclusion of weak lines in a proposed consolidation as it did in the Penn Central and the Norfolk & Western cases. There is, of course, no assurance that the resulting "large systems" will themselves be strong as was dramatically revealed by the bankruptcy of the Penn Central a few months after its formation.

It is not likely that the weak-and-strong-road problem will be solved by any one method, or that it will be completely solved at all in the sense that the problem will entirely disappear. But this does not mean that the problem cannot be alleviated by the various methods that we have described.

Failure to deal with the problem will result in the abandonment of some mileage that still serves a useful purpose, or will throw such lines into the hands of state or local governments which will try to continue their services in the interest of protecting the economy of the areas involved. This has already happened in a few instances.[43] In some cases absorption of railroad deficits by the state or local governments would be necessary if the rail operations were to continue.

SELECTED REFERENCES

The only book devoted to the weak-and-strong-road problem is J. M. Herring, *The Problem of Weak Railroads* (Philadelphia: University of Pennsylvania Press, 1929). Some fundamental economic considerations relating to the problem are set forth in H. G. Brown, "Railroad Valuation and Rate Regulation," 33 *Journal of Political Economy* 505 (1925), pp. 522–29. The problem is also discussed in Charles L. Dearing and Wilfred Owen, *National Transportation Policy* (Washington, D.C.: Brookings Institution, 1949), pp. 324–38.

Recapture of excess earnings and experience with the Recapture Clause are discussed in H. G. Moulton, *The American Transportation Problem* (Washington, D.C.: Brookings Institution, 1933), chap. xviii; and in I. L. Sharfman, *The Interstate Commerce Commission*, Vol. III–B (New York: Commonwealth Fund, 1936), pp. 221–55. Reading on this topic should include *Dayton–Goose Creek Ry. Co. v. United States*, 263 U.S. 456 (1924).

On the division of joint rates as a means of aiding weak lines see *New*

---

[43] See Chapter 38.

England Divisions Case, 261 U.S. 184 (1923); and Sharfman, op. cit., pp. 255–90.

Consolidation as a remedy is discussed in Bird M. Robinson, "The Relation of the Short Lines to Railroad Consolidation," 13 *Proceedings of the Academy of Political Science* 416 (1929); George G. Reynolds, "Consolidation and Equalization," 13 ibid., 425 (1929); L. H. Haney, "Advantages and Disadvantages of Railway Consolidation," 14 *American Economic Review* (Supplement) 89–92 (1924); W. M. W. Splawn, *The Consolidation of Railroads* (New York: Macmillan, 1925), chap. viii. The most complete account of the efforts to bring about railroad consolidation under the Transportation Act of 1920 is W. N. Leonard, *Railroad Consolidation under the Transportation Act of 1920* (New York: Columbia University Press, 1946).

For the pooling plan see J. S. Eaton, "The St. Paul Plan of Rate Relief," 79 *Railway Age* 137 (1925); H. T. Newcomb, "The Potter Plan: A Critical Analysis," 27 *Annalist* 5 (1926). See also J. B. Eastman's dissenting opinion, *Fifteen Per Cent Case, 1931,* 179 ICC 215, 220–36 (1931); the decision of the Commission in *General Commodity Rate Increases, 1937,* 223 ICC 657, 741–45 (1937); and Commissioner Eastman's separate expression in a supplemental report in the same case, 229 ICC 435, 460–62 (1938), and his dissenting opinion in *Property Owners' Committee* v. *Chesapeake & Ohio Ry. Co.,* 237 ICC 249, 580–85 (1940).

Chapter 18

REASONABLENESS OF RATES ON PARTICULAR COMMODITIES

Rate regulation involves more than adjusting rates so that carriers earn a fair return upon the fair value of their property. Rates must be established on particular commodities and between particular points, and these rates must be "just and reasonable." This chapter is concerned with the factors which determine the reasonableness of rates on particular commodities. The following chapter will consider factors determining the reasonableness of rates between specific points, i.e. the spatial element in rate making. Both chapters will be concerned with reasonableness per se and not with discrimination or with undue preference and prejudice. In cases of the latter type the issue becomes one of the differences in rates. Reasonableness per se is concerned with the proper standard to apply on a commodity or on a particular haul, in and of itself. Rates, and not differences in rates, are involved. This is so notwithstanding the fact that reasonableness per se is often determined by means of rate comparisons. In this latter situation, however, the rates with which comparison is made are set up as a standard of reasonableness, and the comparison is not made for the purpose of determining whether one person or commodity has an advantage over another. Cases in which relationships in rates are the primary issue will be considered in Chapter 22.

A knowledge of standards by which the reasonableness of rates is judged is of importance to shippers. It can aid them when adjustments in rates are sought through negotiations with carriers; or if this procedure fails, it will enable them to appraise the possibility of obtaining relief by appeal to regulatory agencies.

FAIR-RETURN DOCTRINE NOT APPLICABLE

When rates on particular commodities are under consideration, the net earnings of the carrier and their relation to property values are largely irrelevant. The rate on a particular commodity may be unreasonably high although the carrier is not earning a fair return. Likewise a rate may be unduly low even though the carrier is earning more than a fair return.

This principle has been recognized by the United States Supreme

Court. "Where the rates as a whole are under consideration, there is a possibility of deciding, with more or less certainty, whether the total earnings afford a reasonable return. But whether the carrier earned dividends or not sheds little light on the question as to whether the rate on a particular article is reasonable."[1] And in interpreting Section 15a of the Interstate Commerce Act, the Court said: "The statute does not require that the net return from all the rates shall affect the reasonableness of a particular rate or a class of rates. In such an inquiry the Commission . . . need not consider the total return at all."[2] Although this principle is widely accepted, it sometimes happens that a certain commodity or group of commodities is such an important item of traffic to the carrier that its net earnings will be greatly affected by raising or lowering the rates thereon. Under such circumstances the earnings of the carrier do have a bearing on the reasonableness of the rate on the commodity or commodities in question.

RATES AND FULLY ALLOCATED COSTS

Although it has sometimes been urged that railroad rates should be based on fully allocated costs, the Commission recognizes that such a method of rate making is impracticable since it would prevent the movement of much traffic that can cover direct or out-of-pocket costs and make some contribution to fixed and overhead costs. Thus rates are not necessarily too low if they are less than fully allocated costs, nor are they necessarily excessive when they are higher than fully allocated costs. The Commission has frequently made this point, which is strictly in accord with traditional theory as outlined in an earlier chapter. In one case the Commission replied to the contention that rates on raw sugar should be based on fully allocated cost by saying:

If rates were made in this manner, it would result in reducing the rates on much of the high-grade traffic transported by the carriers. At the same time, however, it would bring about increases in the rates on most of the low-grade, volume-moving traffic. Rates on the latter have been made in the past under a continuous interplay of economic forces to permit such traffic to move with reasonable freedom and thus to contribute as much as possible to the carriers' overhead or fixed costs. To revise all rates so as to make them reflect exactly or approximately the fully distributed costs, if such a thing were practicable, would tend to dry up much of the traffic moving in large volume, with a consequent reduction in the contribution which this traffic now makes to the carriers' general revenue needs. Such a change would increase rather than reduce

---

[1] *Interstate Commerce Commission* v. *Union Pacific R. R. Co.*, 222 U.S. 541, 549 (1912).

[2] *Dayton–Goose Creek Ry. Co.* v. *United States*, 263 U.S. 456, 480 (1924), and also p. 483.

the portion of the general transportation burden to be borne by the higher-rated traffic.[3]

Although it has long been recognized as economically sound for railroads to charge rates that are less than fully allocated costs on traffic that will not freely move at higher rates, provided direct or out-of-pocket costs are covered and more than covered, a decision of the Supreme Court of the United States in 1915 in *Northern Pacific Railway Co.* v. *North Dakota* seemed to limit greatly the power of regulatory authorities to prescribe rates which do not cover fully allocated costs.[4]

The state of North Dakota had prescribed rates on lignite coal within the state which did not contribute a ratable share of all operating expenses. These rates were set aside by the Supreme Court as confiscatory and in violation of the Fourteenth Amendment of the Constitution. The Court would not recognize the propriety of distinguishing between direct or out-of-pocket costs and fully allocated costs. It said:

> . . . we entertain no doubt that, in determining the cost of the transportation of a particular commodity, all the outlays which pertain to it must be considered. We find no basis for distinguishing in this respect between so-called "out-of-pocket costs," or "actual" expenses, and other outlays which are none the less actually made because they are applicable to all traffic, instead of being exclusively incurred in the traffic in question. Illustrations are found in outlays for maintenance of way and structures, general expenses and taxes. It is not a sufficient reason for excluding such, or other, expenses to say that they would still have been incurred had the particular commodity not been transported. That commodity has been transported; the common carrier is under a duty to carry, and the expenses of its business at a particular time are attributable to what it does carry.[5]

The Court apparently felt that the carrying of some traffic at less than the full cost of the service must necessarily throw a burden on other traffic. Thus the Court said:

> The state cannot estimate the cost of carrying coal by throwing the expense incident to the maintenance of the roadbed, and the general expenses, upon the carriage of wheat; or the cost of carrying wheat by throwing the burden of the upkeep of the property upon coal and other commodities. . . . Certainly, it could not be said that the carrier may be required to charge excessive rates to some in order that others might be served at a rate unreasonably low. That would be but arbitrary action.[6]

---

[3] *U.S. Sugar Corp.* v. *Atlantic Coast Line R. Co.*, 277 ICC 193, 202 (1950). For a somewhat similar statement see *Sugarcane from South Florida to Clewiston, Fla.*, 281 ICC 47, 63 (1951).

[4] 236 U.S. 585 (1915). For comments on this case, see *American National Livestock Assoc.* v. *Atchison, Topeka & Santa Fe Ry. Co.*, 122 ICC 609, 617 (1927); *Grain & Grain Products*, 122 ICC 235, 264 (1927); Robert L. Hale, "Commissions, Rates, and Policies," 53 *Harvard Law Review* 1103, 1127–28 (1940).

[5] 236 U.S. 585, 597.

[6] Ibid., pp. 596–97.

The reasoning of the Court was not wholly sound, as we know, since a low rate on a commodity does not burden other traffic if the rate covers the direct or out-of-pocket costs of the service, makes some contribution to fixed costs, and is necessary to enable the traffic to move. The decision of the Court is open to the interpretation that rates prescribed by a governmental authority must cover fully allocated costs other than return on investment, but the courts now seem to recognize that regulatory authority may require rates that do not cover fully allocated costs.[7]

A more recent decision of the Supreme Court, *Baltimore & Ohio Railroad Co. v. United States*,[8] goes even further since it holds that public authority may require rates that do not even cover out-of-pocket costs provided the carriers are permitted an adequate return from their traffic as a whole. In the Baltimore & Ohio case the Supreme Court said: "And so long as rates as a whole afford railroads just compensation for their over-all services to the public the Due Process Clause should not be construed as a bar to the fixing of noncompensatory rates for carrying some commodities when the public interest is thereby served."[9] In this proceeding the Court approved action by a district court which had dismissed a complaint which alleged that certain rates prescribed by the Commission on fresh fruits and vegetables were confiscatory because they did not cover the cost of the service. The position of the Supreme Court was that even if the rates in question were noncompensatory, that fact did not invalidate the Commission's order.[10]

OUT-OF-POCKET COSTS

Although the language of the Supreme Court in the Baltimore & Ohio Case quoted above implies that rates which do not even cover out-of-pocket costs might be approved or required if the public interest is thereby served, the Interstate Commerce Commission has long condemned rates that did not cover out-of-pocket costs. The Commission has said: ". . . this Commission regards as unreasonable a rate which is so low as to be noncompensatory or which may or does transfer a portion of the cost of transportation to other traffic,"[11] and "it would be unlawful to charge a rate so low as to be noncompensatory or impose a burden upon other

---

[7] This logically follows from the principle stated in the Baltimore & Ohio case discussed in the paragraph which follows.

[8] 345 U.S. 146 (1953).

[9] Ibid., p. 150.

[10] For comments on this decision see 67 *Harvard Law Review* 91 (1953), p. 140; 101 *University of Pennsylvania Law Review* 1228 (1953), p. 1231; and R. W. Harbeson, "A New Judicial Test of Reasonable Rates," 22 *I.C.C. Practitioners' Journal* 789 (1955); Anthony F. Arpaia, "A Noteworthy Drift in the Economics of Transportation—The Implications of Baltimore & Ohio Railroad Co. v. United States," 102 *University of Pennsylvania Law Review* 80 (1953).

[11] *Excelsior from St. Paul, Minn.*, 36 ICC 349, 365 (1915).

traffic."[12] This position has been maintained in decisions since the Baltimore & Ohio Case.[13] We have noted elsewhere that in cases in which a railroad proposes a reduction of rates to meet the competition of another railroad, the Commission will interfere if the proposed rate is not compensatory.[14] The same rule, we shall see, is observed when railroads propose reductions in rates to meet the competition of other modes of transport.[15]

THE COMPARATIVE STANDARD OF REASONABLENESS

Although cost allocations sometimes figure prominently in rate cases, there are hundreds of cases decided each year without any attempt to find the cost of the service in the absolute sense of the word. The usual method of determining the reasonableness of rates on a particular commodity is to compare the rate with the rates on commodities which have similar transportation characteristics. The rates used for purposes of comparison are set up as a standard of reasonableness, and other rates are made to conform thereto unless some difference in the commodities is shown which justifies differences in rates.

ANALOGOUS ARTICLES

The basic principle in the comparative method is commonly stated thus: Analogous articles should ordinarily take the same rates. The term "analogous articles" refers to articles that are alike from a transportation standpoint, that is, alike in the matter of cost of transportation and in value. If the costs of transporting two articles differ, or if differences in value are shown, the articles are not strictly analogous, and different rates are justified. Even if the articles are analogous in the sense defined, differences in conditions of demand for their transportation may warrant differences in rates.

Rate cases can be found by the thousands which illustrate the general rule that analogous articles should normally take the same rates. The Interstate Commerce Commission has held, for instance, that canned evaporated milk should take the same rates as other canned goods,[16] that wooden beer cases should take the same rates as wooden boxes,[17] and that benzol should take the same rates as gasoline.[18] Similarly the Commission

---

[12] *Lumber Rates from the Southwest to Points North,* 29 ICC 1, 15 (1914).

[13] See *Reduced Rates on Pulpwood in Southern Territory,* 297 ICC 735, 747, 749 (1956).

[14] P. 460, infra.

[15] See Chapter 37.

[16] 112 ICC 155.

[17] 25 ICC 249.

[18] 78 ICC 353.

has required that celery take the same rate as egg plant,[19] motorcycles as bicycles,[20] Pluto water as ginger ale,[21] camel's hair as wool,[22] building brick as paving brick,[23] chopped alfalfa as baled hay,[24] lawn mowers as agricultural implements,[25] and fly ash as cinders.[26]

RELATIVE COST OF SERVICE

It will be noted that two commodities are not analogous if there are differences in the cost of transporting them. Differences in rates may then be justified. Sometimes it is possible to measure these differences with some degree of accuracy; sometimes it is not possible to do so. It should be carefully noted that cost of service in the absolute sense is not obtained in such cases. Comparisons of this sort reveal differences in cost, not costs themselves. Relative cost is a more important factor in rate cases than absolute cost.

Since the reasonableness or unreasonableness of rates frequently turns on relative cost of service, it is important to consider the principal factors which cause differences in cost and which therefore justify higher or lower rates on some articles than on others.

PRINCIPAL FACTORS WHICH CAUSE DIFFERENCES IN COST

Loading Characteristics

Freight rates are usually stated in terms of cents per hundred pounds or per ton. At uniform rates per ton or other unit of weight, a carload of a light bulky article would yield the carrier much less revenue than a carload of a heavier commodity. Many elements of transportation cost, however, vary with the number of cars handled rather than with the number of tons handled. In order to obtain reasonable revenues per car, the rates on light and bulky articles must be relatively high, but on heavy-loading articles they may be relatively low. The loading characteristics of an article are therefore important in determining the reasonableness of rates.

Whether an article loads heavily or lightly depends in large measure upon its weight density. This is commonly expressed as weight per cubic foot. In the case of light and bulky articles a difference of a few pounds

---

[19] 5 ICC 663.
[20] 26 ICC 127.
[21] 60 ICC 615.
[22] 78 ICC 178.
[23] 87 ICC 105.
[24] 87 ICC 154.
[25] 109 ICC 465.
[26] 292 ICC 349.

per cubic foot becomes a matter of first importance.[27] Differences in rates on various kinds of lumber and lumber products are determined partly by weight density.[28] Greater weight density explains the common practice of having more favorable rates and ratings on articles "nested" than "not nested" and on articles "knocked down" than "set up." Sometimes the carriers maintain different ratings on the same article which are dependent upon the thickness of the material from which it is made. The Uniform Freight Classification shows that aluminum shipping drums made of material of a certain gauge are rated Class 125, L.C.L.; but if made of a thicker material, they are rated Class 100. The influence of weight density is seen also in the almost universal practice of making higher rates on commodities having low minimum carload weights, and lower rates on articles with high minima. On furniture the Commission once prescribed different ratings according to the weight per cubic foot of the particular article.[29]

A low weight density is not the only explanation of why some articles load lightly. Ability to load the article compactly must also be considered. Articles of odd shapes or large dimensions may not load to advantage. Sometimes, furthermore, carloading is restricted by the impossibility of completely filling a car without causing damage to the contents. Melons cannot be loaded more than a few layers deep without crushing those on the bottom. Crates of fresh fruit shipped in refrigerator cars cannot always be loaded to the top of the car, since the warm air in the car rises to the top and causes the top layers of fruit to spoil. Sometimes the loading of an article is restricted by commercial conditions rather than by physical limitations. If an article is bought and sold in quantities somewhat less than can be loaded in a car, it may be necessary to provide a low minimum carload weight.

There are certain recognized limitations to the practice of adjusting rates to the loading characteristics of the article. In the first place, too minute distinctions cannot be made, at least in the case of classified freight. To do so would destroy the advantages of classification by making the number of classes too great.[30] In the second place, it is not practicable to provide for differing weight densities of the same articles unless the differences are considerable. To make such distinctions often benefits a few shippers and hence tends to discriminate against others. The Commis-

---

[27] See *Better Bedding Alliance* v. *Atchison, Topeka & Santa Fe Ry. Co.*, 148 ICC 66 (1928).

[28] *Rates on Lumber and Lumber Products*, 52 ICC 598 (1919).

[29] *Rate Structure Investigation, Part 5—Furniture*, 177 ICC 5, 109–10 (1931). On furniture weighing 3 pounds per cubic foot and under, the rating was 3 t 1; over 3 pounds and including 3.75, the rating was 2½ t 1. The ratings decreased with increasing weight density, ending in a second-class rating on furniture weighing over 12.5 pounds per cubic foot.

[30] See *Casket Manufacturers' Assoc. of America* v. *Baltimore & Ohio R. R. Co.*, 49 ICC 327 (1918).

sion once refused to require a lower rate on a particular kind of gas heater which loaded more heavily than ordinary gas stoves.[31] There are some cases, however, in which different weight densities of the same kind or class of articles have been held to require different rates,[32] but this is not the usual practice. In one case the Commission refused to lower the rates on cotton compressed to a density of 47 pounds per cubic foot as compared with ordinary cotton bales having a density of 25 pounds per cubic foot. The high-compressed bales would load 50,000 pounds to the car, whereas ordinary bales could be loaded to only 25,000 pounds. The Commission feared that the advantage of the lower rate would accrue only to those who held patents on the machinery for making the high-density bale and that it might lead to a monopoly in the purchasing of cotton.[33] A similar case before the Texas Commission was decided the same way, and the decision was approved by the Texas Supreme Court.[34] The soundness of disregarding such large differences in loading characteristics is highly questionable.[35]

When carload rates are under consideration, the weight density of an article loses its significance if a greater weight density would not permit heavier loading without exceeding the weight-carrying capacity of the car. A weight density which results in complete utilization of the cubic capacity of a car at the same time that the weight limit is reached is sometimes called the "optimum" weight density. A greater weight density than the optimum does not permit heavier loading.

Susceptibility to Loss or Damage

A second cost factor to be considered in determining the reasonableness of rates on particular commodities is the risk of loss and damage. Ocean shipments of freight are usually insured by the shipper against loss and damage, and a regular insurance premium is paid. A railroad company, however, is liable for the safe transportation of the goods it carries. The railroad is, in a sense, the insurer of the goods.[36] No separate insur-

---

[31] *General Gas Light Co.* v. *Alabama Great Southern R. R. Co.*, 102 ICC 181 (1925). See also *Rates on Excelsior & Flax Tow from St. Paul, Minn.*, 29 ICC 640 (1914).

[32] *Edlund Broom Corporation* v. *Boston & Maine R. R. Co.*, 104 ICC 692 (1925).

[33] *Planters Compress Co.* v. *Cleveland, Cincinnati, Chicago & St. Louis Ry. Co.*, 11 ICC 382 (1905).

[34] *Railroad Commission of Texas* v. *Weld & Neville*, 96 Tex. 394 (1903).

[35] See Dissenting Opinion of Commissioner Prouty in the Planters Compress Case, 11 ICC 382, 410–21.

[36] Railroads are liable for loss or damage even though there is no negligence on their part. They are not liable, however, in the absence of negligence, for loss or damage due to an "act of God," an act of the public enemy, an act or default of the shipper, an act of public authority, or the inherent nature or qualities of the goods shipped. For more specific as well as additional causes of loss and damage for which railroads are not liable, see terms of the Uniform Bills of Lading.

ance premium is charged to cover the risk. For this reason the risk of loss or damage is a cost factor which must be considered in making railroad rates.

Commodities differ greatly in the matter of susceptibility to loss or damage. Some, like sand, gravel, brick, and iron and steel articles, are not likely to be damaged. Fragile articles and perishable products, such as fresh fruits and vegetables, are very susceptible to injury. Susceptibility to loss and damage may arise, however, from causes other than fragility or perishability. Grain shipped in bulk tends to leak from cars and is lost. Alcoholic beverages are frequently stolen, and cigarettes are peculiarly susceptible to pilfering. Explosives are easily destroyed and may cause loss and damage to other freight and to the railroad equipment. In a case dealing with rates on dynamite it was pointed out that one half the transportation charge represented compensation for risk.[37] Comparisons of the risk element in the transportation of different articles can be reduced to a statistical basis. Figures showing loss and damage claims on particular commodities in relation to the total freight revenues received from their transportation are often presented in rate cases.

Differences in susceptibility to loss and damage may become the controlling or decisive element in a particular case. In one case the Commission required a lower rate on a new kind of explosive, called "masurite," than was charged on dynamite, because the former was so difficult to explode that it was as safe to transport "as sugar or soap," except in the event that some other explosive in close proxmity also exploded.[38]

In some countries, different rates are provided on articles according to whether they are shipped at carrier's risk (C.R.) or at owner's risk (O.R.). This was the common practice in England, and it was formerly so in the United States. At the present time the railroads in the United States are prohibited (with certain exceptions) from limiting their liability by contract or stipulation in tariffs and classifications. For this reason there are no owner's-risk rates found in the United States. In countries which permit owner's-risk rates the difference between the two classes of rates should compensate for the difference in risk.

The methods by which goods are packed for shipment often affect their susceptibility to loss and damage. Thus canned meats and other foods have usually been charged higher rates when in glass than when in tin containers, although the greater susceptibility of the glass containers to breakage has been hotly disputed.[39] In one case the Commission approved rates on long-type watermelons which were 10 percent higher when loaded lengthwise in freight cars than when loaded crosswise. Susceptibil-

---

[37] *Dupont de Nemours Co.* v. *Central Railroad of New Jersey*, 25 ICC 19 (1912).

[38] *Masurite Explosive Co.* v. *Pittsburgh & Lake Erie R. R. Co.*, 13 ICC 405 (1908).

[39] See *Indian Packing Corporation* v. *Director General*, 64 ICC 205 (1921), and 93 ICC 400 (1924); also *Classification Ratings on Food Products*, 185 ICC 138 (1932), 195 ICC 683 (1933).

ity to loss and damage was found to be greater when loaded lengthwise.[40]

Rule 5 of the Uniform Freight Classification provides a scheme for the establishment of ratings on articles shipped in containers other than those listed with the description of the article in the body of the classification. According to this rule, for instance, articles in crates are charged 20 percent more than when shipped in boxes, L.C.L., and 10 percent more when in carloads. Rule 5 has its justification in the greater risk incurred if the articles are shipped in one form than in another. The Commission, however, does not hesitate to find charges unreasonable if the application of this rule results in the imposition of higher charges on certain shipments than are justified by differences in risk. Thus the imposition of a rating on steel roller chains three classes higher when in bags than when in barrels or boxes was found unreasonable because the article was not easily damaged, even if in bags.[41] Similarly the Commission found unreasonable the imposition of a rating on agate pebbles in bags which was two classes higher than on the same commodity in boxes.[42] Not only are the carriers entitled to higher charges when goods are shipped in forms more likely to result in loss and damage, but they may provide in detail the specifications for the construction of crates, barrels, or other containers used for shipping goods.[43] Under Rule 5 of the *Classification* the carriers are supposed to refuse shipments not properly prepared for shipment. If the goods are accepted when the containers do not conform in all respects to the requirements specified in the descriptions or in the rules, the rates are 20 percent higher, L.C.L., and 10 percent higher, C.L. The Interstate Commerce Commission has held that the carriers have a right to insist upon proper packing but that they have no right to impose higher rates on less substantially packed articles than is warranted by the additional risk assumed.[44]

Amount of the Carrier's Liability

A third factor in determining the relative cost of service is the amount of the liability assumed by the carrier. If the carrier is liable for the full value of the goods it carries, the value of the commodity measures the amount of the carrier's liability. If the carrier exempts itself from liability beyond a certain stated value, this stated or released value measures the amount for which the railroad is liable.

Section 20 of the Interstate Commerce Act makes the railroads liable

---

[40] *Watermelons from Southern Points to U.S. and Canada,* 301 ICC 461 (1957).

[41] *Link-Belt Co.* v. *Pittsburgh, Cincinnati, Chicago, & St. Louis R. R. Co.,* 64 ICC 195 (1921).

[42] *Agate Products Co.* v. *Director General,* 66 ICC 674 (1922).

[43] See Rules 40 and 41 of the *Uniform Freight Classification.*

[44] *Classification of Canned Goods,* 98 ICC 166, 177 (1925).

for the full value of the commodities which they transport, hence the value of the commodity is a factor affecting the cost of service. This should not be confused with the principle of varying rates according to value on the theory that the more valuable goods will stand higher rates. So far as cost of service is concerned, the value of the commodity affects rates only to the extent that it measures the carrier's liability. On this basis, only slightly higher rates are justified on valuable articles than on cheaper ones.

It was common in the past for the carriers to limit their liability by quoting "released rates." These are rates granted on certain articles if the shipper will release the carrier from liability beyond a certain agreed or stated value. Under this system the shipper has his choice of paying a comparatively high rate and having his shipment fully covered by the railroad's liability, or of paying a lower rate but with the carrier's liability limited to a specified amount. Released rates were common on articles varying greatly in value or on commodities the value of which was difficult to determine.

Released rates are made unlawful by Section 20, paragraph 11, of the Interstate Commerce Act. This section makes railroads liable for the full value of commodities carried, "notwithstanding any limitation of liability or limitation of the amount of recovery or representation or agreement as to value in any such receipt, or bill of lading, or in any contract, rule, regulation, or in any tariff filed with the Interstate Commerce Commission." Certain exceptions are permitted, namely: (1) baggage carried on trains carrying passengers; and (2) property, other than ordinary livestock, upon which the Interstate Commerce Commission has specially authorized released rates. The situation may therefore be summarized as follows:

Articles	*Status of Released Rates*
Baggage............................	Lawful
Ordinary livestock.....................	Unlawful
Other-than-ordinary livestock[45].........	}Unlawful unless specifically
All other commodities.................	authorized by the ICC

Two circumstances must exist concurrently before the Interstate Commerce Commission will authorize released rates: (1) the commodity must have a wide range of values, and (2) the commodity must have a high susceptibility to loss and damage.[46] Neither circumstance alone is sufficient to warrant released rates: not a wide range of values by itself, because the loss and damage claims may be negligible; not unusual susceptibility to loss and damage alone, because if the risk is known, the rate can and should be

---

[45] Other-than-ordinary livestock means livestock chiefly valuable for show, breeding, or racing purposes.

[46] See *Released Rates on Stone in the Southeast*, 93 ICC 90 (1924). The same principle was applied to motor-carrier released rates in *Dry Goods, Piece Goods, Dependent on Value*, 53 MCC 157 (1951).

made high enough to cover it. When the two conditions exist together, however, the risk and uncertainty justify the limitation of liability. When released rates are authorized, the difference in rates should represent the difference in cost to the carrier arising from the difference in risk.[47] Although released rates have been authorized on a large number of articles, the Commission considers that its power to permit them "has been used sparingly, as Congress quite clearly intended."[48]

Volume of Movement

The cost of transporting a commodity is affected to some extent by the volume in which it moves over a period of time. If the volume of movement is large, a carrier is in position to organize better its operations and methods of handling the commodity and so reduce the cost of carrying it. We are here referring to costs directly assignable to the commodity in question. The principle should not be confused with the principle that unit costs of transportation decrease as the volume of all traffic increases as a result of spreading the constant or indirect costs over a larger volume of traffic. Sometimes, if the volume of traffic of a single commodity, say coal or coke, is so large as to constitute a substantial portion of the whole traffic, a low rate may be justified because of the relation of volume to overhead.[49] It is the relation between the volume of movement of a commodity and direct costs, however, and not that between total volume and the distribution of general overhead costs, that we are interested in at this point.

Although the volume of movement of an article may affect the direct costs of handling it, this is not true if the larger volume of movement does not permit more economical handling. Thus two articles generally shipped as L.C.L. freight may differ considerably in the quantities offered for shipment, yet this difference may not affect the relative cost of transporting them. "In such a case mere quantity, not measured by a recognized unit of quantity adapted to carriage . . . cannot be allowed to affect rates in the transportation of property."[50] In order for a large volume of movement to justify lower rates on one article than on another, the larger volume should actually lower direct costs. The most striking examples of this principle occur where the volume of traffic in a single commodity permits its movement in solid trainloads.

It is probably true that the Commission has often attached greater significance to volume of movement than is justified by its relation to cost

[47] *Released Rates on Stone in the Southeast*, 93 ICC 90 (1924).

[48] *Released Rate Rules—National Motor Freight Classification*, 316 ICC 499, 509 (1962).

[49] See, for instance, *Tift v. Southern Ry. Co.*, 10 ICC 548, 583 (1905), and *Louisville & Nashville Railroad Coal & Coke Rates*, 26 ICC 20, 31 (1913).

[50] *Harvard Co. v. The Pennsylvania Co.*, 4 ICC 212, 224 (1890).

of service, sometimes giving it weight when cost of service was not affected. Professor Sharfman has justly criticized the Commission on this score.[51]

Regularity of Movement

Regularity of movement is another factor entering into the measurement of relative cost of service. If traffic moves regularly, it can be transported with greater economy. More economical train schedules can be worked out, and empty cars can be supplied with a minimum of expense. Irregularity of movement has the opposite effect. This is often true when there is a distinctly seasonal movement, which taxes the carrier's facilities at certain times and results in idle equipment and facilities at others.

Type of Equipment Required

The type of equipment required for an article affects its relative cost of service. Articles that require refrigerator cars are more expensive to transport than articles that can be carried in ordinary boxcars. Other commodities can be carried in open-top cars or on flatcars. Some articles require insulated cars, and others require lined equipment. Then, too, the dead weight transported is greater when commodities must be transported in the heavier types of equipment.

Special Services

Some commodities transported by the railroads require special services of one type or another. Refrigeration or protection against cold is often necessary. Refrigerator cars may have to be precooled before being loaded with shipments of fresh fruits or vegetables. Caretakers for livestock may be granted free passage. Special sidings or terminal facilities may be provided for the loading or unloading of certain kinds of fruits and vegetables or other commodities. Perishable commodities may be given expedited service. For some of these services, special charges may be made; but if compensation is not provided by extra charges, the regular freight rate must be high enough to remunerate the carrier for the cost incurred.

DEMAND FACTORS

The factors entering into the reasonableness of rates that we have just described concern the relative costs of transporting different articles. We must now turn to a consideration of factors affecting the demand for

---

[51] I. L. Sharfman, *The Interstate Commerce Commission*, Vol III–B (New York: Commonwealth Fund, 1936), pp. 514–18.

transportation service, that is, matters that relate to what the traffic will bear.

The Interstate Commerce Act requires the Commission to consider the effect of rates on the movement of traffic in determining just and reasonable rates. We have already referred to this principle in cases relating to the general level of rates.[52] It applies also in cases involving rates on particular commodities. To consider the effect of rates on the movement of traffic is but to recognize that rates must be limited by the value of the service, or what the traffic will bear, if traffic is to move.[53] The Commission has often said that "the rate level necessary to move a commodity is an element to be weighed in determining a reasonable charge."[54] The Commission, for instance, has recognized that rates on scrap material[55] and on hay[56] had to be low if the traffic was to move; and under certain circumstances it has recognized this principle in fixing rates on fresh fruits and vegetables.[57]

Consideration of the effect of rates on the movement of traffic should not lead to rates that are below the direct costs of transportation. We have seen, however, that it may be sound to make rates less than the full allocated cost of service if such rates are necessary to move the traffic and if they cover something more than the direct costs of providing the service.

Value of the Commodity

It has been customary from the earliest days of railway development to charge comparatively high rates on valuable articles and lower rates on cheaper articles. The relationship between value and rates is based upon a relationship between the value of the article and the value of the service of transporting that article. All too frequently in the literature of railway rates the term "value of service" is used synonymously with "value of the commodity," but the two things are different. It is generally true, as we have elsewhere pointed out, that valuable commodities will stand higher rates than less valuable ones, but the relationship is not always true. Sometimes the valuable commodities will not stand high rates, but the usual relationship clearly warrants the prominence generally given to value comparisons in rate cases. There is no need of giving citations to cases in

---

[52] Pp. 359–60, supra.

[53] Pp. 157–59, supra.

[54] *Half Stage Refrigeration Service*, 256 ICC 213, 221 (1943); *Penick & Ford* v. *Director General*, 80 ICC 152, 156 (1923); *Chicago Heights Mfrs. Assn.* v. *Pennsylvania R. R. Co.*, 92 ICC 194, 198 (1924).

[55] *Waste Material Dealers Assoc.* v. *Chicago, Rock Island & Pacific Ry. Co.*, 226 ICC 683, 691 (1938).

[56] *Hay Rates within Western District*, 195 ICC 461, 477 (1933).

[57] *Fresh Green Vegetables from Idaho & Oregon*, 253 ICC 143 (1942).

which the Commission has acknowledged value of the article as a factor to be considered in determining the reasonableness of rates. Their number is legion. In fact, there is scarcely a case involving rates on particular articles which does not make use of value comparisons. In many cases value becomes the controlling consideration.

The value of the commodity as an indication of ability to pay should not be confused with the value of the commodity as a measure of the liability assumed by the carrier. It has occasionally been argued before the Interstate Commerce Commission that the value of an article is not an element in rate making except to the extent that it measures liability for loss and damage. The Commission maintains, however, that "where two commodities are similar except for a difference in value the difference in rates may and should be more than an amount just sufficient to provide insurance against loss or damage in transit."[58]

If articles are distinguished for purposes of rate making according to differences in value, why should a distinction not be made between the different grades or values of the same article? This is, in fact, sometimes done. Such rates are called "actual-value" rates. When actual-value rates are put into effect, it becomes necessary for the shipper to declare the value of the article before the proper rate or rating can be determined. Actual-value rates should be distinguished from the released rates referred to earlier in the chapter. With actual-value rates the value becomes a part of the description of the property, and misrepresentation of the value is a form of false billing which defrauds the carrier and is therefore subject to a heavy penalty. With released rates, on the other hand, the declared or agreed value is simply intended to limit the carrier's liability, and there may be no pretense that the declared value is the real value of the article. An actual-value rate does not carry with it any limitation of liability, although it may have that effect, since a shipper would hardly dare to claim a value greater than that declared. To do so would be an admission of misrepresentation in order to obtain a rate lower than the legal rate.

Actual-value rates are commonly found on articles having a wide range in values. Examples of actual-value rates may be found in the *Uniform Freight Classification*. Thus "Florist stock: bulbs or tubers" are given an L.C.L. rating of Class 70 when the actual value of the bulbs does not exceed 50 cents per pound, and Class 100 when the value exceeds that sum. Cigarette lighters are rated Class 100, L.C.L., when their value does not exceed 50 cents each, and Class 200 when their value exceeds 50 cents each.

There is one serious difficulty with actual-value rates. The freight agent is not an expert in determining the values and grades of various articles. The carrier must therefore rely upon the statement of value declared by

---

[58] *National Association of Employing Lithographers* v. *Atchison, Topeka & Santa Fe Ry. Co.*, 136 ICC 201, 203–4 (1927).

the shipper. This opens the way for misrepresentation and fraud. Where actual-value rates are quoted, the traffic is apt to move at the lower rates. For this reason the Commission has hesitated to require the carriers to vary rates according to the different grades of particular articles.[59]

The practice of making rates higher on valuable articles than on cheaper articles may be easily abused. It may lead to the exaction of unnecessarily high rates simply because some articles will stand such rates. When low rates are granted on low-grade commodities on the theory that the low rate is necessary to move the traffic but will yield something above the direct costs of transportation, the rates on such commodities will be less than the fully allocated cost of transporting them, and rates on the high-grade articles will exceed their fully allocated costs. At the same time, however, the rates on the valuable articles should be lower, and not higher, than they would be if the low-grade articles were not carried. In other words, the carrying of the low-grade articles at low rates should defray part of the constant or indirect costs that would otherwise be borne by the high-grade traffic alone.[60]

The rise of motor transportation in recent years has forced the railroads to attach less weight to the value of commodities than formerly in fixing rates, and it has brought down the rates on articles that had customarily been charged high rates because of their high value. This was pointed out by the Interstate Commerce Commission in 1945 in *Class Rate Investigation, 1939:*

> Development of competitive transportation agencies with flexible service, and a disregard of the element of value by the competitive agencies in the determination of their charges, have reacted upon the policies of the classification committees with the result that generally weight density is now the dominant consideration in determining classification ratings. This does not mean that value and other principles of classification are completely eliminated from consideration; but it does mean that value of an article does not control the rating to the extent it formerly did.[61]

In an earlier case the Commission noted that motor-carrier competition was undermining the old railroad rate structure and was "rapidly bringing down many of the rail rates on high-grade commodities which were made high because of the weight formerly given to value of the service."[62]

Although the ability of railroads to exact high rates on valuable articles has been greatly restricted by the rise of other modes of transport including private trucking, the inability of low-grade articles to stand rates

---

[59] See *Union Pacific Tea Co.* v. *Pennsylvania R. R. Co.*, 14 ICC 545 (1908); *McCrory Stores Corp.* v. *Director General*, 55 ICC 423 (1919); *Union Made Garment Manufacturers Assoc.* v. *Chicago & North Western Ry. Co.*, 16 ICC 405 (1909); *Silver Plated Iron or Steel Bearings*, 259 ICC 360 (1945).

[60] See pp. 162–63, supra.

[61] *Class Rate Investigation, 1939*, 262 ICC 447, 482 (1945). See also ibid., p. 485.

[62] *Trunk-Line Territory Motor Carrier Rates*, 24 MCC 501, 514 (1940). The term "value of service" is used in this case as synonymous with "value of the commodity."

based on fully-allocated costs must still be recognized. The value of the commodity may no longer be a factor justifying high rates on valuable articles, but it is frequently important in indicating the necessity of low rates on commodities of low value.

Limitations on the Value Principle

There are very definite limitations to the practice of varying rates with the value of the commodity.

The most important one we have already mentioned, namely, that the rise of competing modes of transport has made it impossible to exact very high rates on valuable articles. Even when motor carriers adopt the railroad system of freight classification with high rates on valuable articles, the right of the individual to transport his own commodities in his own vehicles imposes limits on the rates which railroads and for-hire motor carriers can charge for transporting high-grade traffic.

In the second place, even on the lowest grades of traffic the rates should not fall below direct or out-of-pocket costs. Overhead or indirect costs may be ignored in rate making if conditions of demand make impossible the exaction of charges that cover a share of the overhead. But prime costs cannot be ignored; and low-grade commodities, notwithstanding their very low value, ought not to be transported at noncompensatory rates. This is what the Commission has in mind when it disregards value in the case of low-grade commodities and says: "Regardless of the value of the traffic the carriers are entitled to rates which are reasonable for the service which they perform."[63] Transporting commodities at less than direct costs throws an additional burden on other traffic if the carrier is to be adequately supported.

A third limitation arises from the impracticability, in many instances, of distinguishing between different grades of the same commodity. Although this is done to some extent, it is subject to disadvantages already noted.

A fourth limitation on the use of value as a controlling factor in rate making results from the fact, already noted, that conditions other than the value of the commodity may limit the rate that can be charged. We have already pointed out that sometimes articles of high value must take low rates if they are to move.[64] Whenever the value of the service is determined by other factors than the value of the article, value must yield to the more relevant facts.[65]

---

[63] *Sand, Gravel, Crushed Stones & Shells within the Southwest*, 155 ICC 247, 277 (1929). For a similar expression see *Sand, Gravel, Slag, Stone & Chert*, 165 ICC 731, 766 (1930).

[64] See pp. 159–60, supra.

[65] For instances in which the Commission has recognized this point see *Patterson Foundry & Machine Co.* v. *Chicago, Burlington & Quincy R. Co.*, 262 ICC 339, 347 (1945); *Wool & Mohair Rates*, 276 ICC 259, 296 (1949); *Vacuum Cleaner Mfrs. Assoc.* v. *Atchison, Topeka & Santa Fe Ry. Co.*, 276 ICC 783 (1950).

Another limitation on the use of value appears when an attempt is made to distinguish between old and new articles of the same kind. It would be consistent with the use of the value principle to have low rates on used and secondhand articles. The Interstate Commerce Commission has frequently held, however, that lower rates on such articles could not be required.[66] The reason for this departure from the value principle lies in the possibility of misbilling. Goods would be shipped as used or secondhand when in fact they were not. The maintenance of lower rates on used articles leads to attempts to defraud the carrier. For the same reason the Commission has refused to require lower rates on damaged articles than on undamaged ones.[67]

Raw Materials and Finished Products

Whether a commodity is a raw material or a finished product is sometimes considered significant in determining the reasonableness of rates. Finished products generally take higher rates than the materials out of which they are made. The common relationship between rates on raw materials and finished products is a corollary to the rule that valuable commodities have generally taken higher rates than less valuable ones. This is because the manufactured articles are usually more valuable than the raw material. Sometimes the relationship seems to have attained the dignity of an independent rule or principle. The Interstate Commerce Commission has said, however, that "there is in fact no rule or principle of classification which requires that manufactured products be rated higher than the material from which they are made, or, conversely, that raw materials be rated lower than manufactured products."[68]

Although the chief reason for the higher rates on finished products is their greater value, the relationship is supported by other considerations as well. The waste of part of the raw material in the process of manufacture, an important element in some instances, reduces the value of the service per unit of weight transported. Weight-losing raw materials, it will be recalled from a previous chapter, tend to draw manufacturing to them. Manufacturing establishments located at a distance from the sources

[66] E.g., *Continental File Co.* v. *Pittsburgh, Cincinnati, Chicago & St. Louis R. R. Co.*, 93 ICC 373 (1924); *Apex Tire & Rubber Co.* v. *Baltimore & Ohio R. Co.*, 280 ICC 552 (1951).

[67] *Minneapolis Traffic Assoc.* v. *Chicago & North Western Ry. Co.*, 23 ICC 432 (1912); *Danciger* v. *Pittsburgh, Cincinnati, Chicago & St. Louis Ry. Co.*, 29 ICC 99 (1914); *Midwest Waste Material Co.* v. *Canadian National Rys.*, 259 ICC 430, 431 (1945). When articles have a value only for purposes of junk, such as iron and steel articles which can only be used for remelting, they constitute, in fact, junk, and are given low rates. But if they have a value for other purposes, even though actually used for remelting, they are not entitled to the junk rate. See *Alaska Junk Co.* v. *Spokane, Portland & Seattle Ry. Co.*, 98 ICC 551 (1925).

[68] *Aluminum Co. of America* v. *Atchison, Topeka & Santa Fe Ry. Co.*, 146 ICC 363, 366 (1928).

of such raw materials may not be able to survive unless lower rates are given on the raw material than obtain on the finished product. All this is but another way of saying that the traffic will not bear high rates on such raw materials.

On the other hand, when manufacturing or processing is already taking place at the source of a principal raw material, ability to charge higher rates on the finished product may be limited by the possibility of driving the processing to consuming points in order to avoid the high rates. Thus, in a case involving rates on ground sand, the Commission said: "The value of the service or what the traffic will bear is largely determined by the fact that if the rates on ground sand reflect too great a spread over the raw product, the sand may be ground at or near destination instead of being ground at the quarry."[69]

Very frequently, also, the cost-of-service principle supports higher rates on finished products. Manufactured articles are frequently more bulky, more susceptible to loss and damage, and may require more careful handling and protection than raw materials. Cost of service, however, cannot justify the relationship in all instances.

The Interstate Commerce Commission often approves of a differential relationship between the rates on raw materials and finished products, and it has at times required a differential to be established. Thus the Commission has approved of rates on wire brushes higher than on the raw materials from which they were made;[70] and it has similarly required higher rates on brooms than on broomcorn,[71] on malt than on barley,[72] and on enameled pipe than on iron pipe.[73] The Commission has required lower ratings on unfinished bedroom sets than on finished sets,[74] and it has condemned higher rates on pulpwood than on paper.[75] The relationship is not universal, however, and the Commission has often said that a lower rate on a raw material cannot be claimed as a right.[76]

A related practice of varying rates according to the stage of manufacture is illustrated by the rates on many wooden articles. Three different stages of manufacture are recognized: "in the rough," "in the white," and "finished." These terms are defined in Rule 22 of the *Uniform Freight Classification.*

Since there is no reason why raw materials should necessarily take lower rates than finished products unless cost-of-service or value-of-

---

[69] *Industrial Sand Cases, 1930,* 204 ICC 159, 166 (1934).

[70] 13 ICC 109 (1908).

[71] 28 ICC 310 (1913).

[72] 23 ICC 378 (1912).

[73] 26 ICC 472 (1913).

[74] 5 ICC 514 (1892).

[75] 160 ICC 37 (1929).

[76] E.g., *State of Iowa* v. *Atlantic Coast Line R. R. Co.,* 24 ICC 134 (1912).

service factors point to such a rate relationship, it is not strange that there are many exceptions. In many situations the usual relationship of rates would be unnatural and impossible to justify. Sometimes it happens that the raw material is as valuable per unit of weight, or nearly so, as the finished product. Sometimes the finished product is more susceptible to competition from other kinds of transportation agencies than the raw material. This apparently explained higher rates on wood pulp than on paper in one case that came before the Commission. Wood pulp is not a desirable article for water-transportation companies to carry, and it was therefore not subject to the competition encountered in transporting paper, which does move readily by water.[77] Another exception occurs when the finished product is a by-product having low value. In such instances the by-products take low rates, but the main product usually conforms to the general rule. This can be illustrated by the rates on the various products of cottonseed crushing. Cottonseed oil is the most valuable product derived from the seed, and it sometimes takes higher rates than cottonseed. Cottonseed meal and cake are by-products having approximately the same value as the seed. They are generally carried at the rates applicable on seed or at slightly lower rates. Cottonseed hulls and linters are a less valuable by-product and are transported at still lower rates.[78] Another exception to the general practice occurs when a certain raw material constitutes a very small part of the manufactured article. Thus amorphous sulphur is used in small quantities in the manufacture of matches. But this does not mean that amorphous sulphur should take lower rates than apply on matches.[79]

Another cause of departure from the usual rate relationship, even when it could be justified by differences in cost of service, arises from the efforts of carriers to equalize the advantages of producers located near consuming markets and those located near supplies of raw material. The constant struggle between the two groups of producers and the carriers serving them often leads to the equalization of rates on raw materials and finished products. This accounts for the fact, elsewhere pointed out, that in the United States the rates on flour and grain have generally been the same.[80] The Commission, however, has permitted lower rates on wheat than on flour where competition from other modes of transport has forced railroads to lower their rates on wheat but not on flour.[81]

---

[77] *Crown Willamette Paper Co.* v. *Director General*, 78 ICC 273 (1923).

[78] *East St. Louis Cotton Oil Co.* v. *St. Louis & San Francisco R. R. Co.*, 20 ICC 37 (1910).

[79] *Diamond Match Co.* v. *Director General*, 88 ICC 435 (1924).

[80] P. 71, supra.

[81] See *Grain in Multiple-Car Shipments—River Crossings to the South*, 318 ICC 641 (1963); 321 ICC 582 (1963); and *Wheat & Flour, Midwest & Southwest to Gulf Ports & Chicago for Export*, 322 ICC 581 (1964).

Competing Commodities

What the traffic will bear is affected by the competition that may exist between two commodities. Competing commodities should take the same rates unless differences in cost of service are so great as to make equalization impracticable. This principle should not be confused with the principle, previously discussed, that analogous articles should take the same rates. Analogous articles are alike from the point of view of transportation costs and value. Competing articles may not be alike. If two products compete with each other, that is, if one can be used as a substitute for the other, the one burdened with the higher freight rate is at a disadvantage. This may so restrict the volume of traffic that it will be necessary to reduce the rate to that charged on the competing product. Railroads therefore tend to equalize rates on competing commodities, and regulatory authorities recognize that comparisons of rates on competing commodities are of importance in fixing reasonable or proper rates. Upon analysis it will be observed that the principle is but one illustration of the importance in rate making of the elasticity of demand for an article. An article for which there are available substitutes has an elastic demand.

The principle that competing articles should take the same rates, although recognized in cases concerning reasonableness per se, is of even greater importance in cases under Section 3 of the Interstate Commerce Act—the undue-preference-and-prejudice section. Illustrations of cases involving this relationship are given in a later chapter.[82]

Use of a Commodity

The use to which a commodity is put may have a bearing upon the transportation charge which it can be made to stand. This is sometimes because the use made of the article gives some indication of its value. Lime used for agricultural purposes is probably of a lower grade and value than lime used for building purposes, since the former may contain impurities that would render it useless for building. The relationship between use and value has been recognized by the Commission as the reason for giving consideration to this factor in rate cases. In one case the Commission said: "Whenever reference is made in this report to the use of an article, it is for the purpose of reaching some conclusion with respect to its relative value."[83] But the use made of an article may also be of importance in indicating the kind of commodities with which an article may or does compete, or it may aid in determining whether the raw-material-and-finished-product relationship should be considered, or it may for some other reason indicate ability to pay. The Interstate Commerce Commission

---

[82] Pp. 532–33 infra.

[83] *Suspension of Western Classification No. 51*, 25 ICC 442, 499 (1912).

recognizes that the use of an article throws light upon its ability to pay transportation charges and that it is therefore a proper factor to consider in rate making.[84]

On the other hand, the Commission has steadfastly refused to permit different rates on the same commodity depending upon the use which is made of the article.[85] Thus the Commission has condemned the maintenance of lower rates on coke for use in blast furnaces than on coke used for other purposes.[86] It has also objected to higher rates on mussel shells used in making buttons than on shells to be crushed for poultry feed[87] and to different rates on nitrate of soda which depended on whether the product was to be used for the manufacture of gunpowder or for the manufacture of fertilizer.[88]

If different rates on the same commodity depending upon its use are not to be permitted, what is to be done in case a commodity has several uses? Which use is significant in determining the appropriate rate? The Commission has answered this question by holding that the predominant use of a commodity determines its character for transportation purposes.[89]

There seem to be two major reasons for the refusal of the Commission to permit two rates on the same commodity. First, there is no difference in the cost of service. It costs no more, for instance, to haul a given quantity of nitrate of soda that is to be used in the manufacture of gunpowder than a similar quantity that is to be an ingredient in commercial fertilizer. In the second place, if the rate applicable on a commodity depends upon use, the way is opened for misrepresentation. The carrier may not be able to verify the use to be made of the article and must rely upon the statement of the shipper. The shipper is thus in a position to defraud the carrier of a part of the lawful transportation charges.

Although the maintenance of rates depending upon the use to be made of an article is inconsistent with the cost-of-service principle, it is not inconsistent with charging what the traffic will bear. There may be just as much reason for quoting a lower rate on an article when used for particular purposes as there is for quoting a lower rate on a cheap grade than on a valuable grade of the same article. Either the demand for a

---

[84] *Lime from Eastern Trunk Line Points*, 93 ICC 617, 630 (1924); *Crushed Stone from Maryland & Pennsylvania*, 89 ICC 681, 684 (1924); *Classification Ratings on Airplane Seats*, 266 ICC 702, 705 (1946).

[85] *Carter White Lead Co.* v. *Norfolk & Western Ry. Co.*, 21 ICC 41 (1911); *Southwest Steel Rolling Mills* v. *Apache Ry. Co.*, 278 ICC 383, 388 (1950); *Apache Powder Co.* v. *Atchison, Topeka & Santa Fe Ry. Co.*, 299 ICC 649, 651 (1957).

[86] *Anaconda Copper Mining Co.* v. *Chicago & Eastern Illinois R. R. Co.*, 19 ICC 592 (1910).

[87] *Pioneer Pearl Button Co.* v. *St. Louis–San Francisco Ry. Co.*, 93 ICC 599 (1924).

[88] *Fort Smith Traffic Bureau* v. *St. Louis & San Francisco R. R. Co.*, 13 ICC 651 (1908).

[89] *Asphalt from Oklahoma to Omaha, Nebr.*, 308 ICC 223, 225 (1959); *Classification Rating of Spray De-Icer, etc.*, 326 ICC 389, 396 (1966).

commodity for certain uses or the demand for the transportation of the article may be affected by the rate charged. A low rate on nitrate of soda when used in the manufacture of fertilizer may be essential if the commodity is to be used for this purpose, whereas a comparatively high rate on the same product when used in the manufacture of gunpowder might not interfere at all with this use of the article. A lower rate on coke for smelting purposes might be required in order to maintain smelting furnaces located at a distance from a supply of coke but competing with furnaces near a coke supply. The same force would not require a low rate on coke for domestic use. If the value-of-service principle of rate making has any validity whatsoever, there seems to be no reason, in principle, for not permitting rates which vary according to the use to be made of an article. The only sound objection to the practice is the opportunity created for defrauding the carrier.[90]

Although the Commission does not permit rates which depend upon the use made of an article, it does permit something which is very close to the same thing. It sometimes allows the use to be made of an article to determine the proper rate or rating to apply, on the theory that two commodities or grades of commodities, although very much alike in outward appearance, can be distinguished by their uses. The theory is that the differences in use are so great as to constitute the articles different commodities. Thus the Commission has recognized as proper lower rates on horses used for slaughtering than are maintained on ordinary horses.[91] Brick used for facing purposes may be given a higher rate than common brick.[92] Similarly the Commission has recognized that lime suitable for chemical and building purposes and lime having value chiefly for agricultural purposes may be considered as two different commodities.[93] In the same way, sand used in the manufacture of glass is recognized as a different commodity from common sand.[94]

Conditions Existing in an Industry

The ability of a particular commodity to stand a rate is sometimes affected by the conditions of prosperity or depression within the industry

---

[90] For a similar criticism of the Commission's policy on this point see J. F. Strombeck, *Freight Classification* (Boston: Houghton Mifflin, 1912), pp. 90–97.

[91] *Chappell Bros.* v. *Chicago, Burlington & Quincy R. R. Co.*, 161 ICC 677 (1930).

[92] *National Paving Brick Mfrs. Assoc.* v. *Alabama & Vicksburg Ry. Co.*, 68 ICC 213 (1922); *McEwing & Thomas Co.* v. *Chicago & Eastern Illinois Ry. Co.*, 118 ICC 211 (1926).

[93] *Eastern Lime Mfrs. Traffic Bureau* v. *Akron & Barberton Belt R. R. Co.*, 112 ICC 7 (1926).

[94] *American Window Glass Co.* v. *Baltimore & Ohio R. R. Co.*, 155 ICC 301 (1929).

which produces the commodity.[95] If an industry is in a depressed condition, high rates may result in curtailed production. Conversely, if the industry is prosperous, rates may be increased without affecting production. For this reason the Commission has long recognized that the conditions existing in an industry may be taken into consideration in determining the reasonableness of rates. This position has the approval of the United States Supreme Court, for in *Ann Arbor Railroad Co.* v. *United States* the Court said: "In rate making under existing laws it has been recognized that conditions in a particular industry may and should be considered along with other factors in fixing rates for that industry and in determining their reasonableness."[96] The principle received special emphasis in the Hoch-Smith Resolution, passed by Congress in 1925, which declared that the "true policy" to be observed by the Interstate Commerce Commission in adjusting rates was "that the conditions which at any given time prevail in our several industries should be considered in so far as it is legally possible to do so, to the end that commodities may freely move."

The principle that rates should be adjusted in accordance with the economic conditions existing in an industry may easily be abused. It is valid only in so far as it throws light on ability to pay transportation charges. It is not valid when used to help one class of individuals at the expense of another. The Interstate Commerce Commission has emphatically declared that it is not justified in reducing rates on a commodity merely to relieve a distressed industry. This position was taken in a number of cases which came up after World War I, when the agricultural interests argued for lower rates on the products of agriculture on the ground that the industry was in a depressed condition. These pleas were, as a rule, unsuccessful.[97] The soundness of the Commission's reasoning on the question of reducing rates to help a distressed industry cannot be questioned. If the rates are reduced to help out one industry, the burden of the reduction must be borne by the railroads or shifted to other shippers and consumers by increasing the rates on other products. The railroad is not an eleemosynary institution and ought not to be required to forego reasonable compensation for the services it renders. Neither is there any justification for shifting the burden on other groups of people by increasing rates which are reasonable in themselves. The Commission has also pointed out that if rates must be reduced to aid depressed industries, the converse of the proposition must also be true, and carriers ought therefore to be allowed to charge high rates on particular products merely for the reason

---

[95] We are here considering an industry as a whole and not the prosperity or lack of it on the part of a particular shipper or of the industry in one locality as compared with another. This latter situation affects geographical relationships in rates and will be considered in the following chapter.

[96] 281 U.S. 658, 667 (1930).

[97] See *National Livestock Shippers League* v. *Atchison, Topeka & Santa Fe Ry. Co.*, 63 ICC 107 (1921); and *Rates and Charges on Grain and Grain Products*, 91 ICC 105 (1924).

that the industry is prosperous and the carriers wish to absorb part of the profits of the industry. The Commission long ago held that the carriers had no such right,[98] and one of the federal courts has held that "carriers have no right to graduate their charges in proportion to the prosperity which comes to industries whose products they transport."[99]

The Interstate Commerce Commission seems to recognize that the depressed condition of an industry is a proper factor to be considered in determining the reasonableness of rates only to the extent that it indicates ability or inability to pay. Thus in a case involving rates on wool, the Commission said: "If the condition of this industry is such that it can not flourish, that the traffic will not move for the reason that the wool itself will not be produced, that, certainly, is a circumstance which may be considered in comparing this rate with those upon other commodities."[100] In another case the Commission said: ". . . the condition of an industry has an influence upon the ability of a commodity produced by that industry to bear a rate, which in turn may have a bearing upon the reasonableness of the rate charged."[101]

PUBLIC POLICY

We have now completed the discussion of the more important factors affecting the ability of traffic to stand a large or a small share of the constant or overhead expenses of a railroad. But there is one more factor sometimes considered in determining the reasonableness of rates. This is whether the general public welfare requires a high or low rate on the commodity in question. This is not a matter of the ability of the article to stand a high transportation charge but of whether it is deemed desirable, in the public interest, to encourage or discourage the movement of the commodity and bring about some desired social or economic result. The Commission has spoken approvingly of higher rates on luxuries than on necessary articles,[102] and in one case it implied that high rates on tobacco were justifiable on the ground that it is a luxury rather than a necessity.[103]

---

[98] *Tift* v. *Southern Ry. Co.*, 10 ICC 548, 582 (1905); *Central Yellow Pine Assoc.* v. *Illinois Central Ry. Co.*, 10 ICC 505 (1905).

[99] *Tift* v. *Southern Ry. Co.*, 138 Fed. 753 (1905).

[100] *In re Transportation of Wool, Hides & Pelts*, 23 ICC 151, 156 (1912). See also *Wool & Mohair Rates*, 276 ICC 259, 269 (1949).

[101] *Utah-Idaho Millers & Grain Dealers Assoc.* v. *Denver & Rio Grande R. R. Co.*, 44 ICC 714, 726 (1917). See also *Rates and Charges on Grain & Grain Products*, 91 ICC 105, 143 (1924); *Cattle Raisers' Assoc.* v. *Missouri, Kansas & Texas R. R. Co.*, 11 ICC 296, 348 (1905); *Likestock—Western District Rates*, 190 ICC 611, 633 (1933).

[102] *In the Matter of the Investigation & Suspension of Advances in Rates on Coal*, 22 ICC 604, 623 (1912).

[103] *Tobacco Merchants Assoc.* v. *Aberdeen & Rockfish R. R. Co.*, 181 ICC 199, 211 (1931).

The Commission has also maintained that the public interest requires low rates on materials used in manufacturing and in construction.[104] Low rates on fertilizer have been held desirable on account of the "need for continued progress in the use of fertilizer."[105] In another case the Commission admonished the carriers to lower their rates on wastepaper with the observation that the "utilization of waste materials is of economic value to the country."[106] The Commission has been hesitant about permitting any sort of a rate adjustment that would lead to a monopoly in any branch of industry or trade. This factor was mentioned in the Planters Compress Case, where the Commission refused to require lower rates on the special high-density bales.[107]

Although public welfare and social good have apparently been considered in cases like those mentioned, these considerations may not, after all, have been given much weight. In fact, to allow considerations of public policy and welfare to influence a rate case is wholly inconsistent with the common pronouncement of the Commission that the reasonableness of rates on particular articles is to be determined by their "transportation characteristics." The Commission apparently feels that it is on rather insecure ground if it gives weight to public welfare. In many cases the Commission has definitely refused to consider such matters. Thus the Commission has refused to require lower rates on laboratory furniture than on other furniture, notwithstanding the plea that the former was used for educational and research purposes and that the public interest therefore required low rates.[108] In like manner the Commission refused to heed the argument that low rates should be required on schoolbooks.[109] In another case, manufacturers of bedding objected to a proposal for low rates on used matresses because of the danger to health in the use of old bedding. The Commission held that "considerations affecting public health have but little relevancy in determining the reasonableness of freight rates."[110] The Commission is especially loath to consider broad questions of economic and social welfare when the policy involved is one concerning which a prior expression by legislative authority would be more appropriate if the policy is to influence rate making. Thus the Commission refused to require lower rates on grain when the plea was based on the desirability of extending the area of wheat cultivation and thereby in-

---

[104] *Colorado Fuel & Iron Co.* v. *Southern Pacific Co.*, 6 ICC 488, 515 (1895).

[105] *Fertilizers between Southern Points*, 113 ICC 389, 421 (1926). See also *American Potash & Chemical Corp.* v. *Aberdeen & Rockfish R. R. Co.*, 258 ICC 743, 757 (1944).

[106] *Reduced Rates, 1922*, 68 ICC 676, 720 (1922).

[107] 11 ICC 382, 407 (1905).

[108] *Rates Structure Investigation, Part 5—Furniture*, 177 ICC 5, 62 (1931).

[109] *American Book Co.* v. *Ann Arbor R. R. Co.*, 129 ICC 372 (1927).

[110] *American Cotton Waste & Lumber Exchange* v. *Baltimore & Ohio R. R. Co.*, 169 ICC 710, 711 (1930).

creasing domestic production.[111] For a similar reason the Commission once refused to require lower rates on flour for export than on wheat when the purpose of the proposed adjustment was to discourage the direct exportation of wheat and to encourage the milling of the wheat into flour in the United States.[112] The Commission has also refused to prevent rate changes that were opposed on the grounds that they might adversely affect established methods of marketing. "It is not the province of the Commission to determine the relative merits of different sales methods or by rate adjustments to perpetuate any particular system or sales pattern of distribution."[113]

The general conclusion to be drawn from these cases is that although the Commission sometimes recognizes the economic and social effects of certain rates, it is on insecure ground if it modifies rates otherwise reasonable out of deference to these consequences. To give weight to considerations of welfare, economic policy, and the like would hardly be consistent with the statement of the Supreme Court that the standards set up by the Interstate Commerce Act are "transportation standards, not criteria of general welfare."[114]

A contrary policy was apparently followed, however, by the Federal Maritime Commission when it disapproved a proposed reduction in steamship rates on automobiles from eastern United States ports to Puerto Rico, holding that high rates on luxuries were justified to offset low rates needed on imported foodstuffs, certain raw materials, and on outbound products of Puerto Rico in the interest of furthering the economic development of the area.[115] Two commissioners dissented.

Although the Interstate Commerce Commission has been cautious about giving weight to welfare considerations or matters of economic policy when determining the reasonableness of rates, a prior declaration by Congress of a policy will justify, if not require, that it be given consideration by the Commission. A recent example resulted from the National Environmental Policy Act of 1969 declaring a national policy with respect to control and improvement of the environment.[116] In *Increased Freight Rates 1970 and 1971* the Commission was led by the policy of this Act to limit rate increases on scrap metals and waste materials in order not to restrict efforts being made to collect and recycle such materials.[117]

---

[111] *Railroad Commissioners* v. *Butte, Anaconda & Pacific Ry. Co.*, 31 ICC 641, 653 (1914).

[112] *Bulte Milling Co.* v. *Chicago & Alton R. R. Co.*, 15 ICC 351 (1909).

[113] *Transit & Mixing Rules on Foodstuffs*, 270 ICC 157, 175 (1948); and *Transit on Foodstuffs at Toledo, Ohio*, 277 ICC 689, 697 (1950); also *Cotton from Memphis & Helena to New Orleans*, 273 ICC 337 (1948).

[114] *Texas & Pacific Ry. Co.* v. *United States*, 289 U.S. 627, 638 (1933).

[115] *Reduced Rates on Autos—North Atlantic Ports to Puerto Rico*, 8 FMC 404 (1965).

[116] Public Law 91–190.

[117] 339 ICC 125, 207–9 (1971).

RATE MAKING IS A MATTER OF JUDGMENT

Theoretically the reasonableness of rates should be determined by ascertaining the direct expenses involved in moving a certain commodity. Then, after a study of the various demand factors mentioned in preceding pages, the overhead costs should be distributed with careful regard to the principle of what the traffic will bear. But as a matter of fact, the reasonableness of rates is not determined exactly in this way, although the results are often approximately the same. The regulating body, as we have seen, uses the comparative method. Rates on the commodities in question are compared with rates on similar commodities. Cost factors and ability-to-pay factors are compared, and the Commission arrives at a conclusion. The weight accorded to the various factors is not usually stated, and the process by which the conclusion was reached is often not revealed. This gives a mysterious appearance to rate decisions. As one writer has put it: "It may appear that the Commission thrusts its hand into the darkness, and a reasonable rate is plucked back like a rabbit from a conjuror's hat."[118] The recognized principles of rate reasonableness, however, are not difficult to understand when isolated and considered separately. The difficulty comes in reaching a conclusion in a particular case, where many factors, often pointing to divergent results, are combined. In the words of a federal court, ". . . it is beyond the sphere of human ingenuity to establish a rule of mathematical certainty whereby a rate may be ascertained as reasonable or unreasonable."[119]

SELECTED REFERENCES

Literature relating to reasonableness of rates on particular commodities is not extensive. Early treatments of the subject are M. B. Hammond, *Railway Rate Theories of the Interstate Commerce Commission* (Cambridge: Harvard University Press, 1911), pp. 13–69; and J. F. Strombeck, *Freight Classification* (Boston: Houghton Mifflin, 1912). The policies of the Commission in determining the reasonableness of rates on particular commodities are discussed with thoroughness in I. L. Sharfman, *The Interstate Commerce Commission*, Vol. III-B (New York: Commonwealth Fund, 1936), pp. 476–527. There is much material on the subject in Glenn L. Shinn, *Reasonable Freight Rates* (Washington, D.C.: Traffic Service Corp., 1952).

The *Northern Pacific Railway* v. *North Dakota* decision is the basis of an article by Raymond T. Bye on "Social Welfare in Rate Making," 32 *Political Science Quarterly* 522 (1917). The article by H. W. Edgerton entitled "Value of the Service as a Factor in Rate Making," 32 *Harvard Law Review* 516 (1919), although containing some economic fallacies, is a valuable piece of work. Other articles relevant to the subject of this chapter are R. L. Hale, "Commissions, Rates, and Policies," 53 ibid. 1103 (1940); and W. L. Grossman,

---

[118] Henry Hull, "Reasonable Rates," 15 *Michigan Law Review* 478, 486 (1917).

[119] *Hudson & Manhattan R. Co.* v. *United States*, 35 F. Supp. 495, 496 (1940).

"Principles of Carrier Rate Regulation," 26 *New York University Law Review* 475 (1951). An excellent discussion of the implications of the United States Supreme Court decision in *Baltimore & Ohio Railroad Co.* v. *United States* is R. W. Harbeson, "A New Judicial Test of Reasonable Rates," 22 *I.C.C. Practitioners' Journal* 789 (1955).

For an extended review of Interstate Commerce Commission decisions in which value-of-service considerations are emphasized, see Interstate Commerce Commission, Bureau of Transport Economics & Statistics, Statement No. 5912, *Value of Service in Rate Making* (1959).

Chapter 19

REASONABLENESS OF RATES

BETWEEN PARTICULAR

POINTS

The preceding chapter was concerned with the problem of rates on particular commodities in relation to the rates on other commodities; the present chapter deals with rates for particular movements or hauls in comparison with rates for other movements. In both chapters, however, we are concerned with the reasonableness of rates per se rather than with issues of unjust discrimination and undue preference.

RATES TO RESTRICT MOVEMENT

Although the motive of the carrier in adjusting rates is not ordinarily determinative of the reasonableness of the rates charged, the Interstate Commerce Commission recognizes the principle that rates designed to restrict the movement of a commodity are unreasonable. The Commission looks askance at any rate adjustment that seems to have been designed to prevent the normal movement of commodities to market. Cases of this sort frequently arise from the desire of a railroad company to preserve markets on its lines to producers who are also located on its lines. The railroad may therefore attempt to maintain higher rates from producing points located off its lines.[1] Carriers in the western grain-growing states have sometimes maintained higher rates on grain westward than eastward in order to keep the traffic moving to eastern markets, thereby giving railroads a longer haul.[2] Cases have arisen in which a carrier had prohibitive rates on ties or other lumber products from points on its own lines in order to enable it to purchase these products for its own use at a lower price.[3] Rates of this sort have been strongly condemned by regulatory authorities as unreasonable.[4] The Interstate Commerce Commission has said: "A carrier has no right,

---

[1] See *Rates on Plaster and Gypsum Rock*, 27 ICC 67 (1913); *Coal to South Dakota*, 47 ICC 750 (1917); *Wichita Falls System Joint Coal Rate Cases*, 26 ICC 216 (1913).

[2] See *Board of Railroad Commissioners of South Dakota* v. *Atchison, Topeka & Santa Fe Ry. Co.*, 151 ICC 431 (1929).

[3] *Cedar Lumber Products Case*, 3 Canadian Railways Cases 412 (1904).

[4] Such rates are often held to be discriminatory or unduly prejudicial also.

under the guise of reserving to itself the long haul, to restrict the markets of its shippers."[5] In another case the Commission said: "Rates should be a medium for effecting the movement of commerce from one point to another and no carrier has the right, by erecting barriers of prohibitive rates, to restrict the sources from which a consuming point may supply its needs."[6]

CAN CONTINUATION OF PROMOTIONAL RATES BE REQUIRED?

The common railroad practice of granting preferential rates in order to build up a particular industry raises the question of the power of the railroads to increase such a rate at a later date, even though it may be disastrous to the industry in question. The early position of the Commission was that when the investment of capital in an industry was made upon the strength of a particular rate, the rate could not be subsequently increased without a careful consideration of its effects upon the industry. In one case the Commission said: "This Commission has several times held that where a particular industry has grown up under rates voluntarily established and maintained by carriers these rates can not be advanced without considering the effect upon that industry."[7] In 1908 the Commission, acting upon this principle, found increased rates unreasonable on lumber from the Willamette Valley.[8] The carrier had previously granted low rates to the industry, and capital had been invested in the belief that the low rates would continue. The order of the Commission requiring the increased rates to be reduced was set aside by the United States Supreme Court because the order had been "based upon the belief by the Commission that it had the right under the law to protect the lumber interests of the Willamette Valley from the consequences which it was deemed would arise from a change of the rate, even if that change was from an unreasonably low rate which had prevailed for some time to a just and reasonable charge for the service rendered for the future."[9] In commenting upon this decision, the Commission later said that it had always believed that it could, in a proper case, order the continued maintenance of a rate upon which the investment of money had been induced, even though it could not have required the establishment of so low a rate in the first instance.

---

[5] 151 ICC 431, 444 (1929).

[6] *Coal to South Dakota*, 47 ICC 750, 754 (1917). For comments of like purport, see *Cardiff Coal Co.* v. *Chicago, Milwaukee & St. Paul Ry. Co.*, 13 ICC 464–67 (1908); and *Star Grain & Lumber Co.* v. *Atchison, Topeka & Santa Fe Ry. Co.*, 14 ICC 364, 367–68 (1908).

[7] *Beatrice Creamery Co.* v. *Illinois Central R. R. Co.*, 15 ICC 109, 128 (1909). See also *Green Bay Business Men's Assoc.* v. *Baltimore & Ohio R. R. Co.*, 15 ICC 59, 64 (1909).

[8] *Western Oregon Lumber Manufacturers Assoc.* v. *Southern Pacific Co.*, 14 ICC 61.

[9] *Southern Pacific Co.* v. *Interstate Commerce Commission*, 219 U.S. 433 (1911).

The Commission reasserted its right to do this on the grounds that other-wise the property rights of shippers would rest "in the arbitrary whim of the carrier without the right of appeal to any tribunal." The Com-mission declared that it did not consider that the Supreme Court decision in the Southern Pacific Case prevented it from considering this factor. It appears from later cases, however, that the Commission has brought its policy into conformity with the views of the Supreme Court in cases where this issue arises. "However reluctant the Commission may feel to sanction changes in rates which tend to impair or destroy the value of investments made in expectation of their continuance, it can not on that ground deny to the carriers the right to charge rates which are just and reasonable."[10] In some of the cases the Commission has stated that impair-ment of investments made in expectation of the continuance of certain rates may be considered in rate cases, although it cannot be made con-trolling. In other cases the Commission has expressed doubt whether this sort of evidence can be considered at all.[11] It may be taken as settled that the Commission may not prevent the increase of low rates, even when their continuance is necessary to prevent the destruction of an industry which was led to invest capital upon the understanding, expressed or implied, that the low rates would continue.

OUT-OF-POCKET COSTS

In the preceding chapter it was pointed out that the Commission will not ordinarily approve rates on particular commodities which are below out-of-pocket costs. The same principle applies in connection with rates between particular points. As the Commission said in a case involving proposed reductions in rates to the Pacific Coast: "Carriers proposing re-duced rates are subject to the limitation . . . that they may not establish rates which will produce less than the out-of-pocket cost of rendering the transportation and thus unduly burden other traffic."[12]

An exception to this rule occurs when the Commission has approved or prescribed a comprehensive rate adjustment covering a large area and there may be a few specific movements on which the rates prove to be less than out-of-pocket costs when subjected to the usual type of cost analysis.[13] In fact, it is difficult to construct a comprehensive rate structure

---

[10] *Chattanooga Log Rates,* 35 ICC 163, 168 (1915). For similar statements see *1915 Western Rate Advance Case, Part II,* 37 ICC 114, 146 (1915); *Roanoke Railroad & Lumber Co.* v. *Norfolk Southern Ry. Co.,* 41 ICC 431, 433 (1916); *Crawford & Bunce* v. *Pittsburgh, Cincinnati, Chicago & St. Louis Ry. Co.,* 32 ICC 12, 14 (1914).

[11] *Duluth Log Rates,* 29 ICC 420, 421 (1914); *Mercantile Lumber Co.* v. *Illinois Central R. R. Co.,* 53 ICC 663, 666 (1914).

[12] *Reduced Commodity Rates to Pacific Coast,* 89 ICC 512, 530 (1924).

[13] *Wisconsin & Michigan S. S. Co.* v. *Grand Trunk Western R. Co.,* 323 ICC 298, 306 (1964); 325 ICC 244, 246 (1965).

on some commodities which would not produce some instances of this sort.

COST OF SERVICE

Although carriers may, under some conditions, reduce rates between particular points to out-of-pocket costs, the Commission cannot compel them to charge low rates to meet some competitive situation. Normal rates, of course, must cover more than out-of-pocket costs. For this reason, studies of the cost of transportation in a particular area, or on particular lines, or for particular movements are of value in determining reasonable rates. To require a precise adjustment of rates to costs, however, would be to ignore conditions of demand which must sometimes be recognized in any intelligent adjustment of rates. Practical considerations, furthermore, bar the attempt to adjust rates on particular hauls to costs because of the variations in costs that occur within a given area or on different parts of the same railroad. In deference to differences in transportation costs, branch-line rates are often higher than main-line rates, and rates on some sections of a line are sometimes higher than on others; but the courts have held that rates cannot be overthrown as confiscatory if unprofitable on a portion of the carrier's lines. In the words of the Supreme Court: "The company cannot claim the right to earn a net profit from every mile, section, or other part into which the road might be divided, nor attack as unjust a regulation which fixed a rate at which some such part would be unremunerative."[14]

RATE COMPARISONS

Most rate cases are decided without an analysis of cost of service in the absolute sense. Regulatory authorities rely on rate comparisons for the purpose of judging the reasonableness of rates between particular points, just as they do on particular articles. The rates in question are compared with rates for similar distances in the same or in different territories. Sometimes the comparisons are made directly. Sometimes they are reduced to earnings per ton-mile or per car-mile. But in all cases of this sort an attempt is made to judge the rate in question by comparing it with other rates which are set up, tentatively at least, as a standard. Comparisons of one sort or another are used in almost all rate cases. The validity of the comparison depends in large measure upon the similarity of operating and

---

[14] St. Louis & San Francisco Ry. Co. v. Gill, 156 U.S. 649, 665–66 (1895). See also *Puget Sound Traction Co.* v. *Reynolds,* 244 U.S. 574 (1917). The Commission has recognized this principle in numerous cases. *Billings Chamber of Commerce* v. *Chicago, Burlington & Quincy R. R. Co.,* 19 ICC 71, 75 (1910); *Louisville & Nashville R. R. Coal & Coke Rates,* 26 ICC 20, 30 (1913); *Wellington Mines Co.* v. *Colorado & Southern Ry. Co.,* 39 ICC 202, 205 (1916).

traffic conditions in the two areas. The greater the similarity, the greater the value of the comparison.

We may now turn to a consideration of the various cost factors which justify higher or lower rates on one haul than on another.

Distance

Obviously, one of the most important considerations affecting cost of service is the length of the haul. The cost of transportation necessarily increases with distance, although not in direct proportion. For this reason, rates for longer hauls should ordinarily exceed the rates for shorter ones. This accounts for the tendency of the Commission to adjust rates on a distance basis when confronted with a case which involves an entire rate structure. It will be recalled, however, that notwithstanding the extensive use of the distance principle, the Commission has approved the use of group and blanket rates which result in equal charges for distances varying by hundreds or even thousands of miles.[15] The Commission also per mits carriers to ignore differences in distance in meeting the competition of other carriers. The latter tendency is most easily observed in cases involving market competition.

Differences in Operating Conditions

Costs of operation for equal distances over different roads or over different parts of the same road may vary considerably as a result of differences in operating conditions. Frequently the existence of heavy grades and sharp curves makes operating expenses higher in one area than in another and justifies higher rates.[16] Sometimes the existence of numerous or expensive bridges between certain points justifies a difference in rates.[17] Heavy snows and extremely low temperatures in winter likewise increase operating expenses on certain lines.[18] Frequent rains causing washouts; an inadequate supply of fuel or water, which necessitates hauling for great distances; or, in brief, any unusual condition making for higher operating costs may justify higher rates.

Notwithstanding this principle, it is well to recall that in many rate cases the Commission is called upon to determine the reasonableness of rates over a large area and that it customarily makes rates with respect to

---

[15] Pp. 203–6, supra.

[16] E.g., *Railroad Commission of Arkansas* v. *Missouri & North Arkansas R. R. Co.*, 30 ICC 488 (1914); *American Asphalt Assoc.* v. *Uintah Ry. Co.*, 13 ICC 196 (1908); *Cedar Hill Coal & Coke Co.* v. *Colorado Southern Ry. Co.*, 16 ICC 387 (1909).

[17] *Knapp* v. *Big Sandy & Kentucky Ry. Co.*, 62 ICC 345 (1921); *Paducah Board of Trade* v. *Illinois Central R. R. Co.*, 37 ICC 719 (1916).

[18] *New England Lumber Rates*, 43 ICC 641 (1917); *Trimount Bituminous Products Co.* v. *Bangor & Aroostook R. Co.*, 304 ICC 513, 515–16 (1958).

the general transportation conditions in the area or region. The Commission sometimes prescribes a single level of rates on particular commodities which are to apply throughout the entire country or large parts of it.

Multiple-Line Hauls

A special circumstance affecting the cost of service is the number of separate rail lines over which a shipment must move between two points. The Interstate Commerce Commission very frequently permits rates on two-line hauls to be higher than for single-line hauls of equal length.[19] This is particularly true on low-grade commodities moving short distances. When the rates on such commodities are constructed on distance scales, it is not uncommon to have both a single-line scale and a joint-line scale.

The higher costs of joint-line hauls result from the extra switching and billing expense involved. Thus the extra cost incurred on a multiple-line shipment is akin to an extra terminal cost. Like terminal cost its importance diminishes as the length of the haul increases. For this reason the Commission has frequently held that a joint-line arbitrary or differential was not justified for hauls in excess of 500 miles.[20] In the various regional class-rate cases of the 1920s and 1930s the Commission abandoned the use of joint-line differentials or arbitraries in the construction of class rates. This was due partly to a desire to avoid the complications inherent in the system and partly to the fact that the supposed additional costs are not always incurred, or that similar switching and transfer expenses are often incurred on single-line shipments.[21]

Traffic Density

An important factor affecting the cost of particular hauls is traffic density. A large volume of traffic moving over a certain line or portion thereof, or in a certain area, justifies low rates. Conversely, lines or areas with sparse traffic may find it necessary to charge higher rates. A high traffic density reduces the unit cost of transportation, since there is more traffic over which constant operating and capital costs can be spread.

Perhaps the most striking examples of rate adjustments that recognized the effects of traffic density were the regional class-rate cases of the 1920s and early 1930s, in which the Commission differentiated between the areas having a high traffic density and those in which traffic was light.

---

[19] *Investigation of Alleged Unreasonable Rates on Meats*, 23 ICC 656 (1912); *Wichita Board of Trade v. Atchison, Topeka & Santa Fe Ry. Co.*, 25 ICC 625 (1913); *Anthracite Coal Investigation*, 104 ICC 514 (1926).

[20] *Oklahoma Corporation Commission v. Abilene & Southern Ry.*, 98 ICC 183, 248 (1925); *Pacific Guano & Fertilizer Co. v. Southern Pacific Co.*, 91 ICC 228 (1924); *Memphis-Southwestern Investigation*, 77 ICC 473, 516 (1923).

[21] *Southern Class Rate Investigation*, 100 ICC 513, 627 (1925); *Consolidated Southwestern Cases*, 123 ICC 203, 384 (1927).

A number of illustrations were pointed out in a previous chapter.[22] The same principle is recognized when the Commission authorizes arbitraries to be added for movements over short and weak lines. These lines usually have light traffic, and this accounts in large measure for their financial difficulties.[23] Differences in traffic density are recognized in the cases which permit higher rates to branch-line points than to points on main lines.[24]

Empty-Car Movement

The cost of moving traffic is often affected by the unbalanced character of the traffic. If the volume of traffic is greater in one direction than in the other, empty cars must be hauled back. Since these cars must be hauled anyway, it is proper for the carrier to reduce its rates in the direction of the empty-car movement. This practice was recognized as proper by the Commission very early in its history.[25]

SOME SPECIAL RATE COMPARISONS

We have seen that the reasonableness of rates on particular hauls is usually determined by rate comparisons. We have noted some of the factors which affect the cost of movement between particular points and which may justify higher or lower rates than are charged on other hauls. Some comparisons are more convincing than others. There are certain special rate comparisons which require mention because the rate relationships involved are so generally adhered to that they constitute distinct principles of rate making.

Rates in the Opposite Direction

Rates should ordinarily be the same in both directions. In one case the Commission said: "We have repeatedly said that where the transportation conditions affecting the movements in opposite directions between the same points are substantially similar there should be no material disparity in the rates."[26] Cases in which the Commission has required rates to be made the same in both directions are very numerous.[27] It should be care-

---

[22] Pp. 192–95, supra.

[23] *Southern Class Rate Investigation*, 100 ICC 513, 650–55 (1925); *Eastern Class-Rate Investigation*, 164 ICC 314, 422–24 (1930).

[24] E.g., *American National Live Stock Assoc. v. Southern Pacific Co.*, 26 ICC 37, 41 (1913); *Eastern Class-Rate Investigation*, 164 ICC 314, 405–6 (1930).

[25] *James & Abbott v. East Tennessee, Virginia, & Georgia R. R. Co.*, 3 ICC 225 (1889); *Schumacher Milling Co. v. Chicago, Rock Island & Pacific Ry. Co.*, 6 ICC 61, 70 (1892).

[26] *Rates to and from Nashville*, 61 ICC 308, 334 (1921).

[27] E.g., *Hayward Bros. Shoe Co. v. Chicago, Milwaukee & St. Paul Ry. Co.*, 93 ICC 243 (1924); *Parkersburg Rig & Reel Co. v. Union Pacific R. R. Co.*, 136 ICC 327 (1927); *Florida State Improvement Commission v. Atlantic Coast Line R. Co.*, 276 ICC 159, 162 (1949).

fully noted, however, that the rule is applied only when conditions are "substantially similar." There is no rule of law which requires the same rates in both directions. The general rule of the Commission is that any disparity in the rates in the two directions requires justification, at least if the difference in rates is considerable.[28] There are a number of special circumstances which justify higher rates in one direction than the other and which may be pointed out by the carrier in defense of its rates. The direct costs of transporting the goods in one direction may be higher than in the other. This is frequently due to the fact that movement in one direction may be upgrade, and downgrade in the other.[29] Empty-car movement, as already noted, may justify a difference in the rates.[30] If the particular commodity in question moves in large volume in one direction, while the movement in the other direction is sporadic and unusual, higher rates in the direction of sporadic movement are justified.[31] This is particularly true where commodity rates have been granted in one direction on account of the large volume of movement, while class rates are maintained in the other.[32] Sometimes competitive conditions depress the rate in one direction and not in the other.[33]

Rates Higher Than to a More Distant Point

The Commission holds that there is a presumption of unreasonableness if a rate exceeds rates to or from a more distant point on the same line. Section 4 of the Interstate Commerce Act prohibits higher charges for shorter than for longer hauls over the same line and in the same direction as a special form of unjust discrimination. But we are not referring here to unjust discrimination or to the prohibitions of Section 4 but to the policy of the Commission in determining the reasonableness of rates under Section 1. In the words of the Commission a greater charge for a shorter than for a longer haul over the same route is "prima facie unreasonable."[34] The Commission has many times required the reduction of rates under

---

[28] *New Bedford Board of Commerce* v. *Atlantic & West Point R. R. Co.*, 152 ICC 122, 124 (1929); *Garrett & Co.*, v. *New York Central R. R. Co.*, 112 ICC 519, 521 (1926); *Hyman-Michaels Co.* v. *Director General*, 80 ICC 703, 705 (1923).

[29] *Sonken-Galamba Corp.* v. *Chicago & Alton R. R. Co.*, 181 ICC 229, 247 (1932).

[30] This was mentioned in *Weil* v. *Pennsylvania R. R. Co.*, 11 ICC 627, 630 (1906).

[31] *Liggett & Myers Tobacco Co.* v. *Director General*, 58 ICC 196 (1920); *Meridian Cellulose Co.* v. *Director General*, 57 ICC 283 (1920); *Little Rock Freight Bureau* v. *Missouri Pacific Ry. Co.*, 51 ICC 23 (1918).

[32] *Parlin & Orendorff Co.* v. *Southern Pacific Co.*, 42 ICC 29 (1916); *King Bag Co.* v. *Louisville & Nashville R. Co.*, 274 ICC 87 (1949).

[33] *Murray Co.* v. *Alabama Great Southern R. R. Co.*, 168 ICC 795, 797 (1930); *National Automotive Fibres, Inc.* v. *Denver-Chicago Trucking Co., Inc.*, 67 MCC 70, 72 (1956); *Liquefied Petroleum Gas from Canada to Western Trunkline Territory*, 314 ICC 596 (1961).

[34] *Fulton Bag & Cotton Mills* v. *New York Central R. R. Co.*, 139 ICC 225, 227 (1928).

Section 1 because they exceeded rates to or from points beyond.[35] The holding of the Commission on this point seems to be dictated by the pronouncement of the United States Supreme Court in 1925 that: "Apart from statutory enactment it is *prima facie* unreasonable to charge more for a shorter than a longer haul."[36]

The significance of the phrase "prima facie" should not be overlooked in the above expressions. The phrase means that a presumption of unreasonableness is created by the higher charge for the shorter haul, but this presumption may be rebutted by the carrier. It throws the burden of proof upon the carrier to justify the anomalous rate adjustment. It would be absurd to hold that rates in excess of those to more distant points are necessarily unreasonable, for it may be that the low through rate is too low rather than that the intermediate rate is too high. But it is up to the carrier to find adequate justification for the apparent anomaly in the rate structure.

The presumption of unreasonableness attaching to the higher rate may be overcome by showing that the local rate is not unreasonable per se,[37] or that the through rate is less than a reasonable rate or is depressed by competition.[38] The latter point is easily established when it can be shown that the Commission has previously approved the rate relationship by granting the carrier authority to depart from the Long-and-Short-Haul Clause, that is, authority to maintain a lower through rate.[39]

The rule that higher rates for shorter than for longer hauls over the same route are prima facie unreasonable has been applied to motor-carrier rates as well as to rail rates.[40] This action has been approved by the courts.[41]

The Aggregate-of-Intermediates Rule

In an earlier chapter it was pointed out that distance rates are usually constructed on the tapering principle.[42] In other words, although rates usually increase with distance, the rate per mile is less for longer distances.

---

[35] Illustrations are *Southern Scrap Material Co.* v. *Louisville & Nashville R. R. Co.*, 140 ICC 573 (1928); *Schonthal Co.* v. *New York Central R. R. Co.*, 139 ICC 354 (1928); *Cardosi & Co.* v. *Baltimore & Ohio R. R. Co.*, 122 ICC 1 (1927).

[36] *Patterson* v. *Louisville & Nashville R. R. Co.*, 269 U.S. 1, 11.

[37] E.g., *Flaccus Oak Leather Co.* v. *New York, New Haven & Hartford R. R. Co.*, 147 ICC 135 (1928); *Forcum James Lumber & Cooperage Co.* v. *Illinois Central R. R. Co.*, 132 ICC 293 (1927).

[38] *Chicago Mica Co.* v. *Chicago & Eastern Illinois Ry. Co.*, 142 ICC 291 (1928).

[39] *Scharff-Koken Manufacturing Co.* v. *Atchison, Topeka & Santa Fe Ry. Co.*, 151 ICC 270, 278 (1929); *French Lick Springs Hotel Co.* v. *Chicago, Indianapolis & Louisville Ry. Co.*, 148 ICC 737, 739 (1928).

[40] E.g., *New England Motor Carrier Rates*, 8 MCC 287, 322–23 (1938); *Ford Motor Co.* v. *Standard Transportation Co.*, 62 MCC 311, 315 (1953).

[41] *Accelerated Transport–Pony Express, Inc.* v. *United States*, 227 Supp. 815 (1964).

[42] Pp. 188–90, supra.

If the tapering principle is justified, as is generally recognized, the charge for a haul of 500 miles should be less than the charge for two hauls of 250 miles each. It follows, therefore, that a through rate between two points should be less than the sum of the rates to and from an intermediate point. Although the Interstate Commerce Commission does not require a through rate to be less than the sum of the intermediate rates, there is a long-standing rule that through rates in excess of the aggregate of the intermediate rates are prima facie unreasonable. This principle found recognition in early reports of the Commission.[43] The rule is not an absolute one, as is indicated by the phrase "prima facie." The carrier may overcome the presumption of unreasonableness attaching to such rates.

Through rates which are higher than the aggregate of the intermediates not only fall under the Commission's condemnation as unreasonable under Section 1, but they are also specifically prohibited by a clause in Section 4 which provides that railroads may not charge "any greater compensation as a through rate than the aggregate of intermediate rates subject to the provisions of this Act." The Aggregate-of-Intermediates Clause was added to Section 4 by the Mann-Elkins Act of 1910. Relief may be granted from its provisions by the Commission in the same manner as from the long-and-short-haul provisions of the same section.

In 1931 Commissioner McManamy stated that the Commission had rarely granted relief from the aggregate-of-intermediates rule,[44] but his statement hardly holds good at the present time. There are numerous instances in which the presumption of unreasonableness attaching to a through rate in excess of the aggregate of intermediates has been overcome by showing the existence of competition which has depressed rates at intermediate points but which has not affected long-distance through rates. In such situations the Commission has frequently granted relief from the prohibitions of the Aggregate-of-Intermediates Clause of Section 4. The Commission has granted relief from the aggregate-of-intermediates rule when intermediate-point rates were depressed by water competition,[45] by motor-truck competition,[46] and even by market competition.[47] The Commission has said that two general principles are followed in granting relief from the aggregate-of-intermediates provision of the Act. First, the

---

[43] *Savannah Bureau of Freight* v. *Charleston & Savannah Ry. Co.*, 7 ICC 601, 609–10 (1898); *Hardenberg, Dolson & Gray* v. *Northern Pacific Ry. Co.*, 14 ICC 579 (1908).

[44] Dissenting opinion in *Western Salt Co.* v. *Atchison, Topeka & Santa Fe Ry. Co.*, 181 ICC 131, 133–34.

[45] *Printing Paper from Houston, Tex., to Chicago, Ill.*, 251 ICC 507 (1942); *Blackstrap Molasses from Louisiana Points*, 253 ICC 406 (1942).

[46] *Automobiles & Parts to Louisiana & Arkansas*, 211 ICC 323 (1935); *Automobiles & Chassis to Chicago, Ill.*, 215 ICC 495 (1936), 227 ICC 223 (1938); *Vegetables from Florida to Eastern Points*, 219 ICC 206 (1936).

[47] *Baker-Lockwood Mfg. Co.* v. *Alabama Great Southern R. R. Co.*, 198 ICC 401 (1934).

competition relied upon to differentiate the through traffic from that to and from intermediate points must exist at the intermediate points and not at the through point—or must exist in different degrees—and must be beyond the control of the carrier. Second, the rate adjustment must be appropriate to meet the competitive situation, and the competitive rate must not be lower than necessary to meet competition.[48] Under these conditions, departures from the aggregate-of-intermediates rule are logically justified. Any exceptions to the rule, however, may create situations in which some shippers, cognizant of the lower aggregate of intermediates, may defeat the higher through rate by shipping to an intermediate point and reshipping to destination, while other shippers, ignorant of this possibility, may pay the higher through rate. Such a situation would give one shipper an advantage over another and would amount to an unjust discrimination.

DEMAND FACTORS

We now turn to a consideration of factors affecting the demand for transportation service which may modify rates that are reasonable from the standpoint of absolute or relative cost of service.

Competition

It is important to examine the extent to which the reasonableness of rates is influenced by carrier competition.[49] In an earlier chapter it was pointed out that important modifications of the rate structure result from competition among carriers.[50] In the present chapter we have also noted that carriers may voluntarily maintain rates lower than may be prescribed by a commission.

The first point, then, that needs to be noted is that competition frequently causes carriers to establish rates below the normal or reasonable level. Such rates are less than maximum reasonable rates, but they are not necessarily so low as to be unreasonable. The Commission has many times recognized the right of carriers to reduce rates to meet competition if they so desire.[51] Two limitations, however, are placed upon this right: (1) The rates must be compensatory,[52] and (2) they must not give rise to undue

---

[48] *Cement from Metaline Falls, Wash.*, 274 ICC 28, 31 (1949). See also *Commodity Rates in Official Territory*, 209 ICC 702, 704–5 (1935); and *Automobiles & Parts to Louisiana & Arkansas*, 211 ICC 323, 325 (1935).

[49] Strictly speaking, carrier competition is not a value-of-service factor, since it relates not to the ability of traffic to stand a transportation charge, but to the ability of a particular carrier to charge a certain rate without diversion of the traffic to a rival.

[50] Pp. 198–203, supra.

[51] E.g., *La Salle Paper Co. v. Michigan Central R. R. Co.*, 16 ICC 149 (1909).

[52] See pp. 452–53, supra.

preference or prejudice under Section 3 of the Interstate Commerce Act.[53] In addition to these limitations it must be recognized that the Commission may intervene, when necessary, to prevent ruinous rate wars and to protect a rate structure found to be reasonable.[54] Notwithstanding these limitations, the railroads are free, to a considerable extent, to determine whether, for competitive reasons, they will charge rates for particular services which are lower than the basis which the Commission has found to be reasonable.

A second point relating to competition and reasonable rates is that a carrier cannot be compelled against its will to meet competition by reducing rates below a basis found reasonable. In the words of the Commission: "It is the privilege of a carrier, in its own interest, to meet . . . competition, but it is not the privilege of a shipper to demand less than normal rates because of the existence of a competition which the carrier in its own behalf does not choose to meet."[55] In many other cases the Commission has pointed out that in the absence of some unlawful discrimination, it will not undertake to require a carrier to meet competition.[56]

If carriers may meet competition but may not be compelled to do so, a third point seems to follow, namely, that rates dictated by competition are not a good standard for comparison in determining the reasonableness of rates. The Commission has often held that rates compelled by competitive conditions are not a measure of the reasonableness of other rates.[57]

We now come to consider a fourth and more difficult point relating to competition and the reasonableness of rates. May the Commission consider competitive conditions in determining what are maximum reasonable rates? Our previous discussion would imply that it could not. If it is for a carrier to determine whether or not it will meet competition, it would seem that the reasonableness of rates should be judged without reference to competitive conditions that may prevail. To make the rate necessary to meet competition a factor in prescribing maximum reasonable rates would be to require the carriers to meet competition, whether they wished to or not. In fact, the Commission has said: "In fixing maximum reasonable rates, competition is not a factor which we may take into consideration."[58] Regardless of such assertions, however, the competitive

---

[53] These limitations are concisely stated in *Grain Rates from Minnesota & Wisconsin*, 68 ICC 665, 672 (1922).

[54] See pp. 331–32, supra.

[55] *Cohen & Co.* v. *Mallory Steamship Co.*, 23 ICC 374, 377 (1912). See also *Lindsay Bros.* v. *Baltimore & Ohio Southwestern R. R. Co.*, 16 ICC 6, 8 (1909).

[56] E.g., *Iron Ore Rate Cases*, 41 ICC 181, 194 (1916).

[57] See *Boyle Commission Co.* v. *Chicago, Burlington & Quincy R. R. Co.*, 128 ICC 51 (1927); *Oxford Paper Co.* v. *Boston & Maine R. Co.*, 276 ICC 671, 672 (1950); *United States* v. *Oklahoma City-Ada-Atoka Ry. Co.*, 319 ICC 182 (1963).

[58] *Southern Class Rate Investigation*, 100 ICC 513, 611 (1925). See also *Wrought Pipe & Fittings*, 234 ICC 347, 402 (1939); *Bull Steamship Line* v. *Abilene & Southern Ry. Co.*, 251 ICC 475, 480 (1942).

situation is often considered by the Commission in fixing maximum reasonable rates, and the Commission admits this to be so. In the Western Trunk-Line Class-Rate Case the carriers contended that the Commission was without authority to consider motor-truck competition in determining maximum reasonable rail rates. The Commission rejected this contention, holding that truck operations "merely present another element to be given consideration and due weight in arriving at appropriate distance scales."[59] In another case the Commission said: "On many occasions we have given carrier competition controlling weight in determining the level of reasonable all-rail rates."[60] In recent years the Commission has found justification for this policy in the provisions of Section 15a which require it to consider the effect of rates on the movement of traffic as a factor in prescribing rates. Thus, if certain rates will not permit a commodity to move by rail because of the existence of lower rates by competing modes of transport—motor trucks or water carriers, for instance—the Commission may feel compelled to prescribe rates that will permit the traffic to move.[61] In 1941 the Commission prescribed lower rates on petroleum products from the Southwest to points in Western Trunk-Line Territory and Illinois than it had previously established. Its findings were based largely on the fact that lower rail rates were required if the traffic was to continue to move by rail.

Owing to the great changes that have taken place since we last passed upon the rates here under consideration, particularly those which affect the competitive situation, including the increase in the transportation of gasoline by pipe line and by water carriers, and the greatly increased production of crude oil in some parts of the destination territory, we find as a fact that the traffic cannot bear the rates today that were justified at that time. . . . Rates which were reasonable at that time have with the change in conditions ceased to be reasonable.[62]

Here, pipeline competition, water competition, and market competition all influenced the Commission's determination of maximum reasonable rates.

Were it not for the provisions of Section 15a requiring the Commission to consider the effect of rates on the movement of traffic, the legality of considering competition as a factor in setting maximum reasonable rates would be questionable. In *Baltimore & Ohio R. R. Co.* v. *United States*,[63]

---

[59] *Western Trunk-Line Class Rates,* 204 ICC 595, 658 (1934).

[60] *Sugar from Gulf Coast Port Groups to Northern Points,* 220 ICC 623, 642 (1937).

[61] See *Fresh Sea Food from and to the South,* 210 ICC 605, 613 (1935); *Sugar from Gulf Coast Port Groups to Northern Points,* 220 ICC 623, 643 (1937).

[62] *Petroleum Rail Shippers' Association* v. *Alton & Southern Railroad,* 243 ICC 589, 639.

[63] 22 F. Supp. 533 (1937).

Judge Learned Hand noted that certain reduced rates prescribed by the Commission on sugar were made on the theory that a reduction was necessary if the traffic was to move all-rail in competition with barge-rail and barge-truck routes. The Court said:

> Perhaps, the power does in fact exist to make competition control in a proper instance; if it does, it is a corollary of section 15a (2), as amended, which directs the Commission to consider whether rates will move the traffic, and the carriers' need of enough revenue to provide adequate service. In the exercise of that power possibly a rate may be lawfully reduced below what would otherwise be inherently reasonable, when the reduction results in a substantial profit which will strengthen the general resources of the carrier and so enable it to render better and cheaper public service.[64]

We must conclude that the Interstate Commerce Commission has in recent years found rates unreasonable which would not have been found unreasonable had it not been for some competitive situation which required low rates if the traffic was to move. It is probably a safe generalization to say that the more general and widespread the competitive influences, the more likely they are to affect the determination of maximum reasonable rates; while competition of a more limited character, applying to only a limited number of points, may not be allowed to affect the determination of maximum reasonable rates. In the latter situation the rule that "competition is not a factor to be taken into consideration in fixing maximum reasonable rates" tends to retain its force.

Commercial Necessities of Shippers

Almost any rate structure results in excluding would-be producers from a market, particularly if they suffer from some disadvantage of location, such as greater distance from market or high cost of production. It is important to know whether the commercial necessities of a shipper, group of shippers, or a locality can be invoked in an attempt to compel a carrier to reduce its rates. In general the answer is in the negative. A carrier may voluntarily reduce its rates below a normal level to enable shippers to reach a particular market, but it cannot be forced to do so by regulatory authorities. This question is constantly cropping up in cases before the Commission. The Commission has frequently said that it cannot measure the reasonableness of rates "by the commercial necessities of the shipper."[65] The same thought is expressed even more clearly where the Commission has said: "It is not the province of this Commission to prescribe rates to enable shippers to overcome their natural disadvantages

---

[64] Ibid., p. 536.

[65] E.g., in *Green v. Alabama & Vicksburg Ry. Co.*, 43 ICC 662, 676 (1917); *Peninsular Portland Cement Co. v. Director General*, 73 ICC 542, 544 (1922).

of location."⁶⁶ To hold otherwise "would lead to the conclusion that the differential burdens of production arising from natural disadvantages, distance from market, and other economic difficulties of all communities and industries should be neutralized and absorbed by the carriers which serve them."⁶⁷ If the Interstate Commerce Commission were required to adjust rates so as to give rival producers and producing areas a share of the market, it would be making the Commission a sort of economic dictator and would at once precipitate it into the midst of bitter sectional strife. This would embroil the Commission in political controversy and eventually destroy its effectiveness.

We have neither the inclination, the wisdom, nor the power to make or regulate rates for the purpose of determining whether goods shall be bought or sold, produced, manufactured, or consumed in one section or locality, or by one set of persons or another. Such has been the settled policy of the Commission from its creation in 1887 to the present day. We have other well-recognized standards by which the lawfulness of rates have been and are tested, and these standards concern themselves with transportation characteristics. When the standards are applied, the necessary and immediate effect may be to interject into an existing commercial situation new factors, important to those who produce or distribute, buy, or sell, and to their competitors; but such result is neither the cause nor end which has motivated our action.⁶⁸

In spite of these pronouncements of the Commission, decisions may be found in which it appears that the Commission has required a reduction of rates in order that certain groups of producers could reach common markets in competition with those enjoying lower freight rates, even though the rates found unreasonable were not high if strictly transportation conditions were considered.⁶⁹ In some of these cases the Commission has justified its action by pointing out that Section 15a requires it to consider the effect of rates on the movement of traffic.⁷⁰ Where market competition is involved, there may be a conflict between the doctrine that the commercial necessities of shippers are not a factor to be considered in prescribing maximum reasonable rates and the doctrine that the effect of

---

⁶⁶ *National Refining Co.* v. *Missouri Pacific Ry. Co.*, 24 ICC 315, 317 (1912). See also *East St. Louis Cotton Oil Co.* v. *St. Louis & San Francisco R. R. Co.*, 20 ICC 37, 41 (1910); *Baltimore Chamber of Commerce* v. *Baltimore & Ohio R. R. Co.*, 22 ICC 596, 603 (1912).

⁶⁷ *Railroad Commissioners of Montana* v. *Butte, Anaconda & Pacific Ry. Co.*, 31 ICC 641, 644 (1914).

⁶⁸ *Lake Cargo Coal from Kentucky, Tennessee, etc.*, 139 ICC 367, 391 (1928).

⁶⁹ See dissenting opinion of Commissioner Meyer in *Coke from Alabama & Tennessee to Central Territory*, 215 ICC 384, 387–88 (1936); also Commissioner Miller's dissent in *Sugar from Gulf Coast Port Groups to Northern Points*, 220 ICC 623, 644–45 (1937); and Commissioner Eastman's dissent in *State of Alabama* v. *New York Central R. R. Co.*, 235 ICC 255, 333–47 (1939).

⁷⁰ See *Sugar from Gulf Coast Port Groups to Northern Points*, 220 ICC 623, 643 (1937); *Commonwealth of Kentucky* v. *Illinois Central R. R. Co.*, 253 ICC 779, 787 (1942).

rates on the movement of traffic should be considered. As Commissioner Eastman observed in his dissenting opinion in the so-called "Southern Governors' Case": "Where market competition exists, no doubt a reduction in rates for the benefit of one competitor will normally promote the movement of his traffic"; but he went on to say: "I do not believe that we are justified in requiring reductions in rates on this account in disregard of transportation conditions and costs."[71]

The principle that the effect of rates on the movement of traffic should be considered in determining the reasonableness of rates should not be permitted to destroy or weaken the principle that the reasonableness of rates should not depend on the commercial necessities of shippers. Once the principle is established that low rates may be required in order to meet market competition, there is no end to the adjustments in rates that may be required to put producers in common markets. The result would be an enormous amount of wasteful transportation.

One order of the Commission was set aside by the courts on the ground that the Commission had required a reduction in rates in order to permit certain groups of producers to compete in a particular market.[72] The Hoch-Smith Resolution, with its injunction to consider the conditions of prosperity and depression and to adjust rates with a view to a "natural and proper" development of the country, may seem to require the Commission to temper rates to the commercial necessities of shippers and localities. But the pronouncement of a United States district court in the Anchor Coal Case holds to the contrary. "Congress certainly did not intend by this language," said the Court, "to create in the Commission an economic dictatorship over the various sections of the country, with power to kill or make alive."[73] The ruling of the United States Supreme Court in the Ann Arbor Case,[74] to the effect that the Hoch-Smith Resolution did not change existing law or render a rate unreasonable that was reasonable before its enactment, also points to the conclusion that the Resolution does not give the Commission power to adjust rates according to the commercial needs of shippers and localities.

Rates to Offset Locational Advantages

The Commission has denied the carriers the right to maintain high rates to offset the natural advantages of location of particular shippers or communities. "It has never been the view of the Commission that the prosperity of a shipper, a locality, or a state was a reasonable excuse for the imposition of rates conditioned on such prosperity."[75] Although carriers

---

[71] 235 ICC 255, 346 (1939).

[72] *Anchor Coal Co.* v. *United States*, 25 F. 2d 462 (1928).

[73] Ibid., p. 474.

[74] 281 U.S. 658 (1930).

[75] *Investigation of Advance in Rates on Grain*, 21 ICC 22, 35 (1911).

may sometimes maintain less than normal rates to offset disadvantages of location, they may not maintain rates to or from a given point on a higher level than is reasonable "in order to prevent one community from competing with another."[76]

PUBLIC WELFARE

In the preceding chapter we found that considerations of social welfare sometimes affect decisions regarding the reasonableness of rates on particular commodities. In determining the reasonableness of rates on particular hauls, the same thing is true. But here again it is probably true that the Commission is on uncertain ground and gives little weight to such factors. Yet the Commission has spoken approvingly of group rates, on the theory that they promote competition,[77]—a consideration which would seem to be beyond the scope of the Commission's authority. Comments have crept into other decisions of the Commission which indicate that social considerations may have influenced it. The Commission is on shaky ground when it relies on such factors to support its decisions.

SELECTED REFERENCES

Literature on the subject matter of this chapter is not very extensive. The best general discussions are M. B. Hammond, *Railway Rate Theories of the Interstate Commerce Commission* (Cambridge: Harvard University Press, 1911), pp. 70–169; and W. T. Jackman, *Economics of Transportation* (Chicago: A. W. Shaw Co., 1926), chaps. vi and vii. There is some pertinent matter in Edgar Watkins, *Watkins on Shippers and Carriers* (4th ed.; Atlanta: Harrison Co., 1930), parts of chap. iii; and in J. H. Aldredge, *Rate Making for Common Carriers* (Atlanta: Harrison Co., 1929). Many of the principles discussed in this chapter are considered by I. L. Sharfman in *The Interstate Commerce Commission*, Vol. III-B (New York: Commonwealth Fund, 1936), pp. 538–693, although his discussion treats also of cases arising under the undue-preference-and-prejudice provisions of the law. There is material relevant to this chapter in Glenn L. Shinn, *Reasonable Freight Rates* (Washington, D.C.: Traffic Service Corp., 1952); and in W. L. Grossman, "Principles of Carrier Rate Regulation," 26 *New York University Law Review* 475 (1951).

---

[76] *Indianapolis Freight Bureau* v. *Cleveland, Chicago, Cincinnati & St. Louis Ry. Co.,* 26 ICC 53, 58–59 (1913).

[77] *In re Transportation of Wool, Hides, and Pelts,* 23 ICC 151, 164 (1912).

Chapter 20

PERSONAL DISCRIMINATION

Personal discrimination, as that term is used in connection with common carriers, is the practice of charging different persons different rates for substantially the same service, or giving more or less service to one shipper (or receiver of freight) than to another for the same rate. In other words, it is treating shippers unequally in the matter of rates or service. The term ordinarily refers to discrimination between shippers in the same community and not to that between shippers in different communities.

REASONS FOR DISCRIMINATING

Personal discrimination is often the result of competition in an industry which is characterized by a large element of fixed or overhead costs. The carrier can afford to make a concession to a particular shipper if it thereby obtains traffic that would otherwise move over the lines of a competing carrier. This is because the expenses of the railroad are largely constant and will be increased but little by the additional traffic. What the carrier receives as compensation for carrying the traffic will be considered as "velvet." Competition, then, usually provides the motive for personal discrimination, and the peculiar nature of railroad expenses explains how wide the deviations from the normal rate may go in the effort to obtain traffic.

So common was the practice of personal discrimination before 1887 that it was sometimes said that only the unsophisticated paid the published rate. The rates published in the tariffs were but points of departure from which to begin the process of bargaining for special rates. It was not until the public became aroused over the evils of discrimination that legislation was enacted to put a stop to it. The Act of 1887 had this object definitely in view, but not until the law had been strengthened in many ways was the evil brought under control.

OBJECTIONS TO PERSONAL DISCRIMINATION

Personal discrimination is objectionable for a number of reasons. In the first place, it is inconsistent with the democratic ideal of a society com-

467

posed of individuals with equal rights and privileges. The courts have frequently referred to railroads as "public highways." If they are public, each citizen should have equal rights with every other citizen in their use. Former Commissioner Knapp justified the strict rule against personal discrimination in this manner: "The railroads are engaged in a public service, and that service should be impartially performed. They are . . . the purveyors of a public privilege which all are entitled to enjoy on the same terms. They should not be permitted to make differences between individuals on account of their position, their influence or the magnitude of their business. Neither official station, personal prominence nor patronage of unusual volume furnishes any just or defensible ground for giving one man cheaper conveyance than another."[1] The same reason for enforcing the rule of equal treatment was used by a federal court in 1883: "The defendant is a common carrier by rail. Its road, though owned by the corporation, was nevertheless constructed for public uses, and is, in a qualified sense, a public highway. Hence everybody constituting a part of the public, is entitled to an equal and impartial participation in the use of the facilities it is capable of affording."[2]

Personal discrimination is also objectionable because it destroys equality of opportunity in business. Margins of profits are so small in many lines of manufacture and trade that a slight discrimination in freight rates may destroy one man's business and build up that of another. Businessmen object to a practice which places the success or failure of their business at the mercy of a railroad official.

From a social point of view there is another objection to personal discrimination. It destroys the advantages which are supposed to accrue from an industrial society founded upon free enterprise and free competition. Success in business, we have just noted, will come to depend upon one's success in obtaining concessions from a carrier if personal discrimination is allowed. This means that success in business will not depend upon wise, efficient, and economical management. The inefficient and the high-cost producers may be the ones who obtain the special favors, while the efficient and the low-cost producers may be the ones forced out of business. The advantages of the competitive system are thereby lost, and goods are not produced under the most favorable conditions.

Another danger lurking in personal discrimination is the danger of monopoly. The favored industries are able to destroy their competitors and to establish a monopoly in their respective lines of business. Some of the early "trusts" in the United States obtained their monopoly position partly through favored treatment from railroad companies. The Commissioner of Corporations, in 1907, said of the oil trust: ". . . it would be

---

[1] "Government Regulation of Railroad Rates," 51 *Albany Law Journal* 151, 151–52 (1895).

[2] *Hays & Co.* v. *Pennsylvania Co.*, 22 *American Law Register* (New Ser.) 39, 40 (1883).

hardly too strong a statement to say that the railroad rebate was the cornerstone of the success of the Standard Oil combination."[3] A public which is alert to protect itself from the exactions of monopolies will endeavor to remove one of the important aids to their development.

Lastly, personal discrimination is a losing game for the railways themselves. One road may gain by the practice only if others adhere to the regular rates or grant smaller rebates. But one railroad can play the game as well as another; and when they are practically all engaged in the practice, no railroad gains, and all lose. The railroads have very often found themselves at the mercy of the corporations which they first aided by rebates. Many times these corporations were able to exact larger and larger concessions from the railroads by threat of diverting traffic to other lines or, as in the case of the Standard Oil Company, by threatening to build pipelines or other means of transportation of their own. This is why the railroads were themselves anxious to stop rebating and why they sponsored the enactment of the Elkins Act in 1903, which was wholly concerned with personal discrimination.[4] The enactment of legislation which checked the evil of personal discrimination added millions of dollars to the revenues of the carriers.

FORMS OF PERSONAL DISCRIMINATION

Personal discrimination may take so many different forms that it is impossible to enumerate them all. As one of the federal courts expressed it, ". . . discriminations and rebates have ever been sought to be hidden under the most subtle disguises."[5] This has been particularly true since legislation has stopped the simpler and more obvious forms. An enumeration, however, of some of the more common forms of personal discrimination will throw light on the extent of these practices and the difficulty encountered in eliminating them.

Departure from the Published Rate

The simplest form of personal discrimination is the granting of a concession from the published rate in favor of a particular shipper. It should not be understood, however, that all departures from the published rates are discriminations. If there is but one shipper of a certain article at a given point, a departure from the published rate is not a discrimination. There is no one to be discriminated against. If several shippers receive the same concession, there is no discrimination, since all are treated alike. But if one shipper receives a concession and others receive none or receive a

---

[3] *Report on the Petroleum Industry* (1907), p. 55. For another statement to the same effect see ibid., p. 66.

[4] Pp. 228–29, supra.

[5] *Vandalia Railroad Co.* v. *United States*, 226 Fed. 713, 716 (1915).

lesser concession, then there is discrimination. In the effort to prevent discrimination, all departures from the published rate are prohibited.

Bald disregard of published rates rarely occurs at the present time, but such evasion as failure to collect demurrage charges in strict accordance with detailed demurrage rules[6] or failure to observe strictly some limitation or restriction in the tariffs sometimes occurs.[7]

Rebates

One step removed from the simple concession is the rebate. A rebate is a refund of a portion of the rate paid in the first instance. The rebate conceals the fact that a concession has been granted, since the bill of lading and other shipping papers carry the regular charges.

Free Passes

A common form of discrimination in the past was the granting of free passes to shippers whom the company wished to favor. The free pass entitles the holder to transportation on regular passenger trains. The Hepburn Act of 1906 contained specific provisions designed to stop this form of discrimination, but it was not wholly successful. In 1913 the Interstate Commerce Commission made an investigation of the situation then existing in Colorado, where free passes were being given very extensively.[8] The carriers contended that the passes were not in violation of the law, since they were for intrastate journeys; but they were granted to interstate shippers and so fell under the prohibitions of the statute. The carriers were losing large amounts of revenue by the practice and expressed a desire to discontinue it, but they had been unable to do so for fear of offending shippers.

Underclassification

A common form of discrimination results from underclassification. If a shipper, with the connivance of the carrier, misrepresents the nature of shipments and thereby obtains a lower rate than should be charged, the practice is equivalent to direct rebating. In 1898 the westbound inspection bureau of the Trunk-Line railroads found 270,000 misrepresentations by shippers of the contents of packages shipped by rail.[9] These were not all

---

[6] See Appendix A in *Annual Reports* of the Interstate Commerce Commission for many years prior to 1956.

[7] Ibid.; see also *Powell* v. *United States*, 112 F. 2d 764 (1940); and *Boone* v. *United States*, 109 F. 2d 560 (1940).

[8] *The Colorado Free Pass Investigation*, 26 ICC 491.

[9] *Report of the Industrial Commission* (1900), Vol. IV, p. 675.

cases of willful favoritism. It is only when it is done with the knowledge and consent of the railroad or its agents that there is favoritism on the part of the carrier. Underclassification without the consent of the carrier, however, is fully as objectionable, not only because it deprives the carrier of its rightful revenue, but because it gives the dishonest shipper an advantage over the honest one.

False Billing

Another form of discrimination results from permitting the shipper to misrepresent the weight of a shipment or from permitting him to represent a shipment as entitled to a low export rate, or a proportional rate,[10] when it is not so entitled. Sometimes shipments are billed to a false destination but actually move to a different one, where a higher rate should be charged. False billing takes many forms, but the characteristic feature is some misrepresentation which enables the shipper to get a rate to which he is not entitled.[11]

Sudden Changes in Published Rates

One form of personal discrimination which conformed to the letter of the law was to change rates without notice or on very short notice. A few favored shippers would be informed of the change beforehand and would therefore be able to take advantage of it, while their less favored competitors could not. The terms "midnight tariffs" and "flying tariffs" have been used to describe this practice. The device was not wholly stopped by requiring 30 days' notice of changes in rates. The carrier could file notice of a reduction in rates and at the same time or shortly thereafter file notice of the restoration of the old rates. Although notice of the reduction had been properly made, it was likely that only the favored shippers would be aware of the reduction or of the subsequent increase and hence would be in a position to take advantage of the temporary reduction.[12] The power of the Commission to suspend proposed changes in rates enables it to prevent manipulations of this sort.

Excessive Payments for Supplies

Sometimes favoritism is practiced by excessive payments for supplies purchased by the railroad from industries which it serves. The Standard

---

[10] See p. 196, n. 50, supra, for one use of "proportional rates."

[11] For an interesting form of false billing, see *Annual Report* of the Commission for 1932, pp. 49–50.

[12] For an example see Stuart Daggett, *Principles of Inland Transportation* (4th ed.; New York: Harper, 1955), pp. 273–74.

Oil Company received favors in this way. The Commissioner of Corporations said in 1907 that the railroads in the United States paid $2 million per year more for oil than the fair market price because of purchases from the Standard Oil Company.[13] Other instances of the same type of favoritism have been brought to light by the Interstate Commerce Commission.[14]

False Claims

A form of discrimination difficult to detect is the payment of excessive claims for loss and damage. Instances of this practice are constantly appearing.[15] This form of personal discrimination has been particularly common in the fruit and vegetable trade.[16]

Low Rentals for Railroad Property Leased to Shippers

Discrimination has been practiced by the leasing of carrier-owned land for industrial sites or other purposes at extremely low or nominal rentals, sometimes accompanied by an agreement on the part of the shipper to route traffic over the lines of the owning railroads.[17] Discrimination has also taken the form of leasing warehouse space to shippers for storage purposes at rates which do not adequately compensate the carriers for the facilities provided.[18] Lease of locomotives or cars to shippers for intraplant use at less than adequate compensation has also occurred.[19]

Sale of Industrial Sites at Low Prices

Closely related to the lease of railroad-owned property at less than a fair rental is the sale of railroad-owned land to shippers for industrial sites, if sold at less than the fair value[20] or, in some cases, at less than cost to the railroad.

---

[13] *Report on the Petroleum Industry* (1907), Part II, pp. 66–67.

[14] *Reciprocity in Purchasing and Routing*, 188 ICC 417 (1932).

[15] For examples see *Annual Report* of the Commission for 1916, pp. 28–29.

[16] For evidence of this practice see Federal Trade Commission, *Fruits and Vegetables—Agricultural Income Inquiry*, 75th Cong., 1st Sess., Senate Doc. No. 17 (1937).

[17] *Leases and Grants by Carriers to Shippers*, 73 ICC 671 (1922); *Southern Ry.* v. *United States*, 186 F. Supp. 29 (1960).

[18] *Warehousing & Storage of Property by Carriers at the Port of New York*, 198 ICC 134 (1933), 216 ICC 291 (1936), 220 ICC 102 (1937); *Baltimore & Ohio R. R. Co.* v. *United States*, 305 U.S. 507 (1939). See also *Shaw Warehouse Co.* v. *Southern Ry. Co.*, 308 ICC 609 (1959); and *Southern Ry. Co.* v. *United States*, 186 F. Supp. 29 (1960).

[19] *Struthers Iron & Steel Co.—Terminal Services*, 277 ICC 653, 664 (1950).

[20] *United States* v. *Boston & Maine Railroad*, 157 F. Supp. 218 (1957); *United States* v. *General Motors Corp.*, 226 F. 2d 745 (1955).

Extension of Credit to Preferred Shippers

Extending credit to some shippers yet requiring others to pay freight charges in cash also is a form of favoritism that has been practiced.[21]

Allowances for Services or Property Furnished by Shipper

Discrimination may arise from the payment of allowances to shippers for services performed or for property furnished. If a shipper performs some service in connection with shipments that is ordinarily performed by the railroad company, a payment by the railroad to the shipper is wholly proper. Similarly, if the shipper furnishes cars or some other facility ordinarily furnished by carriers, an allowance to the shipper is not wrong. But if the allowance paid for the service or property is excessive, the effect is the same as if a rebate were paid. To avoid discrimination, the payment should not be more than the sum necessary to defray the costs of furnishing the service.

This type of discrimination has frequently arisen in connection with the use of privately owned freight cars. Many special types of freight cars, such as tank cars and refrigerator cars, are furnished by shippers, or by private-car companies which are sometimes controlled by the industries making use of the equipment.[22] Owners of refrigerator cars have sometimes received such generous allowances that the entire cost of the cars plus repairs and expenses of maintenance was repaid in two years.[23] This form of discrimination has been brought under control by vesting the Interstate Commerce Commission with power to determine the proper allowances which private-car owners should receive.[24] The task of prescribing such allowances is difficult, and some writers believe that discrimination of this type can never be removed completely so long as private cars remain in existence.[25]

Allowances to industrial railroads have also been a fruitful source of discrimination. An industrial railroad is one which is owned or controlled by an industry. It has been a very common practice for large manufactur-

---

[21] *United States* v. *Hocking Valley R. R. Co.*, 210 Fed. 735 (1914); *Moshassuck Valley Railroad Case*, 37 ICC 566 (1916).

[22] For an early example, see *Shamberg* v. *Delaware, Lackawanna & Western R. R. Co.*, 4 ICC 630 (1891).

[23] W. Z. Ripley, *Railroads: Rates and Regulation* (New York: Longmans, 1912), pp. 193–94.

[24] Leading cases involving allowances for private cars are *In the Matter of Private Cars*, 50 ICC 652 (1918); *Use of Privately Owned Refrigerator Cars*, 201 ICC 323 (1934); *Allowances for Privately Owned Tank Cars*, 258 ICC 371 (1944); *Mileage Allowances, Tank Cars*, 337 ICC 23 (1970). See also *General American Tank Car Corp.* v. *El Dorado Terminal Co.*, 308 U.S. 422 (1940).

[25] For a general discussion of the private-car problem see L. D. H. Weld, *Private Freight Cars and American Railways* (New York: Longmans, 1908).

ing concerns, like steel companies, to turn over the operation of the many miles of railroad track in and about their plants to a newly organized company which they control. Lumber companies having lines of railroad connecting their mills with regular railroads often organize their transportation system in the same way. The industrial railroad then becomes entitled to a switching charge for the service it performs or for a share in a through rate. Here there is no discrimination if the allowance or division of a joint rate is a proper one. But it is difficult to fix a just remuneration for the services of industrial railroads, and any excess allowance constitutes, in effect, a rebate to the industry owning the railroad. Two instances of gross favoritism resulting from industrial railroads were described by the Interstate Commerce Commission in 1904. The Illinois Northern Railroad Company, owned by the International Harvester Company, received a division of $12.00 per car on certain shipments when a reasonable allowance for the service would not have exceeded $3.50. A similar situation was found to exist because of allowances to the Chicago, Lake Shore & Eastern Railroad Company, owned by the United States Steel Corporation.[26]

In the Tap Line Case the Interstate Commerce Commission held that certain lumber tap lines were plant facilities and not common carriers and hence were not entitled to allowances out of a through rate.[27] The United States Supreme Court annulled the Commission's order on the ground that the tap lines were common carriers and were entitled to compensation.[28] The Court said, however, that it was not only within the power of the Commission, but its duty, to see that the divisions received by the tap lines were not such as to result in rebates to the industries which owned them. The Commission thereupon reopened the proceeding and attempted to deal with the problem by prescribing the divisions which the tap lines might receive out of through rates.[29] This, however, was not an entirely satisfactory manner of dealing with the problem.

A closely related form of discrimination is the payment of allowances to industries for performing switching and spotting services for the railroads serving their plants. The Commission has dealt with this problem by defining the service that the carrier may properly perform at terminals and for which it may pay allowances when the service is performed by industries.[30]

---

[26] *Re Divisions of Joint Rates,* 10 ICC 385 (1904). See also *Transportation of Salt from Hutchinson,* 10 ICC 1 (1904); and *The Industrial Railways Case,* 29 ICC 212 (1924), and 34 ICC 596 (1915).

[27] 23 ICC 277 (1912).

[28] 234 U.S. 1 (1914).

[29] 31 ICC 490 (1914).

[30] *Propriety of Operating Practices—Terminal Services,* 209 ICC 11 (1935). The Commission's action was upheld by the courts. *United States* v. *American Sheet & Tin Plate Co.,* 301 U.S. 402 (1937); *United States* v. *Wabash R. R. Co.,* 321 U.S. 403 (1944).

DISCRIMINATORY TARIFF RATES

Personal discrimination does not always take the form of rebates or more subtle deviations from published rates. Sometimes the rates published in the tariffs, because of their restrictions or the terms of their application, have the effect of discriminating against some shippers and favoring others. Certain kinds of rates which raise the question of possible discrimination among shippers will now be considered.

Rates Varying with the Use of a Commodity

We have elsewhere pointed out that different rates on the same commodity depending on its use have been considered unreasonable under Section 1 of the Act.[31] Such rates may also constitute unjust discrimination. In an early case the Commission condemned a rate on coal for railroad use which was lower than that applicable on other coal.[32] In a more recent case the Commission held that it constituted unjust discrimination to maintain a lower rate on bituminous coal to be used for coking purposes than when it was to be used otherwise.[33]

Rates Based on Size of Shipment

Differences in rates based on the size of a shipment may or may not be unjustly discriminatory. Lower rates on carloads than on less-carloads were early approved by the Commission, in spite of the contention that they favored large shippers and worked to the disadvantage of small shippers.[34]

Approval of lower carload rates has been based partly on recognized differences in costs of transportation and partly on the fact that the carload is a small enough unit to be used by fairly small shippers. Although the Commission early approved of lower carload rates, it refused for a long time to require them. As late as 1910 the Commission said that it had never required the establishment of carload rates.[35] In later years, however, the Commission has often found any-quantity rates unreasonable when applied on carloads, thus in effect requiring the establishment of lower carload rates.[36]

If lower rates on carloads than on less-carloads are justified on the basis

---

[31] P. 442, supra.

[32] *Capital City Gas Co.* v. *Central Vermont Ry. Co.,* 11 ICC 104 (1905). See also *In the Matter of Restricted Rates,* 20 ICC 426 (1911); *Interstate Commerce Commission* v. *Baltimore & Ohio R. R. Co.,* 225 U.S. 326 (1912).

[33] *Ex-River Coal from Mount Vernon, Ind., to Chicago,* 294 ICC 233 (1953).

[34] *Thurber* v. *New York Central & Hudson River R. R. Co.,* 3 ICC 473 (1890).

[35] *Commercial Club of Omaha* v. *Baltimore & Ohio R. R. Co.,* 19 ICC 397, 401.

[36] E.g., *Auto Vehicle Co.* v. *Chicago, Milwaukee & St. Paul Ry. Co.,* 21 ICC 286 (1911); *In re Transportation of Wool, Hides & Pelts,* 23 ICC 151, 168–69 (1912).

of lower costs of providing the service, lower rates on trainload lots, or multiple-car lots, than on single carloads can be justified in the same way. For many years, however, the Commission considered such rates discriminatory, largely because they could be used by only a few shippers.[37] Loss of traffic to water carriers and pipelines finally resulted in efforts by the railroads to recover such traffic by the establishment of "cargo" rates, that is, low rates applying only on multiple-car shipments. In 1939, the Interstate Commerce Commission allowed multiple-carload rates to go into effect on blackstrap molasses in tank cars from New Orleans, Louisiana, to Peoria, Illinois. The rates authorized were 15 cents per hundred pounds on a minimum of 1,800 tons, the equivalent of about 38 cars, as compared with a rate of 17.5 cents in carload lots.[38] Multiple-car rates have been established in numerous other instances.[39]

It is obvious that a proper spread should be maintained between carload rates and multiple-car rates. When the spread only reflects differences in the cost of providing the service the difference can hardly be considered unduly favorable to the large shipper. Even if the spread is greater than can be justified on a cost-of-service basis, it would hardly constitute an undue preference to the large shipper if competition, such as from a barge line, is encountered on volume shipments and not on carload shipments. This is because refusal of reduced multiple-car rates still permits the large shipper to obtain the lower rate by resorting to the other mode of transport. Although the principles underlying the spread between carload and multiple-car rates do not seem to have been spelled out by the Commission, the Commission has frequently disapproved of multiple-car rates when it considered the spread unjustified.[40] In numerous instances multiple-car rates have been approved on the basis of approximately 85 percent of the corresponding carload rates.

An extension of the multiple-carload principle is the train-load rate, usually associated with "unit trains," i.e., trains consisting of permanently coupled cars and operated as a unit. Since the train consists of a single shipment moving from one origin to one destination, it does not require the switching involved in assembling shipments from numerous origins for various destinations. Cost savings make lower rates possible for such movements. Although they work to the advantage of the large shipper or consignee, they can hardly be condemned as unjustly discriminatory if

---

[37] *Paine Bros. & Co.* v. *Lehigh Valley R. R. Co.*, 7 ICC 218 (1897); *Woodward-Bennett Co.* v. *San Pedro, Los Angeles & Salt Lake R. R. Co.*, 29 ICC 664 (1914); *Miller & Lux, Inc.* v. *Southern Pacific Co.*, 41 ICC 617 (1916).

[38] *Molasses from New Orleans, La., to Peoria & Pekin, Ill.*, 235 ICC 485 (1939).

[39] E.g., *Eastern Coal to Chicago, Ill.*, 306 ICC 195 (1959); *Soybean Oil, 40 Tank Car Lots from Iowa to Hammond, Ind.*, 309 ICC 663 (1960); *Multiple-Car Rates on Cement, Evansville, Pa., to New Jersey*, 315 ICC 672 (1962).

[40] E.g., *Limestone to Baton Rouge*, 270 ICC 584 (1948); *Petroleum Products from Salt Lake City to Spokane*, 273 ICC 736 (1949); *Oystershells from Mobile, Ala., to St. Louis, Mo.*, 299 ICC 409 (1956).

the differences in rates are related to the differences in transportation costs. They may also be justified, even with greater rate spreads, on movements that are vulnerable to diversion to a cheaper mode of transport—pipelines or barge lines.

Annual Volume Rates

An arrangement whereby lower rates are granted to shippers offering the carrier a large volume of freight during the year, or other period of time, is ordinarily considered an unjust discrimination against small shippers. Such arrangements were held unlawful before the enactment of the Act to Regulate Commerce.[41] The practice has also been held in numerous cases to be contrary to the provisions of Section 2 of the Interstate Commerce Act. "The fact that one man is a large shipper and another a small shipper does not entitle the carrier to make a difference in the rate, if the property carried in each case is of the same class, and the distance and route is the same."[42] In a very early case the Commission condemned the practice of allowing a discount in the rates on coal to consignees who received not less than 30,000 tons of coal within a year.[43] Reduced rates on shipments of books and drugs which applied only when the consignee had received 150,000 pounds or more of freight in the three preceding calendar months were found discriminatory in recent times.[44] Discounts or reduced rates to large shippers are not ordinarily justified, since the cost of transporting a shipment of a given size is not reduced by the fact that over a period of time the shipper furnishes the carrier with more of such shipments than another does.

What appears to be a departure from the long-established policy of not permitting rates dependent upon the amount of traffic furnished by a shipper or consignee over a period of time occurred in 1959. Division 2 of the Commission approved the establishment of lower rates on bituminous fine coal by the Pocahontas lines to consignees at certain destinations who had received at least 1.5 million tons of coal during a 12-month period preceding.[45] The proposed rates were 35 cents a ton lower than the regular rates and were intended to benefit an electric power company which was considering the establishment of a generating plant nearer the mines, substituting the transmission of electrical energy for the transportation of

---

[41] *Burlington, Cedar Rapids & Northern Ry. Co.* v. *Northwestern Fuel Co.*, 31 Fed. 652 (1887).

[42] *United States* v. *Tozer*, 39 Fed. 369, 371–72 (1889).

[43] *Providence Coal Co.* v. *Providence & Worcester R. R. Co.*, 1 ICC 107 (1887).

[44] *Books, Drugs, & Cotton Goods, New York to Chicago*, 256 ICC 85 (1943). See also *Forwarder Rates Conditioned upon Aggregates of Tonnage*, 258 ICC 635 (1944). See also *Wheat & Wheat Flour, Westbound*, 337 ICC 858 (1971), where the Commission approved certain reduced rates on wheat and flour but required removal of an annual volume restriction.

[45] *Coal—Kentucky, Virginia, and West Virginia to Virginia*, 308 ICC 99 (1959).

coal. The Commission noted that the proposed rates would not result in unjust discrimination since the other receivers of coal at these destinations who would pay the higher rates were not in competition with the public utility company. Commissioner Winchell, however, took the position that the proposed rates were in violation of Section 2 with its prohibition of different rates for like and contemporaneous services.

In another case the Commission approved lower rates on coal from coal-producing areas in the East to the New York Harbor area which were conditioned on annual receipts by consignees of from 500,000 to 5,500,000 tons depending on the destination.[46] The reduced rates were designed to meet the competition of residual fuel oil, mostly imported, in the generation of electricity. There were no competing purchasers of coal at these destinations, hence no injury was suffered by those unable to avail themselves of the low rates for volume users.

Rates subject to annual volume minima were also approved for "unit train" movements of coal from Lynnville, Indiana, to Hammond, Indiana, over an interstate route.[47] The service differed from conventional coal movements and was more economical, hence lower rates were justified. The Commission also noted that there were no shippers or receivers of coal disadvantaged by the lower annual volume rates. The purpose of the reduced rates was to enable coal to compete with natural gas in the generation of electric power.

Examination of the cases described above reveals that the prescription of annual minimum tonnages was a means of selecting out potential traffic movements that would take place only if special rates were provided to meet an unusual competitive situation. In all of the cases, furthermore, either the service provided under the rates was different from that provided at the regular rates, thus justifying a difference in the rates; or the absence of competing shippers or receivers of the commodity at the same points meant that no one was disadvantaged by the rates in question. The special circumstances under which rates of this sort have been approved should be borne in mind.

Guaranteed Rates

The term "guaranteed rates" refers to rates conditioned on an agreement or understanding that the shipper will send all or a certain proportion of his traffic via a carrier or group of carriers. Rates of this type are sometimes called "contract rates" or "agreed rates," the latter term commonly used in Canada where such rates have been legalized.

Rates of this type raise the question of personal discrimination since

---

[46] *Coal to New York Harbor Area*, 311 ICC 355 (1960).

[47] *Natural Gas Pipeline Co. of America v. New York Central R. Co.*, 323 ICC 74 (1964).

they constitute a preferential rate given to shippers who contract to ship all or a certain portion of their traffic by the carrier offering the rate. Shippers who are unwilling to surrender their freedom to ship via any carrier are required to pay higher rates.

The legality of such rates came before the Commission in 1961 in a case involving rates on rugs and carpeting. The New York Central Railroad proposed to establish reduced rates on these articles in carloads from Amsterdam, New York, to Chicago when the shipper executed a contract agreeing to ship at least 80 percent of his Amsterdam-Chicago traffic over the New York Central for a period of one year. The Commission found the rates unlawful, holding that they constituted a destructive competitive practice.[48] The Commission's decision was upheld by the courts.[49] The Commission deemed it unnecessary to consider whether the rates created an unjust discrimination under Section 2 of the Act or undue preference and prejudice under Section 3, although Commissioner Murphy would have found that the rates violated both of these sections. Whether rates conditioned on guaranteeing all or a certain percent of a shipper's traffic constitute a form of unlawful discrimination under the Interstate Commerce Act has therefore not been determined. Rates of this nature have been used by steamship companies for many years. They were ultimately found to be a form of discrimination made unlawful by the Shipping Act of 1916, but they were later legalized by an Act of Congress.[50]

The precedent established in the rug and carpeting case was later followed by the Interstate Commerce Commission in a case in which certain railroads proposed a lower rate on steel and wrought iron pipe and tubing from Sault Ste. Marie, Ontario, to Chicago, conditioned upon the shipment over the railroads involved of 90 percent of the shippers' tonnage moving between these points over a period of 12 months.[51]

LEGISLATION AGAINST PERSONAL DISCRIMINATION

A common-law rule against unequal treatment of shippers existed in the United States as early as 1863,[52] but statutory provisions designed to deal with the problem have occupied a prominent place in regulatory legislation. It is desirable to summarize the more important provisions of the Interstate Commerce Act and related acts which have been aimed at this abuse.

---

[48] *Contract Rates, Rugs and Carpeting from Amsterdam, N.Y., to Chicago,* 313 ICC 247 (1961).

[49] *New York Central R. Co.* v. *United States & Interstate Commerce Commission,* 194 F. Supp. 947 (1961); affirmed 368 U.S. 349 (1962).

[50] See Chapter 32.

[51] *Guaranteed Rates, Sault Ste. Marie, Ontario, to Chicago,* 315 ICC 311 (1961).

[52] Benjamin M. Kline, "The Origin of the Rule against Unjust Discrimination," 66 *University of Pennsylvania Law Review* 123 (1918).

General Prohibitions of Discrimination

Sections 2 and 3 of the Interstate Commerce Act contain broad prohibitions designed to cover all forms of personal favoritism practiced by railroad companies. Section 2 forbids railroads to exact a greater or less compensation from one person than from another for a like and contemporaneous service. Section 3 prohibits undue preference or advantage and any undue prejudice or disadvantage.[53]

Publication of Rates Required

Section 6 of the Interstate Commerce Act requires all rates and fares to be filed with the Commission and obligates the carrier to keep open to public inspection schedules showing its rates and fares. Publicity of rates and fares is the first essential in any attempt to enforce uniformity of charges for the same service. The tariffs must show any special services, privileges, or facilities provided under the published rates.[54]

Notification of Changes in Rates and Fares

No changes may be made in rates and fares except upon 30 days' notice to the Commission and to the public. This provision, coupled with the power to suspend proposed changes in rates, enables the Commission to prevent discrimination through sudden changes in rates for the benefit of preferred shippers.

Adherence to Published Rates Required

Strict adherence to the published rates is required by Section 6 of the Interstate Commerce Act and by the Elkins Act. All deviations, in the form of rebates or otherwise, are forbidden. Section 6 provides that no carrier shall "charge or demand or collect or receive a greater or less or different compensation for such transportation . . . than the rates, fares, and charges which are specified in the tariff filed and in effect at the time." The phrase "different compensation" is to prevent the payment of charges in services or goods, the overvaluation of which might easily lead to discrimination. It has been held contrary to this section for a railroad company to purchase advertising space in a periodical at the regular price and pay for the same by selling transportation at the regular rate.[55] It has also

---

[53] See p. 225, supra.

[54] *Chicago & Alton R. R. Co.* v. *Kirby*, 225 U.S. 155 (1912); *United States* v. *Union Pacific R. R.*, 173 F. Supp. 397 (1959).

[55] *Chicago, Indianapolis & Louisville Ry. Co.* v. *United States*, 219 U.S. 486 (1911).

been held a violation of Section 6 for a carrier to accept promissory notes of a shipper in settlement of freight charges.[56] Payments must be made in cash.[57] The law is very strict in requiring adherence to published rates, even though no discrimination results from the departure. The published rate is the only legal rate. Even if there is a manifest error in the tariff, the published rate, and that alone, must be paid.[58] In one case the Interstate Commerce Commission required adherence to a rate of 1 cent per hundred pounds when a rate of 19 cents was clearly intended.[59] To hold otherwise would open the door to discrimination by making it possible for the carriers to make convenient "errors" in their tariffs. Not only must the regular rate be paid on each shipment, but payments by a railroad company of lump sums to shippers in return for a promise to locate their plants on and route traffic over its lines are held to be departures from the published rate.[60] Likewise a loan of money to a shipper at less than the market rate by a railroad company or companies affiliated with it was held to be rebating.[61] The strictness with which the law requires observance of the published rates is shown by cases in which the railroad is permitted to recover additional charges from a shipper who has paid the freight bill presented to him, and the railroad has later discovered an error in the calculation of the charges.[62] The carrier can collect in such instances even if it results in loss to the shipper, who may have sold the goods at a price that was based on cost plus the freight originally paid. The same rule applies when the shipper, relying upon a carrier's statement of a published rate, enters into a transaction for the purchase and sale of goods but later finds that owing to an erroneous statement of the applicable rate he must pay a higher rate than that on which his calculations were based.[63] To prevent misstatements of applicable rates, the Mann-Elkins Act of 1910 provided that upon written request the railroads must furnish written statements of the rates applicable on described shipments. Failure to do this, or erroneous quotation of the rates, made them liable for a penalty of $250 for each offense. These requirements were repealed, however, by the Transportation Act of 1940. The reason why erroneous quotation of a rate by the carrier does not relieve the shipper of the obligation to pay the

---

[56] *United States* v. *Hocking Valley R. R. Co.*, 194 Fed. 234 (1911).

[57] Checks are held to be payments in cash. *Fullerton Lumber Co.* v. *Chicago, Milwaukee & St. Paul R. R. Co.*, 282 U.S. 520 (1931).

[58] *Tobin Packing Co., Inc.* v. *Baltimore & Ohio R. Co.*, 299 ICC 221 (1956); *Armour & Co.* v. *Atchison, Topeka & Santa Fe Ry. Co.*, 254 F. 2d 719 (1958).

[59] *Ryan Co.* v. *Missouri Pacific R. R. Co.*, 177 ICC 348 (1931).

[60] See *United States* v. *Union Stock Yard & Transit Co.*, 226 U.S. 286 (1912).

[61] *Vandalia R. R. Co.* v. *United States*, 226 Fed. 713 (1915).

[62] *Pittsburgh, Cincinnati, Chicago & St. Louis Ry. Co.* v. *Fink*, 250 U.S. 577 (1919).

[63] *A. J. Poor Grain Co.* v. *Chicago, Burlington & Quincy R. R. Co.*, 12 ICC 418 (1907). See also *Texas & Pacific Ry. Co.* v. *Mugg*, 202 U.S. 242 (1906); *Pettibone* v. *Richardson*, 126 F. 2d 969 (1942).

correct rate is because the contrary rule would enable railroads to favor shippers by intentional misquotations of rates.

Antipass Legislation

The Interstate Commerce Act prohibits the granting of free passes except to certain specified classes of individuals,[64] a measure which is designed to stop this common form of discrimination.

Restrictions on Extension of Credit to Shippers

Paragraph 2 of Section 3 of the Interstate Commerce Act is designed to prevent discrimination through the extension of credit to shippers by railroad companies. The section prohibits railroads from delivering shipments at destination until all transportation charges have been paid, except under such rules and regulations as the Commission may prescribe.[65]

Obtaining Lower Rates by False Billing, etc., Prohibited

Section 10 of the Act provides penalties for shippers who obtain or attempt to obtain transportation at less than the published rates by false billing, false classification, false weighing, and other devices.

Solicitation of Rebates Unlawful

The Elkins Act and Section 10 of the Interstate Commerce Act prohibit the solicitation of rebates and concessions by shippers, or the offering of rebates or concessions by a carrier.

Commodities Clause

The provisions of the Commodities Clause have elsewhere been described.[66] This clause, it will be recalled, prohibits railroad companies from transporting in interstate commerce commodities which they themselves have produced or which they own. The provision was designed to prevent the type of discrimination which is almost certain to develop if carriers are free to manufacture or deal in products which they also transport

---

[64] More fully described, p. 231, supra.

[65] Regulations were prescribed in *Regulations for Payment of Rates and Charges,* 57 ICC 591 (1920). They have been subsequently modified in 171 ICC 268 (1931); 273 ICC 681 (1949); 310 ICC 391 (1960); 313 ICC 97 (1960); and 326 ICC 483 (1966).

[66] P. 232, supra.

for others. Discrimination resulting from such activities of railroad companies had been strongly condemned by the courts before the enactment of the Commodities Clause.[67]

The clause has had the effect of preventing railroads from engaging in manufacturing, mining, and other activities in competition with independent producers served by their lines. The effectiveness of the Commodities Clause has been weakened, however, by court decisions. In 1909 the Supreme Court held that the ownership of stock in a mining company by a railroad company does not give the railroad a legal interest in the commodity mined by the producing corporation such as to come within the prohibitions of the Commodities Clause,[68] although the Court later held that when control of a producing company by a railroad company was so complete that the former was treated as a mere agency or department of the owning railroad, the prohibitions of the Commodities Clause applied.[69] The courts have applied the same principle to situations in which a railroad company and producing companies are controlled by a holding company. Thus in *United States* v. *Elgin, Joliet & Eastern Railway Co.*, the Court found no violation of the Commodities Clause in the transportation of the products of several subsidiaries of the United States Steel Corporation by the Elgin, Joliet & Eastern Railway Company, also controlled by the United States Steel Corporation.[70] The same rule was reaffirmed and followed in *United States* v. *South Buffalo Railway Co.*,[71] where transportation by the South Buffalo Railway Company of commodities produced by the Bethlehem Steel Company was found not in violation of the Commodities Clause, although the stock of the railway company was substantially all owned by the Bethlehem Steel Corporation, which also owned the stock of the Bethlehem Steel Company.[72]

Considerable sentiment has developed for repeal of the Commodities Clause. It is evident, however, that if this is done the sort of discrimination which originally gave rise to its enactment might easily return. In fact, the development of railroad "conglomerates," that is, holding companies controlling a railroad and a number of noncarrier business enterprises, creates a situation in which the type of discrimination sought to be remedied by the Commodities Clause may become more prevalent.

---

[67] *New York, New Haven & Hartford R. Co.* v. *Interstate Commerce Commission*, 200 U.S. 361 (1906).

[68] *United States* v. *Delaware & Hudson Co.*, 213 U.S. 366.

[69] *United States* v. *Lehigh Valley R. R. Co.*, 220 U.S. 257 (1911); *United States* v. *Delaware, Lackawanna & Western R. R. Co.*, 238 U.S. 516 (1915); *United States* v *Reading Co.*, 253 U.S. 26 (1920).

[70] 298 U.S. 492 (1936).

[71] 333 U.S. 771 (1948).

[72] For comments of the Interstate Commerce Commission on the court decisions relating to the Commodities Clause, see *Chesapeake & Ohio Ry. Co. Construction*, 261 ICC 655, 666–68 (1946).

DOES CARRIER COMPETITION JUSTIFY UNEQUAL TREATMENT OF SHIPPERS?

Section 2 of the Act requires equal treatment of shippers for like services performed "under substantially similar circumstances and conditions." The question arises whether differences in competitive conditions create a dissimilarity of circumstances and conditions that justifies a difference in rates. For a long time it was considered that this question had been settled by the 1897 decision of the Supreme Court in *Wight* v. *United States.*[73]

The circumstances of the case were as follows: Mr. F. H. Bruening was a wholesale dealer in beer in Pittsburgh, purchasing his beer in Cincinnati and shipping it by rail to Pittsburgh. His place of business had a siding connection with the Pittsburgh, Cincinnati & St. Louis Railroad, known as the "Pan-Handle." The Pan-Handle could thus deliver shipments of beer at Mr. Bruening's warehouse. The Baltimore & Ohio Railroad also had lines from Cincinnati to Pittsburgh and wished to carry Mr. Bruening's beer. The rate by both roads was 15 cents per hundred pounds, but the Baltimore & Ohio could not deliver beer to Mr. Bruening's warehouse, as there was no siding connection. In order to meet the competition of the Pan-Handle, the Baltimore & Ohio offered to truck the beer from its station to Bruening's warehouse. This was done; but later, after the railroad had found the cost of trucking the beer to be $3\frac{1}{2}$ cents per hundred pounds, it arranged for Mr. Bruening to do the trucking in return for an allowance of $3\frac{1}{2}$ cents from the published rate. Another beer dealer, Mr. Henry Wolf, also shipped beer from Cincinnati to Pittsburgh. He did not have a siding connection with either railroad. He asked for a rebate but was refused one, since he would have to truck his shipments regardless of the road over which they moved. Thus competition forced the Baltimore & Ohio to give a rebate (or trucking service) in order to get Bruening's shipments, but competition did not force it to give a similar rebate to Mr. Wolf. It was contended by the railroad that since it was necessary for it to offer this inducement to Mr. Bruening and not necessary to make a like offer to Wolf, the traffic in the two situations was not handled "under substantially similar circumstances and conditions" and was therefore not in violation of Section 2 of the Interstate Commerce Act. But the Court held that competition did not justify unequal treatment of shippers and that the phrase "under substantially similar circumstances and conditions" referred to the matter of carriage and did not include competition.[74]

To avoid confusion in our later treatment of discrimination between places covered by Section 3 of the Act, it should be pointed out that, although, according to the Wight case, competition does not justify un-

---

[73] 167 U.S. 512.

[74] For application of the principle to a different set of facts see *Seaboard Air Line Ry. Co.* v. *United States,* 254 U.S. 57 (1920).

equal treatment of persons under Section 2, a different rule is followed under Section 3 with its prohibition of "undue preference and prejudice."

The principle of the Wight case in interpreting Section 2 was reaffirmed in a 1920 decision of the Supreme Court. Here, the Court, in referring to the Wight case and others said: "The principle established in these cases is that the statute aims to establish equality of rights among shippers for carriage under substantially similar circumstances and conditions, and that the exigencies of competition do not justify discrimination against shippers for substantially like services."[75] As late as 1968 the Commission reasserted adherence to the principle of the Wight case saying that elements of market competition and carrier competition "are not of any significance whatsoever in determining a case of 'unjust discrimination' under section 2 or its counterpart in section 216(d)."[76]

Notwithstanding emphatic assertions that competition cannot justify a discrimination against persons under Section 2, there are numerous cases in which Section 2 has been less rigidly interpreted and in which competitive circumstances have apparently been found to justify discriminatory rates. This has been particularly true in recent years.[77] The matter was discussed in a 1968 decision where the Commission, after referring to some early court decisions and recent Commission decisions, said: "From the foregoing it is clear that both the courts and the Commission have found that competition and volume of movement can create a dissimilarity in the circumstances and conditions underlying a particular movement of traffic" and that such dissimilarity may be sufficient to preclude a finding of violation of Section 2.[78]

A Circuit Court of Appeals, in reviewing action of the Civil Aeronautics Board involving the establishment of "youth fares" and reduced fares for servicemen by airlines, thereby discriminating against other passengers, made note of the more liberal interpretation that Section 2 of the Interstate Commerce Act had received by the Interstate Commerce Commission in recent years.[79]

Whatever may be the correct interpretation of Section 2, certain observations may be advanced if the matter is considered from the point of view of desirable public policy and not merely as a question of statutory construction.

We see no sound objection to considering competition as a justification for discriminating tariff rates under certain circumstances. First, the com-

---

[75] Ibid., p. 62.

[76] *Reduced Seasonal Household Goods Rates*, 332 ICC 512, 517 (1968).

[77] E.g., *Coal—Kentucky, Virginia, & West Virginia to Virginia*, 308 ICC 99 (1959); and *Coal to New York Harbor Area*, 311 ICC 355 (1960), discussed in this chapter, pp. 477–78, supra.

[78] *Huron Portland Cement Co.* v. *Baltimore & Ohio R. Co.*, 332 ICC 655, 661 (1968).

[79] *Transcontinental Bus System, Inc.* v. *Civil Aeronautics Board*, 383 F. 2d 466 (1967).

petition should be compelling, and not serve as a mere excuse for arbitrary discrimination.

Secondly, in any proceeding involving the establishment of a preferential rate to one group or class of shippers, it should be clearly shown that the parties not enjoying the more favorable rate are not really injured thereby. If, for instance, those to be granted the favorable rate are in a position to avail themselves of a different mode of transport at an equally low rate, no harm is done to other shippers if a carrier, in order to meet such competition, extends comparable rates to those in a position to resort to the other modes of transport. This is assuming that the reduced rates to the special group of shippers are compensatory and not lower than required to meet the competition encountered.

It may be pointed out at this point that the Civil Aeronautics Board has asserted that, under the Federal Aviation Act, competition is a factor which may be considered in determining whether particular rates are unjustly discriminatory.[80]

PERSONAL DISCRIMINATION TODAY

Personal discrimination is much less of a problem today than it used to be. It is not to be assumed, however, that the practice has been entirely stopped. A perusal of the annual reports of the Interstate Commerce Commission, particularly those sections dealing with enforcement activities of the Commission and courts, shows that instances of personal discrimination continue to arise and are vigorously prosecuted. Relaxation of strict enforcement would undoubtedly make personal discrimination a major evil once more.

Neither should it be assumed that personal discrimination is peculiar to railroad companies, although the nature of railroad costs has made the practice more common in the railroad industry than among the other modes of transport. The practice of personal discrimination is equally objectionable when practiced by the other modes of transport and has been prohibited by law as will be more fully shown in the chapters dealing specifically with the other modes of transport.[81]

SELECTED REFERENCES

General discussions of personal discrimination may be found in Eliot Jones, *Principles of Railway Transportation* (New York: Macmillan, 1924), chap. vii; Stuart Daggett, *Principles of Inland Transportation* (4th ed.; New York: Harper, 1955), chap. xiv; H. B. Vanderblue and K. F. Burgess, *Railroads: Rates, Service, Management* (New York: Macmillan, 1923), chap. vi; Truman C. Bigham and Merrill J. Roberts, *Transportation: Principles and Prob-*

---

[80] *Aggregate Rate Rule Proposed by Shulman, Inc.*, Order 68–11–32.
[81] See Chapters, 29, 32 and 34.

lems (2d ed.; New York: McGraw-Hill, 1952), chap. xiii. Especially rich in illustrative material is W. Z. Ripley, *Railroads: Rates and Regulation* (New York: Longmans, 1916), chap. vi.

On the common-law status of personal discrimination there is an excellent article by B. M. Kline, "Origin of the Rule against Unjust Discrimination," 66 *University of Pennsylvania Law Review* 123 (1918).

There is an excellent analysis of cases arising under Section 2 of the Interstate Commerce Act in I. L. Sharfman, *The Interstate Commerce Commission*, Vol. III-B (New York: Commonwealth Fund, 1936), pp. 370–413.

There is much excellent case material on this subject. See especially the following cases: *Handy* v. *Cleveland & Marietta R. Co.*, 31 Fed. 689 (1887); *Wight* v. *United States*, 167 U.S. 512 (1897); *New York, New Haven & Hartford R. Co.* v. *Interstate Commerce Commission*, 200 U.S. 361 (1906); *Chicago, Indianapolis & Louisville Ry. Co.* v. *United States*, 219 U.S. 486 (1911); *The Colorado Free Pass Investigation*, 26 ICC 491 (1913); *The Tap Line Case*, 23 ICC 277 (1913), 234 U.S. 1 (1914), 31 ICC 490 (1914); *The Industrial Railways Case*, 29 ICC 212 (1914); *Vandalia R. R. Co.* v. *United States*, 226 Fed. 713 (1915); *Pittsburgh, Cincinnati, Chicago & St. Louis Ry. Co.* v. *Fink*, 250 U.S. 577 (1919); *Seaboard Air Line Ry. Co.* v. *United States*, 254 U.S. 57 (1920); *United States* v. *American Sheet & Tin Plate Co.*, 301 U.S. 402 (1937); *Baltimore & Ohio R. R. Co.* v. *United States*, 305 U.S. 507 (1939); *General American Tank Car Corp.* v. *El Dorado Terminal Co.*, 308 U.S. 422 (1940); *Union Pacific R. R. Co.* v. *United States*, 313 U.S. 450 (1941); *Tobin Packing Co., Inc.* v. *Baltimore & Ohio R. Co.*, 299 ICC 221 (1956); *Union Pacific R. Co.* v. *United States*, 362 U.S. 327 (1960); *United States* v. *Braverman*, 373 U.S. 405 (1963).

On the Commodities Clause see C. A. Miller, *Legislative and Judicial History of the Commodities Clause* (Washington, D.C.: American Short Line Railroad Assoc., 1946); or for a briefer discussion see H. G. Crafts, "A Study of the Commodities Clause," 20 *I.C.C. Practitioners' Journal* 296 (1953); Eugene D. Anderson, "The Commodities Clause Re-examined," 29 *I.C.C. Practitioners' Journal* 1254 (1962). An article highly critical of the Commodities Clause and of its judicial interpretation is Thomas Leduc, "Carriers, Courts, and the Commodities Clause," 39 *Business History Review* 57 (1965).

For an account of the less rigorous attitude toward personal discrimination in Europe, particularly since the development of motor transportation, see J. P. Carter, "Personal Discrimination in Transportation: A European Technique," 47 *American Economic Review* 372 (1957).

Some attention is given to the possibly discriminatory aspects of volume rates, annual volume rates, and guaranteed rates in Robert F. Lundy, *The Economics of Loyalty-Incentive Rates in the Railroad Industry of the United States* (Pullman, Washington: Washington State University, Bureau of Economic & Business Research, 1963).

Chapter 21

LONG-AND-SHORT-HAUL DISCRIMINATION

The preceding chapter dealt with discrimination between persons. We must now turn our attention to discrimination between places. Discrimination against particular places not only adversely affects particular shippers who may be located in the places discriminated against, but it may seriously affect whole communities. It has been said that the power to make freight rates is the power to turn a wilderness into a city or a city into a wilderness.[1] It is not to be wondered at, therefore, that some of the bitterest contests over freight rates have involved discrimination against places, localities, and regions.

The present chapter is concerned with a special form of place discrimination known as "long-and-short-haul discrimination." This type of place discrimination has been specially legislated against; and a body of well-established principles has been evolved in dealing with it, an understanding of which will aid in considering the broader subject of discrimination between places generally, which is to be considered in the next chapter.

LONG-AND-SHORT-HAUL DISCRIMINATION DEFINED

Long-and-short-haul discrimination consists in charging a larger aggregate amount for the transportation of persons or property for a shorter than for a longer distance when both hauls are over the same line, in the same direction, and the shorter is included in the longer distance.

Long-and-short-haul discrimination may be illustrated by a diagram, as shown in Figure 21–1. If a railroad should charge a rate of $1.00 per hundred pounds for transporting a certain commodity from A to B and $1.25 for carrying it from A to C, the carrier would be guilty of practicing the type of discrimination to which we refer. A similar discrimination would result if the rate from C to A were in excess of the rate from B to A.

This type of local discrimination has been the subject of much heated controversy and considerable confusion of thought. From the earliest days of railroad regulation there has been special legislation designed to pro-

---
[1] J. H. Beale and Bruce Wyman, *Railroad Rate Regulation* (2d ed.; New York: Baker, Voorhis & Co., 1915), p. 657.

hibit it. Long-and-short-haul discrimination is prohibited by Section 4 of the Interstate Commerce Act, known as the "Long-and-Short-Haul Clause." Exceptions may be made, however, by the Interstate Commerce Commission in special cases.

The early prohibition of long-and-short-haul discrimination is to be explained largely by the fact that the practice seemed entirely indefensible and contrary to common sense. If it costs anything at all to move goods from C to B, in the diagram, why should the rates for the longer distance be less than for the shorter? This question was constantly asked in discussions of long-and-short-haul discrimination. The apparent absurdity of this type of discrimination played an important part in the early legislation on the subject.

In addition to this common-sense appeal in behalf of long-and-short-haul legislation, the shippers who were discriminated against voiced their opposition to the discriminatory practices of the railroads. We can imag-

FIGURE 21–1. Long-and-Short-Haul Discrimination

A   C   B
───
                                     $1.25 $1.00

ine the residents of point C saying: "If the rates charged at B are abnormally low, it means that higher rates must be charged at C and other intermediate points; and if the rates at B are not abnormally low but are only reasonable rates, then the rates at C are excessive, yielding the railroad more than a fair profit." Although this reasoning is not unanswerable, it won many advocates to long-and-short-haul legislation.

MOTIVE FOR LONG-AND-SHORT-HAUL DISCRIMINATION

Before proceeding further, it is necessary to understand why long-and-short-haul discrimination has existed so commonly. It should be noted, however, that an explanation of this practice is not necessarily a justification.

The explanation of long-and-short-haul discrimination, like the explanation of other forms of discrimination, is to be found in the nature of railroad expenses. The fact that a large proportion of a railroad's expenses are fixed and do not vary with the volume of traffic, provides the key to the explanation. The railroad rates at the intermediate point C may be reasonable, viewed in the light of all constant or overhead expenses. But if competition makes it impossible to carry traffic from A to B or from B to A at this rate, it is in the interest of the railroad to charge a rate low enough to get a share of the traffic. As long as the through rate more than covers the extra or additional expenses of hauling the additional traffic, it contributes something to constant expenses, and the railroad is better off in carrying the traffic at the low rate than in not carrying it at all. Only when the through rate is forced so low as to make no contribution to indirect expenses does it become unwise for the railroad to carry the traffic. The situation explains why the discrepancy between the low through rate and the higher intermediate rate is often so great. At one time the rate on window-shade cloth from New York to San Francisco was $1.00 per hundred pounds, while from New York to Salt Lake City it was $2.30. Rates from Chicago to Spokane, Washington, were at one time 80 percent higher than to Seattle despite the fact that the latter is hundreds of miles farther west.[2]

OBJECTIONS TO LONG-AND-SHORT-HAUL DISCRIMINATION

We must now examine more critically the case against long-and-short-haul discrimination in order to determine to what extent the discrimination is objectionable and to what extent it is justifiable. The criticism directed against this type of discrimination by the intermedate points rests upon two counts. The first objection is that it tends to increase the rates charged at the intermediate points. The low through rate is alleged to throw an additional burden upon the intermediate points. Expressed in another way, the railroad will make up the inadequate returns received from the very low through rate by increasing the rates at the intermediate points.

The second count against long-and-short-haul discrimination is that an intermediate point is at a disadvantage and cannot compete with the more distant point which receives preferential rates. The issue here is not of the unreasonableness per se of the intermediate rates, but a question of the relative rates. The producer or jobber at C is concerned because his competitor at B has the advantage of a lower freight and can undersell him. He would be as content to have the discrimination removed by increasing the rate at B as by lowering it at C.

JUSTIFIABLE AND UNJUSTIFIABLE DISCRIMINATION

The above objections to long-and-short-haul discrimination are sometimes valid; under other conditions they are not. We shall first give an illustration of long-and-short-haul discrimination which is open to these objections.

Case 1: Discrimination by Two Competing Railroads of Approximately Equal Length

Let us imagine two railroads, *x* and *y*, operating between A and B but serving different intermediate points, as shown in Figure 21–2. Let us

---

[2] These illustrations and many others are given in Eliot Jones, *Principles of Railway Transportation* (New York: Macmillan, 1924), pp. 106–7.

imagine further that the rates under a distance scale are $1.00 on a certain article from A to C and from A to D, and that they are $1.30 by both routes from A to B. The competition between the two railroads for traffic from A to B may soon cause one of the railroads to reduce the through rate to $1.00. If by so doing, it carries more of the through traffic between A and B, it gains by the reduction. Its expenses are increased but little, and its revenues are increased considerably. Railroad *y*, however, will not stand by and allow traffic to be diverted to railroad *x*. So railroad *y* reduces its rates to $1.00, and the traffic is again divided between the two roads. If railroad *x* institutes another cut in the through rate to $0.75 and again carries more than its normal share of the through traffic, a similar cut will likely be made by railroad *y*. As a result of these reductions

Figure 21–2. Unjustifiable Long-and-Short-Haul Discrimination

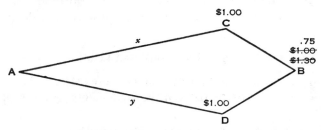

the carriers are now guilty of long-and-short-haul discrimination. Are the two objections stated above valid in this case?

As to the first objection, we find that the railroads have not yet increased the rates at C and D; but since they are carrying the traffic from A to B at less than normal rates, earnings have probably been reduced. An attempt to increase earnings by increasing the rates at intermediate points where the railroad has a monopoly is only natural. There are two situations, however, in which the railroad would refrain from increasing the rates at the intermediate points. In the first place, the low through rate might possibly stimulate enough new traffic to offset the reduction in rates. By "new traffic" we do not mean traffic diverted from the other line, but additional traffic stimulated by the low rates.[3] In the second place, there is the possibility of deriving less profit from the traffic at intermediate points if rates are increased. If the old rates were already at the point which yielded the greatest revenue above direct expenses, it would be poor business to increase rates further. But the above conditions do not necessarily exist. Our conclusion must therefore be that although the railroad may not find it desirable to increase the rates at intermediate points, the latter points have reason to fear that their burdens may be increased.

---

[3] Low rates at intermediate points, of course, would stimulate new traffic equally well.

In fact, the situation may become worse as time goes on. The lower rates at B may stimulate its growth and the decline of C and D. Accordingly the traffic between A and B becomes greater, but the traffic from A to C or D becomes less. Hence more and more traffic will be carried at the reduced rates and less and less at the higher rates. C and D may then be forced to pay still higher rates.

The second objection to discrimination of this type is also valid. Even if the rates at C and D are not increased, the maintenance of the old rates at these points, when B is charged lower rates, must operate to the disadvantage of the intermediate points. Jobbers and manufacturers at C and D are discriminated against, and they cannot compete with their rivals who receive preferential rates.

From this illustration it is apparent that long-and-short-haul discrimination is objectionable and that the intermediate points have just cause for criticizing rates built on this system. There are situations, however, in which the objections voiced by the intermediate towns do not apply.

Case II: Discrimination by a Circuitous Rail Line

In Figure 21–3, railroad *x* forms a direct route between A and B. Railroad *y* is a circuitous route between the same points. Let us suppose that

FIGURE 21–3. Discrimination by a Circuitous Line

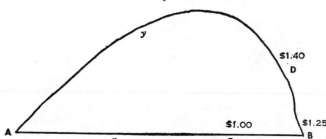

both railroads adopt a distance scale of rates, and that by railroad *x* the rate from A to C is $1.00 and from A to B, $1.25. By railroad *y* the rate from A to D might be $1.40 and from A to B $1.50. Under these conditions all traffic between A and B will move via the direct route, unless the direct line is unable to handle all the traffic. The rate of $1.50 charged by railroad *y* would be a "paper rate," that is, no traffic would move under it. If railroad *y* is to carry any traffic between A and B, it must be at a rate as low as that charged by railroad *x*. It sometimes happens that a circuitous line has to charge less than the direct line in order to divert traffic to the longer route. We shall assume, in the illustration, that railroad *y* can carry a share of the through traffic if it meets the rate set by the direct line. If railroad *y* reduces its rate from A to B to $1.25, it is guilty of long-and-short-haul discrimination. Traffic moves from A through D to B and is charged $1.25; but if it stopped at D, it would have been charged $1.40. Under these conditions, has D a valid objection against the discrimination?

In the first place, will the low rate quoted by railroad *y* from A to B result in a tendency to increase the rates at D? If the railroad should restore the old rate of $1.50, no traffic between A and B would move via its lines. The entire burden of supporting railroad *y* would fall on traffic to, from, or between intermediate points. If the railroad is permitted to reduce its through rate, it will carry competitive traffic. If this rate covers more than the out-of-pocket expenses incurred in carrying the additional traffic, the through traffic is making some contribution to the overhead expenses, and the railroad is better off than it was before. It is conceivable that as a result the local rates at D might even be reduced. Thus the discrimination against D may even be a benefit to it. The first complaint against long-and-short-haul discrimination does not apply in this case.

The second objection raised against the discriminatory rates is not so easily answered. The manufacturers and jobbers at D are not, as we have seen, so much interested in whether rates are $1.25 or $1.40 as they are in knowing that they and their competitors pay the same rate, whether it be $1.25, $1.40, or something else. Under the rate adjustment we have described, the people at B are getting lower rates than those at D. The fact of discrimination cannot be denied. In considering this situation, we must examine two alternative methods of removing the discrimination against D. In the first place, the railroad might remove the discrimination by increasing the charge on goods it carries from A to B. But if it does so, the disadvantage of D is not removed. The people at B will still get their goods for $1.25, but they will be shipped via the direct route. So if we force railroad *y* to observe the Long-and-Short-Haul Clause by increasing the rates at B, we do not relieve the people at D. Point B still has its advantage over D. The other alternative before the carrier, if it wishes to remove the discrimination against D, is to reduce the rate at D to $1.25, thus putting D and B upon an equal basis. But on what grounds can railroad *y* be asked to reduce its rate from A to D? The rate is, as we have seen, a reasonable rate resulting from the adoption of a distance scale, possibly the same scale that is applied on railroad *x*. The distance from A to D via railroad *y* is greater than the distance from A to B via railroad *x*. It is reasonable that the rate from A to D be higher than from A to B. No sound argument can be presented in support of compelling railroad *y* to reduce its rate from A to D. The unhappy fact is that D is handicapped by its location. Point D is farther from A than is B. Point B has the advantage of being located nearer A, and there is no good reason for depriving it of this advantage. Under these circumstances, then, the second criticism of long-and-short-haul discrimination by railroad *y* is not valid. It is assumed in the above case that the direct route between A and B maintains the standard rate. If the direct route began to cut rates, our second illustration would be similar to the first, and the same objections would apply.

The fundamental differences between Case I and Case II, which justify the discrimination in the latter case and not in the former, should be noted. In Case I the competitive point received a subnormal rate; in Case II the competitive point receives a normal rate via the direct route. As a result of the situation just described, point B, in Case I, has an artificial advantage over the intermediate point—an advantage due wholly to the rate cutting of the railroads; but in Case II, point B has a natural advantage over the intermediate point—the advantage of being located nearer A.

It seems clear from the foregoing analysis that the intermediate points are not injured by long-and-short-haul discrimination on the part of a circuitous line competing with a more direct line. The direct line, however—and the shippers served by the direct line—may have something to say about the rate cutting by the circuitous line. The direct route loses traffic to the circuitous; and since the direct route is at less expense in hauling goods from A to B, it has reason to feel that it is entitled to the traffic. The shippers located on the direct line may also have an interest in the matter. If the direct route handled all the traffic moving between A and B, shippers located along its line might get the benefit of even lower rates than is the case when the through traffic is divided with another line. Just as the shippers located on the circuitous line may benefit if the circuitous line is allowed to carry some competitive traffic, so the shippers located on the direct line may lose by the practice. This would clearly be the case if rates were adjusted to give each railroad a fair return; but since it is necessary to consider railroads as a whole or in groups when prescribing a level of rates, it probably makes little difference to the shippers on the direct route if some traffic is diverted to the other line.

Our conclusion regarding long-and-short-haul discrimination by a circuitous line is that the intermediate points are not injured and that the usual complaints directed by them against the discriminatory rates are not valid. The direct line between the competitive points is injured, however, by the discriminatory practice. Under some conditions the shippers located on the direct route may forego rate reductions that would be possible if the direct route could handle all the traffic between A and B.

Case III: Discrimination Caused by Water Competition

Another case in which local discrimination is not injurious to the intermediate points may be worth brief attention. Let us imagine a direct line between A and B, two points which are subject to water competition. (See Figure 21–4.) Let us imagine that under a distance scale of rates the rate from A to C on a certain article is $1.00, and that from A to B it is $1.25. The water rate between A and B, however, is only 80 cents. Under these conditions the railroad will seek to reduce the rate from A to B to 80 cents in order to compete with the water carrier. It might, of course, be unnecessary to reduce the rail rate to the level of the water rate owing to certain advantages in rail carriage; but for the sake of making our illustration as simple as possible, we shall assume that the rail line must meet the water rate in order to divert a substantial amount of the traffic from the water lines. The reduction of the rail rate to 80 cents puts the railroad in the position of violating the prohibition against higher charges for shorter than for longer hauls. Has the intermediate point just cause for complaint?

The case is substantially like Case II. Allowing the railroad to charge 80 cents at B does not tend to increase the charges levied on traffic at C. In fact, the additional traffic carried by the railroad, if it makes some contri-

FIGURE 21–4. Discrimination Caused by Water Competition

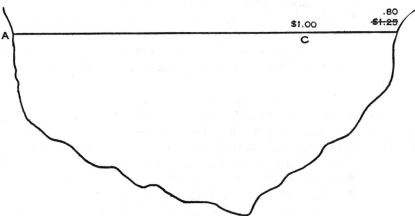

bution to the general or overhead expenses, reduces the burden imposed on local traffic and may enable the railroad to reduce its rates at C. Hence the first objection to the discrimination does not apply. Neither will the second objection stand scrutiny. The disadvantage to C in paying $1.00 while B pays only $0.80 is not removed by forcing the railroad to charge $1.00 or more at B. The people at B will still get their goods from A for $0.80, but they must get them by water. Neither can C reasonably ask for a reduction in its rates to $0.80. The rate of $1.00 at C is a normal rate. It is not unreasonable. The fact is that B is, economically speaking, nearer A than is C; and there is no reason for depriving it of its advantage of location. The real controversy in this case, as in Case II, is between two agencies of transportation. Permitting the railroad to meet the water rates aids the railway and injures the water lines. Requiring the railroad to avoid long-and-short-haul discrimination in this situation injures the railway and favors the water lines. A question of public policy is involved. If the public wishes to encourage water transportation, it will restrict rate reductions designed to meet water competition. On the other hand, if the public finds that there is not traffic enough for both systems of transportation and that the railroad provides service at intermediate points which a water line cannot, a policy will be adopted giving the railroad the through traffic. Circumstances will determine which course is the wiser to pursue.

We have not exhausted, by any means, the circumstances under which long-and-short-haul discrimination does not injure the intermediate points. The above cases, however, are sufficient to demonstrate the test that is to be applied to determine the issue.

Long-and-Short-Haul Discrimination and Economic Waste

Thus far in our discussion we have considered long-and-short-haul discrimination with reference to its effect upon the points discriminated against. Some mention was made also of its effect upon two other interested parties—the carriers which lose traffic, and the shippers they serve. But there is another, if less vocal, party interested in the practice—the general public.

Long-and-short-haul discrimination encourages wasteful transportation, and for this waste the public eventually pays. From a broad social point of view, therefore, it might be better to permit fewer exceptions to the Long-and-Short-Haul Clause. Two examples will serve to illustrate the point. When a circuitous line, like railroad y in Figure 21–3, is granted permission to reduce its through rate in order to compete with the direct route, some of the traffic is being hauled by the less economical route. The actual outlay in labor costs, fuel, and wear and tear on roadway and rolling stock is increased. If railroads x and y were owned and operated by the government, or if they were consolidated into a single system, the folly of transporting goods a roundabout way from A to B would be apparent to anyone. It is just as wasteful if the roads are under separate ownership. If it chanced that the direct route was unable to handle all the traffic from A to B, and the circuitous route was incompletely utilized, it would probably be more economical to permit some of the traffic to move by the circuitous line than to build a second line parallel to x or to enlarge the facilities of x.[4]

Economic waste is also encouraged by granting relief from the Long-and-Short-Haul Clause on account of market competition. In 1924 the Interstate Commerce Commission granted certain carriers authority to establish rates on paper and paper articles from producing points in Wisconsin, Minnesota, and Michigan to New Orleans while maintaining higher rates to intermediate points.[5] It seems that New Orleans could obtain its paper more cheaply by water from producing points in Pennsyl-

---

[4] See H. G. Brown, *Transportation Rates and Their Regulation* (New York: Macmillan, 1916), pp. 120–23.

[5] *Paper and Paper Articles to New Orleans*, 88 ICC 345 (1924).

vania, New York, New England, and Scandinavian countries. New Orleans was therefore tributary to these latter producing areas. Wisconsin paper could not compete in the New Orleans market except by lowering the freight rates below what was reasonable to the various intermediate points. But if relief is granted here, there is no reason why the carriers operating from New England to Chicago should not be granted relief in order to enable New England producers to invade the territory tributary to the Wisconsin producers. If extensive relief from the Long-and-Short-Haul Clause is granted on account of market competition, there will be a large amount of unnecessary and uneconomical hauling of goods. This is what Commissioner Eastman had in mind when he said: ". . . the theory of market competition, if followed consistently, will inevitably lead to all manner of cross-hauling and wasteful transportation for which the country must in the end pay."[6]

HISTORY AND ADMINISTRATION OF THE LONG-AND-SHORT-HAUL CLAUSE

The foregoing analysis of long-and-short-haul discrimination should make more understandable the policy followed by the Interstate Commerce Commission in administering Section 4. We shall now turn our attention to the history and administration of the Long-and-Short-Haul Clause.

The Original Long-and-Short-Haul Clause

The Long-and-Short-Haul Clause as originally enacted read as follows:

That it shall be unlawful for any common carrier subject to the provisions of this Act to charge or receive any greater compensation in the aggregate for the transportation of passengers or of like kind of property, under substantially similar circumstances and conditions, for a shorter than for a longer distance over the same line, in the same direction, the shorter being included within the longer distance; but this shall not be construed as authorizing any common carrier within the terms of this Act to charge or receive as great compensation for a shorter as for a longer distance: *Provided, however,* That upon application to the Commission appointed under the provisions of this Act, such common carrier may, in special cases, after investigation by the Commission, be authorized to charge less for longer than for shorter distances for transportation of passengers or property; and the Commission may from time to time prescribe the extent to which such designated common carrier may be relieved from the operation of this section of this Act.

Two provisions in the section should be noted. In the first place, the Long-and-Short-Haul Clause was not and is not today a rigid prohibition of long-and-short-haul discrimination, since the Commission is authorized, "in special cases," to relieve the carriers from the operation of the section.

---

[6] Ibid., p. 353. See also *Commodity Rates to Pacific Coast Terminals*, 107 ICC 421, 439–40 (1926).

When the Act of 1887 was being debated in Congress, the House of Representatives desired to make Section 4 rigid instead of granting the Commission the power to make exceptions. The Senate, however, insisted on leaving a degree of flexibility in this part of the Act. This was wise, if our analysis of long-and-short-haul discrimination in preceding pages is correct. But Congress has from time to time seriously considered amending Section 4 to make its prohibitions absolute, and some states have rigid long-and-short-haul provisions.

The second point to be noted about Section 4 is that the prohibition against the higher charge for the shorter than for the longer distance applied only when the transportation for the shorter and longer distances was performed "under substantially similar circumstances and conditions." This phrase proved to be a stumbling block in the administration of the Long-and-Short-Haul Clause.

Although the clause was effective for a time, the carriers in the South took the position that any form of competition which existed at through points and not at intermediate points created a dissimilarity of conditions and circumstances such that the prohibition of higher charges for shorter than for longer distances did not apply. They further contended that they could determine for themselves whether conditions and circumstances were dissimilar or not at the through and intermediate points and that they need not, therefore, wait for the Commission to grant them relief from the operation of Section 4 before charging higher rates at intermediate points than at through points when they believed circumstances and conditions to be dissimilar.

Nullification of Section 4

In the Alabama Midland Case[7] in 1897 the Supreme Court accepted the position of the carriers as outlined above. The Court held that any form of competition between carriers might create a dissimilarity of conditions and circumstances such that the prohibitions of Section 4 did not apply. It also held that the carriers could, in the first instance, decide for themselves whether circumstances were dissimilar or not, and that they need not wait for the Commission to grant relief from the operation of the section.

The Commission maintained that this interpretation practically nullified the Long-and-Short-Haul Clause.[8] The Commission pointed out that the evil which the section was intended to remedy was caused by the reduction of rates under the force of competition at certain points. Since it was competition which forced down the through rates, to hold that competition created such a dissimilarity of conditions that the clause did not apply made it impossible to apply the section to the very situations which Con-

---

[7] *Interstate Commerce Commission* v. *Alabama Midland Ry. Co.*, 168 U.S. 144 (1897).

[8] Interstate Commerce Commission, *Annual Report, 1897*, p. 42.

gress desired to remedy. Practically every departure from Section 4 could be explained by dissimilarity of circumstances, and that which the clause was designed to prevent would be lawful. From the date of this decision (November 8, 1897) until the Act was amended in 1910, the Long-and-Short-Haul Clause was a dead letter. Within five days from the Court's decision the Trans-Missouri Freight Bureau filed schedules increasing rates to intermediate points over more than 100,000 square miles of territory.[9] The impotence of Section 4 during the intervening period is shown by the fact that from 1906 to 1910 no applications were filed with the Commission for relief from the section.[10] The reason is plain. Departure from the section could be practiced with impunity, for a dissimilarity of conditions and circumstances could almost always be shown.

Although the Commission declared in 1897 that the decision of the Court had reduced Section 4 to a nullity, some attempt was made to enforce it. In the Alabama Midland Case the Court had said: ". . . we do not hold that the mere fact of competition, no matter what its character or extent, necessarily relieves the carrier from the restraints of the third or fourth sections, but only that these sections are not so stringent and imperative as to exclude in all cases the matter of competition from consideration in determining . . . what are 'substantially similar circumstances and conditions.' " The Commission therefore made some attempt to distinguish between competition that did, and competition that did not, justify departure from the Long-and-Short-Haul Clause. But this attempt was not very successful. In one case that came before the Supreme Court, language was used by the Court which seemed to go even further than in the Alabama Midland Case, for the Court said: ". . . it has been settled by this court that competition which is controlling on traffic and rates produces in and of itself the dissimilarity of circumstances and conditions described in the statute. . . ."[11] Under this interpretation of the Fourth Section it was impossible to differentiate between unjustifiable discrimination, as in our Case I, and discrimination of the justifiable sort, as in Case II. Accordingly it may be truthfully said that the Alabama Midland decision rendered Section 4 nugatory.

Amendments of 1910

Amendments to the Long-and-Short-Haul Clause in the Mann-Elkins Act of 1910 made Section 4 effective once more. This was accomplished by striking the phrase "under substantially similar circumstances and conditions" from the Act. The elimination of this phrase circumvented the

---

[9] Ibid., p. 43.

[10] *Administration of the Fourth Section*, 87 ICC 564, 566 (1924).

[11] *East Tennessee, Virginia & Georgia Ry. Co.* v. *Interstate Commerce Commission*, 181 U.S. 1, 12 (1901), referring to *Louisville & Nashville R. R. Co.* v. *Behlmer*, 175 U.S. 648 (1900).

holding of the United States Supreme Court in the Alabama Midland Case that competition at the through points and not at the intermediate points made the clause inapplicable. As amended, the clause prohibited the higher charges for shorter than for longer hauls, ostensibly at least, whether conditions were similar or not; and the carriers were thus deprived of the privilege of asserting that competition created a dissimilarity of conditions and circumstances. In the second place, the effect of striking out the troublesome phrase was to make the Long-and-Short-Haul Clause applicable unless and until the Commission granted relief from its operation.[12] The Commission has primary control over long-and-short-haul discrimination. Its function is no longer a mere reviewing function.

Another amendment of 1910 permitted the railroads to maintain existing rates which were higher for shorter than for longer hauls if they were protected by applications for Fourth-Section relief filed within five months after the passage of the Act. A moment's consideration reveals the necessity for this provision. We have seen that the carriers paid little attention to Section 4 after the decision of the United States Supreme Court in the Alabama Midland Case. As a result there were thousands of rates in existence in 1910 which were higher for shorter than for longer hauls. If the Long-and-Short-Haul Clause were suddenly made effective, it would be necessary to change all of these rates immediately, even though the discrimination might in many cases be of the type which the Commission considered as justifiable. This provision of the 1910 amendment permitted the existing departures to remain unchanged until the Commission had determined whether or not the rates should be brought into conformity with the Long-and-Short-Haul Clause. As a result of this provision of the law the carriers, within the time authorized, filed 5,031 applications for relief from Section 4. Many of these applications involved thousands of rates in a great many different situations.[13] It was many years before the 1910 applications were disposed of.

Grounds for Fourth-Section Relief

The grounds on which Fourth-Section relief is granted by the Interstate Commerce Commission should now be considered more fully. There are six common competitive situations which the Commission has considered as justifying departure from the Long-and-Short-Haul Clause.

1. Relief has been granted to circuitous lines or routes which are in competition with more direct routes.[14] This is the general situation described in Case II above. In 1925 the Commission said that more than

---

[12] See *Intermountain Rate Cases,* 234 U.S. 476 (1914).

[13] *Administration of Fourth Section,* 87 ICC 564, 567 (1924).

[14] An illustrative case is *Class and Commodity Rates from Pennsylvania,* 115 ICC 331 (1926).

90 percent of all authorizations for Fourth-Section relief came under this heading.[15] So generally accepted is the propriety of Fourth-Section relief under these circumstances that Congress amended Section 4 in 1957 to make it unnecessary for the carriers to obtain special permission for a circuitous route to meet the competition of a direct route while maintaining higher rates at intermediate points. Thus Fourth-Section relief is automatic in situations of this kind.

2. Relief is frequently granted to rail lines which are in competition with water routes.[16] This is the situation described in Case III above.

3. Relief is sometimes granted on account of commercial or market competition or competition of directions. The case concerning the rates on paper and paper articles from Wisconsin and other points to New Orleans, referred to above, is a good illustration.[17]

4. Carriers which are in a poor financial condition or whose costs of operation are high are sometimes granted relief in order that they may meet the rates of stronger lines at the points where they come into competition. In cases of this sort the stronger line sets the rate, and the weaker line must meet it or lose traffic. The Tennessee Central Railroad obtained relief on this ground in one case.[18]

5. In recent years relief has been granted in many cases to permit railroads to compete with motor carriers.[19]

6. Relief has also been granted in numerous instances because of pipeline competition.[20] In some instances relief has been granted on coal, to enable the railroads to meet the competition of natural gas at points served by pipelines.[21]

---

[15] Report on the Gooding Bill in *Hearings on Long and Short Haul Charges*, Committee on Interstate and Foreign Commerce, House of Representatives, 68th Cong., 2d Sess. (1925), p. 702.

[16] E.g., *Commodity Rates from Jacksonville to Miami*, 101 ICC 347 (1925).

[17] Pp. 496–97, supra. For another example see *Iron & Steel Articles from the East to the Southwest*, 310 ICC 587 (1960). When relief is granted on account of market competition, it is not ordinarily granted with respect to origins, that is, to permit a low rate from one origin point to a given destination while maintaining higher rates from intermediate origin points. See *Sugar to Illinois Territory & Cincinnati, Ohio*, 270 ICC 699, 705 (1948); *Liquefied Chlorine Gas to St. Louis & Kansas City, Mo.*, 273 ICC 142, 145 (1948). The reason for this policy, of course, is that the competitive force compelling reduction from one origin must ordinarily apply with equal force from intermediate origins.

[18] *Murfreesboro Board of Trade* v. *Louisville & Nashville R. R. Co.*, 73 ICC 228 (1923).

[19] *Cement from Hudson, N.Y. to Massachusetts*, 186 ICC 8 (1932); *Brick in Southern Territory*, 241 ICC 450 (1940). Fourth-Section relief is not granted to meet motor-truck competition when the force of such competition would seem to operate equally at intermediate points. See *Iron & Steel to Iowa, Minnesota, Michigan, & Wisconsin*, 279 ICC 321, 338–39 (1950).

[20] *Petroleum and Its Products*, 183 ICC 24 (1932); *Petroleum & Petroleum Products*, 245 ICC 33 (1941).

[21] *Coal from Illinois, Indiana & Kentucky*, 192 ICC 586 (1933); *Coal to Sleepy Eye & Springfield, Minn.*, 243 ICC 227 (1941).

In addition to these situations in which Fourth-Section relief is commonly granted, there are a number of more or less technical situations, arising from the peculiarities of rate structures, in which Fourth-Section relief may be justified. One of these situations results from the practice of permitting higher rates, under certain conditions, for joint-line hauls than for single-line hauls. Where this is done, a joint-line route will find itself at a disadvantage in competing with a single-line route between the same points. It may therefore be granted authority to meet the rates of the single-line route without disturbing higher joint-line rates at intermediate points.[22] Another situation which may result in Fourth-Section relief arises on the border between two rate territories having different rate levels. A route which lies wholly or partially in the higher-rated territory may be at a disadvantage with an alternative route through the territory having a lower level of rates. In one case relief was granted to the carriers on the west side of the Mississippi River from St. Louis to Memphis and other crossings to compete with lines on the east side of the river, where the rate level was lower.[23] Perhaps the most frequent of the technical situations which require Fourth-Section relief arises from the existence of group rates. As noted in an earlier chapter, there are many instances in the United States of rates which are made on a group basis.[24] In such instances the rates are the same to or from all points within a certain area or rate group. It sometimes happens, however, that one or more of the roads passes through points in a higher-rated group on its way to or from points in a lower-rated group. Fourth-Section relief may be granted to such lines in order to preserve the group system of rates.[25]

The situations which have been described thus far result in more or less permanent relief from the Long-and-Short-Haul Clause, although relief may be withdrawn if the conditions which originally justified relief cease to exist.[26] Various emergency situations may arise, however, in which temporary Fourth-Section relief is granted. In 1922, for instance, the existence of a drought in New Mexico resulted in the destruction of crops to such an extent that livestock was threatened with starvation. The Commission authorized the carriers to reduce rates on feed shipped into the region without reducing rates at intermediate points. Floods or other abnormal conditions often justify emergency relief of this sort. Temporary relief has sometimes been granted to stop traffic congestion by opening up additional routes of shipment.

---

[22] E.g., *Memphis-Southwestern Investigation*, 77 ICC 473, 522–23 (1923).

[23] *Memphis-Southwestern Case*, 80 ICC 157 (1923).

[24] Pp. 203–6, *supra*.

[25] For illustrations see *Class and Commodity Rates between Western Points*, 104 ICC 578 (1925); and *Liquefied Petroleum Gas, Canada to W.T.L. Territory*, 314 ICC 596 (1961).

[26] *Citrus Fruit from Florida to North Atlantic Ports*, 266 ICC 627 (1946).

Amendments of 1920

The Transportation Act of 1920 contained three amendments to Section 4, two of which require careful explanation.[27] To a considerable degree these amendments merely wrote into the statute policies which the Commission had commonly observed in the administration of the clause. As long as they were not written into the statute, however, they could be applied with flexibility; but incorporated into the law, they deprived the Commission of discretion in their application.

"Reasonably Compensatory." In granting relief from Section 4, the Commission was required to see that the reduced through rates were "reasonably compensatory." This provision was clearly intended to prevent low through rates that would throw a burden on intermediate points. The term "reasonably compensatory" was construed in the Transcontinental Cases of 1922.[28] The Commission held that to be reasonably compensatory, a rate must

(1) cover and more than cover the extra or additional expenses incurred in handling the traffic to which it applies; (2) be no lower than necessary to meet existing competition; (3) not be so low as to threaten the extinction of legitimate competition by water carriers; and (4) not impose undue burden on other traffic or jeopardize the appropriate return on the value of carrier property generally, as contemplated in section 15a of the act.[29]

This definition has been frequently repeated by the Commission in subsequent Fourth-Section cases, and it has been consistently adhered to. It should be noted that a rate, to be "reasonably compensatory," must conform to all of the four requirements laid down in the definition. Because of the importance of the "reasonably compensatory" requirement, the definition requires closer examination.

The first requirement, namely, that the reduced through rate must cover, and more than cover, the extra or additional expenses incurred in handling the traffic to which it applies, is basic and in strict accordance with the theory of rates which was expounded in an earlier chapter. More or less rule-of-thumb methods must sometimes be used to determine whether the through rates meet this requirement. In most cases judgment as to whether the through rates meet this test is based on a consideration of ton-mile or car-mile revenues which the rate will produce. Rates yielding less than 5 mills per ton-mile are quite apt to be considered less than

---

[27] The third amendment, known as the Equidistant Clause, was designed to restrict the discrimination at intermediate points on circuitous routes. It was repealed in 1940. The Commission continued to apply the principle when it seemed appropriate; but since Fourth-Section relief is now automatic for circuitous routes, there is little occasion to apply the principle. For a description of the Equidistant Clause see earlier editions of this book.

[28] 74 ICC 48 (1922).

[29] Ibid., p. 71.

reasonably compensatory.[30] In some instances rates higher than 5 mills per ton-mile have been required.[31] In some instances rates yielding less than 5 mills have been held reasonably compensatory, but in these cases the heavy-loading characteristics of the commodity resulted in satisfactory earnings per car-mile.[32]

The second and third requirements of the definition of "reasonably compensatory" may be considered together. Taken together, they mean that even though the reduced through rates meet the first test, they must not be lower than is necessary to meet the competition encountered; and at least so far as water competition is concerned, they must not destroy such competition. Fourth-Section relief has frequently been denied or restricted where the proposed through rates were lower than necessary to meet the competition encountered at the through point.[33]

The last requirement which must be met before a rate can be found reasonably compensatory is that it will not impose an undue burden on other traffic or jeopardize the appropriate return on carrier property. This requirement is at first puzzling, since it might be argued that a rate which has met the other tests could not possibly cast a burden on other traffic. Careful consideration of the problem, however, reveals that a rate which has been found to be reasonably compensatory by the other tests may cast a burden on other traffic or jeopardize the return on investment because of certain collateral losses of revenue that may ensue from putting the reduced rate into effect. This may happen when a considerable amount of through traffic would have moved under the existing rate. In such instances the gain in revenue from additional traffic that may be obtained under the reduced rate may be more than offset by the reduction in revenue from traffic which would have moved at the existing rate.[34] Collateral losses of revenue figured prominently in a number of the transcontinental Fourth-Section cases in which relief was denied.[35]

"Potential" Competition. A second amendment to the Long-and-Short-Haul Clause in 1920 provided that the Commission was not to au-

---

[30] See *Grain between River Ports on Illinois Central System,* 211 ICC 379 (1935); *Grain & Grain Products,* 197 ICC 441 (1933).

[31] E.g., *Export & Import Rates,* 169 ICC 13 (1930).

[32] *Coal from Southwest Virginia to Memphis, Tenn.,* 264 ICC 398 (1946); *Soda Ash to Georgetown, S.C.,* 269 ICC 475 (1947); *Potash from Carlsbad & Loving, N. Mex.,* 269 ICC 747 (1948).

[33] *Pig Iron from Martins Ferry, Ohio, to Wilder, Ky.,* 270 ICC 783 (1948); *Sulphur to Munising, Mich.,* 245 ICC 171 (1941); *Newsprint Paper from Tennessee & Alabama to Houston, Texas,* 313 ICC 669 (1961).

[34] It may be observed that the requirement that the reduced rates should not jeopardize an appropriate return on the value of carrier property embraces not only the effects on the applicant carriers but the effects on other roads that might be adversely affected.

[35] *Transcontinental Cases of 1922,* 74 ICC 48 (1922); *Commodity Rates to Pacific Coast Terminals,* 107 ICC 421 (1926); *Transcontinental Westbound Automobile Rates,* 209 ICC 549 (1935).

thorize a lower rate to a more distant point on account of "potential" as distinguished from "actual" water competition. There has been some difficulty in interpreting this requirement. When there is a substantial movement of commodities by water, there is no question that the competition is actual. When water transportation facilities are available but actual movement by water routes is absent or negligible in quantity, there is some question as to whether the competition is actual or merely potential. The Commission has held that an actual movement by water is not essential to make the competition actual. It is sufficient that facilities for such movement are readily available.[36]

Although the administration of Section 4 would break down completely if potential water competition, however remote, were permitted to justify Fourth-Section relief, there is some degree of absurdity in a rule which encourages investment in waterways, docks, and barges merely for the purpose of bringing about a reduction in rail rates that cannot be lawfully accomplished until such investment is made. This is particularly true when the water transportation facilities may remain unutilized if the railroad reduces its rates when the competition becomes actual.

The statutory requirement that competition must be actual and not merely potential in order to justify Fourth-Section relief applies only to water competition. Logically, of course, the same rule should be followed when other types of competition are alleged to justify relief. The Commission recognizes this and has applied the principle where other forms of competition were encountered.[37]

The 1957 Amendment

We have elsewhere noted that since 1957 it has not been necessary for the railroads to apply for Fourth-Section relief when they desire to publish reduced rates over a circuitous route in order to meet the rates of a more direct route while maintaining higher rates at intermediate points.[38] This was accomplished by an amendment to Section 4.[39] This change in the law had been recommended by the Interstate Commerce Commission. The Commission had found that the necessity of obtaining Fourth-Section relief in such circumstances had resulted "in disproportionate expenditures of time, labor, and funds in view of the relatively few instances where denial of section 4 relief has been warranted."[40] In 1958 it was stated that

---

[36] *Asphalt to Fulton and Arrowhead, N.Y.*, 238 ICC 531, 534 (1940); *Wood Pulp from St. Marys, Ga., to Gilman, Vt.*, 284 ICC 761 (1952); *Carbon Blacks, Louisiana & Texas to Institute, W. Va.*, 310 ICC 511 (1960).

[37] *Coal from Illinois, Indiana & Kentucky*, 192 ICC 586 (1933); *Petroleum, Colorado & Wyoming to W.T.L. Territory*, 289 ICC 457 (1953).

[38] Pp. 500–501, supra.

[39] 71 Stat. 904.

[40] *Annual Report, 1955*, p. 122; *Annual Report, 1956*, p. 160.

the amendment had resulted in a reduction of Fourth-Section applications by about 50 percent.[41]

The only danger from the liberalized rule is that it could lead to excessively circuitous hauling and the resulting economic waste. It had long been the practice of the Commission to restrict Fourth-Section relief to routes which were not excessively circuitous, frequently to routes that were not more than 70 or 80 percent longer than the direct route. Sometimes when the distance by the direct route was great, say 1,000 miles or more, relief was limited to circuitous routes which were not more than 33⅓ percent longer than the direct route.[42] Under the present law it is possible that routes which are extremely circuitous will attempt to compete for through traffic. Undoubtedly the Commission has authority to interfere in such situations under its minimum-rate and other powers, but there is opportunity under the present law for wasteful competition which the Commission had formerly held in check by its policy in administering Section 4.

Applications for Fourth-Section Relief

The conditions under which Fourth-Section relief is obtained and the limitations imposed by law or by the Commission may now be summarized. This may be done by considering the main points which must be established in every Fourth-Section application.

1. It must ordinarily be shown that the reduced rates proposed are compelled by competitive circumstances beyond the carrier's control. We have already noted the prinicpal competitive circumstances that warrant Fourth-Section relief.

2. It must also be shown that the lower rates for the longer hauls are "reasonably compensatory." The meaning of the term "reasonably compensatory" has already been explained.

3. The third point that must be established in order to obtain Fourth-Section relief is that the rates at the intermediate points are reasonable in themselves.

In addition to these general requirements, an application based on water competition must establish that the competition is "actual" and not merely "potential." This is required by the 1920 amendment relating to potential water competition, which we have previously discussed.

Section 500 of the Transportation Act

We have seen that Fourth-Section relief is commonly granted on account of actual water competition. Since 1920 the granting of relief on

---

[41] *Commodity Rates East of the Rocky Mountains,* 304 ICC 535, 537.

[42] See for example *Class & Commodity Rates from Pennsylvania,* 115 ICC 331 (1926).

this account has been complicated by Section 500 of the Transportation Act. This section reads: "It is hereby declared to be the policy of Congress to promote, encourage, and develop water transportation, service, and facilities in connection with the commerce of the United States, and to foster and preserve in full vigor both rail and water transportation."

What effect Section 500 has had on the administration of Section 4 of the Interstate Commerce Act it is difficult to say with certainty. There are some cases in which it appears to have been a factor in denying railroads Fourth-Section relief to meet water competition.[43] In one of the transcontinental cases the Commission said that the enactment of Section 500 was "Congress' way of saying that we should follow a less liberal policy in dealing with departures from the long-and-short-haul rule than had been followed in former years."[44] In another case the Commission said: ". . . it clearly would defeat the intent of Congress to foster transportation by water as well as rail in full vigor if in any case rail carriers were permitted, at little or no profit to themselves, to operate so as to deprive water carriers of traffic which they now enjoy, and upon which their continued existence depends to some extent."[45]

Notwithstanding these cases in which Section 500 seems to have had an effect on the administration of the Long-and-Short-Haul Clause, the Commission still grants relief to railroads to meet water competition in many cases and has specifically said that Fourth-Section relief to enable rail lines to meet water competition is not inconsistent with Section 500.[46]

ATTACKS UPON SECTION 4

The Long-and-Short-Haul Clause has always been controversial. In the debates that led to the enactment of the Act of 1887 opinion ranged from the belief that a Long-and-Short-Haul Clause was unsound in principle to the opposite view that a prohibition of higher charges for shorter than for longer hauls should be a rigid requirement with no power vested in the regulatory body to make exception. These two points of view, or slight modifications thereof, have asserted themselves at various times since.

A long struggle before the Commission and the courts was carried on by so-called "Intermountain Territory"[47] before the transcontinental commodity-rate structure was finally brought into conformity with the

---

[43] *Transcontinental Cases of 1922*, 74 ICC 48 (1922); *Sulphur to California Terminals*, 100 ICC 369 (1925); *Commodity Rates to Pacific Coast Terminals*, 107 ICC 421 (1926); *Consolidated Southwestern Cases*, 123 ICC 203, 341 (1927).

[44] *Transcontinental Cases of 1922*, 74 ICC 48, 70.

[45] *Tin Plate to Sacramento*, 140 ICC 643, 647 (1926).

[46] *Citrus Fruit from Florida to North Atlantic Ports*, 226 ICC 315, 327 (1938).

[47] Roughly the area between the Rocky Mountains on the east and the Sierra Nevada and Cascade Mountains on the west.

Long-and-Short-Haul Clause in 1918. In the 1920s, Intermountain Territory interests, fearful that their victory might be lost and that the railroads
might be successful in restoring long-and-short-haul discrimination in
transcontinental rates, sponsored legislation which would have deprived
the Interstate Commerce Commission of much of its authority to grant
Fourth-Section relief to the railroads.[48] If our analysis, earlier in this
chapter, of the situations in which long-and-short-haul departures are
justifiable is sound, then it is fortunate that these bills were not enacted.

The railroads, hard pressed for many years by the competition of
other modes of transport, have felt that Section 4 hampered their efforts to
regain traffic and have urged its repeal. Bills to this effect were passed by
the House of Representatives in 1936 and 1937 but did not get through the
Senate.[49] The railroads have gained some support for their proposals to
repeal Section 4 in certain official investigations of the problems of the
railroads.[50]

The competitors of the railroads are very much opposed to repeal of
Section 4. This is particularly true of the coastwise and intercoastal
steamship lines and the barge operators on the inland waterways. They
feel that the Commission has been altogether too lenient in permitting the
railroads to reduce rates to meet water competition, and they fear for
their very existence if Section 4 is repealed.

In so far as railroad criticism of Section 4 is based on the delay and
expense involved in making justifiable reductions in rates to meet competition, they have a valid complaint. Some improvement in this situation has
been made in recent years. The 1957 amendment of Section 4, making
Fourth-Section relief automatic to circuitous routes, has eliminated the
delay formerly involved when relief was requested on grounds of circuity.

If repeal of Section 4 is sought in the belief that less control would be
exerted over this type of discrimination than at present, the proposals
might well be viewed with concern. We have already noted that over the
years the Interstate Commerce Commission has worked out a set of
principles and policies in the administration of Section 4 which recognize
the circumstances under which this type of discrimination is justifiable,
and which at the same time impose limits on the spread between the

---

[48] For a description of these bills, known as the "Gooding bills," see Ralph L.
Dewey, *The Long and Short Haul Principle of Rate Regulation*, Ohio State University, Contributions in Economics, No. 1 (Columbus: Ohio State University Press,
1935), pp. 222–23.

[49] For the committee reports on these bills, known as the "Pettengill bills," see
74th Cong., 1st Sess., House Rep. No. 1560 (1935); 75th Cong., 1st Sess., House Rep.
No. 360 (1938); 75th Cong., 3d Sess., Senate Rep. No. 1768 (1938).

[50] See the so-called "Bricker Report," Domestic Land and Water Transportation Subcommittee of the Senate Committee on Interstate and Foreign Commerce,
Domestic Land and Water Transportation, 82d Cong., 1st Sess., Senate Rep. No.
1039 (1951), pp. 12–13; and the "Weeks Report," Presidential Advisory Committee
on Transport Policy and Organization, *Revision of Federal Transportation Policy*
(Washington, D.C.: U.S. Government Printing Office, 1955), pp. 13–14.

noncompetitive rates and those where competition is met. It is undoubtedly true that by virtue of powers possessed by the Commission under
other provisions of the Act as they now stand, substantially the same
results could be attained even if Section 4 were repealed. It is possible,
however, that the repeal of Section 4 would open the way to long-and-
short-haul discrimination in situations in which it is not justifiable or,
where justified, would result in greater disparities in rates than are
warranted by the circumstances. If injustice is to be prevented at intermediate points, it is important today, as in the past, that long-and-short-haul
discrimination be kept under close supervision.

LONG-AND-SHORT-HAUL DISCRIMINATION BY OTHER MODES OF TRANSPORT

Long-and-short-haul discrimination has been largely a railroad phenomenon. As pointed out earlier in the chapter, the practice arises out of
the nature of railroad costs. Since the costs of other modes of transport are
largely variable, the extent to which these agencies of transport can cut
rates below a normal basis at competitive points is limited. Only occasionally has long-and-short-haul discrimination appeared in the rates of
motor carriers or carriers by water. Water carriers, however, are subject
to the Long-and-Short-Haul Clause; motor carriers are not. The Commission has held that joint rail and motor rates are subject to the requirements
of Section 4.[51]

SELECTED REFERENCES

Long-and-short-haul discrimination is discussed in H. G. Brown, *Transportation Rates and Their Regulation* (New York: Macmillan, 1925), chaps. iv–v;
Eliot Jones, *Principles of Railway Transportation* (New York: Macmillan,
1924), chap. vi; H. B. Vanderblue and K. F. Burgess, *Railroads: Rates, Service,
Management* (New York: Macmillan, 1923), chap. xi; and Stuart Daggett,
Principles of Inland Transportation (4th ed.; New York: Harper, 1955), pp.
411–21. The reports of the Interstate Commerce Commission in *Administration of the Fourth Section*, 87 ICC 564 (1924); and *Fourth Section Order No.
8900*, 88 ICC 765 (1924); and *Rules to Govern Filing of Fourth Section Applications*, 310 ICC 275 (1960) give a good insight into the Commission's policy.
See also the Federal Coordinator's discussion of Section 4 in *Regulation of
Transportation Agencies*, 73d Cong., 2d Sess., Senate Doc. No. 152 (1934), pp.
66–72, and also in *Fourth Report*, 74th Cong., 2d Sess., House Doc. No. 394
(1936), pp. 58–59.

The most extensive study of the Long-and-Short-Haul Clause is Ralph L.

---

[51] *Application of Section 4 Requirements to Joint Motor-Rail Rates*, 326 ICC 453
(1966). This interpretation of the law was rejected by a federal district court in
New York Central R. Co. v. United States, 267 F. Supp. 619 (1967); but was upheld
by another district court, in a later proceeding, in *Atchison, Topeka & Santa Fe Ry.
Co. v. United States*, 300 F. Supp. 1351 (1969).

Dewey, *The Long and Short Haul Principle of Rate Regulation,* Ohio State University, Contributions in Economics, No. 1 (Columbus: Ohio State University Press, 1935). I. L. Sharfman, in *The Interstate Commerce Commission,* Vol. III–B (New York: Commonwealth Fund, 1936), pp. 542–625, intermingles the study of Section 3 and Section 4 cases involving place discrimination. Another analysis of Section 4 cases is "The Interstate Commerce Commission and Long and Short Haul Problem," 45 *Yale Law Journal* 1426 (1936).

Efforts in 1936 and 1937 to repeal Section 4 are discussed in Harold D. Koontz, "Transport Competition and Proposed Repeal of the Long-and-Short-Haul Clause," 46 *Journal of Political Economy* 153 (1938). A challenging study of the administration of the Long-and-Short-Haul Clause, which holds that the Commission has usurped legislative powers in applying the section, is Calvin Crumbaker, *Transportation and Politics—A Study of Long-and-Short-Haul Policies of Congress and the Interstate Commerce Commission* (Eugene: University of Oregon, 1940).

There is an excellent account of the early development of standards to govern Fourth Section cases in Judge Henry J. Friendly's *The Federal Administrative Agencies* (Cambridge: Harvard University Press, 1962), ch. ii. There are pertinent comments on long-and-short-haul discrimination and on Section 4 in U.S. Senate, Committee on Commerce, *National Transportation Policy,* 87th Cong., 1st Sess., Senate Report No. 445 (1961), pp. 146–48.

| Chapter | DISCRIMINATION BETWEEN |
| 22 | PLACES AND COMMODITIES |

In the preceding chapter we studied a particular form of place discrimination, long-and-short-haul discrimination, which is prohibited by Section 4 of the Interstate Commerce Act. In this chapter we are concerned with place discrimination generally and, in the last part of the chapter, with commodity discrimination.

Section 3 of the Interstate Commerce Act makes it unlawful for a railroad to give "any undue or unreasonable preference or advantage to any particular person, company, firm, corporation, association, locality, port, port district, gateway, transit point, region, district, territory, or any particular description of traffic" or to subject any of the above to any "undue or unreasonable prejudice or disadvantage."[1] Unjust place discrimination is therefore included within the scope of Section 3. Although Section 3 uses the terms "preference" and "prejudice" instead of the term "discrimination," the rate disparities referred to in Section 3 are, of course, a form of discrimination in the economic sense. We shall use the terms interchangeably except where there is reason to use the strictly legal terminology.

PLACE DISCRIMINATION DEFINED

From a strictly economic point of view, discrimination between places is unequal treatment of two or more localities in the matter of rates or service when the inequality cannot be justified by differences in the cost of service.[2]

RELATION OF SECTION 4 TO SECTION 3

Before proceeding further in the study of discrimination between places under Section 3, the relation between Section 3 and Section 4

---

[1] The words "port, port district, gateway, transit point" were added in 1935 (49 Stat. 607) following the decision of the Supreme Court in *Texas & Pacific Ry. Co.* v. *United States,* 289 U.S. 627 (1933). The words "region, district, territory" were added by the Transportation Act of 1940.

[2] As will be noted later, discrimination may also consist of equality of rates where differences in distance or transportation costs may justify differences in rates.

should be clarified. The undue preference and prejudice prohibited by Section 3 is broad enough to include the special type of place discrimination prohibited by Section 4. In a Section 3 case, however, the burden of proving "undue preference and prejudice" is upon the complaining party. This is not always easy to do, but the Commission has long held that "undue preference and prejudice must be established by a preponderance of evidence which must make it reasonably clear that the prejudice and preference complained of result from the rate adjustment of which complaint is made."[3] Section 4, on the other hand, prohibits the special type of discrimination covered by that section of the Act, except when the Interstate Commerce Commission, in special cases, grants relief from the prohibition of the section. Here the burden of establishing that conditions are such as to justify the Commission in granting relief rests upon the applicants, and any doubt with respect thereto is to be resolved against them.[4]

REASONABLE RATES MAY CAUSE UNDUE PREJUDICE

To understand fully the nature of Section 3 cases, it is necessary to distinguish clearly between Section 3 cases and those in which it is alleged that rates are unreasonable under Section 1 of the Act.

Rate controversies under Section 3 of the Act relate to rate relationships and not to the reasonableness of the rates themselves. Rates may be unduly preferential or prejudicial under Section 3 although not unreasonable under Section 1. In the words of the United States Supreme Court, ". . . a charge may be perfectly reasonable under section 1, and yet may create an unjust discrimination or an unreasonable preference under sections 2 and 3."[5] And in another case the Court said, "Both rates may lie within the zone of reasonableness and yet result in undue prejudice."[6] Since the injury in a Section 3 case results from a difference in rates and not from the level of rates themselves, orders to remove undue preference are often in the alternative, permitting the carrier to raise the preferential rate, lower the prejudicial rate, or equalize both at some other common level. The Commission has the power, however, under Section 15 of the Act, to prescribe maximum and minimum rates and, if need be, the precise rate to be charged in order to remove any unlawfulness found to exist.

---

[3] *R. C. Williams & Co., Inc.* v. *New York Central R. Co.*, 269 ICC 297, 301 (1947).

[4] *Anthracite Coal to New England Territory*, 277 ICC 569, 571 (1950); *Confectionery to New Orleans, La.*, 273 ICC 264, 265 (1948); *Confectionery to Jacksonville, Fla.*, 272 ICC 240, 241 (1948).

[5] *Interstate Commerce Commission* v. *Baltimore & Ohio R. R. Co.*, 145 U.S. 263, 277 (1892).

[6] *United States* v. *Illinois Central R. R. Co.*, 263 U.S. 515, 524 (1924).

DISCRIMINATION IMPLIES UNEQUAL TREATMENT BY SAME CARRIER

Section 3 cannot remove all discrepancies in rates that work to the disadvantage of one community and to the advantage of another. It can only remove discrepancies caused by unequal treatment of two or more places by the same carrier or carriers. "What Congress sought to prevent by that section," says the Supreme Court, "was not differences between localities in transportation rates, facilities and privileges, but unjust discrimination between them by the same carrier or carriers."[7] This point can be made clear by an illustration. Suppose, as in Figure 22–1, that A and B are localities producing a given commodity to be sold at M. If A and B are served by the same carrier, a rate of 80 cents from A to M and of 60 cents from B to M would, if the cost of transportation was the same in the two

FIGURE 22–1. Unequal Treatment by Different Carriers

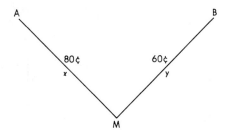

cases, amount to a discrimination against A and a preference to B. But if A is served by railroad x and B is served by y, a finding of undue preference or prejudice cannot be found. Railroad x cannot prefer B, which it does not serve; railroad y cannot discriminate against A, which it does not serve. "It would be quite absurd to charge a railroad with giving preference or advantage to a community which it does not serve, and it is equally illogical to say that it can prejudice or discriminate against such a community."[8] In another case the Commission said: ". . . a carrier can not discriminate within the meaning of the statute except as between those whom it serves or whom it may lawfully be required to serve. . . . The law does not deal in these matters with all carriers collectively as a single unit or system, but its commands are directed to each, with respect to the service which it is required to perform."[9] The Commission has repeatedly

[7] *Central R. R. Co. of New Jersey* v. *United States*, 257 U.S. 247, 259–60 (1921).

[8] *Eau Claire Board of Trade* v. *Chicago, Milwaukee & St. Paul R. R. Co.*, 4 ICR 65, 78 (1892).

[9] *Chicago Lumber & Coal Co.* v. *Tioga Southeastern Ry. Co.*, 16 ICC 323, 332 (1909).

held that a carrier is not guilty of undue preference and prejudice because its rates to a common market are higher than those of other carriers from other points of origin.[10]

The situation is otherwise if the originating lines are different but the delivering carrier is the same. Thus, in the left diagram in Figure 22–2, railroads x and y serve different points of origin but rely upon a common connection to deliver the shipments to M. Here a finding of undue preference and prejudice may be made.[11] The theory is that railroad z should not participate in rates from A and B which unjustly discriminate against one of these points. Railroad z, in effect, serves both A and B, but over the rails of x and y. It is held to be immaterial, furthermore,

FIGURE 22–2. Discrimination When Originating Lines Are Different

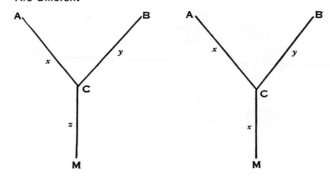

whether the rates from A to M and from B to M are joint rates or a combination of local rates based on C.[12]

A finding of undue prejudice can also be made if, as in the right diagram in Figure 22–2, railroad x extends from A to M, and railroad y delivers shipments to it at C for delivery at M. Here again, railroad x serves B, but over the rails of another line.[13] It is not necessary for a carrier to serve both the prejudiced and the preferred points, or either, over its own rails in order to come under the provisions of Section 3. "Localities require protection as much from combinations of connecting carriers as from single carriers whose 'rails' reach them. Clearly the power of Congress and of the Commission to prevent interstate carriers from practicing discrimination against a particular locality is not confined to those whose

---

[10] *Consumers Co.* v. *Chicago & North Western Ry. Co.*, 36 ICC 259, 261 (1915); *Stone Products Co.* v. *Director General*, 61 ICC 51, 53–54 (1921).

[11] See statement of the United States Supreme Court in *Texas & Pacific R. R. Co.* v. *United States*, 289 U.S. 627, 648 (1933).

[12] *United States* v. *Illinois Central R. R. Co.*, 263 U.S. 515, 527 (1924).

[13] See *Indiana Steel Wire Co.* v. *Chicago, Rock Island & Pacific Ry. Co.*, 16 ICC 155 (1909); also *United States* v. *Illinois Central R. R. Co.*, 263 U.S. 515 (1924).

rails enter it."[14] But if a carrier does not serve both the prejudiced and preferred points over its own rails, it must participate in the rates to both. As the United States Supreme Court has stated it: ". . . a carrier may not be held responsible for undue prejudice or preference unless both of the localities affected are upon its lines, or it effectively participates in the rates to both."[15] The carrier must either serve both points or participate in the rates to both in such manner that it can be said to have power to remove the discrimination. Power to remove the discrimination means power to choose between raising the preferential rate or lowering the prejudicial rate. If only one point is reached, there is no alternative presented to the carrier, and it cannot be said to control the rate relationship.[16]

The requirement that a carrier, to be found guilty of undue preference and prejudice, must serve both the preferred and the prejudiced points or participate in rates to both has been broadened somewhat in recent years. This may be illustrated by a case which involved the rail rates between points in Central and Western Trunk-Line territories and the Atlantic ports on export, import, and coastwise traffic. The Commission found that the failure of the carriers to include the port of Albany in the adjustment, thereby maintaining higher rates to and from Albany than applied at the other ports, unduly prejudiced Albany and preferred the other ports. The railroads contended that a finding of undue preference and prejudice could not be made. To be sure, the New York Central System served Albany, alleged to be prejudiced, and New York and Boston, alleged to be preferred; but it did not serve Philadelphia and Baltimore, also alleged to be preferred. Philadelphia and Baltimore were served by the Pennsylvania and the Baltimore & Ohio, whose rails also reached New York but not Albany; hence it was argued that no carrier or group of carriers controlled the rates to both the preferred points and the prejudiced point. To this contention the Commission replied:

---

[14] *St. Louis Southwestern Ry. Co.* v. *United States*, 245 U.S. 136, 144 (1917).

[15] *Texas & Pacific Ry. Co.* v. *United States*, 289 U.S. 627, 646 (1933). See also ibid., pp. 654–55.

[16] Some writers contend that this rule no longer applies. See especially C. A. Peairs, Jr., "The Golden Eggs: A Study in Tragelaphine Anatomy," 99 *University of Pennsylvania Law Review* 125, 168 (1950). The statement is based on language of the Supreme Court in *New York* v. *United States*, 331 U.S. 284 (1947). There is similar language in *Ayrshire Collieries Corp.* v. *United States*, 335 U.S. 573 (1949). We are inclined to think that more has been read into these decisions than is justified. The Commission has continued to hold that effective participation in the rates to both preferred and prejudiced points is essential to a finding of undue preference and prejudice. See *Whiterock Quarries, Inc.* v. *Pittsburgh & Lake Erie R. Co.*, 280 ICC 143, 153 (1951); *W. C. Reid & Co., Inc.* v. *Boston & Maine R.*, 286 ICC 357, 359 (1952). See also *Union Pacific R. Co.* v. *United States*, 132 F. Supp. 72, 80 (1954); *Utah-Idaho Sugar Co.* v. *Northern Pacific Ry. Co.*, 306 ICC 259, 260 (1959); *Freight, All Kinds, Southern & IFA Territories*, 323 ICC 736, 738 (1965). We shall see later in the chapter, however, that there are situations in which a carrier which serves both preferred and prejudiced points may be said to have no control over the rate relationships and cannot itself remove the preference and prejudice.

Here the cause of the alleged undue prejudice and preference is the entire structure of port rates established by defendants serving the north Atlantic ports and their connections. This structure is not a loose aggregation of separately established rates, but a single entity composed of interrelated rates bound together by the port differentials. . . . This differential rate adjustment was formed by the voluntary joint action of *all* the carriers serving the ports. It depends for its very existence upon the continued participation of *every* such carrier. And so long as this adjustment remains in existence *each* of these carriers effectively participates not only in the rates over its own line, but in every rate in the entire structure.[17] [Italics supplied.]

The rule that carriers which are a part of a complicated structure of rates which they collectively maintain may be considered as parties to discrimination against points which they do not serve has been followed in numerous later cases.[18]

ONLY "UNDUE" AND "UNREASONABLE" PREFERENCE PROHIBITED

The Act, we have already noted, does not prohibit all preferences and prejudices but only such as are "undue" and "unreasonable." Since the Act does not define what shall be due or undue, reasonable or unreasonable, it is for the Commission to decide whether the discrimination is within the law or not. "Whether a preference or advantage or discrimination is undue or unreasonable or unjust is one of those questions of fact that have been confided by Congress to the judgment and discretion of the Commission. . . ."[19] We must now turn our attention to the conditions which determine whether a discrimination is unreasonable or not.

A Competitive Relation between Communities Must Exist

A competitive relation between places is ordinarily essential to a finding of undue preference and prejudice. It is usually because of such a competitive relationship between communities that discrimination affects one community adversely and benefits another.

Two types of cases may be distinguished in this respect: (1) those in which the discrimination is really between particular individuals located at

---

[17] *Albany Port District Commission* v. *Ahnapee & Western Ry. Co.*, 219 ICC 151, 172 (1936).

[18] E.g., *Ohio-Kentucky Associated Industries* v. *Ahnapee & Western Ry. Co.*, 256 ICC 137 (1943); *Oklahoma Corporation Commission* v. *Kansas, Oklahoma & Gulf Ry. Co.*, 266 ICC 495 (1946); *Chrysler Corp.* v. *Akron, Canton & Youngstown Ry. Co.*, 279 ICC 377 (1950). A decision by a federal district court implies that concerted action by groups of carriers in establishing rates through rate bureaus or committees makes them all responsible for rates found unlawful under Section 3. *Illinois Central R. Co.* v. *United States*, 101 F. Supp. 317, 326 (1951).

[19] *Manufacturers Ry. Co.* v. *United States*, 246 U.S. 457, 481 (1918). See also *Texas & Pacific Ry. Co.* v. *Interstate Commerce Commission*, 162 U.S. 197, 219-20 (1896).

different places and (2) those in which the community as a whole is discriminated against. The two classes shade into each other to the extent that the community is affected by the prosperity of a particular industry or business. In the first class of cases the complainant is usually an individual or corporation; in the latter it is often some organization representing the community or business interests of the community. Cases of the latter sort are frequent and have led to the statement that important discrimination cases take on the aspects of "pitched battles between Manufacturers' Associations or Chambers of Commerce of competing localities."[20]

The competitive relationship between communities must be proved in a discrimination case, and the Commission often dismisses cases of alleged undue preference and prejudice because of the absence of a competitive relationship.[21] When the competition is between rival towns for population, industry, or commercial establishments, a competitive relationship is more or less taken for granted. When the case involves rival manufacturers located at different places, more definite proof of the competitive relationship is essential.

Injury Must Be Shown

For prejudice to be undue and unreasonable, the rate relationship must be injurious to the complaining shippers or localities and a source of advantage to the preferred shippers and localities.[22] The evidence must be such "as to make reasonably clear how and where the prejudice and preference result from a rate maladjustment of which complaint is made."[23] Ordinarily, however, if keen competition between shippers or localities alleged to be prejudiced and those favored can be shown, injury is presumed.[24]

If reparation is sought on past shipments because of undue prejudice, the injury shown must be proved with the same degree of certainty and exactness that would be required by a court of law.[25]

The rule that the rate adjustment must injure one locality and benefit another before undue preference and prejudice can be found is not carried so far as to prevent the removal of a rate difference that superficially

---

[20] Anon., "Consideration and Control of Commercial Conditions in Railroad Rate Regulation," 40 *Yale Law Journal* 600, 602–3 (1931).

[21] *Western Carolina Shippers Assoc.* v. *Asheville Southern Ry. Co.,* 174 ICC 353, 358 (1931); *Kistler Leather Co.* v. *Pittsburg, Shawmut & Northern R. R. Co.,* 169 ICC 247, 252 (1930).

[22] *Federated Metals Corp.* v. *Pennsylvania R. R. Co.,* 161 ICC 287, 288 (1930); *City of Moorhead* v. *Great Northern Ry. Co.,* 172 ICC 38, 43 (1931).

[23] *Beneke Corp.* v. *Columbus & Greenville Ry. Co.,* 272 ICC 156, 161 (1948).

[24] See statement of Commissioner Freas in *Stanislaus County* v. *Atchison, Topeka & Santa Fe Ry. Co.,* 315 ICC 459, 467 (1962) and cases cited therein.

[25] See *Matthiessen & Hegeler Zinc Co.* v. *Baltimore & Ohio R. Co.,* 323 ICC 601, 615 (1964).

appears to result in no injury because the prejudiced point has some off-setting advantage, such as a lower cost of production. In such circumstances it might be contended that there is no injury, since ability to compete has not been prevented by the prejudicial rates. The Commission, however, recognizes that a community should not be deprived of equal treatment in the matter of rates merely because it possesses some advantage over its rivals.[26] A patent discrimination in rates is not to be condoned because other competitive advantages and disadvantages wholly unrelated to the service of transportation may favor a shipper complaining of such discrimination."[27]

Proof of actual injury from discriminating rates is perhaps more difficult when the prejudiced point, in addition to suffering a rate handicap, also suffers from some other disadvantage, such as a higher cost of production. Here the removal of the rate disadvantage may still leave the producers at the prejudiced point at a disadvantage in the market. If so, it can be argued that the inability to compete is not caused by the rate adjustment but by other factors. Cases of this sort have sometimes divided the Commission. In some a violation of Section 3 has been found.[28] In others the inability to compete has been laid to the other circumstances and not to the disparity in rates.[29] The preferable rule would seem to be that expressed by Commissioner Eastman in a case in which the Commission failed to find a disparity in rates unlawful because the complainant suffered other disadvantages not related to freight rates. Eastman contended that whatever his other handicaps in the competitive struggle, the complainant was "at least entitled to the opportunity to compete without the unjust and unnecessary handicap of discrimination in freight rates."[30]

Can Equal Rates Be Discriminatory?

In the usual undue-prejudice case the prejudicial rate is higher, in the absolute sense, than the preferential rate, whereas the service in the two cases is alleged to justify equality in rates or at least a smaller difference in rates. The question arises whether equal rates can constitute undue pref-

---

[26] *Meridian Traffic Bureau* v. *Southern Ry. Co.*, 60 ICC 5, 11 (1920); *Allen Manufacturing Co.* v. *Nashville, Chattanooga & St. Louis Ry. Co.*, 98 ICC 405, 407 (1925).

[27] *Consolidated Mining & Smelting Co. of Canada* v. *New York Central R. Co.*, 299 ICC 231, 244 (1956). See also *Washington Potato & Onion Shippers Assoc.* v. *Union Pacific R. Co.*, 300 ICC 537, 555 (1957); *Cudahy Packing Co.* v. *Akron, Canton & Youngstown R. Co.*, 318 ICC 229 (1962).

[28] *Duluth Chamber of Commerce* v. *Chicago, St. Paul, Minneapolis & Omaha Ry. Co.*, 122 ICC 739, 743 (1927); *Indianapolis Chamber of Commerce* v. *Cleveland, Cincinnati, Chicago & St. Louis Ry. Co.*, 60 ICC 67, 73 (1920).

[29] *Barrett Co.* v. *Atchison, Topeka & Santa Fe Ry. Co.*, 172 ICC 319 (1931).

[30] Ibid., p. 336. Although this case involved discrimination between commodities, there is no reason to believe that either the majority or the minority view would have been different in a case involving discrimination between places.

erence and prejudice if the amount of service is different. The question has been definitely answered in the affirmative by the Commission. As Commissioner Eastman once stated it: "Other things being equal, it is as unduly preferential to give one shipper twice as much transportation as another for the same charge as it is to give him the same amount at half the price."[31] The Commission has frequently found equal rates for unequal services to result in undue preference and prejudice.[32] This question was involved in one proceeding which was carried to the courts. In the Texas Port Relationship Case the Commission attempted to break up the practice of equalizing rates to New Orleans and to Texas ports from points in the Southwest when the distances to New Orleans exceeded those to Galveston by more than 25 percent.[33] The Commission's order was upheld by a lower federal court, with one judge dissenting. The dissenting judge said: "I fail to see how the plaintiffs can be guilty of undue preference to New Orleans, or undue prejudice to Texas ports by charging the same rate to both."[34] The Supreme Court reversed the lower court and refused to sustain the Commission; but the case turned on other points, and the Supreme Court said nothing about the allegation that equal rates could not cause undue preference or advantage. But Justice Stone, in a separate opinion, said: "In holding that the Commission is without power to make the order, the Court does not deny that a discrimination which is produced by charging equal rates for unequal service is prohibited by the statute as much as one resulting from unequal rates for equal service."[35]

Can Lower Rates Be Prejudicial as Compared with Higher?

The Commission, however, goes further than to hold that equal rates may be discriminatory. It has held that a community enjoying lower rates than another may still be prejudiced.[36] Here, of course, the lower rates are higher in the relative sense, that is, when distance is considered. One of the lower federal courts, in a case not arising under Section 3, held that a shipper could not be injured if his competitor paid a higher rate. "How could a competitor who is complaining be injured by a rate higher than his

---

[31] Separate opinion in *Dutton Lumber Co. v. New York, New Haven & Hartford R. R. Co.*, 151 ICC 391, 415 (1929).

[32] *Inland Empire Shippers League v. Director General*, 59 ICC 321 (1920); *Milk Producers' Protective League v. Delaware, Lackawanna & Western R. R. Co.*, 7 ICC 92 (1897); *Kansas Grain Assoc. v. Chicago Rock Island & Pacific Ry. Co.*, 139 ICC 641, 670 (1928).

[33] 128 ICC 349 (1927), 160 ICC 345 (1929).

[34] *Texas & Pacific Ry. Co. v. United States*, 42 F. 2d 281, 286–87 (1930).

[35] *Texas & Pacific Ry. Co. v. United States*, 289 U.S. 627, 656 (1933).

[36] E.g., *Northern Potato Traffic Assoc. v. Atchison, Topeka & Santa Fe Ry. Co.*, 178 ICC 237, 245 (1931); *Milk & Cream to New York City*, 45 ICC 412 (1917); *Elk Cement & Lime Co. v. Baltimore & Ohio R. R. Co.*, 22 ICC 84 (1911); *Rich Ladder & Mfg. Co. v. Akron, Canton & Youngstown Ry. Co.*, 241 ICC 475, 482–83 (1940).

rate? . . . He could not be injured by the higher rate. If there be injury, it is because of difference in other conditions, not rates."[37] Admittedly, if a community enjoying lower rates than its rival is unable to compete, it must be under some other disadvantage, such as higher cost of production. But even so, is not the community which is handicapped by a high cost of production still entitled to an equitable rate adjustment?

Rate Differences and "Transportation" Conditions

Differences in rates must be justified by "transportation" conditions if undue preference and prejudice are to be avoided. The phrase "transportation conditions" refers to cost-of-service factors and, to a certain extent, to value-of-service factors also.[38]

Cost-of-Service Factors

A difference in rates which is justified by differences in cost of service is not a discrimination at all. Any cost factor may justify a difference in rates. A difference in distance is probably the most important factor justifying differences in rates to or from rival localities.[39] But distance is not the only cost factor. Thus differences in operating conditions may cause differences in cost, and hence may justify unequal rates even though distances are the same.

Cost of service is also affected by traffic density and by the volume of movement of a particular commodity. It therefore seems proper to take these matters into consideration in determining whether a rate difference is justified. But here a difficulty is encountered. A low traffic density or a light movement of a particular commodity may be caused by the rate disparity. These factors, therefore, are not of much value in attempting to justify differences in rates. This has been frequently recognized by the Commission. In a case relating to livestock rates from Illinois points to Indianapolis as compared with the rates to Chicago, the lower intrastate rates in Illinois were alleged to be justified by the greater traffic density. But the Commission pointed out that the greater density in Illinois was in part caused by "the very condition which this complaint seeks to rectify, namely, the existence of a higher scale of rates mile for mile on livestock from Illinois to Indiana than exists intrastate in Illinois."[40] The same rule

---

[37] *Anchor Coal Co.* v. *United States*, 25 F. 2d 462, 471 (1928).

[38] *York Manufacturers Assoc.* v. *Pennsylvania R. R. Co.*, 107 ICC 219, 229, 230 (1926); *Maritime Assoc., Boston Chamber of Commerce* v. *Ann Arbor Railroad Co.*, 95 ICC 539, 565 (1925).

[39] Although avoidance of undue preference and prejudice may require rates that reflect differences in distance, undue prejudice against a more distant point may sometimes be found even if the higher rates are on a lower per-mile basis than those to the nearer points. See *City of Galveston* v. *United States*, 257 F. Supp. 243, 247–48 (1966).

[40] *Indianapolis Chamber of Commerce* v. *Cleveland, Chicago, Cincinnati & St. Louis Ry. Co.*, 60 ICC 67, 75 (1920).

applies when the volume of movement of a particular commodity is less between some points than others. In one case the Commission found that higher rates on tires eastbound from San Diego, California, than applied westbound from the East were prejudicial to the western producers. The Commission pointed out that while the westbound movement was heavier than that eastbound, the rate relationship itself prevented the free movement of the western product into eastern centers. To permit the difference in volume of movement to justify the rate difference would be to make a preference "justify itself because of the results it produces."[41]

Demand Factors

Similarity in "transportation conditions," we have seen, includes not only cost factors but may also include conditions affecting the demand for transportation service. There are numerous qualifications, however, to the principle that rate discrepancies can be justified by differences in the demand for the service. This will be apparent if we proceed to a consideration of some of the conditions affecting the demand for transportation service.

Disadvantage of Location

If traffic is to move at all from various competing centers of production to a common market, it may be necessary to quote low rates from some points to overcome a natural disadvantage. The disadvantage may be due to greater distance from market or from raw materials, or it may be due to higher production costs. A community, however, cannot demand preferential rates to offset a natural disadvantage of location. "Carriers are not required by law, and could not in justice be required, to equalize natural disadvantages, such as location, cost of production, and the like."[42] In another case the Commission said: "Unjust discrimination by carriers can not be predicated upon their failure or declination to remove, by preferential rates, services, or privileges, the natural disadvantages of location under which one community rests in competition with another that is more favorably located. We have consistently held that it is not our province to adjust rates for the purpose of equalizing natural or commercial advantages."[43]

---

[41] *Spreckles Savage Tire Co.* v. *Atchison, Topeka & Santa Fe Ry. Co.*, 142 ICC 507, 512 (1928). For other cases illustrating the same principle see *Memphis-Southwestern Investigation*, 77 ICC 473, 483 (1923); and *Natchez Chamber of Commerce* v. *Louisiana & Arkansas Ry. Co.*, 58 ICC 610, 618 (1920).

[42] *Elk Cement & Lime Co.* v. *Baltimore & Ohio R. R. Co.*, 22 ICC 84, 88 (1911).

[43] *Port Arthur Board of Trade* v. *Abilene & Southern Ry. Co.*, 27 ICC 388, 402 (1913). See also *Sheridan Chamber of Commerce* v. *Chicago, Burlington & Quincy R. R. Co.*, 28 ICC 250, 262 (1913); *Florida Pulp & Paper Co.* v. *Alabama Great Southern R. Co.*, 266 ICC 331, 334 (1946).

Advantage of Location

The Commission, we have seen, cannot require the establishment of rates to remove disadvantages of location. Sometimes, however, the carriers voluntarily adjust rates to neutralize locational disadvantages. This may be done by giving less favorable rates to localities possessed of some advantage of location or by granting more favorable rates to points possessed of some disadvantage of location. The Commission has held in many cases that a carrier may not deprive a community of its advantages of location. Objections to such a practice are particularly obvious when an advantage of location is taken away by subjecting a community to relatively high rates to neutralize locational advantage. Early in its history the Commission condemned rates constructed on such a principle. Rates on lumber from Eau Claire, Wisconsin, were considerably higher than from other lumber-producing points in the vicinity. Eau Claire possessed certain advantages over its rivals which lowered its costs of production. In order to equalize the competitive advantages of the rival lumber-producing points, the rates from Eau Claire were made higher than from the competing towns. The Commission condemned the principle underlying the adjustment as "radically unsound":

That rates should be fixed in inverse proportion to the natural advantages of competing towns, with the view of equalizing "commercial conditions," as they are sometimes described, is a proposition unsupported by law and quite at variance with every consideration of justice. Each community is entitled to the benefits arising from its location and natural conditions, and any exaction of charges unreasonable in themselves or relatively unjust, by which those benefits are neutralized or impaired, contravenes alike the provisions and the policy of the statute.[44]

In another case the Commission found that higher rates on lumber from Humboldt Bay points on the Pacific Coast than applied from other points on the Coast prejudiced the former and preferred the latter. It was argued that the Humboldt Bay points enjoyed certain advantages over their rivals and that this offset the rate disadvantage. But the Commission replied: "The Humboldt Bay points can not be denied an equality of rates with the coast group points merely because the complainant manufacturers enjoy peculiar natural advantages over their coast group competitors."[45] Elsewhere the Commission has said: "Where the transportation conditions are substantially similar we have never held that a carrier has the right to discriminate against one point in favor of another because a shipper located at the former has a natural advantage over his competitor located at the latter."[46] The Texas Commission was once overruled when it attempted to

---

[44] *Eau Claire Board of Trade* v. *Chicago, Milwaukee & St. Paul R. R. Co.*, 4 ICR 65, 77 (1892).

[45] *Pacific Lumber Co.* v. *Northwestern Pacific R. R. Co.*, 51 ICC 738, 742 (1918).

[46] *Cornell* v. *Lehigh Valley R. R. Co.*, 57 ICC 157, 161 (1920); see also *Ecusta Paper Corp.* v. *Alton R. Co.*, 262 ICC 330, 338 (1945).

require higher rates to Galveston than to Houston. The order was defended on the ground that Galveston had natural advantages not possessed by Houston and could therefore hold its own even if subjected to higher rates. But the court did not consider this a valid defense, and held that the commission was not given the power to offset natural advantages by rate adjustments.[47]

In several of the cases just mentioned, the advantage which the carriers were not permitted to take away was the advantage of lower cost of production. A similar policy has been announced when the advantage is one of distance. Thus in one case, rates on rice from points in Arkansas to points in Central, Southern, and Western territories were found prejudicial as compared with rates from New Orleans, Memphis, and interior Louisiana. Distance had largely been ignored in making the rates. The Commission held that the right of the complainants to the natural advantages of their geographical location could not be taken away from them by rate adjustments and that the wide differences in distance to common destinations must be recognized.[48]

Group Rates and the Advantage of Location

The principle that a carrier may not take away a natural advantage is not wholly consistent with the Commission's approval of group rates. Wherever group rates exist, there is some disregard of distance—a disregard that increases as the size of the groups increases. The Commission in some cases has declared that group rates are not inconsistent with the principle that every community is entitled to its natural advantages.[49] In other cases the Commission has admitted that every system of group rates must occasion more or less discrimination.[50]

If the group rates do not work positive injury to the near points, however, they will not be considered objectionable. There are many cases in which the Commission has definitely refused to break up group or blanket rates, notwithstanding the fact that they tended to deprive some communities of their advantage of location. But there are also many cases in which groups have been broken up to give the nearer points in the group the advantage to which they were entitled.

In some cases of this type an attempt has been made to distinguish between group or blanket rates that open up so much territory in competition with the nearer points that a loss of shipments from the nearer points must occur and, on the other hand, situations in which the market

---

[47] *Railroad Commission of Texas* v. *Galveston Chamber of Commerce*, 51 Texas Civ. App. 476, 485 (1908).

[48] *Stuttgart Rice Mill Co.* v. *Alabama & Vicksburg Ry. Co.*, 93 ICC 517, 530 (1924).

[49] See *Inland Empire Shippers League* v. *Director General*, 59 ICC 321, 341 (1920); *Iron Ore Rate Cases*, 41 ICC 181, 214 (1916).

[50] E.g., *Mitchell* v. *Atchison, Topeka & Santa Fe Ry. Co.*, 12 ICC 324 (1907).

can take the product from all points given the blanket rate. In an early case involving blanket rates on milk to New York City, the Commission dismissed the allegation that the equal rates amounted to an unjust discrimination against the nearby producers and a preference to the distant producers. The decision was based partly on the fact that the costs of transporting milk bore little relation to distance and partly on the fact that the encouragement of milk shipments from the more distant points had not curtailed the output of the nearer producers, since the market could absorb the whole supply.[51] A few years later the same rate adjustment came before the Commission again. The blanket area had now been extended to distances exceeding 300 miles—in some instances to more than 400 miles—from New York City. The Commission found that the extension of the blanket area was opening up more territory than was necessary to supply the market, and that this was operating to the disadvantage of the nearer producers. "The interests of all milk producers, whether located within 50 or 250 miles of New York City on any of the lines, in retaining the share of this traffic to which their nearer location would naturally entitle them, are plainly imperiled under a uniform rate for the transportation service.[52] A similar distinction was made in another early case. Equal rates on coal in disregard of differences in distance were permitted. The Commission held that a considerable disregard for distance to equalize access to markets was permissible in many instances, but that in other cases it might be unreasonable to give equal rates to diversely situated localities. The latter would be the case, the Commission said, if there were insufficient demand for the commodity so that the nearer points had to divide the market with their more distant competitors.[53] These cases would seem to bear out the Commission's statement that when a group-rate system is involved, "dissatisfied producers who would be deprived of their proximity to common markets must show that they probably would be seriously injured by the rate parity."[54]

Another point regarding group rates and undue preference requires mention. The greater the length of the hauls, the greater the actual differences in distance that may be ignored. Stated in another way, groups may be larger for long-distance shipments than for shorter ones.[55]

COMPETITION AND DISCRIMINATION

We now come to consider a much-disputed question—the extent to which carrier competition will justify discrimination between places. May

---

[51] *Howell v. New York, Lake Erie & Western R. R. Co.*, 2 ICC 162 (1888).

[52] *Milk Producers' Protective Assoc. v. Delaware, Lackawanna & Western R. R. Co.*, 7 ICC 92, 167 (1897).

[53] *Imperial Coal Co. v. Pittsburgh & Lake Erie R. R. Co.*, 2 ICR 436 (1889).

[54] *Potatoes from New Brunswick, Canada, to Eastern United States*, 280 ICC 522, 528 (1951).

[55] See *Mutual Rice Trade & Development Assoc. v. International Great Northern R. R. Co.*, 23 ICC 219, 224 (1912).

a railroad grant a preferential rate to one community where it encounters competition with other carriers, and withhold an equally low rate from another point similarly situated but where no competition exists? Three different answers have been given to this question: (1) It has been stated that competition does not afford a valid excuse for discrimination. (2) Exactly the opposite position has been taken, namely, that the existence of competition at one point and not at another is sufficient to justify discrimination. (3) The position has been taken that competition may or may not justify discrimination, depending on the circumstances.

The first position, i.e., that competition at one point and not at another is no excuse for discrimination, was taken by the Illinois Supreme Court as early as 1873.[56] A later Illinois statute specifically provided that the existence of competition at one point and not at another should not be a sufficient excuse or justification for a discrimination against the latter.[57] A similar position to that of the Illinois Supreme Court was taken by the Supreme Court of the state of Washington in a more recent case. In interpreting a statute of that state which forbade undue preferences and prejudices, the Court said: "We think the section of the statute forbidding a carrier from giving undue and unreasonable preferences and advantages to persons, localities, or particular descriptions of traffic, must apply in all instances where no transportation differences intervene, regardless of the question whether the person, locality, or description of traffic is affected by the competition of a rival carrier or not."[58]

In interpreting the Interstate Commerce Act, the federal courts have taken a different position. In general they have declared that competition may, but does not necessarily, justify a discrimination. And since competition *may* offer a sufficient excuse for the preference or prejudice, the Commission must consider the element of competition in reaching its decision. Failure to do so is sufficient to invalidate an order requiring discrimination to be removed. This was the position taken by the United States Supreme Court as early as 1896.[59] The same point was made in the Alabama Midland Case[60] and in a later case.[61]

The foregoing cases establish beyond question that in the estimation of the courts, competition may justify a preference. It has been strongly urged that the existence of competition at one point and not at another necessarily prevents a finding of undue prejudice. The Supreme Court in the Alabama Midland Case took particular pains to point out that its decision was not intended to be so interpreted:

---

[56] *Chicago & Alton R. R. Co.* v. *The People*, 67 Ill. 11, 19 (1873).

[57] See *Illinois Central R. R. Co.* v. *The People*, 121 Ill. 304, 310, 319 (1887).

[58] *Public Service Commission* v. *Northern Pacific R. R. Co.*, 77 Wash. 635, 649–50 (1914).

[59] *Texas & Pacific Ry. Co.* v. *Interstate Commerce Commission*, 162 U.S. 197.

[60] 168 U.S. 144 (1897).

[61] *Louisville & Nashville R. R. Co.* v. *Behlmer*, 175 U.S. 648 (1900).

In order . . . to guard against any misapprehension of the scope of our decision it may be well to observe that we do not hold that the mere fact of competition, no matter what its character or extent, necessarily relieves the carrier from the restraints of the 3d and 4th sections, but only that those sections are not so stringent and imperative as to exclude in all cases the matter of competition from consideration in determining the questions of "undue or unreasonable preference or advantage," or what are "substantially similar circumstances and conditions."[62]

Whether in a particular case a discrimination is justified by the existence of competition at one point and not at another is therefore a question for the Commission to determine. This was put very clearly by a federal court in 1896: "It is to be borne in mind that when competition enters as an element in the determination of a case, this question—whether or not there is an undue preference or advantage—is a question not of law, but of fact. Whether or not the evidence is competent, and must be taken into account, is, of course, a question of law; but with the evidence once admitted, the issue then becomes one of fact."[63]

Although there have been some court decisions which might be interpreted as holding that competition at some points and not at others justifies a discrimination as a matter of law,[64] the Supreme Court has definitely held to the contrary. This was clearly brought out in *United States* v. *Illinois Central R. R. Co.*[65] The Illinois Central Railroad, along with other carriers, had maintained blanket rates on lumber from producing points on its lines in the South. From some points on independent connecting lines the Illinois Central also applied the blanket rates; but from other points on independent connecting lines, higher rates were charged. The Commission found that the exaction of the higher charges from points on the independent short lines was unjustly discriminatory, preferring the points given the blanket rates. The Illinois Central contended that competition forced it to extend the blanket rate to points of origin on independent connecting lines if those points were served by other carriers also, but did not require it when the shipment had to move over the Illinois Central. The United States Supreme Court answered this argument by saying:

---

[62] 168 U.S. 144, 167 (1897).

[63] *Interstate Commerce Commission* v. *Louisville & Nashville R. R. Co.*, 73 Fed. 409, 419 (1896).

[64] *East Tennessee, Virginia & Georgia Ry. Co.* v. *Interstate Commerce Commission*, 181 U.S. 1, 18 (1900). There are a number of other court decisions to the same effect. See *Interstate Commerce Commission* v. *Western & Atlantic R. R. Co.*, 88 Fed. 186, 194–97 (1898), 93 Fed. 83 (1899); *Interstate Commerce Commission* v. *Cincinnati, Portsmouth & Virginia R. R. Co.*, 124 Fed. 624 (1903); *Interstate Commerce Commission* v. *Louisville & Nashville R. R. Co.*, 190 U.S. 273 (1903); *Louisville & Nashville R. R. Co.* v. *United States*, 197 Fed. 58 (1912). See also *Texas & Pacific Ry. Co.* v. *United States*, 289 U.S. 627, 636 (1933), where the Supreme Court said: "The theory of the Act is that the carriers in initiating rates may adjust them to competitive conditions, and that such action does not amount to undue discrimination."

[65] 263 U.S. 515 (1924).

"The innocent character of the discrimination practiced by the Illinois Central was not established, as a matter of law, by showing that the preferential rate was given to others for the purpose of developing traffic on the carrier's own lines or of securing competitive traffic. These were factors to be considered by the Commission; but they did not preclude a finding that the discrimination practiced is unjust."[66]

We may therefore conclude that competition does not necessarily justify a preference in rates. This is the theory upon which the Commission acts:

It is undoubtedly true that when competitive conditions are sufficiently potent to compel lower rates to one locality than are maintained by the same carriers to another locality similarly situated, such competition may be accepted in justification of a resulting preference to the favored locality, which, but for such competition, might be condemned as undue or unreasonable. It is not to be assumed, however, that the mere fact of competition, regardless of its character, will relieve carriers from the limitations of section 3.[67]

If we examine the Commission's decisions relating to undue preference and prejudice, we discover that if the competition encountered at one point and not at others is effective and substantial it will be considered as justifying a difference in rates. In many cases the competition found to justify the discrimination has been from other modes of transport, e.g., water carriers,[68] pipelines,[69] and motor carriers.[70] The burden of establishing that competition encountered at the preferred points is sufficiently greater than that encountered at prejudiced points to justify a rate disparity rests upon defendant carriers.[71]

ANALYSIS OF COMPETITION AS AN EXCUSE FOR DISCRIMINATION

At this point it will be helpful to leave our consideration of the Commission's policy and to analyze the contention that competition justifies preferential rates. It will be helpful to approach the problem with the principle in mind that each community is entitled to the advantages of its location.

---

[66] Ibid., p. 525.

[67] *Chamber of Commerce of Newport News* v. *Southern Ry. Co.*, 23 ICC 345, 353 (1912).

[68] *Connor Lumber & Land Co.* v. *Akron, Canton & Youngstown Ry. Co.*, 40 ICC 111 (1916); *Texarkana Freight Bureau* v. *Illinois Central R. R. Co.*, 38 ICC 55, 58–59 (1916); and many other cases.

[69] *Traffic Bureau, Davenport Chamber of Commerce* v. *Alton & Eastern R. R. Co.*, 167 ICC 276 (1930); *Caddo Central Oil & Refining Corp.* v. *Kansas City Southern Ry. Co.*, 98 ICC 39 (1925).

[70] *Rate Structure Investigation, Part 3—Cotton*, 174 ICC 9, 15 (1931); *Consolidated Southwestern Cases*, 188 ICC 307 (1932).

[71] *Atchison, Topeka & Santa Fe Ry. Co.* v. *United States*, 218 F. Supp. 359 (1962).

We shall first consider a case in which competition seems to justify a discrimination. Suppose, as in Figure 22–3, that A and B compete in the production of an article which is to be sold in M. Railroad *x* serves both A and B. Over the lines of railroad *x*, A and B are equidistant from M. We shall assume the costs of transportation to be the same from both production points. At A, railroad *x* encounters the competition of railroad *y*, a shorter line. The normal rate from A to M via railroad *y* will therefore be lower than that of railroad *x*. Should railroad *x* be permitted to meet the rate of railroad *y* without giving an equally low rate from B? There can be no objection so far as B is concerned. If railroad *x* is forced to maintain a higher rate from A to M than its rival, the traffic will move by the shorter

FIGURE 22–3. Competition with a More Direct Route

FIGURE 22–4. Competition with a Water Carrier

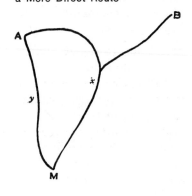
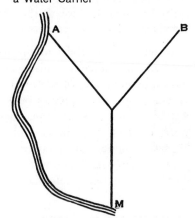

route, and A will retain its advantage over B. Nor can railroad *x* be asked to reduce the rate from B simply because it has lowered the rate from A. To do so would deprive A of its advantage of location. A has a natural advantage over B and should not be deprived of that advantage.

Figure 22–4 represents a different situation, but one which may be analyzed the same way. Here the railroad encounters water competition at A and not at B. It should be permitted to meet the water rate without being accused of unjustly discriminating against B. A has a natural advantage over B. As Acworth once described this situation: "To call upon a railway company to give an inland town rates on the same scale as those which it gives when there is sea competition, simply because it there gives them, is to call upon it, not to maintain equality, but to counteract an inequality for which, not the railway company, but the Author of the Universe is responsible."[72]

---

[72] W. M. Acworth, *The Elements of Railway Economics* (Oxford: Clarendon Press, 1905), pp. 140–41.

Most of the cases in which the Commission finds a discrimination justified by competition can be analyzed with the same results as in the two illustrations above. Occasionally, however, the Commission refuses to permit a discrimination which would seem to be justified by the foregoing reasoning. In one case the carriers proposed an 8-cent rate on iron and steel articles from Chicago to Milwaukee to meet water competition. Producers of steel at East St. Louis, Alton, and other points objected to the reduction, alleging that it unduly preferred Chicago and discriminated against them. Division 2 of the Commission refused to permit the reductions, saying:

> Respondent's desire to divert traffic from the water lines explains, but by no means justifies, the proposed reductions. . . . The fact that shippers located in the Chicago district may ship by water at a rate as low as that proposed does not relieve respondents of their obligations under section 3. . . . There is no provision of the act which gives us authority to relieve the carriers from complying with the provisions of section 3 whenever they desire to divert traffic from their water competitors to their own lines. . . .[73]

The position taken by Commissioner Brainerd in a dissenting opinion would seem to be more in accordance with the policy usually followed by the Commission. He pointed out that unless the rail rate were reduced, the articles would be shipped by water. The disadvantage of producers at East St. Louis and Alton would therefore exist whether the railroads maintained the old rate or reduced it to the water rate.

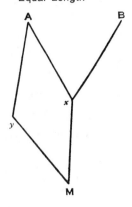

FIGURE 22–5. Competition between Railroads of Approximately Equal Length

An entirely different situation is presented if, as in Figure 22–5, railroad x encounters competition with a railroad of approximately equal length. In this situation a lower rate from A to M than from B to M does not result from the fact that the cost of transportation is less from A to M, but from the fact that the railroads are engaging in competition at A and have reduced rates below a reasonable level; or else it results from the fact that railroad x is maintaining an excessive rate from B to M, where it has a monopoly. As far as the costs of transportation are concerned, B is as advantageously located as A. If A gets lower rates than B, the latter point is deprived of the equal treatment to which it is entitled.

It may be argued that A has an advantage over B—the advantage of having two routes to M, while B has but one. But this advantage is an artificial advantage, not a natural one. If railroads x and y maintained

---

[73] *Iron & Steel Articles from Chicago District*, 163 ICC 369 (1930). The case is complicated by another matter—Section 500 of the Transportation Act, which declares that the policy of Congress is to promote, encourage, and develop water transportation.

normal rates from A to M, A would have no rate advantage over B. There are authorities, however, who have considered the existence of competitive routes as an advantage which should not be taken away. In an English case the court said:

> I cannot see . . . why the advantageous position of the one trader in having his works so placed that he has two competing routes is not as much a circumstance to be taken into consideration as the geographical position of the other trader, who, though he has not the advantage of competition, is situated at a point on the line geographically nearer the market. . . . Of course, if you are to exclude this from consideration altogether, the result must inevitably be to deprive the trader who has the two competing routes of a certain amount of advantage which he derives from the favorable position of his works.[74]

This pronouncement has been quoted approvingly by at least one court in the United States,[75] and a similar position has been taken by one American writer.[76] It must be remembered, however, that a reduced rate due to competition alone, and not to the existence of a cheaper route or means of transportation, results from a depressed rate at the competitive point or from the exaction of monopoly charges at the noncompetitive points. The first partakes of the nature of cutthroat competition—an unwise policy; the second represents an exercise of monopoly power, and is unjust. In either case the point discriminated against has a valid objection to the rate adjustment.

It should be noted that our analysis of competition as a justification for discrimination between places under Section 3 parallels the analysis, in the preceding chapter, of the competitive situations which do or do not justify long-and-short-haul discrimination.

The Ashland Rule

Prior to 1920 the Commission's powers were not adequate to prevent the questionable type of discrimination illustrated by Figure 22–5. Since railroad *y* does not serve B, it cannot be held to be discriminating against B in favor of A. Only railroad *x* serves both A and B, hence only *x* can be found guilty of discriminating against B and of preferring A. If an order were therefore issued requiring railroad *x* to remove the discrimination against B, it could attempt to do so by either lowering the rate from B or raising the rate from A. If the latter course were taken, B would not be benefited as long as *y* continued to maintain the lower rate; and this is within the power of *y* to do. A would continue to have a low rate to M, although it would be necessary to ship via railroad *y* and not via *x*. If, on

---

[74] *Phipps* v. *London & North Western Ry. Co.*, 2 QB 229, 242 (1892).

[75] *Interstate Commerce Commission* v. *Louisville & Nashville R. R. Co.*, 73 Fed. 409 (1896).

[76] W. C. Noyes, *American Railroad Rates* (Boston: Little, Brown, 1906), p. 93.

the other hand, railroad x attempted to remove the discrimination by lowering the rate from B, railroad y could, if it wished, restore the difference in rates by reducing its rate from A. Subject to certain limitations, this is within its power to do.

In such circumstances as those described, the Commission followed the rule, commonly known as the "Ashland Rule," that a finding of undue preference and prejudice could not be made against a carrier unless it effectively controlled the rate from both the preferred and the prejudiced points and so had the power to end the discrimination by its own act.[77] Here, although railroad x serves both A and B, it cannot control the rate relationship so long as railroad y has the right of independent action. Under these circumstances, to require x to remove the discrimination would, to paraphrase a comment by the Supreme Court, be requiring carriers to do what they are powerless to perform.[78]

Although the Ashland Rule still applies to orders issued under Section 3 which require carriers to remove undue preference or prejudice,[79] the broadened powers of the Commission under the Act of 1920 to prescribe the maximum, or the minimum, or the maximum and minimum, or the precise rate to be charged in place of rates found unlawful, would seem to enable the Commission to remove discriminations in rates that the carriers practicing discrimination are not able to remove by their own acts.[80]

All Competitive Points Must Be Treated Equally

We have seen that very often a railroad is permitted to reduce rates to meet the competition of a more direct route or of a cheaper form of transportation, and that it does not constitute a violation of Section 3 to withhold the low rate from points where such competition is not encountered. But if the carrier reduces rates to meet competition at one point, it must make similar reductions at other points where the same competition is encountered. The Commission has said: ". . . carriers are not obligated to meet water competition, nevertheless they may not create an unduly prejudicial situation by meeting it at one point and failing to meet it at a competing point."[81] Similarly the Commission has frequently held that railroads may not reduce rates to meet motor competition at certain points

---

[77] See *Ashland Fire Brick Co.* v. *Southern Ry. Co.*, 22 ICC 115 (1911), and *Texas & Pacific R. Co.* v. *United States*, 289 U.S. 627 (1933).

[78] *New York* v. *United States*, 331 U.S. 284, 342 (1947).

[79] For a later case in which the Ashland Rule was followed, see *H. Samuels Co.* v. *Baltimore & Ohio Chicago Terminal R. Co.*, 299 ICC 793 (1957).

[80] *New York* v. *United States*, 331 U.S. 284 (1947); *Ayrshire Collieries Corp.* v. *United States*, 335 U.S. 573, 593–94 (1949).

[81] *Bunker Hill & Sullivan Co.* v. *Oregon-Washington R. R. & Nav. Co.*, 132 ICC 266, 271 (1927). See also *Spreckles Savage Tire Co.* v. *Atchison, Topeka & Santa Fe Ry. Co.*, 142 ICC 507, 512 (1928).

and fail to reduce them at others where similar competitive conditions prevail.[82] This principle is also of importance when market competition comes into play. A carrier need not reduce its rates to meet the rates of another line extending from another source of supply to a common market; but if it voluntarily makes such a reduction, it must make a similar reduction from all producing points on its lines which are similarly situated.[83]

DISCRIMINATION BETWEEN COMMODITIES

Since the principles recognized in cases involving discrimination between commodities parallel those which we have described in cases relating to discrimination between places, it is necessary to consider them here only briefly.

In the chapter on railway rate theory we used the term "discrimination" to refer to differences in rates not based on differences in cost of service. We found that freight classification is a form of discrimination, for the differences in rates on different commodities are not all to be explained by differences in the direct cost of transporting them; often the differences are due to the commodities' respective abilities to pay more or less toward the indirect or overhead expenses. Here we are not dealing with discrimination in the broad sense of the word, but with unjustifiable discrimination between commodities, that is, discrimination which works an injury to shippers of the articles not given preferences. As we have noted, Section 3 prohibits only undue or unreasonable discrimination.

In cases relating to discrimination between commodities, as in those relating to discrimination between places, the issue is one of differences in rates and not of the rates themselves. Both the preferential and the prejudicial rate may be reasonable per se and yet cause undue preference and prejudice.

Commodities Must Be Competitive

Generally speaking, for a finding of undue prejudice to be made, the commodities concerned must be competing commodities. This is because there can be no finding of undue preference or prejudice unless someone is positively injured by the relationship, and such injury generally arises because the producer of one of the products is unable to sell it in competition with the product granted favored rates. It is difficult to see how a producer of one commodity can be injured by low rates on a

---

[82] *Iron & Steel to Iowa, Minnesota, Michigan, & Wisconsin*, 297 ICC 363 (1955); *Oak Flooring—Pine Bluff, Ark., to Michigan, New York, Ohio, & Pennsylvania*, 315 ICC 77 (1961).

[83] See *Milburn Wagon Co.* v. *Lake Shore & Michigan Southern Ry. Co.*, 22 ICC 93, 100–101 (1911); *North Fork Cannel Coal Co.* v. *Ann Arbor R. R. Co.*, 25 ICC 241, 246 (1912).

different commodity unless the two products compete with each other.[84] The necessity of a competitive relationship between the commodities is frequently pointed out by the Commission.[85]

Cases in which an inequality in rates on different commodities has been found to result in undue preference and prejudice are numerous. Thus it has been found unduly prejudicial to maintain higher rates on zinc ammonium chloride than on sal ammoniac (both commodities being used for galvanizing).[86] It has likewise been found unduly prejudicial to have higher rates on benzol than on gasoline;[87] on cotton-factory sweepings than on rags;[88] on linseed oil than on cottonseed oil;[89] on bran than on middlings;[90] on lard substitutes than on lard;[91] on veneer than on lumber;[92] on gypsum hollow building tile than on clay hollow building tile;[93] on toasted wheat biscuit than on "Cream of Wheat";[94] and on cottonseed oil than on soybean oil.[95]

The competition between two commodities, however, must be real. Findings of undue prejudice are often refused because of the lack of genuine and substantial competition between the commodities concerned. Flaxseed and grain do not compete; hence a disparity in rates cannot result in undue prejudice.[96] Silica sand and common sand are not used for the same purposes; hence higher rates on the former than on the latter can work no injury.[97] Cork board and "Celotex" compete to some extent, but the latter has great tensile strength and the former has not. "Celotex" can therefore be used for many purposes, while cork board can be used only for insulating purposes. The field of competition is accordingly not great enough to permit a finding of undue preference or advantage.[98]

---

[84] Low rates on one commodity, if below out-of-pocket cost, would tend to burden other traffic and hence might discriminate against it even though it is non-competitive with the favored article. But such rates are unreasonably low under Section 1.

[85] *California Walnut Growers Assoc. v. Aberdeen & Rockfish R. R. Co.*, 50 ICC 558, 568 (1918). See also *Boston Wool Trade Assoc. v. Boston & Albany R. R. Co.*, 78 ICC 178, 183 (1923).

[86] 159 ICC 475 (1929).

[87] 156 ICC 444 (1929).

[88] 147 ICC 740 (1928).

[89] 109 ICC 721 (1926).

[90] 101 ICC 14 (1925).

[91] 95 ICC 171 (1925).

[92] 81 ICC 227 (1923).

[93] 53 ICC 46 (1919).

[94] 33 ICC 534 (1915).

[95] 256 ICC 89 (1943).

[96] *Archer-Daniels-Midland Co. v. Great Northern Ry. Co.*, 171 ICC 192, 195 (1930).

[97] *Illinois Sand Traffic Bureau v. Atchison, Topeka & Santa Fe Ry. Co.*, 152 ICC 749, 753 (1929).

[98] *Armstrong Cork Co. v. Akron, Canton & Youngstown Ry. Co.*, 136 ICC 9, 14 (1927).

Actual Injury from Rate Adjustment Must Be Shown

It is not enough to show a competitive relation between two commodities in cases arising under Section 3. A finding of undue prejudice cannot be made unless there is proof that the rate relationship has been the source of actual injury to the complaining party in marketing his product. In one case it was found that a disparity in rates on roofing slate and roofing tile existed, but the Commission said: "It is not shown that the disparities in the rates have affected the movement of roofing slate or that the complainants have been damaged by reason of these disparities."[99] No finding of undue prejudice was made. The same point was brought out in a case involving an alleged preference in the rates on tin and copper to the disadvantage of aluminum.[100] The principle was generalized somewhat in a more recent case, where the Commission said:

> . . . undue prejudice does not exist merely because rates are different and there is some competition between commodities. There must be a further showing that the difference has operated to complainant's disadvantage in marketing its commodity. The character or intensity of the competition, [and] the specific effect of the rate relationship upon such competition . . . must be shown in addition to a difference in the rates.[101]

Exceptions to the Rule of Equality between Competing Products

It should not be inferred that competing products must always be given the same rate by a railway even when a difference in rates works a hardship upon shippers. Differences may be justified on at least three grounds.

Differences in Cost of Service. The cost of transporting one commodity may be greater or less than the cost of transporting the competing commodity. Such differences in cost of service justify differences in the rates charged. Thus the rates on protected metal roofing and hard asbestos roofing need not be the same, although the two products are competitive, since the weight density of asbestos roofing is greater than that of metal roofing. This justifies lower rates on the former.[102] Any other factor affecting relative cost of service[103] will justify a difference in rates on competing commodities, although very minor differences in cost are likely to be disregarded. When a difference is justified by differences in the cost of service, the difference in rates should be measured by the difference in

---

[99] *Arvonia-Buckingham Slate Co. v. Aberdeen & Rockfish R. R. Co.*, 174 ICC 767, 769 (1931).

[100] *Aluminum Co. of America v. Atchison, Topeka & Santa Fe Ry. Co.*, 146 ICC 363, 372 (1928).

[101] *Staley Manufacturing Co. v. Wabash Ry. Co.*, 167 ICC 12, 15 (1930).

[102] *Robertson Co. v. Alabama Great Southern R. R. Co.*, 167 ICC 693 (1930).

[103] For a list of such factors see pp. 426–33, supra.

cost. The Commission very frequently makes a finding of undue prejudice if the differences in rates exceed proper differentials.

Differences in the Value of the Articles. But cost factors are not the only ones that justify differences in the rates on competing commodities. A difference in the values of the two articles has also been held to justify a difference in rates. Thus the Commission has said: "Value of the commodity transported is an important factor in the determination of . . . whether or not discrimination is undue."[104] The value of the commodity is thus considered as one of the "transportation characteristics" held to justify inequalities in the rates on competing articles.[105]

Degree to Which the Articles Are Affected by Carrier Competition. Another factor which may justify differences is the degree to which two articles are affected by competition between carriers. Competition sometimes forces a carrier to charge a low rate on one commodity, but competition may not apply with equal force to the rival commodity. At one time, lower rates on apples than on citrus fruits from the Pacific Coast to eastern points were alleged to prefer unduly the producers of apples to the disadvantage of the producers of citrus fruits. The Commission found that the difference did not result in undue preference and prejudice and pointed out, among other things, that the apples were subject to water competition via the Panama Canal, while citrus fruits were not.[106] In another case the Commission pointed to the competitive forces applying to the transportation of flour and not applying to oatmeal as justifying a difference in rates.[107] Perhaps the most famous example of this principle arose in connection with the relationship in the rates on livestock and packing-house products. In 1905 the Commission ordered the carriers to discontinue charging higher rates on livestock than on packing-house products from Missouri River points to Chicago because the existing

---

[104] *Coke Producers Assoc. of Connellsville v. Baltimore & Ohio R. R. Co.*, 27 ICC 125, 147 (1913). See also *Ogden Packing & Provision Co. v. Atchison, Topeka & Santa Fe Ry. Co.*, 101 ICC 236, 252 (1925); and *Wrigley Jr. Co. v. Aberdeen & Rockfish R. R. Co.*, 161 ICC 41, 44 (1930), where differences in value were considered in Section 3 cases.

[105] The soundness of this rule from an economic viewpoint is open to question if followed as an invariable rule. The usual justification for higher rates on the more valuable commodities is that the greater value indicates greater ability to bear freight rates. But if two articles are truly competitive, the greater cost of one may indicate less ability to pay rather than more, since it must compete with a cheaper article. The higher rate adds to the handicap already suffered by the high-priced commodity in competing with the cheaper. But if the higher price is not an obstacle in the sale of the article, this objection does not apply.

[106] *California Growers' and Shippers' Protective League v. Southern Pacific Co.*, 100 ICC 79, 105 (1925).

[107] *Atlas Cereal Co. v. Atchison, Topeka & Santa Fe Ry. Co.*, 89 ICC 212, 218 (1924). For another example see also *National Veneer & Panel Mfrs. Assoc. v. Aberdeen & Rockfish R. R. Co.*, 195 ICC 411 (1933). For recognition of this principle by the Supreme Court of Nebraska, see *Application of Nebraska Limestone Producers Assoc.*, 97 N.W. 2d 331 (1959).

relationship discriminated against livestock shipments.[108] The order of the Commission was held invalid by the courts on the ground that there was no undue prejudice in view of the fact that keen competition between rival railroads had forced down the rates on packing-house products, whereas no such competition had developed for livestock shipments.[109]

Raw Materials and Finished Products

The raw-material-and-finished-product relationship, already described as a factor in determining the reasonableness of rates under Section 1, is involved in Section 3 cases. Raw materials and finished products are competitive, for the relationship in rates may determine the location of the industry, and that in turn will determine whether the raw material or the finished product is to be transported long distances. It is easy to see, therefore, that the relationship in the rates on a raw material and on the corresponding finished product may discriminate against the producers located near the supply of raw material or those located near the market for the finished product.

Examples of undue prejudice arising from the raw-material-finished-product relationship are numerous. In one case the Commission found that a reduction in rates on roasted coffee from Texas ports to points in the interior without a corresponding reduction in rates on green coffee would unduly prefer coffee roasters in the Houston area and disadvantage those located in the interior.[110] The Commission has found that rates on sash doors and other items of millwork are unduly prejudicial to the extent that they exceed the rates on lumber,[111] and that rates on cottonseed in excess of rates on cottonseed oil result in undue prejudice.[112] More often, perhaps, the rates on the finished product are the higher; but if the proper differential is exceeded, it works an injury to the producers located near the raw materials. In one case the Commission limited the rate on malt to seven cents per hundred pounds over the rate of barley.[113]

When controversies over rate relationships arise between producers located near markets and those located near raw materials, the most logical solution of the difficulty would be to make the differences in rates conform to differences in the cost of service. When this is done, the industry might well be left to migrate to the most advantageous location. This solution of the problem commends itself to one interested in the develop-

---

[108] *Chicago Live Stock Exchange* v. *Chicago Great Western Ry. Co.*, 10 ICC 428 (1905).

[109] *Interstate Commerce Commission* v. *Chicago Great Western Ry. Co.*, 141 Fed. 1003 (1905). Affirmed in 209 U.S. 108 (1908).

[110] *Roasted Coffee from and to Points in Texas*, 292 ICC 777 (1954).

[111] 78 ICC 495, 522 (1923).

[112] 26 ICC 607 (1913).

[113] 23 ICC 378 (1912).

ment of the most efficient methods of production. The Commission has shown a leaning to this view, and the prescription of differentials is governed largely by cost factors. In one of the early livestock and packing-house product cases, the Commission said: "We are of opinion that in the fixing of relative rates upon articles strictly competitive, as these are, the proper relation should be determined from the cost of the service."[114] The Commission has not been able to adhere strictly to this position, and the other modifying factors mentioned above—value, and differences in the extent to which the two commodities are affected by competition of carriers—may affect a particular case. The court decision in the Chicago Live Stock Case, above referred to, requires consideration of the latter factor, at least.

Although relative cost of service is not the only factor considered in prescribing nonprejudicial relationships between rates on raw materials and manufactured articles, it is definitely settled that the relationship ought not to be prescribed for the purpose of equalizing competitive advantage. Proper relationships may exist, but one producer may still have an advantage over another. But if so, the advantage of the one and the disadvantage of the other are due to factors other than a prejudicial rate structure. It is no function of the Commission to prescribe rates to offset a disadvantageous location. This point is well illustrated by a case involving the rates on rough quarried stone and on cut stone. Cut stone is building stone after it has been cut into the proper shapes and sizes for use in the construction of buildings. In this case the conflict was between those who cut stone near the quarries in Indiana and those who purchased the rough stone and cut it in Washington, D.C., and vicinity, where it was being used extensively. The maintenance of the same rates on cut stone as on rough stone was alleged to prefer the cutters in Indiana, who could ship the cut stone as cheaply as the Washington cutters could get their raw material. But another factor entered into the competitive situation. There is an element of waste (about ten percent) in the process of manufacturing the dressed stone. This gave the producer near the quarries an additional advantage, since his competitors had to pay freight on a certain amount of waste. The question arose as to whether the disadvantage of the Washington manufacturers, arising from the necessity of transporting a certain amount of waste material, should be removed by the rate adjustment. The answer of the Commission was in the negative:

. . . it is our duty to remove that undue disadvantage and undue prejudice to complainants which is occasioned by freight rates, but we may not equalize any other advantages or disadvantages enjoyed or suffered by the parties. In order to remove the undue prejudice caused by the rate adjustment, and that adjustment only, the spread established between the rates on rough and dressed stone must be based upon their differences in transportation characteristics. Interveners are therefore correct in their contention that the relationship of the

---

[114] *J. P. Squire & Co.* v. *Michigan Central R. R. Co.*, 4 ICC 611, 626 (1891).

rates involved should not be based upon the amount of waste in dressing stone.[115]

A similar position was taken by the Commission very early in its history and has been consistently followed.[116] The Commission will remove only such disadvantages as arise from inequitable freight rates.

PLACE AND COMMODITY DISCRIMINATION BY OTHER MODES OF TRANSPORT

Section 3 of the Interstate Commerce Act applies principally to railroads, but similar prohibitions against undue preference and prejudice are contained in Part II of the Act, which relates to motor carriers, and Part III, which relates to carriers by water. Likewise, the Federal Aviation Act prohibits undue preference and prejudice by air carriers; and the Shipping Act of 1916 contains similar prohibitions against undue preference and prejudice by the ocean carriers that come under that Act.

SELECTED REFERENCES

References on discrimination under Section 3 are not very numerous. Section 3 is discussed by H. Hull in "Discrimination under the Act to Regulate Commerce," 51 *American Law Review* 166 (1917); and in "What Constitutes Unjust Discrimination in Railroad Rates," 24 *Case and Comment* 873 (1918); and also in Glenn L. Shinn, "Freight Rate Prejudice and Preference," 31 *I.C.C. Practitioners' Journal* 531 (1964).

Interstate Commerce Commission policy in cases of discrimination between commodities is discussed in I. L. Sharfman, *The Interstate Commerce Commission*, Vol. III–B (New York: Commonwealth Fund, 1936), pp. 527–38, and in cases involving discrimination between places on pp. 538–693.

The question of the adequacy or inadequacy of the Commission's power to prevent undue preference and prejudice under all circumstances, either with or without the minimum rate power, is discussed in Nathaniel L. Nathanson, "The Minimum Rate Power and Discriminatory Practices," 59 *Northwestern University Law Review* 1 (1964), pp. 1–17. Legislative history, Commission interpretation, and judicial interpretation of Sections 2, 3, and 4 of the Interstate Commerce Act are analyzed with penetration in Jordon J. Hillman, *Competition and Railroad Price Discrimination* (Evanston, Ill., The Transportation Center at Northwestern University, 1968).

[115] *O'Meara* v. *Baltimore & Ohio R. R. Co.*, 183 ICC 3, 15 (1932).
[116] See the J. P. Squire Case, n. 114, supra.

Chapter 23

ACCOUNTS AND

ACCOUNTING REGULATION

Control over accounts is a prime essential in any attempt to regulate railroads or other transportation agencies. Accounting systems have been prescribed for the various modes of transport by the regulating authorities having jurisdiction over them. In this chapter attention is given to some of the major aspects of accounting regulation, with special reference to the system of accounts prescribed by the Interstate Commerce Commission for railroads.

NECESSITY OF ACCOUNTING REGULATION

A glance at the various regulatory measures, such as are described in preceding pages, which have been undertaken by the government in its attempt to control transportation agencies reveals a close relationship between the system of regulation and control of carrier accounts. The fair-return doctrine, for instance, assumes that the actual earnings of a company can be ascertained. The fair return contemplated by the law is a net return, and this means that operating revenues and expenses must be correctly stated. The determination of the fair value on which a return is to be allowed requires a truthful statement of investment in road and equipment. There are many other regulatory measures which depend upon accounting regulation for their successful administration. Regulation of security issues would be largely impossible without reliable figures showing earnings, fixed charges, property investment, stock outstanding, bonds issued, floating debt, and other pertinent facts. Use is also made of accounts in considering applications for authority to abandon lines.

INCIDENTAL BENEFITS OF ACCOUNTING REGULATION

Although the regulation of carrier accounts is to be explained and justified by its relation to control of railroad rates and practices, it has other benefits of an incidental nature. A uniform and accurate system of accounts, such as is required by law, is of value to the carriers themselves.

The railroads would of course have an accounting system of their own in the absence of a system prescribed by regulatory authorities. Uniformity, however, would probably not be attained without government interference, and there is a distinct gain in a uniform system of accounting which makes comparisons between railroads possible.

Accounting regulation is also of advantage to the investor in railroad securities. It assures him of an accurate and trustworthy statement of earnings and financial position. Before the days of effective accounting regulation, carriers were all too often inclined to misrepresent their accounts, concealing earnings in some instances, and in others making an appearance of earnings where none existed. This practice can be stopped by effective accounting regulation. Incidentally this result of accounting regulation redounds to the advantage of the public in general, for it reduces the risk of misrepresentation in accounts and should lead to the investment of capital in railroad enterprises on more favorable terms.

ESSENTIALS OF A PRESCRIBED SYSTEM OF ACCOUNTS

If we bear in mind the purpose of accounting regulation, it is clear that there are certain things which a system of carrier accounts should provide.

In the first place, the system should be uniform. The greatest confusion would exist if, for instance, the net income of one railroad were not comparable with that of another because of differences in the methods of accounting. Furthermore, when dealing with railroads as a whole or in groups, it is necessary to add together the property investment, net railway operating income, or other items of all or of groups of railroads. Such aggregates would be meaningless if accounts were not kept on a uniform basis. It was for these reasons that the Act of 1887 empowered the Interstate Commerce Commission to prescribe a uniform system of accounts for carriers subject to its jurisdiction. The accounting system prescribed for railroads is uniform except in minor particulars.

A second essential of a system of railroad accounts is a complete separation of carrier and noncarrier business. This is important because of the fair-return-on-fair-value system of regulation. If a carrier is entitled to a fair return on the fair value of the property devoted to transportation purposes, that property must be separated from the other property and investments of the company. Similarly the revenues derived from transportation business and the expenses incurred therein must be separated from other revenues and expenses. The carrier is not entitled to exact more than reasonable rates for the service of transportation to make up for unprofitable undertakings of a noncarrier sort or because of unprofitable investments in other businesses. Neither is a carrier to be deprived of a fair return from its transportation business just because it may have additional sources of income. It will be shown shortly that the system of accounts prescribed by the Commission accomplishes this separation of carrier and noncarrier business.

A third essential of accounting regulation is a careful distinction between expenditures which are chargeable to capital and those which are chargeable to income. Expenditures that represent investment in capital assets should be charged to the appropriate asset account. They do not enter into operating expenses or affect the net income at the time they are made. But expenditures which are properly expenses of doing business and which should be defrayed from current revenues should be charged to income and not to capital. A system of accounting must make the distinction between the two classes of expenditures definite. This is necessary to prevent manipulation of accounts and also to secure uniformity in accounting practice. In the past, carriers have frequently charged to capital what should have been charged as operating expenses, or they have treated as operating expenses what should have been charged to capital. Earnings may be inflated or concealed according to the desire of management if this distinction is not made. But even when there is no desire to falsify returns, the distinction between the two types of expenditures should be insisted upon. This is because accounting practice may differ on different railroads, thereby destroying uniformity in accounts. Some carriers, for instance, might consider all replacements as an operating expense, even if the replacements were accompanied by betterment. Other carriers might carefully distinguish between that part of a certain expenditure which is a replacement in kind and that which represents an improvement and which may therefore be charged to capital. Or again, one carrier might follow the policy of charging replacements in kind to operating expenses, even though the cost of the new property installed was higher than the original cost of the retired unit. Another carrier might charge the difference between the cost of the new unit and the cost of the retired unit to capital.

Under the accounting classifications prescribed by the Interstate Commerce Commission, all additions and betterments must be charged to capital. It was a common practice in the past for railroads to charge additions and betterments to operating expenses in good years. In the case of replacement with betterment the accounting rules provide that the amount representing betterment shall be charged to capital account. The rule with respect to replacements in kind is very specific. When property is retired and replaced in kind, the ledger value of the retired property is deducted from the property accounts and charged to operating expenses.[1] The cost of the new property installed is added to the ap-

---

[1] This is assuming that no depreciation reserve has been set up. In the latter case, part or all of the ledger value of the retired property is charged to depreciation reserve. If the amount to be charged to operating expenses on account of retirements is large, it may, upon approval by the Interstate Commerce Commission, be charged to Profit and Loss.

propriate property account. This means that if the cost of the new unit is greater than the original cost of the retired unit, the difference shows up in an enlarged property investment. Prior to 1914 the amount charged to operating expenses in connection with replacements was the cost of replacing in kind. This meant that if prices had risen, the increase was absorbed in operating expenses, and property accounts were not affected. It is still true that with respect to small units of property like ties and rails, the cost of replacement in kind is charged to operating expenses, regardless of changes in prices.

A fourth requirement of a prescribed accounting system is provision for an accurate statement of the property account. The accounting classifications of the Commission require that the property accounts shall show actual money costs to the carrier. When the consideration given for the purchase of property is other than money, the money value of the consideration at the time of the transaction is charged to the property account. To have the property account show the cost of all property necessitates that additions and betterments be included, whether paid from the proceeds of security issues or out of current resources, and also that the excess cost of replacing property in kind over the cost of the property retired should appear in the account. Abandoned property should be written off if the property account is to give an accurate statement of the cost of property devoted to transportation purposes. The accounting regulations require that a unit of property retired from service must be written out of the property accounts at once.

HISTORY OF ACCOUNTING REGULATION

Probably the earliest system of accounts prescribed for railways by public authority in the United States was that prescribed by the Massachusetts commission under authority of an act passed in 1876. The federal government did not enter this field of regulation until 1907. The original Act to Regulate Commerce empowered the Interstate Commerce Commission to require annual reports of the carriers in such form as it might prescribe. The Commission was also authorized to prescribe a uniform system of accounts. Although the Commission succeeded in obtaining annual reports from the carriers under this law, it made no attempt to prescribe a uniform system of accounting. The enforcement provisions of the law were weak. No penalties were provided in this section of the law, and the Commission was not empowered to investigate or audit the books of the carriers. Under these circumstances little would have been accomplished by prescribing a uniform system.

The Hepburn Act of 1906 enlarged the Commission's powers. Monthly and special reports, in addition to annual reports, might be required of the carriers. Penalties were provided for failure to make reports or for falsifying them. The carriers were required to keep accounts according to the Commission's specifications. The Commission was authorized to appoint examiners to inspect carrier accounts, and the courts were empowered to compel compliance with the accounting provisions of the Act by the issuance of writs of mandamus.

After the strengthening of the Act by these amendments the Commission proceeded to work out a uniform system of accounts. The Commission obtained the cooperation of the Association of American Railway Accountants, and a system of accounting for rail carriers was prescribed in 1907. The system received major revision in 1914, and has been further modified and elaborated from time to time.

BALANCE SHEET ACCOUNTS

The general balance sheet accounts are prescribed by the Interstate Commerce Commission.[2] On the assets side of the balance sheet the most important accounts are "Road and Equipment Property" and "Improvements on Leased Property." These two accounts represent the railroad company's investment in property of a durable character that is devoted to transportation service. "Accrued Depreciation"[3] is shown as a deduction from these investment accounts to give the balance sheet item "Total Transportation Property less Recorded Depreciation and Amortization." Noncarrier property is recorded in other accounts, principally "Miscellaneous Physical Property," "Investment in Affiliated Companies," and "Other Investments." Classified as "Current Assets" are various accounts, the most important of which are "Cash" and "Materials and Supplies."

On the liabilities side of the balance sheet the most important accounts are "Long-Term Debt," "Capital Stock," "Capital Surplus," and "Retained Income." The sum of the last three of these accounts is shown as "Shareholders' Equity." The liabilities side of the balance sheet also includes numerous accounts representing current liabilities, reserves of various sorts, and deferred credits.

INCOME STATEMENT

Income and expense accounts and the form of the income statement are also prescribed by the Commission. A condensed income statement form is shown below. The condensed form reproduced here combines many accounts which are shown separately in more detailed statements:

---

[2] For a detailed description of balance sheet and income statement accounts see Interstate Commerce Commission, *Uniform System of Accounts for Railroad Companies.*

[3] Also an account known as "Accrued Amortization of Defense Projects—Road and Equipment."

Railway Operating Revenues
Railway Operating Expenses
    Net Revenues from Railway Operations[a]
Railway Tax Accruals
    Railway Operating Income[b]
Net Rents[c]
    Net Railway Operating Income[d]
Other Income[e]
        Total Income[f]
Miscellaneous Deductions from Income[g]
    Income Available for Fixed Charges[h]
Fixed Charges[i]
    Income after Fixed Charges[j]
Other Deductions[k]
        Net Income after Fixed Charges and Other Deductions

a Railway Operating Revenues less Railway Operating Expenses.
b Net Revenue from Railway Operations less Railway Tax Accruals.
c An amount added to or subtracted from Railway Operating Income, depending on whether income from rent of equipment and joint-facility rents is greater or less than amounts paid for rent of equipment and as joint-facility rents.
d Railway Operating Income plus or minus Net Rents.
e Includes revenues from miscellaneous operations, rents, dividend income, interest from securities held, etc.
f Net Railway Operating Income plus Other Income.
g Includes expenses of miscellaneous operations, taxes on miscellaneous property, and other expenses not related to railway operations.
h Total Income less Miscellaneous Deductions from Income.
i Includes the following accounts: Rent for Leased Roads and Equipment, Interest on Funded Debt, Interest on Unfunded Debt, Amortization of Discount on Funded Debt.
j Income Available for Fixed Charges less Total Fixed Charges.
k Consists principally of Contingent Interest, i.e., interest payable if earned.

Net Railway Operating Income

The most significant item in the income statement from a regulatory standpoint is "Net Railway Operating Income." This is the figure which, under the fair-return-on-fair-value doctrine, should constitute a fair return on the value of carrier property.

During the years that cost of reproduction had to be given some weight in determining "fair value," the Net Railway Operating Income could not be related to any balance sheet item to determine whether a fair return was being earned or not. Since the Interstate Commerce Commission now relates net railway operating income to "net investment," and since the investment accounts have been adjusted to conform to actual cost, as nearly as is possible,[4] Net Railway Operating Income can be related to book values as a reasonable indication of the rate of return being earned.

DEPRECIATION ACCOUNTING

For many years, even after a system of accounts had been prescribed by the Commission, there was a great variation among carriers in the treatment of depreciation. The Commission had required the railroads to

---

[4] See *Increased Freight Rates, 1968,* 332 ICC 590, 604–8 (1968).

set up depreciation accounts for equipment, but there was no uniformity in the rates of depreciation used. This was not surprising, since differences in climate, in types of equipment, and in conditions of use would naturally result in different rates of depreciation. Differences in the rates of depreciation used, however, were greater than could be justified in this way. In its investigation of depreciation accounting the Commission found that steam locomotives had been given service lives of from 4 to 55 years by different carriers. Wooden freight cars had been given service lives ranging from 3 to 60 years; steel freight cars, from 8 to 50 years; wooden passenger cars, from 5 to 66 years; and steel passenger cars, from 5 to 50 years.[5]

On property other than equipment the railroads were not required to accrue depreciation until 1943, although the carriers had been permitted to set up depreciation accounting for such property if they wished. In general, however, the railroads preferred what is called "retirement accounting" as distinguished from "depreciation accounting." The distinction between depreciation accounting and retirement accounting should be made clear.

Depreciation accounting is based on the theory that the cost of providing a service includes the cost of everything used up in the process. Such things as fuel, gasoline, lead pencils, and paper are used up in a short time and are charged directly to operating expenses. Other things are used up slowly, such as locomotives, freight cars, buildings, and other structures. The using-up of this class of property is a continuous process extending over several accounting periods. The cost of this property ought therefore to be distributed over the service life of the property by periodic charges to operating expenses. These annual charges are accompanied by equal credits to depreciation reserve. By the time the particular piece of property is retired, its entire cost should have been charged to operating expenses, and the depreciation reserve should contain an equal credit.

Retirement accounting is somewhat simpler. When property is retired and replaced with new units, either the cost of the replacement is charged directly to operating expenses with no change in the property investment account, or the cost of the retired unit is credited to the property account and charged directly to operating expenses, while the cost of the new is charged to the property account affected. The advocates of the retirement system of accounting argue that retirements tend to equalize, becoming about the same year after year. For this reason, it is argued, there is no need for annual charges to operating expenses on account of depreciation. The property is maintained at 100 percent operating condition by the process of replacing property as soon as it is worn out.

Theoretically the depreciation system of accounting is the better of the two. Property consumed in service should be charged to operating

---

[5] 118 ICC 295 (1926), pp. 336–37.

expenses as its consumption occurs and not in a lump sum when the property is finally retired. The two methods of accounting, however, have about the same results in the long run if retirements are in fact made at a uniform rate from year to year. But in practice there is rarely this uniformity in the rate of replacements. Since replacements may be delayed or speeded up, the sums spent on replacements do not measure the consumption of the property in service.

Whether the carriers should follow the depreciation system of accounting or the retirement system seems to have been settled by Congress. The Transportation Act of 1920 directed the Commission to prescribe the classes of property for which depreciation charges might properly be included in operating expenses, and required the Commission to prescribe the percentages of depreciation which should be charged for each class of depreciable property.

The Depreciation Order

In 1926 the Commission, seeking to comply with the mandate of the statute, prescribed the classes of property for which the carriers should be required to set up depreciation accounts.[6] Opposition to the Commission's proposals resulted in reopening the case for further hearing. In 1931 the Commission modified its original order in several respects.[7] The system of depreciation accounting prescribed became effective on January 1, 1935, except for road structures. For the latter, depreciation accounting became effective on January 1, 1943.

Classes of Property to Be Depreciated. The original depreciation order of the Commission specified the various property accounts for which depreciation charges should be set up. The list included equipment and nearly all classes of fixed property. Land is not considered as depreciable; neither are the various engineering expenses incident to construction, nor such general expenses chargeable to cost of road as organization expenses, legal expenses during the construction period, and interest during construction. Depreciation accounts are not required for ties, rails, other track material, ballast, and some other property because, although they are depreciable, replacements are normally spread fairly uniformly from year to year and can be adequately treated under the replacement system of accounting.[8] The policy with respect to track property was reviewed and reaffirmed in 1959.[9]

Straight-Line or Sinking-Fund Method. The two most common ways of computing depreciation are the straight-line and the sinking-fund

---

[6] *Depreciation Charges of Steam Railroad Companies,* 118 ICC 295 (1926).

[7] 177 ICC 351.

[8] Interstate Commerce Commission, *Annual Report,* 1943, p. 53.

[9] *Uniform System of Accounts for Railroad Companies,* 309 ICC 289.

methods. Under the straight-line method the cost of a piece of property is divided evenly over its estimated service life. If the property cost $1,000 and has an estimated service life of ten years, the annual depreciation charge (if we disregard salvage value) would be $100. Under the sinking-fund method the annual depreciation charge would be less. It would be the sum which, if set aside each year at compound interest, would, at the expiration of the service life of the unit of property, equal its cost. Assuming the rate of interest to be 5 percent, the annual depreciation charge in our illustration would be $79.50.

The straight-line method of depreciation was adopted by the Commission because of its relation to the rate base. The courts have held that accrued depreciation is to be deducted in arriving at the rate base.[10] This being so, the carrier is entitled to the interest received from the sums recovered through charges to depreciation. These sums represent capital returned to the company. Under the straight-line method, if a piece of property costing $1,000 has lived half its service life, the carrier should have charged to operating expenses and recovered from the users of the service the sum of $500. The carrier can invest this sum and derive income from it. Or the carrier may, if it chooses, use the $500 for additions and betterments to its property, in which case it is entitled to earn a return upon the additional property investment. To use the sinking-fund method of depreciation with a depreciated rate base would be unfair to the carrier. It would, in our illustration, deprive the carrier of a return on the full $1,000, on the theory that part of the amount has been repaid; but it would insist that the amount repaid was not the property of the stockholders but that it must be put at interest to make up the difference between the full cost of the property and the smaller amount which has been recovered through charges to operating expenses. Logically, the straight-line method of depreciation requires a depreciated rate base; the sinking-fund method of depreciation requires an undepreciated rate base.

The Depreciation Base. In its first depreciation order the Commission required the carriers to compute depreciation charges upon the basis of the original cost of the units of property under consideration. This was in conformity with the usual accounting practice. Later the United States Supreme Court, in *United Railways* v. *West*, a public utility rate case, held that the annual depreciation charge should be based upon present values and not on the cost of the depreciable property.[11] In other words, it was not the original cost of a piece of property but its replacement cost that should be distributed over its life and charged to operating expenses.[12] This decision of the Court logically would have required a modification of the Commission's depreciation order if railroad accounts were to be kept in a

---

[10] See p. 389, supra.

[11] 280 U.S. 234 (1930).

[12] See pp. 322–23, supra.

manner consistent with the views of the Supreme Court. The Commission, however, refused to modify its original order on this matter. The Supreme Court subsequently repudiated the views on the depreciation base that had been expressed in the United Railways Case, and has approved of the more common practice of using original cost as the depreciation base.[13]

Rates of Depreciation. The Commission did not attempt at first to prescribe the rates of depreciation for different classes of property but left this largely to the carriers themselves. Later, however, the Commission prescribed for particular carriers the rates of depreciation to be applied to the various classes of depreciable property.

Past Depreciation. When the carriers make the transition from a system of retirement accounting to a system of depreciation accounting, they ought to set up a depreciation reserve account to show the depreciation already accrued upon their property. Only in this way would the accounts indicate the true status of the property. But to set up at once a depreciation reserve of this magnitude would have seriously decreased or entirely wiped out the surplus of many railroad companies. The Commission therefore held, in the second depreciation case, that the depreciation reserve need be credited only with the depreciation accruing after the new system became effective. This meant that the depreciation reserve would not represent the entire accrued depreciation in the property of the railroads until after the lapse of many years.

Depreciation for Income Tax Purposes

Under the provisions of the Internal Revenue Code of 1954, corporations had the privilege of using various methods of accelerated depreciation for income tax purposes. If railroads availed themselves of this privilege, the annual depreciation allowance for tax purposes would be greater, for many years at least, than the depreciation charged to operating expenses under the Commission's accounting regulations. The result would be a lower net income for tax purposes than was shown by the accounts. The Commission did not modify its rules for determining depreciation to correspond to the allowances permitted by the Bureau of Internal Revenue for tax purposes, observing that the accelerated depreciation allowances available for income tax purposes "are not intended to be a standard for measuring the rate at which service loss is incurred."[14] This rule, originally made in 1959, has been subsequently reaffirmed and made to apply to the even greater liberalization of depreciation allowances for income tax purposes provided by the Revenue Act of 1962.[15]

---

[13] *Federal Power Commission* v. *Hope Natural Gas Co.*, 320 U.S. 591, 606–7 (1944).

[14] 24 *Federal Register* 1401 (1959).

[15] *Accounting for Federal Income Taxes*, 318 ICC 803 (1963).

SEPARATION OF FREIGHT AND PASSENGER EXPENSES

The income statement shows the net railway operating income which a railroad earns in a given period from all of its services. It does not show separately the profitableness of the two main classes of service—freight and passenger. For many years, however, the Interstate Commerce Commission has required the railroads to make a separation of freight and passenger revenues and expenses. The separation of expenses involves the assignment to each class of service of the expenses incurred solely for that service and also the apportionment of common expenses on a reasonable basis. The basis for this apportionment has been prescribed by the Commission and varies with the different classes of expenses.

The result of such apportionments is to show that the passenger service has been operated at a loss from 1930 to the present time, with the exception of a few years during World War II. The "passenger deficit" for the year 1970 was about $470 million.[16]

Figures showing the "passenger deficit" can be misleading because a considerable part of the apportioned costs would still be incurred if the passenger services were abandoned. About 75 percent of the passenger operating expenses are solely incurred for this service and presumably would be saved if passenger service were abandoned.[17] The other 25 percent of the passenger operating expenses represent an apportionment of costs incurred in common for both freight and passenger services. Part of the apportioned costs is affected by traffic volume and hence would be reduced if passenger service were discontinued. A large part of the apportioned costs, however, is in the nature of fixed or constant costs and would not be saved if passenger operations were abandoned. The mere fact that a passenger "deficit" is incurred does not mean, therefore, that the railroads would be better off if passenger service were discontinued, nor does it mean that the deficit could be eliminated by increases in fares. Until 1953 the revenues from passenger-train service covered the expenses solely related to that service and covered part of the apportioned costs. From 1953 to the present time, however, revenues from the passenger services have usually failed to cover even the solely related operating expenses. The figures would suggest that the railroads would be better off if passenger operations were abandoned, but caution should be observed before arriving at such a conclusion. The figures are for the railroads as a whole. Individual railroads fare somewhat better. A few railroads have had passenger service revenues that exceed solely related expenses,[18] although none of the larger railroads, with the exception of the Long Island Rail Road Co., have had passenger revenues that covered both solely related and

---

[16] Association of American Railroads, *Yearbook of Railroad Facts, 1971 edition*, p. 19.

[17] *Railroad Passenger Train Deficit*, 306 ICC 417, 423 (1959).

[18] See James C. Nelson, *Railroad Transportation and Public Policy* (Washington, D.C.: Brookings Institution, 1959), p. 302.

apportioned expense. And even on railroads whose passenger service revenues fail to cover solely related expense, there may be individual passenger trains which are distinctly profitable.

Because unwarranted inferences may be drawn from the apportionment of railroad expenses between freight and passenger services, there has been some demand for changes in the rules governing the separation of expenses between the two services, or even for discontinuance of separation. This matter was investigated by the Commission in 1957, but the Commission concluded that no satisfactory proposals for revision had been suggested and that the present rules were adequate for the purpose for which they were intended.[19]

The problem of separating freight and passenger expenses has lost much of its importance, as far as the aggregate amount of money is involved, since Amtrak took over the operation of passenger service over basic routes in 1970 and most other intercity rail passenger operations were discontinued. Separation of freight and passenger expenses will still be required for suburban commuter services and for such intercity passenger operations as the railroads continue independently, and also for determining the cost to the railroads of providing services and facilities for the National Railroad Passenger Corporation.[20]

SELECTED REFERENCES

The best source of information on railroad accounts is Interstate Commerce Commission, *Uniform System of Accounts for Railroad Companies*, revised and reissued from time to time (Washington, D.C.: U.S. Government Printing Office). The history of accounting regulation and a description of the activities of the Commission's Bureau of Accounts is told in Interstate Commerce Commission, Bureau of Statistics, *Interstate Commerce Commission Activities, 1887–1937* (Washington, D.C.: 1937), chap. vi.

Depreciation accounting is discussed at length by the Interstate Commerce Commission in *Depreciation Charges of Steam Railroad Companies*, 118 ICC 295 (1926); 177 ICC 351 (1931); 309 ICC 289 (1959).

The apportionment of expenses between freight and passenger service is considered by the Commission in *In re Separation of Operating Expenses*, 30 ICC 676 (1914); and more recently in *Separation of Operating Expenses, Freight and Passenger*, 302 ICC 735 (1958); and *Railroad Passenger Train Deficit*, 306 ICC 417 (1959). The matter is further discussed in the report of the Commission in *Investigation of Costs of Intercity Rail Passenger Service* (1969).

---

[19] *Separation of Operating Expenses, Freight and Passenger*, 302 ICC 735 (1958).

[20] See pp. 275–77, supra.

Chapter 24 | RAILROAD FINANCE AND FINANCIAL REGULATION

The issuance of securities by railroad companies has been regulated by the federal government since 1920. This chapter is concerned with railroad financial practices and the policy of the Interstate Commerce Commission in regulating the security issues of railroad companies.

Overcapitalization and stock watering were among the chief complaints directed against railroad companies in the years preceding railroad regulation. The Windom Committee, reporting to Congress in 1874, complained of railroad financial practices.[1] The Cullom Committee, which reported to Congress in 1886, charged that stock watering had "imposed a serious and continuous illegitimate burden upon commerce."[2]

RELATION OF CAPITALIZATION TO RATES AND SERVICE

The Cullom Committee assumed that there was a relationship between railroad capitalization and rates, and hence that overcapitalization resulted in imposing an unjust burden on commerce. This was in accordance with popular belief. The railroads, however, insisted that railroad capitalization did not affect rates and hence was of no concern to the shipping public. Neither side was wholly right. There is not the close relationship between capitalization and rates that the public often assumed. On the other hand, railroad capitalization is not a matter of concern to the railway companies alone. Overcapitalization does affect railway service and may affect rates. This matter is important enough to demand closer analysis.

Before discussing the matter further, however, it is necessary to make sure of our terminology. By "capitalization" we mean the amount of stock and long-term debt outstanding. It should be observed that we are not referring to the assets of the company, but to the long-term obligations which are shown on the liabilities side of the balance sheet. By "overcapitalization" we mean a situation in which the capitalization, as above de-

---

[1] *Transportation Routes to the Seaboard,* 43d Cong., 1st Sess., Senate Rep. No. 307, Part I (1874), p. 72.

[2] *Report of the Senate Select Committee on Interstate Commerce,* 49th Cong., 1st Sess., Senate Rep. No. 46 (1886), p. 51.

fined, exceeds the value of the carrier's assets.[3] We may now return to a discussion of the relation of railroad capitalization to rates and service.

The relation of capitalization to service can be easily explained. The overcapitalized road finds the pressure to pay interest and dividends very great. It is inclined to resort to various forms of false economy in order to make these payments, such as the neglect of necessary maintenance. As a result the property gets into a run-down condition and service is impaired. The overcapitalized road may also encounter difficulty in raising new capital. The company is in no position to sell stock if dividends are not paid. Borrowing is resorted to until the fixed charges become too great; then further borrowing is expensive or perhaps impossible. Thus the company is unable to make the improvements, additions, and betterments necessary to provide a high grade of service.

The relation of capitalization to rates is more complicated. Overcapitalization does not necessarily affect rates, even when rates are not regulated by public authority. Clearly, capitalization cannot affect rates when competitive conditions prevail in the industry. The overcapitalized road cannot charge higher rates than its competitors; it must meet the rates set by its rivals. In fact, as we have pointed out elsewhere, if unrestricted competition prevailed, rates would tend to fall to direct or variable costs without regard to a return on legitimate investment in the property.

It may be argued, however, that an overcapitalized road may have a monopoly, or at least a considerable amount of noncompetitive traffic, and that under these conditions it would charge higher rates in order to obtain a return on its inflated capitalization. Or monopoly conditions in the industry may be brought about by agreement among nominal competitors to observe certain rates. But if monopoly conditions prevail, the carrier or group of carriers has the power to exact excessive rates, whether overcapitalization exists or not. Under monopoly conditions a railroad or group of railroads will strive for the greatest profits, overcapitalized or undercapitalized. In such a situation the carriers will charge the most profitable rates in any event. There is one qualification, however, which must be made to this statement. In the struggle for funds to pay interest and dividends, the overcapitalized road or group of roads may follow a rate policy that is not best for itself in the long run. The carrier or carriers may take a shortsighted view of things and charge high rates for immediate revenues, even though this interferes with the future development of the region served.[4]

The discussion of capitalization and rates has thus far proceeded on the assumption that the railroads were free to make their own rates. In so far as regulatory bodies may alter rates, additional factors must be considered.

---

[3] Later in the chapter we shall consider the proper basis of valuing the assets for the purpose of capitalization.

[4] A. T. Hadley, *Railroad Transportation* (New York: Putnam, 1885), pp. 121–22.

When rates are based on fair value, or on actual cost or prudent investment, the rate base is supposed to be unaffected by overcapitalization or undercapitalization. In fact, the fair-value rule was evolved for the very purpose of preventing overcapitalization from resulting in higher rates to the public. If a credit standard of reasonableness were set up, such as has sometimes been used by the Supreme Court in reviewing rates fixed by regulatory commissions,[5] overcapitalization would presumably affect rates, since interest and dividend requirements have to be met if a railroad's credit is to be maintained.

Although overcapitalization would not affect rates if the fair-value rule were strictly observed, there is reason to believe that regulatory commissions have sometimes stretched valuations to cover existing capitalization. In other instances the rate of return permitted may have been influenced by the interest and divided requirements of the company.

Three motives are responsible for the leniency of commissions in sometimes permitting overcapitalization to affect rates. First is the hesitancy about forcing railroads into receivership and reorganization. No commission likes to assume responsibility for throwing a railroad into the hands of receivers, thus causing investors to take a loss in the subsequent reorganization. This motive for allowing existing overcapitalization to affect rates applies, of course, only when the road is excessively burdened with debt, and not when the overcapitalization takes the form of excessive issues of stock.

The second motive is to protect the innocent investor. The securities outstanding, perhaps in large measure watered, are in the hands of innocent purchasers. They are held by savings banks, insurance companies, small investors, and educational institutions, all of which purchased the securities in good faith. The present holders are often in no way responsible for the overcapitalization. Denial of earnings necessary to pay a return upon the inflated securities will not injure those who were responsible for the inflation. The parties who will suffer from a strict regulatory policy are the present security holders.

The third motive that sometimes leads regulatory authorities to permit a return upon inflated securities is the desire to protect the railway's credit in order that adequate service may be rendered. We have alrady pointed out that overcapitalization may impair credit and result in poor service. This result can be avoided if a return is permitted sufficient to pay dividends upon inflated capitalization and to support the credit of the company. As between the two alternatives—high rates or poor service—the public will usually choose the former.

The obvious lesson from our discussion of rates and capitalization is that overcapitalization should be prevented; for if it is not, the public will suffer poor service or pay higher rates than it should.

---

[5] See pp. 354–56, supra.

REASONS FOR OVERCAPITALIZATION

Light may be thrown upon the problem of overcapitalization by considering the ways that it comes about. Very frequently it had its origin in the desire of promoters to reap large profits in the development or expansion of an enterprise. The construction-company device, elsewhere described,[6] was often used for the purpose of enabling insiders to reap large profits from the promotion and construction of a railroad. Likewise, in the building-up of railway systems in the past through acquisition of control of other roads, excessive prices have been paid because of a financial interest by officers or directors of the acquiring road in the properties being acquired.

Even in the absence of efforts to obtain profits for insiders, railroad consolidation and acquisition of control may result in excessive prices being paid for the properties acquired, with the result that capitalization becomes inflated. Whatever the motives that may have been involved, one of the causes of the New Haven debacle, described by the Interstate Commerce Commission in 1913 and 1914, was the purchase of competing companies at excessive figures.[7]

Overcapitalization may arise simply from the issuance of securities at a discount when there is no market for them at par. In an effort to prevent overcapitalization of this sort, many states have prohibited the issuance of stock at less than par.

Overcapitalization has often resulted from financial reorganizations. When a railroad company undergoes a reorganization, it is usually necessary to reduce fixed charges. This is often accomplished by inducing the holders of defaulted obligations to accept inferior types of securities in exchange for bonds having fixed interest requirements. To induce bondholders to accept these inferior securities—income bonds and preferred or common stock—it has sometimes been the practice to offer them securities whose par value exceeded that of the bonds which they were asked to surrender. Thus railroad companies have frequently emerged from a reorganization with a larger capitalization than they had before. This practice has been effectively stopped by Commission control of reorganizations under Section 77 of the Bankruptcy Act.

Sometimes overcapitalization results from prolonged financial difficulties which make it necessary for the carrier to borrow large sums of money to rehabilitate property that has not been properly maintained. Again, it may result from borrowing to pay operating expenses, unpaid interest, or other expenditures which are not properly capitalizable and which should have been paid out of earnings.

Whatever the cause of overcapitalization, it has undesirable conse-

---

[6] Pp. 138–40, supra.

[7] *The New England Investigation*, 27 ICC 560; *Financial Investigation of New York, New Haven & Hartford R. R. Co.*, 31 ICC 32.

quences. It should be avoided, if possible. When it does occur, steps should be taken to eliminate it as soon as possible.

DEVELOPMENT OF SECURITY REGULATION

Although the Cullom Committee in 1886 was strong in its condemnation of railroad financial methods, it was not in favor of federal regulation of railroad security issues. It believed that the states should exercise the necessary control, since railroad corporations were in almost every instance chartered by the states. States had already in some instances attempted such control. Massachusetts had statutory restrictions upon the stock and bond issues of railroads as early as 1852. Texas enacted a statute to regulate railroad securities in 1893. A number of other states enacted similar legislation in the 90s.[8] By 1917, 23 states had some form of control over railroad security issues. There were 25 states, however, which had no form of control. Massachusetts, New York, and Texas were the outstanding examples of strict control. The laws and policies of these three states, however, were very different.[9]

Agitation for federal control over security issues did not become very prominent until 1907. In that year the Interstate Commerce Commission concluded an investigation of the Union Pacific combination and the financial affairs of the Chicago & Alton under the Harriman regime. The Commission, in concluding its report, said: "The time has come when some reasonable regulation should be imposed upon the issuance of securities by railways engaged in interstate commerce."[10] This recommendation was supported by President Theodore Roosevelt and later by President Taft. President Taft's message to Congress in 1910 urged legislation to place railroad security issues under the control of the Interstate Commerce Commission. Congress did not follow the President's suggestion, but incorporated into the Mann-Elkins Act of 1910 a provision authorizing the President to appoint a special commission to investigate the desirability of such legislation. This body was known as the Railroad Securities Commission, sometimes called the "Hadley Commission," since President Hadley of Yale University was chairman.

The Railroad Securities Commission rendered its report in 1911.[11] It opposed federal regulation of railroad security issues. The Commission was very critical of certain practices of the railroads, and it urged the states to impose rather stringent requirements upon financial practices and

---

[8] Mary L. Barron, *State Regulation of the Securities of Railroads and Public Service Companies* (reprinted from *Annals of the American Academy of Political and Social Science*, 1918), pp. 5–6.

[9] The experience of these three states is described in some detail in W. Z. Ripley, *Railroads: Finance and Organization* (New York: Longmans, 1915), pp. 285–306.

[10] 12 ICC 277, 305–6 (1907).

[11] 62d Cong., 2d Sess., House Doc. No. 256.

policies of railroad companies. The Hadley Commission found little public demand for federal security regulation and considerable opposition to it on the part of the railroads and financial institutions. The effect of the report was to discourage the movement toward federal regulation, although the matter again came up in Congress in 1914. By 1919, when Congress was considering needed changes in railroad regulation, practically all opposition to federal regulation of railroad security issues had ceased.

Section 20a

The Interstate Commerce Commission's control over railroad security issues was brought about in 1920 by adding Section 20a to the Interstate Commerce Act. This section provides that no railroad subject to the Act, with the exception of certain electric lines, may issue new securities without first obtaining the approval of the Commission. The Commission is given broad powers in passing upon these applications, and it may attach such terms and conditions to its authorization as it deems necessary or appropriate.

An exception is made to the general requirement in that short-term notes, that is, notes maturing in two years or less, may be issued without the approval of the Commission, unless such notes, together with all other notes outstanding running for two years or less, aggregate more than 5 percent of the par value of all outstanding securities of the corporation. The exemption of short-term notes has been explained by the Commission as a recognition of the necessity of allowing the carriers a certain leeway, a freedom of action within prescribed limits, in the negotiation of short-term loans in order to enable them to meet current financial exigencies more quickly and easily.[12]

The dominant purpose of Section 20a was, in the words of a federal court, "to maintain a sound structure for support of railroad credit to aid in developing a national transportation system" and indirectly "to protect the investing public against faulty or dishonest financing . . . and thus to promote confidence of investors in railroad securities."[13]

The intent of Congress to establish the supremacy of federal authority over state authority in the matter of security regulation is clearly indicated by the words of the Act. The approval of the Commission for the issuance of securities is required "even though permitted by the authority creating the carrier corporation." The Act further provides: "The jurisdiction conferred upon the Commission by this section shall be exclusive and plenary, and a carrier may issue securities and assume obligations or liabilities in accordance with the provisions of this section without secur-

---

[12] *Pledge of Bonds of Baltimore & Ohio R. R.*, 67 ICC 10, 11 (1921).

[13] *Chicago South Shore & South Bend R. R.* v. *United States*, 221 F. Supp. 106, 108 (1963).

ing approval other than as specified herein." The courts have held that state legislation relating to security regulation is no longer applicable. Thus the Wisconsin Supreme Court has said: "We cannot agree with counsel for the state that there is any language in this section which can be construed as . . . recognizing concurrent jurisdiction with the several states."[14] The Act, however, does give the states an opportunity to intervene in an application on behalf of the state or its citizens. When an application is filed with the Commission, a copy must be sent by the Commission to the governor of each state in which the carrier operates so that the state commission or other proper authority may make whatever representations it deems necessary. The constitutionality of Section 20a has been upheld.[15]

OVERCAPITALIZATION

Overcapitalization and Stock Watering

One of the chief objects which the public had in mind in bringing about control of railroad security issues was the prevention of overcapitalization and stock watering. Before proceeding further, it is necessary to distinguish clearly between these terms. Although closely related, they are not the same thing. Overcapitalization, as we have previously defined it, refers to the relation between the total assets of the railroad and its capitalization—stock and long-term debt. If the liabilities of the railroad in the form of capital stock and long-term debt exceed the value of the carrier's assets, there is overcapitalization. Stock watering, on the other hand, refers to the dilution of the carrier's capitalization by issuing new securities without an equal increase in assets. Stock watering often results in overcapitalization, but it does not necessarily do so. If a railroad issues new stock at less than par, its liabilities are increased more than the assets. This would not result in overcapitalization, however, if the carrier had a substantial surplus, i.e., an excess of assets over its capitalization, before the new stock was issued. If the surplus was less than the discount on the stock issued, overcapitalization would result.

Capitalizable and Noncapitalizable Assets

We have defined overcapitalization as an excess of capital stock and long-term debt over the assets of the company, but a qualification must be made to that definition. In the regulating of security issues of railroads and public utilities a distinction is usually made between capitalizable and non-

---

[14] *Minneapolis, St. Paul & Sault Ste. Marie Ry. Co. v. Railroad Commission,* 197 N.W. 352, 356–57 (1924).

[15] *Pittsburgh & West Virginia Ry. Co. v. Interstate Commerce Commission,* 293 Fed. 1001 (1923). Appeal dismissed in 266 U.S. 640 (1924).

capitalizable assets. Noncapitalizable assets are those not used for railroad or public utility purposes. The object of this distinction is to keep the carrier's capitalization down to the value of the property devoted to transportation purposes. This policy discourages but does not prevent the railroad from engaging in noncarrier activities. If a railroad is permitted to capitalize its investments in other undertakings, and these investments fail to yield the expected income, it may be difficult for the railroad to pay interest and dividends on its own obligations. The public would not be under any obligation to pay higher railway rates in order to overcome deficiencies in the railroad's income arising from the unprofitableness of outside investments; but the effect of the situation would be the same as if the railroad were overcapitalized, and its credit would suffer.

This situation is recognized by the Interstate Commerce Commission. "We should authorize the capitalization of those assets of the carrier only which have been provided and which are intended for continuing productive use in the service of transportation."[16] Investments in nonrailroad property are not capitalizable under the Commission's rulings. Investment in the stock of other railroad companies is a capitalizable asset only when "the carrier's holdings are sufficient and essential to give it control of that corporation and it appears that such control will probably be permanent."[17] An exception is made to this rule if the affiliated company is a union-station company, or a bridge or belt line owned by several different railways. Other securities held by a railway are not considered capitalizable except under special circumstances.[18]

What seemed to be a departure from the rule that noncarrier property should not be capitalized appeared in 1962 in a case involving a motor carrier. The Commission in a six-five decision authorized the issuance of stock by Greyhound Corporation for the purpose of acquiring noncarrier property.[19] In a later case, however, the Commission strongly reaffirmed the traditional rule against the capitalization of noncarrier property and pointed out that the *Greyhound* case was not a break with precedent. Although the proceeds of the stock issue by Greyhound were for the purpose of acquiring noncarrier property, the carrier's investment in carrier property was adequate to support the additional stock issued.[20]

Valuation for Purposes of Capitalization

To determine whether or not a carrier is overcapitalized, a valuation must be placed upon the capitalizable assets. This raises the question of the proper basis of valuation to use. Should it be actual cost, cost of reproduc-

---

[16] *Securities of Louisville & Nashville R. R.*, 76 ICC 718, 720 (1923).

[17] Ibid., p. 723.

[18] As when part of working capital, sinking funds, etc.

[19] *Greyhound Corporation Stock*, 90 MCC 215 (1962).

[20] *K. W. McKee Inc. Stock*, 93 MCC 643 (1964).

tion, exchange value, or some other basis? The problem is not the same as the problem of valuation for rate-making purposes. Considerations which affect the choice of a rate base are quite different from those affecting the choice of a basis for capitalization.

Market value, or capitalized earnings, is sometimes set up as a standard of capitalization for industrial or commercial corporations. According to this standard, a company is overcapitalized if it is unable to earn interest and dividends.[21] On the other hand, it may expand its capitalization simply because earnings warrant it. Earning power is hardly a proper basis for use by railroads and public utility corporations, whatever may be said for its use in other types of businesses. The earning power of a railroad is what the public makes it by prescribing the rate level. If the public can reduce the earnings of a railroad to a fair return on the fair value of its property, it would hardly be proper to capitalize on the basis of greater earnings, since the public may at any time step in and reduce rates. On the other hand, it is difficult to accuse a railroad company of overcapitalizing its properties, even when earnings are insufficient to support its capitalization, if the capitalization represents funds actually invested in the property. There is one respect in which earning power does and should affect capitalization. When a railroad is unable for economic reasons to pay a return upon its capitalization, the capitalization should be brought down to what the earnings will support. But certainly it is not proper to charge a company with mismanagement and fraudulent inflation of its capitalization when the securities outstanding represent funds actually invested in the property, even if the enterprise is unable to earn the returns to which it is entitled.

The Interstate Commerce Commission has rejected earning power as the basis of capitalization, except in reorganization cases. It has said: ". . . we do not consider the capitalized value of earning capacity as an appropriate basis for the issue of securities under the provisions of section 20a."[22]

It is sometimes contended that cost of reproduction is the proper basis of capitalization. Even if reprodutcion cost were used as a rate base, it would not be a satisfactory basis for capitalization. The reason is that it fluctuates with the price level, but capitalization cannot easily be changed, at least if a reduction is in order. Under the cost-of-reproduction basis a railroad which is properly capitalized at one time may be overcapitalized at another simply because of changes in the price level.

The basis most frequently used by commissions as a proper standard of capitalization is actual cost. It has the advantage of stability, since actual

---

[21] W. A. Wood, *Modern Business Corporations* (Indianapolis: Bobbs-Merrill, 1906), pp. 32–39; W. H. Lough, *Business Finance* (New York: Ronald Press, 1917), chap. viii.

[22] *Grand Trunk Western R. R. Co. Unification & Securities*, 158 ICC 117, 134–35 (1929). See also *Chicago Junction Case*, 71 ICC 631, 637 (1922).

cost is a historical fact, changing only as the investment in the property changes. The actual-cost basis is also in accordance with the theory of the law that par values represent the amount put into the property by investors and owners.

The Interstate Commerce Commission has used actual cost as the standard by which to determine the amount of securities which a carrier may issue. "We have held in a number of cases that the amount of a carrier's actual investment, not the value of its property, should be the measure by which to determine the amount of securities that may be issued by the carriers."[23]

Are Our Railroads Overcapitalized?

From time to time the charge has been made that American railroads are overcapitalized. In the years during which the public was endeavoring to bring railroads under government control, belief in the existence of overcapitalization was general. The charge was undoubtedly justified during the period of railway expansion and for some time thereafter. In fact, some individual railroads may be overcapitalized at the present time. Taking the railroads as a whole, however, the charge that they are now overcapitalized is not justified by the facts if we accept investment in railroad property as the standard for capitalization. In 1920 the capitalization of the railroads was about equal to investment in road and equipment—101.9 percent, to be exact;[24] but in 1969 the total stock and long-term debt outstanding was only about 47 percent of the total investment in railroad property.[25] Railroad overcapitalization that may have existed in the past has been eliminated over the years by financial reorganizations of bankrupt roads, by reinvestment of earnings in additions and betterments, and to some extent by the retirement of debt out of earnings.

Although the railroads as a whole, and most individual railroads, are not overcapitalized on the basis of investment, it must be remembered that circumstances may exist which prevent a railroad from earning a sufficient amount to support a capitalization that does not exceed actual investment in the property.

Overcapitalization and Regulation

Regulation of security issues may be an effective means of preventing overcapitalization in the future. Cases in which the Interstate Commerce Commission has denied or limited the issuance of securities in order to

---

[23] *Roscoe, Snyder & Pacific Ry. Co. Securities,* 170 ICC 403, 407 (1931).

[24] Interstate Commerce Commission, Bureau of Transport Economics and Statistics, *Transport Economics,* November, 1956, pp. 7–8.

[25] Computed from figures in Interstate Commerce Commission, *Transport Statistics in the United States for 1969, Part I,* pp. 51 and 52.

avoid overcapitalization are numerous.[26] Regulation, however, cannot easily bring about the elimination of such overcapitalization as already exists. New issues of securities cannot be denied on account of overcapitalization if they are to be issued for the purpose of raising funds for needed improvements. To do so would often make improvements impossible. In a number of cases, however, the Commission has denied authority to issue new securities when the proceeds were to be used to reimburse the carrier's treasury for capital expenditures already made therefrom.[27] By this means the Commission may aid in eliminating any overcapitalization that existed before the capital expenditures were made. In effect this policy is to require the carrier to make capital expenditures from earnings, rather than from the proceeds of security issues, until overcapitalization is eliminated. The policy cannot be relied upon to eliminate much existing overcapitalization, because if it came to be the recognized policy of the Commission, the railroads might be unwilling to use current resources for capital expenditures.

Reorganization cases present the best opportunity for seeing that overcapitalization is eliminated. As will be pointed out below, the financial reorganizations under Section 77 of the Bankruptcy Act occurring in the 1930s and 40s resulted in substantial reductions in the capitalization of the railroads involved.

STOCK-WATERING OPERATIONS

The Interstate Commerce Commission is not only interested in preventing overcapitalization; it is also interested in preventing the issuance of securities in larger amounts than necessary. It has sought to prevent stock watering, i.e., the issuance of securities without a commensurate increase in assets.

The Commission has often prevented the capitalization of expenditures that were not properly chargeable to capital account.[28] In connection with new construction the Commission has objected to new issues of securities when the prices paid for the work seemed excessive.[29] It also exercises control over the price to be paid for the stock or the properties of railroads in acquisition-of-control and consolidation cases.[30]

---

[26] *Securities Application of Detroit & Toledo Shore Line R. R.*, 70 ICC 322 (1921); *Securities Application of Apache Ry.*, 71 ICC 245 (1922). For other illustrations and some exceptions as well see D. P. Locklin, *Regulation of Security Issues by the Interstate Commerce Commission*, University of Illinois Studies in the Social Sciences, Vol. XIII, No. 4 (1927), pp. 64–68.

[27] E.g., *Securities of St. Louis–San Francisco Ry.*, 79 ICC 92 (1923), 79 ICC 323 (1923).

[28] E.g., *Bonds of Virginian Ry.*, 71 ICC 383 (1922); *Stock of Albany Passenger Terminal Co.*, 99 ICC 415 (1925).

[29] *Sewell Valley Railroad Notes*, 79 ICC 177 (1923).

[30] *Control of Big Four by New York Central*, 72 ICC 96 (1922).

Stock Dividends

Stock watering may occur through the issuance of stock dividends. By "stock dividends" we mean dividends payable in stock of the corporation. The term should not be confused with the payment of ordinary cash dividends on stock. Although stock dividends have in the past sometimes represented purely fictitious issues to satisfy stockholders when earnings would not permit the payment of cash dividends, the type of stock dividend with which we are concerned here is that which represents reinvestment of earnings in the corporation. Instead of paying out all earnings in the form of dividends, the corporation may retain part of the earnings, which are then invested in additions and betterments.

Technically the issuance of stock dividends is stock watering, for no consideration is received for the stock issued. Actually, however, consideration was received before the stock was issued, because earnings were retained in the business instead of being paid out as dividends. The transaction is not essentially different from the distribution of all earnings in the form of dividends and the sale of new stock to finance further capital requirements, so far as its effect on capital structures is concerned. If earnings are withheld and reinvested, however, the stockholders are forced to contribute new capital; whereas if all earnings are distributed as dividends and new stock is offered for sale, many stockholders would not subscribe to new shares.

If the premise is accepted that the earnings of the company, regardless of their relation to a fair return, may be distributed to the stockholders in the form of dividends (and such is the view of the courts), it follows that there can be no objection to the issuance of stock dividends per se. The only objection that can be made is that it may weaken the carrier's credit and its ability to sell stock at par when new capital is again needed. The payment of a stock dividend reduces the market value of each share of stock outstanding because it reduces the equity behind each share. The issuance of stock dividends may therefore impair the carrier's ability to raise new capital by sale of stock in the future, at least on favorable terms.

It is sometimes argued that the denial of the right to issue stock dividends when earnings have been reinvested denies the stockholders compensation for their sacrifice. But the rights and interests of stockholders in the corporation are in no way increased by the payment of a stock dividend. They are deprived of no right, property, or interest by refusal to permit the stock dividend. If stock dividends are issued, the stockholder can of course convert his new shares into cash; but he no longer has the same proportionate interest in the company as before, and he could have accomplished the same result by selling part of his old shares, which have increased in value because of the reinvestment of earnings.

If a stock dividend does not change the position of the stockholders or give them any rights that they did not have before, it may be wondered what motives lead to the issuance of stock dividends. There are several answers to this question.

First, the stockholder may receive some gain because the total market value of his shares may be increased. This may sound strange in view of the fact that the total equity of stockholders is not increased by the stock dividend. If the company continues the same dividend rate on the increased number of shares, however, the total market value of the stock will rise. Furthermore, stocks tend to sell at more nearly the value represented by the equity behind them if the equity is not much in excess of the par value of the shares. Par value is erroneously set up by investors as a mark of intrinsic worth, and they purchase stock less readily when the price is above par.[31]

A second motive for issuing stock dividends is to facilitate consolidation. Shares of stock can be more easily exchanged on a par-for-par basis. But this is not equitable if market values of the shares in the two corporations differ. The market values of the stock of the stronger corporation can be brought down to par by the issuance of stock dividends. This was one of the motives in the South Georgia stock-dividend case in 1924.[32] The motive is often mixed with the first one mentioned above. If the terms of the exchange of shares in a consolidation are determined largely by the relative market values of the stocks of the consolidating companies, the terms will be more favorable to a strong company if it first increases the total market value of its shares by issuing a stock dividend.

Another motive for stock dividends is to enable cash dividends to be paid out less conspicuously, thereby avoiding the belief that rates are excessive. Issuing a stock dividend increases the dividend base and enables the same sum to be distributed as dividends at a smaller rate per share. Before regulation was effective, the carriers may have concealed excessive earnings by this practice. Under our present regulatory system, earnings cannot be concealed so easily; but if the amount of a carrier's stock outstanding is small relative to its investment in carrier property, earnings may appear to be excessive when in fact they are not. This motive appeared in a stock dividend of the Lake Superior & Ishpeming Railroad, where dividends as high as 50 percent had been paid.[33]

Stock dividends may also be issued to reduce the ratio of bonds to stock. The laws of some states forbid the investment of trust funds or the resources of savings banks and insurance companies in bonds of companies which have too large a ratio of bonds to stock. If this ratio is exceeded, a company may reduce the ratio by issuing a stock dividend. Of course, this procedure is somewhat ridiculous, because a railroad is obviously not in a stronger financial position after the issuance of the stock dividend than before. In fact, it is in a less favorable position; but the bonds may become eligible for investment by insurance companies and savings banks when

---

[31] This motive played a part in a stock dividend issued by the Delaware, Lackawanna & Western Railroad. See brief of the D. L. & W. in Finance Docket No. 65, pp. 11–12.

[32] 86 ICC 713 (1924).

[33] 131 ICC 331 (1927).

they were not before. This motive has appeared in a number of stock-dividend cases that came before the Commission.

The policy of the Interstate Commerce Commission has been to permit the issuance of stock dividends when they represent a reinvestment of earnings in capitalizable assets, provided a substantial uncapitalized surplus will remain.[34] Stock dividends have been denied when the uncapitalized surplus would be too small.[35] In other cases the Commission has endeavored to maintain an adequate surplus by reducing the amount of stock that could be distributed as a dividend.[36]

SALE OF SECURITIES THROUGH COMPETITIVE BIDDING

The Commission has been interested in having the carriers obtain the best possible price for new issues of securities. It had been the common practice of the carriers in the past to float issues of new securities through one of the large firms of investment bankers with whom they had been accustomed to deal, without attempting to resort to competitive bidding. In 1926 the Commission adopted the policy of requiring competitive bidding in the sale of equipment-trust obligations.[37] Later, competitive bidding was required in the sale of bonds of a terminal company.[38] In 1943 the Commission instituted a general investigation into the subject of competitive bidding, and as a result of the investigation it announced in 1944 that competitive bidding would be required as a condition of its approval of the sale of new securities. The rule does not apply to sales of common and preferred stock, and there are other exceptions.[39] The Commission will make individual exceptions to the requirement of competitive bidding if a carrier can show that market conditions are not favorable for competitive bidding or that it can probably obtain a better price for its securities by direct placement.[40]

RAILROAD INDEBTEDNESS

Early railroads in the United States were financed largely by stock issues, but later the practice became general of raising a substantial portion of the capital by the sale of bonds. Over a long period of years funded

---

[34] See *Stock of Chicago, Burlington & Quincy R. R.*, 67 ICC 156 (1921); *Stock of Delaware, Lackawanna & Western R. R.*, 67 ICC 426 (1921); *Richmond, Fredericksburg & Potomac Dividend Obligations*, 79 ICC 465 (1923); *Trona Railway Co. Stock*, 275 ICC 610, 614 (1950).

[35] *Proposed Stock Issue by Pere Marquette Ry.*, 131 ICC 304 (1927); *Chesapeake & Ohio Ry. Co. Proposed Stock*, 254 ICC 653 (1943).

[36] *Stock of Missouri–Illinois R. R.*, 131 ICC 467 (1927).

[37] *Western Maryland Equipment Trust*, 111 ICC 434 (1926).

[38] *Indianapolis Union Ry. Co. Bonds*, 166 ICC 723 (1930).

[39] *In re Competitive Bidding in Sale of Securities*, 257 ICC 129 (1944).

[40] See *Atlantic Coast Line R. Co. Competitive Bidding Exemption*, 282 ICC 513 (1952).

debt has comprised somewhat more than half the total capitalization of the railroads. In 1924 the ratio of long-term debt to total capitalization reached 57.1 percent.[41] Largely as the result of financial reorganizations which followed in the wake of the depression of the 1930s, the ratio of bonds to total capitalization declined to a low of 48.9 percent in 1947.[42] By 1970 the ratio had risen to 64 percent.[43] In recent years the annual reports of the Commission have published the ratio of long-term debt to "total equity and debt" (long-term debt plus stockholders' equity) which is more significant than the ratio of debt to capitalization. In 1970 the ratio of long-term debt to "total equity and debt" was 36.75 percent. Traditionally, however, discussions of the problem of heavy indebtedness have been in terms of the proportion of the total capitalization, or securities outstanding, in the form of long-term debt. It should be noted that this ratio differs widely among individual railroad companies.

The large ratio of bonds to total capitalization has had certain undesirable consequences. First, a railroad with a heavy indebtedness and heavy fixed charges is in danger of receivership or trusteeship in lean years. This danger leads to undermaintenance and skimping to avoid default. If default cannot be warded off, the carrier must go through the process of receivership or trusteeship and reorganization. Second, the credit of a company suffers as the burden of debt increases. The rate of interest on further borrowing becomes high, and it may be difficult or impossible to maintain the stock at par. The weakened credit position of the carrier prevents the raising of new capital for additions and betterments. Third, a large proportion of bonds in the capitalization tends to promote concentration of control and irresponsibility in management. For these reasons students of railroad finance have long deplored the tendency for the ratio of bonds to total capitalization to increase.

There are a number of reasons for the large proportion of borrowed capital among railroad companies.

1. The use of bonds enables the carrier to tap certain sources of capital that could not be reached if only stock were sold. Savings banks, insurance companies, and trustees have commonly not been permitted by state laws to invest in common stocks of corporations, but only in bonds. Then there are many individuals and institutions seeking safety of principal in their investments and regularity of income therefrom. Railroad bonds can be sold to this class of investors when stocks cannot.

2. Borrowing a portion of the capital needed for railroad purposes is profitable to the stockholders. If a railroad company sees an oppor-

---

[41] Interstate Commerce Commission, *Annual Report, 1930*, p. 132.

[42] Interstate Commerce Commission, *Annual Report, 1952*, p. 169.

[43] Computed from figures in Interstate Commerce Commission, *Annual Report, 1971*, p. 120.

tunity to invest a certain sum in additions or improvements that will earn the company 10 to 12 percent on the additional investment, it is obviously to the benefit of the stockholders to borrow the capital at 5 or 6 percent.

3. The legal obstacles in the way of issuing stock at less than par force railroads, as we have seen, to finance by bond issues when their earnings are not sufficient to enable stock to be sold at par.

4. The use of bond issues, particularly of the collateral-trust type, facilitates railroad combination. A carrier seeking to obtain control of another can finance its purchase of stock by selling collateral-trust bonds. The security behind the bonds can be the stock which has been purchased or is to be purchased. Historically this factor has been important during periods in which unification of carriers was taking place on an extensive scale.

5. Retention of control of other lines is made easier if subsidiaries are financed largely by bond issues. If the new capital requirements were to be financed by stock issues, the controlling company would have to take part of the shares to retain control of the company; if bonds are issued, the controlling company will have not have to put up additional funds.

This review of the reasons why railroads have tended to borrow a large portion of their capital reveals the variety of forces that have been at work. The interests of stockholders, the notions and habits of investors, state laws, and a low level of railway earnings have all contributed to this result.

Control of Indebtedness

Although it is desirable to prevent railroads from becoming overburdened with debt, there is no wholly satisfactory method of limiting indebtedness. Some states have attempted to deal with the problem by fixing a ratio of bonds to stock which may not be exceeded by railroads or public utilities.[44] There is probably no one ratio of bonds to stock that is correct, and what is a safe ratio for one railroad may not be so for another. Furthermore, prescribing arbitrary ratios of bonds to stocks may lead to measures which comply with the letter but not the spirit of the limitation, such as reducing the ratio by issuing stock dividends.

A better method of limiting indebtedness is to prescribe a ratio of bonds to investment in the property. But there are objections to this standard. The relation of debt to investment does not measure the burden on earnings created by the indebtedness. The rate of interest on the bonds, and the earnings of the company, must be considered to determine the real burden.

---

[44] See Barron, op. cit., pp. 14–16.

This suggests that the best method of controlling indebtedness is to relate fixed charges to earnings. A limitation of this sort, however, requires the determination of an uncertain element, namely, the probable earnings of the company. For this reason a limitation based on the relation of fixed charges to earnings is unsatisfactory as a statutory rule. The method may be used, however, when security issues are controlled by commissions.

Section 20a of the Interstate Commerce Act contains no limitation upon indebtedness. But the Interstate Commerce Commission, fully cognizant of the dangers of excessive indebtedness, has sometimes restricted the amount of bonds which a carrier might issue in a particular transaction, in order to keep fixed charges within the probable earning capacity of the company.[45] In a few cases the Commission has held that stock should be issued instead of bonds.[46]

The difficulty with requiring stock to be issued instead of bonds is that the company with earnings insufficient to keep its stock at par has to issue bonds or nothing. On the other hand, to require a carrier with good credit and an ample margin of earnings over fixed charges to issue stock seems unnecessarily harsh. The cry of interference with management will be raised if a commission requires stock to be issued instead of bonds when there seems to be no danger in selling bonds. As a result of this situation, regulation has not been able to do very much to reduce railroad indebtedness except in reorganization cases.

The difficulties growing out of a large bond ratio were unusually evident during the depression of the 1930s. In 1932, 122 out of 162 Class I railroads failed to earn their fixed charges. These lines operated nearly 74 percent of the total mileage of Class I roads.

Methods of Reducing Indebtedness

In view of the desirability of reducing debt, it may be well to consider how this can be accomplished. There are four methods by which indebtedness can be reduced. These are (1) by issuing stock to retire or to refund bonds, (2) by retiring bonds out of earnings, (3) by adjustment of debt by agreement with creditors, and (4) by financial reorganization following receivership or trusteeship. Each of these possibilities requires brief examination.

The issuance of stock to replace bond issues is practicable only when earnings and stock market conditions are favorable. Between 1924 and 1929 these conditions were such that many railroads could have taken advantage of the favorable market to effect a reduction of their indebtedness. Some did so. Unless bonds are callable, only maturing indebtedness

---

[45] *Securities of Yankton, Norfolk & Southern R. R. Co.*, 154 ICC 669 (1929); *Acquisition and Operation by Peoria Terminal Co.*, 117 ICC 377 (1926).

[46] *Bonds of Chesapeake & Ohio Ry.*, 105 ICC 748 (1926); *Securities of Houston & Brazos Valley Ry. Co.*, 150 ICC 11 (1928).

can ordinarily be taken care of in this way. To facilitate the refunding or retirement of debt, the Interstate Commerce Commission, in authorizing bond issues, has sometimes required that provision be made for the possible redemption of the bonds prior to maturity.[47]

Retirement of debt from earnings has not been practiced by the railroads to any great extent. The usual practice of the railroads has been to refund maturing issues of bonds and thus to remain in debt. Retirement of debt from earnings may be accomplished in a systematic manner through the use of sinking funds or through the use of serial bonds maturing at regular intervals. It may also be accomplished by the appropriation of available earnings of a particular year to this use if bonds are callable or can be purchased on the market on favorable terms. It has been the practice of the Interstate Commerce Commission for many years, when approving new bond issues by railroad companies, to insist that sinking funds be provided unless good and sufficient reasons appear for not doing so.[48] Insistence upon sinking-fund provisions is designed to bring about a gradual reduction of railroad indebtedness, but it does not always accomplish this purpose. In the past the carriers have reinvested earnings in their business on a large scale. If part of the earnings must go into sinking funds, less is available for additions and betterments. New capital requirements will then have to be met by new issues of securities, and the result may be no net reduction in indebtedness. The appropriation of a portion of the net earnings of a particular year to debt reduction has not been practiced extensively because earnings have not ordinarily been sufficient. During World War II, however, the large earnings of the railroads made it possible for many of them to use part of their earnings for this purpose, but debt reduction in this manner can hardly be expected on a large scale in normal times.

Reduction of indebtedness through voluntary agreement with creditors should be facilitated by the Railroad Modification Act, which was added to the Interstate Commerce Act in 1948 as Section 20b.[49] Some instances of debt reduction through the use of the machinery of this Act have occurred.[50] Other instances of reduction through voluntary reorganizations have taken place under the provisions of somewhat similar, but temporary, legislation that had been enacted earlier.

The most extensive reductions in railroad indebtedness have come from financial reorganizations as a result of receivership or trusteeship. A continuous process of reducing outstanding railroad indebtedness in this fashion has been going on through the years. There are always some railorads in the hands of receivers or trustees and undergoing financial reorganiza-

---

[47] *Bonds of Boston & Albany R. R.*, 138 ICC 727 (1928); *Bonds of Terminal Railroad Association of St. Louis*, 145 ICC 62 (1928).

[48] Interstate Commerce Commission, *Annual Report, 1936*, p. 17.

[49] See p. 269, supra, for an account of this legislation.

[50] See p. 575, infra.

tion. In the 1940 about 30 percent of the railway mileage of the country was operated by railroads in receivership or trusteeship; in 1962 only about 1 percent.[51] The number of companies in receivership or trusteeship in 1940 was 103; the number in 1962 was 6. In 1969 only four railroads were in receivership or trusteeship, but two important railroads were added to the list in 1970, namely, the Penn Central and the Boston & Maine.

The importance of financial reorganizations following receivership or trusteeship in bringing about a reduction in indebtedness is shown by the fact that the railroad reorganizations approved by the Interstate Commerce Commission under Section 77 of the Bankruptcy Act between the time of its enactment in 1933 and April 30, 1948 resulted in eliminating over $2.5 billion of debt.[52]

Fixed charges are sometimes reduced without a redutcion in the face amount of bonds. This may be accomplished by a reduction in the rate of interest on bonds or by refunding maturing bond issues with bonds calling for interest at lower rates. Fixed-interest bonds may be refunded with issues of contingent-interest bonds. Reduction of fixed charges by these methods often involves modification of the legal rights of bondholders, which can be accomplished only as a result of voluntary adjustments or as a result of financial reorganizations following receivership or trusteeship.

The difficulties of reducing indebtedness or fixed charges emphasize the need for preventing an overburden of indebtedness and fixed charges from occurring.

POLICY OF THE COMMISSION IN REORGANIZATION CASES

Early Cases

Prior to 1933 the policy of the Interstate Commerce Commission in reorganization cases was somewhat weaker than might have been expected from its care in preventing undesirable financial practices in other cases. A reorganization affords an opportunity for a thorough revision of the capital structure of a company. It would be reasonable to have expected the Commission to insist that the total capitalization of a reorganized company be not excessive and that the fixed charges be well within the earning capacity of the company. The Commission did, in some cases, insist on the latter requirement, but it permitted other reorganizations in which ability to earn fixed charges seemed highly uncertain. The Commission did not insist on limiting the total capitalization in reorganization cases but looked approvingly upon a reorganization plan if it reduced capitalization and fixed charges. A more vigorous policy was advocated by Com-

---

[51] Interstate Commerce Commission, *Annual Report, 1963*, p. 220.

[52] From mimeographed statement of the Interstate Commerce Commission.

missioner Eastman.[53] The Commission's weak policy in reorganization cases received some explanation in the St. Paul reorganization case, where a particularly unsatisfactory plan was approved.[54] Prior to 1933 the Commission had no real part in the formulation of reorganization plans. After a plan had been worked out by representatives of the various classes of security holders—often a long and difficult process—and after a court had approved the plan, the carrier applied to the Commission for authority to issue the securities necessary to carry out the plan. If the Commission then insisted on a more thorough reorganization, it would undo the labor of the reorganization committees and require the working-out of another plan that would be acceptable to all groups of security holders. Meanwhile the receivership would be prolonged. It was partly to remedy this situation that Section 77 of the Bankruptcy Act was enacted in 1933, which gives the Commission some control over a reorganization plan in its earlier stages.

Section 77 of the Bankruptcy Act

A brief description of the procedures under Section 77 of the Bankruptcy Act will show more clearly the part now played by the Interstate Commerce Commission in railroad reorganizations.

Section 77 provides that a railroad corporation, or creditors having claims which aggregate 5 percent or more of the corporation's indebtedness, may file a petition in the appropriate court, stating that the company is insolvent and unable to meet its debts and that a financial reorganization is desirable. Upon approval of the petition the court must appoint one or more trustees to take charge of the carrier's property. Within six months after approval of the petition the debtor corporation is required to file a plan of reorganization with the court and with the Interstate Commerce Commission. Reorganization plans may also be filed by the trustees, creditors, stockholders, or other interested parties. After public hearings on the reorganization plans the Commission is to render a report approving a plan of reorganization. This plan may be different from that presented by any party. Before approving a plan, however, the Commission must find that it conforms to certain requirements. Among these are the following: (1) The plan must be "compatible with the public interest"; (2) the fixed charges must be within the earning capacity of the carrier; and (3) the plan must be fair and equitable, affording due recognition to the rights of each class of creditors and stockholders, and conforming to the requirements of the law of the land regarding the participation of the various classes of creditors and stockholders. The plan of reorganization

---

[53] See his separate opinions in *Denver & Rio Grande Western Reorganization*, 90 ICC 141, 156 (1924); *Missouri-Kansas-Texas Reorganization*, 76 ICC 84, 108 (1922); *Chicago, Milwaukee & St. Paul Reorganization*, 131 ICC 673 (1928).

[54] 131 ICC 673 (1928).

approved by the Commission is then submitted to the court for its approval. The court is not empowered to approve a plan that has not been approved by the Commission. If the court will not accept the plan approved by the Commission, the matter is referred back to the Commission for reconsideration. After a plan has been approved by the court, it is submitted for approval to such classes of creditors and stockholders as under the circumstances may be necessary. After approval by creditors or stockholders representing two thirds of the amount of such claims or stock, the judge must confirm the plan. Upon confirmation of the plan it is binding upon all parties.

From this statement of the procedures under Section 77 it is clear that the Commission, as promulgator of the plan of reorganization, is in a position to insist that the reorganized company have a sound financial structure.

In view of certain developments that have occurred since the enactment of Section 77 which will be mentioned shortly, it is necessary to draw attention to two other provisions of the section. First, the acceptance of the reorganization plan by stockholders is not necessary if the Commission and the court find that the equity of the stockholders has no value. If the Commission and court so find, the stockholders do not participate in the reorganization; they are "wiped out," as the common expression is. The result is essentially the same as if the railroad's property were sold to satisfy the claims of the bondholders, and it sold for less than the bondholders' claims and nothing was left for the owners.

The second provision of Section 77 to which attention should be called is a provision which enables the court to confirm a reorganization plan even if it has been rejected by a particular class of creditors or stockholders, provided the court is satisfied that the plan makes adequate provision for fair and equitable treatment of their interests, and that rejection of the plan was not reasonably justified. This is commonly known as the "cramdown" provision of the law. It was designed to prevent particular classes of creditors from demanding more favorable treatment as the price of their approval than their legal rights entitled them to.

Reorganization Cases since 1933

The reorganization plans which have been formulated by the Commission under Section 77 of the Bankruptcy Act have been much more thoroughgoing than those which were approved prior to the enactment of Section 77.

The Commission has endeavored to limit the total capitalization of the reorganized companies to an amount which prospective earnings will support. The Commission has refused to base total capitalization on investment, reproduction cost, or value for rate-making purposes, when it seemed unlikely that earnings would support such a capitalization. In the

Western Pacific reorganization case the Commission said: "If this reorganization is to be successful, the capital structure of the reorganized company must be realistically related to its actual earning power, and consideration given to the investment in its property only to the extent that such investment is justified by the probable earnings reasonably foreseeable for the future."[55] Likewise, in the Chicago Great Western reorganization case the Commission held that value for purposes of financial reorganization was basically "dependent upon the present and prospective earning power of the properties."[56] This position of the Commission has been sustained by the Supreme Court of the United States. "The basic question in a valuation for reorganization purposes," said the Court, "is how much the enterprise in all probability can earn."[57] The Court also held that it considered it to be the intent of Congress, when enacting Section 77 of the Bankruptcy Act, to make earning power the primary criterion in valuation for reorganization purposes.[58]

The Commission has also been diligent in keeping the fixed-interest charges of the reorganized companies at a level which would be within their ability to meet, although the margin of earnings over fixed charges has not been large in some of the cases.[59] The reorganization plans approved by the Commission under Section 77 of the Bankruptcy Act up to April 30, 1948, provided for a reduction of the fixed charges of the railroads concerned from $149,973,295 to $38,889,784, a reduction of $111,-083,511.[60]

Criticism of Commission Policy in Reorganization Cases

The policy of the Commission in reorganization cases has been severely criticized. One criticism has been of the use of earning power as the basis of permissible capitalization in disregard of higher investment figures and rate-making values. This point of view led to efforts to prescribe by statute a method of determining the permissible capitalization of reorganized railroads. In 1943 Congress had under consideration a bill which would fix the capitalization of reorganized companies on the basis of the lowest of three figures: (1) existing capitalization, (2) the actual investment in the carrier's properties, and (3) value for rate-making purposes found under Section 19a of the Interstate Commerce Act. The Interstate Commerce Commission expressed opposition to this bill, pointing out that

---

[55] *Western Pacific Railroad Company Reorganization*, 230 ICC 61, 87 (1938). See also 233 ICC 409, 413 (1939).

[56] *Chicago Great Western Railroad Co. Reorganization*, 247 ICC 193, 196 (1941).

[57] *Group of Investors* v. *Chicago, Milwaukee, St. Paul & Pacific Railroad Co.*, 318 U.S. 523, 540 (1943).

[58] Ibid., p. 541.

[59] W. H. S. Stevens, "Railroad Reorganizations under the Bankruptcy Act," 15 *Journal of Business of the University of Chicago* 205, 208–9 (1942).

[60] Figures from Interstate Commerce Commission.

under its provisions the capitalization of a reorganized road would have no relation to earning power and that the road would eventually be in financial difficulties again. Similar bills were before Congress in 1944 and 1945, but did not become law. Railroad reorganizations would be ineffective and useless if they resulted in a capitalization that exceeded an amount which earnings could support. The Commission is on sound ground when it insists that the capitalization of a reorganized railroad should be within the ability of the carrier's earnings to support. A difficulty arises in the application of this principle, however, because of the inability of the Commission or anyone else to estimate the future earnings of a railroad with a reasonable degree of accuracy.

This brings us to a second criticism of the Commission's handling of reorganization cases. The Commission greatly underestimated the future earnings of most of the railroads which were reorganized as a result of the difficulties which they encountered in the depression of the 1930s. Many of these reorganization plans were evolved by the Commission before World War II increased the earnings of the railroads. No one could foresee the events which led up to the war and the increased earnings which it brought to the railroads. Nor would it have been wise to have permitted these railroads to capitalize on the basis of wartime earnings, which were presumably of a temporary nature. As events turned out, however, the postwar earnings of the railroads, although not equal to those of the war period, exceeded the estimates which the Commission had made. The average annual earnings of 15 large railroads which underwent reorganization in this period turned out to be much higher than the Commission had estimated. In some instances, average annual earnings over a period of about 13 years after the Commission's estimate were more than twice the amount estimated.[61]

This underestimation of earnings, combined with the so-called "Boyd Rule," resulted in the stock of many reorganized railroads being declared worthless, although subsequent earnings showed that they need not have been eliminated in the reorganizations. The Boyd Rule, or absolute-priority rule, was originally laid down by the Supreme Court of the United States in 1913 in *Northern Pacific Railway* v. *Boyd*.[62] It is generally interpreted to mean that the creditors of a bankrupt corporation must be taken care of in the order of the priority of their claims before stockholders may share in the reorganization. In the words of one writer: "Neither the courts nor the ICC is permitted to give stockholders anything if the debtor's assets are less than the aggregate of its debts. The holders of senior securities must be compensated in full before any value will be recognized for holders of interests of lesser dignity."[63]

---

[61] *Railroad Reorganization*, 82d Cong., 2d Sess., Senate Rep. (committee print) (1952), pp. 2–3.

[62] 228 U.S. 482.

[63] William Polatsek, "The Wreck of the Old 77," 34 *Cornell Law Quarterly* 532, 535 (1949).

The combined effect of the Boyd Rule and the underestimate of earnings was to wipe out the stockholders' interest in most of the reorganizations effected under Section 77. How the system operates may be seen from a hypothetical example. Suppose that a railroad with a bonded debt of $250 million has been unable to meet its obligations and is undergoing financial reorganization under Section 77. Suppose that the Commission estimates the future annual net earnings of the carrier to be $10 million. If the Commission assumes that 5 percent is a proper rate for capitalizing the earnings of a carrier, it would find that the earnings would support a capitalization of $200 million. This is the sum on which $10 million is 5 percent interest. A capitalization of $200 million would therefore be justified for the reorganized railroad. Since the indebtedness of the road exceeded $200 million, the stock of the bankrupt road would be declared worthless; the value of the property is less than the claims of the creditors, and there is nothing left for the stockholders. Suppose, however, that the Commission has underestimated future earnings and that they turn out to be $15 million per year. These earnings would have justified a capitalization of $300 million, which would have permitted the stockholders to retain an interest in the property and to share in the future earnings. If the reorganization has been completed, however, on the basis of the capitalization of $200 million, no increases in earnings, however large, would give the old stockholders a cent, since their stock was declared worthless and the property has been declared free of all claims of the former stockholders. The combined effect of the Boyd Rule and the Commission's underestimation of the future earnings of the reorganized railroads naturally led to much resentment.[64]

A partial remedy for the situation which we have described was provided by Congress in 1948 through an amendment to the Bankruptcy Act.[65] This amendment requires the Commission, upon petition of any party in a reorganization proceeding which has been approved by the Commission but which is still before the courts, to notify the court of any changes, facts, or developments which make it necessary or expedient to reexamine the plan of reorganization previously approved. In response to such notification the court must return the plan to the Commission for further consideration. Under the provisions of this amendment the Commission took action with respect to the reorganization plan of the Missouri Pacific Railroad, informing the court of various changes and devel-

---

[64] For criticism of the Commission and of the results of reorganization proceedings under Section 77 see Polatsek, op. cit.; Committee on Interstate and Foreign Commerce, U.S. Senate, *Nomination of Charles D. Mahaffie . . . to Be an Interstate Commerce Commissioner*, 82d Cong., 2d Sess., Executive Rep. No. 14 (1952); *Railroad Reorganization*, 82d Cong., 2d Sess., Senate Rep. (committee print) (1952); Justice Frankfurter, *Memorandum in Chemical Bank & Trust Co.* v. *Group of Institutional Investors*, 343 U.S. 982 (1952), and his separate opinion in *Bondholders, Inc.* v. *Powell*, 342 U.S. 921 (1952).

[65] 62 Stat. 167.

opments that had occurred since the plan had been approved.[66] The plan was accordingly returned to the Commission for further action.

Voluntary Reorganizations

We have elsewhere referred to the Railroad Modification Act, enacted as Section 20b of the Interstate Commerce Act in 1948. This Act should enable railroads to make adjustments in their capital structures that may be needed in order to avoid more serious financial difficulties. Under this provision of the Act numerous voluntary readjustments in capitalization or in the terms of securities outstanding have been made. These have included such things as the substitution of income bonds and stock for fixed-interest bonds, the extension of the maturity date of bonds, reduction in the rate of interest on bonds, making interest on certain securities contingent upon being earned, and the funding of unpaid interest or of accumulated dividends on issues of cumulative preferred stock.[67]

Section 20b should enable the railroads to effect financial reorganizations of a moderate sort without resort to Section 77 of the Bankruptcy Act. Some hope has been expressed that Section 20b may supplant Section 77 as the most common method of effectuating financial reorganizations. This may prove to be so; but it must be remembered that Section 20b requires the acceptance of proposals for the modification of the terms of mortgages, stock certificates, and the like, by the holders of 75 percent of the principal amount of such securities. When bondholders or holders of preferred stock can gain more by standing on their legal rights, resort to Section 77 of the Bankruptcy Act, rather than some modification of their rights, may be expected.

FINANCING CURRENT CAPITAL NEEDS

We have elsewhere mentioned that the railroads have made capital expenditures in the form of additions and betterments to their properties, including purchases of new equipment, at a rate exceeding a billion dollars a year in recent years.[68] Doubtless even more would have been spent for the same purposes if the problem of financing had not imposed limitations on such expenditures.

Capital funds may be obtained either from external or from internal sources. The external sources are the capital markets for stocks and bonds or other railroad securities. With the exception of issues of equipment obligations, which ordinarily find a ready market on favorable terms,[69]

---

[66] *Missouri Pacific Railroad Company Reorganization*, 282 ICC 629 (1952).

[67] See *Annual Reports* of the Commission.

[68] Pp. 345–46, supra.

[69] The classic work on equipment obligations is Kenneth Duncan, *Equipment Obligations* (New York: Appleton, 1924). For later developments in equipment

very little new capital has been obtained in recent years from external sources. Little has been obtained from bond issues, and even less from the sale of stock.

Internal sources have become the most important source of capital funds for the railroads. The principal internal sources are depreciation and retirement charges, and undistributed earnings.

Depreciation charges, unlike most charges to operating expenses, do not represent an outlay of cash. It follows that if a railroad collects revenues sufficient to cover its total operating expenses, it has funds available, equal to the charges to depreciation, which may be used for capital expenditures. Annual charges to depreciation by the railroads have averaged more than $600 million in recent years.

The other internal source of capital funds is in net earnings withheld from stockholders. This source of capital funds is limited by (1) the net earnings of the railroads and (2) the willingness of stockholders to permit management to withhold a portion of earnings for reinvestment in the property. We have already noted that it has long been the practice of American railroads to reinvest a portion of their earnings in additions and betterments, and perhaps eventually to issue stock dividends to give the stockholders evidence of their capital contributions through earnings withheld.[70]

The availability of new capital, from whichever of these sources it is obtained, is dependent upon adequate earnings of the railroads. Ability to raise capital by borrowing is affected by prospects of earnings sufficient to cover interest charges by an ample margin; ability to sell stock is dependent upon ability to pay dividends; depreciation charges do not produce capital funds unless operating expenses are recovered; and the level of net earnings after fixed charges, together with dividend policy, determines the amount of net that can be reinvested in the business.

RAILROAD "CONGLOMERATES" AND RAILROAD FINANCING

The rise of railroad "conglomerates" in the 1960s raises certain questions regarding the financing of current capital requirements of the railroads. A number of railroads have organized holding companies which, in addition to acquiring all or most of the stock of the railroad company, acquire a controlling interest in a variety of noncarrier enterprises. The following are the principal holding companies controlling a major railroad and numerous nonrailroad enterprises:

---

financing, see Leonard D. Adkins and De Forest Billyou, "Current Development in Railroad Equipment Financing," 12 *Business Lawyer* 207 (1957); Donald M. Street, *Railroad Equipment Financing* (New York: Columbia University Press, 1959); Hunter Holding, "New Developments in Financing Carrier and Terminal Equipment," *Papers—Third Annual Meeting, American Transportation Research Forum* (1962), p. 221.

[70] P. 562, supra.

Name of Holding Company	*Controlled Railroad*
Bangor Punta Corporation	Bangor & Aroostook
Boston & Maine Industries	Boston & Maine
Illinois Central Industries	Illinois Central
Kansas City Southern Industries	Kansas City Southern
Katy Industries	Missouri-Kansas-Texas
Northwest Industries	Chicago & North Western
Penn Central Company	Penn Central
Rio Grande Industries	Denver & Rio Grande Western
Santa Fe Industries	Atchison, Topeka & Santa Fe
SCL Industries	Seaboard Coast Line
Southern Pacific Company	Southern Pacific
Union Pacific Corporation	Union Pacific

One of the arguments advanced in justification of a conglomerate controlling a railroad and an array of noncarrier business enterprises is that the conglomerate, because of its ownership of prosperous noncarrier companies, can more easily provide the railroad with needed capital. This, of course, is possible, but there is also the possibility that the holding company will exploit the controlled railroad.

Concern over possible detrimental effects of these conglomerates led to an investigation of the matter by the Interstate Commerce Commission.[71] Various practices were discovered which were detrimental to the controlled railroad. Among these were payment of special dividends to the holding company, thus depleting the resources of the carrier; the transfer of nonrailroad property held by the railroad to the holding company at less than its market value; and loans by the holding company to the railroad company to enable it to pay dividends to the holding company. Such transactions indicate that the holding companies are, in some instances, bleeding the railroad company for the benefit of the holding company.

The Interstate Commerce Commission has taken steps to require more information from the railroads on a regular basis that will reveal the transactions between them and the holding companies. It has also recommended that it be given power to control the acquisition of carriers by noncarriers and to exercise some degree of control over such holding companies.[72] No legislative action has been taken on these proposals at time of writing.

FINANCIAL REGULATION OF OTHER MODES OF TRANSPORT

Section 20a of the Interstate Commerce Act applies not only to the railroads, but to motor carriers as well. The security issues of a motor carrier, however, are subject to control only when the amount of securities proposed to be issued, together with its already outstanding issues, exceeds a million dollars. There is no comparable control over the security issues of carriers by water, pipelines, or the airlines.

[71] *Conglomerate Merger Studies* (Washington, D.C.: U.S. Government Printing Office, 1970).

[72] See *Annual Report, 1971*, p. 95.

SELECTED REFERENCES

For early treatments of railroad finance, see F. A. Cleveland and F. W. Powell, *Railroad Promotion and Capitalization in the United States* (New York: Longmans, 1909); and by the same authors, *Railroad Finance* (New York: Appleton, 1912). See also W. Z. Ripley, *Railroads: Finance and Organization* (New York: Longmans, 1915), which is rich in illustrative material.

An excellent discussion of the influence of capitalization on rates and service and of the bases of capitalization is found in James C. Bonbright, *Railroad Capitalization*, Columbia University Studies in History, Economics, and Public Law, Vol. XCV, No. 1 (1920).

Federal regulation of railroad securities under Section 20a is discussed in J. Grodinsky, *Federal Regulation of Railroad Security Issues* (Philadelphia, 1925); J. H. Frederick, *Federal Regulation of Railway Securities under the Transportation Act of 1920* (Philadelphia: University of Pennsylvania Press, 1927); D. Philip Locklin, *Regulation of Security Issues by the Interstate Commerce Commission*, University of Illinois Studies in the Social Sciences, Vol. XIII, No. 4 (1927); J. H. Frederick, F. T. Hypps, and J. M. Herring, *Regulation of Railroad Finance* (New York: Simmons-Boardman, 1930), Part IV. The policy of the Commission under Section 20a is thoroughly treated in I. L. Sharfman, *The Interstate Commerce Commission*, Vol. III–A (1935), pp. 502–617.

The following financial investigations of railroad companies have been made by the Interstate Commerce Commission: *Consolidations & Combinations of Carriers*, 12 ICC 277 (1907); *The New England Investigation*, 27 ICC 560 (1913); *St. Louis & San Francisco R. R. Investigation*, 29 ICC 139 (1914); *St. Paul & Puget Sound Accounts*, 29 ICC 508 (1914); *Financial Transactions of the New York, New Haven & Hartford R. R. Co.*, 31 ICC 32 (1914); *Financial Transactions, Chicago, Rock Island & Pacific R. R. Co.*, 36 ICC 43 (1915); *Financial Relations, Louisville & Nashville R. R. Co.*, 33 ICC 168 (1915); *Pere Marquette & Cincinnati, Hamilton & Dayton Ry. Co.*, 44 ICC 1 (1917); *Denver & Rio Grande Investigation*, 113 ICC 75 (1926); *Investigation of the Chicago, Milwaukee & St. Paul Ry. Co.*, 131 ICC 615 (1928); *Investigation of New York, New Haven & Hartford R. R. Co.*, 220 ICC 505 (1937).

For studies of railroad reorganizations before the enactment of Section 20a of the Interstate Commerce Act, see Henry H. Swain, *Economic Aspects of Railroad Receiverships*, American Economic Association Studies, Vol. III, No. 2 (1898); Stuart Daggert, *Railroad Reorganization* (Cambridge: Harvard University Press, 1908); and by the same author, "Recent Railroad Failures and Reorganizations," 32 *Quarterly Journal of Economics* 446 (1918).

For the Commission's treatment of reorganizations after 1920 see Nathan L. Jacobs, "The Interstate Commerce Commission and Interstate Railroad Reorganizations," 45 *Harvard Law Review* 855 (1932). Section 77 of the Bankruptcy Act and the reasons for its enactment are discussed in Max Lowenthal, "The Railroad Reorganization Act," 47 *ibid.* 18 (1933); and also in Leslie Craven and Warner Fuller, "The 1935 Amendments of the Railroad Bankruptcy Law," 49 *ibid.* 1254 (1936).

The law journals abound in articles and notes dealing with railroad reorganizations under the Bankruptcy Act. Good articles on the subject are

William H. Moore, "Railroad Fixed Charges in Bankruptcy Proceedings," 47 *Journal of Political Economy* 100 (1939); Robert T. Swaine, "A Decade of Railroad Reorganization under Section 77 of the Federal Bankruptcy Act," 56 *Harvard Law Review* 1037, 1193 (1943); and De F. Billyou, "Railroad Reorganization since Enactment of Section 77," 96 *University of Pennsylvania Law Review* 793 (1948). Criticism of Section 77 is set forth in William Polatsek, "The Wreck of the Old 77," 34 *Cornell Law Quarterly* 532 (1949). The latter also discusses the Railroad Modification Act. For additional discussion of this Act, see Chauncey H. Hand, Jr., and G. Clark Cummings, "The Railroad Modification Law," 48 *Columbia Law Review* 689 (1948). The same authors discuss the operation of the Act in "Consensual Securities Modification," 63 *Harvard Law Review* 957 (1950); and in "Funding Arrearages under Section 20b of the Interstate Commerce Act," 65 ibid. 398 (1952). For an analysis of voluntary reorganizations under Section 20b see H. G. Wren, "Feasibility and Fairness in Section 20b Reorganizations," 52 *Columbia Law Review* 715 (1952). For other discussions of Section 77 of the Bankruptcy Act and of Section 20b of the Interstate Commerce Act, see E. S. S. Sunderland, "Suggestions for Improvement in Section 77 of the Bankruptcy Act," 14 *Business Lawyer* 487 (1959); C. H. Hand, Jr., "Railroad Modification Law—Its Use in Comprehensive Changes of Capital Structure," 14 ibid. 470 (1959). Volume VII, No. 3, of *Law and Contemporary Problems*, published in 1940, is a valuable symposium on railroad reorganizations.

On railroad conglomerates, see Interstate Commerce Commission, *Conglomerate Merger Studies* (Washington, D.C.: U.S. Government Printing Office, 1970); Colin Barrett, "Diversification or 'Scatteration,'" 37 *I.C.C. Practitioners' Journal* 198 (1970); Robert W. Harbeson, "Diversification and Transport Investment," 46 *Land Economics* 12 (1970).

Chapter	RAILROAD SERVICE AND
25	SERVICE REGULATION

A railroad derives its income from performing the service of transportation and allied services. Under ordinary conditions, therefore, it is in the interest of the carrier to provide its patrons with an adequate and attractive service. Situations frequently arise, however, in which the motive of self-interest fails to give the public the kind of service which it demands. The public may desire a kind, quantity, or quality of service that the railroad considers unduly expensive to perform. Absence of competition may lead to an indifferent attitude on the part of the carrier and to poorer service than the public expects. Inadequate service may result from a railroad's interest in a competing railroad or transportation agency, or from its wish to favor or discriminate against particular connecting lines.

THE DUTY OF SERVICE

The common law imposed upon common carriers the duty of providing adequate service, and the courts were often called upon to enforce these requirements. The common-law obligations extended to the adequacy of facilities, the duty to accept shipments, transportation with reasonable dispatch, and other matters. Regulatory statutes, both state and federal, have also contained service requirements. Paragraph 4 of Section 1 of the Interstate Commerce Act, for instance, makes it the duty of every common carrier subject to the Act to provide and furnish transportation "upon reasonable request therefor." More specific requirements with respect to service found in the Act will be mentioned shortly. To some extent these provisions merely put in statutory form the common-law obligations; to some extent they modify and extend those requirements. Although the Interstate Commerce Commission and the state commissions are given control over many phases of service regulation, resort is still had to the courts for enforcement of some of the common-law obligations. Our study of railroad service can best be undertaken by considering some of the subject matters involved in service regulation. In so doing, attention will be given to common-law requirements and to pertinent statutory provisions and their interpretation.

COMMODITIES THAT WILL NOT BE CARRIED

Under the common law, common carriers were under a general duty to receive and carry all goods of the kinds they undertake or assume to transport.[1] Carriers were liable for damages due to failure to transport such goods; and the courts, under some conditions at least, would issue writs of mandamus or injunction to force carriers to perform their obligation to the public.[2]

The duty to transport did not prevent a carrier from refusing to transport goods which it did not purport to carry generally. In an early case a certain common carrier by wagon was held to be under no obligation to transport a hogshead of molasses because he did not ordinarily carry the commodity, since his cart was "too small for such freight."[3] Many common carriers by motor vehicle restrict the commodities that they will carry; in fact, many motor carriers are restricted by their certificates to the transportation of certain commodities or kinds of commodities. Railroads do not restrict the commodities that they will carry, except to a very limited extent. Common carriers may refuse to carry explosives or other dangerous articles;[4] in fact, railroads are prohibited by law from transporting certain explosives except in conformity with regulations imposed by the Interstate Commerce Commission (now by the Secretary of Transportation).[5] Extremely valuable articles are commonly refused by carriers. The *Uniform Freight Classification* lists certain items as not acceptable for shipment: principally bank bills, coin, or currency; deeds, drafts, notes, or valuable papers of any kind; jewelry; postage stamps or letters and packets of letters; precious metals or articles manufactured therefrom; precious stones; revenue stamps; antiques; or other old, rare, or precious articles of extraordinary value.[6] The Commission has held that refusal to accept silverware and goldware for shipment was not in violation of Section 1, paragraph 4, of the Interstate Commerce Act.[7] Rule 4 of the *Classification* also gives the carriers the right to refuse freight "liable to impregnate or otherwise damage equipment or other freight."

Cases do not arise very frequently which involve the refusal to carry particular kinds of commodities, but in one case the Commission required the boat lines operating from Lake Superior and Lake Michigan ports to Buffalo and other Lake Erie ports to transport butter, eggs, and poultry products—articles which they proposed, by tariff rule, to refuse.[8] In 1959

---

[1] B. K. Elliott and F. A. Elliott, *A Treatise on the Law of Railroads* (3d ed.; Indianapolis: Bobbs-Merrill, 1922), Vol. IV, p. 635.

[2] See 10 *Corpus Juris* 69–70.

[3] *Tunnell & Short* v. *Pettijohn*, 2 Harrington (Del.) 48 (1836).

[4] *California Powder Works* v. *Atlantic & Pacific R. R. Co.*, 113 Cal. 329 (1896).

[5] Title 18, U.S.C.

[6] *Uniform Freight Classification No. 10*, Rule 3.

[7] *Emporium* v. *New York Central R. R. Co.*, 214 ICC 153 (1936).

[8] *Lake-and-Rail Butter & Egg Rates*, 29 ICC 45 (1914).

the Interstate Commerce Commission warned motor carriers that the practice of refusing shipments of radioactive materials on the grounds that such commodities were excluded from coverage by their insurance policies was unlawful and might lead to proceedings to revoke their certificates.[9] Neither of these examples involves railroads, but they demonstrate the vitality of the rule that common carriers may be compelled to live up to their common-carrier obligation to carry.

REFUSAL OF PARTICULAR SHIPMENTS

If particular shipments consist of commodities which a railroad undertakes to carry, it is supposed to accept them. It may not accept or reject shipments at will. There are numerous situations, however, in which a railroad may reject particular shipments. The more common ones may be noted. If a shipment is improperly packed and is therefore unfit for transportation, the railroad may refuse it.[10] The Interstate Commerce Commission, however, has refused to permit carriers to establish a classification rule providing for the refusal of shipments in containers not conforming to detailed specifications, since the shipments might be reasonably safe when not conforming to the specifications in all particulars.[11] Rule 5 of the *Uniform Freight Classification* provides that articles will not be accepted unless in such condition and so prepared for shipment as to render the transportation thereof reasonably safe and practicable. It also provides that containers must be of sufficient strength and security to afford reasonable and proper protection to the freight which the containers enclose. Specifications for containers and packing requirements are found in the *Freight Classification*. Penalty charges are provided if goods are accepted in containers not conforming to the specifications.

Carriers may likewise refuse shipments which result in violation of law. Thus a railroad cannot be compelled to transport intoxicating liquors for sale into territory which prohibits the sale thereof.[12] The right of a carrier to refuse milk shipments to Chicago was upheld when the temperature of the milk was higher than was permitted by the city ordinance and it was impracticable to lower the temperature of the milk en route.[13]

Carriers may likewise refuse shipments when their safe transportation is endangered by strikes, floods, or other unusual conditions.[14]

---

[9] See *Traffic World*, July 4, 1959, pp. 100–101.

[10] *Atlantic Coast Line R. R. Co.* v. *Rice*, 169 Ala. 265 (1910); *Union Express Co.* v. *Graham*, 26 Ohio St. 595 (1875); *Elgin Joliet & Eastern Ry. Co.* v. *Bates Machine Co.*, 98 Ill. App. 311 (1901).

[11] *Classification Specifications for Fibre-Box Containers*, 77 ICC 713 (1923).

[12] *Gum* v. *St. Louis & San Francisco Ry.*, 198 S.W. 494 (1917); *Leisy Brewing Co.* v. *Atchison, Topeka & Santa Fe Ry. Co.*, 225 Fed. 753 (1915).

[13] *City of Chicago* v. *Chicago & North Western Ry. Co.*, 275 Ill. 30 (1916).

[14] See *Galveston, Harrisburg & San Antonio Ry. Co.* v. *Karrer*, 109 S.W. 440 (1908).

An unusual press of business such that the carrier is unable to handle all the traffic offered is a valid reason for refusing shipments.[15] In fact, carriers frequently declare embargoes on shipments when congestion of traffic occurs. The right of railroads to declare embargoes has been recognized by the courts,[16] but embargoes must be administered without discrimination or favoritism.[17]

CAR SUPPLY AND CAR SERVICE

One of the most common sources of friction between railroads and shippers is failure to furnish a shipper with cars when he wants them. In periods of traffic congestion and car shortage, enormous losses may be suffered by shippers from the failure of the carriers to furnish equipment for the transportation of freight. Under the common law a railroad company was under a legal obligation to provide adequate facilities for the transportation of goods that it holds itself out to carry. Adequate car service is required by the provisions of Section 1 (11) of the Interstate Commerce Act, and "car service" is defined by Section 1 (10) of the Act to include "the use, control, supply, movement, distribution, exchange, interchange, and return" of cars and locomotives. A United States district court once held that a shipper could recover damages for failure of a carrier to furnish cars ordered by the shipper, even when failure to furnish the cars was caused by refusal of the railroad's employees to deliver the cars because of a strike at the shipper's plant.[18]

The Commission has said: "It is the legal duty of a carrier to provide reasonably adequate and suitable equipment for all of the traffic it holds itself out to transport."[19] This obligation extends to special types of equipment if there is a sufficient amount of traffic to justify the requirement. It has long been recognized that the railroads should provide refrigerator cars for perishable products,[20] but the courts once held that the railroads were under no obligation to provide tank cars for oil shipments.[21] The

---

[15] *St. Louis, Iron Mountain & Southern R. R. Co.* v. *Laser Grain Co.*, 179 S.W. 189, 192 (1915).

[16] *United States* v. *Metropolitan Lumber Co.*, 254 Fed. 335, 348 (1918).

[17] *Rogers & Co.* v. *Philadelphia & Reading R. R. Co.*, 12 ICC 308 (1907). For a thorough treatment of the law relating to embargoes, see T. J. Delaney and Tobias Naftalin, "A Study of the Law Relating to Embargoes of Common Carriers Subject to the Interstate Commerce Act," 11 *I.C.C. Practitioners' Journal* 3 (1943).

[18] *Pacific Gamble Robinson Co.* v. *Minneapolis & St. Louis Ry. Co.*, 105 F. Supp. 794 (1952), but other courts have been less strict under circumstances of a similar sort. See Paul S. Katcher, "The Duty of a Common Carrier to Handle Strike-Bound Goods," 24 *I.C.C. Practitioners' Journal* 30 (1956).

[19] *Switching at St. Louis and East St. Louis*, 120 ICC 216, 221–22 (1926).

[20] *In the Matter of Charges for Transportation of Fruit*, 11 ICC 129 (1905); *Baker* v. *Boston & Maine R. R. Co.*, 65 Atl. 386 (1906).

[21] *Chicago, Rock Island & Pacific Ry. Co.* v. *Lawton Refining Co.*, 253 Fed. 705 (1918).

Commission has indicated that railroads probably could not be compelled to provide highly specialized types of equipment.[22] The more specialized types of equipment are usually provided by shippers or by private-car companies. The duty to provide cars includes the duty to have them properly equipped for the transportation of property which the railroad is accustomed to carry.[23] Railroads may be required to furnish cars with heaters or other protection from freezing if there is a substantial movement of the commodities which require such protection.[24]

The duty to furnish cars does not mean that the railroad must own the equipment. In fact, the Interstate Commerce Commission lacks the power to compel a railroad to purchase additional equipment. A railroad may rent equipment from other carriers, shippers, or private-car companies, or may simply use cars of other carriers which may be in its possession, paying the owning railroad the appropriate "per diem" charge for their use.

It should be noted that a carrier is not liable for failure to provide cars when there is an unexpected demand for them. Carriers cannot be expected to have sufficient equipment to meet the peak demands made upon them.[25] Various conditions or circumstances may give rise to car shortages. Such car shortages may be local in nature or may exist contemporaneously over large areas or over the whole country.

In periods of car shortage special problems arise. At such times, opportunity for favoritism and discrimination arises in the distribution of the inadequate supply of equipment. For this reason, rules have been established by the carriers for the distribution of cars in time of shortage. The problem has been particularly acute in the coal-mining industry because ability to operate a mine continuously depends, in many cases, upon ability to move the coal away from the mine as it is produced. Elaborate rules have been set up to deal with this situation.[26] The Transportation Act of 1920 made special mention of the distribution of coal cars and required their distribution according to mine ratings without discrimination of any sort.[27]

The problem of car shortages has been growing more acute in recent years. The number of freight cars owned by Class I railroads decreased

---

[22] *In the Matter of Private Cars*, 50 ICC 652, 690 (1918).

[23] *Forrester & Co. v. Southern Ry. Co.*, 61 S.E. 524 (1908); *Loomis v. Lehigh Valley R. R. Co.*, 101 N.E. 907 (1913).

[24] *Protection of Potato Shipments in Winter*, 26 ICC 681 (1913); *Charges for Protective Service to Perishable Freight—Protective Service against Cold*, 274 ICC 751 (1949).

[25] *Pennsylvania Railroad v. Puritan Coal Co.*, 237 U.S. 121 (1915).

[26] The Commission's treatment of this problem is discussed in D. P. Locklin, *Railroad Regulation since 1920* (New York: McGraw-Hill, 1928), pp. 76–78. The leading cases are 12 ICC 398 (1907), 13 ICC 451 (1908), 80 ICC 520 (1923), and 93 ICC 701 (1924).

[27] Paragraph 12, Section 1.

from 2,427,026 in 1926[28] to 1,488,385 in 1964.[29] Because of increased capacity of cars and increased freight-train speeds, the number of freight cars needed at the present time is less than that required in the 1920s. Notwithstanding this fact, the railroads in 1963 needed 36,000 more boxcars and 19,000 more gondola cars to meet the traffic demands of the period than were available, according to the Interstate Commerce Commission.[30]

In view of the recognized inadequacy of the freight-car supply it is especially urgent that the existing supply be utilized efficiently. This problem has been met, in part, by (1) car-service rules of the carriers, (2) "per diem" charges for the use of cars not on the owning railroads, (3) demurrage charges levied against shippers and consignees for unnecessary car detention, and (4) car-service orders of the Interstate Commerce Commission. Each of these measures requires brief attention.

Car-Service Rules

For many years the railroads have maintained car-service rules designed to promote prompt return of cars to the owning railroads. These rules require that empty cars be returned to the owning railroads without delay, or, if they are to be placed for loading, that they be used for movements in the direction of the owning railroad. Although these rules have been successful to a degree, they tend to be disregarded in times of acute car shortage, and there has been no adequate method of enforcement. In 1969 the Commission required the carriers to observe certain of their car-service rules relating to the return of "foreign cars."[31]

Per Diem Charge

To provide an incentive for the return of cars to the owning carrier and to compensate the owning railroad while its cars are on the lines of another railroad a system of "per diem" charges has been in existence since 1902. Under the system of per diem charges a railroad receives per diem for each car that it owns which is on the line of another railroad and pays per diem for each "foreign" car on its lines. The per diem charge is, or may be, an effective tool to bring about better utilization of equipment. The Interstate Commerce Commission has the power to determine the compensation which a railroad shall receive for its equipment while it is

---

[28] *National Freight Car Supply*, 88th Cong., 2d Sess., Senate Report No. 1192 (1964), p. 7.

[29] 335 ICC 264, 271 (1969).

[30] *Investigation of Adequacy of Freight Car Ownership*, 323 ICC 48, 52 (1964).

[31] Ibid., 335 ICC 264 (1969). This order of the Commission was set aside by a U.S. district court in *Allegheny Ludlum Steel Corp.* v. *United States*, 325 F. Supp. 352 (1971).

on the lines of another railroad. The per diem charge, when first established in 1902, was 20 cents per car. The amount has been increased from
time to time and became $2.88 in 1959. In 1964 the railroads established a
system of graduated per diem charges, the charge depending on the cost
of the car. In 1968 the Commission prescribed the compensation to be paid
for "foreign" cars which consisted of a per-day rate and also a mileage
rate.[32] The mileage charge varied from 1.47 cents per mile for cars worth
$1,000 or less to 4.60 cents for cars costing from $39,000 to $41,000. The
time charge depended not only on the cost bracket in which the car falls,
but also on the age group in which it falls. These charges, under the original finding of the Commission, varied from 63 cents per day for a car
over 30 years old and worth $1,000 or less, to $10.22 for a car 5 years or
less in age and having a value from $39,000 to $41,000.[33] It is believed that
this is a more equitable system of compensating the owners of the freight
cars than a uniform per diem rate and also that it will encourage investment in better equipment.

In the past the per diem charges have been intended to compensate
the owning railroad for the cost of car ownership but no more than this.
In 1947 the Commission authorized an increase in per diem rates with two
objectives in mind: first, to increase the incentive for railroads to get cars
back to the owning railroad, thus promoting greater efficiency in the
use of cars; and second, to stimulate car ownership by the railroads by
providing compensation in excess of the bare cost of car ownership.[34] The
Commission's order, however, was set aside by a court.[35] The court took
the position that the Commission had no authority to inject a penalty
element in the per diem charge to induce railroads to return cars to the
owning railroads more rapidly, and that the Commission could only determine the fair compensation to be received by a railroad while its cars
were in the possession of another. Following this decision, the Commission recommended the enactment of legislation which would either empower the Commission to prescribe penalty per diem charges in time of
car shortage or threatened car shortage, or authorize it to fix per diem
charges which exceeded the mere cost of car ownership.[36]

This was done by amendment of the Interstate Commerce Act in
1966.[37] It was not until 1970, however, that the incentive per diem charges
were prescribed to supplement the basic per diem charges.[38] The order

---

[32] *Chicago, Burlington & Quincy R. Co.* v. *New York, Susquehanna & Western
R. Co.,* 332 ICC 176 (1968).

[33] Ibid., p. 242. Cars are assigned to value brackets on the basis of their original
cost undepreciated. Ibid., p. 217.

[34] *Increased Per Diem Charges on Freight Cars,* 268 ICC 659 (1947).

[35] *Palmer* v. *United States,* 75 F. Supp. 63 (1947).

[36] Interstate Commerce Commission, *Annual Report, 1957,* pp. 136–37.

[37] Public Law 89–430.

[38] *Incentive Per Diem Charges, 1968,* 337 ICC 183 (1969), 337 ICC 217 (1970).

applied only to general-purpose boxcars. The incentive per diem charges were to be levied from September 1 through February 28 of each year, the period when the problem of boxcar shortage is most acute. The amount of the incentive per diem prescribed depended on the age and cost of the cars and reached a maximum of $12.98 on newer cars of the highest values. The order of the Commission was challenged in the courts but was upheld.[39]

Demurrage

Demurrage charges represent another device to insure more efficient use of freight cars. Demurrage charges are levied against the shipper or receiver of freight for detaining cars beyond a certain period of "free time," commonly 48 hours.[40] In 1964 demurrage charges became $5 per car per day for the first four days of detention beyond the free time, $10 per day for the next four days, and $15 for each additional day. During periods of war or other emergency the Interstate Commerce Commission has made demurrage rates steeply progressive. Its power to do this to prevent unnecessary shortages of equipment has been upheld.[41] Because of an acute car shortage in May 1969, the Commission imposed temporary demurrage charges ranging from $25 to $50 per day. The prior basis was restored, however, on September 1 of that year, but increases proposed by the railroads were later permitted to become effective.[42] The resulting demurrage charges were $10 per day for the first four days beyond "free time"; $20 per day for the next two days; and $30 per day for each additional day.

Car-Service Orders

More efficient use of cars and the prevention of traffic congestion and of car shortages are facilitated by the issuance from time to time of car-service orders by the Commission to deal with specific situations that arise. In time of car shortage, traffic congestion, or other emergency the Commission is given rather broad powers to promulgate such measures as may be necessary to cope with the situation. The Act authorizes the Commission in such circumstances to (1) suspend car-service rules of the carriers; (2) require the pooling of equipment; (3) compel joint use of terminals, including main tracks for a reasonable distance outside of terminals; (4) establish embargoes, or require certain commodities to be given priority,

---

[39] *Long Island Rail Road Co.* v. *United States,* 318 F. Supp. 490 (1970). The issue before the court was purely procedural.

[40] On export traffic at ports, free time is commonly seven days. See *Chicago Regional Port District* v. *Atchison, Topeka & Santa Fe Ry. Co.,* 305 ICC 593 (1959).

[41] *Iversen* v. *United States,* 63 F. Supp. 1001 (1946).

[42] *Demurrage Rules and Charges, Nationwide,* 340 ICC 83 (1971).

or require that traffic may only move under a permit system; and (5) route traffic to relieve congestion.[43]

Car-service orders are extensively used to deal with such emergency situations and to implement other powers of the Commission relating to car service.

The Commission has frequently issued car-service orders in the grain-harvest season to get empty boxcars moved promptly into areas where they are needed for moving out the grain crop.

TERMINAL FACILITIES AND SERVICES

The duty to provide adequate facilities includes an obligation to provide adequate terminals for the loading, unloading, and handling of freight.[44]

Terminal services are embraced within the various transportation services over which the Commission has jurisdiction. Some of these services, and the rights of shippers and carriers with respect thereto, require brief consideration.

Loading and Unloading

In the United States it is the usual practice for shippers to load, and for consignees to unload, carload freight, while less-than-carload freight is loaded and unloaded by employees of the railroad. This is one reason for the lower rates on carload than on less-than-carload lots. Under competitive conditions the carriers have sometimes departed from the usual practice and have loaded and unloaded carload freight or have aided in the process.[45] But the Commission has recognized the right of the carriers to exact an additional charge for such service.[46]

An exception to the general practice is also made in case of livestock shipments. Under the Transportation Act of 1920 it is the duty of carriers to load and unload livestock without extra charge at points which have public stockyards.[47] But where no public stockyards are provided, the carrier may refuse to load or unload carload lots of livestock or may make a charge if it does perform the service.[48]

---

[43] Paragraphs 15, 16, and 17 of Section 1.

[44] *Mattoon* v. *Republican Valley R. R. Co.*, 24 N.W. 329 (1885); *Joynes* v. *Pennsylvania R. R. Co.*, 83 Atl. 1016 (1912); *Covington Stock-Yards Co.* v. *Keith*, 139 U.S. 128 (1891).

[45] *Loading and Unloading Carload Freight*, 101 ICC 394 (1928).

[46] Ibid., See also *Unloading Charges, Fruits & Vegetables, New York & Philadelphia*, 272 ICC 648 (1948).

[47] *Livestock Loading & Unloading*, 58 ICC 164 (1920).

[48] *Omaha Packing Co.* v. *Atchison, Topeka & Santa Fe Ry. Co.*, 66 ICC 44 (1921).

Construction of Switch Connections to Private Sidings

Carload freight is ordinarily delivered by a carrier in one of two ways: the car may be placed on public "team tracks," where the consignee may come and get his freight; or it may be placed on a private siding beside which the consignee's establishment is located. The sidetracks and spurs running to particular industries are considered part of a railroad's terminal facilities, even though the tracks may be owned by the industry. Delivery on these tracks is part of a railroad's obligation. Extra charges for this service are not permitted if the service is a substitute for comparable team-track delivery. But if the necessary switching service is an added service performed at an additional expense, appropriate charges may be made for it.[49]

The Interstate Commerce Commission's power over switch connections with private sidings is found in paragraph 9 of Section 1. This paragraph provides that any common carrier subject to the Act "upon application of any . . . shipper tendering interstate traffic for transportation, shall construct, maintain, and operate upon reasonable terms a switch connection with any such . . . private side track which may be constructed to connect with its railroad, where such connection is reasonably practicable and can be put in with safety and will furnish sufficient business to justify the construction and maintenance of the same. . . ."[50]

There are several points to be noted in the above provision of the Act. It does not give the Commission authority to require the construction of sidings, but only the construction of switch connections with sidings already constructed.[51] Nor was the Commission's power in this respect extended by the provision in the Act of 1920 which gave the Commission power to require the construction of extensions, since industrial sidetracks located wholly within one state were specifically excluded from these provisions.[52] The Commission has specifically held that the Interstate Commerce Act does not give it power to require the construction of private sidings.[53]

A second point to be observed in connection with the power to require the construction of switch connections is that certain conditions must be fulfilled before the Commission can issue such an order. First, the switch connection must be "reasonably practicable"; second, it must be where

---

[49] *Associated Jobbers of Los Angeles* v. *Atchison, Topeka & Santa Fe Ry.*, 18 ICC 310 (1910); *Los Angeles Switching Case*, 234 U.S. 294 (1914).

[50] This section also covers switch connections with any "lateral, branch line of railroad."

[51] *Certain-Teed Products Corp.* v. *Chicago, Rock Island & Pacific Ry. Co.*, 68 ICC 260 (1922); *Winters Metallic Paint Co.* v. *Chicago, Milwaukee & St. Paul Ry. Co.*, 16 ICC 587 (1909).

[52] *National Industrial Traffic League* v. *Aberdeen & Rockfish R. R. Co.*, 61 ICC 120, 122 (1921).

[53] *Sioux City Terminal Railway Switching*, 241 ICC 53 (1940).

it can be put in with safety; and third, it must furnish sufficient business to justify its construction and maintenance. When the Commission requires the establishment of switch connections, it may prescribe the compensation which the carrier is to receive for the service.

Switching and Spotting

The switching of cars onto private sidings is one form of delivering shipments. It is in lieu of placing the cars on "team tracks," and we have noted that the carrier can be required to perform the service of placing the cars on industrial sidings. But it is generally recognized that the railroad's obligation is fulfilled when the car is switched onto the private siding, clear of the main tracks.[54] As a usual thing, however, the carriers do more than this. They "spot" the cars, that is, place them in a position for loading or unloading. Compensation for this service, furthermore, is found in the line-haul rate. No extra charge is levied.

The practice of railroads in performing the "spotting" service has led to difficulties in the larger industrial plants which have a complicated system of tracks, with much intraplant switching to perform, and where placing the cars for loading or unloading whenever convenient for the carrier would interfere with plant operations. In such situations the industry often prefers to do its own spotting, with its own locomotives. The industry may then seek an allowance from the railroad company for performing the service which the railroad had been giving. The Commission has held, in a number of cases, that at these large industrial plants the carrier's obligation is fulfilled if it places the cars on interchange tracks, and that it cannot be required to perform the complicated switching operations involved in placing cars for unloading within the plant.[55] If this switching and spotting service cannot be required, it follows that when it is performed by the industry, the industry cannot demand an allowance from the carrier.[56]

JOINT USE OF TERMINALS

Adequacy of service to the public and efficiency in rail operations often require joint use of railway terminals by all railways entering a city. Difficulty has often arisen because of the ownership of valuable terminal

---

[54] See *Industrial Railways Case*, 29 ICC 212, 225–26 (1914).

[55] *General Electric Co.* v. *New York Central & Hudson River R. R. Co.*, 14 ICC 237 (1908); *Industrial Railways Case*, 29 ICC 212, 225–30 (1914).

[56] *Propriety of Operating Practices—Terminal Services*, 209 ICC 11, 44–45 (1935). See also *United States* v. *American Sheet & Tin Plate Co.*, 301 U.S. 402 (1937); *United States* v. *Pan American Petroleum Corp.*, 304 U.S. 156 (1938); *United States* v. *Wabash R. R. Co.*, 321 U.S. 403 (1944); *United States* v. *U.S. Smelting Co.*, 339 U.S. 186 (1950).

properties by individual railroad companies. Some railroads naturally have much better terminal facilities in large cities than others. The railroad having a strategic location, with extensive industries located on its tracks, is in a much better position to obtain traffic than its less fortunate rivals. A carrier naturally guards this competitive advantage and may refuse to allow other railroads to use its terminal facilities, or it may refuse to switch traffic from industries on its own lines to the rival system. The public, on the other hand, prefers open terminals, that is, terminals which are open to the use of all carriers.

There are two common methods of organizing terminal operations in such a way as to make the terminals available for all lines. One is by reciprocal switching; the other is by the creation of terminal companies or associations. Under a reciprocal switching arrangement, traffic brought into a terminal by one railway may be switched to industries on the tracks of another. In the same way, traffic originating at a plant on the tracks of one railway may be turned over to any other for the line haul. Unification of terminals through terminal associations or terminal companies has been accomplished in many cities throughout the United States. Terminal companies or associations may be of several types. They may be independent private organizations; they may be municipally owned; or they may be owned and controlled by some or all of the railroads entering the city. The characteristic feature of this type of organization, however, is the ownership and operation of the terminals in the interest of all of the participating lines. If terminal associations do not include all carriers entering a city, the same difficulties may arise as when each railroad has its own terminal facilities and refuses to permit their use by other lines. For this reason it is preferable that terminal organizations include all the lines entering the terminal or, at least, that there be no discrimination against those not in the organization.

Prior to 1920 the law specifically recognized the right of a carrier to the exclusive use of its terminals and sought to protect that right. The provision of Section 3 requiring carriers to afford facilities for the interchange of traffic between their respective lines was qualified by the proviso that this should not be construed "as requiring any such common carrier to give the use of its tracks or terminal facilities to another carrier engaged in like business." The Commission was therefore powerless to require a carrier to open a terminal to other carriers if the owning carrier insisted upon retaining its exclusive use.[57] But if a carrier had opened its terminals to the use of other railroads, it had to open them to all.[58] These were called "open" terminals, while those used only by the owning line were called "closed" terminals. By opening its terminals to one line, the

---

[57] *Morriss Iron Co.* v. *Baltimore & Ohio R. R. Co.*, 26 ICC 240 (1912); *Kansas City & Memphis Ry. Co.* v. *St. Louis & San Francisco R. R. Co.*, 46 ICC 464 (1917).

[58] *Chicago, Lake Shore & South Bend Ry. Co.* v. *Director General*, 58 ICC 647 (1920); *Switching at Galesburg, Ill.*, 31 ICC 294 (1914).

railroad waived the protection afforded by the provisions of paragraph 3 of Section 3.

Increased control over terminals was vested in the Interstate Commerce Commission by the Transportation Act of 1920. The Act removed the provision which protected the carrier in the exclusive use of its terminals, and it also provided that the Commission could require the joint use of terminals. Regulation of terminal facilities of interstate railroads is now a matter exclusively within the jurisdiction of the federal government and beyond the power of the state,[59] although control over the construction of union stations is still in the states.[60]

Two points must be established before the Commission can issue an order requiring the joint use of terminals. It must be shown that joint use is in the public interest and that it will not impair the ability of the owning carrier to handle its own business. The owning carrier is entitled to compensation for the use of its facilities by another. This is to be a matter of agreement between the carriers, if possible; but if the carriers are unable to agree, the Commission may fix the compensation. This is to be ascertained according to the principles controlling compensation in condemnation proceedings. The latter provision, in the estimation of many students of the problem, will prevent any widespread endeavor of weaker lines to seek the use of the terminals of their more fortunately located rivals.[61]

The desirability of common use of terminal facilities has been strongly urged by the Commission. "All terminal properties should be thrown open to all users on fair and equal terms so that every industry on whatever rails located shall have access to all lines radiating from that terminal, and every line carrier reaching that terminal shall similarly have access to all terminal tracks within the terminal area."[62]

The Commission has required joint use of terminals in a number of cases.[63] In others it has refused to do so.[64] In some of the latter the loss of

---

[59] *Southern Ry. Co.* v. *Shealy,* 18 F. 2d 784 (1927).

[60] *Interstate Commerce Commission* v. *United States ex. rel. City of Los Angeles,* 280 U.S. 52 (1929).

[61] W. M. Daniels, "The Future of American Railroads," 38 *Quarterly Journal of Economics,* 361, 373 (1924); H. B. Vanderblue and K. F. Burgess, *Railroads: Rates, Service, Management* (New York: Macmillan, 1923), p. 278.

[62] *Consolidation of Railroads,* 159 ICC 522, 522–23 (1929); 185 ICC 403, 414 (1932).

[63] *Port Arthur Chamber of Commerce* v. *Texarkana & Fort Smith Ry. Co.,* 136 ICC 597 (1928); *Chicago & Alton R. R. Co.* v. *Toledo, Peoria & Western Ry. Co.,* 146 ICC 171 (1928); *Use of Northern Pacific Tracks at Seattle by Great Northern,* 161 ICC 699 (1930); *Chicago & North Western Ry. Co.* v. *Ann Arbor R. R. Co.,* 263 ICC 287 (1945); *Use by Erie of Niagara Junction Ry. Co. Terminals,* 269 ICC 493 (1947). See also *Florida East Coast R. Co.* v. *United States,* 256 F. Supp. 986 (1966).

[64] *Port Arthur Chamber of Commerce* v. *Texarkana & Fort Smith Ry. Co.,* 73 ICC 361, 364 (1922); *York Manufacturers' Assoc.* v. *Pennsylvania R. R. Co.,* 73 ICC 40, 49–50 (1922); *Hastings Commercial Club* v. *Chicago, Milwaukee & St. Paul Ry.,* 107 ICC 208, 216 (1926); *Jamestown, N.Y., Chamber of Commerce* v. *Jamestown, Westfield & Northwestern R. R. Co.,* 195 ICC 289, 291 (1933).

traffic or revenue that would be suffered by the owning carrier if it opened its terminals to the use of other lines was apparently a factor in the Commission's decision.

INTERCHANGE FACILITIES WITH OTHER CARRIERS

Paragraph 4 of Section 3 of the Act requires carriers to "afford all reasonable, proper, and equal facilities for the interchange of traffic between their respective lines." The Commission has asserted that because of this provision in the law, it is empowered to require railroads to establish connections with other lines.[65] The jurisdiction of the Interstate Commerce Commission over the establishment of interchange facilities between railroads is apparently exclusive, and the states may no longer exercise control over the same matter.[66]

The Interstate Commerce Commission in a number of instances has required the construction of track connections between railroads for the interchange of freight,[67] but such requests have been denied if the volume of traffic to be interchanged did not warrant the expediture[68] or if the resulting interchange would merely divert competitive traffic from one railroad to another.[69]

THROUGH ROUTES AND JOINT RATES

The power to require construction of interchange facilities would be of little value without the power to require railroads to interchange traffic with one another. The principal provisions of the Interstate Commerce Act which relate to this matter are Section 1 (4) and Section 15 (3). The former makes it the duty of common carriers by railroad to establish reasonable through routes with other railroads. Section 15 (3) empowers the Commission to establish through routes and joint rates or fares for the transportation of property and persons by carriers subject to Part I of the Act. The power of the Commission to require the establishment of through routes and joint rates carries with it the power to prevent the closing of through routes and the cancellation of joint rates.

---

[65] *Pittsburgh & West Virginia Ry. Co.* v. *Lake Erie, Alliance & Wheeling R. R. Co.*, 81 ICC 333, 334 (1923); *Breckenridge Chamber of Commerce* v. *Wichita Falls, Ranger & Fort Worth R. R.*, 109 ICC 81, 82 (1926).

[66] *People* v. *Public Service Commission*, 233 N.Y. 113, 119–21 (1922).

[67] *Commercial Club of Faulkton, S. Dak.* v. *Chicago, Milwaukee, St. Paul & Pacific R. R. Co.*, 157 ICC 350 (1929); *Dansville Board of Trade* v. *Dansville & Mount Morris R. R. Co.*, 188 ICC 580 (1932); *Keyes Ry. Committee* v. *Beaver, Meade & Englewood R. R. Co.*, 214 ICC 526 (1936); *Wisconsin Power & Light Co.* v. *Chicago & North Western Ry. Co.* 220 ICC 475 (1937).

[68] *Hilliard Co.* v. *Great Northern Ry. Co.*, 190 ICC 201 (1932).

[69] *Chamber of Commerce of Sapulpa, Okla.* v. *St. Louis–San Francisco Ry. Co.*, 181 ICC 457 (1932).

The terms "through routes" and "joint rates" should be clearly understood before these sections of the law are discussed. As defined by the United States Supreme Court, a through route is "an arrangement, express or implied, between connecting railroads for the continuous carriage of goods from the originating point on the line of one carrier to destination on the line of another."[70] If there is a through route, there is a through rate. This may be a combination rate, that is, the sum of separate rates fixed by the several carriers forming the through route, or it may be a joint rate. A "joint rate" is a single through rate from the point of origin to destination, usually less than the sum of the local rates established by the connecting carriers. Thus there may be through routes with or without joint rates. The power of the Commission extends both to the creation of through routes and to the establishment of joint rates to go with them.

The power of the Commission to require the establishment of through routes is limited somewhat by a provision in the law to the effect that a carrier may not be required to short-haul itself. This limitation is found in paragraph 4 of Section 15. It provides that "in establishing any such through route the Commission shall not . . . require any carrier by railroad, without its consent, to embrace in such route substantially less than the entire length of its railroad . . . which lies between the termini of such proposed through route."[71] This limitation does not apply, however, when its observance would result in a route which is unreasonably long as compared with another practicable through route which could otherwise be established, nor does the limitation apply if the through route which is being proposed "is needed in order to provide adequate, and more efficient or more economic, transportation." Even in these situations, however, the Commission is required to give "reasonable preference" to the carrier which originates the traffic.[72] In a number of cases the Commission has required the establishment of through routes which short-hauled one of the carriers involved.[73] An important instance was when the Commission required the Union Pacific Railroad Co. to establish a through route with the Denver & Rio Grande Western Railroad Co. between points in the Northwest and points south and east of Denver.[74] Such a route would short-haul the Union Pacific. The Commission's order was contested in the courts but was ultimately upheld by the Supreme Court

---

[70] *St. Louis–Southwestern Ry. Co.* v. *United States*, 245 U.S. 136, 139, n. 2 (1917); see also *Thompson* v. *United States*, 343 U.S. 549 (1952).

[71] This rule does not apply if one of the carriers is a water line.

[72] Section 15 (4) of the Act was interpreted by the Supreme Court in *Pennsylvania Railroad Co.* v. *United States*, 323 U.S. 588 (1945).

[73] *Stickell & Sons Inc.* v. *Alton R. Co.*, 255 ICC 333 (1943); *Allied Mills, Inc., of Va.* v. *Alton R. Co.*, 272 ICC 49 (1948); *California Milling Corp.* v. *Atchison, Topeka & Santa Fe Ry. Co.*, 274 ICC 120 (1949).

[74] *Denver & Rio Grande Western R. Co.* v. *Union Pacific R. Co.*, 287 ICC 611 (1953).

of the United States.[75] In other cases the Commission has refused to require the establishment of through routes which would have short-hauled one of the carriers involved. In this group of cases the circumstances did not appear to fall within the statutory exceptions to the rule that the carriers cannot be compelled to short-haul themselves.[76]

The short-hauling limitation on the Commission's power to require the establishment of through routes does not restrict the Commission's power to require a continuance of previously existing through routes which short-haul one of the carriers concerned.[77]

One more point regarding the short-hauling limitations on the Commission's power to require the establishment of through routes should be noted. They do not operate to prevent the Commission from requiring a railroad to treat connecting lines impartially. If a carrier voluntarily short-hauls itself, it cannot refuse to interchange on equal terms with another carrier similarly situated and in a position to interchange and transport traffic equally well.[78]

ABANDONMENTS

Once a railroad has been constructed, industries locate along its line, communities spring up, and homes and business establishments arise. The subsequent abandonment of the railroad will work a hardship upon the industries established along its line and upon the communities that have grown up along it. Property values decline, and losses are imposed upon many individuals. It is natural, therefore, that the people, acting collectively through their government, should endeavor to prevent the abandonment of railroad lines. The theory behind interference with railroad abandonment was stated very clearly by the Supreme Court of Kansas in 1894: "The railway corporation takes its franchises subject to the burden of a duty to the public to carry out the purposes of the charter. The road, when constructed, becomes a public instrumentality, and the roadbed, superstructure, and other permanent property of the corporation are devoted to the public use. From this use neither the corporation itself, nor any person, company, or corporation deriving its title by purchase . . . can divert it without the assent of the state."[79] But although the courts have sometimes enjoined the abandonment of railways, they have held

---

[75] 351 U.S. 321 (1956).

[76] *Adrian Grain Co.* v. *Ann Arbor R. Co.*, 276 ICC 331 (1949); *American National Live Stock Assoc.* v. *Atchison, Topeka & Santa Fe Ry. Co.*, 284 ICC 531 (1952); *United States* v. *Atlantic Coast Line R. Co.*, 287 ICC 487 (1953).

[77] *Cancelation of Rates and Routes via Short Lines*, 245 ICC 183, 185–91 (1941); *Southern Ry. Co.* v. *United States*, 166 F. Supp. 78 (1958).

[78] *Chattanooga Packet Co.* v. *Illinois Central R. R. Co.*, 33 ICC 384 (1915); *Western Pacific R. R. Co.* v. *Southern Pacific Co.*, 55 ICC 71 (1919).

[79] *Naylor* v. *Dodge City, Montezuma & Trinidad R. R. Co.*, 36 Pac. 747, 748 (1894).

that property owners injured by an abandonment cannot recover their losses from the railroad company.[80]

In the decision by the Kansas Supreme Court quoted above, the Court held that the duty of the carrier to operate its road existed whether it operated at a profit or at a loss; but the United States Supreme Court has held that a railroad company cannot be compelled to operate at a loss against its will.[81] In 1921 the Court said: "Apart from statute or express contract people who have put their money into a railroad are not bound to go on with it at a loss if there is no reasonable prospect of profitable operation in the future."[82] To compel a railroad to operate at a loss would be a taking of its property without compensation. But the right to abandon an unprofitable line does not mean that a railroad is free to abandon an unprofitable branch, provided the system as a whole is profitable: "A railway may be compelled to continue the service of a branch or part of a line, although the operation involves a loss."[83] And much more recently a federal court has said: ". . . we hold that no confiscation results from an order . . . denying the abandonment of rail services which are shown to be unprofitable, as long as there is no net loss to the over-all system."[84]

Prior to 1920, control over railroad abandonments was exercised by the states to some extent. The Act of 1920 gave the federal government control over abandonment, although the states were not wholly deprived of their authority over the matter. Paragraph 18 of Section 1 provides that "no carrier by railroad subject to this Act shall abandon all or any portion of a line of railroad, or the operation thereof, unless and until there shall first have been obtained from the Commission a certificate that the present and future public convenience and necessity permit of such abandonment." Another paragraph specifically excludes from the Commission's control the abandonment (and construction) of spur, industrial, team, switching, or sidetracks located wholly within one state. "Abandonment" refers to complete abandonment or cessation of service and not to curtailment of service.[85]

It has taken a number of court decisions to define clearly the relation of state to federal authority over abandonment. In *Texas* v. *Eastern Texas Railroad Co.*,[86] the Court held that the Interstate Commerce Commission

---

[80] *Helena & Livingston Smelting & Reduction Co.* v. *Northern Pacific Ry. Co.*, 204 Pac. 370 (1922).

[81] *Brooks Scanlon Co.* v. *Railroad Commission of Louisiana*, 251 U.S. 396 (1920).

[82] *Bullock* v. *Railroad Commission of Florida*, 254 U.S. 513, 520–21 (1921). See also *Railroad Commission* v. *Eastern Texas R. R. Co.*, 264 U.S. 79 (1924).

[83] *Fort Smith Traction Co.* v. *Bourland*, 267 U.S. 330 (1925). See also *Chesapeake & Ohio Ry. Co.* v. *Public Service Commission*, 242 U.S. 603, 607 (1917).

[84] *Northwestern Pacific R. Co.* v. *United States*, 228 F. Supp. 690, 694 (1964).

[85] *Norfolk & Western Ry. Co. Abandonment*, 187 ICC 66, 72 (1932); *Chicago, Burlington & Quincy R. Co. Control*, 271 ICC 63, 67 (1948).

[86] 258 U.S. 204 (1922).

could permit the abandonment in interstate commerce of purely intrastate railroads but that the state still retained authority over the abandonment of its intrastate operations. It was recognized, however, that if operation of a line in intrastate commerce imposed a burden upon interstate commerce, the federal government could permit abandonment in intrastate commerce. The authority left to the states amounts to very little in practice because if a line abandons its interstate operations, a situation is created whereby complete abandonment of the line can hardly be prevented on account of its unprofitableness.[87] In *Colorado* v. *United States*[88] the Commission was upheld in an order requiring the abandonment of both interstate and intrastate operations of a line located wholly within one state because continued operation would burden interstate commerce.[89]

A few generalizations can be made regarding the Commission's policy in abandonment cases, although each case must be considered as a separate problem.

1. The Commission will not hesitate to authorize abandonments when the railroad no longer serves any useful purpose and when its abandonment will work no great injury to the communities served. Often abandonment is caused by the exhaustion of natural resources upon which the railroad relied for traffic or by the migration of industries to other points. Sometimes the construction of improved highways has made the abandonment of a railroad of little consequence to the communities once dependent upon it. In some instances the Commission has permitted the abandonment of a line on condition that motor-carrier service be substituted.[90]

2. The financial result of operation over the line proposed to be abandoned is an important matter for consideration in an abandonment case. In an early case before the Commission it was argued that the question of profitable or unprofitable operation was largely irrelevant and that the Commission was to pass upon the need for the service afforded by the carrier, regardless of financial results. This view the Commission rejected, holding that the very fact that a line does not pay implies that its services are not greatly needed.[91] But this does not mean that abandonment of a branch that is unprofitable will always be authorized.

---

[87] For an example of this situation see *Railroad Commission* v. *Eastern Texas R. R. Co.*, 264 U.S. 79 (1924).

[88] 271 U.S. 153 (1926).

[89] See also *Transit Commission* v. *United States*, 284 U.S. 360 (1932); *Proposed Abandonment of Detroit & Mackinack Ry.*, 138 ICC 576 (1928).

[90] *Abandonment of Ferry by New York, New Haven & Hartford R. R. Co.*, 150 ICC 413, 415, (1929); *Long Island R. R. Co. Abandonment*, 162 ICC 363, 376 (1930), 166 ICC 671, 678 (1930), 175 ICC 163, 166 (1931).

[91] *Public-Convenience Certificate to Duluth & Northern Minnesota Ry.*, 71 ICC 795, 799 (1922).

3. The Commission recognizes that a branch line can be continued in operation even if operated at a loss, but it has also held that "it is contrary to the purposes of the abandonment provisions and inconsistent with the purposes of the act as a whole to require drains upon the revenue of an interstate carrier flowing from the operation of an unprofitable and unnecessary branch merely because system operations as a whole are profitable."[92] An examination of a number of instances in recent years in which abandonment of unprofitable branches was not permitted reveals that they were cases in which the hardships which would result from abandonment were thought to clearly outweigh the burden on the railway which would result from continued operation.[93] In a large proportion of the cases the Commission also believed that traffic would increase in the future as a result of expected increases in agricultural, mining, or manufacturing output, or, in case of commuter service, as a result of the growth of the area in population.[94] In some instances, the carriers are told that they may renew their application without prejudice if, after a trial period, shipper and community forecasts of increased traffic do not develop.

Since almost every abandonment case requires a careful balancing of the burden imposed upon the railroad by continued operation of a line and the burden upon the public that would result from its abandonment, each case must be decided in the light of the surrounding circumstances and it is not strange that the cases frequently divide the Commission.

From 1920, when the Interstate Commerce Commission was given jurisdiction over railroad abandonments, to June 30, 1969, the Commission has authorized the abandonment of 56,805 miles of line.[95] Statistics of the mileage of abandonments authorized are to some extent misleading. It sometimes happens that after abandonment is authorized, some or part of the mileage involved will be taken over by other existing railroads, or by newly created corporations, or by public authority, and will be kept in operation.

The reasons for abandonment have changed over a period of time. From 1946 to 1955 nonrail competition accounted for 9.8 percent of the abandonments authorized; but between 1935 and 1943 it accounted for 50.7 percent. Exhaustion of natural resources accounted for 14.6 percent of the abandonments between 1946 and 1955; but in the period from 1920 to 1935 it accounted for 65 percent. Between 1935 and 1943 internal ad-

---

[92] *New York Central R. R. Co. Abandonment*, 254 ICC 745, 761 (1944). See also *East Tennessee & Western North Carolina R. Co. Abandonment*, 275 ICC 547, 552 (1950).

[93] *Leelanau Transit Co. Abandonment*, 307 ICC 95 (1959); *Northwestern Pacific R. Co. Abandonment*, 320 ICC 19 (1963).

[94] *Great Northern Ry. Co. Abandonment*, 271 ICC 207 (1948); *Louisville & Nashville R. Co. Abandonment*, 307 ICC 286 (1959); *Missouri Pacific R. Co. Abandonment, Crete Branch*, 307 ICC 189 (1959); *Chicago, Rock Island & Pacific R. Co. Abandonment*, 312 ICC 264; *Southern Pacific Co. Abandonment*, 317 ICC 645 (1963).

[95] Interstate Commerce Commission, *Annual Report*, 1969, p. 132.

justments accounted for 12.4 percent of the abandonments authorized, but the proportion had risen to 36.6 percent between 1946 and 1955.[96]

DISCONTINUANCE OF PASSENGER TRAINS

Traditionally, the railroads have provided both passenger and freight service, and their common-law obligations to provide reasonably adequate service covered both services. The decline of passenger traffic occasioned by the increasing use of automobiles for the intercity movement of persons, and the rapid growth of commercial air transportation for long-distance trips, gave rise to efforts by the railroads to reduce the number of unprofitable passenger trains and thus to reduce losses from this branch of the service. As pointed out elsewhere, state regulatory bodies exercised control over this matter prior to 1958; the federal government did not.[97] The enactment of Section 13a of the Interstate Commerce Act in 1958 was designed to grant relief to the railroads from the obstacles commonly placed in the way of the discontinuance of unprofitable passenger trains by state regulatory bodies. The Interstate Commerce Commission, it will be recalled, could block the discontinuance of passenger trains for a limited period of time upon findings that operation of the trains involved was required by public convenience and necessity and would not cause an undue burden upon interstate commerce.[98]

Section 13a was largely successful in accomplishing its objective since under its provisions the Commission authorized the discontinuance of 768 passenger trains between 1959 and 1970.[99] It should not be inferred, however, that all applications to discontinue such trains have been granted. In fact, during the period 1959 to 1970 the Commission required continuance of 531 passenger trains which the railroads proposed to discontinue.

In view of the changed situation brought about by the Rail Passenger Service Act of 1970, it is unnecessary to examine in detail the policies that the Commission evolved in disposing of Section 13a cases. It is worthwhile, however, to observe the Commission's reaction to the policy of downgrading passenger service that was revealed in some of the proceedings as a deliberate policy adopted to discourage patronage and make the trains so unprofitable that the Commission would permit discontinuance. Often equipment was poorly maintained, toilet facilities were unsanitary or even filthy. In some instances, the railroads eliminated reference to certain trains in their timetables and even instructed ticket agents to deny the existence of the trains on which patronage was to be discouraged. The

---

[96] From Jacob Weissman, "Railroad Abandonments: The Impact of Competition," 44 *Iowa Law Journal* 492, 503 (1959).

[97] P. 272 supra.

[98] For further description of the section see pp. 272–73 supra.

[99] Interstate Commerce Commission, *Annual Report, 1970*, p. 18.

Commission, appropriately enough, condemned such tactics. In one case it said: "The Commission will not find burdens on interstate commerce within the meaning of section 13a of the Interstate Commerce Act to be 'undue' if those burdens are voluntarily created by carrier for the purpose of obtaining a favorable decision from the Commission."[100]

Although the Commission could refuse to authorize the discontinuance of passenger trains when the carrier had deliberately downgraded service, it held that it had no authority to regulate directly the quality of rail passenger operations.[101] Such power, however, appears to have been granted to the Commission by the Rail Passenger Service Act of 1970.[102]

Enactment of the Rail Passenger Service Act renders Section 13a of somewhat less importance in the immediate future than it has been up to the present. Under its provisions, the railroads which have contracted to turn over intercity passenger operations to the National Railroad Passenger Corporation are relieved of the obligation to provide *any* intercity passenger service. If a railroad does not enter into such a contract with the Corporation, it may not discontinue *any* intercity passenger service prior to January 1, 1975. After that date it may discontinue service only in conformity with the procedures prescribed in Section 13a of the Interstate Commerce Act. Thus Section 13a will eventually come into operation again. Furthermore, after July 1, 1973, service provided by the Railroad Passenger Corporation which is part of the "basic system" may not be discontinued except through the procedures of Section 13a, but any of its services which are not part of the "basic system" may be discontinued by the Corporation at any time.

COMPULSORY CONSTRUCTION

Power to prevent abandonment of railroads already constructed is one thing; power to require the construction of a branch or extension is quite another. Paragraph 21 of Section 1 of the Interstate Commerce Act as amended in 1920 provides that the Commission may, after a hearing, "authorize or require by order any carrier by railroad subject to this Act . . . to provide itself with safe and adequate facilities for performing as a common carrier its car service as that term is used in this Act, *and to extend its line or lines.*"[103] A proviso is attached, setting up requirements that must be observed by the Commission before an order may issue. First is the requirement that the extension must be "reasonably required in the interest of public convenience and necessity," and second, "that the ex-

---

[100] *Chicago, Burlington & Quincy R. Co., Discontinuance of Trains,* 330 ICC 742, 760 (1967).

[101] *Adequacy—Passenger Service—Southern Pacific Co. between California & Louisiana,* 335 ICC 415 (1969).

[102] Sec. 801.

[103] Italics ours.

pense involved therein will not impair the ability of the carrier to perform its duty to the public."

Only once has the Commission issued an order requiring a carrier to extend its lines. That was in 1929, when it directed the Oregon-Washington Railroad & Navigation Company—a subsidiary of the Union Pacific—to construct a line about 187 miles long in Oregon, at an estimated cost of $9 million.[104] The Commission's order was set aside by the United States Supreme Court in *Interstate Commerce Commission* v. *Oregon-Washington Railroad & Navigation Company.* The Court, in interpreting paragraph 21 of Section 1, said: "We . . . think the power granted by paragraph 21 is confined to extensions within the undertaking of the carrier to serve, and cannot be extended to embrace the building of what is essentially a new line to reach new territory."[105] Two major considerations led the Court to this conclusion. First was the fact that the phrase "to extend its line or lines" is part of a single sentence giving the Commission power to require carriers to provide safe and adequate facilities for car service. "We should expect, if Congress were intending to grant to the Commission a new and drastic power to compel the investment of enormous sums for the development or service of a region which the carrier had never theretofore entered or intended to serve, the intention would be expressed in more than a clause in a sentence dealing with car service."[106] The second consideration leading to a narrow interpretation of paragraph 21 was doubt regarding its constitutionality if it were interpreted to mean that the Commission could require a railroad to construct a new line against its will. The decision of the Court so restricts the power of the Commission to require railroads to extend their lines that the power is of little practical consequence.

Although the Oregon case was the only instance in which the Commission ever issued an affirmative order requiring new construction, a number of other cases have been before it in which exercise of the power was requested but refused.[107]

SOME SPECIAL SERVICES

The railroads give a large number of special services, some of which are required by the necessities of particular commodities or the characteristics of particular freight movements. It would unduly lengthen this chapter to catalogue even the more common of these. There are two

---

[104] *Public Service Commission of Oregon* v. *Central Pacific Ry. Co.* 159 ICC 630 (1929).

[105] 288 U.S. 14, 40 (1933).

[106] Ibid., p. 35.

[107] *Cooke* v. *Chicago, Burlington & Quincy R. R. Co.*, 66 ICC 452 (1922); *Construction of Lines in Eastern Oregon*, 111 ICC 3 (1926); *Clarkston Chamber of Commerce* v. *Northern Pacific Ry. Co.*, 160 ICC 752 (1930); *Public Service Commission of Wyoming* v. *Chicago, Burlington & Quincy R. R. Co.*, 185 ICC 741 (1932).

services, however, which are so characteristic of railroad freight service as it has developed through the years, and which are so important in the manufacture, sale, and distribution of commodities, that they require brief attention. These are (1) "reconsignment," or "diversion," and (2) "in-transit" privileges.

Diversion and Reconsignment

The terms "diversion" and "reconsignment" are used interchangeably to refer to a change in the destination or billing of a shipment, either before or after it reaches the original destination. An essential feature of diversion and reconsignment is that the shipment moves at the regular published through rate from point of origin to final destination, plus, in some cases, a reconsignment charge. This is what makes the privilege valuable, for the through rate is ordinarily less than the rate to the diversion or reconsignment point plus the rate from there to final destination.

The reconsignment privilege is of considerable importance in the commercial world. Shipments of fresh fruits, of vegetables, or of livestock may be shipped from a distant source of supply and started toward market and then be diverted to the most favorable market as they approach the several destinations to which they might be sent. Brokers and dealers may purchase lumber or other products, sell them while the shipments are en route, and divert them to the ultimate purchaser, thus saving an extra handling of the shipment, eliminating storage, and perhaps saving unnecessary transportation. Other situations are constantly arising in the business world which make the diversion or reconsignment privilege of great value. It is now recognized in the United States as a commercial necessity.[108]

Originally the Interstate Commerce Commission was inclined to treat reconsignment as a privilege which might be extended by the carriers but which could not ordinarily be required of them.[109] In later years the Commission came to regard the denial of the service as unreasonable and to require its establishment or continuance.[110]

Carriers are permitted to make a charge for the diversion or reconsignment privilege. These charges are on a per car basis. The number of diversions that may be made is generally limited in order to prevent the use of freight cars as moving warehouses. If an extra reconsignment is

---

[108] *Central Commercial Co.* v. *Louisville & Nashville R. R. Co.*, 27 ICC 114, 115 (1913). Advantages are discussed in *Detroit Traffic Assoc.* v. *Lake Shore & Michigan Southern Ry. Co.*, 21 ICC 257 (1911).

[109] *Cedar Hill Coal & Coke Co.* v. *Colorado & Southern Ry. Co.*, 16 ICC 387 (1909). See also *Dietz Lumber Co.* v. *Atchison, Topeka & Santa Fe Ry. Co.*, 22 ICC 75 (1911).

[110] *Commercial Exchange of Philadelphia* v. *New York Central & Hudson River R. R. Co.*, 38 ICC 551, 555 (1916); *Doran & Co.* v. *Nashville, Chattanooga & St. Louis Ry.*, 33 ICC 523 (1915).

made, it is considered as a reshipment, that is, the rate applicable is the through rate to the last reconsignment point plus the rate from there to destination. The privilege is also restricted oftentimes to prevent or discourage reconsignment when a back haul is involved.

Transit Privileges

A transit arrangement is the privilege of stopping a shipment en route to enable some process or operation to be performed on the article, and of reshipping to final destination at the through rate applicable from the original shipping point to destination. Milling in transit, as applied to grain shipments, is probably the most common example of this privilege. Grain is also stopped off at intermediate points, under similar arrangements, for cleaning, grading, mixing, and other processes. Transit privileges are often granted on logs and rough lumber. The fabrication-in-transit privilege on iron and steel is common. In 1925 there were said to be some 300 commodities commonly granted transit privileges.[111] The privilege is of great importance to industries not located at rate-breaking points. The general effect of the practice is to equalize the advantages of location of competing manufacturers and to facilitate the decentralization of industry.[112]

The theory of a transit arrangement is that there is but a single shipment from point of origin to final destination, with a stopover privilege. But since two terminal services are performed at the transit point, the cost of the service is increased. Furthermore, additional cost is incurred because of the records made necessary to prevent fraud. For this reason the carriers are permitted to exact an extra charge for the service, although they do not always do so.

A number of points regarding in-transit arrangements should be noted. Usually the materials moving to the transit point and those moving out take the same rates. When they do not, the rate applicable is that of the article with the higher rate. The full local rate to the transit point is ordinarily paid when the article moves into the transit point. When the shipment moves out of the transit point, the rate applicable is the balance of the through rate from the original shipping point to final destination.[113] The identity of each shipment is not preserved, but in order to get the balance of the through rate on a shipment from the transit point, inbound billing must be presented for an equivalent amount of tonnage. The amount which can be shipped out at the balance of the through rate is ordinarily less than the amount shipped in. This is to take care of the

---

[111] G. L. Wilson, *Transit Service and Privileges* (Chicago: Traffic Service Corp., 1925), p. 1.

[112] See p. 76, supra.

[113] For exceptions to this rule, designed to discourage unprofitable circuitous or out-of-line hauls, see description of the "three-way rule," sometimes found in transit rules, in *Transit & Mixing Rules on Foodstuffs*, 270 ICC 157 (1948).

shrinkage in weight due to processing, thereby preventing shipments from moving out which do not represent tonnage shipped into the transit point under a transit arrangement. Under the milling-in-transit privilege the outbound tonnage is usually 1 percent less than the inbound. On barley malted in transit, a deduction of 16 percent from inbound tonnage is commonly made; on corn shipped under a shelling-in-transit arrangement, the deduction is often 20 percent.

The Interstate Commerce Commission has long regarded transit arrangements as privileges which the carriers cannot be compelled to grant. "Transit is a special service which, as a general rule, will be required by us only when necessary to prevent unjust discrimination or undue preference or prejudice."[114] In fact, the Commission is inclined to discourage the extension of the privilege and to criticize the carriers for being unduly liberal in granting it.[115] The Commission has rarely required its establishment except when necessary to do so to prevent discrimination.[116] The Commission is particularly critical of the privilege when it causes back hauls or out-of-line hauls and therefore results in economic waste. "The theory of transit is service at some point between the points of origin and destination of the traffic, and in the direction of the movement of the traffic to the point of final destination. A back haul is contrary to the purpose of transit and should generally be permitted only to meet unusual situations. . . ."[117] The Commission, however, sometimes requires the establishment of the privilege, even if a back haul is involved, if the privilege is given at competitive points which also result in back hauls. This is necessary to prevent discrimination.[118] Railroads very frequently deny the privilege where back hauls will result, or they impose additional charges for the extra mileage.

Some difficulty arises from the tendency to extend the transit privilege to articles which undergo a complete manufacturing process at the transit point. Usually the privilege is extended when there is a mere processing or reworking of the material shipped into the transit point, but not when an entirely new product emerges.[119] Yet flour and grain are quite different

---

[114] *Johnson Coal Cubing Co.* v. *Chesapeake & Ohio Ry. Co.*, 293 ICC 149, 152 (1954).

[115] *Anadarko Cotton Oil Co.* v. *Atchison, Topeka & Santa Fe Ry. Co.*, 20 ICC 43, 47 (1910); *Middletown Car Co.* v. *Pennsylvania R. R. Co.*, 32 ICC 185 (1914). See also *Grain & Grain Products*, 164 ICC 619, 653–54 (1930), and comments of individual Commissioners, pp. 699, 708–9, 743–45.

[116] E.g., *In re Transportation of Wool, Hides & Pelts*, 23 ICC 151 (1922).

[117] *Stock & Sons* v. *Lake Shore & Michigan Southern Ry. Co.*, 31 ICC 150, 153 (1914). See also *Lake Charles Rice Co.* v. *Louisiana Western R. R. Co.*, 69 ICC 508, 513 (1922).

[118] See *Thomas Cotton Co.* v. *Illinois Central R. R. Co.*, 63 ICC 89 (1921).

[119] *Leader Iron Works* v. *Illinois Central R. R. Co.*, 182 ICC 17 (1932); *Atchison, Topeka & Santa Fe R. R. Co.* v. *Union Wire Rope Corp.*, 1 F. Supp. 399 (1931).

commodities, and the milling-in-transit privilege sometimes extends to neatly packed breakfast cereals which move out of transit points.[120]

SERVICE REGULATION AND OTHER MODES OF TRANSPORT

It was noted early in this chapter that the common law imposed upon common carriers the duty of providing adequate service. This obligation applies to common carriers regardless of the mode of transportation in which they are engaged. This chapter has dealt with particular aspects of service and service regulation, some of which, by their very nature, apply only to railroads. In later chapters we shall note more specifically certain service requirements that are imposed on other modes of transport.

SELECTED REFERENCES

Various aspects of railroad service and service regulation are discussed in H. B. Vanderblue and K. F. Burgess, *Railroads: Rates, Service, Management* (New York: Macmillan, 1923); chaps. xiii–xx; Stuart Daggett, *Principles of Inland Transportation* (4th ed.; New York: Harper, 1955), chap. xii; Kent T. Healy, *Economics of Transportation in America* (New York: Ronald Press, 1940), chap. xxiii; and R. E. Westmeyer, *Economics of Transportation* (New York: Prentice-Hall, 1952), chap. xvi.

The terminal problem is discussed in W. Z. Ripley, "The Problem of Terminal Operation," 4 *Harvard Business Review* 266, 385 (1926); M. L. Fair, "The Interstate Commerce Commission and the Railroad Terminal Problem," 44 *Quarterly Journal of Economics* 462 (1930); and S. L. Miller, *Inland Transportation* (New York: McGraw-Hill, 1933), pp. 304–15.

On railroad abandonment see C. W. Needham, "The Rights of the State and Adjacent Owners of Property in the Maintenance and Operation of a Railroad," 32 *Yale Law Journal* 247 (1923); and H. R. Trumbower, "Railroad Abandonments and Additions," 34 *Journal of Political Economy* 37 (1926); Charles Cherington, *The Regulation of Railroad Abandonments* (Cambridge: Harvard University Press, 1948). An excellent analysis of the problem of railroad abandonments is in Emery Troxel, *Economics of Transport* (New York: Rinehart, 1955), chap. xxii. See also J. Weissman, "Railroad Abandonments: The Competitive Ideal," 43 *Minnesota Law Review* 251 (1958); and Michael Conant, *Railroad Mergers and Abandonments* (Berkeley & Los Angeles, University of California Press, 1964), chap. vi.

For a discussion of legal and economic aspects of passenger-train discontinuance, see Eldon Martin, "Legal Problems of the Railroad Passenger Deficit," 54 *Public Utilities Fortnightly* 429 (1954); A. J. G. Priest, "Discontinuance of Railroad Service," 61 ibid. 656 (1958); Michael Conant, "Railroad Service Discontinuances," 43 *Minnesota Law Review* 275 (1958); Michael J. Laird and William E. Thomas, "End of the Line," 15 *Loyola Law Review* 263 (1968–69); George W. Hilton, *The Transportation Act of 1958* (Bloom-

---

[120] See 164 ICC 619, 708.

ington, Ind., Indiana University Press, 1969), chap. iv; also David E. Wells, "A Review of Interstate Commerce Commission Section 13a Decisions," 27 I.C.C. *Practitioners' Journal* 821 (1960).

On the problem of freight car supply, see Committee on Commerce, U.S. Senate, *National Transportation Policy* (The Doyle Report), 87th Cong., 1st Sess., Senate Report No. 445 (1961), chap. xiii, "The National Rail Freight Car Problem."

A thorough study of transit privileges is R. V. Hobbah, "Railroad Transit Privileges," Supplement to Vol. XVII, No. 3, of *Journal of Business of the University of Chicago* (1944).

On reconsignment and reconsignment rules, see Interstate Commerce Commission, *Reconsignment Case,* 47 ICC 590 (1917); *Reconsignment and Diversion Rules,* 58 ICC 568 (1920); *Diversion and Reconsignment Rules,* 61 ICC 385 (1921). *Diversion and Reconsignment Rules and Charges,* 337 ICC 686 (1970).

On service regulation generally, see I. L. Sharfman, *The Interstate Commerce Commission,* Vol. III-A (1935), pp. 55–68; on abandonment, pp. 331–48; on compulsory new construction, pp. 367–85; on joint use of terminals, pp. 410–21.

Chapter
26
PIPELINES

As elsewhere pointed out, pipelines constitute a specialized transportation system used in the transportation of crude oil, gasoline and other liquid products of petroleum, and natural gas.[1] Although pipelines are also being used on a limited scale for the transportation of solids, such as coal, ores, sulphur, phosphate rock, gypsum, wood chips to paper mills, and many other commodities, we are here concerned with pipelines used for the transportation of crude oil and liquid products thereof. The present system of oil pipelines is briefly described in an earlier chapter.[2]

HISTORICAL DEVELOPMENT OF OIL PIPELINES

The first pipeline built for the transportation of crude oil was constructed in western Pennsylvania in 1865. It was laid with 2-inch pipe and was about 4 miles in length. The cost of transporting oil by means of this pipe was considerably less than the charges exacted by teamsters. The success of this line led to the construction of other lines, and in a few years the oil fields in the Appalachian region were connected by pipelines to refineries or to railroads.

The important California, Gulf Coast, and mid-continent oil fields are now supplied with an extensive system of pipelines, extending from the oil fields to the seaboard or to refineries. The cheapness of pipeline transportation facilitated the development of refining at points easily accessible to markets but at great distances from the oil fields.

An important feature of pipeline development has been the close affiliation between the trunklines and the major oil companies. It has been stated that before World War II no one outside the petroleum industry had any substantial financial interest in petroleum pipelines.[3] Pipelines are often considered to be mere plant facilities of the oil companies. In 1956,

---

[1] Pp. 42–43 supra.

[2] Chapter 2.

[3] Surplus Property Administration, *Government-Owned Pipe Lines* (1946), p. 10.

607

70.7 percent of the mileage of crude-oil pipelines was owned or controlled by 20 major integrated oil companies.[4]

During World War II two crude-oil pipelines were constructed which were independent of the oil companies, but these were built by the federal government. The longer of these was the "Big Inch," extending from Longview, Texas, to the New York–Philadelphia refining area, to supply eastern refineries with crude oil without incurring the hazards to which the coastwise tankers were subjected in the war. This line was 1,340 miles long and cost nearly $78 million. Operation of this line was begun in 1943 and continued until 1945. The other crude-oil line constructed by the government was the Southwest Emergency Pipe Line, from Corpus Christi to Houston, Texas.[5] This line was 154 miles long and cost $6.1 million. The "Big Inch" was sold to the Texas Eastern Transmission Company in 1947 and was converted into a natural-gas line.

Pipelines used for the transportation of gasoline or other liquid products of petroleum are called "products lines." The transportation of gasoline by pipeline began in 1930. In that year the Tuscarora Pipe Line Company, controlled by the Standard Oil Company of New Jersey, began using an old crude-oil pipeline for transporting gasoline from its refineries on New York Harbor.[6] The perfection of the process of electric welding led to the rapid development of special gasoline pipelines. Prior to this time the leakage of gasoline at the pipeline joints made extensive use of pipelines for the transportation of gasoline impracticable.

Most products lines, like the crude-oil lines, are owned by or are affiliated with oil companies. The major exceptions have been the wartime pipelines built by the federal government. Of these the "Little Big Inch," or "Little Inch," mostly parallel to the "Big Inch" and connecting the Texas Gulf Coast refinery area with the New York area, was the most important. This line was 1,475 miles long and was built at a cost of $67.3 million.[7] Operation of this line was begun in 1944 but was discontinued in 1945. It was sold by the government, along with the "Big Inch," to the Texas Eastern Transmission Company and was converted into a natural-gas line. In 1957 the Federal Power Commission authorized the abandonment of this line, or a large part of it, and its reconversion to a products

---

[4] Antitrust Subcommittee of the Committee on the Judiciary, House of Representatives, *Report on Consent Decree Program of the Department of Justice* (1959), p. 126.

[5] This line is a converted and reconditioned natural-gas line.

[6] H. G. Moulton, *The American Transportation Problem* (Washington, D.C.: Brookings Institution, 1933), p. 707.

[7] Surplus Property Administration, op. cit., p. 6. Other products lines built by the government were the Florida Emergency Pipe Line (200 miles), across the northern part of the Florida peninsula; the Plantation Extension Pipe Line (179 miles), from Greensboro, North Carolina, to Richmond, Virginia; and the Ohio Emergency Pipe Lines (82 miles) from Tiffin to Doylestown.

line. There are several products lines owned or controlled by railroad companies.[8]

The development of pipelines for the transportation of gasoline and other petroleum products brought a new influence to bear on the location of petroleum refining. Previously the low cost of transporting crude oil and the comparatively high cost of transporting gasoline favored the location of refineries near large consuming markets. The development of gasoline pipelines has removed, in part at least, the disadvantage of refineries located at great distances from consuming markets. It has been asserted that the gasoline pipelines were built for the purpose of relieving the excess refining capacity that had developed near the oil fields of the Southwest.[9] Thus gasoline pipelines were developed to overcome the locational disadvantage of the refineries located near the oil fields but distant from the larger consuming markets.

An important characteristic of pipeline construction since World War II has been the use of large-diameter pipe. In 1941 there were only 170 miles of crude-oil trunk lines that exceeded 12 inches in diameter.[10] In 1968 there were 18,573 miles of such line and a 42-inch pipe had appeared.[11] Pipe of 48 inches in diameter has been recommended for the proposed Trans-Alaska pipeline.

COST CHARACTERISTICS OF PIPELINE TRANSPORTATION

The cost of transporting oil by pipelines varies widely but is considerably less than the cost of railroad transportation. A study by the Bureau of Transport Economics and Statistics of the Interstate Commerce Commission reported the cost of transporting crude oil by pipeline as 1.98 mills per ton-mile in 1942. The cost of transporting crude oil by rail was found to be 10.62 mills and the cost by tank vessels 0.63 mills per ton-mile.[12] The cost of transporting refined products of petroleum by pipeline was found to be 4.39 mills per ton-mile; by rail, 11.19 mills; and by tank vessels, 0.6 mills.[13]

A later study showed costs of transporting crude oil to be 4 mills per ton-mile by rail; 0.5 mills by pipeline; and costs by ocean-going tankers

---

[8] See Chapter 36.

[9] Joseph E. Pogue, "Economics of Pipe Line Transportation in the Petroleum Industry," reprinted in Hearings on H. R. 441, *Petroleum Investigation* (1914), pp. 725–27.

[10] Arthur M. Johnson, *Petroleum Pipelies and Public Policy, 1906–1959* (Cambridge, Mass., Harvard University Press, 1967), p. 352.

[11] U.S. Department of Interior, Bureau of Mines, *Mineral Industry Surveys*, December 23, 1968, p. 2.

[12] Statement No. 4432, *War-Built Pipe Lines and the Post-War Transportation of Petroleum* (Washington, D.C.: 1944), p. 81.

[13] Ibid.

of about 0.3 mills per ton-mile.[14] These estimates are of line-haul costs under favorable conditions. It seems clear that crude oil can be transported most cheaply by tank vessels; that pipelines run a close second; and that rail costs of transporting oil are several times that of pipelines.

One further matter pertaining to pipeline costs requires notice. The unit cost of transporting oil by pipeline decreases as the diameter of the pipe increases, if we assume that the greater capacity of the larger pipe can be utilized. As a result, the pipeline industry can be considered as naturally monopolistic, that is, a single large pipeline in a given market could operate more cheaply than a number of companies with smaller pipe. This explains why there are many multiple-owned pipelines, that is, jointly owned by two or more oil companies.[15]

PIPELINE RATES

The low cost of transporting oil by pipelines is reflected in the charges of pipeline companies. These rates are usually much lower than rail rates. In fact, the railroads make little effort to compete with pipelines for the movement of crude oil. The gasoline rates of pipelines are also usually lower than rail rates, but it appears that there is often competition between railroads and pipelines for the movement of gasoline and other products of the refining process and that rail rates are often depressed by the low rates of pipeline companies.[16]

RELATION OF PIPELINE RATES TO COSTS

Notwithstanding the low rates for the transportation of oil by pipelines, the accusation has often been made that pipeline rates are higher than the cost of the service justifies. The close affiliation between the pipelines and the large oil companies is blamed for the situation, since high pipeline rates work to the advantage of the controlling refineries.

The oil companies which control pipelines gain in three ways from maintaining high rates. First, they may make a large profit from transporting oil for others. Second, they are in effect getting their own oil transported at cost, while their competitors who have no pipelines must pay high rates. This places the oil companies who have no pipelines at a great disadvantage. Third, oil companies owning or controlling pipelines may

---

[14] John R. Meyer and others, *The Economics of Competition in the Transportation Industries* (Cambridge: Harvard University Press, 1959), p. 149.

[15] U.S. Department of Interior, *An Appraisal of the Petroleum Industry of the United States* (1965), p. 37.

[16] E.g., see *Refined Petroleum Products in the Southwest*, 174 ICC 745 (1931); *Petroleum and Its Products*, 183 ICC 24, 31 (1932); *Stanolind Pipe Line Co. v. Alton R. R. Co.*, 225 ICC 693, 695 (1938); and *Petroleum, Los Angeles & El Paso to Arizona & New Mexico*, 287 ICC 731 (1953). See also Interstate Commerce Commission, *Annual Report, 1941*, p. 27.

also gain through the depressing effect of pipelines rates on the price of oil at the wells. Independent producers either pay high pipeline rates to ship oil or sell it at the wells for whatever the large companies with pipeline facilities will offer. The result may be either to make production unprofitable to independent oil producers or to enable the refiners having pipelines to purchase crude oil at low figures.

The high rates of return earned by pipeline companies for many years suggest that pipeline rates have in fact been kept higher than costs of transportation justified. Table 26–1 shows the rate of return on depreciated investment earned from 1921 to 1940 by the pipelines reporting to the Interstate Commerce Commission.

In *Reduced Pipe Line Rates & Charges* the Interstate Commerce Commission found that the average rate of return earned by 35 pipeline com-

TABLE 26–1.   Rate of Return in Investment, Less Depreciation, of Pipeline Companies, 1921–40*

Year	Rate of Return (percent)	Year	Rate of Return (percent)
1921	10.71	1931	23.74
1922	22.92	1932	25.70
1923	20.52	1933	26.72
1924	21.70	1934	22.25
1925	22.37	1935	21.70
1926	23.93	1936	25.37
1927	25.31	1937	28.39
1928	29.15	1938	25.37
1929	30.73	1939	21.70
1930	27.46	1940	21.42

* Figures are calculated from statistics of oil pipeline companies published by the Interstate Commerce Commission.

panies in 1935 was 14.01 percent on the Commission's valuation of their properties. The earnings of individual companies ranged from a deficit of 0.6 percent to a return of 46.86 percent.[17] In this proceeding the Commission found the rates of 21 pipeline companies to be unreasonable and excessive. The pipelines reduced their rates to conform to the Commission's findings, in some instances to an even lower basis, and the Commission then dismissed the proceedings.[18]

In addition to regulatory action by the Interstate Commerce Commission, other forces have been operative to reduce pipeline rates and earnings. Among these have been competition among pipelines for shipments of independent producers in an effort to utilize capacity of the large-diameter lines laid in recent years. Another factor tending to reduce rates is the antitrust "consent decree" described later in this chapter. Notwith-

---

[17] 243 ICC 115, 141–42 (1940).
[18] 272 ICC 375 (1948).

TABLE 26–2. Rate of Return on Investment of Pipeline Companies, 1954–1969*

Year	Rate of Return (percent)	Year	Rate of Return (percent)
1954	16.2	1963	15.9
1955	18.0	1964	14.6
1956	19.2	1965	15.4
1957	17.2	1966	14.8
1958	16.5	1967	14.9
1959	17.5	1968	13.4
1960	17.0	1969	13.6
1961	17.2	1970	14.3
1962	17.7		

* From Interstate Commerce Commission, *Annual Reports*. Rate of return based on net investment in carrier property plus working capital.

standing these circumstances the earnings of pipeline companies continue to be generous. Table 26–2 shows the rates of return earned by pipeline companies on net investment in transportation property plus working capital in recent years.

DEMAND FOR REGULATION

Pipelines, as we have seen, developed as an adjunct of the oil-refining business. The dominance of the Standard Oil Company in the early days of the oil industry was attained partly because of its control over pipelines. The Standard was able to transport crude oil much more cheaply by pipeline than it could be transported by rail. Thus this company had a great advantage over refiners that had to rely on rail transportation. When other oil refiners endeavored to construct pipelines, they met all manner of opposition from the Standard. The railroads, seemingly in league with the Standard, often refused to allow pipelines to cross their rights of way. The few pipelines that were constructed against the wishes of the Standard were eventually brought under its control.[19]

It was this situation which led to the demand for regulation of pipelines. The Hepburn Act of 1906 brought transportation of oil and other commodities by pipeline, except water and natural or artificial gas, under the control of the Interstate Commerce Commission. The Act declared such pipelines to be common carriers.

If pipeline companies were common carriers, they could be forced to carry oil for independent producers or refiners at just and reasonable rates, thereby breaking up the advantage possessed by the Standard or other integrated oil companies. Many of the pipeline companies, however, refused to recognize their common-carrier status and refused to file tariffs with the Interstate Commerce Commission. The companies insisted on

[19] See Commissioner of Corporations, *Report on the Petroleum Industry*, Part I (1907), p. xix; also Interstate Commerce Commission, *Railroad Discriminations and Monopolies in Coal and Oil*, 59th Cong., 2d Sess., House Doc. No. 606 (1907), pp. 5–6.

purchasing all oil which was offered them for transportation by outsiders. Since the oil was the property of the pipelines, the companies contended that they were transporting only their own oil and were not transporting oil for the general public. It became necessary for the Commission to institute an investigation and determine whether it had jurisdiction over these pipelines. The Commission in 1912 decided that these pipelines were within its jurisdiction.[20] It held that the intent of Congress as expressed in the Hepburn Act was to convert interstate pipelines into common carriers. The Commission left to the courts the question of whether Congress could convert pipelines into common carriers by legislative fiat. In The Pipe Line Cases[21] the Supreme Court of the United States upheld the action of the Commission in requiring these pipeline companies, with one exception, to file tariffs. The Court held that the companies were common carriers in fact. "They carry everybody's oil to a market, although they compel outsiders to sell it before taking it into their pipes."[22] The Court considered that the practice of requiring the oil to be sold to the pipeline company was a mere subterfuge. The Court held that Congress "may require those who are common carriers in substance to become so in form."[23] By taking the position that the pipelines were common carriers in substance, although not in form, the Court avoided the necessity of deciding whether Congress could, by legislative fiat, make common carriers out of pipelines that were genuine private carriers. In a more recent case the Court refused to uphold an order of the Commission which directed the Champlin Refining Company to publish and file schedules showing the rates and charges for the transportation of petroleum products, as required by Section 6 of the Act.[24] The Champlin Company used its pipeline solely to carry its own refined petroleum products to market. The Court said that it would be hard to conclude "that Congress intended to apply the sanctions of Sec. 6—imposing the duty of serving the public at regulated rates—on all private pipe lines merely because they cross state lines."[25] It would be strange to suppose, said the Court, that Congress intended that the Commission should make common carriers for hire out of private pipelines "whose services were unused, unsought after, and unneeded by independent producers."[26] The crucial question, yet undecided, is whether the Commission, or Congress itself, can make common carriers out of private pipelines whose services, although unused by independent shippers, *are* sought after and needed by independent producers.

Subjecting pipelines to the provisions of the Interstate Commerce Act,

---

[20] *In the Matter of Pipe Lines*, 24 ICC 1 (1912).

[21] 234 U.S. 548 (1914).

[22] Ibid., p. 561.

[23] Ibid.

[24] *United States* v. *Champlin Co.*, 341 U.S. 290 (1951).

[25] Ibid., p. 297.

[26] Ibid., p. 298.

however, did not eliminate the evils which the control of pipelines by oil companies had brought about, although the rise of independent oil companies brought an end to the monopoly of the Standard Oil companies. But the new oil companies which developed likewise controlled pipelines and possessed some of the advantages over smaller companies which the Standard had so long enjoyed. Two devices in particular have been used by oil companies to retain the advantages which control of pipelines gave them.

The first of these practices is the maintenance of high minimum-tender requirements, which prevent the small oil producer or the small refiner from shipping oil by pipeline. The minimum tender is the minimum amount of oil that will be accepted.[27] There are practically no minimum-tender requirements attaching to the use of gathering lines, but trunklines almost always establish such a minimum. The minimum-tender requirements vary. The most common requirement has been 100,000 barrels, although 25,000 barrels is also common. Sometimes the minimum is as low as 10,000 barrels, and Texas prescribed a 500-barrel minimum for that state.[28] The severity of the minimum-tender requirement is sometimes alleviated by permitting combinations of shipments of different shippers or by other devices. Small oil producers and refiners, however, tend to complain of the minimum-tender requirements of pipeline companies. A complaint before the Interstate Commerce Commission against the Prairie Pipe Line Company resulted in the reduction of the minimum-tender requirement from 100,000 barrels to 10,000 by order of the Commission in 1922.[29] The Commission pointed out that the pipelines were justified in setting up minimum-tender requirements because the transportation of oil by pipelines is essentially a bulk business. "The pipe lines can not be successfully operated on a driblet basis, and there is a reasonable minimum below which they should not be required to accept oil for transportation."[30] But the Commission found that the 100,000-barrel minimum "reserves the pipe lines to a few large shippers and essentially deprives the lines of the common-carrier status with which they were impressed by the interstate commerce act."[31] In the Reduced Pipe Line Rates Case, previously referred to, the Commission again found minimum-tender requirements in excess of 10,000 barrels to be unreasonable.[32]

The second device by which oil companies owning pipelines derive

---

[27] It is not always required that the minimum amount be delivered to the pipeline at one time. See George S. Wolbert, Jr., *American Pipe Lines* (Norman: University of Oklahoma Press, 1952), p. 29.

[28] House of Representatives, Committee on Interstate and Foreign Commerce, *Report on Pipe Lines* (1933), Part I, pp. lxvi–lxvii.

[29] *Brundred Bros.* v. *Prairie Pipe Line Co.*, 68 ICC 458 (1922).

[30] Ibid., p. 466.

[31] Ibid.

[32] 243 ICC 115 (1940).

an advantage over independent producers and refiners is by maintaining high pipeline rates. Mention has already been made of this accusation. The belief persists that by maintaining high pipeline rates, the integrated oil companies depress the price of oil at the wells to the disadvantage of independent producers and at the same time place refiners at a disadvantage who have to rely for oil on pipelines which the large oil companies control. With this accusation constantly made, it is strange that the Interstate Commerce Commission has not been called upon more frequently to determine the reasonableness of rates by pipelines. In only a few instances have cases come before the Commission involving pipeline rates. In 1934 the Commission entered upon a general investigation of pipeline rates for the transportation of crude oil. As a result of this proceeding, known as *Reduced Pipe Line Rates & Charges*, the Commission found the rates of 21 pipeline companies to be excessive, as previously noted.[33] Only two other cases of importance have been before the Commission which have involved the reasonableness of pipeline rates.[34]

The reduction of pipeline rates in recent years and the removal of burdensome minimum-tender requirements have not resulted in extensive use of pipelines by independent oil companies. In the period 1929–38, less than 10 percent of the crude oil shipped by pipelines belonged to non-affiliated shippers.[35] There is evidence, however, that the proportion of "outside" oil transported by the pipelines has increased somewhat in recent years.[36] This is in part the result of the large-diameter pipe laid, particularly since World War II. The pipeline company often needs to obtain outside oil to utilize the larger pipe to capacity.[37]

One reason for the small amount of oil transported for independent shippers is that many of the independent refineries are located in the oil-producing areas. This location may have been dictated by the absence of access to trunkline pipelines on reasonable terms. The extent to which making pipelines serve all shippers at reasonable rates and without burdensome restrictions can improve the opportunities of the independents and change the competitive situation in the oil industry remains in some doubt. But this is no excuse for continuing unjustifiable rates and practices in the pipeline industry.

THE PATTERN OF REGULATION

We have seen that pipelines were brought under the jurisdiction of the Interstate Commerce Commission in 1906. They were made subject to

---

[33] P. 611, supra.

[34] *Petroleum Rail Shippers' Assoc.* v. *Alton & Southern R.*, 243 ICC 589 (1941); *Minnelusa Oil Corp.* v. *Continental Pipe Line Co.*, 258 ICC 41 (1944).

[35] Wolbert, op. cit., pp. 43–44.

[36] Ibid., pp. 44–45.

[37] Arthur M. Johnson, op. cit., p. 387.

various provisions of the Interstate Commerce Act which already applied to railroads. The pattern of pipeline regulation is therefore essentially the same as that applied to railroads. Pipeline rates must be just and reasonable, and they must not create undue preference and prejudice. Personal discrimination is forbidden; rates must be published and strictly observed; and rates must conform to the requirements of Section 4 of the Act. The pipeline companies must make such reports as the Commission may require and must observe a uniform system of accounts prescribed by the Commission.

Differences between Pipeline and Railroad Regulation

There are several respects, however, in which regulation of pipelines is less extensive than control over railroads. The more important of these are as follows: (1) the so-called "Commodities Clause" of the Interstate Commerce Act, which prohibits railroads from transporting commodities in interstate commerce which they have produced or in the production of which they are interested, does not apply to pipelines;[38] (2) there is no control over the construction of new lines or of extensions to existing lines; (3) there is no control over abandonment of pipelines; (4) there is no control over the security issues of pipeline companies; and (5) there is no regulation of consolidations and acquisitions of control, although the pipelines are subject to the antipooling provisions of the law.

Pipelines and the Fair-Return Doctrine

In the few cases involving pipeline rates which have come before it, the Commission has applied the fair-return-on-fair-value doctrine. In so doing, however, the Commission has allowed a somewhat higher rate of return than has been used in applying the doctrine to railroads. The Commission has considered 8 percent to be a fair rate of return for the crude-oil lines.[39] In justification of this rate of return the Commission said: "The hazards and uncertain future of the common-carrier business of the pipelines suggest the fairness of a somewhat larger rate of return than it would be reasonable to expect would be applied in industries of a more stable character, where the volume of traffic is more accurately predictable."[40] For products lines the Commission has considered 10 percent to be a fair rate of return.[41] The Commission has also apparently been more

---

[38] If the principle of the Commodities Clause were applied to pipelines, it might force oil companies to give up their control of pipelines. But see pp. 482–83, supra.

[39] *Reduced Pipe Line Rates & Gathering Charges*, 243 ICC 115, 142 (1940); *Minnelusa Oil Corp* v. *Continental Pipe Line Co.*, 258 ICC 41, 54 (1944).

[40] 243 ICC 115, 142 (1940).

[41] See 258 ICC 41, 53 (1944).

generous in its valuations of pipeline properties, giving more consideration to reproduction costs, than it has in recent railroad rate-level cases.[42]

Pipelines and the Elkins Act

In addition to being subject to Part I of the Interstate Commerce Act, with the exceptions noted above, pipelines are subject to the Elkins Act, which was intended to prevent rebating and other forms of personal discrimination by common carriers.[43] In 1941 the Department of Justice filed a complaint in the District Court of the United States for the District of Columbia alleging that the payment of dividends by pipeline companies to stockholders who were also shippers by pipeline constituted rebating and was unlawful under the Elkins Act.[44] The result of this action was the entrance of a consent decree, agreed to by the pipelines, whereby the pipelines agreed not to pay to any shipper-owner dividends which were in excess of such stockholder's share of 7 percent on the value of the pipeline's property as determined by the Interstate Commerce Commission. If the stock of a pipeline company is all owned by oil companies using the pipeline, dividends are thus limited to 7 percent on the pipeline's valuation. This, of course, is not the same as limiting dividends to 7 percent on the capital stock. Earnings which exceed 7 percent of the pipeline's valuation and which may not be disbursed to shipper-owners must be placed in a special surplus account and may be used only for specified purposes, principally for new construction or the retirement of debt which was incurred for construction purposes. Property constructed from this surplus is not to be included in rate-making value.[45] It should be noted that the consent decree does not reduce actual rates of the pipelines, but its effect is to lessen the advantages to be derived from maintaining them at a high level. In 1957 the Department of Justice sought a court ruling to the effect that the 7 percent return allowable under the consent decree was 7 percent on the stockholders' equity rather than 7 percent on the pipeline company's total valuation. The Supreme Court rejected this contention.[46]

The Antitrust Subcommittee of the Committee on the Judiciary of the House of Representatives has recommended even more drastic restrictions on dividends that may be paid by pipeline companies to the controlling oil companies. It has recommended legislation that would prohibit any payment of dividends by oil pipelines to their shipper-owners that

---

[42] Antitrust Subcommittee of the Committee on the Judiciary, House of Representatives, op. cit., pp. 262–64.

[43] For a description of the Elkins Act see pp. 228–29, supra.

[44] Violation of the Interstate Commerce Act was also alleged.

[45] The consent decree is reproduced in Wolbert, op. cit., pp. 165–69.

[46] *United States* v. *Atlantic Refining Co.*, 360 U.S. 19 (1959).

are derived from transportation charges paid either by the shipper-owner or by competitors of the shipper-owner.[47] It seems to the writer that this is an unduly drastic measure. If the pipeline company's charges are reasonable and permit only a fair return on its investment, the nonowning shipper pays no more than the cost of transporting his oil; the shipper-owner pays the same amount for having his oil transported, and receives back in the form of dividends only a fair return on the investment he has made in pipelines.

The Cole Act

Many states have granted the power of eminent domain to pipeline companies in order that they may not be unduly hindered in obtaining rights of way for their lines. Some states, of which Georgia was one, never granted pipelines this power.[48] Efforts to bring about the construction of pipelines from the Gulf area to the eastern seaboard as part of national-defense measures prior to the Pearl Harbor attack led to legislation by Congress to prevent obstruction of these efforts.[49] The result was the Cole Act, passed in 1941. This Act provided that whenever the President found that the construction of any pipeline for the transportation of petroleum or its products in interstate commerce was necessary for national-defense purposes, and so declared by proclamation, such pipeline company might acquire land or rights of way by the exercise of the right of eminent domain. The Act also authorized the federal government to construct such pipelines. The provisions of the Cole Act were to expire on June 30, 1943, but the Act was twice extended, making its provisions effective up to June 30, 1946.

DIVORCEMENT OF PIPELINES AND THE OIL INDUSTRY

The advantage which oil companies controlling pipelines obtain over their competitors is essentially the same as that which railroad-owned coal mines formerly possessed over independent coal operators.[50] For this reason there has been strong agitation to apply the "Commodities Clause" principle to pipelines and thereby force the separation of oil production and refining from the business of transporting oil.

When the bill which became the Hepburn Act was under consideration by Congress in 1906, there was sentiment in favor of making the proposed "Commodities Clause" apply to pipelines as well as to railroads;

---

[47] Antitrust Subcommittee of the Committee on the Judiciary, House of Representatives, op. cit., p. 296.

[48] *Botts* v. *Southeastern Pipeline Co.*, 10 S.E. 2d 375 (1940); *Harrel* v. *Southeastern Pipeline Co.*, 10 S.E. 2d 386 (1940).

[49] See 77th Cong., 1st Sess., House Reps. No. 602 and No. 685.

[50] See p. 232, supra.

but as finally enacted, the clause applied only to railroads. As early as 1907 the Interstate Commerce Commission said that it would "probably be found necessary to disassociate in the case of oil, as in that of other commodities, the function of transportation from that of production and distribution.[51] In 1917 the Federal Trade Commission recommended the segregation of ownership of pipelines from other branches of the petroleum industry.[52] A later report of the Federal Trade Commission suggested the same remedy, but in a less positive manner.[53] Bills to compel the separation of pipelines from other branches of the industry have been introduced in Congress from time to time. No legislation to this effect has been enacted, but similar proposals continue to come up in Congress.[54] The major oil companies naturally oppose such legislation, whereas small oil operators usually favor it. The previously mentioned recommendation of the Antitrust Subcommittee of the House Committee on the Judiciary to forbid the payment of dividends by pipelines to controlling oil companies would presumably bring about the divorcement of pipelines by indirection.

Advocates of divorcing pipelines from the producing and refining branches of the industry believe that only in this way can real competitive conditions be restored in the oil industry. It is possible, however, that nearly the same result could be attained by vigorous exercise of the Interstate Commerce Commission's powers over rates and practices of the pipelines.

Other students of the problem question whether separation of the pipelines from the oil companies could at this late date in the development of the industry be of any substantial benefit to independent refiners, who have mostly established themselves at locations near the oil fields and who have little occasion to make use of crude oil lines now owned by the integrated oil companies. Fear has also been expressed that there might be some difficulty in getting pipelines laid to new fields if they could not be built by the oil companies interested in the fields. Under the present system the oil companies exploiting a new field proceed at once to build pipelines to carry the oil, regardless of whether the transportation end of the business promises to be profitable. If pipelines were to be kept separate from the oil industry, pipelines would not be built to new fields unless there were good prospects of operating them profitably. For this reason there would be hesitancy and delay in constructing pipelines until a considerable flow of oil was assured.

---

[51] *Railroad Discriminations and Monopolies in Coal & Oil,* 59th Cong., 2d Sess., House Doc. No. 606 (1907), p. 14.

[52] Federal Trade Commission, *Report on the Price of Gasoline in 1915* (1917), pp. 161 and 164.

[53] *Petroleum Industry: Prices, Profits, and Competition,* 70th Cong., 1st Sess., Senate Doc. No. 61 (1928), p. 42.

[54] For a summary of these efforts see Johnson, op. cit., chap. 23.

Regardless of the pros and cons over the policy of forcing a separation of pipelines and the other branches of the oil business, any semblance of excessive rates and unfair practices which tend to discriminate against independent refiners and producers should be eradicated.[55]

SELECTED REFERENCES

A thorough historical treatment of pipelines and the development of public policy in relation thereto may be found in Arthur M. Johnson, *The Development of American Pipelines: A Study in Private Enterprise and Public Policy, 1862–1906* (Ithaca, N.Y.: Cornell University Press, 1956) and *Petroleum Pipelines and Public Policy, 1906–1959* (Cambridge, Mass.: Harvard University Press, 1967).

One of the best discussions of pipelines generally is W. A. Prewitt, "The Operation and Regulation of Crude Oil and Gasoline Pipe Lines," 56 *Quarterly Journal of Economics* 177 (1942). For a good description of pipeline transportation, see G. Lloyd Wilson, "Petroleum Pipe-Line Transportation," in National Resources Planning Board, *Transportation and National Policy* (Washington, D.C.: U.S. Government Printing Office, 1942), pp. 456–69.

For discussion of the problems in the oil industry created by ownership of pipelines by oil companies, see Commissioner of Corporations, *Report on the Transportation of Petroleum* (1906), and *Report on the Petroleum Industry*, Part 1 (1907); see also two reports by the Federal Trade Commission: *Report on Pipe-Line Transportation of Petroleum* (1916), and *Petroleum Industry—Prices, Profits, and Competition*, 70th Cong., 1st Sess., Senate Doc. No. 61 (1927); and Interstate Commerce Commission, *Railroad Discriminations and Monopolies in Coal and Oil*, 59th Cong., 2d Sess., House Doc. No. 606 (1907). This problem is also discussed in two monographs of the Temporary National Economic Committee, namely, Monograph No. 39, *Control of the Petroleum Industry by Major Oil Companies* (Washington, D.C.: U.S. Government Printing Office, 1941), and Monograph No. 39–A, *Review and Criticism on Behalf of Standard Oil Company (New Jersey) and Sun Oil Co. of Monograph No. 39 with Rejoinder by Monograph Author* (Washington, D.C.: U.S. Government Printing Office, 1941). For an excellent discussion of possible methods of forcing the separation of pipelines and other branches of the oil industry, see Forrest R. Black, "Oil Pipe Line Divorcement by Litigation and Legislation," 25 *Cornell Law Quarterly* 510 (1940).

Other good discussions of the problems raised by control of pipelines by the oil companies are William Beard, *Regulation of Pipe Lines as Common Carriers* (New York: Columbia University Press, 1941); Dudley Dillard, "Big Inch Pipe Lines and the Monopoly Competition in the Petroleum Industry," 20 *Journal of Land and Public Utility Economics* 109 (1944); George S. Wolbert, *American Pipe Lines* (Norman: University of Oklahoma Press, 1952);

---

[55] For a positive program of regulation to prevent abuses arising from oil-company control of pipelines, see Dudley Dillard, "Big Inch Pipe Lines and the Monopoly Competition in the Petroleum Industry," 20 *Journal of Land and Public Utility Economics* 109, 115–16 (1944).

Leslie Cookenboo, Jr., *Crude Oil Pipe Lines and Competition in the Oil Industry* (Cambridge: Harvard University Press, 1955).

For those interested in the transportation of solids by pipeline, mention should be made of the extensive literature on the subject, mostly in technical periodicals. See Canadian National Railways, *Bibliography on Pipeline Transportation of Solids, 1962–1965* (Montreal, 1965).

Chapter 27 | HIGHWAY FINANCE

The highway system of the country was described in an earlier chapter.[1] The total mileage of rural highways and city streets in 1969 was 3,710,299. In quality they range from unpaved and ungraded dirt roads to multilane, high-type divided highways of the most modern design. The problem of financing the construction, operation, improvement, and maintenance of our highways is the subject of this chapter.

METHODS OF FINANCING HIGHWAYS

Three general methods of financing the construction, maintenance, and operation of the highway system are possible. These are (1) by general taxation; (2) by a system of "user taxes," such as gasoline taxes, motor-vehicle registration fees, and other taxes that are related to highway use; and (3) tolls levied for the use of particular highways. All three of these methods are in current use. The exclusive use of any one of them would involve difficulties and, in the writer's opinion, inequities.

It might be argued that another method of financing highway construction or improvement is possible, namely, by borrowing. In fact, borrowing for highway purposes is extensively carried on by states and local units of government. If we assume that highway indebtedness is eventually to be retired, it is apparent that resort must ultimately be had to one or more of the three methods of financing highways that we first mentioned.

General Taxation

When highways were used almost exclusively for local transportation, they were financed from the proceeds of local taxation. The provision of highways was considered a governmental function of benefit to the public generally, and properly to be financed like other local government expenditures. To a considerable degree, local roads and streets are

---

[1] Chapter 2, pp. 31–35.

financed in this manner at the present time, and properly so, we believe.

If all highways were to be financed by the proceeds of general taxation at the present time, it would be necessary to broaden the tax base by resorting to state or federal taxation, rather than local taxation. This is because it would be neither possible nor equitable to burden the taxpayers of a particular county to build several miles of high-speed, multiple-lane divided highway that happened to cut across the county but which served long-distance traffic and not the transportation needs of the county, while another county was relieved entirely of contributing to the support of the highway just because no portion of it was located in the county.

Exclusive use of general taxation, whether local, state, or federal, to support the entire highway system would be objectionable because of the competitive inequality that would result in the competition between motor vehicles and railroads for intercity traffic. This point is explained more fully in the discussion of the merits of a system of highway-user charges which follows.

User Taxes

Highway-user taxes consist principally of gasoline and other motor-fuel taxes, motor-vehicle registration fees, and ton-mile or some other form of weight-mile tax imposed on motor trucks by a few states.

The gasoline and other motor-fuel taxes are the most important of the highway-use taxes, yielding the states over $8 billion in 1969. The gasoline tax was introduced by Oregon in 1919, with a rate of 1 cent per gallon. By 1929 every state in the Union had a gasoline tax. As of December 31, 1969, state gasoline taxes ranged from 5 cents in Hawaii, Missouri, and Texas to 9 cents in North Carolina and Washington. The most common rate was 7 cents, applying in 31 states and the District of Columbia.[2]

The federal government also levies a gasoline tax, now 4 cents a gallon. Prior to the enactment of the Federal Highway Act of 1956, when the tax was raised from 2 to 3 cents a gallon, this tax was considered merely as one of many excise taxes, not as a highway-user tax. The proceeds went into general funds, and there was no relation between the amounts raised by the tax and the amounts which might be, or were, appropriated for the federal-aid highways.

Rationale of Highway-User Taxes

As will be pointed out more specifically later in the chapter, the state highway systems are very largely financed today from the proceeds of special motor-vehicle taxes, and local highways are financed in part by allocations from the state highway funds. The tendency to levy special

---

[2] Bureau of Public Roads, *Highway Statistics, 1969*, p. 4.

motor-vehicle taxes for highway purposes is a natural result of the changing use made of the highways. As long as roads were used almost entirely for local transportation, it was natural that they should be financed by local taxes. With the development of motor vehicles and the use of highways for intercity long-distance transportation, new and better facilities were required than had seemed necessary for purely local use. It seemed entirely equitable to finance the building of such highways largely from taxes imposed on those who made use of them.

When financed largely from the proceeds of special motor-vehicle taxes, highways are said to be on a "user basis." The phrase may be a misnomer, however, since to finance some highways from the proceeds of gasoline taxes, registration fees, and the like is to tax those who make little use of them, while to finance certain local roads from the proceeds of general property taxes *is* to tax those who make the principal use of them.

The tendency to shift the burden of financing the more important trunk highways from local taxpayers to operators of motor vehicles, however, is desirable for several reasons. In the first place, it has brought about the improvement of important highways to a degree that would not have been possible if the burden had had to be borne by the local taxpayers. In the second place, the imposition of user taxes puts highway transportation upon a sounder economic basis than when part of the cost is borne by taxpayers rather than by the users of the highway. In other words, transportation is discouraged which is not worth its cost. Lastly, removing or reducing the subsidy to highway transportation that results from the assumption by the taxpayers of part of the costs tends to put motor carriers and railroads on a sounder competitive basis because rates and charges will more nearly reflect the relative costs of transportation by the two agencies. If modern highways were entirely supported by general taxation, while the traffic over them was relieved of any obligation to contribute to their upkeep, the competitive advantage of highway carriers over railroads would appear to be both substantial and unfair. Before the development of the automobile, highways were not competitive with railways, and the imposition of user charges was not required in the interest of a sound distribution of traffic between the two modes of transport.

Exceptions to the User Basis

Because of the importance of the effect of highway-user charges on the competition between railways and highway carriers, the railroads are strong supporters of highway-user taxes. The argument is sometimes made that the cost of supporting the entire highway system should be borne by highway users through motor-vehicle taxes of one kind or another.

Most students of the problem, however, recognize that highways serve other functions than providing a long-distance intercity system of transportation which comes into competition with railroads and other modes of long-distance transportation, and that it is appropriate that taxpayers continue to contribute to their support. Highways continue to perform the functions which highways performed before the development of long-distance over-the-road transport, when no one questioned the propriety of financing them from the proceeds of general taxation. For this reason both theory and practice have approved a mixed system of highway finance, under which highways are financed in part by user taxes and in part by general taxation.[3] To approve the mixed system, however, does not answer the difficult question of what proportion of highway costs should be borne by direct highway users and what proportion should be borne by the general public through general taxation.

To find a logical answer to this question, it is necessary to recognize that highways serve three more or less distinct purposes. One of these purposes is to provide a means of access to land, without which land would be practically unusable and worthless. Thousands of miles of county and township roads principally serve to provide access to farm lands. City streets perform the same function for city property.

A second function of roads is commonly described as a "community-service function." This function cannot be entirely separated from the first, but in this capacity, roads provide for the local movement of persons and property in the performance of the processes of production, market-ing, buying supplies, going to school, and carrying on numerous social and other activities.

The third function of the highway under modern conditions is to provide a means of intercommunity mobility and long-distance transpor-tation. This is the function, as we have noted, that came into prominence with the development of the automobile.[4]

In so far as highways perform the land-access and community-service functions, it is appropriate that they be supported by general tax revenues. It was because they traditionally served these functions that provision of highways has long been considered a proper function of government and that the costs of providing them have been met from the proceeds of general taxation. In so far as highways are used as a means of long-distance intercommunity travel and come into competition with other means of transportation, their support by user charges is appropriate.

Upon the basis of this type of analysis, three methods of determining responsibility for highway support have been advocated. These are some-

---

[3] See Chamber of Commerce of the United States, *Highway Policies* (Washing-ton, D.C., 1944), pp. 7–8; Federal Coordinator of Transportation, *Public Aids to Transportation*, Vol. IV (Washington, D.C.: U.S. Government Printing Office, 1940), p. 45; Board of Investigation and Research, *Public Aids to Domestic Transportation*, 79th Cong., 1st Sess., House Doc. No. 159 (1944), p. 201.

[4] For a further discussion of this type of analysis of highway functions see Charles L. Dearing, *American Highway Policy* (Washington, D.C.: Brookings Insti-tution, 1942), p. 158–63, 209–12.

times called the "predominant-use method," the "relative-use method," and the "earnings-credit method."

The Predominant-Use Method. Under this system those portions of the highway system that are used principally as a means of intercommunity travel and transportation would be financed by means of user charges. On the other hand, those highways which serve as land-access roads and community-service roads would be financed by means of local taxation.[5] Under this system, the state highway system in most states would be financed from user taxes; county and township roads and city streets, except for urban extensions of main highways, would be financed from the proceeds of local taxation. The dependence of local governments on the general property tax, which is borne mostly by real estate, makes it particularly appropriate to finance land-use highways and city streets in this way.

The Relative-Use Method. This method assigns responsibility for particular kinds of highways according to the relative importance of the three functions. It recognizes that every highway serves all three functions to some degree. Instead of financing them according to the predominant function, it asks for support from taxpayers and from users in accordance with the extent to which the highway serves the land-use and community-service functions, on the one hand, and as a means of inter-community travel and transportation, on the other. The greater the degree of use of the highway for intercity transportation, the greater the share of the cost that would be borne by special motor-vehicle taxes. The relative-use theory was adopted by the Federal Coordinator of Transportation in his study of public aids to domestic transportation. The Board of Investigation and Research study, made a few years later, also adopted this theory. The Federal Coordinator considered that for the years 1933–37, motor-vehicle taxes might properly contribute 83 percent of the cost of state highways, 34 percent of the cost of county and local roads, and 30 percent of the cost of city streets.[6] The Board of Investigation and Research study assigned to motor vehicles 85 percent of the annual costs of the primary highway system, 30 percent of the costs of secondary and local roads, and 40 percent of the costs of city streets.[7] Other studies have assigned still different proportions of highway costs to the highway user.[8]

The Earnings-Credit Method. A modification of the "relative-use method" is the "earnings-credit method." Like the former it recognizes that practically all highways perform all three of the highway functions as we have described them, but in varying degrees. The "earnings-credit

---

[5] For strong support of the "predominant-use" method, see Dearing, op. cit., chap. v.

[6] Federal Coordinator of Transportation, op. cit., Vol. I, p. 25.

[7] Board of Investigation and Research, op. cit., p. 283.

[8] For a summary of the results of these other studies, see Charles A. Taff, *Commercial Motor Transportation* (Homewood, Ill.: Richard D. Irwin, Inc., 1950), p. 46.

method" derives its name from the fact that it would credit the cost of supporting land-use and community-service roads with the user-tax revenues that they generate. The theory is that motor vehicles using these roads, whichever highway function they are performing, may well be asked to contribute the same amount per vehicle-mile to support them as they would pay to support the heavily traveled arterial routes.[9] As a matter of fact such vehicles do pay the regular motor-fuel taxes and hence augment highway user revenues. The balance of the cost of the land-use and community-service roads would be defrayed by the general taxpayer.

The "earnings-credit" method is also based on the proposition that some contribution to arterial routes should be made by the general taxpayer. This should be the same amount per road-mile that it would cost to provide the cheaper type of road considered adequate for such uses, since this is what the taxpayers would have to provide if there were no arterial route for them to use.

The "earnings-credit method" and the "relative use method" do not produce widely differing results.

The Department of Commerce Highway Cost Allocation. At the direction of Congress, the Department of Commerce made an elaborate study of highway cost allocation, the results of which were published in 1961.[10] The final findings represented a compromise between the "relative-use method" and the "earnings-credit method." Cost responsibility for the federal-aid highways was allocated as follows:[11]

	To Motor-Vehicle Users	To Other Revenue Sources
Interstate system	94.6%	5.4%
Other primary federal-aid system	92.6	7.4
Secondary federal-aid system	71.6	28.4

It should be emphasized that the study related only to federal-aid highways. A study of local and state highways not in the federal-aid system would show quite different results, presumably with a larger share of the costs allocated to revenue sources other than user taxes.

Financing by Tolls

The third possible method of financing highways is by means of tolls. A flurry of toll-road construction occurred after World War II but has

---

[9] The cost per vehicle mile is much greater for low-type local roads, because of the light density of traffic on them, than the cost per vehicle-mile of more expensive but heavily traveled highways.

[10] *Final Report of the Highway Cost Allocation Study*, 87th Cong., 1st Sess., House Doc. No. 54 (1961).

[11] Ibid., p. 148.

run its course. The special circumstances which led to the construction of toll roads will be discussed shortly. A moment's consideration will reveal that the financing of highways through the collection of tolls, however feasible it may be under special circumstances, could not be relied upon exclusively as a method of financing the highway system. The vast army of attendants and toll collectors, even if automatic toll-collection devices were used, would make the cost prohibitive. Restrictions on entrance and exit to the highways would limit the usefulness of roads for local transportation. Furthermore the vast mileage of thin-density lines could not be supported in this way unless the tolls were burdensomely high; and the interference with the mobility of the population if substantial charges were made for each movement over a highway would be socially undesirable, as well as intolerable, to a population accustomed to a high degree of mobility.

HIGHWAY FINANCE IN PRACTICE

Whatever may be the most desirable basis for dividing responsibility for highway support between general taxpayers and highway users, the actual division of responsibility at a given time is the result of political forces. The ease with which large amounts of money can be raised through motor-vehicle taxes, coupled with the inadequacy of the general property tax as a source of revenue for state and local governments, has contributed to a growing dependence of the states and local units of government on the proceeds of user taxes to finance the improvement and maintenance of highways. The fact that much gasoline is consumed in operating motor vehicles on local roads and city streets lends support for local sharing of the highway revenues raised by state gasoline taxes and motor-vehicle registration fees.

Sources of Highway Revenues

Table 27–1 shows the sources of revenues raised by the state governments for highway purposes in 1969. It will be observed that of the more than $15 billion raised, 54 percent came from highway-user taxes. About 5 percent was raised from tolls; over 27 percent came from federal funds; nearly 9 percent from borrowing.

Table 27–2 shows where local rural governmental units—counties and townships—obtained their funds for highway purposes in 1968. Here nearly 45 percent of the funds represented transfers from state highway-user revenues. Property taxes, special assessments and general fund appropriations accounted for over 35 percent of the highway funds. Borrowing accounted for about 10 percent. Federal funds accounted for less than 2 percent; tolls, less than 1 percent; local highway-user taxes less than 1 percent.

TABLE 27–1. State Highway Receipts, 1969*

Source	Amount	Percent of Total
Highway-user taxes....................	$ 8,238,518,000	54.14
Tolls...............................	772,636,000	5.08
Other imposts and general funds........	236,639,000	1.55
Miscellaneous.......................	300,325,000	1.97
Federal funds.......................	4,190,200,000	27.54
Transferred from local units		
of government....................	134,305,000	0.88
Bond proceeds.......................	1,345,051,000	8.84
Total.......................	$15,217,674,000	100.00

* Bureau of Public Roads, *Highway Statistics, 1969*, p. 107.

TABLE 27–2. Receipts of Counties and Townships for Highways, 1968*

Source	Amount	Percent of Total
Property taxes and special		
assesments......................	$ 652,624,000	24.23
General fund appropriations..........	306,272,000	11.37
Local highway-user taxes............	17,897,000	0.66
Other local imposts.................	17,060,000	0.63
Tolls............................	20,994,000	0.78
Miscellaneous......................	84,948,000	3.15
From municipalities.................	22,521,000	0.84
From state highway-user funds........	1,206,989,000	44.82
Other state contributions............	47,583,000	1.77
Federal funds......................	43,916,000	1.63
Borrowing.........................	272,223,000	10.11
Total.......................	$2,693,027,000	99.99

* Bureau of Public Roads, *Highway Statistics, 1969*, p. 141.

Table 27–3 shows the receipts of municipalities in 1968 for local roads and streets. Property taxes, special assessments, and appropriations from general funds, together accounted for nearly 48 percent of the total. State contributions, mostly from the proceeds of highway-user taxes, amounted to over 22 percent of the total. Local highway-user taxes, however, accounted for less than 3 percent. Borrowing represented 15 percent of the total. Federal funds accounted for less than a fourth of one percent.

Federal Aid to Highways

Table 27–1 shows that the state governments received over $4 billion in federal funds for highway purposes in 1969. Federal interest in improving roads began with the establishment of the Office of Road Inquiry in the Department of Agriculture in 1893.[12] Federal participation in road development between 1893 and 1916 was mostly in the form of educational, promotional, and research work. Grants to the states for highway purposes were not begun until 1917, when the first appropriations were made under the Federal-Aid Road Act of 1916. The federal funds were to be supplemented by the states on a 50–50 basis. The Federal-Aid Road Act was supplemented by the Federal Highway Act of 1921, which provided for the selection of a system of federal-aid highways. During the depression of the 30s, additional funds were made available for highway improvement without the limitations of the Federal Highway Act of 1921. The 50–50 matching basis of financing was restored in 1936. Normal federal-aid work on the highways was stopped late in 1941 as a result of World War II. Such federal funds as were spent on highways during the

TABLE 27–3.   Receipts of Municipalities for Highways, 1968*

Source	*Amount*	*Percent of Total*
Property taxes and special assessments........ $	554,243,000	18.14
General fund appropriations.................	907,002,000	29.68
Local highway-user taxes...................	87,168,000	2.85
Tolls.....................................	84,976,000	2.78
Parking facilities.........................	44,787,000	1.47
Other local sources.......................	161,057,000	5.27
Payments from counties and townships........	67,067,000	2.19
Payments from states......................	686,827,000	22.47
Federal funds............................	4,623,000	0.15
Borrowing...............................	458,345,000	15.00
Total...........................	$3,056,095,000	100.00

* Bureau of Public Roads, *Highway Statistics, 1969*, p. 145.

war were to further the war effort. The regular federal-aid program was resumed in 1946.

The Office of Road Inquiry, which was set up in 1893, was in the Department of Agriculture. It became the Office of Public Roads in 1905, the Office of Public Roads and Rural Engineering in 1915, and the Bureau of Public Roads in 1918. In 1939 the Bureau of Public Roads became the Public Roads Administration in the Federal Works Agency. In 1949 it was placed in the Department of Commerce as the Bureau of Public Roads. It was transferred to the Department of Transportation by the Department of Transportation Act of 1957, becoming part of the Federal Highway Administration.

As we have noted, the federal-aid highway program has usually been financed on a 50–50 basis with the states, but the National System of Inter-

---

[12] Of course, the federal government was active in road building in the early part of the 19th century, when the Cumberland Road was built.

state and Defense Highways is financed on a 90–10 basis, with the federal government paying 90 percent of the cost of developing the system.

Prior to 1956, appropriations for federal aid to highway projects were made from the general funds of the Treasury. In 1956, Congress set up a Highway Trust Fund into which were to be paid the proceeds of the federal motor-fuel tax and certain other taxes. From this fund, payments were to be made to finance the regular federal-aid program, which has a first claim on the amounts in the fund, and to meet the costs of the Interstate System. The Act provided that advances to the states should not exceed the funds available in the Highway Trust Fund, thus putting the road-building program on a pay-as-you-go basis. In 1958 Congress temporarily set aside the pay-as-you-go feature of the plan by authorizing, as an antirecession measure, the expenditure of funds in excess of the amounts in the Highway Trust Fund. In 1959 and again in 1961 provision was made for further augmenting the fund. The Highway Trust Fund is now made up of revenues from the tax of 4 cents per gallon on motor fuel, plus the proceeds of an annual tax of $3 per 1,000 pounds of gross weight on vehicles with a gross weight exceeding 26,000 pounds, plus the revenues from various excise taxes on motor vehicles, tires, tubes, and retread rubber. In the fiscal year 1969 these taxes yielded nearly $5,414,000,000 for the Highway Trust Fund.[13]

Diversion of Highway-User Taxes

A considerable amount of revenue raised from highway-user taxes by the states is diverted to nonhighway uses. About $840 million was so diverted in 1969.[14] Diversion is clearly unjustifiable if the user taxes were imposed for the purpose of financing highways. To divert any of the funds so raised to nonhighway uses under such conditions has been called a "breach of faith" with road users.[15]

In some cases, however, states have deliberately raised gasoline-tax rates to obtain money for some nonhighway purpose, and there was no intention of using the increased revenue for highways. In this situation the tax is just another excise tax, and it should be judged on the basis of the equity or inequity of this particular tax. Generally speaking, such a tax would not measure up very well to the criteria of a good tax. In a few states certain motor-vehicle levies, such as registration fees, have been imposed in lieu of property taxes formerly levied on motor vehicles and are not properly to be considered as highway-user taxes. Not all of the $840 million of highway revenue reported above as "diverted" in 1969, therefore, represents funds that were intended for highway use.

Because the public commonly looks upon highway-user taxes as justifi-

---

[13] Bureau of Public Roads, *Highway Statistics, 1969*, p. 82.

[14] Bureau of Public Roads, op. cit., p. 106.

[15] Dearing, op. cit., p. 179.

able only when the proceeds are devoted to highway purposes, there is strong resentment at the practice of using the proceeds of such taxes for other than highway purposes. Twenty-eight states have adopted constitutional amendments which prohibit, at least partially, the diversion of highway revenues.[16]

Apportionment of Highway Costs among Types of Vehicles

The problem of an equitable system of highway-user charges is not solved when the appropriate share of highway costs which motor vehicles should pay has been determined. Then the problem arises of apportioning that share of highway costs to the different types of vehicles. The problem is too involved for extensive discussion here. Numerous methods of dealing with this question have been proposed; but many, if not all of them, are subject to criticism on theoretical or practical grounds, or both.

It should be recognized, however, that highway-user taxes should reflect to some degree the extent of highway use, or the quantity of service obtained from the highways, and that the taxes should reflect the higher construction, maintenance, and administrative costs, if any, that may be occasioned by a particular class of vehicle or type of operation.

In practice, wide variations exist among the several states in the relative tax burdens imposed on the different classes of vehicles. Studies have been made to determine the total burden of highway-user taxes and property taxes that a vehicle of given size and weight, operating an assumed distance, would pay in the several states.

In all states, passenger automobiles are charged less than freight vehicles. In 1968 a medium-weight passenger car would have paid a registration fee of $3 in Louisiana and South Carolina and $32 in Iowa. The average state registration fee for such a vehicle was $12.89.[17] The registration fee for a five-axle tractor-semitrailer combination in private operation and having a gross weight of 62,000 pounds ranged from a low of $25.50 in Colorado to $1,430.93 in Vermont.

It has not been uncommon for some states to tax for-hire vehicles more than those not operated for hire. Others tax common-carrier trucks more heavily than those operated by contract carriers. When differences in the treatment of for-hire carriers and private carriers, or of common as compared with contract carriers, are based on differences in highway use, the difference in treatment is justified, provided the difference is not greater than can be justified by differences in use. Sometimes, however,

---

[16] Automobile Manufacturers Association, *1970 Automobile Facts and Figures*, p. 68.

[17] This and the following figures on motor-vehicle taxes are taken from U.S. Department of Commerce, Bureau of Public Roads, *Road-User and Property Taxes on Selected Motor Vehicles, 1968* (Washington, D.C.: U.S. Government Printing Office, 1968).

these differences in tax treatment are based on the theory that the use of highways by the owner-operated vehicle is a normal use, but that the use of highways by carriers for hire is a special privilege, and that higher taxes on the latter are justified because the carrier is granted the privilege of using the highway for private profit or as a place of business. It is submitted that whether a person moves his goods over the highway in his own truck or whether he employs a carrier for hire is simply a matter of division of labor. If a carrier for hire is employed, it is the shipper who is the real user of the highway; and his shipments should not be discriminated against in favor of those carried in a private truck.

TOLL ROADS

We have previously mentioned the possibility of financing highways through a system of tolls, and we have pointed out that such a policy would be impracticable as a means of financing all or a major part of the highway system. Under special circumstances, however, the construction of toll roads is an appropriate method of providing needed highway facilities.

A period of extensive toll-road building occurred after World War II, although the first modern toll highway was the Pennsylvania Turnpike, which was built during the depression of the 30s. The success of the Pennsylvania Turnpike led other states to realize the possibility of financing special highway facilities in this manner.

The postwar toll-road movement resulted in a toll-road system of 3,262 miles, with an investment exceeding $5 billion.[18] The toll roads in operation in 1957 are shown in Figure 27–1.

Factors Responsible for Toll-Road Development

Several factors explain the flurry of toll-road construction in the 40s and 50s. The basic reason was the immediate need after the war for vast expenditures on highways, particularly where the traffic density was greatest. During World War II the condition of highways in the United States deteriorated because of lack of adequate maintenance. The normal program of highway modernization was also interrupted. Following the war, a rapid increase in automobile and truck registrations and an increased use of highways made it clear that highway capacity was inadequate and that much of the highway system was functionally obsolete. The toll-road device made it possible to borrow funds for the immediate construction of urgently needed facilities, with the bonds being secured by toll revenues and perhaps also by the guaranty of the state.

A second factor in the situation arose from restrictions on borrowing

---

[18] Bureau of Public Roads, *Highway Statistics, 1957*, p. 114.

FIGURE 27–1. Toll Roads in the United States, 1957

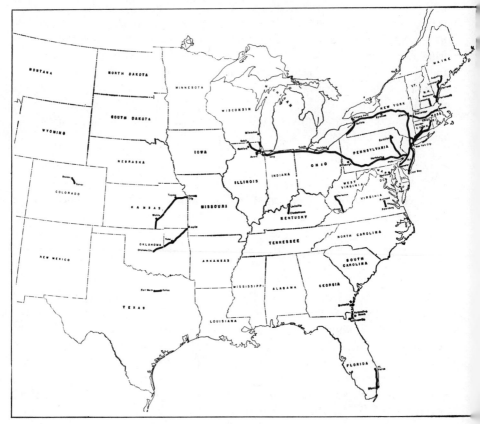

From Bureau of Public Roads, *Highway Statistics, 1957*, pp. 118–19.

by state governments for highway purposes which are found in many states. Turnpike or toll-road "authorities" might be created, however, which had power to issue bonds secured by revenues from tolls.

A third factor which made financing the needed highways in the usual fashion very difficult was that highway funds raised by highway-user taxes frequently had to be shared with local governments on the basis of formulas which left inadequate amounts to the state for financing such expensive roads as were required on the main highway routes. Political pressures, furthermore, made the revision of such formulas very difficult.

Fourth, valid objections can be raised to the spending of a large proportion of state highway funds on "superhighways," even if it is possible, especially when other needed highway improvements would have to be neglected. The facilities required for the heavily traveled routes are expensive. If they are not used by the great mass of motorists of a state, or are used by them only occasionally, the argument that these especially expensive facilities should be paid for by those who use them becomes very convincing.

Lastly, in some instances the decision to improve a through route as a toll road arose from the desire to make the out-of-state user contribute to its cost. Some of the turnpikes are so located as to benefit principally the out-of-state user. Under such circumstances it seemed only just that those who used them should pay for them and that they should not be financed wholly from the state highway fund. This was an important factor in the construction of the Maine Turnpike, which accommodates traffic between southern New England and the Maine summer resorts. On the New Hampshire Turnpike, which is a bridge route between southern New England and the Maine Turnpike, 90 percent of the traffic consisted of out-of-state vehicles.[19]

Some Characteristics of Toll Roads

It will be seen from Table 27–3 that toll roads are high-cost facilities. Many of them represent an investment of more than a million dollars per mile, and the Northwest Tollway in Illinois cost about $3 million per mile.

The toll roads are mostly of the latest designs for the period in which they were built. Nearly all are divided highways, with control of access and with separation of grades at intersections.

The traffic density on most of the toll roads is high. As long ago as 1952 the average number of vehicles per day on the Denver-Boulder Turnpike was 4,600; on the Maine Turnpike, 5,300; on the New Hampshire Turnpike, 8,000; on the Pennsylvania Turnpike, 11,000; and on the New Jersey Turnpike, 20,000.[20] It has been estimated that a traffic volume of about 5,000 vehicles a day is necessary for a toll road to be self-supporting,[21] although of course the figure will vary with the construction cost, the distance traveled, and the tolls charged.

The tolls charged differ on the different toll roads, and they vary with the type of vehicle. The tolls for passenger cars are usually in the neighborhood of 1 or 1½ cents per mile.

Objections to Toll Roads

Numerous objections have been made to toll roads. Some of these objections have proved to be unfounded or of minor importance. Others deserve brief analysis and comment.

---

[19] Harmer E. Davis, Ralph A. Moyer, Norman Kennedy, and Howard S. Lapin, *Toll-Road Developments and Their Significance in the Provision of Expressways,* Institute of Transportation and Traffic Engineering, University of California, Research Report No. 11 (Berkeley, 1953), p. 16.

[20] Ibid., p. 36.

[21] John F. Due, "The Rise and Decline of the Toll Principle in Highway Finance— 1940–1957," 10 *National Tax Journal* 97 (1957), p. 109.

TABLE 27–3. Cost of Major Toll Roads in the United States*

Name and Location	Year Built	Miles	Cost	Approximate Cost per Mile
Denver-Boulder Turnpike...........	1952	17.3	$ 6,237,000	$ 361,000
Connecticut Turnpike..............	1958	129.0	464,000,000	3,597,000
Sunshine State Parkway (Fla.).......	1957	110.0	74,000,000	673,000
Northwest Tollway (Ill.)...........	1958	76.0	289,196,000	3,805,000
Tri-State Tollway (Ill.)............	1959	85.3	106,342,000	1,247,000
East-West Tollway (Ill.)...........	1959	26.0	50,085,000	1,926,000
Indiana Turnpike..................	1956	156.0	280,000,000	1,795,000
Kansas Turnpike..................	1956	236.0	160,000,000	678,000
Kentucky Turnpike................	1956	40.0	38,500,000	963,000
Maine Turnpike:				
Kittery-Portland.................	1947	47.2	20,600,000	436,000
Portland-Augusta................	1955	66.0	58,806,000	891,000
Massachusetts Turnpike............	1957	123.0	239,000,000	1,943,000
New Hampshire Turnpike..........	1950–57	76.2	43,524,000	571,000
New Jersey Turnpike:				
Delaware River to George Washington Bridge...............	1952	117.6	318,952,000	2,712,000
New York Thruway:				
Buffalo–New York City Section...	1956	427.0	675,428,000	1,582,000
Ohio Turnpike....................	1955	241.4	326,000,000	1,350,000
Turner Turnpike (Oklahoma City–Tulsa)....................	1953	88.0	38,714,000	440,000
Will Rogers Turnpike (Tulsa–Missouri State Line..........	1957	88.5	68,000,000	768,000
Pennsylvania Turnpike.............	1940–57	469.8	539,664,000	1,149,000
Dallas–Fort Worth Turnpike........	1957	30.5	58,500,000	1,918,000
Richmond-Petersburg (Va.)........	1958	34.7	75,150,000	2,166,000
West Virginia Turnpike............	1954	87.6	133,000,000	1,518,000

° Data from Bureau of Public Roads, *Highway Statistics, 1957*, pp. 113–14.

First, it has long been considered that a system of free roads is more desirable than a system of toll roads. This undoubtedly accounts for the disfavor with which toll roads have been held by the Bureau of Public Roads, which has been interested in the development of an adequate system of free highways in accordance with long-established tradition. Preference for a system of free roads doubtless explains why, under existing laws, federal funds are not available to aid in the construction of roads on which tolls are to be charged.

Even if we should concede that free highways are *always* preferable to toll roads, it may be pointed out that under the conditions prevailing when most of the existing toll roads were built, the choice was not between toll roads and free roads, but between toll roads and *inadequate* free roads. It is to be assumed, furthermore, that when the existing toll roads are paid for, they will be absorbed into the system of free roads.

A second objection which has been made to toll roads is that they represent a wasteful duplication of highway investment, since free roads must be maintained more or less parallel to the toll roads to serve local traffic. Toll roads, however, are not ordinarily constructed unless the volume of through traffic is so great as to require a separation of the through and local traffic. In other words, it is the volume of traffic that has required the duplication of investment, and the duplication would be necessary if adequate free roads were provided to accommodate the through traffic.

Another objection to toll roads is the extra cost which arises when highways are financed in this way. The extra cost arises from three sources: (1) Since the toll road is built out of the proceeds of a bond issue, interest on bonds must be paid. (2) Higher rates of interest have to be paid when toll roads are financed by revenue bonds than when the state borrows on its own credit. (3) The cost of collecting tolls is expensive.

Interest payments become necessary whenever highways are financed by borrowing. The extra cost is probably more than compensated for by the reduced motor-vehicle operating costs, the reduced number of accidents, and the greater convenience provided by the improved roads which are made possible by borrowing. The higher interest rates resulting from financing toll roads by means of revenue bonds could be avoided by guaranty of the bonds by the state. This practice, however, may be objectionable because of the contingent liability that it imposes on the state. Whether the interest saving would be great enough to offset the disadvantage is a matter that must be determined in a particular case.

The cost of collecting tolls, of course, is a cost that would not be incurred if the road were constructed as a free road. On the heavily traveled routes—and these are the only ones that are likely to be successful as toll roads—collection costs should not be excessive. Collection costs vary with the amount of traffic and with the distance between toll gates. Collection costs on the Pennsylvania Turnpike in 1950 were 3.4 percent of the revenues. The cost on the New Jersey Turnpike in 1952 was 5.3 percent of the revenue. Collection costs on the Maine and New Hampshire turnpikes were 10.4 percent and 11.4 percent of the revenues, respectively, in 1951. On the Denver-Boulder Turnpike in 1952 the collection costs were 15.5 percent of the revenues. In terms of costs per vehicle the above costs were 6.1 cents on the Pennsylvania Turnpike, 4.7 cents on the New Jersey Turnpike, 5.7 cents on the Maine Turnpike, 1.9 cents on the New Hampshire Turnpike, and 3.4 cents on the Denver-Boulder Turnpike.[22]

A further objection to toll roads is the danger that if not financially successful, they will throw an unanticipated burden on the state highway fund. The danger is greatest if the state has guaranteed the bonds of the toll-road authority. If the state has not guaranteed the bonds, failure of the tolls to yield sufficient revenues to pay interest on the bonds and retire them would normally mean that the loss would fall on the investors in the bonds. Under these circumstances, however, pressures would be strong for

---

[22] Davis and Others, op. cit., p. 29.

the state to make up the deficiency in interest and principal payments to save the bondholders from loss.

The Future of Toll Roads

It is not likely that toll roads will be constructed in the future on any extensive scale. The circumstances that gave rise to the toll-road movement of the 40s and 50s have changed. The greatly expanded federal highway program, particularly the construction of the National System of Interstate and Defense Highways, will eventually result in the most modern type of highway facility on the more heavily traveled routes across the length and breadth of the nation.

Nearly 2,300 miles of toll roads have been incorporated into the Interstate System.[23] Tolls will continue to be charged on such roads until the bonds are retired, after which it is contemplated that these roads will become a part of our toll-free highway system.

CONGESTION TOLLS

Thus far in our discussion of tolls and highway-user taxes we have assumed that their purpose was to help finance the construction, maintenance and operation of the highway system. In recent years, however, it has been urged that highway-user taxes or tolls be used as a means of rationing highway use. This view is the product of the serious problem of highway congestion, particularly in metropolitan areas, and the seeming impossibility of keeping ahead of the problem by means of highway construction and improvement. It is therefore suggested that the price system be used as a rationing device, automatically restricting use of congested highways to those who are willing to pay substantial tolls. It is pointed out that throughout the economy the price system functions as a rationing device. Scarce goods and services and productive resources go to those who can and are willing to pay for them.

That the price system operates to ration scarce goods and services is indisputable. Society makes many exceptions, however, such as direct rationing of necessities in times of war, and various forms of poor relief in more normal times. Society also produces many goods and services, such as educational, recreational, and health facilities and services, wholly or partly at public expense. The real question to be faced in considering congestion tolls is whether it would be advisable to restrict use of potentially congested roads to those who are able and willing to pay an extra sum to avoid congestion, however trivial their use of the highway might be, and to deny it to others unless they pay the toll which they might be forced to do by necessity, however burdensome. The social, political,

---

[23] Bureau of Public Roads, *Annual Report*, 1958, p. 7.

and economic implications of such a policy should be carefully examined.

This is not to say that congestion tolls may not have justification in some situations. Their use to discourage highway use in periodic rush hours may be warranted, but even here it will work a hardship on those who *must* use the highway at such times and who may have the least ability to stand the expense. Likewise, it may be justifiable to ration space at all times on highways or segments thereof that are unduly congested, provided there are reasonable substitute routes, or if alternative methods of transport are available. If such alternatives are not present, however, the use of congestion tolls would be a hardship to the less affluent members of society.

We cannot leave the matter at this point, however, since advocates of congestion tolls argue at great length that such tolls are required by the economic principle that prices should cover short-run marginal costs.[24]

The cost of a specific highway trip or journey consists of (1) the operating cost of the vehicle, borne by the vehicle owner, (2) the variable maintenance cost of the highway, and (3) the congestion cost, a cost borne by all users of the congested highway. The congestion cost increases rapidly as congestion occurs, thus causing the marginal cost curve to rise steeply. The marginal cost of a highway trip in a private vehicle consists of the added cost in all three of the above categories.[25]

To justify congestion tolls on the marginal cost principle, it is necessary to include in the cost of a particular highway trip the "congestion cost," that is, the cost which the trip occasions to other users of the highway, principally the cost of delay, but it may include other elements as well such as increased hazard, inconvenience, and the like. Congestion cost is a "social cost," that is, it is imposed on other users of the highway.

"Social costs" occur throughout the economy generally. Almost any manufacturing industry, agricultural or mining operation, creates social costs of one sort or another. Railroads, for instance, impose many social costs on the public, not the least of which is the time and vehicle-miles required to reach an available railroad crossing when one's trip requires it. Similar social costs are occasioned by limited-access highways.

Some social costs could be imposed on the business activity responsible for them and hence become part of the cost of production. This would be true where measurable damages are caused to specific persons or property. Other social costs, like the cost occasioned by air and water pollution, noise, annoyance, and inconvenience cannot practicably be imposed on the industries causing them, although the cost of eliminating, abating, or preventing such social costs can and probably should be imposed on industry. The assumption that social costs ordinarily enter into prices is unwarranted, hence we believe that the argument for congestion

---

[24] This theory is expounded in detail in A. A. Walters, *The Economics of Road User Charges* (Baltimore, Md.: Johns Hopkins Press, 1968).

[25] We are here borrowing from Walters' analysis, op. cit.

tolls which is based on a supposed analogy to pricing throughout the economy is somewhat strained.

We might note also that although an argument can be made on economic grounds for charging highway users for the entire cost of providing highways,[26] congestion costs are not costs of providing needed highways, they are costs of *not* providing needed highways.

Notwithstanding these statements we have recognized that congestion tolls may be practicable and desirable in some special situations if the hardships created are not too great. In such instances it would seem appropriate to fix the toll at such point or points as proved to be necessary to accomplish its purpose rather than to make an attempt to base it on a calculation of the "marginal social cost" of highway use, which might or might not be sufficient to alleviate the congestion.[27]

SELECTED REFERENCES

The best general study of highway policy is Charles L. Dearing, *American Highway Policy* (Washington, D.C.: Brookings Institution, 1942). An excellent study of present highway policy and financing in the United States is Philip H. Burch, *Highway Revenue and Expenditure Policy in the United States* (New Brunswick, N.J.: Rutgers University Press, 1962). An excellent review of highway taxation in the United States is E. M. Cope, "Trends in Highway Taxation in the United States," *American Highways*, October 1970, pp. 8–14. There is a good treatment of highway financing in Charles A. Taff, *Commercial Motor Transportation* (Homewood, Ill.: Richard D. Irwin, Inc., 4th ed. 1969), chap. iii.

On the question of responsibility for highway costs, much has been written. Thorough discussions of the subject may be found in Federal Coordinator of Transportation, *Public Aids to Transportation*, Vol. IV (Washington, D.C.: U.S. Government Printing Office, 1940); Board of Investigation & Research, *Public Aids to Domestic Transportation*, 79th Cong., 1st Sess., House Doc. No. 159 (1944); and Secretary of Commerce, *Final Report of the Highway Cost Allocation Study*, 87th Cong., 1st Sess., House Doc. No. 54 (1961). Helpful discussions of some of the issues involved are: Association of American Railroads, *Highway Benefits and Cost Responsibility* (Washington, D.C., 1957); Hal H. Hale, "Motor Carrier Taxation," 11 *Vanderbilt Law Review* 1081 (1958); George W. Wilson, "The Allocation of Highway Costs," 22 *Current Economic Comment* 13 (1960); James C. Nelson, "The Pricing of Highway, Waterway, and Airway Facilities," 52 *American Economic Review* 426 (1962), pp. 426–32; Robert W. Harbeson, "Some Unsettled Issues in Highway Cost

---

[26] We have pointed out earlier in this chapter, however, that it is generally considered appropriate for part of the costs of highways to be borne by the general taxpayers.

[27] Much more could be said regarding congestion tolls. For an excellent discussion of various aspects of the proposal, see Richard M. Zettel and Richard R. Carll, "The Basic Theory of Efficiency Tolls—the Tolled, the Tolled-Off, and the Un-Tolled," In Highway Research Board, *Traffic Congestion as a Factor in Road-User Taxation*, Highway Research Record No. 47 (1964), pp. 46–65.

Allocation," in Paul L. Kleinsorge, ed., *Public Finance and Welfare Essays in Honor of C. Ward Macy* (University of Oregon Books, 1966), pp. 187–213.

The toll-road movement is appraised in Wilfred Owen and Charles L. Dearing, *Toll Roads and the Problem of Highway Modernization* (Washington, D.C.: Brookings Institution, 1951).

Congestion tolls and issues related thereto are discussed in J. M. Buchanan, "The Pricing of Highway Services," 5 *National Tax Journal* 97 (1952); C. O. Meiburg, "An Economic Analysis of Highway Services," 77 *Quarterly Journal of Economics* 648 (1963); William Vickrey, "Optimization of Traffic," 1 *Journal of Transport Economics and Policy* 123 (1967). The most elaborate exposition of the theory of congestion tolls is A. A. Walters, *The Economics of Road User Charges* (Baltimore, Md., Johns Hopkins Press, 1968). A helpful discussion of the problem is Richard M. Zettel and Richard R. Carll, "The Basic Theory of Efficiency Tolls—the Tolled, the Tolled-Off, and the Un-Tolled," in National Academy of Sciences, Highway Research Board, *Traffic Congestion as a Factor in Road-User Taxation*, Highway Research Record No. 47 (1964), pp. 46–65.

Chapter 28　HIGHWAY TRANSPORTATION

IMPORTANCE OF HIGHWAY TRANSPORTATION

Some indication of the importance of highway transport in the movement of freight was indicated in an earlier chapter.[1] It was shown that in 1970 motor vehicles transported 21.44 percent of the total ton-miles of intercity freight. The corresponding figure for 1940 was 7.91 percent, indicating that the proportion of freight transported by motor trucks has almost tripled since that date.[2] If the proportions shown above had been based on tons carried, instead of ton-miles, highway transport would have shown an even larger percentage of the total movement, since much of the intercity motor-truck transportation is for comparatively short distances, while much of the transportation by rail, water, and pipe-line is for long distances. It should also be pointed out that in certain areas or between particular cities the proportion of the total freight carried by motor truck is larger than is represented by the nationwide figures shown above. Thus studies by the California Public Utilities Commission indicate that in 1946 more freight was transported by truck between the San Francisco and Los Angeles metropolitan areas than was transported by rail.[3]

In the intercity transportation of persons, highways were responsible for 88.73 percent of the total passenger-miles in 1970. Most of this movement was in private automobiles. Intercity buses transported only about 2.14 percent of the total intercity passenger-miles; railroads transported 0.92 percent.[4]

Motor-truck transportation has become extremely important in the transportation of various farm products to markets. A large proportion of the fruits, vegetables, and other farm products received at major markets in the United States arrive by motor truck. The importance of motor-truck transportation, however, is not confined to the movement of agricultural products. Nearly all kinds of manufactured articles are distrib-

---

[1] P. 20, supra.

[2] P. 22, supra.

[3] Decision No. 41470, Appendix A.

[4] Interstate Commerce Commission, *Transport Economics*, Sept.–Oct., 1971, p. 5.

uted by truck to some extent, and some are distributed almost entirely by motor vehicle.

Another indication of the importance of highway transportation in the movement of persons and property is shown by the number of registered motor vehicles. In 1969 there were approximately 86,560,000 passenger automobiles registered in the United States and 17,886,000 motor trucks. Figures showing the growth in motor-vehicle registrations over the years are shown in Chapter 2.

SOME CHARACTERISTICS OF HIGHWAY FREIGHT MOVEMENTS

Length of Truck Hauls

Although there is some trucking for very long distances, there is evidence that comparatively short hauls predominate in motor-truck transportation. A survey of traffic on main rural roads in 1955 revealed that the average length of trip of private carriers was about 24 miles; for carriers for hire authorized by the Interstate Commerce Commission the average trip length was 102 miles, but for other for-hire carriers it was only about 43 miles.[5] The average haul of Class I motor common carriers of property in 1969 was 261 miles. The corresponding figure for railroads was 497 miles; for scheduled air carriers, 1147 miles.[6]

A study of the average length of truck hauls of ten selected fruits and vegetables to eight important markets showed an average haul of 325 miles in 1950. This represented an increase from 275 miles in 1940. Trucks hauled virtually the entire movement to these markets from distances of less than 100 miles. For distances of 500 miles or over, however, trucks hauled only about one tenth of the movement to these markets.[7]

A Bureau of the Census survey of transportation in 1967, confined to shipments by manufacturers, showed the average haul of their shipments by private truck to be 152 miles, and by motor carriers, 270 miles, while the average distance of their rail shipments was 550 miles.[8] For distances under 50 miles 64.8 percent of the tons shipped moved by truck, either private or for-hire, and for distances between 50 and 100 miles 67.5 percent moved by motor truck. For longer distances the proportions moving by truck decreased as distance increased.[9]

---

[5] Interstate Commerce Commission, Bureau of Transport Economics and Statistics, *Truck Traffic on Main Rural Roads, 1955, I.C.C. Authorized, Other For-Hire, and Private Carriers*, Statement No. 5710 (1957), p. 2.

[6] Transportation Association of America, *Transportation Facts & Trends*, 8th ed., (1971), p. 14.

[7] U.S. Department of Agriculture, Bureau of Agricultural Economics, *Length of Haul to Leading Markets by Motortruck, 1941 and 1950, Selected Fruits and Vegetables* (1953), pp. 2–3.

[8] These figures are taken from Automobile Manufacturers Association, op. cit., p. 33.

[9] Ibid.

Emphasis on the short-haul characteristics of motor-truck traffic should not obscure the fact that there is some trucking for very long distances. A Department of Agriculture study of shipments of frozen fruits and vegetables showed that in 1957, although 40 percent of the shipments moved less than 250 miles, and 61 percent less than 500 miles, 21 percent moved over 1,000 miles, and there was a small movement of 3,000 miles or over.[10]

Commodities vary greatly in the distances over which they can profitably be shipped by truck. Commodities that take high rail rates move longer distances by truck than commodities given lower rail rates. Some manufactured articles are less susceptible to breakage or other damage if shipped by motor vehicle, or they require less expensive protection against damage than when prepared for rail shipment. Perishable products commonly move long distances by truck partly because refrigeration is sometimes unnecessary for shipment by truck but would be necessary if they were shipped by rail. The time element is often an important factor in favor of truck shipments of perishables.

Composition of Traffic

The composition of truck traffic is quite different from that of railroads. This is shown by Table 28–1 in which freight traffic of railroads

TABLE 28–1.   Composition of Freight Traffic—Motor Carriers and Railroads, 1963*

	Class I Railroads (Percent of Tons Originated, C.L.)	Class I Motor Carriers (Percent of Tons Originated, T.L.)
Products of agriculture.....................	12.51	2.68
Animals and animal products................	0.73	2.93
Products of mines.........................	51.62	6.66
Products of forests........................	6.10	0.61
Manufactures and Miscellaneous.............	28.68	86.31
Forwarder traffic.........................	0.36	0.81
Total..............................	100.00	100.00

* Data from Interstate Commerce Commission, *Freight Commodity Statistics in the U.S., Class I Railroads; and Motor Carrier Freight Commodity Statistics, Class I Common & Contract Carriers of Property.*

and motor carriers is compared using the broad grouping of commodities formerly used by the Interstate Commerce Commission for statistical purposes. It will be noted that more than 86 percent of the traffic of Class I

[10] U.S. Department of Agriculture, Marketing Research Division, *Interstate Trucking of Frozen Fruits and Vegetables under Agricultural Exemption*, Marketing Research Report No. 316 (1959), p. 18.

motor carriers was in the "Manufactured and Miscellaneous" group, while such traffic constituted slightly less than 29 percent of railroad traffic. Nearly 52 percent of railroad traffic consisted of products of mines, while less than 7 percent of motor-carrier traffic was in this category.

CLASSIFICATION OF CARRIERS

Three types of carriers of property operate motor trucks over the highways, namely: (1) common carriers, (2) contract carriers, and (3) private carriers. The first two groups are carriers for hire. The third class consists of individuals or business establishments transporting their own traffic. In this class are trucks owned and operated by farmers, manufacturers, and commercial establishments. Common carriers are carriers who hold themselves out to serve the public generally, although they may, and commonly do, restrict their business to the transportation of particular kinds of traffic, such as household goods, or liquid petroleum products, or livestock. Others, of course, are carriers of general freight. Common carriers may be further subdivided into regular-route carriers and irregular-route, or "anywhere-for-hire," carriers.

Contract carriers do not purport to transport for the public generally but carry for a very limited clientele under special contracts, which usually cover shipments over a period of time.

Private Trucking

Much of the private trucking is local in character, representing short farm-to-market hauls, or the operation of delivery trucks by mercantile establishments, or operation of service trucks by local industries. There is, however, a large amount of over-the-road private trucking, some of which is competitive with railroads and with for-hire motor carriers. Traffic surveys indicate that about 46.6 percent of the ton-miles of truck traffic on main rural roads in 1955 represented private transportation.[11]

Many industries have large fleets of trucks which are used exclusively in their businesses. This practice is particularly common among large bakeries, food processors and distributors, meat packers, and manufacturers of dairy products. Most of the major oil companies also have large fleets of trucks for distributing gasoline to service stations. Some large industries have so organized their production or distribution systems that it would be difficult or impossible for them to rely on common-carrier services of railroad and trucking companies.

Private transportation may be undertaken by large industries for a variety of reasons. Transportation operations, when performed by the industry itself, can be more closely tied in to the operations of the enter-

---

[11] Thomas B. Dimmick, "Traffic and Travel Trends, 1955," 29 *Public Roads* 97, 103 (1956).

prise. Common carriers do not—and could not, in many instances—provide the specialized type of service required by the industry. Speedier delivery can often be provided by the industry itself than can be obtained by relying on the service of regular common carriers. The motor-carrier rate structure has probably been another factor contributing to the large amount of private transportation. The practice of motor carriers of copying the railroad system of freight classification, with higher rates on valuable articles than are required by cost-of-service considerations, creates an incentive for large industries to provide their own transportation because it is cheaper than to pay high common-carrier rates.

Private transportation by industrial enterprises also has its disadvantages. It is not practical unless there is a sufficient concentration of business to make the operations economical. The small producer or the manufacturer or distributor shipping small orders to a great number of destinations may find it quite impractical to perform his own transportation and must rely on the services of common carriers. Another disadvantage of private transportation is the fact that usually the industries must operate their vehicles empty on the return trip and this tends to increase the cost of private trucking. This disadvantage may sometimes be overcome by transporting on a for-hire basis on the return trips. Commodities so transported, however, must ordinarily be those which have been exempted from regulation under the Motor Carrier Act. This restriction is sometimes evaded by "buy-and-sell operations" which will be described in a later chapter.[12]

Common and Contract Carriers

Common and contract carriers, as we have noted, apparently account for more than half the freight movements over the highways. Common carriers outnumber the contract carriers and transport more of the traffic. Of the 1,311 Class I motor carriers of property in intercity service which reported to the Interstate Commerce Commission in 1969, 1,224 were common carriers and only 87 were contract carriers.[13] According to the American Trucking Associations, common carriers transported 91.1 percent of the intercity tonnage carried by Class I and II motor carriers of property in 1970, and contract carriers only 8.9 percent.[14]

The ordinary shipper must rely on the services of common carriers. Large shippers, however, may find it advantageous to employ the services of a contract carrier. Contract-carrier operations can often be adapted to the needs of a particular industry and hence possess the same advantages as private transportation. They may be economical, however, when private transportation is not, since the contract carrier can serve two or more

---

[12] See pp. 686–87, infra.

[13] *Transportation Statistics in the United States, 1969*, Part 7, p. iii.

[14] *Intercity Truck Tonnage, Full Year, 1970* (Washington, D.C.: American Trucking Associations, Inc.), Table II.

industries at the same time and hence can effect economies which the industry could not obtain in its own trucking operations.

SOME CHARACTERISTICS OF THE MOTOR-CARRIER INDUSTRY

Trucking as a Small-Scale Industry

Commercial trucking, taken as a whole, must be characterized as a small-scale industry, particularly when compared with the railroad industry. Although there are numerous common carriers operating a large number of vehicles, there is a vastly larger number of operators with a few trucks.

The Interstate Commerce Commission classifies motor carriers into three size groups. Class I carriers are those having annual gross revenues of $1,000,000 or more; Class II, those with revenues of $300,000 but under $1,000,000; and Class III, those with revenues of less than $300,000.[15] In 1970 there were 1,571 Class I motor carriers of property required to file reports with the Interstate Commerce Commission. There were 2,061 in Class II, and 11,468 in Class III.[16] In the trucking industry as a whole the proportion of small firms is even greater than in the group reporting to the Interstate Commerce Commission. Many thousands of small trucking concerns are not engaged in interstate commerce, or carry only agricultural products, or for some other reason do not come within the Commission's jurisdiction.

Evidence of the large number of small firms is brought out more strikingly by figures showing the number and size of motor carriers subject to the control of particular state governments. In 1964, of 15,895 motor carriers of property subject to some extent to the authority of the Public Utilities Commission of California, about 24 percent had annual gross revenues of less than $5,000; 46 percent had revenues between $5,000 and $25,000, and only 2.2 percent had revenues in excess of $500,000.[17]

Although the motor-trucking industry is characterized by many small operators, there are a number of large concerns. In 1962 there were 351 common carriers of general freight having revenues in excess of $5 million. There were seven with operating revenues in excess of $100 million. Of these, Consolidated Freightways and Roadway Express had operating revenues which exceeded $200 million.[18]

---

[15] For a number of years prior to 1957, Class I carriers were those with revenues of $200,000 or over; Class II, those with revenues from $50,000 to $200,000; and Class III, those with revenues of less than $50,000. From 1957 to 1968 the line between Class II and Class III carriers was at $200,000.

[16] Interstate Commerce Commission, *Annual Report, 1970*, p. 127.

[17] Public Utilities Commission of California, Transportation Division, *Report on Operations of Carriers of Property, Year 1964.*

[18] Data relating to revenues of individual carriers are from Interstate Commerce Commission, *Transport Statistics in the United States, 1969.* Part 7: *Motor Carriers.*

Size of Firms in the Motorbus Industry

In the intercity motorbus industry there is much greater concentration than in the trucking industry. In 1970 there were 107 Class I motor carriers of persons engaged exclusively in intercity service. The various Greyhound companies and the operating divisions of the Greyhound Corporation, which together make up the Greyhound system of bus lines, constitute the dominant organization in intercity bus transportation.

The Question of Economies of Scale

If economies of large-scale enterprise were evident in the motor-carrier industry, a tendency toward the formation of a few large firms would doubtless appear unless restricted by regulation. This would come about through mergers and consolidations and the elimination of small concerns through the competitive process.

Whether or not there are economies of large size in the motor-carrier industry is a matter of dispute. Certain statistical studies that have been made point to the conclusion that there are no economies due to size.[19] These studies, however, have been criticized as not conclusive.[20] One study finds a general association between small scale and high truck-mile costs, but concludes that these high costs are due to the prevalence of shorter hauls and less intensive exploitation of their routes, as evidenced by truck-miles per route-mile. These, the study asserts, are not necessary characteristics of small carriers.[21] These characteristics, however, seem to be associated with small firms.

There is little positive evidence that points to economies of scale in the motor-carrier industry, although a British writer asserts that Britain's experience with nationalization of the trucking industry showed that there are technical economies of large-scale operation.[22]

---

[19] Robert A. Nelson, "The Economic Structure of the Highway Carrier Industry in New England," in New England Governors' Committee on Public Transportation, *Motor Freight Transport for New England* (1956), pp. 34–35; Merrill J. Roberts, "Some Aspects of Motor Carrier Costs: Firm Size, Efficiency, and Financial Health," 32 *Land Economics* 228 (1956).

[20] E. W. Smykay, "An Appraisal of the Economics of Scale in the Motor Carrier Industry," 34 *Land Economics* 143 (1958). See also Gary N. Dicer, "Economies of Scale and Motor Carrier Optimum Size," 11 *Quarterly Review of Economics & Business* 31 (1971).

[21] Roberts, op. cit.

[22] J. R. Sargent, *British Transport Policy* (Oxford: Oxford University Press, 1958), p. 73. Of the same view is L. A. Schumer, "Road Transport," in Australian Institute of Political Science, *Australia's Transport Crisis* (Sydney: Angus & Robertson, 1956). That there are economies of scale up to a moderate size is asserted by P. S. Henman, "The Economics of Goods Transport by Road," 29 *Institute of Transport Journal* 259 (1962). Other British authorities inclined to the view that there are economies of scale in the road haulage industry are Gilbert Walker and A. A. Walters. See Walter's "Economies of Scale in Road Haulage," 13 *Oxford Economic Papers* (n.s.) 116 (1961). Eric Schenker, on the other hand, concludes that British

We are inclined to the conclusion that the existence of substantial economies in large-scale operations in the motor-carrier industry has not been
established, although there may be small economies resulting from size.
On the other hand, it has not been established that small firms in the industry are more economical than large ones.

The point also needs to be made that concentration in the trucking industry, with resulting large-scale firms, may naturally occur even if there
are no substantial economies of scale. This is because of the service advantages inherent in geographically extensive operations and hence the
greater ability of the large carrier to get traffic. There is an abundance of
evidence that shippers prefer to ship by a motor carrier which provides a
one-carrier service, that is, provides a complete service to the ultimate
destination of the shipment. Shippers are reluctant to make shipments that
involve interchange with one or more connecting carriers when it can be
avoided. In fact, many motor carriers refuse to interchange traffic with
others. Problems of tracing shipments and of collecting loss and damage
claims account for the reluctance to employ the services of carriers who
cannot complete the movement of the shipment to destination. This difficulty could be overcome by improvements in interchange arrangements;
but as long as single-line service is preferred, the large carrier operating
over an extensive area has an advantage over smaller concerns.

It is possible that large-scale firms will naturally come to dominate in
the long-distance movement of general commodities, while small concerns
will continue to provide more localized services and some specialized services for longer distances.

Proprietorship in the Motor-Carrier Industry

Because of the large number of small concerns in the trucking industry
the single proprietorship and the partnership forms of organization are
common. In 1939 about 70 percent of the intercity carriers of property
subject to the jurisdiction of the Interstate Commerce Commission were
single proprietorships; 12 percent were partnerships; and 17 percent were
corporations.[23] Of the intercity bus lines, however, about 50 percent were
incorporated, 42 percent were single proprietorships, and about 8 percent
were partnerships.[24] Although the proportions may be somewhat different
today, the prevalence of single proprietorships and partnerships still characterizes the motor-carrier industry. This situation may change as the size
of motor-carrier firms increases.

---

experience indicates no economies of large size in trucking. See "Nationalization and
Denationalization of Motor Carriers in Great Britain," 39 *Land Economics* 219 (1963).

[23] C. S. Morgan, E. V. Breitenbach, and J. O. Riley, "The Motor Transport Industry," in National Resources Planning Board, *Transportation and National Policy*
(Washington, D.C.: U.S. Government Printing Office, 1942), p. 407.

[24] Ibid., p. 405.

Capital Requirements of the Motor-Carrier Industry

There are two aspects of the capital requirements of the motor-carrier industry that have significance for our discussion. The first is that not much capital is required to start a small-scale motor carrier business. The thousands of very small operators having only a few vehicles testify to this point. In California, for instance, there were over 4,300 motor carriers for hire in 1964 who operated only one truck, and over 3,000 with but two trucks. These two classes of carriers comprised more than half of the for-hire carriers in the state.[25]

The second aspect of the capital requirements of the motor-carrier industry that needs to be noted is that the capital invested is small in relation to the volume of business done. In other words, the ratio of capital investment to gross revenue is small. The contrast between motor carriers and railroads in this respect is striking. The net investment in carrier property of Class I line-haul railroads in 1969 was $24,538,333,000. Their operating revenues were $11,450,325,000. Thus the investment was over twice the operating revenues. The investment of Class I motor carriers of property in intercity service in 1969 was $2,002,147,000. Their operating revenues were $10,723,430,000. Thus the investment was less than 20 percent of the operating revenues. These relationships are sometimes expressed in terms of "capital turnover," that is, the ratio of revenues to investment. Thus the capital turnover of the motor carriers in 1969, computed from the figures shown above, was 5.36. In other words, the revenues were more than five times the investment in carrier property.

Motor-Carrier and Railroad Operating Ratios

Because the amount of capital invested in the motor-carrier industry is small relative to the amount of business done, only a small margin of revenues over expenses is necessary to pay a return on invested capital. In the railroad industry, on the other hand, the margin of operating revenues over expenses must be substantial to pay an adequate return on investment. This difference between the motor-carrier industry and the railway industry is shown in the differences in the operating ratios which characterize the two industries (see Table 28–2). In the motor-carrier industry an operating ratio of 95 may provide a sufficient margin to pay a generous return on the capital invested. In the railroad industry such a high operating ratio would probably leave the company with earnings insufficient to pay interest charges, and, as Table 28–2 reveals, operating ratios in the 70s provide them with only a meager rate of return.

---

[25] Public Utilities Commission of California, Transportation Division, op. cit., p. 13.

TABLE 28–2. Operating Ratios and Rate of Return on Investment, Class I Railroads and Class I Intercity Motor Carriers of Property, 1960–1970.*

	Railroads		*Motor Carriers*	
	Operating Ratio	*Rate of Return*	*Operating Ratio*	*Rate of Return*
1960..........	79.52	2.21	97.51	11.53
1961..........	79.16	2.04	96.11	17.83
1962..........	78.59	2.77	95.87	19.22
1963..........	77.95	3.07	95.90	18.53
1964..........	78.50	3.22	95.46	20.22
1965..........	76.90	3.73	94.80	22.56
1966..........	76.19	3.92	95.04	20.90
1967..........	79.15	2.48	96.36	15.07
1968..........	79.05	2.52	95.16	21.18
1969..........	79.18	2.38	95.96	17.44
1970..........	80.56	1.75	93.12	13.90

* Interstate Commerce Commission, *Annual Report, 1971,* pp. 121, 122, 126, and 127.

Financing the Motor-Carrier Industry

The comparatively small size of firms in the motor-carrier industry and the fact that the capital requirements are small make it possible for the industry to be financed in large part without resort to the capital markets. The larger firms, of course, may issue securities which are sold to the public; but the capital for the smaller operators is often provided by a very few individuals, and in many cases a large part of the capital invested represents reinvested earnings of the business.

Constant and Variable Costs

Unlike the railroad industry the motor-carrier industry is not characterized by a substantial element of fixed or constant costs.[26] The costs incurred by motor carriers are of a sort which tend to vary with the volume of traffic carried. This difference between motor carriers and railroads arises largely from the fact that motor carriers do not have to provide and maintain their own highways. The substantial contributions which motor carriers make for the use of public highways, furthermore, tend to vary with the use made of the highways. The contributions made through gasoline taxes vary with road use; mileage and ton-mile taxes vary with the amount of traffic carried; and to a certain extent, registration fees also vary with the volume of traffic, since they vary with the amount of equipment used.

The Bureau of Transport Economics and Statistics of the Interstate

---

[26] For discussion of fixed costs in the railroad industry see pp. 143–46, supra.

Commerce Commission considered that not more than 10 percent of motor-carrier operating costs can be considered as constant.[27] These conclusions are based on the fact that the equipment and other facilities used by motor carriers can be readily adjusted to the volume of business done. Mr. John R. Turney, an attorney who long represented the motor-carrier industry, contends that all motor-carrier costs are variable, although the "expansion of the facilities and personnel of a motor carrier, as distinct from the expansion of its traffic, develops by steps and plateaus, and not in a straight line."[28]

If motor-carrier costs can be considered as largely variable, the rate-making policies of motor carriers should tend to be quite different from the rate-making policies of railroads. The limits within which motor carriers can reduce rates below fully allocated cost in order to meet competition is much more restricted than in the case of railroads. Similarly there is less scope for the play of value-of-service factors in motor-carrier rate making. Likewise, personal and place discrimination are likely to be less extensive in the motor-carrier industry than in the railroad industry.

It will be noted that the conclusion that motor-carrier costs are mostly variable is based on the fact that the equipment used can be readily adjusted to the volume of traffic. In terms of economic theory we are dealing with the "long-run" period, since that term is defined as one in which plant can be adjusted to changes in the volume of business. In the motor-carrier industry, however, the long run is short in terms of calendar time, unlike the situation in industries which have difficulty in adjusting their plant and equipment to changes in the volume of output.

In the short run, however, motor carriers have a substantial proportion of their costs fixed or constant. This can be seen by considering the case of an individual who undertakes to engage in for-hire transport with only one or two vehicles. If he finds it difficult to obtain business, he is tempted to take any business that he can get at a cut-rate price, which may be a price that will give him some revenue above gasoline and oil costs and any other immediate outlay. Under these circumstances he recognizes that interest on investment in vehicles, property taxes on the vehicles, motor-vehicle registration fees, and at least part of the depreciation on the vehicle are fixed costs and are incurred whether he moves any traffic or not. Short-run variable costs, rather than long-run variable costs, will determine what rate he charges. The situation which we have described often occurs in the trucking industry and shows that as a practical matter, short-run pricing sometimes becomes a problem for the industry.

---

[27] Interstate Commerce Commission, Bureau of Transport Economics and Statistics, Statement No. 4616, *The Meaning and Significance of the Out-of-Pocket, Constant, and Joint Costs in Motor Carrier Operation* (mimeographed; Washington, D.C., 1946), p. 12.

[28] Brief for Hayes Freight Lines, Inc., before the Interstate Commerce Commission in Docket No. I. & S. M–2333, p. 24.

Ease of Entry and Its Consequences

A characteristic of the motor-trucking industry is the ease with which one can, in the absence of regulatory controls, enter the business, at least on a small scale.

This characteristic of the industry has given rise to two conflicting claims about its consequences. Ease of entry, coupled with ease of exit resulting from ability to dispose of trucks without great financial sacrifice, leads some observers to the conclusion that the trucking industry is one in which competition should work satisfactorily, and that government regulation is unnecessary. This view was stated clearly by Walter Adams and James B. Hendry in a report prepared by them on trucking mergers for the Select Committee on Small Business of the United States Senate in 1957. "Here is an industry where there appears to be no substantial economies of scale, where the number of firms is large, and where, in the absence of restriction, entry would be brisk. In short, here is an industry where competition is structurally feasible and technologically possible."[29] In fact, the authors of the study consider that the trucking industry "epitomizes the classical model of 'perfect' competition."[30]

Ease of entry is claimed by others to create a condition of overcapacity in the industry which does not correct itself through withdrawal of the unsuccessful because there is a constant influx of newcomers into the industry to take the place of those who have failed. This view, based on the experience of the 1930s, had much to do with the establishment of federal regulation of motor carriers in 1935. Although there has been a tendency to discount the overcapacity or "excessive-competition" contention as merely the rationalization of the desire of the railroads and the existing motor carriers to obtain protection from additional competition, the matter cannot be dismissed so easily. The phenomenon of overcapacity does occur in the industry. The same tendency has been observed in other countries and recognized as a problem.[31] There are indications that the unregulated segments of the industry in the United States are sometimes confronted with a similar situation. In the words of two British students of the problem: ". . . competition cannot succeed if facilities are so plentiful that operators generally are obliged to quote prices on short-term specific costs."[32]

[29] *Trucking Mergers, Concentration, and Small Business: An Analysis of Interstate Commerce Commission Policy, 1950–56* (Washington, D.C.: U.S. Government Printing Office, 1957), p. 7.

[30] Ibid.

[31] E.g., A. W. Currie, *Economics of Canadian Transportation* (Toronto: University of Toronto Press, 1954), p. 491; A. M. Milne and Austen Laing, *The Obligation to Carry* (London: Institute of Transport, 1956), pp. 83–84; J. Williams, "The Coordination of Road and Rail Transport in New Zealand," 14 *Economic Record* 191 (1938), p. 196; L. A. Schumer, op. cit., p. 144; Francisco Botteri, "Exposicion de Motivos para Nueva Ley de Transporte Caminero," in *Boletín de la Biblioteca del Congreso de La Nación* (Argentina), Enero–Abril, 1960, pp. 119–55 at p. 133.

[32] Milne and Laing, op cit., p. 83.

The suggestion has been made that the problem of chronic overcapacity, resulting from ease of entry, is less important now than formerly, and will become even less so in the future.[33] The special conditions that made the problem serious in the 1930s, namely, depression and wide-spread unemployment, were not permanent. It is also argued that the increased size and cost of motor-carrier equipment brought about by technological change, together with the fact that several vehicles are needed for economical operations, make the cost of entering the industry sufficiently high to eliminate the one-man firm, the source of much of the undesirable competitive conditions in the industry in the 1930s. Undoubtedly there is some truth in this position, but the tendency for excess capacity to develop has not been confined to the depression period of the 1930s, nor has pricing below full costs in the competitive struggle been confined to the one-man firm.

Comparative Cost of Transport by Rail and Motor Truck

It is generally conceded that motor carriers can transport freight for short distances at lower costs than railroads, but that for long distances the railroads have a cost advantage. In the movement of small shipments in less-than-carload lots the motor carriers have a cost advantage even over long distances.

The advantage of motor carriers for shorter distances arises from the lower terminal costs, or perhaps it would be better to say that the railroads necessarily labor under a cost disadvantage arising from expensive terminal facilities and high terminal costs. For the line-haul movement, however, motor-carrier costs build up more rapidly with distance than the line-haul costs of railroads. The result is that the railroad usually has a distinct cost advantage on long-haul shipments, and the motor carrier has a cost advantage for short distances.[34]

The situation described is brought out in cost studies which have been made.[35] Studies of comparative costs of rail and motor-carrier movements are frequently used in cases before regulatory bodies involving the establishment of rates of competing rail and motor carriers. Generalizations concerning the distance at which motor-carrier costs exceed rail costs are difficult to make and not very meaningful unless they relate to specific movements of specific commodities.

---

[33] J. R. Meyer, M. J. Peck, John Stenason, and Charles Zwick, *The Economics of Competition in the Transportation Industries* (Cambridge: Harvard University Press, 1959), p. 216.

[34] Ernest W. Williams, Jr., "Some Aspects of the Problem of Intercarrier Competition," 11 *Vanderbilt Law Review* 971 (1958), p. 977.

[35] *Comparison of Rail, Motor, and Water Carrier Costs,* 79th Cong., 1st Sess., Senate Doc. No. 84 (1944), pp. 3–5.

MOTOR-CARRIER RATES

Because fixed costs are less important in the motor-carrier industry than in the railroad industry, we should expect to find differences in the motor-carrier and railroad rate structures. Such differences do exist, as will be pointed out shortly, but to a considerable degree the common carriers of freight by motor vehicle have followed the pattern of railroad rates. This is due in part to the fact that the motor carriers were required by the Motor Carrier Act of 1935 to publish and file rates in a comparatively short time, and it was easier to adopt the pattern of railroad rates than to construct an entirely independent structure of rates. They were also in competition with rail carriers and could not charge rates much higher than rail rates. On the other hand, they could charge above-cost rates where the railroad rates permitted.

Motor-Carrier Freight Classifications

The motor-freight classification most widely used throughout the United States is the *National Motor Freight Classification*. The ratings in the *National Motor Freight Classification* originally followed the railroad classification ratings very closely.[36] As time goes on, however, there have come to be more differences between the ratings in the motor and rail classifications.

The *National Motor Freight Classification*, as originally set up, contained different ratings on many articles in the East, South, and West, respectively, following the railroad ratings for Official, Southern, and Western classifications. After the establishment of the *Uniform Freight Classification* by the railroads in 1952, a *National Motor Freight Classification*, with one set of ratings for most articles, was set up. This classification is now in general use where the railroads use the *Uniform Freight Classification*.[37]

In New England two motor-freight classifications developed which were constructed on somewhat different lines than the *National Motor Freight Classification*. These classifications were the *Official Motor Freight Classification* and the *Coordinated Motor Freight Classification*. The former was subsequently absorbed by the latter. The distinguishing feature of the New England classifications was that the ratings were based largely on the weight densities of the various articles, and were designed to produce approximately the same revenue per truckload from all commodities carried. In general, commodities weighing 20 pounds or more per cubic foot were rated fifth class; those weighing less than 20 but more

---

[36] See *New England Motor Carrier Rates*, 8 MCC 287, 292–93 (1938); *Minimum Class Rate Restrictions*, 44 MCC 367, 369–70 (1945); *Motor Carrier Rates in New England*, 47 MCC 657, 658 (1948).

[37] For a discussion of the *Uniform Freight Classification* see pp. 172–74, supra.

than 15 pounds per cubic foot were rated fourth class; those weighing from 10 to 15 pounds, third class; those weighing from 6 to 10 pounds, second class; and those from 3 to 6 pounds, first class.[38] Articles weighing 3 pounds and under are now rated either 1½ times or 2½ times first class. The rating determined by this formula, however, was not always the rating finally adopted. Articles having unfavorable transportation characteristics, such as exceptional fragility or susceptibility to theft, were given a rating one or two classes above that which would have resulted from the weight-density factor alone; and on some desirable traffic, lower ratings were applied when necessary to meet railroad competition.[39] The Interstate Commerce Commission once pronounced the New England system of classification a sounder method of classifying motor-carrier freight than that adopted elsewhere, but expressed some doubt as to its practicability if the railroads adhered to their traditional method of classifying freight.[40] In *Motor Carrier Rates in New England* the American Trucking Associations, Inc., contended that the classification in New England should be brought into line with that used elsewhere in the country. The Commission refused to require that this be done.[41] The *National Motor Freight Classification*, however, generally applies on shipments between New England and the rest of the country.

In addition to the *National Motor Freight Classification* and the New England classification, the railroad classifications, either the *Consolidated Freight Classification* or the *Uniform Freight Classification*, sometimes apply to motor-carrier shipments. This is because a large number of motor carriers have adopted the railroad classifications.

Motor-Carrier Rates and Rail Rates

Not only did the motor carriers throughout the country, except in New England, tend to follow the rail system of freight classification, but they have tended to base their class rates on railroad class rates.[42] The general equality of rail and motor-carrier class rates was upset as a result of the numerous rate-level cases following World War II. We have seen elsewhere that the railroads were granted increases in rates in several nationwide rate-level proceedings following the war.[43] Motor carriers felt

---

[38] *Motor Carrier Rates, New York City Area–New England*, 62 MCC 427, 432 (1954).

[39] *Motor Carrier Rates in New England*, 47 MCC 657, 661 (1948).

[40] *New England Motor Carrier Rates*, 8 MCC 287, 321 (1938).

[41] *Motor Carrier Rates in New England*, 47 MCC 657, 663 (1948).

[42] *Rates over Freight Forwarders, Inc.*, 4 MCC 68, 74 (1937); *Stoves from Alabama & Tennessee to Interstate Points*, 4 MCC 641, 643 (1938); *Central Territory Motor Carrier Rates*, 21 MCC 473, 474 (1940); *Minimum Class Rate Restrictions*, 44 MCC 367, 370; *Transcontinental Motor Rates—Increases*, 49 MCC 211, 213 (1949); *Class Rate Investigation, 1939*, 281 ICC 213, 252 (1951).

[43] See pp. 371–72, supra.

the effects of the same inflationary forces that made increases in railroad rates necessary, and there have been numerous proceedings involving increases in motor-carrier rates in different parts of the country. Railroad rate increases and motor-carrier rate increases have not occurred at the same time or in the same amounts; hence the motor-carrier rates have been higher than rail rates at times or in certain areas, while at other times or in other areas they have been left on a lower level than the rail rates.

Classification exception ratings and commodity rates are important in the motor-carrier industry, although a larger proportion of the traffic of motor carriers than of railroads moves on class rates. No valid generalization can be made with respect to the relation of motor-carrier commodity rates to corresponding rail rates.

Rail versus Highway Distances

When motor-carrier rates are based on distance, highway distances are sometimes used, but in other instances railroad distances are used. Logically, of course, highway distances should be used. The use of rail distances, however, produces rates that are more competitive with the railroad rates and avoids the various difficulties encountered in the use of highway distances.

California bases intrastate rates on the shortest highway route, but uses "constructive distances" to reflect differing costs on different highways.[44] In 1963 the Florida Railroad and Public Utilities Commission required the use of highway distances because of the inequities arising from the use of rail distances.[45] In 1950 the Michigan Public Service Commission required the use of the shortest trunkline highway distance, but in 1957 it rescinded the order because of the difficulties encountered. Highway distances were approved by the Interstate Commerce Commission in a case involving rates in the Pacific Northwest.[46] The use of rail distances, however, was approved in a case involving class rates between Middle Atlantic and New England territories.[47] Rail distances were also approved in *Iron & Steel Articles—Eastern Common Carriers*,[48] over the opposition of Commissioners Arpaia and Walrath.

"Weight Breakdowns"

A feature of some motor-carrier rates, less often found in the railroad rate structure, is the use of "weight breakdowns," that is, different rates

---

[44] See Eric A. Mohr, "Constructive Mileage," 18 *Traffic Quarterly* 433 (1964).

[45] Traffic World, July 6, 1963, p. 76.

[46] *Seattle Traffic Assoc.* v. *Consolidated Freightways, Inc.*, 301 ICC 483 (1957).

[47] *Class Rates between Middle Atlantic & New England Territories*, 67 MCC 741 (1956).

[48] 306 ICC 369 (1959).

per hundred pounds depending on the size of the shipment, even if the quantity is less than a truckload. Class rates in New England, for instance, provided different fifth-class rates on six weight groups, namely, under 1,000 pounds, 1,000 to 6,000 pounds, 6,000 to 12,000 pounds, 12,000 to 20,000 pounds, 20,000 to 28,000 pounds, and 28,000 pounds and over. This system of rates, the Commission has stated, "is designed to pass on to the shipping public the benefit of a carrier's lower costs, especially for pickup and delivery, in the handling of larger shipments."[49]

Volume Minimum Weights

Railroads have long made a distinction between carload and less-carload shipments and have provided lower rates on carload lots. The motor carriers, for the same reasons, may properly distinguish between truckload and less-truckload shipments. The motor carriers, however, have in many cases adopted minimum weights which are substantially greater than the weight which can be loaded into a truck. Minimum weights which are in excess of the weight which can be loaded into a truck are sometimes called "volume minima." In one case the Commission explained the term by saying: "A volume minimum is distinguished from a truckload minimum in that the volume rate applies when a shipper tenders the volume minimum weight of a commodity for transportation at one time, even though it may exceed the carrying capacity of the largest vehicle available and must be transported in two or more vehicles, whereas a truckload minimum is generally understood to be the quantity which a carrier can transport in a single vehicle."[50]

The use of minimum weights in excess of the weight which can be carried in a truck cannot be justified by cost-of-service considerations. Such shipments cannot ordinarily be transported at a lower cost per hundred pounds than a truckload shipment. The use of volume minima, however, can be explained in terms of the competition between motor carriers and railroads. The Commission condemned the use of volume minima in a number of cases. The leading case is *Rugs & Matting from the East to Western Trunk Line Territory*.[51] The decision of the Commission in this case, however, was reversed by the Supreme Court in *Eastern-Central Motor Carrier Association* v. *United States* in 1944.[52] The implication of the Court's decision is that volume minima may not be condemned merely because they do not conform to cost-of-service standards but that they

[49] *Multiple Deliveries—New England*, 69 MCC 77, 78 (1956).

[50] *Stoves, Alabama & Tennessee to Interstate Points*, 4 MCC 641 (1938), n. on p. 643.

[51] 31 MCC 193 (1941), 34 MCC 641 (1942). For other instances see *Paper from Mechanic Falls, Maine, to Boston, Mass.*, 28 MCC 196 (1941); *Activated Carbon from Texas to Kansas City*, 31 MCC 597 (1942).

[52] 321 U.S. 194.

may be justified, within limits at least, on the grounds that they are necessary to meet the competition of rail carriers. In a subsequent decision the Commission approved volume minimum weights, saying: "In many instances, the minimum weights to which motor-carrier rates are subject are greater than the amounts which can be transported in a single vehicle; and such minima are not necessarily unlawful, particularly if they are compelled or warranted by carrier or commercial competition and, in connection with the rates to which they are applied, yield adequate earnings."[53]

Minimum Rate "Stops"

As previously pointed out, most motor carriers adopted a freight classification similar to the railroad freight classification and initially published class rates which were substantially the same as the railroad class rates. It soon became apparent, however, that the motor carriers could not carry the lower-rated commodities profitably, particularly for the longer dis-

TABLE 28–3.   Average Revenue per Ton-Mile, Railroads and Motor Carriers, 1959–69[*]

	Class I Railroads (Cents)	Class I Motor Common Carriers (Cents)
1959	1.44	6.28
1960	1.40	6.31
1961	1.37	6.30
1962	1.35	6.41
1963	1.31	6.38
1964	1.28	6.66
1965	1.27	6.46
1966	1.26	6.34
1967	1.27	6.65
1968	1.31	6.93
1969	1.35	7.21

[*] Bureau of Economics, Interstate Commerce Commission, *Transport Economics*, January 1971, p. 6.

tances. The device of minimum rate "stops" was introduced to remedy this difficulty, whereby the rates on the low-rated freight were made the same as on a higher class. Thus the fifth-class rate might be the lowest rate which a motor carrier would charge, even though the article in question might be rated sixth class or below. In some tariffs, rates would not be published for the lower classes of freight; but a tariff rule would provide that on articles given ratings for which no class rates were published, the rate would be that applicable on the lowest class for which rates were

[53] *Iron or Steel, Minimum 80,000 Pounds from Chicago District*, 54 MCC 413 (1952).

published. The Commission rather reluctantly approved of minimum rate stops in 1945.[54]

That motor carriers have found it necessary to resort to rate stops demonstrates that the greatest field of usefulness of motor carriers is in the transportation of high-class traffic and that they cannot compete with the railroads for low-rated traffic, particularly on the longer hauls. That motor carriers are predominantly carriers of high-class freight is borne out by a comparison of the average revenue per ton-mile received by the railroads and by motor carriers. In recent years the average revenue per ton-mile received by railroads has been a little over 1 cent, while the amount received by motor common carriers of property in intercity service has been between 6 and 7 cents, as shown by Table 28–3.

SOME EFFECTS OF MOTOR-TRANSPORT DEVELOPMENT

We now turn to a brief consideration of some of the effects of the development of motor transportation.

Modern highway transport has brought about significant changes in the economic life of the country. Even if we dismiss from consideration the many and revolutionary effects of the private automobile and confine our attention to the changes brought about by the movement of commodities by motor vehicle, the changes are profound. Many changes have occurred in the methods and organization of marketing and merchandising, in food processing, in manufacturing, and in the location of manufacturing industries, which are dependent upon motor-truck transport over a system of highly developed roads.

Of more immediate concern, so far as the problems discussed in this book are concerned, are the effects of motor-vehicle transport upon railroads, and the response of the railroads thereto.

Diversion of Traffic from Railways

Motor-truck transportation has made serious inroads on railroad traffic, particularly less-carload traffic. The decrease in less-carload traffic began before car-load traffic had reached a peak prior to the depression of the 30s, and the later decline was greater than that of the carload traffic. In 1963 the Class I railroads originated only 1,679,000 tons of L.C.L. freight, compared to 22,500,000 tons in 1947.[55] The loss of traffic by railroads, however, has not been limited to the L.C.L. traffic. Some commodities handled in carload lots and formerly considered almost exclusively rail traffic have been extensively diverted to trucks. Steel is an outstanding example.

---

[54] *Minimum Class Rate Restrictions*, 44 MCC 367 (1945).

[55] Interstate Commerce Commission, *Freight Commodity Statistics, Class I Railroads, 1963*.

Mention has already been made of the use of motor trucks in transporting fruits, vegetables, and livestock to market. Over the years, with the exception of the period of World War II, the proportion of receipts of farm products at principal markets arriving by truck has tended to increase.[56] Loss of traffic to motor carriers is revealed in hundreds of rate proceedings before the Interstate Commerce Commission involving many different commodities.

Some attempts have been made to indicate the diversion of traffic from railway to trucks by the divergence between indices of the physical volume of production and indices of railroad freight traffic. The Bureau of Transport Economics and Statistics of the Interstate Commerce Commission made studies of this sort.[57] The studies show that except for the war period the railroads have been carrying a smaller proportion of the total physical volume of goods produced than they formerly did. These studies point to the conclusion that there has been a large diversion of tonnage from the railroads to other forms of transportation. They may also indicate that changes in the location of industries and a breaking-down of geographical division of labor are occurring in an effort to avoid high transportation charges.

From a revenue standpoint the diversion of traffic from the railroads to other modes of transport is more serious to the railroads than figures showing loss of tonnage reveal. This is because much of the traffic diverted paid relatively high rates, and also because reductions in rates on some traffic have been made to lessen or prevent further diversion.

Abandonment of Railroad Lines

Reference has been made elsewhere to the problem of railroad abandonments.[58] Thousands of miles of rail line have been abandoned since the advent of motor-vehicle transportation. A study of railroad abandonments occurring from 1921 to 1937 in New England showed that 43 percent of them were caused by highway competition.[59] A later study of abandonments over the whole country showed that highway competition was responsible for 58 percent of the mileage in abandonments which had been

---

[56] U.S. Department of Agriculture, Bureau of Agricultural Economics, *Trucks Haul Increased Share of Fruit and Vegetable Traffic* (Washington, D.C., 1953); "Rail and Truck Shares in the Hauling of Perishables: Some Recent Developments," in U.S. Department of Agriculture, Agricultural Marketing Service, *The Marketing and Transportation Situation*, July, 1958, p. 40.

[57] See Statement No. 6301, *Fluctuations in Railway Freight Traffic Compared with Production, Class I Line-Haul Railroads, 1958, 1959, and 1960.* (Washington, D.C., 1963).

[58] Pp. 595–99 supra.

[59] Charles R. Cherington, "Railroad Abandonment in New England, 1921–37," 14 *Journal of Land & Public Utility Economics* 40 (1938).

authorized by the Interstate Commerce Commission from 1920 to 1943.[60] Another study holds that highway competition was an element in 700 abandonment cases decided between 1920 and 1941, involving 15,000 miles of road, and was the primary factor in 153 cases involving the abandonment of 4,824 miles of road.[61]

There is reason to believe that thousands of miles of additional railway line have been made redundant by the development of highway transport and that a restructuring of the railway system is necessary.

Vanishing Rail Passenger Service

The development of highways has been a major cause of the near demise of intercity railroad passenger traffic. The gradual curtailment of railroad intercity passenger traffic is described in earlier chapters, particularly in discussing the events leading to the enactment of the Rail Passenger Service Act of 1970.[62] Suffice it to say here that the principal means of intercity travel, especially for shorter distances is the private automobile.[63] The improvement of highways and the construction of the National System of Interstate and Defense Highways has extended the length of trips commonly taken in the private automobile. The development of air transport, however, is the principal reason why long-distance travel has deserted the railroads. To what extent "Railpax" will restore passenger movement by rail remains to be seen.

Decline of Railroad Less-Carload Service

We have already mentioned the decline in the volume of less-carload traffic handled by the railroads to 1963. The burden of unprofitable less-carload traffic caused the Pennsylvania Railroad to discontinue less-carload freight service in 1962. Most other railroads followed suit during the next few years and the nation-wide L.C.L. service formerly provided by the railroads has virtually ceased to exist. This means that such traffic has been diverted principally to motor trucks, either private or for-hire, to freight forwarders, and to some extent to airlines. Motor carriers and freight forwarders can handle much of the small-shipment traffic more economically than the railroads. Even the motor carriers, however, frequently seek to avoid transporting small shipments, which they also find to be unprofitable.

---

[60] Interstate Commerce Commission, Bureau of Transport Economics and Statistics, *Railroad Abandonments, 1920–1943* (Washington, D.C.: 1945), p. iii.

[61] Charles R. Cherington, *The Regulation of Railroad Abandonments* (Cambridge: Harvard University Press, 1948), pp. 110, 117.

[62] Pp. 275–76 supra.

[63] Note figures shown in Table 2–3, p. 21 supra.

Reductions in Railroad Rates

Motor-truck competition has brought about many reductions in railroad rates. An examination of railroad rate cases before the Interstate Commerce Commission will reveal hundreds of instances in which railroads have deemed it necessary to reduce rail rates to meet competition from common and contract carriers and, in some instances, from private trucking. A study of the rate structure on any important commodity will, with but few exceptions, provide illustrations of modifications in the general level or in the structure of rates that are the result of highway competition. In the 1940s and 1950s the great majority of rate cases which came before the Interstate Commerce Commission involved competitive reductions.

The railroads, feeling that the Commission had unduly restricted their efforts to reduce rates to meet competition of other modes of transport, prevailed upon Congress, in 1958, to amend Section 15a of the Act in such manner as to permit them greater freedom in this respect. The provision of the law has been explained in earlier pages.[64] This action of Congress has led to even more aggressive action on the part of the railroads to prevent further diversion of traffic to highway carriers and to recover some already lost.

The use of "all-commodity" or "all-freight" rates for application on carload mixtures represents an attempt on the part of railroads to meet motor-truck competition on high-grade traffic that is particularly susceptible to diversion to highway carriers. These rates, usually on carloads, apply regardless of the ratings provided by the freight classification on the particular articles included in the mixture. All-commodity rates were first introduced in 1932 and were made 70 percent of first class. Lower all-commodity rates have since been established, but the Commission does not ordinarily approve of them if they are on a lower basis than 45 percent of first class.[65] In 1959 the New York, New Haven & Hartford Railroad established all-commodity rates between certain New England points and Chicago and St. Louis which applied on straight carloads as well as on mixed carloads. The Commission eventually held that these rates were unlawful, but its order was set aside by the courts.[66]

General Improvements in Railroad Service

Many improvements in railroad service have been brought about in the attempt of railroads to recover traffic. There has been a general speed-

---

[64] See pp. 273–74, *supra.* The Commission's policy in cases involving rates of competing modes of transport is discussed in Chapter 37.

[65] *All Commodities, Mixed Carloads, in Official Territory,* 306 ICC 29, 35 (1959).

[66] *All States Freight, Inc.* v. *New York, New Haven & Hartford R. Co.,* 379 U.S. 343 (1964).

ing-up of merchandise traffic and the establishment of overnight service for distances within which a comparable service is provided by truck. Among the more spectacular developments has been the introduction of tri-level cars for the transportation of new automobiles by means of which the railroads recovered a large part of this important traffic which had been lost to specialized highway carriers. In 1959, the railroads carried only 7.8 percent of shipments of motor vehicles; motor carriers, 88.0 percent. In 1969, the railroads carried 37.3 percent of this traffic and the motor carriers 62.0 percent.[67] Other innovations have been introduced by the railroads to move particular commodities, but not all of them are related to motor-carrier competition.

Trailer-on-Flatcar Service and "Containerization"

A device which the railroads have introduced quite extensively in recent years is trailer-on-flatcar service, commonly referred to in the industry as "TOFC," but more popularly known as "piggy-back." TOFC service represents an attempt to utilize railroads for long hauls, where the railroad has a cost advantage, with short hauls at origin and destination and pick-up and delivery service performed by motor truck. Closely related to TOFC service is "containerization," the handling of shipments in large containers that can be readily transferred from flatcars to motor vehicles and ships.

Both TOFC service and container service represent a form of coordinated intermodal transport and are referred to again in a later chapter.[68] In 1969 over 2 million trailers or containers were terminated by Class I railroads in these services, representing over 33 million net tons of freight.[69]

SELECTED REFERENCES

Two early studies of the motor-carrier industry are by the Interstate Commerce Commission, namely, *Motor Bus and Motor Truck Operation*, 140 ICC 685 (1928), and *Coordination of Motor Transportation*, 182 ICC 263 (1932).

Books devoted entirely to highway transport are Charles A. Taff, *Commercial Motor Transportation* (4th ed.; Homewood, Ill.: Richard D. Irwin, Inc., 1969); and William J. Hudson and James A. Constantin, *Motor Transportation: Principles and Practices* (New York: Ronald Press, 1958).

The matter of economies of scale in the motor-carrier industry is discussed in Merrill J. Roberts, "Some Aspects of Motor Carrier Costs: Firm Size, Efficiency, and Financial Health," 32 *Land Economics* 228 (1956); and E. W. Smykay, "An Appraisal of the Economies of Scale in the Motor Carrier In-

---

[67] Bureau of Economics, Interstate Commerce Commission, Monthly *Comment*, June, 1970, p. 2.

[68] Chapter 37.

[69] *Transport Economics*, August–September 1970, p. 3.

28 / Highway Transportation

dustry," 34 *Land Economics* 142 (1958); also R. A. Nelson, "The Economics of Scale in the Motor Carrier Industry: A Reply," 35 *Land Economics* 180 (1959), and Gary N. Dicer, "Economies of Scale and Motor Carrier Optimum Size," 11 *Quarterly Review of Economics & Business* 31 (1971).

On the nature of competition in the motor-carrier industry, see George W. Wilson, "The Nature of Competition in the Motor Transport Industry," 36 *Land Economics* 387 (1960).

DEVELOPMENT OF MOTOR-

CARRIER REGULATION

In the preceding chapter we made certain observations concerning motor-vehicle transportation over highways. This and the following chapter are concerned with the regulation of such carriers.

In studying the control of motor transportation, three types of regulation must be distinguished: (1) regulation to protect the highway, (2) safety regulation, and (3) regulation of the business of transporting goods for hire over the highways, sometimes called "economic regulation."

REGULATION TO PROTECT THE HIGHWAY

Under the first type of regulation are the weight limitations imposed upon vehicles to prevent destruction of bridges and road surfaces. There is little question concerning the need for regulation of this type, and it is appropriate that control over the weight of motor vehicles should rest in the first instance with the states. The states have built highways at great expense, and it is fitting that they impose such restrictions as may be necessary to prevent their destruction.

Although it is conceded that regulation of this type is desirable, there is frequent controversy over just what restrictions should be imposed. The railroads have been interested in having weight limitations imposed on motor vehicles that will reduce the competitive threat of motor transportation. It is clear that weight limitations should be imposed for the purpose of protecting highways and not for the purpose of making truck transportation unprofitable or for driving traffic back to railroads.

Weight limitations are of various types. Gross weights may be fixed in order to limit the weight of the load as a whole; maximum weights per axle or per wheel may be used to limit the concentration of loads; and weight per inch of tire width may be used to assure that vehicles are equipped with tires of sufficient size to sustain the load without damage to the highway.

Some states have been much more strict in limiting weights of vehicles than others. These differences may result from differences in the highways and bridges; but as standards of highway construction have become more nearly uniform for main traveled roads, there is less justification for wide variations in weight limitations. For many years Kentucky permitted a gross weight of only 18,000 pounds, although most states permitted weights of from 30,000 to 40,000 pounds.

The diversity in state requirements relating to maximum weights of motor vehicles has been a handicap to long-distance transportation by motor vehicle that must cross state boundaries. Efforts to remedy this situation have proceeded along different lines. The American Association of State Highway Officials recommended an axle-load limit of 18,000 pounds, but the establishment of uniformity by voluntary action of the states is likely to be slow, if not impossible.

Efforts have also been made to overthrow the excessively strict weight requirements through judicial proceedings in which it is alleged that the unreasonable weight restrictions of some states impose an unconstitutional burden on interstate commerce. These efforts have met with little success, since the courts are loath to interfere with the judgment of the state legislatures concerning appropriate weight limits.[1]

A third method of dealing with the problem is by means of direct federal invasion of this field of regulation. This could take various forms, representing varying degrees of federal control.

An extreme form of federal interference would be for the federal government to occupy entirely this field of regulation, so far as interstate commerce is concerned, substituting federal for state restrictions. The constitutionality of federal invasion of this field to such an extent, however, has been questioned.

A lesser degree of federal interference is represented by the rcommendations made by the Interstate Commerce Commission in 1941. The Commission was directed by the Motor Carrier Act of 1935 to investigate and report on the need for federal regulation of the weights and sizes of motor vehicles engaged in interstate and foreign commerce. The Commission's report did not recommend that the federal government attempt to oust the states completely from control over weights of trucks engaged in interstate commerce. It did recommend, however, that it be empowered to hear complaints against specific state limitations that were alleged to be an unreasonable obstruction to interstate commerce and that it be given the power to prescribe limitations in such instances in lieu of state restrictions found burdensome.[2] Federal interference would thus be limited to particular situations in which the state restrictions were found to be unreasonable and to constitute an undue burden on interstate commerce. The Commission believed that interference with state control to this extent would not be unconstitutional, since it is recognized that Congress

---

[1] See *South Carolina State Highway Department* v. *Barnwell Bros.*, 303 U.S. 177 (1938).

[2] *Federal Regulation of the Sizes and Weight of Motor Vehicles*, 77th Cong., 1st Sess., House Doc. No. 354 (1941).

has the power to remove unreasonable restrictions on interstate commerce. Legislation along the lines suggested by the Commission was not enacted, and it was vigorously opposed by state officials.

A certain degree of federal control over weight limits was provided by the Federal Aid Highway Act of 1956 so far as the National System of Interstate and Defense Highways is concerned. The Act provided that appropriations for this system are to be withheld from any state that permits the portion of the Interstate System within its borders to be used by vehicles carrying a weight in excess of 18,000 pounds per axle,[3] or such maximum weights as were permitted by the state on July 1, 1956, whichever is the greater. In 1964 the Secretary of Commerce recommended a scale of maximum weights on the Interstate System varying from 32,000 to 104,000 pounds, depending on the number of axles and the distances between the extreme axles.[4] Bills to accomplish this result were introduced in Congress in 1969 but were not enacted.

SAFETY REGULATION

Included in this type of regulation are the numerous measures designed to protect the general users of the highway. These measures specify limitations on the width of trucks and buses; maximum heights; maximum lengths of vehicles and of combinations of vehicles; speed limits; requirements to insure the equipment of vehicles with safety appliances such as speedometers, adequate brakes, horns, lights, windshield wipers, mirrors, and bumpers. Under this type of regulation also is included the requirement that motor-vehicle operators carry liability insurance against personal injuries and property damage caused in the operation of vehicles. Insurance for the protection of passengers and cargoes, however, does not come under this type of regulation, but under the third type.

The desirability of safety regulation is generally admitted, but such regulations should be made with careful consideration of their purpose and should not be imposed with the object of rendering highway transportation unprofitable. Diversity of state requirements undoubtedly operates to some extent as a hindrance to the use of the highways in interstate commerce.[5] The extent to which the federal government has invaded this field of regulation will be discussed later.

---

[3] Or with a tandem axle weight in excess of 32,000 pounds, or with an overall gross weight in excess of 73,280 pounds, or with a width exceeding 96 inches.

[4] *Maximum Desirable Dimensions & Weights of Vehicles Operated on the Federal-Aid Systems*, 88th Cong., 2d Sess., House Doc. No. 354 (1964).

[5] For a description of some difficulties encountered by interstate truck operators because of diversity of weight limitations or of safety requirements, see Hearings before Committee on Interstate and Foreign Commerce, House of Rep., 73d Cong., 2d Sess., on H.R. 6836, *Regulation of Interstate Motor Busses and Trucks on Public Highways* (1934), pp. 404–7.

REGULATION OF THE BUSINESS OF TRANSPORTATION FOR HIRE

Regulation of this type includes the control of rates and services, the requirement that certificates of convenience and necessity or permits to operate be obtained by operators for hire, and that common carriers obtain liability protection for shippers and passengers. It is this type of regulation that gives rise to the greatest controversy and the most difficult problems.

IS REGULATION NECESSARY?

We have elsewhere pointed out that the motor-carrier industry has economic characteristics quite different from railroads. The characteristics of the railroad industry which made regulation necessary do not apply to the motor-carrier industry to the same degree. It was pointed out in an earlier chapter[6] that competition was not an adequate regulator of the railroad rate level because of the huge investment required in fixed and specialized facilities. The railroad industry can operate at high profits without inducing a duplication of facilities; it will also operate for long periods of time with little or no return on the capital invested because capital cannot be readily withdrawn from the industry. The motor-carrier business, on the other hand, does not require a large investment in fixed and specialized capital. The highway is provided by the state, and the investment of the motor-vehicle operator is largely an investment in equipment, in garage facilities, and possibly in terminal property. Motor trucks are not fixed capital, nor are they so specialized as to be of use only for common-carrier purposes. They are movable and readily salable. The result is that the trucking concern can expand or contract its facilities as traffic conditions require, or it can withdraw from the industry entirely. The motor-carrier industry would appear to be one in which a flow of capital into and out of the industry would readily occur. It is logical to suppose, therefore, that motor carriers would not long operate without a return on capital, nor would they earn excessive profits for long.

We also noted in an earlier chapter that the railroad industry is one in which increases in the volume of traffic result in lower unit costs,[7] and hence that the industry is one in which there are substantial economies of scale. We have noted in the preceding chapter that any very marked economies of scale in the motor-carrier industry are not evident. It would seem to follow that an economical organization of the motor-carrier industry does not require a single operator or a limited number of operators

---

[6] Pp. 142–43, supra.

[7] Pp. 146–47, supra.

in a given transportation market, but that a number of competing carriers could operate as efficiently.

The large proportion of fixed or constant expenses in the railroad industry has also been mentioned as the source of discrimination in rates and the cause of rate cutting on the out-of-pocket-cost theory.[8] For this reason railroad competition was held to be "ruinous" in character unless restrained in one way or another. Since the motor-carrier industry has a much smaller proportion of fixed or constant costs and a larger proportion of direct or variable costs, it would seem that both discrimination in rates and the ruinous type of competition would be much less likely to appear.

These comparisons of the railroad and motor-carrier industries point to the thesis that motor transport need not be subjected to the type of regulation that is characteristic of railroad regulation, particularly rate regulation and restriction of entry into the industry.[9] The conclusion, however, must be qualified by recognition of the fact, mentioned in the preceding chapter, that the special conditions existing in the motor-carrier industry have resulted in a tendency for overcapacity to develop and to persist,[10] and that under these conditions competition does not function as the theorist assumes. The ruinous type of competition does develop; discrimination in rates does appear; the condition of overcapacity does not correct itself automatically; and the struggle for survival in the face of inadequate revenues leads to deterioration of safety standards, evasion of safety regulations, financial irresponsibility, and generally unsatisfactory service.

A study of conditions in the motor-carrier industry prior to the establishment of regulation reveals that the results of noninterference were far from satisfactory. The Supreme Court of the United States, in describing the circumstances which brought about the enactment of the Motor Carrier Act, pointed out that the motor-carrier industry "was unstable economically, dominated by ease of competitive entry and a fluid rate picture," and that "it became overcrowded with small economic units which proved unable to satisfy the most minimal standards of safety or financial responsibility."[11] Similar conditions have been experienced in many other countries as motor-vehicle transportation has developed.

It was to remedy this state of affairs, and also to afford some protection to railroads, that regulation was undertaken in the United States, first by

---

[8] Pp. 150–51, supra.

[9] A strong argument that the motor-carrier industry is naturally competitive and does not require regulation, at least to the extent that it is presently regulated, is made by Dudley F. Pegrum, "The Economic Basis for Public Policy for Motor Transport," 28 *Land Economics* 244 (1952). A similar argument was made by James C. Nelson in "New Concepts in Transportation Regulation," in National Resources Planning Board, *Transportation and National Policy* (Washington, D.C.: U.S. Government Printing Office, 1942), particularly pp. 216–37.

[10] P. 653, supra.

[11] *American Trucking Associations* v. *United States*, 344 U.S. 298, 312 (1953).

the states and later by the federal government. Similar motives explain the development of regulation in other countries as well.

OBJECTIVES OF MOTOR-CARRIER REGULATION

We may now turn to the more specific objectives which were sought by subjecting motor carriers to regulation. For the most part these objectives reflect the standards of service, responsibility, and rate practice which the public had come to expect of common carriers.

Stability of Rates

The shipping public has long sought a certain degree of stability in rates charged by common carriers. Unstable rates inject an element of uncertainty into business transactions that is disconcerting to shippers. Business transactions are constantly entered into which involve calculations based on freight rates at a given time, usually in the immediate or near future. Calculations of this sort are impossible if freight rates are fluctuating. Rates can be stabilized by a requirement that they be published and that they cannot be changed except on due notice. Although motor-truck rates, if unregulated, will not vary as widely as rail rates under similar circumstances because of the difference in the nature of transportation costs, desirable stability cannot be attained without some degree of control.

Prevention of Discrimination

Personal discrimination and unjust discrimination between places and particular descriptions of traffic are objectionable regardless of the transportation agency which resorts to the practice. Again we may note that the motive for discrimination is not so strong among highway carriers, because their expenses are largely direct expenses. But discrimination by motor carries has not been entirely absent. In fact, experience under the Motor Carrier Act indicates that as much vigilance is required to prevent motor carriers from engaging in discriminatory practices as to prevent railroads from doing so.

Financial Responsibility

Means of insuring financial responsibility on the part of motor carriers in order that they may be able to meet court judgments against them arising from motor-vehicle accidents, from loss or damage to goods carried, or from injury to passengers, is a problem that is peculiar to the industry. The problem arises in part from the large number of small-scale operations in the industry and the small amount of capital required to embark on such operations. Regulation has attempted to remedy this situation by requiring the posting of bonds or the carrying of insurance by motor carriers to cover judgments against them.

Dependable Service

Regulation has been considered desirable in order to insure dependable service. Common carriers by highway should assume the responsibilities which are ordinarily imposed upon other common carriers. Prior to the establishment of federal regulation of motor carriers, complaints against truck operators on this score were not uncommon. The Federal Coordinator of Transportation stated in 1934 that there was a feeling that trucking concerns did not measure up in all respects "to the standards of responsibility expected of a public servant."[12] He also referred to the fact that the motor-transport industry did not assume responsibility for complete coverage of the transportation needs of the area which it served in the same manner as railroads. Regulation may be necessary to enforce upon common carriers by motor vehicle the responsibilities which have traditionally been required of common carriers.

Reasonable Rates

Regulation may be necessary to insure just and reasonable rates, even though competitive conditions are more likely to prevail in the motor-carrier industry than in the railroad industry. In many instances there may be little or no competition between motor common carriers over a given route. The policy of requiring certificates of convenience and necessity may result in excluding or limiting competition on a particular route. Even in the absence of restriction of entry into the industry, conditions of monopoly, duopoly, or oligopoly are more likely to prevail over a given route than conditions approaching perfect competition. Agreement among motor carriers, tacit or otherwise, is to be expected. Rail rates are often adopted by motor carriers, and this practice may result in rates higher or lower than motor-transportation costs warrant. The competition afforded by contract carriers may enable large shippers to avoid high common-carrier rates, or it may induce common carriers to maintain lower rates on certain traffic; but the business of small shippers is not sought by contract carriers, hence many shippers may be at the mercy of the common carriers. Similarly the right to transport one's own goods as a private carrier may limit the charges of both common and contract carriers; but only the large shipper can resort to this practice, hence the small shipper has no alternative but to patronize common carriers. Under the circumstances, therefore, it seems wise to give commissions the power to

---

[12] *Regulation of Transportation Agencies,* 73d Cong., 2d Sess., Senate Doc. No. 152 (1934), p. 23.

determine the reasonableness of motor-carrier rates and to prescribe reasonable charges when circumstances require it.

Financial Stability

Adequate and dependable motor-carrier service cannot be obtained unless the earnings of the operators are adequate. This may require some degree of control over the rates and competitive activities of motor carriers. It has already been suggested that competition between trucking concerns should work more satisfactorily than competition between railways because of the absence of a large element of fixed costs. Rate cutting of the ruinous type, however, has not been absent in the motor-carrier field. Prior to the establishment of regulation, established carriers were frequently complaining of ruinous rate cutting, particularly by new and inexperienced operators who were ignorant of real costs. The situation was aggravated by the ease with which one could enter the industry, as we have previously noted. The absence of any legal restrictions and the small amount of capital required enabled many persons with little training or experience to enter the industry. After regulation was established, numerous cases arose in which it seemed necessary or desirable for the regulatory body to step in and put a stop to rate cutting of the disastrous type.

To aid in the attainment of greater financial stability in the motor-carrier industry, two control devices are commonly used. The first is restriction of entry into the industry through requiring certificates of public convenience and necessity or permits for new operations. The second is the prescription of minimum rates. Both of these powers carry with them grave dangers of abuse, and they should be exercised with caution. The inclusion of both of these controls in state and federal legislation indicates that unrestricted competition in the motor-carrier industry was deemed incompatible with the attainment of financial stability in the industry.

Transport Coordination

Regulation is necessary to aid in bringing about coordination of rail and motor transportation. By coordination we mean fitting each mode of transportation into its proper place in the transportation system. This requires control over competitive relations. It does not require the elimination of competition, yet each mode ought to be prevented from invading the field of operation in which another mode is clearly superior.

STATE REGULATION

State regulation of motor carriers preceded federal regulation by several years. By 1928 the transportation of passengers by motor vehicle was regulated in 43 states and the District of Columbia, and the transportation of property in 33 states and the District of Columbia.[13] In 1932 the Interstate Commerce Commission was able to say that all states except Delaware attempted to regulate the transportation of passengers and that 29 states had laws regulating the transportation of property by motor vehicle.[14]

State laws have varied widely in their content and in the degree of success with which they have been administered. Many states have revamped their regulatory statutes one or more times. Following the enactment of the federal Motor Carrier Act of 1935, a number of states enacted new regulatory laws patterned after the federal statute. Thus federal regulation has had the effect of bringing about greater uniformity in state regulation. Substantial differences among the states continue to exist, however, in the kind and degree of regulation imposed on motor carriers.

The States and Contract Carriers

State experience demonstrated that contract carriers had to be regulated as well as common carriers. There are two reasons for this. First, if common carriers are regulated and contract carriers are not, there is a possibility that common carriers will resort to subterfuge for the purpose of escaping regulation. There are many cases on record in which common carriers have altered the nature of their business to give plausibility to the claim that they were not subject to regulation. The line between common carriers and contract carriers is not always easy to draw. The second reason for regulating contract carriers is that the latter can often make common-carrier service unprofitable. Common-carrier service is of greater benefit to the public than contract-carrier service because it serves the whole public. The contract carrier can often take the traffic of the common carrier's best customers and render the common carrier's service unprofitable and perhaps destroy it. In so far as the costs of operation are lower for the contract carrier, it may be proper for it to obtain the business of the large shippers by quoting lower rates than common carriers do. But if there is not traffic enough for both common and contract carriers, protection of the common carrier may be justified.

The first attempts of the states to regulate contract carriers fared badly in the courts. In three different cases the Supreme Court of the United States held state statutes unconstitutional which attemped to regulate contract carriers by motor vehicle.[15] The difficulty encountered arose from the fact that contract carriers were not businesses "affected with a public

---

[13] *Motor Bus & Motor Truck Operation*, 140 ICC 685, 741 (1928).

[14] *Coordination of Motor Transportation*, 182 ICC 263, 371 (1932).

[15] *Michigan Public Utilities Commission* v. *Duke*, 266 U.S. 570 (1925); *Frost* v. *Railroad Commission of California*, 271 U.S. 583 (1926); *Smith* v. *Cahoon*, 283 U.S. 553 (1931).

interest."[16] The state of Texas, however, devised a scheme of regulation of both common and contract carriers that the Supreme Court upheld in *Stephenson* v. *Binford*.[17] This plan of control imposed one system of regulation upon common carriers and a slightly different system upon contract carriers. Contract carriers were to obtain "permits," not "certificates of public convenience and necessity." The Texas law gave the commission power to prescribe the minimum rates of contract carriers, but not their maximum rates. The minimum rates were in no event to be less than those of rail carriers. Permits were not to be issued to contract carriers unless the commission was of the opinion that the proposed operation would not impair the efficient public service of any authorized common carrier then adequately serving the same territory.

After the decision in *Stephenson* v. *Binford* a number of states followed the lead of Texas and enacted legislation that distinguished between contract carriers and common carriers, applying to contract carriers only such control as was deemed necessary to make the control of common carriers effective. This set the pattern for the Federal Motor Carrier Act of 1935.[18] It is interesting to note that the basis for the requirement that contract carriers be treated differently from common carriers seems to be destroyed by the subsequent repudiation by the Supreme Court, in *Nebbia* v. *New York*,[19] of the doctrine that there are two categories of businesses—those "affected with a public interest" and those not so affected.[20] From a practical standpoint, however, it is desirable to continue the difference in treatment of common and of contract carriers.

DEMAND FOR FEDERAL LEGISLATION

Prior to 1925 the states exercised some degree of control over the affairs of interstate carriers operating in the state. But in *Michigan Public Utilities Commission* v. *Duke*, a case to which we have already referred, the Supreme Court held that a permit could not be denied an interstate operator. A similar position was taken in other cases, although the right of the state to impose regulations upon interstate operators was upheld when the regulations related to protection of the highways and the promotion of safety. The inability of the states to control the operations of interstate buses and trucks led to the demand for federal legislation. After the Duke decision in 1925 the National Association of Railroad and Utilities Com-

---

[16] For the discussion of this concept see pp. 217–19, supra.

[17] 287 U.S. 251 (1932).

[18] The federal statute does not restrict contract carriers to the extent that the Texas statute did.

[19] 291 U.S. 502 (1934).

[20] See statement of Judge Frank in *Fordham Bros. Corp.* v. *United States*, 41 F. Supp. 712, 715 (1941).

missioners sponsored federal regulation in the belief that without it, state regulation was largely ineffective. Bills to this end were introduced in Congress in 1925 and during every succeeding session of Congress until the Motor Carrier Act finally became a law. The railroads supported the legislation in the belief that it would benefit them. The motor-carrier industry was divided, but there was a tendency for the older and better-established concerns in the industry to support the legislation because it promised them some protection from the competition of "irresponsible" operators.

Opposition to the legislation came particularly from farm organizations, which feared that regulation would hamper and restrict trucking operations and tend to restore a railroad monopoly. There was also some opposition among contract carriers.

The Interstate Commerce Commission kept in close touch with developments in the motor-carrier industry. In 1928 the Commission made a thorough investigation of motor-vehicle transportation and recommended federal regulation of buses but not of trucks.[21] In 1932, after another investigation, the Commission recommended federal regulation of trucks also.[22] Further stimulus to action resulted from the report of the Federal Coordinator in 1934, which urged the need for the regulation of interstate motor-vehicle operations.[23] The bill finally enacted closely followed the one drafted by the Coordinator.

THE MOTOR CARRIER ACT

The Motor Carrier Act of 1935 was approved by President Roosevelt on August 9, 1935. In 1940 it became Part II of the Interstate Commerce Act, and the former Interstate Commerce Act became Part I of the enlarged Act. We shall speak of the provisions relating to motor carriers as "Part II of the Interstate Commerce Act" or as the "Motor Carrier Act." Various amendments to the original Motor Carrier Act have been made, and the description which follows is of the amended Act unless otherwise indicated.

The Act places under the jurisdiction of the Interstate Commerce Commission carriers by motor vehicle engaged in interstate and foreign commerce. This includes purely intrastate operators handling shipments that move in interstate and foreign commerce. The Act, however, gave carriers operating solely within a state under a state certificate the right to transport between points within the state persons or property which are moving in interstate or foreign commerce. An amendment to the Act in 1962 removed the automatic authorization of intrastate carriers to also

---

[21] *Motor Bus & Motor Truck Transportation,* 140 ICC 685, 746 (1928).

[22] *Coordination of Motor Transportation,* 182 ICC 263, 386–87 (1932).

[23] *Regulation of Transportation Agencies,* 73d Cong., 2d Sess., Senate Doc. No. 152 (1934).

engage in interstate commerce. It provided that in the future a carrier operating within a single state must, in order to transport in interstate or foreign commerce, be specifically authorized to do so by the state authority upon an affirmative finding that the public convenience and necessity so require.[24]

Exemptions

There are numerous exemptions from the provisions of the Act. It is important to note, however, that the exempt carriers are not exempt from those provisions which empowered the Commission, now the Secretary of Transportation, to prescribe qualifications and maximum hours of service of employees or to make rules relating to safety of operation and standards of equipment.

One exemption is transportation by motor vehicle by or for railroads, water carriers, or freight forwarders in the performance of transfer, collection, or delivery service in terminal areas. Such transportation is regulated as part of the railroad, water-carrier, or freight-forwarder service of which it is part.

A second group of exemptions covers carriers whose operations are local in nature. Included in this group are school buses, taxicabs, hotel buses, trolley buses, and motor vehicles under the control of the Secretary of the Interior and used principally in transporting persons in or about national parks or monuments.

There is another group of exemptions put in at the behest of agricultural groups who were inclined to oppose regulation of motor transportation. These exemptions include: (1) motor vehicles owned and operated by a farmer and used in the transportation of his agricultural commodities and products thereof or in the transportation of his supplies to the farm; (2) motor vehicles controlled by a cooperative association as defined in the Agricultural Marketing Act; and (3) motor vehicles used in carrying ordinary livestock, fish (including shellfish), or agricultural commodities (not including manufactured products thereof), if such motor vehicles are not used in carrying any other property, or passengers, for compensation. By amendment of the Act in 1952, horticultural products were included in the agricultural exemptions.[25]

It is doubtful whether any real exemption is granted by listing motor vehicles owned and operated by farmers among the exemptions. Such vehicles are private carriers and are subject, therefore, only to the provisions relating to safety; and as we have noted, exempt carriers are not exempt from the safety provisions anyway. The exemption of motor carriers used exclusively in carrying livestock, fish, or agricultural and horti-

---

[24] Public Law 87–805. The background and purpose of this amendment is discussed in *Dugan Extension—Certificate of Registration*, 99 MCC 557 (1965).

[25] Public Law 472, 82d Cong., 2d Sess.

cultural commodities is a real exemption, since it includes common and contract carriers which would otherwise be subject to the provisions of the Act. This exemption does not include carriers which haul agricultural products from farms and have a return load of nonagricultural products. Controversy that has arisen with respect to the agricultural exemptions and later amendment of the provisions relating thereto will be discussed in the following chapter.[26]

Another exemption consists of trucks engaged exclusively in the transportation of newspapers. This represents a concession to newspaper publishers, who were opposed to the enactment of the law if their trucking operations were to be included in its provisions.

An amendment to the Act in 1938 added another exemption, namely, motor vehicles used exclusively in the transportation of persons or property when incidental to transportation by aircraft.

In addition to these exemptions there are two qualified or conditional exemptions: (1) transportation "wholly within a municipality or between contiguous municipalities or within a zone adjacent to and commercially a part of any such municipality"; and (2) the "casual, occasional, or reciprocal transportation" for compensation by any person not engaged in transportation by motor vehicle as a regular occupation or business. To transportation falling in these two categories the provisions of the Act do not apply unless and to the extent that the Commission finds regulation is necessary to carry out the policy of Congress. The second exemption is for the purpose of excluding unimportant transportation for hire. The exemption of transportation within a municipality, between contiguous municipalities, or in a zone adjacent to and commercially a part of a municipality is for the purpose of excluding purely local transportation which may be interstate in character because of the proximity of the cities to state boundaries.[27]

Transportation Agencies Regulated

Part II of the Interstate Commerce Act deals with four types of transportation agencies by motor vehicle: (1) common carriers, (2) contract carriers, (3) private carriers, and (4) transportation brokers. The reader should be familiar already with the distinction between the first three classes of carriers. Transportation brokers are individuals or organizations which arrange with shippers for transportation service but own no vehicles themselves and therefore arrange with others to perform the

---

[26] See pp. 690–93, infra.

[27] For examples of cases in which the Commission has defined the boundaries of commercial zones, see *New York, N.Y., Commercial Zone,* 1 MCC 665 (1937), 2 MCC 191 (1937); *Chicago Ill., Commercial Zone,* 1 MCC 673 (1937); *Philadelphia, Pa., Commercial Zone,* 17 MCC 533 (1939). A general rule for determining commercial zones was announced in *Commercial Zones and Terminal Areas,* 46 MCC 665 (1946).

actual transportation service. An appropriate system of regulation is set up for each of these groups.

Common Carriers

As might be expected, the system of regulation that is provided for common carriers is the most complete. Its major provisions may be summarized as follows:

1. The Commission may require reports of the carriers and may prescribe a uniform system of accounts.
2. Carriers must obtain certificates of public convenience and necessity before engaging in business or extending their operations to additional points or over additional routes. An appropriate "grandfather clause" accompanied this provision, which entitled carriers to a certificate as a matter of right who were in bona fide operation on June 1, 1935, and had operated continuously since that date. Certificates remain in effect indefinitely but may be suspended or revoked for willful violation of the Act or of an order of the Commission.
3. Consolidations, mergers, and other forms of control of motor carriers are made subject to Section 5 of Part I of the Act, which formerly applied only to combinations of rail carriers. A consolidation, merger, or unification must be approved by the Commission as "consistent with the public interest." Exemption from the requirements of this section was originally provided when the total number of vehicles involved was not more than 20. (For later change see p. 706, infra.) The purpose of this exemption was to simplify the Commission's task by confining its jurisdiction to the larger concerns, where questions of public interest are more likely to be involved. Special requirements are set up to govern acquisitions of control of motor carriers by railroads.[28] The Commission's approval of combinations and acquisitions of control carriers with it relief from the antitrust laws to the extent necessary to carry out the transaction.
4. The issuance of securities by motor carriers is made subject to the provisions of Section 20a of Part I of the Interstate Commerce Act, but here again exception is made in favor of the small concerns. Only if the securities proposed to be issued, together with those outstanding, exceed $1 million is the Commission's approval of new issues necessary.[29]
5. Surety bonds or insurance is required of all common carriers in such

---

[28] These requirements are discussed in a later chapter. See Chapter 36.

[29] Under the original Act the exemption was $500,000. The increase of the exemption to $1 million was made in 1952 in Public Law 492, 82d Cong., 2d Sess.

amounts as the Commission may require. Insurance protection may cover claims for loss or damage to shipments as well as injuries to, or damage to the property of, third parties. Self-insurance may be permitted under such rules as the Commission may prescribe.

6.   Rates and fares must be reasonable and not unjustly discriminatory.

7.   Publication of rates and fares is required, and there must be strict observance of tariffs.

8.   Notice of 30 days is required for changes in rates and fares.

9.   Proposed rates and fares may be suspended by the Commission for a period not exceeding seven months. The Commission, however, was not permitted to suspend the initial schedules of rates filed by the carriers when the Act became effective.

10.   The Commission has power to prescribe the maximum, minimum, or actual rate to be charged in lieu of a rate found unreasonable or otherwise unlawful.

11.   The Commission has jurisdiction over the adequacy of service of motor carriers.

Under the original Act, the Commission was empowered to establish requirements concerning the qualifications of employees of carriers, maximum hours of service, safety of operation, and standards of equipment. These matters all related to safety. By the Department of Transportation Act of 1966 these powers relating to safety were transferred to the new Department of Transportation. The Commission, therefore, no longer has jurisdiction over these matters.

Contract Carriers

Many provisions of the Act apply to contract carriers as well as to common carriers. Among such are those relating to the prescription of accounts, the making of reports to the Commission, control over consolidations and acquisitions of control, and the regulation of security issues.

There are differences, however, between the regulatory system that is applied to contract carriers and that which applies to common carriers. The more important of these differences are as follows:

1.   Contract carriers do not have to obtain "certificates of public convenience and necessity," but they must obtain "permits." The difference between a permit and a certificate is not a difference in name only. A permit is issued upon a showing that the proposed operation "will be consistent with the public interest." Presumably this is a less exacting requirement than proof of "public convenience and necessity," required for common-carrier operations.

2.   Contract carriers, unlike common carriers, do not have to provide bonds or insurance to cover loss and damage to goods carried. This is because contract carriers are not liable, as are common carriers, for the safe transportation of goods committed to their care. Contract

carriers, however, must provide bonds or insurance to cover liability for death or injury to persons, or damage to property, arising in the operation of motor vehicles.
3. The Commission has power to prescribe the minimum rates of contract carriers, but it may not prescribe maximum rates for them.

Under the original Act contract carriers were not required to publish their actual rates, but only their minimum rates or charges. An amendment to the Act in 1957 required contract carriers to publish their actual rates and to adhere to them.[30] This amendment resulted from complaints of common carriers that they were at a disadvantage in competing with contract carriers. Contract carriers knew what rates they had to meet because common-carrier rates were published; common carriers did not know precisely what rates they had to meet since the actual rates of the contract carriers were not published.

The somewhat lesser requirements imposed by the Act on contract carriers than on common carriers reflect the fact that they do not have the duties and obligations to the public which have long been imposed on common carriers. The theory of the Act is that contract carriers are to be regulated only so far as this may be necessary to make common-carrier regulation effective, or to prevent contract carriers from unduly interfering with the business of common carriers.

Private Carriers

By "private carriers" the Act means the not-for-hire carriers, that is, those transporting goods for their own use or as an incident to their business or occupation. No regulation is provided for private carriers beyond the requirement that they are subject to such regulations as the Commission, now the Secretary of Transportation, may prescribe regarding qualifications of and maximum hours of service of employees, safety of operation, and standards of equipment.

Transportation Brokers

Transportation brokers may not operate without a license from the Commission. The Commission may require accounts and reports, and may also prescribe rules and regulations to be observed by brokers for the protection of the public. Bonds or other security to insure financial responsibility are required.

The Use of Joint Boards

A novel feature of Part II of the Act is its provision for obtaining the aid of state officials. The Act provides that if an application or complaint

---

[30] Public Law 85–124.

filed with the Commission involves not more than three states, it shall be referred to a joint board consisting of a representative of the state commission of each state affected. Joint boards may be used at the discretion of the Commission in proceedings which involve more than three states. The members of joint boards are appointed by the Commission from nominees made by the state regulatory body or by the governor. A decision of a joint board becomes final if exceptions to its report are not made within twenty days after the service of the report upon the interested parties, or if the Commission does not review the case. If exceptions are filed to the report of the joint board, the Commission must consider the same and, either upon the same record or upon the record as supplemented by further hearing, make such order as may be appropriate.[31]

Two reasons may be given for calling upon state officials in this manner to help administer a federal law. In the first place, it relieves the Commission of much work. The number of applications and complaints under the Act has been very large and will continue to be so. It expedites the disposition of these cases to have them referred to joint boards. In the second place, the joint-board device is a means of decentralizing the administration of the Act and of placing responsibility for decision upon those closer to the matter involved. The operations of many interstate bus and truck operators are essentially local in nature.

DIFFERENCES BETWEEN RAILROAD AND MOTOR-CARRIER REGULATION

A comparison of the provisions of Part II of the Act with those of Part I reveals differences between the regulatory systems set up for motor carriers and for railroads. Certain of these differences should be mentioned.

1. The regulation of motor carriers is more complicated because of the existence of contract carriers, private carriers, and transportation brokers in addition to the common carriers. Railroads are practically always common carriers; hence one system of regulation can be applied to all of them.
2. Many motor carriers are exempt from regulation.
3. The large number of small concerns in the motor-carrier field makes the partial exemption of small operators necessary if regulation is not to be too cumbersome. This, as we have seen, is the reason for the exemption of small carriers from the requirements concerning security issues and from those relating to consolidations and acquisitions of control.

---

[31] For discussions of joint boards see Paul G. Kauper, "Utilization of State Commissioners in the Administration of the Federal Motor Carrier Act," 34 *Michigan Law Review* 37 (1935); James C. Nelson, "Joint-Board Procedure under the Motor Carrier Act," 13 *Journal of Land and Public Utility Economics* 97 (1937).

4. Part II of the Act contains provisions requiring motor carriers to obtain insurance or other liability protection. No such requirement is imposed on rail carriers. The reason for the difference is that many of the small motor carriers, of which there are thousands, are financially weak and sometimes unable to meet judgments against them; railroads are larger concerns and are ordinarily able to meet judgments which may be rendered against them by the courts.

5. The Commission has no power to prevent the abandonment of operations by a motor carrier if the carrier desires to discontinue operations entirely.[32]

6. The Act does not require motor carriers of property to establish through routes and joint rates with other motor carriers,[33] although such through routes and joint rates may be voluntarily established. Motor carriers of persons, however, may be required to establish through routes and joint fares with one another.

7. Motor carriers are not subject to a long-and-short-haul clause. This is not a discrimination against rail carriers in favor of motor carriers, as is sometimes alleged. The difference in treatment arises simply from the fact that long-and-short-haul discrimination has been a rare occurrence in the motor-carrier industry. The reason for this lies, of course, in the absence of a large mass of constant expenses in the motor-carrier business. If long-and-short-haul discrimination makes its appearance in the motor-carrier industry, there will be a demand, and justly so, for the enactment of a long-and-short-haul clause.

8. The Interstate Commerce Commission is denied any power to control intrastate rates. It will be recalled that after the Minnesota and Shreveport cases in 1913 and 1914, the power of the Interstate Commerce Commission to change purely intrastate rail rates when necessary to remove discrimination against a point outside the state was recognized by the courts.[34] The Transportation Act of 1920, furthermore, empowered the Commission to raise the general level of intrastate rail rates to the level of interstate rates when the former were so low as to amount to a discrimination against interstate commerce.[35] Part II of the Act contains no similar provision. In fact, it provides that "nothing in this part shall empower the Commission to prescribe, or in any manner regulate, the rate, fare, or charge for intrastate transportation . . . for the purpose of removing discrimination against interstate commerce or for any other purpose whatever." This prevents the application of the Shreveport doctrine to motor-carrier rates.

---

[32] *Towns of Bristol & Hill, N.H.* v. *Boston & Maine Transportation Co.*, 20 MCC 581 (1939).

[33] *Hausman Steel Co.* v. *Seaboard Freight Lines*, 32 MCC 31 (1942).

[34] See pp. 286–87, supra.

[35] See pp. 249–50, supra.

9. Congress did not originally empower the Commission to award reparations to shippers on account of unreasonable rates charged, but this
preferred treatment of motor carriers was later removed. (See p. 717,
infra.)

ADMINISTRATION OF THE ACT

The large number of carriers has made the task of regulating motor
carriers a burdensome one. The Commission had to dispose of more than
89,000 applications for certificates or permits under the "grandfather
clause," and since then it has handled many thousands of cases involving
motor carriers. Cases involving applications for new operating authority,
consolidation and merger cases, and cases involving rates of motor carriers have been the most numerous. In the following chapter we shall examine some of the problems that have arisen in the administration of the
Act and discuss the policies which the Commission has adopted on major
issues that have come before it.

SELECTED REFERENCES

There is a good discussion of the motor-carrier problem as it appeared in
the 1930s, together with a description of state regulatory experience, in the
Federal Coordinator's report, *Regulation of Transportation Agencies,* 73d
Cong., 2d Sess., Senate Doc. No. 152 (1934), particularly pp. 13–35, 45–49, and
Appendix B.

Good descriptions of the Motor Carrier Act of 1935 are James C. Nel-
son, "The Motor Act of 1935," 44 *Journal of Political Economy* 464 (1936);
John J. George, "The Federal Motor Carrier Act of 1935," 21 *Cornell Law
Quarterly* 249 (1936); Edward A. Haid, "Regulation of Motor Carriers," 23
Washington University Law Quarterly 1 (1937); Russell E. Westmeyer, *Economics of Transportation* (New York: Prentice-Hall, 1952), chap. xix; Stuart
Daggett, *Principles of Inland Transportation* (4th ed.; New York: Harper,
1955) chap. xxxi. For the legislative history of the Act, see Warren H. Wagner,
A Legislative History of the Motor Carrier Act, 1935 (Denton, Md.: Rue Publishing Co., 1935). There is also a discussion of the legislative background of
the Act in Warren G. Magnusson, "The Motor Carrier Act of 1935: A Legis-
lator Looks at the Law," 31 *George Washington Law Review* 37 (1962).

The development of state and federal regulation is described in William J.
Hudson and James A. Constantin, *Motor Transportation: Principles and Practices* (New York: Ronald Press, 1958), chap. xix; and Charles A. Taff, *Commercial Motor Transportation* (Homewood, Ill.: Richard D. Irwin, 4th ed.,
1969), chap. xvii.

Chapter 30

PROBLEMS AND POLICIES IN
MOTOR-CARRIER REGULATION

In treating the problems encountered in the administration of the Motor Carrier Act, and in describng the policies which have been formulated by the Commission in carrying out its provisions, we shall confine ourselves to matters of particular importance, or to problems which are peculiar to the motor-carrier industry, and to instances in which different policies have been followed than have commonly been applied in the regulation of railroads.

DISTINGUISHING BETWEEN PRIVATE AND FOR-HIRE TRANSPORTATION

Private carriers are not regulated, except as to matters which are related to safety, while carriers for hire are regulated as either common or contract carriers. At first thought it would seem that no difficulty should be encountered in distinguishing between private and for-hire transportation. The private operator is not in the business of transporting property for hire; he is ordinarily transporting commodities which he owns in the furtherance of his business or occupation. Mere ownership of the load, however, does not make one a private carrier under all circumstances. Some early cases came before the Commission in which the owner of a truck took orders for coal, purchased it at the mine, transported it to his customers, and charged them the mine price plus an amount as compensation for hauling. In these cases the Commission held that the trucker was a common carrier, since his main interest was in the transportation of the coal and in the compensation which he received for this service.[1]

Carriers for hire, seeking to restrict the transport operations of industries performing their own transportation service, contended that whenever a concern transporting its own goods clearly receives compensation for the transportation, it is a carrier for hire and not a private carrier. Transportation for compensation is clearly involved, they argued, when the goods transported by the industry are sold to a customer at

---

[1] *Carpenter Common Carrier Application*, 2 MCC 85 (1937); *Monninger Common Carrier Application*, 2 MCC 501 (1937).

factory price plus the regular railroad or motor-carrier rates or any other amount which varies with the quantity of transportation service performed. The Commission refused to apply this "compensation test" in determining the status of an operator. In other words, the Commission refused to hold that the status of a carrier is determined by whether or not he receives compensation in some form for the transportation service performed. Instead the Commission applied what is called the "primary-business test." If the primary business of the operator is the manufacture or sale of goods, and if the transportation service which he performs is incidental thereto, the transportation is private and not for hire. The leading case in establishing the primary-business test is known as the *Woitishek Case*.[2] The principle was later reaffirmed in the *Lenoir Chair Case*, where the Commission said:

> If the facts establish that the primary business of an operator is the supplying of transportation for compensation then the carrier's status is established though the operator may be the owner, at the time, of the goods transported and may be transporting them for the purpose of sale. . . . If, on the other hand, the primary business of an operator is found to be manufacturing or some other noncarrier commercial enterprise, then it must be determined whether the motor operations are in bona fide furtherance of the primary business or whether they are conducted as a related or secondary enterprise with the purpose of profiting from the transportation performed.[3]

The policy of the *Lenoir Chair Case* was upheld by the courts.[4] In fact, the principle was written into the statute by a 1958 amendment to the Act which provided that no person engaged in a business enterprise other than transportation could transport property in interstate commerce by motor vehicle unless such transportation was "within the scope, and in furtherance, of a primary business enterprise" of such person.[5]

Pseudo-Private Transport. The Commission has been plagued by efforts of for-hire carriers to masquerade as private carriers and thus to avoid regulation. Two devices to accomplish this purpose are pertinent to our discussion at this point. One is through "buy-and-sell operations" previously mentioned. This practice has been common on the part of legitimate private carriers who are seeking return loads of otherwise empty vehicles. Since private carriers are not ordinarily permitted to engage in for-hire operations, they sometimes purchase commodities that may be available for a return movement and carry them back to the locality of their primary business operation where the goods are sold. Any profit realized over the purchase price serves to reduce the cost of returning the vehicles to the base of operations. It is not always easy to

---

[2] *Woitishek Common Carrier Application*, 42 MCC 193 (1943).

[3] *Lenoir Chair Co. Contract Carrier Application*, 51 MCC 65, 75 (1949).

[4] *Brooks Transportation Co. v. United States*, 93 F. Supp. 517 (1950), 340 U.S. 925 (1951).

[5] Sec. 203 (c).

distinguish between such spurious buy-and-sell operations and the transportation of goods as part of a bona fide commercial enterprise. In one highly controversial case a Commission decision finding a buy-and-sell operation to be unlawful was reversed by a federal court[6] and the court's decision was sustained by the Supreme Court.[7]

A second device for disguising for-hire transportation as private transportation is through leasing of vehicles and drivers to shippers. The transportation services then performed have the appearance of bona fide private transportation.

In attempting to prevent wholesale evasion of regulation through such arrangements, the Commission early established the rule that the shipper must have control over the vehicles and the drivers if the operation is to be genuine private transportation. If control remained in the parties furnishing the vehicles or drivers, the transportation service was in reality that of a for-hire carrier.[8] Later the Commission developed a further requirement, namely, that the shipper must have assumed the risks normally involved in private transportation. If he has shifted these risks to the owners and lessors of the vehicles, he has contracted for transportation services, and the operations are not those of a private carrier.

In one case involving this principle, the Commission held that the leasing arrangement entered into by a furniture manufacturer did not constitute private transportation because substantial risks had been shifted to the lessors.[9] The company had leased vehicles from owner-operators who acted as drivers. They were paid on a fixed mileage basis. The Commission noted that the furniture company had shifted the risks associated with ownership of the vehicles. It was also protected from the risks of increased gasoline and fuel costs as well as other costs related to operation of the vehicles. The owner-operators bore the risks of nonutilization of the equipment since they received neither rent nor wages when the vehicles were not in use. The decision of the Commission in this case was sustained by the Supreme Court in *United States* v. *Drum*.[10]

The principle approved in the *Drum Case* presages future difficulty. Any lease of equipment by a manufacturer involves a shifting of some risks to the owner of the vehicles that would be borne by the manufacturer if he owned the equipment. The courts and the Commission, however, apparently do not intend to carry the "assumption of risk" test that far. The Commission recognizes that there are leasing arrangements compati-

---

[6] *Shannon* v. *United States*, 219 F. Supp. 781 (1963).

[7] *Red Ball Motor Freight* v. *Shannon*, 377 U.S. 311 (1964). For a case illustrating the difficulties involved in applying the "primary business" test, see *Martin E. Hansen —Investigation of Operations*, 113 MCC 362 (1971).

[8] The leading case in the establishment of this principle is *H. B. Church Truck Service Co.*, 27 MCC 191 (1940).

[9] *Oklahoma Furniture Mfg. Co.—Investigation of Operations*, 79 MCC 403 (1959).

[10] 368 U.S. 370 (1962).

ble with private-carrier operations.[11] Border-line cases are bound to arise in which the private-carrier status of the operation will be in doubt. This is likely to remain true as long as the "assumption of risk" test is not rigidly applied or definitely qualified.[12]

CONTRACT CARRIER OR COMMON CARRIER

Since contract carriers are regulated differently than common carriers, a clear distinction between the two types of operation is necessary. In the last analysis, the essential attribute distinguishing common carriage from contract carriage is the presence or absence of a holding-out to serve the public generally. "Each case requiring a determination whether or not common carriage exists, when brought to its irreducible minimum, turns finally on the question whether or not a holding out to the public generally is shown."[13] The Commission found, however, that the line of distinction between common and contract carriage was "of necessity, indefinite, inexact, and difficult to fix in many individual instances."[14] In dealing with the problem the Commission attempted to lay down certain criteria that would aid in the proper classification of a particular operation.

In one proceeding the Commission described contract carriage as follows: "A contract carrier is essentially an independent contractor whose undertaking is defined and limited by an individual contract which calls for a service specialized to meet the peculiar needs of a particular shipper or a limited number of shippers and operates to make the carrier virtually a part of each shipper's organization."[15] In this description it will be noted that, in addition to the individual contract requirement, two features of contract carriage are mentioned: (1) the specialized nature of the service and (2) the limited number of shippers served.[16] Both of these characteristics have played an important part in determining whether an operator was a common carrier or a contract carrier.

Specialization in type of service, the Commission said, may be evidenced "(*a*) by the use of special equipment required by the commodities transported or adapted to the convenience of the shipper, (*b*) by the transportation only of certain commodities or of commodities the transportation of which requires the use of special equipment, equipment accessories, or specially trained personnel, (*c*) by the strict observance of

---

[11] *Lovell—Investigation of Operations*, 92 MCC 728 (1963).

[12] An interesting case involving the "assumption of risk" test is *Keller Industries, Inc.—Declaratory Order*, 103 MCC 520 (1966), 107 MCC 75 (1968), 311 F. Supp. 384 (1970).

[13] *Craig Contract Carrier Application*, 31 MCC 705, 708–9 (1941).

[14] *Fischbach Trucking Co. Common Carrier Application*, 61 MCC 539, 546 (1953).

[15] *Transportation Activities of Midwest Transfer Co.*, 49 MCC 383, 390 (1949).

[16] Specialized nature of services does not preclude a finding of common-carrier service, as specialized service may be offered to the public generally.

shipper-designated loading and unloading hours, or by other similar practices."[17]

The number of contracts held by a carrier has also been significant in determining whether a carrier was a contract carrier or was in fact a common carrier. In one proceeding the Commission found that Contract Steel Carriers, Inc., holding authority to operate as a contract carrier, had unlawfully converted its operations into those of a common carrier.[18] In the course of a few years it had increased the number of contracts held from 13 to 69. This decision was carried to the courts and ultimately to the Supreme Court of the United States, which held, with Justices Frankfurter and Harlan dissenting, that the Commission had erred and that "A contract carrier is free to aggressively search for new business within the limits of his license."[19]

This decision precluded a consideration of the number of contracts in determining whether a carrier was a bona fide contract carrier or was in reality a common carrier. The Commission considered that this decision practically obliterated the distinction between common and contract carriage, since a contract carrier, by negotiating an unlimited number of contracts, would be offering his services, in fact, to the general public. The Commission accordingly recommended to Congress that the Act be amended to define more precisely the term "contract carrier."[20]

Congress responded to the Commission's request by an amendment to the Act in 1957 specifying that a contract carrier must be transporting "under continuing contracts with one person or a limited number of persons either (*a*) for the furnishing of transportation services through the assignment of motor vehicles for a continuing period of time to the exclusive use of each person served or (*b*) for the furnishing of transportation services designed to meet the distinct need of each individual customer."[21] The definition thus emphasizes that specialized services and a limited number of patrons are necessary for qualification as a contract carrier. The amendment also provided that the Commission may specify in a permit issued to a contract carrier "the person or persons and the number or class thereof for which the contract carrier may perform transportation service." The amendment also required the Commission to examine each outstanding permit and to revoke the permit and issue a certificate of public convenience and necessity as a common carrier to those carriers who, on the effective date of the Act, were found to have been operating as common carriers.

Although a "limited number" of contracts is an essential for qualifica-

---

[17] 49 MCC 383, 396–97 (1949).

[18] *Motor Ways Tariff Bureau* v. *Steel Transportation Co., Inc.,* 62 MCC 413 (1954).

[19] *United States* v. *Contract Steel Carriers, Inc.,* 350 U.S. 409, 412 (1956).

[20] *Annual Report, 1956,* pp. 162–64.

[21] Public Law 85–163.

tion as a contract carrier, Congress did not specify the number permissible.[22] The matter is left to the discretion of the Commission. The Commission recognizes that the number of contracts permissible in order to retain one's status as a contract carrier must vary with the circumstances. It has held that a large number of shippers which are members of a limited class may be regarded as a "limited number of persons" if the service is highly specialized to meet the particular needs of members of that limited class.[23] For less specialized services the policy which the Commission intends to pursue was set forth in the *Umthun Case*, where the Commission said: "Those contract carriers whose services do not possess such a high degree of specialization . . . are hereby put on notice that their attempts to expand their operations by offering service to more than six or eight separate shippers will be scrutinized with great care to insure that they are not thereby placing themselves in a position to serve more than a limited number of persons . . ."[24] In several cases the Commission has found certain contract carriers to have exceeded the "limited number of shippers" requirement and has required them to bring their operations within the limitations or apply for certificates to operate as common carriers.[25]

THE AGRICULTURAL EXEMPTIONS

We noted in the preceding chapter that the for-hire movement of agricultural commodities is exempt from the Act under some conditions. This exemption, as it stood after some minor amendments, applied to "motor vehicles used in carrying property consisting of ordinary livestock, fish (including shell fish), or agricultural commodities (not including manufactured products thereof), if such motor vehicles are not used in carrying other property, or passengers, for compensation." By amendment in 1952, horticultural commodities were also brought within the exemption. We shall speak of these exemptions as the "agricultural exemptions," although they are somewhat broader than that term implies.

The agricultural exemptions have raised difficult questions of interpretation as well as the fundamental issue of whether or not the exemptions are justified at all. Problems of interpretation have involved the question of what are "agricultural commodities," and also the distinction between agricultural commodities, which are exempt, and "manufactured products thereof," which are not exempt. The qualification to the exemption found in the clause "if such motor vehicles are not used in carrying any other

---

[22] Some states prescribe the maximum number in the statute. Connecticut specifies four as the limit. See *Anthony Angliera, Inc.* v. *Loughlin*, 181 A 2d 596, 599 (1962).

[23] *Connell Transport Co. Extension—New York, N.Y.*, 91 MCC 113 (1962).

[24] *Umthun Trucking Co. Extension—Phosphatic Feed Supplements*, 91 MCC 691, 697 (1962).

[25] E.g., *Contractors Cargo Co.—Extension of Operations*, 96 MCC 306 (1964); *Gallagher & Sons* v. *Cleveland General Transport*, 98 MCC 356 (1965).

property, or passengers, for compensation" has been held by the courts to mean "if such vehicles are not used *at the same time* in carrying any other property, or passengers, for compensation."[26] Any other interpretation would have led to absurd results.

The term "agricultural products" has been defined rather broadly by the Commission as "all products raised or produced on farms by tillage and cultivation of the soil (such as vegetables, fruits, and nuts); forest products; live poultry and bees; and commodities produced by ordinary livestock, live poultry, and bees (such as milk, wool, eggs, and honey)."[27]

The greatest difficulty in interpreting the agricultural exemption provisions of the Act has involved the distinction between agricultural commodities and manufactured products thereof. At first the Commission was inclined to interpret the terms in such a way as to exclude from the exemption products which had undergone very simple packaging or processing operations. Thus washed vegetables packaged in cellophane bags were at first held not to be within the exemption.[28] The Commission contended also that beheaded shrimps were not within the exemption because they were not in the original form in which they were taken from the water. The courts refused to sustain the Commission in the latter position, however.[29] The Commission thereupon broadened the application of the exemption to include even quick-frozen packaged shrimp and other fish.[30]

The Commission also broadened the scope of the term "agricultural commodities" to include treated or processed commodities, provided such processing had not given them new forms, qualities, or properties, or resulted in combinations. In *Determination of Exempted Agricultural Commodities*, commonly known as the Determination Case, the Commission enumerated many commodities which it considered to be exempt, and others which it considered not exempt because they were manufactured products.[31] Subsequent court decisions forced the Commission to include some commodities as exempt which it had considered to be manufactured products.[32] Finally, in a case involving dressed or frozen poultry the Supreme Court held that these products were within the exemption.[33] In so doing, the Court adopted a new test for determining when an agricultural

---

[26] *Interstate Commerce Commission* v. *Dunn*, 166 F. 2d 116 (1948); *Interstate Commerce Commission* v. *Service Trucking Co.*, 91 Fed. Supp. 533 (1950), 186 F. 2d 400 (1951).

[27] *Determination of Exempted Agricultural Commodities*, 52 MCC 511, 519 (1951).

[28] *Harwood Contract Carrier Application*, 47 MCC 597 (1947).

[29] *Interstate Commerce Commission* v. *Love*, 77 Fed. Supp. 63 (1948), 172 F. 2d 224 (1949).

[30] *Monark Egg Corp. Contract Carrier Application*, 52 MCC 576 (1951).

[31] 52 MCC 511 (1951).

[32] E.g., *Interstate Commerce Commission* v. *Wagner*, 112 Fed. Supp. 109 (1953); *Interstate Commerce Commission* v. *Yeary Transfer Co.*, 104 Fed. Supp. 245 (1952), 202 F. 2d 151 (1953); and reports of the Commission on reconsideration in the Determination Case, 62 MCC 87 (1953) and 74 MCC 549 (1958).

[33] *East Texas Motor Freight Lines, Inc.* v. *Frozen Food Express*, 351 U.S. 49 (1956).

commodity was exempt and when it was a "manufactured product thereof" which came to be known as the "substantial identity test." "[Where] the commodity retains a continuing substantial identity through the processing stage we cannot say that it has been 'manufactured'. . . ."[34] In conformity with the substantial identity test, quick-frozen fruits and vegetables were later found within the exemption.[35]

Before the decision of the Supreme Court in the *Frozen Food Express Case*, the Commission had recommended that the agricultural exemptions be limited to the movement of the commodities from producing point to market or first processing point.[36] Congress, however, responded in a different way to the suggestion. It decided simply to call a halt in the expansion of the list of exempt commodities. This was done in the Transportation Act of 1958 by "freezing," with some modification, the list of exempt commodities which the Bureau of Motor Carriers had issued in 1958. Returned to regulation, however, were frozen fruits, frozen berries, frozen vegetables, cocoa beans, coffee beans, tea, bananas, hemp, imported wool, wool tops and noils, and wool waste which has been carded, spun, woven, or knitted. On the other hand, specific exemption was granted to fish or shellfish, cooked or uncooked, frozen or fresh, but not treated for preserving. Presumably any processed agricultural commodities not listed by the Bureau of Motor Carriers or specifically mentioned in the statute will continue to be subject to the substantial identity test.

The application of the substantial identity test brought many additional commodities under the agricultural exemption. Since many of these consisted of processed agricultural products, the exemptions covered extensive movements from processing points and factories to distributors and retailers.

Justification of the agricultural commodity exemptions rests upon the nature of the movement of agricultural products from farm to market or processing point. These commodities are often perishable; their movement is seasonal; they require a large number of vehicles in the crop-moving season, which is often of short duration. Operations of this kind do not lend themselves to the type of regulation that is appropriate for carriers of general merchandise over regular routes, or even for specialized carriers whose operations are not seasonal. Exemption of agricultural commodities from regulation when moving from farm to first market or processing point is justified. The movement of processed agricultural products from processing points in the regular channels of commerce does not seem to require special treatment. We have already noted that the Interstate Commerce Commission has recommended such a limitation of the exemptions. In 1961 the Commission suggested that this could be

[34] Ibid., p. 54.
[35] *Home Transfer & Storage Co.* v. *United States,* 141 Fed. Supp. 599 (1956).
[36] *Annual Report, 1955,* p. 128; *1956,* p. 162; *1957,* pp. 138–39.

accomplished by restricting the exemptions to movements in vehicles or combinations of vehicles having three axles or less.[37] It is thought that this would automatically limit the exemptions to farm-to-market movements since the economics of the situation demands that movement from markets and processing points be in vehicles having more than three axles.

The existence of the agricultural exemptions, insofar as they exempt the flow of these commodities beyond the first marketing or processing point, tends to weaken common carriage. It does so partly because of the traffic diverted from common carriers, and partly because the exempt commodities are a source of back-haul traffic for many private carriers of manufactured commodities. As the Commission has observed, "Private carriage would not, in many instances, be financially feasible without such backhauls."[38]

Agricultural interests stoutly defend the agricultural exemptions, even to the movement of processed agricultural products in the channels of commerce. In part, this is based on the belief that unregulated transportation is cheaper, as it may be, and that the farmer benefits therefrom. Any conclusions regarding the desirability of maintaining the agricultural exemptions in their present form that rest upon lower costs to the shipper should be accompanied by an analysis of the reasons for lower costs. Lower costs may be due to the nature of the operation, and irrelevant so far as the issue of regulation is concerned; they may be due to causes which point to the desirability of regulation; they may be due to causes which indicate defects and shortcomings in the regulatory system which should be remedied.

Believing that it may be politically impossible to eliminate the agricultural commodity exemptions, some parties have advocated that the same exemptions be extended to rail and water carriers in the interest of equal treatment of all modes of transport. This policy was recommended by President Kennedy in his Transportation Message of 1962,[39] and was embodied in bills introduced in Congress thereafter. The proposal has not been enacted. This solution of the problem of the agricultural exemptions could easily lead to other and serious problems.[40]

EXEMPTION OF AGRICULTURAL COOPERATIVES

Motor-vehicle operations of agricultural cooperative associations are exempt from regulation. Since such operations are akin to private trans-

---

[37] *Annual Report, 1961,* p. 185. See also *Annual Report, 1962,* p. 203.

[38] *Annual Report, 1962,* p. 202.

[39] 87th Cong., 2d Sess., House Doc. No. 384 (1962), p. 4.

[40] Particularly the weakening of the Commission's control over competition between railroads as well as over interagency competition, and the weakening of the Commission's power to deal with unjust discrimination and undue preference and prejudice.

portation it is logical that they be exempt. If agricultural cooperatives confined themselves to the transportation of exempt commodities, no special exemption would be necessary. It is customary, however, for cooperatives to transport farm supplies on return hauls and such commodities are not included in the commodity exemptions.

The agricultural cooperative exemption has been used to cloak illegal for-hire operations. So-called agricultural cooperative organizations have been created to engage in transportation operations when they were not real cooperatives. Likewise, some genuine cooperatives have engaged in general for-hire transportation services for nonmembers.

In order to qualify for exemption from regulation an agricultural cooperative must conform to the requirements of a farm cooperative as defined in the Agricultural Marketing Act of 1929. This means, among other things, that (1) its members must be producers of agricultural products; (2) it must be controlled by its members; (3) it must be engaged in marketing farm products of, or furnishing farm business services to, its members; (4) it may not deal in farm products, farm supplies, or farm business services for nonmembers in an amount greater than the amount of such business transacted for members.

There have been numerous cases in which the cooperatives did not conform to these requirements and so did not qualify for exemption.[41]

Agricultural cooperatives often find themselves with a back-haul problem. To some extent they transport farm supplies and other commodities for the use of members. There is no controversy about this. But if such traffic is insufficient to utilize their vehicles when returning from a haul of farm products they may seek other traffic on a for-hire basis, thus coming into competition with common carriers. The Commission, in addressing itself to this problem in *Machinery Haulers Association* v. *Agricultural Commodity Service*, said: "Neither the express language of the act nor the legislative history thereof . . . warrants the conclusion that Congress intended to allow agricultural cooperatives to become general transportation companies by performing for-hire transportation for anyone or for any purpose."[42] The Commission took the position that such movement must be incidental to and necessary for the farming activities of its members, that is, the permissible back-haul traffic must be "functionally related" to the members' agricultural activities. In effect, the Commission's interpretation of the agricultural cooperatives exemption was to the effect that the cooperative could not transport commodities unrelated to farm operations on a for-hire basis. In *Northwest Agricultural Cooperative Association* v. *Interstate Commerce Commission*, a United States Court of

---

[41] E.g., *Interstate Commerce Commission* v. *Nelson Cooperative Marketing Association*, 209 F. Supp. 697 (1962); *Agricultural Transportation Association of Texas Investigation*, 96 MCC 293 (1964), 102 MCC 527 (1966); *Interstate Commerce Commission* v. *Southwest Marketing Association*, 315 F. Supp. 805 (1970).

[42] 86 MCC 5, 24 (1961).

Appeals, although accepting the "incidental and necessary" test of the legitimacy of for-hire transportation by a cooperative, held that the transportation of commodities on a for-hire basis that were unrelated to farm activities were "incidental and necessary"—incidental because limited to back-haul traffic, and necessary "because it is not economically feasible to operate the trucks empty on return trips, and because the additional income obtained is no more than that required to render the performance of the cooperative's primary farm transportation service financially practicable."[43] The Commission believed that this decision opened the way for farm cooperatives to enter the general transportation business without Commission authorization and to the detriment of common carriers. The Commission asked Congress to address itself to the problem. Congress eventually responded by amending the statute in 1968.[44]

The 1968 amendment provided that nonmember transportation by a cooperative "shall be limited to that which is incidental to its primary transportation operation and necessary for its effective performance and shall in no event exceed 15 percentum of its total interstate transportation services in any fiscal year, measured in terms of tonnage." The Commission has interpreted the "incidental and necessary" requirement to mean that the for-hire transportation for nonmembers "must, as a minimum, be rendered so as to equalize or prevent an economic loss which would have resulted from an otherwise empty movement of a vehicle employed on the prior or subsequent trip in member transportation."[45]

The 1968 amendment thus fell short of limiting the transportation for nonmembers to farm products, farm supplies, and other farm-related traffic as the Commission had originally proposed. It recognizes the principle of the *Northwest Agricultural Cooperative Case* that cooperatives may transport nonfarm traffic for nonmembers as a back-haul, thus reducing the cost of transportation of the farm cooperative traffic. As interpreted, however, the amendment does not authorize general for-hire transportation services merely because the cooperative's activities would otherwise be unprofitable.[46] The nonfarm nonmember traffic must be coordinated with membership shipments in the reverse direction.

"GRANDFATHER-CLAUSE" CASES

Under the "grandfather clause," certificates or permits were to be granted upon a showing of "bona fide" operation on the "critical" date— June 1, 1935, in the case of common carriers; July 1, 1935, in the case of contract carriers—and continuously since, except for interruptions of

[43] 350 F. 2d 252, 255 (1965).

[44] Public Law 90–433.

[45] *Implementation of Public Law 90–433*, 108 MCC 799, 827 (1969).

[46] See *Interstate Commerce Commission* v. *Milk Producers Marketing Co.*, 405 F 2d 639, 641–42 (1969).

service over which the carrier had no control. No proof of public convenience and necessity or of consistency with the public interest was required under the "grandfather clause." The object of the "grandfather clause," of course, was to protect carriers who were already in operation at the time the Act was passed.

For several years after the passage of the Motor Carrier Act the principal activity of the Commission under the Act was disposing of applications for operating authority under the provisions of the "grandfather clause." Since this phase of the Commission's activities is over, we shall consider the Commission's policies in "grandfather" cases only in so far as they have a bearing on the present condition of the industry.

It was natural that carriers applying for certificates under the "grandfather clause" should seek as broad and extensive operating authority thereunder as possible. It was within the spirit and intent of the Act, however, to hold such operating authority to the operations that were actually carried on by the applicant on the "grandfather" date and subsequent thereto. The Commission interpreted the Act rather strictly to prevent the granting of operating authority more extensive than that acually exercised on and after the "grandfather" date. In the case of regular-route common carriers it was naturally the practice to restrict operating rights under the "grandfather clause" to the routes and to the points which the carrier had served.

Some difficulty was encountered in connection with "grandfather" applications of irregular-route or anywhere-for-hire carriers. If they had held themselves out to transport over an extensive area but had actually transported to and from a limited number of points, should their operating rights under the "grandfather clause" be restricted to the points actually served, or should they extend to other points? If a carrier had held himself out to transport general commodities but had, in fact, transported only a limited number of commodities, should his operating authority embrace commodities generally or only those which he had actually carried? It can be seen that some restriction was necessary to prevent wide-open authorization far beyond the service which an irregular-route carrier had performed. On the other hand, it might be unduly restricting the operations of an anywhere-for-hire carrier to confine his operations to points to or from which he had actually transported goods.

The Commission was upheld in restricting operating authority under the "grandfather clause" to areas or to points actually served.[47] If the nature of the carrier's business, however, was such as to require rather broad authorization, even to points not actually served in the past, such authorization was granted by the Commission. The Supreme Court in one

---

[47] *Loving* v. *United States*, 32 Fed. Supp. 464 (1940). See also *United States* v. *Carolina Carriers Corp.*, 315 U.S. 475 (1942), where territorial restrictions of an irregular-route operator were upheld.

case upheld the Commission, over the protest of railroads, in granting authority under the "grandfather clause" to a transporter of motor vehicles by the "drive-away," or caravanning, method to serve all points within a state, although but few points had actually been served. "While the test of 'bona fide operation' within a specified 'territory' includes 'actual rather than potential or simulated service,' it does not necessarily restrict future operations to the precise points or areas already served," said the Court. "The characteristics of the transportation service rendered may of necessity have made trips to any specified locality irregular or sporadic."[48]

Although the Commission was upheld in imposing territorial restrictions on irregular-route operators, it received a setback in connection with certain commodity restrictions which it included in a certificate under the "grandfather clause."[49] The Commission had confined the authority of an irregular-route operator to the transportation of certain commodities which it had previously handled, although the carrier had held itself out as a general carrier of freight. In the words of the Court, ". . . if the applicant has carried a wide variety of general commodities, he cannot necessarily be denied the right to carry others of the same class merely because he never carried them before."[50] The Court went on to say: "The Commission may not atomize his prior service, product by product, so as to restrict the scope of his operations, where there is substantial evidence in addition to his holding out that he was in *'bona fide* operation' as a 'common carrier' of a large group of commodities or of a whole class or classes of property."[51]

In granting permits under the "grandfather clause" to contract carriers, the Commission refused to limit such carriers to the service of particular shippers,[52] but it commonly limited contract carriers to the same general class of shippers, such as retail food stores,[53] chain department stores,[54] or packing houses.[55] This type of restriction is commonly known as a "Keystone restriction," from the leading case which involved the Keystone Transportation Company.[56]

Although a rather strict limitation of operating authority under the

---

[48] *Alton R. R. Co.* v. *United States*, 315 U.S. 15 (1942), p. 21.

[49] *United States* v. *Carolina Freight Carriers Corp.*, 315 U.S. 475 (1942), and the companion case, *Howard Hall Co.* v. *United States*, 315 U.S. 495 (1942).

[50] 315 U.S. 475, 483.

[51] Ibid., pp. 483–84.

[52] *Motor Convoy, Inc., Contract Carrier Application*, 2 MCC 197 (1937).

[53] *Keystone Transportation Co. Contract Carrier Application*, 19 MCC 475 (1939).

[54] *Koelker Contract Carrier Application*, 22 MCC 474 (1940).

[55] *Clancy Common Carrier Application*, 24 MCC 727 (1940).

[56] See n. 53, supra. When granting permits for new operations, the Commission may, under the Act as amended in 1957, impose restrictions or limitations respecting the person or persons for whom a contract carrier may provide service.

"grandfather clause" is doubtless necessary in order to prevent wholesale evasion of the requirement that public convenience and necessity or consistency with the public interest be shown in connection with new operations, these limitations and restrictions undoubtedly interfere with efficient operation of motor carriers. Commodity restrictions may also interfere with efficient operation. Regular-route common carriers are sometimes compelled by restrictions on their operating authority to operate over circuitous routes and are barred from more direct routes. Others may not be authorized to serve intermediate points on their routes, while others may be authorized to carry traffic to, from, or between intermediate points but not between their termini. Some carriers may carry traffic in one direction but have no authority to transport return loads. The Keystone restriction, by confining contract carriers to the service of a particular class of customers, may prevent an economical expansion of a carrier's business. These situations are the inevitable result of restricting operating authority under the "grandfather clause" to services rendered on the "grandfather" date and continuously since. They would be difficult to justify if an effort were being made to promote the most economical organization of the industry. Carriers may sometimes overcome the effect of these restrictions by purchasing the operating rights of others or by seeking an expansion of their operating authority under other provisions of the Act. In the latter case, however, difficulty may be encountered, since public convenience and necessity would have to be shown for the additional service if the carrier is a common carrier, and consistency with the public interest would have to be shown if the carrier is a contract carrier. This is particularly difficult to do when the additional operating authority sought would encroach upon the vested interests of other operators having "grandfather" rights in the territory or between the points involved.

We have previously noted that the definition of a "contract carrier" was changed in 1957 and that the definition reinstated the number of shippers served as a criterion for contract carriage. The Commission was directed to examine outstanding permits to determine whether the operations performed thereunder were in conformity with the new definition. If they were found to be those of a common carrier, the Commission was to issue a certificate authorizing such operations as a common carrier of "the same commodities between the same points or within the same territory as authorized in the permit." Cases under this section are known as "conversion proceedings." They raise some of the same issues as the original "grandfather clause." In one case the Commission carried over into the certificate a Keystone restriction found in the permit being superseded.[57] Commissioner Brown, dissenting, took the position that a Keystone re-

---

[57] *J. B. Montgomery, Inc. Conversion Application*, 98 MCC 262 (1956).

striction in the certificate of a common carrier was incompatible with a common carrier's obligation to serve the public.[58]

CERTIFICATES AND PERMITS FOR NEW OPERATING AUTHORITY

The statute provides that certificates for new common-carrier operations be granted to an applicant "if it is found that the applicant is fit, willing, and able properly to perform the service proposed and to conform to the provisions of this part and the requirements, rules, and regulations of the Commission thereunder, and that the proposed service . . . is or will be required by the present or future public convenience and necessity." Permits to contract carriers are to be granted "if it appears . . . that the applicant is fit, willing, and able properly to perform the service of a contract carrier by motor vehicle, and to conform to the provisions of this part and the lawful requirements, rules, and regulations of the Commission thereunder, and that the proposed operation . . . will be consistent with the public interest and the policy declared in this act."

It will be noted that a certificate for common-carrier service may not be issued except upon a showing that the proposed service will be *required* by "public convenience and necessity." The Commission has pointed out that the word "necessity" must be liberally construed, "for there are comparatively few things in life which can be regarded as an absolute 'necessity,' and it was surely not the intent of Congress to use the word in so strict and narrow a sense."[59] It is apparent, however, that an affirmative showing must be made that the proposed service "will serve a useful public purpose, responsive to a public demand or need."[60]

To obtain a permit as a contract carrier a showing of public convenience and necessity is not required, but only that the proposed operations will be consistent with the public interest and the national transportation policy. That these requirements are less exacting than those for obtaining a certificate of public convenience and necessity to operate as a common carrier was brought out clearly by the decision of the Supreme Court in *Interstate Commerce Commission* v. *J–T Transport Co.* in 1961.[61] The Commission had denied a permit to J–T Transport Co., largely on the grounds that the existing common-carrier service was adequate and hence the contract-carrier service was not needed. The Supreme Court, in reviewing the case, held that adequacy of existing services was a criterion to be considered by the Commission but that it was not determinative. In the words of the Court, the standard is not whether existing services are "reasonably adequate." It is whether a shipper has a "distinct need" for

[58] Ibid., pp. 269–72.

[59] *Pan-American Bus Lines Operation*, 1 MCC 190, 202 (1936).

[60] Ibid., p. 203.

[61] 368 U.S. 81 (1961).

the different, or more select, or more specialized service which the contract carrier proposes.[62]

Protection of Existing Carriers against Competition

One of the most important questions arising in the administration of the Act is the extent to which existing motor carriers should be protected from new competition. Obviously any limitation on the freedom of entry into the motor-carrier field operates to protect those already in the field from additional competition. If unlimited freedom to enter the business had been considered desirable by Congress, no certificate requirements would have been set up. The Commission has recognized an obligation to protect existing carriers. In an early case the Commission said: ". . . the maintenance of sound economic conditions in the motor-carrier industry would be jeopardized by allowing new operators to enter a field in competition with existing carriers who are furnishing adequate, efficient, and economical service.[63] In numerous cases the Commission has asserted that existing carriers are entitled to transport all of the traffic which they can handle adequately, efficiently, and economically without the competition of new services.[64]

Such pronouncements as the above, taken by themselves, leave the impression that protection of existing carriers from additional competition is the main consideration of the Commission in new certificate cases, which only yields to findings of inadequacy of existing service. Such a conclusion might be warranted if grants of operating authority could only be given when existing services were shown to be inadequate. But such is not the case. In fact, one decision of the Commission which denied a certificate for new operations because existing service was not shown to be inadequate was set aside by a district court. The Commission had said: ". . . since no inadequacy was shown in protestants' services, it is clear that the application must be denied." To this court replied: ". . . we understand the Commission to have thereby enunciated a rule of law to the effect that a showing of inadequacy of the present service of protestants is an element indispensable to the ultimate finding of public convenience and necessity of proposed . . . service."[65] The court then said: "While there is some authority for this view . . . we feel that the better rule is embodied in the more numerous cases to the contrary.[66]

---

[62] Ibid., p. 88.

[63] *Clark Common Carrier Application*, 1 MCC 445 (1937), citing *C. & D. Oil Co. Contract Carrier Application*, 1 MCC 329 (1936).

[64] See *Walter C. Benson Co., Inc., Extension*, 61 MCC 128, 130 (1952); *New York Cenrtal R. Co. Extension*, 61 MCC 457, 462 (1953); *Jones Trucking Co. Extension—Utah*, 69 MCC 273, 276 (1956); *Willman Contract Carrier Application*, 77 MCC 535 (1958).

[65] *Nashua Motor Express, Inc.* v. *United States*, 230 F. Supp. 646, 653 (1964).

[66] For cases cited, see ibid., p. 653.

A great many cases can be cited in which grants of new certificates have been upheld by the courts although there was no finding of inadequacy of existing service.[67] Although adequacy of existing service is a factor to be considered in grants of operating authority there are other elements to be considered. Among these are the desirability of a different kind of service, improved service, and the desirability of competition.

The desirability of competition has been specifically recognized by the Commission. Thus in one case the Commission said: "We believe that when the available traffic permits it, competition should be encouraged."[68] And in another case the Commission said: "It has been our view that in order to develop a healthy transportation system in a territory, a certain degree of competition should be encouraged."[69] To draw the line between desirable competition, on the one hand, and protecting existing carriers, on the other hand, from excess capacity and diluted revenues is not an easy task. If service inadequacies seem to result from a monopoly position, the Commission is particularly inclined to allow new competition on a route.[70]

An interesting difference between federal policy and that of some states is found in the matter of granting certificates for new operations when existing service is found to be inadequate. Under these circumstances, some states give the existing carriers an opportunity to improve their service before authorizing new entrants into the field. A federal district court once set aside an order of the Commission because it failed to do this.[71] The Supreme Court reversed the decision of the district court, holding that no such policy had been established by the Commission's decisions or by the courts.[72]

As we have previously noted, most states regulate motor carriers operating in intrastate commerce. State policy on the question of competition versus protection of established carriers varies widely. In some states, as shown above, the certification of added services is forbidden unless and until existing carriers have had an opportunity to establish needed service. Such is the situation in Florida, Nebraska, Arizona, Virginia, Mississippi, Kentucky, Louisiana, Colorado, and Texas.[73] In Pennsylvania, on the other

---

[67] Some recent ones are: *Petroleum Carrier Corp.* v. *United States*, 258 F. Supp. 611 (1966); *Morgan Drive-Away, Inc.* v. *United States*, 268 F. Supp. 886 (1967); *Younger Bros., Inc.* v. *United States*, 289 F. Supp. 545 (1968).

[68] *Balch & Martin Motor Express Common Carrier Application*, 47 MCC 75, 78 (1947).

[69] *Associated Transports, Inc., Extension—Kansas*, 54 MCC 528, 529 (1952).

[70] See *P. C. White Truck Line, Inc., Extension—Northwest Florida*, 102 MCC 204, 212–14 (1966).

[71] *Dixie Highway Express, Inc.* v. *United States*, 208 F. Supp. 239 (1967).

[72] *United States* v. *Dixie Highway Express, Inc.*, 389 U.S. 409 (1967).

[73] Florida: *Redwing Carriers* v. *Mack*, 73 So. 2d 416 (1954), and *Alterman Transport Line* v. *Carter*, 88 So. 2d 594 (1955); Nebraska: *Application of Moritz*, 43 N.W. 2d 603 (1950); Arizona: *Corporation Commission* v. *Southern Pacific Co.*, 191 Pac. 2d 719 (1948), and *Whitfield Transportation Co., Inc.* v. *Tucson Warehouse &*

hand, the question of whether competitive services shall be authorized is left to the judgment and discretion of the commission, as is the case under the federal law.[74] The same is true in Wisconsin, where the Supreme Court of the state has held that the statute "does not create any presumption in favor of, or against, either monopoly of motor carrier service or competition, but the commission is free to determine which of the two will best serve the public interest.[75]

Alternate-Route Authority

A special type of case arises when a carrier authorized to provide service between two points over a given route seeks authority to use an alternate and perhaps more direct route for operating convenience.

FIGURE 30–1.   Alternate-Route Authority

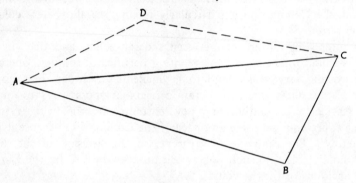

The problem arising out of this type of case may be illustrated by the diagram in Figure 30–1. Suppose that a carrier is authorized to operate between A and B, and also between B and C. This authority enables him to operate between A and C via B. A direct highway route between A and C may be available, over which the distance is less and which might have other operating advantages. The carrier therefore seeks authority to operate between A and C over the direct route. He may encounter opposition,

Transfer Co., 276 Pac. 2d 954 (1954); Virginia: *Seaboard Air Line R. Co.* v. *Commonwealth,* 71 S.E. 2d 146 (1952); Mississippi: *West Bros., Inc.* v. *H. & L. Delivery Service,* 70 So. 2d 870 (1954); *F. & W. Express, Inc.* v. *Delta Motor Line, Inc.,* 78 So. 2d 887 (1955); Kentucky: *Jones* v. *Webb Transfer Line, Inc.,* 328 S.W. 2d 407 (1959); Louisiana: *Herrin Transportation Co.* v. *Louisiana Public Service Commission,* 127 So. 2d 541 (1961); Colorado: *Ephraim Freightways, Inc.* v. *Public Utilities Commission,* 380 P. 2d 228 (1963); Texas: *Railroad Commission* v. *National Transport Corp.,* 363 S.W. 2d 360 (1963).

[74] *Follmer Trucking Co.* v. *Pennsylvania Public Utilities Commission,* 90 Atl. 2d 294 (1952); *Motor Freight Express* v. *Pennsylvania Public Utility Commission,* 119 Atl. 2d 661 (1956).

[75] *Motor Transport Co.* v. *Public Service Commission,* 56 N.W. 2d 548, 552 (1953).

however, from another carrier or group of carriers who have authority to operate between A and C over the direct route. Whether or not alternate-route authority should be given to operate between A and C over the direct route, but not to serve intermediate points, sometimes raises difficult questions. If the applicant actually carries traffic between A and C over the indirect route and is an effective competitor of those operating over the direct route, there is no reason why alternate-route authority should be denied. Operation over the direct route would be conducive to greater economy and efficiency in operation, would reduce wasteful hauling, and might redound to the public's advantage through lower rates. If, however, the applicant does not actually carry traffic between A and C, or is not an effective competitor for the traffic, authorization of alternate-route authority would be equivalent to establishing a new service which, if granted, could lead to overcapacity, especially if there are other carriers operating between A and C via another circuitous route who also demand the right to operate between A and C over the direct route.

As a federal court pointed out, two recognized principles of regulation come into conflict in situations of this sort. The first is that if there is only traffic enough for one carrier, only one should be certificated; the other is that if economies in operation are possible, the public interest requires such economies.[76] How the conflict will be resolved ought to depend upon the circumstances.

The policy of the Commission in alternate-route cases is to require proof of three conditions before alternate-route authority will be granted for operating convenience. These are (1) that the applicant is presently operating between the involved points over a practicable and competitively feasible route, (2) that it is handling a substantial amount of traffic in effective competition with existing carriers between these termini, and (3) that the competitive situation will remain relatively unchanged if the authority sought is granted.[77] Possibly the Commission can be criticized for giving too great weight in some cases to the effect of alternate-route authority on other carriers, but in at least two instances the courts have remanded a case to the Commission for granting alternate-route authority without adequate consideration of the effect on other carriers or without finding that additional direct service was needed.[78]

Use of Interstate Highway System

A certificate issued to regular-route common carriers by motor vehicle specifies the routes over which they may operate, the termini between

---

[76] *Clarke* v. *United States*, 101 Fed. Supp. 587 (1951).

[77] *Hayes Freight Lines, Inc., Extension—Ohio,* 69 MCC 205 (1956); *St. Johnsbury Trucking Co., Inc., Extension, Alternate Route,* 76 MCC 709 (1958).

[78] *Interstate Common Carrier Council of Maryland* v. *United States,* 84 Fed. Supp. 414 (1949); *Clarke* v. *United States,* 101 Fed. Supp. 587 (1951).

which they may operate, and intermediate and off-line points to be served. The development of the National System of Interstate and Defense Highways and other "superhighways" raised the question of the use of these highways by regular-route carriers for any portion of their routes when it is convenient for them to do so. Many savings accrue to a truck line when it is practicable to make use of one of the superhighways over a segment of its authorized route. Speedier service is also made possible. On the other hand, unrestricted right to use the superhighways may result in neglect of service at intermediate points not on a superhighway, and may also affect the competitive relationship between rival carriers, some of which are able to use the superhighway practicably and others not.

In 1968 the Commission laid down rules to govern the use of super-highways by regular-route carriers.[79] For carriers of property the basic provision is that a certificated regular-route carrier may use any super-highway on its route provided either that (*a*) it is wholly within 25 airline miles of the authorized regular route or routes, or that (*b*) the distance from the carrier's point of receipt of a shipment to its point of release over the superhighway route (including connecting highways) is not less than 85 percent of the distance between the same points over the regular route. Provision is made for discontinuance or modification of such service if it results in inadequate service at points on the carrier's authorized route or if it results in "destructive" competition.

Thus, by general rule the Commission has sought to give regular-route motor carriers of property the advantages flowing from use of the Interstate Highway System and other "superhighways" without impairing service at intermediate points on the carriers' originally certificated routes, and without jeopardizing other carriers. The question may be raised whether these rules are too much concerned with preserving the competitive status quo, and not enough with the promotion of the cheapest and most efficient movement of goods.

For carriers of passengers the problem is approached on a case-by-case basis rather than by general rule.

For-Hire Service by Private Carriers

The Commission has been inclined to deny certificates and permits to private carriers who desire to engage to some extent in for-hire operations. The principle was established in *Geraci Contract Carrier Application.*[80] The Commission there explained why it considered it objectionable to mix contract and private carriage. "If private carriers generally were permitted to engage in contract-carrier operations in the manner here proposed, it is clear that the results might seriously affect the maintenance of

---

[79] *Motor Service on Interstate Highways,* 107 MCC 95 (1968).
[80] 7 MCC 369 (1938).

adequate and efficient service by the motor common carriers upon whom the general public must depend, and by the contract carriers who do not also engage in private carriage."[81] The *Geraci Case* involved contract-carrier operations by a private carrier, but the principle has also been applied to proposed common-carrier operations by private carriers.[82] The principle of the *Geraci Case* has been followed in many cases, but there are exceptions. Particularly where the for-hire services proposed were not competitive with regular for-hire carriers, or where no adverse effects on common-carrier operations would result, the Commission has authorized private carriers to engage in for-hire operations.[83]

In 1963, in the *Veon Case*, the Commision reaffirmed the doctrine of the *Geraci Case*, noted that case-by-case exceptions over the years had weakened its authority, and announced that in the future the exceptions to the policy of the *Geraci Case* "will be rare indeed."[84]

Dual Operation

The Act specifically provides that a carrier shall not hold both a certificate as a common carrier and a permit as a contract carrier. This prohibition of dual operation, however, is not absolute, since the Commission may, "for good cause shown," grant both a certificate and a permit to the same carrier.

The principal objection to dual operation is that it creates an opportunity for personal discrimination. Some shippers may be charged common-carrier rates; others, whom the carrier wishes to favor, may by reason of contracts entered into, receive substantially the same service at lower rates.[85]

The cases in which dual operation as both a common and a contract carrier have been authorized represent situations in which the two services were so different as to be noncompetitive or were between different points or in different areas, and hence there was little possibility that the undesirable consequences of dual operation could arise.[86]

---

[81] Ibid., p. 372.

[82] *Bales Common Carrier Application*, 9 MCC 709 (1938).

[83] E.g., *Zeisloft Common Carrier Application*, 12 MCC 13 (1938); *Villaume Contract Carrier Application*, 30 MCC 92 (1941); *Stanley & Reedy Contract Carrier Application*, 82 MCC 270 (1960). For a short analysis of exceptions to the general policy of not authorizing for-hire service by private carriers, see Frederick M. Porter, "Federal Regulation of Private Carriers," 64 *Harvard Law Review* 896, 906 (1951).

[84] *Ralph A. Veon, Inc., Contract Carrier Application*, 92 MCC 248, 250–52 (1963).

[85] See *Gallot—Purchase—Holst*, 45 MCC 1, 4 (1946); *La Casse Extension*, 79 MCC 222 (1959); *Telishak Trucking, Inc., Extension—Concrete Slabs and Beams*, 92 MCC 553 (1963).

[86] E.g., *McCormick's Express, Inc., Common Carrier Application*, 12 MCC 632 (1938); *Klann Moving & Trucking Co. Contract Carrier Application*, 29 MCC 409 (1941); *Oil Carriers Co. Extension*, 79 MCC 169 (1959).

Revocation and Suspension of Certificates

The Commission may revoke a certificate upon application of the holder; or it may suspend or revoke a certificate for willful failure to comply with the Act, or with an order, rule, or regulation of the Commission, or with terms or conditions of the certificate. Except upon application of the holder, a certificate may not be revoked until the holder has been given a reasonable time to comply with an order of the Commission commanding obedience to the Act, or to a rule or regulation of the Commission, or to the terms and conditions of the certificate.[87] The same rules govern the revocation or suspension of a permit.

CONSOLIDATIONS, ACQUISITIONS OF CONTROL, AND PURCHASES

Consolidations and all forms of unification of motor carriers came under the provisions of Section 5 of Part I of the Act, as previously noted, if more than 20 vehicles were involved.[88] In 1965 Congress amended the Act, abolishing the 20-vehicle test, but exempting motor-carrier consolidations if operating revenues did not exceed $300,000.[89] Actually the Commission's control over combinations was not limited to cases involving more than 20 vehicles under the original Act since Section 212 (b) of the Act gives the Commission power to prescribe rules governing the transfer of certificates and permits, and the Commission has promulgated a rule requiring its approval of the transfer of any operating rights.[90]

Although consolidations of motor carriers, acquisitions of control through lease or stock ownership, and the purchase of operating rights of another have occurred in large numbers since the Motor Carrier Act was passed, the industry is still characterized by a large number of small operators, as we have previously pointed out. Consolidations continue, however, in substantial numbers. One writer, close to the industry, holds that the bases for such mergers "are that there is a competitive advantage to be gained from being able to offer a shipper one-carrier service to more points, while exposure to a larger share of the total traffic market offers greater opportunities for growth."[91]

---

[87] Section 212 (a).

[88] In determining the number of vehicles involved, those of both the acquiring carrier and of the carrier to be acquired were counted. A tractor and trailer, or tractor and semitrailer, constituted one vehicle, and one trailer might be combined with a semitrailer and tractor as one vehicle; but tractors and semitrailers in excess of those paired with a tractor were counted as vehicles.

[89] Public Law 89–93.

[90] See *United States* v. *Ressler*, 313 U.S. 57 (1941).

[91] See remarks of A. Joseph Debe of Chase Manhattan Bank in *Traffic World*, April 3, 1965, p. 24. See also Eugene T. Liipfert, "Consolidation and Competition in Transportation: The Need for an Effective and Consistent Policy," 31 *George Washington Law Review* 106, 132 (1962).

Monopoly versus Competition

The most important issue that is likely to arise in consolidation cases concerns the elimination of competition. The Commission considers this factor; but it is not controlling, as the disadvantage to the public of eliminating competition might be offset wholly or in part by various advantages, such as the possibility of more economical operation and better service.

The issue of competition versus monopoly in motor-carrier unification cases was clearly presented in the *Associated Transport Case*. The Commission authorized Associated Transport, Inc., to acquire control of several large carriers in the East, even though there would be no other motor carrier of similar size to compete with it throughout the same area.[92] The Commission found, however, that there would remain ample competitive motor-carrier service throughout the territory involved and that, in addition, one or more rail carriers would offer substantial competition at all principal points. The Commission also found that the consolidation would result in improved service. In *McLean Trucking Co.* v. *United States* the Commission's order was upheld by the Supreme Court[93] against the contention that it should be set aside on the grounds that the Commission had failed to give consideration to the policy of the antitrust laws in authorizing the unification. It is obvious that Congress would not have made consolidations approved by the Commission exempt from the Sherman Antitrust Act if the Commission could not authorize combinations that might run counter to that Act. There can be little doubt, said the Court in upholding the Commission, "that the Commission is not to measure proposals for all-rail or all-motor consolidations by the standards of the anti-trust laws."[94] On the other hand, the Court held that Congress had not authorized the Commission, in passing on a proposed merger, to ignore the policy of the antitrust laws. The task before the Commission apparently is to weigh the advantages of preserving competition between independent carriers and the advantages of improved service, lower costs, and the like which may result from a particular consolidation.[95] This, we believe, is what the Commission would do as a common-sense matter, even if it were not legally required to recognize the policy of the antitrust laws. There may be some advantage, however, in establishing the principle that the Commission is under compulsion to recognize public policy as it has found expression in the antitrust laws.

Effect of Consolidations on Connecting Carriers

A consideration that has assumed considerable importance in certain consolidation cases is the effect of a consolidation of connecting carriers on

---

[92] *Associated Transport, Inc.—Control & Consolidation,* 38 MCC 137 (1942).
[93] 321 U.S. 67 (1944).
[94] Ibid., pp. 84–85.
[95] Ibid., p. 87.

other carriers with whom the acquiring carrier has formerly interchanged traffic. This was a factor in the Commission's refusal to authorize the control of Keeshin Freight Lines by Pacific Intermountain Express. The Pacific Intermountain Express had interchanged traffic at Chicago and St. Louis with a number of eastern truck lines, including Keeshin. The acquisition of Keeshin by Pacific Intermountain Express, thus establishing a single-line transcontinental route, would have adversely affected the other eastern truck lines with which Pacific Intermountain Express had formerly interchanged traffic.[96] Adverse effect of a consolidation on other carriers, through loss of interchanged traffic, is not a controlling factor in a consolidation case and may be outweighed by other considerations.[97]

Cases of this sort bring out clearly that end-to-end consolidations may affect the competitive situation as much as the consolidation of carriers competing over the same routes. The carrier providing a single-system service to many points has a distinct competitive advantage over small carriers with shorter routes who must rely upon connecting carriers to provide service to more distant points. This situation, as elsewhere pointed out, suggests an economic basis for large firms in the motor-carrier industry despite the fact that there may be no substantial economies in large size.[98]

Sale of Dormant Operating Rights

The Commission has often refused to permit the transfer of dormant operating rights, that is, operating rights under which no service has been performed for some time. Objection to the sale of dormant rights arises from the adverse effect that the resumption of operations would have on existing carriers, who have often expanded their operations to fill the gap resulting from the abandonment of operations by another. "We have repeatedly said that carriers which have expended their funds and energies in developing and maintaining facilities to handle all available traffic are entitled to protection against the purchase of operating rights under which operations have been abandoned, for the institution of a new service in competition with them."[99] In another case the Commission said that when seeking to acquire dormant rights "it is incumbent upon applicants to show

---

[96] *Pacific Intermountain Express Co.—Control & Purchase,* 57 MCC 341 (1950), 57 MCC 467 (1951). See also *Super Service Motor Freight Co., Inc.—Purchase—Hayes Freight Lines, Inc.,* 58 MCC 137 (1951).

[97] *Ringsby Truck Lines, Inc.—Control—Northern Transportation Co.,* 58 MCC 594 (1952); *Gateway Transportation Co.—Purchase—Aztec Lines, Inc.,* 59 MCC 89 (1953).

[98] P. 649, supra.

[99] *Herrin Transportation Co.—Purchase—Mobile Express, Inc.,* 58 MCC 59, 61 (1951). See also *Burlington-Chicago Cartage, Inc., Purchase—Smith,* 56 MCC 739 (1950); *L. Nelson & Sons Transportation Co.—Purchase—White's Express,* 59 MCC 675 (1953).

that the carrier proposing to acquire such rights would meet some transportation need not being met by existing carriers."[100]

RATE-LEVEL CASES

In studying the regulation of railroads, we found that the Commission is occasionally faced with proceedings in which the railroads throughout the country, or in parts of it, seek a general increase in rates. A similar situation arises in the regulation of motor carriers, and many cases have come before the Commission involving general increases in rates throughout extensive areas.

The Operating-Ratio Standard

For many years the operating ratio was the principal, if not sole, standard used by the Commission to determine the adequacy of motor-carrier earnings. No effort was made to apply the fair-return-on-fair-value or return-on-investment standard traditionally used in railroad rate-level cases. An operating ratio of 93 was found reasonable in a considerable number of cases.[101]

The operating-ratio standard has also been used commonly by state regulatory commissions in regulating the rates of motor carriers. Its use instead of a return-on-investment standard arises from the peculiarities of the motor-carrier industry. Investment is so small relative to the volume of business done that the margin of revenues over expenses required to pay a normal rate of return on capital invested would be so small that a slight miscalculation of probable revenues or expenses could leave the carrier with revenues insufficient to pay operating expenses. One writer has noted that a 10 percent return on investment would mean an operating ratio of 98 for a motor carrier.[102] Such a close margin between operating revenues and expenses is in danger of disappearing entirely if either revenues or expenses turn out to be different than was anticipated. As one writer has stated it: "The risk inherent in the bus industry is involved not so much in the investment as in the expenses that are underwritten by the operator."[103] The important thing to consider in regulating the rate level of either bus companies or trucking concerns is whether the

---

[100] *Atlanta Motor Lines Control—Atlanta-Ashville Motor Express*, 93 MCC 160, 165 (1963).

[101] *Increased Common Carrier Rates in the East*, 42 MCC 633 (1943); *Increased Common Carrier Rates in New England*, 43 MCC 13 (1949); *Increases, Middle Atlantic & New England*, 49 MCC 357, 367 (1949); *Increased Motor Carrier Rates in New England, 1949*, 49 MCC 477, 488 (1949).

[102] Edgar S. Idol, "Railroad and Carrier Cases," 48 *Public Utilities Fortnightly* 678, 679 (1951).

[103] Robert Driscoll, *Rates and Fares in the Intercity Bus Industry* (mimeographed, 1948) p. 12.

margin of revenues over expenses is sufficient to survive a decline in revenues or an increase in expenses. This is the thought that the Commission had in mind in *Middle West General Increases,* when it said:

> In industries where the amount of investment is large in relation to total costs, the rate of return on investment generally has been accepted as appropriate for determining revenue needs. In such industries the risk is related more to the amount of the investment and less to costs. On the other hand, where the amount of the investment is relatively small in relation to total costs, investment is not the primary factor in determining revenue needs. . . . The owners of motor carriers can hardly be expected to look to the return on the amount of their investment as an incentive where the principal risk is attached to the substantially greater amount of expense.[104]

The operating-ratio standard has been criticized as no standard at all, since the operating ratio required in one industry to pay a return on capital invested is quite different from that required in another industry.[105] The argument overlooks the purpose of using the operating ratio. The particular operating ratio deemed reasonable is not chosen for the purpose of providing an adequate return on capital invested, but for the purpose of providing a margin of revenues over expenses that is not in danger of disappearing entirely if changes in revenues or expenses occur. The reasonable operating ratio required should therefore have some relation to the variability of net revenues and to any other factors that indicate the degree of risk that operating expenses may not be covered. An operating ratio so selected may or may not provide an adequate return on investment. If it does not, then the fair-return-on-fair-value standard rather than the operating-ratio standard should be applied.

Although the operating-ratio standard is useful in judging the reasonableness of earnings in the motor-carrier industry, or in any regulated industry which is characterized by a small investment in relation to operating revenues, it is possible to use the conventional return-on-investment standard in such industries. If this is done, however, a sufficiently generous rate of return must be allowed to cover the risk that operating expenses will not be covered and also to permit the accumulation of adequate reserves out of the earnings of good years to supplement inadequate revenues of poor years.

In response to numerous attacks upon the operating ratio standard, the Commission cautioned against its uncritical and more or less mechanical use.[106] A look behind the operating ratio is made necessary by the prevalence of subsidiary corporations and affiliates of motor carriers from which the carrier may purchase supplies and services at excessive prices. This

---

[104] 48 MCC 541, 552–53 (1948).

[105] Laurence S. Knappen, "Transit Operating Ratio—Another View," 51 *Public Utilities Fortnightly* 485, 488 (1953).

[106] E.g., *General Increases—Eastern Central Territory,* 316 ICC 467 (1962); *General Increase—Middle Atlantic & New England Territories,* 319 ICC 168 (1963).

situation led the Commission, in a 1963 decision, to say: "In view of the recurring attacks on the use of operating ratios to justify revenue needs —attacks which have substance particularly with respect to the effect on such ratios of transactions between carriers and their affiliates or subsidiaries—the carriers are admonished that in the future, expense items of representative carriers should be shown in greater detail, and all pertinent information regarding carrier-affiliate relationships should be disclosed."[107] This problem, of course, is not peculiar to use of operating ratios as a standard of adequacy of revenues. The same critical examination of operating expenses may be necessary when the fair-return-on-investment standard is used.

Beginning in the 1960s, the Commission has not only looked more critically at operating ratios under the circumstances just described, but has also required that financial data of various sorts be introduced in rate-level cases to show the carriers' needs for revenue. In other words, operating ratios are being supplemented by other data indicative of the revenue needs of the carriers. In numerous cases evidence of return on net investment, and return on equity capital, has been introduced.[108]

In part at least, the new policy seems to have been the result of a decision by the Court of Appeals for the District of Columbia Circuit in which a decision of the Washington Metropolitan Area Transit Commission was set aside. The Transit Commission used the operating-ratio standard as required by the statute under which it functioned. The court held, however, that matters other than bare operating ratios should have been considered by the Transit Commission. The court mentioned specifically interest requirements, dividend payments sufficient to continue to attract investors, and additional amounts to create a surplus sufficient to provide financial strength and stability. This is practically the "credit standard" of which we have spoken in an earlier chapter.[109] Concerning the operating-ratio standard, the court said: "An enterprise's operating ratio— the arithmetical ratio of its expenses to its gross revenues—may *suggest* that its rates are too high or too low, but whether they are too high or too low in fact depends in the final analysis on the degree of their correspondence to the items mentioned above."[110] The court added: "A rate fixed without particularized reference to these needs does not satisfy any standard of rate making of which we are aware . . ."[111]

If this decision of the District of Columbia District Court of Appeals

---

[107] *General Increases—Transcontinental,* 319 ICC 792, 803 (1963).

[108] *Increased Rates and Charges, Middlewest Territory,* 335 ICC 142 (1969); *Increased Rates, New England Territory,* 335 ICC 185 (1969); *Rate Increases and Charges, Southwestern States,* 335 ICC 361 (1969).

[109] See Chapter 15.

[110] *D.C. Transit System, Inc.* v. *Washington Metropolitan Area Transit Commission,* 350 F. 2d 753, 778 (1965).

[111] Ibid.

is to be accepted as the law of the land, we may expect to see the motor-carrier rate-level cases before the Interstate Commerce Commission assume the characteristics of typical public utility rate cases with use of not only return-on-investment data, but other financial information bearing on the question of ability to attract equity capital. Operating ratios will continue to be relevant but will assume a less definitive role than they have in the past.

Inequality of Earning Power

We have found that in the regulation of the general level of railroad rates, difficulty has been encountered because of the inequality in the earning power of different railroads.[112] The same problem is encountered in the regulation of motor-carrier rates on a territory-wide basis. In *Increased Common Carrier Rates in the East*[113] the Commission noted the wide range in the operating ratios of the carriers and pointed out that some carriers were earning substantial profits and some were operating at a loss. The Commission pointed out that rates could not be raised sufficiently to give all of the carriers adequate revenues. It pointed out that if that were possible in light of competitive conditions, most of the carriers would earn excessive profits. The Commission dealt with the carriers as a whole and said that the carriers with operating ratios substantially higher than the others had the right to propose higher rates if such would improve their earnings.[114] In a New England case the same situation appeared. The Commission again called attention to the necessity of dealing with the carriers as a whole, and added: "It is inevitable that any general increase, determined upon a consideration of average conditions, benefits some which are not in need of improved net revenues and fails to render profitable the operations of all respondents."[115]

RUINOUS COMPETITION AND MINIMUM RATES

We have noted elsewhere that the large element of fixed expenses in the railroad industry provides the explanation of the tendency for competition among railroads to become "ruinous" in character, and that the absence of a large element of fixed expenses in the motor-carrier industry would seem to indicate that ruinous competition would not be as likely to develop among motor carriers.[116] We have also noted, however, that conditions of overcapacity seem to develop quite commonly in the motor-

---

[112] See Chapter 17 on the weak-and-strong-road problem.

[113] 42 MCC 633 (1943).

[114] Ibid., p. 648.

[115] 43 MCC 13, 17–18 (1943). See also *Transcontinental & Rocky Mountain Increases*, 54 MCC 377, 384–85 (1952).

[116] See pp. 651–52, supra.

carrier industry and that under such conditions short-run variable costs rather than long-run variable costs tend to determine rates.[117]

Rate wars and unremunerative rates have occurred in the motor-carrier industry, and the Commission has found it necessary in a number of instances to prescribe minimum rates to put a stop to what appeared to be disastrous rate cutting. This was done on a territory-wide basis in five cases between 1937 and 1941.[118] In the case which involved the motor carriers in the Middle Atlantic states, the Commission said: "The record shows plainly that the motor carriers here concerned found themselves in a competitive struggle which was undermining their rates and depleting their revenues at a time when costs of operation were rising rapidly. Their reserves, to the extent that they had any, were nearing exhaustion and financial ruin loomed ahead."[119]

In a later case the struggle between conference and nonconference carriers for traffic between New York and Philadelphia made it necessary for the Commission to interfere in order to stop what it called a "vicious circle" of rate reductions. In justifying its action, the Commission said: ". . . the important considerations here are that there is a rate war, that carriers have lost and are losing traffic because of rates which as a whole are substantially lower than necessary to yield adequate revenues, and that to regain and retain traffic they are engaging in destructive competitive practices. We know of no other way of correcting this situation than by placing a floor below which rates may not go without our prior approval."[120]

The difficulty of motor carriers in maintaining remunerative rates under highly competitive circumstances is revealed in other cases where the Commission has found it necessary or desirable to step in and stabilize rates by a minimum-rate order.[121]

Although the Commission has not hesitated to issue a minimum-rate order when it was convinced that the circumstances required it, the Commission is fully cognizant of the fact that general minimum-rate orders are objectionable if they remain in force for a considerable period because they freeze the rate structure and interfere with "the normal processes of ratemaking by negotiations between carriers and shippers."[122] "It is not our policy," says the Commission, "to keep such orders in force

---

[117] P. 652, supra.

[118] *Middle Atlantic States Motor Carrier Rates,* 4 MCC 68 (1937); *Central Territory Motor Carrier Rates,* 8 MCC 233 (1938); *New England Motor Carrier Rates,* 8 MCC 287 (1938); *Trunk Line Territory Motor Carrier Rates,* 24 MCC 501 (1940); *Midwestern Motor Carrier Rates,* 27 MCC 297 (1941).

[119] 4 MCC 68, 77 (1937).

[120] *Class & Commodity Rates, New York to Philadelphia,* 51 MCC 289, 298–99 (1950).

[121] *New England Motor Rate Increases, 1955,* 66 MCC 215 (1956); *Iron & Steel Articles—Eastern Common Carriers,* 68 MCC 717 (1957), 305 ICC 369 (1959).

[122] *New England Motor Rate Increases, 1955,* 67 MCC 75, 77 (1956).

any longer than necessary to achieve stabilization of the particular rate structure which is the subject of the order."[123]

It will be noted that the Commission has exercised its minimum-rate power only in circumstances where competition of the ruinous type had appeared, that it has confined its minimum-rate orders to the specific situation involved, and that it intends to keep such orders in effect no longer than is necessary to effect a stabilization of the rate structure. This policy should be contrasted with that of some of the states which have prescribed a general floor of rates for motor carriers subject to their jurisdiction.[124]

If minimum rates are prescribed, particularly for general application, either by regulatory bodies or, as in some countries, by the industry through trade associations, care should be taken not to make them so high that an excessive number of carriers is attracted into the industry. If the latter situation develops, it will dilute the traffic unnecessarily and create a demand for still higher rates. In fact, prescription of minimum rates may require control over entry even when the rates prescribed are no higher than are justified by long-run costs in the industry.

REASONABLENESS OF RATES ON PARTICULAR COMMODITIES AND HAULS

The same general principles are followed by the Commission in determining the reasonableness and lawfulness of motor-carrier rates on particular commodities and hauls as have long been followed in determining the reasonableness and lawfulness of railroad rates. This statement does not mean, however, that the Commission disregards such special characteristics of the motor-carrier industry as may require or justify different rate practices and different rate levels. Thus the Commission has held that because of the limited capacities of motor trucks as compared with railroad freight cars, weight density should be given more consideration in determining classification ratings for motor carriers than it has customarily been given in making rail classifications.[125] The Commission, however, has disapproved of motor-carrier classification ratings applicable on light articles generally which were based on differences in density, because that would ignore other factors recognized as appropriate in determining classification ratings of specific articles.[126]

---

[123] Ibid.

[124] See Public Utilities Commission of Connecticut, *In the Matter of Investigation & Stabilization of Rates of Motor Common Carriers* (1959); Michigan Public Service Commission, *General Investigation of Rates & Charges for the Transportation of Property by Intrastate For-Hire Motor Carriers* (1964). California experience is reviewed in Harold W. Nicholson, "Motor Carrier Cost & Minimum Rate Regulation," 72 *Quarterly Journal of Economics* 139 (1958).

[125] *Incandescent Electric Lamps or Bulbs*, 47 MCC 601, 603 (1947).

[126] See *Classification Ratings Based on Density*, 337 ICC 784 (1970).

There is some evidence, likewise, that the Commission has placed more emphasis on fully allocated costs in prescribing minimum rates for motor carriers or in restricting reductions in rates proposed by motor carriers than has been the practice when dealing with railroad rates.[127] Such a policy would seem to be justified in view of the fact that motor-carrier costs are mostly variable, if we assume that equipment can be readily adjusted to the volume of traffic; and there is therefore normally little justification for rates that do not cover fully allocated costs.

Back-Haul Rates

In discussing the reasonableness of railroad rates, we noted that railroads are commonly permitted to maintain lower rates in the direction of empty-car movement.[128] In the case of motor-carrier rates, however, the Commission has repeatedly refused to authorize back-haul rates on a subnormal level.[129] Usually this is done with a mere assertion that rates made on an added-traffic basis are not warranted.

At first glance, refusal to permit lower back-haul rates seems an unsound policy because the empty vehicles must be moved anyway and the traffic moving in the predominant direction is properly chargeable with the cost of returning the vehicles. The condition which justifies the Commission in refusing to authorize low back-haul rates in motor-carrier cases is found, however, in the case commonly cited as a precedent for the Commission's policy.[130]

An unbalanced condition of truck traffic, because of the greater number of operators, is apt to be somewhat of an individual matter. That is to say, the traffic of one truck operator may preponderate in one direction, whereas that of a competing operator may preponderate in the other. As between operators, therefore, the application of the "out-of-pocket" cost method of making rates might well result in a break-down of the rate structure in both directions.[131]

As the matter is sometimes popularly expressed: "One man's back haul is another man's living."

It should be recognized that if one carrier has an empty-truck movement from A to B, and another carrier an empty movement from B to A, there is excess capacity over the route. In the absence of regulation, the

---

[127] See D. P. Locklin, "Rates and Rate Structures," in National Resources Planning Board, *Transportation and National Policy* (Washington, D.C.: U.S. Government Printing Office, 1942), particularly pp. 110–14. See also *Alcoholic Liquors from Ohio, Indiana & Kentucky to St. Louis,* 49 MCC 703, 707–8 (1949).

[128] Pp. 456 and 457, supra.

[129] *Eggs & Poultry from Topeka, Kansas, to Chicago, Ill.,* 53 MCC 30 (1951); *Plastics from Chicago, Ill., to New York, N.Y.,* 66 MCC 203 (1955); *Glass Containers from Ada, Okla., to Chicago, Ill.,* 306 ICC 275 (1959).

[130] *Refrigerator Material, Memphis, Tenn., to Dayton, Ohio,* 4 MCC 187 (1938).

[131] Ibid., p. 189.

excess capacity would ultimately be eliminated. Out-of-pocket-cost rates in both directions would eventually eliminate one or both of the competitors; a single carrier would replace the two; capacity would be adjusted to the volume of traffic; rates would be placed on a normal basis. Before this process was completed, however, a consolidation of the two carriers might be accomplished, or a pooling of traffic or other agreement arranged, and again normal rates would eventually prevail. A regulatory body is amply justified in warding off this distressing sequence of events and stabilizing rates on a normal basis, but in so doing it should not underwrite excess capacity by excessive rates.

There are two situations in which rates for a back haul may properly be based on an added-traffic theory. One occurs where the traffic of the motor carriers as a whole is unbalanced. If the Commission were confronted with a situation in which the predominant movement of truck traffic as a whole, or for one type of equipment, was in one direction, making the return of empty vehicles necessary, the Commission would be fully justified in allowing back-haul rates on an out-of-pocket-cost basis. This is the situation usually found when railroads encounter an unbalanced movement of traffic.[132]

The other situation in which back-haul traffic may properly be sought on an incremental-cost basis is where the traffic sought is not to be diverted from other for-hire carriers, but is traffic that would not move at all except for the reduced rates, or would move in private transportation. The Commission has sometimes authorized such back-haul rates when the traffic to be obtained was moving as proprietary traffic of manufacturers or of other enterprises.[133]

In at least two cases the Commission, in divided opinions, has permitted back-haul rates on a reduced basis by motor carriers when the traffic sought would be diverted from railroads.[134] These cases involve intermodal competition, a subject considered in a later chapter.

Unreasonable Rates and Reparation

We have elsewhere pointed out that at first the Motor Carrier Act did not give the Commission power to award reparation to shippers for injury sustained as a result of having been charged rates which were unreasonable or otherwise unlawful.[135] It was believed for a long time, however, that a shipper who alleged that a rate charged on a past shipment was unreasonable had a right to bring action in a court for recovery under the common law. If this were done, the Commission, rather than the court, would have

---

[132] For recognition of this point in air transport see Chapter 33.

[133] *Aluminum Extrusions from Miami to Chicago*, 325 ICC 188 (1965).

[134] *Animal Feed from Kansas City, Mo., to Chicago*, 325 ICC 147 (1965); *Carbon Blacks, Southwest to Indiana, Ohio, & Missouri*, 325 ICC 138 (1965).

[135] See p. 684, supra.

to determine whether or not the rate had been unreasonable, since under the doctrine of the Abilene Cotton Oil Case[136] the reasonableness or unreasonableness of a rate is a question which the Commission and not the courts must determine.[137] Armed with a determination by the Commission that the rate had been unreasonable in the past, the shipper could ask the court to award reparation. But in 1959, in *T.I.M.E.* v. *United States*,[138] the Supreme Court of the United States, in a 5-to-4 decision, held that the common-law right of recovery did not survive the enactment of the Motor Carrier Act. Thus the shipper who felt that he had been charged an unreasonable rate by a motor carrier on a past shipment had no remedy whatsoever. Amendments to the Interstate Commerce Act made by Congress in 1965 included one which enables shippers to recover damages resulting from unreasonable or otherwise unlawful rates charged by motor carriers.[139] Action for recovery must be brought in court and not before the Commission. Before a court can award reparation, however, the Commission must determine whether the rate is unreasonable or otherwise unlawful.[140]

Relation between Contract Carrier and Common Carrier Rates

Since the power to prescribe minimum rates for contract carriers was given to the Commission as a means of protecting common carriers, upon whom the general public must rely, the relation between contract carrier rates and common carrier rates was bound to arise. The Texas statute regulating motor carriers, which was upheld in *Stephenson* v. *Binford*,[141] required contract carriers to charge no less than common carriers for equivalent service. In fact, the statutes of some 16 states make a similar requirement.[142] In some other states, the regulatory agency has imposed a similar rule as a matter of policy. This has been true of Washington[143] and Minnesota.[144]

The Interstate Commerce Commission, however, has followed no such policy. To require contract carriers to charge common-carrier rates would be inconsistent with the declaration of policy found in the amended

---

[136] See pp. 291–92, supra.

[137] *Bell Potato Chip Co.* v. *Aberdeen Truck Line*, 43 MCC 337 (1944); *United States* v. *Davidson Transfer & Storage Co., Inc.*, 302 ICC 87 (1957).

[138] 359 U.S. 464 (1959).

[139] Public Law 89–170.

[140] *Informal Procedure for Determining Motor Carrier Reparation*, 335 ICC 403 (1969).

[141] See p. 675, supra.

[142] Donald V. Harper, *Economic Regulation of the Motor Trucking Industry by the States* (Urbana: University of Illinois Press, 1959), pp. 202–3.

[143] See *Prater* v. *Department of Public Works*, 60 Pac. 2d 238, 239 (1936).

[144] *Minnesota–North Dakota Motor Carrier Rates*, 43 MCC 289, 303 (1944).

Interstate Commerce Act[145] and with other provisions of the Act. Contract carriers can frequently transport at lower costs than common carriers. Recognition of the inherent advantages of contract-carrier transportation would therefore seem to require that they be allowed to charge lower rates than common carriers. The Commission's policy on this issue was established in 1941[146] and has been consistently followed.[147]

SERVICE REGULATION

One of the complaints against motor carriers in the preregulation period was that they did not fully assume the responsibilities which have traditionally been expected of common carriers. This was one of the reasons advanced for regulation. It is not strange, therefore, that regulatory action in this field has sometimes been necessary.

Perhaps the most common dereliction of duty results from efforts of motor carriers to rid themselves of unprofitable operations. A common action has been refusal to handle less-truckload traffic. In fact, the certificates under which many motor carriers have operated limited their services to truckload business. In *Removal of Truckload Lot Restrictions*,[148] the Commission, in 1968, required the removal from certificates of all restrictions which limited service to truckload traffic. The Commission said: "The question of the consistency of truckload lot restrictions with the basic concepts of common carriage has been dealt with by this Commission in several cases, and it has been observed that such restrictions violate the basic tenets of common carriage."[149] The action of the Commission in this proceeding was sustained by a federal court.[150]

The Commission has also ruled against tariff provisions which limit the motor carriers' services to less than that authorized by their certificates.[151] Common tariff provisions have restricted service on small shipments or to and from points in rural areas. One device has been to provide weight limitations on the size of shipments that will be accepted, thus ruling out acceptance of shipments of small size.

In instituting an investigation of these practices in 1969, the Commission said: "Common carriers by motor vehicle are a public institution upon which the general public must depend for adequate, economical, and efficient transportation. They are engaged in what has always been

---

[145] See pp. 265–66, supra.

[146] *New England Motor Rate Bureau, Inc.* v. *Lewers & McCauley*, 30 MCC 651 (1941).

[147] *Roofing from Elizabeth, N.J., to Norwood, Mass.*, 51 MCC 258 (1950); *Catalogs & Paints between Chicago and Denver*, 67 MCC 463 (1956).

[148] 106 MCC 455 (1968).

[149] Ibid., p. 484.

[150] *Regular Common Carrier Conference* v. *United States*, 307 F. Supp. 941 (1969).

[151] *Restrictions on Service by Motor Common Carriers*, 111 MCC 151 (1970).

regarded as a public calling, and by reason of that fact they are subject to specific legal obligations. They must, according to their abilities, serve all who seek their services, and serve them equally and fairly. They may not pick and choose."[152] As a result of this investigation, the Commission ruled that motor carriers could not publish in their tariffs any provisions which restricted service to less than the carrier's full operating authority. On minimum-weight restrictions, however, the Commission laid down, not as a rule, but as a guideline, that tariff provisions might restrict shipments of less than 500 pounds.

Another service inadequacy of motor carriers arises out of their refusal, in many instances, to interchange or "interline" traffic with connecting motor carriers. It will be recalled that motor carriers of property may establish through routes and joint rates with other carriers but may not be compelled to do so. The Commission is therefore without power to remedy this inadequacy of motor-carrier service. The Commission has repeatedly asked that it be given power to require the establishment of through routes and joint rates between connecting motor carriers. The Commission was upheld, however, in one case in which it found it unlawful for a motor carrier which had established through routes and joint rates on traffic generally, to exclude certain traffic from the arrangement. The case arose when a motor carrier cancelled through routes and joint rates on furniture between Central states and the South although maintaining such an arrangement on other commodities.[153]

CRITICISMS OF MOTOR-CARRIER REGULATION

The purpose of this chapter and the preceding one has been to describe motor-carrier regulation as it has developed and to determine how specific problems of regulation have been met. In so doing, an effort has been made to explain the reasons for the statutory provisions and the reasons for some important policies that have been adopted by the Interstate Commerce Commission in the administration of the Act. It is natural that the Act and its administration should have been subjected to some criticism, as well as that regulation as a whole should be attacked.

The greatest amount of criticism has been directed at the policy of controlled entry and the exercise of the minimum-rate power to stabilize rates and check rate cutting. The position is taken by some critics, as we have previously noted, that regulation is totally unnecessary and that the forces of competition in the industry are adequate to protect the public interest.

Against these contentions must be posed the experience with free

---

[152] *Notice of Proposed Rulemaking and Order, Ex Parte* No. MC-77.

[153] *National Furniture Traffic Conference* v. *Associated Truck Lines,* 332 ICC 802 (1968); upheld in *Associated Truck Lines* v. *United States,* 304 F. Supp. 1094 (1969).

competition in the industry prior to the enactment of regulatory legislation, recognition of undesirable conditions that still appear in the unregulated segments of the industry, awareness of conditions in the regulated segment of the industry which regulation has been able to remedy, and the experience of numerous other countries in the world in dealing with similar problems. Undoubtedly regulation in some of its aspects has been too detailed, too restrictive, and annoyingly slow, cumbersome, and expensive; but to hold that a laissez-faire policy would produce satisfactory results to the public appears to disregard the lessons of experience.

SELECTED REFERENCES

For a discussion of various aspects of the administration of Part II of the Interstate Commerce Act, see the following: James C. Nelson, "Joint-Board Procedure under the Motor Carrier Act," 13 *Journal of Land and Public Utility Economics* 97 (1937); W. H. Wagner, "Common, Contract, and Private Motor Carriers Defined and Distinguished," 9 *I.C.C. Practitioners' Journal* 119 (1941); John J. George and J. R. Boldt, Jr., "Certification of Motor Common Carriers by the Interstate Commerce Commission," 17 *Journal of Land and Public Utility Economics* 82, 196 (1941); John J. George, "Authorization of Contract Motor Carriers by the Interstate Commerce Commission," 26 *Cornell Law Quarterly* 621 (1941); Board of Investigation and Research, *Federal Regulatory Restrictions upon Motor & Water Carriers*, 79th Cong., 1st Sess., Senate Doc. No. 78 (1945); John Coggins, "The Private Motor Carrier Definition of the Interstate Commerce Act: An Economic-Legal Battleground," 19 *George Washington Law Review* 1 (1950); John E. Altazan, *Interstate Commerce Commission Policy Concerning Consolidations and Acquisitions of Control in the Motor Carrier Industry* (New Orleans: College of Business Administration, Loyola University, 1956); Fritz R. Kahn, *Principles of Motor Carrier Regulation* (Dubuque, Iowa: Wm. C. Brown Co., 1958); Drew L. Carraway, "Motor Carrier Operating Authorities," 11 *Vanderbilt Law Review* 1029 (1958); Howard W. Nicholson, "Motor Carrier Cost and Minimum Rate Regulation," 72 *Quarterly Journal of Economics* 139 (1958); Eugene T. Liipfert, "Consolidation and Competition in Transportation: The Need for an Effective and Consistent Policy," 31 *George Washington Law Review* 106 (1962); Carl H. Fulda, *Competition in the Regulated Industries* (Boston: Little, Brown & Co., 1961), chap. v; Byron Nupp, "Control of Entry as an Economic and Regulatory Problem," 35 *I.C.C. Practitioners' Journal* 591 (1968).

On the operating ratio as a standard of adequacy of earnings, see Charles A. Wright, "Operating Ratio—A Regulatory Tool," 51 *Public Utilities Fortnightly* 24 (1953); Laurence S. Knappen, "Transit Operating Ratio—Another View," 51 *Public Utilities Fortnightly* 485 (1953); Charles W. Knapp, "Economics of the Transit Operating Ratio," 56 *Public Utilities Fortnightly* 467 (1955); Paul Weiner, "The Use of the Operating Ratio—Revisited," *Public Utilities Fortnightly*, August 5, 1971, p. 33.

For a review of state regulation, see Donald V. Harper, *Economic Regulation of the Motor Trucking Industry by the States* (Urbana: University of Illinois Press, 1959).

On the agricultural exemption provisions of the Motor Carrier Act, see the following: Richard W. Southgate, "Certain Implications of the Agricultural Exemptions," 22 I.C.C. *Practitioners' Journal* 3 (1954); James F. Pinkney, "Exemption of Agricultural Commodities from Motor Carrier Regulation," 58 *Public Utilities Fortnightly* 498 (1956); Carl Helmetag, Jr., "Judicial Expansion of the Agricultural Exemptions in the Motor Carrier Industry," 43 *Virginia Law Review* 211 (1957). See also, Clem C. Linnenberg, Jr., "The Agricultural Exemptions in Interstate Trucking: Mend Them or End Them," 25 *Law & Contemporary Problems* 139 (1960); Thomas C. Campbell, "Agricultural Exemptions from Motor Carrier Regulation," 36 *Land Economics* 14 (1960); Committee on Commerce, U.S. Senate, *National Transportation Policy* (Doyle Report), 87th Cong., 1st Sess., Senate Rep. No. 445 (1961), pp. 516–26.

For a critical discussion of motor-carrier regulation, see James C. Nelson, "New Concepts in Transportation Regulation," in National Resources Planning Board, *Transportation and National Policy* (Washington, D.C.: U.S. Government Printing Office, 1942), pp. 197–237; and Dudley F. Pegrum, "The Economic Basis of Public Policy for Motor Transport," 28 *Land Economics* 244 (1952).

Chapter 31

WATER TRANSPORTATION

The total domestic waterborne commerce of the United States amounted to 927,379,000 tons in 1969. This was equal in volume to about 72 percent of that hauled by the railroads. About 41 percent of the water traffic consisted of petroleum and its products; 16.5 percent was coal and coke; 12.5 percent consisted of sand, gravel, and stone; and 9.5 percent consisted of iron ore and iron and steel.[1]

COASTWISE AND INTERCOASTAL TRANSPORTATION

In discussing domestic transportation by water, it is desirable to distinguish between coastwise and intercoastal shipping, on the one hand, and transportation over inland waterways and the Great Lakes, on the other.

The term "coastwise transportation" refers to transportation along the seacoasts, i.e., between the various Atlantic ports, or the Gulf ports, or the Pacific Coast ports, or between the Gulf and Atlantic ports. Transportation between the Pacific Coast and the Atlantic or Gulf ports is known as "intercoastal transportation." The principal ports through which coastwise and intercoastal traffic moves are shown in Figure 31–1.

Intercoastal commercial traffic, as measured by the domestic traffic passing through the Panama Canal, amounted to 3,851,326 tons in fiscal year 1969. Of this, 2,580,644 tons moved from the East Coast to the West Coast (including Alaska and Hawaii); 1,270,682 tons moved from the West Coast to the East Coast.[2]

History of Coastwise and Intercoastal Transportation

Coastwise transportation antedates railroads; in fact, the ocean routes were the only routes by which trade was carried on between the different

---

[1] Corps of Engineers, U.S. Army, *Waterborne Commerce of the United States, 1969*, Part 5.

[2] Figures on intercoastal traffic are from Panama Canal Co. and Canal Zone Government, *Annual Report, 1969*.

FIGURE 31–1.   Principal Atlantic, Gulf, and Pacific Coast Ports of the United States Mainland

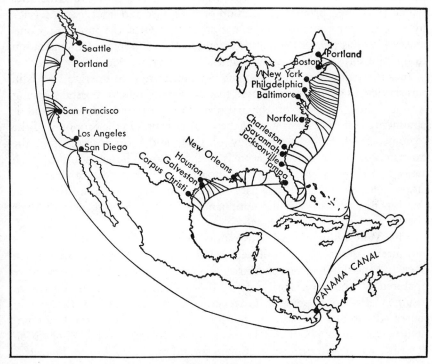

National Resources Planning Board, *Transportation and National Policy* (Washington, D.C.: U.S. Government Printing Office, 1942), p. 48.

ports in the colonial period. Although the building of railroads which connected important seaports brought railroads and coastwise vessels into competition with each other, coastwise shipping has always been important in the commerce of the country.

Prior to the opening of the Panama Canal in 1914, intercoastal shipping was by way of Cape Horn or the Straits of Magellan. In fact, until the opening of the first transcontinental rail route in 1869, trade between the Atlantic seaboard and the Pacific Coast was nearly all via the South American route or via a shorter water-rail-water route made possible in 1854 by the construction of the Panama Railroad.[3] The opening of the Panama Canal greatly increased the amount of intercoastal commerce. Traffic from as far west as Chicago has moved to New York or Philadelphia for shipment to the Pacific Coast by the Panama Canal route.

World War II brought an end to substantially all coastwise and intercoastal shipping. This was the combined result of the hazards of the

---

[3] U.S. Maritime Commission, *Economic Survey of Coastwise and Intercoastal Shipping* (Washington, D.C.: U.S. Government Printing Office, 1939), p. 3.

trade, arising from submarine attacks, and the requisition by the government of most of the vessels engaged in these trades. Because of difficulties which prevented prompt restoration of coastwise and intercoastal service by former operators after the cessation of hostilities, the Interstate Commerce Commission, in 1945, authorized the War Shipping Administration to operate ships in the coastwise and intercoastal services.[4]

In authorizing the War Shipping Administration to operate vessels in this service, the Commission stated that coastwise and intercoastal shipping was an "integral part of the national transportation system,"[5] and it commented on the importance of these water routes in the economy of the regions served. "The dependency of ports and coastal areas upon the existence of water transportation is well known. The economy of such areas, to a large extent, is founded upon the availability of such transportation, without which a large part of their economy would not have been developed, and with the discontinuance of which a large part of their normal activity will cease to exist."[6]

The War Shipping Administration operated ships in the coastwise and intercoastal services until September 1, 1946, when they were taken over by the United States Maritime Commission.[7] The services were operated by the latter until July 1, 1947, when private operations were resumed.[8] Private operations, however, were handicapped by the greatly increased costs of operation in the postwar period and by the low competitive rail rates which had been instituted to meet water competition at a time when water transportation costs and rates were lower. The latter situation has been changed somewhat by postwar increases in rail rates. Neither coastwise nor intercoastal shipping, however, has regained its prewar importance. In 1939 there were 235 dry-cargo vessels operating in coastwise service; by 1949 the number had been reduced to 78.[9] According to the Interstate Commerce Commission, there were 180 ships operating in the intercoastal trade as common carriers in 1935; by 1952 the number had been reduced to 60.[10] In 1957 the Commission pointed out that of the 15 common carriers authorized to operate between Atlantic and Pacific ports, only 10 were providing any service at all.[11]

Efforts have been made to overcome the high loading and unloading costs and excessive turnaround time involved in operating the conventional

---

[4] *War Shipping Administration Temporary Authority Application,* 260 ICC 589 (1945).

[5] Ibid., p. 593.

[6] Ibid., p. 591.

[7] Interstate Commerce Commission, *Annual Report, 1946,* p. 34.

[8] Interstate Commerce Commission, *Annual Report, 1947,* p. 46.

[9] Committee on Interstate and Foreign Commerce, U.S. Senate, *Merchant Marine Study and Investigation,* 81st Cong., 2d Sess., Senate Rep. No. 2494 (1950), p. 28.

[10] *All Water Rates, Sacramento to Atlantic Ports,* 286 ICC 695, 698 (1952).

[11] *Pan-Atlantic Steamship Corp.—Extension—Intercoastal,* 303 ICC 163, 168 (1957).

general-cargo ships by transporting loaded highway trailers by ship. Two methods of operation—the "roll-on, roll-off" type and the "lift-on, lift-off" type—are in use. The use of highway trailers as containers, or the development of special types of containers which are less wasteful of cargo space than trailers, may prove sufficiently successful to restore coastwise and intercoastal shipping to its former importance. Attempts to revive coastwise and intercoastal shipping by these methods, however, may be countered by rate reductions by railroads where this type of service is instituted.[12]

INLAND WATERWAY TRANSPORTATION

The system of inland waterways in the United States was described in Chapter 2.[13] Before considering the historical development of the system and issues of public policy relating thereto, a glance at the present volume of inland water transportation is helpful. It was pointed out in Chapter 2 that 16 percent of the total freight transportation service performed in 1970 was over the inland waterways including the Great Lakes.[14] In 1969 the total ton-miles of freight service carried by inland water-ways was 302,901,008,000. This traffic was distributed among the various parts of the waterway system as follows:[15]

	Ton-Miles
Atlantic Coast Waterways	26,602,679,000
Gulf Coast Waterways	27,807,696,000
Pacific Coast Waterways	8,060,940,000
Mississippi River System, including Ohio River and tributaries	125,195,008,000
Great Lakes System (excluding traffic between foreign ports)	115,234,683,000
Total	302,901,008,000

HISTORICAL DEVELOPMENT OF INLAND WATERWAYS

Although inland waterways underwent extensive development in the prerailroad era and then suffered a decline after the coming of the railroads, a movement for revival of inland water transportation started in the last decade of the 19th century. In 1901 the first National Rivers and Harbors Congress convened at Baltimore. In 1903 the people of the state of New York voted $101 million to transform the Erie Canal into a modern barge canal. In 1907 President Theodore Roosevelt appointed

---

[12] See *Commodities—Pan-Atlantic S.S. Corp.*, 313 ICC 23 (1960); and *Interstate Commerce Commission* v. *New York, New Haven & Hartford R. Co.*, 372 U.S. 744 (1963).

[13] Pp. 37–40 supra.

[14] P. 20 supra.

[15] Corps of Engineers, U.S. Army, op. cit., p. 29.

a commission, known as the Inland Waterways Commission, to prepare a plan for improving inland waterways. This Commission made a report in 1908, which recommended, among other things, "that the Congress be asked to make more suitable provision for improving the inland waterways of the United States at a rate commensurate with the needs of the people as determined by competent authority."[16] This Commission was succeeded by the National Waterways Commission, which was created in 1909. The report of this body in 1912 contained specific recommendations for legislation to aid water transportation and to bring about greater cooperation between railroads and water carriers.[17]

There were several reasons for the revival of interest in inland water transportation during the early years of the 20th century. First, inland waterway development was part of the program for conservation of natural resources, a movement that was strong during the administration of Theodore Roosevelt. Second, the rising freight rates after 1910, and particularly after the outbreak of World War I, created a demand for cheaper forms of transportation. In the effort to throw off the burden of rising freight rates, the possibilities of water transportation were not overlooked. A third reason for the revival of interest was the belief that the development of waterways would keep rail rates down. Water transportation was seen as an automatic regulator of railway rates. A fourth cause of interest in the movement was the belief that waterways were needed to relieve traffic congestion on the railroads. Recurring periods of traffic congestion were responsible for this belief. Lastly, waterway projects were pushed with vigor by the communities and interests which hoped to gain by the policy. Sectional interests and the ambitions of rival cities have always played an important part in the consideration of specific waterway projects. The true national interest has often been obscured by the struggle between those interests that would gain and those that would lose by the development of a particular waterway.

Development of Waterway Policy

Although the federal government began to aid in the improvement of harbors as early as 1789, there was hesitation by the states before they surrendered control over harbor improvements to the federal government. The first Rivers and Harbors Act was passed in 1823. In the following year an appropriation of $75,000 was voted for the removal of sand bars and other obstructions to navigation in the Mississippi River.[18] After the Civil War the federal government took a more active part in the development of

---

[16] *Preliminary Report*, 60th Cong., 1st Sess., Senate Doc. No. 325, p. 26.

[17] *Final Report of the National Waterways Commission*, 62d Cong., 2d Sess., Senate Doc. No. 469 (1912).

[18] Emory R. Johnson, *History of Domestic and Foreign Commerce of the United States* (Washington, D.C.: Carnegie Institution, 1915), Vol. II, p. 321.

waterways. Since 1866 Congress has made appropriations for rivers and harbors either annually or at intervals of two or three years.

A number of undesirable features characterized federal appropriations for waterway improvements, particularly in the 19th century. In the first place, many projects were authorized which were of little or no benefit to the commerce of the country as a whole. Many waterway appropriations were maneuvered through Congress by logrolling tactics, and waterway appropriations came to be considered as "pork-barrel" legislation. Each congressman was interested in obtaining appropriations for rivers and harbors in his district, regardless of the economic justification of the project. Often the sole benefit sought was the expenditure of public funds in the district, with little expectation that the waterway would prove of value even to the communities concerned.

Another objectionable feature of the federal appropriations was that no plan for the development of a waterway system was formulated. Appropriations were for isolated projects, regardless of their place in a national system.

A third weakness in the method of appropriating money for waterways was piecemeal construction. The National Waterways Commission complained in 1912 that "with the 295 navigable streams and 200 harbors requiring improvement there has been a disposition to distribute river and harbor appropriations over a large number of projects instead of concentrating them upon those which expert investigation showed to be worthy of undertaking."[19]

An effort was made to remedy these features of our policy as early as 1902. The Rivers and Harbors Act of that year provided for the organization of a board in the office of the Chief of Engineers of the Army to be known as the "Board of Engineers for Rivers and Harbors." The Board originally consisted of five engineers, but the number was later increased to seven. The function of the Board is to review, from both an engineering and an economic standpoint, the surveys of waterway projects undertaken by the Corps of Engineers at the direction of Congress. In recent years, too, the practice has been followed of making lump-sum appropriations for rivers and harbors, and this sum is then allotted to various authorized projects by the Chief of Engineers. Each year the Chief of Engineers presents to Congress plans for the development of the waterways, and an effort is made to see that moneys appropriated for waterway improvement are spent where they will be most effective in developing a coordinated system of waterways.

Notwithstanding the careful study of particular waterway projects before they are recommended by the Chief of Engineers for inclusion in an omnibus rivers and harbors bill as an authorized project, there has been much criticism of the resulting program of waterway improvements.

---

[19] Ibid., p. 514.

There is a general belief that waterway projects are approved which cannot be justified by purely economic considerations.[20] Political pressures of interested groups affect the final determination of the waterway projects that are to be included in any rivers and harbors bill.

Waterway Expenditures

Total federal expenditures on waterways to the end of 1971 amounted to over $9.5 billion, state and local expenditures are estimated at approximately $6.4 billion; thus the total public expenditures on waterway facilities amount to approximately $16 billion.[21] Unfortunately, we are unable to say what portion of this expenditure represents investment in waterways facilities, and what portion represents maintenance and operating expenses. The investment in present water transportation facilities cannot be accurately determined from records of expenditures. Capital and maintenance expenditures have not always been clearly distinguished; expenditures for flood control or power development are not always separated from expenditures for navigation; and many sums expended undoubtedly represent work that is no longer used or useful for transportation purposes and ought to be written off.

The Federal Barge-Line Experiment

For many years the federal government operated a barge service on the Mississippi, Illinois, Missouri, and Warrior rivers. The federal barge line was started during World War I and was operated by the United States Railroad Administration, which was then operating the railroads of the country. At the termination of federal operation of railroads in 1920 the barge line was turned over to the War Department. In 1924 the Inland Waterways Corporation was organized to take over the operation of the line. The stock of the Inland Waterways Corporation was all owned by the federal government.

The purpose of the federal barge lines was to demonstrate the practicability of barge operations and to develop a barge service that could later be turned over to a private operator. In 1953 the federal barge lines were sold for $9 million to the Federal Waterways Corporation of Delaware, a subsidiary of the St. Louis Shipbuilding & Steel Co. The name of the purchaser was later changed to Federal Barge Lines, Inc. The terms of sale of the government-owned barge line required the purchaser to continue a barge service substantially similar to that which the government had provided. A minimum number of yearly trips was required between

---

[20] This problem receives further attention in a later chapter. See Chapter 36.

[21] Association of American Railroads, Bureau of Railway Economics, *Government Expenditures for Highway, Waterway, and Air Facilities, etc.* (Washington, D.C., 1971), Table 6.

the various ports served and a minimum amount of less-than-bargeload shipments was to be handled. These restrictions proved burdensome and were removed by act of Congress in 1963.[22]

SOME CHARACTERISTICS OF WATER TRANSPORTATION

We now turn to a consideration of certain characteristics of water transportation which are significant in connection with controversial questions of public policy. Some of these characteristics have already become obvious from what has been said, but their significance requires elaboration.

Government Improvement and Maintenance of Waterways

As has become apparent from preceding pages, waterways are provided by the government to the extent that they are not usable in their natural condition. The federal government and, to a minor degree, the state governments have made the necessary expenditures to construct or improve water transportation facilities. State and local governments have also provided terminal facilities to a considerable extent.

The federal government's jurisdiction over the control and improvement of navigable rivers stems from the power to regulate interstate commerce and was early established by decisions of the Supreme Court of the United States.[23] By later decisions the jurisdiction of the federal government has been found to extend to streams which are not navigable in their natural state but which require improvement before navigation is possible.[24] The federal government's jurisdiction extends, furthermore, to the nonnavigable stretches of a river in order to preserve and promote commerce on the navigable portions.[25]

Water transportation, like highway transportation but unlike railway transportation, is a mode of transport in which the "way" is provided and maintained at public expense. With the exception of the service formerly provided by the Inland Waterways Corporation, transportation service over inland waterways has not been provided by the government. The policy has been to leave the provision of transportation service over waterways to private enterprise.

The provision and maintenance of waterways by governments is significant in that the expansion of water-transportation facilities and the maintenance of existing waterways are to some extent political questions, since decisions regarding the expenditure of public funds on waterways

---

[22] Public Law 88–67, repealing the Inland Waterways Corporation Act.

[23] *Gilman* v. *Philadelphia*, 3 Wall. 724 (1866); *The Daniel Ball*, 10 Wall. 557 (1870); *South Carolina* v. *Georgia*, 93 U.S. 4 (1876).

[24] *United States* v. *Appalachian Electric Power Co.*, 311 U.S. 377 (1940).

[25] *Oklahoma* v. *Atkinson Co.*, 313 U.S. 508 (1941).

are ultimately made by Congress or, in the case of state and local governments, by other legislative authority.

The building and maintaining of waterways by governments also means that part of the cost of water transportation is borne by the taxpayer unless tolls or other special charges are imposed upon waterway users. This point will receive further attention in subsequent paragraphs.

Waterways as Public Highways

Since waterways are provided by the government, it is natural that they be considered as "public highways" which may be used by anyone. Such has been the general policy throughout our history, although the state of New York in the early days of steamboats granted to Robert R. Livingston and Robert Fulton the exclusive right to navigate the waters of the state with boats "moved by fire or steam." This grant was invalidated by the Supreme Court of the United States in 1824, however, as repugnant to the Commerce Clause of the Constitution.[26]

If waterways are considered as public highways for anyone to use, it follows that competition in the establishment of for-hire transportation services over a waterway may be expected. Such has usually been the case. Competing carriers may operate over the same waterway or water route. Freedom to establish competitive water-carrier service, however, has been restricted in recent years by statutory provisions requiring certificates of public convenience and necessity or permits before new for-hire service may be offered.

Classes of Operators on Waterways

Because waterways are public highways, they are used by private individuals and corporations for the transportation of their own property as well as by carriers for hire. For-hire carriers, in turn, are of two kinds: common carriers and contract carriers. The same classification of carriers, it will be recalled, is found in connection with highway transportation.

Private carriers by water are frequently called "proprietary" carriers or "industrial" carriers. Contract carriers by water are frequently referred to as "tramps" or "charterers," the former term being used generally when referring to vessels operating as contract carriers on the high seas. Some carriers operate both as common and as contract carriers. Industrial carriers sometimes transport for hire, particularly when the proprietary traffic is unbalanced.

The public derives the greatest benefit from waterways if common-carrier service is available, since common carriers hold themselves out to serve the public generally, while contract carriers usually confine their

---

[26] *Gibbons* v. *Ogden*, 9 Wheaton 1.

services to those who ship in large lots or quantities. Furthermore, only the larger private concerns with a large volume of traffic can afford to provide themselves with ships or barges to operate as proprietary carriers. When industrial carriers make use of waterways, the benefit of the cheaper transportation that may be afforded by the waterway goes to the industries concerned and not to the general public, except as the cheaper transportation may be reflected in lower prices for the products of those industries or may in some other way be diffused throughout society.

We have already noted that two or more common carriers may compete with each other over a given waterway or water route. The common carriers may also find themselves in competition with contract carriers for the traffic of large shippers, and both common and contract carriers may find their charges limited by the possibility that shippers may obtain ships and barges and perform their own transportation service.

Free Use of Waterways

We have noted that waterways are improved and maintained by the government. With the exception of the Panama Canal and the St. Lawrence Seaway, the waterways under the control of the federal government are free of toll. In the Rivers and Harbors Act of 1882 a provision was incorporated prohibiting the collection of tolls or operating charges for the use of any canal or other improvement of navigation belonging to the United States.[27]

As a result of this situation the taxpayer bears part of the costs of water transportation, and the rates charged by common and contract carriers making use of publicly provided facilities do not reflect the entire cost of the transportation. In some instances, therefore, water transportation seems to be cheaper than railroad transportation when it may not actually be so. The fact that water transportation often appears superficially to be cheaper than other modes of transportation leads to a demand for the expansion of waterway facilities on the ground that they provide cheaper transportation than railroads. Pressure of shippers who stand to gain by the use of free, publicly provided transportation facilities may also lead to the development of waterways that may not really provide a more economical form of transportation if all costs are considered.

Cost of Transportation by Water

To the shipper the one advantage which water transportation has over rail transportation is its cheapness. A study by the National Resources Planning Board in 1942 showed that contract-carrier rates for transporting grain on the Great Lakes were from 0.7 mill to 1 mill per ton-mile.[28] Iron-

---

[27] 22 Stat. 209.
[28] National Resources Planning Board, op. cit., p. 97.

ore charges yielded about 0.8 mill per ton-mile; and coal, 0.5 mill.[29] These rates have been so low that railroads have not attempted to compete for the traffic. Few commodities transported by rail yield less than 5 mills per ton-mile, and the average revenue per ton-mile for the railroads at that time was between 9 and 10 mills. On improved rivers the cost of transportation is greater than on the Great Lakes or on the ocean, but it is lower than by rail. The National Resources Planning Board study showed that contract carriers on the Mississippi River System transported coal at rates as low as 2.3 mills per ton-mile,[30] petroleum at rates which yielded 2.85 mills per ton-mile,[31] grain at 2.1 mills,[32] and sugar at 3.6 mills.[33] Common-carrier rates tend to be higher than the rates of contract carriers, but they are commonly maintained at differentials below the corresponding rail rates.

The lower rates charged by common and contract carriers by water than are charged by rail carriers are to be explained in part by lower costs. The lower costs in turn rest upon two major circumstances. First, the tractive effort required to move a given weight in floating equipment is less than that required to move the same weight on wheels. This holds true, however, only when the movement is slow, for the expenditure of energy to propel a boat through the water increases rapidly as speed is increased. Sometimes, however, the lower cost of moving freight by water is partly offset by the greater distance between two points by water than by rail. This is important on meandering streams like the Mississippi and its tributaries.

The second reason for the lower cost of water transportation is that there is no maintenance or capital charge for the use of the waterway. If the waterway is a natural one, no capital investment was made to provide it. Maintenance expenditures may also be comparatively small or nonexistent. If the waterway is artificial, it was built and is maintained at government expense without charge to the users. In the latter case, water transportation may or may not be cheaper than rail transportation, but it appears to be cheaper because the shipper is not charged with the full cost of the service.

If costs which are borne by the taxpayer were included in the calculations of the cost of water transportation, it would be seen that the real cost is often much greater than is indicated by the charges which are made by common and contract carriers. The study of public aids to transportation made by the Board of Investigation and Research made an attempt to calculate the "unit Federal costs" of transportation on all active waterways for the year 1940. The "unit Federal cost" is the sum of the annual operating and maintenance cost borne by the federal government,

---

[29] Ibid.

[30] Ibid., p. 436.

[31] Ibid., p. 437.

[32] Ibid.

[33] Ibid.

interest on investment, and amortization of investment in the waterway over a fifty-year period, divided by the ton-miles of freight transported over the waterway. As might be expected, these costs vary greatly from one waterway to another. On the Mississippi River from the mouth of the Ohio River to New Orleans the ton-mile cost borne by the taxpayer was only 1.7 mills per ton-mile;[34] from the mouth of the Missouri River to the mouth of the Ohio River it was 4.9 mills.[35] On the Missouri River from Kansas City to its mouth the cost was 107.8 mills, while from Kansas City to Sioux City it was 319 mills.[36] On the Illinois Waterway the unit federal cost was 3.1 mills per ton-mile.[37] Although these computations raise a number of debatable issues,[38] they serve to show that the full economic cost of water transportation must include the costs which are ultimately borne by the taxpayer.

Disadvantages of Water Transportation

Water transportation, particularly on inland waterways, operates under certain disadvantages which make the service less attractive to shippers. The more important of these require mention.

Slowness. Water transportation is normally slower than rail transportation. This is not always the case, however, as the delay incident to switching freight cars at junction points and terminals sometimes more than offsets the greater speed at which freight trains are operated.

Seasonal Character of the Service. Water transportation is impossible on inland waterways during the winter months in the northern parts of the country. Navigation on the Great Lakes is at a standstill during the winter. The New York Barge Canal is open about seven months of the year. In the southern states this difficulty is not experienced, since the waterways can be used throughout the year.

Interruption of Service Due to Drought or Floods. Water transportation upon improved rivers is often interrupted by floods or drought. This difficulty has frequently been experienced on the Mississippi River System.

Transfer of Freight. When freight traffic originates at points which are not on waterways, a transfer of freight from trucks or freight cars to ships or barges is necessary if use is to be made of the waterway. This often absorbs the saving made by the lower costs of water transportation.

[34] Board of Investigation and Research, *Public Aids to Domestic Transportation*, 79th Cong., 1st Sess., House Doc. 159 (1954), p. 584.

[35] Ibid.

[36] Ibid., p. 585.

[37] Ibid.

[38] Among the debatable points is the propriety of amortizing the total capital investment in waterways over a 50-year period. The results must also be qualified by recognition that high unit cost, in some cases, may be due to diversion of traffic from the waterway as a result of rate cutting by railroads.

The same difficulty is encountered if industries are not located at the water front and must haul goods to and from the waterway. Rail service, on the other hand, extends to the industrial plant of the consignor or consignee if siding connections with the railroad are provided. With respect to some types of freight, this disadvantage of water transport is being overcome, in part, by the use of containers or of truck trailers that can be readily transferred to and from ships and barges without handling the contents.

Liability for Loss and Damage.   Under the Harter Act of 1893 the liability of water carriers for loss and damage to goods shipped is less than that of rail carriers. This sometimes makes necessary the purchase of insurance if the shipper is to be adequately protected. This disadvantage of water carriage is not always present, however, as some water carriers provide full insurance for their cargoes, even insuring against losses caused by an "act of God"—losses for which even railroads are not liable.

Railroad Obstruction of Water Transportation

Railroads have naturally led the opposition to the development of waterways which might divert traffic from the rails. They have also engaged in various practices which have tended to limit the development of water transportation. Important among these measures have been failure to establish facilities for the interchange of traffic with water carriers, refusal to establish through routes and joint rates with water lines, discrimination against connecting water carriers in various ways, and rate cutting—even to an out-of-pocket-cost basis or below—where competition with water carriers is encountered. Legislation designed to prevent these practices will be described in a later chapter.

ANALYSIS OF WATERWAY POLICY

The extent to which waterways should be further developed has always been open to argument. Waterway advocates have been energetic in their efforts to encourage further improvement of water transportation facilities. The railroads, on the other hand, have vigorously opposed further expenditures on expansion of the waterway system. The principal arguments advanced on both sides of the controversy require critical examination.

Is Water Transportation Cheaper?

The major argument in behalf of developing waterways is that they afford cheaper transportation than can be provided by railroads. The reduction of transportation costs to a minimum is socially desirable. If water transportation is really cheaper than rail transportation, every effort should be made to develop it.

Water transportation is cheap on natural waterways because the waterway is a gift of Nature. It represents no capital investment on which a return must be earned. Maintenance costs may also be negligible. But not all our waterways are provided by Nature. At the other extreme are the waterways which are largely artificial, like the New York Barge Canal. For the construction of these waterways a large capital expenditure is necessary, and large sums are also necessary to keep the property in condition. When these costs are taken into consideration, water transportation often proves to be more costly than rail transportation. Between these two extremes are waterways requiring varying amounts of expenditure to make them serviceable. For this reason it is impossible to generalize concerning the cost of water transportation.

It is important that proposals for the improvement of waterways be examined carefully for the purpose of determining whether the expenditures are justified. Waterways which do not provide cheaper transportation, all costs considered, have little to justify them from a purely economic standpoint. Waterways which can reasonably be expected to provide cheaper transportation than other modes of transport are presumably justified, and their development should not be prevented in order to protect special interests which may be adversely affected. It should be recognized, however, that to determine whether a waterway will provide cheaper transportation is by no means easy. It involves not only an estimate of capital and maintenance costs but, what is more difficult, a forecast of the traffic which is available for movement over the waterway. The principle stated by former Commissioner Eastman, however, seems basically sound as a guide in the determination of the economic soundness of a proposed waterway project: "In determining whether a new waterway should be constructed, the essential question, it seems to me, is whether, assuming no reduction in the normal rates of competitors, it would make available new means of transportation which could function, taking *all* costs into consideration, more economically than existing means."[39] It should be recognized, however, that there may be situations in which traffic will not support both rail and water transportation facilities and in which water transportation cannot take the place of essential rail transportation service. Under such circumstances it may be the wiser public policy to forego the development of the waterway in order to support necessary rail transportation facilities; but it is doubtful that this should be done at the expense of those who could avail themselves of the cheaper mode of transport if it were developed. The latter, in other words, would seem to be entitled to some concessions from the normal rail rates.

---

[39] Federal Coordinator of Transportation, *Public Aids to Transportation*, Vol. I (Washington, D.C., U.S. Government Printing Office, 1941), p. vii.

Waterways to Relieve Railroad Congestion

Another argument frequently urged in behalf of waterway development is that the waterways are needed to relieve traffic congestion on the railroads. Periods of car shortage and traffic congestion have at times lent strength to this argument. The entrance of the federal government into the barge-line business on the Mississippi and Warrior rivers during World War I was an outgrowth of such a situation. Between the two world wars, however, the argument had little application, since there seemed to be an excess rather than a shortage of transportation facilities. The overloading of the transportation system during World War II revived the argument, however. The contention that inland waterways should be developed to relieve railroad congestion may be applicable in particular situations, but it does not justify indiscriminate expansion of water transportation facilities. The argument needs to be examined with reference to each particular waterway project proposed.

Waterways as Regulators of Railway Rates

One of the most common arguments in behalf of developing waterways is that they have a beneficial effect upon the level of railroad rates. The Windom Committee, which reported to Congress in 1874 on the transportation problem, emphasized this point. It stated that water routes were "the natural competitors and most effective regulators of railway-transportation."[40] It advocated the development of waterways for this reason. The Cullom Committee, reporting to Congress in 1886, made a similar observation about waterways, claiming that they would continue "to exercise . . . an absolutely controlling and beneficially regulating influence upon the charges made upon any and all other means of transit."[41] Anyone familiar with railroad rate structures in the United States will admit that water rates have sometimes had a controlling influence on rail rates. Since this is the case, the demand for water transportation to lower rail rates is very natural. The argument had particular force before railroad regulation had been set up to protect the public from unjust and unreasonable rates. Waterway opponents maintain that the argument is no longer sound, since regulation is competent to keep rates down. Thus H. G. Moulton says: "It is economically indefensible to spend millions of dollars for the purpose of providing 'potential' competition when we have available an infinitely less costly means of regulation."[42] But the contention assumes that a regulatory body can force rates as low as water rates.

---

[40] Select Committee on Transportation Routes to the Seaboard, *Report*, 43d Cong., 1st Sess., Senate Rep. No. 307, Part I, p. 243.

[41] Senate Select Committee on Interstate Commerce, *Report*, 49th Cong., 1st Sess., Senate Rep. No. 46 (1886), p. 170.

[42] H. G. Moulton and Others, *The American Transportation Problem* (Washington, D.C.: Brookings Institution, 1933), p. 437.

Rarely can this be done. Confronted by low water rates, railroads will often reduce their rates to meet the water rates, since it is in their interest to do so. But such rates are subnormal; they are less than "reasonable" rates. Commissions cannot require railroads to charge less than "reasonable" rates. Moulton, in referring to the argument that the St. Lawrence waterway would lower rail rates to the seaboard, suggested direct legislative action as a means of bringing about the same reductions. "Lower rates," he says, "might . . . be secured through legislative means at an infinitesimal expenditure of public money as compared with what would be involved in constructing the waterway."[43] He goes on to say that relief could be made effective by granting low rates on commodities originating in the interior and intended for export, and by granting low import rates on certain other commodities needed by the Middle West. The contention fails to recognize that even a legislative body, less hampered than a commission in its powers, is still limited in its power to require rate reductions. It is highly doubtful whether a legislative body could reduce rates by statute to a basis as low as they would be reduced voluntarily by a railroad confronted with effective water competition. Statutory rates on such a low basis would likely be set aside by the courts as confiscatory.

Although the argument that waterways should be developed to keep rail rates down is not satisfactorily answered by asserting that regulation could accomplish the same purpose, there are other and sounder reasons for questioning a policy of expanding the waterway system to force low rail rates. Under some circumstances such a policy is open to the charge of unfairness. It is not unfair to develop a waterway, and thereby force rail rates to the level of the water rates, when the water rates cover the full cost of the service; but it is another thing to force railroads to meet water rates when the latter do not cover the full cost of the service because the taxpayer is paying part of it.

Subsidized Competition

The railroads argue that since water transportation is subsidized, a condition of unfair competition is created. The water carrier can quote lower rates than the railroad because no charges are made for the use of the waterway. The railroad, on the other hand, has to maintain its road and pay a return on the capital invested in it. Waterway transportation has been developed on the theory that it is proper for the public to pay part of the costs of transportation, since the benefits are so widely diffused. Railroad transportation, on the other hand, has developed on the theory that the users should pay the costs. When the two modes of transport come into competition with each other, the one which is supported in part by public funds has a competitive advantage which is not due to its inherent supe-

---

[43] H. G. Moulton, C. S. Morgan, and A. L. Lee, *The St. Lawrence Navigation and Power Project* (Washington, D.C.: Brookings Institution, 1929), p. 187.

riority. It is clear that the assumption of part of the costs of water transportation by the taxpayer places the railroads at a competitive disadvantage, and that it may result in an allocation of traffic between the two modes of transport that is not based on real differences in transportation costs.

The remedy for this situation would appear not to be the refusal to develop waterways when they will really provide a cheaper mode of transport, all costs considered, but rather to place water transportation upon a "user basis," in so far as that would be possible. This could be done by levying tolls for the use of publicly provided water transportation facilities, thereby shifting from the taxpayer to the user of the waterways the costs associated with providing and maintaining waterways.

Do Waterways Benefit All the People?

Opponents of waterway development frequently allege that the improved waterways benefit only the communities situated on the waterways, and that even there the use of the waterways primarily by private carriers creates a situation in which a few enjoy the benefits paid for by the many. Our waterway policy, it is argued, creates private benefits at public expense.

There is some truth to this argument, but it cannot be accepted without substantial qualification. It is true, of course, that the greatest benefits accrue to the communities located on a waterway. It is also true that there may be changes in industrial location brought about by waterway development. Some communities will obtain a competitive advantage that they did not have before, and other communities will suffer a handicap. But it does not follow that waterway improvement benefits only the communities on the waterway. If a common-carrier service is provided on waterways, and if through routes and joint rates are made with connecting railroads, the benefits of the cheaper transportation by water accrue to all portions of the country. Shipments which move over common-carrier barge lines on the Mississippi River come from nearly every state in the Union. Traffic from distant points is carried over the waterways at a rate which represents the same saving for the water portion of the haul as if the traffic moved only between points on the waterway.

The whole public may gain through waterway expenditures in another way, even if such expenditures bring cheaper transportation to only a limited number of communities. If cheaper transportation of raw materials is made possible for certain industries, and these industries become concentrated on the waterways, the lower costs of production will, under strictly competitive conditions, be reflected in lower prices to consumers.

In so far as waterways are used largely by industrial carriers, it is true that the benefits accrue in the first instance to the industries which use them. Whether the resulting savings simply increase the profits of the favorably located industries, or whether they are passed on to the public in lower prices for the products of the industries concerned, or are in other ways diffused throughout the whole economy, admits of no general answer, for it depends upon the extent to which competitive conditions exist in the industries concerned and upon the resulting price policies which prevail in those industries.[44] Any broad assertion that the benefits resulting from the development of waterways are passed on to the public at large or that they accrue to a limited group of special interests is too simple a statement and cannot stand analysis.

It should be noted also that an argument against improving waterways based on the fact that only a small portion of the public is benefited is not really an argument against developing waterways but is one against developing them at the taxpayers' expense. In so far as our waterway policy has been objectionable on the grounds that the benefits have accrued to a limited group of individuals, an appropriate remedy would be to impose a system of tolls and thereby to transfer to the users the burden of supplying such facilities.

Should Tolls or Other Charges Be Levied on Waterway Users?

From time to time it has been urged that tolls should be levied for the use of waterways which are provided at public expense. We have suggested in previous paragraphs that certain objections to our waterway policy could be overcome by levying tolls, thereby shifting from taxpayers to shippers the cost of providing these facilities. Railroad spokesmen have urged such a policy.[45] The Federal Coordinator favored the imposition of tolls on a moderate scale.[46] The Board of Investigation and Research study of public aids to transportation was also favorable to the proposal,[47] although one member of the Board was opposed.[48]

The principal advantages of a policy of levying tolls for the use of waterways may be summarized as follows: (1) It would remove the charge of unfairness and competitive inequality arising from the present subsidization of water transportation. (2) The rates of water carriers would more nearly reflect the real cost of transportation by water; hence

---

[44] For an extended discussion of this problem, see Federal Coordinator of Transportation, op. cit., Vol. III, pp. 101–10.

[45] *Report of Committee Appointed by the President of the United States to Submit Recommendations upon the General Transportation Situation* (1938), pp. 18–19. (This Committee was known as the "Committee of Six.") See also Statement of the American Short-Line Railroad Association to the House Committee on Interstate and Foreign Commerce in *Investigation of National Transportation Policy* (1945), p. 8; and Association of American Railroads, *Federal Policy Relating to Inland Waterway Transportation* (Washington, D.C., 1950), pp. 27–29.

[46] Federal Coordinator of Transportation, op. cit., Vol. 1, p. vii.

[47] Board of Investigation and Research, op. cit., pp. 47–48, 413–27.

[48] Board Member C. E. Childe, ibid., pp. 38–39.

competition between railroads and water carriers would tend to distribute traffic between waterways and other modes of transport more nearly in accordance with their relative economy and fitness. (3) A more careful scrutiny of proposed waterways, in order to determine their economic soundness, would likely result. (4) The charge that the improvement and maintenance of waterways by the government results in private benefits at public expense would be removed.

In opposition to levying tolls on waterways, it is sometimes argued that such a policy would make the public pay for waterway improvements twice—once as taxpayers and again as users, since user charges must eventually be passed on to the consuming public. Even if tolls were designed to amortize the past investment in waterways—and such is by no means a necessary feature of the policy—it would be more appropriate to recognize the tolls as a reimbursement of the taxpayer for funds advanced to improve the waterways.

There are certain dangers, however, in a policy of levying tolls. Tolls should not be levied that would prevent the use of waterways already in existence. On these waterways, funds have already been expended. Doubtless such projects should be abandoned if the tolls will not defray maintenance costs, but the fact that the traffic will not stand tolls sufficient to yield a normal return on the cost of the waterway is not proof that the waterway should be abandoned. Furthermore, all tolls should be adjusted somewhat in accordance with the ability of the traffic to stand the charge. Canal tolls, before the days of railroads, were adjusted according to the ability of the traffic to bear them. Railroads follow the same practice in fixing their rates. Much rail traffic, we have seen, is carried at rates which are less than the cost of the service if all overhead and constant costs are prorated over the traffic. It is just as sound to levy waterway tolls on this principle as for railroads to make concessions to low-grade traffic. Such a system of levying tolls for the use of waterways would probably fall short of the demands of those who hope, by levying tolls, to drive water traffic back to the railroads.

To advocate the levying of tolls for the use of waterways is not to deny that noneconomic considerations and indirect economic benefits may in particular cases justify the use of public funds for the construction of waterways, even though the waterway would not support itself from tolls. National-defense considerations, for instance, might justify such an expenditure, or indirect economic gains through the development of the resources of an area might warrant the expenditure in the same way that indirect economic benefits sometimes justified public contributions to the construction of railroads in the early days of railroad building. This fact, however, does not lessen the desirability of levying tolls for the support of waterway facilities to the extent that it is possible.

Tolls are not the only form of charge that could be levied for the use of waterways improved by the federal government. An excise tax on fuel consumed on the waterways could be imposed. President Kennedy made such a proposal in 1962,[49] and the recommendations were renewed by President Johnson in 1965.[50] A fuel tax avoids some of the difficult problems necessarily involved in a system of tolls and it would undoubtedly be less expensive to collect. On the other hand, revenues raised by fuel taxes would bear little relationship to expenditures on particular waterways. Tolls, however, can be adjusted to the expenditures on particular waterway facilities.

RATES OF WATER CARRIERS

We now turn from a discussion of waterway policy to a consideration of some aspects of water-carrier rates.

The rates of contract carriers, as we have noted, are generally lower than those of common carriers. The contract carriers, principally because they do not operate on regular routes or according to fixed sailings, and also because they usually carry commodities in large lots, operate with lower costs and hence are able to charge lower rates.

The rates of common carriers by water are frequently patterned on railroad rates, and the railroad freight classifications are generally used. Much of the traffic, however, moves on commodity rates. Some barge lines transport bulk commodities only and publish no class rates, and hence have no need for a freight classification. Water-carrier rates are sometimes established as fixed differentials below rail rates.

In the coastwise and intercoastal service, port-to-port rates often disregard great differences in distance. In the intercoastal trade the rates have commonly been the same from all Atlantic ports—Jacksonville, Florida, to Portland, Maine, inclusive—to all Pacific Coast ports—San Diego, California, to Vancouver, Washington.[51] This disregard of great differences in distance results in part from the fact that many of the costs of water carriers are unrelated to distance. The Interstate Commerce Commission has recognized this characteristic of water-transportation costs.[52]

In the coastwise and intercoastal trade, as well as on foreign-trade routes, steamship lines have generally been organized in "conferences," which endeavor to control rates and competitive practices of the steamship lines engaged in a particular trade. In the intercoastal trade the practice of the conferences has sometimes been to recognize two classes of steamship lines, known as Class A and Class B lines.[53] The Class B lines, because of their less frequent sailings and slower service, have been per-

[49] 87th Cong., 2d Sess., House Doc. No. 384 (1962), p. 6.

[50] 89th Cong., 1st Sess., House Doc. No. 173 (1965), p. 8.

[51] National Resources Planning Board, op. cit., p. 372.

[52] *All Rail Commodity Rates between Calif., Oreg., & Wash.*, 277 ICC 511 (1950).

[53] At times Class C lines have also been recognized.

mitted to maintain rates on some commodities slightly lower than the Class A lines.

On the Mississippi River System and other inland waterways it has been the practice for the common carriers to maintain port-to-port rates which are 80 percent of the corresponding rail rates, i.e., 20 percent lower than the rail rates.[54] The rule is not invariable, however, and there are many exceptions. Extensive joint rail-barge rates are also in effect, and these rates were originally made by deducting from the all-rail rates the 20 percent differential on the water portion of the haul. Thus the joint rail-barge first-class rate between Chicago and New Orleans was originally made $1.15. The first-class rail rate between St. Louis and New Orleans at the time was $1.125; the port-to-port barge rate between St. Louis and New Orleans was 80 percent of this amount, or 90 cents. The difference between the rail and the barge rate was, therefore, 22.5 cents. To arrive at the barge-rail rate from Chicago to New Orleans, this 22.5 cents was deducted from the Chicago–New Orleans rail rate of $1.375, thus making the barge-rail rate $1.15.[55] In constructing these joint rates, the differential represented by the saving on the water portion of the haul was deducted from the direct all-rail rate between origin and destination rather than from the all-rail rate via the port at which the railroad interchanged traffic with the barge line. More recently a system of joint rail-barge rates for application on the Mississippi and Warrior rivers and their tributaries was prescribed by the Interstate Commerce Commission, but the basis on which they were constructed was not explained.[56]

Interaction of Rail and Water Rates

Water-carrier rates are sometimes affected by the corresponding rail rates; in other cases rail rates are affected by water rates.

When water-carrier rates are made differentials under all-rail rates, the water-carrier rates are definitely tied to the rates which the railroads maintain. We have already noted that many common-carrier water rates are constructed on this basis.

On the other hand, we have seen that rail rates are frequently affected by water rates. This is particularly true on low-grade commodities moved in bulk which can be transported cheaply by water. In some cases the railroad rates are affected by the cost at which commodities may be transported by industrial carriers. In an earlier chapter the importance of water competition in explaining departures from the Long-and-Short-Haul Clause by railroads was noted.[57] Many other examples of the effect of water competition on rail rates might be given. Figure 31–2 shows how

---

[54] See *Rail and Barge Joint Rates*, 270 ICC 591, 597 (1948).

[55] Ibid., n. 24.

[56] *Rail and Barge Joint Rates*, 270 ICC 591 (1948), 274 ICC 229 (1949).

[57] Pp. 494–96, supra.

FIGURE 31–2. All-Rail Carload Rates on Green Coffee from New Orleans, January 1, 1937, Showing Effect of Barge Rates on Rail Rates

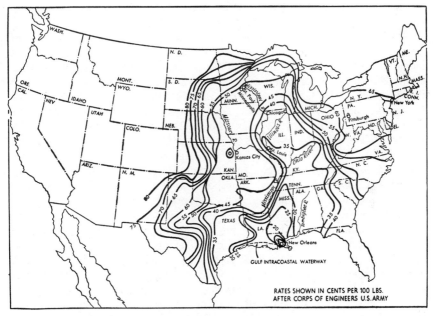

RATES SHOWN IN CENTS PER 100 LBS.
AFTER CORPS OF ENGINEERS U.S. ARMY

Map from National Resources Planning Board, op. cit., p. 445.

the all-rail carload rates on green coffee from New Orleans have been affected by barge transportation on the Mississippi River. Green coffee is a commodity which is well adapted to barge transportation and which cannot be held to the rails where barge transportation is available without substantial reductions in rates.

Questions of principle relating to the adjustment of rates between competing modes of transport are discussed in a later chapter.[58]

SELECTED REFERENCES

A number of periodical articles are valuable for the reader interested in water transportation. Among these are the following: Lytle Brown, "Water Transportation in the United States," 9 *Harvard Business Review* 202 (1931); G. L. Wilson and H. S. Perry, "Intercoastal Shipping," 171 *Annals of the American Academy of Political and Social Science* 211 (1934); I. M. Bettman, "The United States Intercoastal-Shipping Conference," 12 *Harvard Business Review* 116 (1933); Yates Catlin, "By Barge—River Transportation's Confluence," 345 *Annals of the American Academy of Political & Social Sciences* 89 (1963).

Water transportation is discussed in Federal Coordinator of Transportation, *Regulation of Transportation Agencies*, 73d Cong., 2d Sess., Senate Doc. No.

---

[58] Chapter 37.

152 (1934), particularly pp. 5–13 and Appendix A, Part I. Waterway policy is discussed in President's Water Resources Policy Commission, *A Water Policy for the American People*, Vol. I (Washington, D.C.: U.S. Government Printing Office, 1950), chap. xiv.

Much factual material relating to water transportation and a discussion of some of the controversial issues involved are in the two official investigations of public aid to transportation, namely, Federal Coordinator of Transportation, *Public Aids to Transportation*, Vol. III (Washington, D.C.: U.S. Government Printing Office, 1939), summarized in Vol. I (1941), pp. 20–25, 47–49, 52, 54–60; and Board of Investigation and Research, *Public Aids to Domestic Transportation*, 78th Cong., 1st Sess., House Doc. No. 159 (1945), pp. 65–74, 323–427. Waterway policy is critically considered in Senate Committee on Interstate and Foreign Commerce, *Domestic Land & Water Transportation*, 82d Cong., 1st Sess., Senate Rep. No. 1039 (1951), pp. 28–38. See also Senate Committee on Commerce, *National Transportation Policy*, 87th Cong., 1st Sess., Senate Report No. 445 (1961), the "Doyle Report," pp. 197–209.

Factual material relating to inland waterways and barge transportation may be found in Braxton B. Carr, "Inland Water Transportation Resources," in National Academy of Sciences, National Research Council, *U.S. Transportation: Resources, Performance & Problems* (Washington, D.C., 1961), p. 269.

Private studies of the water transportation problem are: H. G. Moulton et al., *The American Transportation Problem* (Washington, D.C.: Brookings Institution, 1933), Part V; Marshall E. Dimock, *Developing America's Waterways* (Chicago: University of Chicago Press, 1935). See also Charles L. Dearing and Wilfred Owen, *National Transportation Policy* (Washington, D.C.: Brookings Institution, 1949), chap. v.

Some problems of coastwise and intercoastal shipping in the postwar period are analyzed in U.S. Department of Commerce, Maritime Administration, *A Review of the Coastwise and Intercoastal Shipping Trades* (Washington, D.C., 1955); and John L. Hazard, *Crisis in Coastal Shipping: The Atlantic-Gulf Case* (Austin: Bureau of Business Research, University of Texas, 1955).

An analysis of water transport costs is found in John R. Meyer et al., *The Economics of Competition in the Transportation Industries* (Cambridge: Harvard University Press, 1959), pp. 111–26.

Chapter 32 | REGULATION OF WATER TRANSPORTATION

Chapter **REGULATION OF WATER**

32 **TRANSPORTATION**

The present system of regulation of coastwise, inter-coastal, and inland transportation by water was set up by the Transportation Act of 1940. Prior to this time the Interstate Commerce Commission had very limited jurisdiction over certain water carriers. Some other water carriers were under the jurisdiction of the United States Maritime Commission; others were not regulated at all. In order to understand the present system of regulation, it is necessary to relate some of the history of regulation prior to 1940.

HISTORY OF REGULATION PRIOR TO 1940

The Act of 1887

The Act to Regulate Commerce, passed in 1887, gave the Interstate Commerce Commission jurisdiction over carriers engaged in the transportation of persons or property "partly by railroad and partly by water when both are used under a common control, management, or arrangement for continuous carriage or shipment." Some difficulty was experienced in determining what constituted an "arrangement for continuous carriage or shipment," and judicial interpretation of the Act was necessary.[1] When the Interstate Commerce Commission gained jurisdiction over a water carrier under this provision of the statute, its control was limited to joint rail and water traffic and did not extend to port-to-port traffic of the water carrier,[2] although the Commission could require accounts and reports of the carriers covering their entire operations.[3]

The Panama Canal Act, 1912

The Interstate Commerce Commission also derived jurisdiction over certain water carriers by the provisions of the Panama Canal Act of 1912.

---

[1] *United States* v. *Munson Steamship Line*, 283 U.S. 43 (1931).

[2] *In the Matter of Jurisdiction over Water Carriers*, 15 ICC 205, 211 (1909).

[3] *Interstate Commerce Commission* v. *Goodrich Transit Co.*, 224 U.S. 194 (1912).

This Act, which will be discussed more fully elsewhere,[4] provided that railroads may not have any interest in a common carrier by water with which the railroad does or may compete for traffic. The Act then provided that the Commission might under certain conditions permit railroads to operate competing boat lines. When the Commission granted such authorization, the water carrier controlled by the railroad was to be subject to the jurisdiction of the Commission in the same manner and to the same extent as the rail carrier. In this situation, therefore, the Interstate Commerce Commission even had control over the port-to-port rates of the water carrier.[5]

The Shipping Act, 1916

Additional carriers by water were subjected to regulation by the Shipping Act of 1916. This Act created the United States Shipping Board and gave it jurisdiction over common carriers by water operating in interstate or foreign commerce on the high seas and upon the Great Lakes. Although the Shipping Act brought an important segment of water transportation under regulatory control, the limited jurisdiction of the Board needs to be emphasized in order to understand later developments. (1) The Board had no control over contract carriers. (2) Water carriers operating upon inland waterways other than the Great Lakes did not come under the Act. (3) By specific provision the Board did not have concurrent jurisdiction with the Interstate Commerce Commission over such carriers as were under the jurisdiction of the latter; thus water carriers coming under the Commission's jurisdiction as a result of the Panama Canal Act were not subject to the Shipping Board.

The Shipping Act represented an attempt to legalize a certain amount of self-regulation in the shipping industry and at the same time to protect the public against the partial monopoly resulting. It also sought to forbid certain objectionable competitive practices which had developed in the industry, some of which might easily lead to monopoly.

Conference Agreements and the Shipping Act

Control of competition in the shipping industry had been practiced for many years through so-called "conferences" and "conference agreements." The House Committee on the Merchant Marine and Fisheries declared in 1914:

It is the almost universal practice for steamship lines engaging in the American foreign trade to operate . . . under the terms of written agreements,

---

[4] See Chapter 36.

[5] For assertion of authority over port-to-port rates in this situation, see *Changes in Schedules to Meet Water Competition,* 176 ICC 217, 222–23 (1931); *Rail and Water Rates from Atlantic Seaboard,* 63 ICC 267, 275 (1921); *Reduced Rates from New York Piers,* 81 ICC 312, 330 (1923).

conference arrangements or gentlemen's understandings, which have for their principal purpose the regulation of competition through either (1) the fixing or regulation of rates, (2) the apportionment of traffic by allotting the ports of sailing, restricting the number of sailings, or limiting the volume of freight which certain lines may carry, (3) the pooling of earnings from all or a portion of the traffic, or (4) meeting the competition of non-conference lines.[6]

Eighty of these agreements were examined by the Committee. Similar conferences have existed in the coastwise and intercoastal trade. Such agreements have been partially, but not wholly, successful in stabilizing rates and controlling competition. It is clear that agreements of this sort are in restraint of free competition and might easily run afoul of the Sherman Antitrust Act.

The Shipping Act of 1916 legalized conference agreements. It required all common carriers by water, whether engaged in foreign or domestic trade, to file with the Shipping Board all agreements "fixing or regulating transportation rates or fares; giving or receiving special rates, accommodations, or other special privileges or advantages; controlling, regulating, preventing, or destroying competition; pooling or apportioning earnings, losses, or traffic; allotting ports or restricting or otherwise regulating the number and character of sailings between ports; limiting or regulating in any way the volume or character of freight or passenger traffic to be carried. . . ."[7] The Board had authority to approve, disapprove, or modify any of these agreements. Any agreement approved by the Board was lawful and was exempt from the prohibitions of the Antitrust Act. Agreements not approved by the Board were unlawful and might not be carried out.[8] The Board and its successors have approved many conference agreements.

Conference agreements which were not under the control of a regulatory body would be undesirable. In so far as the agreements were successful in eliminating competition they would give the carriers a certain degree of monopoly power; but such power would be limited somewhat by the existence of contract carriers and by the possibility of private carriage. After a careful consideration of the subject in 1914 the House Committee on the Merchant Marine and Fisheries reached the conclusion that the conference agreements were useful and should not be prohibited but that they should be brought under government control.[9] This was in accordance with other expert opinion,[10] and it accounts for the provisions

---

[6] Committee on Merchant Marine and Fisheries, House of Representatives, *Report on Steamship Agreements and Affiliations in the American Foreign & Domestic Trade*, 63d Cong., 2d Sess., House Doc. No. 805 (1914), p. 415.

[7] Section 15.

[8] Except that agreements existing at the time of the organization of the Board were to be lawful unless and until disapproved by it.

[9] House Committee on Merchant Marine and Fisheries, op. cit., pp. 416–18.

[10] See E. R. Johnson, "Competition versus Cooperation in the Steamship Business: Proposed Legislation," 55 *Annals of the American Academy of Political and Social Science* 1, 7 (1914).

of the Shipping Act which placed conference agreements under the supervision of the Shipping Board.

The Shipping Act and Unfair Competitive Practices

There were a number of provisions of the Shipping Act which were designed to curb objectionable competitive practices among water carriers.

1. Section 19 of the Act was intended to prevent what is sometimes described as "cutthroat" competition. It provided that "whenever a common carrier by water in interstate commerce reduces its rates . . . below a fair and remunerative basis with the intent of driving out or otherwise injuring a competitive carrier by water, it shall not increase such rates unless after a hearing the board finds that such proposed increase rests upon changed conditions other than the elimination of said competition."

2. In an effort to prevent another objectionable practice, the Shipping Act made it unlawful for any common carrier by water to persuade or influence any insurance company or underwriter not to give a competing carrier by water as favorable a rate of insurance on its vessels or cargoes as is granted to it or to another carrier.[11]

3. Deferred rebates were also prohibited. The term "deferred rebates" was defined in the Act as

    a return of any portion of the freight money by a carrier to any shipper as a consideration for the giving of all or any portion of his shipments to the same or any other carrier, or for any other purpose, the payment of which is deferred beyond the completion of the service for which it is paid, and is made only if, during both the period for which computed and the period of deferment, the shipper has complied with the terms of the rebate agreement or arrangement.[12]

    Deferred rebates had commonly been given by steamship lines to such shippers as would agree to give all their shipments to a given line or to lines in a certain conference. This is a device which common carriers by water have used to fight the competition of tramp steamers which do not provide a regular service. There was some question regarding the desirability of permitting the practice to continue. The carriers were inclined to defend it, but Congress decided to prohibit it.[13]

---

[11] Section 16.

[12] Section 14.

[13] The United States is the only country which prohibits deferred rebates. Although American-flag steamship lines may not use deferred rebates, the carriers have developed a "dual-rate" system, or "contract-noncontract rate" system, which accomplishes about the same objective as deferred rebates. This device is discussed later in this chapter.

4. The Shipping Act prohibited the use of "fighting ships." The term was defined in the Act as "a vessel used in a particular trade by a carrier or group of carriers for the purpose of excluding, preventing or reducing competition by driving another carrier out of said trade." "Fighting ships" have sometimes been put in service by the larger steamship lines. They were able to quote ruinously low rates to drive out competing lines. The larger lines had more frequent sailings and maintained remunerative rates, except when the smaller operators were trying to obtain cargoes; at such times the "fighting ships" of the larger lines would appear and cut rates to prevent the independent from obtaining any traffic.[14]

5. The Shipping Act also forbade retaliation against shippers who had patronized other lines. The Act prohibited retaliation in the form of "refusing, or threatening to refuse, space accommodations when such are available, or resort to other discriminating or unfair methods, because such shipper has patronized any other carrier. . . ."

Regulation to Protect Shippers

Although the regulatory measures which we have described were directly or indirectly of benefit to the shipper, their first object was to protect the carriers from ruinous competition and to prevent unfair competitive practices. In addition to these measures the Shipping Act contained provisions designed to protect the shipping public against real or possible monopolistic practices. The following provisions fall into this class:

1. Common carriers by water engaged in interstate commerce were required to publish and file with the Board their maximum rates. The carriers were required to charge no more than these maxima, which were not to be changed except upon ten days' notice. It is to be noted that the Act did not require water carriers to publish and file their actual rates and to adhere to them. In this respect the law was much less strict than the provisions of the Interstate Commerce Act applicable to railroads.

2. It was provided that all rates of interstate common carriers by water should be just and reasonable. The Shipping Board was empowered to determine the reasonableness of rates and might prescribe maximum reasonable rates when existing rates were found unreasonable. However, the Board did not have power to prescribe minimum rates.

3. The Act forbade undue or unreasonable preference and advantage "to any particular person, locality, or description of traffic," or any unjust discrimination.

---

[14] For an example, see House Committee on Merchant Marine and Fisheries, op. cit., pp. 393–94.

The Shipping Board and Its Successors

The Shipping Board originally consisted of five members, appointed by the President with the advice and consent of the Senate. It was not a purely regulatory body, since it had other functions as well. The Act which created the Shipping Board was entitled: "An Act to establish a United States Shipping Board for the purpose of encouraging, developing and creating a naval auxiliary and naval reserve and a merchant marine to meet the requirements of the commerce of the United States with its Territories and possessions and with foreign countries; to regulate carriers by water engaged in the foreign and interstate commerce of the United States; and for other purposes." The developmental functions of the Board in connection with the establishment of a merchant marine occupied more of its time and attention than the regulatory functions. The Shipping Board was enlarged to seven members in 1920. In 1932 the "Economy Act" reduced the number to three; and in 1933 the Board lost its independent status when, by executive order, it became the United States Shipping Board Bureau of the Department of Commerce. By the Merchant Marine Act of 1936 the United States Maritime Commission, consisting of five members, was created to take over the administration of the Shipping Act and related Acts. In 1950 the Federal Maritime Board, consisting of three members, was created by executive order under the provisions of the Reorganization Act of 1949 to take over the functions of the Maritime Commission.[15] The Federal Maritime Board was placed in the Department of Commerce. By another Reorganization Plan, the Federal Maritime Board became the Federal Maritime Commission in 1961.[16] The membership was increased to five, and the Commission became an independent agency and not a part of the Department of Commerce.

Intercoastal Shipping Act, 1933

As a result of intense competition in the intercoastal trade after World War I, due partly to overtonnaging of this service, Congress enacted the Intercoastal Shipping Act of 1933 to strengthen controls over competition in this service. The Act applied only to carriers operating in intercoastal commerce via the Panama Canal. The Act applied, however, to contract carriers as well as to common carriers. This result was accomplished by making the Act applicable to all common carriers, but common carriers were defined as "every common and contract carrier" by water. The Act required carriers to file their actual rates with the Shipping Board, rather than maximum rates only, and required them to adhere strictly to such rates. Thirty days' notice was required for any change in rates, either

---

[15] See *Reorganization Plan No. 21 of 1950,* 81st Cong., 2d Sess., House Doc. No. 526 (1950).

[16] *Reorganization Plan No. 7 of 1961.*

upward or downward. The Board, however, was not given the power to prescribe minimum rates.

Amendments to the law in 1938[17] extended the provisions of the Intercoastal Shipping Act to common carriers in the coastwise service and on the Great Lakes, but apparently only to common carriers in the strict sense, and not to contract carriers. The same amendments gave the Maritime Commission power to prescribe minimum rates of carriers subject to its jurisdiction in intercoastal and coastwise service, but not to those operating on the Great Lakes.

WHY REGULATION OF WATER CARRIERS?

The description of the evolution of control over water carriers reveals that regulation developed more slowly than railroad regulation and that it had not, by 1940, become as comprehensive in its coverage or as complete in its controls as had railroad regulation.

The reasons for the situation just noted are not far to seek. In the first place, competitive conditions have prevailed in the water-transport industry to a considerable degree, since the carriers make use of natural waterways, or waterways improved or provided by the government. Common carriers by water can operate over the same routes in competition with each other, and common carriers encounter competition from contract carriers and private carriers. The opportunity for monopoly charges is thus remote, and complaints of excessive rates are infrequent.

In the second place, the circumstances which gave rise to various abuses among railroads do not exist to so large a degree among water carriers. If we assume that the supply of ships or barges can and will be adjusted to the volume of traffic available, we shall find that water carriers do not have the large mass of fixed costs that characterize railroads. This is due largely to the fact that water carriers do not have to provide the waterway or maintain it. Fixed costs in the railroad industry, it will be recalled, arise largely from the huge investment in the railway and from the necessity of maintaining a large physical plant.[18] Since fixed costs are relatively small in the water-transport industry, we should not expect to find the industry characterized by the practices which ordinarily arise from the existence of such costs, namely, competition of the ruinous type, discriminating rates, and the pressure to combine in order to control competition. There are some students of transportation who seriously question whether regulation of water carriers is necessary, at least to the extent to which it was finally established in 1940.[19]

---

[17] 52 Stat. 953, 964.

[18] See pp. 143–45, supra.

[19] Ralph L. Dewey, "The Transportation Act of 1940," 31 *American Economic Review* 15 (1941), pp. 18–21; James C. Nelson, "New Concepts in Transportation Regulation," in National Resources Planning Board, *Transportation and National*

Our account of the development of water-carrier regulation up to the time of the enactment of the Transportation Act of 1940, however, reveals that such regulation as we had at that time had developed in an effort to prevent certain undesirable practices. In the ocean-shipping industry, particularly, conditions have commonly existed which create overcapacity, or overtonnaging, and which lead to rate cutting, discrimination, and undesirable practices. This has been particularly true on foreign-trade routes where the ships of many nations compete, sometimes on a subsidized basis. Furthermore, during periods of war, huge shipbuilding programs are undertaken as a war necessity. At the end of hostilities there is left a supply of ships greatly in excess of the tonnage needed for peacetime commerce. Although domestic shipping, with which we are primarily concerned in this book, is less likely to be affected by overcapacity than international shipping, because foreign vessels are excluded from engaging in coastwise and intercoastal trade, our coastwise and intercoastal shipping has been overtonnaged at times partly as a result of our wartime shipbuilding programs.

When overtonnaging occurs, or even when a shrinkage in traffic or a temporary excess of shipping space occurs on a given route, the carriers are likely to engage in drastic rate cutting and undesirable practices in the scramble for cargo. Once a ship is committed to sail, most of the expenses of operating the ship are fixed. Expenses will be nearly the same whether the ship is fully loaded or only partly loaded. Any freight that can be obtained at a rate which covers something more than mere handling costs will be taken. Short-run variable costs dominate rate making at this point.

It is this situation which has led to the almost universal organization of steamship operators into "conferences" to stabilize rates and prevent the ruinous type of competition. Belief in the necessity for such conferences led to the legalization of steamship conferences by the Shipping Act of 1916, as we have previously pointed out.

In international shipping, regulation must be self-regulation by the industry, rather than government regulation, since no nation has effective control over the shipping of other nations. In domestic water transportation, however, direct government control through rate regulation, certificate requirements, and the like, can be substituted for the self-regulation represented by conference agreements, or it can supplement such regulation. The Intercoastal Shipping Act of 1933 and its later amendments represented a move in this direction. Direct government control to stabilize rates and practices is superior to regulation by the industry itself; and to the extent that self-regulation is permitted, it should be under the close supervision of the government, or abuses will arise resulting from the monopoly power given.

Policy (Washington, D.C.: U.S. Government Printing Office, 1942), pp. 197–237; John C. Spychalski, "On the Nonutility of Domestic Water Transport Regulation," 37 *I.C.C. Practitioners' Journal* 7 (1969).

Although the conditions of overcapacity, short-run pricing, and various attendant abuses have occurred most commonly in ocean shipping, a similar situation can make its appearance on inland waterways, giving rise to a demand for regulatory action in this branch of the water-carrier industry.

In the extension of regulation to water carriers operating in the coastwise and intercoastal service and on inland waterways, another factor has been of importance. If unregulated water carriers are competitive with railroads, or if some water carriers are regulated and others are not, the regulated carriers are at a competitive disadvantage. The regulated carriers are required, quite properly, to publish their rates and to adhere to them, while the unregulated carriers are free to charge whatever rates may be expedient at the moment and to discriminate between persons. Recognition of this situation was important in bringing about the extension of regulation to inland water transportation in 1940.

DEMAND FOR FURTHER REGULATION

It will be observed that the regulatory situation with respect to water carriers was somewhat confusing just prior to the enactment of the Transportation Act of 1940. Authority over water carriers was divided between the Interstate Commerce Commission and the United States Maritime Commission. Many water carriers were not regulated at all. Both the Maritime Commission and the Interstate Commerce Commission had different degrees of control over different carriers subject to their respective jurisdictions, and certain controls were entirely lacking.

With this situation existing, and with the railroads becoming more concerned with competition from water carriers, it was not strange that there was agitation for further control of water carriers and that the railroads should be among the supporters of additional control. The Federal Coordinator of Transportation gave careful consideration to the problem in 1934 and came to the conclusion that more effective regulation of water carriers was desirable.[20] This recommendation was renewed, with further analysis, in 1936.[21] The Coordinator considered that the essentials of effective regulation were (1) control over the amount of competitive service afforded, (2) control over minimum rates, (3) control over the operations of private and contract carriers, (4) adherence to published schedules and prevention of unjust discrimination, and (5) coordination with other forms of transportation.[22] The proposal that water carriers be further reg-

---

[20] Federal Coordinator of Transportation, *Regulation of Transportation Agencies*, 73d Cong., 2d Sess., Senate Doc. No. 152 (1934), pp. 10–13.

[21] *Fourth Report of the Federal Coordinator of Transportation*, 74th Cong., 2d Sess., House Doc. No. 394 (1936), pp. 7–22.

[22] *Regulation of Transportation Agencies*, pp. 11–12.

ulated also met with the approval of the Interstate Commerce Commission.[23]

Opposition to regulation of water carriers came largely from those who feared that it might result in regulation in the interest of the railroads rather than in the interest of the shipping public. This fear was doubtless intensified by the eagerness of the railroads to have water carriers brought under the control of the Interstate Commerce Commission.

TRANSPORTATION ACT OF 1940

Congress responded to the agitation for more effective regulation of water carriers by including provisions in the Transportation Act of 1940 which set up a new and expanded form of regulation of water carriers. The Act transferred to the Interstate Commerce Commission the jurisdiction over domestic water transportation which had been under the Maritime Commission; it brought additional water carriers under regulation; and it enlarged the regulatory powers to be exercised. The Maritime Commission, however, retained jurisdiction over water transportation in foreign commerce and also over commerce between points in continental United States and the territories of Hawaii, Alaska, and the various possessions of the United States. The control retained by the United States Maritime Commission is now exercised by the Federal Maritime Commission. The acts of Congress which provided for the admission of Alaska and Hawaii into the Union in 1958[24] and 1959,[25] respectively, specifically provided that the Federal Maritime Board, now the Federal Maritime Commission, should retain its jurisdiction over water carriers engaged in transportation between any port in those states and other ports of the United States, and that jurisdiction was not transferred to the Interstate Commerce Commission.

By the Transportation Act of 1940 the new provisions relating to water transportation were added as Part III of the Interstate Commerce Act. In addition to adding Part III to the Interstate Commerce Act, the Transportation Act of 1940 made water carriers subject also to certain provisions of Part I of the Act.

Provisions of Part 1 of the Interstate Commerce Act Applicable to Water Carriers

1. Water carriers were made subject to Section 4—the Long-and-Short-
   Haul Clause. This was done notwithstanding the fact that water-

---

[23] Interstate Commerce Commission, *Annual Report, 1937*, p. 105. See also comments in *Annual Report, 1940*, pp. 14–15.

[24] Public Law 85–508.

[25] Public Law 86–3.

carrier rates have very rarely violated the long-and-short-haul principle.

2. Water carriers were also brought under the provisions of Section 5, paragraph 1, which relate to pooling agreements.

3. Water carriers were made subject to the provisions of Section 5 of Part I, relating to consolidation, merger, or other forms of unification. Thus water carriers are now subject to the same requirements as railroads in so far as consolidations and unifications are concerned.

4. The provisions of Part I relating to the granting of free passes, free transportation, and transportation at reduced rates were made applicable to carriers by water.

5. In 1948, when Congress passed the Reed-Bulwinkle Act, relating to the control of rate bureaus and agreements among carriers, its provisions were also made applicable to water and motor carriers.[26]

Part III of the Interstate Commerce Act

Part III of the Act relates specifically to water carriers. It applies to common and contract carriers by water engaged in interstate or foreign commerce, but the treatment of contract carriers is somewhat different than that of common carriers, as will be noted in more detail in a subsequent paragraph.

Exemptions

There are numerous water carriers which are made exempt from the provisions of the Act. In fact, the exemptions are so numerous and important that the Interstate Commerce Commission has said that its jurisdiction "is limited to a small portion of the total transportation by water performed in the United States."[27] One estimate is that only about 10 percent of all tonnage shipped by water is subject to regulation.[28] An enumeration of the principal exemptions will indicate why so little water transportation comes under the Commission's control.

1. The transportation of commodities in bulk is exempt "when the cargo space of the vessel in which such commodities are transported is being used for the carrying of not more than three such commodities." The statute then specifies that "two or more vessels while navigated as a unit shall be considered to be a single vessel." Thus if more than three bulk commodities are transported in a single tow consisting of numerous barges, the exemption of the bulk commodities is lost. The Commission held, furthermore, that regulated or nonexempt com-

---

[26] For provisions of the Act see pp. 269–70 and 325–26, supra.

[27] Interstate Commerce Commission, *Annual Report, 1943*, p. 128.

[28] Interstate Commerce Commission, *Annual Report, 1946*, p. 36.

modities could not be transported in the same tow as bulk commodities without the latter losing their exemption.[29] This restriction, however, was removed for an experimental three-year period by an amendment to the Act in 1970,[30] thus permitting the transportation of general commodities and bulk commodities in the same tow without loss of the bulk cargo exemption.

2. Transportation of liquid cargoes in bulk in tank vessels is also exempt from regulation.

3. Transportation by contract carriers is exempt when "by reason of the inherent nature of the commodities transported, their requirement of special equipment, or their shipment in bulk," it is not actually and substantially competitive with transportation by any common carrier which is subject to Parts I, II, or III of the Act. Contract carriers claiming exemption under this provision must make application to the Commission for such exemption.[31]

4. Private transportation is exempt, since the Act applies only to common and contract carriers; and there is a further exemption of carriers transporting property of a person who owns all or substantially all of the voting stock of such carrier.

5. There is an exemption provided for transportation which is incidental to transportation by railroad, motor carrier, or express company and which is in the nature of transfer, collection, or delivery services in terminal areas or has to do with the performance of floatage, car ferry, lighterage, or towage.

In addition to the above exemptions there are certain other conditional exemptions. The conditional or qualified nature of these exemptions arises from the fact that the carriers are exempt except to the extent that the Commission shall find, and by order declare, that application of the Act "is necessary to carry out the national transportation policy declared in this Act." The conditional or qualified exemptions are (1) transportation in interstate commerce by water solely within the limits of a single harbor or between places in contiguous harbors, when not a part of a through movement to or from places beyond; (2) transportation by small craft of not more than one hundred tons carrying capacity, and certain other small craft;[32] and (3) ferries and certain other special types of operations.

The exemption of bulk cargoes was based in part on the belief that such transportation was not competitive with railroads or motor carriers. As a matter of fact, much of the bulk commodity movement by water is competitive with the railroads. The latter are at a serious disadvantage in com-

---

[29] *Portland Tug & Barge Co. Extension,* 265 ICC 325, 335 (1948).

[30] Public Law 91–590.

[31] For an example and the grant of an exemption, see *Bulk Food Carriers, Inc.— Exemption Application,* 326 ICC 106 (1965).

[32] The Commission has found that certain types of small craft should be regulated. See *Application of Part III to Transportation by Small Craft,* 260 ICC 155 (1943).

peting for it, since they must adhere to published rates while the exempt carriers are free to make whatever rates are necessary to obtain the traffic. For this reason considerable sentiment has developed for repeal of the bulk cargo exemption.[33] For many years the Interstate Commerce Commission recommended such action. These recommendations were strongly seconded by the Doyle Report, made for the Senate Committee on Commerce in 1961.[34] Failure of Congress to respond has led to an alternative proposal, namely, to extend the bulk commodity exemption to railroads. The Doyle Report concluded that such action would deregulate approximately 70 percent of railroad carload tonnage and would make regulation so generally ineffective that it would necessarily be abandoned.[35]

Common-Carrier Regulation

The pattern of regulation applied to common carriers by water follows closely that applied to railroads and to common carriers by motor vehicle. For this reason it is unnecessary to give the provisions of the Act in detail. The familiar provisions are found requiring that all rates must be just and reasonable and free from unjust discrimination or undue preference and prejudice. Through routes and joint rates with other water carriers and with railroads may be required by the Commission.[36] Rates must be published and strictly observed, and 30 days' notice of changes in rates is required. The Commission has the power to prescribe maximum, minimum, or maximum and minimum rates, and the power to suspend proposed changes in rates. The Act contains a "Rule of Rate Making" in Section 307 (f) which is very similar to Section 15a in Part I of the Act. The Commission may prescribe a uniform system of accounts for water carriers and require reports of the carriers.

Certificates of Public Convenience and Necessity

As in motor-carrier regulation the provisions relating to control of entry into the business of common carriage are important. The Act requires certificates of public convenience and necessity of water carriers, but a "grandfather clause" entitled a common carrier to a certificate who was in bona fide operation as a common carrier by water on January 1,

---

[33] Senate Committee on Interstate and Foreign Commerce, *Domestic Land & Water Transportation*, 82d Cong., 1st Sess., Senate Rep. No. 1039 (1951), pp. 15–17; Presidential Advisory Committee on Transport Policy and Organization, *Revision of Federal Transportation Policy* (Washington, D.C.: U.S. Government Printing Office, 1955), pp. 16–17.

[34] *National Transportation Policy*, 87th Cong., 1st Sess., Senate Report No. 445 (1961), pp. 529–32.

[35] Ibid., p. 533.

[36] In this respect water carriers are treated more strictly than motor carriers of property. See p. 683, supra.

1940, and who had so operated since that time. A certificate granted under the "grandfather clause" covers operations over the routes the carrier had served or between the ports it had served.

When a certificate is sought which is not covered by the "grandfather clause," the carrier must prove that it is "fit, willing, and able" properly to perform the service proposed and to conform to the requirements of the Act and the rules and regulations of the Commission thereunder and that the proposed service "is or will be required by the present or future public convenience and necessity."

Differences between Regulation of Common Carriers by Water and Railroad Regulation

Although the regulatory system prescribed for common carriers by water follows the earlier pattern of railroad regulation, there are certain differences which ought not to be overlooked. The more important of these are as follows:

1. There is no control over abandonment of operation by water carriers.
2. Water carriers are not subject to financial regulation.
3. Federal interference with intrastate water rates to remove discrimination against interstate commerce is prohibited, since Section 303 (k) provides that "nothing in this part shall authorize the Commission to prescribe or regulate any rate, fare, or charge for intrastate transportation . . . for the purpose of removing discrimination against interstate commerce or for any other purpose."

Regulation of Contract Carriers

The regulation provided for contract carriers differs from that provided for common carriers. The principal differences are as follows:

1. Contract carriers are not required to publish their actual rates and adhere to them but must publish and file with the Commission their minimum rates. Rates lower than the published minima may not be charged. Thirty days' notice is required of any change in these rates. The Commission has held that the minimum rates filed by a contract carrier by water must be the lowest rate or charge actually maintained.[37] The published minimum, therefore, cannot be a more or less arbitrary figure below which the carrier has no intention of going.
2. The Commission may prescribe reasonable minimum rates but not maximum rates.
3. Contract carriers must obtain "permits" to operate instead of "certificates of public convenience and necessity." The difference between the requirements necessary to obtain a permit and the requirement

---

[37] *Atwacoal Transportation Co.—Minimum Rates*, 283 ICC 647 (1951).

imposed on common carriers to obtain a certificate is that the latter requires a showing of public convenience and necessity, while the former requires only a showing that the proposed operations "will be consistent with the public interest and the national transportation policy declared in this act."

The lesser degree of control over contract carriers than over common carriers is to be explained, as was the case in motor-carrier regulation, by the belief that the contract carrier needs to be regulated only to the extent necessary to protect common carriers. Attention should be called to a difference in the treatment of contract carriers by water and contract carriers by motor vehicle. As pointed out above, contract carriers by water are only required to publish minimum rates; contract carriers by motor vehicle have been required, since 1957, to publish their actual rates and to adhere to them.[38]

Dual Operation

The Act forbids a carrier to hold both a certificate as a common carrier and a permit as a contract carrier, although the Commission is empowered to make exception to this prohibition when shown that such dual operation is consistent with the public interest and with the national transportation policy. The prohibition of dual operation was designed to prevent discrimination against shippers by carrying for some at common-carrier rates and for others at lower rates as contract carriers, and also to prevent evasion of the published rates. The Commission has permitted dual operation (1) when the common- and contract-carrier services were entirely different and did not compete to any substantial extent[39] and (2) under other special circumstances.[40] Where there is a possibility of discrimination if a carrier holds both a certificate and a permit, the Commission will not permit dual operation.[41]

Water-Carrier Regulation to Protect Railroads

Since one of the fears expressed by those who were opposed to the further regulation of water carriers in 1940 was that the Commission was "railroad-minded" and would regulate water carriers in the interest of the railroads instead of in the interest of the public, it is well to point out that certain provisions in the Transportation Act of 1940 were designed to prevent that result.

---

[38] See p. 681, supra.

[39] *John L. Goss Corp. Contract Carrier Application,* 250 ICC 101, 104 (1941); *Isthmian S. S. Co. Common Carrier Application,* 250 ICC 359, 360–61 (1942).

[40] *Pope & Talbot, Inc., Common & Contract Carrier Application,* 250 ICC 117 (1941).

[41] *S. C. Loveland Co., Inc., Application,* 250 ICC 571, 573–74 (1943); *Shamrock Towing Co., Inc., Contract Carrier Application,* 250 ICC 788 (1943).

One of the most important of these provisions was the Declaration of Policy inserted in the Act before Part I and designed to indicate the general policy which was to be observed by the Interstate Commerce Commission in administering the whole statute.[42] The declared policy calls for the "fair and impartial" regulation of all modes of transportation subject to the Act; and what is more important, it directs the Commission to administer the Act so as "to recognize and preserve the inherent advantages" of each mode of transport. These requirements are clearly designed to prevent the Commission from regulating water carriers, or other carriers, primarily for the purpose of protecting another form of transport.

Another provision in the Act which reveals a similar purpose is found in the Rule of Rate Making. This provision requires the Commission, in prescribing rates of water carriers, to consider the effect of rates on the movement of traffic "by the carrier or carriers for which the rates are prescribed." The quoted phrase is apparently designed to prevent the Commission from regulating water-carrier rates for the purpose of protecting the traffic of other carriers. The amendment of Section 15a in 1958, which was made applicable to all modes of transport, reinforces this policy.[43]

Another provision designed to prevent regulation of water carriers in the interest of rail carriers is Section 305 (c), which contains a statement that "differences in the classifications, rates, fares, charges, rules, regulations, and practices of a water carrier in respect of water transportation from those in effect by a rail carrier with respect to rail transportation shall not be deemed to constitute unjust discrimination, prejudice, or disadvantage, or an unfair or destructive competitive practice. . . ."

ADMINISTRATION OF PART III OF THE ACT

We may now turn to a consideration of the administration of Part III of the Interstate Commerce Act, which, for convenience, we shall call the Water Carrier Act. The early decisions mostly involved the granting of certificates or permits under the "grandfather clauses" or the interpretation of exemption provisions. We may profitably note certain problems, however, that have arisen in the administration of the Act and give some attention to policies that have been formulated by the Commission in carrying out its provisions. We reserve for later chapters those aspects of regulation that relate primarily to the relations between water carriers and other transportation agencies.

Common or Contract Carrier

Since the Act treats common and contract carriers differently, the distinction between the two is important; and it sometimes proves to be a

---

[42] See pp. 265–66, supra.

[43] Paragraph 3 of Section 15a. See pp. 273–74, supra.

troublesome question, as was found to be true in the regulation of motor carriers. The Act defines a common carrier by water as one "which holds itself out to the general public to engage in the transportation by water in interstate or foreign commerce of passengers or property or any class or classes thereof for compensation. . . ." A contract carrier is one which, "under individual contracts or agreements," engages in transportation other than as a common carrier. The Act furthermore specifically provides that one who furnishes vessels, other than to a carrier, when such vessel is to be used by the person to whom it is furnished for the transportation of his own property, shall be considered a contract carrier.

The Commission has said that the test of common carriage is the holding-out to serve the public generally.[44] As in motor-carrier cases, the Commission has also made use of the specialization test in determining whether one may properly be classified as a contract carrier.[45]

The "Grandfather Clause"

Common carriers in bona fide operation on January 1, 1940, and who had operated continuously since that date, except for interruptions caused by conditions beyond their control, were entitled to a certificate under the "grandfather clause." Contract carriers meeting the same condition were entitled to a permit.

In granting certificates and permits under the "grandfather clauses" of Part III, the Commission has imposed fewer restrictions than has been done in administering the comparable provisions of Part II of the Act which relate to motor carriers.[46] In 1944 the Commission said: "The common-carrier certificates are not restricted to the transportation of the particular commodities formerly carried, or to the specific points actually served, by the holders thereof. As a general rule, common carriers have been authorized to transport commodities generally and to serve all intermediate ports on the waterways traversed by them."[47] This is in contrast with commodity and point restrictions sometimes imposed in motor-carrier cases.[48] The greater liberality in the treatment of water carriers than of motor carriers may be due to the somewhat different nature of their operations, including the fact that water carriers frequently hold themselves out to serve ports at which calls are made only on request; and it may also be due to the fact that the commodities actually carried by water carriers are sometimes limited, although the carrier stands in readiness to carry others

---

[44] *Wilson Line, Inc., Common & Contract Carrier Applications,* 250 ICC 411, 415 (1942); *Cornell Steamboat Co. Contract Carrier Application,* 250 ICC 301, 314 (1942).

[45] See *Martinson Contract Carrier Application,* 265 ICC 586, 587 (1949).

[46] See the statement of the Commission's policy in *Nicholson Transit Co. Contract Carrier Application,* 260 ICC 301 (1944); and in *Nicholson Universal S.S. Co. Applications,* 260 ICC 393 (1944).

[47] Interstate Commerce Commission, *Annual Report, 1944,* p. 24.

[48] See pp. 696–98, supra.

as well. The liberality of the Commission in granting carriers authority under the "grandfather clause" to serve ports which were not actually served on and since January 1, 1940, has not been without protest from within the Commission.[49]

Certificates and Permits for New Operations

The most important question of public policy likely to arise in applications for new service is the extent to which competitive service should be permitted or encouraged, or the extent to which existing carriers should be protected from new competition. It is obviously the purpose of the Act to prevent an excess of water transportation facilities and services in order to introduce stability into the water-carrier industry and to permit existing carriers to operate with some degree of profitability. Congress would not have required proof of public convenience and necessity for the inauguration of new water-carrier services if it had desired unlimited competition. The Act, however, does not require that certificates for new operations be denied just because the new operations might divert traffic from existing carriers. In fact, the Act specifically provides that no certificate "shall confer any proprietary or exclusive right or rights in the use of public waterways."[50]

The Commission has refused to authorize additional services when it was clear that there was insufficient traffic to support them. In one case the Commission denied a certificate for operations that would compete with two existing carriers, pointing out that the additional service "might so diffuse the available traffic as to result in uneconomical operation detrimental to all concerned."[51]

Where the traffic will support additional services, or where there are prospects of new traffic in the future, certificates have been granted, notwithstanding the opposition of existing carriers who might be adversely affected.[52] The Commission has been upheld by the courts in this policy. In at least three instances existing water carriers sought unsuccessfully to have orders of the Commission set aside which had authorized the institution of competing operations.[53]

---

[49] See dissent of Commissioner Mahaffie in *Schafer Bros. S.S. Lines Contract Carrier Application*, 250 ICC 353, 356–58 (1942); and of Commissioner Miller in *Isthmian S.S. Co. Common Carrier Application*, 250 ICC 359, 367–68 (1942); and *McLain Carolina Line, Inc., Common Carrier Application*, 250 ICC 521, 523–24 (1942), and *Valley Barge Line Contract Carrier Application*, 250 ICC 566 (1942).

[50] Section 309 (e).

[51] *Arrow Line Extension*, 265 ICC 347, 360 (1948). See also *Commercial Barge Lines, Inc., Extension—Grain*, 285 ICC 549 (1954).

[52] See *McCarthy S.S. Co. Common Carrier Application*, 250 ICC 550 (1942); *Pan-Atlantic S.S. Corp. Extension—Intercoastal*, 303 ICC 163 (1957).

[53] *United States v. Detroit & Cleveland Navigation Co.*, 326 U.S. 236 (1945); *Newtex S.S. Corp. v. United States*, 107 Fed. Supp. 388 (1952); *Luckenbach S.S. Co. v. United States*, 122 Fed. Supp. 824 (1954).

Revocability of Certificates

Originally, certificates and permits granted by the Commission could not be revoked.[54] This created a problem when service had been abandoned but the right to operate remained outstanding. The existence of the dormant rights, which might be revived at any time, deprived the Commission of effective control over the amount of water-carrier service. If operations were resumed—particularly if existing carriers had expanded their service—a surplus of available shipping capacity might be created. The existence of unused operating rights was also a deterrent to the institution of new operations, since the old operations might at any time be resumed.[55] In 1965 Congress remedied this situation by empowering the Commission to revoke certificates for failure to provide service thereunder.[56]

Private Carriers and For-Hire Service

Whether private carriers should be permitted to carry for hire, either as common or as contract carriers, was a question raised in the regulation of motor carriers. The same issue comes up in the regulation of water carriers. As noted in the preceding chapter, industrial carriers have frequently taken cargo on a for-hire basis when proprietary traffic was absent or insufficient to obtain a full load. The practice makes for the economical use of shipping facilities of industrial carriers and may provide needed shipping capacity when the facilities of other carriers are inadequate. On the other hand, if a regular common-carrier service is considered to be of the first importance from a public standpoint, there is some point in restricting the practice of industrial carriers of taking nonproprietary traffic. The common carriers consider that carrying for hire by private carriers is unfair and that it jeopardizes the ability of the regular common carriers to provide satisfactory service at low rates.

The Water Carrier Act contains no provision which prohibits private carriers from carrying goods for hire. Under the "grandfather clauses," furthermore, private carriers operating also as common or contact carriers on January 1, 1940, and since that date, had their rights so to operate protected if their operations were shown to be bona fide.[57]

When proposed for-hire services of industrial carriers are not protected by the "grandfather clause," and public convenience and necessity must be proved, the Commission can deny industrial carriers certificates or permits. This was done in one case involving the performance of for-hire

---

[54] *United States* v. *Seatrain Lines*, 329 U.S. 424 (1947).

[55] Interstate Commerce Commission, *Annual Report, 1947*, pp. 50–51; *Annual Report, 1949*, pp. 53–54.

[56] Public Law 89–170.

[57] E.g., *E. K. Wood Lumber Co. Contract Carrier Application*, 250 ICC 499 (1942), and dissenting opinion of Commissioner Miller.

transportation by a chemical corporation which operated barges primarily for the transportation of raw materials for its own use.[58] On the other hand, a certificate or permit will be granted to a private carrier to engage in common-carrier or contract-carrier operations if the proposed for-hire service is needed.[59]

Service Obligations of Common Carriers

A water carrier which is authorized to operate as a common carrier must assume the obligations which the Act imposes, such as the duty of providing transportation upon reasonable request therefor. This was brought out in a case involving barge lines on the Mississippi River. Because of the unprofitableness of less-than-bargeload traffic, certain barge lines had placed an embargo on such traffic in 1948, thereby refusing to handle it. This action was found unlawful by the Commission, notwithstanding the fact that water carriers may abandon their operations without the approval of the Commission.[60]

Rate Regulation

The Rule of Rate Making in Section 307 (f), following the language of Section 15a of Part I of the Act, requires consideration of the revenue needs of the carriers in determining the reasonableness of rates. The close relationship that, as a practical matter, must be maintained between water and rail rates makes it impossible for the Commission to deal with the general level of water-carrier rates separately and to adjust them in accordance with the financial needs of the carriers. In the railroad rate-level cases that have arisen since World War II, the water carriers have sometimes sought and obtained the same increases as were granted the railroads. Water carriers have encountered increases in their operating costs comparable to those experienced by the railroads. This fact, coupled with the necessity of maintaining somewhat the same relations between water and rail rates, has justified this treatment of water-carrier rates.

The impossibility, in some instances, of adjusting the level of water-carrier rates independently of rail rates was shown in a proceeding relating to the Pacific coastwise rates in 1950. A cost study showed that the steamship rates were in many cases less than sufficient to cover cost plus a fair return to the water lines. The excess of cost over revenues for some of the traffic was from 7 to 29 cents per 100 pounds. The Commission noted that the rates could not in practice be increased unless there were corresponding increases made in the rates of the rail carriers.[61]

---

[58] *Davison Chemical Corp. Applications*, 250 ICC 291 (1942).

[59] *McGehee Contract Carrier Application*, 285 ICC 107 (1951).

[60] *New Orleans Traffic & Transportation Bureau v. Mississippi Valley Barge Line Co.*, 280 ICC 105 (1951).

[61] *All Rail Commodity Rates between Calif., Oreg., & Wash.*, 277 ICC 511 (1950).

The close relationship that must be maintained between rail and water rates, as well as the highly competitive situation resulting from the competition of the regulated and unregulated carriers, undoubtedly accounts for the comparatively small number of shipper complaints about the rates on particular commodities or for particular movements. In so far as questions of reasonableness of particular rates have come up for consideration, the Commission has followed the same general procedures and policies that have been developed in railroad rate cases.

Not only has the Commission had little occasion to prescribe maximum reasonable rates of water carriers, but it has likewise had little occasion to prescribe minimum rates. In 1940, prior to the enactment of the Transportation Act of 1940, the United States Maritime Commission had found it necessary to prescribe minimum reasonable rates for common carriers by water in westbound intercoastal commerce, where serious rate cutting was threatened.[62] After the transfer of jurisdiction over these rates to the Interstate Commerce Commission the Commission made numerous modifications of the original order to permit steamship lines to charge lower rates on particular commodities, usually to enable them to meet the competition of transcontinental rail lines.[63] In 1950 the Commission, finding that the competitive situation had been stabilized and that it could deal with any future outbreaks of rate cutting through its rate-suspension power, vacated the earlier minimum-rate orders.[64] There has been no other instance of a general outbreak of rate cutting among water carriers subject to the Commission's jurisdiction such as to require extensive use of the minimum-rate power.

ADMINISTRATION OF THE SHIPPING ACT AND RELATED ACTS

We have noted that the provisions of the Shipping Act of 1916 and related acts, which provide a certain amount of regulation to ocean carriers operating between the United States and its possessions and foreign countries, and also between ports in the states of Alaska and Hawaii and the rest of the United States, are now administered by the Federal Maritime Commission. Certain policies of the Federal Maritime Commission and its predecessors require brief mention.

Conference Agreements

We have also noted that the Shipping Act of 1916 legalized steamship "conferences," but that conference agreements were subject to the approval of the Shipping Board, now the Federal Maritime Commission. An important feature of the Commission's policy, and that of its predecessors,

---

[62] *Intercoastal Rate Structure*, 2 USMC 285 (1940).

[63] E.g., 246 ICC 555 (1941).

[64] *Intercoastal Rate Structure*, 277 ICC 328 (1950).

is that conferences shall be "open," i.e., that any carrier operating over the route or routes involved shall be admitted to the conference if it desires.[65]

The Dual-Rate System

The Shipping Act of 1916 outlawed "deferred rebates,"[66] a device by which shipping conferences attempted to suppress competition from nonconference members. The carriers have developed another device, that of "dual rates" or "contract-noncontract rates," to accomplish the same purpose. Under the dual-rate system, shippers who agree to ship exclusively by conference lines are given lower rates than other shippers. Failure on the part of a shipper to live up to the agreement means that he becomes liable for damages, the amount usually related in some way to the revenues lost by the conference lines.

The dual-rate system differs in one important respect from the deferred-rebate system. The deferred-rebate system is self-enforcing, since rebates can be withheld if a shipper fails to patronize the conference lines exclusively; but enforcement of the dual-rate system, if a shipper violates his agreement, may require bringing suit against him to recover the damages.

In 1958, in *Federal Maritime Board* v. *Isbrandtsen,*[67] the Supreme Court of the United States held that the dual-rate system maintained by the Japan–Atlantic and Gulf Freight Conference was in violation of the provisions of the Shipping Act which make it unlawful for a water carrier subject to the Shipping Act to "retaliate against any shipper by refusing, or threatening to refuse, space accommodations when such are available, or resort to other discriminating or unfair methods, because such shipper has patronized any other carrier. . . ." The dual-rate contract involved in this case provided that the shipper signing the exclusive-patronage contract would receive rates $9\frac{1}{2}$ percent below the noncontract rates. Breach of the contract by the shipper would result in loss of the right to reduced rates in the future and obligate the shipper to pay "liquidated damages" equal to 50 percent of the contract rates. In its decision the Supreme Court said: "It would be anomalous for Congress to strike down deferred rebates and at the same time fail to strike down dual-rate contracts having the same objectionable purpose and effect."[68] Although the Supreme Court decision relates to the particular dual-rate contract that was before it in

---

[65] See *Phelps Bros. & Co.* v. *Cosulich-Societa,* 1 USMC 634 (1937); *Waterman S.S. Corp.* v. *Arnold Bernstein Line,* 2 USMC 238 (1939); *Olsen* v. *Blue Star Line,* 2 USMC 529 (1941); *Black Diamond S.S. Corp.* v. *Compagnie Maritime Belge,* 2 USMC 755 (1946); *Pacific Coast European Conference Agreement,* 3 USMC 11 (1947).

[66] P. 748, supra.

[67] 356 U.S. 481 (1958).

[68] Ibid., p. 495.

the *Isbrandtsen Case*, it is difficult to see how any dual-rate contract of the conventional type could escape the same fate. The steamship lines consider that the dual-rate system is essential to the preservation of the conference system of rate control and the prevention of ruinous competition among steamship lines.

In 1961 Congress amended the Shipping Act of 1916 to legalize the dual-rate system.[69] Dual-rate contracts, however, must be approved by the Federal Maritime Commission and must be available to all shippers and consignees on equal terms and conditions. The Act imposes certain specific requirements and limitations on dual-rate contracts. These are as follows:

1. The contract must provide for prompt release of the shipper from the contract with respect to shipments for which the conference lines cannot provide, on reasonable notice, as much space as the shipper requires.
2. The contract rate may not be increased in less than 90 days from its effective date.
3. The contract may cover only those goods of the shipper for which he has the right to select the carrier, but there is provision for preventing this clause from being used to evade obligations under the contract.
4. The contract may not require the shipper to divert shipments from natural routings.
5. Damages recoverable for breach of the contract must be limited to actual damages, but the contract may specify damages in an amount not exceeding the freight charges at the contract rate less cost of handling.
6. The spread between the contract and non-contract rate may not exceed 15 percent of the ordinary rate.
7. The contract must permit the shipper to terminate the agreement without penalty on 90 days' notice.
8. Bulk cargo, with certain exceptions, may not be included in the contracts.

It should be noted that dual-rate contracts are only used in international shipping. In domestic commerce the Federal Maritime Commission, or its predecessors, has not permitted their use since the enactment of the Intercoastal Shipping Act of 1933. The dual-rate system is not considered necessary in domestic shipping, because the carriers are required to publish their rates and adhere to them, and because the regulatory authority can also prescribe minimum rates for such carriers if the need arises.[70]

---

[69] Public Law 87–346.

[70] See statement of Chairman Morse of the Federal Maritime Board in Hearings before the Special Subcommittee on Steamship Conferences of the Committee on Merchant Marine and Fisheries, House of Representatives, *Steamship Conference Study*, Part I (1959), p. 66.

Rate-Level Cases

Limited use of the fair-return-on-fair-value rule has been made in cases involving the rates of water carriers. In a case involving rates between United States ports and the then territory of Hawaii, the Federal Maritime Board measured the reasonableness of the proposed rates by the needs of Matson Navigation Company, the dominant carrier in the trade and the recognized rate maker.[71]

In a number of cases the Federal Maritime Board, predecessor of the Federal Maritime Commission, refused to use depreciated original cost in the valuation of ships, holding that such a valuation was unrealistic since the ships had a greater market value in case of liquidation. The Board used depreciated original cost, however, in valuing property other than ships.[72] The present Federal Maritime Commission, as pointed out in a previous chapter, has adhered to a prudent investment standard in the valuation of the properties of steamship lines.[73]

SELECTED REFERENCES

The most thorough discussion of the extent of the Interstate Commerce Commission's jurisdiction over water carriers prior to 1940 is in I. L. Sharfman, *The Interstate Commerce Commission*, Vol. II (New York: Commonwealth Fund, 1931), pp. 17–57.

The Federal Coordinator's analysis of water-carrier regulation prior to 1940 and the need for further regulation may be found in *Regulation of Transportation Agencies*, 73d Cong., 2d Sess., Senate Doc. No. 152 (1934), particularly pp. 5–13, 41–45, and Appendix A, Parts 2 and 3; and in *Fourth Report*, 74th Cong., 2d Sess., House Doc. No. 394 (1936), pp. 7–22.

On regulation under the Transportation Act of 1940, see Stuart Daggett, *Principles of Inland Transportation* (4th ed.; New York: Harper, 1955), chap. xxxii; Erle J. Zoll, Jr., "The Development of Federal Regulatory Control over Water Carriers," 12 *I.C.C. Practitioners' Journal* 552 (1945); Russell E. Westmeyer, *Economics of Transportation* (New York: Prentice-Hall, 1952), chaps. xxiii–xxiv; and critical of regulation, John C. Spychalski, "On the Nonutility of Domestic Water Transport Regulation," 37 *I.C.C. Practitioners' Journal* 7 (1969).

A detailed analysis of the regulation of water carriers under Part III of the Act, made by Dr. C. S. Morgan of the staff of the Interstate Commerce Commission, was published in 1946 by the Commission under the title of *Problems in Regulation of Domestic Transportation by Water*.

The most thorough treatment of shipping conferences is Daniel Marx, Jr., *International Shipping Cartels: A Study of Industrial Self-Regulation by Shipping Conferences* (Princeton: Princeton University Press, 1953). The subject is

---

[71] *General Increase in Hawaiian Rates*, 5 FMB 347 (1957).

[72] Ibid.; also *General Increases in Alaskan Rates and Charges*, 5 FMB 486 (1958); and *Atlantic-Gulf/Puerto Rico General Rate Increases*, 6 FMB 14, 34 (1960).

[73] See p. 392, supra.

also treated in Robert N. Kharasch, "Conferences of Carriers by Sea: Freedom of Rate Fixing," 25 *Journal of Air Law and Commerce* 287 (1956), and John S. McGee, "Ocean Freight Rate Conferences and the American Merchant Marine," 27 *University of Chicago Law Review* 191 (1960). The dual-rate system is excellently treated in an anonymous note entitled "The American Shipping Industry and the Conference System," 11 *Stanford Law Review* 136 (1958). The dual-rate system and its legal status is discussed in Carl A. Auerbach, "The Isbrandtsen Case and Its Aftermath," *1959 Wisconsin Law Review* 224 and 369. The subject is also well treated in E. Robert Seaver and Edward Schmeltzer, "The Role of Conferences and the Dual Rate System in Ocean Foreign Trade," 34 *Law and Contemporary Problems* 605 (1959).

Chapter 33   AIR TRANSPORTATION

Air transport is the most recent form of transportation to develop; it is also the most rapidly growing. In the fiscal year 1958 the airlines exceeded the railroads for the first time in volume of passenger business as measured by passenger-miles.[1] The situation is quite different, however, so far as the movement of freight and express is concerned. The volume of express and freight moved by air, although a substantial amount in the aggregate, is an insignificant proportion of the total intercity movement of property,[2] but technological advances, which occur rapidly in the industry, may change this situation in the future. It is the purpose of this chapter to trace the development of air transport, describe its present status, and point out some of the characteristics of the industry which are significant and which have a bearing on questions of public policy.

HISTORICAL DEVELOPMENT

The first airplane flight was in 1903, when the Wright brothers made their trial flights at Kitty Hawk, North Carolina. Even before World War I sufficient progress had been made in the development of aircraft to indicate its possibilities as an instrument of warfare. During that war, immense strides were made in aircraft development, and at the close the United States had built nearly 17,000 planes and taught some 10,000 men to fly.[3] After the war, many pilots became civilan aviators. Surplus government planes were purchased and used for stunt flying, carrying sight-seeing passengers, giving flying instruction, taking aerial photographs, and for various other purposes. Experimentation with airmail service was begun by the government in 1918. Transcontinental airmail service was established in 1919. Continuous day-and-night service for transcontinental air mail was established in 1924. The early airmail routes were operated by the government, but the Kelly Act of 1925 authorized the Post Office

---

[1] Civil Aeronautics Board, *Annual Report, 1958*, p. 2.

[2] See p. 20, supra.

[3] U.S. Department of Commerce, Bureau of Air Commerce, Aeronautics Bulletin No. 1, *Civil Aeronautics in the United States* (1937), p. 3.

Department to contract with private companies for the transportation of mail. The first contracts were let in 1926, and government operation of airmail routes ceased entirely in 1927. Since then, air mail has been transported by private air-transport companies except for a period of about three months in 1934. The contract system stimulated the development of commercial air transportation. Airmail carriers were required by the government to provide facilities for the transportation of passengers in order to reduce the cost of transporting mail.

Air transport received additional stimulus during World War II. Demands upon the airlines for the transportation of military personnel and property and of civilians engaged in the war effort brought greatly increased volumes of traffic to the airlines, some of it transported under special contract with the government. This, in turn, brought years of prosperity and high earnings to the airlines.

The stimulus of wartime activity was felt even after the close of the war and resulted in an expansion of air-transport services in the years immediately following. Among the important developments of this period were the expansion of route mileages by the trunklines, the establishment of a group of feeder or local lines, the institution of an air freight service by the scheduled air carriers which was independent of the service already provided through the air express service of the Railway Express Agency, the mushroom growth of nonscheduled air transportation, the establishment of a group of all-cargo airlines, and the institution of "air coach" service by regular scheduled airlines. In 1958 and 1959 turboprop and turbojet planes were introduced. The decade of the 1960s may be characterized as the decade of conversion to jets. Late in the 1960s and early 1970s jets of still greater size were put in operation. Among these were the "stretched-out" version of the DC-8, with a capacity of 250 passengers, the wide-bodied "jumbo jets," carrying around 300 passengers, and the Boeing 747 capable of transporting as many as 490 passengers.

At time of writing, supersonic transport (SST) is in the offing. France and England together have developed the *Concorde*, a 1400 mph plane; and Russia has developed the *Tu-144*. The United States has suspended its financing of the development of a SST plane as a result of Congressional action in May 1971, although over $800 million had been expended by the government and $58.5 million advanced by the airlines. Among the factors leading to the abandonment of the program were: (1) the extremely high cost involved; and (2) fear of the environmental effects of supersonic flight.[4]

Some indication of the growth of scheduled domestic air transportation in the United States is shown by Table 33–1.

Air transport provides a superior type of service that other modes of

---

[4] A good discussion of the problems of SST transportation is John R. Montgomery, "The Age of the Supersonic Jet Transport: Its Environmental and Legal Impact," 36 *Journal of Air Law & Commerce* 577 (1970), particularly pp. 577–95.

transport cannot, in most instances, hope to equal. Airlines have become the major carrier of passengers, except for short distances, and the near demise of long-distance rail passenger service is to be explained primarily by airline development. Some freight, particularly the movement of high-value commodities, has been diverted to air; but air freight constitutes only a very minor share of the total movement of freight, as we have already noted.

It should be recognized that air transportation has created new traffic, both in the freight and passenger fields. Much business travel, for instance, would not have occurred at all if air transport had not made a quick business trip possible; much vacation air travel has been stimulated

TABLE 33–1. Growth of Scheduled Domestic Air Transportation in the United States*

Year	Passenger Originations[a]	Express and Freight Ton-Miles[b]
1930	385,000	....
1935	763,000	1,098,000
1940	2,523,000	3,476,000
1945	6,541,000	22,175,000
1950	17,468,000	152,223,000
1955	38,221,000	229,966,000
1960	52,375,000	386,933,000
1965	84,460,000	943,128,000
1969	142,340,000	1,971,088,000

* *Source:* Federal Aviation Agency, *FAA Statistical Handbook of Aviation.*
a Figures for 1930, 1935 & 1940 not strictly comparable to later figures.
b Excludes freight carried by all-cargo and irregular or supplemental air carriers.

by the possibility of a trip to distant places without consuming too much travel time; and the long-distance movement by air of cut flowers and other perishable products is new traffic, not traffic diverted from surface carriers.

AIRWAYS AND THEIR FINANCING

Air transport requires an elaborate system of aids to flying known as the airway system which is provided by the federal government and is under the control of the Federal Aviation Agency. The airway system was described in more detail in an earlier chapter.[5] At this point, however, we need to note the method by which the airway system is financed.

From 1925 through 1967 approximately $11.929 billion had been spent

[5] Pp. 40–42, supra.

on the establishment, maintenance, and operation of the federal airways system.[6]

Until 1961 no taxes especially designed as user taxes had been levied on users of airway facilities. The first step in that direction was taken in 1961 when Congress left a tax on air passenger fares of five percent when a similar tax of ten percent was removed from passenger tickets of all other modes of transport. The retention of a tax on air passenger travel was intended to serve as a user tax. There was also in effect a tax of two cents a gallon on aviation gasoline, originally imposed as part of the general excise tax on gasoline and not considered as a user charge.

The Airport and Airway Development Act of 1970

Further steps were taken toward placing the financing of airways on a user basis by the enactment of the Airport and Airway Development Act of 1970.[7] This Act imposed taxes on airway users as follows:

1. a tax of five percent on air freight;
2. a tax on domestic air passenger tickets of 8 percent;
3. a $3 per person "head tax" on most overseas flights;
4. a $25 per year registration fee on all aircraft;
5. an annual registration fee of 3.5 cents per pound on all jet aircraft, and 2 cents a pound on all piston aircraft weighing over 2,500 pounds; and
6. a tax of 7 cents a gallon on aircraft fuel except that used by commercial aviation.

The proceeds of these taxes go into an "Airport and Airway Trust Fund" created by the Act and are to be used only to finance planning, development, construction, operation, and maintenance of the airway system, and also to meet obligations incurred in airport development in accordance with the Act.

To what extent the funds provided by the user taxes above described will be sufficient to defray the costs of constructing, operating, and maintaining the airway system cannot be told at this time. It should be recognized, however, that not all the cost associated with airways should be borne by airlines and private aircraft since the military establishment makes very extensive use of them. A portion of the costs of the airway system and its operation may properly be borne by the general taxpayer as are other defense expenditures. This was recognized by Congress, since the Airport and Airway Development Act of 1970 directed the Secretary of Transportation to allocate costs of the airport and airway system

---

[6] Bureau of Railway Economics, Association of American Railroads, *Government Expenditures for Highway, Waterway and Air Facilities* (Washington, D.C.: 1971).

[7] Public Law 91–258, 84 Stat. 219.

among the various classes of users,[8] and likewise to recommend what revisions of the user taxes should be made to insure an equitable distribution of the tax burden among various classes of users and beneficiaries.[9]

AIRPORTS

In 1969 there were 9,909 airports in the United States exclusive of heliports, seaplane bases, and strictly military airports. Of these airports, 817 were served by commercial airlines.[10] The latter are commonly called "air carrier airports" and they are the ones with which we are particularly concerned in this discussion.

Unlike the airway system, airports are not owned by the federal government, with the exception of Washington National Airport and Dulles Airport which serve the Nation's capital. Instead, airports are owned by cities, counties, states, or "airport authorities" representing two or more cities or other governmental units, or by private interests. Few air carrier airports, however are owned by private individuals or corporations; most are owned by some governmental unit. As we shall see, however, the federal government has extended financial aid to governmental units for the construction and improvement of airports.

Three factors explain why airports of the type used by commercial airlines are generally provided by municipalities or other governmental units. First, airport construction has been motivated, not by a desire to obtain profits from airport operation, but from the desire of a community and the business interests therein to obtain various benefits, direct and indirect, which will be derived from the existence of airport services in the community. Second, federal aid has been available for the financing of publicly owned airports, but not for private airports. The third reason for municipal ownership is that airports are not ordinarily profitable, and hence private capital will not provide the airport facilities which a city wants.

Federal Aid in Airport Building

Prior to 1933 airports were largely financed by local governments. The Air Commerce Act of 1926 barred the federal government from direct construction and operation of airports. This was accomplished by a provision in the Act which authorized the Secretary of Commerce "to establish, operate, and maintain . . . all necessary air navigation facilities except airports." As a relief measure, however, large sums of money were advanced by the federal government for the construction and improvement

---

[8] Sec. 4.

[9] Sec. 209.

[10] *FAA Statistical Handbook of Aviation, 1970 Edition*, p. 45.

of airports during the depression of the 30s through various relief agencies. The Civil Aeronautics Act of 1938 removed the limitations on federal participation in airport development and specifically empowered the Administrator to engage in a plan of airport development and improvement. The Act directed the Civil Aeronautics Authority to make a survey of airports and to make definite recommendations as to whether the federal government should participate in the construction, improvement, and development of a national system of airports and, if federal participation was recommended, as to the extent and manner of its participation. The Civil Aeronautics Authority made its report in 1939 and recommended federal participation in the development of an adequate system of airports, including financial assistance.[11] Appropriations were made by Congress from time to time for the construction and improvement of airport facilities under the supervision of the Civil Aeronautics Administration. In 1944 further expansion of airports through a federal-aid program was recommended by the Civil Aeronautics Administration and the Secretary of Commerce.[12] This led to the enactment of the Federal Airport Act of 1946.

The Federal Airport Act of 1946 ushered in a period of more systematic participation by the federal government in airport development. Since the Act has been superseded by Part II of the Airport and Airway Development Act of 1970, we need not describe the provisions of the former. It should be said, however, that the Airport and Airway Development Act of 1970 incorporates many features of the earlier Act.

Airports and the Airport and Airway Development Act

The major features of the 1970 Act in so far as they relate to airports may be summarized as follows:

1. The Secretary of Transportation is directed to prepare a national airport system plan for the development of public airports, and to review and revise it as necessary.
2. The Secretary, in formulating a plan, must cooperate with various federal, state, and other agencies and interests.[13]
3. Funds available for grants to airport sponsors must be apportioned among the several states according to a formula which is based on

---

[11] *Airport Survey*, 76th Cong., 1st Sess., House Doc. No. 245.

[12] *National Airport Plan*, 78th Cong., 2d Sess., House Doc. No. 87 (1945).

[13] Among those specified are the Civil Aeronautics Board, the Post Office Department, the Department of the Interior, the Federal Communications Commission, the Department of Defense, the Secretary of Health, Education and Welfare, the Secretary of Agriculture, the National Council on Environmental Quality, the Federal Power Commission, planning agencies, airport operators, air carriers, aircraft manufacturers, and a specially created Aviation Advisory Commission of a temporary nature.

both population and area, but provision is made for a "discretionary fund" not subject to the apportionment formula.

4. An airport project, in order to be eligible for federal funds, must be included in the national airport system plan.

5. The federal government's share of the cost of airport improvements may not, with some exceptions, exceed 50 percent of the "allowable costs."

6. "Allowable costs" are not to include public parking facilities, or any part of airport buildings except such as are intended to house facilities or activities directly related to safety of persons at the airport.

7. Federal funds advanced are to be from the "Airport and Airway Trust Fund," previously described.[14]

8. The sponsors of an airport development project must assume certain responsibilities to the satisfaction of the Secretary of Transportation before the project is approved. Among these, we note particularly the following:[15]

   a) that the airport will be available for public use on "fair and reasonable terms and without unjust discrimination";

   b) that the airport and facilities will be suitably operated and maintained;

   c) that aerial approaches to the airport will be adequately cleared and protected;

   d) that appropriate action will be taken, including adoption of zoning laws, to restrict the use of land in the vicinity of the airport to uses compatible with normal airport operations;

   e) that the airport will be available for use by government aircraft without charge except under special circumstances;

   f) that the owner will furnish space in airport buildings to the government for air traffic control and weather reporting without charge;

   g) that a system of fees and rental charges will be established for services and facilities provided for airport users "which will make the airport as self-supporting as possible under the circumstances. . . ."

The Future of Federal Aid to Airports

In 1958 when extension of the Federal Airport Act of 1946 was under consideration, a difference of opinion developed between Congress and the Administration over the propriety of further federal aid in airport financing. Congress passed a bill to continue the Act with an increased level of expenditure. President Eisenhower vetoed the bill, saying: "I am

---

[14] See p. 773, supra.

[15] Stated here in abbreviated form.

convinced that the time has come for the federal government to begin an orderly withdrawal from the airport grant program."[16] He pointed out that aviation had achieved a state of maturity in which users should be expected to pay an increasing share of airport costs. Previously the Under-secretary of Commerce for Transportation had opposed the bill, taking the position that the construction, maintenance, and operation of civil airports was primarily a matter of local responsibility.[17] Congress, how-ever, remained convinced that federal aid is necessary if airport facilities are to be expanded to meet the needs of the rapidly growing air-transport industry. "[The] committee is convinced that the capital investment re-quired to bring airport facilities up to the present and future needs of this Nation is far beyond the financial capacity and capabilities of local com-munities without continued effective assistance and encouragement from the Federal Government."[18] A bill was subsequently passed by Congress and approved by the President which extended the Act.

Considering the tremendous growth in air transportation since 1958 and the serious congestion that has developed at major airports, it has be-come clear that a large input of capital to expand airport facilities is re-quired and it is difficult to see how such funds can be raised by local gov-ernments for airport purposes without federal help. Since 1947, under the federal-aid airport program nearly $2 billion has been made available by the federal government to state and local governments for airport devel-opment.[19]

In addition to providing financial aid for airports, the federal govern-ment performs other functions in connection with airport development under the present system of federal aid. Since the requirements of an adequate national system of air transport should be the dominant consider-ation in airport planning, participation of the federal government in air-port planning is necessary to insure that airport facilities are meeting the needs of an expanding air-transport system, and also to prevent the waste of capital that would result from independent and uncoordinated airport planning by a host of local authorities with local interests in mind. Fed-eral participation in airport development is also required to insure ade-quate standards in airport design and construction.

Airport Income and Expense

The statement that airports do not ordinarily pay their way requires further discussion. Public airports derive income from landing fees, rent-als, sale of aviation fuel, concessions to persons permitted to provide res-

[16] Reported in *Traffic World*, September 6, 1958, p. 32.

[17] Reported in *Traffic World*, April 19, 1958, p. 48.

[18] Senate Committee on Interstate and Foreign Commerce, *Amendments to the Federal Airport Act*, 86th Cong., 1st Sess., Senate Rep. No. 49 (1959), p. 8.

[19] *FAA Statistical Handbook of Aviation, 1970 Edition*, p. 45.

taurant or other facilities, and from various other sources. Although many airports derive sufficient income from these sources to cover actual costs of operation and maintenance, there are many which do not, and there are very few which derive sufficient income to cover depreciation and interest on investment.

The study of public aid to transportation made by the Board of Investigation and Research revealed that in 1936 the ratio of income to expense of about 200 publicly owned airports, most of which were used by scheduled air carriers, was 57.4 percent.[20] By 1940, however, the ratio had risen to 77.1 percent. Another study, using data of the latest year then available—1943, 1944, or 1945 in most instances—showed 14 that failed to meet annual out-of-pocket operating costs.[21] There were 16 which covered such costs; but if depreciation, interest on investment, and an in-lieu-of-taxes charge were included, only one could be said to show a profit. A California study showed that for the fiscal years 1954 and 1955 the airports at Los Angeles, Oakland, San Diego, and San Francisco had an excess of revenues over operating and maintenance expense.[22] Of 9 airports of medium-sized cities, 5 showed operating revenues in excess of expenses; 4 showed a deficit. Of 19 airports at smaller cities, 7 covered their operating and maintenance expenses; 12 operated at a deficit. Some later studies, although limited in scope, reinforce the conclusion that few airports do more than cover maintenance and operating expenses from airport revenues, and many can not do that.[23]

It is advisable that airports be made self-supporting where that is possible. At the same time it must be recognized that social and economic benefits to the communities involved may be sufficient to create a willingness on the part of local taxpayers to assume the burden of airport deficits.

Airport Congestion and Airport Adequacy

A serious condition of congestion developed at major airports in the late 1960s, one result of which was intolerable delays at airports—with incoming planes sometimes "stacked" for an hour or more and unable to land. The Civil Aeronautics Administration found it necessary in 1968 to

---

[20] Board of Investigation and Research, *Public Aids to Domestic Transportation*, 79th Cong., 1st Sess., House Doc. No. 159 (1944), p. 496.

[21] Lynn L. Bollinger, Alan Passen, and Robert E. McElfresh, *Terminal Airport Financing and Management* (Boston: Graduate School of Business Administration, Harvard University, 1946), pp. 128–30.

[22] Richard Zettel and Robert Horonjeff, *The Practice and Theory of Airport Financing Based on a Survey of California Airports* (Berkeley: Institute of Transportation and Traffic Engineering, University of California, 1956), p. 26.

[23] Richard Nelson, "Airport Development and Operation Problems," 24 *Journal of Air Law & Commerce* 49 (1957); California, Senate Fact Finding Committee on Transportation & Public Utilities and Assembly Interim Committee on Commerce, *Preliminary Report on California Airport Development & Other Aviation Matters* (1964).

restrict the number of flights permitted at certain of the most seriously congested airports. A Civil Aeronautics Board study in 1969 reported five major airports that had reached a saturation point, with others that would reach that point in a few years.[24] Various steps taken by the Civil Aeronautics Board to alleviate congestion at airports will be mentioned in a later chapter.[25] Some cities require additional airports; others require the enlargement of existing airports and airport facilities. Estimates of the amount of new investment necessary in airports vary widely but the Federal Aviation Administration is reported to have estimated that total airport investment requirements between 1970 and 1980 would be about $8.5 billion.[26]

CLASSIFICATION OF AIR CARRIERS

Carriers by air may be classified into private, contract, and common— a classification already familiar to the reader from our description of transportation by highway and waterway. Although much of the private air travel in the United States is for pleasure, there is an increasing use of private planes for business travel. So far as the transportation of property by private air carriers is concerned, there is nothing comparable to the extensive movement of property in motor trucks by farmers, industries, and commercial establishments, although there is some movement of property in industry-owned planes. No statistical information is available concerning the amount of such traffic, but it is apparently unimportant in amount.

There is some transportation of property by air by contract carriers; but since contract carriers are not subject to the Federal Aviation Act except in matters relating to safety, no statistics are available concerning the volume of traffic which they carry.

Certificated Route Carriers

The principal airlines of the United States, designated by the Civil Aeronautics Board as "certificated route carriers," are classified by the Board for statistical purposes into seven groups as follows: (1) domestic trunklines; (2) local-service carriers; (3) helicopter carriers; (4) intra-Alaska carriers; (5) intra-Hawaii carriers; (6) domestic all-cargo carriers; and (7) international and territorial carriers.

Domestic Trunklines. These are the major airlines and serve primarily the larger communities and heavy-density routes. There are 11 domestic

---

[24] Civil Aeronautics Board, *Problems of Airport Congestion by 1975* (1969).

[25] See p. 818, infra.

[26] John H. Crooker, "Congested Airports and the CAB," *Public Utilities Fortnightly,* Sept. 25, 1969, p. 64.

trunklines. The four largest of these are commonly known as the "Big Four." They are:

American Airlines	Trans World Airlines
Eastern Air Lines	United Air Lines

Of the Big Four, American, United, and TWA are transcontinental lines. The Big Four accounted for over 60 percent of the total operating revenues of the domestic trunklines in 1968. The other domestic trunklines are:

Braniff Airways	Northeast Airlines
Continental Airlines	Northwest Airlines
Delta Air Lines	Western Air Lines
National Airlines	

Local-Service Carriers. The local-service lines are those which operate over routes between smaller cities, and between such cities and the larger traffic centers. At time of writing there were nine such lines, namely:

Allegheny Airlines	Ozark Air Lines
Frontier Air Lines	Piedmont Aviation
Hughes Air West	Southern Airways
Mohawk Airlines	Texas International Airlines
North Central Airlines	

Merger of Allegheny and Mohawk was conditionally approved in 1972.

Helicopter Carriers. There are four carriers certificated to operate as helicopter carriers. They are:

Chicago Helicopter Airways
Los Angeles Airways
New York Airways
San Francisco & Oakland Helicopter Airlines

Intra-Alaska Carriers. There are four carriers in this group, namely:

Kodiak Airways	Western Alaska Airlines
Reeve Aleutian Airways	Wien Consolidated Airlines

Intra-Hawaii Carriers. There are two certificated airlines which operate in Hawaii, namely, Aloha Airlines and Hawaiian Airlines.

Domestic All-Cargo Carriers. This group consists of carriers which transport freight only, although in charter operations they sometimes carry groups of persons. There are three carriers in this group:

Airlift International
Flying Tiger Line
Seaboard World Airlines

International and Territorial Airlines. These airlines operate to, from, or between points outside the territory of the United States, or between United States points which are separated by foreign territory or by major expanses of international waters. Some of our domestic airlines engage in substantial international or territorial operations, but there are several airlines engaged exclusively in these operations. The largest of these is Pan American World Airways.

Supplemental Air Carriers

There is a group of carriers which at various times in the past have been designated as "nonscheduled" or "irregular" air carriers, and which are now known as "supplemental" air carriers. The history and present status of these carriers is discussed in the following chapter. In 1970 there were 14 carriers holding authority to operate as supplemental air carriers.[27]

Air Taxi Operators

The name of this group indicates the type of services that they provide, or originally did at least. This class of operators is permitted to use light planes only. The usual limitation has been planes not exceeding 12,500 pounds maximum certificated takeoff weight; under some conditions 27,000 pounds; and even larger by special exemption. Air taxi operators are not regulated, except that they are required to register with the Board and maintain a certain level of liability insurance. In 1969 there were 1500 air taxi operators registered with the Board. A special group within this class are known as *commuter air carriers,* and unlike other air taxi operators provide service on a scheduled basis. There were 168 commuter air carriers in 1969.[28]

Indirect Air Carriers

The Civil Aeronautics Board recognizes a class of "indirect" air carriers. They differ from any of the carriers mentioned above in that they do not own or operate any aircraft, but have arrangements with regular airlines to transport for them. Indirect air carriers, however, deal with shippers and consignees in the manner of direct air carriers and assume responsibility for the transportation of freight committed to their care. The Railway Express Agency is such an indirect air carrier because of the air express service which it provides for shippers. Air-freight forwarders, of which there were 201 in 1970,[29] are also in the class of indirect air

---

[27] Civil Aeronautics Board, *Annual Report, 1970,* p. 10.
[28] Ibid., p. 7.
[29] Ibid., p. 14.

carriers. Of these 201 air-freight forwarders, 38 held domestic authority only; 36 held international authority only; and 127 held both types of authority.

SOME CHARACTERISTICS OF AIR TRANSPORT

Speed

Air transport's great advantage over other modes of transport is speed. By 1930 the airlines were using planes having a speed of 100 miles per hour. In 1936 and 1937 the DC–3's were introduced, which were capable of speeds in the vicinity of 200 miles per hour. This greatly exceeded the speed of the fastest railroad passenger trains. Various four-engine planes, like the Constellation, the Douglas DC–6, and the Boeing Stratocruiser, were introduced between 1947 and 1949. These planes had cruising speeds of about 300 miles per hour. Between 1950 and 1954 still larger and more powerful planes were introduced which were capable of speeds in excess of 300 miles per hour. The turboprops and jet props introduced in 1958 and 1959 are capable of cruising speeds between 500 and 600 miles per hour. SST aircraft will presumably have a cruising speed in the vicinity of 1800 miles per hour.

For short distances, particularly those of less than 100 miles, the advantage of high speed in airport-to-airport flight is often lost in whole or in part by the time consumed in getting to and from business centers or residential areas of a city. The average ground transportation mileage from airports to cities for 125 cities in the United States is 8.7 miles, and for the 25 largest cities in the United States the average is almost 14 miles.[30] O'Hare Airport is 23 miles out of Chicago; Willow Run Airport is 31 miles from Detroit; and Friendship Airport is 32 miles from Washington, D.C.[31] It is claimed that the average ground time involved in an ordinary airline trip is one hour and forty minutes.[32] It follows that the advantage of speed in air transportation is greatest on long-distance flights. It should also be noted that the greater the number of stops at intermediate points, the less the time advantage in air transport because of the time consumed in landing, loading and unloading passengers, and taking off.

The speed advantage which air transportation has over surface transportation has made air travel particularly worth while for business trips. The speed advantage of transportation by air is also very important in the transportation of certain kinds of express and freight.

---

[30] *Motor Transportation of Passengers Incidental to Transportation by Aircraft,* 95 MCC 526 (1964), Appendices B and C.

[31] Ibid., p. 542.

[32] Wm. A. Burden, *Airports—The Foundation of Aviation Progress* (mimeographed, 1946).

Availability to Remote and Thinly Settled Areas

An important feature of air transport is that it can be made available to many areas which are not provided with surface transportation facilities. The airplane can be used to reach remote and inaccessible places, and also areas which are so sparsely settled that the volume of traffic will not support surface transportation agencies. This advantage of air transport arises from the fact that it is less hampered by topography than any other form of transport and that it requires no large investment in "way" comparable to that required by railroad and highway transport and sometimes by water transportation. The importance of air transport in Alaska is to be explained both by the nature of the topography of the area and by the fact that it is very thinly populated. Sparsity of population in Australia, outside of a few coastal cities, explains the importance of air transport on that continent.

High Costs and High Rates

Air transport, up to the present at least, has labored under the disadvantage of high costs as compared with surface transportation, and these high costs are reflected to some extent in rates and fares. Air passenger fares are generally higher than rail fares; air freight rates are much higher than rail freight rates.

Differences in the levels of passenger fares are reflected in the average revenue per revenue passenger-mile received by the different modes of transport. For 1970 the average revenues per revenue passenger-mile of the different modes were as follows:[33]

	Cents
Domestic scheduled airlines, first class	8.27
Domestic scheduled airlines, coach	5.42
Class I railroads, first class	4.27
Class I railroads, coach	3.98
Class I motor buses	3.60

In the case of first-class travel by rail there is an additional cost to the passenger, namely, the price of a seat, roomette, or other accommodation. Air transport also has a cost which is not reflected in fare comparisons, namely, the cost of transportation to and from the airports, and this frequently adds several dollars to the cost of the trip.

The spread between air and rail freight rates is greater than the spread between air and rail passenger fares. In 1969 the average revenue per ton-mile of the different modes of transport was as follows:[34]

---

[33] Figures taken from Air Transport Association of America, *Air Transport 1971*, p. 42.

[34] From Civil Aeronautics Board, *Annual Report, 1970* and Bureau of Economics, Interstate Commerce Commission, *Transport Economics*, January 1971, p. 6.

	Cents
Domestic trunk airlines.............	24.61
Domestic all-cargo airlines.........	18.75
Class I intercity motor carriers....	7.21
Class I railroads...................	1.35

Hazard

Formerly air transport was characterized by a much greater degree of hazard than existed in other forms of for-hire transportation, but this condition appears to have greatly improved in recent years. Table 33–2 shows

TABLE 33–2. Passenger Fatalities per Billion Passenger-Miles, Railroads and Domestic Scheduled Airlines 1940–1949 and 1960–1969*

Year	*Railroads*	*Airlines*	*Year*	*Railroads*	*Airlines*
1940..............	3.4	30.0	1960..............	1.6	9.3
1941..............	1.4	23.0	1961..............	1.0	3.8
1942..............	1.7	37.0	1962..............	1.4	3.4
1943..............	3.1	13.0	1963..............	0.7	1.2
1944..............	2.6	22.0	1964..............	0.5	1.4
1945..............	1.6	22.0	1965..............	0.7	3.8
1946..............	1.8	12.0	1966..............	1.6	0.9
1947..............	1.6	32.0	1967..............	0.9	2.9
1948..............	1.3	13.0	1968..............	1.0	2.8
1949..............	0.8	13.0	1969..............	0.7	1.3

* *FAA Statistical Handbook of Aviation* and *World Almanac.*

the fatalities per billion passenger-miles of the domestic scheduled airlines and of the railroads in two different periods—1940 to 1949 and 1960 to 1969. The table shows that the airline record has greatly improved from the decade of the 1940s. In the earlier decade airline fatalities per billion passenger-miles were many times those of the railroads; in the more recent decade the airline fatality rate approaches the railroad rate.

AIRLINE PASSENGER BUSINESS

In 1968, the passenger revenues of the domestic trunk airlines, excluding the all-cargo carriers, comprised slightly over 89 percent of their transportation revenues, and freight only 5.6 percent. By way of contrast, the railroads in their year of greatest passenger traffic, the war year of 1944, derived less than 19 percent of their operating revenues from passengers; and in 1969, the year before Amtrak, less than 4 percent of their operating revenues.[35] It is clear that the airlines are primarily carriers of passengers.

[35] Airline figures from FAA, *Handbook of Airline Statistics, 1969*, pp. 80 and 92; railroad figures from Interstate Commerce Commission, *Transport Statistics in the United States, 1962*, pp. 105 and 106; and *Annual Report, 1970.*

The Air Traffic Pattern

A characteristic of air passenger traffic is that a large proportion of it is generated by a few large cities. In 1958 more than 72 percent of the air passengers originated at 14 cities. New York and its vicinity alone accounted for 23.6 percent of the passengers.[36]

The air traffic pattern has been likened to a series of wheels, of which the hubs are the traffic centers, like New York, Chicago, Washington, Los Angeles, San Francisco, and a number of lesser cities.[37] The heavy-density traffic moves from hub to hub, but a significant amount also moves between the hubs, on the one hand, and smaller cities not too greatly distant from the hub, on the other, thus forming the spokelike pattern. Very little traffic moves between any two small cities.

"Coach" and "First-Class" Service

Prior to 1948 the airlines offered what was essentially a one-class service, although special fares were sometimes given for special occasions or to special groups. Air coach service by the scheduled air carriers began in 1948 and seems to have been induced by the low fares and less expensive accommodations offered by the irregular air carriers.[38] Capital Airlines was the first of the scheduled airlines to establish the service. The idea spread rapidly throughout the industry. The fares were originally established at a level of approximately 4 cents per passenger-mile, as compared with almost 6 cents for regular-fare flights. Service was provided only over high-density routes, during off-peak hours, and in planes of high seating capacity. Meals were not provided in flight. Coach rates were later placed on a level of 4½ cents per mile on most routes. In a policy statement issued in 1953, the Civil Aeronautics Board declared that fares for coach service should not exceed 75 percent of the first-class fares. The early restriction of coach service to off-peak hours was later removed. The effect of providing air coach service at reduced fares was to increase the volume of air travel. It was estimated at one time that about 70 percent of the coach travel was additional traffic to the airlines, and about 30 percent was diverted from first-class flights.[39]

The two-class system has not been universally accepted by the industry. Some airlines have experimented further with a single-class sys-

---

[36] U.S. Department of Commerce, Civil Aeronautics Administration, *Air Commerce Traffic Pattern, Fiscal Year 1958* (Washington, D.C.: Superintendent of Documents, 1958).

[37] D'Arcy Harvey, "Airline Passenger Traffic Pattern within the United States," 12 *Journal of Air Law and Commerce* 157 (1951), p. 164.

[38] Harold A. Jones and Frederick Davis, "The 'Air Coach' Experiment and National Air Transport Policy," 17 *Journal of Air Law and Commerce* 1 (1950), pp. 2–4.

[39] Ibid., pp. 426–27.

tem; others with a three-class system. It is possible that practice may be standardized as a result of Civil Aeronautics Board action.

Promotional Fares

In addition to the two-class system of fares generally maintained, there are all sorts of special fares of a promotional nature which have been instituted from time to time by the airlines. Among these are "family fares," "youth fares," "Discover America fares," and group fares of various sorts. Legal questions involved in some of these fares are considered in a later chaper.[40]

Promotional fares illustrate price differentiation based largely on conditions of demand or "value of service." They are designed to utilize unused capacity and increase revenues by tapping sources of traffic that are lower on the demand curve. To be successful they must not divert too much traffic from first class.

AIR EXPRESS SERVICE

Air express service began soon after the contract air-mail service was established. In 1927 the American Railway Express Company entered into contracts with a number of airlines to establish an air express service. In 1929 this service, along with the railway express service, was taken over by the Railway Express Agency, which was owned by the railroads. In 1932 another organization, General Air Express, was formed as a rival of the Railway Express Agency in the field of air express. General Air Express was an interline association of airlines, about six in number. It was in operation only a few years. By 1937 all of the airlines had joined the Railway Express Agency system and have continued in the system to the present.

Agreements between the Express Agency and the airlines provided for the deduction from air express revenues of the expenses incurred by the Agency in handling air express and for a division of the remainder between the airlines and the Agency on the basis of 87½ percent to the airlines and 12½ percent to the Railway Express Agency.[41]

Control of air express service by a railroad-controlled agency naturally aroused some apprehension lest the development of the service might be restricted to protect the rail express service of Railway Express Agency. The Civil Aeronautics Board, in 1948, said that there was no evidence that the service had been inhibited or restricted in any way as a result of railroad control.[42]

---

[40] See p. 837, infra.

[41] *Railway Express Agency, Grandfather Certificate*, 2 CAB 531, 532 (1941).

[42] *Air Freight Forwarder Case*, 9 CAB 468, 485 (1948).

There were certain advantages which arose from having air express service provided by the Railway Express Agency, now known simply as REA. Among these was the fact that REA had an organization for pickup and delivery which it used for railway express and which it could also use for air express. Another advantage was that REA covered the whole country and hence could provide a one-company service, which no individual airline could do. Another advantage of this arrangement was that REA was in a position to forward shipments by rail to expedite movement when flight cancellations interfered with the movement of shipments by air. Lastly, REA had offices at many points not served by airlines; hence it could easily provide air express service to and from points not served directly by airlines.

Modification of Express Contracts

In 1939 the Civil Aeronautics Board instituted an investigation of the contracts between the Railway Express Agency and the airlines to determine whether any of the provisions were adverse to the public interest. As a result of this proceeding the Board suggested modifications of the contracts in certain respects.[43] Four provisions in the contracts were found objectionable. These were (1) that the air carrier would not accept express business from any person other than the Express Agency; (2) that the Express Agency would not make an agreement with another air carrier for similar service except under certain conditions; (3) that air express rates would not be reduced to a point below twice the rail express rates without the consent of the Express Agency; and (4) that the Express Agency would not enter into the air express transportation business by operating its own aircraft in competition with the airline. New contracts entered into by the Express Agency and the airlines eliminated the objectionable features.

The first provision virtually gave the Express Agency a monopoly and prevented air carriers from transporting property for shippers directly. The third provision mentioned above was often pointed out as evidence that the Express Agency was interested in maintaining high air express rates in order to prevent air express from becoming too competitive with railway express. The Board said that the provision in the contract had not been of practical importance, since air express rates had been maintained by the airlines at a point higher than twice the rail express rates. The Board wisely held, however, that the provision should be eliminated "in order that air express rates could find their own proper level without regard to those being charged for the transportation of express by rail."[44]

In 1948, in the Air Freight Forwarder Case,[45] the Civil Aeronautics

---

[43] *Railway Express Agreements*, 4 CAB 157 (1943).

[44] Ibid., p. 158.

[45] 9 CAB 473.

Board made further criticisms of the contracts between REA and the air-lines, and directed the Agency to negotiate revised contracts. The Board found that the deduction of the Agency's "out-of-pocket expenses" from air express revenues before division with the airlines was a source of fric-tion and did not provide the Agency with sufficient incentive to keep its costs down. The Board specified that the new contracts should provide that REA pay the airlines a definite amount for carrying express and that this should be related to the costs of performing the service. This would remove the source of controversy over the propriety of certain of the Agency's deductions which characterized the existing arrangement and would provide the Agency with an incentive to reduce costs. The Board also held that the air express rates should be fixed by REA and not, as in the past, by the airlines. The Board said that this change would provide a remedy for "an anomalous situation which permits the air carriers to set tariff rates for REA and at the same time compete with REA for air cargo traffic."[46]

AIR FREIGHT SERVICE

As suggested above, the airlines not only transport air express for REA, but they also provide an independent air freight service. The term "air express" generally refers to commodities transported by air through the medium of REA, and the term "air freight" to the property transported by the airlines for the shipper directly.

Independent air freight service was instituted by American Airlines in 1944. By 1947 all of the trunklines had established a similar service. Air freight and air express are to some extent competitive, but there are differences in the service offered and the rates charged which may de-termine whether air express service or air freight service is utilized for a particular shipment. Rates are considerably lower for air feight; air ex-press receives a more expedited service, particularly in ground service; and an extra charge is usually made by the airlines for pickup and delivery of air freight, while this service is provided by REA without a separate charge.

Air freight service is provided not only by the scheduled air carriers but by supplemental air carriers and by the all-cargo carriers. In 1969 the volume of domestic air freight, including express, amounted to over 2.5 billion ton-miles, of which 74 percent was carried by scheduled "combi-nation" carriers, that is, regular airlines which transport passengers, freight, and express; 16 percent was carried by the all-cargo carriers; and 10 percent by supplemental carriers.[47]

---

[46] Ibid., p. 486. New agreements between REA and the airlines were made in 1959; but from available information it does not appear that the method of com-pensating the airlines has been changed.

[47] Computed from figures in *FAA Statistical Handbook of Aviation, 1970*, p. 135.

The volume of air freight has not grown as rapidly as was commonly predicted a number of years ago. Some early estimates forecast over five billion ton-miles by 1950; later forecasts have been more cautious, but most of them have predicted greater volumes than have actually materialized.[48] The introduction of jet aircraft may result in lower ton-mile costs and rates, and thus provide the basis for a great expansion of air traffic in the future.

CHARACTERISTICS OF AIR FREIGHT AND EXPRESS TRAFFIC

As might be expected, the traffic which moves by air consists of articles having high value in relation to their weight or bulk, or of shipments for which speed is highly important for one reason or another. This fact is demonstrated by the articles listed in Table 33–3, which shows the commodities comprising the bulk of air shipments.

TABLE 33–3. Percentage Distribution by Commodities of Air Freight Carried by Major Airlines, 1951*

Commodity Group	Percentage of Total Volume
Electric and electronic equipment and parts	14.3
Wearing apparel	12.1
Machinery and parts	11.6
Advertising and printed matter	7.7
Cut flowers	7.1
Auto parts and accessories	6.8
Aircraft parts and accessories	5.7
Drugs and biologicals	4.9
Metal products, hardware	4.7
Luggage and personal effects	3.5
Livestock, chicks, fish	3.4
Cameras, film, photo equipment	2.9
Professional and scientific instruments, engines, and parts	2.4
Plants and nursery stock	2.2
Paper and paper products	1.5
All other	9.2
Total	100.0

* *Source:* Program Planning Staff, Office of the Administrator of Civil Aeronautics, *Staff Study, Domestic Air Cargo Forecast, 1955 and 1960* (1952), p. 45.

Since air freight consists so largely of high-valued manufactured articles, and these articles are manufactured most extensively in the North and East, a preponderance of air freight moves from the East and North to the West and South, creating a serious imbalance of traffic.[49]

---

[48] For a summary of various estimates see U.S. Department of Commerce, Civil Aeronautics Administration, *Staff Study, Domestic Air Cargo Forecast, 1955 and 1960* (1952), p. 16.

[49] For analysis of this situation see *Air Freight Rate Investigation—Directional Rates*, 11 CAB 228 (1950), particularly pp. 229–31.

Both air freight and air express tend to move long distances. This is to be expected, since the speed advantage of air transport becomes greater as the length of the haul increases. In fact, air freight ordinarily has little advantage over surface transportation for those distances within which railroads and motor carriers can provide overnight delivery. The average length of haul of air freight by the domestic certificated airlines was 1,147 miles in 1969.[50]

AIR FREIGHT AND EXPRESS RATES

Freight Classification

Much less use is made of freight classification by airlines than by other transportation agencies. Railroads and motor carriers, we have seen, maintain an elaborate system of freight classification, with widely varying rates on the different classes of freight. The air express service provided by REA takes all commodities, with few exceptions, at the same basic rates. One exception consists of newpapers, which have been given 60 percent of the regular rate.

Although air express handled by REA is substantially on a one-class basis, a rule is maintained to the effect that 250 cubic inches are considered as a pound regardless of the actual weight. Higher rates on light and bulky shipments are provided in this manner instead of by placing such articles in separate and higher-rated "classes," as is done by the railroads. The airline method of dealing with this matter is not new, however, since steamship lines have long made use of the same device to some extent.

In the air freight service maintained by the airlines independently of REA, freight classification has been used in varying degree, but not so extensively as in the railroad and motor-carrier field. The American Airlines air freight service which was established in 1944 made use of a freight classification in which articles were classified into four classes. In addition, commodity rates were provided on certain articles. Somewhat later, United Air Lines and others established a one-class system of rates, but since special rates are published for specific commodities or categories of commodities, the system may be more appropriately described as one of specific commodity rates plus a general commodity rate, the latter applying on everything not given a specific commodity rate or not falling in a group or category of articles which are given a specific rate.

Graduated Quantity or Volume Rates

Another characteristic of air freight rates has been the use of graduated quantity or volume rates, that is, rates that vary in cents per pound or per

---

[50] Transportation Association of America, *Transportation: Facts & Trends, 1971,* p. 14.

hundred pounds with the size of the shipment. Thus the United Air Lines rate structure, established in 1946, provided rates averaging 26.5 cents per ton-mile on shipments weighing from 100 to 499 pounds, 25.6 cents on shipments weighing from 500 to 999 pounds, 24.7 cents on shipments weighing 1,000 to 1,999 pounds, 23 cents on shipments weighing from 2,000 pounds to 2,999 pounds, and 21.2 cents on shipments weighing 3,000 pounds and over.[51]

In 1947 the scheduled airlines adopted a consolidated freight tariff which abandoned the system of graduated rates on shipments weighing less than 16,000 pounds.[52] The all-cargo lines, however, retained the system of varying rates with the size of the shipment. Thus the tariff of Slick Airways provided volume breaks at 1,000, 3,000, and 10,000 pounds. The Flying Tiger Line did likewise, but with an additional break at 20,000 pounds.[53]

The abandonment of weight breakdowns on shipments of less than 16,000 pounds by the combination carriers was based in part on the hostility of the scheduled air carriers to air freight forwarders. The existence of weight breakdowns provides an opportunity for freight forwarders to consolidate small shipments into larger ones and to profit from the spread between the rates charged their patrons and the lower rates charged for the movement of the larger consolidated shipments.

Tapering Principle

Air freight rates are based on distance. Some of the early tariffs, furthermore, did not make use of the tapering principle. Tapering on a moderate scale was subsequently introduced and now characterizes the air freight-rate structure.[54]

"Directional Rates"

Because of the unbalanced freight movement, which has been previously noted, the airlines have established, with the approval of the Civil Aeronautics Board, a system of lower rates from the West to the East and from the South to the North than prevail generally.[55] By this means it was hoped to stimulate additional traffic in an easterly and northerly direction and overcome the traffic imbalance. No reductions below previously prescribed minimum rates were permitted on eastbound movements for distances up to and including 650 miles. Beyond 650 miles the "direc-

---

[51] Harold W. Torgerson, "History of Air Freight Tariffs," 15 *Journal of Air Law and Commerce* 47 (1948), p. 50.

[52] The Pennsylvania-Central Airlines retained the volume breakdowns.

[53] See *Air Freight Rate Investigation*, 9 CAB 340, 342 (1948).

[54] Ibid., pp. 340, 341–43.

[55] *Air Freight Rate Investigation—Directional Rates*, 11 CAB 228 (1950).

tional" rates were graded from 99.88 percent of previously prescribed minima to 60 percent at 1,300 miles and over. Northbound, because of the lesser distance involved, the reduced rates began at 551 miles, becoming 60 percent of the previously established minima at 1,100 miles. The lower directional rates were not permitted on certain commodities which would move at or above the generally established minima.[56]

AIR-TRANSPORT SUBSIDY

The railroads have long complained that air transportation is subsidized and hence that shippers and travelers do not pay as high rates and fares as would be necessary if the industry were self-supporting. Subsidy to the airlines takes three forms: (1) Airlines for many years were given free use of the airways which are established and maintained by the federal government; (2) Airlines may be making inadequate payment for the use of publicly owned airports; (3) The payments made by the government to the airlines for the transportation of mail may contain a substantial subsidy. Each of these forms of subsidy will be examined in turn.

Earlier in the chapter we recognized that there was an element of subsidy to air transport arising from the use of the federal system of airways. The cost of providing, operating, and maintaining the airway system is a cost of providing air transportation service. To determine the amount of subsidy to commercial transportation arising from this source, however, is not an easy task. An attempt to measure the amount of subsidy from use of airway facilities was made by the Board of Investigation and Research and published in 1944.[57] The amount of subsidy was determined by taking the annual cost of operating and maintaining the airway system, interest on investment in the airways, and depreciation or amortization of investment, and by determining the share of such costs which would be charged to scheduled air carriers on the basis of the use which they make of the airways in comparison with other users. The 1941 subsidy figure was approximately $35 million[58] or about 5.6 percent of the total revenues of the domestic airlines. These figures, of course, have only an historical value and do not describe the present situation. A later study, using similar methods of calculation, was made by the Federal Aviation Agency in 1961 in connection with the proposal to impose user charges for the use of the federal airway system.[59] The Federal Aviation Agency estimated that the annual cost of the federal airway system would be $479 million

[56] Art works, cut flowers, gold coins and bullion, household goods, human remains, ladies' hats, live animals, negotiable securities, paper currency, personal effects, platinum and precious metals, wearing apparel on racks or hangers.

[57] Board of Investigation and Research, *Public Aids to Domestic Transportation,* 79th Cong., 1st Sess., House Doc. No. 159 (1944), chap. vi.

[58] Ibid., p. 480.

[59] *A Study of User Charges for the Domestic Federal Airway System* (1961).

in 1963, and that the civil aviation share of the cost would be $335 million. Since "civil aviation" includes more than use by commercial airlines, it is not to be supposed that the share of the cost assigned to civil aviation should all be borne by commercial airlines.

The user charges levied under the Airport and Airway Development Act of 1970 are expected to provide sufficient funds by January 1, 1972 to defray the costs of the airport and airway program. If that should happen, we still could not say whether there was now a subsidy to the airlines through use of the federal airway system. An excess of airway expenditures over the revenues from user charges would not prove existence of a subsidy since actual expenditures include a large amount of capital outlays not properly chargeable to a single year. On the other hand, actual expenditures less than user revenues would not prove the absence of a subsidy since actual expenditures do not include interest on past capital outlays, or depreciation, both of which are a part of the annual cost properly chargeable against users in determining subsidy.

The amount of subsidy that may exist because of inadequate payments by the airlines for the use of publicly provided airports is an unknown amount. The Board of Investigation and Research staff report reached the conclusion that subsidy from this source for the year 1940 was $3,780,-000.[60] This was 5.7 percent of the revenues of the domestic airlines in that year. The computation of annual airport costs, as in the case of airways, included maintenance and operation, interest on investment, and depreciation or amortization of investment. To determine the amount of subsidy, it was necessary to deduct from annual airport costs the amount which airlines had paid for the use of airport facilities. We have no way of knowing what a similar study would reveal as the amount of present subsidy to the airlines arising from inadequate airport charges. Even if landing fees were substantially increased it is not likely that they would greatly affect the level of airline fares. It has been estimated that landing fees constitute about 1.5 percent of airline operating expenses.[61]

Air-Mail Payments and Subsidy

There has sometimes been misunderstanding about the relation between air-mail payments and subsidies to the airlines. It is sometimes assumed that the entire sum paid by the government for the transportation of air mail constitutes a subsidy, but this ignores the fact that the government is receiving a valuable service for the payments made. Again, it is sometimes claimed that the subsidy is the difference between the amounts paid the airlines for carrying mail and the amount of postage receipts from air mail. But an excess of payments to the airlines over the air-mail postage receipts

---

[60] Board of Investigation & Research, op. cit., p. 503.

[61] Adele Schwartz, "Airport Use Charges: the High Cost of Landing," *American Aviation*, Feb. 1965, p. 18.

would only prove that air mail is subsidized, not that air transportation is subsidized. In other words, such an excess of payments to the air carriers would show that the air-mail branch of the postal service did not pay its own way. Conversely an excess of air-mail postage receipts over payments to the airlines would merely prove that the government was making a profit from this branch of the postal service.

There is subsidy in the air-mail payments if the amount of such payments exceeds a reasonable price for the service performed. Any payment to the airlines for carrying mail that exceeds a reasonable compensation for the service is subsidy. The determination of the subsidy, therefore, first requires the determination of a reasonable price or rate for transporting mail. Since airlines that carry mail also carry passengers, freight, and express, the determination of a reasonable mail rate is similar to the problem of determining reasonable rates for transportation of any particular commodity or class of commodities by a transportation agency that performs other transportation services at the same time.

That subsidy might be expected to exist in the air-mail payments is clear when the provisions of the Civil Aeronautics Act relating to air-mail compensation are recalled. The compensation is to be determined by the Civil Aeronautics Board in accordance with standards laid down in the Act. The Act specifically requires that the compensation be based on the carrier's needs after considering its revenues from other sources. It was recognized that the payments should be made on such a basis as might be necessary to keep the airlines going.[62]

Acting in response to considerable agitation for a separation of the fair-compensation and subsidy elements in air-mail payments, the Civil Aeronautics Board in 1951 announced an "administrative separation" of the two elements.[63] We shall not at this point examine the methods used by the Board to separate the subsidy element from total mail compensation.[64] For several years the Board published the separation, showing for groups of carriers and for carriers individually the total mail compensation, the amount which it considered to be reasonable compensation for the service performed, called "service mail pay," and the amount which it considered to be subsidy. Prior to 1953 the payments to the airlines for carrying mail, including whatever part thereof was subsidy, were paid by the Post Office Department out of its appropriations. By Reorganization Plan No. 10 of 1953 President Eisenhower transferred from the Post Office Department to the Civil Aeronautics Board the function of paying the subsidy portion of the mail compensation.[65] This means that the Post

---

[62] For further discussion of the determination of air-mail compensation see pp. 830–31, infra.

[63] *Administrative Separation of Subsidy from Total Mail Payments to Domestic Air Carriers* (1951).

[64] The method is briefly referred to on p. 834, infra.

[65] The reorganization plan and the President's statement accompanying it are printed in 20 *Journal of Air Law & Commerce* 210 (1953).

Office Department is now charged only the "service mail pay," while the subsidy element is paid by the Civil Aeronautics Board from appropriations made for the purpose. Theoretically, at least, the total amount of compensation which the airlines will receive for transporting mail is not affected, since the basic rules by which the compensation is to be determined are in the statute and have not been changed.

Since the subsidy portion of the air-mail payments must now be made from appropriations made for the purpose, failure of Congress to appropriate the necessary funds would create a difficult situation. Payments could not be made if the funds had not been appropriated, but the airlines,

TABLE 33–4. Air Mail Subsidy Payments to Airlines, 1959–1968*

	In Thousands					
Year	*Domestic Trunklines*	*Local Service Lines*	*Helicopter Carriers*	*Intra-Alaska Lines*	*Intra-Hawaii Lines*	*Total*
1959........$	—	$42,179	$4,915	$3,611	$ —	$50,705
1960........	—	54,126	4,931	4,852	109	64,018
1961........	—	62,937	5,258	6,352	697	75,243
1962........	—	67,948	5,518	5,139	355	78,960
1963........	988	78,623	4,641	5,317	716	79,543
1964........	3,408	65,779	4,300	5,590	878	79,955
1965........	3,508	66,012	2,712	5,266	1,124	78,623
1966........	2,110	54,924	584	5,124	1,124	63,866
1967........	2,822	50,961	—	4,729	—	58,512
1968........	—	40,950	—	3,190	—	44,139

° From Civil Aeronautics Board, *Handbook of Airline Statistics, 1969.*

under the law, are entitled to the air-mail compensation determined by the Board and based on their need. Under these circumstances it would seem that the airlines would have grounds for suing the government for the amounts legally due them. Requiring the subsidy element in air-mail pay to be paid out of special appropriations for the purpose has created a situation whereby Congress can pressure the Board in determining subsidy need, thus interfering with what was intended to be determined administratively. Although it may be argued that Congress rather than the Civil Aeronautics Board should determine the extent to which the airlines shall be subsidized through air-mail payments, that was not the plan provided for in the Civil Aeronautics Act. Unless the courts should hold that airlines are entitled to the air-mail compensation determined by the Board without Congressional interference, the Board has been wrested of the power to determine air-mail compensation.

SELECTED REFERENCES

A general book on air transport is John H. Frederick, *Commercial Air Transportation* (5th ed.; Homewood, Ill.: Richard D. Irwin, 1961).

On the early history of air transport, see E. P. Warner, *The Early History of Air Transportation* (Northfield, Vt.: Norwich University, 1938). There is much information about the history of air transport in Paul T. David, *The Economics of Air Mail Transportation* (Washington, D.C.: Brookings Institution, 1934); and in Francis A. Spencer, *Air Mail Payment and the Government* (Washington, D.C.: Brookings Institution, 1941).

For a good description of airway facilities and an analysis of the problem of user charges, see Federal Aviation Agency, *A Study of User Charges for the Domestic Federal Airway System* (1961).

The most extensive study of airport problems is Lynn L. Bollinger, Alan Passen, and Robert E. McElfresh, *Terminal Airport Financing and Management* (Boston: Graduate School of Business Administration, Harvard University, 1946). For later material, see Richard Zettel and Robert Horonjeff, *The Practice and Theory of Airport Financing Based on a Survey of California Airports* (Berkeley: Institute of Transportation and Traffic Engineering, University of California, 1956); and Richard Nelson, "Airport Development and Operation Problems," 24 *Journal of Air Law and Commerce* 49 (1957).

A very informative article on the passenger traffic pattern is D'Arcy Harvey, "Airline Passenger Traffic Pattern within the United States," 18 ibid. 157 (1951). The development of air coach service is detailed in Harold A. Jones and Frederick Davis, "The 'Air Coach' Experiment and National Air Transport Policy," 17 ibid. 1 and 418 (1950). A most detailed study of passenger-fare policy is Paul W. Cherington, *Airline Price Policy* (Boston: Graduate School of Business Administration, Harvard University, 1958).

On economic analysis of the airline industry, see John B. Crane, "The Economics of Air Transportation," 22 *Harvard Business Review* 495 (1944); Harold D. Koontz, "Economic and Managerial Factors Underlying Subsidy Needs of Domestic Trunk Line Carriers," 18 *Journal of Air Law & Commerce* 127 (1951); Jesse W. Proctor and Julius S. Duncan, "A Regression Analysis of Airline Costs," 21 ibid. 282 (1954); John R. Meyer et al., *Competition in the Transportation Industries* (Cambridge: Harvard University Press, 1959), pp. 133–44; Richard E. Caves, *Air Transportation and Its Regulators* (Cambridge: Harvard University Press, 1962), particularly Parts I and III.

Chapter 34

DEVELOPMENT OF AIR TRANSPORT REGULATION

The present system of federal regulation of air transportation was established by the Civil Aeronautics Act of 1938, although the present statute, essentially the same as the Civil Aeronautics Act except as it relates to safety regulation, is known as the Federal Aviation Act of 1958. Prior to the enactment of the Civil Aeronautics Act in 1938, however, there were three statutes which imposed a limited amount of regulation on the industry by the federal government.

REGULATION PRIOR TO 1938

The first of these statutes was the Air Commerce Act of 1926. The Air Commerce Act provided for the construction, maintenance, and operation of the federal airways system by the Department of Commerce which was also given research and development functions relating to aeronautics. Thus the Act was promotional rather than regulatory in nature, but it did provide for the following matters related to safety regulation: the registration of aircraft; the rating of aircraft as to airworthiness; examination and rating of airmen, navigation facilities, and aviation schools; the rating of airlines and the establishment of minimum safety standards; and the establishment of air traffic rules.

A second statute affecting air carriers was a 1936 amendment to the Railway Labor Act of 1926. This amendment brought employees of commercial airlines under the provisions of that Act, thus providing a certain amount of regulation of labor relations in the industry as well as machinery for the settlement of labor disputes.[1]

The third statute to be mentioned was the Air Mail Act of 1934,[2] amended in 1935. This Act gave certain regulatory powers over air transportation to the Post Office Department and to the Interstate Commerce Commission. Grant of such powers to the Post Office Department grew out of the fact that the airlines transported mail for the Department. The

---

[1] For provisions of the Railway Labor Act see pp. 257–58, supra.

[2] This was the last of several acts, beginning with the Kelly Act in 1925, which dealt with air-mail contracts and control over the air-mail contractors.

Postmaster General could prescribe the number and frequency of schedules, intermediate stops, and the time of departure of planes carrying mail. He was also empowered to prescribe a system of accounts for air-mail contractors. In addition to these regulatory powers given by the Act, the Postmaster General, because of his power to award air-mail contracts and to extend the routes of existing contractors, exercised in fact a considerable amount of control over the establishment of air transportation routes and in large measure determined who should operate them.

The Air Mail Act also contained a number of provisions relating to intercorporate relations of air-mail contractors designed to prevent holding-company control and also to keep the air-transport industry independent of other branches of the aeronautics industry, such as the manufacture and sale of planes and the furnishing of materials, accessories, and the like.

Under the Air Mail Act the Interstate Commerce Commission had certain powers and duties in the determination of reasonable rates of compensation to be received by the airlines for transporting mail.

It is unnecessary to review the provisions of the Air Mail Act in detail or to discuss the difficulties encountered in administering them, since the Act was soon replaced by the more comprehensive system of regulation provided by the Civil Aeronautics Act of 1938.

In view of later developments, however, one other provision of the Air Mail Act of 1934 should be noted. It provided for the appointment of a Federal Aviation Commission to make recommendations to Congress, not later than February 1, 1935, concerning appropriate policy with respect to all phases of aviation. Many, but not all, of the recommendations of the Federal Aviation Commission were incorporated into the Civil Aeronautics Act of 1938.

REPORT OF THE FEDERAL AVIATION COMMISSION

The Federal Aviation Commission,[3] after an intensive study of all phases of aviation, and after compiling an extensive record of testimony and statements, made its report in January of 1935.[4] The more important recommendations of the Commission which are pertinent to the subject matter of this chapter may be summarized as follows:

1. The Commission recommended a comprehensive system of regulation of air carriers.
2. The Commission recommended against giving the Interstate Commerce Commission jurisdiction over air carriers and favored the creation of a separate "air commerce commission" to exercise the regula-

---

[3] The Commission consisted of Clark Howell, Chairman; Edward P. Warner; Albert J. Berres; Jerome C. Hunsaker; and Franklin K. Lane, Jr.

[4] *Report of the Federal Aviation Commission*, 74th Cong., 1st Sess., Senate Doc. No. 15 (1935).

tory powers given. The Commission was not averse, however, to a plan whereby the regulatory commission would ultimately become a division of an over-all commission or group of commissions which embraced all forms of transport. In deciding against regulation of air transport by the Interstate Commerce Commission, the Federal Aviation Commission said:

There would seem to us to be great danger that through the placing of an additional burden upon an already heavily loaded agency delay might be caused where promptness and certainty of action are of the utmost importance, and that in the formative stage of a new regulatory doctrine there might be an inevitable feeling for analogies with other forms of transportation where such analogies may be superficially attractive but valid only in a very limited degree and actually misleading beyond that point.[5]

3.   The Commission recognized that air transport could not exist, at its then stage of development, without some form of direct government aid.

4.   The Commission favored a competitive organization for the airline industry, believing that the high quality of American air transport was due in large part to the competitive spirit that had existed throughout its development. It held that there should be no arbitrary denial of the right of entry of newcomers into the field where they could make an adequate showing of their readiness to render a better public service than could otherwise be obtained. The Commission cautioned against a system that would freeze the present air-transport map with respect either to the location of routes or to the identity of operators, saying that "present operators of air lines have no inherent right to a monopoly of the routes that they serve."[6]

5.   Notwithstanding its advocacy of competition among airlines, the Commission believed that the competition should be a carefully controlled competition. Too much competition, it said, can be as bad as too little. "To allow half a dozen air lines to eke out a hand-to-mouth existence where there is enough traffic to support one really first-class service and one alone would be a piece of folly. To try to maintain a multiplicity of services in such a case by giving direct governmental aid to all of them would be folly thrice compounded."[7] The Commission therefore recommended that no airline should be allowed to operate without obtaining a certificate of public convenience and necessity from the regulatory body. Whether or not routes would be paralleled should be left to the discretion of the regulatory body, in the light of all the circumstances. The Commission was of the view that every airline operating on December 1, 1934, should be con-

---

[5] Ibid., p. 244.
[6] Ibid., p. 62.
[7] Ibid., p. 61.

sidered to have a presumptive right to a certificate of public convenience and necessity.

6. The Commission recommended that payments for the carrying of mail should be quite separate from the direct financial aid given to the airlines. This recommendation was not followed by Congress, as we shall see, but was subsequently achieved by action of the President.[8]

7. Other matters over which the regulatory body should be given control, according to the Federal Aviation Commission, were accounts and reports, rates and fares, control of airlines by outside interests, intercorporate relationships among airlines, and financial structures.

When President Roosevelt transmitted the report of the Federal Aviation Commission to Congress, he stated that he was unable to concur in the recommendation that a separate air commerce commission be created but that he favored giving a division of the Interstate Commerce Commission control over air transport pending the creation of a consolidated agency with jurisdiction over all forms of transport. This attitude created somewhat of an impasse between the President and Congress because Congress favored the creation of a separate regulatory agency. Eventually, however, President Roosevelt withdrew his opposition to a special regulatory agency for the airlines.[9]

THE CIVIL AERONAUTICS ACT OF 1938

The Civil Aeronautics Act was passed by Congress after a long and complicated legislative history, and it was signed by the President on June 23, 1938.[10] The Act set up a system of regulation of air carriers comparable to that which had been provided for railroads and motor carriers. The Act, furthermore, transferred to the newly created Civil Aeronautics Authority the functions formerly carried on by the Department of Commerce under the Air Commerce Act of 1926. These functions included safety regulation and the construction, maintenance, and operation of the federal airways. The Act also empowered the Civil Aeronautics Authority to determine the compensation to be received by the airlines for the transportation of mail and relieved the Interstate Commerce Commission of such powers and duties as it had over this matter under the Air Mail Act of 1934 and 1935.

The Civil Aeronautics Authority

The Civil Aeronautics Authority was to be composed of five members, appointed by the President with the advice and consent of the Senate. The term of office was six years; members of the Authority might be removed

---

[8] Pp. 794-95.

[9] Charles S. Rhyne, *The Civil Aeronautics Act Annotated* (Washington: National Law Book Co., 1939), pp. 52-53.

[10] 52 Stat. 973. The Act is reproduced in Rhyne, op. cit., Appendix C.

by the President for inefficiency, neglect of duty, or malfeasance in office. Not more than three members were to be appointed from the same political party.

The Civil Aeronautics Authority was intended to be an independent regulatory agency, comparable to the Interstate Commerce Commission, and free from executive interference so far as its quasi-legislative and quasi-judicial powers were concerned. Within the Authority, however, were set up two agencies which were to be responsible to the President. These were the Administrator and the Air Safety Board.

The Administrator was to be appointed by the President with the advice and consent of the Senate; but unlike the members of the Authority he might be removed by the President at will. In general the Administrator was to take over the promotional and developmental functions formerly performed by the Bureau of Air Commerce in the Department of Commerce. These included the establishment and the maintenance and operation of the airways and air navigation facilities, and the collection and dissemination of information relative to civil aeronautics. The Administrator might also exercise such powers and duties as were assigned to him by the Authority.

The Air Safety Board consisted of three members, appointed by the President with the advice and consent of the Senate. The Board had no regulatory powers other than the power to make rules and regulations governing the reporting of accidents involving aircraft, and these were subject to the approval of the Authority. The Air Safety Board was a fact-finding body set up to investigate aircraft accidents and to make recommendations to the Authority concerning measures to prevent accidents.

Congress was very careful to make the Air Safety Board independent of the five-man regulatory body or of the Administrator. This was because there had been some criticism of the investigation of accidents by the Department of Commerce under the Air Commerce Act of 1926. It was felt that the investigation of accidents should not be made by the agency which made the safety rules or which provided and operated the airways. An independent body, it was thought, would be less likely to gloss over any failure to make and enforce adequate safety rules or failure to have provided and to have properly operated aids to navigation on the airways.

Some confusion arose because the term "Civil Aeronautics Authority" could be used in two senses. It might be used to designate either the five-man regulatory body or the over-all organization which included the regulatory agency, the Administrator, and the Air Safety Board.

Reorganization of 1940

Important changes in organization of the Authority, using that term in the broad sense, were made as a result of two executive orders of President Roosevelt in 1940. These changes were as follows:

1. The name of the five-man regulatory body was changed from "Civil Aeronautics Authority" to "Civil Aeronautics Board."
2. The Administrator became Administrator of Civil Aeronautics. This change would appear to be necessary to make clear what the Administrator was administrator of, since he was no longer a part of a "Civil Aeronautics Authority" nor attached to the Civil Aeronautics Board. Presumably the change gave the Administrator of Civil Aeronautics greater freedom of action than the Administrator had enjoyed as a part of the old Civil Aeronautics Authority.
3. Both the Civil Aeronautics Board and the Administrator of Civil Aeronautics were placed in the Department of Commerce. The Administrator of Civil Aeronautics was made responsible to the Secretary of Commerce; but the Civil Aeronautics Board was to retain its complete independence, without interference from the Secretary of Commerce. It was sometimes said that the regulatory body was placed in the Department of Commerce for "housekeeping purposes" only. Placing the Civil Aeronautics Board in the Department of Commerce, however, was inconsistent with the tradition of independent regulatory agencies,[11] and raised fears that it would fall under the domination of the Executive. Eventually, as we shall see, the Board was again made an "independent" establishment like the other regulatory agencies.[12]
4. Certain administrative functions formerly performed by the Authority were transferred to the Administrator of Civil Aeronautics. These included administration of the civilian pilot-training program; issuance of aircraft, airmen, and other certificates required in the interest of safety; and the administration of safety regulations, but not the prescription of safety rules and standards.
5. The Air Safety Board was abolished, and its functions were transferred to the Civil Aeronautics Board.

It should perhaps be noted that the organization built around the Administrator of Civil Aeronautics came to be known as the Civil Aeronautics Administration.

ECONOMIC REGULATION

We may now turn to a consideration of the system of regulation provided by the Civil Aeronautics Act. In so doing, we shall be concerned with the regulation of the business of transporting persons, property, and mail by air, commonly described as "economic regulation," rather than with safety regulation. The latter is important but is beyond the scope of the present volume. The provisions of the Act relating to economic regulation are largely found in Title IV of the Act. Since these provisions

---

[11] See p. 288, supra.
[12] P. 806, infra.

have been reenacted as Title IV of the Federal Aviation Act of 1958 and are presently in effect, they will be referred to in the present tense. Economic regulation is patterned on the system of regulation of railroads and motor carriers, although there are significant differences. Economic regulation is provided only for common carriers by air and carriers of mail, while safety regulation extends to all flying, including that by common carriers and contract carriers, and private flying also. At first glance the Act would seem to apply economic regulation to "air carriers" rather than only to common carriers by air, but the definitions of "air carrier" and "air transportation" are such as to confine economic regulation either to common carriers[13] or to other carriers of mail. Thus, contract carriers by air are not regulated at the present time.

The Pattern of Regulation

The major provisions of the Act establishing the general pattern of regulation show a close resemblance to statutory provisions applying to the other modes of transport. They may be summarized as follows:

1. Certificates of public convenience and necessity are required of air carriers, although an appropriate "grandfather clause" protected carriers which were in operation from May 14, 1938, to the date the Act became effective. When a certificate authorizes the transportation of mail, an air carrier must provide necessary and adequate facilities therefor and he must also transport the mail whenever required by the Postmaster General.
2. Rates and fares are to be published, and tariffs containing such charges must be open to public inspection and filed with the regulatory authority. Strict observance of published rates is required.
3. Notice of 30 days is required of changes in rates, and the regulatory body has power to suspend proposed changes in rates for 180 days.
4. Carriers are to charge just and reasonable rates, and are to provide safe and adequate service, equipment, and facilities.
5. Undue preference and prejudice are prohibited.
6. The regulatory agency has power to prescribe the "lawful" rate or charge in lieu of a rate found unreasonable or otherwise unlawful. Or it may prescribe the maximum or minimum, or the maximum and minimum, rate. On overseas traffic[14] the regulatory authority may prescribe the maximum or minimum, or the maximum and minimum, but not the exact rate. Prior to 1972 the Board had no power over rates and fares to or from foreign countries but this lack was remedied in 1972 (Public Law 92–259).

---

[13] See *Railway Express Agency, Grandfather Certificate*, 2 CAB 531, 535–36 (1941).

[14] "Overseas traffic" means traffic between points in the United States proper and points in territories or possessions of the United States or between two points in possessions or territories of the United States.

7. The abandonment of routes is prohibited except upon approval of the regulatory authority.

8. The regulatory authority may require reports from air carriers and may prescibe the system of accounts.

9. Consolidations, mergers, and acquisition of control of air carriers by other air carriers, or by carriers of any type, or by persons engaged in any other branch of aeronautics are made unlawful unless approved by the Board. The scope of these provisions was broadened in 1969 by including acquisition of control of an air carrier "by any other person" within the prohibition.[15]

10. Interlocking relationships between air carriers, or between air carriers and other common carriers, or between air carriers and other branches of the aeronautics industry are prohibited unless approved by the regulatory authority.

11. Pooling or other agreements among air carriers or between air carriers and other carriers must be filed with and approved by the regulatory body.

12. The regulatory authority is empowered to investigate alleged "unfair or deceptive practices or unfair methods of competition in air transportation," and to order the carriers to cease and desist from any such practices. This power extends to foreign air carriers operating to and from points in the United States.

In addition to the provisions enumerated above, which establish a familiar pattern of regulation, there are certain other provisions of the Act to which attention should be drawn.

Power of Exemption

An unusual provision of the Act is that the regulatory authority is empowered to exempt any air carrier or class of carriers from any of the provisions of Title IV, with certain exceptions, if it finds that enforcement of such provisions would be an undue burden on the carrier or carriers. This is a much broader exemption authority than is found in other regulatory legislation.[16]

Joint Board

Another novel provision of the Act provides that cases involving through services and joint rates and fares established with carriers under

---

[15] Public Law 91–62. The amendment was apparently aimed at acquisition of airline control by conglomerates, and also at rumored take-over of certain airlines by "underworld" elements. For a discussion of some of the legal issues involved, see Raymond J. Rasenberger, "Control of an Air Carrier by 'Any Other Person,'" 37 *Journal of Air Law & Commerce* 65 (1971).

[16] For a good discussion of this point see Neal Pilson, "The Exemption Provision of the Civil Aeronautics Act," 29 *Journal of Air Law & Commerce* 255 (1963).

the jurisdiction of the Interstate Commerce Commission may be referred
to a joint board consisting of an equal number of members from the
Interstate Commerce Commission and the Civil Aeronautics Board. In
such cases the joint board has the same power that the Civil Aeronautics
Board itself would have.

Rule of Rate Making

The Act contains a rule of rate making, comparable to Section 15a of
the Interstate Commerce Act and to a somewhat similar section in Part II
of the Interstate Commerce Act relating to motor carriers. In the Civil
Aeronautics Act the rule of rate making reads as follows:

In exercising and performing its powers and duties with respect to the determination of rates for the carriage of persons or property, the Authority
shall take into consideration, among other factors—(1) The effect of such rates
upon the movement of traffic; (2) The need in the public interest of adequate
and efficient transportation of persons and property by air carriers at the lowest cost consistent with the furnishing of such service; (3) Such standards
respecting the character and quality of service to be rendered by air carriers
as may be prescribed by or pursuant to law; (4) The inherent advantages of
transportation by aircraft; and (5) The need of each air carrier for revenue
sufficient to enable such air carrier, under honest, economical, and efficient
management, to provide adequate and efficient air carrier service.

Declaration of Policy

The Civil Aeronautics Act contains a declaration of policy which
makes it evident that Congress was desirous of encouraging the development of air transportation and did not intend that regulation should be
used for the purpose of hindering its development in the interest of older
transportation agencies. Since the declaration of policy expresses the will
of Congress with respect to the policies which should govern the administration of the Act and is a direct charge to the regulatory agency, it may
well be quoted in full. The section reads as follows:

In the exercise and performance of its powers and duties under this Act,
the Authority shall consider the following, among other things, as being in the
public interest, and in accordance with the public convenience and necessity—
(*a*) The encouragement and development of an air-transportation system
properly adapted to the present and future needs of the foreign and domestic
commerce of the United States, of the Postal Service, and of the national defense;
(*b*) The regulation of air transportation in such manner as to recognize
and preserve the inherent advantages of, assure the highest degree of safety in,
and foster sound economic conditions in, such transportation, and to improve
the relations between, and coordinate transportation by, air carriers;
(*c*) The promotion of adequate, economical, and efficient service by air

carriers at reasonable charges, without unjust discrimination, undue preferences or advantages, or unfair or destructive competitive practices;

(d) Competition to the extent necessary to assure the sound development of an air-transportation system properly adapted to the needs of the foreign and domestic commerce of the United States, of the Postal Service, and of the national defense;

(e) The regulation of air commerce in such manner as to best promote its development and safety; and

(f) The encouragement and development of civil aeronautics.

THE FEDERAL AVIATION ACT OF 1958

The Federal Aviation Act of 1958[17] created the Federal Aviation Agency to replace the Civil Aeronautics Administration and take over its functions. The Act was largely concerned with matters of safety regulation. In addition to transferring to the Federal Aviation Agency the functions with respect to safety which were formerly exercised by the Civil Aeronautics Administration, the Act gave the Agency the power to establish air safety regulations, a power previously exercised by the Civil Aeronautics Board. The Civil Aeronautics Board, however, continued to have responsibility for the investigation of air accidents. In 1966, the Department of Transportation Act[18] transferred both the air safety powers of the Federal Aviation Agency and the accident investigation powers of the Civil Aeronautics Board to the National Safety Board in the newly created Department of Transportation.[19]

So far as economic regulation of air carriers is concerned, the Federal Aviation Act provided for the continuation of the Civil Aeronautics Board as the regulatory agency, and it reenacted without substantial change the provisions of the Civil Aeronautics Act of 1938 relating to economic regulation. There was no intent on the part of Congress to change the substance of the statute relating to economic regulation or to change the policies of the Board in administering it. It should be noted that the Civil Aeronautics Board became an independent agency, not attached to the Department of Commerce as it had been since 1940.

DIFFERENCES BETWEEN AIR AND RAIL REGULATION

We have noted that air-carrier regulation has many of the features of railroad regulation. It is desirable, however, to call attention to some of the more important differences.

1. The Civil Aeronautics Board, as has been mentioned, may exempt any carrier or class of carriers from any of the provisions of the Act relating to "economic regulation of air carriers" except regulations

---

[17] Public Law 85–726.
[18] Public Law 89–670.
[19] See p. 275, supra.

relating to maximum flying hours of pilots and copilots, and certain labor provisions of the Act. The Interstate Commerce Commission does not have equal authority to make broad exemptions from the provisions of the Interstate Commerce Act.

2. The Federal Aviation Act contains no long-and-short-haul clause.
3. There is no control over the issuance of securities of air carriers. The Civil Aeronautics Board, however, has recommended that it be given control over the issuance of securities by air carriers in order to prevent the development of unsound capital structures.[20]
4. The Civil Aeronautics Board does not have power to award reparations to shippers for injury resulting from the charging of unreasonable or otherwise unlawful rates.

STATE REGULATION

The regulation of air transportation described up to this point has been federal regulation. There is some regulation of air transportation, however, by the states. In discussing state regulation, it is necessary to distinguish between safety regulation and economic regulation, since the line between state and federal jurisdiction at the present time is different in the two fields of control.

By means of a broad definition of "air commerce," the safety provisions of the Federal Aviation Act apparently extend to the navigation of aircraft within the limits of any federal airway or any operation or navigation of aircraft which directly affects, or which may endanger safety in, interstate, overseas, or foreign air commerce.[21] It will be observed that any navigation of aircraft on a civil airway or any flying which might endanger the safety of interstate, overseas, or foreign air commerce comes under the federal Act. The Federal Aviation Agency has power to regulate all flying, interstate or intrastate, to the extent that may be necessary to protect interstate, overseas, or foreign air commerce. This greatly restricts the authority of the states in safety regulation—at least if state regulations should conflict with federal regulations.

The power of the federal government to prohibit the flying on any federal airway of a plane which does not have a federal airworthiness certificate has been upheld, even when applied to a purely intrastate flight, and even though the craft was licensed by the state in which it was flown.[22] In another case the power of the federal government to prohibit intrastate flight unless both the plane and the pilot held a federal certificate was upheld even when the flight was not on a federal airway.[23]

In the field of economic regulation the federal government's regulation

---

[20] *Annual Report, 1942,* p. 14. This recommendation has been renewed in some later annual reports also.

[21] Section 101 (4).

[22] *Rosenhan v. United States,* 131 F. 2d 932 (1942).

[23] *United States v. Drumm,* 50 Fed. Supp. 451 (1943).

extends to interstate, overseas, and foreign transportation and to transportation of the mails. Except for transportation of mail, therefore, it would seem to leave the field of intrastate commerce by air to the jurisdiction of the states.

The right of states to regulate intrastate fares of airlines has been upheld.[24] It is quite possible that the Shreveport doctrine[25] would be applied if state regulation of intrastate rates interfered with effective federal regulation, since there is no provision in the Civil Aeronautics Act which specifically rules out its application to air transportation, such as is found in Part II of the Interstate Commerce Act, which rules out its application to motor carriers.[26]

The right of a state to issue certificates for intrastate airline operations has been upheld. The Texas Supreme Court held that "Congress has not preempted the field of economic regulation of air carriers, and the states have the power to act so long as there is no conflict with federal law."[27] But Nebraska failed in an attempt to compel an interstate air carrier to continue service over an intrastate segment of a route which the Civil Aeronautics Board had authorized the carrier to discontinue.[28] The Supreme Court of Nebraska said:

It appears that Congress has preempted the field of interstate air transportation in regard to the routes and points to be served by interstate air carriers to the exclusion of conflicting regulation by the states. . . . It follows that the Nebraska State Railway Commission lacks authority to compel a carrier licensed by the Civil Aeronautics Board to continue operations over a segment which that board has authorized to be discontinued, since the federal authority is paramount in this area and the conflicting directive of the state's agency interferes with the national policy.[29]

According to a member of the Pennsylvania Public Utility Commission, 28 states exercised some regulatory control over intrastate transportation by air in 1969.[30] In most states this has resulted from legislation specifically bringing air carriers under state control; in some, the control has been exercised under statutory or constitutional provisions covering the regulation of "common carriers" or of "public utilities"—terms which are broad enough to include common carriers by air.[31]

---

[24] *People* v. *Western Air Lines*, 268 Pac. 2d 723 (1954); appeal dismissed by Supreme Court of the United States, 348 U.S. 859 (1954).

[25] See pp. 286–87, supra.

[26] See p. 683, supra.

[27] *Texas Aeronautics Commission* v. *Braniff Airways, Inc.*, 454 S.W. 2d 199, 200 (1970).

[28] *Application of Frontier Airlines, Inc.*, 122 N.W. 2d 476 (1963).

[29] Ibid., p. 488.

[30] Reported in *Traffic World*, August 2, 1969, p. 33.

[31] See *State ex rel. State Ry. Commission* v. *Ramsey*, 37 N.W. 2d 502 (1949); *People* v. *Western Air Lines*, 268 Pac. 2d 723 (1954).

The air carriers and the Civil Aeronautics Board have tended to oppose state regulation of air cariers. Efforts have been made to get legislation enacted which would give the federal government exclusive jurisdiction over air carriers and thereby deprive the states of the power to regulate even the intrastate operations of airlines.

The position of the air carriers is that air transportation is mostly interstate in character and that the federal government should have exclusive control. They also contend that state regulation of intrastate operations of the airlines would interfere with the successful administration of the federal law in various ways. Certificates to provide intrastate service might be denied interstate carriers in favor of intrastate carriers, thereby depriving major airlines of needed revenues; or conversely, interstate carriers might be required to provide intrastate service that was unprofitable to the airlines and a burden on their operations. This in turn might make heavier mail payments necessary to subsidized lines. Other difficulties might arise over rates. Intrastate rates and fares might be prescribed by the states which were lower than interstate rates and fares, thus preventing intrastate business from contributing its share of the support of the airlines.

State authorities, on the other hand, believe that the intrastate operations of airlines are primarily of state and local interest and should be controlled by state authorities. The fact that the business of the airlines is mostly interstate is considered irrelevant. State authorities argue that there is no need for departing from the pattern of regulation followed in the railroad and motor-carrier field, which acknowledges the propriety of state control of intrastate rates and service.

There seem to be good reasons for retaining in the state governments control over intrastate commerce by air, provided it does not interfere with the successful carrying out of the purposes and objectives of the Federal Aviation Act. It seems clear that the courts will check state action which interferes with federal control, following the tradition and reasoning of the Minnesota and Shreveport Rate Cases.[32] Certainly the principle of these cases should be recognized and not legislated away, as was done in the Motor Carrier Act.[33]

SELECTED REFERENCES

The background of the Civil Aeronautics Act and a meaningful analysis of its legislative history and subsequent modification by Presidential and Congressional action is Howard C. Westwood and Alexander E. Bennett, "A Footnote to the Legislative History of the Civil Aeronautics Act of 1938 and Afterward," 42 *Notre Dame Lawyer* 309 (1967). Other references to the background of the Act and its history are Claude E. Puffer, *Air Transportation* (Philadelphia: Blakiston, 1941); C. S. Rhyne, *The Civil Aeronautics Act An-*

---

[32] See pp. 286–87, supra.
[33] See p. 683, supra.

notated (Washington, D.C.: National Law Book Co., 1939); John W. Gelder, "The Federal Aviation Act of 1958," 57 *Michigan Law Review* 1214 (1959).

On state regulation and its relation to federal control, see Oswald Ryan, "Economic Regulation of Air Commerce by the States," 31 *Virginia Law Review* 479 (1945); F. G. Hamley, "Appropriate Areas of State Economic Regulation," 11 *Law and Contemporary Problems* 488 (1946); Ben H. Sheppard, Jr., "State-Federal Economic Regulation of Commercial Aviation," 47 *Texas Law Review* 275 (1969); Gene R. Beaty, "Air Carriers—Intrastate Regulation—Limits of Federal Jurisdiction," 35 *Journal of Air Law & Commerce* 663 (1969).

Chapter

35

PROBLEMS AND POLICIES IN
AIR TRANSPORT REGULATION

In this chapter we turn to a consideration of policies which have been evolved in the regulation of air transportation, and some of the controversial problems that have arisen.

CERTIFICATE CASES

One of the most important duties of the Board is to dispose of applications for new services. Certificates of public convenience and necessity are required before new routes may be flown or before additional points may be served. The questions involved in such cases are succinctly stated by the Board in 1941 as follows:

The primary questions to be considered in the disposition of cases involving applications for new service are, in substance, whether the new service will serve a useful public purpose, responsive to a public need; whether this service can and will be served adequately by existing routes or carriers; whether it can be served by the applicant without impairing the operations of existing carriers contrary to the public interest; and whether any cost of the proposed service to the Government will be outweighed by the benefit which will accure to the public from the new service.[1]

Applications for new services often result in bitter conflicts between airlines. An application may be for the establishment of a service competitive with another airline. Sometimes there are several applicants for the right to operate over a route, and it may be impracticable to authorize operations by more than one of them because of the limited amount of traffic available. The granting of the certificate to one of the applicants may have certain advantages to the public, while granting it to another line would have other advantages. There is often a conflict between large and small lines, with the question in the background of whether it is in the interest of the public to permit large lines to become larger or to encourage the development of smaller lines.

In considering certificate applications, the Board is obviously under

---

[1] *Delta Air Corp., Service to Atlanta and Birmingham,* 2 CAB 447, 452 (1941).

some obligation to protect existing carriers from new operations. If Congress had not intended some protection to be given them, it would not have required certificates of public convenience and necessity but would have permitted unrestricted entrance into the industry. One of the objectives of the Act was to prevent excessive competition which would jeopardize the successful operation of the airlines. It must also be recognized that the government subsidy to airlines through air-mail payments would presumably be increased if an attempt were made through air-mail payments to keep more lines in operation than were necessary. The effect of proposed operations on other carriers is always a factor which receives careful consideration in certificate cases.

The principle that existing carriers are entitled to some protection from new operations that would jeopardize their earnings may come into conflict with another principle, namely, that a certain amount of competition between air carriers is in the public interest. This brings us to the important question of the extent to which competition in the industry should be encouraged.

Competition versus Monopoly

That Congress wanted some degree of competition to be maintained in the air-transport industry is clear from two provisions of the Civil Aeronautics Act. The declaration of policy, previously quoted,[2] mentioned "competition to the extent necessary to assure the sound development of an air transportation system properly adapted to the needs of the foreign and domestic commerce of the United States" as in the public interest and in accordance with the public convenience and necessity. The other provision of the Act which evidenced a desire on the part of Congress to preserve competition in the industry is found in the sections dealing with the consolidation and combination of airlines. The Act provided that the Board "shall not approve any consolidation, merger, purchase, lease, operating contract, or acquisition of control which would result in creating a monopoly or monopolies and thereby restrain competition. . . ."[3]

In the early years of air-transport development it was natural that the Board should exercise a cautious policy and not authorize competing services if there were doubts about the sufficiency of traffic to support the airlines. In 1940 the Civil Aeronautics Authority said:

Congress intended the Authority to exercise a firm control over the expansion of air transportation routes in order to prevent the scramble for routes which might occur under a "laissez faire" policy. Congress, in defining the problem, clearly intended to avoid the duplication of transportation facilities and services, the wasteful competitive practices, such as the opening of non-

---

[2] Pp. 805–6, supra.

[3] Section 408 (b).

productive routes, and other uneconomic results which characterized the development of other modes of transportation prior to the time of their governmental regulation.[4]

The Board, however, has not been unmindful of the statutory provision which stated that competition was in the public interest. In the period of increasing load factors during World War II, when a feeling of optimism about the future growth of air traffic was widespread, the Board, in a series of cases, authorized competing services over routes that had been served by a single carrier. TWA was authorized to provide service between Los Angeles and San Francisco.[5] Later, Western Air Lines was also permitted to enter this market.[6] In another proceeding National Airlines was allowed to establish a route between New York and Florida in competition with Eastern Air Lines.[7] Still later, Eastern and Northeast were authorized to serve the New York–Boston market in competition with American, which had previously had the route to itself.[8] In these cases the Board was following a policy which came to be called "the presumption doctrine," namely, that there was a presumption in favor of competing air-carrier services where there appeared to be sufficient traffic to support them. The doctrine was originally stated in the California North-South Case in 1943 as follows:

> While no convenient formula of general applicability may be available as a substitute for the Board's discretionary judgment it would seem to be a sound principle that, since competition in itself presents an incentive to improved service and technological development, there would be a strong, although not conclusive, presumption in favor of competition on any route which offered sufficient traffic to support competing services without unreasonable increase of total operating cost.[9]

The doctrine was reaffirmed and explained in the other cases mentioned above.

The Board encountered strong criticism for adopting the "presumption doctrine," much of it based on the legalistic reasoning that it would require those objecting to the award of competitive routes to prove that additional service was unwarranted, instead of requiring the applicants to prove that additional service was needed. It is extremely doubtful if the Board ever meant to carry the presumption doctrine that far.

The Board, however, soon began a retreat from the "presumption

---

[4] *Northwest Airlines, Duluth–Twin Cities Operation,* 1 CCA 573, 577–78 (1940).

[5] *Transcontinental & Western Air, North-South California Service,* 4 CAB 254 (1943).

[6] 4 CAB 373 (1943).

[7] *Colonial Airlines, Atlantic Seaboard Operation,* 4 CAB 552 (1944).

[8] *Northeast Airlines, Boston Service,* 4 CAB 686 (1944).

[9] *Transcontinental & Western Air, North-South California Service,* 4 CAB 373, 375 (1943).

doctrine." A hint of it appeared as early as 1944, when the Board said: "The mere fact that a particular route develops a large volume of traffic does not of itself afford sufficient justification for finding that the public convenience and necessity require establishement of an additional competitive service exactly duplicating an existing operation."[10] This and later cases seem to indicate that substantial benefits from competitive service in a particular case would have to be proved before the additional competing service would be authorized.[11] In 1951 the Board said that the provisions of the Act declaring that competition to the extent necessary to assure the sound development of air transportation was in the public interest constituted "no mandate to seek competition merely for the sake of having competition."[12] The "presumption doctrine" had been abandoned. In its stead appeared the doctrine that the establishment of competitive operations required a showing that competition in the particular case was necessary to improve a service which was not up to adequate standards. "Undoubtedly, where it appears on the record of a particular case that an air carrier is failing to attain the high standards of public service contemplated by the Civil Aeronautics Act, and where only provision for an economic competitive service would contribute effectively to the assurance of such standards, a case is made for competition."[13] One member of the Board dissented from the view just quoted, saying that "it changes the policy of the Board from one that favors competition wherever it can be justified to one that opposes it wherever its refusal can be justified."[14] The Board justified its policy during this period by emphasizing the requirement of the Act that it foster "sound economic conditions" in air transport. It was hesitant to authorize additional competitive service that might create excess capacity and weaken the carriers and perhaps result in increasing subsidies to the airlines.

The protective policy of the Board where the question of new competition arose was soon to be reversed once more. In a series of cases beginning in 1955, the Board embarked upon a policy of authorizing greatly expanded air service, much of which was competitive with other airlines and, in effect, returned to the "presumption doctrine" although careful not to use that term.[15] In the Southwest-Northeast Service Case the Board noted that it had in recent years authorized the expansion of the air transportation system in such manner as to bring "more and more competitive

---

[10] *Northwest Airlines, Chicago–Milwaukee–New York Service*, 6 CAB 217, 228 (1944).

[11] See *West Coast Case*, 6 CAB 961, 970 (1946).

[12] *Southern Service to the West Case*, 12 CAB 518, 532 (1951). See also *Reopened Southern Service to the West Case*, 18 CAB 234, 239 (1953).

[13] 12 CAB 518, 533 (1951).

[14] Ibid., dissenting opinion of Josh Lee, p. 586.

[15] Leading cases are *New York–Chicago Service Case*, 22 CAB 973 (1955); *Denver Service Case*, 22 CAB 1178 (1955); *Southwest-Northeast Service Case*, 22 CAB 52 (1955); *New York–Florida Case*, 24 CAB 94 (1956).

service to more and more communities." The Board said that in taking such action, it had not been guided "by the negative concept of determining first whether the existing services met minimum standards of legal adequacy," but rather "by the concept that competitive service holds the greatest prospect for vigorous development of our national air transport system . . ."[16]

As a result of the Board's liberal policy in authorizing competitive services, the number of transport markets (pairs of cities) in which two, three, or more carriers compete for the traffic greatly increased. In 1956, competitive service had been authorized in 348 of the 400 most important travel markets, and there were 115 markets with 3 or more authorized carriers, of which 12 were served by 5 or more carriers.[17] Even more competitive service has been subsequently authorized. The Board's policy brought forth some expressions of apprehension from within the Board itself,[18] as well as from outside sources.[19] Although the Board has authorized competitive services on a large scale, the new services authorized have been by existing carriers; the Board has not granted certificates to any new trunklines.

The expansion of competitive services in the 1950's again brought charges that the Board had authorized "excessive competition." Furthermore, the introduction of jet aircraft in the latter part of the 50s brought a new element into the picture which presages a more conservative policy on the part of the Board one more. In *Southern Transcontinental Case*, in 1961, the Board said:

The operation of jet aircraft must have an important bearing upon the question of creating additional duplicating service. The increased capacity and speed inherent in jets means that the amount of traffic which might have supported duplicating operations with piston aircraft will not necessarily support the same level of duplicating service with jet equipment.[20]

The changed situation was emphasized again in the *New York–Florida Renewal Case*, and appears to have been a factor in denying a renewal of Northeast Airline's certificate to serve the New York–Florida route.[21]

Notwithstanding the pronouncement concerning the changed situation

---

[16] 22 CAB 52, 60 (1955).

[17] Paul W. Cherington, *The Status and Economic Significance of the Airline Equipment Investment Program* (1958), p. 10.

[18] See dissenting opinion of Minetti in *Eastern Route Consolidation Case*, 25 CAB 215, 225 (1957); of Gurney in *St. Louis–Southeast Service Case*, 27 CAB 342, 358 (1958); and of Durfee and Denny in *New York–San Francisco Nonstop Service Case*, 29 CAB 811, 825 (1959).

[19] Gilbert L. Bates, "Current Changes in Trunkline Competition," 22 *Journal of Air Law and Commerce* 379 (1955), p. 393.

[20] 33 CAB 701, 715 (1961).

[21] 41 CAB 404, 420–21 (1964).

introduced by jet aircraft, the Board seems to have continued a policy of authorizing additional competition when a more cautious policy might have been anticipated. It should be pointed out, however, that the Board has frequently refused to authorize "multiple competition" in many markets.[22] In the *Service to Omaha & Des Moines Case,* in 1970, the Board showed that it was influenced by the financial stringency of the airlines existing at the time. ". . . in view of the nationwide slowdown in air traffic growth and the financial pinch in which a number of carriers currently find themselves—new multiple competition should be authorized only in markets which . . . are clearly large enough to support such competition without inflicting seriously harmful losses on any carrier, and only where the relevant public convenience and necessity factors clearly call for such multiple awards."[23]

Changes from time to time in the Board's policy toward authorizing competitive services can be explained partly by changes in the membership of the Board, and partly by changes in the actual and prospective traffic and revenue position of the airlines. Generally speaking, the Board has been more liberal in authorizing additional competitive services when the earnings of the airlines have appeared favorable; a more cautious policy has been followed when the airlines were having difficult times or the outlook was unfavorable.

From a strictly economic standpoint the question of whether competition or monopoly should prevail over the principal air routes depends on the relation between size and costs in the air-transport industry. If unit costs decline substantially as the volume of traffic increases, then the service can be provided at the lowest cost if one carrier is allowed to carry all the traffic over the route. If unit costs do not decline substantially with increased volume of traffic, there is little justification for excluding additional carriers. Such evidence as is available indicates that there are no substantial economies of size after a moderate size has been attained.[24] If there is sufficient air traffic over a given route to utilize planes of large size, any additional traffic will require additional flights, with a resulting increase in direct flying costs. Although certain ground and overhead costs exist which may be spread over the greater volume of traffic, there is

---

[22] E.g., *Service to Omaha & Des Moines Case,* 70-7-24 (1970); *Phoenix-Seattle/ Portland Nonstop Case,* 70-8-13 (1970); *Service to Salt Lake City Investigation,* 70-8-1 (1970).

[23] 70-7-24 (1970), p. 4.

[24] John B. Crane, "The Economics of Air Transportation," 22 *Harvard Business Review* 495, 501-5 (1944); Harold D. Koontz, "Economic and Managerial Factors Underlying Subsidy Needs of Domestic Trunk Line Air Carriers," 18 *Journal of Air Law and Commerce* 127, 133-49 (1951); Stephen Wheatcroft, *The Economics of European Air Transport* (Manchester: Manchester University Press, 1956), pp. 76-93; John R. Meyer, Merton J. Peck, John Stenason, and Charles Zwick, *Economics of Competition in the Transportation Industries* (Cambridge: Harvard University Press, 1959), p. 135; Richard E. Caves, *Air Transport and Its Regulators* (Cambridge: Harvard University Press, 1962), pp. 57-61.

not such a clear-cut reduction in unit costs with increasing traffic as occurs in the railroad industry.

If it could be shown that substantially lower costs of providing transportation service would result from the exclusive occupancy of a route by a single airline, then the justification for protecting the existing carrier would be clear. If, on the other hand, two or more carriers on a given route can handle the traffic at as low a unit cost as a single carrier, there is justification for authorizing competing services in order to provide a stimulus to good service and economical operation. Where there would be some, but not large, savings in unit costs by granting one carrier the exclusive right to serve a given route, the advantages of competition in the particular case must be weighed against the disadvantages before a wise decision can be reached. It needs to be pointed out, furthermore, that the issue of the amount of competition to be authorized is sometimes subordinated to other considerations, such as the desire to strengthen a weak carrier—a matter discussed below.

In view of the fact that there seem to be no substantial economies of size in the air-transport industry after a certain moderate size has been attained, we may conclude that the policy of authorizing competitive services over a given route is superior to a policy of granting a carrier a monopoly of the route. The policy should not be carried too far, however, for the establishment of services in excess of what the traffic will support can only lead to dangerously low load factors, impaired earnings, and the jeopardizing of the carriers' ability to provide safe and adequate service. Also, if air carriers are to be subsidized, through air-mail payments or otherwise, it is necessary to prevent more carriers on a given route than the traffic will support. The airline industry complains that the Civil Aeronautics Board tends to authorize too many competitive services thereby creating a condition of overcapacity in the industry.

Strengthening Small Lines

In awarding certificates for new operations, the Board has shown a tendency to favor the building-up or expansion of smaller lines in an effort to strengthen them.[25] This policy was conspicuously followed in several of the cases involving expansion of route mileage in 1955 and 1956. In the Southwest-Northeast Service Case the Board said: "It is vital, in our opinion, to so develop the national air route structure as to tend to decrease rather than increase the gap between the relative size of the Big Four carriers and the smaller trunks."[26] The Board went on to say: "Our objectve is to so strengthen the smaller trunks as to insure that they will in the future be able to continue operations without subsidy even during

---

[25] See *West Coast Case*, 8 CAB 636, 639 (1947).
[26] 22 CAB 52, 56 (1955).

periods of economic adversity."[27] Some question has been raised, however, as to whether the Board has succeeded in all instances in strengthening the smaller and weaker carriers by this policy.[28] One difficulty with attempting to strengthen the weaker lines by "cutting them in" on the profitable routes served by other carriers is that sometimes the latter will not make room for them. In fact, the charge is sometimes made that the stronger lines will overschedule the route themselves in order to make it more difficult for the newcomer.[29]

Airport Congestion and Route Patterns

A new element has been injected into some certificate cases by the serious airport congestion that developed in the late 1960s and early 1970s. The Board has attempted to alleviate the problem in several ways, one of which is through changes in the service pattern of airlines. In some instances the Board has required the use of satellite airports by some carriers or some flights in order to divert air traffic away from the more congested airports. Another device has been to authorize flights that bypass congested transfer points. Thus Milwaukee was provided direct service to Boston, Baltimore, and New York instead of through Chicago to help reduce congestion at Chicago's O'Hare Airport.[30]

Revocation, Suspension, and Modification of Certificates

A certificate of public convenience and necessity under the Act may be revoked, against the holder's wish, only for intentional failure of the holder to comply with the provisions of the Act, or with orders of the Board, or with the terms, conditions, or limitations in the certificate. Revocation is a penalty measure which is designed to insure compliance with the Act.

The permanence of operating authority granted by a certificate limits the power of the Board to modify the route pattern, or to correct errors of judgment that may have been made in granting certificates, or to make adjustments called for by changes in conditions and circumstances.

Although the Board may not revoke a certificate except for the reasons mentioned, it may "suspend" a certificate "if the public convenience and necessity so require." This gives the Board some power to modify the route pattern on account of changes in conditions and circumstances.

---

[27] Ibid.

[28] See statement of Clarence M. Young in a separate opinion in *North Central Case, Twin Cities Service*, 8 CAB 477, 483–84 (1947); also Vice-Chairman Gurney's dissent in *St. Louis–Southeast Service Case*, 27 CAB 342, 358 (1958).

[29] See *Complaint of Northeast Airlines against Eastern Air Lines*, 39 CAB 556 (1964), and particularly the dissenting opinion of Murphy and Minetti, p. 566.

[30] See Civil Aeronautics Board, *Annual Report, 1970*, p. 4. Other examples are mentioned there also.

Suspension, however, is presumably temporary, and there is a question whether a certificate could be suspended indefinitely or for so long a period as to constitute revocation in effect. An examiner of the Board has said: ". . . it would seem that a suspension may continue in effect as long as the factors of public convenience and necessity requiring the original suspension prevail."[31] The Board may also "alter, amend, or modify a certificate" if the public convenience and necessity so require. The Board has exercised the power to suspend or to modify certificates on many occasions, particularly to add or to take away the right to serve certain points.[32] The power of the Board to do this has been upheld by the courts.[33] The Board may not "terminate" a certificate; it attempted to do so in one case, but was reversed by a court which held that "terminating" a certificate was equivalent to "revoking" and could not be done except for violations of the Act.[34]

Compulsory Extension of Routes

Whether the power to alter, amend, or modify a certificate empowers the Board to compel an air carrier to extend its routes or to serve additional points against its will was raised by the Board in 1944. The Board said:

We are of the opinion that this section of the Act does authorize the Board to add new points or services to the certificate of a carrier on the Board's own initiative and without an application by, and the consent of, the carrier; but this authority does not include the addition of new service which would be so extensive as to amount to a new air transportation route, or of such a kind as to substantially change the character of a carrier's system.[35]

Local and Feeder Airline Service

We noted in the previous chapter that there is a separate class of airlines known as local-service lines. The establishment of this group of airlines stems from a decision of the Board in 1944. Because of the large number of applications before it for the establishment of local and feeder air service, the Board instituted a general investigation of the subject in 1943. The investigation brought out the fact that the traffic potential at the

---

[31] *Southwest Renewal—United Suspension Case*, 15 CAB 61, 89 (1952).

[32] E.g., *Caribbean Area Case*, 9 CAB 534 (1948); *Frontier Renewal Case*, 14 CAB 519 (1951); *North Central Route Investigation*, 14 CAB 1027 (1951).

[33] *United Air Lines* v. *C.A.B.*, 198 F. 2d 100 (1952); *Western Air Lines* v. *C.A.B.*, 196 F. 2d 933 (1953).

[34] *Pan American World Airways* v. *Boyd*, 207 F. Supp. 152 (1962). Reversed but on other grounds in *Alaska Airlines, Inc.* v. *Pan American World Airways, Inc.*, 321 F. 2d 394 (1963).

[35] *Panagra Terminal Investigation*, 4 CAB 670, 673 (1944).

small cities was very limited and that local and feeder airlines, if established, would' be competing with highly developed surface transportation agencies in a field in which the outstanding advantage of air transportation—namely, speed—would count for the least. Air transportation fares, furthermore, would have to be at a comparatively high level in local and feeder service, and failure of local and feeder passenger and express traffic to develop would throw a substantial burden on the government in the form of air-mail payments.

Notwithstanding these adverse circumstances, the Board concluded that local and feeder services should be established on a temporary and experimental basis where there seemed to be "a justifiable expectation of success at a reasonable cost to the government."[36] The Board proceeded to dispose of the individual applications for this type of service in a series of "area" cases, in which all of the applications involving service in well-defined areas were considered together.[37] As a result of these cases, 23 local-service lines were established. Because of subsequent abandonments and mergers the number has been reduced to the present nine.

The decision to establish a group of local-service lines as opposed to authorizing trunklines to provide local service was based partly on the belief that a carrier whose sole interest was in developing this kind of service was more likely to be successful in developing the market than would trunkline carriers, whose primary interest was in long-distance traffic.[38] The Board also noted that the type of plane adapted to trunkline operations was not well suited for local service.

Even before the Board had completed the original area cases, some opposition to the establishment of additional local-service lines arose within the Board. As early as 1946, Clarence M. Young, a member of the Board, urged that enough feeder lines had been established to enable the Board to formulate a sound policy for the future and that there was no need for authorizing additional lines.[39] Mr. Harllee Branch took a similar position in the Great Lakes Area Case, maintaining that no additional services should be authorized pending the outcome of experiments already authorized.[40] The Board went on authorizing local-service lines until a

---

[36] *Local, Feeder, and Pick-up Air Service*, 6 CAB 1, 4 (1944). See also *Service in the Rocky Mountain States Area*, 6 CAB 695, 731 (1946).

[37] The more important area cases were *Service in the Rocky Mountain States Area*, 6 CAB 695 (1946); *Florida Case*, 6 CAB 765 (1946); *West Coast Case*, 6 CAB 961 (1946); *New England Case*, 7 CAB 27 (1946); *Texas-Oklahoma Case*, 7 CAB 481 (1946); *North Central Case*, 7 CAB 639 (1946); *Southeastern States Case*, 7 CAB 863 (1947); *Great Lakes Area Case*, 8 CAB 360 (1947); *Mississippi Valley Case*, 8 CAB 726 (1947); *Arizona–New Mexico Case*, 9 CAB 85 (1948); *Middle Atlantic Area Case*, 9 CAB 131 (1948).

[38] *Rocky Mountain States Area Service*, 6 CAB 695, 737 (1946).

[39] *Texas-Oklahoma Case*, 7 CAB 481, 536 (1946).

[40] 8 CAB 360, 419 (1947). See also *Mississippi Valley Case*, 8 CAB 726, 775–76 (1947).

substantial system of such lines was established throughout the country.

The second policy which was followed by the Board in the local-service cases was to impose restrictions on local-service lines to prevent them from competing with trunklines. In one case the Board said: ". . . we have neither the disposition nor the intention to permit local air carriers to metamorphose into trunk lines competitive with the permanently certificated trunk lines."[41] One of the restrictions commonly imposed on the local lines was that they must serve all points on their routes on all flights.[42] This restriction was intended not only to insure adequate service at the smaller communities served by the airline, but to make the through service, which is often competitive with trunklines, from becoming too attractive. Restrictions of this type proved too drastic in some instances, preventing the local-service line from providing extra flights over heavily traveled segments of its routes. For this reason early restrictions of this nature were later modified in a number of instances.[43]

A third policy adopted by the Board in the local-service cases was to grant certificates initially for only a three-year period because of the experimental nature of the operations. In so doing, the Board was in a position to terminate the experiment by refusing to renew the certificates if the carriers did not develop sufficient traffic to justify their continuance.

When the renewal of the three-year certificates came up for consideration in a series of "renewal" cases, the Board declared that "Only certificates covering routes which offer substantial public benefits and hold promise of future economic soundness will be further extended by the Board."[44] Most of the certificates were renewed, some for three years, others for five and even seven years. Certificates were renewed for some carriers which had little prospect of self-supporting operations and which were therefore dependent upon mail subsidies indefinitely. One member of the Board, Mr. Harold A. Jones, strongly objected to the renewal policy that seemed to be shaping up. In the Trans-Texas Certificate Renewal Case, Mr. Jones pointed out that the Board was virtually committed to a renewal of nearly all of the certificates of the local-service carriers if it renewed that of Trans-Texas, one of the least promising of the local-service lines. The real issue, according to Mr. Jones, was whether there should be established two separate domestic air-transport systems, one to be made up of the so-called "trunkline carriers," which would serve only the larger, profitable communities and would operate without government financial assistance, and the other to be made up of secondary short-haul or local-service airlines, serving the smaller communities and perma-

---

[41] *Bonanza–TWA Route Authorization Transfer*, 10 CAB 893, 897 (1949).

[42] See *Service in the Rocky Mountain States*, 6 CAB 695, 732 (1946).

[43] *Middle Atlantic Area Case*, 10 CAB 41 (1949); *North Central Case*, 7 CAB 639 (1946); *Pioneer Air Lines, Amendment*, 7 CAB 473 (1947).

[44] *Pioneer Certificate Renewal Case*, 12 CAB 1, 4 (1950).

nently subsidized with public funds.[45] It is clear that the issue was decided in favor of the second alternative.

The local-service lines were not content with the renewal of their certificates for a limited period of time and sought to obtain permanent certificates. Unsuccessful in their attempt to induce the Board to grant permanent certificates, they appealed to Congress to amend the law and grant them certificates of a permanent nature. Congress responded by an amendment to the Act in 1955 which substantially granted their request.[46] The Board was empowered, however, to limit the duration of certificates at not over one half of the intermediate points named in a carrier's certificate if the Board found that the intermediate points did not generate sufficient traffic to justify permanent certification. The Board considered that an intermediate point should show an average of at least five enplaned passengers per day over a test period to warrant authorization for permanent service.[47]

In the Seven States Area Investigation, the first of a series of "area" cases in which the Board undertook a review of local-service operations, the Board authorized a substantial increase in local-service operations but anounced a policy called the "use-it-or-lose-it" policy. Under this policy service was to be withdrawn from points which, over a test period, did not enplane a sufficient number of passengers to warrant continuance of the service. A minimum of five passengers a day was required, or the Board would institute proceedings to suspend or delete service at such points.[48] This policy was reaffirmed in later cases.[49]

In the Seven States Area Case the Board introduced another policy, one which was intended to reduce the subsidy requirements of local-service lines. Where new routes were authorized, it provided that "skip-stop" service between terminals would be permitted after each intermediate point had received two daily round trips, except that where a trunkline carrier provided service between the terminals, the local-service carrier would be required to make one intermediate stop, and in some instances, two.[50] This was a liberalization of restrictions commonly imposed to prevent local-service carriers from becoming competitive with trunklines.

We noted in an earlier chapter that local-service carriers are heavily subsidized by means of air-mail payments in excess of the "service"

---

[45] 12 CAB 606, 619 (1951).

[46] Public Law 38, 84th Cong., 1st Sess.

[47] *West Coast Airlines, Permanent Certificate Case*, 22 CAB 565, 583 (1955).

[48] 28 CAB 680, 756 (1958).

[49] *South Central Area Local Service Case*, 29 CAB 425 (1959); *Pacific Northwest Local Service Case*, 29 CAB 660 (1959); *Montana Local Service Case*, 29 CAB 1046 (1959).

[50] 28 CAB 680, 758–62 (1958).

rate.[51] President Kennedy, in his Transportation Message to Congress in 1962, called upon the Civil Aeronautics Board to present a plan for the reduction of subsidies to airlines over a period of years.[52] In response to this directive the Board, in 1963, submitted a plan designed to accomplish this result.[53]

In the ensuing years, various policies have been adopted to reduce the necessity of subsidy to the local-service lines, some of them mentioned in the Board's report to the President, others developed subsequently. Among the measures adopted we would like to mention the following:

1. A reduction in the number of flights that would be entitled to subsidy. This policy was designed to force the airlines to bring their schedules more into conformity with demand.
2. Enforcement of the "use-it-or-lose-it" policy. As of June 30, 1965, this had resulted in full deletion of service at 37 cities, and partial deletion at 30.[54]
3. Extension of service of local-service lines, often on a nonsubsidy basis, to important traffic hubs even though it involved service competitive with trunklines. Two illustrations are the extension of some of Ozark's routes to New York and Washington, and extension of Southern to serve New York and Washington.
4. Transferring from trunklines to local-service carriers certain routes which could be operated more economically by the latter. The introduction of large planes by the trunklines had made it unprofitable for them to serve light density, short-, and medium-length routes. As a result, the trunklines were willing to turn these routes over to local-service lines, an arrangement of advantage to both.
5. Authorizing the abandonment of service at numerous small cities which could only be provided at a loss.

The cessation of service at small cities naturally aroused the opposition of the communities involved. To some extent, the air-taxi operators, particularly the commuter lines, have filled the gap created by the withdrawal of local-service carriers. In numerous instances where the Board has permitted the withdrawal of service by the local-service lines, it has approved of agreements between the local-service carriers and the commuter lines whereby the latter agreed to substitute a specified amount of service, and the local-service line agreed to underwrite the operations of the commuter line by some sort of guaranty arrangement. Since the local-service line is under obligation to restore service if the commuter line

---

[51] See p. 795, supra.

[52] 87th Cong., 2d Sess., House Doc. No. 384 (1962), p. 7.

[53] *Report to the President on Airline Subsidy Reduction Program* (1963).

[54] Civil Aeronautics Board, *Annual Report, 1965*, p. 20. Still other cases were pending.

does not fulfill its obligation, a case can be made for including such payments to the commuter line as a legitimate expense of the local-service line in determining its subsidy needs, although it is not clear at present whether this will be done.

Efforts to reduce subsidy payments to the local-service lines bore fruit, although it has been at the expense of the service provided the public in some instances. Table 33–4 in an earlier chapter[55] shows that the subsidy payments to the local-service lines decreased each year after 1963, except in 1965, and reached a low in 1968. Adverse conditions affecting all airlines in 1970 and 1971 made it necessary to increase the subsidy payments made to the local-service lines.

It is interesting to note that if local service had been made an obligation of trunkline carriers, profits from high-density passenger routes could have been used to finance the unprofitable local operations. This would be similar to what happens when railroads are required to continue unprofitable local services. In situations of this kind, whether on railroads or airlines, it could be said that unprofitable operations were being subsidized, though the subsidy is not paid by the taxpayer but by the users of the profitable transportation services. Senator Johnson of the Committee on Interstate and Foreign Commerce once suggested that the profitable airlines should assume some of the burden of the unprofitable operations of the local-service lines and small trunklines.[56] Mr. Gilliland, a member of the Civil Aeronautics Board, once suggested the merger of trunklines and local-service carriers to accomplish the same purpose.[57]

All-Cargo Carriers

In 1949, in the Air Freight Case,[58] the Board granted five-year certificates of public convenience and necessity to four airlines to provide an exclusively air-freight service. The four all-cargo carriers granted certificates were the Flying Tiger Line, Slick Airways, U.S. Airlines, and Airnews, Inc. These four carriers were already in operation at the time of the decision in the Air Freight Case. They had originally developed as nonscheduled carriers, exempt from regulation by reason of an early order of the Civil Aeronautics Authority, shortly to be mentioned, which exempted nonscheduled carriers from regulation. In 1947 the all-cargo carriers had been granted temporary authority to operate without the restrictions which the Board was attempting to impose on irregular air carriers.

The main issue in the Air Freight Case was whether a group of all-

---

[55] See p. 795 supra.

[56] 20 *Journal of Air Law & Commerce* 203 (1953).

[57] *Remarks at American Airlines Annual Meeting of Regional Vice Presidents and City Managers* (Washington, D.C., 1969).

[58] 10 CAB 572.

freight carriers should be certificated to operate in competition with the air freight service of the scheduled airlines. The scheduled carriers objected to the grant of certificates to all-cargo carriers. The Board was convinced that the potential volume of air freight was so great that the all-cargo carriers would not seriously affect the volume carried by the scheduled airlines. The Board also felt that the all-cargo carriers, operating without air-mail subsidies, would be forced to develop an efficient service, which would provide a yardstick of efficiency and costs. The Board was also of the view that the competition would be good for the scheduled air carriers. Two members of the Board, however, were of the view that all-cargo carriers should not be certificated because of the adverse effect that they would have on the revenues of the scheduled carriers.

Two of the all-cargo carriers originally certificated soon disappeared from the scene—U.S. Airlines and Airnews, Inc. Slick ceased operations in 1966. Two all-cargo carriers subsequently certificated were AAXICO and Riddle, but AAXICO became a "Supplemental air carrier" in 1962; Riddle became Airlift International in 1964. As elsewhere pointed out, the three all-cargo lines in operation at time of writing are Airlift International, Flying Tiger Line, and Seaboard World Airlines.[59]

In the Air Freight Case the newly certificated all-cargo carriers were not authorized to carry express for the Railway Express Agency nor to carry mail. These restrictions were for the purpose of protecting the combination carriers, which do carry both mail and express.

In granting certificates to the all-cargo carriers, the Board emphasized that they would not be subsidized and would "live and prosper only through their ability to develop an economic business and by constant search for new techniques, new business, and new equipment."[60] In reply to the contention of Josh Lee, a dissenting member of the Board, that certification would be a first step toward subsidy payments to them, the majority said: "We have made it abundantly clear . . . that in this present proceeding we find the public convenience and necessity *not* to require certification of the applicants for carriage of mail, and have further specifically stated that one important factor in our determination to grant temporary authority is that the freight carriers which will be certificated herein will not receive support in the form of mail pay."[61] In 1955 the Board authorized Riddle and AAXICO to transport express,[62] and in 1956 the same privilege was granted to Slick and Flying Tiger.[63] This action provided the cargo carriers with an additional source of revenue. Also in 1956 the Board, with Mr. Gurney dissenting, authorized all four

---

[59] P. 780 supra.

[60] 10 CAB 572, 589 (1949).

[61] Ibid., p. 592.

[62] *North-South Airfreight Renewal Case,* 22 CAB 253.

[63] *Airfreight Certificate Renewal Case,* 23 CAB 186.

cargo carriers to transport mail for a one-year period on a *nonsubsidy* basis.[64] In 1958 the Board denied a request to put the all-cargo carriers on a mail-subsidy basis.[65]

An effort to strengthen the all-cargo carriers was made by the Board in 1964. All-cargo carriers were to be given the exclusive right to sell "blocked space." This is an arrangement whereby reduced rates are given if the shipper reserves, and agrees to pay for, a specified amount of space on a recurring basis for a period of not less than 60 days.[66] This service would be available to ordinary shippers, freight forwarders, and combination carriers. Its probable effect would be to give the all-cargo carriers the large-volume shipments and leave the smaller shipments to the combination carriers. The latter contested the Board's decision, carrying the matter to the courts. The Board's decision was ultimately upheld.[67] When it became evident, however, that the Board might extend the same privilege to the combination carriers, Flying Tiger Line, the only carrier which had actually offered the service, withdrew its tariffs which provided for the service.[68] Flying Tiger Line feared that the establishment of this service, if the combination carriers could do likewise, would precipitate a costly rate war.[69]

NONSCHEDULED CARRIERS

One of the most troublesome problems which faced the Civil Aeronautics Board after World War II was the treatment of nonscheduled carriers. Soon after the enactment of the Civil Aeronautcs Act of 1938, the Civil Aeronautics Authority granted nonscheduled carriers exemption from regulation under its authority to exempt any carrier or class of carriers from most of the provisions of the Act. At that time, nonscheduled carriers were of the type commonly known as "fixed-base" operators. To the extent that they carried passengers their operations were in the nature of air taxi services. There was no reason for subjecting the nonscheduled carriers to the type of regulation provided for regular airlines.

After World War II, large numbers of ex-servicemen who were trained as pilots entered the nonscheduled transport field with large transport-type planes that were obtainable from the government. These carriers began to provide services which in some cases were scarcely distinguishable from the services of scheduled airlines. They tended to concentrate flights over the most heavily traveled routes and between the major traffic centers and hence posed a threat to the scheduled carriers.

---

[64] Ibid.

[65] *Applications of Riddle, Slick, AAXICO, and Flying Tiger Line*, 28 CAB 15.

[66] PS-24, 29 Fed. Reg. 11589, and *Blocked Space Service*, 41 CAB 774 (1964).

[67] *American Airlines* v. *Civil Aeronautics Board*, 359 F. 2d 624 (1966).

[68] See *Traffic World*, December 30, 1967, p. 62.

[69] Ibid.

The fundamental question raised by the existence of the nonscheduled carriers was whether an unlimited and unregulated system of nonscheduled air carriers was consistent with a controlled and regulated system of air transport designed to provide reasonably adequate airline service between the major cities of the country. With no obligation to serve the less important traffic centers, the nonscheduled carriers were in a position to take much of the most profitable traffic of the scheduled airlines, thus threatening their existence or making larger mail subsidies necessary to keep them in operation.

The first efforts of the Board to deal with this problem were directed toward keeping the services of the nonscheduled carriers from becoming so frequent and regular that they would seriously affect the traffic and revenues of the scheduled airlines. In 1947 the Board classified these carriers as "irregular air carriers" to emphasize the fact that the distinguishing feature of their operations was irregularity of service.[70] The irregular air carriers were divided into two groups—the large and the small. The former were those operating larger aircraft of the transport type. It is this group with which we are concerned in the following discussion. The small irregular air carriers posed no problem for the scheduled air carriers as their services continued to be of the air-taxi type. The Board, in attempting to deal with the large irregular air carriers, spelled out in considerable detail what constituted "irregular" service and what constituted "regular" service similar to that provided by the regular airlines. Later the Board also attempted to restrict the number of flights that an irregular air carrier might make between any two cities.[71]

Because of the generally unsatisfactory situation created by the operations of irregular air carriers and the efforts of the Board to control them, a general investigation of irregular air carriers was instituted by the Board in 1951. One purpose of the investigation was to determine the proper role of irregular air carriers in the air transport system. As a result of the investigation the Board found that the services of irregular air carriers were needed to supplement the service of the regular airlines.[72] Because they were unhampered by schedule and route requirements they were able to provide service wherever and whenever the services of the scheduled airlines were unable to meet the demand. The Board therefore designated these carriers as "supplemental air carriers," and it liberalized its restrictions on their operations. In addition to authorizing unlimited charter operations domestically, a service which was not generally opposed, the Board authorized individually ticketed and individually waybilled opera-

---

[70] *Large Irregular Carriers, Exemptions,* 11 CAB 609 (1950).

[71] Between 13 specified pairs of cities, where air traffic was the heaviest, the irregulars were to be permitted only three flights in each direction in a period of four successive weeks. Between other cities eight flights were to be permitted. This rule, known as the 3-and-8 rule, was never put into effect.

[72] *Large Irregular Air Carrier Investigation,* 22 CAB 838 (1955).

tions between any two points, provided the individual carrier did not exceed 10 trips per month in the same direction between any single pair of points. This authorization of supplemental service was accomplished by granting exemption from the certificate requirements of the Act. Two members of the Board, Gurney and Denny, dissented vigorously, holding that the right granted supplemental carriers to provide service between any cities, provided no individual carrier exceeded 10 flights per month between any two cities, was creating almost unlimited competition for the scheduled airlines and was inconsistent with the provisions of the Act which provide for certificating air service over regular routes according to the requirements of public convenience and necessity.

The Board's decision in the above-mentioned proceeding was carried to the courts; and its order was set aside on the grounds that, under the Civil Aeronautics Act, the Board could not exempt carriers from the requirements of the Act except upon a showing that compliance with the Act would place an undue burden upon the carriers, and the Board had made no such finding.[73] The case was therefore remanded to the Board. In 1959, the Board in a supplemental decision substantially reaffirmed the position that it had taken in the earlier decision, but granted the carriers operating authority, not through exemption from the certificate requirements of the Act, but by granting them certificates of limited duration.[74] Again the Board's decision was appealed to the courts, and again the court found that the Board had exceeded its authority.[75] The court noted that the Act requires that certificates specify terminal and intermediate points, whereas the certificates granted in this case were for authority to operate between any points in the country. The court also found that the Board's action was unlawful because it limited the number of flights to 10 per month in each direction between any two points, although the Act provides that no condition or limitation of a certificate shall limit the right of an air carrier to add or change schedules.

The action of the courts in setting aside both the exemption orders of the Board and the certificates issued later left the supplemental air carriers without any operating authority. At this point Congress stepped in and temporarily validated the certificates issued by the Board while Congress studied the situation to determine what action, if any, it should take with respect to the matter.[76]

In 1961 Congress enacted amendments to the Federal Aviation Act which provided a basis for certificating supplemental air carriers in the future on a restricted basis.[77] The most significant feature of the amend-

---

[73] *American Airlines* v. *Civil Aeronautics Board*, 235 F. 2d 845 (1956).

[74] *Large Irregular Air Carrier Investigation*, 28 CAB 224 (1959). Certificates were granted to 23 applicants, denied to 23, and action deferred on 8 applications.

[75] *United Air Lines* v. *Civil Aeronautics Board*, 278 F. 2d 446 (1960).

[76] *Public Law* 86–661.

[77] *Public Law* 87–528.

ments is that the supplemental air carriers were eventually to be restricted to charter operations, although individually ticketed and individually waybilled operations might be authorized for a two-year period in order to permit an orderly transition from their existing operations to all-charter operations.

Because of past instances in which supplemental air carriers failed to complete services which had been contracted for, the 1961 amendments to the Act provide that the Board may require supplemental air carriers to file a bond to assure compensation to passengers and shippers for failure to perform services in accordance with agreements therefor. Another feature of the 1961 amendments is that supplemental air carriers are made ineligible for subsidy.

CONSOLIDATIONS, MERGERS, AND ACQUISITIONS OF CONTROL

As we have noted, the Civil Aeronautics Board has control over consolidations and mergers of air carriers or the purchase, acquisition of control, and lease of air carriers by other air carriers. The Board is required to grant applications for such consolidations or other form of unification unless it finds that the proposed unification "will not be consistent with the public interest"; but the Board may not approve of any unification "which would result in creating a monopoly or monopolies and thereby restrain competition or jeopardize another air carrier."

In a consolidation or merger case, therefore, the primary considerations are the effect of the proposed consolidation or other form of unification on competition and the effect that the unification would have on other carriers. The Board is also mindful of the advantages of consolidations such as more economical operation, less dependence on subsidies, and the service advantages to the public that may result. In considering the effects of consolidations on other carriers, the Board pays careful attention to the general airline pattern. The Board has shown an interest in preventing large carriers from dominating an area to the disadvantage of smaller lines, and has favored expanding and building up smaller lines if there is a possibility of strengthening them by this means.[78] The Board has no authority, however, to compel the consolidation of air carriers.

The Board has control over the transfer of certificates of public convenience and necessity; and such transfer applications have some of the aspects of a consolidation or merger case and involve substantially the same considerations, since transfers of operating authority from one car-

---

[78] For policy considerations in consolidation and unification cases, see *Acquisition of Mayflower Airlines by Northeast Airlines,* 4 CAB 680 (1944); *American Airlines, Acquisition of Control of Mid-Continent Airlines,* 7 CAB 365 (1946); *United Air Lines–Western Air Lines, Acquisition of Air Carrier Property,* 8 CAB 298 (1947); *Monarch-Challenger Merger Case,* 11 CAB 33 (1949); *Delta-Chicago & Southern Merger Case,* 16 CAB 647 (1952); *Northwest-Northeast Merger Case,* Order 70–12–162 (1970), Order 71–3–8 (1971).

rier to another can radically alter the competitive relations among the airlines.

The provision of the Act which requires the Board to deny consolidations that would result "in creating a monopoly or monopolies" raises some problems of interpretation. Any consolidation of major carriers is likely to create a monopoly between certain pairs of cities. If approval of such a consolidation is foreclosed by the antimonopoly provision of the Act, very little consolidation among airlines could take place. In the *United–Capital Merger Case*[79] the Board more or less avoided the monopoly issue by invoking the "failing-business doctrine." This is a doctrine enunciated by the Supreme Court of the United States in 1930 in a case arising under the Clayton Act. There the court held that acquisition of a failing competitor did not violate the Clayton Act.[80] The circumstances existing at the time that the United–Capital merger proposal was before the Board were such that refusal to approve the absorption of Capital by United would result in Capital's demise. The Board could conveniently invoke the 'failing-business doctrine" and approve the merger, notwithstanding some elimination of competition that would result. On appeal to the courts the decision of the Board was sustained, but the court pointed out that it was not necessary to consider the propriety of relying on the "failing-business doctrine," because to permit Capital to fail and go out of business would result in more monopoly than if its merger with United were permitted. This was because Capital competed with other airlines between certain cities and these carriers would be left without competition over these routes if Capital were permitted to disappear.[81]

There need not be too much concern over the elimination of competition between particular city pairs as a result of airline mergers. The Board has the power to authorize other carriers to come in on the routes that would be left without competition. This the Board did when it permitted other airlines to serve four markets, or city pairs, from which competition had been eliminated by the United–Capital merger.[82]

AIR-MAIL COMPENSATION

An important duty of the Civil Aeronautics Board is the determination of the compensation to be received by the airlines for transporting air mail.

The "Need" Basis

The Civil Aeronautics Act provided that in determining the fair and reasonable compensation to be paid an air carrier for transporting air mail

---

[79] 33 CAB 307 (1961).

[80] *International Shoe Co.* v. *Commission,* 280 U.S. 291 (1930).

[81] *Northwest Airlines, Inc.* v. *Civil Aeronautics Board,* 303 F. 2d 395 (1962).

[82] *United Air Lines, Competitive Service Investigation,* 40 CAB 772 (1964).

the Board should take into consideration the "need" of the carrier for compensation sufficient "together with all other revenue of the air carrier" to enable it, "under honest, economical, and efficient management, to maintain and continue the development of air transportation to the extent and of the character and quality required for the commerce of the United States, the Postal Service, and the national defense." This provision was carried unchanged into the Federal Aviation Act of 1958. It is clear from these provisions of the Act that Congress intended that the carriers be paid for carrying air mail whatever might be necessary to give them adequate revenues. In 1942 the Board said: "The Civil Aeronautics Act has established the rule that where the other revenues of an air carrier do not suffice to meet the expenses of developing and maintaining air transportation as required in the national interest, the air-mail compensation shall be given the marginal role, and shall be established at such a level as is necessary to build the total revenues up to the required level."[83]

The general procedure for determining air-mail compensation prior to 1942 was to estimate the expenses that would be necessary to provide a reasonable amount of service, including a return on investment, and then deduct anticipated revenues from passengers and express, and later from freight. The balance represented the carrier's "need" and constituted the amount which would be paid it by the Post Office Department for carrying air mail.

In carrying out this method of determining air-mail compensation numerous questions of policy and procedure necessarily arose. Certain of these require mention at this point.

First, if air-mail compensation is to be determined on a need basis, it follows that a close scrutiny of operating expenses, charges to depreciation, managerial policies, and the like is required in order to protect the public's interest. Practically every mail case illustrates this practice; and in many instances some readjustments of accounts, or disallowance of certain items of expense, or refusal to underwrite some managerial decisions, is found. An example of the last of these practices is found in the refusal of the Board in one case to underwrite the increased expenses of an airline resulting from the change-over to a different type of aircraft. The carrier was a feeder or local-service carrier, and the equipment adopted was more suited for trunkline operations.[84]

Second, in determining the "need" of a carrier in fixing its mail rates, the Act requires the Board to consider "all other revenue" which the carrier may obtain. In a case involving mail rates of Western Air Lines, the Board refused to consider as "other revenue" the profit derived by Western when it sold its Denver–Los Angeles route to United Air Lines. In other words the Board refused to consider that the profit from the sale of this route reduced the "need" of Western in determining mail pay for

---

[83] *Pennsylvania–Central Airlines, Mail Rates,* 4 CAB 22, 51 (1942).
[84] *Pioneer Air Lines, Mail Rate,* 17 CAB 499 (1953).

the period in which the transaction took place. The position of the Board was that allowing such profits as an extra gain to the carrier would encourage a revision of the route pattern by giving carriers an incentive to dispose of routes which might be operated more advantageously by others. The Supreme Court refused to sustain the Board on this point, holding that this profit was "other revenue" which reduced the subsidy needs of the airline.[85] In accordance with the holding that "other revenue" includes revenue from whatever source derived, profits on the sale of equipment would be "other revenue" which must be taken into consideration in determining "need" of an airline. In order to aid the airlines in financing their program of purchasing new flight equipment, Congress enacted a law in 1958 which provided that profits from the sale of flight equipment should not be considered as "other revenue" by the Board in mail-pay proceedings if the Board was notified that an amount equal to the net gain from the sale of flight equipment had been, or would be, used for the purchase of flight equipment.[86] Except under these special conditions, however, profits from the sale of flight equipment must still be considered as "other revenue" in determining a carrier's "need" in air-mail cases.[87]

Third, the Board recognizes actual investment as the sum on which the carrier is entitled to earn a fair return, and the Board has rejected the use of cost of reproduction. "We believe that the ascertainment of the capital cost of producing the air transportation service requires that the rate of return should be predicated upon the funds which have been actually and legitimately invested in the transportation enterprise rather than upon any valuation of the carrier's property, and we shall continue to adhere to this method in the future as we have in the past.[88]

Fourth, in determining the fair rate of return to be used in air-mail cases the Board for a long time used 8 percent after federal income taxes when prescribing mail rates for the future.[89] In adjusting mail rates for past periods, however, 7 percent was considered adequate in view of the fact that the element of risk is reduced, if not eliminated, since the rates in such instances are being made retroactively.[90] Since the Board in the General Passenger Fare Investigation in 1960 found 10.5 percent as a fair rate of return for the domestic trunklines,[91] it presumably would use the same or a closely related rate of return in an air-mail case. For local-

---

[85] *Western Air Lines* v. *Civil Aeronautics Board*, 347 U.S. 67 (1954).

[86] Public Law 85–373.

[87] *Capital Gains Proceeding*, 27 CAB 79 (1958).

[88] *American Airlines, Mail Rates*, 3 CAB 770, 789 (1942).

[89] *Colonial Airlines, Mail Rates*, 4 CAB 71, 86 (1942); *Northeast Airlines, Mail Rates*, 4 CAB 181, 189 (1943); *All American Aviation, Mail Rates*, 4 CAB 354, 368 (1943).

[90] *Delta Air Lines, Mail Rates*, 9 CAB 645, 656–57 (1948); *Chicago & Southern Air Lines, Mail Rates*, 9 CAB 786, 804 (1948).

[91] See p. 838, infra.

service carriers, the Board decided in 1960 that the appropriate rate of return should depend on the capital structure of the individual carriers, subject to a minimum of 9 percent and a maximum of 12.75 percent.[92]

Fifth, although the Act contemplates that mail rates will ordinarily be prescribed for future periods, and not retroactively to cover past periods, revised mail rates are customarily made retroactive to the time of the application for the increased rate or to the time that the investigation of mail rates was instituted. In 1947 the Board was requested by certain airlines to make a mail-rate adjustment retroactive for a period prior to the application for increased rates. This the Board refused to do, and it was upheld by the Supreme Court.[93] The Court noted that prescribing rates retroactively was contrary to the traditions and practices of rate making and that it was unwilling to read a broader meaning into the Act unless clearly intended by Congress. The Court also noted that retroactive rate regulation would put rate making on a cost-plus basis, which was not consistent with the apparent design of the Act. Even the rule that rates may be made retroactive to the time of the institution of the rate proceeding can, and sometimes does, result in putting mail rates on a cost-plus basis if the carrier keeps a rate case before the Board constantly. The fixing of temporary rates as an emergency measure after World War II also created a situation, for a time, in which earnings were virtually guaranteed, since the temporary rates were subject to retroactive adjustment when a final rate was established.

"Service" Mail Rates

In the years before World War II the determination of air-mail compensation on a need basis was workable. During World War II the larger airlines were operating very profitably and the method of determining air-mail compensation by deducting from anticipated costs the anticipated revenues from passengers and express would have left some airlines transporting mail for nothing. In these circumstances the Board came to recognize two kinds of mail rates: a "need" rate which continued to be determined as before and which was applied to carriers which had not attained a condition of self-sufficiency in their commercial operations; and a "service" rate which was based largely on an allocation of costs between passenger, express, and mail services, and which resulted, of course, in a figure which could be considered the "cost" of transporting air mail. The "service" rate fixed in these cases was first established on the basis of 0.3 mill per pound-mile, or 60 cents per ton-mile.[94] In 1944 the Board noted that

---

[92] *Rate of Return, Local-Service Carriers*, 31 CAB 685 (1960).

[93] *T.W.A.* v. *Civil Aeronautics Board*, 336 U.S. 601 (1949).

[94] *Eastern Air Lines, Mail Rate Proceeding*, 3 CAB 733 (1942); *American Airlines, Mail Rates*, 3 CAB 770 (1942); *Pennsylvania-Central Airlines, Mail Rates*, 4 CAB 22 (1942).

this "service" rate had been fixed for 11 carriers operating 80 percent of the domestic route-miles.[95] In 1945 the air-mail rates of the Big Four were reduced from 60 cents to 45 cents per ton-mile.[96] Financial difficulties of the airlines in the period immediately after World War II made it necessary to resort to certain expedients in connection with air-mail compensation to avoid immediate financial disaster to some of the companies. One expedient was to grant mail-rate increases on a temporary basis pending a more careful investigation of the carrier's needs, with a retroactive rate adjustment when final rates were determined. By 1945, however, the Board had returned to a 45-cent rate for the Big Four.[97]

The 45-cent rate was determined by a cost-allocation process, although express, freight, and half-fare family-plan passengers were treated as by-products and not assigned their full share of common costs, thus increasing the share of costs to be borne by air mail. The 45-cent rate was considered by the Board to be free of any element of subsidy.

Following the compulsory separation of air-mail pay into the subsidy and nonsubsidy elements under Reorganization Plan No. 10,[98] the Board prescribed the nonsubsidy element as the "service" rates to be paid by the Post Office Department. These rates were prescribed for groups of carriers, with the Big Four—Group I—paid on the basis of 45 cents per ton-mile. Other groups were paid on a higher basis. The result was that the air-mail rates between two cities served by two or more airlines might be different by the different carriers.

In 1953 the Assistant Postmaster General announced that when the air-mail rates between two cities were different by different carriers the Post Office Department would send mail over the line with the lowest charges when the air-mail service would not be impaired thereby. This practice would have worked havoc with the efforts to relate air-mail compensation to differences in costs by the different airlines and might have deprived the high-cost lines of much of their mail traffic over certain routes. This situation forced the Board to revise the "service rates," the rates which the Post Office Department pays, in such manner as to give a uniform rate between any pair of cities. This was accomplished in 1955, so far as the trunklines were concerned.[99] The Board set up a "two-part" rate, consisting of a uniform ton-mile rate as a line-haul charge, and a terminal charge per pound of mail enplaned which varied by class of airport. Airports were grouped into four classes, with the larger airports handling a large volume of traffic given the lowest terminal charge per pound of mail enplaned. The terminal charge applied for any movement was the rate applicable at the originating station. The line-haul rate was determined by

---

[95] Civil Aeronautics Board, *Annual Report, 1944*, p. 20.

[96] Civil Aeronautics Board, *Annual Report, 1945*, pp. 9–10.

[97] *American Airlines, Mail Rates*, 14 CAB 558 (1951).

[98] See p. 794, supra.

[99] *Domestic Trunklines, Service Mail Rates*, 21 CAB 8 (1955).

costing techniques similar to those used in the Big Four Case in 1951, with some modifications. The line-haul charge eventually prescribed in this proceeding was 30.17 cents per ton-mile. The terminal charge ranged from 3.32 cents per pound at the largest airports to 33.21 cents at the smallest airports. These rates were prescribed as the service rates for the 13 domestic trunklines.[100] These rates were later prescribed for the local-service lines also.[101] Thus all the airlines, local service lines as well as the trunklines, are paid the same service-mail rate, but the local-service lines receive additional mail pay based on their "need," and this is known as their "subsidy mail rate."

In 1967 the service-mail rates became 24 cents per ton-mile, plus a terminal charge ranging from 2.34 cents per pound at the largest airports to 9.36 cents at airports emplaning less than 5,000 tons of all traffic per year.[102]

Class Subsidy Rates for Local-Service Lines

Prior to 1961 the subsidy mail rates were determined according to the "needs" of the individual lines. In that year, however, the Board adopted a formula for fixing the subsidy rates of the local-service lines in which the subsidy rate will be less for the carriers with more favorable traffic densities.[103] The formula has been revised several times to effect improvements in its operation and to meet changed conditions, becoming more complex as time goes on.

A revision in 1967 provided an automatic revenue-growth adjustment that reduces the subsidy payment to an individual line as its passenger revenues increase.[104] This was expected to bring about a gradual reduction in the subsidy payments to the local-service lines. When the local-service carriers encountered financial difficulties in 1970, the Board in effect suspended the revenue-growth adjustment. Further changes were made in the class subsidy rate in 1971, and the rates were increased temporarily.[105]

Since the Federal Aviation Act provides for air-mail payments on the basis of the "need" of each carrier, it might be suggested that the rates, based on the operations of the carriers as a group failed to conform to the requirements of the Act, and that the formula might result in some carriers getting more and others less than their individual needs. The Board, however, strongly argued that it has the requisite authority to establish "need" rates for a class of carriers. The major advantage of the "class" rate is that it leaves the individual carrier with incentives for greater effi-

---

[100] Ibid.

[101] *Service Mail Rates for Allegheny Airlines, et al.,* 21 CAB 894 (1955).

[102] *Domestic Service Mail Rate Investigation,* E-25610 (1967).

[103] *Local-Service Class Subsidy Rate Investigation,* 34 CAB 416 (1961).

[104] *Annual Report, 1969,* p. 30.

[105] *Investigation of the Local Service Class Subsidy Rate,* 71-1-143 (1971).

ciency, better cost controls, and economical scheduling instead of depending entirely on subsidy payments.

RATE REGULATION

We shall now turn to a consideration of some practices and policies observable in cases relating to freight rates and passenger fares.

Minimum Rates to Restrict Rate Cutting

In 1947 competition between the certificated carriers and the noncertificated carriers brought about reductions and counterreductions in airfreight rates that threatened the ability of the all-cargo carriers to remain in existence. This led the Board to institute an investigation of the rates of both the certificated and the noncertificated carriers. In a competitive struggle between the noncertificated or all-cargo carriers and the certificated or "combination" carriers, the advantage lies with the latter. The combination carriers transport much of the freight on passenger planes on regular flights practically as a by-product. Even if they transport freight in cargo planes, as do the cargo carriers, the certificated airlines could outlast the all-cargo carriers in a competitive struggle because of the revenues which the combination carriers derive from passengers, express, and mail.

As a result of its investigation the Board concluded that "an unsound competitive condition" existed in the air-freight industry because the rates were so low as to result in substantial operating losses.[106] Accordingly a system of minimum rates was prescribed, the minima depending upon the length of the haul and the size of the shipment. To prevent an undesirable freezing of the rate structure, the way was left open for modification of the order to permit justifiable exceptions.

Minimum air cargo rates were also prescribed in 1966 between eastern ports and San Juan, Puerto Rico, as a rate war had developed because of overcapacity on the route.[107] In imposing minimum rates the Board said: "Experience indicates the importance of relieving the air carriers of the burden of operating under a minimum rate order as soon as possible in the circumstances of each case and allowing the carriers to resume their statutory responsibility for establishing just and reasonable rates. . . ."[108] The order was to remain effective for seven months, in the hope that the situation would then stabilize.

Promotional Rates and Unjust Discrimination

Most promotional rates and fares raise the issue of "unjust discrimination" since they grant certain groups or classes of traffic special and pref-

---

[106] *Air Freight Rate Investigation*, 9 CAB 340 (1948).
[107] *New York–San Juan Cargo Rates Investigation*, E-23431 (1966).
[108] Ibid., pp. 121–22.

erential rates and may thereby unjustly discriminate against others. They seem to violate the rule of equality which is firmly embedded in transportation and public utility law.

Differences in rates or fares may ordinarily be justified if differences in the cost of providing the service can be shown. A reduced fare for groups of persons could be justified on the basis of the cost saving to the carriers. But reduced fares for groups of 25 or more *students* was found unlawful by the Board because it discriminated against groups of nonstudents.[109]

Unjust discrimination occurs when there is different treatment of "like traffic" for like and contemporaneous service under substantially similar circumstances. Difficulty lies in determining in a particular case whether the traffic receiving the preferred and that receiving the regular rates is "like" or not and whether or not it is handled "under similar circumstances." In connection with the latter, there is the further question whether carrier competition for one kind of traffic and not for other traffic creates a dissimilarity of circumstances, and also whether differences in the conditions of demand, or what the traffic will bear, create a dissimilarity of circumstances. These questions have perhaps not been finally answered by the courts.[110] It should be noted that they are the same questions that have arisen in the interpretation of Section 2 of the Interstate Commerce Act.[111]

The issue of unjust discrimination has been raised in connection with service-men's fares, youth standby fares, youth reservation fares, family fares, and the "Discover America" fares. Competing bus lines have objected to these features of airline fares. The legality of these fares was made part of the Domestic Passenger Fare Investigation instituted by the Civil Aeronautics Board in 1970. The initial decision of the Board's examiner in the proceeding found these fares not unjustly discriminatory as such, but would require certain changes and limitations in them to avoid unlawfulness.[112]

Rate Levels and Airline Earnings

Inquiry into the reasonableness of the levels of passenger fares has, of course, involved the question of the adequacy of airline earnings. The most intensive study of the appropriate level of airline earnings has been in two passenger-fare investigations on a nationwide scale. The first of

---

[109] *Capital Group Student Fares,* 25 CAB 280 (1957).

[110] For good discussions of the legal principles involved in determining whether discriminatory tariffs are permissible, see *Transcontinental Bus System, Inc.* v. *Civil Aeronautics Board,* 383 F. 2d 466 (1967), particularly pp. 474–91; and *Trailways of New England* v. *Civil Aeronautics Board,* 412 F. 2d 926 (1969), particularly pp. 932–36.

[111] See pp. 484–86 supra.

[112] Initial Decision of Arthur S. Present in Docket 21866–5, *Domestic Passenger-Fare Investigation—Discount Fares* (1970).

these was concluded in 1960;[113] the second reached the stage of tentative findings in 1971.[114]

In the 1960 proceeding the Board rejected a proposal that an operating ratio standard be used to determine the adequacy of airline earnings and adopted a return-on-investment standard. The 1971 investigation continued the traditional policy. An unusual feature of the 1971 case, however, was the projection of investment into the future, doubtless because of large capital commitments and investment plans for the immediate future.

In both general fare investigations the appropriate rate of return was based largely on cost-of-capital studies in accordance with the common practice of public utility commissions. In determining the cost of equity capital the Board relied largely, but not exclusively, on earnings-price ratios, i.e., the ratio of earnings per share to the market values of common stock. We have elsewhere noted certain limitations of cost-of-capital studies and of earnings-price ratios in determining a fair rate of return.[115] In the 1960 decision the Board concluded that the industry should have a return of 10.5 percent. To this conclusion Board member Minetti dissented, noting that the rate of return adopted by the Board was, so far as he knew, higher than had been allowed by any other regulatory agency in history.[116] Minetti believed that the data on earnings-price ratios overstated the rate of return needed by the industry. In the 1971 decision the Board established 12 percent as a fair rate of return for the trunklines and 12.35 percent for the local-service lines.[117]

The 12 percent established for the trunklines was based on a cost of 6.2 percent for borrowed capital and 16.75 percent for equity capital. These rates were applied to an "optimum" capital structure rather than to the actual capital structure as had been done in the 1960 proceeding. The Board used a 45/55 ratio of debt to equity capital. A hypothetical capital structure was used, over the opposition of Murphy and Minetti, because existing capital structures were overweighted with debt. This excessive reliance on debt was the combined result of heavy capital requirements and inadequate earnings which made financing through equity capital impractical if not impossible.

One other feature of the 1971 investigation should be noted since it represents an innovation made necessary or desirable by special conditions. The Board established a standard load factor to be used in computing the necessary level of revenues. This grew out of the fact that there is overcapacity in the industry, resulting in low load factors and high costs per passenger-mile. The overcapacity has resulted from the introduction of larger planes, overoptimistic estimates of the future growth of traffic, and

---

[113] *General Passenger-Fare Investigation,* 32 CAB 291 (1960).

[114] *Domestic Passenger-Fare Investigation,* Docket 21866.

[115] Pp. 397–98 supra.

[116] 32 CAB 291, 332 (1960).

[117] *Domestic Passenger-Fare Investigation—Phase 8—Rate of Return,* 71-4-58.

the efforts of competing airlines to maintain or increase their respective shares of the market. There is no reason why the public should pay fares necessary to support capacity greatly in excess of that required to accommodate the traffic. Accordingly, the Board established 55 percent as a load-factor standard for the trunklines and 44.4 percent for local-service airlines.[118] The revenue needs of the airlines are calculated on the basis of these standard load factors.

In the regulation of rate levels of transportation agencies it is always

TABLE 35–1.   Return on Investment, Domestic Trunk Airlines, 1939–70*

Year	Rate of Return	Year	Rate of Return
1939[a]	2.3	1955	11.8
1940[a]	13.2	1956	9.3
1941[a]	4.5	1957	4.8
1942	20.3	1958	6.5
1943	17.1	1959	7.1
1944	17.5	1960	2.6
1945	9.4	1961	1.0
1946	1.5	1962	3.7
1947	2.9	1963	3.9
1948	1.7	1964	9.1
1949	6.1	1965	11.2
1950	11.2	1966	9.7
1951	14.6	1967	6.9
1952	14.2	1968	4.9
1953	11.3	1969	4.2
1954	10.4	1970[a]	1.5

* Civil Aeronautics Board, *Suspended Passenger Fare Case,* 25 CAB 511 (1957) for figures before 1957; later figures from Air Transport Association of America, *Facts & Figures—Air Transportation,* and not strictly comparable with the earlier figures.
a Fiscal year ended June 30.

necessary to recognize that earnings will fluctuate from year to year and that it is impossible to adjust rates so that the desired rate of return is earned each year.[119] This matter is of particular importance in the airline industry since the earnings of the airlines fluctuate widely. This is shown in Table 35–1, which gives the return on investment of the domestic trunk airlines from 1939 to 1970.

The Board recognized in both the 1960 and the 1971 investigation that fares cannot be varied in such manner as to stabilize annual earnings. In the 1971 case, the Board noted that while short-term considerations need not always be ignored, fare levels should be designed to produce a reasonable return over an extended period of time.[120]

---

[118] *Domestic Passenger-Fare Investigation—Phase 6B—Load Factor.*
[119] See pp. 361–62 supra.
[120] *Domestic Passenger-Fare Investigation—Phase 7—Fare Level,* p. 72.

In both the 1960 and 1971 cases, the Board also noted that the adequacy of the rate level must necessarily be based on the industry as a whole and not on the needs of the lowest-cost or the highest-cost firms. This problem, it will be recalled, has faced the Interstate Commerce Commission in railroad rate-level cases, and gives rise to the weak-and-strong-road problem.[121] The inequality in earning power among the trunklines is shown by figures of estimated earnings. The Board estimated that with no fare changes the rate of return of the trunklines as a group would, at the standard load factors, be 6.6 percent in 1972, but that the rates of return of the individual airlines in the group would be as follows:[122]

American	8.9%
Eastern	5.7
TWA	2.1
United	3.2
Braniff	9.2
Continental	8.4
Delta	12.0
National	4.3
Northeast	−13.8
Northwest	16.7
Western	2.0

CRITICISMS OF REGULATION

Criticism of air-transport regulation has largely centered around control of entry into the air-transport industry. Some of the criticism relates to Board policy. The Board has been taken to task for awarding additional routes to existing carriers instead of certificating new airlines.[123] The Board has been criticized frequently by the airlines for certificating too much competitive service and thereby fostering overcapacity in the industry and contributing to the financial difficulties of the airlines.

The position is taken by some writers that the whole system of control of entry in the industry is unnecessary and unwise and that competitive forces should be allowed to work themselves out in this field.[124]

It is clear that the framers of the Civil Aeronautics Act considered the problem and were convinced that control of entry into the air-transport industry was essential if the public was to enjoy safe and adequate transportation service provided by financially sound and reliable carriers. As

---

[121] Pp. 363–65 and Chapter 17.

[122] *Domestic Passenger-Fare Investigation—Phase 7—Fare Level*, p. 75.

[123] For an example of this criticism, see Hardy K. Maclay and Wm. C. Burt, "Entry of New Carriers into Domestic Trunkline Air Transportation," 22 *Journal of Air Law and Commerce* 131 (1955).

[124] Perhaps the strongest arguments along this line from a theoretical standpoint are Lucile S. Keyes, *Federal Control of Entry into Air Transportation* (Cambridge: Harvard University Press, 1951), and by the same author, "A Reconsideration of Federal Control of Entry into Air Transportation," 22 *Journal of Air Law and Commerce* 192 (1955).

we previously noted, the Federal Aviation Commission, which reported to Congress in 1935, and out of whose report came many features of the Civil Aeronautics Act, believed that control over the amount of air-transport services was essential. The Commission said: ". . . there should be a certain measure of control by the government of the right of entry into the business in order that proper standards may be enforced and irresponsible campaigns of mutual destruction on the part of operators averted."[125] In another place the Commission said: "The arguments for control over entry into the field seem to us compelling."[126]

In considering the question of abandoning control over entry, it should be recognized that such action would make it necessary to abandon the policy of subsidizing airlines that are unprofitable but are considered essential. If airlines are to be subsidized to provide essential or desired services, the public needs to protect itself by limiting the number that it will support, and also by restricting the diversion of traffic from subsidized to nonsubsidized lines.

Even if complications arising from our subsidy policy were removed, it by no means follows that unrestricted competition would produce desirable results. If overcapacity developed, as would be quite likely, the temptation to out-of-pocket-cost rate making would appear; and even if it did not, earnings would likely be depressed below a remunerative level. Competition would soon give way to some form of monopolistic or semi-monopolistic control.

Another factor which should be considered is the possible effect of unrestricted freedom of entry on safety standards. The high degree of hazard in the air-transport industry makes it imperative that competitive pressures and the resulting struggle for survival do not lead to inadequate safety measures. This is a matter which cannot be controlled entirely through strict safety regulations imposed by public authority.

One other probable result of unrestricted entry should be recognized before a decision is made to abandon present regulatory controls. It would substantially change the airline pattern in the United States. More competitive services might be available between important traffic centers; but air service at smaller cities, and on some routes, would likely disappear. The carriers would be under no obligation to provide service to cities that enplaned or deplaned little traffic. In fact, if traffic between the major cities was spread too thin among competing carriers, the airlines could not afford to provide service at the smaller communities. It may be argued that from a strictly economic standpoint, this very thing should happen, and that profitable services should not be burdened with carrying unprofitable ones. To do so constitutes an internal subsidization of unprofitable opera-

---

[125] *Report of the Federal Aviation Commission,* 74th Cong., 1st Sess., Senate Doc. No. 15 (1935), p. 52.
[126] Ibid., p. 54.

tions. The fact remains, however, that the carrying of some unprofitable services by the more profitable has long been a characteristic of public utilities and of transport agencies, and is an almost inevitable consequence of requiring reasonably acceptable public utility and transport services. Abandonment of entry controls of air transport should not be adopted unless the public understands and is willing to accept the resulting change in the pattern of air-transport services.[127]

SELECTED REFERENCES

For criticism of restriction of entry generally in air transportation, see Lucile S. Keyes, *Federal Control of Entry into Air Transportation* (Cambridge: Harvard University Press, 1951); also "A Reconsideration of Federal Control of Entry into Air Transportation," 22 *Journal of Air Law and Commerce* 192 (1955). For defense of control over entry, see Stuart G. Tipton and Stanley Gewirtz, "The Effect of Regulated Competition on the Air Transport Industry," 22 ibid. 157 (1955); Robert L. Clark, "Freedom of Entry in Air Transportation," 58 *Public Utilities Fortnightly* 532 (1956); Stephen Wheatcroft, *Air Transport Policy* (London: Michael Joseph, 1964), chap. iii.

On the Board's policies in certificate cases, see George B. McMillan, "Factors Considered by C.A.B. in Certifying Air Carriers," 14 *George Washington Law Review* 611 (1946); Howard C. Westwood, "Choice of Air Carrier for New Air Transport Routes," 16 ibid. 1 and 159 (1947 and 1948); Gilbert L. Bates, "Current Changes in Trunkline Competition," 22 *Journal of Air Law and Commerce* 379 (1955); Hardy K. Maclay and Wm. C. Burt, "Entry of New Carriers into Domestic Trunkline Air Transportation," 22 ibid. 131 (1955); Aaron J. Gellman, "The Regulation of Competition in United States Domestic Air Transportation: A Judicial Survey and Analysis," 24 ibid. 410 (1957). The most extensive studies of this phase of regulation are Samuel B. Richmond, *Regulation and Competition in Air Transportation* (New York: Columbia University Press, 1961), particularly chaps. v and vi; and Richard E. Caves, *Air Transport and Its Regulators* (Cambridge: Harvard University Press, 1962), chaps. viii and ix. For criticism of the Civil Aeronautics Board for lack of standards in route certification cases, see Henry J. Friendly, *The Federal Administrative Agencies* (Cambridge, Mass.: Harvard University Press, 1962), chap. v.

Revocation and suspension of certificates and other problems affecting the modification of the airline-route pattern receive attention in the following: Oswald Ryan, "The Revocation of an Airline Certificate of Public Convenience and Necessity," 15 *Journal of Air Law and Commerce* 377 (1948); Norman E. Johnson, "Suspension of Certificates of Convenience and Necessity under the Civil Aeronautics Act of 1938," 15 ibid. 512 (1947).

On feeder or local-service airlines, see James G. Ray, "The Feeder Airline

---

[127] For a statement by the Civil Aeronautics Board in defense of the present system of restriction of entry, see *Materials Relative to Competition in the Regulated Civil Aviation Industry, 1956: A Statement Transmitted by the Civil Aeronautics Board to the Select Committee on Small Business, U.S. Senate* (Washington, D.C.: U.S. Government Printing Office, 1956), particularly pp. 10–11.

Story," 16 ibid. 379 (1949); Paul D. Zook, "The Certification of Local and Feeder Air Carriers," 7 *Southwestern Law Journal* 185 (1953); Craig Mathews, "Certificated Air Service at Smaller Communities: The Need for Service as a Determinant of Regulatory Policy," 34 *Journal of Air Law and Commerce* 27 (1968); Robert W. Harbeson, "Economic Status of Local Service Airlines," *Journal of Transport Economics and Policy*, Vol. 4, No. 3 (1970), p. 1. See also Virgil D. Cover, "The Rise of Third Level Air Carriers," *Transportation Journal*, Fall 1971, p. 41.

The Board's efforts to deal with irregular air carriers are related in John P. Moore and K. Robert Hahn, "Regulation of Irregular Air Carriers," 35 *Cornell Law Quarterly* 48 (1948); Victor S. Netterville, "The Regulation of Irregular Air Carriers: A History," 16 *Journal of Air Law and Commerce* 414 (1949); F. James Kane, "Air Law—Supplemental Air Carriers," 34 *Notre Dame Lawyer* 439 (1959).

Air-mail pay and the determination of subsidy in air-mail payments are discussed in George M. Goodrick, "Air Mail Subsidy of Commercial Aviation," 16 *Journal of Air Law and Commerce* 253 (1949); Joseph J. O'Connell, "Air Mail Pay under the Civil Aeronautics Act," 25 *Indiana Law Journal* 27 (1949); D. Philip Locklin, "A Critique of Proposals to Separate Subsidy from Air Mail Pay," 18 *Journal of Air Law and Commerce* 166 (1951); Raymond J. Rasenberger, "Legislative and Administrative Control of Air Carrier Subsidy," 25 *George Washington Law Review* 397 (1957); Gilbert L. Gifford, "The Evolution of Air Mail Rate Making," 22 *Journal of Air Law and Commerce* 298 (1955).

On passenger fares, see Harold A. Jones and Frederick Davis, "The 'Air Coach' Experiment and National Air Transportation Policy," 17 *Journal of Air Law and Commerce* 1 and 418 (1950); Lucile S. Keyes, "Passenger Fare Policies of the Civil Aeronautics Board," 18 ibid. 46 (1951). A good history of the part played by the Civil Aeronautics Board in passenger-fare changes is in Paul W. Cherington, *Airline Price Policy* (Boston: Graduate School of Business Administration, Harvard University, 1958), chap. iii. See also Richard E. Caves, op. cit., chap. viii.

On consolidation in the airline industry, see Anon., "Merger & Monopoly in Domestic Aviation," 62 *Columbia Law Review* 851 (1962); David H. Marion, "The American–Eastern Application: Crucial Test of CAB Merger Policy," 111 *University of Pennsylvania Law Review* 195 (1962); Anon., "Merger in the Domestic Air Transport Industry," 48 *Virginia Law Review* 1428 (1962); Marvin L. Fair, "Problems of Airline Mergers." In *Papers—Fourth Annual Meeting of the Transportation Research Forum, 1963*, p. 1; A. H. Travers, Jr., "Examination of the CAB's Merger Policy," 15 *Kansas Law Review* 227 (1967); Robert E. Gallamore, "Observations on the Domino Theory of Airline Mergers." In Papers—*Eleventh Annual Meeting of the Transportation Research Forum, 1970*, p. 237; Lucile S. Keyes, "Airline Mergers," 37 *Journal of Air Law and Commerce* 357 (1971).

For overall analysis of CAB regulatory policy, see Richard E. Caves, op. cit.; William A. Jordan, *Airline Regulation in America* (Baltimore: Johns Hopkins Press, 1970).

Chapter 36

TRANSPORT COORDINATION

AND INTERAGENCY

COMPETITION

In earlier chapters of this book the different modes of transport have been described and their characteristics noted. The regulatory system that has been developed for each has been explained; the regulatory problems of each have been discussed; and the principles and policies which have been developed by regulatory agencies in the administration of the legislation have been recounted. Little has been said, however, about the relations between the different modes of transport or about the problems to which these relations give rise. To these latter we must now turn our attention.

TRANSPORT COORDINATION

The term "coordination" has assumed a prominent position in recent years in the literature on the transportation problem. By "coordination of transportation" is meant the fitting of each form of transport into its proper place in the transportation system. In the words of another writer: "Coordination is the assignment, by whatever means, of each facility to those transport tasks which it can perform better than other facilities, under conditions which will insure its fullest development in the place so found."[1]

The term is often used in a much narrower sense than is implied in the above definition. Sometimes it is used in the sense of joint services by two or more agencies of transportation such as result from the establishment of through routes and joint rates by rail and water lines or by any two transportation agencies. This we shall speak of as "coordinated service"; and we shall give it further attention in the next chapter, recognizing that the full benefits of a coordinated transportation system cannot be enjoyed unless joint services by two or more modes of transport are available. At other times the term "coordination" is used in the sense of avoiding unnecessary duplication of transport facilities, whether of the same or of different forms of transport. This is too narrow a definition of "coordina-

---

[1] G. S. Peterson, "Transport Co-ordination: Meaning and Purpose," 38 *Journal of Political Economy* 660, 680 (1930).

tion," although the attainment of coordination in the sense in which we have defined it may sometimes require the elimination of unnecessary duplication or the imposition of restrictions to prevent it from occurring.

Coordination, defined as fitting each mode of transport into its proper place in the transportation system, epitomizes the transportation problem as it exists today. This is because the transportation problem at the present time is primarily one of adjustment between the different forms of transport. The problem of transport coordination is not new, for the relation of rail transportation to water transportation has been a problem ever since railroads have existed. The problem of coordination, however, has assumed a new importance in recent years. This is explained by the growth of inland water transportation, the rapid expansion of motor-vehicle transportation, and the development of air transport. The place of highways in the transportation system was clearly fixed when they were used principally by horse-drawn vehicles; but with the development of motor vehicles and paved roads, highway transportation assumed a new importance and became competitive with the railroads. Thus the problem of the relationship of highway transportation to railroads was raised anew. In lesser degree the development of pipelines and air transport has given rise to the question of their respective places in the transportation system.

If a coordinated transportation system is desirable, the question of how to attain it becomes important. The problem would be simpler if the precise field of operation in which each form of transport was superior to, or cheaper than, other forms could be marked out distinctly. This cannot easily be done. In fact, there is probably much overlapping of the fields in which various forms of transportation can operate effectively. The problem, therefore, is one of creating the conditions under which the proper place of each form of transport can be determined experimentally, with such restrictions as may be necessary to keep each from invading fields of operation in which others clearly prove superior.

TRANSPORT COORDINATION AND PROMOTIONAL POLICY

The attainment of a properly coordinated system of transportation may require a reexamination and reconsideration of the promotional policy which has been followed with respect to the various modes of transport. The railroads have contended from time to time that governmental action has promoted the expansion of water, highway, and air transportation facilities without adequate attention to their economic justification or to their effect upon railroads. This policy, it is argued, has had three unfortunate results. First, it is claimed that it has resulted in excess capacity in the transport industry, that is, in more transportation facilities than are needed. Second, it is claimed that this policy sometimes encourages less efficient modes of transport—a claim that is directed particularly against the expansion of water transportation facilities. Third, the policy of promoting the expansion of water, highway, and air transportation has intensified the railroad problem by making it more difficult for the railroads to obtain adequate revenues. It can be seen that all three of these results are easily possible, particularly if there is a more or less indiscriminate expansion of the various modes of transport.

Whether or not we have excessively promoted the expansion of the various modes of transport through public expenditures, and whether or not changes in policy may be desirable, can be determined only by examination of our policy with respect to the three modes of transport against which the charge of excessive promotional activity has been directed.

Highway Policy

Responsibility for local highways rests with local and state governments; responsibility for the primary intercity highways rests primarily with the state governments, with a certain amount of federal participation, particularly in financing.[2]

Highways are demanded for the convenience of the millions of owners of private automobiles who use them for both local and long-distance travel. Much of this use is not competitive with the railroads. Another important use of highways is to move products from farm to market and from city to farm. This traffic is competitive with the railroads only to a limited extent. Of course, the highways are used to a considerable extent for intercity movements of traffic that are directly competitive with railroads. This is particularly true of the Federal-Aid Primary System and the National System of Interstate and Defense Highways. The motor-carrier services made possible by such highways, however, are frequently more convenient than rail service. Under the circumstances, few would contend that highway development should be checked just because the highways divert considerable amounts of traffic from the railroads. The public needs and demands an adequate system of highways, and this need overshadows the adverse effects that highway improvement may sometimes have on the revenues of the railroads. It would be too much to expect the public, in this day of automobiles and other motor vehicles, to do without an adequate system of highways, even though these highways may divert traffic from railways and intensify the difficulties which railways have to face. We should recognize, however, that an overexpansion of the highway system is easily possible, and certain features of present methods of financing highways may lead to such a result.

Air Transportation Policy

We have noted elsewhere that the federal government has provided the system of airways and that municipalities have generally provided air-

---

[2] See pp. 629–31, supra.

ports.[3] The federal government, under the Federal Airport Act of 1946, and presently under the Airport and Airway Development Act of 1970, has actively engaged in encouraging airport construction and improvement and in aiding the financing of airports. Although there could be an overexpansion of air transportation facilities, it is likely that an adequate system of air transportation requires an expansion of airway and airport facilities far beyond those that we now have. The service provided by air carriers is a high-class service which surface transportation agencies cannot provide. Although air carriers will undoubtedly become more and more competitive with surface transportation agencies, it is doubtful if the public would accept a policy of retarding air transportation development in an effort to protect older modes of transport. In view of the unique service which air transportation can provide, it is distinctly in the public interest to encourage the development of air transportation facilities.

Waterway Policy

Waterway policy has been discussed in an earlier chapter.[4] It was there pointed out that there has been an extended argument between those who advocate an expansion of our system of inland waterways and those who strongly oppose the expenditure of public funds for the development of additional water facilities. Waterway policy in the past has been open to the criticism that insufficient attention has been given to questions of economic justification from a national standpoint. Not all waterway improvements that are suggested are economically sound. On the other hand, not all projects for improvement of waterways can be condemned as unsound or unwise. As stated elsewhere, the criterion suggested by former Commissioner Eastman for determining whether a waterway should be improved or not is basically sound: "In determining whether a new waterway should be constructed, the essential question . . . is whether, assuming no reduction in the normal rates of competitors, it would make available new means of transportation which could function, taking *all* costs into consideration, more economically than existing means."[5]

It should be noted that Commissioner Eastman's suggested comparison is that of the relative costs of the two modes of transport. In the past, comparisons have often been between cost *to the shipper* of the two modes of transport. In such a comparison, transport costs that are borne by the taxpayer are ignored. Furthermore, the comparison is with railroad rates, not costs. The rates may be more or less than transport costs, as we know from

---

[3] See pp. 772–76, supra.

[4] Chapter 31.

[5] Federal Coordinator of Transportation, *Public Aids to Transportation*, Vol. I (Washington, D.C.: U.S. Government Printing Office, 1940), p. vii. We will shortly suggest a qualification of Eastman's rule under certain circumstances.

a consideration of the principles on which rates are made.[6] Of course from the shipper's point of view, the comparison of costs to him is the important thing, since he is looking for means of reducing *his* transport costs. From the point of view of the economy as a whole, however, the significant thing is a comparison of water transport costs, all costs considered, with rail transport costs, irrespective of rates charged. This would be quite obvious in a planned economy where an effort was being made to economize on the use of resources.

Another question arises in a policy decision with respect to the development of a waterway that would be competitive to some extent with an existing railway. Should the cost to society of developing the waterway include the increased rail transport costs that may result from diversion of traffic from the railway to the waterway? Stated in another way, should calculation of the benefits to be derived from the proposed waterway in the form of lower transport costs take into account the negative benefits of increased rail transport costs? In a competitive free-enterprise economy, with both modes of transport being provided by private enterprise, it is clear that the investment would be made in the waterway if it would result in lower-cost transportation even if persons necessarily dependent on rail transport would have to pay higher rates. In a socialist economy, doubtless the negative as well as the positive benefits would receive consideration. If the state provides water transport facilities, but not rail transport facilities, as is the situation in the United States, it would seem appropriate for the government to give attention to the effect of the proposed waterway on rail transport users. Somewhat of a dilemma is presented. Failure to develop the waterway will deprive shippers who could use it of the benefit of a cheaper mode of transport; developing the waterway will increase transport costs to those dependent on rail transport.

These considerations should make it clear that determining whether a particular waterway should be improved is not an easy decision even when costs of developing the waterway, and future traffic volumes that will utilize it, can be determined. When these basic facts are not known with any degree of certainty, and such is usually the case, the problem becomes more difficult.

Coordination of Planning and Promotional Activities

In the past, different federal agencies have been responsible for the promotion of the different modes of transport and the provision of transportation facilities which are financed in whole or in part by the federal government. For many years the Corps of Engineers, U.S. Army, exercised control over the improvement of waterways; the Federal Aviation

---

[6] See Chapter 7.

Agency and its predecessors provided the federal airway system and administered the Federal Airport Act of 1946; the Bureau of Public Roads, in the Department of Commerce in later years, administered the federal-aid highway program.

As a result of this system, the construction and development of government-provided transport facilities have proceeded without much regard for overall needs or for the effect that the creation of the proposed facilities would have on other agencies of transportation. For this reason it has been urged that the promotional activities of the federal government relating to highway, water, and air transport should be centralized in one agency.[7]

There is much merit in the proposal, although there is danger that too much emphasis would be put on the effects of expanding such facilities on the other modes of transport. It is extremely doubtful, as we have noted, whether the effect on other modes of transport should be the major consideration in the provision of highway and air-transport facilities. So far as water transport is concerned, we have elsewhere maintained that proposed waterway improvements should be carefully scrutinized to determine whether or not they would provide a really cheaper mode of transport. Where they would not, there is certainly little reason for making the expenditure. Where they would provide a cheaper mode of transport, the expenditure would ordinarily be justified.[8] An exception to this rule should be made, however, in instances in which the development of the waterway would threaten the existence of a railroad whose services would still be needed. Railroads can serve some points and areas and provide some transportation services that waterways cannot. We have also noted that reduced transport costs made possible by the improvement of a waterway may result in increased transport costs to those dependent on rail transport, and this is a factor which might well be considered before a waterway project is undertaken.

Transport Planning and the Department of Transportation

A step toward coordinated planning of public expenditures on transportation facilities was provided by the Department of Transportation Act of 1966, since it directed the Secretary of Transportation to develop standards and criteria "consistent with national transportation policies, for the formulation and economic evaluation of all proposals for the investment of Federal funds in transportation facilities or equipment. . . ."

The power of the Secretary of Transportation in the formulation of

---

[7] Charles L. Dearing and Wilfred Owen, *National Transportation Policy* (Washington, D.C.: Brookings Institution, 1949), pp. 353–56; Secretary of Commerce, *Issues Involved in a Unified and Coordinated Federal Program for Transportation* (Washington, D.C.: U.S. Government Printing Office, 1950), p. 20.

[8] See pp. 734–35 supra.

standards, however, is severely restricted by various provisions of the Act. The more important of these are as follows:

1. The standards and criteria developed by the Secretary must be approved by Congress. This provision is reinforced by a further declaration that "Nothing in this Act shall be construed to authorize, without appropriate action by Congress, the adoption, revision, or implementation of—

   a)   any transportation policy, or

   b)   any investment standards or criteria."

2. Standards and criteria for the evaluation of water resource projects are not to be established by the Secretary of Transportation but by the Water Resources Council, although the Secretary of Transportation is made a member of the Council on matters pertaining to navigation facilities of water resource projects.

3. Standards for measuring benefits of water resource projects are laid down in the Act and defined as "the product of the savings to shippers using the waterway and the estimated traffic that would use the waterway; where the savings to shippers shall be construed to mean the difference between (*a*) the freight rates or charges prevailing at the time of the study for the movement by the alternative means and (*b*) those which would be charged on the proposed waterway; and where the estimate of traffic that would use the waterway will be based on such freight rates, taking into account projections of the economic growth of the area." These are essentially the standards that have been used by the Corps of Engineers in recommending waterway improvement projects. They are open to criticism from an economic standpoint because they are based on relative transportation *rates* rather than on relative *costs*.

4. The power of the Secretary of Transportation over transportation investment standards is also limited by provisions of the Act which exclude various proposals from his jurisdiction in this matter. Among these are grant-in-aid programs established by law, which of course include federal-aid highway projects.[9]

These provisions of the Act clearly demonstrate the intention of Congress to retain control over transportation investment policies, and not to delegate such power, except in an advisory capacity, to any government bureau, or to any department of the Executive branch of the government.

Under a democratic form of government it is to be expected that the

---

[9] Other projects excluded from the Secretary's consideration are the acquisition of facilities or equipment by federal agencies in providing facilities for their own use; an interoceanic canal outside the contiguous United States; defense features required by the Defense Department in transportation projects; and programs of foreign assistance.

people, acting through their elected representatives, will insist on retaining ultimate control over the expenditure of public funds for particular transportation facilities, however unwise their actions may sometimes be when measured by economic criteria.

The Airport and Airway Act of 1970 advanced a step further in centralized planning of transportation development. The Secretary of Transportation, as elsewhere pointed out,[10] was directed by this Act to formulate a plan for the coordinated development of all modes of transportation with the priority to be assigned to the development and improvement of each mode. Although the Act makes no reference to the investment standards required by the Act of 1966, presumably the standards established thereunder would apply so far as pertinent in the establishment of priorities.

THE SUBSIDY PROBLEM

The position which any one of the modes of transport will occupy in the national transportation system will depend in part on the extent to which it or its competitors are subsidized. As the term "subsidy" is used here, any mode of transport is subsidized if part of its costs are borne by taxpayers and not by the users. The railroads have long complained of the subsidies extended to their competitors.

Before discussing in greater detail the extent and effects of subsidizing various forms of transportation, it should be pointed out that it is no answer to the railroad complaint to say that railroads were subsidized in the early days of railroad building. That they were subsidized admits of no doubt.[11] Such subsidy, however, is of little significance at the present time. Land donated to railroads for rights of way has entered into present valuations and rate base in the same manner as if it had been purchased. Funds originally donated to railroads for construction purposes have been converted into physical property which enters into the rate base. Very little, if any, of the subsidy granted to railroads has relieved shippers of paying any part of the current expenses of operating and maintaining the railroad system or has relieved them of the burden of paying, if possible, a return on the capital invested in railroads. Part of the cost of water, highway, and air transport, however, is borne by the general taxpayer and not by those whose goods are transported by these agencies.

Water transportation, highway transportation, and air transportation are the forms of transportation concerning which the issue of subsidy arises. Although the question of subsidy to each of these modes of transport has been discussed in earlier chapters, a review of the situation is required at this point.

---

[10] P. 275, supra.

[11] See pp. 126–38, supra.

Subsidy to Water Transportation

Water transportation is subsidized, since part of the costs of water transport are borne by the taxpayers and not by the users of the waterway. We have pointed out in a previous chapter that waterways are improved and maintained principally by the federal government and that no charges are imposed on users to defray such expenditures, except for use of the Panama Canal and the Great Lakes–St. Lawrence Seaway.[12]

Although there can be no disputing the fact that water transportation is subsidized by taxpayers, controversy arises the moment an attempt is made to measure the amount of the subsidy in a particular year. Obviously the total expenditures on waterways made in any one year are not chargeable to that year, since part of the expenditures are in the nature of a capital investment which will be useful for many years. Actual expenditures must be classified according to whether they are operating and maintenance expenditures or whether they are capital expenditures. Capital expenditures must be distributed over the life of the improvement. This means that the total investment in waterways must be determined and that a rate of depreciation or amortization must be set up in order to determine an annual depreciation or amortization charge. There is ample opportunity for argument over the prospective service life of various waterway improvements. Controversy also arises over the question of whether interest on the investment in the waterways should be included in the calculations.[13] Then, if the subsidy is to be expressed in terms of cents per ton or per ton-mile of traffic, should the cost be divided by the actual traffic over the waterway, or may allowance be made for various circumstances? Thus, if the waterway is incomplete, the traffic now handled may be small, although it may reasonably be expected to be greater when the entire waterway is completed. Furthermore, if railroads are allowed to reduce rates to meet the competition of water carriers, thus diverting traffic from the waterway, is it proper to charge the remaining traffic with the whole amount of the public expenditure?

The amount of subsidy or public aid found in water transportation will depend upon how these and other questions are answered. The study of public aids to transportation made for the Board of Investigation and Research found the subsidy to water transportation in 1940 averaged 2.2 cents per ton on traffic handled at ports, port rivers, and connecting channels. On the longer rivers and canals, federal aid amounted to 3.1 cents per ton-mile on the average, ranging from two tenths of a mill for the lowest-cost group of waterways to 90 cents per ton-mile for the highest-cost group.[14]

---

[12] See p. 731, supra.

[13] This question will be discussed later.

[14] Board of Investigation and Research, *Public Aids to Domestic Transportation,* 79th Cong., 1st Sess., House Doc. No. 159 (1945), p. 21.

Subsidy to Highway Transportation

Highways are provided and maintained by state and local governments, as we have previously noted. Annual highway costs can be determined by the same method that is used to determine annual waterway costs, that is, by determining annual operating, administration, and maintenance costs, setting up an annual depreciation or amortization charge based on the estimated service life of highways, and, if interest is to be included, computing it on the unamortized investment in the highways. The all-important question of what portion of the annual cost of various classes of highways may properly be charged against motor vehicles must be answered, and the motor-vehicle share of the highway costs must then be compared with the payments made by vehicle owners for the use of the highways through special motor-vehicle taxes. There is much room for difference of opinion in making computations of this sort; hence there is bound to be disagreement as to whether highway transportation is subsidized or not, or, if subsidized, as to the amount of such subsidy.

Two careful investigations of this question by government agencies reached the conclusion that motor vehicles as a whole were not subsidized. The Federal Coordinator of Transportation found that motor-vehicle users as a class had paid their way since 1926.[15] The study made for the Board of Investigation and Research found that motor-vehicle users as a class "have contributed amounts fully adequate to meet an equitable share of total annual costs of roads and streets."[16] The wide variation in special motor-vehicle taxes in the different states suggests that there may be subsidy in some states and not in others. The railroads refused to accept the findings of either the Federal Coordinator's study or that made for the Board of Investigation and Research, contending that there was still a substantial element of subsidy to highway transport.[17]

Conclusions concerning the existence of a subsidy to highway transportation depend to a considerable extent on judgment as to the proportion of road costs which motor-vehicle users as a class should pay. It has been pointed out in a previous chapter that many highways are primarily land-access highways that are used very little by the average motor-vehicle owner. The annual costs of such highways may well be borne in large part by the local property owner and the general taxpayer. City streets are usually financed, and quite properly so, by special assessments on benefiting property and by local taxation. All streets and roads, furthermore, serve certain community functions which justify the assumption of part of the cost of building and maintaining them by the general taxpayer. For

---

[15] Op. cit., Vol. I, p. 26.

[16] Op. cit., p. 293.

[17] C. S. Duncan, J. C. Greenway, Chester K. Smith, and Earl R. Feldman, *A Review of "Public Aids to Domestic Transportation"* (mimeographed; Washington, D.C.: Association of American Railroads, 1946), p. 22.

these reasons it seems to us that it would be unfair to make the motor-vehicle operator pay the entire annual cost of providing and maintaining such roads and streets. Just what proportion of these costs should be borne by motor-vehicle operators, however, cannot be determined by any statistical formula yet devised. It is a matter of judgment on which differences of opinion are bound to exist. The Federal Coordinator's study assigned to motor vehicles 83 percent of the annual cost of state highways, 34 percent of the cost of county and local roads, and 30 percent of the cost of city streets for the period 1933–37.[18] The Board of Investigation and Research study assigned to motor vehicles 85 percent of the annual costs of the primary highway system, 30 percent of the costs of secondary and local roads, and 40 percent of the costs of city streets for the year 1940.[19] The railroads have contended that a larger share of highway costs, even the entire costs, should be assigned to motor vehicles.[20] Various methods of assigning highway costs to immediate users and others have been discussed in an earlier chapter.[21]

Although both the Federal Coordinator's study and the Board of Investigation and Research study concluded that motor vehicles as a class had paid their share of highway costs in recent years, both recognized that certain types of vehicles had not paid their share. The apportionment of the motor-vehicle share of road costs among the different classes of motor vehicles involves many controversial questions which cannot be discussed here. The conclusion of the Board of Investigation and Research study was that farm trucks, other trucks having a capacity of a ton or more, and intercity buses having 25 seats or more did not pay their share of highway costs and were in effect being subsidized by other motor-vehicle owners.[22] This conclusion was unacceptable to the trucking industry.

Subsidy to Air Transportation

In the past, subsidy to air transportation has arisen from the use of publicly provided airports without adequate payment therefor; from the free use of airway facilities; and from generous compensation for carrying mail. A beginning in placing airports and airway facilities on a user basis was made in the Airport and Airway Development Act of 1970, since federal expenditures for the development and improvement of airports and for the construction, maintenance, and operation of air navigation facilities are to be made from the proceeds of special aviation user charges.[23] It

---

[18] Op. cit., Vol. I, p. 25.
[19] Op. cit., p. 283.
[20] Duncan et al., op. cit., p. 54.
[21] See pp. 625–27, supra.
[22] Op. cit., pp. 61–62, 313.
[23] Pp. 773–75, supra.

is not possible to determine at this time to what extent the element of subsidy will be removed by these taxes.

Direct subsidies to airlines through air-mail payments are shown in an earlier chapter.[24] Mail subsidy accruals, as estimated by the Civil Aeronautics Board, reached a peak of $82,909,000 for the fiscal year 1963, declined to $46,955,000 in 1970, but was estimated at $63,246,000 for 1971.[25]

Objections to Subsidy

We have seen that water transport is subsidized. Air transport is presumably subsidized through inadequate payments for the use of publicly provided airports and airway facilities. It is also subsidized through direct mail subsidy payments to needy airlines. There is disagreement over the question whether highway transportation is subsidized, but it is likely that the heavier vehicles pay less than their share of highway costs. The objections to such subsidies need to be stated more definitely.

1. Subsidy places the railroads at an unfair disadvantage in competing with the subsidized forms of transport. It is obvious that the difficulties of the railroads are increased if part of the costs of water, air, and highway transportation are borne by the taxpayer.
2. The existence of subsidy to some modes of transport and not to others results in an uneconomic allocation of traffic. It is obvious, for instance, that if waterways are provided and maintained by the taxpayer, the rates charged by carriers operating on the waterways do not cover the full cost of water transportation. The artificially low rates, therefore, may divert traffic from other transportation agencies, even though the real cost of transportation by water is greater. If the rates of each form of transport more nearly covered its full cost, traffic would be distributed more nearly in accordance with relative economy and fitness.
3. A corollary of the point just made is that subsidizing some modes of transport and not others makes it more difficult to determine the proper place of each in the transportation system. If subsidy were removed, the relative economy of the different forms of transport would be more clearly revealed.
4. Subsidy to some modes of transport and not to others stimulates the overexpansion of the subsidized transportation facilities. If water transport or highway transport appears to be cheaper because the taxpayer pays part of the costs, there will be a tendency to overexpand these transportation facilities even though they may not provide a cheaper or a superior means of transport when all costs are considered.

---

[24] See p. 795 supra.

[25] Civil Aeronautics Board, *Subsidy for United States Certificated Air Carriers,* 1971 ed., Appendix No. 1.

Methods of Removing or Reducing Subsidy

Subsidy to water transportation could be removed by a system of tolls or other charges for the use of publicly provided water transportation facilities. Many difficulties would be encountered, however, in an attempt to figure out reasonable tolls.[26] Subsidy to highway transportation, in so far as it may exist, could be removed by increasing motor-vehicle taxes on the types of vehicles subsidized. Subsidy to air transportation could be removed by seeing that aviation user taxes together with airport fees and charges were sufficient for that purpose, and by reducing or eliminating air-mail subsidy payments.

Some Controversial Questions over User Charges

Discussions of alleged subsidy to water, highway, and air transport often become involved in controversy over (1) the propriety of including interest on investment in publicly provided facilities as part of the subsidy, (2) the question of whether hypothetical taxes on highways, waterways, and other publicly owned property should be included in the calculations, or (3) whether depreciation or amortization of investment in publicly provided facilities should be included. Divergence of opinion on these questions is often due to a failure to distinguish between the ascertainment of the amount of subsidy or public aid as a fact and the related but not identical question of public policy to be followed in imposing special user charges.

Those who object to the inclusion of some or all of the controverted items mentioned above may be objecting explicitly or implicitly to a tax policy which makes the users of publicly provided facilities pay more than is necessary to cover the actual cash outlays made by the government in the provision of these facilities. They do not necessarily deny that the controversial items are an element in the determination of the relative costs of the different modes of transport in the economic sense. Those who have argued for the inclusion of the controverted items in calculations of the amount of subsidy are thinking in terms of the real costs of highway, water, and air transportation and the determination of the portion of those costs borne by taxpayers as distinguished from users. They may recognize that the question of whether all such costs should be shifted from taxpayers to users of publicly provided facilities is another question, or they may take it for granted that sound public policy requires all of these costs to be borne by the users.

The question of the proper compensation which users of publicly provided transportation facilities should be asked to pay is approached by

---

[26] For a discussion of this problem, see Board of Investigation and Research, op. cit., pp. 421–27.

different individuals with different underlying purposes or objectives in mind. Frequently these purposes and objectives are not clearly defined; but the conclusions regarding the treatment of interest, tax equivalents, and some other matters will depend on the purposes and objectives adopted. Let us consider three common purposes or objectives held in mind by those seeking to determine proper user charges, in order that we may see to what conclusions they lead concerning the inclusion of the disputed items.

User Charges to Equalize Competitive Conditions. User charges may be levied with the object in mind of equalizing competitive conditions between privately owned and publicly owned facilities. If this objective is kept in mind, an effort will be made to offset, by special user charges, any advantage that grows out of the fact that some transportation facilities are provided by the public instead of by private enterprise. Interest on investment will be included, because private enterprise must include interest on investment in its costs. In fact, interest would be included not at the rate which a government would have to pay if funds were borrowed, but at the rate which a private business would have to pay. A tax equivalent would be included on the theory that if the facilities were privately owned, they would be subject to taxation. On this basis, also, the investment in highways would include the value of lands used for rights of way, whether they were paid for by the state or not.[27]

User Charges to Cover Full Actual Cost. User charges may be imposed for the purpose of making users pay the full economic cost of the service. This shifts to the rate payer those costs which are initially borne by the taxpayer. If the determination of user charges is approached with this objective in mind, interest on the investment in highways, waterways, and air-transport facilities will be included in the cost. These are elements of cost, irrespective of who provided the capital facilities or who owns them. Of course, it is true that unless the government borrowed the funds to build the transportation facilities, interest is not an actual cash outlay. It is a cost, nevertheless. This cost has been borne by those who contributed the funds to provide the facilities. In the case of waterways, airways, and airports, the taxpayer contributed the funds. In the case of highways the general taxpayer and those who aided in financing the highways through the payment of special motor-vehicle taxes provided the funds.

Whether a tax equal to that which would be paid on the transportation facilities if they were privately owned is properly a cost has been hotly debated. The Federal Coordinator did not consider such tax equivalents to be a cost.[28] The Staff of the Board of Investigation and Research took

---

[27] The railroads criticized the Board of Investigation and Research study for not including the value of highway rights of way in highway investment unless the rights of way were purchased. See Duncan and Others, op. cit., p. 36.

[28] Op. cit., Vol. I, p. 6; Vol. IV, p. 52; Vol. III, pp. 24–25.

the same position.[29] The railroads contend that "escaped taxes" are a cost.[30]

User Charges to Finance Publicly Provided Facilities. User charges may be levied for the purpose of financing new transportation facilities or improvements thereto, in addition to the cost of operating and maintaining them, or for the purpose of reimbursing the government for the actual outlays incurred in the past to create the facilities. If this is the objective, user charges must include first or last the cost of constructing them—the capital costs. Interest, however would be included in the costs only to the extent that the government agency has borrowed to finance the construction.

User Charges and Public Policy

User charges may be levied with any of the above objectives in mind. The policy of levying user charges simply to equalize competitive conditions seems the least justifiable if it is carried to the point of making such charges cover costs which are not actually incurred but which would have been incurred if the facilities had been built as private business enterprises. It appears as a form of protectionism, handicapping the public enterprise to protect the private, and should be resorted to only when necessary to preserve essential private operations.

A strong argument can be made, however, for a system of user charges that seeks to place upon users of publicly provided transportation facilities the full economic cost associated with the provision and maintenance of those facilities. Under this system, transportation rates by the various modes of transport would be more likely to reflect actual transportation costs, and each mode of transport could more easily be assigned to its most useful place in the transportation system. Under this system, also, there would be less tendency for overexpansion of transportation facilities, and the railroads could not complain that the terms of competition were unfair. This basis of levying user charges is particularly appropriate for any public undertaking in which the benefits accrue to very limited groups in society rather than to a large segment of the population.

It should be recognized, however, that to treat highways, waterways, and air transportation facilities in this way is to depart radically from the usual method of managing these public undertakings as well as other public enterprises which have been undertaken to render a service to the general public. If user charges were levied to recover the entire economic cost associated with the provision of publicly provided facilities, including interest on investment, these enterprises would be put on an income-pro-

[29] Op. cit., pp. 100–101, 231–32.

[30] C. B. Breed, Clifford Older, and W. S. Downs, *Highway Costs* (a report to the Association of American Railroads) (1939), p. 34; Association of American Railroads, *What Is Public Aid to Transportation?* (Washington, D.C., 1940), p. 131; and Duncan et al., op. cit., pp. 25 and 36.

ducing basis. The states would derive large amounts of revenue from the highways in the form of interest on investment; the federal government would derive a cash income from the ownership of waterways; and municipalities would derive an income from airports in excess of their immediate outlays. It has not been customary to look upon such investments as sources of revenue. These facilities have been provided by the people acting collectively through their governments in order that they might enjoy the services which these facilities make possible. The public looks for a return on its investment in the form of these services and benefits.

The argument for departing from the traditional treatment of publicly provided facilities arises from the competitive relation between these facilities and privately owned railroads. If there were no railroads, and if the public were wholly dependent on the publicly provided transportation facilities, it is doubtful if anyone would suggest that user charges should yield the government a cash return on its investment. Railroads are admittedly at a disadvantage in competing with publicly provided transportation facilities when user charges for the latter do not cover interest on investment; but whether this situation is serious enough to require that all publicly provided facilities be put on a completely commercial or income-producing basis, contrary to usual practice in public undertakings, may be questioned. If the competition of highway, waterway, and air transportation should threaten the existence of needed rail transportation facilities, attention should doubtless be given to this method of reducing the competitive disadvantage of the railroads.

Defense of Subsidies

We have discussed the railroad claim that highway, water, and air transport is subsidized; and we have noted the undesirable consequences that result from such subsidy as may exist. We have also suggested that attempts at complete removal of subsidies through the adoption of user charges might lead to results so much at variance with traditional policies as to be unacceptable to the public. At this point, therefore, it may be well to recognize that under some conditions the subsidization of transportation services or facilities can be justified.

A common justification for subsidy of air transportation is that it is a comparatively new industry, promising to provide us with a valuable type of transportation service, but which could not be expected to be self-sufficient in its early years. Subsidy to railroads was justified on similar grounds in the early years of railroad building. The same argument is used to justify subsidization of any new and promising industry. It may well be argued, however, that the air-transport industry has long passed the stage in which subsidy can be justified on grounds of infancy.

Subsidy to transportation may be defended also on the grounds that social, political, national-defense, or other noneconomic benefits justify it.

These factors have played a part in the early subsidization of railroads, the support of a local highway system from the proceeds of taxation, federal financial aid to highways and airports, and government provision of waterway improvements and, until recently, airway facilities without charge to the user.

Indirect economic gains have also played a part in the subsidization of transportation agencies. Cities and the business interests located in them may find the indirect benefits from airport facilities and airline service of sufficient importance to justify the levying of taxes to provide and maintain an adequate airport. Indirect economic gains may also result from the construction or improvement of highways and the development of water transportation facilities. Railroad history reveals that indirect economic gains provided much of the motivation for the heavy subsidies granted railroads by local, state, and federal governments. Referring to early railroad construction, one writer said: "No line of ordinary importance was ever constructed that did not, from the wealth it created, speedily repay its cost, although it may never have returned a dollar to its share or bondholders."[31]

Conclusion on Subsidies

The fact that subsidization of transportation agencies may be justified in the developmental period of a transportation agency, or that social, political, or other noneconomic benefits may be of great value, or that the subsidized transportation agencies may bring indirect economic gains to the persons or areas which they serve, is not a justification for maintaining unnecessary subsidies. Social and political benefits and indirect economic gains also flow from self-supporting industries. To the extent possible, subsidies should be removed and the transprotation agencies made self-supporting. However, if particular transportation services or facilities cannot be made self-supporting, the question of whether indirect economic gains and social or other noneconomic benefits are sufficient to warrant their support from public funds becomes an important issue. In some cases the answer will be in the affirmative; in others, in the negative; and in many the decision will be difficult.

COMMON CONTROL OF COMPETING MODES OF TRANSPORT

The various modes of transport are to some extent competitive with each other. An important question is whether one agency of transporta-

---

[31] Henry V. Poor, *Influence of the Railroads of the United States in the Creation of Commerce and Wealth* (New York: Journeymen Printers' Co-operative Association, 1869), p. 42. See also P. P. Sveistrup, "Some Problems in Planning Transportation," 6 *Transport and Communications Review* 24 (1953); and Moses Abramovitz, "The Economic Characteristics of Railroads and the Problem of Economic Development," 14 *Far Eastern Quarterly* 169 (1955), p. 171.

tion should be permitted to obtain control of transportation agencies of another kind. Similarly, should one agency of transport be permitted to expand its operations and engage in other forms of transport? As a practical matter the question usually appears in the form of efforts by railroad companies to acquire control of other forms of transport or to engage directly in highway, water, or air operations. The issue has also arisen because of the efforts of steamship lines to develop air-transport services.

A number of arguments may be advanced in favor of permitting railroad companies to engage freely in other forms of transport. These may be stated as follows:

1. Railroad participation in other modes of transportation would permit "coordination" of the various modes of transport, in that a railroad company could utilize water transport, highway transport, and air transport, whichever was cheapest or provided a superior service. Coordination would thus become largely a managerial matter. In support of this view it may be pointed out that railroads have frequently found it possible to effect important economies in their operations by substituting other forms of transport, particularly highway transport, for more expensive rail operations. Sometimes they have abandoned unprofitable passenger-train operations and substituted bus service or have given up expensive way-freight trains and substituted motor-truck service.

2. Permitting railroads to operate highway, water, or air services would in some situations eliminate wasteful struggles for competitive traffic. When the various modes of transport compete with each other for traffic, there is a tendency for each to reach out for traffic that can more economically be carried by its competitor. These practices might be eliminated if other modes of transport came under the control of a railroad, although there is no assurance that wasteful competition would disappear unless a monopoly were established over a particular route. If independent carriers by water, highway, or air continued to exist, wasteful struggles for traffic might continue.

3. Allowing railroads to engage in highway, water, and air transportation would mitigate to some extent the competitive inequalities between railroads and the "subsidized" forms of transportation, since railroads, as well as others, would be deriving some benefit from public expenditures on highways, waterways, and air transportation facilities.

Against railroad participation in, or control of, other modes of transport, four arguments are of major importance:

1. A more rapid development of highway, water, and air transportation will be likely to occur if the different modes of transport are kept independent. This is because such carriers have an undivided interest in

the form of transport in which they engage, whereas the interest of the railway companies would be divided. This argument was of more significance when motor transport and air transport were in their infancy.

2. An actual conflict of interest may appear between the railway operations of a carrier and its highway, water, or air operations. The investment of the company in railroad transportation facilities is so great that it would be more interested in keeping traffic on its rails and protecting its investment there than in developing a new and competing mode of transport. Railroads in control of a competing mode of transport, therefore, may be inclined to keep rates high for nonrail service, and the service poor, in an effort to hold traffic to the rails.

3. Competition among the different modes of transport, it is alleged, would give the public better service, since there is an incentive for each form of transport to win the favor and patronage of the public.

4. Lastly, competition between railroad-controlled waterlines, bus lines, truck lines, or airlines, on the one hand, and independent water, highway, or air carriers, on the other, could result in the elimination of the independents through unfair competitive practices. Water, highway, or air carriers controlled by a railroad could cut rates to an unprofitable level and drive out the independents, since the losses of the railroad-controlled operations can be absorbed by the railroad, while the independents, having no other source of income to fall back on, could be forced out of business. With adequate minimum-rate powers, however, and with control over adequacy of service, a regulatory body should be able to prevent abuses of this sort.

Railroad Control of Water Carriers

The policy of Congress has been to maintain competition between railways and carriers by water. The Panama Canal Act of 1912, now part of Section 5 of the Interstate Commerce Act, contained provisions designed to break up the control of boat lines by competing railways. This provision of the Interstate Commerce Act, as it now stands, makes it unlawful for a railroad "to own, lease, operate, control, or have any interest whatsoever (by stock ownership or otherwise, either directly, indirectly, through any holding company, or by stockholders or directors in common, or in any other manner)" in any common carrier by water or any vessel with which the railroad does or may compete for traffic. The Act gives the Commission authority to determine the fact of competition or possibility of competition.

The Commission is also empowered to permit railroad control of water carriers if it finds that such control "will not prevent such common carrier by water or vessel from being operated in the interest of the public and with advantage to the convenience and commerce of the people" and that "it will not exclude, prevent, or reduce competition on the route by water under consideration." The Commission is not empowered, however, to permit railroad control of competing boat lines which operate through the Panama Canal. Here the prohibition of the statute is absolute.

In order to conform to the provisions of the Panama Canal Act, certain railroads were forced to give up their control of steamship lines operating on the Great Lakes. The Commission found that the railroads had maintained high steamship rates to divert traffic to the rail lines and that independent water lines had been driven out of business.[32] In numerous situations, however, the Commission has permitted railroad control of, or interest in, competitive water lines,[33] but in 1962, acquisition of control of a barge line operating on the Mississippi River and other waterways in the Middle West, South, and Southwest by the Illinois Central Railroad Company and the Southern Pacific Company was prevented by the provisions of the Panama Canal Act.[34]

It should be emphasized that permission for a railroad to operate a competing boat line rests upon a showing that the operation "will not exclude, prevent, or reduce" competition by water. At one time the railroads sought to have the provisions of the Panama Canal Act repealed. They argued that the need of the present is coordination of the various agencies of transportation and that coordination is impossible if the railroads are not allowed to own steamship lines. It must be remembered that the Panama Canal Act does not prohibit railroad ownership or control of all water carriers, but only of competing lines. In view of the possibilities of harmful practices if railroads are allowed to control competing water carriers, the general prohibition of railroad control of competing water carriers is wise. The prohibition prevents a situation from arising in which a conflict of interest between the railroad and the water line would lead to discrimination against water transportation, and it prevents the unsound competitive practices so likely to arise when a railroad-controlled water line is competing with independent water carriers.

The power of the Commission to make exception to the prohibitions of the Panama Canal Act introduces some flexibility into the statute. The requirement that the Commission may not authorize railroad control of competing water lines unless such control will not "exclude, prevent, or reduce" competition by water would appear to limit greatly the possibil-

---

[32] *Lake Line Applications under the Panama Canal Act*, 33 ICC 700 (1915). For a later application of the Panama Canal Act, see *Nicholson Universal S. S. Co. Ownership*, 248 ICC 43 (1941).

[33] See *Central Vermont Boat Lines*, 40 ICC 589 (1916); *Ocean Steamship Co. of Savannah*, 37 ICC 422 (1915); *Steamer Lines on Long Island Sound*, 183 ICC 323 (1932); *Missouri Pacific R. R. Co. and Texas & Pacific Ry. Co., Service by Water*, 245 ICC 143 (1941). The Administration of the Panama Canal Act is discussed in detail in Federal Coordinator of Transportation, *Regulation of Transportation Agencies*, 73d Cong., 2d Sess., Senate Doc. No. 152 (1934), Appendix I.

[34] *Illinois Central R. Co.—Control—John I. Hay Co.*, 317 ICC 39 (1962).

ity of relief from the provisions of the section. The Commission, however, has interpreted this requirement rather loosely.[35] It would be preferable for Congress to amend the law so as to permit railroad control of a water line if such control is shown to be in the public interest and if it will not unduly restrict competition.

Railroad Control of Motor Carriers

Prior to the enactment of the Motor Carrier Act of 1935, many railroads had instituted motor-carrier operations either directly or through subsidiary companies. The Federal Coordinator of Transportation reported that in 1933 there were 209 steam or electric railways which were engaged to some extent in motor-vehicle operations.[36] Line-haul motortruck service was performed by rail carriers over 469 routes with an aggregate length of 16,394 miles.[37]

Although such operations were protected by the "grandfather clause" in the Motor Carrier Act, special tests were provided to govern the granting of authority under the Act for railroads or any "carrier other than a carrier by motor vehicle" to acquire control of motor carriers. This special test or requirement, with some change in language, was incorporated by the Transportation Act of 1940 into the broadened Section 5, which relates to consolidations and acquisitions of control of the various classes of carriers subject to the Act. The Act provides that if a carrier by railroad, or any person controlled by such a carrier or affiliated therewith, seeks authority to acquire control of a motor carrier, the Commission shall not issue an order authorizing such control unless it finds that the transaction will be consistent with the public interest and "will enable such carrier to use service by motor vehicle to public advantage in its operations and will not unduly restrain competition."

The Commission, in referring to this provision of the law, said that Congress intended "to protect each mode of transportation from the suppression or strangulation thereof which might follow if control thereof were allowed to fall into the hands of a competing transportation agency."[38] At the same time Congress was aware that motor vehicles could often be used as a subordinate instrumentality for the improvement of rail transportation service, and it therefore permitted railroads to acquire control of motor carriers when it would enable the railroad "to use service

---

[35] See dissenting opinion of Commissioner Anderson in *Steamer Lines on Long Island Sound*, 50 ICC 634, 647–51 (1918), and of Commissioner Eastman in the same proceeding on further hearing, 183 ICC 323, 349–52 (1932).

[36] *Regulation of Transportation Agencies*, 73d Cong., 2d Sess., Senate Doc. No. 152 (1934), p. 264.

[37] Ibid., p. 274.

[38] *Rock Island Transit Co.—Purchase—White Line Motor Freight Co., Inc.*, 40 MCC 457, 461 (1946).

by motor vehicle to public advantage in its operations" and would not "unduly restrain competition."

The leading case in the early development of policy under this provision of the Act is known as the Barker Case. In this case an affiliate of the Pennsylvania Railroad sought authority to acquire control of a motor carrier.[39] The Commission said: ". . . we are not convinced that the way to maintain for the future healthful competition between rail and truck service is to give the railroads free opportunity to go into the kind of truck service which is strictly competitive with, rather than auxiliary to, their rail operations."[40] The Commission pointed out that the language of the Act was evidence that Congress was of the same view. The Commission also remarked that in its opinion, truck service would not have developed to the extraordinary extent to which it had developed if it had been under railroad control.[41] The Pennsylvania Railroad affiliate was allowed to acquire the motor carrier, but the Commission laid down a number of conditions to keep the motor-carrier operations strictly auxiliary to rail service, such as the substitution of truck service for that of way-freight trains. One restriction imposed in the Barker Case was that no service should be given to or from a point not a station on the line of the acquiring railroad. The Commission expressed particular disapproval of railroad-controlled motor-carrier operations (1) which would compete with the railroad itself, or (2) which would compete with an established motor carrier, or (3) which would invade a territory already adequately served by another rail carrier. The policy of the Barker Case has been followed in subsequent acquisition cases. Such conditions are imposed as may be necessary to insure that the motor-carrier operations are auxiliary or supplementary to rail operations.

Applications of railroads to acquire control of existing motor carriers are covered by the provisions of the Act which we have just discussed, but applications of railroads to institute new service by motor vehicle directly or through an existing subsidiary are subject to the provisions of Section 207 which relate to the issuance of certificates of public convenience and necessity. No special requirements are imposed by the statute for a certificate when the applicant is a rail carrier or is affiliated with a rail carrier. Public convenience and necessity must of course be shown, but no showing that the motor-carrier operations will be auxiliary or supplemental to rail transportation is required by the statute. The Commission, however, has usually granted certificates for rail-controlled motor-carrier operations only when the service would be auxiliary or supplemental to rail service, thus recognizing the objections to participation by a railroad in motor-carrier operations competitive with itself. This action also makes

---

[39] *Pennsylvania Truck Lines, Inc.—Control—Barker Motor Freight,* 1 MCC 101 (1936), 5 MCC 9 (1937), 5 MCC 49 (1937).

[40] 1 MCC 101, 111–12.

[41] Ibid., p. 112.

the Commission's policy under this section of the Act consistent with the policy required by Section 5 of the Act in acquisition cases. The railroads have criticized the policy of the Commission, saying that there is no statutory authorization for imposing more difficult conditions on a railroad than on any other applicant for a certificate of public convenience and necessity to operate motor-carrier services. The Commission commented on this charge in 1946, saying:

We appreciate, of course, that section 207, unlike section 5, does not require of a railroad, undertaking to prove that public convenience and necessity require a motor service which it proposes, any greater measure of proof than is required of any other applicant. But this does not mean that it is as easy for one applicant, as for another, to prove need for a proposed service or that this Commission considering an application by a railroad for authority to perform an all-motor service, not in aid of its rail service but in competition therewith and with other motor carriers, can ignore the circumstance that such applicant is a railroad whose operation as proposed would ordinarily be inconsistent with the principles underlying the national transportation policy.[42]

The leading case establishing the above policy was the Kansas City Southern Case.[43] Here, as in the Barker Case, the Commission imposed various conditions to restrict the service to that which was auxiliary or supplemental to the rail service. One such condition was that the railroad-controlled motor carrier should transport only traffic having a prior rail haul or traffic which was to have a subsequent rail haul. This restriction was later found to be objectionable under some conditions because it did not permit the railroad-controlled motor carrier to transport local freight between two small stations on its line, thus requiring the continuance of lightly loaded way-freight trains. The Commission has therefore commonly substituted what came to be known as "key-point" restrictions.[44] A key-point restriction does not permit railroad-controlled motor service between larger cities, called "key points." The key points are, in fact, concentration and distribution points. Between them rail service is economical, and railroad-controlled motor-carrier operations are not permitted. Railroad-controlled motor service is confined to traffic moving from local points to key points, from key points to local points, or between local points. In transporting traffic between local points, the carrier may not transport it by motor vehicle through more than one key point. The key-point restrictions allow traffic to be moved by motor vehicle between local points regardless of whether there has been a prior rail haul or whether there will be a subsequent rail haul on the traffic. Since the Commission's decision in the Kansas City Southern Case, most grants of motor-

---

[42] *Rock Island Motor Transit Co.—Purchase—White Line Motor Freight Co.*, 40 MCC 457, 473-74 (1946).

[43] *Kansas City Southern Transport Co., Inc. Common Carrier Application,* 10 MCC 221 (1938), 28 MCC 5 (1941).

[44] 28 MCC 5 (1941).

carrier operating authority to railroads or railroad affiliates have been made with restrictions similar to those imposed in the Kansas City Southern Case. The power of the Commission to impose such restrictions has been upheld by the courts.[45]

In special circumstances, the Commission may grant operating authority to a motor-carrier subsidiary of a railroad without the usual restrictions.[46] According to a federal court, the only "special circumstances" which have led the Commission to relax its restrictions on motor service by rail subsidiaries have been "the unavailability of independent motor carrier service for the area involved."[47]

It is apparent that the "prior-or-subsequent-rail-haul" and "key-point" restrictions are designed to protect independent motor carriers, but, at the same time, to enable the railroads, through motor affiliates, to provide a more efficient and economical service than can be provided by rail alone.

The railroads would like to have a broader authority to engage in motor-carrier operations than is permitted under the principle of the Barker and Kansas City Southern cases. The motor carriers, on the other hand, object to even this much participation by railroads in motor-carrier operations.

Control of Air Carriers by Surface Carriers

The law relating to control of airlines by railroads or by any surface carrier is quite similar to the law relating to railroad control of motor carriers. Section 408 (b) of the Civil Aeronautics Act required approval of the Civil Aeronautics Board for the acquisition of control of an air carrier by another carrier. The section further provided that when control of an air carrier is sought by "a carrier other than an air carrier" or by a person controlled by such carrier or affiliated therewith, the Board may not approve of such consolidation or acquisition of control unless it finds that it "will promote the public interest by enabling such carrier other than an air carrier to use aircraft to public advantage in its operation and will not restrain competition." Following the Interstate Commerce Commission's interpretation of similar language in the Motor Carrier Act, the Civil Aeronautics Board interprets this restriction to mean that the services of an air carrier controlled by a surface carrier must be auxiliary or supplemental to the surface-carrier operations.[48] It was under this provision of

---

[45] *United States* v. *Rock Island Motor Transit Co.*, 340 U.S. 419 (1951). A variation of the "key-point" restriction, known as a "key point zone" restriction has been adopted in some cases. It is designed to accomplish the same objectives, and the technical difference need not concern us here. See *New York Central Transport Co. —Modification*, 89 MCC 389 (1962).

[46] *American Trucking Association* v. *United States*, 355 U.S. 141 (1957).

[47] *Pennsylvania Truck Lines* v. *United States*, 219 F. Supp. 871, 875 (1963).

[48] 3 CAB 631, 636 (1942).

the Act that American Export Lines, a steamship line, was required to divest itself of control of American Export Airlines.[49] Control of Northeast Airlines by three railroads—the Maine Central, the Boston & Maine, and the Central Vermont—was not found in violation of this provision of the law, however, since control antedated the effective date of the Civil Aeronautics Act, and the degree of control had not been increased since that date.[50]

The Civil Aeronautics Act did not specifically impose any restrictions on the grant of a certificate of convenience and necessity to a surface carrier to engage in air transportation; but in the American Export Case the Board expressed the opinion that the legal restrictions imposed on acquisition of an airline by a surface carrier must be applied, as a matter of law, to the grant of a certificate to a surface carrier or its subsidiary to engage in air transportation. This view reiterated in certain later cases.[51] In 1947 the Board reconsidered this view of the law and concluded that the restrictions imposed on acquisition of control of an air carrier by a surface carrier were not, *as a matter of law*, applicable to cases in which surface carriers were applying for certificates to engage in air operations.[52] The Board, however, took the position that the policy of the Act, as shown by the statutory restrictions on acquisitions of airlines by surface carriers, should be considered in a certificate case in determining public convenience and necessity. This means that the Board is not likely to grant certificates to surface carriers to engage in air transportation unless the service will be auxiliary or supplemental to surface-carrier operations. The Board recited the familiar objections to surface-carrier participation in air transportation, saying: "Surface carriers engaging in air transportation would at times be under a strong incentive to act for the protection of their investment in surface transportation interests. Again, by reason of their superior resources and extensive facilities for solicitation, such carriers would often be the possessors of powerful competitive weapons which would enable them to crush the competition of independent air carriers."[53]

Railroad Control of Pipelines

There is no legislation relating specifically to railroad control of pipelines. In 1969 there were ten pipeline companies owned or controlled by

---

[49] *American Export Lines, Control of American Export Airlines*, 4 CAB 104 (1943).

[50] *Railroad Control of Northeast Airlines*, 4 CAB 379 (1943). Control of the airline was later given up voluntarily by the railroads.

[51] *Latin American Air Service*, 6 CAB 857, 904–7 (1946); *Local, Feeder, and Pick-up Air Service*, 6 CAB 1, 8 (1944).

[52] *American President Lines, Petition*, 7 CAB 799 (1947).

[53] Ibid., p. 803.

railroads or railroad holding companies.[54] The railroads involved were the Southern Pacific, the Union Pacific, the Penn Central, the Santa Fe, and the Burlington Northern.[55]

Conclusions on Railroad Control of Other Modes of Transport

The policy of Congress has been neither to prohibit absolutely, nor to permit freely, the control of other modes of transport by railroads. Congress has recognized that under some circumstances railroads may to their advantage and to the advantage of the public engage in other modes of transport. It has also recognized that special dangers lurk in such control. Safeguards have therefore been set up to prevent railroad control of water, highway, and air transport except in special circumstances. This policy is superior to one which absolutely prohibits railroads from engaging in other modes of transport, or to one which makes no effort to prevent the peculiar abuses which are latent in such a situation. We are inclined to the view, however, that nonrail operations of railroads need not be restricted or limited to the degree that they frequently have been under existing legislation.

Intermodal Ownership by Nonrail Carriers

The previous discussion of intermodal ownership of transportation agencies has related primarily to control by railroad companies either directly or indirectly. These are the forms of intermodal ownership that have been of public concern and have led to special statutory provisions.

Unlike the railroads, the water carriers, motor carriers, pipelines, and air carriers are not faced with specific prohibitions of, or restrictions on, control of other transportation media. The difference in treatment is not difficult to explain. Restrictions on intermodal ownership are based on the belief that in the absence of such restrictions the railroads would come to dominate the other modes of transport and that this would not be in the public interest. That the other modes of transport might come to dominate the transportation scene by control of carriers of a different type has not seemed to be a realistic danger.

We have stated above that air carriers, along with other nonrailroad transportation agencies, are not specifically restricted in acquisition of control of other modes of transport. The Civil Aeronautics Board, however, has interpreted the Federal Aviation Act broadly enough to bring under its control the acquisition of surface carriers by airlines. This matter came before the Board in 1971 in connection with the effort of Trans World Airlines to obtain control of Sun Line, an ocean-cruise ship enter-

---

[54] Robert C. Lieb, "Intermodal Ownership—A Limited Reality," *Quarterly Review of Economics and Business*, Summer 1971, p. 73.

[55] Ibid., p. 74.

prise.[56] TWA sought the Board's approval or else a disclaimer of jurisdiction. The Board asserted jurisdiction over the case, reiterating a position taken in 1948 in the Air Freight Forwarder Case,[57] that although the Civil Aeronautics Act (now the Federal Aviation Act) did not literally cover the acquisition of a surface carrier by an air carrier, nevertheless "the plain policy" of the Act required Board approval before there could be unified control of surface and air carriers, "whether that be in the form of a surface carrier acquisition of an air carrier, or an air carrier acquisition of a surface carrier, or an acquisition of common control by a third person."[58] The Board, however, approved TWA's application. It held, again citing the Air Freight Forwarder Case, that the special statutory restrictions imposed on control of air carriers by surface carriers did not apply to control of surface carriers by air carriers, nor in the instant case was the control objectionable "since in neither form nor substance will the acquiring or dominant entity be the surface carrier."[59]

Integrated Transportation Companies

It has often been suggested that intermodal ownership of transportation companies should not only be encouraged but that present *railroad* companies should become *transportation* companies engaging in all modes of transport.[60] Such "transportation companies" might evolve naturally if restrictions on intermodal ownership were removed, but probably not on the grand scale apparently envisaged by some proponents of the plan.

The arguments for and against this proposal are substantially the same as those which we have stated for and against railroad control of or participation in other modes of transport. This is particularly true since it seems likely that in most instances nonrail operations would be secondary to rail operations, and rail interests would become dominant in the integrated company.

Probably the most crucial question to be raised in considering the desirability of so-called integrated transportation companies is their effect on competition. The integrated company would certainly have an advantage over independent motor and water carriers, particularly on shipments that originated or terminated on the rail line and moved partly by

---

[56] *Trans World Airlines, Inc., Acquisition of Sun Line Companies,* 71-1-4 (1971).

[57] 9 CAB 473 (1948).

[58] Op. cit., p. 2.

[59] Ibid., p. 3.

[60] For example, H. G. Moulton, "Fundamentals of National Transportation Policy," 24 *American Economic Review* (Supplement) 33 (1933); and *The American Transportation Problem* (Washington, D.C.: Brookings Institution, 1933), pp. 889–90; Lee J. Melton, "Transport Coordination and Regulatory Philosophy," 24 *Law & Contemporary Problems* 622 (1959); James E. Suelflow and Stanley J. Hille, "The Transportation Company: An Argument for Intermodal Ownership," *Land Economics,* August 1970, p. 275.

rail. The independents would have little chance to compete for such traffic.

Theoretically there could be competition between integrated transportation companies but, on intermodal traffic, only if the rail lines themselves were competitive. Two integrated companies could hardly be said to be competitive with each other on intermodal shipments, unless the rail services of both companies were competitive, i.e., unless both provided rail services at the same points. Competition between integrated companies would therefore only be effective where there was considerable duplication of rail lines.

In view of the limited extent to which integrated transportation companies would be competitive with each other, it seems likely that the most important result of their creation would be to stifle independent nonrail carriers and allow the integrated companies to dominate a major part of the transport system. If it should be considered desirable, in the interests of economy or of transport coordination, to encourage integrated transportation companies, strict control would be necessary to protect the public from abuses. Competition could not be relied upon as much as at present to provide that protection.

SELECTED REFERENCES

An excellent discussion of the concept of transport coordination is G. S. Peterson, "Transport Coordination: Meaning and Purpose," 38 *Journal of Political Economy* 660 (1930). A good general article on the subject is Lee J. Melton, Jr., "Transport Coordination and Regulatory Philosophy," 24 *Law and Contemporary Problems* 622 (1959).

The subject of highway promotional policy is treated extensively in Charles L. Dearing, *American Highway Policy* (Washington, D.C.: Brookings Institution, 1941). Promotional policy with respect to water transportation is critically discussed in Board of Investigation and Research, *Public Aids to Domestic Transportation*, 79th Cong., 1st Sess., House Doc. No. 159 (1944), pp. 393–413. Policy with respect to the addition of new transportation facilities is discussed at length in Federal Coordinator of Transportation, *Public Aids to Transportation*, Vol. I (Washington, D.C.: U.S. Government Printing Office, 1940), pp. 75–96. A critical consideration of promotional policy with respect to all modes of transportation may be found in Charles L. Dearing and Wilfred Owen, *National Transportation Policy* (Washington, D.C.: Brookings Institution, 1939), chaps. i–viii and xvi.

The literature on subsidy to transportation agencies is voluminous. The most authoritative treatment is in two reports on the subject by government agencies, namely, Federal Coordinator of Transporation, op. cit. (4 vols.; Washington, D.C.: U.S. Government Printing Office, 1938–40); and Board of Investigation and Research, op. cit. See also James C. Nelson, "Policy Issues and Economic Effects of Public Aids to Domestic Transport," 24 *Law and Contemporary Problems* 531 (1959).

On railroad control of water carriers under the Panama Canal Act, see

Philip F. Welsh, "The Right of Railroads to Engage in Water Transportation," 24 *I.C.C. Practitioners' Journal* 139 (1956). The most complete account of policy with respect to railroad control of motor carriers and motor-carrier operations is Carl H. Fulda, "Rail-Motor Competition: Motor-Carrier Operations by Railroads," 54 *Northwestern University Law Review* 156 (1959). For the Civil Aeronautics Board's interpretation of the provisions of the Civil Aeronautics Act relating to control of air-transport operations by surface carriers, see *American President Lines, Petition*, 7 CAB 799 (1947). In favor of permitting control of one mode of transport by another is George L. Buland and Frederick E. Furhman, "Integrated Ownership: The Case for Removing Restrictions on Common Ownership of the Several Forms of Transportation," 31 *George Washington Law Review* 156 (1962); and James E. Suelflow and Stanley J. Hille, "The Transportation Company: An Argument for Intermodal Ownership," *Land Economics*, August 1970, p. 275. Opposed to integrated ownership is Peter T. Beardsley, "Integrated Ownership of Transportation Companies and the Public Interest," 31 *George Washington Law Review* 85 (1962); and Carolyn C. Stitt, "Common Ownership of Rail and Motor Carriers: The Case against the Railroads," 48 *Texas Law Review* 460 (1970). The problem is discussed in Senate Committee on Commerce, *National Transportation Policy* (The Doyle Report), 87th Cong., 1st Sess., Senate Report No. 445 (1961), pp. 219–228.

Chapter 37

TRANSPORT COORDINATION

AND INTERAGENCY

COMPETITION—*CONTINUED*

In this chapter we shall consider further aspects of transport coordination, particularly controls that have been used to bring about a better coordinated transportation system. The controls which we must consider are (1) restriction of entry into the business of transporting persons or property for hire, (2) regulation of the rates of competing modes of transport, and (3) various measures designed to facilitate the establishment of coordinated transport services, that is, joint services involving two or more modes of transport.

RESTRICTION OF ENTRY

Certificates of public convenience and necessity (or "permits," in some cases) are required before anyone may engage in transportation by rail, highway, water, or air. Certificates of public convenience and necessity are not required for the construction of pipelines used for the transportation of crude oil or its products. Restriction of entry as a form of control was established chiefly for the purpose of controlling competition between different carriers of the same type rather than for the purpose of controlling competition between the different modes of transport. Railroads, however, were hopeful that the establishment of certificate requirements, particularly for highway carriers and water carriers, would operate to restrict to some extent the establishment of service by highway and by water which would be competitive with railroads. This hope explains why railroads were strong advocates of regulation of motor carriers and water carriers.

Restriction of Entry to Protect Railroads

Under state legislation, certificate provisions have sometimes been used to protect railroads from the establishment of competing motor-carrier services. State motor-carrier laws, and practices thereunder, however, have varied widely. In some states the statutes require that the effect of proposed motor-carrier operations on railroads must be considered before new motor-carrier services are authorized; in most states, consideration of the effect of the motor-carrier operations on other carriers is required, but without specific mention of railroads. The Federal Coordinator of Transportation pointed out in 1934 that in a few states the statutes specifically forbade consideration of the effect of motor-carrier operations on railroads.[1] The courts of some states have held that the regulatory authority must give consideration of existing rail services before authorizing motor-carrier operations.[2] The Michigan Supreme Court, however, has held that in the absence of any language in the statute which would require it, there should be no consideration of the effect of the proposed service upon railroad companies but that the commission should consider only its effect on other motor carriers.[3]

It is difficult to generalize regarding the proper policy to adopt on this question. Undoubtedly a commission should take into consideration the effect of proposed truck services upon rail carriers, and statutes should permit this to be done. Certainly, if the public cannot support two transportation systems, it must choose which one it will have, and in this situation the rail service is often preferred. On the other hand, some states have undoubtedly gone too far in protecting railroads from motor-vehicle competition.

There are two objections to the policy of denying certificates to motor carriers for the purpose of protecting the railroads. First, such a policy, if effective, deprives the public of a service that is often superior to and sometimes cheaper than rail service. The two classes of service are so different that the existence of seemingly adequate rail service does not always justify the denial of truck service. No artificial restrictions should be imposed that will prevent the development of a cheaper or better transportation service. The second difficulty with this policy of protecting rail carriers from highway carriers is that it is largely futile unless private transportation is also restricted. If common carriers and perhaps contract carriers are denied the right to operate, the shipper who has substantial and frequent shipments to make can perform his own transportation service. As long as the individual has the right to operate his own trucks on the highway, the highway will be used when truck transportation is cheaper or more convenient than rail transportation. The railway is competing with the highway, not simply with carriers for hire operating over the highway. Only the small shipper who cannot afford to do his own trucking is forced to patronize railways if certificates are denied to motor common carriers.

---

[1] Federal Coordinator of Transportation, *Regulation of Transportation Agencies,* 73d Cong., 2d Sess., Senate Doc. No. 152 (1934), p. 181.

[2] *Chris Vander Werf* v. *Board of Railroad Commissioners of South Dakota,* 237 N.W. 909 (1931); *Seaboard Air Line Ry. Co.* v. *Railroad Commission of Florida,* 100 Fla. 1027 (1930); *Application of Hvidston,* 48 N.W. 2d 26 (1951).

[3] *Rapid Ry. Co.* v. *Michigan Public Utilities Commission,* 225 Mich. 425 (1923).

The Motor Carrier Act does not specify that the effect of a proposed motor-carrier operation on competing railroads shall or shall not be considered in an application for a certificate. Of course, the Act requires a showing of public convenience and necessity, and obviously the existence of rail service may have a bearing on the matter. In a multitude of cases, however, the Commission has authorized motor-carrier service over the opposition of railroads that would be adversely affected.[4] What seems to be the prevailing view was expressed by the Commission in one case as follows: "We agree . . . that motor service has certain inherent transportation advantages not found in rail service, and that these advantages warrant a grant of authority even where certain amounts of traffic may be diverted from existing rail carriers."[5] This does not mean that an application for motor-carrier service will be granted merely upon a showing that only rail service exists. The Commission has refused to hold that as a matter of law an application must be granted in the absence of motor-carrier service.[6] Inadequacy of rail service or superiority of the proposed motor-carrier service must ordinarily be shown. Effect of proposed motor operations upon railroads has been a factor of greater or lesser importance in a number of cases in which applications have been denied.[7]

In one case the Commission seems to have gone too far in protecting railroads from motor transportation. The Commission had refused to grant a certificate to a motor carrier to transport granite between various points on the grounds that existing rail service was adequate. The Commission was reversed by the courts on the grounds that it had not adequately considered the "inherent advantages" of motor transport as required by the National Transportation Policy. Included among the advantages of motor transport in this case was the ability of the motor carrier to operate at a lower rate than was charged by the railroads.[8]

We conclude that the certificate requirements of the Motor Carrier Act have afforded the railroads some protection from the establishment of competing service by motor vehicle, but that the comparative ease with which advantages in motor-carrier service over rail can be shown has resulted in the authorization of motor-carrier service competitive with rail service on a very extensive scale. In general it may be said that the

---

[4] E.g., *Williams Motor Transfer, Inc., Extension—Granite*, 67 MCC 735 (1956); *Karl E. Momsen Extension—Joliet, Ill.*, 69 MCC 491 (1957); *Ligon Extension—Warrick County, Ind.*, 71 MCC 695 (1957); *Dallas & Mavis Forwarding Co., Extension—Lumber*, 76 MCC 245 (1958).

[5] *Carl Subler Trucking, Inc., Common Carrier Application*, 77 MCC 395, 397–98 (1958).

[6] *Hitchcock Common Carrier Application*, 54 MCC 16, 19 (1952); *International Transport, Inc., Extension—Tractors & Farm Machinery*, 66 MCC 241 (1955).

[7] *Hitchcock Common Carrier Application*, 54 MCC 16 (1952); *Wilson Extension—Dairy Products*, 61 MCC 51 (1952); *California Express, Inc., Extension—Wichita, Kans.*, 77 MCC 118 (1958).

[8] *Schaffer Transportation Co. v. United States*, 355 U.S. 83 (1957).

certificate requirements of the Motor Carrier Act have not resulted in suppression of motor transport in the interest of the railroads to any significant extent.

It may be noted that many, if not most, countries of the world that have developed a system of rail transport have imposed greater restrictions on motor transport than has the United States. In some countries the restrictions on highway transport to protect the railroads extend to restrictions on private transportation of goods by motor vehicle. New Zealand and most of the Australian states are good examples. Private transportation of goods by motor vehicle requires licensing in these countries, and often mileage limitations on private trucking force traffic to the rails. Countries following this policy are commonly countries in which the railroads are government owned, and in which traffic densities are light. Under these circumstances restriction of road haulage is defended on grounds of unused rail capacity and the burden of railway deficits on the taxpayer.

In granting certificates for water-carrier service, the Commission has shown even less inclination to protect railroads from competition than it has in the motor-carrier cases. In numerous cases the Commission has said that available rail service does not warrant a denial of an application for water-carrier authority.[9]

Protection of rail or other carriers from competition has even been sought in cases involving the grant of certificates of public convenience and necessity to air carriers. The Civil Aeronautics Board, when faced with the question of whether it should consider the effect on railroads of proposed air-transport operations, said: "It is our view that the Board is not required to consider ordinary competitive impact upon the railroads as a public interest factor. . . ."[10] However, it reserved judgment on whether it would consider it a factor in an extreme case.

Each mode of transport has certain advantages over others, and the public should not ordinarily be deprived of these benefits. Only when the development of the newer modes of transport threatens the existence of other needed transportation services, or when the diffusion of the traffic among too many transportation agencies would unduly increase the unit cost of all transportation services involved, does a policy of restricting one form of transport to protect another seem to be justified.

INTERAGENCY COMPETITION AND RATE REGULATION

We must now turn to a consideration of one of the most difficult problems which has faced regulatory bodies in recent years, namely, the ad-

---

[9] E.g., *Yankton Barge Line Common Carrier Application*, 265 ICC 271, 276 (1948); *Newtex S. S. Corp. Extension—Sulphur*, 285 ICC 260 (1953); *Yazoo Barge Line Common Carrier Application*, 305 ICC 17 (1958); *Coyle Lines, Extension—Chattahoochee & Flint Rivers*, 323 ICC 386 (1964).

[10] *New York–Florida Case*, 24 CAB 94, 119–20 (1956).

justment of rates between competing modes of transportation. A large proportion of the rate cases which have come before the Commission in recent years have involved this issue. The extent to which we shall attain a coordinated system of transportation, in the sense of each mode of transport performing the services for which it is best fitted, will depend in large measure on the policies developed by the Interstate Commerce Commission in cases of this type.

We will first consider a number of possible policies that might be observed in dealing with the adjustment of rates between different modes of transport, after which we will turn to a consideration of policies which have been worked out by the Interstate Commerce Commission.

Unrestricted Out-of-Pocket-Cost Rate Making

Under this policy, competing modes of transport would be permitted to reduce competitive rates to direct or variable costs.[11] The regulatory body would not interfere unless and until the rates were below the direct costs incurred. This policy would be little different than no regulation. In the absence of any control whatsoever, competing transportation agencies would tend to reduce rates to this basis. Direct or variable costs, rather than fully allocated costs, tend to control rate making under the stress of competition, since any traffic carried at a rate which covers direct costs and a little more leaves the carrier better off than if it allowed the traffic to go to another agency.

It may be argued with some persuasion that this is a sound policy, considering the economy as a whole, because if the traffic is carried by the agency with the lowest direct costs, it is carried with the least expenditure of resources, whereas sharing the traffic with carriers incurring a higher direct cost represents an unnecessary expenditure of resources. The argument is valid to a degree, but if the policy is considered with reference to its long-time results some qualification may be in order.

In the first place, unrestricted competitive rate making might threaten the viability of the railroad industry. If all traffic of the railroads were carried at direct or variable costs, total costs would not be covered and the carriers would be operating at a loss. Not all railroad traffic is competitive with other modes of transport, so there is little danger that all rates would be put on the basis of direct or variable costs, but if the competition facing the railroads is as all-pervasive as is sometimes claimed, and if competitive rates gravitated toward direct or variable costs, the position of the railroads might well become critical. This is particularly true since there are limits to the extent to which the remaining noncompetitive traffic could carry the burden of the fixed costs.

The conclusion seems warranted that it may be necessary at times to

---

[11] For many years the Commission used the term "out-of-pocket cost" in the sense of direct or variable costs. In recent years it has expressed preference for use of the term "variable cost" as more descriptive of what is meant. See p. 143 supra.

prevent competitive rates from falling to direct costs in order to maintain a viable transportation industry.

A second result of unrestricted competitive rate cutting appears when one mode of transport has lower direct costs than others. The mode with the lowest direct costs would be able to drive its competitors out of business. From a strictly economic point of view this may sometimes be desirable; in others it is not. If it eliminates high-cost carriers and reduces the total consumption of resources in providing a given transportation service, it can be said to be desirable, at least if we disregard effects of losing certain noncompetitive services of the high-cost carrier. On the other hand, if it eliminates carriers capable of performing the transportation service at lower unit costs, both direct and indirect costs included, the policy is more questionable. The public may well be dubious about a policy that destroys the transportation agency having the lowest total costs, particularly when it may give or restore a monopoly of the transportation service involved to the agency with the higher total costs.

"Umbrella" Rate Making

A highly objectionable rate policy that might be adopted is that of making rates sufficiently high to protect the high-cost agency. This is substantially the method of rate making which the carriers would undoubtedly adopt if they sought by agreement among themselves to prevent competition of the ruinous type. It is the pricing policy which is frequently adopted in cartelized industries.

The majority of cases in which the Commission had occasion to speak on this matter contain very positive statements against a policy of holding up rates of low-cost carriers to a level necessary to protect high-cost carriers. In a 1940 decision involving rates on petroleum and its products the Commission positively rejected the contention of motor carriers that the railroads should be required to maintain rates at a level which would enable the motor carriers, the high-cost carriers in this case, to remain in competition. The Commission said that such a policy "would be regulation in the interest of the high-cost agency rather than in the public interest."[12] The 1940 amendments to Section 15a, it will be recalled, modified the language which requires the Commission to consider "the effect of rates on the movement of traffic" by adding the phrase "by the carrier or carriers for which the rates are prescribed."[13] The Commission interpreted this phrase, and similar language in the rules of rate making for motor and water carriers, to mean that "no carrier should be required to maintain rates which would be unreasonable, judged by other standards, for the purpose of protecting the traffic of a competitor."[14] And in *New*

---

[12] *Petroleum and Petroleum Products, California to Arizona,* 241 ICC 21, 43 (1940).

[13] See p. 267, supra.

[14] *Seatrain Lines, Inc.* v. *Akron, Canton & Youngstown Ry. Co.,* 243 ICC 199, 214 (1940).

Automobiles in Interstate Commerce, a frequently cited case, the Commission said: ". . . there appears no warrant for believing that rail rates, for example, should be held up to a particular level to preserve a motor-rate structure, or vice versa."[15]

A policy of "umbrella" rate making would not only be inconsistent with the revised rules of rate making in the Interstate Commerce Act; it would also be inconsistent with the national transportation policy, which requires that the "inherent advantages" of each mode of transport be recognized in regulating the various types of carriers subject to the Act.

Notwithstanding the pronouncements of the Commission against "umbrella" rate making, it has sometimes been assailed for having engaged in the practice. Opinion on this point depends in part on one's definition of "umbrella" rate making. We have used the term in the sense of requiring a carrier to maintain rates higher than would otherwise be deemed reasonable with the object of protecting a high-cost carrier. By this definition, most of the Commission's decisions are in conformity with its pronouncements. If "umbrella" rate making is deemed to include any interference with rate cutting above the out-of-pocket-cost level in order to prevent elimination of competition, then it would have to be said that the Commission had indulged in the practice. The policy which we wish to condemn is a policy of requiring a carrier to maintain rates at a higher level than would ordinarily be deemed reasonable, with the object of protecting high-cost carriers.

Rates Based on Fully Allocated Costs

This policy would require each mode of transport to base rates on its own fully allocated costs. This would be the only sound policy if all costs were direct or variable. Under such circumstances, to permit any transportation agency to charge less than cost would be of no benefit to the carriers concerned and would represent a social loss. Since each mode of transport has some fixed or overhead costs, however, a policy of requiring each mode of transport to adhere to rates based on its fully allocated costs would deny carriers the right to increase the utilization of their plants by differential charging. The practice of charging rates where necessary that are less than fully allocated cost, but higher than direct or variable costs, and thus inducing a more complete utilization of plant, has been recognized elsewhere in this volume as a sound policy.[16] Requiring carriers to charge no less than fully allocated cost would thus seem to be too harsh a policy.

Direct Costs plus a Uniform Increment

This basis of adjustment would require each mode of transport to fix particular rates on the basis of its direct costs plus a fixed increment, pre-

---

[15] 259 ICC 475, 538 (1945).

[16] See Chapter 7.

sumably on a ton-mile basis.[17] There are two advantages to this solution
of the problem. First, it would insure that the traffic would move by the
agency with the lowest direct costs, except where some service advantage
led shippers to use the other mode of transport. This method of rate making would automatically allocate the traffic to the agency that could transport it with the smallest consumption of resources. A second advantage
of this policy is that it overcomes the chief objection to pricing on the
basis of out-of-pocket costs by making some provision for covering fixed
costs.

In spite of these advantages, this method of adjusting rates is open to
serious objections. It precludes any competition between the different
modes of transport. The high-cost carrier is completely excluded from the
market unless service advantages give it some of the traffic. The scheme is
therefore completely at variance with the spirit and intent of the revised
Section 15a of the Act. Another weakness in this solution of the rate
problem is that determination of the "fixed" amount to be added to direct
or out-of-pocket costs is arbitrary, like any apportionment of fixed costs
on the basis of averages.

Full Costs of Low-Cost Mode with Right of Others to Compete

This policy is to base rates on the fully allocated cost of transportation
by the low-cost agency but to permit the high-cost carriers, if they so
desired, to meet the rates of the low-cost carrier so long as their own
direct costs were covered. This policy not only assures the public of rates
based on the low-cost transportation agency, but it assures the public of
competitive services that some other policies would deny; it also benefits
the high-cost carriers by enabling them to utilize their plants more fully;
and it may conserve resources, since it may be more economical to permit
the high-cost carrier to carry some of the competitive traffic at out-of-
pocket-cost rates than to expand the facilities of the low-cost carrier
sufficiently to carry all the traffic.

There are two difficulties with the policy which we have just described.
The first is that unless the low-cost carrier is utilizing its facilities to capacity, a certain amount of economic waste is encouraged. Economic
waste is involved if the high-cost carrier is allowed to share in traffic that
could be handled at a lower direct cost by the low-cost agency. This,
however, may not be a serious matter; the economic waste involved may
be a low price to pay for the benefits of competition, not unlike the situation, almost universally accepted, in which two or more railroads share
competitive traffic, although none of them may be utilized to full capacity.

A second and more serious difficulty with this policy arises from the

---

[17] This method of adjusting rates has been advocated for Great Britain. See J. R.
Sargent, *British Transport Policy* (Oxford: Clarendon Press, 1958), chap. iv.

fact that some rates of the low-cost carrier may quite properly be either higher or lower than fully allocated costs. Some may be lower than fully allocated costs because they have to be if the traffic is to move, yet the low rates make some contribution to fixed and overhead costs. Some rates may be higher than fully allocated costs, though lower than they would have to be if no low-rated traffic were carried to contribute a portion of the fixed and overhead costs. When the low-cost transportation agency, therefore, has set up a system of discriminating rates, as the principal transportation agencies do, it is not feasible or sound to require the low-cost agency to put all of its rates on the basis of fully allocated costs.

Normal Rates of Low-Cost Mode—Right of Others to Compete

This is a modification of the policy described above and is designed to get around the second difficulty which we mentioned. This policy would be to start with a normal rate structure on the part of the agency normally charging the lower rates, whether it be railroad, water carrier, or motor carrier, and then to allow the disadvantaged carriers to meet these rates, provided their own out-of-pocket costs are covered.

Policy of the Commission before 1958

Basically, the policy of the Commission in the cases that came before it involving competitive rate reductions before the amendment of the Act in 1958 was to recognize the low-cost carrier as the rate-making line and to permit other carriers to meet the competition provided the rates proposed covered out-of-pocket costs and something more. The Commission, however, often added another requirement in approving rate reductions. This was that the reduced rates be no lower than necessary to meet the competition encountered.

Whatever the merits of this requirement, and there are some, it laid the Commission open to the charge that it was determining the "fair share" of traffic that each mode should have in a particular situation, and that it was "allocating traffic." Also, the railroads felt that the Commission's policy was preventing them from exploiting their advantage of low direct costs and that the water and motor carriers were the recipients of unwarranted protection at the hands of the Commission. As a result, the railroads staged a prolonged campaign for greater freedom in rate making. In this they were joined by the Executive branch of the government.

In 1955 a bill was introduced in Congress and strongly supported by the railroads which provided that in determining whether a rate is unreasonably low the Commission "shall not consider the effect of such charge on the traffic of any other mode of transportation; or the relation of such charge to the charge of any other mode of transportation; or whether such charge is lower than necessary to meet the competition of any other mode of transportation. . . ." These proposed provisions came to be known as "the three shall-nots." This bill died in committee. It was considered too drastic, although the Senate committee considering the bill was of the view that the Commission had not given the railroads sufficient latitude in adjusting rates to meet the competition of other modes of transport.

The amendments to the Interstate Commerce Act enacted in 1958 contain the provision that "Rates of a carrier shall not be held up to a particular level to protect the traffic of any other mode of transportation," but adds the clause, "giving due consideration to the objectives of the national transportation policy declared in this Act."[18] Reference to the National Transportation Policy, with its mention of "sound economic conditions . . . among the several carriers," "unfair or destructive competitive practices," recognition and preservation of the "inherent advantages" of each mode of transport, and a transportation system "adequate to meet the needs of the commerce of the United States, of the Postal Service, and of the national defense" opened the door to serious qualification of or exceptions to the first part of the section. The amended Section 15a was a compromise that by reason of its ambiguity enabled the railroads, on the one hand, and water carriers and motor carriers, on the other, to read into the provisions about what they wished. Obviously, judicial interpretation of the Act would be required before its real significance could be determined. Even within the Commission itself there was some belief that the law had not been essentially changed by the enactment of Section 15a (3).

The New Haven Case

Enactment of Section 15a (3) in 1958 appears to have had no immediate effect on Commission decisions relating to intermodal rate competition.[19] The Commission's policy and the meaning of the 1958 amendment to Section 15a were to come before the courts as a result of a Commission decision in 1960. In *Commodities—Pan-Atlantic Steamship Corporation*,[20] the Commission required rail trailer-on-flatcar (TOFC) rates on selected commodities from the East to certain Texas points to be at least six percent higher than the rates of the so-called "Sea-Land" service (trailers on ships) and on "Seatrain" service (railroad cars on ships) maintained by certain coastwise water lines. The proposed rail TOFC rates found unlawful were on a substantial parity with the Sea-Land and Seatrain rates. They were, with minor exceptions, above the out-of-pocket costs of the rail lines, and many of them above fully distributed costs. The Commission's order requiring the rail TOFC rates to be at least six percent above

---

[18] See p. 273, supra.

[19] See Robert W. Harbeson, "The Regulation of Interagency Rate Competition under the Transportation Act of 1958," 30 *I.C.C. Practitioners' Journal* 287 (1962).

[20] 313 ICC 23 (1960).

the water rates was enjoined by a federal court which held that the Commission had not observed the provisions of Section 15a (3) in requiring a rate differential to protect the water lines.[21] This decision was affirmed by the Supreme Court in *Interstate Commerce Commission* v. *New York, New Haven & Hartford Railroad Co.*[22]

The Commission, in requiring the rail TOFC rates to be at a level above the Sea-Land and Seatrain rates, had invoked the provision of Section 15a (3) which requires that the section should be administered with due regard to the objectives of the National Transportation Policy, noting particularly its duty to prevent "unfair or destructive competitive practices." The Commission considered that the proposed reduction in rail rates, by threatening the destruction of the coastwise water-carrier industry, would constitute an "unfair or destructive competitive practice." The Supreme Court, however, in interpreting Section 15a (3) said: "If there is one fact that stands out in bold relief in the legislative history of [Section] 15a (3), it is that Congress did not regard the setting of a rate at a particular level as constituting an unfair or destructive competitive practice *simply* because that rate would divert some or all of the traffic from a competing mode."[23]

The Commission, in the Pan-Atlantic Case, had also justified disapproval of the proposed rail rates and the threatened demise of the coastwise shipping industry by citing the phrase in the National Transportation Policy which refers to the maintenance of a national transportation system adequate to meet "the needs of the commerce of the United States" and "the national defense." The Supreme Court held that the Commission's reliance on these factors was not supported by adequate findings or substantial evidence. To justify resort to this language in the National Transportation Policy, the court said, ". . . we believe it must be demonstrated that the proposed rates in themselves genuinely threaten the continued existence of a transportation service that is uniquely capable of filling a transcendent national defense or other public need."[24]

The Ingot Molds Case

The Supreme Court decision in the New Haven Case in 1963 seemed to grant the railroads nearly, but not quite, the freedom in rate making which they had sought in urging Congress to enact "the three shall-nots" previously mentioned. Another Supreme Court decision in 1968 further interpreted Section 15a (3), enacted in 1958, and definitely upheld the right of the Commission to interfere with railroad rate cutting in order to protect a low-cost carrier, a right implied in the New Haven Case. In a case

---

[21] *New York, New Haven & Hartford Railroad Co.* v. *United States*, 199 F. Supp. 635 (1961).

[22] 372 U.S. 744 (1963).

[23] Ibid., p. 759.

[24] Ibid., p. 762.

involving ingot molds the Commission had found that a reduced rate published by the Pennsylvania and the Louisville & Nashville railroads from Neville Island and Pittsburgh, Pa., to Steelton, Ky., was unlawful. The rate had been reduced from $11.86 to $5.11 per ton to meet the competition of a barge-truck rate of $5.11. The fully distributed cost to the railroads was $7.59 per ton, but the out-of-pocket cost was $4.69. Thus the new rate exceeded the railroad out-of-pocket cost, but it was admittedly below the barge-truck fully distributed cost of $5.19. The barge-truck interests contended that they were the low-cost carrier and that the reduced rail rates deprived them of their "inherent advantage." The Commission, following its customary practice, measured "inherent advantage" by fully distributed costs, against the railroad contention that inherent advantage should be measured by direct or out-of-pocket costs which would make the railroads the low-cost mode. The reduced rail rate was condemned because it deprived the barge-truck interests of their low-cost advantage since it would have forced them to charge a rate below their full cost in order to compete with the railroads.[25] A federal district court set aside the Commission's order,[26] but the Supreme Court reversed the lower court and upheld the Commission in *American Commercial Lines v. Louisville & Nashville Railroad Co.,*[27] commonly called the Ingot Molds Case.

In upholding the Commission's practice of measuring "inherent advantage" by fully distributed costs rather than by "out-of-pocket" costs, the Court did not say that inherent advantage *must* be measured by fully distributed costs, but merely that the Commission had the right to determine what measure should be used. The Court's pronouncement would seem to give the Commission the right to use "out-of-pocket" cost, fully distributed cost, or some other measure of cost in an appropriate proceeding. However, in rejecting the railroad contention that Section 15a (3) of the Act *required* the use of out-of-pocket costs, the Court said that such an interpretation would be inconsistent with the purpose of Section 15a (3) and the intent of Congress. Such an interpretation would give the railroads virtually what they had asked in the proposed "three shall-nots" which Congress had rejected. It appears unlikely, therefore, that the railroads will get unlimited right to out-of-pocket-cost rate making as long as Section 15a (3) remains in its present form.

Present Control over Competitive Rate Cutting

We are now in a position to summarize the extent to which competitive rate cutting between the different modes of transport can be controlled by regulatory action.

---

[25] *Ingot Molds from Pa. to Steelton, Ky.,* 326 ICC 77 (1965).

[26] *Louisville & Nashville R. Co.* v. *United States,* 268 F. Supp. 71 (1967).

[27] 392 U.S. 571 (1968).

If we put the matter negatively, we can say that the power of the Commission to interfere with competitive rate making is limited, and that, contrary to its practice before the amendment of Section 15a in 1958, the Commission may not now prevent a competitive rate reduction on the grounds that the rate is lower than necessary to meet competition.[28]

If we state positively the extent to which the Commission may and does interfere with competitive reductions in rates, we find the following principles.

1. Proposed reductions in rates will be disapproved if they are below the out-of-pocket costs of the proponent. The power of the Commission to do this was unaffected by the amendment of Section 15a in 1958, and the Commission has continued to disapprove rates which were below out-of-pocket costs.[29] Occasionally the Commission has approved rates that would appear to have been below out-of-pocket costs, if the costs were calculated by the usual methods. In some instances, special consideration was given to the back-haul characteristics of the movement in question which justified not charging the back-haul traffic with the full cost of hauling; in others, it was deemed appropriate to exclude any part of return on investment and an allowance for federal income taxes from the calculation of out-of-pocket costs. This is more in line with economic theory, in the short run, than the cost-accounting formula which had usually been used by the Commission.[30]

2. A low-cost carrier is entitled to protection from rate cutting by a high-cost carrier. This is because the Act requires recognition of the "inherent advantages" of each mode. The low-cost carrier is entitled to protection, however, only (a) if the rates of the high-cost carrier are below its own fully allocated costs, and (b) if they would force the low-cost carrier to charge an unprofitable rate.[31] Both of these conditions must be met before protection is forthcoming. The Commission has frequently refused to interfere with rate reductions to protect the low-cost carrier when the proposed rates covered the fully distributed costs of the proponent.[32] It has also refused to inter-

---

[28] There may be an exception to this if rates lower than necessary to meet competition in a particular situation create undue preference and prejudice in violation of Section 3 of the Act.

[29] *Cast Iron Boilers, Boyertown, Pa., to Points in Texas,* 319 ICC 319 (1963).

[30] *Carbon Blacks, Southwest to Indiana, Ohio, & Missouri,* 325 ICC 138 (1965); *Animal Feed from Kansas City, Mo., to Chicago,* 325 ICC 147 (1965); *Coal from Southern Mines to Tampa & Sutton, Fla.,* 318 ICC 371 (1962); *Baltimore & Ohio R. Co. v. Chicago & Eastern Illinois R. Co.,* 322 ICC 572 (1964).

[31] An example is *Grain from Idaho, Oregon & Washington to Ports in Oregon & Washington,* 319 ICC 534 (1963).

[32] *Aluminum Articles from Sandow, Tex., to Pennsylvania & New York,* 319 ICC 431, 439 (1963); *Agricultural Insecticides—Heyden, N.J. to Houston, Texas,* 319 ICC 493 (1963).

fere with rate reductions when they could be met by the low-cost carrier without forcing it to charge an unprofitable rate.[33]

3. In determining which carrier is the low-cost carrier and hence entitled to protection from rate cutting, the Commission normally uses fully distributed cost as the appropriate measure.[34] In this the Commission was upheld in the Ingot Molds case as previously noted.

The Commission apparently feels that it has no obligation to extend protection from out-of-pocket-cost rate making to unregulated carriers even though they might be the low-cost carriers in a particular situation.[35] This is because such carriers are not subject to the provisions of the Interstate Commerce Act.

4. When protesting a rate reduction and demanding protection as the low-cost carrier, the carrier must show its cost or otherwise establish that it is, in fact, the low-cost carrier. If it does not do so, no protection is extended to it.[36]

5. In determining which is the low-cost carrier in cases of intermodal competition, the matter of "public costs" has arisen, particularly if the carrier alleged to be the low-cost one is a carrier by water. From a strictly economic standpoint, the "public costs," that is, those defrayed by the taxpayer in the provision and maintenance of navigable waterways, should be included in costs. They are a part of the "cost" of water transportation. Division 2 of the Commission, in one case, held that the "public costs" should be considered in determining which mode of transport was cheaper and therefore entitled to invoke the protection of its "inherent advantages." This contention was overruled by the full Commission, however, largely on the grounds that to include "public costs" would neutralize the efforts of Congress to develop water transportation by the improvement of waterways at government expense.[37]

6. The Commission may reject a proposed rate reduction on the grounds that it will leave the carrier worse off than before. This may happen when the amount of traffic to be gained by the rate reduction is small relative to the competitive traffic already being carried at the higher rate. A United States District Court upheld the Commission when it

---

[33] E.g., *Plastics from Texas to the East*, 319 ICC 379 (1963); *Export Grain & Grain Products—WTL to Gulf & Lake Ports*, 321 ICC 88 (1963).

[34] See *Grain from Idaho, Oregon, and Washington to Ports in Oregon & Washington*, 319 ICC 534, 560 (1963).

[35] *Grain in Multiple-Car Shipments—River Crossings to South*, 321 ICC 582, 589 (1963); 325 ICC 752, 772 (1965).

[36] See *Steel Bars from Lemont, Ill. to Iowa, Kansas, Missouri, Minnesota, & Nebraska*, 319 ICC 292, 303 (1963); *Cement within Southern Territory & from Hagerstown to South*, 319 ICC 465, 480 (1963). See also *Interstate Commerce Commission v. New York, New Haven & Hartford Railroad Co.*, 372 U.S. 744 (1963), p. 760, note 12.

[37] *Grain in Multiple-Car Shipments—River Crossings to the South*, 321 ICC 582 (1963). The prior report by Division 2 is reported in 318 ICC 641 (1963).

acted on this principle in refusing to approve reduced rates on phosphate rock where it appeared that the lower rates would result in a reduction in net revenues.[38] This principle was followed in a later case.[39] The power of the Commission to do this rests on its obligation under Section 15a and under the National Transportation Policy to see that the carriers obtain adequate revenues.

7. Lastly, the Commission may prevent a rate reduction that genuinely threatens to destroy a transportation system or service definitely shown to be required in the interests of national defense or the needs of commerce. This, it will be recalled, was one of the considerations which led the Commission, in the Pan-Atlantic Case, to protect the coastwise shipping industry. The Supreme Court, in the New Haven Case, found that there was not sufficient evidence to support that position. It is important to note, however, that the power of the Commission to hold up rates for this purpose was recognized by the Supreme Court, provided that the service was "uniquely capable of filling a transcendent national defense or other public need."

COORDINATED SERVICE

If the public is to enjoy the full benefits of a coordinated transport service, there must be an opportunity for the interchange of traffic between different modes of transport without the imposition of unnecessary obstacles. Various aspects of this problem require attention.

Establishment of Facilities for Interchange of Traffic

Rail carriers have sometimes refused to establish the necessary physical facilities for interchange of traffic with other agencies of transportation, particularly with water carriers. By this means railroads have sought to keep traffic on the rails which might otherwise have moved partly by water. This practice inconveniences the public and also interferes with the normal development of water transportation. A provision in the Panama Canal Act of 1912 empowered the Interstate Commerce Commission to require the establishment of a physical connection between rail and water carriers.[40] The rail carrier, or the water carrier, or both, may be required to construct tracks between the docks of water carriers and the lines of rail carriers.[41]

---

[38] *Atlantic Coast Line R. Co.* v. *United States,* 209 F. Supp. 157 (1962).

[39] *Tractors—T.L. & W.T.L. Territories to S.W. & W.T.L. Territories,* 319 ICC 758 (1963).

[40] Now Paragraph 11 (a) of Section 6 of the Interstate Commerce Act.

[41] See *City of St. Paul* v. *Chicago, Milwaukee, St. Paul & Pacific R. R. Co.,* 160 ICC 227 (1929).

Through Routes and Joint Rates

It is not uncommon for carriers of one type to refuse to establish through routes and joint rates with carriers of another type. By a "through route" we mean an arrangement between connecting carriers for the continuous carriage of goods on a single billing from a point on the lines of one carrier to a point on another. By a "joint rate" we mean a single rate from point of origin to destination rather than a combination of the rates of the separate carriers. Through routes may exist without joint rates, but the two commonly go together. Failure of carriers to establish through routes with carriers of another type deprives the public of the advantage of a coordinated transport service involving two or more modes of transport, and it may also restrict and hamper the development of one agency of transport.

The Interstate Commerce Act gives the Interstate Commerce Commission authority to require the establishment of through routes and joint rates involving railroads and water carriers. Dissatisfaction with the progress made in the establishment of joint rail-water rates with barge lines under the provisions of the Interstate Commerce Act led Congress, in 1928, to enact the Denison Act, which practically forced the railroads to establish through routes and joint rates with barge lines on the Mississippi River and its tributaries. In numerous proceedings under the Denison Act an extensive system of joint rail-barge routes and rates was established.[42] The Denison Act was repealed by the Transportation Act of 1940, but it had served its purpose by bringing about the establishment of through rail-barge routes and rates.

The Interstate Commerce Commission has no authority to require the establishment of through routes and joint rates involving railroads and motor carriers, or motor and water carriers. Through routes and joint rates, however, may be established voluntarily by such carriers. Some truck-water through routes and joint rates are in effect. Railroads have often been unwilling to establish through routes and joint rates with motor carriers, except in connection with certain trailer-on-flat-car operations. At one time the railroads which are members of the Association of American Railroads had an agreement not to establish through routes and joint rates with motor carriers. This agreement was attacked by the Department of Justice as a violation of the Sherman Antitrust Act.[43] As a result of this action a "consent decree" was entered by the court, which

---

[42] E.g., *Through Routes & Joint Rates*, 156 ICC 724 (1929); *Application of American Barge Line Co.*, 167 ICC 41 (1930), 182 ICC 521 (1932); *Inland Waterways Corp.* v. *Alabama Great Southern R. Co.*, 151 ICC 126 (1929); *Application of Mississippi Valley Barge Line*, 167 ICC 41 (1930), 178 ICC 224 (1931). The joint rail-barge rates were reexamined by the Commission in *Rail & Barge Joint Rates*, 270 ICC 591 (1948), and revised rail-barge differentials were prescribed. This decision was upheld by the Supreme Court in *Alabama Great Southern R. Co.* v. *United States*, 340 U.S. 216 (1951).

[43] 64 *Traffic World* 1034 (1939).

was agreed to by the Association and the railroads involved, breaking up the agreement and enjoining similar action in the future.[44]

The establishment of coordinated service involving two or more modes of transport, as well as a more natural development of motor transportation, might occur if the Commission were empowered to require the establishment of through routes and joint rates involving all modes of transportation subject to its jurisdiction when such through routes and joint rates were shown to be required in the public interest.

The Federal Aviation Act authorizes, but does not require, air carriers to establish through routes and joint rates with other common carriers. Some joint air-truck rates have been established, as well as other air-truck arrangements for providing a coordinated air-truck service.[45] When through routes and joint rates are established between airlines and modes of transport subject to the jurisdiction of the Interstate Commerce Commission, controversies over these rates may be referred to a joint board consisting of an equal number of members of the Interstate Commerce Commission and of the Civil Aeronautics Board. This joint board is empowered to take such action as the Civil Aeronautics Board might exercise over joint rates between air carriers.

Discrimination against Connecting Carriers

Carriers sometimes discriminate against connecting carriers of another type in the interchange of traffic or in the establishment of rates. Railroads have been inclined to resort to this practice in order to keep traffic on the rails and prevent its conveyance by water or motor carriers.

Paragraph 4 of Section 3 of the Interstate Commerce Act contains provisions which are aimed at discrimination of this sort. The paragraph provides that railroads shall "afford all reasonable, proper, and equal facilities for the interchange of traffic between their respective lines and connecting lines, and for the receiving, forwarding, and delivery of passengers and property to and from connecting lines; and shall not discriminate in their rates, fares and charges between connecting lines. . . ." The paragraph defines "connecting lines" to include any common carrier by water subject to Part III. An obligation similar to that placed on railroads by Section 3 (4) is placed upon water carriers by Section 305 (d) of the Act.

Section 3 (4) of the Act received application in a case involving reshipping rates on grain from Chicago to eastern points. In *Interstate Com-*

---

[44] 68 *Traffic World* 229 (1941).

[45] See Whitney Gilliland, "CAB Coordination of Unlike Modes of Transportation," *Public Utilities Fortnightly*, Sept. 2, 1965, pp. 23–24; and "Administration of the Federal Aviation Act with Respect to Coordination of Unlike Modes of Transportation." Panel discussion remarks at Fifth Workshop Conference on Coordinated Transportation at The American University (1966).

merce Commission v. *Mechling*[46] an order of the Commission authorizing
higher rail rates on ex-barge grain from Chicago to the East than on ex-rail
or ex-lake grain was set aside by the Supreme Court as contrary to Section
3 (4) of the Act. Ex-barge grain was grain which was brought into
Chicago by barge over the Illinois waterways. Ex-rail grain came into
Chicago by rail; ex-lake grain, by lake steamers. The higher out-bound
rates authorized on ex-barge grain would have discriminated against the
barge lines which bring grain into Chicago and preferred rail lines and
lake carriers performing the same function.

The Supreme Court has adhered to the doctrine of the Mechling case
under somewhat different circumstances.[47] Following the precedent of
these cases, a lower federal court set aside an order of the Commission
which had permitted the railroads to charge higher rates on ex-barge grain
from Tennessee River ports to southeastern points than applied on ex-rail
grain from the same ports. This practice of the rail carriers discriminated
against grain brought to the river ports from the Middle West by barge
in favor of grain brought in by rail. The Court said: "We construe the
Supreme Court decisions in Mechling and Dixie as making unlawful any
rate-making device which deprives barge transportation of its rightful
place in the National transportation system or which deprives shippers of
any part of the economies resulting from the use of barge transportation."[48]

Techniques of Traffic Interchange

Transfer of freight from one mode of transport to another usually involves handling costs and delay. Efforts have been made to reduce such
costs and delays by improved techniques. The use of car floats or ferries to
transport loaded freight cars across rivers, harbors, or lakes has long been a
feature of transportation in the United States which makes possible the
utilization of water transport without unloading freight from freight cars.
The use of steamships on which loaded railroad cars are transported has
long been a novel feature of Seatrain Lines which operates in coastwise
service and formerly carried freight in this manner between United States
ports and Cuba.

In recent years the practice of transporting loaded truck trailers or
semitrailers on flatcars has developed on an extensive scale. Trailer-on-
flatcar service (TOFC), commonly known as "piggy-back" service,
makes possible a coordinated railroad and highway service with a minimum of freight handling.

---

[46] *Interstate Commerce Commission* v. *Mechling*, 330 U.S. 567 (1947).

[47] *Dixie Carriers* v. *United States*, 351 U.S. 56 (1956).

[48] *Arrow Transportation Co.* v. *United States*, 176 Fed. Supp. 411, 421 (1959);
affirmed *per curiam* in 361 U.S. 353 (1960).

At the present time, trailer-on-flatcar service is provided under five basic plans, commonly referred to as "Plan I," "Plan II," etc.

Under Plan I the railroad transports the loaded trailers or semitrailers of motor carriers. Shipments move on a motor-carrier bill of lading and are charged motor-carrier rates. The railroad receives either a "division" of the rates or makes a flat charge per trailer.

Under Plan II the freight moves on railroad billing at railroad rates in trailers furnished by the railroad. The service includes picking up the loaded trailer at point of shipment and delivering it to the consignee's place of business at destination.[49]

Plan III provides for TOFC service to shippers or freight forwarders using their own trailers. In this case, trailers are moved to and from the railroad by the shipper or forwarder. Rates may depend upon the commodity transported or may be a flat charge per trailer. In 1964 the Commission ruled that rail TOFC service should be made available to for-hire motor and water carriers as well as to private shippers.[50]

Plan IV is like Plan III except that the flatcar, as well as the trailer, is furnished by the shipper. The railroad makes a charge for the movement of the flatcar and trailer, loaded or empty.

Plan V, which has more recently developed, provides for the movement of commodities in TOFC service on joint rail-truck rates. Either the motor carrier or the railroad may solicit and accept freight and issue bills of lading therefor under this plan. In effect, this extends the territory of each carrier into that served by the other.

There are numerous variations in the details of the above plans, and some railroads operate under two or more plans. Plan II, which is a completely railroad-provided service, has been the plan most widely used.

Trailer-on-flatcar service has suffered from lack of standardization of flatcars and of tie-down methods, and also from lack of general rules governing the interchange of trailers. The Interstate Commerce Commission has exercised no compulsion to extend this type of service.

It should be noted at this point that the movement of loaded highway trailers is also performed quite extensively by water carriers.

Containerization

In TOFC service, and in the "roll-on, roll-off" type of ship operation, trailers are being used as shipping containers. Other containers are being developed which have advantages over the trailer or semitrailer as a container and which can be used by all modes of transport. This development is in an experimental stage, but it holds out considerable promise for more effective coordinated transport service. The Interstate Commerce

---

[49] Under a variation of Plan II, known as Plan II½, shippers and consignees move the trailers to or from the railroad.

[50] Ex Parte No. 230, *Substituted Service—Piggy-Back*, 332 ICC 301.

Commission has asserted that all forms of transportation "should adopt a uniform container size which would be interchangeable for carrier use on land by rail and truck lines, on water by inland barge and oceangoing ship operators, and in the air by freight-lifting cargo planes."[51]

Freight Forwarders and Transport Coordination

Freight forwarders often provide the shipper with a coordinated transport service under a single billing. Freight forwarders have existed for many years. They accept small shipments, consolidate them into larger lots, and ship them by railroad or other mode of transport, deriving their income from the difference between the rates charged the shipper and the rates charged for the movement of the larger shipments by the carriers that they utilize. Although freight forwarders are generally associated with a particular mode of transport—railroads, motor carriers, or air carriers—they can be an instrumentality for sending a shipment by the mode or combination of modes that is most appropriate under the circumstances. The Civil Aeronautics Board has authorized certain surface carriers to engage in air freight forwarding,[52] and the Interstate Commerce Commission has authorized air freight forwarders to utilize the services of motor carriers in serving points not on air routes.[53] Both of these actions promote an intermodal transportation service that should be advantageous to the shipping public.

TRANSPORT COORDINATION—AN OVERALL LOOK

In the preceding chapter we defined transport coordination as the fitting of each mode of transport into its proper place in the transportation system. In that chapter and this one we have examined some special aspects of the problem in detail. We may note that transport coordination involves a more rational approach to the promotion of those transport facilities that are provided by government. It also involves the removal of subsidies to transport in so far as that can be done without interfering with broad social, political, and economic ends which require financial support from the government. Transport coordination requires regulatory action to prevent one mode of transport from stifling or unduly interfering with the development of other modes of transport. At the same time, it requires prevention of unnecessary and wasteful duplication of facilities that would increase the total cost of transportation services. Coordination requires the maintenance of some degree of competition between different modes of transport and between carriers of a particular mode in order to provide the spur for improved service and facilities and help determine the proper

---

[51] *Annual Report, 1959,* p. 71.

[52] *Motor Carrier-Air Freight Forwarder Investigation,* 69-4-100.

[53] *Emery Air Freight Corp., Forwarder Application,* 339 ICC 17 (1971).

place of each mode in the transport system. At the same time, competition must be controlled lest it lead to unfair tactics that will result in monopoly or destroy needed transport facilities. Lastly, transport coordination requires the establishment of joint facilities and services involving the different modes of transport, with close watch by the government to prevent discrimination by one mode of transport against another.

SELECTED REFERENCES

The literature on the adjustment of rates between competing modes of transport is extensive. Only a limited number of referencs can be given here. We include the following: Merrill J. Roberts, "The Regulation of Transport Price Competition," 24 *Law & Contemporary Problems* 557 (1959); Lee J. Melton, "Transport Coordination and Regulatory Philosophy," 24 *Law & Contemporary Problems* 622 (1959); Wm. J. Baumol et al., "The Role of Cost in the Minimum Pricing of Railroad Services," 35 *Journal of Business of the University of Chicago* 357 (1962) and 36 ibid. 348 (1963). The subject is discussed in Senate Committee on Commerce, *National Transportation Policy* (The Doyle Report), 87th Cong., 1st Sess., Senate Report No. 445 (1961), part vi. The problem with special reference to Interstate Commerce Commission policies is treated in numerous places, especially Ernest W. Williams, Jr., *The Regulation of Rail-Motor Rate Competition* (New York: Harper, 1958); Jervis Langdon, Jr., "The Regulation of Competitive Business Forces: The Obstacle Race in Transportation," 41 *Cornell Law Quarterly* 57 (1955); Robert W. Harbeson, "The Regulation of Interagency Rate Competition under the Transportation Act of 1958," 30 *I.C.C. Practitioners' Journal* 287 (1962); Henry J. Friendly, *The Federal Administrative Agencies* (Cambridge: Harvard University Press, 1962), chap. vi; and Nathaniel L. Nathanson, "Administration Proposals for Revision of Our National Transportation Policy— Herein of Intermodal Competition and the Minimum Rate Power," 58 *Northwestern Law Review* 583 (1963) and 59 ibid. 1 (1964); Joseph R. Rose, "Regulation of Rates and Intermodal Transport Competition," 33 *I.C.C. Practitioners' Journal* 11 (1965); B. J. McCarney, "ICC Rate Regulation and Rail-Motor Carrier Pricing Behavior: A Reappraisal," 35 *I.C.C. Practitioners' Journal* 707 (1968); Robert W. Harbeson, "The Supreme Court and Intermodal Rate Competition," 35 *I.C.C. Practitioners' Journal* 1487 (1969); J. J. Coyle, "The Ingot Molds Case and Competitive Ratemaking," 36 *I.C.C. Practitioners' Journal* 1654 (1969).

On trailer-on-flatcar service, see Harold L. Johnson, *Piggyback Transportation—An Economic Analysis,* Georgia State College of Business Administration, Studies in Industry and Economics, Bulletin No. 1 (Atlanta, 1956); Interstate Commerce Commission, *Annual Report, 1959,* pp. 69–71. For a discussion of some legal questions involved, see *Movement of Highway Trailers by Rail,* 293 ICC 93 (1954), and *Substituted Service—Piggy-Back,* 322 ICC 301 (1964).

A comprehensive study of legal and policy aspects of transport coordination, particularly coordinated service, is Samuel P. Delisi, "Coordinated Freight Transportation Service: Legal and Regulatory Aspects," 34 *ICC Practitioners' Journal* 379 & 548 (1967).

| Chapter | TRENDS AND CHOICES |
| 38 | IN TRANSPORT POLICY |

In this chapter we wish to take a broad look at the changes in our transport system that have developed, principally since 1920, and to observe the main features of regulatory policy that resulted; and finally, to take a look at choices that lie in the future.

THE TRANSPORTATION REVOLUTION

Developments in the field of transportation that have occurred since 1920, principally technological in nature, have constituted a virtual revolution. The period marks the development of modern highways and motor-vehicle transportation, a great increase in the improvement and use of waterways, the appearance and rapid development of air transport, and an expanded system of pipeline transportation. Nonrail transport was stimulated by large government expenditures on highways, waterways, and air transport facilities.

Effects of the Transportation Revolution

The developments which we have noted have been of great benefit to the nation. The newer modes of transport have brought transportation services that were not possible before. They have brought these services, furthermore, to communities and areas that could not support rail transportation facilities.

The effect on persons, communities, and areas which had been served by rail transport was not an unmixed blessing. On the benefit side have been certain improvements in railroad service instituted to retain traffic threatened by the newer modes of transport; stimulation of technological developments from which the public has benefited, and reductions in railroad rates brought about by injection of a competitive element which had not existed before. On the debit side has been a general deterioration of railroad plant and some services; loss of extensive railroad mileage, depriving communities of service for which the newer modes of transport were not an adequate substitute; and impoverishment of the railroads, which, in turn, has prevented modernization of plant.

Transport Policy of the Period

We have elsewhere described in some detail the regulatory legislation of the period.[1] Some provisions of this legislation were for the purpose of protecting the newer forms of transportation and water carriers from suppression by the railroads. Such legislation included restrictions on railroad control of other modes of transport; establishment of through routes and joint rates between rail and water carriers; and legislation to prevent discrimination by railroads against connecting carriers of a different type.

Other measures enacted during this period were designed to help the railroads meet the new conditions with which they were faced. Among such measures were amendments to make it easier for the railroads to abandon unprofitable rail lines; measures to facilitate curtailment of burdensome passenger trains; measures to make it easier for railroads in financial difficulties to effect a financial reorganization or to readjust financial structures without resort to bankruptcy procedures.

Legislation was also enacted obligating the Commission to promote "fair and impartial regulation" of all modes of transport and to recognize and preserve the "inherent advantages" of each mode of transport.

We mention these provisions for the purpose of showing that Congress was addressing itself to the problems created by the transportation revolution.

PROPOSED CHANGES IN REGULATORY POLICY

We now turn to a consideration of changes in regulatory policy which have been advocated in recent years. These are, of course, the product of the changes in transportation that have developed and of the problems to which they have given rise.

Deregulation—Complete or Partial

Throughout the period that we are considering, particularly after 1950, there developed a movement to liberalize regulation and give the carriers more freedom of action, particularly in rate making and in the abandonment of unprofitable operations. This movement was the natural result of the development of motor transportation, air transportation, and the increased extent and effectiveness of inland waterway transportation.

A number of official studies and inquiries into the transportation problem in the 1950s and 1960s have given support to varying degrees of deregulation.[2]

---

[1] Chapter 12.

[2] See Presidential Advisory Committee on Transport Policy and Organization, *Revision of Federal Transportation Policy* (Washington, D.C.: Government Printing Office, 1955); U.S. Department of Commerce, *Federal Transportation Policy and Program* (Washington, D.C.: Government Printing Office, 1960); U.S. Department of Commerce, *Rationale of Federal Transportation Policy* (Washington, D.C.: Gov-

Most of the discussions of deregulation center on rate control; restriction of entry, particularly in the motor-carrier industry; and regulatory provisions which have hindered railroads in their attempts to abandon unprofitable operations. Some proposals, however, have extended to complete deregulation, with the exception of the application of the antitrust laws, and a return to free competition in the industry.[3]

The deregulation movement has already had some legislative results in modification of the Interstate Commerce Act. The principal legislative response is found in the following legislation which has been detailed elsewhere:

1. the amendment of Section 15a in 1958 which was intended to restrict interference by the Commission with competitive reductions in rates;[4]
2. the enactment of Section 13a, also in 1958, making it even easier for railroads to discontinue unprofitable passenger trains;[5] and
3. the Rail Passenger Service Act of 1970 permitting discontinuance of nearly all rail long-distance passenger service except that to be operated under contract with the National Railroad Passenger Corporation—"Amtrak."[6]

It is interesting to note that other countries which have felt the impact of the newer modes of transport on an extensive railroad transportation system that had developed earlier have responded to the changed situation by giving the railroads, even if government owned, more freedom in adjusting rates to a new competitive situation, and have authorized widespread discontinuance of unprofitable services and line abandonments. This has happened in Canada, Great Britain, and many countries on the continent of Europe.

President Nixon's Council of Economic Advisers, in 1971, supported eventual deregulation, but emphasized the necessity of gradualism in the process in view of "the magnitude of the changes that would be brought about by such deregulation."[7]

---

ernment Printing Office, 1960); Committee on Commerce, U.S. Senate, *National Transportation Policy* (The Doyle Report), 87th Cong., 1st Sess., Senate Report No. 445 (1961).

[3] See George W. Hilton, *The Transportation Act of 1958* (Bloomington, Indiana: Indiana University Press, 1969), chap. vi; and "The Two Things Wrong with the Interstate Commerce Commission," Transportation Research Forum—*Papers, Eleventh Annual Meeting, 1970,* p. 299; Merton J. Peck, "*Competitive Policy for Transportation,*" In Paul W. MacAvoy, *The Crisis of the Regulatory Commissions* (New York: Norton, 1970).

[4] See pp. 273–74 supra.

[5] See pp. 272–73 supra.

[6] See pp. 275–77 supra.

[7] *Economic Report of the President* (Washington, D.C.: Government Printing Office, 1971), p. 126.

Additional Controls

Although increased sentiment toward relaxation of some controls has characterized the period that we are considering, there are also proposals that move in the opposite direction. The proposals for additional controls are quite specific in nature and grow out of the situations with which we have been confronted. Without attempting to mention all of the legislative proposals or demands for more vigorous exercise of existing regulatory powers we may indicate what seem to be the major ones. These are:

1. positive action in the area of freight car supply and car utilization;
2. removal of some of the exemptions from regulation, particularly the agricultural commodity exemptions in the Motor Carrier Act, and the bulk commodity exemption in the Water Carrier Act;
3. prevention of evasion of common-carrier service obligations by railroads, motor carriers, and airlines;
4. granting to the Interstate Commerce Commission of power to require the establishment of through routes and joint rates by motor carriers of property, and through routes and joint rates for rail-motor movements;
5. more adequate treatment of shippers by the carriers in handling loss and damage claims;
6. stricter supervision of railroad financial transactions in order to prevent debacles like those which accompanied the Penn Central financial difficulties and subsequent bankruptcy;
7. control over railroad conglomerates to prevent the abuses to which they are prone.

These are areas in which federal regulation is absent or inadequate at the present time. The conditions giving rise to these demands for additional controls do not speak well for a policy of laissez-faire in the industry. Although it could be said that some of the practices complained of are the consequence of past regulatory policies, it does not follow that decontrol would bring them to an end.

COMPETITION AND COMMON-CARRIER OBLIGATIONS

We have seen that the increased competitiveness of the transportation industry has brought many benefits to the public, and that it has given rise to the belief that competition alone can bring about an adequate and satisfactory transportation system. There is one respect, however, in which an all-out competitive system in transport would be less than satisfactory, judged by accustomed standards.

The ability of carriers to fulfill the traditional obligations of common carriers is diminished as competition in transport increases. Competition in transport and common-carrier obligations are to a certain extent incompatible. Common carriers, like public utilities generally, may be expected to provide some specific services that are not profitable by themselves.

Railroads, motor carriers, water carriers, and airlines have in varying degrees been expected to provide certain unprofitable services as part of their common-carrier obligations. These services are supported from an overall level of rates that is sufficient to maintain all services deemed essential. A protected position in the market is necessary to enable this to be done. If competition reduces rates to a cost basis, or perhaps to an out-of-pocket cost basis, where costs are low, the carrier's ability to support other services is impaired.

It may be argued at this point that no carrier or public utility should be required to provide a service that does not pay its cost. This argument ignores the fact that there may be a collective demand for transportation services of a broader range, and a collective willingness to pay the costs through an overall higher level of rates. We may recall at this point the words of Chief Justice Taft years ago in upholding the fixing of railroad rates on the basis of a group of carriers considered as a whole, when he said that the individual shipper may "properly be required in the rate he pays to share with all other shippers of the same section the burden of maintaining an adequate railway capacity to do their business."[8] Such a policy would be impossible if rates on high-density low-cost railroad routes were reduced to a bare cost basis.

This so-called "public utility principle" has a solid legal basis. The legality of requiring a railroad to continue operation of an unprofitable branch line has long been recognized,[9] or to operate unprofitable passenger trains,[10] and the Supreme Court of the United States has upheld the principle that rates on particular commodities or services may be required which are even below out-of-pocket cost, provided the carriers are permitted an overall return that is adequate.[11]

Of course the ability of a railroad, motor carrier, or airline to carry unprofitable operations is limited; the point is that under a competitive organization of the industry this ability is more severely restricted. The result would be abandonment of many services considered to be an essential part of the transportation system. To prevent the abandonment of such operations the public will be forced to resort either to subsidy or to taking over responsibility for providing these services and facilities. This situation will have an effect on future transport policy.

---

[8] *Dayton-Goose Creek Ry. Co.* v. *United States,* 263 U.S. 456, 481 (1924).
[9] See p. 596 supra.
[10] See pp. 578–79 of sixth edition.
[11] See p. 424 supra.

POLICY CHOICES

We now turn to a consideration of recent proposals for changes in regulatory policy. In general, three different lines of action have been proposed, and each has variations and modifications. The three diverse lines of action are (1) deregulation and a return to unrestricted competition in the industry, both intermodally and intramodally; (2) assumption by the government of the responsibility for providing adequate transportation service directly, i.e., some form of public enterprise; and (3) retention of the existing system of controls with such changes therein as changed circumstances may make necessary or appropriate. Although these lines of action seem opposed to each other, they are not mutually exclusive unless each is pursued to its ultimate. In other words, some features of each might find an appropriate place in overall policy, as will be made clear in our discussion.

Deregulation

We shall take the policy of deregulation to mean *complete* deregulation with the exception of the application of the antitrust laws to the transportation industry. We cannot here devote the space necessary for a full analysis of the problem. We would like, however, to make certain observations about the policy.

First, the policy is based on the assumption of the "all pervasiveness" of competition, which is an overstatement of the competitive situation. In the railroad field there are many commodities for which motor transport or transportation by water is not a substitute, particularly for longer hauls. The list of such commodities is on the increase because of the development of various kinds of specialized freight cars adapted to carrying particular commodities more economically than they can be carried by motor vehicle. There is a considerable body of traffic for which motor carriers cannot compete, and in this area the railroads have as much monopoly power as they did before motor transport appeared.

Secondly, the extent to which competition would work satisfactorily in the motor-carrier and air-carrier industries has long been a matter of dispute, and we will not attempt to resolve the issue here.

Thirdly, we would like to point out that so much is at stake in deregulation that it behooves those in responsible positions to proceed cautiously in this area. Billions of dollars invested in agriculture, mining, manufacturing, and other business activities would be placed in jeopardy by the resulting changes in individual rates that might occur. The survival of particular industrial enterprises and the welfare of particular communities and whole areas would be endangered if freight rates were subject to an unrestricted right of individual carriers to make them and change them at will. We do not mean to imply that rate patterns are inviolate or that established patterns of production and distribution must always be preserved, but rather that the potential effects of unrestricted rate-making power are so great that a policy of caution should be observed, and that some form of governmental restraint is required.

In the fourth place, we repeat the point which we previously made that even if competition worked out in conformity with theoretical models, the resulting transportation system would not be satisfactory. The public demands some transportation services that are not strictly "economic" according to the standards of the marketplace. For reasons of national or regional development, or for social or political reasons, transport systems and services are demanded which must be supported in part by taxation, or by a noncompetitive price system that permits some degree of "cross subsidization."

That the public is willing to provide direct subsidy for some transport operations which are not self-supporting is shown by subsidies to local service airlines, and by state and local subsidies to local transit operations and rail commuter services. In some instances state governments have taken over bankrupt or distressed railroad properties in order that service might be continued. Examples are the purchase of the Long Island Railroad by the State of New York, and the purchase of some portions of the abandoned Rutland Railroad by the State of Vermont.[12] Amtrak represents an attempt to continue hitherto unprofitable railroad passenger service by a semipublic corporation. Legislation was introduced in Congress in 1971 to insure continued operation of railroad services threatened by railroad bankruptcies, and, if necessary, to provide for a take-over by the government.

Government Provision of Transportation Services

Under this policy the government would engage in the business of carrying persons and property, although not necessarily by all modes of transport. With the exception of local transit systems commonly owned by the municipalities in which they operate, this system has not been generally used in the United States.[13]

If this policy were adopted, it would involve ownership and operation of the railroads by the federal government. Of course there could be government operation of railroads which were privately owned, or there could be private operation of railroads which were owned by the government. Usually, however, government ownership and government opera-

---

[12] Vermont does not operate these lines but has leased portions to two newly created corporations for operation.

[13] Exceptions are the Alaska Railroad, owned by the United States government, and the Federal Barge Lines owned and operated by the government from 1917 to 1953. During World War I and until March 1, 1920, the railroads were operated by the federal government although remaining in private ownership.

tion go together. Such is the policy of practically all nations except the United States. In Canada, however, which has two major railroad systems, one is government owned—the Canadian National—; the other is privately owned—the Canadian Pacific.

In some countries government ownership is extended at least to a limited extent to other modes of transport. The major airlines in most countries of the world are owned by the government or by companies in which the government has a substantial interest. Some countries also provide road services, particularly, the transportation of passengers by bus. In 1947, Great Britain nationalized long-distance "goods transport" by motor vehicle but the policy was later reversed and denationalization of truck transport was undertaken in 1953.

One advantage, from the public's point of view, of government ownership of transportation systems is that they can be operated as a public service without too much regard to whether various parts are self-supporting. The cost of providing the services is to some extent spread over all users of the system. The experience of Great Britain and Canada, however, is that this practice may involve too much of a burden on users, and they accordingly seek to abandon unprofitable services, as a private concern would, or to seek a direct subsidy for the unprofitable operations.

Another advantage of government ownership and operation of railroads is that the system can be planned, and the plans executed more effectively than when the system is privately owned. Wastes and duplication inevitable in an unplanned system are thereby avoided.

Under government ownership, it would presumably be easier to obtain capital for improvement and modernization of the railroad system. Inability to raise sufficient capital for improvements in railroad plant has handicapped the railroads in recent years. Of course this situation would be remedied by government ownership only if the government is able and willing to provide the necessary capital in one way or another.

Government ownership, whatever may be its advantages, has certain disadvantages. First, there is a group of disadvantages commonly associated with public enterprises. They include (1) inefficiency due to lack of the competitive spur; (2) a tendency for public enterprises to be overstaffed; (3) politics in administrative appointments and in hiring at all levels; (4) less incentive to introduce innovations and technological improvements; and (5) political pressures for unwarranted services and preferential treatment. These difficulties, however, could be overcome with determination to do so. Although these problems have doubtless arisen in all countries, it is still true that many government-owned railways are well managed and efficiently operated.

Although most government-owned railroads incur deficits in operation, this is not necessarily an indication of poor management or inefficiency. It may be the result of a conscious policy of keeping rates and fares low; or it may result from operating lines or service for developmental or other purposes which are not profitable in themselves. The success of a government-owned enterprise is not to be measured solely by profits.

Even though this is so, someone has to stand the burden of unprofitable operations. Under government ownership the burden falls on the taxpayer. Under private ownership the burden falls on investors who were unfortunate enough to have invested in the enterprise. When a private enterprise fails, investors take their losses; the enterprise goes out of existence, or more often in the case of railroads, continues in operation with a lightened capital structure. But a government cannot as easily rid itself of the debt created in the construction or acquisition of the railroad if it wishes to be in a position to borrow in the future.

Government ownership of railroads in the United States would pose a problem of organization that is more difficult than in other countries. Few countries have an area as extensive as the United States, and none have as great a railway mileage. Undoubtedly the system could be broken up into parts for the purposes of operation, but this does not entirely solve the problem and some inefficiencies might occur which were solely the result of size.

Government ownership of railroads is not likely to come in the United States if the railroads can be maintained as viable enterprises. If widespread bankruptcies occur with threatened loss of essential services then there may be no practical alternative to government ownership. This process might not involve taking over the whole railroad system, but only those railroads whose services would otherwise be discontinued or impossible to maintain in an adequate manner.

Ownership of railroads by state governments, particularly of small lines, is also a possibility. We have already mentioned in this chapter two instances of acquisition of bankrupt railroads by state governments in recent years. The wholesale abandonment by large railroads of branch lines considered unprofitable is likely to lead to other instances of this sort. Acquisition of such lines of railroad by state or local governments is an appropriate means by which a community or area can protect its economy.

Continuance of Regulation, but Adapted to New Conditions

We now turn to a consideration of the third direction which policy might take—the continuance of regulation, modified or expanded as developments may require. This might be called "evolutionary regulation," as emphasis must be placed on its adaptability to new conditions and circumstances.

This policy involves the least break with the past; it involves the least risk, i.e., it has a better chance of success than either of the other two courses of action.

It does not bar deregulation in certain aspects of regulation, if a convincing case can be made for it; it does not bar the imposition of additional controls or more strict application of existing regulatory powers, as circumstances may require. It does not bar assumption of responsibility for providing transportation service by federal, state, or local governments where that appears to be the appropriate manner of dealing with particular situations.

For the present at least, an evolutionary process in transportation regulation, as in other institutions, seems preferable to the more extreme courses of action which have been proposed.

SELECTED REFERENCES

Among the official reports dealing with transport policy in recent years the following provide excellent discussion of the problem but recommendations vary considerably: Presidential Advisory Committee on Transport Policy and Organization, *Revision of Federal Transportation Policy* (Washington, D.C.: Government Printing Office, 1955); U.S. Department of Commerce, *Federal Transportation Policy and Program* (Washington, D.C.: Government Printing Office, 1960); U.S. Department of Commerce, *Rationale of Federal Transportation Policy* (Washington, D.C.: Government Printing Office, 1960). The most extensive report on the subject, more than 700 pages in length, and dealing with many specific aspects of regulation and promotional policy is the Doyle Report, Committee on Commerce, U.S. Senate, *National Transportation Policy*, 87th Cong., 1st Sess., Senate Report No. 445 (1961).

Advocacy of deregulation, wholly or in considerable degree, is found in George W. Hilton, *The Transportation Act of 1958* (Bloomington, Ind.: Indiana University Press, 1969), particularly chap. vi; and also by the same author, "The Two Things Wrong with the Interstate Commerce Commission," in Transportation Research Forum, *Papers, Eleventh Annual Meeting* (1970), p. 299; Merton J. Peck, "Competitive Policy for Transportation," in Paul W. MacAvoy, ed., *The Crisis of the Regulatory Commissions* (New York: W. W. Norton & Co., 1970), p. 72; Ann F. Friedlander, *The Dilemma of Freight Transport Regulation* (Washington, D.C.: The Brookings Institution, 1969); and "The Social Costs of Regulating the Railroads," *American Economic Review*, May 1971, p. 226. A brief discussion of the subject, advocating gradual deregulation, is in *Economic Report of the President* (Washington, D.C.: Government Printing Office, 1971), pp. 122–30, and more specific changes in regulation are proposed in the 1972 report, pp. 130–35.

Other discussions of deregulation, generally more moderate in tone, are George W. Wilson, "The Effect of Rate Regulation on Resource Allocation in Transportation," in Paul W. MacAvoy, op. cit., pp. 57–71; also "The Goals of Transportation Policy," in Ernest W. Williams, Jr., ed., *The Future of American Transportation* (Englewood Cliffs, N.J.: Prentice-Hall, 1971), chap. i; Dudley F. Pegrum, "Restructuring the Transport System," in Ernest W. Williams, Jr., op. cit., chap. iii; and also "Should the I.C.C. Be Abolished?" *Transportation Journal*, Fall 1971, p. 5; James C. Nelson, "Toward Rational Price Policies," in Ernest W. Williams, Jr., op. cit., chap. v.

Transport policy is reviewed extensively in Hugh S. Norton, *National Transportation Policy: Formation and Implementation* (Berkeley, Calif.: McCutchan Publishing Corp., 1966).

INDEX

905

This book has been set in 10 and 9 point Janson, leaded 2 points. Chapter numbers are in 16 point Helvetica italic; chapter titles are in 16 point Helvetica caps. The size of the type page is 27 × 46½ picas.